THE TIGERS TALE

THE OFFICIAL HISTORY OF LEICESTER FOOTBALL CLUB 1880-1993

By STUART FARMER & DAVID HANDS

Published by
ACL & POLAR PUBLISHING (UK) LTD

DEDICATION
To Mum and Dad in your Golden Year
S.F.

First published in Great Britain by
ACL Colour Print & Polar Publishing (UK) Ltd
2, Uxbridge Road, Leicester LE4 7ST
England

Text Copyright Stuart Farmer & David Hands

Design Copyright ACL & Polar 1993

ISBN No. 0 9514862 5 X

Edited by
Julian Baskcomb

Designed and Printed by
ACL Colourprint & Polar Publishing (UK) Ltd
2, Uxbridge Road, Leicester LE4 7ST
Telephone: (0533) 610800

Dust jacket design: Leigh R. Pearce

Interior design: Eamon C. Heighway

Photographs are courtesy of:
Leicester Football Club, Colorsport, George Herringshaw/ASP, Leicester Mercury, Neville Chadwick Photography,
David Munden Photography, AllSport, Empics, Andrew Maw.
Many of the photographs reproduced are from original material in the files at Leicester Football Club who retain the rights to all official
photocall pictures. Most of the remaining photographs are from the private collections of the authors or from albums owned by various
Tigers supporters or players. We have been unable to trace the sources of these pictures, but any photographer involved is cordially
invited to contact the publishers in writing providing proof of copyright.

Cover Photographs:
Front: (Clockwise): A jubilant **Rory Underwood** (main pic) raises the Pilkington Cup to the fans after Leicester beat Harlequins in the
1993 final at Twickenham. *(Photo: Press Association).*
Tom Crumbie - Tigers long-serving Secretary; **Edward Redman** depicted on an 1895 beer-mat; **'Dusty' Hare** in action
(Photo: Colorsport); and Tigers star England international captain of the 1930's **Bernard Gadney**.

Back: The Tigers **Welford Road** ground in 1959; a 1930's cigarette card caricature of Tigers' **George Beamish** in his Irish international
shirt; **Tigers 1988 team** group with the inaugural Courage Clubs Championship trophy *(Photo: AllSport)*; **H.L.V. Day** takes a place-kick
during the 1920's; influential fly-half **Les Cusworth** *(Photo: Colorsport)*; an even earlier beer-mat from 1892 featuring the Tigers;
leading Tigers and England hooker **Peter Wheeler** *(Photo: Colorsport)*.

By Dean Richards
(Leicester, England and British Isles)

I FELT honoured when asked by Stuart Farmer to write an introduction to *"The Tigers' Tale"*, the most recent and most comprehensive history book to be written on any rugby club. I am particularly proud that the publication coincides with my year as captain of Leicester Football Club.

For those of you who know me, you will readily acknowledge that I too am a statistician. I made my debut for the Tigers on Easter Saturday 1982 at Neath and I am enjoying my thirteenth season with the club. At the time of writing I have made 218 first-team appearances - or is it 219? - for the club. I have scored 96 tries - or is it 97? I can't be sure. I never will be sure.

That is why I want to congratulate Stuart Farmer for all the painstaking research he has carried out and for all the facts and figures which this book presents. I know that his research has extended not only to all parts of the United Kingdom but also to many other countries throughout the world. No one would appear to be safe when Stuart is around and wanting some information. This is another first for Leicester Football Club.

My thanks also go to David Hands for updating and adding on another thirteen years of rugby on to the history of "Leicester Football Club."

I look forward to the hours of enjoyment I shall have when browsing through this book. I hope that you will too, because after all, everything about rugby football, especially rugby football at Leicester is about enjoyment.

Thank you Stuart and David and everyone associated with *"The Tigers' Tale."*

October 1993

An attractive picture montage of early Tigers taken from the souvenir produced by Leicester Football Club at the turn of the century to commemorate the winning of the Midland Counties Cup three times in succession during seasons 1897-98, 1898-99 and 1899-1900.

CONTENTS

Tthis book is the result of a personal wish to turn my research work on the history of the
Tigers into a quality, comprehensive work of reference recounting the heritage and
achievements of Leicester Football Club, so that it could be shared and enjoyed by one and
all. In doing so I wanted to chronicle the events which shaped the club into what we see today,
recognising that during the last few years not only are there literally thousands of members who
are new to the club, but also that many of them are indeed new to the sport of rugby union
football.

To conceive of such a project is all well and good, but to "deliver the goods" requires the co-
ordination of a complete team of professionals and fellow collaborators (and their various
computers). Here is my "roll of honour" to the main individuals who have given immense amounts
of time and effort, and burnt so much 'midnight oil.'

Firstly an enormous thank-you to the officials of the Leicester Football Club who have freely
opened their superb archives to my inquisitiveness, and to the players for their good humour in the
face of my never ending barrage of questions. In the words of Rory Underwood in his book "Flying
Wing" - 'What a family'. Special thanks are due to Mr Tudor Thomas the 1993 President, whose
limitless enthusiasm and boundless energy was a thorough inspiration to me. Also thanks to Stuart
Roscoe for his encouragement, Graham Willars with his Past Players Association, Bob Barker with
his statistics, Bill Moore, Haydn Thomas, Ken Nicholas, Peter Thorneloe, Peter Konig, Nick Hughes,
George Vallance, Eric Lacey, Bill Bottrill, Denis Bolesworth, 'Dosser' Smith, Steve Hackney, Miss
Atkins, Mrs Jerwood, Ann Laverack, Mrs Greenlees, David and Geoff Penny, Freda Wallace, and so
many players, ex-players and old players' families too numerous to mention, and of course to
'Deano' for his foreword.

Recognition is due in no small part to my co-author David Hands, who took on the project and
agreed to my impossible deadlines with such vigour, and to his son Robert in the capacity of sub-
editor. Also to my network of researchers, helpers and friends; to Gillian and Brian Bates of King's
Norton, thanks for your valuable assistance and ongoing friendship, to Janet Berry for her hard
work and patience, and to the ever reliable Welshman John Jenkins for your diligence and attention
to detail; the 'Who's who' section would have been nowhere near as comprehensive without your
work. Credit is also due to Nick Cross of the Harlequins for hours spent looking through dusty old
newspapers on my behalf, Dennis Keen of Rugby RFC, Jack Pope of Bedford RFC, Robert Gate of the
Rugby League, the Zimbabwe Rugby Union, Martin Potter the enthusiastic Tigers fan, and to my old
employers Safe Computing for the loan of yet another computer, so that I could cajole someone else
to word process my research work!

Thanks to the employees of the Leicester Mercury, especially Steve England and his staff at the
Library for your company during my 'take-over' of your offices. To Chris Goddard for the loan of
his notebooks, and his help with publicity. The staff of the National Newspaper Library at Colindale
and the Central Reference Library in Bishop Street.

For illustrations and photographs, I would like to express my gratitude to Alan Wells and Van
Hopkins of the Leicestershire Rugby Union, the Leicester Mercury archives, the Leicestershire
Records Office at Wigston Magna, Neville Chadwick Photography, Eric Ballard of Nuneaton RFC,
and to Tim Auty for the loan of his personal collection of scrapbooks and photos. Leonard Jenkinson
for the first-day cover, Alan Jackson for his old Tigers programmes, Andrew Maw, Colorsport and
Associated Sports Photography. For some of the photographs used I have been unable to establish a
clear copyright. The publishers would be pleased to hear from anyone whose copyright has been
unintentionally infringed.

Finally thanks are due to the publishers ACL & Polar Publishing. To Julian Baskcomb for having
the foresight to back the project, and allocate so many resources to its successful completion. To Julia
Byrne for her administrative expertise, and Eamon Heighway and his studio team for their
presentation skills.

A sincere thank-you one and all,

Stuart Farmor
September 1993

WHEN you write a centenary history you do not expect, in the nature of things, to write another - at least, not for the same club. One hundred years is enough for most people, and the second hundred must of necessity be left to someone else. So when Leicester Football Club 1880-1980 was completed I imagined that was the end - as far as I was concerned - of the Tigers' history.

I moved away from Leicester, from the sports department of the *Leicester Mercury* which had brought me into contact with the Tigers in the early 1970s - not without some regret since it was midway through the club's three-year domination of the John Player Cup. Working for the sports department of *The Times*, however, has allowed me to return to Welford Road every now and again and thus to keep in touch with the many developments which have taken place over the last decade.

What I reckoned without was the affection and enthusiasm which exists in so many people for the Leicester club; in this case of Tudor Thomas who contributed so much towards the original centenary history is now, the club President, and Stuart Farmer, a club member with a statistical bent which has been given huge scope by the onslaught of the computer age.

Both of them wanted to bring Tigers up to date - in a literary sense - so that a new generation of Leicester followers could appreciate the history of the club whose activities they follow with such avidity. The wealth of detail Stuart has amassed, and has at his fingertips will satisfy any sporting brain of Britain currently resident in Leicestershire and his research has allowed earlier errors to be corrected: the club's all-time record try-scorer, for example, is confirmed as Percy Lawrie, the centre who played before and after the First World War and scored 206 tries. Tudor appreciated the immense changes which have overtaken rugby union during the 1980s and believed there to be a case for chronicling those changes and how they have affected Tigers. In addition they have uncovered additional material which was not available at the time the original centenary history was written.

The combination of their enthusiasm and a willing (and local) publisher proved overwhelming. What follows is not a complete re-write of the centenary history; the work of 13 years ago has hardly had time to be invalidated, although it has been possible to add some considerable detail to the original work. But so much has happened during the 1980s and early 1990s that there is no shortage of new material to add to what went before. In addition the club itself seized the time: in 1993 the players added fresh laurels by winning the Pilkington Cup with a vibrant young team which seems set to become a major force in English rugby during the decade.

The face of the game has been changed since the publication of the centenary history: the world has grown smaller and Leicester have availed themselves of touring opportunities in a way that they did so seldom during the first 100 years. World Cups and League Rugby have produced a completely new climate in which the game prospers in a public sense, although the amateur ethic - which has been perennially abused - is under intolerable strain. Through it all, however, Leicester, the club and its officials, have preserved an enviable reputation for honourable dealing and high standards of performance, on and off the field. The Leicester crowd, which now averages around 8,000 per match, provides an atmosphere which is the envy of all clubs - even those such as Bath whose success has been the dominant theme of the last decade in England.

Yet it is worth recalling the words written in the foreword of the 1980 history by two club players, Bleddyn Jones and John Duggan, who never won caps but whose achievements during the 1970s linger in the memory. "A hundred years of history is based on the actions of many people," they wrote. "Their loyalty and cheerful service in changing circumstances have contributed to the well-being of the Leicester Football Club." It is the many who make a club, not the few, and that is worth remembering at a time when club loyalty has seldom been so severely tested.

One of the great strengths of the leading clubs in the English provinces is the constant recycling of players-turned-administrators, which provide not only continuity but a sense of tradition. The wisdom of one generation may be handed down to another, to provide a bedrock on which the manners and customs of today may be tried and tested. Thus it is that, for example, no sooner have players such as Ian Smith and Paul Dodge stopped playing then they have started coaching while such contemporaries as Steve Kenney join the committee. That is a direct link with the customs of the Leicester of the nineteenth century, when players also helped run their club. Long may it remain.

David Hands
August 1993

... to Present Day Triumphs

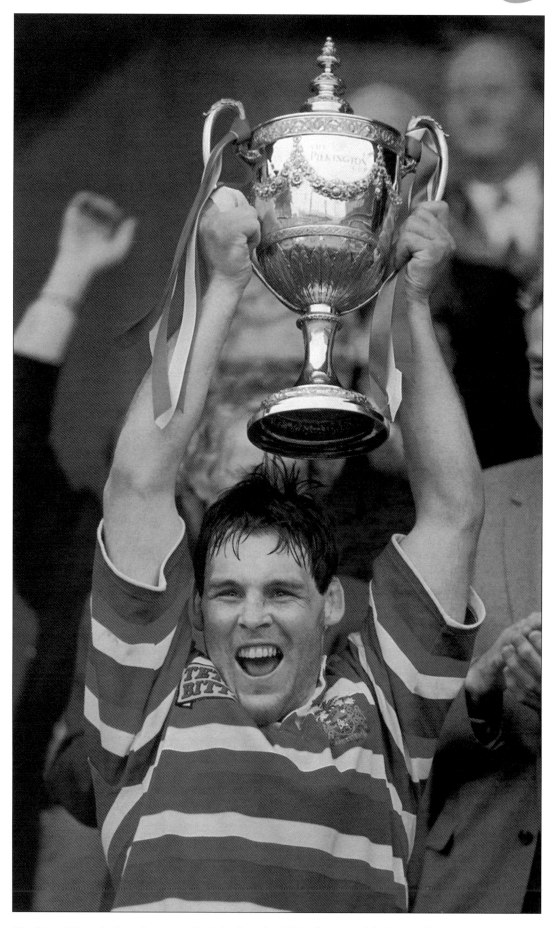

The latest Tigers' triumph came at Twickenham in 1993 when they lifted the Pilkington Cup. Here skipper John Wells is a picture of delight as he shows off the trophy to the massed ranks of Tigers' supporters celebrating the splendid victory over Harlequins.

8 THE TIGERS TALE

THE PIONEER DAYS
1880-1892

THE official attendance at the 1993 Pilkington Cup final between Leicester and Harlequins at Twickenham was 56,500. If all those from the Leicester area who wanted tickets had been able to get them, and Twickenham had been able to accommodate them, the crowd which watched Leicester win the cup for the fourth time in their history would surely have passed 70,000 - the sort of numbers which used regularly in the 1950s and 1960s to watch internationals.

Of those who were there that May day, unofficial estimates suggest that two-thirds were supporting Leicester; during the summer that followed, the club's membership list expanded to 10,000 to become the first club in England with a five-figure membership. There is a magic attached to the club which is, perhaps, unparalleled in England and which is matched in the United Kingdom only by the two Welsh giants, Cardiff and Llanelli.

Why should this be so? Leicester itself is not the most romantic of cities. Its fortunes are based firmly on trade and the wheels of industry still whir busily in a complex, multi-cultural society. Football, England's strongest sport, has a well-respected place in that society and Filbert Street, the headquarters of Leicester City, is little more than a stone's throw from the Tigers' clubhouse on the busy Aylestone Road. Other sports, team and individual, prosper yet the hold that the rugby club now exerts on people in the city and county is as strong now - and probably stronger - as it has ever been, closely bound up as it is with the business and social life of Leicester.

Part of the magic, I believe, derives from the sense of ambition which has always been a feature of the Tigers. In a physical sense that is exemplified by the club ground, with the two stands which have long made anything else in English rugby (Twickenham excepted) seem small beer; the proximity to the city centre is important too, because the club is in no sense cut off from the day-to-day life of Leicester. But that ambition also extends to the playing of the game: the club's administrators have always striven for the best for their players and have expected the best in return, on the playing field. Today's supporters have seen for themselves how well the current team has repaid that trust, but how many of them are aware of the tradition which the team of the 1990s is sustaining and how it all began?

It may come as no surprise that one of the first actions of the committee which formed the Leicester Football Club in 1880 was to decide the date of an inaugural dinner. Indeed, the dinner was held well before the club played its first game. Socialising has always been an integral part of rugby union and the new club had something worth celebrating, because

WIDE PITCH
In October 1881 the pitch on the Edgbaston Cricket ground was marked out 30 yards wider than normal, in order that the Edgbaston Crusader backs had more room to run! It obviously worked, they won by one goal and two tries to nil.

from the grass roots of several junior clubs, players and administrators had emerged to try and put Leicester on the map as a rugby-playing city. The game that earned its name from Rugby School had crossed the twenty miles to Leicester comparatively slowly if we take the iniquitous actions of William Webb Ellis in 1823 as the starting point. But at least the intervening half-century gave rugby the chance to establish itself as a credible sporting activity, to put down formal roots not only in England but in Scotland, Ireland and Wales, wherever university students and teachers and young captains of trade and industry carried the handling game.

Before the inaugural club meeting on August 3, 1880, at the George Hotel, there was already a useful nucleus of clubs in Leicester and Leicestershire, though sadly most of them no longer exist or have merged under a new name. The first in the city were Leicester Athletic Society and St Margaret's, both formed in 1869, two years before the formation of the Rugby Union itself. Records exist at Twickenham of a Leicester club formed in 1872, but this was an irregular team representative of various junior clubs, equivalent to a Leicestershire XV of today.

Burton had a club, as did Nottingham, while Moseley Harriers had got off the ground in Birmingham. Further south Harlequins, Richmond, Blackheath and several more had been growing apace. Leicester as a city could offer nothing comparable until 1880, when Leicester Societies AFC, Leicester Amateur FC and Leicester Alert decided to amalgamate to form a club representative of the city. W A Wheeler, an enthusiastic player during the 1870s whose home was in Lancaster Street, was elected the first president of the new Leicester Football Club. By a vote of 14-2, A E Brice, who lived in Mill Hill Lane off the London Road, was elected captain ahead of J W Symington who, though nominated vice-captain, found no place in the opening game, against Moseley. J A Lakin and John Parsons became joint secretaries and, at the George Hotel that night, 46 players went on the books of the new club.

In the light of the reputation Leicester restored during the late 1970s and 1980s, it was a not inappropriate moment. Rugby union was undergoing considerable change during the 1870s and 1880s; hacking had been abolished, teams had been reduced from 20 to 15-a-side and Oxford University were in the process of showing the world that backs could play a vital part in the game.

The new Leicester club, however, had still to establish its identity. The inaugural meeting went some way towards this by laying down the name, the Leicester Football Club (later to cause some confusion for followers of the association code), the subscriptions of five shillings a year, and the club colours of black. The bye-laws were drawn up at the first committee meeting 24 days later and they were: 1, the club was to be called the Leicester Football Club; 2, the club was to play under Rugby Union rules (the laws of the game came later); 3, colours were to be black; 4, the officers and the committee were to be chosen annually at an April meeting; 5, the club was to be managed by a committee comprising the president, captain, vice-captain, treasurer, secretary and six other members;

6, two general meetings were to be held each year, in April and September; 7, all elections were to be by ballot; 8, teams were to be chosen weekly by the committee; 9, anyone wishing to become a member had to be proposed, seconded and voted for by a majority at a general committee meeting; 10, subscriptions had to be paid by October 31 each year; 11, anyone wishing to resign had to give written notice to the secretary before September 1 each season.

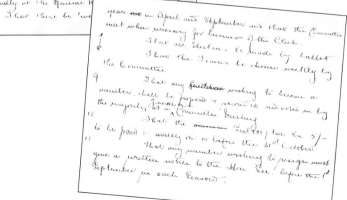

The original rules of the club taken from the 1880 minute book.

A meeting a month later decided that anyone carded to play who failed to reply should be fined sixpence and anyone promising to play and failing to do so should be fined two shillings and sixpence. Again as an experiment for the inaugural season the committee decided to give a prize to the player with the highest points total, though since there is no indication who won it six months later, it seems possible this idea was quietly forgotten. The first practice was held on the Welford Road Recreation Ground on October 2, 1880, and 10 days later two teams were selected against Moseley. The senior squad chosen for the club's first game was:
A E Brice, L Young, W A Wheeler, J A Lakin, T D Hart, A T Porter, C E Worthington, F Sheen, J T Lovett, A Turner, T R Pickering, H J Barwick, J Rhodes, W F Watts, W R Porter, H S Biggs, J Gilbert, A J Burford.

The club's ground in this first season was the Belgrave cricket and cycle ground, a little out of the centre of the city but obviously a popular leisure centre. The first game produced a draw, though Moseley expressed some dissent at the Leicester score - setting the tone for some acrimonious encounters during the next 20 years! But not all of the committee were satisfied with this early venue and only three months after formation, an application was made to the Leicestershire County Cricket Club for the use of the Aylestone Road ground, with any gate money to be divided between the two sporting bodies. However the cricket ground company, belying the close associations which were to grow between the city's main sporting clubs, declined the offer.

Early in the New Year, Leicester applied for membership of the Midland Counties Football Association and a fortnight later, issued a challenge to a Midland Counties XV to play them at Coventry. This may have been a rash move for in March 1881, Leicester had to pay Northampton one pound because the Saints had advertised a game and Leicester had failed to raise a side. In that first season, however, the club won 19 games, lost four and drew seven. They also fielded a side playing association football which won seven games, lost two and drew two.

It was a good start, particularly since the first XV lost only three of their 17 games, the other defeats being suffered by the second, or A, XV. There was a charge of two pence for admission and income for the season was £36.19s.10d. But even after so short a time, considerable changes were made for the second season. The club's doings had attracted very little public attention, the main sports taking up space in the local newspapers being horse racing, walking and cycling. So they officially moved to play at Victoria Park (they had in fact been playing there since the new year), in the centre of the city,

where it cost nothing to watch and where they hoped to build up a useful following. Cash flow remained an irritant though, and the secretary was reduced to applying to the city's estates committee for a reduction in the charges made for playing on Victoria Park.

H W Salmon became secretary and, after Brice's resignation through illness, A T Porter became club captain. After five months, however, the club had a third captain, Porter resigning because he felt "unable to play and fulfil the duties of captain." The leadership went to L Young and over the season the three sides (including the association team) won 24 games, lost 19 and drew four. They had entered the Midland Counties Senior Cup competition, whose games were always held at the end of each season, and in his first report Hedley Salmon said: "Although knocked out by a second rate club (Edgbaston) in the first round of the cup ties...I think it will take the premier club (Moseley) all its time to knock us out in the final (if we do not meet before) in the forthcoming season." Certainly an optimist was at the helm, even if his prediction took some while to come true.

The major games in these early days were those with Moseley, Northampton and Coventry, while the only Leicestershire teams encountered were Leicester Victoria and Market Harborough. Soon they were joined by Nuneaton, and Bedford Grammar School which was invariably a hard game occupying much the same sort of space then, perhaps, as Loughborough Students have in recent times in Tigers' fixture lists. In 1883, the Leicester Association Football Club was formed (better known in subsequent years as Leicester Fosse and then Leicester City) and the club dropped their association side, developing instead a third, or B, XV. But they recognised the challenge that the new football club threw down: they, too, were angling for support - what would now be called their share of the market - and the next five years proved an anxious time as gate receipts dwindled upon the return to Belgrave Road. Therefore they reverted to Victoria Park and found that the competitive edge required for the Midland Counties Cup added to their public appeal. It is hard not to think of the last decade and appreciate that things do not always change quite as much as we believe.

At the same time Leicester were going through a very 'colourful' phase. The black strip with which they began gave way to a chocolate and yellow confection which almost certainly is the origin of their famous nickname, Tigers. It is hard to be certain because of the connection they had already established with officers of the Leicestershire Regiment, whose own soubriquet was Tigers. The earliest reference to the name Tigers appears to bear out the first explanation: the *Leicester Daily Post*

states "the Tiger stripes were keeping well together", in their match report of the game against Bedford Grammar School in February 1885. However, if it was, then the name stuck but the shirt did not, for they changed to claret and French grey and then to red, green and white stripes (hoops followed in 1895) which, though there was a hiatus in the early 1900s when they wore white, proved to be the most lasting of the lot and the colours by which they are now known to rugby followers all over the country.

Having established themselves in the public's esteem, Leicester returned to the Belgrave ground in 1888 and their supporters went with them, becoming paying customers. A season ticket cost five shillings (25p) or two shillings and sixpence (12 and a half pence) while non-members could pay threepence (just over 1p) for entry and a further threepence for a seat in the stand. Ladies were not charged admission, though they may not have been unduly enthused by the club's disappointing record between 1888-90.

The 'Death or Glory' boys in black had given way to the Tigers in stripes and, in accordance with their enhanced standing, they branched out, striking up fixtures with clubs from the north and from Wales. They reached the final of the Midlands Cup in 1889 but lost to Moseley, and two years later they were back again, losing this time to Coventry by 8-0. But that 1890-91 season was the best so far, for they could look back on 18 wins, two draws and just five defeats.

It was also their penultimate season at Belgrave Road. When, in April 1891, Leicester sought a further lease with the Belgrave Road Ground Company they found the company's new terms to be unacceptable. Members of the ground committee were instructed to look for alternative sites, among them the Evington Lane ground used for training. A plethora of committee meetings took place at the Clarendon Restaurant, Wyggeston School and the offices of Parsons and Co but it was not until December 1891 that the problem was resolved.

With finances ticking over happily, Leicester accepted the offer of a 10-year lease from the city corporation on land between the Welford and Aylestone Roads, close by the city centre. The lease was signed in spring 1892 and permission obtained for the ground to be "artificially levelled and drained" at a maximum cost of £200. In all £1,100 was spent in preparing an entirely new playing area, a considerable sum at the time.

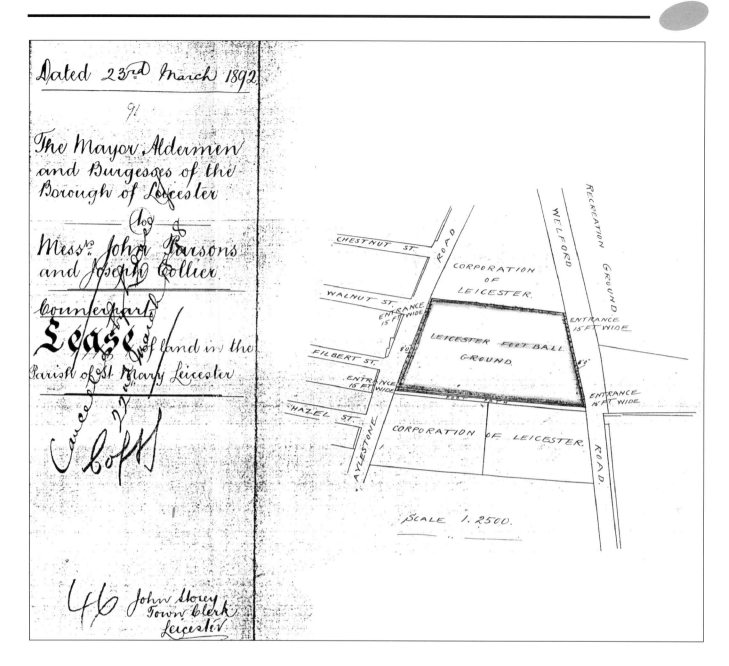

Part of the original Welford Road lease.

The club placed an advertisement in *Athletic News* to alert the public to the new arrangements, emphasising their desire to play any team of good standard and hinting at a sound financial base from gate takings of £50 a match. Indeed they were sufficiently solvent to offer Old Edwardians from Birmingham a guarantee of £50 if they came to Leicester in March 1891 (though such an offer meant admission charges doubled from sixpence to one shilling); the usual guarantee was £10 or half the gate, though the treasurer obviously worked a sliding scale depending on the opponents and whether they were touring or not. Meanwhile work on the new ground continued: tiered seating was installed and the stand erected at the Belgrave Road ground was transferred to Welford Road.

After a practice match the preceding week, the new Welford Road ground was opened on the 10th September, 1892, with a game against a Leicestershire XV. Although it was agreed that railings were needed to keep the playing area clear, the new facilities were much admired and, in keeping with the occasion, W H Sturges led

Leicester to a 17-0 victory. One hundred years later the same two teams met again, in celebration of an investment which has paid the club ample dividends.

A NEW HOME
1892-1895

THE acquisition of a new ground, of course, brought attendant administrative problems. The regular monthly committee meeting became a weekly one as autumn of 1892 turned to winter and the workload on individuals grew. The ground committee ordered the installation of fencing at Welford Road and then discovered their new commercial role: applications for perimeter advertising came flooding in and, in some trepidation, the club turned to the city estates committee, expecting to be accused of making money by illegal means. However, they were assured that advertising was entirely legitimate and, confidence growing, received an offer from Messrs Scott and Pearson to distribute an advertisement sheet including the names of the contending teams on match day - the first club programme?

Leicester being the thriving commercial centre it was and is, the committee advertised matches in the local newspapers on Fridays and Saturdays and, for 15 shillings a week, posted slips on the cars and buses of the Tramways Company. Few in the city could not be aware of the young sporting body and various requests to hire the new ground were received: the YMCA applied successfully for Easter Monday, the county rugby union played there and the Press and Panto Company as well, though what the latter body got up to history does not record.

To sustain their boast of a ground protected against frost the ground committee spent their Octobers in search of straw. At 37 shillings a ton they were authorised to spend no more than £50 while they also lashed out on a 30-foot flagpole at sevenpence a foot with a flag costing 35 shillings. Consideration was even given to floodlighting, for training purposes, but the committee baulked at the cost of 12 naphtha lamps and turned the idea down.

On the field, however, all was not entirely well. The local press complained of "reprehensible" tactics by the Lancashire club Pendleton in a 9-2 defeat ("such brutality was never intended to be introduced to our sports") while already Tigers were drawing on students from Cambridge University and occasionally faced problems when the youngsters were not available. For the home game with Moseley that season for instance, three-quarter Hugh Bryan, it was reported, "in company with his fellow collegians, had been gated for a week and so could not leave the Alma Mater." Moseley won that match by three goals and six tries to nil and there is a tolerably familiar ring to the report of the Gloucester game in which "the Westerners pushed the scrum in the easiest manner possible" and won by two goals and three tries to nil. Against Coventry, however, Leicester introduced the Reverend C H Wilkinson, late of the Leeds Parish

Church Club, and resorted to the four three-quarter system. With two more reverends, Ley and Wynne, at half back, God was on their side and they forced a draw. Incidentally the Reverend Robert George Ley was reported by *The Wyvern* newspaper to be "the "People's Idol', never known to be out of form and when he wears the scarlet, green and white jersey it adds 25% to the gate receipts!"

In the New Year came the first visitors from London, Guy's Hospital, playing the Tigers in January, 1893. The Tigers' initial visit to London had been the preceding year when they came away from Blackheath a thoroughly chastened side, beaten 37-0. Guy's were the first of four London sides in a season dominated by home games, although most opposition came from the Midlands and the north. The derby matches produced attendances up to 7,000 and club membership tickets rose to six shillings; by the end of the season F J Brett, the treasurer, was not entirely unhappy with a deficit of £476 and five shillings considering the costs of preparing the new ground.

There were rumours that this might be the last year of Midlands Cup competition, that there might soon be a Midland Counties league - this is 1893, remember - but they came to nothing. Indeed, although Cardiff Harlequins became the first Welsh club to visit Leicester and included a handful of internationals, the game of the season was the second-round Midland Counties Cup match with Coventry: the Leicester committee speculated by doubling admission charges and accumulated £220, 17 shillings and elevenpence from a gate of more than 10,000 which, unhappily, saw Leicester beaten 12-0. Extra seating, then as now, was required and

George Jones joined Leicester from Malvern in 1894. He played for the Midlands and was reckoned to have been one of the best forwards ever to have played for the club.

CHAPTER 2

THE LUCK OF THE IRISH

A nil-nil draw is a fairly rare event these days but back in January 1895 it was a reasonably frequent occurrence. So what was odd about the game against Irish champions Bective Rangers?

Well, Bobby Lewis dropped a goal for Leicester mid way through the first half, and there being no more scoring a win for the Tigers by four points to nil should have ensued. However, prior to the kick-off both captains had come to a mutual agreement that the result would be a draw, due to the frost-bound condition of the pitch.

even so the accommodation was not sufficient. Leicester ended their longest season yet with 16 wins from their 36 games.

However the work load on the club officials had increased hugely and the annual meeting in 1893 pondered whether to appoint a paid secretary at an annual salary between £20-£25 with bonuses for increased membership! At the subsequent half-yearly general meeting on September 15 (held in the Temperance Hall) members heard that J H Harcock had taken over as secretary and 250 new members had already been "elected"; there is no record of the new official's bonus. Seating accommodation was being expanded as the club pushed forward its ambitious plans, which included hosting some kind of forerunner of the divisional championship, a match between the Midlands and the Western Counties.

This season the club moved from the Bedford Hotel to the George Hotel for their headquarters - there was no clubhouse at the ground then - though they continued to change at the Bedford and trot

Edward Redman

across to the ground pursued by small boys and admiring female glances! A professional trainer was appointed to alleviate their aches and pains and he seems to have worked wonders, for they made an excellent start to the 1893-94 season. Shrewdly the season opened against a Leicestershire XV (who included in their ranks one T H Crumbie, of whom more later) and Leicester Crusaders, a recognition of local talent and useful training matches for the club before the first visit to Welford Road of Kent Wanderers; seven London teams were included on the fixture list as well as Penygraig from Wales and Bective Rangers from Dublin, the first Irish opponents.

A favourite of the crowd was the centre, W R Hesmondhalgh, known for reasons which must remain obscure as 'Clasher'; whether he was as well favoured by Mrs Hesmondhalgh is not revealed, for a few hours after their marriage at St Andrew's church on April 14, 1894, 'Clasher' was playing against Manchester Free Wanderers, helping his club to a 9-0 win rather than being locked in nuptial bliss. Such sacrifice doubtless contributed to the testimonial match which was contemplated on his behalf.

Again Tigers reached the Midlands Cup final but lost to Coventry and there were complaints from members that none of the cup ties had been at home, which had hit finances. There were also letters to the local press complaining that Tigers players had been overlooked for representative honours by the Midland Counties while the president pointed out to members how they should "keep their feelings in bound and not be led to make uncharitable remarks during the game." One committee minute unlikely to recur these days is the one which agreed to "consult Mr Field as to the probable cost of repairing Mr Akers' teeth." 'Tough' Akers was also a boxer of some repute and there is no indication of which sport he was engaged in when the damage was suffered.

These were difficult days for rugby because the Northern Union, later to become the Rugby League, had just been formed. There were circulars regarding professionalism from the Rugby Football Union and many fixtures were lost, such as Warrington and Stockton at the start of the 1895-96 season. Nevertheless, in their first seven matches Tigers scored 103 points and conceded only eight. It was not untypical of the mores of the time, however, that William Yiend, who had been capped for England while with Hartlepool Rovers, played for the club this season when he was available, once at least to the exclusion of Akers who had been pencilled in against Coventry because Yiend had said that he would not be available but turned up at the last moment looking for a game.

Some outstanding players were filtering in and out of Leicester's sides now and Edward Redman captained in 1895 a first XV which included scrum half Billy Foreman, who came to Leicester with the Kent Wanderers, was found a public house to manage and promptly stayed. The Nottinghamshire cricketer A O Jones made his debut at the end of the 1894-95 season, at full back, just in time to see Leicester pass 500 points, having conceded less than 100. The second game of that season, indeed, had been quite an occasion for it was against Burfield

Rangers, holders of the Leicestershire Senior Cup. It was intended as a warm-up for more serious affairs and at the end of it Tigers ran out winners by 71-0, for many years their record score, though equalled against a Bedford XV during the 1918-19 season. To be fair, the local press could only make it 69-0, a conversion having gone astray somewhere in a match when 17 tries were scored. The referee made it 71 though and his word was law - as that official pointed out afterwards, there wasn't really any doubt who had won!

It had been a tremendous season, tempered only by the failure to win the Midlands Cup, Tigers going down to Moseley in the semi-finals. Off the field Leicester had grown in stature too, helping to form the Leicester Schools League and establishing a midweek team, the Leicester Thursday, for players unavailable at the weekend. The schools league arose as the result of a letter published locally from an enthusiastic member, F St Clair Pain, of Forest House in Clarendon Park, who called for an annual dinner and the introduction of "a cup to be presented among the public elementary schools, the final to be played at the ground." After appropriate debate Leicester agreed to guarantee £25 towards the cost of forming a schools league and two club members, W A Wheeler and A Jackson, were appointed to the organising committee. It was only the first of several significant alliances with the youth of the city and the club.

The organisation for the team and supporters to away games was remarkable: the club booked trains with the Midland Rail Company, the North-Western, the Midland and Great Northern Railway and the South and NW line to games at Rugby, Coventry, Northampton and Nuneaton respectively, though kick-off times tended to fluctuate depending on arrival of the trains. The club even issued free rail passes to away games for the local rugby writers - well, it is never a bad thing to have the press on your side. Moreover the welfare of the players was looked after by an insurance policy against injury while training or playing. The policy permitted the payment of twenty shillings a week to an injured player but no more than £10 for any one accident. In due course the (inaptly named for Leicester) Ocean Insurance Company insured the club's three teams for an annual premium of £25, though since it was raised by 50 per cent the following year there would seem to have been rather too many claims.

Public relations were uppermost in the committee's minds too: various local associations were allowed to hire the ground while the Friar Lane Sunday School's annual children's treat went ahead free of charge. All these activities served to reduce the debt on the ground, if only by £64, but since spending amounted to a further £1,600 the bank clearly had faith in the club as a going concern.

A newcomer to the team, from Richmond, had been F A Jackson, reputedly one of the fastest wingers in the Midlands. Looking back on those days 60 years later, Frank Jackson said: "There was a lot more scrummaging and to my way of thinking it was a more skilful part of the game than it is now. Scrums lasted longer but although this made play rather dull for the spectators it was far more interesting for the players [heaven knows what Frank would have made of the 1992 law changes].

"I remember how Leicester were the first club to spread sand on the pitch during frosty weather. The sand was used so that a match against Coventry should not be cancelled because a large gate was expected. One of the Tigers' officials, Tom Pettifor, promised me a new hat if I scored a try. I scored the try alright but I never got the hat!"

T W Pettifor had succeeded J Wykes as secretary, after Mr Salmon had resigned through pressure of business, but another appointment was in the offing. Thomas Henry Crumbie had played for Leicester Swifts and for Tigers' 'A' side, (plus three games for the First XV) and had also been the 'A' team secretary before he became Leicester's secretary on August 2, 1895, at the age of 27. He was to occupy that post for the next 33 years and his influence on the club's fortunes went far beyond that.

"Seven members of the club playing for the Midlands in 1894-95."

Back (Standing):
W.F. Lincoln, *A. Henshaw,*
G. Jones, *J.J. Robinson,*
W. Adams, R.S. Millward,
E. Redman, F.A. Jackson,
W.R. Hesmondhalgh.
Seated:
F.A. Byrne, F.R. Loveitt,
R.H. Cattell, J.F. Byrne (Capt),
W. Jackson, W.J. Foreman.

THE CRUMBIE ERA
1895-1914

IT would be difficult to overstate Tom Crumbie's contribution to rugby in the city and county. He had his own printing and stationery business in Leicester's Halford Street and much of the money he made there - as well as the duties of the staff - must have been directed at Welford Road. He was a man whose sole purpose in life would appear to have been the welfare and prestige of the Leicester Football Club; many criticisms could be, and were, levelled at him, that he was dictatorial, that he ignored local talent, but nobody could ever doubt the impact he made.

He regarded the players as part of his family - "my boys", he called them - and nothing was too much for them. In return he expected certain standards and he inspired immense loyalty in those who worked for him and played for him. It was his practice to call individual players into his reserved compartment on the train to away games to have a little talk to them before the game. But his demands for discipline had to be met: travelling to play in the West Country he ordered a bottle of beer for every player but when he heard that one player had asked for a second he found out who it was, gave him the return half of his ticket to Leicester, and put him off the train at Birmingham (having ensured initially that he had a reserve travelling).

A teetotaller himself, he was also a diabetic but he seldom let ill-health get on top of him. He was accustomed to running the line for his club and continued to do so well into the 1920s, even when his eyes were beginning to fail. His kindness and entertainment of his own players, referees and guests of the club, combined with his flair for organisation, made him in many ways the perfect secretary-manager, a title which betrayed his professional approach to his job, even if it was never bestowed on him during his life.

It was Crumbie who dragged Tigers into national prominence, by discontinuing the 'B' team during the 1890s and the 'A' team in 1905, making Leicester an invitation club and introducing players into the side from all over the country. It was a policy which did not make for consistency since frequently teams playing away went without the "stars" who only made the trip to Welford Road for home games. But it ensured that the Leicester public saw, as near as possible, the best rugby on offer in the country and explained why the club had gates of anything from 6,000 upwards every Saturday. During the Crumbie era, over 30 players from the club were capped and Leicester came to dominate the Midland scene.

In his initial season Crumbie had fertile ground in which to work and his secretaryship happened to coincide with the beginning of the senior career of one Sid Penny, whose name occupies an honoured place in the club's history. Penny had played for the local club, St Peter's, and for Leicester 'A' before making his debut early in 1896: his first class career did not end until 14 years later, after 491 first-team appearances for Tigers and caps for the Midland Counties and England. His number of games for Leicester has been passed by only one other player,

David Matthews, who recorded his 502nd game in 1974.

Penny was also the first in a long and distinguished line of Leicester hookers. Whatever else the club may have lacked at any time, it has seldom lacked a first-class hooker, and the likes of George Ward, Doug Norman, E S Nicholson, and Peter Wheeler have all followed Penny into England's national side.

After reaching what was thought at the time to be 500 games for the first-team, Leicester gave Penny a special dinner in honour of his achievement, at the Leicester Constitutional Club, on December 29, 1910. It was the evening following the Barbarians game, so there was a notable gathering to see the club's president, James Collier, present the player with a magnificent inscribed picture and describe how invaluable Penny had been to the club: "He seems good enough for another quarter of a century," said the president, to which the modest Sidney replied that, pleased though he was to be there, he would rather have been pushing in the scrum.

Penny was asked to go to Australia and New Zealand with the Anglo-Welsh party of 1908 but he was playing in the days when touring overseas was the good fortune of the monied gentry. An employee in the shoe trade, there was never any prospect of him being able to accept the invitation, and there were doubts in his family at one time that he would be able to play for England against Australia in 1909 - his best suit was not fit for travel. He made the game, however, and though he won no more caps, there can have been few honours so genuinely earned.

In his first full season, injuries and unavailability militated against Leicester and even the climate came in for blame: against Gloucester it struck a local reporter as more like the tropics with a quoted temperature of 112 degrees - which made it pretty hot. "In spite of the great heat and in the consequent terrible perspiration it caused players, the game was fast and vigorously fought from start to finish", the story ran. Brave boys. Two months later heavy showers on the day before the game with Northampton meant Leicester did not have to call upon the Fire Brigade to water the ground!

There was huge local mirth at the demise of Rugby (who, the season before, had declined to play on what they described as sand). Some 7,000 spectators saw Rugby collapse in the second half to a 33-0 defeat, though the return in the new year was far harder, a 3-0 win to Leicester. There were a couple of notable wins, by 44 points in successive matches, over Bridgwater Albion and St Bartholomew's Hospital, Jackson scoring three tries in the first game and six in the second. As the Midlands Cup approached there was a sardonic reference in *The Leicester Mercury*: "So far as we have been able to ascertain the cup is, at the time, really in existence, having escaped the perils which appear to surround trophies of this kind when they are lodged for a brief period in the city of Birmingham." (an obvious allusion to the loss of soccer's FA Cup.) There was ill-feeling at that time between the club and Moseley, who had broken off fixtures, and between the club and the Midland Counties committee, who had hinted at professionalism on Leicester's part over the transfer of the full back, A C Butlin, from Rugby to Leicester, though a Rugby Football Union hearing

completely cleared Leicester and laid any blame for mismanagement at the Midlands' door (a subsequent letter to the Mercury suggested it was high time Leicester seceded from the Midland Counties Rugby Union and "threw in their lot with the Northern Union, which would furnish a greater attraction and better football for their supporters.").

Ironically enough, it was Moseley who dispatched Leicester from the cup competition in the third round, by a penalty to nil at The Reddings. It was a grave disappointment but there was still the end-of-season tour to the West Country to come. *The Leicester Mercury* waxed lyrical about the train journey from Leicester to Devonport: "The attractive scenery en route, the passing glimpses of the Malverns, the picturesque heights and bosky slopes of Devon all aroused admiration - as also did the appetising luncheon baskets provided for the team by the kindly forethought of the committee." Devonport Albion spoiled the Sunday School atmosphere by beating them 11-3 but there was little time to speculate on what might have been; trips had been organised for the players, visits to the dockyards, tours of warships, steamboat trips up the Tamar among a fleet of ironclads and torpedo boats. Buoyed up by this martial spirit, the lads gallantly beat Bridgwater Albion the next day, by 3-0.

Things were moving in the right direction, though. In 1897, after strictures from the Midland Counties who said Leicester's pitch would not be used for cup ties unless the surface was relaid, the ground was returfed; not, one imagines, without regret, for the sandy surface had permitted Leicester to play when other clubs were forced by frost to cancel. The following year the 'B' team was discontinued but by then Tigers had ensured their best playing season to date, culminating in their triumph in the Midland Cup for the first time. The captain in 1897-98 was A O Jones, who distinguished himself by playing centre, full back and scrum half before New Year and then leading his team to wins over Rugby (31-0), Burton (17-0), Coventry (12-5) and, in the cup final, Moseley, whom they beat 5-3 at Coventry. Unfortunately a change of dates forced Jones to miss the final when the team was: A C Butlin; H Wilkinson, P W Oscroft, H P Atkins, F H Jones; W J Foreman, J Braithwaite; E Redman, R N Campbell, A Akers, J W Garner, S H Penny, G H Keeton, M E Whitehead, W Jackson.

The only try of the final came from the centre, Oscroft, with Frank Jones, younger brother of A O, converting. Fred Byrne kicked a penalty for Moseley but after three near misses Tigers had brought home the bacon. Thousands lined the streets between Leicester station and the George Hotel as the Highfield brass band led the team from the station playing "See the conquering heroes come". There were speeches and receptions before the inevitable comeuppance, when they rashly toured in Wales and lost to Swansea and Llanelly (before the days when the 'y' became an 'i'). Nevertheless it was the start of a marvellous run in the Midlands Cup, which Leicester retained for the next eight years.

It is surprising how frequently the club undertook short tours in those days, to South Wales, the West Country and the North. The 1898-99 season saw them start with eight home games - always good for morale - and the playing surface "under the influence of scythe and roller was in first-class condition and looked not unlike a cricket pitch. All vestiges of sand had disappeared and the ground lost its erstwhile seaside appearance." The first tour that season was to Wales in November, the team and a few supporters leaving Leicester at 5.28 on a Friday evening and reaching Swansea soon after midnight. Despite what was described as "a strict training lunch" they lost 20-0 at St Helen's, but took comfort in a 5-3 win over Treherbert the next day.

After the usual heavy Christmas programme - never less than three games in four days and soon to become four in five - the second tour was to Devonport Albion (lost 10-7) and Exeter (won 3-0) before retaining the Midlands Cup with a 20-3 win over Nuneaton.

The turn of the century brought new honours as Leicester's name, and their facilities after the expenditure of a further £1,300, drew national attention. An estimated 12,000 watched the 4-0 win over Northampton, "inspired by the Highfield Band," as one report put it, and there was a successful campaign for the Midland Counties Cup: the game against Old Edwardians was remembered with little affection after injuries to 12 players, including a twisted knee for F A Jackson which ended his season. The final (at Coventry) brought a 13-4 win over Moseley, those deadly rivals, and the Highfields Band met the team's train when it returned and played them back to the George Hotel in triumph.

There must have been a disappointed response from the crowd which arrived to watch the November match with Swansea in 1901 when, after Mr.Ashton the referee had declared the ground playable, the Swansea captain refused to play because it was too hard but compensation was at hand: Leicester went to Kingsholm and beat Gloucester 3-0, the first team to win there for three seasons, while on February 8, 1902, the Welford Road ground was honoured with an international, England beating Ireland 6-3. There were no Leicester players involved but a crowd of around 14,000 watched - among them the correspondent of *The Athletic News*, who complained; "I don't know what kind of thin people write for the Press in Leicester but if the authorities had measured a local scribe and found he measured only 13 inches across the bust, it is time that journalist took a course of Mellin's food." If Mellin's food was

IN MEMORY OF THE
DEATH OF MOSELEY.

Poor old MOSELEY, your chances are blighted !
Like your followers, you could not keep cool ;
And now they are dead, it may truly be said—
The CUP will go to the good old TIGERS.

"LOST! BUT NOT FORGOTTON."

Satirical postcard reflecting The Tigers first Cup win over Moseley.

to journalists what spinach was to Popeye, then the result must have been noted for it was not long before the Press box at the ground became a degree more commodious.

Membership by now had reached 1,200 and the experiment of granting season tickets to the cheap sides of the ground at a nominal cost of three shillings increased receipts from £15 to £60. Relationships with Moseley improved to the extent that, in the 1902-3 season, "friendly" fixtures were resumed after a gap of eight years though there may have been subtle irony in the granting of the proceeds (over £194) from the second match to the Leicester Infirmary! Nor was friendly the word used to describe the match with Llanelly (before a crowd of 11,000 with gate receipts of £122): "Certain of Llanelly's players included foul and off-side play...and the Welshmen can consider themselves lucky that penalty goals are not added to Tigers' score of 15-3," wrote the local scribe censoriously.

John Miles became the first home-produced international from the club when he played on the wing against Wales in 1903 (he went to Medway Street School and played for Medway Athletic and Stoneygate before joining Leicester) but there were complaints at the start of the following season when four of the first five games were lost: "The heavy fixture list of the club will not permit neglect of training and without training, proficiency cannot be attained," stormed *The Leicester Daily Post*.

Injuries and absentees did not help the cause though things were not quite as bad as they seemed the day a full back, W Gale, played twice for the club. Having distinguished himself for Leicester 'A' on Victoria Park one Saturday morning, he turned out against Treherbert in the afternoon when A O Jones missed his rail connection over the Christmas period. He can't have done too badly because Leicester won 18-3, assisted also by the Cardiff international centre 'Pussy' Jones who happened to be on holiday in Leicester at the time. So taken was Jones with the Leicester organisation that he even toured with them to Hartlepool a few days later.

The local press made a pertinent point, too, after the match with Bristol when the timekeeping of the referee became an issue: during the first half no more than 31 minutes were played, according to unofficial clock watchers who were expecting two 35-minute halves. However the second half lasted 42 minutes the assumption being that, allowing for an injury to Miles, the referee was making up for the earlier deficiency. A voice from the stand cried out: "It will be morning soon," and the reporter observed how strange it was that people who paid to see a game so often wanted the end to be signalled.

The club retained the Midlands Cup for the seventh consecutive year, beating Moseley 13-3 but their overall record in 1904 was indifferent. The following year, however, came one of those major

events that happen now and again in every sport - the tour of Dave Gallaher's New Zealanders. In 1904 one of the club's forwards, George Keeton, a former Oakham School student, had been capped against the three other home countries by England but he was missing when Leicester took on the All Blacks in the fifth match of the tour, the New Zealanders having scored 55, 41, 41 and 32 points in their previous four games.

They had taken a rather complacent country by storm and they did the same to Leicester, winning 28-0 on September 30 before 16,000 people - a gate which produced £392 of which 70 per cent was said to have gone to the visitors. Interesting, is it not, to see how touring teams subsisted in those days. Leicester's team, the first time they had met a touring side, was: A O Jones; A O Parsons, N McFarlane, J W Bainbridge, A E Hind; B Hills, J Braithwaite; S Matthews (captain), S H Penny, T Goodrich, A Goodrich, R F Russell, F S Jackson, D B Atkins; H P Atkins. The Tigers, unbeaten before the game, held the tourists for half an hour before G W Smith scored the first of six tries. W J Wallace, H L Abbott, G A Tyler, H J Mynott and G W Nicholson scored the others, Wallace converting five times. The club XV was clearly outclassed and there was some objection - as there was all through the tour - of Gallaher's role as a "rover". But at the reception after the match Gallaher paid tribute to Leicester: "When we were down south we were told that when we got to Leicester we should know about it. Well, we do know about it. You gave us one of the hardest games I have ever played in."

He may have been in a generous mood but the remark was at least indicative of Leicester's standing in England and that season four Tigers were capped by England: half-back Jacky Braithwaite, three-quarter Ernest Hind, full back John Jackett and forward Richard Russell played against New Zealand (for Braithwaite and Russell it was their only cap) and forward Alfred Kewney (then with Rockcliff) won the first of 16 caps against Scotland. A month after playing the club, the All Blacks returned to Welford Road to play a Midland Counties XV containing seven Tigers. At that stage the tourists had scored 429 points and conceded 10,

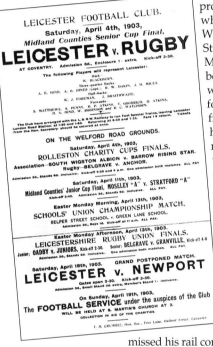

so the Midlands did well to hold them to 21-5, Russell scoring the Midland try.

It was not the last the club were to see of some of the New Zealanders (the international apart). On January 13 they lost 20-0 at Gloucester who fielded three New Zealanders (two of them, Mynott and McGregor, were responsible for all the Gloucester tries). Apparently the touring side had offered to help Leicester out, but even though they had only five regulars, the offer was not taken up. In 1906, Jackett was in the England side beaten 16-6 by Ireland at Leicester and as the season neared its end there was dissent in the camp, as Hind, then vice captain and scorer of 37 tries in 1902-03, left to play for Nottingham and there was criticism of the club's

failure to raise strong sides for away fixtures. In addition, the proud Midlands Cup run ended because the Tigers had opted out of the competition, to give someone else a chance.

During the season various clubs, among them Leicester, had experimented with the New Zealand style of play, packing seven forwards, but without conspicuous success. Against Devonport Albion, in a 3-3 draw, Leicester packed down with a 2-3-2 scrum formation and H P Atkins at "wing forward". The following season, 1906-07, Leicester met Hartlepool Rovers in the first game and both clubs imitated the New Zealanders, playing three three-quarters, two five-eighths, a scrum half and a rover. It was not a happy experiment and in October Tigers reverted to four three-quarters, two half backs and eight forwards against Richmond. They won 11-0 and it was, according to *The Leicester Mercury*, "a triumph for the old style of play."

Meanwhile another touring side was in Britain, the first South African visitors, captained by Paul Roos. They visited Welford Road on September 29 and beat a Midland Counties XV containing seven Tigers by 29-0, not so much because of any innovative style of play but by sheer athleticism. The

Leicester players in that match were Bainbridge, Braithwaite, Russell, Penny, Matthews, Alf Goodrich, and Percy Atkins, a crowd of between 13 and 14,000 producing a gate of £500. Russell was captain of Leicester that season and, in an age when specialisation had reached only a short distance into rugby, he left his usual place in the pack to play on the wing for a few games, such was the injury situation around Christmas.

Leicester v West Hartlepool at Welford Road, 15th September, 1906.

It was not a vintage season, with bad weather forcing seven cancellations including the Christmas tour of the north but a promising scrum-half emerged in George Wood, known as 'Pedlar', in succession to Braithwaite. An interesting statistic from the season was the number of penalties kicked, which aggregated seven. This was not untypical. When you remember that four or five penalties in one match is not uncommon today it speaks volumes for the players' control and knowledge of the laws, or suggests that there were few outstanding placekickers. The latter explanation is possibly the more credible, for there seems to have been several Leicester players who had their chance as goalkickers - moreover, the drop kick may still have been regarded as more worthy of attention, particularly as it was worth four points.

At the start of 1907-08 another young player emerged from that rugby nursery in Leicester, Medway Street School. Then 19, Frederick 'Tim' Taylor formed a long and profitable half-back combination with 'Pedlar' Wood which culminated in their both winning caps in 1914, against Wales. It was the second outstanding half-back pairing the club had produced, following Braithwaite and

Leicester v Nottingham at Coventry in the Midland Counties Cup Final, 1st April 1905.

Tom Smith in lineout action during 1907.

and F S Jackson had been obtained by Leicester in violation of the laws regarding professionalism.

It was not the first time allegations of veiled professionalism had been levelled at Leicester, though it is not clear who were responsible for bringing the charges. The names of two members of the RFU's committee, Messrs Byrne and Adams, were apparently connected with this latest allegation at a time when the President of the Union, Arnold Crane - who represented the Midlands - was desperate to ensure that the game preserved an amateurism of unashamed virginity. He was at odds with many members of his executive committee during his second year of office and, indeed, resigned after a sub-committee had completed its inquiries into the management of the Leicester club.

Smith and Jackson had not yet returned from New Zealand before they were suspended by the RFU, along with Leicester's captain, Matthews, following inquiries into "breaches of the professional laws". Matthews' offence was said to have been committed nine years before when, in 1897, he had signed a form for Hull but never committed himself to playing for them. At the time he had received out-of-pocket expenses of £1, but it was claimed that what he had done did not infringe the rules regarding professionalism as they then stood. At a meeting of the Rugby Football Union on October 5, Smith, Jackson, Matthews and F W Hardiman were all declared professionals and an inquiry was ordered into the affairs of the Leicester club.

Foreman, and it was by no means the last. Neither player was very big - Taylor in particular was very slight while Wood was short but stocky - but they soon became favourites with the Leicester crowd.

These were hard times though. "Leicester on the down grade" said one newspaper headline which was as near to screaming blue murder as newspapers allowed then. Against Oxford University "too many of the men...showed the white feather and absolutely refused to go down to a ball to stop the rushes of the opposition." Tigers lost 27-6, suffered a poor tour to the West Country and were then drubbed on their own pitch by London Scottish 39-0. The tide turned over Christmas with a win over Coventry - always good for a celebration - and at the season's end, E J Jackett, F S Jackson and T W Smith were invited to tour New Zealand and Australia with the Anglo-Welsh party, the first Leicester players to go abroad with a major touring side, although Hind had been to South Africa with Mark Morrison's team in 1903 while he was still at Cambridge University.

Predictably, strong words were uttered in the local press and there were suggestions that another split - such as the one 15 years before when the Northern Union was formed - was imminent.

T C Pring, A Hartley and F Hugh Fox, all of whom had either been or became presidents of the RFU, were appointed to conduct the inquiry. As the season wore on, it transpired that Hardiman and Jackson - recalled by the RFU midway through the tour - had indeed gone north, and that Smith had been approached in Queenstown on the way home from the tour and later signed for Broughton Rangers. The unlucky Matthews remained the victim of an indiscretion committed nearly a decade before.

It was Leicester's contention, however, that all these individuals had formed connections with the Northern Union without giving the Leicester club any indication of the fact. It has been said too, on good authority, that Jackson's name was in fact Gabe, that he was Welsh, and that he had played for the Northern Union for three years before coming south. Despite these smears, Leicester still found their players picked for England and in January, 1909, France were due to play England at Leicester.

The concluding phase of the RFU inquiry was held at Leicester's Grand Hotel on January 14-15, 1909, and a fortnight later came an eventful day, both for the club and the union. On the morning of the

Tom Smith, F.S. Jackson and John Jackett, Leicester's first tourists to Australasia and New Zealand in 1908.

The troubles of one season, however, were as nothing when compared with the troubles of 1908-09. Professionalism was still a very sore point with the Rugby Football Union and in October, 1908, the RFU had before them a motion that Leicester should be expelled from the union, for just that offence. It was suggested that T W Smith, F S Jackson and S Matthews had played for the club either after signing forms for the Northern Union or receiving money from the same direction, and that the services of A L Kewney, T B Hogarth, E J Jackett,

England-France game the RFU general committee met at the Grand and their sub-committee issued a complete vindication of Leicester with the following statement:

"With regard to the first charge (against Smith, Matthews and Jackson) your committee could obtain no evidence of this, and consequently dismissed the charge. With regard to the second charge (against Kewney and the other three players), after hearing the evidence of Kewney, Hogarth, Jackett and others, your committee was quite satisfied that there had been no breach of the professional laws. They were much struck with the way evidence was given, especially that by Kewney and Hogarth, whose sincerity it was impossible to doubt, and whose presence in the ranks of the Leicester club was quite satisfactorily accounted for.

"Various doubtful items on the accounts, especially relating to travelling expenses, were satisfactorily explained and your committee endorses the findings of the previous committee on this head.

"Your committee is strongly of the opinion that the allegations against the Leicester club are largely due to the fact that the club, having a strong team with a good match list, attracts players who are unable to get such good football in other localities, but that, however undesirable this may be, the players have not benefited pecuniarily thereby."

It was a more than satisfactory conclusion for Leicester, whose anxious committee must have adjourned in high spirits to Welford Road where they watched England beat France 22-0. For, despite the worries the inquiry must have caused, the playing side of the club's affairs had gone well. They had acquired Hogarth from Hartlepool Rovers at the start of the season - he had travelled down with the Rovers for the opening game at Welford Road but to play in Leicester's pack - and another useful newcomer was a young prop, W G 'Gil' Hopkins, whose hard training and enthusiastic play quickly earned him plaudits.

The Australians were touring (at the end of the season a dozen of them were banned from Rugby Union for having played for the Kangaroos who were touring the Northern Union clubs at much the same time) and when they came to Welford Road the Midlands beat them 16-5. Kenneth Wood, a centre who got very near a cap, played from Leicester and scored the game's first try, and with him were clubmates Sid Penny and A J Hobbs. Penny and Kewney were picked by England against the Australians. Kewney was retained for the France match and was joined by Jackett and Frank Tarr, then at Oxford University.

And, as if to refute suggestions that Leicester's teams were made up entirely of imported talent, there were 12 local players in the team which beat Coventry in the Midlands Cup Final, the outsiders being Jackett (who went to Northern Union club Dewsbury in 1911), Hobbs and Hogarth. The season ended with an important decision: to spend £1,150 on a new clubhouse, and the work was done so quickly that the new building was opened on September 4, 1909, before the first game of that season, against Stratford. Strengthening Leicester's claims to an above board reputation was the fact that the opening ceremony was performed by George Rowland Hill, a former president of the Rugby Union and still generally regarded as one of the most influential men to hold that office. The same year Leicester reverted to the colours which they had worn before and which they still wear today.

'Gil' Hopkins had made his debut in 1908, thanks to the vacancies left by the trio of banned forwards. At much the same time a young winger from Wyggeston School and Stoneygate, Percy Lawrie, was making himself noticed and he was to become Hopkins' brother-in-law. Seventy years on, Hopkins recalled some of the personalities of his era and the spirit which existed in the club: "Percy was one of the finest wingers I've ever seen," Hopkins said, comparing Lawrie with the powerfully-built New Zealander of the 1970s, Bryan Williams, who subsequently became coach to Auckland and then the Western Samoan World Cup squad. "Percy was almost the spitting image of Williams, build and everything. Tarr was a lovely player and as for the forwards, well, it will give you an idea what they were like when you think that in 1913, when the Midland Counties won the championship, there were 10 Leicester players in the side and five of the club's forwards went for an England trial.

*One of Gil Hopkins'
most memorable games.*

8 POINTS ALL.
LEICESTER v CARDIFF
AT CARDIFF ARMS PARK
SATURDAY, APRIL 10TH 1909.

"Tim Taylor and Pedlar Wood, I reckon, were the best pair of halves in the country, in their day and, compared with some of today's teams, our three-quarters seemed to go more smoothly. There's too much kicking today [a remark passed in 1979 though it might still apply]. When I was playing the club always played 15-man rugby although I remember one game down at Swansea when Wood, who had an enormous swing, went to pass the ball one way, the whole of the Swansea back division went the same way and he went round the other side and scored under the posts. I've never seen a lot of fellows look so silly. He was a crafty devil. But then, in my day there was none of this tapping at a lineout, you had to catch the ball and there was old Pedlar waiting for it.

"And we had a lot of fun among ourselves, on the train when we went on tour. One time when we were in Swansea - you know how popular laver bread is down there - well, we got some of this black stuff and put it in some of the beds. There was one hotel in Plymouth where we were barred. It had one of these open staircases and Coventry had been there before us, chucking a lot of bedding down the stairs, so we had to go to the Albion instead. It was in the West Country and Wales though we had our hardest games - we always used to get the ball when we played London sides. Once [March 1912] against the Harlequins, we were getting loads of ball and the referee, from London, kept penalising us, so Adrian Stoop (the Harlequins captain) went up to his player who was taking the free kicks and told him to put it directly into touch, not to gain any advantage.

"At half-time Stoop went across to Mr Crumbie who was standing on the touchline and told him that if he wanted to take the whistle, there would be no objection from Harlequins. Stoop, of course, was an exceptionally fine player and a gentleman. I think that it was this same match that the referee sent Harry Lawrie (Percy's brother who played in the pack) off and no-one knew what it was for so Stoop sent off one of his own men, J V Rees, to level things up. (What is more, Stoop afterwards went and explained to the Press exactly what had occurred and why.)

"In Wales we expected the referees to be against us. At Neath we slammed in a couple of tries in a very few minutes and the crowd came storming onto the ground, shaking their fists at the referee and of course he was intimidated. We seldom came away from Wales with the spoils, though we drew with Cardiff on two occasions.

"In my time it was a fairly local side. We trained Tuesdays and Thursdays and during the four years before the war we were about the best English side, without a doubt. When we played Moseley it was a certain win, and it was much the same against Coventry and Northampton." Hopkins was only 20 when he played in the club's first match with the Barbarians: "We won three of the five games I played against the Baa-baas, one was drawn and we lost the other by a conversion. I always admired the Baa-baas' style because they played the open game

but it's team spirit that wins matches and that's what we had. There was very little dirty play and I remember Tom Crumbie saying once to Sid Penny after he'd seen him hit someone on the field: "As many games as you've played for Leicester, if you do that again you'll never play another one".

"We played clean football. If you play dirty football, you're not playing football at all. There was a marvellous atmosphere at the club. There was one occasion when we'd lost unexpectedly to Headingley and the next time we played them we were determined to win. On the train north I was talking to Pedlar Wood and I said we should throw the ball around. We won that game 32-6. I've seen so many international games when the players kicked so much you couldn't have called it a handling code."

That first game with the Barbarians, drawn 9-9, marked the beginning of a proud relationship which Leicester have treasured down the years as the only club side to have a regular fixture with the famous nomadic team in England. It began because the previous season a regular fixture with Fettes-Lorettonians had fallen through and the Barbarians were invited to take up the vacant date in Tigers' Christmas rugby festival. That 1909 Christmas the club had beaten Cinderford, Birkenhead Park and Penarth before the Barbarians arrived on December 28 and two late tries by Pedlar Wood and George Greasley, with an earlier effort from Burdett, produced the draw. The game was refereed by A O Jones, who also officiated at the next four games: it is not recorded whether there were complaints about the referee being a "homer".

Conditions for the game were very poor, nevertheless both teams contrived to play a match which was a credit to Mr Crumbie's men and to the guest XV led by W C Wilson, at that time an officer in the Leicestershire Regiment who had played for Tigers and whose relationship with the club and with the Barbarians no doubt helped to bring the game about. Leicester's team for the game was: L D Ellwood; J Dickens, K B Wood, J W D Smith, E J Jackett; J R Watson (captain), G W Wood; T B Hogarth, J C Burdett, S H Penny, G Greasley, W G Hopkins, W J Allen, C Gimson, W S Ellis.

In 1910 Percy Lawrie got the first of his two caps, against Scotland, and there were many in Leicester who said he deserved more. Another honour for the club was the selection of Kenneth Wood to go to South Africa with the British touring side, his club's only representative on tour.

At the end of the year came Sid Penny's proud moment when, on December 26, he played what was reported at the time to be his 500th game for the club against Birkenhead Park. Another veteran, A O Jones, made a brief comeback in the same game and Penny was chaired off after the club's 25-5 win. That year the Barbarians were dismissed 29-3, giving the Tigers an aggregate of 106 points against 16 in their four Christmas games. Two days later they went on tour and lost to Headingley and Hartlepool Rovers before beating Manchester - seven matches in ten days!

Pedlar Wood finished the season with 15 tries, exactly the same number he had scored in the previous season, but Tigers lost the Midlands Cup. They had re-entered the competition two years

before and beat Coventry 8-3 in the final. They beat Coventry 8-6 in 1910 but lapsed in 1911 before resuming their winning ways in 1912, beating Coventry 16-0 after a competition in which they had beaten Newbold-on-Avon in the semi-final by 65-0. Four of their 17 tries in that match - all tries, mark you, no penalties or dropped goals - went to Percy Lawrie and three each to Tim Taylor, O J Hargrave and Harry Lawrie.

To the delight of all their supporters, the club began the 1912-13 season with eight wins (seven of them at home), including the scalps of Bridgend, Neath, Aberavon, Newport and Llanelly. But it was to a Welsh club that their unbeaten record fell when they lost 26-13 at Swansea. This was the season of the second Springbok touring team, captained by Billy Millar, and they played a Midland Counties XV at Leicester on November 9, eleven Tigers turning out on their home ground: P W Lawrie, F N Tarr, S A Hunter, G W Wood, F M Taylor, H S B Lawrie, W J Allen, W G Hopkins, G Greasley, W A Dalby and G Ward. The Midlands, beaten up front, lost 25-3, Dalby getting the try in a game marked by fireworks during the interval and great interest in the filming of proceedings. But Leicester's first home defeat did not come until January 4, 1913, when Gloucester won 13-8; it was Leicester's sixth game in 10 days.

Whatever Tigers' reputation in other respects at this time they were certainly popular with the fair sex. A local writer was moved to comment: "There is one most striking characteristic of the Leicester club. More ladies attend the Leicester matches than is the case in any other centre - either rugby or association - in the kingdom. The presence of the ladies tends to maintain a high tone and not only in the club itself but amongst the spectators generally." No doubt the author had toured every football ground in the country to pronounce with such authority: he does not say whether the club were chivalrous enough to extend a welcome to the ladies after the game.

George Ward and Frank Tarr were in the England side that season but Ward, the former Belgrave forward, after winning three caps, opted not to represent his country against Ireland in Dublin on the grounds that international rugby did not appeal to him. Happily the selectors forgave him the slight and he won three more caps in 1914, continuing to play rugby after the war until he was past 40. For the first time in the Midlands Cup competition two clubs from the same town contested the final when Leicester played Belgrave Premier Works at Welford Road. Belgrave had beaten Syston Street OB, Rugby and Newbold in a superb season but predictably they suffered a beating in the final by 39-8. It was Leicester's 12th win in 16 years.

This season won Leicester the reputation of champion club in England but in 1913-14 they lost their third game 8-3, when Pontypool paid their first visit to Leicester. They subsequently paid the penalty of success by losing players to international trials, which affected their performance, although they lost by only 3-0 against Gloucester with 10 regulars missing. Seven of the 10 played in the England v The Rest game and Ward, Tim Taylor and Pedlar Wood played against Wales - the only time the outstanding half-back pair were capped.

The Baa-baas game was postponed, because of bad weather, to February but the club's list was evidently still crowded for, in their fourth game in nine days, they went down to the guest side by 5-3. Yet they could claim a moral victory, for they provided the Barbarians with two late replacements, Harry Lawrie and Steve Farmer, and it was Farmer, formerly of Aylestone St James, who scored the Baa-baas' try. Surprisingly Leicester went out of the Midlands Cup in round two, beaten by Coventry, and the season ended poorly, Pedlar Wood being sent off in the last game (for "wrong scrum tactics"; persistent infringement?) as his club lost for the first time to Birkenhead Park.

Before the First World War brought rugby to a halt, however, there was time for the reconstruction of the Members' Stand, which had been moved in 1899 (when the ground could accommodate 19,800, over 3,000 seated). It was the beginning of the ground as it looks today, for two years after the war ended, the New - later the Crumbie - Stand was opened by the then president of the Rugby Union, Ernest Prescott. Already four internationals had been played there, England v Ireland (1902 and 1906), England v Wales (1904) and England v France (1909) as well as numerous schools internationals. There was to be one more major international there, in 1923, when England beat Ireland 23-5, before the prolonged gap to 1991 when the World Cup brought New Zealand and Italy as welcome visitors to Welford Road.

CHAPTER 4

THE WAR AND GLORY YEARS 1914-1923

THE OUTBREAK of the First World War in August, 1914, brought another upsurge of activity at Welford Road, whose objective was purely military. Rugby activities ceased, many of the players joined up, and Tom Crumbie turned his attention to raising as many men as possible for active service. The club premises were loaned for army and auxiliary purposes and formed the headquarters for two artillery units and a pioneer corps. It was not difficult to imagine Crumbie overseeing recruitment in much the same way he oversaw the rugby club - and conceivably exercising similar authority - and all told 3,500 officers and men joined the colours as testimony to his efforts.

Not all of them came back in 1918. When the Armistice was signed in November of that year, several Tigers had lost their lives, including that outstanding centre, Frank Tarr. Several more had been injured but recovered to help Leicester to an outstanding decade. It seems incredible but only six weeks after the guns had finally ceased on the Continent, a Leicester XV - and a good Leicester XV - was in action again at Welford Road.

The reconstructed Members' Stand, completed before war broke out, was officially opened over Christmas, 1918, and on Boxing Day Percy Lawrie led out Tigers for their first game in three and a half years, against the 4th battalion of the Leicestershire Regiment. George Ward, A G Bull and Pedlar Wood, all of whom had made their names before the war, were there to help Leicester to a 6-5 win over the service unit, Lawrie scoring two tries before a crowd of 4,000.

Also on call at that time were two men destined to make lasting names for themselves, H L V Day and Frank 'Sos' Taylor, while in the pack was Captain J Woolley. The good captain plays no part in the club's history but it is worth noting a declared ambition of his, to plant Leicester's flag at the South Pole when he became a member of Ernest Shackleton's next Antarctic expedition. Even Mr Crumbie's powers of recruitment might have failed him there.

Of necessity most of Leicester's 19 fixtures in what remained of the 1918-19 season were against service sides but the rugby-starved Leicester public got the best of what was available. Apart from attracting sides like the South African and New Zealand Armed Forces to play the club, Leicester helped host the services tournament which played a notable part that season, in a variety of venues up and down the country, in putting rugby back on its feet.

Against the New Zealand Forces, captained by 'Ranji' Wilson, Tigers lost 19-0 with the following team: F Read; H L V Day, C D Carter, M Abraham, P W Lawrie; E Myers, G W Wood; C D Ferris, G Vears, W P Collopy, A G Bull, J Woolley, F Taylor, W J Allen, G Ward. Of that side Lawrie, Wood, Bull and Ward had already been capped by England, and Collopy by Ireland. Day, Myers and Taylor were to

join them as English caps within a couple of years, which indicated the strength of Leicester's line-up and also a possible reason why, on February 15, 1919, they equalled the club's existing record of points scored in one match when they beat a Bedford XV 71-0.

It is perhaps a little hard on Bedford that they should have entered Tigers' record book this way, since they were represented largely by players from service depots in the area and boys from the school. There, however, it stood for more than sixty years as Leicester ran in 19 tries, seven of them converted. Teddy Haselmere collected five tries on one wing, Harold Day four on the other, while centre Norman Coates and fly half Alf Bates each scored three. Since the game was played for just over an hour there was fractionally over a point a minute in which the crowd could revel.

The following week the Llanelly and Wales centre, Willy Watts, made his debut against the Australian Armed Forces (lost 6-8) and twice before the season ended, Wavell Wakefield played at Welford Road, for the RAF against the club and against the Canadian Armed Forces. In another four years he was to captain Leicester, so at the time allowing the club to claim him as their most capped player - a distinction they shared with Harlequins, Wakefield's original club, until his feat was overtaken by Peter Wheeler and then Rory Underwood during the 1980s.

The season ended with 12 wins and seven defeats but during the summer Leicester lost the services of one of their most enthusiastic supporters, their treasurer of the past 15 years, F St Clair Pain. His active connection with the club had begun 25 years earlier when he initiated, by his lively correspondence in the local press, the formation of the Schools League whose administration must have contributed to the foundation by Leicester schoolmaster Joseph Cooper in 1904 of the English Schools Rugby Union. The club recognised new talent and Mr St Clair Pain served them long and well before his death in 1919, doubtless happy to see that a £3,000 debt on the Members' Stand had been cleared by a public appeal coupled with gate receipts.

The first full season after the war, 1919-20, opened against Bath when each club fielded three survivors from pre-war days. For Leicester it became a record-breaker in many ways. The club scored more points, 756, than they had ever scored before or were to do again for 50 years, and the minute, nine-stone wing Haselmere scored the staggering total of 59 tries - no-one else before or since has even reached 40.

Haselmere, from Rugby, had been introduced to the club by 'Jumbo' Allen, one of their leading forwards, when the game resumed after the war and he was the first to pay tribute to his centres in helping him to his record number of tries. Inside him he had the dependable Norman Coates who joined Leicester from Bath, Willy Watts and more of a similar ilk, while he also benefited from Tigers' new style of play. For this was the season they began to play with seven forwards and eight backs, largely due to the return from service of the pre-war fly half, Tim Taylor.

Leicester had acquired the services of another outstanding fly half, Alf Bates, who could turn on a

Leicester v Cardiff in grim
wintry conditions at
Welford Road in 1919.

sixpence and whose individual running captivated the crowds - even if he not infrequently lost his own players in the intricacies of his side-stepping. Crumbie therefore decided that he could afford to play a man short in the forwards, in order to accommodate Taylor and Bates, the one at fly half, the other at five-eighth. It was a novelty that must have taken a lot of clubs by surprise and, provided the midfield players always ran straight, it meant the wings inevitably had an overlap.

Haselmere was the first to benefit from this, his exceptional speed bringing him tries in 27 of his 40 games. Twice he scored five times, against Burton and Headingley, and against Burton he aggregated 31 points in a 58-0 win, since he also kicked six conversions and a dropped goal, this remained the individual record in a game until beaten by 'Dusty' Hare in 1981. Curiously enough, however, the club had an even better all round player on the other wing in A M Smallwood, one of the outstanding players of his time.

Alistair Smallwood was educated at Newcastle Royal Grammar School and went to Gonville and Caius College, Cambridge, on an organ scholarship. A man of many parts he won his blue in 1919, dropping a goal in Cambridge's 7-5 win over Oxford - the first Varsity Match to feature a penalty goal - and he then took up a teaching appointment at Uppingham. The first of his 14 caps came in 1920, when he was picked at centre in the 8-3 win over France, and he was never in a losing England team until his last game, when Scotland won 14-11 at Murrayfield in 1925.

A man who placed considerable emphasis on the running game, it is slightly ironical that two of Smallwood's high spots in his career revolved round drop goals. The first won the only Varsity Match in which he played; the second won the 1923 international against Wales 7-3 when L J Corbett

flicked a pass between his legs to Smallwood who overcame his surprise sufficiently well to drop a goal from 45 yards.

That was the match in which H L Price scored a famous try straight from Wakefield's kick-off at the start of the game. Price caught the ball from the kick-off, dropped for goal, followed up his own kick and touched down for a try. Since Price was also playing for Leicester at the time, the club's players were responsible for all the points.

It is Smallwood too, who holds Leicester's record for the number of tries scored by an individual in one match. In the last match of the Christmas holiday in 1922, against Manchester at Welford Road, he scored seven tries in a 36-0 win, his hand-off and swerve baffling the opposition on a day when Tigers were fielding a severely weakened team. In the book which many players of a past generation regarded as something of a bible, *"Rugger"*, by W W Wakefield and H P Marshall, Smallwood was described thus:

"He...was always experimenting and attempting new methods of attack. Certainly he was one of the most enterprising, as well as one of the cleverest, post-War backs. It was he who started the wings throwing in from touch instead of the scrum half, with a view to getting a swift return pass from a short throw-in and thus having a clear run along the line before the defence was in position.

"He also had a useful habit of bluffing the opposition and I shall never forget once when he had raced back, apparently to touch down, but picked up the ball instead and quietly walked right up to the opposition players who were following up instead of trying to dodge them. When he nearly reached them he handed out the ball as if he were giving it to them and so taken aback were they that he was able suddenly to slip round them and go all out to start an attack.

George 'Pedlar' Wood in action at Welford Road during 1921-22.

"Of course it was risky but it came off for Smallwood could always size up the possibilities of the situation accurately...He always insisted that his centre should let him have the ball early to give him plenty of time and room in which to manoeuvre and he had the invaluable knack of keeping in touch with his centre so that real combination between the two was possible."

Also capped in 1920 was 'Sos' Taylor, the former Medway Street Old Boys forward who had received such serious wounds on active service with the Leicestershire Regiment that he had been told he would never play rugby again. His sterling efforts brought him international honours, at the age of 29, against France and Ireland, while during that season the Leicester pack also had the services of J E 'Jenny' Greenwood, captain of England that year and later an outstanding president of the RFU. Greenwood distinguished himself by kicking 10 conversions in the 62-3 win over Richmond, and another debutant that season was a schoolboy international full back of pre-war days, D J Norman, now a forward and 11 years later to win his cap for England as a hooker.

If the club's playing members should seem to take the limelight it is not entirely surprising, considering the personnel Tom Crumbie called on. Yet much good work was going on off the field, with the erection of a new stand - appropriately enough, called the New Stand and later to be renamed the Crumbie Stand following the death in 1928 of the secretary. It was part of Crumbie's aim to make the club's facilities the best in the country and attract regular internationals to the Midlands, blithely ignoring the development of the Twickenham ground.

In that respect it could be said that the Welford Road playing arena became one huge white elephant, for England (for whom it was primarily designed) played only one international there following the completion of the New Stand. Yet again, later generations can only admire Mr Crumbie's ambitions on Leicester's behalf, for his efforts gave the city a stadium second only to four national playing arenas in the British Isles, and the atmosphere engendered on special match days -

when the Barbarians or touring sides visit - is something to be savoured. It is certainly the envy of many other provincial clubs and, now that the profile of the game is so much higher and league rugby is drawing such big attendances, Crumbie's foresight is once again being rewarded.

It had been hoped that the stand would be ready for the start of the 1920-21 season but the official opening was made on October 2 by the President of the RFU, Ernest Prescott, before the game against Headingley. The stand, and additional improvements, cost over £21,000 and saddled the club with a debt that was to plague them for years. But that was all in the future - the wife of the club president, Mrs Hedley Salmon, presented a new flag and the players obliged with a 33-3 win, featuring a line-up at three-quarter of Haselmere, Smallwood, Tim Taylor, Percy Lawrie and Day, a back division to match any in the country. Of that quintet Lawrie, who started to play for Leicester in 1907 as an 18 year-old, went on until 1924 and accumulated the staggering total of 206 tries - far and away the club record. Since he captained the club before and after the war (during which he served a lieutenant in the Royal Artillery) his influence was far-reaching.

It was to be another outstanding season. Newport, with a 22-3 win, deprived the club of their unbeaten record in the ninth game and there was a degree of criticism of the eight-backs formation - not surprising since, no matter how good a collection of forwards could be recruited, there had to be occasions when seven men were thoroughly outplayed by eight. Interestingly enough, Leicester reverted to eight forwards for the game with the Barbarians, which they won 8-6 thanks to two tries from Tim Taylor.

Leicester was the venue for the England v The South game, during which there were trials for Haselmere, Smallwood, 'Sos' Taylor and Day, while the club helped Leicestershire to the final of the County Championship. The Midland Counties Union had been disbanded after the War and this was the first season of the new county

Herb Sharratt's Easter tour Itinerary 1922.

groupings, the fourth system tried for the County Championship. Yorkshire were beaten 8-5 in the semi-final at Welford Road and it was an all-Leicester team that represented the county in the final against Gloucestershire at Kingsholm. The XV was: J Wilkinson; F Mellor, P W Lawrie, J R Markham, E E Haselmere, F M Taylor, G W Wood, F Taylor, G Ward, C W Cross, D J Norman, W J Allen, Wal Buckler, J Wickson,

E Ward. Unfortunately the dream faded as Percy Lawrie scored Leicestershire's only points with a dropped goal in a 31-4 defeat.

One of the forwards, Charlie Cross, who had made his debut the season before, was to distinguish himself in another way before the season ended. On the way from Chester for the game in which the Tigers took Birkenhead Park's ground record, he leapt from the leading car and pulled up a runaway horse and cart - a feat which no doubt inspired his team-mates in the game that day. Times, of course, had changed, and the team no longer travelled in style by train. Motor cars were now so common that they had taken over from the train for away games - just as well, since that day a coal strike had prevented many of the trains from running!

It had long been decided to make the last game of the season a charity match, in aid of the Royal Infirmary in Leicester, a laudable habit which was maintained up to the Second World War. To begin with this match was against a London XV - subsequently it was generally the match with Blackheath and it was in the 1921 Infirmary Match that Wakefield made his debut for Leicester, scoring two tries in a 20-5 win which gave the Tigers the admirable record of 31 wins, eight defeats and two draws. The same match the following season meant that £950 of the required £1,000 had been raised, allowing the consecration of a memorial bed at the Infirmary commemorating players killed during the Great War.

More ground improvements were carried out during the summer of 1921, terracing being built up in front of the New Stand and the extension to the Members' Stand giving a seating capacity of 10,250. Subscriptions for the stand seats were now 25 shillings (15 shillings for ladies and boys) and the unemployed were allowed in free at each end of the ground (on production of their out-of-work cards). But the new season began on an unhappy note with the death in an airship disaster over Hull of G M Thomas, who had played three-quarter off and on during the previous two seasons.

Nevertheless there were 12,000 there for the opening match against Bath, there were caps for Day and Smallwood, and Leicester became the first English club to win at Swansea for 26 years. It was the last season for scrum-half Pedlar Wood, however. Having made his debut in 1906 and played 388 games for Leicester he was to join Nuneaton the following season where he concluded his career.

Day's first cap had come against Wales in 1920 and two years later he played against Wales and France, a fourth cap coming his way in 1926 when he was called into the side at a late hour against Scotland. Fondly remembered by some of his contemporaries as one of the slowest wingers to represent his country, Day made up for this by his phenomenal place-kicking and it was not uncommon to see him landing goals from his own half at Welford Road.

In the course of eight seasons he scored over 1,000 points for the club, regularly topping 100 points in a season, and if that does not sound much by contemporary standards, it should be remembered that the old leather balls were far heavier than today's flighty affairs, that there were far fewer

opportunities for penalty kicks and that Day, a schoolmaster at Felsted, Essex, missed quite a lot of games either because of representative calls or because he was unable to travel away on any regular basis.

Recalling his days as a Tiger 30 years later, Day commented on the team's formation of eight backs: "I have preserved four foolscap pages from E H D Sewell (the noted rugby critic), addressed to me as captain, proving that it could never work. We won our next game by 40 odd points against Moseley. I received a postcard from him suggesting we took on stronger opponents.

"Our success was due to a supply of great half backs. At scrum-half, following that fearless box of tricks Pedlar Wood we had J C Russell, whose neglect by Scotland was a mystery, Guy German and E J Massey. For fly-halves there were P G Scott, R A Buckingham and H D Greenlees."

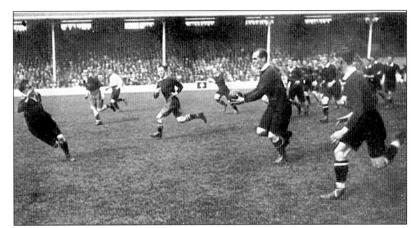

Norman Coates (with ball), Alf Bates (left) and Teddy Haselmere (right) take on Bradford in 1920.

This of course was after the retirement of Tim Taylor and the loss, in 1922, of Bates who joined the professional ranks with Oldham. But little, it seemed, could halt the Leicester points machine. In the 33-5 win over Nuneaton, Day scored 15 points and in the following match, a 46-5 success over Headingley, he registered 20 points from two tries, four conversions and two penalties. He may have lacked a degree of pace at international level but there was no doubting his worth at club level. There was an interesting addition to the three-quarter line in the shape of Andrew Roxburgh, a former Leicester City player who did well enough with the oval ball to win a regular place over the next two seasons.

Over the Christmas period Leicester entertained their first guests from France, Racing Club de France, and won 4-0 with a Haselmere dropped goal on an occasion graced by the presence of the French consul and attaché, both representing their country's embassy in London. But there was nothing like the high jinks that occurred in the game against London Irish, when an aghast *Leicester Evening Mail* reporter recorded: "An incident which convulsed the crowd followed. Wright [the Leicester wing] had received the ball but was grasped by Stanley. The two players struggled for a time and then the Tiger broke away but left his knickers in the hands of the Irishman. Wright commenced to run, unaware of the disaster which had overtaken him. He quickly realised his position and collapsed to the ground where he was quickly surrounded by the rest of the players until

he was supplied with a new garment." Tigers won 22-3 and Wright got his try - would players today collapse in the same modest heap?

There were caps this season for Smallwood and Price while Scotland capped the Melrose forward, J R 'Jock' Lawrie, who was to join Leicester the next year. The club's two England players were in the XV which beat Ireland 23-5 in the last home international to be played at Welford Road, on 10th February,1923. A crowd of around 20,000 saw both men score a try in a game dominated by the half-back expertise of Kershaw and Davies.

Four days later the club made their first trip to foreign parts, returning the visit of Racing Club de France. It was quite a tour, for after the game in Paris they were due to return to play US Portsmouth and Plymouth Albion. Perhaps the best way to describe the trip is through the eyes of one of the club's forwards, Henry Grierson, who was not only a useful player but a man of words who, in 1924, published an entertaining anecdotal book, called *"The Ramblings of a Rabbit"*.

The party left Leicester for London on the Sunday and crossed the Channel the following day, via Folkestone-Boulogne, and so to the Hotel St James and Albany in Paris. The game was on the Tuesday and, according to Grierson, "was a real bad show. They were a fine side and just about good enough to beat us without any outside assistance, but they were packed with it in the form of a French referee. He was mustard and nearly blew us off the field."

Tigers, with some of their leading players unable to travel, lost 19-9 but it seems reasonable to assume that their evening at the Folies Bergéres the night before may not have helped form! The post-match dinner was held at Maxims and it must have been a bleary-eyed bunch of rugby players who assembled for departure on Wednesday. Indeed, some of them may have been fortunate to depart at all, for the practical joker, Norman Coates, and little Tim Taylor had an altercation with a French taxi driver during the night and wound up in the police cells. It is not known whether Coates' allegation to the gendarmerie that Taylor was a "gendarme anglais" was the main reason for their release or not.

Little, it seemed, could keep Coates down and as the tour party passed through customs at Dover the *Leicester Mercury* reporter, who had omitted to declare some scent, became the butt of his humour. Coates knew nothing of the perfume residing in the reporter's bag but happily informed officials: "Don't you believe him, he's a prevaricator. His grip is packed with contraband, search him!" The scent was discovered and the extra duty made it an expensive present at 25 shillings. Maybe the Mercury's expense account footed the bill. When his playing days were over the irrepressible Coates ran the line for many seasons and became one of the well known characters at Welford Road, along with the pre-war forward, Tom Goodrich, who became groundsman in 1922.

That particular tour continued at Portsmouth on the Thursday with a game against the services side (drawn 3-3) and then to Plymouth for the match with the Albion on the Saturday (lost 5-15). The next day they returned, via Bristol, to Leicester.

In the same season 13 Tigers played in the Leicestershire side beaten 8-6 at Bridgwater by Somerset in the County Championship final and only a couple of points prevented Tigers from beating Newport in the Welsh club's invincible season. Day kicked two penalties but Leicester lost 7-6 before a crowd of 16,000 people - they were to make up for that later in the year.

Travelling to an away game in the Twenties. Note the smart line in Tiger mittens!

"WAKERS" AT WELFORD ROAD 1923-1929

THE season 1923-24 has to be known as Wakefield's season, even though it was very far from the most successful one in terms of mere statistics. One of the most distinguished players ever to represent his country, WW Wakefield had made a name for himself as an all-round athlete at Sedbergh school, and later in the RAF, with Harlequins and at Cambridge University. First capped in 1920, he came to the Midlands to work for Boots in Nottingham, and made his home in Leicester.

He was, naturally, a notable capture for Tom Crumbie and made his first appearance of the season in the third game, scoring a try in an 8-3 win over Neath. He won fame as a back row player but Tigers happily used him at centre in his next game, when he again scored a try in the 24-9 away win over Headingley. In October he took over the captaincy of the side from George Ward and it was under his leadership that Leicester finally stopped Newport's unbeaten run, when they came to Welford Road and lost 7-5, Percy Lawrie scoring the winning try.

It must have been a frustrating experience for him, however, to play in a seven-man pack. As the architect of a style of back row play which helped England to dominate the 1920s and always one of the game's leading tacticians, he found himself in a side which not infrequently did not possess a back row. Sometimes the Leicester scrum packed three-four, sometimes three-two-two; sometimes, indeed, they played four-three before the laws laid down the exact number of players to constitute a front row. He

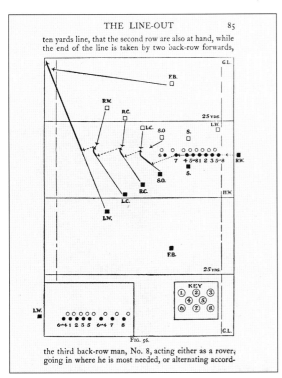

THE LINE-OUT 85

ten yards line, that the second row are also at hand, while the end of the line is taken by two back-row forwards,

FIG. 56.

the third back-row man, No. 8, acting either as a rover, going in where he is most needed, or alternating accord-

Diagram of lineout play from WW Wakefield's 1927 book, "Rugger and How to Play it".

was unhappy, too, with the eight backs, feeling that too frequently players were crowded out on the wings but, as a man of considerable tact, refrained from offending Crumbie, who originated the pattern of play. His feelings must have been reflected elsewhere though, for the former scrum-half Billy Foreman suggested a return to the conventional style of play in committee without achieving anything.

During his one season with Leicester, Wakefield also captained England and there is little need here to remind readers of his subsequent outstanding career, both in public life and as an administrator of the game. As Lord Wakefield of Kendal, he had fond memories of Leicester and recalled vividly that success against Newport:

"They were a well-drilled and disciplined side captained by Jack Wetter, the Welsh international half back, who was not only a fine player but an excellent tactician. I am pleased to say we took away their unbeaten record and we deserved to win, but in my view Wetter and his side had the moral victory.

"When Newport were in the lead and I wanted to open up the game, and he wanted to close it up and keep it tight, then the game became closed up. When we got into the lead and I wanted to close the game and he wanted to open it up, then in spite of all we could do the game became open.

"In another match I remember that we started an attack from our own goal-line. Eventually the ball was passed to me and, as I was rounding the opposition full back on the half way line, in a despairing clutch my shorts were torn off and I had to run the length of the field with no shorts and no jock strap. I sat on the ball behind the goal posts until another pair of shorts arrived. Tom Crumbie later observed that on the next Saturday he had never had such a good gate!

"Another character was our hooker, George Ward. There was not much he did not know about front row play in general and hooking in particular. Before I joined Leicester, when I was captain of Cambridge in 1922, after Leicester had played the university I arranged for him to give the university some coaching and it was most valuable.

"The season I played with Leicester was most enjoyable. England won all her matches and the Tigers, with the strongest fixture list in the UK, had a good and balanced side of talented players...it was a happy side, with a wonderful team spirit inspired by dear old Tom Crumbie, who insisted on taking the touchline although he was nearly blind and could hardly walk, let alone run.

"Except when there was a quick throw-in, there was a gentlemen's agreement by both sides that we would line up where we reckoned the ball went into touch and the side entitled to throw in the ball would get ready to throw it in so that when dear old Tom arrived to put up his flag there was no problem, although if the ball happened to go into touch somewhere near where Tom happened to be, then the home side invariably had the advantage of a yard or two.

EXAM PASSES

D J Thomas son of the vicar of Desford, played on the left wing in the 1923 game against Llanelly. A student at Lampeter College, he received a wire telling him he had passed as a senior scholar whilst he was in the dressing room before the game.

"He was exceedingly kind to me when I came as a stranger to Leicester and he dispensed his genial hospitality to everyone connected with the game. He looked after the members of the team as if they were his children; nothing was too much trouble for him and he kept an open house for all players who wished to take advantage of his friendliness."

Again there were international honours for the club: apart from Wakefield, Price and Day were capped by England and Jock Lawrie by Scotland, while Leicester's consistent full back, Claude Sambrook, was an England reserve. The club renewed their acquaintance with the Racing Club de France, winning 24-5 but going down at the Stade Bergeyre by 22-3.

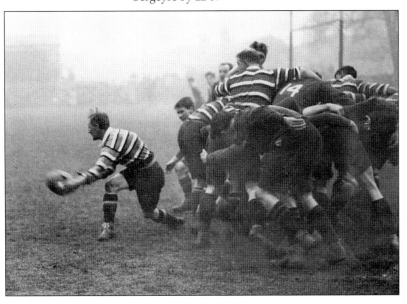

'Pedlar' Wood in the days before letters appeared on the back of the players' shirts.

Off the field, however, there were intimations of mortality from Crumbie. His efforts on the club's behalf had taken their toll and he was, anyway, suffering from diabetes. In March, 1924, he notified the committee of his impending resignation but other counsels prevailed and, to no-one's surprise, he was still at the helm when the new season, and the New Zealanders, arrived. This was the year of C G Porter's "Invincible" All Blacks and Leicester had lost the services of Wakefield, who had resumed his club career with Harlequins, and Bob Usher, unfortunately killed in a flying accident.

The ground was packed to the seams with 35,000 people for the game between Leicester and the tourists on October 4, but they were in for a disappointment. Leicester lost 27-0 with the following XV: L C Sambrook; O C Bryson, M S Holden, P G Scott; A M Smallwood, H L Price; E J Massey, J C Russell, J R Lawrie, J C R Buchanan, G Ward, F D Prentice, W B N Roderick, H Sharratt, J E Davis. The hallmark of the New Zealanders' win was their cover in defence, support for the man with the ball and the way they hustled the Leicester halves into error. Aided by some poor Leicester tackling they ran in tries through L F Cupples, J Richardson, J Steel, F W Lucas, A White and K S Svenson, Mark Nicholls kicking three conversions and a penalty.

The best to be said of the game, from the local viewpoint, was the profit of £1,000 but there was some consolation that season. For Leicestershire,

represented entirely by Leicester players, won the County Championship, for the first, and so far the only, time. The XV included two more players who were to become great favourites with the Welford Road crowd, George Beamish and Ralph Buckingham, and was: L C Sambrook; A M Smallwood, H L V Day, O C Bryson, H A Sambrook; M S Holden, R A Buckingham; G J German, G Ward, J R Lawrie, G R Beamish, H Sharratt, F D Prentice, D J Norman, N T Thorneloe.

Beamish, Bryson and Holden scored tries, Day landing a conversion and a penalty, in the 14-6 win over Gloucester at Bristol and, coupled with the caps awarded to Massey and Smallwood (England) and Beamish (Ireland) helped turn a disappointing start into a proud finish. The season was rounded off, as usual in those days, with the Easter tour to Wales and a sample itinerary was: April 10 - leave Leicester in cars, dinner at the Grand Hotel, Bristol; April 11 - visit zoological gardens (a.m.), game v Bristol, leave for Monmouth and dinner at the Beaufort Arms.

April 12 - motor through the Wye Valley to Chepstow and back; April 13 - leave for Llanelly, lunch at the Stepney Hotel, game v Llanelly, back to Monmouth in time for an 8.15 p.m. dinner; April 14 - leave for Bath, lunch at Ye Olde Red House, game v Bath, leave for dinner at the Swan's Nest Hotel, Stratford; leave for Leicester. How strictly the timetable was adhered to remains an unknown factor and the fact that only 45 minutes was allowed for dinner on the final day means the tour party should undoubtedly have arrived back in Leicester with a severe bout of indigestion.

Another fine crop of players had now taken root in the Leicester side. There was the RAF connection (happily sustained in recent years by Rory Underwood), when players posted to Cranwell and Midland stations generally tended to head for Leicester. C E H Medhurst, Oliver Bryson, Bob Usher, John Russell, all were servicemen but the best known of the RAF players to come to Leicester at that time has to be George Beamish, whose three brothers also played for the Tigers at one time or another.

Outside the service ranks came Edward Massey, capped three times in 1925, a pupil at Ampleforth College who played the last hour of his first international, against Scotland, with a broken collarbone and a partially dislocated shoulder. There were some notable local products too, in Doug Prentice and Ralph Buckingham, the first a pupil of Wyggeston School who joined Westleigh before coming as a back row forward to the Tigers in 1923; the second born in Blaby and educated at Stoneygate School and Rossall, before returning to the Stoneygate club and playing for Leicester first in 1925.

It was, however, a time of transition. No club can go through a decade without the graph indicating their success ratio taking a downward curve now

MUD-DLED CONFUSION
The game against United Services in 1924 was played on a very wet day and became "quite ludicrous at times, owing to the similarity in the jerseys of the teams. They became very mud-spattered, and in the general excitement, the players could not always tell friend from foe, resulting in the spectacle of team mates tackling each other".

and then, and Leicester were no exception. The very fact that they could call on so many servicemen told against them when duty demanded these same players should be elsewhere - during the 1925-26 season John Russell was not regularly available, George Beamish played only 10 games and Massey had gone abroad. Several youngsters had to be introduced and there was increasing criticism of the seven-man pack.

1925 Match Programme.

No doubt the service presence accounted for an increase in the social side of the club's doings: the Tigers Ball at the Junior Training Hall over Christmas 1925 attracted 450 revellers, who were entertained by the La Veeda orchestra and the songs of the visiting Barbarians. In strict contrast a fortnight later, the 500 visiting Swansea supporters provided entertainment before, during and doubtless after the game by their hymn singing (they brought their own conductor), climbing the goalposts and a would-be George Formby who played the ukulele in the committee box.

The Welford Road crowd had the novelty, too, of a couple of New Zealanders introduced into the side around the turn of the year, two straight-running, forthright backs in R E S Fitzgerald and C B Tate, and a newcomer at fly-half who was to make a considerable impact, Harry Greenlees. And later in that year, in November 1926, came more New Zealanders, the Maori party captained by W P Barclay.

This particular touring team had created something of a storm by refusing to play under Welsh referees in Wales earlier in the tour, but they had an enjoyable game at Welford Road when they beat the Tigers 15-13 before a crowd of 20,000. It was not an entirely typical Leicester performance for their speedy wings, Ewart Farndon and Ted Flewitt, got few opportunities and Day inside them at five-eighth was suffering from a leg injury and should not have played.

The team was: L C Sambrook; W E Farndon, O C Bryson, E C A Flewitt; H L V Day, R A Buckingham; H D Greenlees, J C Russell; F D Prentice, D J Norman, E G Coleman, A H Greenwood, M G Christie, F V Beamish, G J German. The club XV led 8-3 at the interval, Farndon scoring a try which Prentice, who also kicked a penalty, converted. Potaka scored the Maoris' try but in the second half Falwasser got an

interception try and a dropped goal by Wilson put the tourists ahead. Prentice scored a try, which he converted himself, to restore Leicester's lead but a try by Gemmell, converted by Love, tipped the balance.

Farndon, who scored 13 tries in 1925-26, said of the sides he played in: "We were a great team together, wonderfully friendly and on tours we stuck together. We used to play tricks on Tom Crumbie of course, in spite of his general insistence on strict discipline. He wouldn't allow a Tigers player to turn out for the Barbarians - he felt that playing for the club and county was enough football for anyone. On one occasion Trevor Thorneloe did defy his injunction and turned out for the Barbarians, and Tom promptly dropped him."

But the days of the great administrator were drawing to a close. Prematurely aged and nearly blind, Crumbie recovered from illness in time for the 1927-28 season and it doubtless warmed his heart to see Leicester score exactly 100 points in their first four games, aided now by George and Victor Beamish. He also saw an all-Leicester XV represent the county against the touring side from New South Wales, the Waratahs of A C Wallace who left such a lasting impression in this country. The XV was L C Sambrook; W E Farndon, R A Buckingham, H L V Day, F E Wood; H D Greenlees, J C Russell; F D Prentice, D J Norman, E G Coleman, G R Beamish, D W R Ryley, M G Christie, S F Lawrence, T H Briers.

The Australian side led 9-3 at halftime and won 20-8, Day scoring a first half try for the county XV and converting a later try by Farndon. That made it 9-8 but then Russell left the field with a broken collarbone and the Waratahs took full advantage to score three more tries. There were further honours for the club when Buckingham and Farndon played in the first England trial, held at Welford Road, while Greenlees received a Scottish trial and went on to win caps against the Waratahs, Wales and France that season.

Buckingham had already been capped the season before, against France. It was, in fact, his only cap and he was unlucky that it came on a day when England were hard pressed (they lost 3-0) and the backs were on the defensive. A dependable and

FULL BACK FAR FORWARD
In 1924 it was still somewhat unusual for a full-back to score a try. Against Cambridge University Harold Day picked up the ball in a tight corner on his own 25, and scored far away on the other wing. His first intention was to run it out to the right and kick into touch, but when he got there he decided to go on. At the half way line he passed inwards to Scott, who was tackled before he could pass back, however the ball rolled loose, and Day got it again and worked across to the other side of the ground. He still had enough speed to get past two tackles, before he fell over the line, a winded but delighted Tiger. Unfortunately he failed to convert.

WW Wakefield, Russell Davis, Jock Lawrie and 'Sos' Taylor do battle with Llanelly during 1923.

versatile player, he was travelling reserve for his country 10 times and recalled what the club was like shortly before the death, in March 1928, of Tom Crumbie:

ECLIPSE
There was an eclipse of the sun during the 1925 game against the Army. When half time came it was reportedly beginning to grow dark and during the second half the sun threw a queer light over the ground.

"It was different from any club I had known. Normally you were proposed, seconded and worked your way up from the lower sides. It was rather like playing for the Barbarians when you were invited to play for Leicester. And after the match we used to go to the 'Big Window', a room at the Prince Leopold on the corner of Welford Road. We had Tom Goodrich to look after our kit and he was the kindest man possible. Nothing was too much for him, he polished the boots, soles and all.

"I think football today is probably better but in the mid-20s we produced play almost as good. But the wing forward was the man who ruined open rugby: it started with Voyce and Blakiston in 1924 and gradually developed from the days when, basically, there were two scrums whose only job was to get the ball for the backs."

Buckingham it was who was involved in a light-hearted incident with his great friend, Ted Flewitt, after a sailing excursion on the Norfolk Broads. Flewitt was the man who 'took the rap' to the glee of the local press when he was fined £5, with four shillings and sixpence costs, for holding up a motorist and playing football in the highway at Purgh St Margaret's. A group of men, in yachting clothing, threatened to put a car driven by a journalist from Attleborough in the river, after the overbearing scribe broke up their impromptu game on the road. It was said in court that "the young man who kicked the ball was not present...he had played against France". The chairman of the bench

NO PENALTIES
It must be almost unprecedented for a game to be finished without the referee once blowing his whistle for a penalty kick, but this happened on 7th November 1925 against Cambridge University. In fact the only stoppages were for "the torn shorts of the Cambridge forwards!"

delivered himself of the opinion that he was sorry to see young men making fools of themselves. Three years later the unfortunate Flewitt was killed in an aeroplane crash at Castle Bromwich.

With the club well on the way to another successful season the man who made so much of it possible, Tom Crumbie, died. Although his health had been deteriorating for several years he still maintained his record of never missing a club match - even when serving on Rugby Football Union committees in London - until November 1927. Then the strain of travelling told and though he passed his 60th birthday in February, 1928, a few weeks later, on March 13, he died.

It is not too much to say that, for Leicester, it was the end of an era, for in many ways Crumbie had been the club for 33 years. Particularly this was true when Leicester became an invitation side, for then the club was, in essence, the 15 players who happened to turn out each Saturday. Crumbie was the cog around which it all revolved.

The Leicester Mercury's rugby critic, A C Tole, who reported under the pseudonym Cyrus, wrote: "He was more than a mere secretary-manager of the club; in a sense he epitomised the Tigers in his own genial personality...His house at Smeeton Westerby was "Liberty Hall" and seldom a Sunday went by without a group of Tigers foregathering there to talk over tactics and prospects...He had a knack of getting people to do what he wanted."

St Peter's Church was packed for the funeral service, not only by friends he had made in the rugby world but by trade acquaintances, for he had been at one time a vice-president of the Leicester Master Printers' Association. One of the original Leicester players and administrators, James Collier, attended the funeral and the following Saturday the Tigers paid their own special tribute. Crumbie's

Leicester v United Services on 6th November 1926. Tigers players pictured are: DJ Norman, AH Greenwood, JM Dykes, EM Barlow and MG Christie. Tigers won 15-5.

John Russell receives the ball against London Scottish at Richmond in February 1929. Tigers won 28-3.

usual seat in the committee box was left vacant and the Imperial Band played "Solemn Melody" as Leicester and Penarth took the field wearing black armbands.

Day kicked the penalty which gave Leicester a 3-0 win though they were without Prentice, who was playing for England against Scotland that day, for this was the season when he won his three caps. It would doubtless have pleased the late secretary to know that Doug Prentice was to captain the British Isles to Australasia in 1930, to manage a British tour to the Argentine in 1936 and to become secretary of the Rugby Football Union between 1947 and 1962.

It was Day and Prentice who shared the scoring honours at the end of the season. Although Frank Wood, younger brother of Pedlar, headed the try-scorers with 19, Day totalled 123 points and Prentice 105, while the indefatigable Doug Norman only missed the last game of the season.

Leicester concluded their playing season with a win in the inaugural Leicestershire seven-a-side competition. Organised in aid of the Infirmary, the Tigers beat Aylestone Athletic 30-3 in the final and not unnaturally were to dominate the tournament for the next few years. They also concluded the season with a new secretary, J E Thorneloe, who was appointed on April 4.

WAR CRY

Lt C F Hallaram, who was the 1925 heavy-weight champion boxer of the Navy, did his best to encourage the United Services forwards with his famous war-cry. This did not however measure up to the encouragement the Tigers had from their own spectators, who stood up in their seats every time Bryson got the ball.

Eric Thorneloe was to do as much for Leicester in his own quiet way as his predecessor. Stocky and tough, with a resonant voice, Mr Thorneloe had emerged from the First World War with a distinguished record and the Military Cross. He resumed playing with Westleigh but had one season, 1920-21, when he played on several occasions for Leicester as a wing or full back. A knee injury forced him to retire in 1925, by which time he

had become secretary to Westleigh (1920) and to Leicestershire (1923).

Among his first duties was to help decide on a fitting memorial to Crumbie. The club set up a committee to debate the problem and six months later recommended that the New Stand be renamed the Crumbie Stand and that a Memorial Fund be established to help pay off the debt on the stand. But inevitably there were problems as the new administration felt its way. Crumbie, after all, had been very much a one-man band and had done his printing firm no good at all by subverting much of its time and effort to rugby matters.

The transitional period began to be reflected on the field and the 1928-29 season was the worst since the war. Day played only five matches and was one of a maddening crop of injuries. Tigers had the services of the Old Laurentians forward, Philip 'Pop' Dunkley who was to win six England caps in the 1930s and a new name appeared ten times at full back, the 21 year-old Westleigh player R J (Bobby) Barr. There was a rift too with Tigers' long standing link with Cardiff. Early in the season Leicester beat the Welsh club 8-5 at Welford Road, when two Cardiff forwards were sent off for arguing with the referee. But in the return Tigers lost by a similar score in what was to prove to be the last match between the clubs for several years. Cardiff had been in the habit of playing two '1st XVs' on occasions and Leicester felt they were getting the second best of the two teams. Their objections were not met and the fixture was dropped - it was a disheartening note on which to end.

WHAT NO OPPOSITION !

The 29th January 1928 was the first time a team (Richmond) had failed to turn up since Tigers started taking gates 35 years previously. However, the mystery was solved when it transpired that a telegram cancelling a minor match was wrongly re-directed to M L Maley a former student at St Bartholomew's Hospital, and the acting captain of Richmond. It should have gone to a student at St Bart's named Malley.

TIGERS REBUILD
1929-1931

A NEW DECADE was at hand. Some of the great names of the 20s had gone, like Day and Russell, others, like Prentice, were approaching the end of their careers. Leicester were anxious to resume their pre-eminent position of the early 1920s and new stars were beginning to adorn the firmament, perhaps the foremost of them being Bernard Gadney.

Gadney, born in Oxford and educated at Stowe where he captained the school XV, played for English Public Schools in 1929 before joining Richmond. But the London club had F M T Bunney as their scrum-half and, upon taking a teaching appointment in Brackley, Gadney joined Leicester and made his debut in November, 1929, in a 4-3 win over Nuneaton.

He was one of a reserve pair of halves, the Scottish cap Greenlees suffering from a wrist injury and the first choice scrum-half, Langley Burton, also on the casualty list. Gadney, it was said, "started well but fell away in the second half...He should be a useful substitute when Burton, as so often happens, is unable to accompany the team away." It was a hasty judgement by the local rugby reporter, but not more hasty than that made by no less a personage than *The Times'* rugby correspondent, who took it upon himself to inform others that Gadney was too big and too slow and would never make a first class footballer. It is hoped that both these gentlemen made due apology as Gadney became one of the brightest lights in the England teams of the 1930s.

As ever a touch of humour remained, even when the team was struggling for form: one (un-named) Tiger took the field in an away game without removing his false teeth and dashed hastily back to the changing room to thrust them into his coat pocket. The match over, bath taken, equilibrium restored, the player looked for his teeth and found that, since they were not in his own pocket, he must have placed them in the wrong coat. Eric Thorneloe was forced to circulate the other 14 players the next day before the errant molars were restored to an embarrassed owner.

Another debutant in the second half of the season was D A Kendrew, an Uppingham School pupil destined to become Major-General Sir Douglas Kendrew, enjoy an outstanding service career and to become the Governor of Western Australia. He was only 21 when he was posted to South Wigston Regimental Headquarters but England had already capped him in their pack - it was Leicester's misfortune that his Army duties prevented him from playing with any great regularity and England's that he was available to win only 10 caps.

There were more international honours for Greenlees and George Beamish with their respective countries and Doug Norman and the promising ex-Aylestone St James forward S H (Stan) Saunders were given trials. Gadney, now noted for his breaks from the scrum, was voted the most improved player of the season and three of the club's members, Prentice, Beamish, and Kendrew went to Australasia with the 1930 British Isles party, Prentice

as captain after Wavell Wakefield had been unable to accept the invitation.

The season ended with three wins from three games on tour, and with 26 wins against 10 defeats, the future looked rosy. But off the field financial matters were causing the committee a headache. A meeting in June decided on a series of economies, to help with the running of the club and to reduce the debt on the stand. The band was to be discontinued at a saving of £90 p.a., grants to the referees' society and the Leicester Alliance were to be decreased, season ticket prices were increased, against a background of falling gate receipts and declining members' subscriptions.

Significantly too, there had been a suggestion during the season that the 'A' team should be revived. It was perhaps the first sign of a definite change from the policies instituted by Crumbie, although the local clubs were still comparatively happy to supply Leicester at short notice. Bill Parker, from South Leicester, was one such. A back row player, he represented the Tigers off and on for four years and not infrequently turned up for a game, only to find a full complement of players already present: "We accepted being turned away," he said, "because it was an honour to be considered by the Tigers - although we didn't like missing a game." But the smooth organisation on away trips remained - typical may have been the game at Blackheath in which Parker played, when the team took the train to London, the bus to Blackheath and returned for dinner at Simpson's in The Strand. Afterwards there was a ticket each for the Palladium, coffee and sandwiches on the train home and a free taxi from the station at Leicester to each player's home.

Major-General Kendrew, affectionately known at the club as 'Joe', also recalled with fondness his playing days with Leicester as a Second Lieutenant with the Royal Leicestershires: "There were many outstanding players but the real personality and the man that mattered was Eric Thorneloe. He stamped his mark on the side. He ran the club and nothing was too much trouble for him and he set a very high standard.

"We were welcomed when we turned up to play. We had our rugger clothes laid out in the changing rooms, the equipment provided was of the very highest standard. I retain a very vivid impression of the tremendous enjoyment which everyone seemed to get out of taking part in a game. It was always hard and vigorous yet there was a certain "joie de vivre" feeling and not the desperate sense of earnestness which seems to possess players these days.

"Eric was a clever secretary. One day when I was playing A L Novis and C D Aarvold (both leading England players) were with me and were travelling down south and decided to watch the Tigers play. I introduced them both to Eric. He was delighted to

PLAYING DOCTORS
W Mills playing in the 1930 game for Plymouth was injured in a rush just before end of the game and was carried off unconscious. Half an hour after the game finished he was taken to the Infirmary and when he woke up the first person he saw was Dr R A K Wiener the Tigers player whom he had just been playing against.

see them and immediately pressed them to take part in the game! They both accepted and a placard was paraded around the ground for everyone to see, saying that Novis and Aarvold were playing instead of so-and-so and so-and-so. I felt a bit sorry for those who had stood down but the club and spectators enjoyed Eric's new recruits.

"He was a great secretary for collecting players. If he could include anyone who was in the Leicester area who had a reputation he would prevail upon him to wear the Tigers jersey.

"Another enjoyment was the way we played. We were a good side with a few weak links. We played attractive rugger, giving the ball plenty of air and the leadership on the field was well-directed and well-planned. I cannot remember a dirty game or any unpleasant moments. We played for the love of the game and the great enjoyment we got out of it all and the quality of the team members who understood the basic skills. With men like George Beamish, Harry Greenlees and Doug Norman you knew that we could hold our own in any company."

It was Greenlees, the former Rossall and West of Scotland player, who took over the captaincy of the club in 1930-31, but it was not a very happy season for him since injury caused him to miss the second half. For the second year running Tigers featured a New Zealander in their backs; the previous season it had been I McNicol, a fly half, now it was to be a powerful winger, G R White, a serviceman in the RAF.

The side was affected, however, by injury to Farndon, leading try scorer the previous season with 23, and Gadney who underwent an operation for appendicitis. Kendrew, Prentice and Beamish were all late starters after returning from New Zealand where Prentice had contracted an irritating ear infection. But the presence of such luminaries at the club no doubt assisted the BBC in their decision to broadcast the match against Waterloo on November 29, 1930, the first radio commentary on a Leicester match which, happily, was won 21-5. Less happily, in the New Year the club President, Sir Samuel Faire, died and the team honoured his memory by wearing black armbands in the game with Richmond on January 24. Ralph Buckingham was having another injury-plagued season and the club was forced to sound a rallying call to their waning support.

Despite these upsets the record was a good one, 23 wins against 12 defeats, and in an attempt to raise extra money, Prentice brought an English Touring XV to Welford Road in April, 1931, to play Leicester. It was not a very good game but the club were better off by £286 and it was as good a way as any for Prentice to retire from the game, having recorded 575 points for Tigers - not bad for a man who began life as a soccer player before picking up rugby during service with the ANZACs during the war, when he was wounded sufficiently badly for doubts to be cast on his ability to play again. His final match was that against Blackheath when he took over the captaincy from Doug Norman (himself a replacement for Greenlees) and, under the refereeing eye of Wavell Wakefield, kicked three conversions and a penalty.

Greenlees led the side again in 1931-32 and the first five games were won without conceding a

point. But the popular Scotsman could not escape the injury hoodoo which followed him around and he was out of action again in October, Leicester calling on the Nuneaton fly half R V M Odbert who had been capped by Ireland against France three years earlier. Another Irishman to come into the side on a more permanent basis was P B Coote, inevitably known as 'Paddy', an RAF serviceman who was to prove himself a superb centre before his career was cruelly cut short by injury.

Money problems were still evident. An application to run greyhounds at the ground had been refused that year - well, there are limits! - but gates were still poor and members' subscriptions had gone down by £7,600 over the last 10 years. Since 1914, £40,000 had been spent on the ground but the strength of support had changed radically. Eric Thorneloe complained that "no other club caters for its supporters in the way of members' subscriptions and season tickets at such a cheap rate as is offered by the Leicester club." Members were permitted to take guests into the Crumbie Stand for the normal admission charge, a facility extended to the reserved section of the Members Stand. It should be remembered, though, that this was a time of abnormal recession and Leicestrians, like any other, were short of cash.

The club began to sell programmes at one penny each and, for the first time, pondered the possibility of a supporters' club. To help identification backs, as well as forwards, were lettered. But whatever the trials being endured by the treasurer, W N (Billy) Bradshaw, there is no doubting that everything else this season paled beside the achievement of the Leicestershire and East Midlands XV which became the only side to beat Bernie Osler's touring South African party.

It has been called the greatest game to have been played at Welford Road and seven Leicester players took part, one of them, George Beamish, captaining the combined side. It was possibly Beamish's finest hour, even though the big lock had already collected 18 of his 25 Irish caps and was well known as not only a rumbustious forward but a talented captain.

The Springboks arrived in Leicester on the morning of the match, November 14, 1931, and in the afternoon cars stretched all the way up Welford Road and spilled into the sidestreets as 25,000 people made their way to the ground. It was, said *The Leicester Mercury's* Cyrus, "one of those games we dream about but very seldom see."

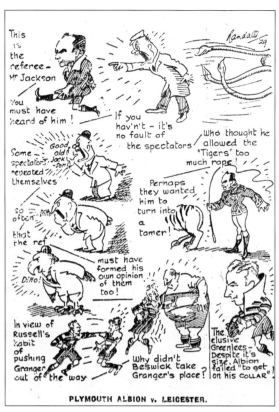

PLYMOUTH ALBION v. LEICESTER.

A cartoon in the Western Evening Herald mocking the Tigers loss to Plymouth Albion in 1929.

TRIBUTE
Before the game against Gloucester in October 1930 there was a tribute to victims of the R101 airship disaster. A minutes silence was followed by the "Last Post" played by a bugler from the Leicestershire Regiment.

WHO'S IN CHARGE
Soon after the start of the second half of the 1931 game against the RAF, the referee was hit in the face by a ball from Llewellyn. He controlled the game for the next 30 minutes without the faintest consciousness of what was going on, and when he "came to" had to ask a player the score!!!

The combined side was: R J Barr (Leicester); J T Hardwicke (Leicester), R A Buckingham (Leicester), R C Brumwell (Bedford), L G Ashwell (Bedford); C F Slow (Northampton), B C Gadney (Leicester); A H Greenwood (Leicester), D J Norman (Leicester), R J Longland (Northampton), T Harris (Northampton), A S Roncoroni (West Herts), W H Weston (Northampton), G R Beamish (Leicester), E Coley (Northampton).

Osler rested himself for the game, which must have helped the counties' cause since so much of the Springboks' play revolved around his kicking, and the tourists fielded: J C Tindall; F D Venter, J C van der Westhuizen, B G Gray, M Zimerman; M G Francis, D H Craven; L C Strachan, J N Bierman, P J Nel, J B Dold, S C Louw, G M Daneel, S R du Toit, P J Mostert.

The Midlands team which beat the Springboks 30-21 at Leicester on 14th November 1931.
Back:
JB Minahan (Chairman), FH Richards (Touch Judge), AH Greenwood, RJ Longland, AS Roncaroni, BC Gadney, WH Jackson (Referee), WN Bradshaw (Hon.Tres), JE Thorneloe (Hon.Sec).
Middle:
CF Slow, RA Buckingham, E Coley, GR Beamish (Capt), T Harris, DJ Norman, RC Brumwell.
Front:
RJ Barr, WH Weston, LG Ashwell, JT Hardwicke.

Barr, brave and solid as a rock, had now established himself as Leicester's last line of defence while Hardwicke had impressed as a clever winger since joining from Stoneygate two years before. Buckingham's quality was well known and Gadney was on the threshold of a brilliant international career. Beamish and Norman were established players both while Henry Greenwood had earned his position with his hard, no-nonsense play.

In the game itself the counties went into an early lead thanks to a dropped goal by Charles Slow, and they never lost it. To many people this has always remained Slow's match and after the Springbok wing Zimerman had crossed for the first of his four tries, the Northampton fly-half went through for a try which was converted. Louw left the field for treatment to a knee injury, returning just before half-time, but by then the counties led 19-6.

A dribble and pick-up by Buckingham had laid on a second try for Slow, Weston converting and though Zimerman scored again, a punt ahead by Slow enabled Hardwicke to cross for the counties' third try, to which Weston again added the goal points. Zimerman opened the second half scoring but then Weston broke away and sent Beamish off on a run to the line for a try greeted with

tremendous enthusiasm and converted by the faithful Weston.

Down by 24-9 the Springboks responded but Barr survived all the pressure placed on him. Nevertheless the tourists scored through Gray, following a dribble, and then Francis dropped a goal to narrow the gap to eight points. Gray made the break for Zimerman's fourth try and a conversion by Francis made it 24-21. It is not difficult to imagine how tense a moment it must have been, for the players and the crowd, willing their team on. The counties shook off their lethargy, with Buckingham in exceptional form, and Weston kicked the only penalty of the game. Then Slow dribbled through and Buckingham crossed in the corner to put his side out of reach, the counties winning 30-21.

Beamish had to make a speech before the crowd dispersed and four days later the counties received due tribute from the South Africans in the shape of the Springbok head which was the trophy played for by Leicestershire and the East Midlands for many years. For the Tigers' players a more tangible reward came in the form of trials for Barr, Gadney, Greenwood and Norman and subsequently caps for all of them save Greenwood. The 30 points scored by the counties was a record for a British team against any major touring side.

Although Slow - a late addition to the original XV after Greenlees and Coote dropped out because of injury - was the man of the match, the plan of the match was Beamish's. He had played for the Combined Services against the Springboks the week before (and was to captain Ireland against them) and Bernard Gadney recalled vividly the build-up to the game: "I had watched the Springboks play against London and I thought they were unbeatable. But Beamish said our forwards would have to shake them up, and when the ball came out it never got beyond the centre, but was always played back inside.

"And our forwards were colossal. Mind you, Osler didn't play in this game and the Springboks may have been a little more open than usual. Before the game Beamish said to me: "Understand one thing - no loose play, because if there is, they'll score." I remember, quite early in the game I threw out a bad pass which they seized on and almost got away and I thought George was going to kick me off the field!

"The Springboks were superb coverers and we thought we wouldn't have much chance if we tried to play it out to the wings. So we kept the ball coming back to the pack and they kept going extraordinarily well all through the game, men like Ray Longland, Bill Weston, they were superb."

Buckingham, too, remembered his pre-match instructions: "Beamish said to Brumwell and me: "I don't mind if they have the ball but I want you two centres to hit them so hard they won't know what's going on. As soon as they got the ball, we did just that. I've never known anything like the atmosphere of that match. It was so close and after I had scored the last try I could hardly get off the ground I was so tired."

KEEPING THE FAITH
1931-1934

ON THE STRENGTH of the tumultuous game played by the East Midlands, Barr and Norman got their first caps for England, in the side beaten 12-5 by Wales at Swansea. They played sufficiently well to go through to the next game, against the Springboks, which the tourists won 7-0 and Barr, though he played well in most respects, had the misfortune to be concerned in both the Springbok scores. In fielding a kick ahead of his own line the ball went loose and he slipped in turning to touch down, the referee awarding a try to Bergh. And it was from a kick of his that Brand collected near touch in front of the West Stand and fired over a huge dropped goal which made the match safe.

He won a third cap that season, against Ireland, but Norman was dropped following the Springbok game. It was, nevertheless, a major achievement for the hooker. Having been capped at schoolboy level as a full back before the First World War, he had served in Mesopotamia and made his debut for Leicester in 1919. His first trial came in 1921 but he had to wait until he was 34 for his cap and few begrudged him the honour.

On the domestic front Leicester's unbeaten home record survived until the last day of October when Cambridge University won 26-6 and Gadney, unlucky with injuries this season, ignored offers to play rugby league from the two Hull clubs. Leicester encountered a particularly butter-fingered referee in the January game with Rosslyn Park, since twice the official dropped his whistle in the mud and, despite all the assistance of Norman Coates from touch, it was so clogged up that he had to finish the game by waving his hands wildly to indicate no-side. The giant Beamish played his final game against Blackheath before taking up an RAF posting in the Middle East.

The 1932-33 season, his 12th, Norman captained the club but was unlucky enough to be injured in the second game of the season, against Old Blues. Ernie Coleman was recalled to the colours in his absence and Kendrew tried his hand at hooking before Norman resumed, in a 6-3 win over Gloucester. The permutations in the front row were particularly interesting in view of an International Board circular then going the rounds, which urged clubs to "return to honest scrummaging" and cut out specialisation in the forwards. In other words, back to the old, first up, first down days of before the war.

The spirit of the game as it was then may have been captured by a booklet which the Leicestershire Schools Union had compiled, with articles by Norman, Buckingham, Barr and Greenlees, called *"Hints on Rugger for Schools and Clubs"*. Among the technicalities dealt with appeared this passage: "The essence of rugby football is that it is played by those who believe that a game should be played for the love of the game itself, and not for what they can make out of it; that is, by true amateurs. As soon as money matters become involved in a game, there is always a loophole for all sorts of abuses to creep in. Players commence to consider their own immediate value, and very soon the aim of true sportsmanship is apt to become lost."

"Never descend to such tricks as holding a player in a tackle long after he has parted with the ball, or tackling a player deliberately after he has kicked a ball to prevent him from following up, knowing that the referee will be following the flight of the ball. These actions and the practice of stealing up off-side behind the referee's back are tricks which no gentleman would consider for a moment. In other words, always play the game in such a spirit that at any time afterwards you will never be able to recall any incident of which you might be ashamed. There is much more abiding value in an honourable defeat than in a victory gained by shady means."

Written 60 years ago, the validity of the message still holds good in an increasingly professional sporting world but Leicester in 1932 had other problems, besides upholding the traditions of the game. The financial position was still shaky, despite an increase of £900 in gate receipts and season tickets and another economy was introduced when after match tea was switched from the nearby Granby Halls to the upstairs room of the clubhouse. It seems curious that the committee had not thought of it before! Gallant as ever, the committee were considering the needs of their lady guests, but estimates for a new ladies' lavatory were too high and the matter was deferred.

New talent was still becoming available and in October 1932, Leicester played an all-Irish centre pairing against Coventry, Paddy Coote and Morgan Crowe, who helped in a 16-4 win. Dr Crowe had come to work at Leicester's Royal Infirmary, following the footsteps of medical men like R A K Wiener, J C R Buchanan, H N Knox and J H Moore, all of whom had helped Leicester since the war. A Dubliner, he was to prove one of the most popular players at Welford Road during his three-year stay, famed for his practical jokes as well as his abstention from tobacco and alcohol.

When he joined Leicester he had already been capped 10 times by Ireland and he was joined, not quite so regularly, in the side by another cap, S S C Meikle, from Waterloo. Stephen Meikle won his only England cap at fly-half in 1929 but he turned in some exceptional performances for Leicester on the wing.

The 1932-33 season, at club level, held great promise early on when Leicester went 12 games without defeat. Number 13 proved their undoing when they lost at Cambridge University, a day when the Leicester scrum packed in the 3-4-1 formation and there were local complaints that, if Albert Freethy, the referee, had applied the advantage law correctly Leicester would have won. 'Twas ever thus. Their ground record fell to Old Merchant Taylors in the next game and, with players called away for trials and Gadney unavailable through injury for most of the first half of the season, form slumped. Representative honours continued to come the club's way, however, among them an invitation to play for England to the

Tigers team at Coventry, 7th October 1933.
Mr Bradshaw (Hon Tres), Wormleighton, Hughes, Bennett, Edmiston, Adams, Jackson, Mr Thorneloe (Hon Sec).
Coote, Crowe, Gadney, Buckingham (Capt), Vallance, Berry, Manson, Slow, Harris.

hard working lock, George Vallance, who had joined Leicester from Notts in 1930.

Vallance, Kendrew, C G R Lewis and Gadney had all been picked for trials, although Gadney could not play and when everyone was expecting Kendrew to be picked against Wales, he was omitted and Vallance was called up. Unfortunately for him influenza put him out of action for a time and, though he played in a game for Richmond so that the selectors could see whether he was fit, Vallance asked them not to consider him because he felt he could not give 100 per cent. He never had another chance of representing his country, Tony Roncoroni of Richmond coming in and holding his place all season.

When England played Ireland, though, Gadney was in for his first cap, and Kendrew was restored to the front row. With George Beamish on the Irish side, Leicester were well represented and Gadney scored a try, Kendrew kicked a conversion and England won 17-6. For their game with Scotland, Ireland called up Crowe and gave Coote his first cap. And in March, there was another significant recruit to the club in the form of Charles Slow, whom so many at Welford Road remembered fondly. He had lost his place in Northampton's side, missing the 21-3 defeat they gave Leicester, and switched allegiance, making his debut in a 31-12 win over London Welsh.

It was during the 1933-34 season that Slow's partnership with Gadney really began to blossom

though not at Swansea, since Slow missed the Cardiff connection. But Leicester lost Coote in much unhappier circumstances: in that same game at St Helen's, Coote, a fearless tackler, collided with one of the Welsh three-quarters, who had to leave the field. Coote carried on but collapsed in the train on the way home and was rushed to the RAF hospital at Uxbridge with a severely damaged neck. He was on the dangerously ill list for a long time and though he finally recovered he never played rugby again.

For the 1933 game against the Barbarians, G W C Meikle joined his brother Stephen in Leicester's line up and became only the second Tigers player to score three tries against the Baa-baas. Usually a centre, Graham Meikle was on the wing for his first appearance in Leicester colours and he had inside him that fine Bath centre, Ron Gerrard, whom the selectors wanted to see prove his fitness before picking him for England.

After helping Leicester to a 21-10 win, the next day Graham Meikle was playing for Waterloo against Tigers, who included in their ranks five of the beaten Barbarian XV. It may have been nice for the spectators but there can be little doubt that it must have rankled with those players whom the club dropped and there is little question that Tigers' somewhat cavalier treatment of the local men did them little good in the long term.

At least it was a Leicester regular, Bernard Gadney, who really dominated the headlines this season. He and Kendrew were both picked against

Wales, with Kendrew expected to get the captaincy, but when he pulled out it was Gadney who was given the leadership of his country, and his half-back partner Slow was named a reserve for the match. It was a singular honour for the club, for though J E Greenwood and W W Wakefield had captained England while playing for Leicester, Gadney was the first home-produced player to captain his country.

His first outing as skipper - only his fifth cap - was crowned with success, for Wales were beaten (though it was suggested that a representative Leicester XV could have beaten Wales that day). He then led England to the Triple Crown, being joined in the Calcutta Cup-winning XV by Kendrew and Slow. For the fly-half it was his only England cap but for Leicester it was the second time they had provided England's halves, Wood and Taylor having done the job once before the war. In addition to captaining England successfully, Gadney captained the East Midlands - again with Slow as his partner - to the County Championship.

SUGAR WHISTLE

Mr Scorer the referee, could not make his whistle work at the start of a game in 1934 against Bristol. Thinking he had repaired it, he tried it out only for the two parts to break away. He then borrowed another whistle which had been in the hands of a child and was found to be blocked with a sweet!

The 1933-34 season ended with a successful tour of the West Country, on which they were joined by the Northern back row forward, Jack 'Mac' Hodgson, who had toured with the 1930 Lions and was capped by England in 1932 and 1934. It was on this tour, under the guidance of Hodgson (Northern's youngest captain at the age of 19), that Leicester changed their scrum formation very successfully from 3-2-3 to 3-4-1. The eight forwards had been restored shortly after Crumbie's death but this latest change, despite earlier experimentation, had been picked up from Guy's Hospital and Leicester found that their scrummaging greatly improved. The club had been invited to play in the Middlesex Sevens but they decided to stay loyal to the Leicestershire event.

THURSDAY'S MAN

Whilst stationed in Ireland 'Joe' Kendrew would commute between Londonderry and Leicester, on one occasion staying at Glen Parva Army Depot. Leicester Thursday, if a man short, would ring the officers mess and ask if anyone wanted a game. Kendrew accepted, and during a lift to the game this conversation took place:-

X   Where do you play?
K   (trying to be helpful)- It is very kind of you to give me a game. I will play wherever you like.
X   (rather confused) - When did you play your last game?
K   Last Saturday
X   What position did you play then?
K   Forward
X   Where was it played?
K   Twickenham
X   Who were you playing for?
K   Er, England

Upon which X (Harry Bryan) very nearly crashed his car!

Tigers (in white) chasing Tom Clay of Nuneaton at Welford Road on 24th November 1934.

CHAPTER 8

PAUPERS AND THE PRINCE
1934-1939

DEBT still hung heavily over the club. Support had not picked up as much as Leicester needed and those who came regularly seldom, if ever, saw the same XV do service from one week to the next. Leicester were using between 60 and 80 players a season which could hardly make for continuity and besides, there was a growing amount of alternative attractions. At the club's annual meeting, the joint treasurer, Mr Bradshaw, declared: "It is up to the supporters if they want to save the club."

The supporters responded. The Leicester Rugby Supporters club was formed, under the presidency of the former forward, Charlie Cross. Grants to the Leicester Alliance were ended and the ladies of the club took over serving the teas. It is not very surprising at this traumatic stage in the club's life that the committee turned down an invitation from Amatori Club, Milan, to make a tour in Italy - they had to concentrate on the home front (The same Milan club helped Leicester celebrate their ground centenary in 1992).

The idea of the supporters' club had come from the other joint treasurer, Mr J G Grahame, whose three daughters had taken out a permanent loan on the rugby world by marrying Harry Greenlees and the brothers Stephen and Graham Meikle. The club's function, it was stressed, was to support rugby throughout the city and county but their primary fund-raising efforts, dances, socials, fetes and funfairs, were directed towards Leicester's coffers and in the five seasons before the Second World War

they raised £2,225 for the Tigers. Over 300 people attended the inaugural meeting, at the Granby Halls, while another source of income was developed in the letting of Welford Road for professional boxing shows.

The 1934-35 season began with the decision of the former Coalville forward, G N Harris, who had improved spectacularly during 1934, to join Salford Rugby League Club (he was to be followed North a year later by another ex-Coalville player, centre I Lloyd, who joined Barrow). But on the credit side Leicester had the services of Lancashire's Roy Leyland at centre, Hodgson in the back row, and a useful Scottish fly-half, John McLean. When asked why he preferred to play for Leicester when his work was in London, Hodgson is reputed to have replied: "I haven't got a bowler hat and an umbrella so I can't join 'Quins and I certainly haven't got a sports car to admit me to Blackheath so I'm happy to have a couple of hours on the train and play for Leicester."

Hodgson, whose business interests subsequently took him to Johannesburg and then Turkey, later became the brother-in-law of another player then on the fringe of Leicester's regular side, J T W Berry, a back row forward from the Market Harborough area who played his first game in Tigers' colours in 1932. In the early 30s Tom Berry played a lot of his rugby for Market Harborough, near his farm, but he was to win a reputation as an immensely hard-working forward which brought him three England caps before the outbreak of the Second World War. His administrative qualities were to take him further than that, for he became manager to the first England side to go on a short tour in 1963 and subsequently the first Leicester member to become President of the Rugby Football Union.

At this stage, however, Berry was still hoping for a regular spot with the club, in what was to be the consistent Ralph Buckingham's last season. It was a memorable swansong, however, Buckingham formed part of a back division that would have done any England side proud: in the game against Harlequins it was hoped to field an all-international back division when Barr, Graham Meikle, Leyland, Crowe, Buckingham, Slow and Gadney were named, but Slow dropped out.

In addition Buckingham, along with Barr, got his first game for the Barbarians, against the East Midlands, and he became the club's first choice goal-kicker after 10 years when he had never place-kicked at all. "Anyone ought to be able to kick goals, Bernard," said Buckingham to his captain, Gadney, one day when the kicks were not going over at all. "You have a shot then," said Gadney and Buckingham did so well that for the first time in his career he became the club's leading scorer.

In his last home match, against Blackheath, he scored 15 points in a 39-8 win and in his last match for Tigers, on tour against Exeter, he passed 100 points. His attitude to the game can perhaps be encapsulated in the remark he once made: "We all like to win but to lose well if we can't." He got a good send off from the Press too, for Dai Gent, writing in *The Sunday Times* said: "Quite one of the best club players any side in the country has ever had. Versatile, skilful and always cheerful, Buckingham has rendered his club grand service."

![SUPPORTERS' CLUB PERSONALITIES - caricatures including J.G. Grahame The Founder, Coun. Mrs Swinfen Vice-Pres Ladies Section, Oliver Holmes Hon. Sec., Charlie W Cross - President, B.R. Baxter Hon. Treas. Publicity Comm., E.O. Waller Chairman Whist Comm., H. Wreford Chairman Excursion Comm., F.W. Taylor Hon. Treas., Coun. D.E. Morris Vice-Pres. Chairman Membership Comm., R. Jacob Chairman Dance Comm., D.J. Norman Chairman Publicity Comm., J.M. Higgs Hon. Sec. Membership Comm. 1934 Page 10]

The Tigers Supporters' Club 1934.

During the 1934-35 international season Gadney found himself for once on the sidelines, as his old rival Jimmy Giles of Coventry was given a chance by the selectors. Perhaps a selector attended the club game against London Welsh in December when, firstly, the opposition were delayed on their journey by a train and had to be ferried to the ground by a fleet of taxis then, secondly, Gadney sent a telegram to say he was held up at Banbury; at 2.45 pm a second telegram arrived from the hapless scrum-half (expense no object): "Engine broken down - fill my place." But 35 minutes later, the player arrived, Buckingham moved to the wing and Newton Adams back to the pack and the two clubs played 25 minutes each way with no interval. Enough to confuse any selector! But Gadney returned for England in the Calcutta Cup game, with Headingley's Dick Auty as his half back partner. Auty had played several games for Leicester and was well known as a brilliant attacker, even if his defensive qualities were not quite so marked. Kendrew had taken over from Gadney as England's captain and the 22-year-old Leyland played in all three games, the only caps of a distinguished career, though he was to go with the British Lions to South Africa in 1938.

Bill Bottrill in action against Coventry on 28th March 1936.

Another youngster made his bow for Tigers this season too, an 18-year old product of Trent College, Prince Alexander Obolensky. Playing on the wing over the Christmas period he scored two tries in an 11-8 defeat against Birkenhead Park. It was remarkable then that a Russian prince, born in St Petersburg, should have been playing first class rugby but Obolensky's subsequent career for Oxford University and England showed just what a talented performer he was.

In 1935 Crowe returned to Ireland and Leyland left to join Richmond, which left something of a hole

in the centre, but on the credit side was the acquisition of the Oxford University and England hooker, Edward Nicholson. He joined a club still the best part of £6,000 in debt but still to the forefront as far as the England selectors were concerned. For this was the season of Jack Manchester's All Blacks and Obolensky's match against them.

The Russian prince, the RAF centre S G Walker and Charles Beamish had all played for the Midlands XV beaten 9-3 by the All Blacks at Coventry and seven more Leicester players appeared in the Leicestershire and East Midlands XV beaten 16-3 by the tourists before a 27,000 crowd at Welford Road. In the backs were Barr, Slow, Gadney, John Charles and John Fox - the latter two both products of Stoneygate, the one a wing, the other a hard tackling centre - while the pack included Nicholson and M A Robinson. Also in the side was Morgan Crowe but this time there was no repeat of the famous win four years previously.

Slow, the hero against the Springboks, pulled a leg muscle in the first quarter and left the field, Bill Weston coming out of the pack to cover for him. Reduced to 14 men for most of the match, the combined side had to concede the game although Gadney and Charles both went close, and Longland scored the counties' try.

On the club scene there were rumbles that Leicester rugby was on the way down, with six defeats in nine games. There was a 0-0 draw with the Barbarians and a rash of honours tended to gloss over some indifferent results. Gadney, Kendrew, Nicholson and Obolensky were picked for England against the All Blacks, with Gadney captaining the side, and although years later that match is remembered for Obolensky's spectacular brace of tries in a 13-0 win, Gadney was more inclined to recall the contribution of England's pack early in the game: "We had a very heavy pack - just like Leicestershire did against the Springboks - and we decided to shove very hard in the first two or three scrums, to make the New Zealanders feel worried. After the match Jack Manchester told me: "That first scrum, I knew we were up against it. When we got the ball I tended to break, as I did with Leicester, which made them think we were trying to go through that way."

However, most people remember the game for Obolensky's second try, when he turned up on the wrong side of the field - a not infrequent occurrence - and took advantage of a slight hesitation by Peter Cranmer to run diagonally through the All Blacks' defence. For Kendrew it was his fifth appearance against these particular tourists, having done duty against them for Combined Services, London Counties (twice), Ulster (where he was stationed) and England. Later in the season, against Ireland, he was picked at hooker when Nicholson was dropped and Hodgson was picked against an Irish XV including Charles Beamish. But only Gadney and Obolensky survived through the season to play against Scotland.

The season ended with only 15 wins and 20 defeats and the club established a special committee

Tigers match programme against Bristol on 30th November 1935.

TRAINING
Unlike in the modern game, fitness has not always been a priority. In December 1935 a special request had to be made for players to attend training!!!!

to look for talent in Leicester. Of the 84 players used that season, 41 were local and a game against a Rest of Leicester XV in April left Tigers with an unimpressive 13-3 win. There were calls for the revival of the 'A' team as a stepping stone for local talent, and it was obvious that change was in the air.

Three Leicester members spent the summer with a British team in the Argentine, Gadney (as captain), Charles Beamish and Obolensky, with a fourth Leicester man, Doug Prentice, acting as manager. While they were still away the club's talent scouts came up with a list of names of local players worth consideration by Leicester, 70 of them being invited to pre-season training at Welford Road. Among other things Tigers were short of a hooker, having lost Nicholson to Guy's Hospital the previous season, and the consistent Melton Mowbray farmer S A Loxton having retired.

But it was not an auspicious opening to the 1936-37 season. Bedford won the first game 18-12, the first time since the war they had won at Leicester and the first time since 1919 that Tigers had lost their initial game. The experiment of playing a back row forward, Rodney Willcox, at centre, was discontinued fairly rapidly and form picked up. Gadney returned to action to help in a fine 18-18 draw at Newport and Leicester became the first club to beat Oxford University - including Obolensky - and they then beat a full-strength Gloucester 7-3.

The Hinckley hooker T G Ridgway, despite being sent off in a county match for persistent foot-up, was picked for Major R V Stanley's XV against Oxford and then won a reserve place for England's first trial. Another newcomer to make a distinct impression - as much for his youth as anything else - was the Wyggeston School captain, J R Preston, who played centre against Birkenhead Park over the Christmas holidays. All but one of the six December fixtures were lost, including that against the Barbarians which began with a minute's silence in memory of their founder, Percy Carpmael, who had died that year.

Once more the club had hit a low spot: there was a run of 12 defeats in the space of 13 matches and though Berry and Barr were called on as reserves for England against Wales, Tigers could make no excuses about losing a large number of players to trial and international games. To add to their depression, their leading player, Gadney, accepted a post at a school in Leeds and this was to be his seventh and last season with Leicester. Another, the former Aylestone St James and RAF prop George Greaves, joined the Rugby League club Castleford and for the first time in 17 years, Leicester lost all three games on their West Country tour at Easter.

No longer were they cock of the Midlands roost. After the defeat at Coventry there were numerous complaints about the tactics of the Coventry wing

forwards, who allegedly spent much of the match virtually offside. A fortnight later the Rugby Football Union approved an experiment in the game with Northampton at Welford Road, law 17(b) being tampered with so that players were prohibited from advancing at a set scrum in front of their own forwards until the ball had gone. The result was, according to *The Leicester Mercury*, "a gloriously open game", won by the Saints 11-4.

But overall the results were the worst in the club's history, with 14 wins and 23 defeats, even if a very young Leicester XV beat Bristol and Blackheath in the last two games. The crowning insult was defeat in the first round of the Leicestershire Sevens, against Aylestone Athletic, a competition in which Leicester had been in the final every year since its inception.

Obviously the policy of picking players who would be regularly available - which meant in practice more home-based players - was going to take time to come good. But the 1937-38 season brought another useful crop of promising youngsters, among them the Hinckley forward Denis Bolesworth, a former Uppingham School pupil Bill Bainbridge who had played a couple of games the previous season as a schoolboy and whose father had played for the club before the war, and the Aylestone St James full back, Ernest Watkin.

Slightly better known, at the time, was the Welsh trials centre Gwyn Thomas, who joined from Burton, but sadly he spent most of the season out of action through injury. Honours were comparatively few, Berry and Ridgway becoming non-travelling England reserves against Wales and Berry being forced to turn down a place in the Barbarians XV against the East Midlands because of injury. The Baa-baas, incidentally, had done Leicester no favours by picking Gadney and Auty at half back against them over Christmas. The two were now in harness for Headingley and assisted the guest side to a record 34-0 win, Auty scoring three tries. Only twice since then have the Baa-baas won by bigger margins, 35-0 in 1969 and 43-4 in 1974.

Bainbridge distinguished himself by playing every game during the season and travelling some 10,000 miles to do so since he lived in Warrington. Curiously, having played 41 consecutive games for

George Greaves

the club, the following season he joined Birkenhead Park since Leicester were better off for locks and could afford to ignore his qualities. Another son of a famous father found his way into the side this season, in the shape of Gordon Lawrie, son of Percy, who made his debut against Blackheath.

It was a 16-0 win for Leicester but the limelight undoubtedly went to former Newbold back row player, Fred Doe, who scored four tries. In 13 games he scored nine tries and played regularly the next season, sufficiently well to get an England trial, though Warwickshire never picked him for their county side. Cecil Beamish played on tour, following in the well trodden footprints of George, Charles and Victor, and the season ended on a hopeful note with a 27-0 win over Bath, the best win of the season.

It had also been a good year for the Stoneygate winger S F Herbert, who topped Leicester's points chart with 77. Frank Herbert scored 12 tries during 1937-38 in a comeback which must have caused some blushes at Welford Road. He made his Leicester debut as far back as 1931 but he never won a regular place until the two seasons which preceded the Second World War - certainly a case of better late than never.

The stormclouds were gathering over Europe as Leicester went into the 1938-39 season, which was unfortunate because prospects for a fairly young side looked bright. Tom Berry captained a team which included the Scottish cap from Dunfermline, M M Henderson, who had become a PE instructor at Loughborough Colleges, and the England trials centre Francis Edwards, who joined from Birkenhead Park. But for the Second World War, Francis would surely have become a senior cap for he was a very fine player but he had to make do with a wartime international selection. Another centre, R A Squibbs, who had spent much of the previous year injured, joined from Loughborough and did enough to win a Welsh trial while the Leicester pack included Peter Jerwood, who had played against them the previous season while he had been a student at Cambridge University.

In fact Tigers had a strong link with the Light Blues this season, and when the two clubs met in a game refereed by Wavell Wakefield, Leicester had E R Knapp - then a student at Cambridge - at fly-half while the University had Jim Parsons at scrum-half. Parsons had first played for Leicester four years earlier while still at Rydall School and he fought a protracted battle with the Old Wyggestonians scrum half D E Bevins for the right to succeed Gadney. On the day the students had the edge, winning 28-22.

For the first time since 1934 Leicester beat Coventry 6-0, despite an injury to Bevins which reduced them to 14 men, and they did remarkably well to beat Northampton 5-3 on the last day of the old year: snow prevented the Hinckley men, Bolesworth and Ridgeway, reaching Northampton and Leicester started with a six-man pack, to be reinforced during the game by York and Lees, both of whom were spectating. Berry, Edwards, Ridgway, Doe and S E A Anthony, another back row forward, played in England's first trial and there were Scottish trials for Henderson and the former Loughborough Colleges centre W G Young, while Squibbs had to turn down a Welsh trial because he

had influenza. Another newcomer, Keith Downes, a centre from Cambridge who joined Leicester over Christmas, was named in a Welsh trial despite the fact that he had been born to Scottish parents at Birkenhead and lived most of his life in England. His Welsh 'qualification' was that he had gone to Rydall School in North Wales, but, probably confused by it all, he withdrew from the trial.

Edwards scored two tries from the wing to help the Tigers to an 8-6 win over the Barbarians and the club were delighted to see their skipper, Berry, picked at last for England in the back row, even though he spent much of the season in the second row. Kept out for so long by Northampton's consistent Bill Weston, Berry played in all England's games while Edwards and Downes were reserves for their respective countries - Downes had opted for Scotland. Obolensky, now with Rosslyn Park, made a final appearance in Leicester colours against Richmond, at the request of the England selectors and Gadney was available to tour at the season's end. Tragically his old Leicester and East Midlands partner, Charles Slow, missing from the first-class game for two seasons, was killed in a motoring accident returning from playing the last game of the season with Stony Stratford.

Nevertheless, in all respects it had been a much improved year. The Supporters' Club, working away in the background, had played an immense part in bolstering the club's finances and the players responded by winning 20 of their 36 games. In a year when Loughborough reached the Universities Athletic Union final, Leicester had received a lot of help from Colleges members and a curious statistic from that season was that Tigers used ten fly-halves.

There was every reason to suppose that the new decade would be a bright one. Fixtures were due to be renewed with Cardiff and Gadney was hoping to be available again. The Australians were to tour but no sooner had they set foot in this country than war was declared against Germany - it was a long way to come to play no rugby. The first game of the 1939-40 season should have been against Bedford but only one member of the opposition, the Irish international wing V J Lyttle, appeared so a hurriedly organised Rest XV played Leicester and lost 20-6. The Territorial Army had called up its members and, for the second time in 25 years, rugby closed down.

Tigers VII's line-up in 1935-36. Adams, Charles, Willcox, Parsons, Berry, Hodgson, Vallance.

FALSE ALARMS
When Leicester made the trip to Newport for the game in 1938 there was a large crowd in the station upon their arrival. Unfortunately it was not for the Tigers; it turned out Gracie Fields was expected!!

TIGERS REFORM
1940-1948

"WE NEVER CLOSE" may have been the motto of London's famous Windmill Theatre during the war but it could very well have been true for rugby in Leicestershire. Obviously regular fixtures had gone by the board but Thorneloe spared no efforts to keep the game going by raising a side to play other Midland teams and bringing Barbarian XVs to Leicester to raise money for charity.

His endeavours were boosted by a new organisation, the Leicestershire Harlequins, formed to give a game to servicemen passing through the county, local players home on leave and anyone still in the area who wanted to play. Four enthusiasts, Doug Norman, R C Nun, C G Smith and C A Davis, ran the Harlequins who played their first game on October 4, 1941. Several times they were able to field as many as three XVs and when the war ended, 34 members of the Harlequins figured in Tigers' teams.

Under normal circumstances 1940 would have been a gala occasion for Leicester, since it was the year of their diamond jubilee. In fact it was the year the club suffered the first of its war casualties, when Obolensky was killed in a flying accident. By the end of the war Leicester, like many other clubs up and down the country, had the melancholy duty of recording the deaths of several more players - Victor Beamish, Wilfred Young, A P Hughes, J G Llewellyn, Paddy Coote, and A H Greenwood. On a happier note Bobby Barr, who was taken prisoner at Dunkirk by the Germans and spent most of the war as a POW, won the Military Cross and Colonel Guy German the Distinguished Service Order.

It is conceivable that there was more rugby in Leicester during the war than in any other centre in the country and when hostilities ended, a grateful letter arrived from the Army Rugby Union thanking the Leicestershire officials for their work in raising over £10,700 for service charities.

The war in Europe ended on May 5, and 18 days later the Tigers committee held their first meeting to contemplate the future. They had a lot to think about - they were still some £1,800 in debt and likely to be more so in view of the work to be done to the ground, which had been damaged during the war, the repair to the collapsed wall at the Welford Road end and renovation of the stands.

A select committee was formed to launch a public appeal for funds while the affairs of the club were in the capable hands of Billy Bradshaw, the President, R L Bedingfield, the treasurer, with Thorneloe remaining as secretary and Ralph Buckingham becoming team secretary. During the summer there were several meetings between the secretary and Doug Norman, since it was envisaged that the Leicestershire Harlequins would form the basis for the post-war Tigers.

And so it turned out. During the 1945-46 season it was decided to run two teams, the first to be called the Leicester Football Club, the second to be called the Leicestershire Harlequins. The selection committee comprised three Leicester members and three Harlequins members and the arrangement, after some initial hiccoughs, settled down well enough. There were only four defeats after Christmas and in January, 1946, a Leicestershire and East Midlands XV played Charles Saxton's Kiwis at Welford Road, the New Zealand Army touring side which did so much to put rugby back on its feet after the war.

There was an excellent nucleus of experienced players to build round. Tom Berry, now considerably nearer 40 than 30, captained the side and with him he had Watkin, Bolesworth, W H Richards and Cecil Beamish. In due course Francis Edwards, who had played in service internationals during the war, returned from Burma while a former Wyggestonian schoolboy who was still serving in the Royal Navy, W K T Moore, did so well at scrum-half that England picked him in two Victory internationals.

Ironically enough, Moore, the grandson of the former Leicester half-back Billy Foreman, played only eight games for Tigers that season, none of them at scrum-half. Seven of his appearances were at centre, the eighth at fly-half, but he played at scrum-half for Devonport Services, for the Navy and Leicestershire and the East Midlands. But much of the credit for a successful resumption had to go to the two 'old hands', Berry and Edwards, even though they knew few of their playing colleagues at the start of the season.

Berry, in a reserved occupation during the war, had played no rugby for five years: "It was quite amazing when I turned up for pre-season training how few of the players I recognised," he said.

"I felt almost as if I were starting playing for the Tigers all over again. Soon we all got to know each other and I was asked to lead the side for the next two years which, on reflection, I think were the most enjoyable rugger-playing days of my life." The first game of the newly-constructed club played on September 8, 1945, could hardly have been harder; it was against Cardiff, the first between the clubs

Wartime Leicestershire Harlequins at Bristol on 29th April 1944 where they lost 12-3.

since the rift some 15 years earlier. Leicester lost 12-6 at the Arms Park and in the pack was a 22-year old back row forward from Alderman Newton's School in Leicester, one Jerry Day, who thus began a period of service to the club maintained for the next 37 years.

While the players did their utmost to recapture the lustre of pre-war days, the committee had to iron out more damage, to the clubhouse which had been used by the Army during the war. The occupying military had the delightful habit of boring holes in the floor, so extensive repairs had to be made. No doubt the treasurer welcomed the funds brought by another group of servicemen, the Kiwis, when they played Leicestershire and the East Midlands at Welford Road on January 31, 1946, before an enthusiastic crowd.

Leicester had eight players in the combined XV, with a claim on M M Henderson, who joined Bedford after the war. The team was: C E Watkin (Leicester); A G Butler (Harlequins), F G Edwards, H Thomas (both Leicester); R O Pell; J M Pell (both Northampton); W K T Moore; A D Bolesworth (both Leicester), G A Kelly (Bedford), R J Longland (Northampton), H P Hughes (Leicester), R Willshire (Bedford), J T W Berry, C H Beamish (both Leicester), M M Henderson (Bedford). Berry captained the side in the only game he ever played against a touring party, having been kept out of all the regional games before the war by Northampton's consistent Bill Weston. But the Kiwis took the honours 14-0, tries coming from J Sherratt, P K Rhind and E G Boggs, with a penalty and a conversion from H E Cook, and the locals were left with the memory of some good runs from Edwards, Haydn Thomas and J M Pell, with some outstanding work in the loose from Henderson.

The 1945-46 season ended with the very precise record of 16 wins, two draws and 16 defeats, and at the annual meeting that year it was decided that the Harlequins XV should be replaced by an 'A' XV, a decision which was to have lasting consequences. It was 40 years since Leicester had fielded a second string and it was a move that met with considerable hostility from clubs on whom Tigers had previously relied, like Stoneygate, Westleigh and Old Wyggestonians.

Junior clubs such as these had supported Leicester staunchly when called upon for players but they felt disinclined, not unnaturally, to see their players go to Leicester's second team when Tigers were still, in essence, an invitation club. There was hot division too, among the Leicester committee, some of whom looked back fondly to the Crumbie era of one team, and those who looked forward and saw that sooner or later Leicester would have to conform and become a proper members' club running two or three XVs. The arguments began to rumble back and forth, and were to do so, with increasing vehemence, for another 10 years - the long-term consequences were still being felt in the 1970s.

On a happier note, in June, 1946, Leicester began their old players' membership. The qualification for this, which has not altered, was a minimum of 20 games for the senior side which earned the individual his player's tie. It is also the reason why such esteemed players as Tony O'Reilly of Ireland and Alan Old of England fail to appear on the club's

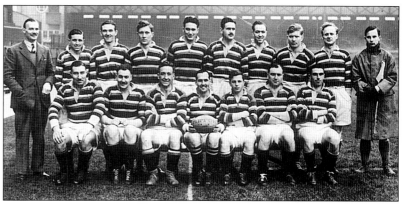

honours board, for neither played 20 games during their time with Leicester, even though both were members for two seasons.

The controversial 'A' XV made its bow on September 21, against Rolls Royce, while the senior side had already got off the ground with a 12-0 win over Bedford. It was virtually a brand new three-quarter line and Tigers scored four tries, three of them coming from a 22-year-old South African then serving in the RAF at Cosford, M R Channer. Mel Channer had played a handful of games the previous season, first in the centre and then at fly-half. His brilliance was to be of considerable importance to the club's playing record during the next eight years.

A useful start to the season was spoiled somewhat when Waterloo, with John Heaton and his cousin Dickie Guest in their three-quarter line, won 34-19 at Welford Road, the highest aggregate score at the ground since Richmond were beaten 62-3 in 1919 and equalling the highest total ever scored at that point against Leicester, by the Barbarians in 1937. In those days club games were played over two 35-minute halves, although when Leicester played Cambridge University, the referee agreed to two 40-minute halves (to help Cambridge's preparation for the university match) which allowed Leicester to kick the winning penalty in the 36th minute of the second half.

The long-standing connection of the Goodrich family with the club ended when Albert Goodrich, who had succeeded his uncle Tom as groundsman, left. A proposed Christmas fixture with the Racing Club de France fell through when the French club decided not to travel, so Leicester played Rugby instead and enjoyed a comfortable 24-3 win.

Then winter took a hand. Billy Moore just had time to play his first game of the season, and earn his first full England cap, when the weather brought all sport in the country to a standstill. Snow and ice halted proceedings for two months and there were nine cancellations before the season was finally completed and Tom Berry retired from the first-class game. He had played 275 games for Leicester and his last two seasons must have been among his most valuable. Happily he retained an active connection with the club by agreeing to lead and coach the 'A' team, who had won 14 of their 21 games in their first season back.

The captaincy of the 1947-48 side passed to another pre-war player, Peter Jerwood, who was able to welcome two newcomers into his three-quarter line. They were A C Towell and D E B Rees, both of whom made an immediate impact. Allan

Tigers line up at Twickenham against Harlequins on 6th December 1947.
Back:
RJ Barr (Team Hon.Sec), WJ Herbert, TM Jones, DEB Rees, P Herbert, JR Scott, JR Stapleford, AC Towell, FMT Ashley, W Freer (Touch Judge).
Front:
AD Bolesworth, WH Brown, LG Dermott, CE Watkin (Capt), RE Tudor, HP Hughes, HW Sibson.

Towell had won an England trial with Middlesbrough and was coming to study at Loughborough Colleges, while Danny Rees, from Bridgend, came to the club from Colleges. In the first match of the new season, against Bedford, Towell scored a try from centre in a 22-3 win, but was outshone by his captain who registered two tries. In the next match, a 31-11 win over Bath, Rees made his debut, also at centre, and was twice among the try-scorers in a match during which Channer dropped three goals.

Another newcomer that season was a hefty lock from Leicester Thursday and the club's 'A' side, Eric Lacey, who made his bow in a 6-5 defeat against Neath. But there was much activity off the field too as Leicester found themselves forced to organise a meeting with five junior clubs, Oadby, Old Newts, South Leicester, Stoneygate and Westleigh, over the 'A' team controversy. That their discussions were inconclusive is indicated by the deathly silence which followed the meeting.

In the meantime the Australians, having missed out badly in their 1939-40 tour, were back in the country under the leadership of Bill McLean. It was not the happiest of tours and the Wallabies found themselves involved in several incidents, particularly in Wales, but nothing marred their 17-11 win over Leicestershire and the East Midlands at Welford Road on November 15, 1947.

The worst aspect of the day, from a local point of view, was that Berry took a weakened club XV to Cardiff where they received a 50-5 battering (the only time they have ever conceded fifty points) when Cardiff visited Leicester a fortnight later the Welshmen won 8-4. Meanwhile there were 25,000 at Welford Road to watch Jerwood captain the combined side, which was: C E Watkin (Leicester); R Jones, L B Cannell, T Gray, N Bailey; E Knapp, E J O'Mullane (all Northampton); A D Bolesworth, A E Neal (both Leicester), G A Kelly (Bedford), H P Hughes (Leicester), W R Hamp, D F White (both Northampton), H P Jerwood (Leicester), R G Furbank (Bedford). Danny Rees had been picked on the wing but injury prevented him from playing, while Moore too was unavailable.

Tom Berry, Doug Norman and Bill Moore in 1947.

The Australians, an extremely fit combination, eased their way into a commanding lead. By half-time they had run up an 11-0 lead, their acting captain, Colin Windon, having scored two tries, a third coming from T K Bourke with A K Walker converting the first of Windon's tries. J O Stenmark had run in a fourth try before Ernie Watkin kicked a penalty and then Knapp dropped a goal. Windon's third try made it 17-7 but a dropped goal from over 40 yards by Watkin ensured the counties were not disgraced.

The club side, however, was struggling, with Channer on leave in South Africa, Moore out of action with a septic leg, Rees also injured and Towell on call for Yorkshire. The victory over Harlequins on December 6 was the first since September 20 but there were better things against the Barbarians, who won by only 15-10. Towell, who had moved to fly half, was outstanding. He had made the switch from centre in October and his impressive play over the season as a whole won him first a reserve place for England in the Calcutta Cup match and, on Easter Monday, his first cap at centre against France. He partnered another debutant, Northampton's Lew Cannell, but on the day France were much the better side and won 15-0 in Paris.

On the club front it was unfortunate that the grand gathering of old players on April 16, 1948, had to discuss a season ruined by injuries and outside calls. But at least they were all there the following day when Berry finally called it a day as a player by leading the senior side against Blackheath, being chaired off after a 6-5 win. Watkin became the first club player to pass 100 points in a season since 1935 (his aggregate was 102).

LEICESTER FOOTBALL CLUB

TELEPHONE No. 65330
HOME TEL. No. OADBY 541

BARR RADCLIFFE LTD.,
RYDAL STREET, LEICESTER.

You have been selected to play

versus   Blackheath

at   Leicester   on Saturday

the   17th April, 19 48 Kick off 3 p.m.

Please note Club photograph will be taken before the match. It is, therefore, important that you should be ready at 2.50 p.m.

Train leaves   Station at

Yours faithfully,

R. J. BARR, Hon. Team Sec.

Tom Berry's card for his 277th and final game.

Another who had come to the end of his playing career was the RAF Squadron Leader, H P 'Nick' Hughes, who had played for Waterloo before moving to Leicestershire during the war. He was to become president of the club in 1969 but on his first encounter with Leicester he found life quite different from that he had known in the north-east: "At Waterloo I remember standing next to Jack Heaton in the bar and if I spoke to him I felt chuffed. They ran several sides of course. There was none of that at Leicester.

"Eric Thorneloe was very opposed to a bar. The upstairs clubroom at Welford Road was a tea-room and hardly anyone came. There were no teas for members or spectators while being a member of the supporters' club meant nothing more than paying half a crown for a badge." The social side of life at Leicester consisted of a couple of barrels of beer - not conspicuous for its quality - for the two first XVs upstairs before they adjourned to the "Big Window". Ladies, by common consent, were strictly forbidden before the magic hour of 8pm when they might join their husbands or boyfriends, assuming by then that they wanted to.

It was not for another ten years, after Bobby Barr had become secretary, that the club were decadent enough to run a bar, following some strong lobbying by Francis Edwards. And it was nearly another 10 years later before the club really began to utilise the assets at its disposal and hold regular functions in the clubhouse - but by then the essential nature of the Leicester Football Club had undergone a dramatic change.

SEEDS OF GROWTH
1948-1954

PETER Jerwood was absent through illness early in the 1948-49 season and that consistent hooker, Eddie Neal, retired, to be succeeded by the diminutive (five feet two inches tall) Ronnie Tudor. The Welsh influence in the back division from Rees, Ken Nicholas from Newbridge and Gwynne Lawrence, a native of Swansea but educated at Alderman Newton's School in Leicester, failed to have the desired effect and for the second season running victories were outweighed by defeats.

Jerwood announced his retirement from first class rugby, having achieved an England trial and a Barbarians tie after the war, but the following season he was persuaded back into harness for several games, which enabled him to watch the progress of two new forwards, Peter Thorneloe (nephew of the secretary) and the thickset, former Aylestone St James player, R V Stirling.

Bob Stirling, a regular RAF officer, had spent most of the war in India where he met his wife, a cousin of Tom Berry's. He returned to this country late in 1947, was posted to Cranwell and, on Berry's recommendation, joined the 'Jimmies' before progressing into Leicester's 'A' side. Although his experience was confined to station rugby he quickly made an impact and, though only five feet ten inches tall, Leicester played him in the second row as much for his line-out ability as anything else.

It was the former Leicester player and Ireland cap, George Beamish, who suggested to Stirling that he should play prop for the RAF and in that position he won all his 18 England caps, though when he became a regular for Leicester in 1948 he was only a year short of his 30th birthday. The last year of the decade, however, gave no indication that the clouds over the club's playing record were lifting. The committee decided against electric floodlighting at the ground (too expensive) and the division over the 'A' team continued. On the field the record at the end of 1949-50, of 15 wins against 23 defeats, remains the worst tally since the war.

For all that, the season was by no means featureless. It began with rumours that J C Windsor, one of the 1947-48 Australian party who had played at Welford Road, was to join the club after coming to work at Leicester General Hospital. In fact he did not play and so missed the first post-war victory over Newport, only the 12th win over the Gwent club since fixtures between them began. Towell was leading the side and for the last two months of 1949, he experimented by playing himself at wing forward, by no means unsuccessfully.

A new recruit joined over Christmas, from Loughborough Colleges, the centre George Cullen, and immediately lifted the club morale. He distinguished himself against Nuneaton by scoring in every possible way in a 16-8 win and enjoyed a very successful Easter tour. Billy Moore was capped three times by England and, on the odd occasion, Tigers enjoyed the services of the RAF and Scotland forward, S T H Wright.

The seeds of rapid improvement were there, with players of the quality of Stirling, Moore and Cullen available, while there was the strength and consistency of the pre-war forward Denis Bolesworth and the promise of back row men like Harry Sibson and Leicester University College student Tom Bleasdale to look forward to. Even though Towell moved to Bedford during the close season, under the captaincy of Moore the 1950s opened well.

The 33-9 win over Plymouth was Leicester's biggest for years, the back row was reinforced by England international Bob Weighill - later to be secretary to the Rugby Football Union; Cullen was in fine form both in general play and as a kicker, while in Stan Pratt Leicester had unearthed yet another talented hooker. There were trials for Moore, Cullen and Stirling while Bleasdale and Sibson got reserve cards, though only Stirling was capped, playing all four internationals.

By now Leicester had formulated a policy to try and make their 'A' team acceptable to junior clubs in the county. They circulated a statement of intent, that their aim was to encourage local players, and that local clubs should release players for up to six games. A nucleus would be retained as 'A' team regulars while, in return, Leicester would make their facilities and playing experience available.

Seven clubs, Leicester Thursday, Belgrave, Lutterworth, Aylestonians, Loughborough, South Wigston O B and Melton Mowbray, went along with the policy, but the five who had

Bill Moore (Royal Navy), Peter Jerwood and Francis Edwards (RAF) in training in 1948.

Bill Moore is collared by Micky Steele-Bodger against the Barbarians in 1949.

itself to the admirable work of the Midlands team. Gwynne Lawrence, who was enjoying such a notable season for Leicester, took the eye in the early stages but inevitably the main battle was fought up front, Lacey losing his jersey in the struggle. At halftime there was no score but a penalty by Basie Viviers was enough to see the tourists through.

Lawrence and Moore were Leicester's ever-presents that season, Moore's final season since he retired following the 25-3 win over Sale, chaired off the field. Cullen once again scored over a century of points, despite going through a slightly sticky patch at the end of 1951, and retains fond memories of the Easter tour to the West Country which formed the regular end-of-season climax:

"At this time we were still on friendly terms with the management of the Rougemont Hotel in Exeter, though how they survived the weekend mystified us all. Their stirrup pump fire extinguishers, left over from the war and placed strategically at various levels on a wide spiral staircase and landings surrounding the main lounge, disappeared quickly after one tour when they had been used freely by one player, clad in a jock strap only, to keep Tigers players, guests and management at bay for fully 30 minutes."

Cullen, of course, had joined the club at a time when they were still able to preserve some of the pre-war features and were eagerly watched by crowds starved by the war of live sport. Gradually counter attractions were eroding the numbers of supporters and it was clear as 1952 developed that a crisis was looming. Early in the year the president, Billy Bradshaw, had tendered his resignation but had been persuaded to stay on. At an emergency committee meeting in June Mr Bradshaw warned that considerable economies were necessary, in view of falling gates and the way county rugby on Saturdays was hitting the club. The best way out, he suggested, was to disband the 'A' XV. The majority of the committee disagreed: they decided the club should pay for no drinks, cheaper travel should be investigated and the 'A' XV retained by an 8-5 vote. The following month Mr Bradshaw resigned in protest and Charlie Cross was elected president.

Perhaps it was not surprising that the 1952-53 season should have proved mediocre, though it was a pity from the point of the veteran prop Bolesworth, who had been elected captain. Anyone looking for signs of optimism might have noticed the emergence of two very promising back row forwards, the Cambridge blue John Jenkins and Peter Konig from Moat Old Boys. The season started well enough and included the first win at Coventry for four years following five successive home games: "A good indication of the ferocity of the game was the number of times play was stopped to replace players' shorts," commented the local scribe - a case of post-war shortages?

But then the rot set in and even the recall of the officially retired Moore could not stop it. Leicester lost at Blackheath for the first time since the war and Stirling's commitments allowed him to play only infrequently though England still benefited from his remarkable consistency - he was to captain the national side in 1954, after he had left Leicester for Wasps. The consequences of having too many services players were heavily rubbed in when the

originally stood out against the 'A' team did not. Yet again there was stalemate. Better news for the backroom boys was that Berry was asked to act as an England selector while the club received an invitation to guest in the Middlesex Sevens. It was the Tigers' first appearance in the tournament and they put out the following VII: C G S Lawrence, W K Nicholas, H Thomas, W K T Moore, T Bleasdale, S Pratt, A D Bolesworth. Unfortunately the abbreviated game was not their forte and they went out in the first round, beaten 8-5 by Harlequins 2nds, Moore scoring a try which Nicholas converted.

But 23 wins against 13 defeats was a distinct improvement on the past few years so nobody grumbled too much. And, for the first time, Leicester were televised in action, against London Scottish at Richmond. Ironically enough, that same season, the club had refused to allow the BBC to film the Baa-baas match, fearing that the gate would be down.

At the other end of 1951, Leicester welcomed back the mercurial Channer from South Africa and were delighted to acquire the services of the international wing, Ian Botting, capped by England against Ireland and Wales in 1950 having toured South Africa with New Zealand the previous year though he was not selected for any of the tests. Channer, of course, was not the only rugby-playing South African in the country that season, for Basil Kenyon's Fourth Springboks were sweeping all before them (save the London Counties).

Stirling played against them three times - for the Combined Services, England and the Barbarians - but not at Leicester when they played a Midland Counties XV drawn from Leicestershire, East Midlands and Oxfordshire. On December 29, on a glutinous Welford Road playing surface, the following Midlands XV put up a brave display before going down 3-0: A Smailes (Richmond); N Bailey, L B Cannell (both Northampton), A C Towell (Bedford), C G S Lawrence (Leicester); R H Haynes, E M Fletcher (both Bedford); M J Berridge, T Smith, I H Whiting (all Northampton), E C Lacey (Leicester), J F Bance (Bedford), H W Sibson, T Bleasdale (both Leicester), D F White (Northampton, captain).

It was the only time on tour that the Springboks failed to cross their opponents' goal-line, a tribute in

RAF beat Tigers for the first time since the war, Channer collecting eight points for the airmen who won 12-11. This was one of the major reasons for the poor showing during the season though the club were very unlucky with injuries: Lacey broke an ankle in pre-season training and was not able to play once, Sibson and Bleasdale both sustained nagging injuries which kept them out. Compared with the previous season's total of 34, the club used 45 players in the senior side and it was obvious that a new-look Leicester was in the making.

Tigers in action against Newport on 2nd February 1951.

It was with considerable reluctance that Stirling left the Tigers, a direct consequence of his posting to the Air Ministry in London where he was involved in Saturday morning work. "There was an excellent spirit at the club," he said of his days at Welford Road, "and to get into the Tigers first XV was a great thing. We always tried to play open, aggressive rugby." Not so aggressive though as the story Stirling told against himself of an Easter tour game at Bristol might indicate.

He had been on an RAF ground defence course before joining the tour party and, up to the eyebrows in supposed corpses, could not prevent himself from attracting the referee's attention during the game to an injured player by calling out: "Referee, man wounded." There was also the problem of representing two sides, the club and the force, so that when he found himself playing for the RAF against Leicester, it may not have been entirely inexcusable that, at the first scrum, Stirling was seen to pack down in the Leicester second row.

The improvement during the 1953-54 season was radical, 22 wins against 13 defeats, and speaks much for the qualities of John Jenkins who was the new captain. There was evidence of the new broom at work in the first game, when the former Moseley centre S M Duff, the Loughborough Colleges centre John Elders and the West Countryman David Hazell, all made their debuts against Bedford at full back, centre and prop respectively.

Lacey was back in action and Channer had a new partner at scrum half in A W Black. Gus Black, capped six times between 1947-50 for Scotland, was on the same RAF station as Channer and had played

a couple of games the previous season but now he was to prove a tower of strength before being posted during the 1954-55 season to the West Country, when he joined Bristol.

Elders had played for Leicestershire in 1952 before going to teach in South Wigston and he gave Tigers magnificent service, joining that band of players who, in other circumstances, might well have been capped for their country but who in the end missed out. He was unlucky to coincide with the likes of Lew Cannell, Jeff Butterfield and Phil Davies, but on his day he was as good a centre as most in the country. Hazell, another Loughborough Colleges product, was more lucky for he was capped four times in 1955. He had broken a Colleges points-scoring record in 1951-52 by registering 162 points - including 54 conversions as against 12 penalties which must be considered typical of Colleges rugby.

Perhaps inspired by the suggestion at the annual meeting that year, that the "Tiger Rag" should be played before the teams came onto the field at every home game - marginally better than "The Entry of the Gladiators", one supposes - the team began well, early victories including the first win over Coventry at Welford Road since the war, by 14-3. The escutcheon was promptly blotted when Moseley were allowed their first win in Leicester since 1895-96 (fixtures, it should be remembered, had not been continuous) but honour was partially restored by handing Northampton their first defeat of the season, again at Welford Road.

As the year neared its end their were two displays at Welford Road, completely contrasting in nature, which stood out. The first was the performance of the Midland Counties against Bob Stuart's All Blacks, when the combined side held the tourists to

THE PORTERS TRUCK

Haydn Thomas tells the tail of an Easter Tour to the West Country in the late '40's. " On arrival at Exeter railway station the team loaded their luggage onto a large porters truck (about the size of a mini). They were making their way to the double decker 'bus which was to take them to their hotel when someone had the bright idea of taking the truck with them because it had made life so much easier at the station! By a process of jiggery pokery to equal that of any line out, it arrived (round the bend) upstairs!

"Messrs Thorneloe and Bedingfield laid down the law the following morning, and the truck was duly trundled through the streets of Exeter back to the station."

Stan Pratt (with ball) during the 1951 Barbarians game.

a 3-0 margin, a penalty kicked by Ron Jarden being sufficient to win the game. Five Leicester players were in the side, Cullen (playing on the wing), Elders, Hazell, Bleasdale and Jenkins who was also captain.

Shortly before the game three of Northampton's internationals, Don White, Lew Cannell and John Hyde were forced to drop out and the side which represented the Midlands was: J Hodgkins; D McNally (both Northampton), R W Hosen (Loughborough Colleges), J Elders, G H Cullen (both Leicester); A C Towell (Bedford), J W Hobbs (Gloucester); C R Jacobs, T Smith (both Northampton), D St G Hazell (Leicester), R C Hawkes (Northampton), J M Jenkins, T Bleasdale (both Leicester), V H Leadbetter (Northampton), P S Collingridge (Bedford).

There were 20,000 in the ground to watch Jarden put his side in front after only six minutes but, with the Midlands pack working hard, the All Blacks found themselves pressurised and owed much to the steadiness of that outstanding full back, Bob Scott. Allan Towell had a splendid game, in defence and attack and only an outburst of spleen by the crowd, when Scott was aiming for goal after a controversial penalty, marred the occasion. A letter from the tour manager, J N Millard, to Eric Thorneloe, illustrated what the tourists thought of Leicester:

"I am very glad indeed that we altered our programme to allow us to have a longer stay in your city. I wish to congratulate all those who had any part in staging the match on Saturday. The crowd was handled very efficiently and I realise the demonstration made when Scott was kicking a goal was no fault of yours. Your team played a very fine game and they made a magnificent attempt during the last few minutes to pull the match out of the fire."

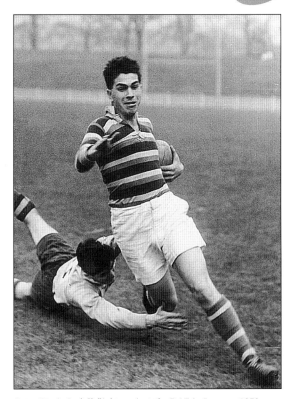

Peter Konig in full flight against the RAF in January 1953.

Three weeks later anyone in that crowd who regretted the lack of scoring received compensation as the Barbarians hammered Leicester 39-11, the chief architects of what was then the Baa-baas' highest points tally against the club (it was passed in 1974) being Ken Jones with three tries, Butterfield and Davies with two each. Black and Hazell worked hard for Leicester with the prop scoring a try, penalty and a conversion.

January and February of 1954 were bleak months, however. For the first time in seven seasons Leicester failed to achieve the double over Bath and the first win since Boxing Day came on February 20 as service calls took their toll. But spring brought doubles over Coventry and Harlequins, a 6-6 draw with Swansea whose try was scored, ironically, by Gwynne Lawrence, and the retirement after the final game, with Sale, of that consistent prop Bolesworth, after 18 years in the game. Hazell scored 102 points, easily leading the scoring charts, and Leicester looked ahead to the season when they would celebrate their 75th birthday.

Derek Ashurst and Freddy Doore in action versus Loughborough Students in October 1954.

TIME TO CHANGE
1954-1957

LEICESTER were no nearer to a solution regarding the 'A' team and the leading local junior clubs but, on the administrative side, there was a major change with the appointment of a paid official in the shape of Major Albert Chilton, to work as general secretary at £250 a year. It had long been obvious that the burden of detail in running the club put such a strain on the honorary secretary and his business affairs that a full-time official was required and Major Chilton fitted the bill. A regular officer who had been serving at South Wigston, his appointment signified an end to the near monopoly of power which had been invested in the secretary ever since Tom Crumbie occupied that post.

Among his first duties would have been to assist in organising the club's 75th anniversary dinner, fixed for the Bell Hotel the following April, and check the last details of the programme that went out on BBC Radio on September 6, commemorating Leicester's distinguished past. A host of famous names took part in the programme, among them Wavell Wakefield, Bernard Gadney, Tom Berry and Bob Stirling, and it probably pained them slightly to see how the current pack was struggling.

There were frequent changes among the forwards, including the introduction of the 1950 British Lions and Ireland captain, Karl Mullen, who hooked against Moseley. Mullen had an appointment at Derby Hospital and it was hoped that he would become regularly available, but it was not to be. At the same time, ironically, as the Tigers were in the toils, Leicestershire had found a winning combination. An 8-0 win over Notts, Lincs and Derby made them Midlands champions for the first time since 1927 and later in the year a single penalty prevented them from progressing to the county championship final, Lancashire - with Tom Bleasdale in their ranks - winning 3-0 at Blundellsands.

Elders captained the county XV and gradually several of the successful Leicestershire players found their way into the Leicester ranks, though not the young M J K Smith who helped Oxford University to an 18-0 win over the club. It was one of those 'chicken and egg' situations: was the club making hay out of the county's victorious run or were the individual players imbued with the desire to play a higher standard of rugby week after week, which meant leaving their junior clubs and joining Tigers? In any event, Stoneygate lock John Ford, who had been asked as a reserve for an England trial after his county displays, made his debut against Blackheath. Two more December debutants, against Birkenhead Park, were the Westleigh full back Brian Small (then studying at Cambridge University) and the Hinckley hooker John Stevens.

Stevens, in particular, showed immense promise, as did another newcomer, John Thompson, who made his debut at lock against London Scottish after service with Aylestone Athletic and Leicester 'A'. Confirmation of the promise shown by this new material came when Tigers beat Swansea at St

Helen's for the first time in 31 years, Elders and Peter Thorneloe scoring the tries which helped the club to an 8-5 win. At the end of the 1954-55 season, Hazell, Channer and Irish scrum half Tom O'Connor were invited to play for the Midland Counties against a Dublin combination at Lansdowne Road, which was doubtless a pleasant way for Hazell to end the season.

The Nottingham schoolmaster had played in all England's games, kicking two penalties against France and one against Scotland. He had been the club's only cap, although back row man Ron Smith had won a trial place. The points total for the season of 454 was a post-war record, very satisfying for the skipper, John Jenkins, who had played in every game.

Three months later the club had cause to wonder just what the future had in store. At the July annual meeting in 1955, the 'A' team was discontinued. According to the club president, Charlie Cross, it had "served its purpose but had now become an expensive luxury." There would be no problems filling positions, said Mr Cross, because Leicester had the support of all the local teams. But the committee remained divided on the appropriate way to guide the club; the older members saw the move as a return to the great days of the Crumbie era. A younger member of the committee, more prophetically, said: "Within three years you will form yourselves into a club with three or four sides."

In the meantime it was apparent that a certain number of players would be leaving the club - if it is possible to "leave" an invitation club - since there was only one XV to play for. Lacey, in any event, had retired from first-team football after 175 games and as one stalwart made his way out, another made his way in. For although the first game of the 1955-56 season, against Bedford, was lost 11-20 there was a newcomer to the back row who was to leave a distinct mark on the club, the 18-year old David Matthews who, the previous year, had been captaining Oakham School. It was to be 19 years and more than 500 games later that Matthews ended his first class career, though by no means his connection with Leicester.

In another respect it was to be quite a season for youth, for Leicestershire chose to overlook the talents of Cullen and named a Wyggeston schoolboy, Michael Wade, against Warwickshire - the start of a distinguished career for the 18-year old Wade which was to bring him three England caps. The younger generation must have been watched with approval by two distinguished visitors and ex-players to the game with Coventry, George Beamish - now knighted, an Air Vice Marshall and serving with Transport Command - and Denis Morris, ex-Conservative councillor and now director of BBC Midlands. Nevertheless Cullen, who had scored a try in Leicester's notable 6-3 win over Cardiff (the first against a Welsh club since 1946) and reached a landmark when he passed 500 points for the club in a game against Old Blues.

TRAPPED TRAINER
The biggest laugh of the afternoon in the 1955 game against Rosslyn Park at Welford Road came when play resumed after a player had been treated for injury. The rival packs were so keen to get down to business that they formed up for a scrum with the Tigers trainer caught inbetween them. There then followed the spectacle of the trainer having to fight his way out!

Action from the Tigers v RAF game of 1955.

He was subsequently recalled by the county who won the Midland group with a 17-0 success over East Midlands.

In general, however, Leicester's backs were not playing well, though Bleasdale from the forwards got an England trial. Maybe it added more point to the new training lights which came into operation in December, 1955, while in the same month Wade made his debut for Tigers. He took part in a 0-0 draw at Bedford, playing opposite one of his masters from school, Ken Nicholas, who had moved to Bedford two years earlier.

Wade kept his place for the Christmas game against the Barbarians because the club captain, Elders, was injured and played against Birkenhead Park to complete the four-day Christmas programme. The Barbarians match was to be Mel Channer's last game for Leicester before returning to South Africa and, as if in his honour, the Tigers played superbly against a guest XV composed - with one exception - of 1955 British Lions. Tries by Tony O'Reilly (two) and Robin Roe helped push Leicester to a 12-3 defeat but it was a memorable moment for Channer who was playing on the wing. He scored 327 points for the club during his years with them but the nearest he came to a cap was a Scottish trial in 1954.

All the more regrettable, therefore, was the subsequent 3-0 defeat by Rugby, their first win at Welford Road this century. It marked something of a decline in form and the first three months of 1956 went by with only two wins. Leicester were never able to field the same XV in successive matches but at least they could hold their heads high after a remarkable game at Llanelli, when they were beaten 24-20, three goals and three tries against a goal, four tries and a penalty. Better goal-kicking might have won them the game, which made the departure of Hazell for Somerset at the season's end the more poignant.

There had been some credits from the season, though. Elders had led Leicestershire, including ten Tigers, to the county championship semi-final when they were beaten 9-3 by Devon at Welford Road, while for both county and club, Wade had been the man of the moment. A useful fly half, Mike Freer from Kibworth, had come into the club side late on and there was every reason to suppose that the 1955 Lions captain, Robin Thompson of Ireland, would join during the summer. He trained with the club as they prepared for the 1956-57 season but then spoiled it all by joining Warrington as a rugby league player.

Further blows came when Wade and the new captain, Bleasdale, were injured in pre-season training and the scrum half, Tom O'Connor, who had been given a trial by Ireland the previous season, joined Northampton because of the lack of opportunity in a club running only one side. It did not help when Nicholas, their former winger, scored the winning points for Bedford in the first match of the new season.

If supporters wanted something fresh to take their minds off this melancholy news, they got it in the shape of a Romanian touring side which played at Welford Road on September 8. Bleasdale had visited Romania at the end of the previous season, guesting with Harlequins, though the visit had been arranged in 1955. It was a XV representing the combined clubs of Bucharest and they met the following Leicester side: B T C Small; P T Baker, J Elders, B A F Smith, R D Matthews; M E Freer, M G Lubbock; F Chawner, J Stevens, J S Thompson, R H Smith, J G Ford, A D Ashurst, J T McCormack, P H Konig.

The visitors proved tough customers. After presenting scarves to the Leicester players and throwing flowers into the crowd, they gave nothing away in terms of tackling, cover defence and man-to-man marking. Their main weakness was the failure to exploit openings but they scored in each half, I Dobre and A Marinache each dropping a goal. In reply, back row forward Derek Ashurst kicked two penalties (though he had no previous reputation as a goalkicker) and the match ended as a 6-6 draw. Peter Thorneloe gave each of the Romanians a model tiger with a cub and they also went away with a club tie each and an official history of the club, which had been written by Brian Thompson, formerly rugby correspondent of *The Leicester Mercury* and later the newspaper's board chairman.

The first two months of the year brought little reward, however. Two wins from eleven games was hardly what the Leicester public were accustomed to, even if there was an interesting newcomer from Westleigh in the shape of a New Zealand-born back row man, Colin Martin, who made his debut against Newport in September and also solved something of a goal-kicking problem, since Ashurst was unable to maintain the performance he had shown against the Romanians.

Off the field though, things were starting to hum. During the summer the club had appointed a sub-committee to investigate the constitution of the club, following suggestions at the annual meeting that the 'A' XV should be reformed. The committee, chaired by Doug Norman, consisted of Tom Berry, Tom

ACCIDENTS GALORE
The last week of the year 1955 was hardly a lucky week for the Tigers visitors. Birkenhead Park met with a road accident motoring back on Monday night; Tony O'Reilly (who played for the Barbarians) was involved in an accident going to the Television studios in Birmingham the following evening; then Robin Thompson, (skipper of the British Lions side in South Africa) who led the Barbarians at Leicester was operated on for appendicitis on his return to Ireland.

Bleasdale, Francis Edwards, Alistair Smallwood and W H Richards, all of them men with immense experience both in the playing side of the game and its administration.

The result of their endeavours was a report with nine suggestions which, since it was adopted by the main committee by an overwhelming majority, helped establish the direction the club was to take in the foreseeable future. It is therefore worth giving their findings in some detail: the main recommendation was that the Tigers should be a club in the real sense of the word, running three XVs and leaving behind any idea of being an invitation club which, the committee pointed out, had alienated many local players. The second XV was to be known as the Extra Firsts and the third as the Colts.

The Colts XV was regarded as a "must", for herein, said the committee, lay the future of the club. In view of this it is somewhat ironic that later developments modified the colts XV into a Swifts XV (with an intended emphasis upon youth) and the Leicester club had to wait another 16 years for a genuine youth side.

It was hoped that neither of the proposed new sides would become a financial burden, therefore a finance sub-committee was recommended in order to investigate new ways of raising extra cash. Taking note of the attitude of several local clubs while the 'A' XV had been in existence, the sub-committee stressed that "under the new arrangements, the club, being based on three XVs, and the likelihood of players being attracted from outside districts, in due course, the new working should not handicap local clubs or players, any of whom can play for the premier XV."

Perhaps the most essential recommendation was that every member of the general committee had to be 100 per cent behind the new arrangements, as distinct from the divided loyalties during the running of the 'A' XV.

The report was outlined, as well, to a meeting of the old players whose help was to be vital. To give further point to the sub-committee's endeavours Ron Smith (after seven years with the club) and Ashurst (five years) joined Northampton and Coventry respectively after losing their places. It was obvious that Tigers had to reshape their entire way of life, for they could not afford to have players of this quality leaving the club. The upshot was the adoption, virtually in its entirety, of the report with the Extra First XV to begin in 1957-58 and the Colts the following season.

The last season under the old regime wound its way to a close, and even if it was far from memorable, it was by no means uneventful. Having entertained Romanians at its beginning, Leicester paid their first visit to Ireland in November, 1956, where they lost 17-16 to Lansdowne and 23-3 to an Old Belvedere XV which included Tony O'Reilly. They impressed Irish observers with their open style of play and the heavy defeat in the second match was at least partially due to open-handed Irish hospitality the night before.

Elders was given an England trial, where he had the big Wasps wing Ted Woodward as a co-centre, and was regrettably dropped for the second trial. Eight Tigers helped Leicestershire to become Midlands champions again though once more they were to go

down to Devon in the semi-final at Torquay, beaten 11-6. The public were getting more for their money as Leicester began to play 40 minutes each way, when the opposition agreed, rather than 35 - though the club's comparative lack of success may not have made this seem a progressive step.

England winger Peter Thompson scored five tries against the club for the Barbarians, who won 23-6 and on the same day, as if to emphasise the passing of the old order, Percy Lawrie died, having retired from committee work only two years earlier. One of his contemporaries, 'Sos' Taylor, had died only a couple of months earlier. And in March, 1957, Eric Thorneloe informed the committee of his decision to resign as secretary. He had not been well for some time but it meant the end of a term of office which lasted 28 years and had seen two dozen internationals pass through the club. Bobby Barr, the first team secretary, succeeded him and two months later, Thorneloe became the club's president when Charlie Cross died in office.

Tigers playing at Twickenham against Harlequins in September 1956. Here Peter Konig tackles 'Quins RJN Leonard.

At least the players were able to give Thorneloe something of a "going away" present as the season drew to a close. They beat Newport for the first time in eight years at Welford Road and achieved the not inconsiderable triumph of fielding the same side in successive games for the first time in two years when the team that did duty against Newport went in en bloc against the British Police. Home matches ended with a 19-3 win over Llanelli and lock forward John Thompson became the only ever-present for the season. But tempering this successful conclusion was the news that Elders (later to coach England) was to leave the club after four years, for an appointment in Newcastle. With Cullen, who had been plagued by an ankle injury all season, also nearing the end of his career with Leicester, it was, in so many ways, the end of an era.

MASTER & PUPIL
Ken Nicholas and Mike Wade turned out for Leicestershire together in 1955-56 when Mike was one of Ken's pupils at Wyggeston School. The first time they had opposed each other was for Leicester against Bedford in December 1955 after Ken had changed clubs.

TIGERS ABOUT-TURN
1957-1958

THE EFFECT of the steps taken in 1957 was to change Leicester from a club hanging on grimly to memories of the years between the two World Wars to an organisation with a bright future and new traditions to establish. And if any one man could be said to have moulded that future in a very definite way it was probably the 24-year old New Zealander, Colin Martin, whose influence on the club in the 1960s was of paramount importance.

A graduate in engineering, he played in 'A' grade rugby in Auckland and for the New Zealand Universities. But it looked as though a promising career was to be nipped in the bud when he suffered severe back injuries following an accident when the car in which he was travelling was hit by a train on a level crossing. He recovered to join the Shell Oil Company, who promptly dispatched him to Holland where he watched sufficient rugby to encourage him to take up the game once more.

With no ill effects and deciding that drilling for oil in Indonesia or Kuwait was unlikely to provide a boost to his rugby career, he came to England to seek a job, on a temporary basis, arriving in Leicester to work with English Electric at Whetstone. "My first visit to Tigers was on a summery Thursday evening in July," recalled Martin. "I remember being overawed by the size of the ground and the stands, reminiscent of provincial grounds in New Zealand.

"Training commenced with a wild game of soccer and was dominated by a strapping 17-stone speedster, later to be identified as Tom Bleasdale. After a few beers in the bar I started to understand the organisation and realised I may well be out of my depth, having not played serious rugby for

nearly two years." Martin was advised to join Westleigh and played several games for that club before receiving an invitation to play for Leicester, whose organisation and fixture list, he found, closely resembled that of a New Zealand provincial side.

"My first impression of playing with Leicester was that, in spite of vigorous individual training, we had little team training, simply because less than half the team turned up for practice. My first game, against Newport, soon demonstrated that the Welsh clubs did not suffer from this weakness. We seemed to have many talented individuals to call on but frequently they were unable to play and often lived miles from Leicester.

"It was apparent, talking to many of the senior players, that this approach, while extremely successful in the past, was increasingly inadequate for the needs of the day." The times, of course, were changing. Reviewing the situation before the 1957-58 season, the club found itself in debt by £1,766 and decided to imitate the county cricket club and raise funds via a football competition, guided by a well known Leicester entertainer and sports enthusiast, Billy Butler, who had done so much for the cricket club. Ken Kinder, president of the club 20 years later, worked hard with him to get the scheme off the ground and it proved very successful.

Also successful was a meeting with local clubs in September to explain Leicester's plans on a revised team structure. At the same time it was agreed that the proposed Colts XV should be called the Swifts, enabling older players to be picked although the accent was to be on youth. With Barr now in office as club secretary, Jerry Day and Rodney Willcox became the new team secretaries. It was obvious there were going to be some rough edges to be smoothed over: accusations of poaching from junior clubs were made but this is hardly an uncommon feature in any day or age. There was the integration of the three teams and the worry about how much money would be needed. There was also the very real counter-attraction just across the road, for Leicester City were in the First Division of the Football League.

With this in mind Tigers welcomed with open arms a new recruit, Scottish international wing 'Ian' Swan, who joined from Coventry. John Spence Swan, then 26, had already won 16 of his 17 caps and had been with Coventry for two years before moving. With him came Derek

Ian Swan awaits an Oxford University break in the match against the Dark Blues at Welford Road in October 1957.

CHAPTER 12

THE TIGERS TALE

Ashurst while Ron Smith returned from Northampton and a new scrum half, Herbert Victor White, who had captained Camborne in 1957-58, took up a teaching appointment in Nottingham and joined Leicester. 'Chalkie' White was to have a certain amount of influence on his new club, too.

Swan made his debut in the 1957-58 season's first game, against Bedford, and a month later must have been highly delighted to run in two tries against Coventry, but it was sad that no place could be found for Cullen who, not surprisingly since he had lived and worked there for some time, gave his last season to Bedford. Players nowadays may complain of too much rugby but it was reported that Wade looked exhausted against Cheltenham: the youngster, then on national service, played against Richmond the previous Saturday, for his unit on the Wednesday, for the county the next day and then Tigers.

The Extras, captained by John Taylor, won their first five games and scored over 100 points in the process but the senior XV found it difficult to field a settled back division. They were trying to play an open game but lacked cohesion, and their first away win did not come until the end of November, at Moseley. In the meantime the local press speculated during the November match against Old Blues, in the light as it were of Leicester City's brand new floodlights, that maybe it was time for Tigers to make a similar investment. The Scottish lock and 1955 British Lion, Ernie Michie, found a place in the side in December - reminiscent of the good old, bad old days - but there was a depressing showing on December 21 when the touring Australians beat Leicestershire and East Midlands at Welford Road by 18-3.

The combined XV was J Hetherington (Northampton); J S Swan (Leicester), M R Wade (Leicester), R Leslie (Sale), J P Hyde (Northampton); R G Smith (Northampton), L G Karseras (Loughborough Colleges); C R Jacobs (Northampton), G Franklin (Bedford), J P Fellows-Smith (Northampton), C P Daniels (Northampton), T Bleasdale (Leicester), D J Hayward (Cardiff), M A L Tansey (Hinckley), D F White (Northampton, captain). Of the forwards, Bleasdale, Hayward and White distinguished themselves but the backs lacked punch and the game proved a triumph for the Australian full back Jim Lenehan who scored two tries and three conversions. A further try came from Alan Morton while Ron Harvey kicked a penalty, the Midlanders' only reply coming from a penalty by White.

Over Christmas John Elders, on holiday in Leicester, played three games in three days for the club and back row forward Bob Small joined brother Brian in the team against Birkenhead Park. Also back in the side was David Matthews, following a two year break with Stoneygate, but seven wins from 20 games in the first half of the season was hardly the stuff dreams are made of. To add to the depression as 1958 opened was the knowledge that the RAF were to claim Wade and wing Richard Rawson, while Scotland claimed Swan for his last cap, against France.

There was speculation in the new year that Ireland's Tony O'Reilly might join the club, since it was rumoured that he had been given a business appointment in the Midlands, but for the present life for the senior side was decidedly hard. The halves and back row were unsettled, though the introduction of the dynamic Kibworth flanker, Gordon Almey, proved a successful step.

Loughborough Colleges gained their first win over the club by 6-3 in March, which had the effect on Leicester of bringing out their best the next day, against Swansea. The Welsh club went down 20-8, their first defeat in England of the season, and the hero was a Yorkshireman studying at Loughborough, Linford Tatham, who scored a try and a dropped goal even though he was reduced to a passenger on the wing by injury.

The 1957-58 season ended on a high note, with the first hat-trick of victories on the Easter tour since the war. That included a 5-3 win over Bristol, then noted as one of the best sides in the country. Maurice Key, a full back from East Anglia, gained plaudits for his general play while Elders was also back in circulation. For the second season in succession Thompson played every game, giving him 87 consecutive appearances.

Wade, who never played as many games for Leicester as the club might have liked because of national service, studies at Cambridge University, business commitments and injury, has vivid memories of Easter tours and all that led up to them. Now working in the USA, he recalled his career with Leicester thus: "There was the tradition and pageant of the Barbarians game, starting with lunch at the Bell Hotel. The nervousness and awe of meeting the rugby legends in the Baa-baas party, the bus journey to Welford Road now totally consumed by nerves, the astonishment at the size and mood of the holiday crowd milling around outside the ground.

"The uplift from the crowd cheering the home team. Too busy now for nerves - trying like hell to get a few quick points on the board in order to be still in the game when the inevitable deluge of Barbarian attacks began in the second half. The utter exhaustion of the last 15 minutes, trying to stay on one's feet and trying to make one's legs move fast enough to make just one more tackle.

"The post-game celebrations...the reluctant move to the Sportsmen's Club or other institutions naive enough to agree to put on a rugby dinner...a prolonged dinner guaranteed to produce irate wives and girlfriends waiting impatiently to be summoned to the dance...the agony of the next day, not so bad as a student but horrendous later in one's career when it meant a return to work.

"The post Baa-baas let-down...enthusiasm picking up again rapidly after a few unexpected losses, especially if accompanied by a few demotions to the Extra Firsts...the slow build-up to the Easter Tour, zenith of the season...the relatively

SHORTS SHORTAGE
In the first match that Tigers played against British Police in 1957, the game was repeatedly held up by players requiring a change of shorts. Eventually Mike Freer had to don a new pair of shorts in a different colour to the remainder of his side!

Tigers unbeaten Easter tour squad of 1958.
Back:
Bolesworth, Small, Thompson, Muddimer, Elders, Almey, Matthews, Wade, Chawner, Key, Kinder, Lacey, Lubbock.
Front:
Shephard, Skelton, Swan, Bleasdale (Capt), Walker, Freer, White.

serious beginnings of the tour with the game against Bristol...the warm-up for the tour starting after the game in the Bristol clubhouse.

"Easter Sunday, determined to have a good time despite the seemingly serious efforts of the local populace to put a damper on proceedings by daring to observe a religious holiday. The Easter Monday morning trip to Plymouth...the almost equal mix of white and green faces on the bus...the dread of having to play before noon...the first half of the game taking place as if being played by bodies other than our own...the mocking exhortations of those team members lucky enough not to have to play.

"Half-time...suddenly compos mentis again, looking up at the scoreboard and finding that we are only 20 points down...the mad scramble in the second half to win the game despite the deficit...the realisation that we would have to do it playing up a slope which now seemed as steep as Everest...did we really win the toss and choose ends? Who the hell is captain today anyway?

"The festivities continue...a trip to the races, a few wins, many, many losses... Tuesday morning, the most disorganised muster ever for the trip to Exeter...a mountain of hotel guests' shoes in the foyer of the hotel, inextricably interlaced...the fear/panic on the faces of some of the guests, the utter contempt of the remainder, the obvious relief of the hotel staff at the prospect of our final departure. The trip to Exeter...a few half-hearted

water-pistol battles and games of liar dice.

"Rejuvenated at lunch...a vague recollection of being pressed into service as a pro tem cleric to bless the food...a repeat performance of the contempt of the other hotel guests. The game over against Exeter and a hurried departure followed by the long trip home to Leicester. The bus disgorging its zombie-like passengers, complete with crumpled blazers and flannels into the Welford Road car park. Finally creeping into bed in the early morning. Is it still Easter? The end of the season arriving mercifully before the body is totally destroyed."

Players of twenty or more years ago will have the same recollections of their Easter Tour, even if the venue was different. Certainly the West Country visit has a hallowed place in the memories of those players lucky enough to make it - possibly an equally hallowed place in the memories of those hotel managers unlucky enough to host it. But, many would say sadly, the Easter tour is not what it was - another casualty of the competitive structure introduced during the 1980s.

THORNELOE'S PASSING 1958-1960

IAN SWAN was elected captain for the 1958-59 season, the first season for the Swifts XV. Leicester were making their intentions plain by running a three-week coaching course for promising schoolboys and local club players, under the guidance of Alistair Smallwood who had put so many Uppingham schoolboys on the right road and who was now president of the Leicestershire Schools Rugby Union. Doug Norman was president of the County R U so it could hardly be said that the club did not have friends in the right places, though obviously local clubs were able to benefit from the use of Leicester's experience and facilities.

There were several interesting newcomers, among them Leighton Jenkins who was capped five times by Wales in 1954 and 1956 as a number eight. He had played for Leicestershire in 1955 while at Loughborough and was now taking up a teaching appointment at Oakham. Another ex-Loughborough Colleges and Leicestershire debutant was the wing Harry Jessop who could generally be distinguished on the field because he played in a scrum cap. Michael Gavins, a product of Leeds University and Loughborough, came into the side on a regular basis at full back and among the younger elements to join were the former Wyggeston School prop John Bailey and the Lutterworth Grammar School centre Trevor Allen.

a member in October. It is always nice to have internationals coming to a club, though the appearance of Horrocks-Taylor put even more pressure on the fly-half spot where Leicester already had Lyn Tatham, Mick Freer and another newcomer, Gordon Blackett from Newcastle.

In the event Tatham opted to play for Loughborough Colleges and, since Horrocks-Taylor was a Yorkshireman from Halifax, it was obvious that Leicester would not have his services during the county championship season. With Wade going up to Cambridge, there was also a gap in the centre, which offered a partial solution to the problem of too many fly-halves.

There was a new, and rather special game at the season's start. It had been agreed the previous season that Leicester should play a XV raised by the former Welsh international Watcyn Thomas, in order to raise funds for the English Schools Rugby Union - the union had, after all, been founded in Leicester at the start of the century. The money was aimed at boosting 15 group rugby and the result of the first game, apart from bringing Leicester an 18-3 win, was £250 into the union's coffers. The fixture was to be maintained for 11 years, Leicester losing just twice to sides which frequently resembled Barbarian XVs in strength.

For the first time since the 1935-36 season, Leicester went through September undefeated, even if Coventry provided their come-uppance in Horrocks-Taylor's debut game. Later in October came O'Reilly's first game in Leicester's colours, against Northampton, and it is a matter of record that that game too was lost, the Irishman conceding a penalty try. At that time O'Reilly, who first played at centre for Leicester, had made 17 appearances for Ireland as well as collecting rave reviews for his 1955 tour of South Africa with the Lions - and he was still only 22. His displays for the 1959 Lions in Australia and New Zealand confirmed his place in rugby legend, even had he not gone on make a huge impact on the business world as chief executive with the Heinz Corporation.

Certainly the club was not short of colour, even if they lost O'Reilly's services temporarily when touring in Ireland again, for in the second game the

Tigers prop Frank Chawner takes on Bath in September 1958.

The first week of the season brought even better news when the rumour spread that Philip Horrocks-Taylor, capped by England twice the season before, was to join the club and that O'Reilly would become

Irishman swapped sides to represent his old club, Old Belvedere. Not surprisingly gates were going up and there was talk that another international, Irish scrum-half Andy Mulligan, might be joining, though this was one rumour that proved groundless. That willing lock John Thompson

CHAPTER 13

Mick Freer playing against the Harlequins in 1959.

established a club record of 103 consecutive games and, away from Welford Road, Wade won his blue for Cambridge on the wing and scored two tries in the Light Blues' 17-6 win over Oxford University.

The 19-year old former schools international Gordon Blackett made his debut in December against Bristol and though he was to appear comparatively few times for Leicester, he left an indelible impression on many of his contemporaries. Martin described him as one of the most talented uncapped players he had ever played with: "His touchline punting was almost unbelievable in accuracy and it is difficult to recall him dropping a pass. In fact it was Gordon who brought it home to me the positive influence of schoolboy soccer on English rugby players, particularly backs." White was another immensely impressed with the ability of the young northerner.

Unfortunately several of the leading players were unavailable for the Barbarians game, played for a change on Boxing Day. O'Reilly had a broken shoulder bone, Horrocks-Taylor had influenza and Swan was absent but this did not prevent the Tigers collecting their first win since 1951. Matthews, winger Cliff Shephard and Jenkins scored the tries in a 9-3 win and Blackett was superb while the pack boasted an exceptionally mobile back five, with Martin and Bleasdale in the second row, Matthews, Jenkins and Almey in the back row.

Although he was injured, O'Reilly impressed many Leicester regulars with the work he was prepared to put in off the field, helping to bring fresh approaches in training and new attitudes towards the game in general. Lower down the line Ron Smith was doing an exceptionally valuable job in bringing on the Swifts. O'Reilly returned to score his first try for the club against London Scottish before the internationals claimed him and another comeback man was the retired Eric Lacey. Horrocks-Taylor failed to appear after being best man at a wedding in the morning when Wasps paid their first visit to Leicester so Almey moved out to the three-quarters and Lacey was called from his shop to play in the pack. Leicester won 22-0 against a side containing five caps.

It had not been an entirely successful season, one of the problems having been the availability - or otherwise - of leading players. The internationals from the four home countries, for instance, Swan, Horrocks-Taylor, O'Reilly and Jenkins, never played in a side together.

Another invitation to play in the Middlesex Sevens resulted in an entry to the Oxford Sevens, in order to prepare a reasonable squad. Leicester reached the semi-finals of the Oxford tournament, where they lost to Wasps, but at the Middlesex it was defeat in the second round, again at the hands of Wasps. In the first round White scored a try in the 3-0 win over Old Colfeians and repeated the effort in the 6-3 defeat by Wasps. The Leicester VII was: J S Swan, M R Wade, J P Horrocks-Taylor, H V White, D J Matthews, A Jones, L H Jenkins (Bleasdale played in the first round but was injured).

On the credit side Gavins established a post-war points record of 145, passing Cullen's 128 (1950-51) with 14 points from the 23-9 home win over Llanelli. It was eleven points short of Harold Day's haul in 1925-26 and nearly 100 short of Teddy Haselmere's club record.

And for the first time since the war, a current Leicester player was picked by the British Lions, even if Tigers could hardly claim too much of the credit for Tony O'Reilly. Gus Black had toured with the 1950 Lions before joining Leicester but O'Reilly was a bona fide playing member. He was to be joined midway through the tour by Horrocks-Taylor, who replaced the injured Irishman Mick English. Bev Risman was the tour's first choice fly half but O'Reilly played in all six Tests, two in Australia and four in New Zealand where he scored a record 17 tries in 17 appearances.

There was satisfaction, too, from the records of the Extras and the Swifts. The Extras won 24 games, losing five times, and scored 432 points. The Swifts won 14, drew four and lost eight, which was a very respectable tally for an entirely new side finding its way to the right strength of fixture. The first team had 19 wins against 14 losses and three ever-presents in Bleasdale, Almey and the former Old Wyggs prop, Rex Skelton, while Freer missed only one game which made it a pity that a change in his job during the summer meant he would not be regularly available.

That same summer saw the resignation of Eric Thorneloe as president, Rodney Bedingfield succeeding him and Ron Gerrard taking over as treasurer. Thorneloe had not been well and his death in August, 1959, was as much the passing of an era as Tom Crumbie's had been. His attitude to the club had been very similar to Crumbie's and of course he had been a direct link to the halcyon days of the 1920s. He was, in the words of the club's first historian, Brian Thompson, "a scrupulously fair man. He probably did as much for Tigers, in a different way, as Crumbie did. He gave them the sort of consolidation they needed and he was a man of unfailing wisdom."

A sub-committee was appointed to consider a permanent memorial to him and their recommendation was for a framed picture of Thorneloe, to hang in the clubhouse, honours boards commemorating officers, captains and internationals, and clocks for the stands. These were duly commissioned and a year later, in October, 1960, were unveiled by the president of the Rugby

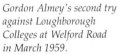

Gordon Almey's second try against Loughborough Colleges at Welford Road in March 1959.

Football Union, Tom Voyce.

There was a minute's silence before the first game of the 1959-60 season, against Bedford, but the club were unable to give their former secretary the kind of memorial they would have preferred, since they lost 11-20. The game marked the debut of the burly Headingley and England trials winger David Senior, who had moved to work in Nottingham and had joined Leicester, while another debutant was Brian Wigley from Lutterworth.

Change was in the air, for though Leighton Jenkins had been elected club captain he was taking a commission in the RAF and was away on a refresher course in the Isle of Man. He subsequently resigned the post and Bleasdale took over once more. Neither O'Reilly nor Horrocks-Taylor were available before Christmas and Swan's firm were moving him to the south of England. Wade of course was still at Cambridge (he had toured with a combined Oxford and Cambridge party to the Far East during the summer) and the promising Hartlepool Rovers centre John Dee, later capped by England, failed to get a place at Loughborough and did not join. One significant newcomer, however, was the 1950 British Lion and Wales prop, John Robins, who had received a lecturing appointment at Loughborough.

Robins' stay with Leicester, as a player, was comparatively short and much of his rugby was played in the Extras but he proved one of the most consistent place-kickers since the days of H L V Day besides retaining much of his old ability and added one of the foremost intellects in the game to the club's strength. His name is still held in high esteem at Loughborough and though he had an unhappy tour as assistant manager to the 1966 British Lions, his service to the game went on in his work for student rugby in England.

Another newcomer was the Moat Old Boys flanker, Graham Willars, who made his debut against Cheltenham in October and then distinguished himself in his next game, against Oxford University, by falling offside and giving the Dark Blues the penalty which won the match 6-3. With competition for back row places always fierce it was some time before Willars became a regular but it was his vision for the game which helped the club develop so well in the late 60s and early 70s.

Spectators at the Nuneaton game included Joe Erskine, the Welsh boxer then training in Leicester for his British and Empire title fight against Henry Cooper, though it was not hard men that Leicester sought. Their problems were at half-back, for though White was settled at scrum-half after battling it out with Mike Lubbock for some seasons, he had a succession of different partners including Blackett, Freer, Tatham, Horrocks-Taylor and John Berry, eldest of Tom Berry's four rugby-playing sons.

There was great joy though at the 8-3 win over Llanelli at Stradey Park, tempered slightly by the sending-off of Almey for fighting. It was the first away win over the Welsh club since the 1900-01 season and Peter Konig, recalled to the back row, got a try, Gavins converting it and dropping a goal. A proposed trip to play Lourdes in France was called off because the French wanted more than just the one game and, as 1960 dawned, Leicester had their first experience of playing under floodlights,

Robins, Jones and White close in on a Newport forward at Welford Road in April 1960.

losing 9-19 at Newport who were inspired by two will o'the wisp half-backs, Brian Jones and Billy Watkins. On the credit side was the 6-3 defeat of Gloucester, who arrived at Welford Road with a club record of 13 consecutive victories behind them.

O'Reilly, who damaged a shoulder in the Golden Jubilee match with the Barbarians, was back in the side until Ireland called on him as a late replacement for the unfit Michael Flynn against England in February. The telegram which arrived on the Friday from the Irish RFU was alleged to have read: "Situation desperate, you are needed." O'Reilly's reply ran: "Arriving 11.45, De Gaulle," which, even allowing for the famed O'Reilly sense of humour, must have made the selectors ponder.

Records fell with a rush as the 1959-60 season neared its end, success after Christmas being much assisted by the regular presence of Horrocks-Taylor. Gavins became the club's second highest points scorer ever with 153 while Senior shattered the post-war record for tries, held jointly by George Cullen and Haydn Thomas at 16, by running in 23. Newport were beaten 17-11 at Welford Road, Robins kicking four penalties and a conversion, but that marked one of O'Reilly's last performances, for his firm were moving him to southern Ireland. It also occasioned the admirable *Daily Mail* headline "Man bites Tiger" when two teeth had to be removed from Almey's head, left there after a collision between him and Geoff Whitson, the Newport forward!

O'Reilly made 16 appearances in two seasons but was able to play in the Leicester VII which qualified for the Middlesex Tournament. The club seemed determined to wipe out the memory of their two previous visits and fielded the following team: D Senior, A J F K O'Reilly, J P Horrocks-Taylor, H V White, G Cherry, A Jones, T Bleasdale. In the first round Senior scored three tries as Leicester dispatched the holders Loughborough Colleges, 19-0. O'Reilly and George Cherry also scored tries, Horrocks-Taylor converting twice, but their second round game with St Luke's College, Exeter, was drawn 10-10 at full time and they lost to a sudden death try. Senior and O'Reilly had scored tries which Horrocks-Taylor had converted, but unhappily the fly-half missed a penalty at the end of proper time which might have won the match.

CHAPTER 14

MARTIN TAKES THE HELM
1960-1962

COLIN Martin was elected captain for the 1960-61 season, a position he had never dreamed of occupying but an indication of his standing within the club. The pressure on back row places was eased with the decision of David Perry (later capped by England from Bedford), who had come into the side just prior to the 1960 Easter tour, to rejoin Harlequins and there were more additions from Lutterworth Grammar School, where Tatham was a master. John Allen, a scrum-half of whom more later, joined his brother Trevor, the Cooper brothers, Richard and John (better known as a 400 metre hurdles Silver medallist at the Tokyo Olympics before his sad death in the 1974 Paris air disaster) came straight from school to join Wigley and David Bird at the club.

On October 22, before the game with Northampton, Tom Voyce 'unveiled' the clocks on each stand which were to be the main memorials to Mr Thorneloe. Northampton rather spoiled the occasion by winning 9-0 though there may have been one or two Tigers with sore heads since the club's 80th birthday dinner had been held the night before.

Then, a fortnight later, Avril Malan's Fifth Springboks were in town. It was to be another historic match at Welford Road, for though the Midland Counties XV could not beat the tourists as did their predecessors of 1931, their 3-3 draw was the best result of any British side until the Barbarians beat South Africa 6-0 in the last match of the tour.

"What a little concerted team practice did for that XV who, with a simple and single-minded approach...played the Springboks at their own game and produced a result and a game few of those

present will forget," said Martin, who captained the combined side. It was the fifth game of the tour and the Midlands XV was: M N Gavins (Leicester); K Chilton (London Welsh), B K Williams (Bedford), J Butterfield (Northampton), R Leslie (Northampton); I H P Laughland (London Scottish), D T Stevens (Blackheath); C R Jacobs, A Johnson, R Wilkins, C P Daniels (all Northampton), J S Thompson (Leicester), D P Rogers (Bedford), C G Martin (Leicester, captain), D F White (Northampton).

It was a major achievement for Don White, who had played against every touring side since the war, but unluckily it was his fumbling of a loose ball near the Midlands line which gave the Springbok lock, 'Stompie' van der Merwe, the chance to seize a try early on. Before half-time, however, the South African centre, Benjamin van Niekerk, pulled a leg muscle and though he played on after treatment, Doug Hopwood was withdrawn from the pack to cover for him. The Midlands proceeded to set about the Springbok seven, giving their halves the chance to progress up the touchline.

But it was from their own 25 that the counties equalised. Budge Rogers gathered a missed place kick and opened up play, the centres putting Keith Chilton away across the right wing. Just over halfway he kicked ahead but the bouncing ball eluded him and the Springbok cover as White, whose run must have started 100 yards away, arrived for the try. It was not a difficult conversion but Gavins, who had played a magnificent game, missed his kick and the match was drawn.

"We had four kickers in the team," said Martin. "Don White, Keith Chilton, Mike and myself but I was in no doubt who should take it at such a late stage in the game - the full back." At the post-match reception the Springboks manager, 'Ferdie' Bergh, described the Midlands pack as the most rugged they had encountered and he had little cause to change his mind as the tour progressed. Even though it was a Midland Counties XV in name, it was in fact the old Leicestershire and East Midlands combination and both bodies received a memento in

John Allen throws out a pass from scrum-half as Gordon Almey looks on against Plymouth Albion in September 1961.

the shape of a shield and a plaque.

Although it had been an indifferent first half of the season for Leicester, the results of Martin's captaincy were beginning to show. "I set out to build on what Tom Bleasdale had already achieved," said the New Zealander. "More particularly I endeavoured to combine the spearhead-style of New Zealand forward play with the swift flanking attacks characteristic of English rugby. My task was made much less difficult by the presence of one of the game's great generals, Phil Horrocks-Taylor, at fly-half."

There were signs of this when Leicester went down 14-5 to the Barbarians, O'Reilly making a guest appearance for Leicester. In the opposing XV was another international, Ken Scotland, whose name had already been linked with Leicester when he had completed his course at Cambridge. Not that Leicester had any lack of faith in their current full back, Gavins, who received the reward his consistency merited when picked by England against Wales at Cardiff.

Unfortunately he became one of the many players to have been capped once, against Wales, when England lost, in a season when England obviously did not know who was the best full-back in the country, having played Don Rutherford, Gavins and John Willcox in succession. Gavins was Leicester's first new England cap since Hazell six years before, though it had been whispered in previous seasons that Ireland might have played him since a great-grandparent had been Irish.

At much the same time Leicester decided to try out their promising half-backs, Richard Cooper and John Allen, against the RAF on the Welford Road Recreation Ground. In an atmosphere seldom conducive to good rugby the youngsters came up against that wily Rugby League fly half Alex Murphy and the nuggety Gloucester scrum-half Micky Booth, and the servicemen won 11-6.

Before the season's end there were two landmarks. Bleasdale, who made his debut in 1949, played his 300th game for the club against Newport and Horrocks-Taylor was recalled by England for the Calcutta Cup match. His tactical kicking put considerable pressure on the Scots and he placed a penalty in England's 6-0 win. In the 22 matches he played for Leicester that season, they won 17. Without him they won 7 out of 20, an impressive statistic.

The 24 wins that season were a post-war record and the 15 tries by David Matthews was the best by a forward since the war. Off the field there was, though, an element of sorrow at the disbanding of the Supporters' Club. It had performed prodigies in its early days but of late it had been rather less meaningful, and the Leicester committee took over its main functions of organising programmes, teas and the like. Perhaps not surprisingly the committee turned down the idea of floodlighting (the cheapest estimate was £6,000) since the rent for the ground was going up, from £225 to £1,000, although the city council had always borne in mind the part played by Leicester in attracting people to the city.

It was also, as it happens, an unhappy decision when Tigers agreed to play the first match of the 1961-62 season away. It had always been their custom to open the season at home but Bedford were opening their new clubhouse and marked the occasion by winning 21-13, a match whose second half was screened live by BBC Television cameras.

Making his debut that game was former Bedford and RAF centre Malcolm Greenhow, and two games later, against Bath, Ken Scotland made his first appearance, having moved to work at Tamworth. At this time Scotland had won 18 of his 27 caps and had proved himself a player of quite outstanding ability. A pupil from the famous George Heriot School, he had captained Cambridge University - as did Wade a year later - and toured with the Lions in 1959. During his career he showed himself capable of playing anywhere behind the scrum but, regretfully, his debut game marked Bath's first win at Welford Road for 42 years.

Leicester were badly in need of some inspiration. They had lost Gavins to Moseley (which was nearer the full back's Wolverhampton home) and the pre-Christmas period brought them little success. Several changes were made in the pack and John Allen and the RAF's Mike Dymond were challenging White for the scrum-half position. The Yorkshire contingent, Horrocks-Taylor, former Northampton centre Ian Gibson and Senior were missing for long periods. Interestingly, in the light of recent law changes, Leicester and Bristol played an experimental line-out variation which obliged the forwards to stand a yard apart but clearly the refereeing was not strict enough. The contemporary report said there was no obvious difference and certainly no clear tunnel between the players.

Wade was leading an unbeaten Cambridge to success in the Varsity Match and, upon his return to the club at Christmas, he brought with him the Light Blues' promising prop, Nick Drake-Lee. Nevertheless it was just as well the Barbarians game was postponed until March because of frost, despite the efforts of some spaceship-like heaters hired by the secretary from the Syston firm of En-Tout-Cas. Drake-Lee made his debut in the first month of the New Year, on the occasion when Bath performed the

These curious hot air machines were kept burning overnight at Welford Road in 1961 in a vain attempt to save the match against the Barbarians.

The Tigers pack closes in on Newport hooker Bryn Meredith at Welford Road in September 1961.

double over Tigers, and in the same month Wade won the first of his three caps for England, playing in an incredibly dull 0-0 draw against Wales.

It should be added that his next game, a 16-0 win over Ireland, was very much better, Wade scoring a try. The big centre was the first Leicestershire-born player to be capped from Tigers since Bill Moore and the 16th international to have played for the club since the war - though that total was inflated with the likes of Mullen and Michie who played the odd game.

Wade, however, was dropped for the Calcutta Cup game, in which Horrocks-Taylor made his fourth England appearance. In the opposing ranks was Scotland who had played in all his country's internationals, severely limiting his club appearances (in addition he missed the encounter with Rosslyn Park to ensure that his wife gave birth in Scotland and that the child would thus be eligible for his native country!). Nevertheless, the full back topped the points scorers' list, with 138 from 24 games in what had been a remarkably inconsistent season.

There had been some interesting newcomers after Christmas, the former Wyggeston School and Loughborough Colleges product Michael Harrison playing centre in the side that lost to Bath and also when they beat Northampton for the first time in five years. A new lock forward from Hull University and Loughborough, Robert Errington Rowell, had scored a try in his debut against the Colleges and, though already thinning on top, at 22 had a long future in the game. The veteran prop Frank Chawner had made a remarkable comeback while David Bird, on the wing, was confirming the good impression he had already made. Behind the scenes Tom Berry had been named chairman of the England selectors, at much the same time that Doug

Prentice was being forced by ill health to retire as secretary to the Rugby Football Union. He died in October, 1962.

The points total for the 1961-62 season beat the previous year by six, so 496 was the target now for would-be record breakers. But before play resumed for a season which heralded the first visit by the Canadians to this country, changes were being made. Bobby Barr succeeded Rodney Bedingfield as club president and the secretary's post was filled by Ron Gerrard, the new treasurer being the quiet but efficient Stan Thorpe. There was considerable debate over the development of the clubhouse, particularly in view of the city council's scheme to widen the Aylestone Road which would have led to an arterial highway running through the existing changing rooms.

It came to nothing, fortunately, and the same fate met the suggestion that the club should purchase underground electric heating for the pitch (perhaps no-one wanted a repetition of the postponed Barbarians game of 1961-62, a dreadfully dull match won by the Baa-baas 5-3).

THE BIG FREEZE
1962-1968

THE 1962-63 season began with four Berrys on the club's books, though not even father Tom could have hoped to see them all appear in the same senior XV. It was, still, a proud moment for the senior Berry who was preparing to go as manager on England's first short tour overseas, to New Zealand in 1963.

After a storming climax to the opening game with Bedford - trailing 13-6 with five minutes to go Wade scored one try and was knocked unconscious in the process then Small crossed for the decisive score - the club went on to win its first five games before going down to Harlequins at Twickenham, a match in which England wing John Young (later a national selector) proved chivalry was not dead by refusing to run in a try after the referee had failed to spot a Harlequin knock-on.

Fixtures resumed with Swansea after a gap of five years and Leicester celebrated with a brilliant 29-6 win at St Helen's. The forward play was exceptional, the backs incisive, and Horrocks-Taylor went over for two tries while Scotland registered 17 points. The following week the club received a letter from Swansea secretary David Price which ran: "I have been asked by my committee to write to you concerning the very fine game at St Helen's. It was a great pleasure to see Leicester back...and the quality of your football pleased our members greatly. I believe our spectators expressed their evident satisfaction as the teams left the field. Well done." One illustration of the high regard Welsh clubs in general held for Leicester then, and now.

For the second year running bad weather forced the postponement of the Barbarians' game although Scotland travelled 600 miles and the lock Mike Jones 400 miles for a game which was not played. Scotland returned the next day for a national game and was subsequently asked to captain his country. At the same time he moved back to Edinburgh to work and joined Heriot's FP (Former Pupils) in January 1963. It was a surprise blow for Leicester who thereby lost a great entertainer, who scored 240 points in the 40 matches he played.

Not that Leicester had to rush around for a replacement, for Graham Pulfrey from Newark was playing well at full back after making his debut in September 1962, and the weather had taken a grip on sport up and down the country. It was the big freeze-up which hit the club's hopes of a record number of wins (before the break they had won 14 from 19 games). Twelve weeks went by without a game although there was satisfaction when England gave Drake-Lee the first of his eight caps - against Wales at Cardiff in England's last win in the Principality for 28 years.

Play resumed on March 2 against Harlequins in the somewhat surreal surrounds of Teddington where some 300 watched two of England's most successful clubs free of charge. The Baa-baas came on March 28 with, among others, Gordon Blackett in their ranks. Blackett was now with Gosforth and was later to turn professional. The Leicester back row of Martin, Matthews and Bob Small was in tremendous form and the club won 16-9. But April brought disappointment: with Horrocks-Taylor, Gibson, Senior and Dymond unavailable, Leicester scratched from the Middlesex Sevens, lost every match on tour and came home to lose to Rugby at Welford Road. Having lost only five games before that, they emerged from the abbreviated season with 21 wins and nine defeats. For the second successive season, Matthews had played in every game.

While their seniors were crumbling, the Swifts had been carving their own niche in the club's record book. Well marshalled by the experienced Peter Konig, they had gone through the season unbeaten, with 21 victories, 626 points for and 85 against. No-one could have complained if they had taken receipt of the tiger skin which was presented to the club at the 1963 annual meeting by a former player of the 1920s, C T (Charles) Cramphorn, whose brother had brought it specially from India.

Martin's three years as captain came to an end when Wade was elected to the post for the 1963-64 season. He had lost the services of Senior and Jones who had moved away but Cambridge blue Malcolm Bussey had come to teach at Uppingham and was available on the wing, while London Welshman Keith Chilton, who had been working for two years just outside Leicester, at Whetstone, also joined.

It was to be another significant season, for where Martin had concentrated on honing the forwards into a force to be feared, Wade began to work on the backs. He introduced new ideas at training, at pre-match preparation and, off the field, gave the lead to the move for Saturday dances in the largely neglected upstairs clubroom. The players became increasingly involved in the running of club functions although the state of the clubroom was not impressive. It had metal rafters in the roof, a wooden floor, and if you fell down the chances of collecting splinters in an uncomfortable part of the anatomy were very good.

For all that it had atmosphere - a bit too much on occasions, though at least in a rugby club there is seldom a shortage of bouncers. And it helped to make players and members feel that it was really their club, rather than the monopoly of two or three individuals.

Initially, on the field, there were experiments. Horrocks-Taylor, who had played in four of England's six tour games, including the three Tests against New Zealand (twice) and Australia, returned to his native Yorkshire in September, so a fly-half was required. Richard Cooper was tried there before his return to Hull University, then Harrison, before Wade decided to play there himself. The move was a distinct success but at the same time Matthews' long run of successive games ended. He passed John Thompson's record 103 and finally wound up with 109 before being rested.

It was also the season of Wilson Whineray's Fifth All Blacks, who came to Welford Road three days after Christmas, giving local enthusiasts a surfeit of good rugby, since they had been able to watch the Barbarians beat Leicester 13-6 on Boxing Day. It was to be another epic Midland performance against a touring side with Leicestershire and the East Midlands fielding the following XV: J Smith (Bedford); D W Bird (Leicester), R Leslie (Northampton), L R Drury (Bedford), M R Wade

Gordon Almey halts Lewin, the Bedford scrum-half in his tracks during the match at Leicester in September 1963.

(Leicester); F Hawkins, R C Ashby (both Wasps); C R Jacobs (Northampton, captain), A Johnson (Northampton), N J Drake-Lee (Leicester), R E Rowell (Leicester), C P Daniels (Northampton), D Coley (Bedford), C G Martin (Leicester), D P Rogers (Bedford).

For Bird - known inevitably as Dickie - it was to be the outstanding game of his career. A fast, elusive runner who ended the season as the club's leading try-scorer with 14, he was robbed of a try in the second half when the referee failed to allow the combined side advantage after an All Blacks knock-on. Another Leicester player, Bob Rowell, had a significant match, trading blow for blow - sometimes literally - with his opposite number as the Midlands forwards showed no inclination to knuckle under to Whineray's pack.

Kevin Briscoe kicked two first half penalties to put the tourists six points up at half-time but offside against Earle Kirton gave Coley a successful penalty. A try from Malcolm Dick made it 9-3 but a magnificent solo try by Wasps fly-half Fred Hawkins put the Midlands XV right back into contention. It was not until injury time that the All Blacks made the game safe with a try by Alan Stewart, converted by Briscoe, but the Midlands forwards had shown they could be held and Colin Martin must have been delighted with their performance against his fellow countrymen.

Drake-Lee had already been picked for England against New Zealand but Rowell had not. The selectors, impressed with his showing at Leicester,

rectified that by capping him against Wales which meant that the lock had reached international status without ever playing in a trial game. England achieved a 6-6 draw and Rowell was unfortunately dropped for the next game, although he did achieve a second cap the following season, again against Wales.

With Wade and John Allen combining well at half-back the season for Leicester proved the best for 30 years. Chilton chalked up 135 points and there were 26 wins, including an unbeaten Easter tour. The club had proved they were capable of more expansive football, with Harrison and Gibson combining well in the centre. During the summer, work finally began on the erection of floodlights at Welford Road, despite criticism at the annual meeting that they were merely an attempt to increase club prestige. No, said the committee, they were an amenity for club, for members and for Leicestershire and they organised a game against a Midlands XV on October 8 to mark the official "lighting-up" time.

The annual meeting also threw up the subject of rats. There were, a member claimed, too many rat holes and too many rats at the ground and was told by Bobby Barr that the efforts of the local pest exterminator had proved in vain; the president endeavoured to lighten the proceedings by describing the appearance of a dead rat in one scrum during a Barbarians match though discussion of the sewer running beneath the ground from the cattle market must have kept subsequent questions to a minimum.

New laws had come into operation for the 1964-65 season, restricting the activities of wing forwards and making the backs lie back. Obviously it was to encourage more open play after some of the dull games of the early 60s but Leicester's hopes of profiting from it took a knock when 10 regulars went on the casualty list during the first month, among them the captain, Wade. Feeling his responsibilities he may have tried to return to action too early but his knee injury eventually forced him to have a cartilage operation and, effectively, ended his playing career at the time when he was proving so valuable to the club.

In the first seven weeks of the season Wade, Harrison, Martin and Drake-Lee captained the club before Harrison stepped into the breach in November, following Wade's enforced resignation. It was Harrison who had distinguished himself in the inaugural floodlit game with three tries as Leicester won 31-8 following the 'switch on' by the Rugby Football Union's treasurer, Bill Ramsay. The Midlands XV included the exceptional Llanelli teenager, Terry Price (then at Leicester University, but sadly killed in a road accident in 1993), and the Wyggeston School scrum half, D R Elliott.

Richmond claimed their first win in 33 years in October but the following month, Leicester enhanced their reputation in Ireland in a splendid game against Old Belvedere. The Irish club won 16-14, Chilton scoring in every possible way to notch 11 points himself, but Bussey almost won the match with a late run and their hosts were loud in their praise. There were trials for Harrison and Rowell but Tigers were having problems at fly-half again, in Wade's absence. Another Berry, David, was given

an opportunity there and, with Martin increasingly unavailable because of his business commitments, another Antipodean made his bow in the back row against Headingley in December, Australian No 8 John Quick, alongside David Matthews playing his 250th match - the halfway stage for the flanker.

A few days later the Barbarians succumbed 12-11, Bird scoring a try despite difficulties when his contact lenses became steamed up. There were caps for Drake-Lee and Rowell against Wales, in both cases their last, and a new recruit to the club in the shape of Kevin Paul Andrews, a lock from Bath who had moved to Burton-on-Trent. Andrews, who had played for Hampshire in the County Championship final of 1962, made his debut in a 10-30 defeat against Newport but overall the season proved mediocre, a reflection perhaps on the difficulties over injuries and the consequent problem of being unable to field a settled side.

There was, however, a significant merger of talents for 1965-66. Matthews was elected captain and Martin, his playing career now over, offered to help coach the players. "The experiment of a coach other than the captain was a relatively new concept in English rugby," said Martin. "In my view it faced up to the times. Captains were men with family and business responsibilities and needed support, competition was increasing year by year and certainly no longer could 15 brilliant individuals defeat a well-organised team.

"In addition I had always held the view that players liked to play the game well and a coach/captain combination could more readily achieve that objective, with one important rider - the captain is ultimately in charge, the coach has a supportive role."

Matthews, then 28, thought his opportunity of captaining the club had gone although he had always hoped for the chance: "I wanted Leicester to be top of the rugby world and I like to think what people may recall about my time as captain was the organisation. The club had struggled for so many years and I had to decide the best way of improving things. So I tried to play as much of the game in the opposition 25 as I could, although that was foreign to my innermost thoughts on the game."

A lot of Martin's thinking had rubbed off on Matthews and the new captain spent considerable time discussing the game with Wade, too. "I never wanted to do more on a rugby field than play running rugby," said Matthews. "But success had to come first." There can be no doubt that Matthews achieved that goal: in his first season as captain, the team won 30 games, in the second they won 33 to break the club record which had stood at 31 (1897-98 and 1920-21).

During 1965, Drake-Lee took up an appointment at Stonyhurst and moved to Manchester but a glut of fly-halves joined the club, Bill Coutts from Loughborough Colleges, Bevis Martin Bedggood from Moseley and Rod Coady, another Australian. Both Quick and Coady were from Sydney, the back row man having played for Randwick before coming to this country to practise dentistry at Market Harborough, where he had initially joined the junior club Kibworth. Coady, an Eastern Suburbs player down under, was a master at Bushloe School, and the two first played together in

David Matthews takes on the Barbarians in 1964. Tigers won 12-11.

a 14-3 win over Plymouth Albion.

Quick's finest moment was to come at Christmas time against the Barbarians. On a day when the Leicester back row of Matthews, Quick and Bob Small were in commanding form, the Australian scored three tries in a 14-10 win, joining the elite group to have run in a hat-trick against the Baa-baas. It was a fitting honour for an outstanding back row and an equally outstanding captain when Matthews was invited to represent the Barbarians that season in the Mobbs Memorial Match.

There were trials for John Allen and Kevin Andrews, who was proving a very successful pack leader, but that was the nearest two very fine players came to being capped. Allen had the misfortune to be injured during one trial but it must have been a bitter pill to see England play three scrum-halves that season, Jeremy Spencer, Trevor Wintle and Clive Ashby, and feel that he had perhaps missed the boat.

Off the field it was Doug Norman's first year as president but the general secretary, Major Chilton, announced his resignation in November 1965, because of ill-health. For the same reason the groundsman, Bill Nash, resigned and his place went to the energetic Fred Cox. The post of general secretary was advertised at £1,100 a year, though a clerical error in the committee minutes made it £11,000 which would have had considerable appeal even to captains of industry.

The successful applicant was Air Commodore S G Walker, who took over at much the same time as Jerry Day became club secretary in succession to Ron Gerrard who had retired. Day had appeared at intervals for the senior side during the five years following the war but had not held down a regular place. He had played loyally for the 'A' XV before ending his career with Aylestone St James. When the club was reformed he became team secretary for the Extra 1sts and subsequently for the senior XV.

His election was known at the annual general meeting of 1966, when the club gleefully reviewed the progress made on the field during the previous

season. Quick headed the try scorers with 15 and Chilton's 181 points (22 of them came in a massive 43-3 win over London Irish) was the best since Haselmere in 1920. Oxford and Cambridge Universities had been beaten in the same season for the first time in 11 years though on the debit side Bob Rowell was moving away from the area to work in Manchester. And another famous name from the past, 'Tim' Taylor, had died, not long after the death in May, 1965, of Sid Penny.

In fact Rowell continued initially to travel from Burnley to play with Leicester as the 1966-67 season got under way, though he later joined Fylde. The club was bursting with wingers in September and could afford to play two England triallists, Roy Sleigh and Mike Brownhill, in the Extras since Bird and Bussey were holding down the first team spots. Another England triallist on the strength was the former Bristol prop, Roger Grove, but Leicester's front row man contending for honours early on was Field Walton, one of five Leicester players named in the Midland Counties (East) XV which met the Australians captained by John Thornett in the second game of their tour at Welford Road, on October 22.

The combined XV was: B Page (Northampton); W M Bussey, K Chilton (both Leicester), K F Savage, D T Robertson; J R Cooley, T C Wintle; D L Powell, A Johnson (all Northampton), F L J Walton (Leicester), P J Larter (Northampton), P W G Tom (Leicester), D P Rogers (Bedford, captain), J N Pallant (Notts), D J Matthews (Leicester).

It was not the most memorable display by the combined side. The Australians won 17-9 and it was only the East Midlands' back row and full back Brian Page who came out of the match in credit. Page collected all his side's points and began the scoring with a penalty. A try by John Brass made it 3-3 at halftime then heavyweight winger Alan Cardy got another. Page dropped a fine goal to level matters before Phil Hawthorne dropped a goal and Stewart Boyce scored the third Australian try. Page banged over another penalty but Boyce's second try, converted by Phil Gibbs, gave the tourists a comfortable margin.

Andrews also played against the Australians, for Midland Counties (West), but it was Harrison and Matthews who were given trials by England while in December, 1966, a Welshman named David Lyons had one of his few first-team games at centre, against Bristol. It was Lyons who, six years later, played such an important part in establishing a Leicester Youth side. The club gained the services, at the same time, of an England triallist from Loughborough Colleges, hooker John Elliott, and a couple of months later a raw youngster from the Loughborough Town club, Garry Adey, made his debut at lock against the Colleges.

The wins continued to roll in - among them victory over Northampton in new scarlet shirts purchased for use under the new lights - and, for the second season running, the club passed 500 points. Andrews won his Barbarians tie and, on the Easter tour, was accorded the singular honour for an

John Allen tackles a Northampton forward during the match against the Saints in February 1966.

uncapped player of captaining the Baa-baas, against Penarth. To round matters off, Harrison and Matthews were picked for a Midlands XV against a London and Home Counties XV, as the English regions girded their loins for the coming encounter with the 1967 All Blacks.

Matthews was elected for a third successive year as captain, despite his personal misgivings, and the 1967-68 season started off magnificently, all three teams going through September unbeaten. During the summer there had been a slight change in the administrative style, when 'Ranji' Walker left the area and the post of general secretary was left unfulfilled. It had not been an entirely happy marriage of the differing functions of the secretary's job and Jerry Day, like his famous predecessors, Crumbie and Thorneloe, a man who ran his own business, gathered everything back under the one hat.

The senior XV won their first seven games before drawing with Coventry and then losing to Richmond, but, sadly, there were no Leicester players on view when the next touring side came to Welford Road. Brian Lochore's New Zealanders were the first of the International Board countries to make a shortened tour of the British Isles and a revised fixture list had to be worked out. Accordingly the Midlands joined forces with the Home Counties and played the following team on October 28, 1967: R Hiller; J T Cox (both Harlequins), R D Hearn (Bedford), R H Lloyd (Harlequins), R E Webb; A James, W J Gittings (all Coventry); P E Judd (Coventry, captain), H O Godwin (Coventry), A L Horton (Blackheath), J E Owen (Coventry), P J Larter (Northampton), D P Rogers (Bedford), G A Sherriff (Saracens), R B Taylor (Northampton).

The All Blacks won 15-3 but the match will be remembered more for the tragic injury to the England centre Danny Hearn, who broke his neck in a tackle on Ian MacRae. The combined XV played the bulk of the match with 14 men and Budge Rogers and George Sherriff performed prodigies about the field, while Bob Taylor deputised well in the centre. There was no score at half-time but the outcome was inevitable, Fergie McCormick kicking three penalties, Malcolm Dick scoring a try and Mac Herewini dropping a goal. Bob Lloyd scored a fine try for the counties.

Meanwhile the club's form was patchy although one individual, Graham Willars, was consistency itself and had at last won a regular back row spot. After two successful seasons it was not entirely surprising that the club was having difficulty living up to its own standards, and their form had made them a marked team wherever they went. The

Line-out action under floodlights against Nuneaton in 1966. (Tigers are in white).

absence of a place-kicker, Chilton having left the area, may have had a lot to do with it and meant another burden for Matthews, since he took over the kicking role.

In the second half of the season, however, the hard-pressed captain had some of the weight lifted from his shoulders. Martin had returned to New Zealand in 1967 (after an intended stay of two years had turned into 11) and the task of coaching, still an unofficial job, devolved upon H V 'Chalkie' White and Rex Skelton. Both players had been overtaken by time and younger, more promising men in terms of first-team appearances but they stayed with the club, involved themselves in committee work and were happy to lend some new ideas in the general approach to the game at a time when Matthews was under considerable pressure.

It was some time before their influence - more particularly that of White - was felt. In the meantime Leicester made their way to a respectable aggregate of wins, helped by a new recruit from Cardiff, Michael Evans, who, as well as being a useful centre or fly half, could kick goals too. Matthews injured a knee towards the end of the season and Quick took over the captaincy, but returned to Australia at the end of the season.

Plans were afoot to change the sequence of Easter tours, after years of visiting the West Country. After 1968-69; tours were to be undertaken in alternative years, in order to give Leicester fans something to look forward to in the holiday period and to try and draw bigger crowds. It was to change the emphasis of the season for Leicester, even if barmen in the West heaved a collective sigh of relief.

TEARAWAY TIGERS
1968-1970

BRITISH rugby was changing. After years of being kicked around by Springboks, All Blacks and, latterly, Frenchmen, players and administrators were taking a new, more critical look at their game. The Australians, no doubt to their amazement, found their kicking restrictions accepted by the International Board and players were no longer able to kick to touch on the full outside their own 25-yard lines. It was a major breakthrough and the statuesque variety of full back became obsolete overnight.

Leicester, in the person of their new captain, Graham Willars, embraced the changing atmosphere with delight. A constructive, intelligent flanker who must have been a joy to play with, and in many respects against because he was such an honest footballer, Willars wanted a game in which all 15 players could participate fully, in which they could find their own entertainment as well as providing enjoyment for spectators. Since he worked in telecommunications, Willars was also able to get his message across, as captain and, subsequently, as coach and president.

It was also to be a formative season off the field. For the first time Leicester provided the President of the Rugby Union in the person of Tom Berry (whose service as a national selector had ended two years before) and he was able to launch an appeal to improve club facilities. The target was £30,000, the object being to turn the clubhouse into a worthwhile social centre which could be used all year.

A natural consequence of such an appeal, however, was the wish for a successful side, a side that would draw larger crowds, a money-spinning side if you like. Not that the last few years had been unsuccessful in terms of results, far from it; but there was considerable scope for development of the club's game. "I decided we had to use our backs more," said Willars. "It didn't matter what standard they were, we had to use them.

"Once they started developing, using the ball in all situations, if you scored two tries and the opposition scored one, that to me was good. I always felt it didn't matter how many points the opposition got, if we got more then I was quite happy."

To assist Willars in his endeavours was 'Chalkie' White, who had become the unofficial club coach - not without a degree of resentment from committeemen who thought it was vaguely unsporting and senior players who had been used to working things out for themselves - because of his close relationship with Matthews. After illness had effectively terminated his playing career by keeping him out of action for 18 months White had been invited to join the committee, with no particular role. "My forte at the time was to associate closely with the players. I never thought about coaching but the opportunity occurred because David asked me to help."

Leicester were exceptionally lucky to have the right man available at the right time. Although he had been a fairly unexceptional player as a scrum-half, White had a great variety of experience, having played schools and colleges rugby (at Borough Road), service rugby, club rugby in the south-west and Midlands, and county championship rugby in the north. His job as a teacher at Nottingham High School allowed him sufficient time to devote to the task of coaching a first class club (not to mention a captive squad of schoolboys available as a testing ground) and the tremendous encouragement of his family allowed him to develop that task.

White saw, and still sees, himself as a visionary. The problem for such men, of course, is always to convince others that their road is the right one, and White and Willars were lucky to have each other during that opening period of coaching, when they were of necessity working from game to game, although it did not take long before White realised there had to be long-term objectives.

"I did not mind laying down fairly tight guidelines," said White. "Some players, capable of more, did not respond, they had no sympathy with what I was doing. And in all fairness, I don't think I ever went to the trouble of making it clear - there was no avenue to do so, no need, I was creating a precedent."

Precedent or not, the Willars/White team was successful, for the 1968-69 season produced 657 points, second only to the 756 of 1919-20. Drake-Lee rejoined the club briefly at the start of the season and so did Gavins, although as far as the full back position was concerned there was a young Scotsman from Hawick and Jordanhill, Robin Money, who was beginning to press for a place.

Matthews, relieved of the burden of captaincy, celebrated with 21 tries, the best individual total since Senior in 1960 and the record for a forward until surpassed by Simon Povoas who scored 25 during the 1989-90 season. It rapidly became the season of the comeback men: in addition to Drake-Lee and Gavins, Harrison, having retired at the end of the previous season to concentrate on his work at Wyggeston School, rejoined the club while Rowell returned at the start of 1969. Newcomers included a promising back row man from Loughborough Colleges, Christopher Baynes, and a centre who could also play wing, Bob Barker from Stoneygate.

It was not a season for individual honours, although Elliott, the hooker from Nottingham who played a key role as selector during England's grand-slam era of 1990-2, won an England trial. This was just as well since it enabled the captain and the coach to concentrate on building the side, knowing they would not lose a vital player halfway through the season. Matthews and Allen played in all 43 games and the Easter tour, the last to the West Country, was a memorable one. Doug Norman, who played in 1929-30, the first time Tigers had enjoyed an unbeaten tour, and White, who had played in the last unbeaten touring side, that of 1958, were both

NEEDLE WORK
A letter in the local paper of 1969 "to whom it may concern" suggested that the club invest in a new stylus for the record player used for pre-match broadcasting. Apparently before every home game that season numerous tunes had been ruined by the constant repetition of a few bars when the needle had obviously "stuck".

there to see the club go through their three games unbeaten, Matthews scoring his 100th try for the club against Bristol.

Regrettably the appeal fund's success did not match the football. Outside consultants had been brought in to suggest ways and means of raising cash, then their services were dispensed with. It seemed apparent that a lack of enthusiasm from the general public would mean a cutback in the club's ambitious plans. There were complaints from members that they did not feel part of the club and, with the season half gone, only some £7,000 had been raised. That total doubled by the end of the season but it was still less than half the projected amount.

The committee decided to hang on for the rest of the year to see whether the appeal fund was going to grow any more and, in the meantime, sanctioned the formation of a 200 club, another fund-raising entity which proved immediately more successful. Other topics were in the air: leagues, a knockout competition, and the club president, Nick Hughes, was on record suggesting zone competitions. He must have derived a certain ironic satisfaction when such competitions were introduced eight years later. In general, Leicester favoured competition within regional pools, the leaders from each pool going forward to a knockout competition.

All of this made certain that the summer months passed quickly, for the 1969-70 season which was approaching produced a problem British rugby had never previously faced: a Springbok tour with demonstrations. The anti-apartheid forces in this country had laid their plans with considerable care to make sure that 'Dawie' de Villiers' Sixth Springboks never settled to the task of actually playing rugby, and the game against the Midland Counties (East) at Welford Road on November 8 was the second of the tour.

The Leicestershire Rugby Union laid their counter plans, in conjunction with the police, while the Leicester club privately congratulated itself on undertaking no alterations or improvements to the ground before the Springboks passed through. It must have come as a rude surprise, however, to the canine supporter labelled Tigers' keenest fan in the local press: Bruce, a boxer dog, was in the habit of leaning paws up against the railings in front of the stand to watch every game, alongside his master, Walter Hardy, a supporter for over forty years. "He gets really excited sometimes," Mr Hardy was reported as saying. "You can almost see the smile on his face when someone kicks a penalty goal." Clearly Bruce was a product of the drab sixties.

Kevin Andrews, the 29-year-old lock, was captaining the club in what was his last season and there were several newcomers in the wings, notably the former Rosslyn Park fly half or full back, Arthur Chapman, who made an important points contribution in his 17 games. Perhaps the most obvious success of the season, however, was to be a new centre who joined from Headingley, Michael Yandle. Yandle, a Welsh schools cap, had learned to play his rugby in Llanelli before his job as a research chemist took him to "foreign" parts. His first game for the club was not auspicious: Bedford recorded their biggest win over the Tigers, by 39-5, though there was some comfort in the 33-21 win over the

John Allen makes a blind-side break at Welford Road against Watcyn Thomas' XV in September 1968.

Irish Wolfhounds and a 48-6 defeat of Gosforth, in which Chapman scored 18 points.

There were others who were to become mainstays during the 1970s: John Duggan, a winger with Irish qualifications who, though a student at Loughborough Colleges, preferred to play his rugby with Oakham; a young Welshman from Brynramman, Bleddyn Jones, who had taken up a teaching post in Leicester; a couple of props from the Colleges, Philip Vesty and Chris Owen, and a blond hooker from Old Brockleians whose job with an insurance company had brought him to Leicester, Peter John Wheeler.

They all began their Leicester careers in the Swifts, though in October the club had the interesting situation of Elliott hooking for Notts, Lincs and Derby, Richard Berry for Leicestershire and Wheeler for Kent. So much new blood jostling for a place,

Boxer Bruce is Tigers' keenest fan

BRUCE is a rugger enthusiast. Every Saturday when Leicester Tigers play at home he leans against the railings on the terraces below the main stand at the Welford Road ground, and watches the game intently.

Which does not seem unusual — until you consider that Bruce is a seven-year-old Boxer dog who really does lean against the railings, he stands on his hind legs and puts his front paws up, and really does watch the game—every minute of it.

Bruce has been following the fortunes of the Tigers nearly all his life, like his master, Mr Walter Hardy, a regular supporter for over 40 years.

Before Bruce, Mr. Hardy who lives at 66, Knighton Fields Road East, Leicester, had another boxer — the oval ball fascinated him too.

"Bruce never misses a match. We always stand on the 25-yard line and he always follows the ball. He gets really excited sometimes," said Mr Hardy.

And Bruce's love for rugby extends further than being a spectator. At home he lets off steam by playing with a rugger ball.

"He could dribble round all 30 players on this field with ease," said Mr Hardy, at the game against Gloucester on Saturday.

Dogs are supposed to be like their masters, and as far as rugby football goes this is certain

Bruce the Boxer dog eagerly watches the action with his master Walter Hardy, a Tigers supporter for 40 years.

however, gave the selection committee problems so it was not entirely surprising that only three Leicester players were included in the combined XV which met the Springboks in front of a 15,000 crowd. The side was P G S Pulfrey (Leicester); R E Morris (Hinckley), P R Sweet (Northampton), D J Small (Bedford), G T Robertson (Northampton); P D Briggs (Bedford, captain), J A Allen (Leicester); P S Onyett (Bedford), A G Johnson, D L Powell (both Northampton), J Harrison (Boston), P J Larter (Northampton), D J Matthews (Leicester), B West, R B Taylor (both Northampton).

The tourists had begun by losing 6-3 to Oxford University and they only just got home, by 11-9, at Welford Road, in a match interrupted by abuse from demonstrators and intrusions onto the pitch. Piet Visagie opened the scoring with a penalty before Larter levelled with a huge kick from a penalty on halfway. Playing with the gusting wind, the Midlands took advantage of the tourists' uncertainty to score tries through Glenn Robertson and Peter Sweet, a dropped goal by Visagie making the score 9-6 at halftime. It was backs to the wall in the second half for the East Midlands, with the back row working overtime, but with only 10 minutes left, Visagie made the break to give Piet van Deventer a try, Visagie's conversion winning the game.

Groundsman Fred Cox and assistant Ralph Boulter somehow manage a smile during the strenuous straw-clearing operations necessary for the previously postponed Barbarians game in 1969.

With the South Africans gone, Leicester totalled up the amount of cash they had raised and embarked on phase one of their planned redevelopment. The ground floor of the clubhouse was restructured to include an extra changing room, a foyer and an office for the secretary. Upstairs was redesigned as an all-purpose room for general functions, as well as the usual post-match imbibing, and a kitchen was added. Just outside the clubhouse, the banking at the Aylestone Road end of the ground was levelled to give car parking space, though this did cut down the amount of standing room available at big matches.

At much the same time Doug Norman resigned as fixture secretary, the task passing to Robert Beason. It was an indication of changing times that Beason, still playing well after nearly ten years with the club, should become an office holder too. It was not many years before that the idea of a player holding such a post had been virtually unthinkable.

With the team struggling to make an impact there was much discussion of playing policy and whether a club coaching panel should be instituted. Those who wished to see the Swifts scrapped were over-ruled, though it was agreed that a greater emphasis should be placed on young players in the Swifts. November, 1969, saw Jones make his debut at fly-half instead of the injured Chapman, against Wilmslow, but his first game was overshadowed by the first appearance in a Leicester shirt of the Scotland and British Lions flanker, Rodger Arneil.

Arneil, then 25, had made his name on the 1968 Lions' visit to South Africa and had won seven of his 21 caps. He played little more than a dozen games for the club during his two seasons at Welford Road but while there he gave them what so many back rows lack - height, weight and speed. At six feet four inches tall and nearly 15 stone he was a considerable asset, apart from the prestige attached to an international then at the summit of his powers.

In the same month Wheeler made his first appearance in the senior side, against Moseley, but it was not until the new year that Leicester managed to climb out of the doldrums in which they had settled. At that stage they had to recover from the indignity of a 35-0 defeat at the hands of the Barbarians, the highest score the guest XV had put together. It was the 50th encounter between the two sides (excluding two WW1 games) and the Baa-baas turned in a golden display, with David Duckham scoring five tries and equalling Thompson's effort of 1956. Keith Fielding scored two tries, John Jeffrey and Bob Phillips one each, and a young full back called J P R Williams kicked four conversions.

There was some consolation for the club when they achieved the "double" against Gloucester, Barker scoring all the points in the second victory at Kingsholm. The former Stoneygate winger had become a regular member of the side, and a useful place-kicker, even though he was the only player who could, in the words of the club coach, make the ball turn three different directions before it crossed the bar. A canny footballer with the knack of turning up in the right place at the right time, he was to score 158 tries for Leicester, a post-war record until beaten by Barry Evans in 1989-90, though still well short of Percy Lawrie's 206.

For the first time since 1895, Leicester stayed home at Easter and entertained Liverpool, Fylde and Manchester over the holiday period. Even though all three games were won, however, the attendances were disappointing. Equally disappointing was the decision at the season's end of the captain, Andrews, to retire, leaving behind this epitaph on the club: "They are without doubt the best club I have played for...They have the right attitude to the game and this is why they will always be a great club." A self-confessed Tigers addict, Andrews continued to work off the field as hard as he always worked on it.

Another leading forward, Bob Small, was retiring and though they won for the first time in 16 years at Coventry, Leicester completed a not entirely happy season, when they crashed 43-11 at Llanelli with Rowell being sent off for questioning the referee's decisions. The last Leicester player to have been sent off during a game had been Almey, also at Llanelli, 10 years before.

A NEW LOOK
1970-1972

GOING into the 70s, Leicester decided there had to be a fresh outlook on relations with local clubs. They had appointed a coaching panel of White, Small and Lyons for their own purposes; now they organised another panel, headed by Andrews, to visit the junior clubs in Leicestershire and discuss moves to and from the county's senior club. It was hard to break down the accumulation of prejudices which had built up, on both sides, but the attempt had to be made and similar ventures continued, in one form or another, during the next eight years. The immediate response, in general, from the junior clubs was that they felt two sides would be sufficient for Leicester's purposes but that they would support a youth XV.

In the meantime there were problems enough restoring the image of the 1st XV. Allen had been elected captain but the scrum-half did not see eye to eye with the coach, White, and the element of discord in their views of the game may have been reflected in the results. The season was notable in one respect, for one of White's contemporaries as a player, the full back Gavins, returned for one more season, and re-appeared with a bang. He played in 14 games which was enough to make him top scorer with 115 points.

Among the newcomers was a centre from Nottingham, Brian Hall, who was to form a profitable partnership with Yandle, and a full back from the West Country who was studying at Leicester University, David Whibley. Ten Tigers played in the Leicestershire XV which beat Durham 25-14 in the county's jubilee game and there were six in the Midland Counties (East) XV which lost to the

Mike Gavins kicking against Harrogate in September 1970.

touring Fijians at Welford Road on November 7, 1970, among them an athletic lock, Eric Bann, who had joined the club two seasons before. A player of immense potential and probably the best line-out exponent Leicester had over the last two decades before the arrival of Martin Johnson, Bann never reached the heights which his talent suggested he should.

The Midland XV was: P Jenkins (Loughborough Colleges); M J Duggan, M J Yandle, B P Hall (all Leicester), B Oldham; J R Cooley (both Northampton), V J Lewis; P S Onyett (both Bedford), A G Johnson (Northampton), D L Powell (Northampton, captain), E E Bann (Leicester), P J Larter, R B Taylor (both Northampton), G J Adey, C J Baynes (both Leicester).

The local side lost 24-14, after leading 11-8 at halftime. Tikoisuva and Kurisaru scored tries for the tourists, Cooley got one back for the Midlands and Jenkins kicked a conversion, a penalty and a dropped goal. After the break Sovau scored a try, converted by Barley, and the game took an ugly turn, fists flying, and the Midlands lost Cooley, injured. His place at fly-half was taken by a teenager from Notts, W H 'Dusty' Hare, who had only recently broken through from junior football. Jenkins kicked another penalty but tries by Sikivou, Kurisaru and Sovau, one improved by Barley, put the game well out of reach.

There was some compensation in the selection of Adey for the first - and so far the only - England under-25 side to play the Fijians. Wheeler was a replacement for the match which was played in miserable conditions; Adey had been suffering from influenza during the week and may not have done himself justice, since he was the only member of the side who did not to go on to get a trial.

It was, though, the start of an exceptional decade for Wheeler. He got the slice of luck everyone needs, even the good players, when Elliott dropped out through injury and missed the Barbarians game. Wheeler, not without a blush, recalls that it was he who delivered the injury during a training evening but, having got the first-team place, he kept it, to such good effect that Elliott eventually moved clubs and joined Notts.

As well as being a good hooker, Wheeler was a remarkably fine all-round footballer. In his first season he proved a useful addition to the place-kicking strength; fast and hard, he could also tackle, distribute the ball and kick well out of hand. Sufficient of these qualities came through for him to be chosen, with Matthews, for the London, Midland and Home Counties XV which played the RFU President's XV at Welford Road on April 7, 1971, as part of the Rugby Football Union's centenary celebrations.

The President's men won 18-13 in a game notable for a remarkable try by the Springbok lock, Frik du Preez, but Wheeler was on his way. On the club tour in the north-west, he scored 32 of 47 points recorded against Liverpool, Fylde and Manchester, and 29 of those came from the boot. And though there was no fairy story ending with a place in the British Lions side to Australasia that summer - Arneil was chosen from Leicester (as replacement for Mick Hipwell), the club's first Lion since 1959 - Wheeler was picked for England's tour to the Far East.

What had started as a thoroughly mediocre year was turning out to be quite eventful. Thinking ahead ten years, the club elected their own centenary committee (Tom Berry, Doug Norman and Bob Beason) and decided to undertake, for the first time, a pre-season training weekend. Chalkie White took his troops to Cromer in August for a valuable couple of days, although the value of the trip took some time to appear. The new season, marked by the appearance of a new-look, 16-page programme, was clouded by five successive defeats, attendance at training was poor, Arneil joined Northampton and the England wing, Keith Fielding, after joining the club from Moseley, hastily returned there after Leicester decided he was not good enough for their first XV.

The turning point came against Gloucester previously undefeated by an English club who crashed 31-9 at Welford Road. Money, the full back, had taken the afternoon off to attend a wedding and Whibley seized his opportunity with both hands to become the goal-kicker the club desperately needed and turn in such a consistently high standard that he very nearly went from Leicester Extras to a full cap in one season. After only nine first-class games he won an area trial and in the new year there were senior trials.

Bob Rowell takes on Gloucester in 1971.

Unfortunately he could not help Leicester win their first venture in the Rugby Football Union's national knockout competition. Drawn against Notts, the game was played on a Sunday at Beeston, the home side having Hare to help them to a 10-3 win. It was another 18 years before Nottingham, as they became, repeated that success. There was compensation at Christmas in a splendid 20-14 win over the Barbarians, Barker joining the ranks of the few by scoring three tries. The game was a fitting tribute, too, to Doug Norman, who died early the same day. 1971 had also seen the death of two stalwarts, Rodney Bedingfield and H L V Day, the latter after a distinguished career as a referee and rugby correspondent.

In the meantime the club were planning a step which ranks as one of their most important decisions since the war. An article had appeared in *The Leicester Mercury*, written by the paper's rugby correspondent, Paul Neale, describing the activities of a schools side, the Leicester Ravens, composed of some of the best 14 and 15 year-olds in the county. It was organised by David Lyons who had a genius for bringing the best out of young players, and the article mooted the possibility of the Ravens becoming, in effect, a Tigers youth side.

It was a gift horse which Jerry Day, for one, was

not going to look in the mouth and he threw all his support behind the project. A special club sub-committee recommended Leicester to seek the advice and co-operation of leading rugby-playing schools, to constitute a youth sub-committee for the side's management, to organise as many fixtures as possible outside Leicestershire, but not more than 20 in a season, to charge a subscription of £1 with full membership rights and, in particular, that the youth team should train separately and should not be used to fill gaps in the three senior sides.

In March, 1972, a former Leicestershire RU president, Joe Pickup, became secretary of the junior football sub-committee and Lyons, a teacher at Roundhill School, Syston, and Michael Deathe, a Hinckley schoolmaster, were appointed youth coaches and joined the club's coaching committee. On April 15, 1972, Leicester Youth took the field for the first time and beat Nottingham Cubs 78-9. They followed this up with a 76-0 win over Derbyshire Youth and the first report on the team's activities in the club committee minutes noted, somewhat drily in the circumstances: "This was felt to be a promising start."

Of the side that played the Cubs, the scrum-half, Stephen Kenney, was to make the most impact, winning England colts and under-23 caps with his exciting, running style which was worth, in the opinion of many outside observers, even higher honours. The team was: M Hellyer; R Lett, M Wyatt, S Dexter, K Smith; J Flint, S Kenney; P Hemsill, M Briggs, C Siwek, J Fraser, R Hull, J Krych, A P Collington, P Bennett. Both on the playing and administrative side, the youth side has made emphatic progress since then.

In several seasons the quality of the youth rugby has been exceptional but the most valuable aspect of the side's creation has been the insight into the future of the senior side. With a coach already keen on long term planning, the youth team enabled Leicester to think in terms of the next decade rather than the next two or three seasons. Within six short years the youth had produced their first full international in Paul Dodge, one of the boys directly influenced by Lyons in those formative years of the early 70s.

While the youth side was coming into being, their seniors were not standing still. Casting aside the disappointments of the early part of the 1971-72 season they scored fifty points for the first time since the 1919-20 season (against the RAF) and went out in a blaze of glory, winning at Newport for the first time in 39 years and, in the same match, passing the previous highest points tally of 756, recorded in 1920. They wound up with 789 points, Whibley scored 200 points (the best since Haselmere in 1920) and Barker 26 tries (the best since Haselmere in 1921). To cap it all, Whibley was named in the England party to tour South Africa, the assistant manager of the party being John Elders.

Another tourist was the Middlesbrough fly-half, Alan Old, capped in all the home internationals and against South Africa and the scorer of a record number of points (24) in England's 60-21 win over Griqualand West. An appointment to the teaching staff at Worksop College brought Old south and he joined Leicester, along with a New Zealander who had played in the centre for Auckland, Gary

Weinberg, who was in this country on business.

A G B Old, one of the best, and certainly one of the most under-rated, fly-halves capped by England during the seventies, helped bring a new confidence to the club's back division which was not exactly lacking in it anyway, with characters like Hall and Yandle playing. The pity of it was that he was available for so few games, because of his commitments to Yorkshire in the county championship and the demands made on him by England. He and Bleddyn Jones alternated for the fly-half position, and occasionally they played in the same side, with Old at centre.

Graham Willars in 1970.

CHAPTER 18

HEADING FOR THE HEIGHTS
1972-1974

FROM the outset of the 1972-73 season Graham Willars, the captain, and White were determined on a target of 30 wins and 1,000 points; failure was relative, in that the side finished with 29 wins and 988 points, with 683 against. It was the highest points aggregate in the club's history, yet twice Leicester conceded 40 points.

It was a season of change as long-serving prop Roger Grove retired, Whibley had to concentrate on his studies and, halfway through the season, moved to London along with the talented reserve hooker, David Pickering, the players joining Richmond and London Scottish respectively. Old was lost to the side after injuring a leg in the Barbarians match and Willars too fell by the way through injury, which provided an opportunity for a young student from Madeley College who had been playing with Nottingham, Paul Ringer, to come in on the back row. A hard, no-nonsense flanker, Ringer was subsequently troubled by a chest complaint and there were few at Leicester who anticipated that, six years later, he would be capped by Wales.

A local centre, John Ingleby, played 23 games during the 1972-73 season and scored 200 points, all but 12 of them from the boot, while Barker scored 29 tries. Neither, however, was in the Midland Counties (East) side which played Ian Kirkpatrick's All Blacks at Welford Road on January 13, 1973, for which they were duly grateful, no doubt, when the tourists ran out winners by 43-12. There were eight Leicester players in the combined XV which was coached by White and was: D F Whibley; M J Duggan, M J Yandle (all Leicester), G Phillips, R Morris (both Northampton); B Jones, J A Allen (both Leicester); D L Powell (Northampton, captain), P J Wheeler (Leicester), P Duffy, P J Larter (both Northampton), R M Wilkinson (Cambridge University), C J Baynes, G J Adey (both Leicester), I Clayton (Nottingham).

It was one of the few occasions on tour when the All Blacks cut loose, prompted by Lyn Colling at scrum half. Duggan and Yandle sent in Allen for the counties' try which Whibley converted, besides kicking two penalties. Against that was a flood of tries from Robertson, Batty, Hurst, Burgess, Colling, Stewart, Sutherland and Kirkpatrick, Karam converting four times and landing a penalty. With Jones having to leave the match injured (he was replaced by Nottingham's Alan Davies who subsequently won greater fame as a coach, to Nottingham, England B and Wales), it was not a good day for the locals.

In the knockout cup competition it was Leicester's best season and remained so until 1977-78. They beat Bedford away (21-17) then Hinckley (16-4) before losing disappointingly in the quarter finals at Sale (7-0). But plans for bettering what had been a record season in terms of points took a knock in summer 1973 when Yandle, who had been elected club captain, moved to work in Swansea. Wheeler was elected instead, to be faced with a schedule which included two touring sides in the first eight games.

The first visitors were Fiji, invited to this country to help Swansea celebrate their centenary. They drew a crowd of 12,000 to an evening match at Welford Road on September 11, 1973, and home pride was considerable when Leicester, with the following team, beat them 22-17: R S Money; R G Barker, J Ingleby, B P Hall, M J Duggan; B Jones, J A Allen; P N Vesty, P J Wheeler (captain), M R Mortimer, E E Bann, R Watson, D J Forfar, G J Adey, P Ringer. Leicester stayed in the game through Ingleby kicking four penalties to go with Wheeler's try but, with 10 minutes left, the Fijians led 17-16. But a blind side move put Barker over for a try improved by Ingleby and the 1973-74 season was off to a tremendous start.

The second touring side, delightfully known as the 'Galloping Greens', were Randwick from Australia, winners the previous season of the Sydney senior grade final. They began their British tour at Welford Road on October 3 and again Leicester proved triumphant with a 15-10 win in a

John Duggan and John Ingleby chase Coventry's David Duckham in October 1973.

hard encounter. Wheeler kicked two penalties, Money dropped a goal and, in injury-time, a superb try by Jones, converted by Ingleby, made sure.

If anything more were needed to make it possibly the most cosmopolitan season the club had yet enjoyed, the Japanese played the Midland Counties at Welford Road a

John Allen and Graham Willars in action.

week later. Wheeler, Adey and Ringer played for the Midlands but it was a poor game, won by the local side 10-6. It heralded a series of reverses: in the third defeat of the season, at Northampton, Ringer was sent off and Adey carried off; seven penalties by Peter Butler helped Gloucester to a 29-6 win at Welford Road and, in the first round of the knockout competition, Leicester went down 22-6 at Northampton, Arneil rubbing salt into the wound by scoring against his old club. The only mitigating feature as 1974 approached was Old's selection for England against the touring Australians and Wheeler's elevation as deputy hooker to England's John Pullin.

Old achieved a notable treble by playing in the 20-3 win over Australia, becoming one of the few players to have shared in wins over South Africa, New Zealand and Australia, all within the space of 18 months. He had been the only Leicester player on the short trip to New Zealand in August and September, which culminated in the 16-10 win over the All Blacks. He was to play in all the internationals during 1973-74 and earn selection for the 1974 British Lions who toured South Africa, captained by Willie John McBride.

After the flying start, the season tended to tail off for Leicester. There was a quirky incident at Rosslyn Park when a new centre, Ted Holley, tripped over a step emerging from the dressing room and had to be replaced before the game began; there was an unhappy moment when the club suspended one of their props, Mike Mortimer, after a fracas during the home game with Bedford. Both club and player aired their views on the incident which ended with neither side entirely happy. Much more pleasure was derived by the celebration, on February 23, 1974, of David Matthews' 500th game for Leicester, against Northampton, which ended with the veteran flanker being carried from the field shoulder high after Leicester had won 15-9.

Matthews' own, wry comment on his achievement was: "You've got to have a lot of willpower and luck as well - I was very lucky with injuries." Perhaps more to the point was Matthews' belief in himself as a player; he never won a cap but this did not mean he ever considered himself second best to any rival

he played against. It was entirely fitting that the man to pay tribute to Matthews at a special dinner, and present him with an engraved cigarette box, was his great back row rival from Bedford, D P 'Budge' Rogers, later to become the chairman of the England selectors. Matthews made two more senior appearances before calling it a day.

Before the season's end there were three more causes for celebration: Wheeler played his first game for the Barbarians, against the East Midlands, and scored three tries which created a Baa-baas record. Allen was also chosen for the Barbarians for the first time, playing against Penarth and Newport on the Easter tour. And, at Stradey Park, Leicester played superbly to deprive Llanelli of their ground record with an 11-10 win.

That game at Llanelli when, ironically, Leicester's two tries came from Welshmen, Bleddyn Jones and Frank Jones, would have warmed the cockles of the recently-reformed Supporters' Club, which was revived that winter. Also off the field, Tom Berry handed over as president to Rodney Willcox; another Leicester member, Peter Jerwood, became president of Leicestershire, and Fred Cox resigned as groundsman, his position going, after several hiccoughs, to Derek Limmage who has worked unstintingly ever since to ensure that the playing surface remains among the best in the country.

Wheeler was due to serve his second term as captain but the club lost the services of Old during the summer. The fly-half was unlucky enough to suffer severe ligament damage after a late tackle in the seventh match of the Lions' tour, against the Proteas - this when he had set a Lions record by scoring 37 points in the 97-0 win over South West Districts (from a try, a penalty and 15 conversions) and looked a more likely bet for the test spot than Phil Bennett. He returned home after a spell in hospital and returned to Yorkshire, later joining the Sheffield club and continuing to oversee, in his county team, the progress of several potential internationals.

CHAPTER 19

BACK TO THE DEPTHS 1974-1977

THERE was little indication at the start of 1974-75 that it was to be the worst season for 17 years, for on September 1, 1974, Leicester won the inaugural Midland seven-a-side tournament, sponsored by Carlsberg. It was held at Welford Road and on the way to the final, Leicester disposed of the Middlesex Sevens winners, Richmond. In the final they beat a brave, inexperienced Moseley VII by 18-16 with the following team: R S Money, J Reeve, B P Hall, B Jones, M Marshall, P J Wheeler, G G Willars.

Among the newcomers to the club was an England reserve prop, Robin James Cowling, who had been a member of the Gloucester side which won the first knockout competition (not that Leicester, this year, had an interest in the competition since they had failed to qualify the previous season). A hard, very competent player, Cowling gave added bite to the Leicester front row: as the season progressed another new face was that of 'Jock' Millican, capped by Scotland as a flanker three years previously but now seeking to re-establish himself after a badly broken leg had kept him out of action for a season.

In December the first player from the youth team to graduate to the senior XV, a flanker turned front row, Jez Krych, made his debut against Blackheath and he was followed later in the season, against Moseley, by a back row forward, Andrew Collington. Both Krych and another player who was still in the youth XV, Paul Dodge, were in the squad for the Barbarians match but in the event, neither played in the overwhelming 43-4 defeat. Nine tries were scored against Leicester as the Barbarian backs ran riot, though the score does no justice to the efforts of the home forwards. It was the biggest total the Baa-baas had ever recorded.

In a miserable December, Leicester lost four successive games, but took solace from the gradual progression of their captain, Wheeler, towards his first cap. He had been a replacement for the Barbarians in their 13-13 draw with New Zealand, he played for England against the Rest in the final trial (with Cowling in the opposing front row) and both he and Cowling were on the bench against Ireland. Cowling remained there for the rest of the season but Wheeler replaced Pullin against France, and won his second cap against Wales at Cardiff, a match in which he sustained a neck injury which, initially, looked as though it might wreck his career, though as it turned out, only meant a lay-off for the rest of the season.

In the new year Willars retired from first team rugby, though he could not be prevented from making several one-game comebacks. Changes in the centre and back row meant the side could never settle down and John Allen was nearing the end of a distinguished career at scrum-half. A black statistic against the season was the sending-off of three players: lock Nick Joyce against Northampton, and Cowling and Rowell together in the game at Fylde.

In the latter game Leicester redeemed themselves by winning 21-19 despite having only 13 men for an hour. The Youth scrum-half, Kenney, won an England Colts cap against the Welsh Youth and Bleddyn Jones, apart from playing in every game, was named director of mini-rugby for Leicestershire, with Frank Jones and Duggan assisting him.

It had been more than a decade since the club had recorded more defeats than victories (20 against 19) and the improvement the following season was only marginal, since 1975-76 brought 23 wins and 21 defeats. Yet the circumstances for the side captained by Money were much changed: for this was the season when a group of original youth team members "came of age" and qualified for senior rugby. Money outlined his requirements for success thus: "Correct attitude of the players; healthy competition for all positions; blending together the talent we have available in the club, both youth and experience." In the latter case, easier said than done: two of the youngsters, John Flint at half-back and Dodge in the centre, were picked for the first match, against Bedford, and though Bedford won 24-12 Leicester had at least discovered a kicker of talent in Flint who landed four penalties.

Kenney came into the side for the next match but the strain began to tell on the youngsters when they ran into the "heavy brigade", Coventry, Richmond and Northampton in October. Cowling broke a leg in one of England's regional training sessions and the forwards as a whole were not sufficiently on top of their game to be able to afford much protection to their young halves. It was the tragedy of the season that Flint, a footballer of genuine ability, suffered such a battering in carrying out defensive duties that his confidence drained away, he was injured, and though he played again in the club's lower sides, it was virtually the end of his first class career, before it had even begun.

Dodge, on the contrary, went from strength to strength. Physically bigger than Flint and not in such an exposed position as fly-half, Dodge was able to show all the skills of passing, running and kicking which had caught the eye of club officials when he was in the youth. As well as playing centre for the club, he played full back for Leicestershire and, still only 17, was pitched into representative rugby on November 12 when he was a member of the Midland Counties (East) XV which achieved a notable, and entirely unexpected, 11-8 win over the touring Australians, led by John Hipwell, at Welford Road under lights - the first time the Wallabies had played a floodlit game.

Wheeler captained a side containing three current Leicester players and, in Hare, Rod McMichael and Nigel Gillingham, three future ones. The combined XV was: W H Hare (Nottingham); K Parker (Northampton), P W Dodge (Leicester), N French (Wasps), B Oldham (Northampton); R D J McMichael (Westleigh), I George (Northampton); J Pearce (Nottingham), P J Wheeler (Leicester), W Dickinson (Nottingham), R M Wilkinson (Bedford), N K Gillingham (Loughborough Colleges), G Phillips (Northampton), G J Adey (Leicester), P Sweet (Northampton).

Ian Clayton of Nottingham replaced Bob Wilkinson after only 20 minutes but despite the disruption, the Midland XV played sound, effective

football, Parker scoring two tries and Hare kicking a penalty against tries by Hipwell and Laurie Monaghan. Another group of touring Australians, from the Sydney club Eastern Suburbs, brought Leicester relief when Tigers were able to end a dismal run of eight successive defeats with a 22-15 win but alas for hopes of success in the knockout competition (now sponsored and renamed the John Player Cup), the following week Leicester went down 10-7 at Liverpool in the first round in a match dominated by their forwards.

It was, essentially, a season of individual achievement rather than team success, although there were three notable games, against the Barbarians, Nottingham and Northampton. All three featured the Loughborough Grammar School full back, Marcus Rose, then 18, who had come into the side against Bristol the week before Christmas because Money had hamstring trouble which effectively wrecked his season. Rose provided a spark of inspiration sadly lacking, playing with flair and originality, kicking goals when least expected and showing all the easy poise which made many Leicester folk feel they had another international on their hands. "I had an invitation to play in London on Boxing Day but I turned it down and just intended to go and watch the Baa-baas," Rose said. Instead he found himself playing in the match which, though lost 20-11, was a distinct improvement on the season before. Two months later, in only his fifth game, Rose scored 13 points against Northampton to bring his aggregate to 52; it was as well Leicester were away from home that day since, during the match between the Swifts and Norwich at Welford Road, a cavity appeared in the middle of the pitch. It turned out to be the club's old friend, the sewer, though no rats were reported this time!

Rowell took over the leadership of the side and helped tighten up the forward play which may have contributed to the two caps won by Adey that season. He and Wheeler had both played in the trials, Wheeler going through to play in all the internationals save the last, against France, when a foot injury kept him out. Adey made his England debut against Ireland and stayed to play in a poor performance against the French.

It was an honour applauded by back row forwards up and down the country, who recognised in Adey one of the game's grafters. Unspectacular, often unseen, Adey took an immense amount of work on his broad shoulders, appropriate for one who worked in the family construction firm in Loughborough: his reward was two caps, and selection for the Barbarians, both on their Easter tour and their 1976 summer visit to Canada when he was accompanied by Wheeler. The hooker, incidentally, had captured a unique record by playing three times against the Australians, for the Midland Counties (East), for England and the Barbarians, and each time on the winning side (scoring a try in the Barbarians game). He was the only Englishman to do so, indeed the only Englishman in the Baa-baas XV against the tourists. At a lesser level, Dodge emulated Kenney by winning an England Colts cap, scoring eight points against Wales in a 12-13 defeat.

There was a strong contingent of Leicester support for Adey in Paris, since the club had decided to accept an invitation to play a French second division club, CASG, whose ground at the Jean Bouin Stadium is next door to the Parc des Princes. It was Leicester's first trip abroad (excluding Ireland) since 1923, an amazing record considering how easy travel had become. Not every first-team regular was available but Leicester still beat the French club 20-8, with the knowledgeable Willars making a brief return to duty. The weekend visit was in every sense a success, off the field as well as on: at the post-match reception the Leicester president, Rodney Willcox, made the entente even more cordiale with a speech which was not quite English and not quite French (Franglais perhaps?) but which, assisted by generous amounts of vin rouge, went down exceptionally well.

Bleddyn Jones in action during the 1974 Leicester against Barbarians game.

Back home Leicester had been going through the traumatic experience (for a senior club of their traditions) of playing in the Midland Cup to qualify for the following season's John Player Cup. It is the only time they have had to do so and they had to survive games with Nottingham (easily), Westleigh (by a whisker) and Kettering (uncomfortably) before making sure of a place in the last 32. Off the field there had been a flurry of action: Allen's playing career ended in December, 1975, after a massive 457 appearances and he promptly took over as club treasurer from Stan Thorpe, who retired gracefully after 14 years of dedicated assistance.

In January, 1976, an ad hoc committee was established with the following brief. To examine, report and make such recommendations as they think fit on the structure and organisation of the Leicester Football Club and the Leicester FC social club with particular reference to: a) the playing structure of the club; b) the relationship of the club to other major clubs, the constituent body and local clubs; c) the administration of the club in its entirety; d) the financial objectives of the club.

Such self-examination had been in the air a long time and it proved a profitable exercise, even if no radical reorganisation of the club resulted. Functions of the officers and various committees were

redefined and the post of club chairman created, while the presidential term was established at two years instead of three. The first chairman, in due course, was Bob Beason, who handed over the duties of fixture secretary in June, 1976, to John Berry, eldest son of the club's former president.

There was also a recommendation that Messrs Allen, Beason and Willars should meet a delegation of local club representatives, under the chairmanship of the Leicestershire RU secretary, John Simpson. Late in the year there were several meetings which helped contrive a better atmosphere than had existed for a considerable time, although the main bone of contention, the Swifts, received another vote of confidence from the ad hoc committee.

In the meantime it was entirely fitting that, at the end of a long and incredibly hot summer, new visitors to Welford Road (which had hosted, for the first time, in April that year, a game between the England under-23 XV and the English Students) should be a Caribbean touring side which played a Leicester XV composed largely of Extras and Swifts players, the tourists going down 18-15. The new captain, in his 38th year, was Rowell and, in what turned out to be his last season, he went out with a bang. Determined to drag the side back to its position of pre-eminence, he worked hard on the forwards and by the season's end he was able to retire a happy man.

John Reeve supported by Paul Dodge and Marcus Rose in 1976.

Early in the 1976-77 season there were fresh honours when Dodge won his under-23 cap against Cornwall, subsequently playing against Japan, and the club celebrated with their biggest ever defeat of Northampton, by 40-13. Dodge was joined by Wheeler, Adey and the flanker, David Forfar, in the North and Midlands XV which, coached by Chalkie White, beat the touring Argentines 24-9 at Welford Road on October 9. It was the first defeat of their short tour and the combined XV was: W H Hare (Nottingham); J Carleton (Orrell), P W Dodge (Leicester), A M Bond (Broughton Park), M A C Slemen (Liverpool); J P Horton (Bath), S J Smith (Sale); C White (Gosforth), P J Wheeler (Leicester), F E Cotton (Sale, captain), R Trickey (Sale), W B Beaumont (Fylde), D J Forfar (Leicester), G J Adey (Leicester), A Neary (Broughton Park).

The man of the match was undoubtedly Hare, who kicked five penalties and converted a try by Slemen, while Horton dropped a goal. Beccar Varela (two) and Sansot kicked penalties for the Argentines but the manner of the English side's win brought criticism from a variety of quarters for White, because he had instructed his players to keep the game tight, playing to their own known strengths. The criticism seemed then, and still does today, quite unrealistic but not entirely divorced from the reasons why English rugby struggled throughout the 70s.

The following week Hare, who had been capped by England in their win over Wales in 1974, joined Leicester amid allegations of poaching and scored 22 points in his first senior game, a 46-8 win over Oxford University. It was a significant change of allegiance, for Leicester had never possessed such a points accumulator as the Newark farmer and, considering the world record he established, seem unlikely to do so again. Although good enough full back to be capped by his country, it was his ability as a place-kicker which gave Leicester the freedom to play the expansive style of game with which they have become associated, a style which also involved Hare (who began life as a fly-half) as a runner.

In a good December, five Leicester players went for England trials:

Wheeler, Adey, Forfar, Hare and Cowling, and two of them played throughout England's season, the front row men, Wheeler and Cowling. It was a particularly delighted Cowling who made his international debut against Scotland, for he had been only a replacement in the first trial but, at the age of 32, he had seized his opportunity, going on to win eight caps, a number which would have been increased but for injury. "I am not happy with anything I do in life unless I can be successful," the farming prop said. "To be second best is not sufficient for me. In rugby football I don't enjoy playing unless I win, but I haven't forgotten that at the grass roots of the game one can't win all the time."

The Barbarians were beaten 12-8 though there was an unhappy note when the club's promising teenage prop, Steve Redfern, was sent off with Chris Howcroft of London Welsh, on the Exiles' first visit to Welford Road for nearly forty years. Since the club put out an SOS to members of the public to come in and help clear the artificial covers spread over the pitch to ensure the match went ahead, there must have been some who wondered if it was worth it.

Nevertheless the momentum was sustained in a 17-6 win over Wakefield in a much postponed John Player Cup first round game which eventually had to be played at Headingley. Alas for high hopes, the second round of the cup brought only a 23-9 defeat at Moseley but the season was by no means done. There was a return visit by CASG, who played a night match in a torrential downpour, the game being abandoned 11 minutes from time with Leicester leading 28-4.

Rowell and Cowling made first appearances for the Barbarians, Hare and Cowling going on the Easter tour. Redfern and reserve hooker John White joined Dodge as under-23 players when they played on their home ground against the English Students. For White, a product of Linwood Old Boys in Leicester and overshadowed by the formidable presence of Wheeler, it was a joyful moment; he had been a replacement for the under-23s against Japan while still in Leicester's third team and now he had won an under-23 cap proper without ever having played regularly in his club's senior side.

White was in the party Leicester sent to Twickenham when they guested in the Middlesex Sevens at the season's end but, in common with their forerunners, they failed to distinguish themselves. In the first round they beat Old Reigatians 16-12, thanks to a sudden death try by Money, the earlier scores coming from Reeve and Dodge, who also converted the tries. But they crashed out 34-0 to the eventual winners, Richmond. The VII was: J Reeve, P W Dodge, R S Money, S Kenney, K Steptoe, J R White, G G Willars. In a rash of end-of-term honours, two youth players, a lock, Rupert Precious, and a wing, Derek Butler, won England Schools (16 group) caps and Dodge and Redfern were named for the England under-23 tour to Canada.

The proliferation of representative sides to play for, and to play against, had already become apparent during the 70s as travel became easier. But the major honour in a senior player's career was still a British Lions place, and Wheeler achieved that when he was selected for the 1977 party to tour New Zealand and Fiji. He went as the number two hooker to Bobby Windsor (Pontypool) but he returned firmly established as the number one in possibly the best test pack ever put out by a Lions party.

Unfortunately, however, Dodge and Redfern were to enjoy their trip to Canada somewhat more than Wheeler. Dodge was an automatic choice against Canada but Redfern paid the penalty for being the cover for both tight and loose head props, playing in three of the provincial games. In New Zealand Wheeler was recognised as being one of the most consistent members of an occasionally inconsistent party and, after being passed over for the First Test, played in the next three, forming a formidable front row with Fran Cotton and Graham Price. He also became one of the most photographed players in the country when he stuffed the match ball up his jersey after the Lions had won the Second Test. Overall, however, it was not the happiest of tours and few of the players were sorry when it ended.

Peter Wheeler and Steve Redfern.

THE CUP IS SPILLED
1977-1978

PETER Wheeler returned from his Lions tour to a well-earned rest from rugby as Brian Hall took up the captaincy from the now retired Rowell. Business commitments prevented Cowling from recommencing on time and, not for the first time, the season opened with defeat at Bedford. But the next four years were to see the establishment of a side whose success was unparalleled in the club's history. The 1977-78 season saw Leicester to the John Player Cup final, and the following three seasons they won the trophy to confirm their standing as the leading club side in England.

The season opened with a new scoreboard at the Welford Road end - the gift of the Loughborough building materials firm run by the Adey family - and a new wing, 'Tim' Barnwell, who had made a reputation for himself with Coventry as a consistent try-scorer. But it was an old wing, Barker, who sealed a niche for himself in the club's history when he reached 1,000 points with the first of two tries in a 23-17 win over the Harlequins. He was followed into the record books by Duggan on the opposite wing, who passed 500 points against Sale and all of them scored in tries.

A notable recruit from the youth team was the former Wyggeston schoolboy, Ian Smith, a flanker who made his senior debut when he was still 18. 'Dosser' Smith, like his predecessors, Matthews and Willars, was to become captain and, latterly, coach to the club. With over 50 points against Nuneaton and Nottingham, and more than 500 overall going into December, the season looked like being a memorable one. Eight Leicester players were chosen for the Midlands East XV in the inter-divisional tournament, then in its inaugural year: Hare, Dodge,

Barker, Hall, Cowling, Smith, Kempin and Adey, with Hall captaining the side. Wheeler had been chosen but withdrew with injury while Barnwell, still qualified for Warwickshire, played for Midlands West, who won a dreary game 12-6 at Coventry. On the same day the club side beat Waterloo 14-3, an indication of the reserve strength.

The Leicester ground record eventually succumbed to the Barbarians before a crowd numbered at 19,000 but three players were chosen for England against France: Wheeler, Cowling and Hare, who had waited four years for his second cap. Although England lost 15-6 in Paris, the game was notable for a display of exceptional courage by Cowling, who dislocated a shoulder in the second half after tearing a shoulder muscle in the first half. With both England replacements used up after injuries to Andy Maxwell and Peter Dixon, Cowling stayed on the field when every scrum was agony for him. It was the end of his season.

There was some solace, however, when Dodge who, with Hare, had played in an England XV against the USA the previous October, was picked for his first cap against Wales. He joined Wheeler (Hare had been dropped) in the side beaten 9-6 at a muddy, wet Twickenham. It was the first time since the early 1930s that four Leicester players had appeared for England during the same season.

At the same time the John Player Cup run began. For the first time since the competition's inception, Leicester were drawn at home and, as if to make up for past misfortunes, they received home draws all the way through to the final. Three penalties by Hare saw them through round one, 9-3 against Hartlepool Rovers. Round two saw a brilliant display against Rosslyn Park, who were beaten 25-16 thanks to tries by Barker, Kenney and Forfar, Hare converting twice and kicking three penalties. The quarter-final round brought a 20-11 win over Northampton, Joyce and Duggan scoring tries while

Action from the 1978 John Player Cup Final against Gloucester.

Hare and Dodge shared four penalties.

During the game, however, the captain, Hall, broke two ribs and was missing when Leicester beat Coventry 25-16 in the semi-final. Dodge scored the try that finally ensured victory and allowed Leicester a chuckle at the thought that now the BBC would have to televise them - something the corporation was alleged not to enjoy because Leicester's lettering made identification more difficult for commentators.

That game came just after Easter when Leicester had taken another change of direction in respect of their touring habits; the north-east was left behind and, as so many times sixty, seventy years previously, they went to Wales, losing to Neath but beating Maesteg. They were just the kind of pressure games to help Tigers prepare mentally for Coventry: Jones scored Leicester's other try, Hare kicked three penalties, a conversion and a dropped goal, and a newcomer from Sheffield, Bill Reichwald, playing instead of Hall, dropped a goal.

The final, at Twickenham on April 15, was against Gloucester, winners of the first knockout competition. It was touch and go whether Hall would lead the side out but, with the co-operation of Stoneygate and Oadby Wyggs, who allowed him to play in their game during the week of the final, he declared himself fit. In the event, the match was something of a let-down. The attendance was 24,000, double the previous highest for a cup final, but Gloucester, with a virtual monopoly of possession, closed the game down. The result perhaps justified their decision, since they won 6-3 (a try by Richard Mogg, converted by Peter Butler, against a penalty by Hare). But the feeling remained that they could have won by considerably more had they not kicked so much ball away.

Leicester's team was: W H Hare; M J Duggan, P W Dodge, B P Hall (captain), R G Barker; B Jones, S Kenney; R E Needham, P J Wheeler, S P Redfern, N J Joyce, A Hazlerigg, S R Johnson, G J Adey, D J Forfar. There was a moment, late in the game, when Leicester had a faint sniff of victory: they managed to work an overlap for Barker some 40 metres out but Mogg appeared from the opposite wing to close him down just as a try looked a possibility. It was to be the last chance of cup glory for the likes of Jones, Hall and Barker; for the following season Jones retired, after 333 games, easily the most by a fly-half for the club, while Hall and Barker found younger players jostling them for positions. It was Steve Kenney who declared, in the unnaturally quiet Twickenham changing room after the final: "We wanted to win today for the blokes who won't have another chance."

Their success in reaching the final was recognised with receptions from both the Lord Mayor of Leicester and the chairman of the county council. From a playing point of view, the form of Steve Johnson, a recruit two seasons before from the Leicestershire Police side, and Forfar brought them selection for the first England 'B' side, which visited Romania at the start of the close season, while Dodge, as captain, and Rose, went with the under-23s to Holland. Rose had not appeared for the club since early in the season because he was a student at Durham University but he had continued to do them proud in student representative sides.

Forfar, however, who had made his first appearance for the club back in 1971 after joining from Syston and had not been far away from under-23 honours two years later, had to drop out of the 'B' party because of a thigh injury which was to linger on and prevent him from playing at all during the 1978-79 season. Johnson played in both games in Romania which suggested that, had he played first class rugby at an earlier age - he was then 29 - he might have gone all the way to a full cap.

Hare ended the season with 304 points, a club record by a long way, but it was his predecessor, Robin Money's, last season with the club after 258 appearances, since business moved the little Scot to Wilmslow. Always a popular player, one of Money's trademarks had been to head high, bouncing balls into touch on the basis that, owing to his size, it was as easy to do that as adopt a more conventional method. Rounding off the season's honours list was another Colts cap, this time awarded to the young lock, Precious, who played against Wales and France.

Success in the John Player Cup, of course, meant welcome additions to the club's funds, although there was also an appeal to members to help defray the cost of re-roofing the Crumbie Stand, the work being carried out during the summer of 1978. There were also changes in hand to the main clubhouse, with a new annexe, toilets and secretarial room being built on to the ground floor, and a new President's Room upstairs. The work was completed in time for an official opening by the president of the Barbarians, Herbert Waddell, before the annual game in December that year.

1977/78 Season Programme.

THE CUP THAT CHEERS 1978-1980

PETER Wheeler was elected captain for the new season with the club riding the crest of a wave of popularity, reflected in the increase in membership which doubled in the space of 12 months and, at the end of 1979, was verging on 2,000, having been around 750 at the start of 1978. In the second game of the season, against Nuneaton, Dodge completed 100 games for the club while still only 20.

In the opening game the former Loughborough Colleges captain, Nigel Gillingham, had made his debut and became regularly available, save when duty for the RAF prevented it. For a player of 6ft 5in and nearly 17 stone, Gillingham was exceptionally mobile and a fine ball handler and his introduction to the second row added welcome weight and height.

The pack, even when every regular was available, was never notable for sheer physique so there was more reliance on technique, with younger players like Redfern and Smith learning from the senior 'pros' - Wheeler, Cowling and Adey. In September, however, one of the seniors behind the scrum, Jones, was injured and announced his retirement. This may have helped prompt a move of some significance, that of England 'B' fly-half Les Cusworth, from Moseley to Leicester.

Cusworth had gained a reputation while with Wakefield as an expert at dropping goals but there was much more to his play than that. He had a creative spark which quickly helped give the Leicester midfield more penetration, once he had decided that it was not worth continuing the battle with Martin Cooper for the fly-half berth at The Reddings. His first game came against Swansea and was hardly a triumph but he soon settled into the Leicester side, becoming one more player to derive considerable benefit from White's coaching.

There was some consolation for the cup final defeat when Leicester came away from Kingsholm in November with a 9-7 win over Gloucester and a few days later, on November 18, the All Blacks were at Welford Road again. Graham Mourie's side, under-rated before and after the completion of their tour despite the achievement of winning all four internationals, had a hard game against the Midlands XV which contained eight Leicester players, with three more among the replacements.

The Midlands XV was: W H Hare; M J Duggan, P W Dodge, B P Hall (all Leicester), P F Knee (Coventry); M J Cooper, C J Gifford (both Moseley); R J Cowling (Leicester), P J Wheeler (captain, Leicester), W Dickinson (Richmond), B F Ninnes (Coventry), N E Horton (Toulouse), J Shipsides (Coventry), G J Adey, I R Smith (both Leicester). Among the six replacements were Rose, Cusworth and White. The tourists won 20-15, by taking the chances offered them in the way which had become their trademark. Bryan Williams, Mourie and Mark Taylor scored tries and Richard Wilson collected a penalty, a conversion and a dropped goal. Against that the Midlands put together four penalties and a dropped goal by Hare, a performance that consolidated his place in the England team the following week. The tight forwards did particularly well for the Midlands but a couple of slim chances for tries were ignored.

Gillingham captained the Combined Services against the New Zealanders four days later and at Twickenham the following Saturday, Hare was joined by Wheeler, Cowling and Dodge in a disappointing game which England lost 16-6, Hare dropping a goal and kicking a penalty. On the domestic side Leicester moved merrily on, not perhaps as consistent as they might have been but capable, at their best, of playing rugby unparalleled by another English club side. The Barbarians found that out on an appalling day at Welford Road when the Tigers, with Kenney in superb form, gave possibly their best display of the season to win 18-6.

The second half of the season brought the cup competition and a home draw with Northampton, who were beaten as convincingly as 29-3 might suggest. With frost and snow about there had been grave dangers of the match being postponed but members and supporters rallied round to clear snow off the pitch and Northampton duly succumbed to reward their efforts, tries coming from Terry Burwell, Tim Barnwell, Adey and Hare, who also

Beating the freeze - Robin Cowling in action against Northampton in the 1979 John Player Cup first round.

converted twice and kicked two penalties. The other points came from a Burwell dropped goal. Broughton Park went much the same way in the second round, again at Welford Road, when Dodge, Adey, Cusworth and Smith scored tries and Hare

kicked a conversion, three penalties and a dropped goal in a 30-7 win.

The club's achievements had been recognised already by the council but it was acknowledged further in a thoughtful leader in the *Leicester Diocesan News and Views* - not, perhaps, the most likely vehicle for sporting acclaim. "Vive le sport!", cried the editor, for its provision of recreation after the cares and worries of everyday life. It was time, he opined, for Leicestershire to awaken to the fact that its fine rugby team was worthy of greater support, week in and week out. Hear, hear, cried the club and, suitably inspired, went on to greater things.

After being drawn at home on six occasions, however, it had to happen sooner or later that Leicester went away and they did so to Bedford in the quarter-finals. It was an important game because they had to prove to themselves, if nobody else, that they could play well away from Welford Road when it mattered. They did, Hare turning on his own particular magic with a try, a conversion and four penalties - Burwell scored the other try - in a 22-12 win. A fortnight later they were away again, to Wasps in the semi-final, and under the beady eye of the BBC's cameras, they utterly overwhelmed the home club 43-7.

It was a performance without equal in the competition's admittedly brief history: that so many points should have been scored in a semi-final, and coming before an audience augmented by television viewers it boosted Leicester's image to new heights. Perhaps Wasps made a mistake by scoring first; whatever the cause, Leicester cut loose, with Cusworth in brilliant form, and they ran in tries by Mick Newton (two), Barnwell (two), Redfern, Hare, Collington and Burwell, Hare converting four times and kicking a penalty.

In the meantime Moseley were beating Gosforth 6-3 to reach the final at Twickenham on April 21. It was important to Leicester that, before the final, they played Neath and Maesteg over Easter at home; the Welsh clubs gave them the opportunity to tune up in two hard games, both of which were won. The next week Twickenham, it seemed, belonged to Leicester. The crowd of 18,000 was not as big as the previous year but it seemed they were nearly all from Leicester, who even managed to produce a jazz band led by Bob Beason, playing their own inimitable, and almost unidentifiable, version of "Tiger Rag".

The unlucky Duggan, who had been in the losing final a year previously, failed to recover from a broken arm in time so the young winger, Newton, a youth team product, kept his place. Cowling, whom injury had prevented from appearing against his old club, Gloucester, was there, as was Barnwell; both had previously been on the winning side in the final, for Gloucester and Coventry respectively.

The Leicester side was: W H Hare; M J Newton, P W Dodge, T R Burwell, R C Barnwell; L Cusworth, S Kenney; R J Cowling, P J Wheeler (captain), S P Redfern, N J Joyce, A Hazlerigg, S R Johnson, G J Adey, I R Smith. It was a final unmatched for excitement if not for technical excellence. For an hour the Moseley forwards played with great skill, dominating the match, and if their backs had taken every chance offered, they might

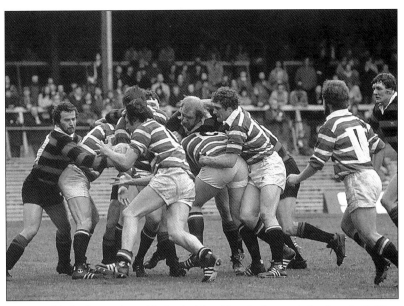

Action from the thrilling John Player Cup Final victory against Moseley at Twickenham in 1979.

have established an unbeatable lead. After Hare had dropped a goal in the eighth minute, Moseley went ahead through a fine try by Rob Laird, converted by Akenhead and a dropped goal by Cooper made it 9-3 to Moseley at half-time.

Akenhead kicked a penalty but missed another and the match was entering the final quarter when Hare kicked his first penalty. By that time Moseley had lost Barrie Corless and Nutt through injury and though they had very adequate replacements for centre and back row, their forward effort was waning. Another penalty by Hare made it 12-9 and wave upon wave of Leicester attacks surged towards the Moseley line - which held. There were just three minutes of official time left when Leicester won a scrum five metres out, on their own put-in, and Kenney broke round to dive in for the decisive try which Hare converted.

It was a win as much for character as anything else. From the technical point of view Moseley had been better in several departments but Leicester, with the disappointment of 12 months previously nagging at them, would not allow victory to slip away this time. They had also picked up the important All Black habit of being a full 80-minute side. So it was back to Leicester with the spoils, a civic reception (the Lord Mayor had been at Twickenham but had been obliged to leave at half-time) and the knowledge that if anyone should ask "Where do we go from here?", the answer was: the club centenary.

The excitement of the cup win overshadowed events elsewhere; Hare had been dropped yet again after the New Zealand match, and Cowling suffered the same fate after playing against Scotland and Ireland. Dodge and Wheeler played through the international championship (the same two players had appeared for an England XV against Argentina early in the season) and both were named for England's tour to the Far East, together with Hare.

Under-23 honours went to the young flanker, Smith, to Redfern again and, at last, to Kenney. The last two named went on a short close season tour of France and Italy with the under-23s but Kenney was unlucky enough to be injured in the opening stages of the game against the French junior side. In the Far East the senior threesome had mixed fortunes and it

is fair to say that none of them came home with an enhanced reputation, in so far as any player from Europe could make a name for himself in the context of Japanese football. Dodge was overplayed and his form in the opening games of the new season was such as to suggest that he had played too much rugby in too short a space of time.

Such are the problems success brings. Another occurred at the beginning of the 1979-80 season when the club selectors decided not to pick the XV which won the John Player Cup for the first game of the season, at Bedford. Forfar, after a season's absence through injury, reclaimed a back row spot from Johnson and a newcomer, Clive Woodward, was paired at the centre with Dodge at the expense of Burwell. There were murmurs in and around the club, even though the selected XV 'scraped' home by 34-12!

The new man, Woodward, was not unknown to Leicester since he had been a student for four years at Loughborough University and had captained the side. Already an England Colts and under-23 cap, he had played fly-half and centre with considerable success and was one of few midfield players in the country possessed of both the eye for a break and the speed to exploit it. He swiftly added an England 'B' cap to his honours when he played against France 'B' at the end of September, while Forfar was also given the 'B' cap he would have got had he been fit enough to go to Romania in 1978. Redfern occupied a position on the replacements' bench which may have been the best place to be in a match which England lost 25-9.

But the thoughts of the club had turned firmly towards retention of the cup, with Jerry Day accurately forecasting a third successful season, and arrangements for the centenary season in 1980-81. Two years earlier the idea of a world tour had been proposed as one way of celebrating the centenary and this was adopted, though the fixture-making proved a little difficult.

Originally a grandiose sweep through Australia, New Zealand, Fiji and the USA had been envisaged. With the tour due to be made in August, 1980, however, it proved awkward to find fixtures in New Zealand, whose domestic season would be reaching its peak, and the eventual arrangements produced three games in Australia and three in Fiji - considerably better than a training weekend in Cromer and a major achievement for a club which had never before been further afield than France. The Queensland state side, Randwick and Eastern Suburbs were to provide the Australian opposition and in Fiji the club were to meet two regional selections and a Fijian RU chairman's XV.

Plans for celebrations nearer home were also developing while within the club the advances of the last few seasons brought members flowing in

and increased revenue via a club shop, selling mementoes, jerseys, ties and more, so successfully that on one occasion during the season the "take" for the day entered four figures. It was sad that the membership secretary, the former full back Ernie Watkin, did not live to see the club to its 100th birthday. He died a fortnight before the club's third successive appearance in the John Player Cup final.

In an increasingly professional sporting world, Leicester's amateur organisation was coping well, on all fronts. In the playing context there had been a slight hiccough when Bath won 10-9 at Welford Road in the third match of the season. More significant was the defeat, again at home, at the hands of Swansea by 27-12 who went on to prove themselves the outstanding club combination in Britain by the season's end. Nevertheless, club form was quite good enough for nine players to be picked in the Midland Counties XV against yet another New Zealand touring side, again captained by Graham Mourie. Among early-season tourists to this country had been the Canadians and a South African Barbarians party but neither had played in the Leicester area.

The Midlands-All Blacks game was the third of the New Zealanders' short tour but there was to be no glory at Welford Road this time. Moved perhaps to heights they otherwise failed to reach on this tour by the death of their former coach, Jack Gleeson, the All Blacks disposed of the Midlands by 33-7, making hay with the mistakes contrived, mostly behind the scrum, by the local XV which was: W H Hare (Leicester); M Perry (Moseley), P W Dodge, C R Woodward (both Leicester), P F Knee (Coventry); L Cusworth (Leicester), I G Peck (Cambridge University); R J Cowling, P J Wheeler (captain), S P Redfern (all Leicester), N E Horton (Toulouse), R Field (Moseley), G N Phillips (Bedford), G J Adey, D J Forfar (both Leicester).

The Midlands worked well at the tight pieces, less well in the loose, and poorly amongst the backs. Woodward made holes in the New Zealand defence but lost his support in the process and with Hare not having one of his best kicking days, the Midlands were 23-0 down before they scored. Richard Wilson kicked three penalties before halftime, Fraser, Burgoyne and Mexted scored tries, the last of them converted by Wilson. At this stage Hare kicked a penalty and Paul Knee ran in a good try, which prompted further All Black tries from Fraser and Fleming, the second converted by the faithful Wilson. It was not a good day.

Three weeks later, on November 24, three Leicester players faced the All Blacks again, this time for England at Twickenham. With Hignell out of the running through injury, Hare was called up at full back; Cusworth won his first cap at fly-half and Wheeler retained the hooking berth but Dodge, after eight successive games, was dropped. Again it was not a good day, the All Blacks scraping home 10-9 and England doing little to encourage their supporters for the forthcoming home championship. Hare kicked England's three penalties but Cusworth, called upon to play a game similar to that demonstrated by Alan Old when the Northern Division had decisively beaten the All Blacks the previous week, was unable to do so with sufficient accuracy.

Meanwhile, apart from representative calls, injuries were afflicting the club side and the number of players used in the senior side moved rapidly into the 30s. The side was playing inconsistent rugby but even in the troughs they were quite capable of beating most opposition, in itself the sign of a class team. One of their most enjoyable outings was the 42-4 win at Northampton, another step along the road to the top of the Midland merit table. The Barbarians came and went over Christmas, beating the club 9-8 in a match played in a quagmire but with great intensity of spirit on both sides. Leicester scored two tries to one but could convert neither; it was a heartening performance with the cup approaching once more and immediately afterwards Duggan scored his 150th try for the club in a 55-3 romp against Headingley.

The holders had been drawn at home to Orrell, the Northern merit table leaders, and Leicester were happy enough to begin the defence of the cup with a 16-7 win, Smith scoring a try, Hare kicking two penalties and Cusworth two dropped goals. One of the most impressive aspects of Leicester's win was their scrummaging, and this feature was to be repeated in the subsequent rounds.

Before the second round, however, there was to be more pleasure derived from Woodward winning his first England cap. While Dodge had begun the season indifferently, and Woodward on a high note, the two centres had swapped positions in terms of club form, for Dodge was now back at his best and Woodward seemed to have lost touch somewhat. However, England had decided to call him up as a replacement for the game with Ireland, retaining Hare and Wheeler but replacing Cusworth with John Horton of Bath. During the game, won 24-9 by England, Sale's Tony Bond broke a leg and Woodward went on for his first cap. He was retained against France and was joined by Dodge for the game against Wales, an appalling match which Hare's three penalties permitted England to win 9-8 against a Welsh team reduced to 14 men when the former Leicester flanker, Paul Ringer, now with Llanelli, was sent off.

In a far more appealing finale against Scotland, Woodward was quite outstanding in broken play as England achieved their first triple crown and grand slam for 23 years. It was another feather in the club's cap that four Leicester players should have participated in the country's triumph and that a fifth should also have represented England, reminiscent of the balmy days of the 1900s and the 1930s.

The John Player Cup second round brought together the 1979 finalists, Moseley and Leicester, at The Reddings but there was seldom much doubt of the outcome this time, Dodge excelling himself in a 17-7 win. He scored one try, Burwell another, Hare kicked two penalties and Cusworth again dropped a goal. As if in celebration, Leicester scored 108 points in the next two games, exactly divided against the Royal Navy and the Harlequins. Cusworth, who had scored 23 points from seven penalties and a conversion in an early season game against London Welsh, registered 30 points against the Harlequins from two tries, three penalty goals, five conversions and a dropped goal, a virtuoso performance bettered only once before.

It was Cusworth who stole the honours in the third round cup tie, against London Scottish at Welford Road. The game had virtually been decided by half-time, even though only seven points had been scored, and the tries came from Smith and Cusworth, who also dropped a goal. Hare added three penalties and a conversion. A fortnight later Hare, after only three and a half years with the club, eased gently past Leicester's individual points scoring record of 1,117, held by Bob Barker, with 12 points against Sale. He recorded another dozen in the cup semi-final the following week, with four penalties in the 16-9 defeat of Harlequins at Twickenham. A try by Dodge made up the tally but it was by no means an emphatic win in a game spoiled by a strong wind.

Nevertheless, Leicester were in the final for the third year running, and were everybody's favourites to beat London Irish - except, naturally enough, the Irish. And had it not been for the fact that they won the cup, April would have been a poor month for Leicester since they lost four more games, failed in their effort to score 1,000 points for the season and to establish a record number of wins.

That is looking at it coldly. Ironically, had they had taken into account the 20 points scored against an International XV in a fund-raising match at Welford Road on April 1, it would have made the round 1,000. But that game, an attractive affair designed to add cash to the tour fund and won by the star-studded guest XV 22-20, was not included in the first-class fixtures. Two hard games in Wales followed over Easter, a scrappy win over Neath

distinguished only by a marvellous 90-metre try from Burwell and a 21-13 defeat at Pontypool Park where the local side kicked five penalties and two dropped goals against a goal, a try and a penalty, leaving something of a sour taste in Leicester mouths - though not quite as sour as the taste left in Steve Johnson's mouth earlier in the year when he played for the British Police against their French opposites and was raked so severely that the lacerations to his head required forty stitches.

Leicester came through Easter without Wheeler and Woodward, both of whom had been picked for the British Lions tour to South Africa in the summer of 1980. It was a splendid conclusion to Woodward's season, even if it did confuse arrangements for his

Ian Smith scores against Orrell. Tigers began their 1980 defence of the John Player Cup with a 16-7 win.

wedding in July. The honours were not confined to the seniors, however, for two youth players, Stuart Redfern, brother of the 1st XV prop, and Rob Tebbutt, won England Colts caps at prop and flanker respectively, against Wales and France.

There was one match that Wheeler and Woodward could not miss though, the John Player Cup final at Twickenham on April 19. Leicester were at strength but, sadly, could not include their experienced wing, Duggan, who had damaged a hamstring against Neath. Had selection been made two days later, Duggan might have passed a fitness test; instead he was doomed, for the second year running, to take a back seat through injury. The Leicester team was: W H Hare; R C Barnwell, C R Woodward, P W Dodge, T R Burwell; L Cusworth, S Kenney; R J Cowling, P J Wheeler (captain), S P Redfern, N J Joyce, N K Gillingham, S R Johnson, G J Adey, I R Smith.

Cusworth having opened matters with a neat drop goal and Hare having kicked three penalties. Hare dropped his goal and kicked another penalty before Meanwell landed an Irish penalty but Cusworth popped over another drop to conclude the scoring. It had been an efficient display, Leicester exerting control whenever they needed to, and it gave them the opportunity of going into their centenary season as cup holders and the chance of keeping the trophy in perpetuity if they could win again in 1980-81.

Coincidentally, the win at Twickenham was also the 33rd of the season, equalling the record established by the 1966-67 side, but the 34th eluded them in lackadaisical displays against Moseley and Rosslyn Park. Still, it was not a bad way to end the decade and to begin the next 100 years and, as an indication of how success had permeated the club's other sides, the records in 1979-80 for the four XVs were:

Joyce and Johnson contest a line-out during Tigers efficient 21-9 victory over London Irish at Twickenham in the 1980 John Player Cup final.

There was a 27,000 crowd, including a vast Leicester contingent, which established a record gate for the final. If they were expecting a classic, they were disappointed but the Leicester contingent were happy enough to see the Tigers triumph 21-9, thanks to four penalties and a dropped goal by Hare, and two dropped goals by Cusworth. There was none of the excitement of the previous year, largely because it was always obvious that Leicester would win. London Irish, basing their game around the unflagging efforts of their back row and scrum-half, covered and disrupted to the extent that they preserved their record of keeping their line intact in all cup games, and they had the satisfaction of scoring a try themselves, through the lock, Smythe. Meanwell's conversion made the interval score 12-6,

	W	D	L	For	Against
1st XV	33	0	9	980	420
Extras	26	1	8	897	373
Swifts	25	2	3	876	214
Youth	18	3	3	614	171

Hare had raised the record for points scored in one season to 319 and, for once, there was a second player well into three figures, since Cusworth totalled 173, including 13 dropped goals. Duggan ended his 11th full season equal with Bob Barker's post-war club mark of 158 tries and, not merely a statistical quirk, Graham Willars, whose career was alleged to have ended five years previously, made his 336th senior appearance when coming on as a replacement in the last game of the 1979-80 season,

giving him two complete decades of playing service to the club.

The year, however, had something more to offer before the centenary celebrations began. The Lions, hit by injuries throughout their 18-match tour in South Africa in the summer of 1980, called upon eight replacements, among them Dodge who joined the tour party when the Welsh centre, David Richards, was injured. With a month of the tour remaining, Dodge stepped straight into the international side when he was chosen for the third Test, joining both his club colleagues. Wheeler was first choice hooker throughout the series and played in all four Tests while Woodward, centre in the second Test, played on the wing in the third.

The prospect of seeing three Tigers playing for the Lions was too much for Chalkie White, who promptly dipped into his savings and flew to Port Elizabeth for the third Test: "If I live for another 100 years this will not happen again," White declared (though in 1993 the Lions took four Leicester players on tour, to New Zealand). Sadly the Lions lost 12-10, Woodward's failure to cover a quick throw-in conceding the crucial try; thus the series was lost 3-1 but Dodge retained his place for the last Test, won by the Lions 17-13, and gave every indication in his five tour games that he should have been an original selection.

Woodward gave way to John Carleton for the fourth Test but ended the tour as second highest points scorer behind Ollie Campbell. Campbell totalled 60 points and Woodward 53 from four tries, five conversions, eight penalties and a dropped goal. Wheeler and Dodge contented themselves with a try apiece. Woodward's emergence as a place-kicker was of considerable significance to the tour results and, while not entirely a surprise, his consistency was unexpected in view of the lack of practice he had both at Leicester, where Hare and Cusworth looked after the kicking duties, and at college where he had been only an occasional kicker. One of the most elusive runners on the tour, he also made a success as a wing despite his lack of experience in that position which brought him perhaps an unfair measure of criticism after that crucial third Test. Nevertheless, three players on a major tour was something Leicester had not achieved since the 1908 Anglo-Welsh tour to Australasia.

Clive Woodward breaks clear for the British Lions during the second Test against South Africa at Bloemfontein in 1980.

CENTENARY
1980-1981

LEICESTER'S departure for Australia in August 1980 could hardly have found the club in better heart though even now, Peter Wheeler was thinking ahead: a convinced campaigner for more competitive rugby and improving the players' lot, Wheeler believed that a tour of this magnitude was essential to a progressive club, every three years or so with lesser tours in between. It was not a view which found uniform agreement from those who felt that the money raised for tours could be better spent on the fabric of the club.

Wheeler's argument was that the players are the club and, if they are well-prepared and enthusiastic, then the club will prosper anyway. Enthusiastic they were as they embarked on the three-week, six-match trip and evidently well-prepared since during the stopover in Vancouver three of the players (aptly Nick Joyce, the lock and a policeman, was one) disarmed a woman apparently intent on stabbing her husband to death with an eight-inch knife.

The high point of the Australian section of the tour was the meeting with Randwick, Sydney's champion club, which perhaps left Leicester under-prepared for the opening encounter against the might of Queensland at Ballymore: cluttered with internationals such as Paul McLean, Andrew Slack, Roger Gould and Peter Grigg the state side proved too strong for a team just off the 'plane and won 22-12, Gary Adey scoring both Leicester's tries and Hare converting twice.

Eastern Suburbs, in Sydney, proved easier meat and Leicester, buoyed by tries from Kevin Williams, Kenney and Barnwell, all converted by Cusworth who also kicked two penalties, won 24-3. If the backs dominated that game it was forward power which beat Randwick 31-19 at Coogee Oval in the clash of champions: Ian Smith and John White scored tries while Hare lobbed over five penalties, a dropped goal and a conversion and Cusworth threw in another dropped goal.

Suitably heartened Leicester flew to Fiji and won all three games, against Lautoka 12-6 (Smith try, Hare conversion and two penalties), Combined Fijian Services 8-4 with tries by Barnwell and Cusworth and a Fiji Chairman's XV 12-0 (Hare three penalties and a Cusworth dropped goal). The final game was the only one in which Wheeler played, a neck injury having limited his activities to those of tour leader rather than tour captain. But all in all it proved valuable experience and, under the eagle eye of coach White, admirable preparation for the season ahead.

Those at home had not been idle either. Gate takings during the previous season had risen by £15,000 and season-ticket returns doubled, a reflection both of the club's mounting popularity and the capacity of their own voluntary workers to deal with it. When the domestic season opened Welford Road was in prime condition with over 1,000 new seats in the Members' Stand, new floodlighting and enough new paintwork to satisfy a sergeant-major, all after the expenditure of some £50,000.

The fixture list was an exotic one, including in the first two months visits from the Irish Wolfhounds - a guest side with whom Cusworth, for one, enjoyed many happy moments playing sevens - Romania and Queensland. Hare and Woodward scored tries against the Wolfhounds in a slim 10-6 win but the work of the tour was not immediately apparent in the early-season defeat at Bath which brought a critical blast from Jerry Day. Worse was to come in October when the Romanians arrived at the end of their tour of Ireland during which they had drawn 13-13 with what was in all but name the full Irish XV: Tigers crashed 39-7 against forwards whose strength matched the oak leaves on their jerseys and Florica Murariu, the visiting flanker, scored four tries. Leicester's limited response came from Kevin Williams' try and Hare's penalty.

Spirits were briefly raised by the return match with Queensland, who found Leicester less accommodating on home soil and lost 21-9, the only defeat of their five-match tour of England and Scotland. But when the defence crumbled against

Tigers in action in Fiji during the 1980 tour.

Gloucester at Kingsholm by 31-4 it was evident hard work was going to be necessary if the centenary was not going to be something of a whimper; adding point to such thoughts was the knowledge that the Rugby Football Union committee headed by John Burgess, the former England coach, was going the rounds of the country discussing the way ahead, in particular a revised competitive structure including league rugby. The Burgess Report had its critics and Jerry Day warned against their possible

CHAPTER 22

consequences: "If a club wanted to compete with any success in a league system it would have to become almost professional - with all the inherent risks that entails....the pressure to win would, of course, produce more inhibited rugby." As we have since seen there was considerable perception in Day's vision although set against that was Wheeler's opinion that "leagues are long overdue. Either we have a successful international side or we simply carry on as we are. Players would benefit by having that extra competitive edge."

Wheeler's return to action, after injury forced him to make a belated start to the season, assisted a revival while the captain himself, together with Woodward, represented England and Wales against Scotland and Ireland in one of the Welsh Rugby Union's centenary celebration games, Woodward scoring a try and dropping a goal in his XV's 37-33 win (for good measure Wheeler played in the WRU's final centenary game the following April, when Wales beat a Welsh President's XV). Wheeler also captained the Midlands in a somewhat dreary revival of the divisional championship, then played on a knockout basis in which the North took the trophy by virtue of their 6-0 win over a Midland XV including five Leicester backs.

The Barbarians match produced a breathless 28-24 win for the visitors and more points in the fixture than ever before; it also helped project Williams, the young PE teacher at City of Leicester School who had taken over from Duggan on the wing, into the Welsh squad though his only reward did not come until the next season when he played for Wales 'B' against the Australians.

Four Leicester players appeared on the senior side in the England trial against a Rest XV including a past Tiger in Marcus Rose, now winning blues at Cambridge University, and a future one in Nick Youngs, then with Bedford and recently a dominant force in the successful England Schools side coached by Mike Davis. The same quartet - Hare, Dodge, Woodward and Wheeler - went forward to the opening international, against Wales which was a triumph for Hare in that he scored all England's 19 points but a disaster for Woodward in that his accidental offside in midfield gave Steve Fenwick the chance to kick the winning goal in Wales's 21-19 win. Unlike a year earlier Hare could not convert the late penalty which would have restored England's fortunes.

In what was to prove a disappointing England season, after the euphoria of 1980, England retained the services of their Leicester players in the 23-17 win over Scotland (in which Woodward scored a try and Hare kicked 11 points) but then dismissed Hare and called up, instead, Rose which was a bittersweet pill for the club. The young full back responded by scoring a try against Ireland, in Dublin, and then setting up another for Dodge in a 10-6 win; but he could not prevent a French grand slam at Twickenham despite kicking four penalties as France, aided by a palpable refereeing error which allowed a try for Pierre Lacans, won 16-12.

Back at Welford Road Leicester embarked on the cup trail in the knowledge that this would be the last season for two great stalwarts, Garry Adey and Robin Cowling: an ankle injury, increased work commitments and the demands of a young family

led to Adey's announcement in January, while Cowling's job as a farm manager was taking him back to his native Ipswich (and subsequently to Cornwall where he continued to follow Leicester's progress with enthusiasm). Before he left Cowling expressed his typical pithy view of the influence of coaching: "The most successful sides have been those with strong captains. Since Gloucester and Coventry acquired coaches they have been less successful. Top-class players should always make a point of passing on their knowledge and expertise to younger players...that, to me, is the only real way in which skills can be passed on to the younger player."

The club opened with a 34-3 win at Roundhay, a victory as comfortable as it sounds, and followed up with a 27-14 win over Bristol though their inconsistent form was emphasised by a horrid 46-10 mauling by London Welsh in an intervening friendly. Hare kicked seven goals from eight attempts on a slippery surface against Bristol,

TRAINER PULLS A MUSCLE
The long casualty list after the game against London Welsh in 1981 also had two rather humorous additions. Trainer Bill Michelmore made so many excursions onto the pitch that he finally pulled a muscle, and Nick Joyce's encounter with a bar of changing room soap led to an ungainly double axle and a severe headache.

Terry Burwell, Mick Merriman, Chris Tressler and Robin Cowling in action against Gloucester in 1980-81.

including five of the nine points in the closing minutes which made the result safe. Conditions were not much better against Sale in the quarter-final: earlier in the week Welford Road had been almost under water but it drained sufficiently well to allow Leicester their 21-7 win in which, again, Hare's place-kicking was outstanding with five goals out of five.

If Leicester had found the going hard before, they had to redouble their effort in the semi-final at London Scottish. This proved to be the first extra-time cup tie when, at the end of full time, the score stood locked at 12-12 and no-one could have been feeling the pace more than Wheeler, Woodward and Cusworth, who had returned only 24 hours earlier from Hong Kong where they had helped the Barbarians become the first, and so far the only, northern-hemisphere side to win the Cathay Pacific sevens.

The *Leicester Mercury* described the Leicester changing room as resembling a scene from M.A.S.H. (the television black comedy centred round a hospital unit during the Korean War) after the semi-final: they used two replacements, Woodward suffered concussion and thought he was still in

Hare kicks his first penalty to put Tigers 3-0 ahead against Gosforth in the 1981 John Player Cup Final at Twickenham.

Hong Kong, Johnson and Wheeler finished with various wounds after an unrelenting yet gripping struggle in which two dropped goals by Cusworth finally settled the issue. The club were through to an unprecedented fourth successive final, against Gosforth who beat Moseley 24-3, and those Leicester supporters who made the trip (many did not as a protest against unreasonably high ticket charges at Richmond) must have thought their money well spent.

The following climactic month contained more than even the most romantic novelist could have wished for: first came the emergence from retirement of Adey as the club, anxious about the well-being of 'Angus' Collington who damaged a shoulder against the Scottish, asked their No 8 for one more effort. Adey's best was so good that the unlucky Collington, so often a bridesmaid on the big occasion, found himself a replacement yet again for a cup final. Then came Hare's assault on the world points-scoring record, that of 3,651 established by the late Sam Doble, of Moseley and, briefly, England, in the middle 1970s.

Ironically it was to Moseley that Leicester went in mid-April: Hare, then 28, needed six points. He scored 14 to conclude the game with 3,658 of which 1,800 were scored for Nottingham, 1,532 for Leicester and the remainder from international and other representative games. "I couldn't tell anyone else how to kick," Hare said. "All you can say is, get the run-up right. It's like a fast bowler, you must have the right approach and you must keep your head down. If I'm having a poor spell it's usually because the rhythm has gone, what's happening when I get to the ball to kick it."

Everything was coming together at the right moment: centenary, world record and a cup final at Twickenham on May 2 with a team which read:
W H Hare; A K Williams, P W Dodge,
C R Woodward, R C Barnwell; L Cusworth, S Kenney;
R J Cowling, P J Wheeler (captain), S P Redfern,
N J Joyce, N A Jackson, S R Johnson, G J Adey,
I R Smith. It was Wheeler's last match as captain after three magnificent years; it was the last appearance in Leicester colours for Adey and Cowling (who led the team out) before 24,000 people of whom 15,000 were estimated as coming from Leicester - confirmation of the city's contribution towards turning the cup final from an end-of-season sideshow to the event it has become in its own right.

Chalkie White had warned beforehand about the effect of nearly two years of continuous rugby but he need not have worried as Leicester, against a Gosforth team whose forwards, critics predicted, would take charge of the match, produced the most remarkable of three consecutive cup wins. In the days to come Wheeler emphasised how he had used dismissive headlines to inspire his players: the front row was rock-like and though Steve Bainbridge presented problems in the line-out they were not insuperable. The midfield organisation was watertight and

Cusworth, as he was to do throughout the 1980s, pulled the strings like a conjurer. Even when Gosforth had pulled back to 12-9 and dominated possession in the third quarter they lacked the guile - and perhaps the big-match experience which was Leicester's - to use it effectively.

Hare, on his way to a club record of 358 points for the season, kicked two first-half penalties and converted a try by Kenney against David Johnson's two penalties. Brian Patrick's penalty from fifty yards narrowed the gap and Johnson might have levelled the scores with a penalty but he missed: Leicester's response was to throw everything into attack, Steve Johnson made the extra man and Woodward sent Barnwell speeding on his way to the try-line. Going into injury-time Hare pursued his own chip ahead to score a try which he converted; the result was secure and Johnson 'limped' off (the exact injury remained a closely-guarded secret!) to allow Collington to leave the replacements and take a place in the side for which he had worked so hard during the season - a gesture appreciated by every Leicester supporter present. It mattered little that Rob Cunningham scored late in the day for Gosforth; Leicester had equalled their record for wins in a season by their 22-15 success and the cup was at their lips.

Moreover it was theirs for keeps. John Player, the sponsors, had offered it as a permanent trophy to any side good enough to win three times in a row and though Day suggested it should remain for competition by all clubs, his was a lone voice. "Just looking at the cup reminds you not only of the matches but the good times afterwards," Wheeler said. "It also means a lot to the people of the city and our way of thanking them for their support will be to show the cup off at pubs and clubs so there's no question of it gathering dust."

Six days later 700 gathered at the De Montfort Hall for almost the final act of a memorable centenary season (that it was not the final act was only because Leicester had agreed to send a team to the Middlesex sevens the following day; although they overcame Loughborough Students it was hardly surprising, in view of the night before, that they then succumbed to Saracens). The centenary dinner was a night of tributes, a night for sentiment for Eric Lacey, the president, and good humour from Max Boyce, the Welsh humorist and self-confessed rugby nut, and fellowship during which the only false note was the lack of a public acknowledgement for the work achieved for Leicester by Jerry Day. The club had already undertaken the publication of a centenary history which, finally, hit the streets, better late than never. It had 100 years to be proud of.

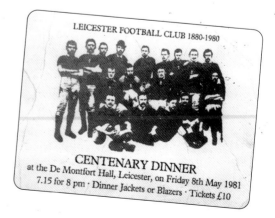

LEICESTER FOOTBALL CLUB 1880-1980

CENTENARY DINNER
at the De Montfort Hall, Leicester, on Friday 8th May 1981
7.15 for 8 pm · Dinner Jackets or Blazers · Tickets £10

END OF THE DAY
1981-1983

WHATEVER followed such an overflowing season was bound to bring a sense of anti-climax. Peter Wheeler, to no-one's surprise, declared his unavailability for England's summer tour to Argentina although Dusty Hare, Clive Woodward and Paul Dodge all travelled, Woodward scoring two tries in the drawn first Test and Hare kicking seven and eight points respectively in the two internationals.

In Leicester there was a sad start to the 1981-82 season with the death of Ken Kinder, president in the first cup-winning year and a committeeman since 1958. Chalkie White lamented that the club's success had not attracted more new talent - although Nick Youngs had joined the club from Bedford - but existing members quivered at the news of Wheeler's elevation to Justice of the Peace, the law bench being an arena not unknown to rugby players the worse for wear, notably on tour.

A touring team composed largely of players from the Extras and the Swifts returned in good heart from a close-season tour of Florida and Steve Johnson, the new captain, was full of optimism for the new season. He had every reason to be as Leicester brushed aside a series of opponents, including Bath by the margin of 44-6, and Jerry Day pondered whether playing standards elsewhere in the country were declining. Following up the thought, he asked the newly-formed Senior Clubs Association whether they would care to constitute their own criteria for a "first-class" club. "We are so far in front of everyone else that we can play at half-pace and still win," Day opined, on the eve of a 49-12 demolition job on Harlequins at Twickenham.

Even that was as nothing compared with the club's then record win of 78-8 over Birmingham at the Portway, Hare scoring three of their 14 tries and converting 11 of them for another club record tally of 34 points. Pride goes before a fall: Richmond forced a draw and Leicester's unbeaten record fell in mid-October to Northampton on a day when seven club players appeared for the Midlands against the

touring Australians at Welford Road and two more were on the bench. Remarkably one of those two was Hare because Marcus Rose was preferred at full back and kicked two penalties and a conversion in the 16-10 defeat which got the touring side off to a thoroughly bad start.

The Midlands team was: W M H Rose (Cambridge University); S Holdstock (Nottingham), G H Davies (Cambridge University), C R Woodward, R C Barnwell; L Cusworth (all Leicester), S P Thomas (Coventry); S P Redfern (Leicester), P J Wheeler (captain, Leicester), S Wilkes (Coventry), N J Joyce (Leicester), V Cannon (Northampton), N C Jeavons (Moseley), G L Robbins (Coventry), I R Smith (Leicester). Dodge would have played but his withdrawal with a hamstring injury on the morning of the match meant the removal of Huw Davies from fly-half to centre and Cusworth's inclusion in a match where the tries came from Steve Holdstock and Nick Jeavons.

The Australians struggled in their next four games, including a 10-9 win over a Wales 'B' side including Kevin Williams, although when Youngs played against them for London they were building up a head of steam. They beat Ireland in the first international and returned to Leicester on November 25 to play the club, an unusual honour granted in recognition of the outstanding achievements of the past three seasons. Not that Leicester were in wonderful shape: defeats against Swansea and Gloucester and the loss of Tim Barnwell with a broken jaw had seen to that. Moreover, Steve Kenney injured a leg against Nottingham and Williams had sustained an eye injury playing for Wales 'B', which gave scope for a youngster from Hinckley, Barry Evans, just 20, to come into the side.

Williams recovered in time to play a further 'B' international, against France, but Evans remained, his speed impressing everyone who saw it. Youngs, the squat, powerful son of a farmer, made his debut at scrum-half although by the time the Wallabies returned to town, Kenney had recovered. Leicester's team was: W H Hare; B J Evans, C R Woodward, P W Dodge, R C Barnwell; L Cusworth, S Kenney; J Deacon, P J Wheeler, S P Redfern, N J Joyce, N A Jackson, S R Johnson, D J Forfar, I R Smith. With only a half-hour gone Leicester had already lost the experienced Dave Forfar, who was badly trampled on the leg and had to be replaced by a youngster, Duncan Black.

But the Tigers lived up to their nickname. They roared into an Australian side including Paul McLean, Michael O'Connor, Mark Ella, Greg Cornelsen and Mark Loane to such an effect that

they led 6-3 at the interval and 15-12 with only two minutes remaining. Hare had kicked dropped goals from 45 and 50 yards, and two penalties with Cusworth dropping another goal from a heel against the head. McLean kicked two penalties and the conversion to Mick Martin's try and the full back levelled matters with a third penalty before Ella, to local anguish, dropped the goal that made the score 18-15 to the Australians. There was even more anguish when, in the sixth minute of injury-time, Hare's long-range penalty scraped the outside of an upright.

Not that such a brave performance influenced the England selectors unduly: as the Australians left for Wales and Scotland both Cusworth and Hare were overlooked for the December trial, behind respectively Huw Davies, John Horton, Marcus Rose and Nick Stringer. Davies and Rose played in the international against Australia on January 2 alongside Dodge, Woodward and Wheeler who contributed to a 15-11 victory (Dodge recalling his goal-kicking skills by converting Jeavons' try) as well as expressing amazement at the exploits of the legendary Twickenham streaker, Erika Roe, and congratulating a young Yorkshire flanker on his international debut, Peter Winterbottom. There was a degree of comfort for Cusworth, too, since he was

elevated to the replacements and remained there for the 9-9 draw against Scotland in which his three colleagues played.

It was as well some people were playing rugby regularly because the weather took a hand, forced the postponement of the Barbarians match (and of Australia's tour finale against the Baa-baas) and sent Leicester scurrying down to Torquay in search of a match to prepare their defence of the John Player Cup. The Devon Riviera toned them up sufficiently for a 53-19 win over Hartlepool Rovers in the opening round (although the unfortunate Rovers had not played for seven weeks).

Meanwhile there were fateful events on the international front: a head injury in the county championship final terminated Bill Beaumont's playing career and though there was speculation that Wheeler might succeed him as England captain, that role went to Steve Smith against Ireland. A hamstring injury removed Dodge from that game at Twickenham (in which Wheeler equalled Wavell Wakefield's club record of 31 caps), which might have been significant since the Irish, heading for a triple crown, won 16-15; such a disappointing first half of the championship caused the selectors to reflect and when they had done so, Dodge and Cusworth both joined Wheeler and Woodward in

Dean Richards leaps against Gloucester's Adrian Turton at Welford Road in January 1983.

the side to play France in Paris. It was a major *volte-face* and earned Cusworth only his second cap after the one-off against New Zealand in 1979: "This time I'm sure I'll be asked to play my natural game," he said with feeling.

Even better from the club's point of view was the restoration of Hare after the withdrawal through injury of Stringer, bringing to five the Leicester players who shared in the 27-15 victory over France - a tally to which Hare contributed (for the second time in his international career) 19 points from five penalties and two conversions, one of them of a try by Woodward. To general approbation the same XV did duty in a 17-7 win over Wales, Hare kicking three penalties.

Steve Redfern against the Barbarians in 1983.

Things were looking up. Leicester disposed of Northampton 23-10 in the cup and then went through a re-run of the 1981 final, though this time Gosforth subsided 18-9. Hare passed his own club record for a season against the RAF, having passed 5,000 career points against Wales, and all seemed set fair for the semi-final against Moseley. Alas, after 18 consecutive cup wins, the dream died at The Reddings, kicked to death by Mike Perry's penalties and dropped goals against a Cusworth try in a 12-4 defeat.

White blamed poor preparation, with players away in Hong Kong and others on business courses: "It's all very well people saying what a good run we've had and it had to end some time. That's the sort of attitude that gets you beaten. You're only as good as your last game - and we were bad." Moseley's satisfaction must have been even more intense, given the long history of rivalry between the clubs, and they went on to the only drawn cup final, against Gloucester.

All of a sudden it seemed as though the wheels were being removed from the Leicester chariot: out of the cup and two leading officials resigning their posts: Jerry Day and the chairman of selectors, Bob Rowell. Both pleaded pressure of business and, in the case of Day, perhaps a slight sense of disenchantment with the game. As someone who, running his own business - like Tom Crumbie - had put his all into Leicester for so long, Leicester owed Day a debt that could never be repaid; outspoken and opinionated, he also recognised that the game was changing and, rightly, realised that he did not necessarily want to go with it.

He stayed to see heavy defeats by Bristol and Moseley (again) offset by a spectacular 36-32 victory over the Barbarians and an Easter tour to Wales in which, almost unnoticed at Neath, a young No 8 called Dean Richards made his debut. He was so unknown that the *Leicester Mercury* (though we could be charitable and call it a copy-taking error) referred to him in the team list as T Richards.

At the annual meeting that summer John Allen moved from the post of treasurer to secretary and members discovered that White, too, was soon to leave. After thirty years in teaching, the abrasive, intense, hugely influential coach had accepted a post with the Rugby Football Union, as one of the newly-created divisional technical administrators - in his case for the South and South-West Division, based in Taunton. In some ways it was a most unlikely marriage since White had at times been immensely critical of rugby's establishment (and has not always been the model establishment man since) but part of his motivation was the realisation that he would not be invited to coach England, an ambition which hit the buffers in 1979 when he was passed over for Mike Davis, the Sherborne School master.

But the creation of new, professional posts within the game offered an opportunity to one who cared so deeply about the game and White was encouraged to change roles by Don Rutherford, England's technical administrator and another deep thinker where the game's future was concerned. "I reckon," White said before he left, "that if, at the end of a season, I have given every player the opportunity to play to his potential, I'm satisfied. There's not a lot of original thought I've been capable of: I crib and I steal and I plagiarise. But I tell players that if they cheat me on the training field, they'll cheat their team-mates in the game and in all other aspects of life. Players have to be themselves - I am the catalyst for others.

"Our game is part of society, it cannot be isolated from what is happening in society. We cannot operate our game in a vacuum. The standards of society, morality, all the bits we like and don't like, must be part of our game. In our own right at Leicester, we have to be trendsetters because there is so much more going for us. We work harder, we think more and some of us care."

White's opinions have brought him at times into conflict with administrators, coaches, press, players but no-one who knows him has ever doubted his commitment to his view of the game. His departure from Leicester to take up his new post in January 1983 was of enormous significance though it has always been the club's strength that when one baton is dropped, someone is always waiting to pick it up: from Day to Allen, from Allen to Bob Beason as treasurer, from White to, in this case, Graham Willars.

Meanwhile Hare, Woodward, Cusworth and Wheeler took themselves off on a fairly undemanding tour of the USA and Canada with England, Barry Evans made off to the Far East with England Students and a young man called Rory Underwood, then with Middlesbrough, began to spread his wings on an England under-23 tour to Italy. In a crowded summer the four England men, plus Dodge, also accepted places in an invitation party to play three games in South Africa to mark the re-opening of the Ellis Park Stadium in Johannesburg - a decision with political consequences locally while the club, again under Johnson's captaincy, made a five-match visit to Zimbabwe.

The portents for a good start to the 1982-83 season were not good since several first-teamers were unavailable - some because of work, some resting from their summer labours while Woodward was trying to throw off a troublesome shoulder injury. Results were uneven, though that was scarcely reflected in selection for the Midlands against the touring Fijians at Welford Road on October 6: although the seven Tigers who played included Brian Hall, now only an occasional in the club's senior side, and Terry Roberts, that hardy annual lock from Gosforth who established a brief connection with Leicester.

The team was: W H Hare (Leicester); S Holdstock (Nottingham), P W Dodge (Leicester), G H Davies (Coventry), J Goodwin (Moseley); L Cusworth

Tim Barnwell is helped from the field, seriously injured in the John Player Cup Final against Bristol in 1983.

(Leicester), S P Thomas (Coventry); L Johnson (Coventry), P J Wheeler (Leicester, captain), G S Pearce (Northampton), T Roberts (Leicester), V Cannon (Northampton), R Salmon (Nottingham), S R Johnson (Leicester), G W Rees (Nottingham). It was not the happiest of tours for Fiji, who lost all ten games, but this was one of their better performances, aided by the goal-kicking of Sevaro who landed four penalties. Unfortunately for him Hare was more than equal in this department, scoring a try, kicking two conversions and three penalties to go with Lee Johnson's try and a penalty try.

A week later Barry Evans scored two tries against the hapless tourists when England Students beat them 26-9 at Bristol, so there was little surprise when England ran all over them to the extent of 60-19 in a non-caps match: Hare kicked six conversions, Dodge and Cusworth were among the try-scorers which meant that, of the club's representatives, only Wheeler missed out.

Domestically the first was heard of a youngster from Loughborough Students, John Wells, who scored two tries against Harlequins and indicated a long-term successor to Johnson, now in his last season. But perhaps Leicester were saving their best for the Barbarians: that match marked White's final game with the club and his players did him proud, winning 36-16 and scoring five tries before a capacity 17,000 crowd. Three of the tries fell to Evans, whose speed left as experienced a wing as Mike Slemen opposite looking very reflective and helped the Leicester player to an England trial. There were kind words, too, for the play of Richards at No 8 and experienced judges looked forward to the day when his hard, grafting play would benefit England.

Leicester saw White off with a dinner at the Grand Hotel and Willars, assistant to Leicester Youth for two years but coach for only one, quietly slotted in: "I'm prepared to put the work in if the players are," he said. "It may be an amateur game but the rewards - victory, pride and prestige - are worth working for." That attitude earned Leicester a 21-9 win over Bath despite playing the second half without Nick Jackson, the lock, who became the first club player in five years to be sent off after retaliating against Roger Spurrell, the Bath flanker. Richards moved up to replace him in the second row and his contribution caused Martin Johnson, the *Leicester Mercury* man in prescient mood, to note that he had "the potential one day to play for his country."

That was for the future. The present brought the selection of five Leicester players in the England team to play France with two more, Evans and Redfern, named in a extended training squad. But Woodward withdrew because of his shoulder problems, thereby missing a 19-15 defeat in which Hare (four penalties) and Cusworth (dropped goal) kicked all England's points, and then Wheeler's ankle ligaments, damaged in the cup win over High Wycombe, would not sustain him for the match with Wales.

In that game England came as close to winning in Cardiff as at any time since 1963, a Leicester move called the 'Chattanooga Choo-choo' earning John Carleton a try in a 13-13 draw. Hare (two penalties

took him past Bob Hiller's England record of 138 points) and Cusworth (dropped goal) kicked the other points, not that it did the fly-half much good because he and Steve Smith, the scrum-half, were promptly dropped for the Calcutta Cup match. A sequence of injuries led to Smith's restoration but England's fortunes plummeted: Hare, Dodge and Wheeler were in the side beaten 22-12 by Scotland and though they were joined for the Irish match at Lansdowne Road by Woodward and Nick Youngs, winning his first cap to great local glee, a disorganised English XV crashed 25-15. Hare's five penalties gave him 42 of the 55 points England scored in the championship, a somewhat melancholy record at the time and brought him selection for the 1983 Lions tour to New Zealand.

There had been considerable speculation, not only in Leicester, that Wheeler would captain the Lions: in the event he was not chosen at all, the captaincy going to Ciaran Fitzgerald on the back of Ireland's successful season and the other hooking place going to Colin Deans of Scotland. Nor did Dodge receive the call though Woodward, whose form and fitness had been in doubt all season, did. In view of the controversies which surrounded the tour one could only wonder at the decisions made in March by the Lions selectors: Deans was clearly the better hooker but could not oust the captain whose leadership qualities, apt enough for Ireland, could not prevent a 4-0 whitewash by New Zealand. Since three different centre pairings appeared in the Tests it is reasonable to suggest that Dodge might have had a contribution to make too.

It was Hare's selection for the Lions that caused him to miss the 1983 cup final. Leicester opened with an easy 47-18 win over a spirited High Wycombe and then saw off Cusworth's old club, Wakefield, 30-14; Youngs scored two tries in a tight 18-4 win over Harlequins (who had beaten Leicester in a friendly a week earlier) but the club then showed that they had not lost their capacity for running rugby by dismissing London Scottish 30-9 in the semi-final. Cusworth scored one of five tries in a series of displays which appeared to become better and better in the wake of his England disappointment.

As they rolled back to Twickenham Leicester also filed away a 34-0 win over the RAF, whose ranks included Pilot Officer Underwood, but their greater concern was the side to play Bristol in the cup final: in the end it included Woodward, who felt he needed the match practice, but not Hare whose desire not to risk his Lions place met with a sympathetic view at Welford Road and gave an unexpected place at full back to young Ian Dodson.

Steve Johnson's 207th and last appearance was in a marvellous game, quite the best final in the 12 years of the competition, which Bristol won 28-22

before a then record crowd of 33,000. Yet in the midst of the back-slapping for both clubs there was grave concern for Tim Barnwell, the Leicester wing helped off late in the first half after a heavy collision with David Palmer, Bristol's hooker. Barnwell was taken to hospital and later underwent a five-hour operation to remove a blood clot on the brain; it was the end of his career, during which he proved himself one of the most elusive - if not most disciplined - runners to appear in a Leicester shirt. Happily he made a complete recovery and, apart from resuming a successful business career, also made a name for himself as a commentator on Leicester matches for local radio.

The match itself brought together the two most attractive teams in England, neither of them inhibited by the occasion. Leicester's team was: I R Dodson; B J Evans, P W Dodge, C R Woodward, R C Barnwell; L Cusworth, N G Youngs; Stuart Redfern, P J Wheeler, Steve Redfern, N K Gillingham, M V Foulkes-Arnold, S R Johnson (captain), D Richards, I R Smith. Cusworth took over Hare's role as goal-kicker and immediately scored two of four first-half penalties to which Stuart Barnes replied with one of his own. Barnes, in his final year at Oxford University, was in transition; he remained with Bristol for the 1984 cup final, against

Bath whom he subsequently joined.

Evans scored the first try of the match which took Leicester past 1,000 points for the season for the first time and a second loomed for the wing had Barnwell's pass gone to hand; but it went down and John Carr, the big Bristol wing, kicked on to score his second try which Barnes converted, as he did a further penalty to leave the interval score locked at 16-16. Ian Bates had replaced Barnwell but Bristol's power was growing: Simon Hogg shredded the midfield defence and Bob Hesford smashed into the corner, Barnes converting twice and leaving Leicester only the consolation of the last word, by Ian Smith which Cusworth converted. Cusworth's, too, was the last word on the match: "This was the best final I've played in and we lost. What more is there to say about the game?"

Action from the superbly entertaining 1983 John Player Cup Final against Bristol at Twickenham which Tigers lost 28-22.

CHAPTER 24

WHEELER'S WAY
1983-1986

IF ANYONE imagined it would be a quiet summer, the Lions tour apart, they were wrong. There was intense speculation that a professional touring circus would be established by an Australian journalist, David Lord, and since Leicester had so many members of the England squad their names were inevitably linked - on whatever tenuous grounds - with the potential party of 200 players. Large sums of money were bandied around and late in the year a fixture schedule was even published but it came to nothing - though it did serve to emphasise the degree to which the game was changing that the project was taken very seriously indeed.

While Hare and Woodward shared the trials and tribulations of New Zealand, Wheeler, Cusworth and Youngs took themselves off to South Africa in an international squad which helped Western Province celebrate its centenary. Wheeler was, too, in the throes of writing an autobiography which duly appeared in the autumn entitled *"Rugby from the Front"* - a year later Hare followed him into print with *"Dusty"* - the proceeds from both books going to help different sporting organisations, Leicester among them.

As things turned out Wheeler's book, designed partly to be the diary of the Lions captain, was premature: 1983-84, his final international season, was also the one in which he captained England. During the summer Budge Rogers, the chairman of selectors, resigned, as did Mike Davis, the coach, and two other selectors; Derek Morgan took over as chairman and Dick Greenwood as coach and among their first actions was Wheeler's appointment to lead England against Canada, a match organised as preparation for the November international against the touring All Blacks. At 35 the honour came late but no less merited as England struggled to extract themselves from the malaise of the previous season.

Hare, Dodge and Youngs joined him in the non-caps match at Twickenham which England won in foul conditions 27-0; though the rain did not stop, Hare achieved a perfect six kicks out of six, three conversions and three penalties. Selection for the game against New Zealand, however, did not happen until after the Midlands had played the touring side in a game at Welford Road on November 8, 1983, which surely matched that memorable day in 1931 against the South Africans.

The All Blacks, captained by Stuart Wilson, were a curious team, neither fish nor fowl. Five of the tight forwards who had swept aside the Lions in the summer were unable to tour, nor was David Loveridge, the influential scrum-half. The inexperience of those who did showed throughout the visit to England and Scotland and their opponents, burning from the shame endured by the Lions, were not about to treat them lightly in consequence; indeed the England selectors co-ordinated their plans closely with the four divisional sides so that all could contribute to the style of rugby Greenwood sought when it came to the international.

Nevertheless New Zealand won their first four games and arrived in Leicester as exponents of a wonderfully proud tradition. Under the Leicester lights (New Zealand's first ever floodlit game), though, they met their match against a team including Stuart Redfern, the 22-year-old younger brother of Steve, the tight-head prop, and winner of an England under-23 cap the previous season. The Midlands team was: W H Hare (Leicester); S Holdstock (Nottingham), P W Dodge, C R Woodward (both Leicester), J Goodwin (Moseley); L Cusworth, N G Youngs; S B Redfern (all Leicester), P J Wheeler (Leicester, captain), G S Pearce (Northampton), R M Wilkinson (Bedford), V Cannon (Northampton), N C Jeavons (Moseley), G L Robbins (Coventry), G W Rees (Nottingham).

Wheeler, the captain, acknowledged his team faced a "mammoth task" but added that, "if Dusty bangs over all his kicks we may sneak it by a point or two." Never a truer word. Two immense kicks, one a penalty, one dropped, from his own half by Hare gave the Midlands a famous 19-13 win, only the fifth by an English team over New Zealand since they started touring in 1905. The New Zealanders were only four days away from the international with Scotland and did not field their strongest available XV (though the pack was little short of international strength) but nothing should detract from the way the Midlands hurled themselves into their task, notably Gary Rees, the Nottingham flanker whose tackling was of the highest quality.

Robbie Deans opened the scoring for the All Blacks with the first of two early penalties, which enveloped a close-range try by Graham Robbins, Coventry's No 8 who was replaced late in the game by Dean Richards. The Midlands bombarded their opponents with high kicks from half back but fell further behind early in the second half to Deans' third goal before Hare closed the gap with a penalty. Steve Pokere, pursuing a speculative kick through, scored a try which kept the Midlands at arm's length but when Rees made the extra man the Leicester centres were able to work space for Steve Holdstock to cross and Hare's conversion levelled matters.

Then Wheeler's team went for broke. They attacked from long range, Bob Wilkinson and Vince Cannon stayed in the lineout contest and, roared on by 17,000, they battered away at the New Zealand half. Yet it was from their own territory that they clinched matters: Hare missed his easiest penalty attempt of the night before he took aim from around 55 metres and landed a mighty kick which gave his team the lead. Then, when Murray Mexted failed to find touch with a clearance, Hare gathered on his own 10-metre line and let fly at the distant posts with the dropped goal which disbelieving New Zealanders watched descend over the bar.

It was a mighty match and it earned caps for six Leicester players - Hare, Dodge, Woodward, Cusworth, Youngs and Wheeler - 11 days later. At Twickenham they won again, by 15-9, Hare kicking three penalties and converting Maurice Colclough's try though the match cost Wheeler five weeks away from the game with a broken bone in his hand. Older Leicester supporters could happily reminisce about England's previous home win over

New Zealand, in 1936, when Leicester's Bernard Gadney was the captain.

Meanwhile the club itself was not doing badly. Under the captaincy of Ian Smith, the former Wyggeston School student, they established a club record of 16 successive wins from the start of a season until the massed ranks of England players at Twickenham cost them defeat against Wasps. In September they beat the touring national team from Zimbabwe 29-12 and, a month later, Rory Underwood - who joined the club at the start of the season after his posting to RAF Cranwell - made his first-team debut against Birmingham, and his second game was a 25-0 victory over Northampton. "I noticed the step up in class," Underwood said, "but it was a tremendous education to train and play with the Leicester back division, all of whom were internationals except Barry Evans and me. I don't think I could have had a more unblinkered, unstereotyped experience at such a young age."

Dusty Hare and Peter Wheeler after the famous Midlands victory over the All Blacks in 1983.

Underwood, already a 'B' international from the previous season, served notice of intent with three tries in the 61-10 win over Saracens and two more tries in the 30-26 win over the Barbarians earned him a place in England's training squad. Meanwhile calamity had struck: Smith broke a thumb and missed a month while, against Blackheath at the Rectory Field, Dodge suffered a spiral fracture of the leg. It wrecked his entire season, although he was able to tour South Africa in the summer, and to many observers it took an indefinable edge from his game, even though he recovered to play international rugby again and to give the club another seven years.

Piling on the agony Leicester, without the injured Cusworth, lost their first John Player Cup outing, to Coventry 13-9. Denied possession by their neighbours Leicester might still have won had not Woodward, after a 70-metre run, stumbled in changing direction to avoid pursuit just short of the posts. This, John Allen said, would be a test of the supporters: "Many have been attracted by our cup success but we hope we've also persuaded them that our style of rugby is worth watching every Saturday afternoon."

Perhaps not surprisingly the remainder of the season was inconsistent, with Leicester turning on the power against mediocre sides but struggling against the better ones. Even so there was some compensation from the international scene: although Dodge was absent Leicester were able to offer a club record of seven players to the game against Ireland at Twickenham. After defeat in Scotland, Underwood was called up for his first cap on the left wing, joining Hare, Woodward, Cusworth, Youngs, Wheeler and, in the second half, Steve Redfern who came on for what proved to be his only cap as a replacement for the injured Colin White. But that 12-9 win was England's only success of the season: although Underwood and Hare scored tries against France, and Hare converted both as well as kicking two penalties, England lost 32-18 and all they could offer against Wales was Hare's five penalties in a 24-15 defeat.

It was a sad conclusion to Wheeler's distinguished international career of 41 caps. Not that the hooker announced his retirement, but he was not available for the summer tour to South Africa and acknowledged that, at his age, it would be surprising if England did not start to look elsewhere. In fact neither Steve Mills of Gloucester nor Coventry's Steve Brain made an outright claim on the number two shirt on an unsuccessful tour but events early in the 1984-85 season proved Wheeler's final downfall.

Amid much controversy the Rugby Football Union voted to go ahead with the visit to South Africa and England departed with Hare, Dodge and Youngs in their ranks, leaving behind a simmering row between Leicester and the Labour-controlled city council which wished to

Dusty Hare, Nick Youngs, Les Cusworth, Paul Dodge, Peter Wheeler (captain) and Clive Woodward helped England beat the All Blacks 15-9 in November 1983.

Tigers galore! - the England v Ireland programme for the match at Twickenham in February 1984.

prevent the club using the Recreation Ground - later renamed Mandela Park - for training and playing purposes because they opposed sporting links with South Africa.

Indeed in August that year the council banned Leicester from using the Recreation Ground for a 12-month period because their response to a council questionnaire was deemed inadequate: included in the club's considered response, which joined with the council in a condemnation of apartheid, was an emphasis that the same objective may be achieved in different ways. "Rugby union players, as amateur sportsmen, have individual choice as to when and where they play, subject only to the constraints of the RFU rules and club loyalty," their statement read. The club's appeal went all the way to the House of Lords where five law lords ruled unanimously against the council; that the ban was due to expire two months after the hearing was not the point and Lord Templeman, giving judgement, said: "The laws of this country are not like the laws of Nazi Germany. A private individual or a private organisation cannot be obliged to display zeal in the pursuit of an object sought by a public authority and cannot be obliged to publish views dictated by a public authority."

While such weighty matters were being considered, Evans, Stuart Redfern, John Wells and the young hooker, Chris Tressler, toured Spain with

A formidable front-row! Two Redferns and a Wheeler in 1983.

England under-23 while Leicester themselves departed for the uncontroversial venue offered by the United Arab Emirates where they played matches in Bahrain and Dubai and heard from afar the decline of their colleagues elsewhere: Dodge returned home early with an ankle injury, Youngs lost his international place to the ginger-headed dynamo from Bath, Richard Hill, and Hare, though he kicked four penalties in the first international and three in the second, played out his final two England appearances in undistinguished circumstances.

He announced his retirement from international rugby in September, having played more times at full back for England (25) than any previous encumbent and having scored more points (240), though Jonathan Webb has since surpassed both

milestones. Hare was always under-valued by England, who dropped and recalled him five times, and his decision, taken at 31 for "family and business reasons" was probably a case of jumping before being pushed: the following weekend England's first squad of the season included Marcus Rose, Nick Stringer and Chris Martin as full backs. Happily Hare continued to ply his trade with Leicester and Stringer was given first shot at filling his boots in an England XV which played an RFU President's XV to celebrate 75 years of rugby at Twickenham: Underwood, unavailable for the South African tour, Woodward and the younger Redfern joined him in a low-key match lost 27-10.

It soon became apparent that Leicester's stock was declining: the early-season confrontation with Bath, new holders of the cup, ended in favour of the West Countrymen and Tigers had to scramble around for a scrum-half, Youngs having decided to play out the South African season in Durban and Kenney being injured. Ian Smith, captain once more, suffered further damage to his hand and the protracted, and potentially costly, wrangle with the council cast a gloom over proceedings. Even worse was the prospect of losing Cusworth to a Manchester-based building society, a situation relieved when he started a new career as a trainee insurance broker with the Leicester firm of P & G Bland, who have since become close allies of the club.

Still, there was the prospect of the touring Australians to look forward to. Leicester had already formed valuable links with down under, and a healthy respect for their achievements, though no-one was aware of quite how much Andrew Slack's Wallabies would achieve in Britain. It was significant that their England representation had declined in the space of seven months from seven to one, when only Underwood (who played against the Australians four times, for the Combined Services, the North and the Barbarians) was named in a very raw England XV beaten 19-3 on November 3, and Leicester supporters looked forward to their Midland players proving a point three days later at Welford Road.

All seven of their heroes were there in a Midland team which read: W H Hare (Leicester); S Holdstock (Nottingham), P W Dodge, C R Woodward (both Leicester), J Goodwin (Moseley); L Cusworth, N G Youngs (both Leicester); L Johnson (Coventry), P J Wheeler (Leicester, captain), G S Pearce, V Cannon (both Northampton), N Mantell, P W Cook (both Nottingham), G L Robbins (Coventry), I R Smith (Leicester). It was a stage from which Wheeler conceivably could reclaim his England place, having rebuffed the challenge at home of young Tressler, but not by the time the match had finished.

Alan Jones, the Australian coach, described the Midlands as "the other England side, if only they were selected" but by the end of a match which he was relieved his team had won 21-18, Jones was incandescent with rage at the sending-off by Winston Jones, the Welsh referee, of Mark McBain, his reserve hooker, and Wheeler. It was the turning point of a match the Midlands might have won since they led 18-9 at that stage through Hare's five penalties and a dropped goal by Simon Hodgkinson, the replacement for the injured Cusworth, with less

than 12 minutes left; but in the resulting confusion Peter Grigg crossed for a try and James Black, nerve holding remarkably well under the Welford Road lights, kicked the conversion and two penalties.

At that time any English player sent off, at whatever level, was automatically barred from consideration for the national side for the remainder of the season, a ruling to which Wheeler objected - not so much on his own behalf as for younger players with their way to make - owing to its arbitrary nature. The following season it was discarded. But Wheeler, who had never been sent off in his lengthy career, was also fuming that the referee had acted on something he did not witness: he and McBain had niggled at each other throughout the game and they did so once more with arm-swinging gestures which did not connect. They were dismissed for punching and though Wheeler subsequently produced video evidence purporting to show that no blows had landed, the mandatory 30-day suspension stood.

There was more than a suspicion that the referee reacted to the roar of the crowd rather than any physical violence witnessed, having spoken to both players earlier in the game. "We weren't having a stand-up brawl and what went on was insignificant both in terms of the game and in terms of the two of us," Wheeler said. Sadly, though Wheeler appeared at the disciplinary hearing in Dublin, along with McBain and his management, Winston Jones submitted only a written report which could not be challenged at the time. It was an unnecessary cloud which tarnished the career of one of Leicester's most remarkable players though, to his credit, Wheeler faded with dignity from the playing scene, playing as and when he could and in whichever team Leicester chose to pick him.

But he had remained long enough to see the beginning of fundamental change to the domestic competitive structure: England and the English were beginning to tire of being cannon fodder and there was talk of a new divisional championship, of a national club merit table if not leagues, of husbanding the country's playing resources far more effectively. Leicester had long since agreed that a merit table might be beneficial and were building for the future: at the start of the season a five-year sponsorship was agreed with Ind Coope, the brewers, designed to help offset the costs of refurbishing Welford Road, the most expensive ground outside Twickenham. In the new year plans were unveiled for ground improvements costing £100,000: the changing rooms and additional facilities were to be moved

underneath the Crumbie Stand for the 1985-86 season and the room created in the Aylestone Road clubhouse turned into a members' bar and lounge. In the wake of the fire which destroyed the Bradford City Football Club stand, in which several people died, later in the season a further £60,000 was set aside to comply with safety requirements.

By the time Christmas came, Wheeler had regained his place in the side which gave the Barbarians their biggest drubbing in the series, by 35-11. Dodge had been recalled to the England squad and even the unwelcome news that Steve Redfern had decided to turn professional with the new Sheffield Eagles rugby league club did not cast too great a shadow. Redfern, then 26 and with 241 appearances to his credit since joining Tigers from Coalville, was the first England international to go to rugby league for eight years and it was a move he subsequently regretted. It was not a success and at various stages during the 1990s, as rugby union progressively relaxed the laws on amateurism, he hoped for reinstatement as a player; so far, however, his involvement with rugby union has been only as

a coach after the International Rugby Football Board approved his reinstatement in 1991.

The new year also brought word that Dodge had been invited to captain England against Romania. Nigel Melville, who led England in his debut international against Australia, had damaged his knee and Dodge offered experience and solidity to a team desperately in need of it. He was the fourth captain in ten months, Wheeler having been briefly succeeded by John Scott, and was given a side including five newcomers - among them Rob Andrew and Wade Dooley. Dodge had been sounded out by Derek Morgan during the South African tour but the selection came, nonetheless, as a surprise to a player whose only previous leadership experience had been an undemanding game

Steve Redfern takes possession for Tigers in a maul against Cambridge University in November 1984. It was one of his last appearances before turning professional.

between England under-23 and Holland.

He retained the role for seven games, including the two internationals in New Zealand during the summer. 1985, though, was Dodge's international swansong: he became England's most-capped centre with 32 games (a record subsequently bettered by Will Carling) but his more subtle skills were seldom appreciated at international level. At 6ft 2in he had physical presence but far more than that, he had a footballing brain and handling skills which could have been far better used than they were; his organisational powers were always more clearly understood by those who played alongside him (or against him) than those who watched.

Underwood, who thought his RAF career would keep him out of top-class rugby this season, was alongside him though unable to tour in the summer. But again England made hard work of a season disrupted by bad weather: one try in the 22-15 win over Romania, a surprise draw with France, a

Underwood, with four tries, was the chief surgeon. Hare kicked four conversions and four penalties, Wheeler took three heels against the head, Woodward popped over a dropped goal and Cusworth was at his most impish.

When Liverpool were beaten 37-9 hopes rose even higher, only to be flattened when Leicester could only draw 10-10 at Coundon Road, Coventry going through to the semi-finals by virtue of scoring two tries to one. Ironically Coventry went out in the same way, by the same score, to London Welsh. The season tailed off in a welter of injuries, one of them to Wheeler who damaged elbow ligaments, and even the two matches played on a brief visit to France, at St Claude and Chambéry, were lost. Barry Evans played in the end-of-season 'B' international against Italy at Twickenham but otherwise Leicester looked forward to life under Cusworth in 1985-86.

Life, that is, in the John Smith's merit table, division 'A'. This was the first, tentative dabble with a structured season though the tables themselves were worked on a percentage basis since half the competing teams did not play each other: thus, in a 12-club table, Leicester played 10 matches, more than anyone else including Gloucester, the eventual winners and in some cases 50 per cent more. Just to complicate matters (and, given the events of 1992-93, one can see how history repeats itself), new laws came into force including scrum and tackle laws, designed to keep players on their feet rather than creating pile-ups on the ground.

As if to emphasise change the club bade farewell to Clive Woodward who, after some months of speculation, announced that he had accepted a business move to Australia. He had won 21 England caps and proved himself a player of immense flair: he and Dodge complemented each other perfectly, Dodge offering the security for the will o' the wisp Woodward to go where his fancy took him. Yet Woodward was also a tremendous support player because he had the vision to see what was possible - if not always what was probable. He led the side out for his final match, against Bath, who failed to acknowledge the occasion by winning 40-15, and after settling in Sydney he spent three good seasons with Manly.

Nick Youngs in action at Twickenham against Harlequins in the John Smith's merit table match during September 1985.

snatched victory over Scotland but they could not deny Ireland the triple crown. Although Dodge set up a try for Underwood with his cross-kick, a late dropped goal gave the Irish the verdict 13-10 at Lansdowne Road and Wales made off with the spoils at Cardiff as usual on the day that Jonathan Davies took to the international stage.

Underwood may well have thought club rugby came slightly easier, judging by the start Leicester made to the John Player Cup. Two years earlier Bristol had taken the trophy, the previous season they were beaten finalists: but on January 26 Tigers erased them from the competition with a dazzling 43-4 victory at Welford Road. It was a quite clinical dissection of a good Bristol side, in which

There was no shortage of competition to partner Dodge: Ian Bates had been joined by Steve Burnhill, a tourist in South Africa with Dodge in 1984, and Tim Buttimore, a Coventry centre with some of Woodward's mercurial talent. Meanwhile Dodge himself, after captaining England to a narrow 18-13 defeat in the first international with New Zealand in the summer (six penalties by Kieran Crowley accounted for England's loss) and an unpleasant, in every sense, 42-15 defeat in the second, found himself omitted from the first England training squad. In a party of 37 Leicester had only two: Underwood, whose flying duties affected his

availability, and Richards whose attitude to training made even the relaxed Graham Willars grumble: "One day I might turn him into a fitness freak but at the moment I can't see it," Willars said while extolling the England potential of the young No 8.

Enter the divisional championship, which was a genuine regional competition or an extended trial, depending on your viewpoint. The Midlands team was dominated by Nottingham and Coventry players, which rankled somewhat at Leicester since they had beaten both: only Dodge and Cusworth played in the team that won the title by beating the North and London at home and the South-West away, their mauling style projecting Graham Robbins, the Coventry No 8, into the England team.

Leicester meanwhile rolled forward reasonably comfortably, running up substantial wins against London Welsh, Coventry, Oxford University and enjoying an 18-10 triumph over Swansea before Cardiff brought them to ground. But they remained not entirely convincing, the mauling by Bath taking time to work its way from the corporate system. Underwood played his first club match of the season in the 19-16 defeat by the Barbarians but clearly the club was saving itself for the cup in the new year.

Certainly there was little prospect on the international front: Underwood retained his place but even he missed the game with Scotland because of an ankle injury, the first time in 54 internationals and 11 years that Leicester had not been represented in an England side. It may have been a judicious one to miss: England crashed 33-6, the second time in eight months they had lost by the record margin of 27 points. The effect was to introduce Richards to international rugby: the 22 year-old policeman from Hinckley replaced Robbins against Ireland and marked the occasion by scoring two tries in a 25-20 win. Even Clive Norling, the Welsh referee, congratulated him on his debut and both he and Underwood remained for the final match, a defeat by France.

Richards was then, and subsequently remained, a mould-breaker: Wheeler, for example, was an outstanding forward in the breed of the modern hooker, who had many of the ball skills of a back-row forward but was identifiable as one of a type. Richards was entirely his own man: loose-limbed, unathletic in build but a man of immense presence even though he was not the tallest of No 8s. Socks round ankles, shirt flapping wildly, with considerable mauling power, he conformed in no way to the textbook of back row play - he just turned up wherever the ball happened to be. And, happily for Leicester, international rugby was never the be-all and end-all for him: Richards was as happy playing with his club as he was to turn out for England at Twickenham. Rugby was his hobby and had its place in his life, but no more.

For some obscure reason he and Underwood were both included, at the season's end, in an England under-23 side against Spain. A week later Underwood, leaping up the scale, was playing for the British Lions against the Rest of the World in the first of the two special matches celebrating the centenary of the International Rugby Football Board. Seven of that side in Cardiff - Underwood, Gavin Hastings, Brendan Mullin, Robert Jones, Wade Dooley, Donal Lenihan and John Jeffrey

subsequently joined forces in the 1989 Lions tour party to Australia. On this occasion they lost and Underwood was in the defeated side three days later when a Five Nations XV played the Overseas Unions at Twickenham.

Richards was on hand when Leicester began their John Player Cup campaign by extracting revenge from Coventry for the disappointment of the previous season: they had to work hard for a 21-14 win at Coundon Road, losing Underwood with an ankle injury on the way, and then had to wait for the vagaries of the weather before scoring eight tries (three to Richards) in a 46-6 victory over Broughton Park in a Sunday cup tie. In fact it was hard to keep Richards out of the news: he scored again, his 18th try of the season, when Leicester beat Harlequins 15-8 in the quarter-final at the Stoop memorial ground, paving the way for a dramatic semi-final against Bath - the club whose ebullient young forwards had treated Tigers with such disrespect the previous September.

Everyone in Leicester, it seemed, wanted a ticket for the match but for those who obtained one there was only disappointment: the club's first cup defeat at Welford Road. Bath won 10-6 (a scoreline that was to return to haunt Leicester three years later) and deserved to, their juggernaut pack rolling back the Leicester forwards. The contest at scrum-half between Youngs and Hill failed to materialise after Youngs left the field in the first quarter and the side that scored the try (through Simon Halliday) won the match, and went forward to beat Wasps in the final. Since Leicester also finished fourth in the new merit table their standing in English club terms was confirmed: nearly but not quite.

Dean Richards celebrates his first international try against Ireland in March 1986.

CHAPTER 25

A CHANGING WORLD 1986-1989

ENGLISH rugby braced itself for change in the second half of the 1980s: though the merit tables continued during 1986-87 all the talk was of a new league system, to be introduced the following season and involving more than 1,200 clubs - the biggest of its kind in the world. And a World Cup, to be played in New Zealand and Australia in the summer of 1987. What was the world coming to?

Leicester was as well prepared for the future as any club in England, and better than most, thanks to changes in the club administration over the previous decade and the success which had brought a new generation of supporters into a ground already the envy of all for its ability to host big matches. Membership had risen to 4,500, a profit on the previous season was announced at over £46,000 and the club was prepared to spend a further £100,000 on ground improvements, mostly to comply with the Safety of Sports Grounds Act (a year later, as developments continued, the Welford Road bank, that mound of ash and gravel hated by players who had sweated up and down it in the pursuit of greater fitness, was levelled).

Newcomers to the club included Harry Roberts, a hooker born in Zambia, brought up in Zimbabwe and finished (in rugby terms) in the Transvaal where he had played provincial rugby. Roberts, strong and mobile, had a chequered career with the club in his restless pursuit of international honours, hindered by a recurring shoulder problem; six years

later he returned to Welford Road as part of the first South African tour party to visit Britain in 23 years but even then he was doomed to miss the cap he so desperately sought.

Cusworth was captain again, hoping for a return to the expansive rugby he so enjoyed, although not even he would have anticipated a club record so early in the season: in the final fixture against the Birmingham club, Leicester won 95-6 and Hare established an individual record of 43 points, which carried him past 6,000 for his career. Nick Youngs led the 15-try romp with four and though the club promptly tripped up at Harlequins, they were at it again when London Welsh visited Welford Road: this time the margin was 69-4, the worst defeat in the long and proud history of the Welsh, twelve tries of which Underwood scored four and Evans two.

Not that anyone doubted Leicester's quality behind the scrum but Willars, as coach, was keen to develop the forward strength: his degree of success was indicated by victory at Swansea and that momentum was sustained against the touring Fijian Barbarians who crashed 39-14 at Welford Road. The Fijians were making a world tour on a shoestring and their best contribution to the evening's entertainment was their singing in the clubhouse afterwards: they were also impressed by Tom Smith, the young Leicester lock, and extended an invitation - happily accepted - for him to play for them in a subsequent game against West Hartlepool (doubtless Smith would have been even more delighted to have played for them in Fiji!).

Even so Cusworth was less than happy: "Rugby should take a hard look at itself and ask what spectators are being offered," he said. "We [and he was not referring only to Tigers] are playing a negative, stop-start game with little good second-

Nick Youngs powers forward during the 69-4 crushing of London Welsh in September 1986.

phase ball and this leads to hardly any decent handling moves. The problem is that these days a side's initial thought is to go out and stop the other playing whereas it should be to create and make something happen. Leicester are as guilty as anyone. We used to play a high-risk game which was entertaining. Now results have become all-important."

In other words, Leicester could play only when the opposition was of insufficient stature to stop them: against the better clubs, the Baths and Wasps, they adopted defensive mode. For what it was worth, their style gave them six representatives in the divisional championships, though the Midlands did not distinguish themselves and Dodge broke a bone in his hand during the first game. At much the same time a young prop from Reading, Paul Burnell, made his debut as a replacement against Saracens though it was not until he moved to London Scottish that Scotland decided here was a potential international - and, as it turned out in 1993, a British Lion.

One of the problems of competitive rugby, of course, was the knock-on effect from representative calls and the divisional championship left Leicester in no doubt that they should "de-merit" their game with Bristol in December. Bristol were aggrieved that Leicester should not have done so much earlier, knowing of the clash with the divisional game, and promptly made their feelings known by administering a 39-9 defeat; the same thing happened against Gloucester, who also won heavily at Kingsholm and added interest by winning the merit table game at Leicester 14-12.

Adding injury to insult, Dean Richards damaged medial ligaments in his knee (playing against his police colleagues when bad weather forced Leicester to re-arrange their fixtures and meet Metropolitan Police). He and Underwood had been try-scorers in an England XV's win over Japan in October and both were regarded as automatic choices for England for the five nations championship and the World Cup: but the injury kept Richards out of three of the four championship matches, leaving Underwood to battle on alone through a season of gloom unrelieved until the 21-12 victory over Scotland in the final match. Leicester could though, take vicarious pleasure from the return to international rugby of Marcus Rose, now playing his rugby with Harlequins.

They could even call upon a player of unstinting enthusiasm to fill Richards' boots: Simon Povoas, then 20, has spent a career in the giant shadow of the England No 8 but his quality allowed him to surpass Richards' record for tries scored by a forward and took him to the England 'B' squad. Here he stepped up to score in a much-postponed John Player Cup game against Rosslyn Park in which Leicester were taken to the wire at 18-15. Evans, too, returned after a season adversely affected by a damaged Achilles tendon and scored in the next cup round, a 19-6 win over Gosforth. Cusworth nudged the England

Simon Povoas - a quality forward for Tigers despite a career in the giant shadow of Dean Richards.

selectors with a try and dropped goal in the 17-7 quarter-final win at Bristol, at a time when the national number ten shirt seemed to be in limbo after the sour international against Wales in Cardiff, but again they looked elsewhere.

Richards returned for the Calcutta Cup match but Cusworth's disappointment was mirrored by the 13-6 semi-final defeat at Wasps: again a case of so far but yet no farther. Another Barbarian side, this time from New Zealand on a world tour with something not far short of a complete All Blacks party, brought further gloom to Leicester with a comprehensive 33-3 win at Welford Road: men such as John Kirwan, David Kirk, Steve McDowell and the then uncapped Michael Jones were to win fame a few months later when New Zealand won the Webb Ellis Cup at the end of the inaugural World Cup - a tournament in which Richards and Underwood played for an England team of no great distinction and which departed at the quarter-final stage, beaten by Wales.

Leicester had the limited comfort of finishing second to Bath in the John Smith's merit table 'A' but were now more concerned about their assault on the first league season proper: to which end the club set out, yet again, on a tour down under. The end of the season was a clutter of minor cameos: of Willars coming on as a replacement in the match with Waterloo, of three Leicester players (Hare, Wells and Buttimore) playing in a charity match organised by Steve Burnhill and finding themselves on the same pitch as three rugby league players, of Hare missing his club points record for the season by three.

Meanwhile Leicester's forward planning committee was looking at recruitment: "The player market has become very competitive because there are so few talented players around," Cusworth, retiring as captain, said. "But the situation has to be very carefully monitored to make sure we get the best for the club without losing sight of what the game is all about." That is an equation which some leading clubs have still not got right, and there was little encouragement from the Leicestershire AGM that summer, which reported that few youngsters played rugby regularly and at any standard in the city schools.

Cusworth's successor was Paul Dodge, who led Leicester off to Australia where they made a slightly lower-key entry than seven years earlier, losing to Western Australia 26-19 but then beating a Western Australian president's XV, a Manly side including Clive Woodward at fly-half, and Ponsonby in Auckland, New Zealand. They returned to Brisbane to lose 37-13 to a Queensland side fielding nine internationals and collected an easy win over Singapore Cricket Club on the way home.

Rory Underwood during the 1987 World Cup match against Australia at Concord Oval, Sydney.

The pre-season preparation paid dividends: Leicester's first match in the newly-formed Courage Clubs Championship was against England's acknowledged top club, Bath, merit-table winners and cup holders. Not since 1983 had they won and both their England players, Richards and Underwood, were absent but Dodge denied any inferiority complex: "We know we are there or thereabouts. It's just a question of lifting our game one notch higher." Lift it they did: in a wonderful advertisement for league rugby, completely absorbing and full of skill, Leicester won 24-13, Cusworth scoring a try, dropping a goal and setting up a try for Jez Harris, the replacement wing.

In a sense that one game teed up the whole season, regardless of the fact that Tigers promptly went walkabout and lost to London Welsh in the absence of the maestros, Cusworth and Hare, both at Underwood's wedding. It gave Leicester the belief that they could compete with anyone, a belief sustained throughout a season which saw them take the inaugural league title. It was not that they were unbeatable - as the Welsh had already proved - but that they had the inner resolve which could carry them through games against apparently better-

equipped clubs: only once did it let them down in the league, against Orrell who thereby began a run of success against Leicester.

That resolve had to survive various vicissitudes: Willars was unwell and had to stand back from the regular coaching duties which allowed Peter Wheeler to expand in that direction. In fact later in the year Wheeler took the "hands-on" role with Willars heading a coaching panel as Leicester appreciated the difficulties for one man of running the whole show. Dodge, too, suffered a setback with a broken kneecap which kept him out of action for three months.

Against that was the promise of a new acquisition from Nottingham, Peter Thornley, a flanker who went on to win an England 'B' place the next season before a persistent back injury ended his first-class career prematurely. Thornley doubtless enjoyed himself in the 22-13 win over Nottingham, the early-season league leaders by virtue of having played more games than anyone else, and Leicester hit the top of the first division by beating Moseley 21-3 with a forward performance as dominant as anything they produced that season. Yet throughout it was the direction given by Cusworth and Hare that permitted Leicester to turn the screw: there were few good decision-makers in the country at the time and Leicester had two of them. "Les is the most experienced and skilled attacking fly-half in the country," Geoff Cooke, the new England team manager, said after he watched Cusworth orchestrate the win at the Reddings.

Remarkably the Midlands found room for only three Tigers (they added a fourth, Buttimore, for the final game) in the divisional championship but four were called up for England's trial, all on the senior side: Underwood, Cusworth, Richards and the deserving Wells. The blind-side flanker had made a name for himself in an unspectacular way but on the day the Rest XV, prepared by Alan Davies, overturned the England XV 13-7 and the selectors went for the height of Mickey Skinner: save for an appearance for an England XV against Italy two years later, it was the nearest Wells got to a cap.

A few days earlier Leicester had rattled up nine tries in a remarkable 48-30 win over the Barbarians: over the last ten years some cherished Barbarian fixtures have become devalued but never the Christmas game at Welford Road. That was then, and remains, a competitive match played out before a full-throated house and the adventure and skill of both sides (the Barbarians included the two mercurial Welshmen, Jonathan Davies and Mark Ring, whose father Brian played for Leicester) gave the enthusiastic crowd everything it could wish for.

Leicester's cup ran over when England picked Cusworth to play fly-half against France in Paris. It was a remarkable comeback, at 33, though fully deserved on form: the sad aspect was that Cusworth's 12 caps should have been won over a nine-year period. What might he have achieved with the continuity which has been the hallmark of England selection over the last four years? He,

Richards, and Underwood played in the Parc des Princes while, next door in the Jean Bouin Stadium, Wells helped England 'B' to victory over their French counterparts. Alas, a mistake by England's captain, Mike Harrison, led to the try which gave France their 10-9 win and Cusworth could only wonder that he, such a talented drop-kicker, should have missed four such goals.

In their absence another Underwood made his debut in an easy win over Bedford: Tony Underwood, nearly six years younger than Rory and a student at Leicester University, failed to score then but has missed few such opportunities since. His time was still to come: Evans and Rory Underwood held down the places in the first cup game of the season, a 15-0 win over Rosslyn Park, which earned them a fourth-round tie with none other than Bath. It was the West Countrymen's second bite at the cherry and this time they did not miss: Leicester were eased out of the cup 13-6 on their own ground.

February, Leicester would claim, was a wicked month: a week earlier their three representatives had been in an England side beaten 11-3 by Wales at Twickenham; then came the cup exit; and that was closely followed by the loss of their 100 per cent league record in a 30-6 defeat at Orrell. All they needed was what the England selectors duly provided: the dropping of Cusworth in favour of Rob Andrew for the Calcutta Cup match in Edinburgh (if Leicester felt battered that was as

nothing compared to the Calcutta Cup's fate after being removed from the post-match banquet by two players who then proceeded to play rugby with it. To Leicester's embarrassment, one of the guilty men turned out to be Richards who was duly suspended for one international by the Rugby Football Union for his part in a stupid prank).

Northampton offered an unlikely aid to recovery when Leicester beat them 35-9 and Rory Underwood, requiring practice on the right wing after England had switched him from his normal left-wing position, scored four tries. It was a switch with which Underwood was not entirely happy but a 35-3 victory over Ireland in which he ended a try-drought by scoring twice was considerable solace.

Leicester, in need of the same, found it over Easter weekend: a fortnight earlier they had played Lansdowne after a 90-year gap and another Irish club, Ballymena, gave Cusworth the chance to become the 26th player to appear 300 times for Leicester. Two days later, after a 39-15 win over Waterloo, the league title was theirs and, happily, in front of their own supporters. Though many players contributed significantly during the season, the XV which did a lap of honour with the new trophy was: W H Hare; B J Evans, I Bates, T J Buttimore (replaced by P W Dodge), R Underwood; L Cusworth, S Kenney; S B Redfern, H Roberts, W P Richardson, T Smith, M V Foulkes-Arnold, J M Wells, D Richards, P T Thornley.

Referee Fred Howard lays down the law to Chris Tressler and Brian Moore, then of Nottingham, in 1987.

It was a happy coincidence that Dodge was able to share in the final league match, at the end of an injury-wrecked season. Yet again Hare laid the foundations with four penalties and four conversions, alongside tries by Evans, Underwood, Thornley and a penalty try, and a dropped goal by Cusworth. After the celebrations were over Wheeler outlined the reasons for success: "We had problems in other positions but no other club in England could match the spine in our side - Harry Roberts, Dean Richards, Steve Kenney or Nick Youngs, Les Cusworth and Dusty Hare....The teams with the half-backs are the ones that did best in the Courage league."

Tigers even managed to retain their equilibrium for the final weeks of the season: they ended a record Bristol run of 21 games and passed 1,000 points for the season after dismissing Gosforth 65-0, Underwood and Richards each scoring three tries. Hare would doubtless have established a personal record had he not carelessly dropped a five-bar gate on his foot while out farming and broken his toe: the emergency sent Jez Harris haring down the road to Leicester from Hinckley and he arrived, breathless but in time to score 25 points against Gosforth and round off the season with 17 points in the 41-3 victory over Moseley which carried Leicester to a season's aggregate of 1,077 points and 32 victories.

Richards and Underwood departed with England on their tour of Australia and Fiji where they were joined by both Evans and Buttimore. Evans received a late call-up when Mike Harrison was injured and Mark Bailey proved unavailable and, in due course, received the caps which many in Leicester believed he should have won earlier: no-one doubted his try-

Paul Dodge with the 1988 Courage Clubs Championship Trophy.

scoring capacity - there were few quicker wings than the former student at Hinckley's John Cleveland College - but his handling and defensive skills occasionally let him down. However, he was called up for his international debut in the second international against Australia and won a second against Fiji at the tour's end.

Buttimore had planned to go to Australia anyway and play with Woodward at Manly but when John Buckton, the Saracens centre, was injured against Queensland, Buttimore was brought into the England party to cover. Although it was not an outstandingly

successful tour, Underwood (who began the tour by playing in a World XV against Australia) continued his try-scoring feats with one in each of the internationals against the Wallabies and two against Fiji.

At home Leicester were not sitting back and basking in reflected glory: Kevin Andrews, the club chairman, called for hard work to maintain the club's standing and more money was committed to ground improvements - this time £150,000 to remove the old Nissen hut (erected as a "temporary" measure in 1947) alongside the clubhouse and replace it with the existing sponsors' facilities. The club had announced a profit of more than £24,000 but they were delighted to start a new season with a new sponsor - Ansells, the brewers, who were prepared to commit £100,000 to Leicester over a five-year period in what was then believed to be the most substantial agreement in English club rugby.

Nevertheless it was disappointing to lose players of potential - Buttimore in Australia, Burnhill to Sale, Rob Tebbutt to Northampton and Paul Burnell to London Scottish (later in the season he was called into Scotland's squad). Leicester knew well the value of strength in depth and, on the eve of a new season, Wheeler called for greater investment in the playing squad: regular tours, the capacity to ensure that players did not suffer financially because of their involvement in the game and the consideration of a paid Director of Rugby.

It was even more disappointing to lose to Orrell so early in the league season: no doubt the representative of *The Sun* who took his seat in the press box under the impression he was about to watch Leicester City against Brighton would have spotted his mistake sooner or later but if he was bemused, so were Leicester's supporters as the Lancashire club ran in three tries to none. Even the reorganisation consequent upon an injury to Nick Youngs - Cusworth went to scrum-half, Hare to fly-half and a new recruit from Wakefield, John Liley, came in at full back - could not entirely explain Orrell's success. Another newcomer, Aadel Kardooni, a scrum-half of Iranian descent who had played for England Schools and Wasps, made his debut against Swansea.

What Leicester were suffering from, of course, was the backlash which those at the top always suffer: teams try harder against the league champions and the quality of the club's reserves was being tested. At the same time there were difficulties behind the scenes: Wheeler had discovered there were not enough hours in the day for family and sport while trying to establish a new insurance business and had to step down as coach. A month later, despite speculation that Chalkie White might return, the club had brought in an old favourite, David Matthews, the former flanker, with Allen Foster, a 37-year-old PE officer in the Prison Service as fitness and conditioning coach; once again the long-term commitment of individuals to Leicester was paying dividends.

As the club struggled to cope with the increasing pressures placed on an amateur organisation, their leading players were doing battle once more with the Australians. Six of them, including the whole back row, played in a side captained by Cusworth for the Midlands: S D Hodgkinson (Nottingham);

B J Evans, P W Dodge (both Leicester), G J Hartley, S T Hackney (both Nottingham); L Cusworth (Leicester), S P Thomas (Coventry); L Johnson, B C Moore, G Mosses, P W Cook (all Nottingham), M C Bayfield (Metropolitan Police), J M Wells, D Richards, P T Thornley (all Leicester). It was by no means the most powerful combination the Midlands could field but, struck down by injuries as they were, they did well to hold the Australians to 25-18.

Indeed victory came as a great relief to the visitors who had lost to the other three divisions on a tour in which Underwood again played against them four times - for the North, England, the Combined Services and the Barbarians. The Midland backs were short of penetration and they lost Steve Hackney - later to join Leicester - in the first half, replacing him with Clifton Jones, the Nottingham centre. Richards wrenched himself over for a close-range try which Simon Hodgkinson converted, as well as kicking four penalties, but tries by Nick Farr-Jones, James Grant and Brad Girvan, alongside the goal-kicking of the recently-arrived Michael Lynagh (two conversions, three penalties) earned victory.

A week later, after David Campese had taken apart an England Students XV including Tony Underwood, it was a different story. England, beaten twice in the summer, turned on an exciting open style of rugby under the captaincy, for the first time, of Will Carling to win at Twickenham 28-19. It was a magnificent, fluid game in which two tries within six minutes by Rory Underwood tilted the balance: the first after deft play by Rob Andrew, the second after a forward drive sparked by Richards, both coming in the same north-west corner.

The Australians left and the divisional championship came, bringing with it places for eight Leicester players in the Midland ranks but to no great effect. Harris made one appearance at full back while the Underwood brothers both turned out for the North, Tony for the first time. Indeed the younger Underwood was not only called into the divisional ranks but, in the new year, made the England 'B' side against France on his home club ground.

The league title, meanwhile, was slipping inexorably away: held to a draw by Nottingham and then beaten by Harlequins on a day when neither

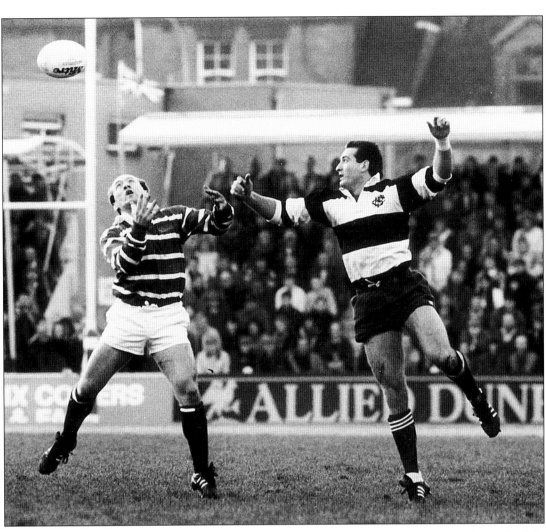

Rory Underwood nor Richards could play, not even Hare's kicking could save Leicester. The Barbarians brought no relief: Campese, the Australian wing and by a distance one of the greatest entertainers in world rugby, did everything except a juggling act and scored one of seven tries in a 36-19 victory, the heaviest loss Leicester had suffered for 14 years.

A pick-me-up was required: it came from two sources, one the unusual direction of Buckingham Palace. The new year's honours included an MBE for William Henry Hare for his contribution to rugby and Hare celebrated in style: on the last day of the old year, at the age of 36, he converted his own try to pass 7,000 career points in a 39-13 victory over Nuneaton. The stage may have been less grandiose than the achievement but he received a wonderful reception from the crowd at the Harry Cleaver Ground and champagne in the dressing room.

The wine, though, went a bit flat in the course of a 28-0 league drubbing by Gloucester and it took the cup - now the Pilkington Cup after a change of sponsorship - to lift Leicester. A 37-6 victory over Liverpool St Helens was just the tonic: three tries for Kardooni but four dropped goals by Cusworth who also scored a try for good measure. For the third successive year Rosslyn Park lay in wait but their challenge petered out in a 23-9 defeat with Richards the rock on which Leicester built.

He and Rory Underwood had taken their by now customary places in England's championship team

Les Cusworth and the remarkable David Campese compete for the ball in the 1988 Barbarians game.

and, after a disappointing draw with Scotland, victories over Ireland and France left them with hope of the championship title. That hope foundered in the rain of Cardiff, though both had done enough to win selection in the British Lions tour party to visit Australia during the summer, under the captaincy of Finlay Calder, the Scottish flanker.

In February a young schools cap, Martin Johnson, made his senior debut at lock against the RAF before deciding to see the world and winding up in New Zealand, where he developed so well that he found a place in their national under-21 side. Leicester, though, were focusing their thoughts on the cup quarter-final with Wasps and were disappointed to discover that a knee injury sustained playing against Ireland would keep Rory Underwood out of it. That, though, let in brother Tony and it was his try that made the difference in a 22-18 win, erasing the memory of the semi-final defeat two seasons earlier.

Cusworth landed two more dropped goals and Hare kicked four penalties in what looked suspiciously like a scripted conclusion to his marvellous career: it was by now common knowledge that Hare was to retire and that added zest to the semi-final against the cup holders, Harlequins, at the Stoop. Sure enough the full back made sure of a finale at Twickenham: not only did he kick a couple of goals he latched on to a cross-kick by Cusworth to score a try in a 16-7 win. Kardooni scored another and Cusworth dropped his 30th cup goal to ensure another meeting with Leicester's Nemesis, Bath.

It was Leicester's sixth final and Bath's fifth and before they reached it Hare had time to pass 400 points in a season for the first time, scoring 17 against Ballymena. Retirement dinners were planned, and eaten, and the opportunity taken to

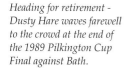

Heading for retirement - Dusty Hare waves farewell to the crowd at the end of the 1989 Pilkington Cup Final against Bath.

welcome Ian Smith to the 300 club in the match with Moseley. Coincidentally, the week before the cup final, Leicester and Bath met in the league, having failed to win permission for the final to count towards both competitions. Since Bath had already won the title and Leicester were comfortably placed in mid-table the result was of little consequence and both clubs fielded second XVs, Leicester winning 15-12.

When it mattered, however, they did not and Hare's magic moment was denied him. The 1989 cup final was a titanic struggle, decided only two minutes from time when a battered and weary Tigers defence finally let Stuart Barnes over for the decisive try. Leicester's team was: W H Hare; B J Evans, P W Dodge (captain), I Bates, R Underwood; L Cusworth, A Kardooni; S B Redfern, T A Thacker, W P Richardson, M V Foulkes-Arnold, T Smith, J M Wells, D Richards, I R Smith. A world record for a club game of 58,000 people packed Twickenham and those from Leicester cheered themselves hoarse when Hare kicked two penalties to give his club the half-time advantage.

The second half was a different story: Bath waxed stronger and stronger up front, with Damian Cronin having a storming game. Barnes kicked a penalty and Leicester, denied possession, could win no relief; a second penalty, with barely 12 minutes left, pulled Bath level and Leicester were like a boxer clinging to the ropes. Barnes's knockout punch, making the score 10-6, came too late for them to organise any kind of rally and Bath recorded English rugby's first double. Hare, with hardly a backward glance, left the scene with a club record of 438 points for the season, 4,507 for Leicester and 7,191 throughout a career which began at 17 and closed nearly twenty years later.

"We owe him a great debt," Cusworth said of his departing colleague. "Without him we would not have been able to play such attractive 15-man rugby over the years. By guaranteeing us, on average, nine points a game, he relieved the pressure, allowed us to relax and play football. There will never be another like him and his record points haul will never be broken. The best tribute I can pay him is that if my life depended on a kick, I'd give it straight to him, no question."

LIFE AFTER HARE
1989-1991

DUSTY Hare having ridden off into the sunset (to re-emerge at various intervals, running the line as a Barbarians committeeman at Christmas until, in 1992, he took up the post of director of rugby at Nottingham, his old club), Rory Underwood and Dean Richards departed for Australia with the Lions. Both players appeared in all three internationals as the Lions won the series 2-1 and Richards would have captained the team in the final match, against an ANZAC XV, but for injury; four years later, against Canterbury in New Zealand, he enjoyed that honour.

Indeed Richards's powerful, mauling play was the bedrock of the Lions success and his combination with Mike Teague, the England flanker, created a momentum that the Australians, in the second and third internationals, found hard to counter. He came home to lead Leicester into a new season: it was a brief flirtation with authority because, in the first league match of the season (at Wasps) Richards damaged his shoulder so badly that it effectively terminated his season, Cusworth taking over the captaincy.

The club, meanwhile, had warmed up for the season with a tour to the USA (during which they played the national team) and now watched with interest to see how Hare's successor at full back would go. It was an unenviable position for John Liley, since invidious comparisons were bound to be made, but in the event he could not have wished for a better first full season. Liley, a swimming pool attendant in Wakefield but who turned to accountancy in Leicester, announced himself with two tries, two conversions and five penalties in an ugly 41-18 win over Pontypridd.

It was the Welsh club's first visit to Leicester since the previous century and, sadly, they lived up to a reputation for violent play which preceded them. Nigel Benzani, their prop, was sent off and Leicester subsequently dropped them from their fixture list. When defeat against Wasps followed, Leicester may have felt that life after Hare was not going to be easy, except that nothing could stop Liley. A genuinely two-footed goal-kicker, Liley's receding hairline even gave him a vague resemblance to Hare and he certainly enjoyed the chance to counter-attack, just like his predecessor.

There were difficulties, too, in keeping three outstanding wings happy: the Underwood brothers and Evans constituted a formidable trio but the last named felt that he was being overlooked too frequently for comfort. Even so the trip to Orrell was a good one to miss: yet again Leicester crashed, this time 33-10, and already their league expectations were looking thin. The situation was not improved when it was discovered that Dodge required an exploratory knee operation, though the question of too many wings was (temporarily) resolved when Tony Underwood broke his jaw playing for the North in the divisional championship.

On the representative front, however, matters were far more satisfactory: Rory Underwood played in Paris when the Lions, reformed on the occasion of the bicentenary of the French Revolution, beat France and when the touring Fijians arrived in England, the wing positively blasted them out of the international with England. He scored five tries in his 34th international, equalling the record set by "Dan" Lambert in 1907 for one match and catching up the 66-year-old record held by Cyril Lowe as England's leading try-scorer with 18. Moreover, to their great delight, the brothers appeared together for the Barbarians at Twickenham in the finale to the New Zealand tour of Wales and Ireland. Although the Baa-baas lost 21-10, Tony Underwood's flair for

Dean Richards in action for the Lions in Australia in 1989.

attack shone so brightly that confident predictions were made that he was ready to follow his brother into the national team.

Leicester as a unit, however, found it hard to put their act together. Kardooni's form had slipped which gave Steve Kenney the chance to play his 350th game against Saracens and there was local criticism when four players - Evans, Ashley Johnson, Tebbutt and Buttimore (the latter two having rejoined the club during the summer) - went to play sevens in Dubai only for three of them to find they were required for the league match with Harlequins. Evans and Buttimore made frantic efforts to return to London in time to play but, inevitably, their indifferent preparation saw Leicester slip to defeat. A fortnight later Harry Roberts left the club, for "business reasons", and joined Richmond (when the two clubs met later in the season Roberts scored Richmond's only try in a 44-12 defeat).

posts with the London divisional side, the new England under-21 side and England Students; indeed those latter two appointments gave him a very good appreciation of the young talent available up and down the country, including a blond flanker from Barkers Butts, Coventry, who played in England's first under-21 international, against Romania - Neil Back.

Russ's role differed from that of Corless in that there was no commercial element involved: "This is the first job which is 100 per cent rugby and there is no-one to look for as a role model," Russ said, accepting that status for himself when he took up his £20,000 position in August 1990. John Allen, stressing the duality of rugby in the nineties, said: "We involve a lot of our members in various sub-committees and we need to retain those people, the same as we need to retain the sort of people who are coaching our teams at the moment. I think it's very important we don't lose those who want to be involved, without thinking of payment. But what we do need is someone whose job it is to prepare a framework, so that when the amateurs come to the club the way has been prepared for them to make their contribution more effective."

Aadel Kardooni launches a rare Tigers attack during the defeat by Cardiff in September 1990.

At least the players emerged from the doldrums to make a point against the Barbarians: Rory Underwood scored two tries in a 32-16 victory, Wells and Thacker vying for the title of man of the match. Indeed it had not been a bad month for Troy Thacker, since he played through the divisional championship: had injury not hindered his career a bright future appeared to lie ahead. Moreover a new, young second-row partnership was settling together: Matt Poole and Alex Gissing, who had won England honours at under-21 and colts level, gave promise of solidity in an area where Leicester had seldom been dominant.

After much debate Leicester decided to take the paid road and advertised for a director of coaching. It was a road which Northampton, their near-neighbours, had already taken when they appointed Barrie Corless, the former England centre, and other clubs, at various levels of the game, were finding it a necessary step, to relieve the amateur administrators of an increasingly onerous burden. It was a major step, partly because the club committee were aware of Leicester's long and proud tradition of self-help and partly because of the sheer economic burden imposed by a salaried official; from the beginning, though, it was made clear that the newcomer would be an adjunct to the existing (unpaid) coaches rather than a replacement.

Three months later Leicester had their man: Tony Russ, 43, a teacher from Thorpe Hall School in Southend but who came from Burton and went to school locally in Ashby-de-la-Zouch. Russ had done wonders as coach to Saracens, his success in earning them promotion to the first division helping him to

Still the club could not get it right in the league so they turned to the cup: Povoas, increasingly effective as Richards' replacement, scored three tries in the 43-3 demolition of London Welsh and then it was Liley's turn to rattle the scoreboard: the full back scored 27 points in the 43-15 win over West Hartlepool in the fourth round. But Leicester faltered at the quarter-final stage at Franklins Gardens: the second-division leaders, Northampton, largely in the person of John Steele, removed them from the competition with a conclusive 23-7 victory.

Although the selectors rang the changes and produced an improved performance in the league against Bristol, Leicester's spirits were not lifted when they lost for only the second time to their northern neighbours, Nottingham. That match was on the eve of the grand-slam decider between Scotland and England at Murrayfield, the result of which must have completed a disastrous weekend

for any fervent Leicester and England supporter.

Up to that point everything had gone so well for England, and Rory Underwood. Expansive wins against Ireland, France and Wales, with the Leicester wing scoring in each match to extend the national try-scoring record; moreover when he played against Wales he became England's most-capped back with 37 and celebrated (despite a dose of 'flu) with two tries. But in Edinburgh the wheels came off the England bus: against an implacable Scottish defence they lost 13-7, a result which had long-term consequences in terms of style and attitude.

Four Barbarian Tigers in the 1990 Mobbs Memorial game. Ian Smith, Simon Povoas, Tony Underwood and captain Les Cusworth.

In a different scoring key, Barry Evans landed five tries in a 70-4 club win against the RAF which erased the post-war try-scoring record of 158 held jointly by Bob Barker and John Duggan and helped carry Evans to a career total of 169 before he left to join Coventry. Liley, too, was closing on Hare's record set only 10 months earlier: 18 points in the 66-12 win over London Scottish (in which Underwood scored five tries) did him no harm and the target was further reduced in substantial wins over Ballymena and Gosforth which helped Leicester to a record points aggregate for the season of 1,109 and Povoas to a record tally for a forward of 25 tries. It is worth recording, too, that the most successful team in the club was the Extras, who lost only once and suggested strength in depth for the future.

Ironically the climax of the season was to come at Bath - Liley required 15 points to pass Hare's 438 and Cusworth bade the game farewell. Few players have been held in greater affection at Leicester than the little balding fly-half: "Over the years he, more than anyone else, has persuaded people to continue supporting the game," Chalkie White said. "If you were in two minds about sitting in front of the television or going to watch Les Cusworth, you'd go to the match. The perfect player doesn't exist and Les's imperfections were conspicuous but also misunderstood. His fingertip tackling left people

wondering who was doing what but his intelligence, his nous, more than compensated."

Dusty Hare, too, paid tribute to Cusworth: "Les has been so important to Leicester because he makes us tick. Apart from, perhaps, Stuart Barnes, he is the only fly-half in England who can take the game by the scruff of the neck and dictate it." In Leicester's final home game of the season, against Gosforth, Kardooni gave Cusworth the final try and he was chaired off; typically Cusworth himself recalled the player with whom he had been so long associated and who was also retiring, Steve Kenney, both of them having played 365 games for the club. They were an alliterative pair, Cusworth and Kenney, both of them with distinct gifts which, happily, were allowed to blossom at Welford Road.

Kenney, a fiery-tempered performer in his youth, was possessed of one of the quickest breaks from scrum-half most people have seen; disappointment matured him and he would surely have played well over 400 games but for the presence at the club of Nick Youngs in the middle 1980s. His unswerving loyalty to Leicester created a great well of sympathy among Leicester members, all of whom were delighted to see it sustained when he was elected to the committee.

Cusworth, meanwhile, received a warm welcome in his final match at Bath though the generosity of the applause did not extend to the result: Bath won 26-15 but Liley got his record by scoring a try (his eighteenth of the season), converting it and kicking three penalties - it carried him to 439 points for the season, a quite outstanding achievement and one which allowed Liley himself to emerge from the long shadow cast by Hare. Indeed his form carried Liley into the England touring team to Argentina in the summer, alongside Tony Underwood and Matt Poole.

Not that it was the happiest of tours for the Tigers trio. The touring party was a mixture of youth and experience since several senior players chose to take the summer off, knowing what 1991 would bring. There were caps to be won but Underwood, plagued by injury at home, could not find his best form away and had a muted trip, being overtaken by Nigel Heslop; Liley, too,

The dynamic Neil Back in action for the Barbarians against an England XV at Twickenham in 1990.

found the step up in class demanding while Poole, as a youngster, was there to learn from such as Wade Dooley and Nigel Redman. The party lurched from one crisis to another, losing four of the seven games and seldom coping with the indifferent local refereeing.

Back in Leicester the club were pondering how best to replace Cusworth, knowing that this was likely to be Paul Dodge's last season. The national divisions of the Courage league had been extended from 12 to 13 clubs and the introduction of the Heineken League in Wales meant considerable adjustment to the fixture list, including the loss of the prized game with Llanelli. At least Richards was fit again to take over the reins of captaincy and the fly-half problem appeared solved when Brian Smith, the talented Australian studying at Oxford University, joined the club: controversy tended to dog Smith, a protege of the former Wallabies coach, Alan Jones, and who played international rugby in every position behind the scrum. Not everyone approved when he was selected for Ireland and even less when, near the end of the season, he chose to accept a rugby league offer with the Sydney club, Balmain, coached by Jones.

The scoreboard tells the story as Leicester beat Bath at the Recreation Ground in the 1990 Pilkington Cup. It was Bath's first home Cup defeat since 1982.

Jez Harris had entertained reasonable hopes of replacing Cusworth but Smith's arrival altered the perspective. Amid a clutch of other newcomers one stood out: Neil Back, who arrived from Barkers Butts via Nottingham with a reputation as one of the fittest flankers in the country. Back seemed destined for the game's top honours: with his distinctive lock of floppy blond hair, his irrepressible energy and ball-handling skills he seemed made for the style of play which was traditionally Leicester's.

In fact, while the Underwoods and Richards played for an England XV in a game designed to celebrate the centenary season of the Barbarians, Back emerged as a replacement for Karl Janik in the Baa-baas back row and almost stole the show in an 18-16 England win. Leicester, for their part, enjoyed a cosmopolitan start to the season with a match against the touring Romanian national side: ten

years earlier they had suffered a rude shock at the hands of the Romanians but this time, though their forwards found themselves struggling, Leicester emerged with a slightly fortuitous 15-12 win thanks to four penalties and a dropped goal by Liley.

Nonetheless the league campaign opened well: Back claimed the headlines as Gloucester were beaten and then Wasps, the 1990 champions, fell 22-12 on their own patch. Victory over Nottingham made it three out of three until Leicester tripped over at the unlikely venue of Roehampton: Rosslyn Park ran up a 17-6 lead and had the strength to hold off a late rally which left Leicester 17-15 losers.

The representative honours were returning too: Argentina, having drawn their series 1-1 with England in the summer, now came for the "return" and lost to an Ireland side containing Smith only to an injury-time penalty. A week later their limitations were underscored by England, who won 51-0, Rory Underwood scoring three tries and Richards returning at No 8. It was a heavy international weekend, for Liley and Evans played in an England 'B' XV which beat Namibia 31-16 at Welford Road (Liley kicking five penalties and two conversions) and, two days later, a different 'B' XV drew 12-12 with an Emerging Australians team at Wasps. Tony Underwood, now at Cambridge University, played on the wing and Back at flanker: "We'd have won if it hadn't been for the little blond guy," Peter Slattery, the Australian captain, said admiringly.

But not even the little blond guy could stop Bath in the league: 9-3, all penalties, may not sound the most entertaining of matches but when these two clubs have met over the last decade, the intensity of the occasion has made for gripping viewing. Bath's forwards took a grip on the game they never relaxed and it would have been a bold man who predicted that, a week later in the Pilkington Cup (a restructuring process of the competition had moved the entry of the first-division clubs in the third round to a pre-Christmas date) at the Bath Recreation Ground, that result would be reversed.

Yet it was, and without Back. A bizarre training accident left him with a back strain while neither of the first-choice wings nor Gissing at lock was available: yet on a filthy day Leicester had the character to put the league result to the back of their minds and remove the holders from the cup competition 12-0. Back's replacement, Rob Tebbutt, played an utterly inspired game and Martin Johnson showed how much his experience in New Zealand had advanced his play in a game which precipitated him into the divisional team; it was the first cup tie Bath had lost at home since 1982. Smith scored the try from a kick-and-chase, and Liley kicked the goals, and Richards was aptly described by Stuart Barnes as not merely a mountain but an entire Himalayan range.

Four other Leicester players joined Johnson in the Midlands team but, sadly, the young lock missed the second half of the season with the recurrence of a shoulder injury. It came as no surprise that the

Barbarians match was sold out well in advance, reflecting a membership now just short of 7,000; the league match with Bath had drawn over 11,000 and at Christmas, with temporary seating at the Welford Road end, 17,500 people were able to watch Leicester (led on the day by Rory Underwood in the absence through injury of Richards) lose 26-21. But there were no post-Christmas blues: when the league resumed in the new year Leicester went to resurgent Northampton and mauled them 28-18, Rory Underwood scoring three tries of which the last was an utter gem, indicative of the confidence and skill with which the England wing was now playing.

Not only Underwood: Kardooni, at scrum-half, had accepted the increased responsibility bequeathed by the retiring Cusworth and was able to carry his team forward with or without the assistance of Smith. The development of young forwards like Johnson and Gissing provoked debate over a new "golden era" for the club, which was promptly squashed when Wasps arrived at Welford Road in the cup and departed with a 15-13 victory. Although Tony Underwood scored the only try of the game Rob Andrew kicked five penalties, the fifth after a controversial decision against the Leicester front row for dropping the scrum - and also after a delay of ten minutes while a spectator in the crowd received treatment after he had collapsed.

Coinciding with news of the death at the age of 71 of the former Leicester and England prop, Bob Stirling, it made a gloomy weekend for the club. There was some comfort in that Liley and Back were regulars for England 'B' for much of the season and that England, with Rory Underwood and Richards to the fore, should be progressing towards a grand slam. Given the rock of Simon Hodgkinson's place kicking, England disposed of Wales and Scotland but needed all the steadying influence of Richards and a quite brilliantly taken try by Underwood to beat the fighting Irish in Dublin. The outcome rested on the final match with the other unbeaten country, France, and to the unrelieved joy of players, management and supporters, England won 21-19.

The French scored three tries, one of them from their own goal-line qualifying as the try of this or any other tournament, but England offered traditional qualities of organisation and determination, embellished by Hodgkinson's goal-kicking and another try by Underwood.

Leicester still hoped for an impact on the Courage league but narrow defeats against Bristol and Harlequins terminated such optimism; in between

Dusty Hare returns as the Barbarian touch judge in 1990.

those games they also lost Smith to rugby league amid a shower of recrimination from Ireland who had hoped to build their World Cup back division around him. Smith's time at Welford Road had been brief; quite unlike Paul Dodge who played his 436th and what was intended to be his final game for the club in a 43-19 victory at Moseley, alongside old friends in Ian Smith and Malcolm Foulkes-Arnold who were also retiring.

At 33 Dodge had been afflicted by a variety of injuries over the previous three years, perhaps the body's way of reminding him that he had been playing first-class rugby since he was 17 and that it was time for a rest. Chalkie White called him 'Colossus'. Peter Wheeler, recalling his own disappointment when he was omitted from the 1983 Lions, described how he went down to training at Leicester after the fateful announcement and found Dodge - whose disappointment at his treatment must have equalled Wheeler's - there before him, as industrious as ever: "He was 25, at the peak of his career," Wheeler said. "The tour would have been just right for him; he deserved to go far more than I because he was so far ahead of the rivals for his position in terms of ability, compared with my own situation. He was training faithfully: Mr Reliable."

'Alas Smith and Dodge!'
Ian Smith and Paul Dodge in 1991, the coach and assistant for a new Tigers generation.

It is not exaggerating to say that, at his peak, Dodge could do it all: that he scored his 93rd try in his final match speaks volumes for his ability as a strike force in the centre but it was the service he gave his wings that marked him out. If he became known in representative circles for the length of his left-footed kicking, that is not how his club colleagues saw him. His timing of the pass, his tackling and midfield organisation stamped him as a player of uncommon class. But as well as being a quality player he was a thoroughly likeable man: journalists found him difficult to talk to because he never enjoyed discussing himself but his ability to analyse a game is now being gently drawn out as assistant coach to Ian Smith. In these two Leicester recognised more gems of complementary ability and had no hesitation in using them.

BACK TO THE FUTURE
1991-1993

WITH the retirement of Paul Dodge, the last link with the Leicester of the 1970s, with those early cup finals, had been severed. The 1990s are new-age, hi-tec, computer-based, business-orientated: they are faster, fitter, more time-consuming than ever and clubs are finding themselves running just to maintain a place among the elite. League rugby had ensured a place in the sun for some while other, famous names have found themselves floundering - London Welsh, for example, descending to area league status, Coventry and Richmond and Blackheath struggling and eventually failing to save themselves from third-division rugby.

Leicester had cause to look back to the mid-1970s and their own internal reorganisation and be grateful, for the foresight of their administrators and the devotion of those who succeeded them. Nor was their vision blurred: in 1991 Leicester decided the time was ripe to drop the Swifts, their third team, and replace it with an under-21 team to bridge the gap more effectively between youth and senior rugby. Steve Solomons, a full back with the club during the 1970s, returned from a successful coaching spell with Vipers to help run the under-21s and Dodge had scarcely retired before he was coaxed back to help.

Then there was the World Cup. Leicester had long known that they were to host one of the pool games during the 1991 tournament, the first full international to be played on the ground since 1923, but the price for clubs up and down the country during the first two months of the new season was a collapse in interest while the drama and spectacle of the World Cup swept the country. Leicester had sent a squad on tour to Canada to get themselves in shape and youngsters like Graham Rowntree - who had made his debut at prop against Oxford University the previous season - Laurence Boyle and Richard Wareham all found first-team places in the opening match against Bedford.

Meanwhile the World Cup rolled into the country. England, with Rory Underwood and Dean Richards, had prepared by touring Australia and Fiji during the summer, without conspicuous success. Those preparations were sustained in matches during September against the USSR, Gloucester and England Students before the event itself got under way with defeat in the opening match against New Zealand. It was the All Blacks, too, who came to Leicester to play Italy in a Pool One match of a competition spread throughout the four home unions and France: nor did they find life easy, the Italians scoring three tries against four and losing only 31-21 as it became apparent that the inaugural winners of the World Cup were not at their best.

England marched forward to the quarter-finals by beating the USA and Italy but, against France in Paris, sprang a shock of seismic proportions (in Leicester anyway) by dropping Richards. "Dean has been struggling to find his form, he knows he has not come up with the goods," Geoff Cooke, the team manager, said though he admitted it was one of the most difficult decisions he had ever taken. Richards, keeping his own counsel as usual, accepted the disappointment and got on with a tournament which he never claimed to enjoy unduly: a total rugby environment was not what he yearned for and the concept of touring in his own country seemed unnatural.

Even so England could claim the move was justified; they beat the French, Underwood led out the side in the semi-final against Scotland to mark his fiftieth cap and success at Murrayfield took England to the World Cup final with a back row of Peter Winterbottom, Mickey Skinner and Mike Teague at No 8. That they subsequently failed to beat Australia was due in part to the high quality of their opponents but also a failure to mix their tactics effectively and it was impossible not to wonder whether Richards' presence might have afforded a calming influence amid the helter-skelter style which won many friends but which was the complete antithesis of the means by which they had reached Twickenham.

At least dropping Richards left him raring for rugby with his mates when the World Cup ended. Leicester needed him: their start had been unimpressive, attention apparently elsewhere and disrupted during October by the divisional championship which the Midlands, with half a dozen Leicester men (among them Steve Hackney, the former Nottingham wing), won. The club sought support from local business too, in the vital matter of recruitment of players, while John Wells, the new captain, and Ian Smith, the new coach, struggled to find a pattern of play which would work once league rugby resumed in November: five defeats in nine games was not the stuff of champions, with Smith having to emerge from retirement (and not long after a bad car accident) against Sale when Neil Back missed the coach. Since Smith scored a try in the 12-9 defeat he may have wondered whether his retirement was not premature.

The Tuesday following the World Cup final Richards was back in action, against Cambridge University. Underwood, sated with the preparation that modern rugby requires (as he admitted in his autobiography, *"Flying Wing"*, published the following year) took longer to return to action but was happy to be among the scorers in the second league match of the season, a win over Wasps, during which Jez Harris dropped three goals. With the Pilkington Cup calling, Leicester beat Fylde 34-6 and when Tony Underwood scored a critical try to help Cambridge beat Oxford at Twickenham and Back joined Richards and Rory Underwood in the five nations championship England squad, the future looked brighter.

Indeed, as if to emphasise that, seven Leicester players were named in an England development squad. Tony Underwood and Back took up semi-permanent residence in the England 'B' team during the new year and Tigers even went to the top of the league table when they beat London Irish. It was, though, a false dawn: reality hit home when Bath demolished Leicester's pretensions 37-6, a hard debut for Gerry Ainscough, a recent recruit from Orrell and favoured ahead of Jez Harris.

In the old year Mickey Steele-Bodger, president of the Barbarians, officially opened the Barbarians Room, reserved for sponsors in the new addition to the clubhouse but also a showcase for the club's collection of memorabilia. In the new year Leicester found that, try as they might, no fresh items were likely to find their way to the new facility: they worked their way past Waterloo and Newcastle Gosforth (as their old friends from the north-east were now called) in the cup only to founder against Harlequins at the Stoop.

In the league they were consistent only in their inconsistency: Orrell's victory ensured no prospect of the title and though Bristol were beaten, the occasion was soured by accusations from Back that he had been gouged in the eyes. They promptly lost to Harlequins a week before the cup semi-final, and lost the services for that cup match of Kardooni through a knee injury. It was some consolation that Richards was able to get back from playing in a ten-a-side tournament in Hong Kong for the cup game but he was clearly carrying an injury and left the field during a contest dominated by David Pears, the Harlequins fly-half, who scored all their points in a 15-9 win.

was required against the French, that match in Paris marred by the dismissal of two French forwards. Underwood scored his 35th international try and was looking for a full hand of tries in every championship game against the Welsh but though England won 24-0 to clinch a second successive grand slam, the wing could not do it.

That was a source of keen regret because Underwood had decided to retire from the international game, at the age of 28, in the interests of his family and his flying career. Indeed he announced as much on the day of the game, only to undergo a change of heart during the summer - the first rest he (and other England players) had enjoyed from the game since the summer of 1990. Six months later came the announcement that Underwood senior remained very much in the running to extend both his record number of England caps and tries.

However, speculation about his future and that of Richards - who was said to be losing his appetite for the international game - served as an unwanted distraction for Leicester during their league programme. Three days after their cup semi-final they lost a mighty battle with Northampton 22-19 but that game served to demonstrate the character

John Wells in action for an England XV against Italy at Rovigo in May 1990.

Still, it had not been a bad season for Richards as an individual. He started the five nations championship as a replacement but emerged in the second half against Scotland when Tim Rodber was injured to play a critical role in England's 25-7 win - an occasion marked for Rory Underwood by his first try against the Scots. Rodber returned against Ireland but it was the durability of Richards that

and resilience at the club as a back division of Liley, Hackney, Key, Boyle, Tony Underwood, Harris and Darren Grewcock could scarcely have played better. Four days later they were able to relax and, for the first time in their history, scored 100 points in a match: the unfortunate contributors to the Leicester record book at Welford Road were Liverpool St Helens, against a Tigers team at something like half-

strength. Tony Underwood scored six tries, failing by one to equal Alistair Smallwood's achievement against Manchester seventy years earlier; in all they registered 19 tries, equalling another record, and Ainscough scored 26 points.

The end of a season so demanding that Wells, the captain, questioned the place of a two-match Easter programme, arrived with nothing tangible to show for it: even in the national sevens at Bath, Leicester had to settle for runners-up and two splendid servants in the front row, Stuart Redfern and Chris Tressler, announced their retirement after 324 and 264 games respectively. Significantly both cited the demands made by the game on their business and family as reasons for finishing at, for tight forwards, relatively young ages.

Not that it was over for some, since Tony Underwood, Back, Hackney and Kardooni were chosen to tour New Zealand with England 'B'; Johnson would have gone too but for his shoulder injury which required yet another operation. All four of them played in the two games against a New Zealand XV and Kardooni responded splendidly to the workload thrown at him after an injury to the party's other scrum-half, Dave Scully from Wakefield. Underwood junior at last offered convincing proof that he had thrown off all the doubts that had arisen about his capabilities when he toured Argentina with the senior side in 1990; so well did he play that the New Zealand rugby almanack elected him one of their five players of the year, a rare honour for a northern-hemisphere player.

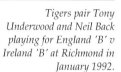

Tigers pair Tony Underwood and Neil Back playing for England 'B' v Ireland 'B' at Richmond in January 1992.

Graham Rowntree and Steve Wills both played for England's under-21 team and Boyle played in the students world cup in Italy for an England side now coached by Les Cusworth. So many honours for so many young players was encouraging, as was the form of the youth team who lost only four games and who were a credit to Paul Stone, coach for the final season before moving on to Nuneaton as senior coach. Despite a mid-season financial hiatus caused by the weather, the club's profit on the season was an outstanding £109,000 and membership, far and away the biggest in England, stood at 7,400 and rising; moreover Ansells were happy to renew their sponsorship of the club for a further five-year period, a deal worth in excess of £180,000.

Yet all the time Leicester were aware, as were so many others, of strains to come: new laws, including a five-point try, were approved for the 1992-93 season and a home-and-away league formula had been approved by the Senior Clubs Association for 1993-94. It was not a formula with which John Allen, for one, concurred: Leicester had voted for eight-club national divisions but ten clubs were agreed, thereby creating a league season of 18 matches rather than 14. "You'll have 18 league games; with a good cup run that becomes 24. Take three divisional matches, five internationals, that's 32. A couple of squad weekends leaves only one spare Saturday. There's no way some of these lads are going to go through

John Liley

Action from the Pilkington Cup semi-final defeat against Harlequins at the Stoop in April 1992.

relieve the main pitch at Welford Road. Oadby Wyggs remained there but the ground, with extended clubhouse, floodlights and regraded pitches, was renamed Oval Park and was officially inaugurated in December with a match between the Droglites, the old Tigers XV, and a Rugby Union Writers' Club XV; given the imbalance in the scoreline in favour of the Droglites perhaps the word "match" is a misnomer but the players seemed happy to have put one across the journalists. The writers, too, were happy that the old weights room under the Crumbie Stand had been converted into a press working area while at the far end of the ground, in the clubhouse, the Tiger Room was opened as an illustrated record of differing stages in the club's development. To enjoy the

the whole season doing that. With these extra six games, clubs are going to have to look very carefully at how they use players." Allen pointed out, too, that bad weather could throw the whole competitive programme into confusion.

A more pressing problem for Leicester was to find a fitting way to celebrate 100 years of rugby at Welford Road: the club's answer was to host a morning of rugby for youngsters, in conjunction with Tim Wood, the county's youth development officer, and a match against England the same day. This was followed by a midweek meeting with Leicestershire (commemorating that other match against the county 100 years earlier) and a glamorous encounter with Mediolanum Milan, the Italian club side to which those two remarkable Australian players, David Campese and Mark Ella, belonged.

Fittingly Leicester seemed on the verge of a new era: several youngsters had already made their mark and more arrived during the summer (though one famous name, Craig Chalmers, the Scotland and British Lions fly half, did not). Richard Cockerill, the England under-21 hooker, joined from Coventry, Stuart Potter and Wayne Kilford, centre and full back respectively, from Nottingham. Ainscough returned to Orrell but Richards had recovered from Achilles tendon trouble and was (comparatively) happy to fill in at second row while Johnson recovered fully from his shoulder operation.

Moreover a new facility was opened at Wigston Road, Oadby: Leicester had invested over £400,000 in a new training ground, the playing area used by the Oadby Wyggestonian club, to

future it is worth being aware of the past. With such heavy expenditure it was no wonder that the club announced a three-year contract with the local insurance and sports marketing firm, P & G Bland, to act as its commercial advisors: Roy Jackson, who had done so well for several seasons as Leicester's commercial manager on a part-time basis was being overwhelmed by the volume of work and a call for professional assistance was inevitable. That the new advisors had as a managing director Peter Wheeler and included Les Cusworth, Graham Rowntree and Steve Hackney among their employees kept the appointment within, as it were, the family.

England, with pre-Christmas internationals against Canada and South Africa to come, were happy to warm-up against Leicester but deprived the club of two key players, Back and Tony Underwood, by choosing them in white: Leicester had very adequate replacements in Hackney and Nigel Richardson, the young Loughborough University captain and flanker, and it was Hackney

LEICESTER FOOTBALL CLUB
OFFICIAL OPENING OF OVAL PARK
Their New Training Complex

With a Grand Charity Match
DROGLITES (Old Tigers) v THE RUGBY WRITERS CLUB
Sunday 6th December 1992 – K.O. 2.00pm
at Oval Park, Wigston Road, Oadby
All Proceeds to The Cardiothoracic Unit, Glenfield Hospital – the charity of the Lord Mayor of Oadby & Wigston Borough
SOUVENIR PROGRAMME £1.00

who scored their try in an 18-11 defeat whose somewhat scruffy nature did not quite do justice to the occasion. The new ruck-maul laws and a propensity for kicking dominated post-match discussion: England, shaking the rust out of their system, scored two tries through Nigel Heslop, the Orrell wing who later in the season went to rugby league, with Jonathan Webb kicking a conversion and a penalty and Rob Andrew dropping a goal. Liley added a couple of penalties to Hackney's try and it was generally felt that the best feature of Leicester's game was their spritely front row of Rowntree, Cockerill and Darren Garforth, the tight-head prop who

had joined the previous season from Nuneaton. However, the game cost them the services of Back who departed with a damaged shoulder.

Something close to an Extras XV beat Leicestershire 40-20 before the arrival of Milan, littered with Italian and Argentinian internationals (though without Campese who was still in Australia). This was by far the best of the ground centenary games, full of vivid passages of play: Leicester won 40-24, Liley converting all four tries and kicking four penalties, and the positive sides of the new laws could be seen to better advantage, emphasising the need for constant support and greater thought in tactical kicking.

The party over, the serious business of league rugby began in a season complicated not only by new laws but by a restructuring of the national divisions themselves. Agreement on home-and-away for 1993-94 meant a reduction in the size of the national divisions, from 13 clubs to ten: four clubs were to be relegated from the first division, seven from the second division and eight from the third to form a new fourth division. It was almost a case that, if you were not sitting at or near the top of your division, you were in danger of going down: Gloucester, for example, spent much of the season fending off relegation but concluded the season in fifth position.

Leicester began well enough, beating London Irish and Gloucester (if only by a point in a game where Gloucester played with 14 men after the dismissal of the flanker, Paul Ashmead). But a one-point defeat at Wasps was discouraging, despite the return of

Back, and it took Tony Underwood to lift the club, with a gem of a try against West Hartlepool and selection for his first England appearance, against Canada at Wembley (Twickenham's East Stand was being rebuilt at the time). Although brother Rory had announced his comeback he was not available for this game but Richards, too, won selection despite less than amiable noises coming from him about life in the second row.

As it happened it was Richards's only international of the season; England's most-capped No 8 was overlooked in favour of Bath's Ben Clarke in subsequent internationals, as England concluded they needed greater pace and height from their back row. Richards's nose for the ball, mauling strength (particularly relevant under the new laws) and sheer experience were not enough for England, though curiously they were welcomed when the British Lions sat down to choose their team to visit New Zealand in 1993. Not that Richards himself much favoured the new law: "You can't control a game any more," he said. "The law helps a small, or less-skilled, side disrupt a game."

The Midlands, too, had confidence in the No 8 and asked him to captain the side against the South Africans at Welford Road on November 4. These South Africans, captained by 'Naas' Botha, were the first to make a major tour since 1981, and the first to visit Britain since the 1969-70 season which had been so disrupted by political demonstrations. They arrived in England from France, where they had not enjoyed themselves even though they shared the two-match international series; having been absent

Alex Gissing during Leicester's record 37-6 defeat in the Courage League versus Bath in January 1992.

from world rugby for 11 years they were understandably rusty and short of confidence.

Not that it showed in a 32-9 win over the Midlands who fielded the following team: J G Liley; S T Hackney, I Bates, S Potter (all Leicester), H S Thorneycroft; J Steele (both Northampton), A Kardooni (Leicester); M S Linnett (Moseley), C J Olver, G S Pearce, M C Bayfield (all Northampton), M O Johnson (Leicester), P Shillingford (Moseley), D Richards (Leicester, captain), R S Tebbutt (Northampton). That selection was influenced by a hand injury to John Wells and the absence of three players, including Back, who were due to appear three days later for England 'B' against the touring team but the South Africans, with the local knowledge provided by Harry Roberts - now their number two hooker - were clearly happy to be in England where the food and the language was more familiar.

They dominated the line-out, if not the loose ball, and the Midlands offered no cutting edge in midfield; even when they did find space they ran into an unforgiving defence. Liley kicked two penalties (but missed five others) and John Steele a dropped goal but the South Africans responded with two tries from 'Faffa' Knoetze, the little centre, one from his burly partner, Danie Gerber, and a fourth by Deon Oosthuysen, the wing. Botha kicked three conversions and two penalties to complete a sound night's work, and his team was even happier after beating England B at Bristol 20-16 in a splendid match, during which Tony Underwood scored a try.

A week later the South Africans received their come-uppance at Twickenham: for the first time since 1938 England fielded brothers, Rory on the left wing and Tony (who replaced the injured Ian Hunter of Northampton) on the right. Although the tourists led 16-11 at one stage they were outclassed in the second half at a dank and gloomy Twickenham, illuminated by the glee with which Rory fielded a fly hack and acted as pivot for his brother to score his first international try. Victory by 33-16 suggested, falsely as it turned out, that England were on the verge of another distinguished championship season.

Talking of false dawns, Leicester were perched on top of the first division by virtue of having played one more game than unbeaten Wasps. After their meeting with Bath, however, they had slithered back to third, over 10,000 people at a rain-drenched Welford Road watching Bath win 13-3 on their way to yet another league title. Neither Richards nor Wells was fit for the match which hardly came at an ideal time: the week before the third round of the Pilkington Cup, in which Leicester were due to play London Scottish at Richmond Athletic ground.

As it happened Leicester came through 20-11 on a weekend when five former cup holders (among them Bath at Waterloo) lost. It was not their most disciplined game but a huge advantage at the line-out by Johnson and Poole paved the way for victory in which Hackney and Liley scored tries with Liley kicking two conversions and a penalty and Harris, with what was to become something of a trademark, dropped a goal. Although he had been with the club the better part of 12 years this was Harris's first full season at fly-half and the Market Harborough boat builder made every game count.

Leicester's form projected eight players, including Potter and Garforth, into the Midlands divisional team but club glee was tempered by the announcement of England's training squad to go to Lanzarote and prepare for the five nations. The Underwoods were included, as was Johnson, but no Back nor Richards (who was said to be unavailable). The omission of Neil Back provoked huge ire; it appeared that his footballing qualities were overlooked because of his lack of inches. At 5ft 10in Back was deemed too short for the highest reaches of the game; that he could play international rugby was not in question but against the best in the world England felt they had to find a new model at open-side flanker, pencilling in such players as Steve Ojomoh from Bath or Justyn Cassell from Saracens, both of them well over 6ft.

"It is becoming harder for the good little 'un to survive at the highest level," Geoff Cooke, England's manager, said. "I think Back could play for England in several games and do very well. We are not discarding him but we are looking at a different way forward. He plays right to the edge of his game and it is unfortunate for him the way we are viewing it at the moment." Tony Russ described the decision as "appalling" and Back himself offered the view that his size was an advantage in that he was more agile at playing the ball on the ground than bigger men.

The argument rumbled on most of the season, with fuel added to the debate when Back was omitted from the England 'A' side (as England 'B' had now become) midway through the representative season. Predictably both Back and Richards played marvellously in a 41-23 victory over the Barbarians, during which Rory Underwood continued to demonstrate a broader vision for the game - in defence as well as attack - than at any previous time in his career.

A new year, fresh plans. Leicester unveiled a long-term project to transform their ground, taking into account the boom that rugby was enjoying and the likely increase in interest for league rugby. "We have to look to the future and develop the ground, which again will benefit players and members," said Graham Willars, now the club president. That a rugby club could contemplate developments costing over £1m, thereby increasing capacity to 25,000 - quite like the old, between-the-war days - was a sign of the times.

It was a sign of what was to come, too, when the league season resumed with a 13-12 win over Northampton at Franklins Gardens. Both clubs had to win to have any chance of keeping pace with the league leaders, Wasps and Bath, and for an hour Northampton looked likely to carry all before them; but in the final quarter the game was turned on its head and, in injury-time, Back scored the try which allowed Liley to win the game with the conversion. A resolute character was growing within the Leicester team which, though it lacked the maturity to make a convincing challenge for the league title this season, was to come to the fore in the cup.

International rugby returned to Welford Road with the 'A' match between England and France, in which Tony Underwood, Back and Johnson were due to play. But, on the morning of the match, Johnson was required to up sticks and join the full England team at Richmond: Wade Dooley had

John Wells drives on against London Irish in 1992.

pulled out of the game with France because of a thigh strain and Johnson, at 22, was to win his first cap at Twickenham. It was a wonderful moment for his family: his great grandfather had been an amateur football international and his mother, Hilary, was an international ultra-distance runner.

His colleagues looked after the 'A' team, Underwood scoring in a 29-17 win, and Johnson helped look after the senior French team: although he had taken no part in the main squad practices, he grew into the match and became a significant influence in the line-out in the second half as England grasped a slim 16-15 win. Although Dooley returned for the final three internationals of the season it was a performance which interested the Lions selectors. Johnson spent the rest of the season playing for England 'A' where he was joined against a weak Italian side by Underwood, Potter and Back (all of whom scored two tries apiece); although Back was dropped for the games with Spain and Ireland, Garforth stepped up a level too.

Would that the rest of the international season had been as successful for England's championship side. Rory Underwood kept his place although there were calls for his head after a disastrous error of judgement let in Ieuan Evans for the decisive try against Wales. Instead the selectors dropped Rob Andrew and Ian Hunter and called in Stuart Barnes and Tony Underwood for the games against Scotland and Ireland; the first was a triumph, in which both Underwoods scored and their mother, Annie, was seen on television by the nation performing a jig of triumph in the West Stand at Twickenham. The second was a palpable disaster as Ireland swept what could only be described as an ageing England away 17-3.

Leicester's cup campaign was going far better. The visit to Beeston, where Dusty Hare was hard at work bracing his Nottingham charges for the fray (though seven months later Hare and Nottingham parted company), ended with a 28-3 win in which the Underwoods and Back scored tries and Liley kicked

Tony Underwood playing for an England XV against Leicester in 1992.

the goals. In the quarter-finals Exeter, from the third division, were summarily dismissed 76-0; Tony Underwood scored three tries, Richards and Liley two, with Povoas, Back, Cockerill, Potter, Grewcock and Rory Underwood all contributing tries. Though he also kicked 14 points Liley missed nine conversions and the chance of a cup record.

The league may have brought diversions - victory over Orrell (welcome), inglorious defeat at Bristol, dismissal of a below-strength Harlequins - but the scent of Twickenham was strong in the air. For three Leicester players, too, the scent of New Zealand was equally strong: the Lions named a party in March that included both the Underwoods and, for all the ups and downs of the previous 18 months, Dean Richards. At one stage Richards had seemed out of the running, a clerical error having delayed his availability card from the Rugby Football Union. But the hand of Ian McGeechan, the Scottish coach, could be seen in the selection which brought together 13 of the players who had worked so hard for him in Australia in 1989. For Leicester it was the second time that three players from the club had reached this apogee of British rugby, following in the steps of Wheeler, Woodward and Dodge in 1980.

Moreover five further players - Back, Garforth, Hackney, Johnson and

Rowntree - were chosen by England to tour Canada in May, an important staging post in the development of a side for the 1995 World Cup in South Africa and where they were subsequently joined by Potter. It was apt recognition of the club's achievements and, as important, development of players as individuals. For those who missed representative honours there was a tour to come too: Tony Russ had been hard at work organising a five-match club trip to South Africa in August 1993, including games against development teams in Cape Town and Durban.

First, though, there was the little matter of the cup and Northampton in the semi-final. Leicester were not entirely happy that the game at Welford Road was to be televised live because of a lack of consultation and the precedent set but there were few fears about the effect on the crowd: for the first time in the history of the cup the game was sold out. And by half-time the tie was, effectively, over. Leicester led 23-3 with a performance which any of their great sides of the past would have been proud of. That they could not sustain it in the second half was no surprise but the yawning 28-6 margin surprised all who expected a repeat of the tense league match. Northampton wanted to reach Twickenham for the sake of Wayne Shelford, their New Zealand No 8 in his last season with them but they were out-run, out-fought and out-thought. Richards, Back and Laurence Boyle (the replacement for Liley) scored tries, two of them converted by Liley who also landed two penalties while Harris, across a swirling wind, dropped a lovely goal.

Their opponents in the final at Twickenham on May 1 were Harlequins, victors over Wasps in their semi-final. It was to be the last game for the London club of Peter Winterbottom, that marvellously consistent England flanker into whose shoes Back was trying so desperately to step. Winterbottom's position was one Leicester knew well, from the 1989 final in which Hare played - not that they were more sympathetic as a result. Their major concern was that Back and Poole should have recovered from injury and that Kardooni's grumbling appendix would settle down; on a broader front Leicester were dismayed that there should be as few as 14,500 tickets available from the Rugby Football Union, who admitted their error in selling their portion of tickets before the two finalists were known. From past experience Leicester were confident of selling upwards of 20,000 tickets for a stadium reduced in capacity to 56,500.

Come the day all those places were taken and on a warm, hazy May Day Leicester fielded the following team in their seventh final: J G Liley; T Underwood, I Bates, S Potter, R Underwood; J C Harris, A Kardooni; G C Rowntree, R Cockerill, D J Garforth, M O Johnson, M D Poole, J M Wells (captain), D Richards, N A Back. Harlequins, their form uneven throughout the season, were without the injured David Pears (as they had been all season) and chose not to play Andrew Harriman, the once-capped wing who had led England to victory in the World Cup sevens in Edinburgh a fortnight earlier. On the morning of the match Brian Moore, the England hooker, withdrew with a groin strain, which was a psychological blow as well as upsetting to their set-piece play.

Dean Richards in the thick of the action during the stirring 1993 Pilkington Cup semi-final victory over rivals Northampton. Tigers won 28-6.

To say the quality of a final which Leicester won 23-16 was not that of their two losing finals, in 1983 and 1989, is as much a commentary on a long and demanding season as anything. Not that that mattered to Leicester: the cup was back and, in the long term, an important step had been taken in the maturing of a side for the 1990s. "We have a group of young players who have gained a vast amount of experience in a short time," Ian Smith said. "On this performance they have a long way to go. The side lacks a degree of consistency....when we have that we can challenge the best in the country." Since in Smith and Dodge - who had become assistant coach during the season - Leicester had an equally young pair of coaches, the two sides of the game seemed well-matched.

Both teams might have preferred a running game: neither produced one, partly because control of the ball was difficult, partly because of the quality of the defences. Harlequins took the initiative through Rob Glenister's try from a ruck, converted by Paul Challinor, but Leicester promptly levelled through a wonderful attacking excursion by Liley. The full back veered out of his own half and, from the ruck,

Harris and Back sent Potter dummying through the shredded defence for a try which outshone anything else during the afternoon.

Liley converted but Leicester had still to play catch-up rugby when Challinor kicked the first of three penalties. Harris provided a timely dropped goal but Harlequins still led 13-10 at the interval before Liley levelled matters again with a penalty. Ten minutes of the second half had passed before Back kicked a splendid diagonal ball into the north-east corner and when Leicester took a free kick, three dummy runs left space for Johnson to thunder through to the line for a try converted by Liley. But, with Harlequins forwards growing in strength, Leicester could not confirm their lead: Challinor kicked a third goal and Chris Madderson, their young wing, went on a long and powerful run before Liley chipped over a close-range penalty in injury-time.

Wells, who nearly missed the game because of a thigh strain, received the cup amid great enthusiasm and then went on to dismiss comparisons with previous cup-winning sides. He was right to do so: this Leicester team was, and is, a product of its time,

Martin Johnson thunders over to claim the winning try in the 1993 Pilkington Cup Final against Harlequins.

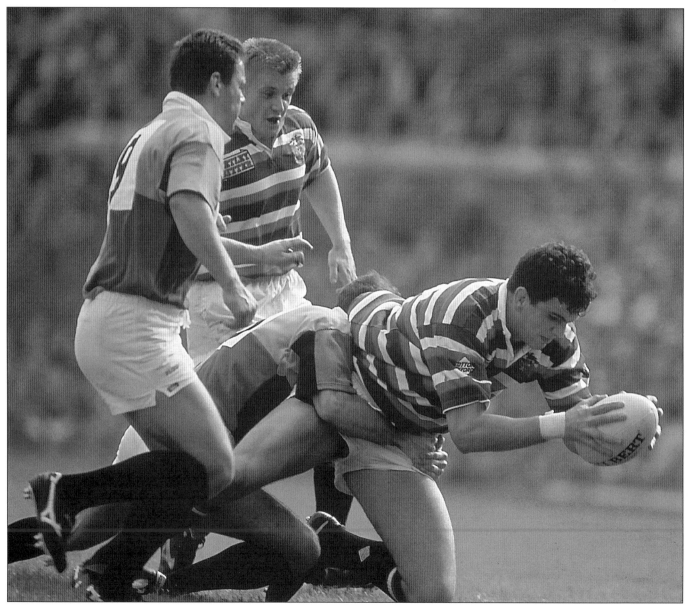

not to be compared with conditions in which the Cowlings and Woodwards, the Wheelers and Cusworths, had plied their trade. But the new-age Tigers have also sprung from a long and distinguished line; they are merely proud inheritors of a mighty tradition, to which they can bring their own particular honours.

There were postscripts to the season: in these hectic days of world-wide rugby, there always are but one was a sad occasion for the club: during the summer Tom Berry died aged 82. He had played for his country, chaired the national selectors, managed England overseas and presided over the Rugby Football Union. His work for Leicester has been sustained by his sons, as players and administrators, a family connection for which the Tigers have long been grateful.

Meanwhile the Lions left for New Zealand while England's 'A' team headed for Canada and England's under-21 team, who included the young Leicester hooker, Chris Johnson, prepared to visit Australia. All three touring sides came away with a mixed bag of results: England, including Rowntree, Martin Johnson, Back and the newly-arrived Potter, contrived to lose the first of their games with Canada 15-12 before girding their loins and winning the second game more easily than the 19-14 result suggests.

Scarcely was Johnson off the field than he heard he was required by the Lions as a replacement for Wade Dooley, who returned home because of the death of his father. Some more-or-less continuous 56 hours of travelling later he was in New Zealand's South Island and was even spoken of as a possibility for the imminent first Test in Christchurch as doubts remained about the fitness of Martin Bayfield: in the event Bayfield played in the 20-18 defeat by the All Blacks, as did Richards and Rory Underwood. Both the Underwood brothers had been in spritely form early in the tour but so was Ieuan Evans, the Welsh wing; his experience deservedly brought him the Test place ahead of Tony Underwood, whose tour declined in a midweek XV considerably inferior at forward to the Test combination.

In direct contrast, Johnson's year grew better and better: a good display against Taranaki, then against Auckland, hoisted him into Test contention and he joined Bayfield in the second row for the match in Wellington by which the Lions tour stood or fell. In the event it stood, the two Midland locks proving a decisive factor in the 20-7 victory, the biggest ever by a Lions team over New Zealand. Moreover Rory Underwood scored the Lions' try, a dazzling 40-metre effort in which he flashed past John Kirwan and beat the cover into the corner, effectively putting the match out of reach. But victory in the series was not to be: the three Leicester players retained their places for the deciding game in Auckland but this time the desperate desire was with the All Blacks, who won 30-13. The Lions were left with a mediocre record of won seven, lost six, the Underwood brothers contributing five tries (Rory three, Tony two) to the statistics and Richards one.

But the tour did serve to point the way for a promising young England team in 1993-94, in which Leicester players seem sure to play a key role. The national under-21 team added to that feeling when, with Chris Johnson hooking, they concluded their visit to Australia with a 22-12 win in Sydney over an Australian team including one senior cap and several with experience at state level.

The benefits gained by two-thirds of a Leicester team on national tours, added to the preparations which the club's August tour of South Africa permitted, ensured that the club began 1993-94 in good heart under the captaincy of Dean Richards. It is a season which threatens to be the most demanding yet in competitive terms for English club players: "With the advent of the home-and-away [league] system of 18 games next season, it [is] important to strengthen the squad of players to provide cover," John Allen told the club's annual meeting in June. He added: "It is important and significant that players wish to join to play good rugby and to improve their own skills," facets of the game which have always loomed large at Leicester.

During the summer an all-weather surface was added to the facilities at Oval Park in Oadby and the club's officials, paid and unpaid - that balance of professional and amateur which is so hard to achieve in a game so firmly rooted in the past - prepared for another season of sustained public interest amid the spotlight which an increasingly inquisitive media invariably holds over the cup holders. There are few challenges which Leicester have not met in their distinguished history; it is hard not to believe that they will do so again.

A WHO'S WHO OF CELEBRATED TIGERS

It would not be possible to profile here all of the 1,897 men who have pulled on a Tigers jersey (an alphabetical index is at the back of this section), we have therefore chosen to focus on 227 of these players under the title of "Celebrated Tigers". As we are then forced to have a selection criteria the most equitable way seemed to be on a purely statistical basis, thus allowing a cross-section of players to be profiled from all eras. Therefore qualification is either to have played in 100 or more first-class Tigers fixtures, or be an international player for any country who has played for the Tigers more than ten times. Of course this excludes prominent players such as Arthur Hazlerigg and Dave Whibley, and many players who had a large part of their careers disrupted by the wars, but unfortunately the line for inclusion had to be drawn somewhere. One good point is that Matt Poole made his 100th appearance in the first game of the 1993-4 season, and although is strictly speaking out of the scope of this volume, he has been included.

Entries are listed in alphabetical order; those of the same surname are listed in order of their initials, not their first forenames. Where all relevant details are known, each "Celebrated Tiger" entry is keyed as per the following example:

SURNAME, FORENAME(S): *Note: The forenames given are those on their birth registration, if a player later adopted an additional name then this is shown in brackets.*	***BOTTING, Ian James***
Birthplace, birthdate: Place and date of death: *Note: If exact dates and places are not known then registration details are given with place, year and quarter of year registered.*	*b. Dunedin, New Zealand, 18.5.1922* *d. Merivale, Christchurch, New Zealand, 9.7.1980*
Senior school and colleges attended including universities:	**Educated:** John McGlashan College, Christ's College (New Zealand), Ashburton College, Otago University, Worcester College Oxford
Rugby clubs including junior clubs; universities and the years if Blues were attained; Barbarians season of debut, and club at that time:	**Clubs:** Otago, Oxford University (Blues 1949-50), Blackheath, Leicester, Barbarians (1949/50, Oxford University)
Leicester debut details, and scoring: Leicester last appearance details, and scoring: International caps, including British Isles:	**Debut:** *1.12.1951 v Harlequins(A), Lost 3-9* **Last Game:** *7.4.1953 v Exeter(A), Won 13-5* **CAPS:** England (2) 1950
Career biography:	Ian Botting represented Notts, Lincs & Derbys and the RAF. He played on the wing for England against Wales and Ireland while at Oxford University, and made nine appearances for New Zealand, though not in internationals. He toured South Africa with the All Blacks in 1949 and scored his only two tries on his last appearance of the tour against Orange Free State at Bloemfontein on August 27. During the Second World War, Botting served as a lieutenant in the New Zealand Army and a Flying Officer in the Royal New Zealand Air Force. On his return to New Zealand he represented Otago University at athletics, cricket and rugby. He then entered holy orders (Church of England), and became chaplain at Christ's College and later St Margaret's College. He was later precentor at both colleges and at Christchurch Cathedral. He died from injuries received in a road accident. His bicycle collided with a bus near his home in Merivale, and he was thrown under the wheels of a passing car.
Total of Leicester appearances and points scored: *Note: Where appearance totals incorporate a 'plus'(+) sign, the following figure represents games where the individual was a playing replacement.*	*Apps: 38* *Points: 45*
Detailed scoring analysis: T-tries, C-conversions, PG-penalty goals, DG-drop goals, GM-goals from a mark:	*Scoring: 15 T*

ADAMS, Newton

b. Leicester, 29.11.1912
Educated: Mill Hill School
Clubs: Westleigh, Leicester
Debut: *11.3.1933 v Northampton (H), Lost 3-21*
Last Game: *17.12.1938 v Rosslyn Park (H), Won 14-5*

Newton Adams, a back-row forward, retired from the Royal Air Force as a group captain. He played for Leicestershire, for the Possibles against the Probables in an England trial in 1936 and was reserve for England v Scotland at Murrayfield in 1937.

Apps: 126
Points: 78
Scoring: 26 T

Garry
Adey

ADEY, Garry John

b. Loughborough,, Leics, 13.6.1945
Educated: Humphrey Perkins Grammar School, Barrow-on-Soar; Loughborough Technical College
Clubs: Loughborough Town, Leicester, Barbarians (1975/76)
Debut: *8.3.1967 v Loughborough Colleges (H), Won 14-6*
Last Game: *2.5.1981 v Gosforth (John Player Cup Final at Twickenham), Won 22-15*
CAPS: England (2) 1976

Born "via Nick Hughes' surgery", as he once put it, Garry Adey played for the county under-15s as a prop and as a lock for the under-19s and colts. While at school he also putt the shot for the county

athletics team. He toured as a lock with Leicester over Easter 1965 but moved to No 8 after John Quick left the club. Adey won numerous representative honours for Leicestershire and for the Midlands against Fiji, the All Blacks (twice), Argentina, Australia and Japan. He also played for England under-25s against Fiji in 1970.

A powerful mauling forward, he replaced Andy Ripley in the England back row against Ireland and France in 1976 and went on the Barbarians tour of Canada in the same year. An ankle injury in the game against Cambridge University in November 1980, and increased work and family commitments, led Adey to announce his retirement after 15 years with the club. His place in the team was taken by Angus Collington; however, injuries sustained by Collington and Ian Smith later that same season forced Tigers to ask Adey to reconsider. He stipulated that, if selected for the first XV, it should be on merit, and then demonstrated he had lost none of his skills during the last three games of the season including the John Player Cup final against Gosforth where Collington yet again sat on the bench.

He is now managing director of Adey Steel in Loughborough. His father was a keen footballer and cricketer, and presented the club with a new scoreboard in readiness for the start of the 1977-78 season.

Apps: 381
Points: 215
Scoring: 57 T

AKERS, Arthur

b. c 1869
d. Leicester, 8.10.1899
Educated: Not available
Clubs: Leicester
Debut: *25.11.1893 v Rugby (A), Won 8-7*
Last Game: *15.4.1899 v Gloucester (H), Won 6-4*

Arthur Akers, a forward rejoiced in the nickname "Tough 'un" which he picked up on the boxing circuit. *The Saturday Herald* of October 31, 1891, previews a fight between Lachie Thompson of Glasgow and Arthur Akers "Tough 'un", to be held in London, under the Marquis of Queensbury rules, at a weight of 10st 8lbs. As the stake money was £400, Akers must have been upset that he lost the fight, much to the surprise of the local press. He helped Leicester win the Midland Counties Cup in 1898 and 1899, and it was a great shock when he died suddenly of pneumonia in October of that year. The memorial service at Leicester

Cemetery was attended by the first XV, and the lesson read by the three-quarter, the Reverend Cary-Elwes.

Apps: 160
Points: 32
Scoring: 10 T, 1 C

John
Allen

ALLEN, John Albert

b. Leicester, 29.7.1942
Educated: Lutterworth Grammar School
Clubs: Leicester, Barbarians (1973/74)
Debut: *26.1.1961 v Royal Air Force (H at the Rec), Lost 6-11*
Last Game: *13.9.1975 v Bath (H), Won 37-7 (1T, 4 pts)*

John Allen is a chartered accountant, and a partner in Grant Thornton. His brother, Trevor, was also a Tiger from 1957-61 while John played in the same Lutterworth GS side as fellow Tigers Richard and John Cooper. Allen represented Leicestershire at scrum half at under-15 and under-19 level, and went on to make 45 appearances for the senior county side. Leicester was his only senior club and he was captain in 1970-71. He had trials for England at under-15 and under-18 level and for England's senior team in 1969 and 1973 but was, as he puts it, "always the bridesmaid, never the bride". A hard-working player who enjoyed an effective relationship with a series of talented back-row forwards, Allen has been tireless in his efforts for the club; when his playing career ended he became treasurer and he has been the honorary secretary of Leicester Football Club since 1982, following the long and distinguished line of devoted officials in that post.

Apps: 457
Points: 297
Scoring: 58 T, 27 C, 17 PG, 2 DG

ALLEN, W.J.

Clubs: Rugby, Leicester
Debut: *20.11.1909 v Newport (A),
Lost 3-23*
Last Game: *12.4.1921 v Nuneaton (A),
Won 19-3*

Jimmy 'Jumbo' Allen played at forward for Rugby from the age of seventeen and was the Rugby Lions captain for the 1909-10 season when he was invited to tour with Leicester. After this he immediately resigned the captaincy and joined Leicester. He played regularly for the Midlands Counties and played once for The Rest against England in a 1911 trial. He appeared in three Midland Counties Cup-winning teams in 1910, 1912 and 1913, and became the Leicester captain in 1919-20.

Apps: 209
Points: 170
Scoring: 37 T, 25 C, 3 PG

ALMEY, Gordon Arthur

b. Market Harborough, Leics, 16.8.1936
Educated: Welland Park School,
Market Harborough
Clubs: Kibworth, Leicester,
Market Bosworth
Debut: *21.12.1957 v Bristol (A), Lost 6-12*
Last Game: *14.3.1964 v The Army (H),
Won 14-3 (1T, 3 pts)*

Gordon Almey, a fiery back row forward and very occasional wing three-quarter, was a policeman in Market Harborough and Hinckley, and is now retired. He was also the police officer who showed Dean Richards "the ropes" at Hinckley police station.

Apps: 150
Points: 93
Scoring: 31 T

ANDREWS, Kevin Paul

b. Southampton, Hampshire, 28.4.1939
Educated: Downside School
Clubs: Trojans, Burton-on-Trent, Bath,
Leicester, Barbarians (1966/67)
Debut: *13.2.1965 v Newport (H),
Lost 10-30*
Last Game: *25.4.1970 v Halifax (H),
Won 31-8*

Kevin Andrews, a lock, joined the Tigers after taking up a position with Marstons Brewery in Burton-on-Trent. He played for Trojans in Southampton before

moving for six years to Bath, whom he captained. Andrews played for Hampshire, including their county championship final against Warwickshire in 1962; while with Burton he skippered Staffordshire from 1964-67. He appeared for London Counties and captained the Midland Counties XV to a win against the Australians at Coventry. Kevin was also captain of Leicester.

He enjoyed for many years the distinction of being the only uncapped Englishman to have captained the Barbarians twice (against Penarth in 1967 and Swansea in 1968), and was picked in a final England trial in 1965-66 but had to withdraw due to injury sustained in the club's Christmas fixture with the Barbarians. He was elected President of the club in 1987. His uncle, W H R (Bill) Andrews, bowled Don Bradman when playing for Somerset in 1938, and his father played for Hampshire at rugby and cricket. Andrews is a national account manager with Marstons Brewery.

Apps: 191
Points: 36
Scoring: 12 T

ARNEIL, Rodger James

b. Edinburgh, Scotland, 1.5.1944
Educated: Edinburgh Academy, Scottish Woollen College
Clubs: Edinburgh Academicals,
Leicester, Northampton, Barbarians
(1965/66 Edinburgh Academicals)
Debut: *15.11.1969 v Wilmslow (H),
Lost 13-23 (1T, 3 pts)*
Last Game: *24.4.1971 v Sale (H), Won 3-0*
CAPS: Scotland (22) 1968-72,
British Isles (4) 1968

Rodger Arneil was a hard-tackling flanker and his 22 Scottish international caps were all won in consecutive games, starting in 1968. He was chosen as a reserve for both the British Isles tour to South Africa in 1968 and to Australia and New Zealand in 1971, and uniquely was called upon to play after injuries to other team members. On the 1968 tour he joined on the eve of departure, and became the success of the tour, playing in all of the Test matches, making twelve appearances in all. He was late joining the tour in 1971 and although turning in some good performances his challenge did not result in any more Lions caps; he played in five provincial games.

Arneil also toured South Africa with the Barbarians in 1969; he played against the Springboks for the Barbarians at Twickenham on January 31, 1970, when they lost 12-21. The same year he toured Australia with Scotland, having been a Scottish tourist in Argentina in 1969. His international career ended against the All Blacks at Murrayfield in December 1972, as his business commitments increased. He is now a company director in Oxfordshire.

Apps: 25
Points: 12
Scoring: 4 T

Rodger Arneil

ASHURST, Alfred Derek B.

b. registered in Leicester, December qtr, 1932
Clubs: Leicester Thursday,
Aylestone Athletic, Leicester, Coventry
Debut: *27.10.1951 v Northampton (A),*
Lost 11-13
Last Game: *15.9.1962 v Plymouth Albion*
(H), Won 11-6

Derek Ashurst, a back row forward, was
at one time a chicken farmer on the
Narborough Road near Cosby. He was
never what could have been described as
a regular player though, his 112
appearances being spread over 12
seasons, and in only one of those seasons
did he play in over twenty games; 28 in
1955/6. Derek also turned out once on the
wing at Gloucester in 1954, and twice at
full-back on the Easter tour of 1959.

Apps: 112
Points: 57
Scoring: 14 T, 3 C, 3 PG

ATKINS, Dudley Beaumont

b. Hinckley, Leicestershire, October 1879
d. Abergele, North Wales, 17.10.1945
Educated: Bedford School
Clubs: Hinckley, Leicester
Debut: *7.9.1901 v Nuneaton (H), Won 27-3*
Last Game: *31.10.1908 v Cardiff (H),*
Won 7-0

Dudley Atkins, a strong forward, was in
Leicester's Midland Counties Cup-
winning teams from 1902 to 1905. He was
for a time a member of the Imperial
Yeomanry in South Africa. The youngest
son of John Atkins of The Hall, Hinckley,
he worked in the family business - Atkins
Brothers, and was a member of the
Hinckley Amateur Operatic society. For a
time he ran a sheep farm in New Zealand,
and was a generous benefactor of the
Hinckley & District Hospital. Atkins was
a founder member of Hinckley Cricket
Club and Hinckley RFC and was
President of the latter from 1919-39.

Apps: 147
Points: 30
Scoring: 10 T

ATKINS, Hugh Percival

b. Hinckley, Leicestershire, 13.3.1877
d. Burbage, Leicestershire, 19.4.1958
Educated: Bedford School
Clubs: Hinckley, Leicester, Nuneaton
Debut: *5.4.1897 v Llanelly (H), Drew 0-0*
Last Game: *6.10.1906 v Devonport Albion*
(H), Lost 0-8

Percy Atkins, a centre or wing, was the
captain of Nuneaton in the 1895/96
season. He played in 15 Midland Counties
Cup ties winning them all, including four
finals, three of them with his cousin
Dudley. He also had a trial with England,
and was secretary of Hinckley RFC from
1893-1914.
Atkins, the owner of the shoe
manufacturers, W Johnson's, in Upper
Bond Street, Hinckley, was a member of
the Hinckley Amateur Operatic Society.
He was an expert marksman with a rifle
and often represented the Army in
tournaments at Bisley. He became a major
in the First World War where he was chief
instructor in charge of sniping; in that
capacity he went to the United States to
instruct their soldiers in modern warfare
when the USA entered the war. In the
Second World War he commanded the
Wolvey Home Guard. Percy was a
founder member of both Hinckley Cricket
and Rugby Clubs, as was his cousin
Dudley.

Apps: 186
Points: 126
Scoring: 42 T

AUTY, Joseph Richard

b. Batley, Yorkshire, 19.8.1910
Educated: Mill Hill School
Clubs: Old Millhillians, Batley,
Headingley, Leicester, Barbarians
(1934/35 Headingley)
Debut: *30.1.1930 v Royal Air Force (H),*
Won 23-11
Last Game: *9.11.1938 v Oxford University*
(A), Won 17-3
CAPS: England (1) 1935

Dick Auty represented Yorkshire 24
times, and captained Headingley to 29
wins in the 1933/34 season. He played fly
half for England against Scotland in 1935
and subsequently had the distinction of
scoring a hat-trick of tries in the
Christmas Barbarians fixture of 1937, only
this feat was against the Tigers. He came
from a successful rugby family: his uncle,
Joseph Speight Auty, played for
Headingley and Yorkshire and was a
reserve for England in 1905; his father,
F W H Auty, played for Batley and
Yorkshire as an amateur. Auty is a retired
company director in the woollen industry
and his son, Tim, is a well-known rugby
historian.

Apps: 19
Points: 24
Scoring: 8 T

BANN, Eric Edward

b. Lynmouth, Devon, 17.10.1946
Educated: City of Leicester Boys'
Grammar School,
Alsager College of Education
Clubs: Leicester,
St. Mary's College (Ireland),
Dolphin (Ireland),
Stoneygate
Debut: *27.4.1968 v Manchester (H),*
Won 13-6
Last Game: *1.11.1975 v Gloucester*
(H), Lost 12-22

Not many Tigers can claim to have
played for Leicester at both Welford
Road and Filbert Street but Eric
Bann, an athletic second row
forward, did. His goalkeeping
abilities took him to both Notts
County and the reserves at Leicester
City. He was persuaded at Alsager
College to change to rugby by Alan
Black, ex-Gosforth and Wasps and
now the RFU's promotions officer,
and Mick Mahoney, now commercial
manager of Newcastle Gosforth. An
all-round athlete, Bann was a
member of Leicestershire's AAA
team and finished fourth in the UAU
decathlon event. A county high
jump, triple jump and 110 metres
hurdles champion, he also gained an
England under-21 basketball cap,
and was interested in swimming and
sailing.

Apps: 163
Points: 188
Scoring: 26 T, 18 C, 18 PG

BARKER, Robert George

b. Leicester, 23.10.1944
Educated: Alderman Newton Grammar School, Scraptoft Training College
Clubs: Stoneygate, Leicester
Debut: 19.10.1968 v Northampton (H), Drew 17-17 (1T, 3 pts)
Last Game: 23.11.1979 v Moseley (A), Lost 6-13

Initially a centre, and later a wing, Bob Barker played for Leicestershire at under-15 and under-19 level - captaining both age groups - and for England under-15 against Wales. He represented Leicestershire's senior team and played for the Midlands East. An all-round sportsman, Barker ran in five All-England Athletics Championships with a best time of 22.9 seconds for the 220 yards, once running the 100 yards in 9.9 seconds, "with a strong wind behind him". He has played for the Leicestershire Young Amateurs at cricket, and is also a qualified tennis coach.

At one time the post-war record holder for the number of tries scored, until overtaken by Barry Evans, Barker's 1,000th point for the club was scored in the memorable setting of Twickenham with a try in a game against the Harlequins. A reliable, if somewhat eccentric goal-kicker, his post-war individual points record was overtaken later by Dusty Hare. Barker is one of only five Tigers to have scored a hat-trick of tries in the annual fixture with the Barbarians, in 1971. He specialised in PE and geography when he qualified as a teacher but he also gained a diploma of education to teach the physically and mentally handicapped. He is now head of special needs at Rushey Mead School in Leicester.

Apps: 318+2
Points: 1,117
Scoring: 158 T, 92 C, 107 PG, 2 DG

Bob Barker

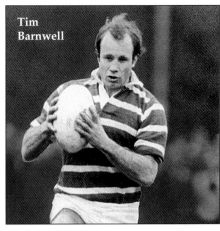

Tim Barnwell

BARNWELL, Richard Charles

b. Coventry, Warwickshire, 31.1.1953
Educated: Warwick School, Loughborough Colleges
Clubs: Loughborough Colleges, Coventry, Leicester
Debut: 14.9.1977 v Birmingham (A), Won 28-9 (2T, 8 pts)
Last Game: 30.4.1983 v Bristol (John Player Cup Final at Twickenham), Lost 22-28

'Tim' Barnwell, a wing three-quarter, gained six caps for England schools at under-19 level between 1970 and 1972, and played for England under-23 in 1974. He played four seasons for Coventry before joining Leicester in 1977, and won Cup-winners' medals with Coventry (for whom he scored a try against London Scottish in the 1974 final) and Leicester (three times). Tim also represented both Warwickshire and the Midlands.

His playing career was brought to an abrupt end when, after a clash of heads during the 1983 John Player Cup final against Bristol, he was forced to leave the field. He was taken to West Middlesex Hospital for examination and kept in for observation. During the night he lapsed into a coma and was rushed across London to the Central Hospital where he underwent six hours of surgery to remove a blood clot from his brain. Barnwell spent 24 hours on a life support system before a long period of recovery, first in London, then in Leicester Royal Infirmary.

Though he did not play again he was restored to health and now works for the local tour operators, Page and Moy; he can also be heard commenting on Tigers' games on *Leicester Sound* radio. An elusive player, Barnwell's biggest disappointment was the fact that despite sitting on the bench and wearing a Barbarian shirt in 1983, he never actually played for the famous invitation club.

Apps: 188+1
Points: 382
Scoring: 95 T, 1 C

BARR, Robert John

b. Blisworth, Northamptonshire, 26.5.1907
d. Great Oxendon, Northamptonshire,
22.9.1975
Educated: Stamford School
Clubs: Westleigh, Leicester, Barbarians
(1934/35)
Debut: *3.11.1928 v Cambridge University*
(A), Lost 3-20
last game: *15.4.1939 v Blackheath (H),*
Lost 10-23
CAPS: England (3) 1932

Bobby Barr was one of only two people
(the other being John Parsons) to hold all
three senior positions at Leicester - as
Captain, Secretary and President. A full
back he played for Leicestershire and East
Midlands in the famous victory over the
South Africans in 1931 and went on to
win his three England caps that same
season - including another appearance
against the Springboks. He captained
Leicestershire and demonstrated the
power of his kicking in successive games
for Leicester when he dropped goals from
over 40 yards, no mean feat with the
heavy leather ball then in use - the second,
against Gloucester, secured victory.

R·J·BARR FULL·BACK

During the Second World War he
served in the Army as a Territorial officer
in the Leicestershire searchlights unit. He
was captured in a rearguard action at
Bologne and spent five long years as a
prisoner of war. In an interview in 1959 he
recalled some of his escape attempts, such
as the occasion when the German
Commandant advised the senior British
officers: "Your men haven't made much
progress with the tunnel, I find they have
only done two yards since
yesterday...may I suggest that they might

do better if they go westwards instead of
east as they will strike less water that
way." When moved to Ulm in the Black
Forest, he was one of 24 prisoners who
escaped through a tunnel, only to be
recaptured four kilometres short of the
Swiss border; ironically the German
troops were not looking for him but
French prisoners escaping from work
farms. After his first two years of captivity
it was decided that it was more important
to help recent arrivals to get out so he
spent the rest of his time planning and
helping others escape. When he was
repatriated he was awarded the Military
Cross.

Barr was a member of the Worshipful
Company of Framework Knitters and
founded the hosiery brand label
manufacturing firm of Barr, Radcliffe &
Co at Sileby and Oadby. He had two
daughters, one of whom Judith, married
Roger Clark the international car rally
driver. Barr also played occasionally for
Leicestershire County Cricket Club
second XI.

Apps: 241
Points: 66
Scoring: 12 C, 6 PG, 6 DG

Ian Bates

BATES, Ian

b. Earl Shilton, Leicestershire, 16.5.1963
Educated: Heathfield High School, Earl
Shilton Community College, Hinckley
College
Clubs: Market Bosworth, Leicester, Manly
(Australia)
Debut: *5.2.1983 v London Scottish (A),*
Won 18-12

Ian Bates, a self employed carpenter in
Shearsby, is a product of the Leicester
youth team, which he joined as a scrum
half from Market Bosworth, but Graham
Willars (then the youth coach) converted
him to centre. Bates played for
Leicestershire, for the Midlands under-23
and Midlands. He was selected for
England's under-23 squad during 1984-86.
A strong runner and defender, he served
his apprenticeship behind two England
centres, Clive Woodward and Paul
Dodge.

Apps: 274+1
Points: 154
Scoring: 38 T

BAYNES,
Christopher James

b. Gillingham, Kent, 24.11.1946
Educated: Gillingham Grammar School,
Loughborough Colleges
Clubs: Loughborough Colleges, Leicester,
Nottingham
Debut: *19.3.1969 v Coventry (H), Won 15-6*
Last Game: *24.4.1973 v Wilmslow (A),*
Lost 10-16

Chris Baynes, a back row forward, was a
schoolteacher at Trent College when with
Leicester, but is now a financial consultant
with the Royal Bank of Scotland. Chris

was captain of Notts, Lincs and Derbys,
and twice played for the Midland
Counties (East) against the touring Fijians
and All Blacks in 1970 and 1973
respectively.

Apps: 116
Points: 125
Scoring: 37 T

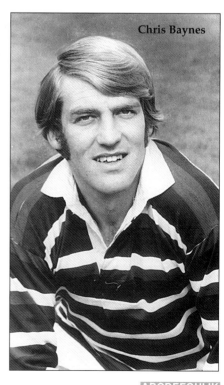

Chris Baynes

BEAMISH, Charles Eric St John

b. Cork, 23.6.1908
d. Templemore, County Tipperary, 18.5.1984
Clubs: North of Ireland (NIFC),
Harlequins, Leicester, Barbarians (1933/34)
Debut: 11.12.1926 v Blackheath (A), Lost 6-18
Last Game: 1.2.1936 v London Scottish (H),
Drew 3-3
CAPS: Ireland (12) 1933-38

Charles Beamish, a prop or hooker, was
brought up in Ireland, joined the RAF and
was commissioned in 1927. He played for
Ulster against New Zealand in 1935 and
toured Argentina with Ireland; he also
represented the RAF. Serving throughout
the Second World War he was awarded the
DFC in 1940, and retired from the RAF
eight years later, as a group captain. He
then returned to his native Ireland where
he took up farming in Tipperary. He was
the brother of Sir George, Cecil and Victor
Beamish, the only family which has
produced four Tigers brothers.

Apps: 17
Points: 6
Scoring: 2 T

BEAMISH, George Robert

b. Dunmanway, County Cork, 29.4.1905
d. Castlerock, Ireland, 13.11.1967
Educated: Coleraine Academical Institute
Clubs: Coleraine, Leicester, London Irish,
Barbarians (1927/28)
Debut: 27.12.1924 v Heriotonians (H),
Won 22-0
Last Game: 17.4.1933 v Plymouth Albion
(A), Won 11-6 (1T, 3 pts)
CAPS: Ireland (25) 1925-33,
British Isles (5) 1930

George Beamish represented RAF
Cranwell, the RAF, and Leicestershire &
East Midlands. In 1930 he went on the

British Isles tour to Australia and New
Zealand. During a five-year period
beginning in 1928 he missed only one
international for Ireland, that against
England at Lansdowne Road in 1930;
during that period he gained 22 of his 25
caps. His record number of appearances in
the middle of the back row stood for nearly
fifty years.

A powerful back-row forward with a
magnificent
physique, he
instilled his
players with a
restraint which
permitted them
to play a
constructive,
disciplined
game, seldom
the forte of Irish
packs. He
captained the
Irish side which
shared the
championship
in 1932 but one
of his finest
moments came
when Leicestershire and East
Midlands won the Springbok head
awarded by the 1931/32 South Africans
beaten at Welford Road. A commentator at
the match described the Springboks as
giants but added that "no-one could dwarf
the huge Beamish".

G. R. BEAMISH
[R.A.F. & IRELAND]

He was a Battle of Britain pilot who
made history in 1942 by becoming the first
RAF officer to be promoted to the rank of
air commodore; awarded the CBE in 1942
and the KCB in 1955, he retired in 1958. In
January 1959 he was nominated as Unionist
candidate for North Belfast but was
defeated by the then sitting MP. He was the
RAF officers' golf champion in 1925, and
the RAF heavyweight boxing champion in
1929, and in 1932 he lost the final to Welsh
international prop Cecil Davies.

Apps: 118
Points: 74
Scoring: 24 T, 1 C

Bob Beason

BEASON, Robert

b. Leicester, 1.9.1938
Educated: Dixie Grammar School, Market
Bosworth; Nottingham University
Clubs: Old Bosworthians, Leicester
Debut: 3.9.1960 v Bedford (H), Drew 9-9
Last Game: 9.9.1972 v Bath (H), Won 34-4

Bob Beason, a prop forward big enough to
play lock, represented England Schools
against Wales at Twickenham in 1954. He
was captain of Old Bosworthians for three
years from their foundation and went on
to represent Leicestershire whom he both
captained and, in 1973, coached. Beason's
two sons, Richard and Michael, have both
been captains of Old Bosworthians. He
was President of Leicester Football Club
from 1985-87 and is now managing
director of Beason-Cooke Ltd.

Apps: 203
Points: 9
Scoring: 3 T

Tom Berry

BERRY, Joseph Thomas Wade

b. Slawston, Leicestershire, 17.7.1911
d. Market Harborough, Leics, 1.7.1993
Educated: Eastbourne College
Clubs: Market Harborough, Leicester,
Barbarians (1938/39)
Debut: 5.3.1932 v Harlequins (H),
Won 13-11 (1T, 3 pts)
Last Game: 17.4.1948 v Blackheath (H),
Won 6-5
CAPS: England (3) 1939

Tom Berry farmed at Ashley, near Market
Harborough virtually all his life. He was a
good sportsman, playing cricket for the

Gentlemen's Cricket Club but it was at rugby that he excelled, representing the Tigers, Leicestershire, and England. He won three full caps as a back row forward as well as making two appearances in war-time Red Cross internationals. He captained Leicester both before the Second World War and immediately afterwards. Subsequently Berry became a leading administrator: he represented Leicestershire on the RFU committee from 1953 to 1968 and was an England selector from 1951-1966, during which time he became manager of the first England side to tour abroad, to Australia, New Zealand and Fiji in 1963. He was President of the RFU in 1968/69, the first Leicestershire representative to enjoy that honour. He was the brother-in-law of 'Mac' Hodgson, and his wife Margaret represented England at golf. Three of their sons went on to become Tigers: John, and the twins David and Richard, while another son, Michael, also played for the Extras.

Apps: 277
Points: 45
Scoring: 15 T

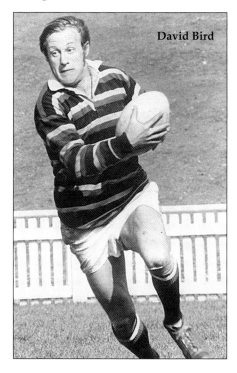

BIRD, David William

b. Broughton Astley, Leicestershire, 26.8.1940
Educated: Lutterworth Grammar School, Loughborough Colleges
Clubs: Hinckley, Leicester
Debut: *3.9.1960 v Bedford (H), Drew 9-9 (1T, 3 pts)*
Last Game: *21.4.1973 v Broughton Park (A), Won 10-9*

David Bird, a wing, was a PE teacher at various Leicester schools during his

Tigers career. He is now a mathematics and careers teacher at Judge Meadow School, Leamington Spa. Because of war-time bombing, Bird was born in the same house as his cousin, M J K Smith, the former England and Warwickshire cricket captain. He took up the family trait and played cricket for Loughborough Colleges, before turning his hand to rugby. His twin sister Diane was an England hockey player, and coached the Great Britain women's hockey team to a bronze medal at the Barcelona Olympics.

Apps: 285
Points: 258
Scoring: 86 T

BLACK, Angus William

b. Dunfermline, Scotland, 6.5.1925
Educated: Dollar Academy, Edinburgh University
Clubs: Edinburgh University, Dunfermline, Leicester, Bristol, Barbarians (1945/46 Edinburgh University)
Debut: *21.3.1953 v Swansea (A), Lost 3-8*
Last Game: *28.12.1953 v Barbarians (H), Lost 11-39*
CAPS: Scotland (6) 1947-50, British Isles (2) 1950

Gus Black was one of several players of substantial pedigree to have a regrettably brief career with Leicester. A scrum-half, he made his mark immediately after the Second World War, playing for the Combined Services and in two services and five Victory internationals. He toured Australia and New Zealand with the 1950 British Lions. He graduated in medicine, and became a consultant psychiatrist with the RAF.

Apps: 16
Points: 9
Scoring: 2 T, 1 DG

BLEASDALE, Tom

b. St. Anne's, Lancashire, 9.6.1930
Educated: King Edward VII School, Lytham; Leicester University
Clubs: Fylde, Leicester, Barbarians (1957/58)
Debut: *5.11.1949 v Gloucester (A), Lost 6-18*
Last Game: *4.1.1964 v Bath (A), Lost 0-11*

Tom Bleasdale played at flanker for his native Lancashire, Leicestershire, Buckinghamshire and the Midlands during a distinguished career. He came to Leicester as a student, after a season with Fylde, but during his first season played only 10 games for the Tigers, as the

Tom Bleasdale

University had first call on him as captain. He had his first England trial in the 1951/52 season, when he also played for the Midland Counties against South Africa, and was travelling reserve for the England v Wales match. After gaining his degree he joined the RAF on a short service commission, and went on to captain both the RAF and the Combined Services in 1955, leading the RAF team against the Tigers in January that year. He had another England trial in the 1955/56 season but a full cap eluded him. He returned to Leicester, playing for several more seasons, and became captain. He emigrated to America in 1973, sat the Harvard Advanced Management Programme, and is now a trustee for the Colonial Group of Mutual Funds, in Massachusetts, USA.

Apps: 340
Points: 159
Scoring: 53 T

BOLESWORTH, Arthur Denis

b. Hinckley, Leicestershire, 2.9.1916
Educated: Ratcliffe College, Sileby
Clubs: Hinckley, Leicester, Nuneaton, Barbarians (1945/46)
Debut: *4.11.1936 v Oxford University (A), Won 16-13*
Last Game: *12.3.1955 v Coventry (H), Drew 11-11*

Denis Bolesworth captained Leicester and Leicestershire. An energetic prop, he played for the Midland Counties against the Barbarians in 1940, in a special game in aid of Army Recreational and Comforts Funds, but had to wait until February 28, 1946, before making his Barbarians debut

Denis Bolesworth

against the East Midlands. In 1952/53 he was an international triallist and played for the RAF in the inter-services competition, as well as captaining Leicester. He announced his retirement at the end of the 1953/54 season and was carried off shoulder-high after the final game against Sale. However, he returned for the game at Coventry in March 1955, to replace David Hazell who withdrew through illness. He was a hosiery manufacturer, and now lives in Cornwall. Bolesworth was nicknamed 'Milord' after an Easter tour to Wales when he entered two Grand National sweepstakes and picked the 100-1 shot, Russian Hero, both times. Taking it as an omen he had a bet on it as well, and the horse won. On the return journey every time the team coach passed a big house, Francis Edwards would ask if Bolesworth was going to buy it, coining the phrase 'Milord', which promptly stuck.

Apps: 330
Points: 69
Scoring: 23 T

BOTTING, Ian James

b. Dunedin, New Zealand, 18.5.1922
d. Merivale, Christchurch, New Zealand, 9.7.1980
Educated: John McGlashan College, Christ's College (New Zealand), Ashburton College, Otago University, Worcester College Oxford
Clubs: Otago, Oxford University (Blues 1949-50), Blackheath, Leicester, Barbarians (1949/50 Oxford University)
Debut: *1.12.1951 v Harlequins (A), Lost 3-9*
Last Game: *7.4.1953 v Exeter (A), Won 13-5*
CAPS: England (2) 1950

Ian Botting represented Notts, Lincs & Derbys and the RAF. He played on the wing for England against Wales and

Ireland while at Oxford University, and made nine appearances for New Zealand, though not in internationals. He toured South Africa with the All Blacks in 1949 and scored his only two tries on his last appearance of the tour against Orange Free State at Bloemfontein on August 27. During the Second World War, Botting served as a lieutenant in the New Zealand Army and a Flying Officer in the Royal New Zealand Air Force. On his return to New Zealand he represented Otago University at athletics, cricket and rugby. He then entered holy orders (Church of England), and became chaplain at Christ's College and later St Margaret's College. He was later precentor at both colleges and at Christchurch Cathedral. He died from injuries received in a road accident, when his bicycle collided with a bus near his home in Merivale, and he was thrown under the wheels of a passing car.

Apps: 38
Points: 45
Scoring: 15 T

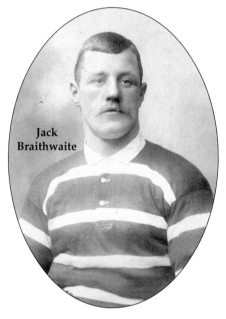

Jack Braithwaite

BRAITHWAITE, John

b. Leeds, Yorkshire, 21.4.1873
d. West Humberstone, Leicester, 14.11.1915
Clubs: Holbeck, Vulcan Rovers, Leicester
Debut: *12.10.1895 v Bedford (A), Lost 3-8*
Last Game: *22.12.1906 v Coventry (A), Drew 0-0*
CAPS: England (1) 1905

Jack 'Nipper' Braithwaite began his rugby career at the age of 13, playing for Leeds St Cuthbert's; during his time with them, they were winners of the Leeds Junior League for two consecutive seasons. In his first season with Leicester he was a member of the successful 'A' team which won the Nuneaton Cup, scoring the

winning try against Nuneaton. The next season he played in the senior side and went on to represent the Midland Counties, all by the age of 22. A small man (he was only 5ft 2in and 9st), he was a clever and resourceful player, but a quiet, unassuming character. Dave Gallaher, the All Blacks captain of 1905, paid Braithwaite a great compliment after playing against him in his only international, by stating that he was one of the most determined little men he had ever met. Braithwaite was only once on the losing side in 34 Midland Counties Cup ties, including eight successive cup final wins from 1898-1905. He was an engineer by trade, and a serious accident at work almost led to him losing a leg but he made a complete recovery. A very tough character, it was a great shock when pneumonia claimed his life at the age of only 42; only one week earlier he had expressed his intention of enlisting to fight in the First World War.

Apps: 359
Points: 361
Scoring: 67 T, 45 C, 2 PG, 15 DG, 1 GM

BREAM, J.W.

Clubs: Aylestone St James, Leicester, Northampton, Bedford
Debut: *28.1.1911 v Moseley (H), Won 21-5 (1PG, 3 pts)*
Last Game: *21.3.1914 v Newbold-on-Avon (A) (Midland Counties Cup 4th round), Won 27-0 (3C, 2PG, 12 pts)*

J W Bream, a full back, won two Midland Counties Cup-winners' medals with the Tigers in 1912 and 1913. In the game against Llanelly on November 1, 1913, Bream was reported to "have returned to his goal-kicking mood. He converted all of the tries and landed a penalty goal, several of the kicks being of a difficult character." He played in an England trial in 1913 and went on to appear in 16 games for Northampton in 1921-22, scoring 38 points; he played twice for Bedford the following season.

Apps: 101
Points: 332
Scoring: 4 T, 125 C, 22 PG, 1 DG

BROWN, William Henry

b. Hinckley, Leicestershire, 4.6.1915
Educated: Hinckley School, Alma Road
Clubs: Hinckley, Coventry, Leicester
Debut: *13.10.1945 v Nuneaton (H), Won 8-3*
Last Game: *19.4.1949 v Bath (A), Won 8-3 (1T, 3 pts)*

Bill Brown, a second-row forward, also represented Leicestershire. He introduced Dean Richards to the Tigers when he was a scout in Hinckley. Now retired and living in Sapcote.

Apps: 106
Points: 6
Scoring: 2 T

BUCKINGHAM, Ralph Arthur

b. Blaby, Leicester, 15.1.1907
d. Stoneygate, Leicester, 10.4.1988
Educated: Rossall School
Clubs: Stoneygate, Leicester, Barbarians (1934/35)
Debut: *10.9.1924 v Rugby BTH (A), Won 24-0*
Last Game: *23.4.1935 v Exeter (A), Won 42-0 (3C, 6 pts)*
CAPS: England (1) 1927

Though Ralph Buckingham played once for England, his outstanding game was as part of the Leicestershire and East Midlands team which beat the South Africans in 1931. Buckingham played football at Stoneygate School and earned his colours for cricket and boxing while at Rossall. An elegant centre, he won his cap against France in 1927 (when England lost 3-0 in Paris) and was unfortunate not to win further honours - he was a travelling reserve ten times. He captained Leicester in 1933/34 and, in his final season, became first-choice goal-kicker and scored over 100 points. When he retired he was elected a vice-president of the club.

During the Second World War Buckingham served with the Civil Defence Force, and later in the RAF as a flight-lieutenant. He was awarded the British Empire Medal in 1942 for gallantry. He was the company director of the shoe merchandisers, Sowter and Buckingham. During the 1920s he was also a member of the Leicester Rowing club and of the Kirby Muxloe Golf Club. His England cap and boots are still displayed in the Stoneygate club house.

Apps: 325
Points: 443
Scoring: 117 T, 38 C, 4 PG, 1 DG

BULL, Arthur Gilbert

b. registered in Newport, September qtr, 1890
d. Chandlers Ford, Hampshire, 15.3.1963
Educated: Bedford Modern School, King's College Hospital
Clubs: Old Bedford Modernians, Bedford, Northampton, Leicester, Barbarians (1915)
Debut: *26.12.1918 v 4th Leicestershire Regiment (H), Won 6-5*
Last Game: *12.11.1919 v Oxford University (A), Lost 8-16*
CAPS: England (1) 1914

Arthur Bull, a prop forward, also played for the Barbarians against Leicester in March 1915, and captained the East Midlands in the first ever Mobbs Memorial game against the Barbarians at Northampton in February, 1921.

Apps: 17
Points: 8
Scoring: 2 T, 1 C

BURDETT, J.C.

Clubs: Stoneygate, Leicester, Barbarians (1912/13)
Debut: *5.12.1903 v Coventry (H), Won 14-5*
Last Game: *5.10.1912 v Aberavon (H), Won 18-0*

Jimmy Burdett, a forward, played in two games for the Barbarians in December 1912, against Cardiff and strangely Leicester, considering he was a Leicester player at the time. He helped Leicester in two Midland Counties Cup-winning finals in 1910 and 1912.

Apps: 108
Points: 36
Scoring: 12 T

BURNELL, Andrew Paul

b. Edinburgh, 29.9.1965
Educated: Bluecoat School, Reading; Leicester Polytechnic
Clubs: Marlow, Harlequins, Leicester, London Scottish, Barbarians (1989/90 London Scottish)
Debut: *29.11.1986 (replacement) v Saracens (H), Won 19-16 (1T, 4 pts)*
Last Game: *16.1.1988 v Bedford (H), Won 42-9*
CAPS: Scotland (25) 1989-93, British Isles (1) 1993

Paul Burnell, a tight-head prop forward, represented Berkshire Schools at under-16 and under-18 level, and gained his county cap for Buckinghamshire. He played at junior level for Harlequins before joining

Paul Burnell

Leicester. He scored on his Tigers debut (as a replacement for Ian Smith) and on his Scotland 'B' debut in the 26-3 win over Italy in L'Aquila in 1989. Burnell maintains that the Leicester World Tour brochure of 1987 caught the attention of the London Scottish and, hence, Scotland selectors since it mentioned he was born in Edinburgh. He went to Zimbabwe in 1988 and New Zealand in 1990 with Scotland. He missed tours to Japan (1989) and Australia (1992) due to injury. Prior to injury against Wales in the 1992 five nations championship he had played in 24 of the previous 26 full internationals, including all six World Cup games in 1991 (when he switched to loose-head for the 51-12 win over Zimbabwe). He represented Scotland 'A' in the 36-16 win over Spain on December 28, 1991, and toured with the British Lions to New Zealand in 1993, where he made seven appearances including the first Test. Burnell is a sales director with Anglo Scottish Finance, based in Reading.

Apps: 12+1
Points: 8
Scoring: 2 T

BURWELL, Terrence Raymond

b. Northampton, 27.7.1951
Educated: Northampton Grammar School, Bournemouth School, Loughborough Colleges
Clubs: Loughborough Colleges, Leicester
Debut: *18.1.1975 v Bedford (A), Lost 19-23*
Last Game: *26.3.1983 (replacement) v London Scottish (A) (John Player Cup semi-final), Won 30-9*

Terry Burwell, a centre or wing, played for British Universities in 1971 before

Terry Burwell

Malcolm 'King' Bussey, a wing, played twice for England Schools under-19 against Wales and France in 1960, and went on to become an England triallist in 1962. He represented his native Yorkshire, and Leicestershire, and toured South Africa in 1963 with the combined Oxford and Cambridge universities team. He was also an athlete, winning the All England Schools 440 yards championship at Northwich in July 1959 with a time of 50.5 seconds. Bussey, who gained an honours degree in natural sciences from Downing College, Cambridge, joined Tigers after taking up a teaching post at Uppingham School, where he is now a senior master.

Apps: 121
Points: 117
Scoring: 38 T, 1DG

Malcolm Bussey

Alfred Butlin

November 1895 amid accusations of poaching. The matter was reported to the Midland Counties Rugby Union, who suspended him until an enquiry (the costs of which were paid by Rugby), allowed the transfer to go ahead. He was described in 1896 by the *Wyvern* newspaper as a "most resourceful player", who also appeared for the Midlands Counties. Between 1898 and 1902 he appeared in five successive Midland Counties Cup-winning teams. He was an engine cleaner who lived in East Union Street, Rugby.

Apps: 252
Points: 118
Scoring: 19 T, 11 C, 1 PG, 9 DG

joining Leicester. He represented England Students and English Universities at full back but most of his rugby was at centre, where he also appeared for East Midlands in the county championship and, in 1979, on the winning side against the Barbarians. He believes the high point of his career was Leicester's defeat of Randwick on tour in 1980, in a match billed in Sydney as the "World Club Championship".

After a period of teaching at his old school, Northampton Grammar, Burwell left to become a building society manager. When his playing career ended he took up coaching at Northampton and then became one of the earliest paid directors of coaching in England, with Newbury RFC which also involves player-development and commercial management.

Apps: 111+9
Points: 111
Scoring: 27 T, 1 DG

BUSSEY, William Malcolm

b. Halifax, Yorkshire, 19.2.1941
Educated: Heath Grammar School, Halifax; Downing College Cambridge
Clubs: Halifax, Cambridge University (Blue 1960-62), Leicester, Irish Wolfhounds.
Debut: *2.9.1963 v Torquay (A), Won 18-5*
Last Game: *4.10.1967 v Nuneaton (H), Won 17-8*

BUTLIN, Alfred Charles

b. registered in Rugby, Warwickshire, December qtr, 1872
d. details not available
Clubs: Rugby, Leicester
Debut: *23.11.1895 v Swinton (A), Lost 0-13*
Last Game: *13.12.1902 v Northampton (A), Won 12-6 (1DG, 4 pts)*

Alfred Butlin played full back for the Rugby second XV in 1892/93, and displaced W H Webb in the first team the following season. There was controversy about his transfer to Leicester in

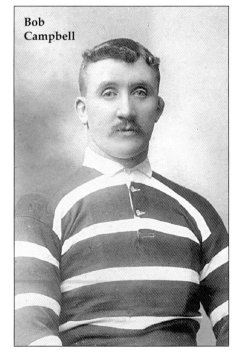

Bob Campbell

CAMPBELL, Robert N.

b. Carnforth, Lancashire, c 1875
d. details not available
Clubs: Morecambe, Leicester
Debut: 21.9.1895 v Nuneaton (H),
Won 24-0 (1T, 3 pts)
Last Game: 21.9.1901 v Bristol (H), Lost 3-6

Bob Campbell played for London and Universities against the Rest of the South, in the trial game of 1899. When he lived in Morecambe he was unfortunate not to gain a county cap, being selected only as a reserve for Lancashire. A player described as "always on the ball", he appeared in four successive Midland Counties Cup-winning teams.

Apps: 207
Points: 25
Scoring: 7 T, 1 DG

Mel Channer

CHANNER, Melville Ramsay

b. Uitenhage, South Africa, 4.9.1924
Educated: Muir College, South Africa
Clubs: Leicester, Orange Free State
Debut: 16.3.1946 v Bedford (H),
Won 10-9 (1T, 3 pts)
Last Game: 27.12.1955 v Barbarians (H),
Lost 3-12

Mel Channer was a fly-half from a famous rugby family, as his grandfather had founded the South African regional team, the Swifts. He served with the South African Air Force during the Second World War and came to Eric Thorneloe's attention when he was stationed at Market Harborough. Channer was then moved to RAF Cosford which seemed to play havoc with his timekeeping as he was reported 10 minutes late for the game against Oxford University on October 30, 1946, and failed to appear for the game against Blackheath later in the same season.

He played for Rhodesia in 1950, and his final game before returning to South Africa was against the Barbarians over Christmas 1955 when he surprised the crowd by playing on the wing. He played for the RAF and for the Combined Services team which met Australia; he was also the RAF long jump champion. Channer became one of South Africa's leading rugby journalists and is now a freelance sports reporter in Port Elizabeth.

Apps: 127
Points: 327
Scoring: 33 T, 19 C, 35 PG, 26 DG

CHAWNER, Frank

b. Leicester, 11.7.1927
Clubs: Vipers, Leicester
Debut: 19.2.1949 v Swansea (H), Won 14-3
Last Game: 18.4.1964 v Saracens (H),
Won 9-3

Frank Chawner was a lock forward on his debut, but then moved to prop. He was due to play his 300th game over Christmas 1962, but the weather did not take account of this landmark as it was the winter of the big freeze and all games

Frank Chawner

were suspended for two months. At the time it was reported that Chawner was the longest-serving member of the Tigers and still scoring tries - 23 in his career. Chawner is now retired; his cousin, Len, also played for the Tigers.

Apps: 331
Points: 69
Scoring: 23 T

CHILTON, Keith

b. Ogmore Vale, Glamorgan, 28.5.1938
Educated: Christ's Hospital
Clubs: Old Blues, London Welsh, Leicester
Debut: 2.9.1963 v Torquay (A), Won 18-5 (3C, 6 pts)
Last Game: 22.4.1967 v Aberavon (H), Won 9-0 (1DG, 3 pts)

Keith Chilton, a centre, was educated at Christ's Hospital and went on to play for their old boys club, the Old Blues, whom Leicester used to have a regular fixture against between 1924 and 1958. At school he was influenced by W P C Davies, the former England centre, and N T Friar, the English and Welsh triallist. Chilton was a Welsh triallist himself on three occasions. In November 1964, playing for Leicester against Old Belvedere in Dublin, he scored in every possible way with a try, conversion, penalty goal and drop goal. He worked for English Electric at Whetstone while playing for Tigers but is now managing director of Oakland Elevators in Oadby. A keen sportsman he still enjoys a round of golf with the Tigers' golfing society.

Apps: 144
Points: 551
Scoring: 26 T, 91 C, 95 PG, 2 DG

COATES, Norman

b. Bath, Wiltshire, 25.9.1892
d. Moulsford-on-Thames, Oxfordshire, 22.12.1953
Educated: Haileybury School, Cambridge University, Edinburgh University
Clubs: Bath, Cambridge University, Wallingford, Leicester, Barbarians (1923/24)
Debut: 8.2.1919 v Gloucester (H), Won 15-0
Last Game: 16.4.1927 v Bristol (A), Lost 6-26

Norman 'Sam' Coates came from Bath, the second son of a doctor whose other son, Vincent Middleton Hope Coates, played for England. Norman played at both centre and in the pack for Leicester;

he also represented Leicestershire, and played for the Barbarians against the Tigers on December 27, 1923, and against the East Midlands at Bedford in 1924. He came to Leicester after serving in the First World War and established a motor business in Market Street. He later became manager at Leicester Speedway for three years before founding a New Walk pub, then moving to an hotel at Wallingford-on-Thames. He served with the RASC in the Second World War, becoming commanding officer of a corps formation covering the south of France. After the war he returned to Wallingford before moving to a small hotel in Bath; in 1951 he became manager of the old coaching inn, The George, in Hinckley.

Apps: 203
Points: 194
Scoring: 62 T, 4 C

COLEMAN, Edgar George

b. Leicester, October 1899
d. Evington, Leicester, 30.7.1983
Clubs: Westleigh, Leicester, Nuneaton
Debut: 27.10.1921 v Cambridge University (A), Won 13-11
Last Game: 11.3.1933 v Northampton (H), Lost 3-21

'Ernie' Coleman played for the Tigers and Warwickshire as a front-row forward, and kept up his social links with the club after his playing career ended. An engineer, he worked for the Standard Engineering Company in Evington Valley Road, until the outbreak of the Second World War. He then became a chief instructor at the Government Training Centre in Humberstone Lane, where he worked until his retirement in 1965. Upon his death Stan Saunders commented "he was a great player, and one of the most unlucky men not to have been capped."

Apps: 260
Points: 56
Scoring: 18 T, 1 C

COLEMAN, James George Sherrard

b. registered in Leicester, December qtr, 1860
d. 1909
Club: Leicester
Debut: 30.10.1880 v Leicester Victoria (H), Won 10-0
Last Game: 2.1.1892 v Gloucester (A), Lost 0-6

Sherrard Coleman, a three-quarter back,

worked as a clerk in the hosiery trade for Riley & Co. He was captain of the club from 1882-85, and appeared in Leicester's first Midland Counties Cup final, losing to Coventry at Rugby on March 31, 1894.

Apps: 140
Points: 52
Scoring: 31 T, 7 DG

COLLINGTON, Andrew Peter

b. Leicester, 2.2.1956
Educated: Wyggeston Grammar School
Clubs: Leicester, Westleigh, Old Bosworthians, Leicester Thursday
Debut: 19.2.1975 v Moseley (H), Lost 9-27
Last Game: 31.3.1986 v Pontypool (A), Lost 6-39

'Gus' Collington (he was known at school as Angus because his mother came from Aberdeen) joined the Leicester club straight from school, graduating to the 1st XV through the youth side. An industrious No 8, he gained exceptional strength from his work as a demolition contractor but much of his career was spent in the shadow of Garry Adey. Collington played for the county at all levels - under-15, under-19, colts and seniors, and was on the replacements bench for England colts in 1975. He was also a replacement in four John Player Cup finals before appearing in the closing minutes of the 1981 final against Gosforth at Twickenham. He still plays rugby for Leicester Thursday, and also squash and cricket. He runs his own builders supply business in Leicester.

Apps: 112+18
Points: 88
Scoring: 22 T

Ted Cooke

COOKE, A.E.

b. Painswick, Gloucestershire, 1870
d. Canada
Educated: Painswick Grammar School, Gloucestershire
Clubs: Leicester Nelson, Leicester Swifts, Leicester
Debut: 28.9.1889 v Stratford-on-Avon (A), Lost 0-7
Last Game: 11.9.1897 v Nuneaton (H), Won 22-8

Ted Cooke, the brother of Rupert, also a Tiger came from a family of Quakers. He learned the rudiments of the game in Gloucestershire. His effective play at three-quarter helped the Leicester Swifts win the Leicestershire Senior Cup in 1890/91 under the leadership of Tom Crumbie. He played for Leicester as a forward and captained the club in the 1893/94 season when they were runners-up in the Midland Counties Cup. He also played for Midland Counties for four seasons. He was described as a "sterling forward, who does a lot of work in the scrummage and is very quick on the ball when it comes out." In later years he emigrated to Canada.

Apps: 158
Points: 163
Scoring: 31 T, 18 C, 6 PG, 3 GM

COOTE, Patrick Bernard

b. Eton, 7.1.1910
d. Killed in action 13.4.1941
Club: Leicester
Debut: *10.10.1931 v Gloucester (A),*
Lost 6-12
Last Game: *18.11.1933 v Swansea (A),*
Lost 6-8 (1PG, 3 pts)
CAPS: Ireland (1) 1933

Paddy Coote represented RAF Cranwell, the RAF (whose squash champion he became in 1931 when he beat his uncle in the final) and Surrey. He played centre, and was capped by Ireland against Scotland on April 1, 1933, when his fellow centre was another Tiger, Dr Morgan Crowe. A fearless tackler, his playing career was sadly abbreviated when he suffered a severely damaged neck in tackling W D Williams, the Swansea wing (who ended up with concussion) in November 1933. He collapsed on the train home from Swansea but was cared for by Dr Crowe before being taken to the RAF hospital in Uxbridge. He was not discharged for three months.

Apps: 27
Points: 96
Scoring: 12 T, 13 C, 6 PG, 4 DG

CROSS, Charles Woodrow

b. registered in Norwich, March qtr, 1887
d. Leicester, 23.4.1957
Clubs: Stoneygate, Leicester
Debut: *9.4.1910 v London Welsh (H),*
Won 11-3 (1T, 3 pts)
Last Game: *26.12.1923 v Birkenhead Park (H), Won 17-3*

Charlie Cross, a forward, was involved in a famous incident when Tigers were travelling to the game at Birkenhead Park in April 1921: a group of players came across "a runaway horse attached to a cart near Eastham Ferry. Cross, who was in the foremost car, jumped out and after a short sprint overtook the runaway and stopped it before much damage was done." In 1958 Stoneygate Rugby Club presented the Charlie W Cross Memorial Trophy, to be awarded annually to the winners of the referees' and club secretaries' match. Cross was President of Leicester Thursday, and a vice-president of South Leicester and Oadby RFC, and became President of Leicester in 1949, an office he held until his death. He was also the first President of the Tigers Supporters' Club.

Apps: 131
Points: 57
Scoring: 19 T

CROWE, Morgan Patrick

b. Dublin, Ireland, 5.3.1907
d. Nutley Park, Ballsbridge, Ireland, 8.4.1993
Educated: Blackrock College, Royal College of Surgeons of Ireland (RCSI)
Clubs: Lansdowne, Leicester, Barbarians (1931/32 Lansdowne)
Debut: *1.10.1932 v Coventry (H), Won 16-4*
Last Game: *23.4.1935 v Exeter (A), Won 42-0 (1T, 1C, 5 pts)*
CAPS: Ireland (13) 1929-34

A dashing centre, Morgan Crowe won international honours before seeing his brother (Philip Martin, in 1935) and son (James Fintan, in 1974) capped for Ireland. He was an outstanding schools player and captained the Blackrock side that won the Leinster Schools' Senior Cup for the 25th time in 1925. After leaving school, he joined the Lansdowne club with whom he won the Leinster Cup in 1928, 1929, 1931 and 1933. He was selected for the British Lions tour to Australia and New Zealand in 1930, but missed the trip because of an injury sustained playing in a Hospitals Cup match while he was studying to become a doctor.

He joined Leicester after coming to work at the Royal Infirmary (prior to this he used to commute from Dublin every

COWLING, Robin James

b. Ipswich, Suffolk, 24.3.1944
Educated: Sidcot School, Weston-super-Mare; Royal Agricultural College, Cirencester
Clubs: Gloucester, Leicester, Barbarians (1976/77)
Debut: *7.9.1974 v Bedford (H), Won 19-12*
Last Game: *2.5.1981 v Gosforth (John Player Cup Final at Twickenham), Won 22-15*
CAPS: England (8) 1977-79

Loose head prop Robin Cowling, the son of a headmaster, was taken to Painswick in Gloucestershire when a year old as his home area in Suffolk was subjected to wartime bombing. His paternal grandfather was a Gloucester player, while on his mother's side an uncle, J G A'Bear, captained Gloucester for five seasons and went on the 1936 British tour to Argentina. After leaving school he started farming, first in England and then for two years in Scandinavia and Germany. On his return he qualified at the Royal Agricultural College, Cirencester, and worked at the college farm. A fellow student, John Pullin, who preceded him into the England front row, encouraged Robin to play for Gloucester whom he joined as a hooker before moving to prop.

He represented Gloucestershire in five consecutive county finals (twice on the winning side) and was a member of the Gloucester side that won the first RFU club knockout competition against Moseley in 1972. He also played for the Western Counties against Ian Kirkpatrick's All Blacks.

He moved to Market Harborough and joined Leicester but, although always respected by his own and opposing front rows as a superb craftsman, it was three years before he gained the first of his eight caps for England, against Scotland in 1977. An heroic performance against France in 1978, when he stayed on the field with a badly-damaged shoulder, undoubtedly cost him further caps. He gained four John Player Cup winners' medals with Gloucester (one) and Leicester (three).

After his retirement from the game his job as a farm manager took him back to his native Ipswich and subsequently to Cornwall, where he now coaches the Hayle club in his spare time. An experienced sailor of near-international standard, his love of the sea has been inherited by his sons.

Apps: 184
Points: 32
Scoring: 8 T

Saturday) and became well known for his practical jokes and his abstention from tobacco and alcohol. He was appointed to the City Isolation Hospital in February 1934, but returned to Ireland in 1937 to become deputy medical officer of health for Dublin.

Morgan Crowe was also proficient at golf - he was a long standing member of Elm Park, and he was in the Marlborough Hockey Club side that won the Midlands Cup in 1939. He captained the Claremont Tennis Club and played cricket for the now defunct Monkstown club. He served as an Ireland selector in the 1950s and was President of Lansdowne in 1956/57.

Apps: 72
Points: 160
Scoring: 18 T, 36 C, 9 PG, 1 DG, 1 GM

George
Cullen

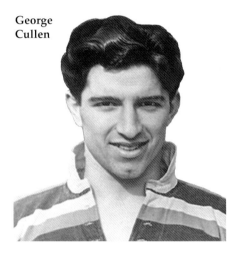

CULLEN, George Henry

b. Newark, Nottinghamshire, 28.2.1928
Educated: Magnus Grammar School, Newark; Loughborough Colleges
Clubs: Newark, Nottingham, Loughborough Colleges, Leicester, Bedford
Debut: *26.12.1949 v Birkenhead Park (H), Lost 0-5*
Last Game: *23.4.1957 v Exeter (A), Lost 10-14*

George Cullen, a fly-half, was originally a schoolteacher in Windsor before moving to Bedford Modern School where he taught PE and English until his retirement. He represented Notts, Lincs & Derbys while still at school. He scored 13 of the Tigers' 16 points in the October 1955 game against Moseley, and but for an unfortunate bounce of the ball would have scored the lot, the last try going to John Elders.

Apps: 180
Points: 550
Scoring: 66 T (including a penalty try), 77 C, 57 PG, 9 DG

CUSWORTH, Leslie

b. Normanton, Yorkshire, 3.7.1954
Educated: Normanton Grammar School, West Midlands Teacher Training College, Walsall; Birmingham University
Clubs: Wakefield, Moseley, Leicester, Barbarians (1980/81)
Debut: *28.10.1978 v Swansea (A), Lost 12-21 (1DG, 3 pts)*
Last Game: *28.4.1990 v Bath (A) (Courage League), Lost 15-26*
CAPS: England (12) 1979-88

Les Cusworth, the son of a miner, was one of the most talented fly halves of his era, though the vagaries of selection restricted him to twelve England caps. At Normanton Grammar School he came under the influence of the games master, Alan Jubb, a former Harlequin and great exponent of sevens play. This obviously encouraged Cusworth, who went on to earn a world-wide reputation as a sevens player, especially for the Barbarians and the Irish Wolfhounds at the annual Hong Kong tournament. This was the perfect pedigree for coaching England's winning team in the inaugural World Cup Sevens in Scotland during April 1993.

In his long career Cusworth played for England colts, British Colleges and the UAU, Yorkshire, North-East Counties, North Midlands and went on the England 'B' tour to Romania in 1978. His first cap came against New Zealand the following year but he was promptly dropped and his other 11 caps came over a period of six years, though Leicester supporters never doubted his rare ability both as entertainer and decision-maker.

In 1974/75, while with Wakefield, Cusworth established a world record of 25 for drop goals in a season, breaking the record of

22 set by Keith James (Newport) in 1971/72. He still holds the Leicester club record of four drop goals in a match in the Pilkington Cup tie at Liverpool St Helens in 1989, ironically almost a year to the day after he had missed four on his penultimate appearance for England against France in Paris. He also held the club record for points scored in one match by an individual (30), until overtaken by Dusty Hare. He played in three successive John Player Cup finals with Leicester, and the losing 1983 and 1989 finals. He was named *Leicester Mercury* Sports Personality of the Year in February 1988. Formerly a schoolmaster, he is now a sales director with the insurance brokers, P & G Bland.

Apps: 365
Points: 947
Scoring: 66 T, 100 C, 65 PG, 96 DG

DAY, Harold Lindsay Vernon

b. Darjeeling, India, 12.8.1898
d. Hadley Wood, Hertfordshire, 15.6.1972
Educated: Bedford Modern School
Club: Leicester
Debut: *11.1.1919 v New Zealand Services (H), Lost 0-19*
Last Game: *26.1.1929 v Richmond (A), Lost 3-12*
CAPS: England (4) 1920-26

Harold Day won a national reputation as a goal-kicking wing (though Wavell Wakefield once observed that a slower wing never played for England) and a shrewd observer of the game. He served as a lieutenant with the Royal Artillery during the First World War, and was severely wounded in France. After the armistice he was stationed in the Midlands and came to play for Leicester. After resigning his commission, he became a teacher at Felsted School and while there he was involved in a controversial incident when playing for Leicestershire against the North Midlands at Moseley on November 4, 1925: Leicester won 6-3 but later the match was declared void by the RFU, as Day was ineligible to play being neither resident nor employed in the county. (The game was replayed on February 3, 1926, without Day, and the North Midlands won 6-3.) He captained the all-Tigers Leicestershire side that

won the county championship in 1925, and the Tigers themselves from 1924-28.

He played for the Army against the Royal Navy in 1920, 1922 and 1923; against the RAF and French Army in 1922 and he captained the Army side once. He also represented the Midlands, Hampshire and Leicestershire, as a burly, strong-running wing; though in the game against Cambridge University in November, 1924, Day, playing as full back, picked the ball up on his own 25 and instead of kicking into touch, spotted an opening and ran in a try. It was reported at the time that it was "somewhat unique when a full back scores a try". Slightly winded, however, he failed to convert. Day's England debut was unusual as the original choice, W M Lowry, was left out after the team photograph had been taken as it was thought conditions would better suit Day. He went on to score all of England's points in a 19-5 defeat by Wales. It was his kicking skill, in borrowed boots, that saved England from defeat in the match with France at Twickenham in 1922 - after which he was dropped from the side! Later in his career he became an international referee, taking charge of the game between Scotland and Wales at Murrayfield on February 3, 1934.

Day played cricket for Bedfordshire before joining Hampshire and playing 78 first-class games for them between 1922 and 1931, scoring 1,000 runs in his first season. He also played cricket for the Army, and was invited to tour South Africa in 1924 with Sol Joel's team, but declined. In 1968 *The Cricketer* magazine erroneously carried his obituary, though the first Day knew of this was when a friend called his wife. "She told him I certainly wasn't dead although I was on the compost heap!", Day, who had been in the garden, was later quoted as saying. The writer of numerous newspaper articles, he was also the author of *"Rugby Union Football"*.

Apps: 212
Points: 1,151
Scoring: 108 T, 281 C, 81 PG, 4 DG, 2 GM

Paul Dodge

DODGE, Paul William

b. Leicester, 26.2.1958
Educated: Roundhill School, Syston; Wreake Valley Upper School
Clubs: Leicester, Barbarians (1977/78)
Debut: *6.9.1975 v Bedford (A), Lost 12-24*
Last Game: *3.4.1993 (replacement) v Richmond (A), Won 29-15*
CAPS: England (32) 1978-85, British Isles (2) 1980

Paul Dodge, one of the finest and certainly one of the most dependable centres ever to play for Leicester, became the youngest Tiger to win his player's tie, which he was awarded after playing against the Barbarians in 1975 at the age of 17 years 305 days - only 112 days after his debut. He capped the day with a try! By then he had already played for the Midland Counties (East) against John Hipwell's touring Australian XV and was on the winning side. He completed 100 games for the club before his 21st birthday.

Dodge came under the influence at Roundhill School of Dave Lyons, a former Tiger who was influential in establishing the Leicester Youth team in 1972. He suffered a broken leg early in his playing career but the next season played for Leicestershire's under-15 side (when still under 14); he also captained the under-14 side. He joined Leicester's youth side and played in the county colts team which won the Midlands Championship, in company with Steve Kenney and Andrew Collington. In 1976 he gained his only England colts cap against the Welsh youth and, later that year, appeared for the Midlands and North against Argentina at Welford Road. In 1977 he toured Canada with England under-23, eventually winning six under-23 caps, and appearing in the England XV which beat the American Eagles.

A tall, powerfully-built player with a raking left-footed kick, and a useful goal-kicker, Dodge won the first of his 32 caps for England in 1978 against Wales. In 1979 he toured the Far East with England and also played for an England XV against the USA and Argentina. He missed selection for the first two games of the grand slam year of 1980, but returned to play against Wales and Scotland alongside his club colleague, Clive Woodward. He remained a regular choice until he broke his leg playing against Blackheath in 1983 but toured South Africa in 1984 (returning home early because of injury) and became captain of England in 1985 for the five nations championship and the summer tour to New Zealand. He ended his international career as England's most capped centre. Dodge was a replacement for the Lions tour to South Africa in 1980, when he scored a try in his first game and played in the last two tests, making five appearances in all.

A bookbinder in the family business in Syston, Dodge was one of the mainstays of the Tigers in the 1980s, helping them to six John Player and Pilkington cup finals (as captain in 1989). He was also captain in 1988 when Leicester became the inaugural winners of the Courage Clubs' Championship. When he retired, he became coach to the club's newly-formed under-21 side before moving up to assist Ian Smith as first-team coach.

Apps: 434+3
Points: 567
Scoring: 93 T (including a penalty try), 33 C, 40 PG, 3 DG

Paul Dodge

DRAKE-LEE, Nicholas James

b. Kettering, Northamptonshire, 7.4.1942
Educated: Stonyhurst College, Downing College Cambridge
Clubs: Kettering, Cambridge University (Blues 1961-63), Leicester, Manchester, Waterloo
Debut: *6.1.1962 v Bath (A), Lost 5-8*
Last Game: *23.11.1968 v Moseley (A), Lost 3-16*
CAPS: England (8) 1963-65

Nick Drake-Lee won the first of his three blues for Cambridge University as a freshman and went on to become the youngest prop to play for England when he made his international debut against Wales in 1963. He also represented East Midlands and Lancashire.

While at Cambridge he approached both Leicester and Northampton which led to him being picked to play for both clubs on the same day, but as Northampton had not contacted him, he made his debut for Leicester. His two brothers played, respectively, for St Thomas's Hospital, and for Rosslyn Park and Plymouth Albion. Drake-Lee had the unique distinction of playing in all three front-row positions for England in the same international season (1963), being picked twice at loose-head prop, twice at tight-head prop, and hooking for ten minutes against France when John Thorne was injured.

He also played for Kettering Cricket Club. He read history at Cambridge and became a schoolmaster but is now a chartered surveyor in Rothwell, specialising in the Licence Trade. His son, Bill, is a current Tigers flank forward.

Apps: 73
Points: 21
Scoring: 7 T

DUGGAN, Michael John

b. Dublin, Ireland, 5.6.1948
Educated: Oakham School, Loughborough Colleges
Clubs: Oakham Town, Loughborough Colleges, Leicester
Debut: *3.1.1970 v Bath (A), Lost 9-13*
Last Game: *16.8.1980 v Lautoka, Fiji (A), Won 12-6*

John Duggan was born in Dublin but since his father was Irish and in the RAF he spent many of his early years travelling the world, especially the Far East, including Malaya and Singapore. The family eventually settled in Oakham

Peter Edwards

where he went to Oakham School. He studied physical education and biology at Loughborough Colleges and qualified as a teacher. Unlike most of the Loughborough students he opted to play for Leicester, having previously played for Oakham Town from 1963-70.

A powerful and gymnastic wing, Duggan invariably had the crowd on its feet when he had the ball. He played for Leicestershire, and Midlands East against Fiji and New Zealand; for the Midlands against New Zealand; and toured with the Irish Wolfhounds to Scotland and Ireland in 1975. At one time he was offered a trial for England, but declined, thinking he had an Irish qualification. It transpired however that to be selected for Ireland at the time, an individual had to play provincial rugby. He was offered a position at Dublin Wanderers but was unable to take the post.

John Duggan

He is keen on all sports, especially sailing, canoeing and rock climbing and is now a lecturer next door to the Welford Road ground, at Southfields College, where he specialises in fitness and exercise. At one time he was honorary secretary of the Leicester Schools Gymnastic Association, and has produced international gymnasts from his school squad. He also won a silver medal at the "World Welly-wanging Championship" at the Liverpool Royal Show in 1977!

Apps: 302
Points: 608
Scoring: 158 T (including a penalty try)

DUNKLEY, Philip Edward

b. Charwelton, Northamptonshire, 9.8.1904
d. 17.6.1985
Educated: Royal Wolverhampton School
Clubs: Old Laurentians, Leicester, Harlequins, Rugby, Congleton, Barbarians (1931/32 Harlequins)
Debut: 21.1.1928 v London Welsh (H), Won 22-0 (2T, 6 pts)
Last Game: 26.12.1934 v Birkenhead Park (H), Lost 8-12
CAPS: England (6) 1931-36

Philip 'Pop' Dunkley, a second-row forward, made a record number of appearances for Warwickshire whom he captained for several seasons. He also captained Harlequins between 1933-36 and was a member of their winning squad in the 1935 Middlesex sevens. A strong line-out forward, he had a reputation as a dribbler of the ball in an era when a forward foot-rush was a fearsome thing. He played in the three home internationals of 1936, including the celebrated victory over New Zealand, and toured Argentina with a British team in the same year.

Dunkley was a bank manager for National Provincial; a strict teetotaller, he was a very religious man and strong supporter of the Toc H charity organisation. During the 1950s, until his retirement in 1964, he worked in Warwick which allowed him more time to devote to his county RFU.

Apps: 32
Points: 26
Scoring: 8 T, 1 C

EDMISTON, James Henry (FOWNES)

b. West Derby, 6.6.1905
d. West Wittering, Sussex, 26.8.1962
Educated: Haileybury, Brasenose College Oxford
Clubs: Blackheath, Oxford University (Blues 1926-27), Leicester
Debut: 20.3.1926 v Old Blues (H), Won 21-5
Last Game: 13.10.1934 v Bridgwater Albion (A), Drew 0-0

Harry Edmiston was the brother of J G who occasionally played for Tigers, but was better known as a Blackheath player. Harry played for Kent and London against the All Blacks in 1935/36. He was the director of Grosvenor and Company, a jointing and packaging company.

Apps: 112
Points: 62
Scoring: 9 T, 8 C, 5 PG, 1 DG

EDWARDS, Peter G.

Clubs: London Welsh, Leicester
Debut: 16.9.1961 v Plymouth Albion (H), Lost 9-11
Last Game: 20.4.1968 v Llanelli (A), Lost 5-14

Peter Edwards took over the regular hooking duties for the Tigers when Mick Walker was injured in November 1963, he then did not miss another first-team game for 21 months (70 games). Prior to joining Leicester Peter had turned out once for the London Welsh first-team at Blackheath on 12th March, 1960.

Apps: 145
Points: 6
Scoring: 2 T

ELDERS, John

b. Middlesbrough, Yorkshire, 18.12.1930
Educated: Acklam Hall Grammar School, Middlesbrough; Loughborough Colleges
Clubs: Loughborough Colleges, Leicester, Northern, Barbarians (1958/59 Northern)
Debut: 5.9.1953 v Bedford (H), Won 12-6
Last Game: 27.12.1958 v Birkenhead Park (H), Drew 8-8 (1T, 3 pts)

John Elders, one of several Leicester centres during the 1950s and 1960s who came close to international honours, played for Leicestershire and Northumberland and received several England trials. He captained Tigers and began a distinguished coaching career with Northumberland in 1968. He coached England between 1972-74 and was a national selector the following year, before taking over England schools from Mike Davis in 1979.

John Elders

During his Leicester career Elders taught mathematics and physical education at South Wigston and Alderman Newton's schools. He then went on to teach at the Royal Grammar School in Newcastle for 25 years but in 1981 he emigrated to Australia where he became sports master at Downing College in Toowoomba, Queensland; during his time there he coached the current Wallaby centre, Tim Horan. He returned to England in 1990, and is now director of rugby at Northern Football Club.

Apps: 144
Points: 126
Scoring: 38 T, 3 PG, 1 DG

John Elliott

ELLIOTT, John James

b. Nottingham, 10.6.1943
Educated: High Pavement Grammar School, Nottingham; Loughborough Colleges
Clubs: Old Paviors, Loughborough Colleges, Edinburgh Wanderers, Leicester, Nottingham, Barbarians (1975/76 Nottingham)
Debut: *18.2.1967 v Wasps (H), Won 6-3*
Last Game: *19.12.1970 v Bristol (A), Lost 0-10*

John Elliott, one of several talented hookers in Tigers' ranks during the late 1960s, represented Notts, Lincs & Derbys at under-19 level during his final year at school. When he went to Loughborough he continued playing for his school old boys, Old Paviors, until he gained a first-team place in the Colleges side of 1963. He played for Notts, Lincs & Derbys at senior level, the North of England and the Midlands, and in various England trials between 1966-1976; he was an England reserve in 1976.

Elliott became an England selector in 1987, working alongside Geoff Cooke and Roger Uttley, and was assistant manager on the England tour to Argentina in 1990. The same management panel helped England to the World Cup final in 1991 and Elliott has remained a national selector while also managing the England under-21 team, with whom he toured to Australia in 1993. He was confirmed as England's assistant manager in autumn 1993. He is now head of marketing for the East Midlands Electricity Board in Nottingham.

Apps: 126
Points: 60
Scoring: 20 T

EVANS, Barry John

b. Hinckley, Leicestershire, 10.10.1962
Educated: John Cleveland College, Hinckley; Derby Lonsdale Teacher Training College
Clubs: Hinckley, Leicester, Coventry, Barbarians (1982/83)
Debut: *31.10.1981 v Saracens (A), Won 34-14 (1T, 4 pts)*
Last Game: *16.11.1991 v Gloucester (A) (Courage League), Lost 3-21*
CAPS: England (2) 1988

Barry Evans represented Leicestershire schools at under-14, -16 and -19 levels as a centre, and England under-16 as a centre before switching to the wing at under-19 level. He toured with the schools to Portugal, with England Students to Japan and the under-23s to Spain. One of the fastest wings to play for Leicester in the modern era, he appeared for the Midlands at all levels and added four 'B' international caps to his representative honours; he won his two full England caps in 1988 on the tour of Australia and Fiji after being called into the squad at the eleventh hour.

Evans, whose father played for Nuneaton Old Edwardians, is Leicester's leading post-war try scorer and one of only five players to score a hat trick of tries in the Christmas fixture against the Barbarians (the others being Percy Lawrie, Graham Meikle, John Quick and Bob Barker). He trained as a teacher of physical education and mathematics, but became an office systems executive. He is now a global account manager with British Telecom, and captain of Coventry RFC.

Apps: 264+1
Points: 678
Scoring: 169 T, 1 C

FARNDON, William Ewart

b. Market Harborough, Leics, 29.12.1901
d. Bognor Regis, Sussex, 27.4.1982
Clubs: London Welsh, Stoneygate, Leicester, Nuneaton
Debut: 18.4.1925 v Birkenhead Park (A), Won 11-5
Last Game: 21.11.1931 v Swansea (A), Lost 0-11

Ewart Farndon, a wing, joined the Tigers in 1924, and in 1925/26 he topped the list of try scorers with 14. In his first game at Welford Road he was said to have given a "wonderful exhibition of speed and football brains". An all-round sportsman, he represented Warwickshire at rugby, he also played cricket and competed for the Amateur Athletic Association. At the time of his wedding in 1927 it was reported that the "honeymoon was of short duration" as he was married on a Wednesday but had to turn out for Tigers on the Saturday for the game against Birkenhead Park.

A liveryman of the Worshipful Company of Framework Knitters, he was the managing director of Dorothy Perkins until his retirement in 1967. He lived for a long time in Central London before retiring to Bognor Regis.

Apps: 183
Points: 258
Scoring: 86 T

FLEWITT, Edward Charles Ansell

b. Sutton Coldfield, Warwickshire, December qtr, 1907
d. Castle Bromwich, Warwickshire, 12.7.1931
Educated: Dunchurch Hall, Brighton College
Clubs: Leicester, Moseley
Debut: 26.12.1925 v Birkenhead Park (H), Won 16-3 (2T, 6 pts)
Last Game: 5.11.1930 v Oxford University (A), Won 16-9

Ted 'Buller' Flewitt, one of the best wings to play for Leicester between the wars, died tragically at Castle Bromwich Aerodrome when his own Gypsy Moth aeroplane crashed shortly after take off. The aeroplane, piloted by his companion, Roderick Baker, dived from 100 feet and crashed near the Chester Road, a main thoroughfare into Birmingham. Flewitt had purchased the aeroplane two years earlier and kept it at Castle Bromwich, although he was a frequent visitor to Leicestershire Aero Club at Desford. He was also an ardent motorist, travelling

many long journeys to away games accompanied by his colleague, Ralph Buckingham, while the rest of the team went by train.

The son of Dr C Y Flewitt, he represented Warwickshire and on December 12, 1928, played alongside Buckingham for the Possibles against the Probables in an England trial, opening the scoring with a try. When he died, Leicester officials described him as "a strong, thrustful player who, on his day, was one of the best wing three-quarters the Tigers have had. His full-hearted dashes for the line will not easily be forgotten." Though he held a position with a Birmingham brewery he had independent means and left £19,681 in his will.

Apps: 129
Points: 221
Scoring: 73 T, 1 C

Billy Foreman

FOREMAN, William James

b. Farnham, Surrey, June qtr, 1866
d. Oadby, Leicester, 15.7.1945
Clubs: Walthamstow, London Caledonians, Kent Wanderers, Leicester
Debut: 7.10.1893 v Gloucester (H), Lost 3-8
Last Game: 3.2.1906 v Coventry (A), Lost 3-12

Billy Foreman played his first game at the age of 15 for Woolwich Clarendon against Roans School, Greenwich, scoring seven tries as a three-quarter. In senior rugby he became captain of the London Caledonians, then moved to Kent Wanderers and played at half back for Kent County for three seasons. While in Leicester with Kent Wanderers, Tom Crumbie persuaded him to stay - and found him a job as a mechanic at Gimson & Sons. In his second season at Leicester he appeared for the Midland Counties against Kent, an action which caused some comment in the London press.

He had the distinction of being the first captain to bring the Midland Counties Cup home to Leicester, having to step in when A O Jones was absent due to illness, and it was his pass which put Percy Oscroft in for a sensational try to beat Moseley 5-3 in 1898. He was also in the cup-winning side for the following five seasons. In 1895 the *Wyvern* reported "for tricky play around the scrum, Foreman takes some beating." Another newspaper article towards the end of his career noted that he was a remarkably fit man and a most consistent player for the club, but his season had been marred by "a dislocated thumb, strained leg, and broken collarbone." Before his move to Leicester he had been a member of the Polytechnic Boxing club, and had more than average success in running.

He was approached several times by the Northern Union but preferred to stay at Leicester because of "the good feelings that existed between himself, the committee and the people of the town", so much so that he became landlord of the Marlborough Head public house on Welford Road. In the 1901/02 season Foreman helped Northampton on two or three occasions when W Patrick was disabled. Always a keen golfer, he was a founder member of the Glen Gorse Golf Club in Oadby, and indeed died on the first hole there whilst playing a round of golf. His grandson was the Leicester and England scrum half, W K T Moore.

Apps: 358
Points: 263
Scoring: 85 T, 4 C

David Forfar

FORFAR, David John

b. Salford, Lancashire, 6.9.1951
Educated: Stonehill High School, Longslade College
Clubs: Syston, Leicester
Debut: 13.4.1971 v Manchester (A), Won 17-9
Last Game: 25.11.1981 (replaced) v Australia (H), Lost 15-18

Dave Forfar, a flanker, played for the county at under-19 and senior level. He also appeared for the Midlands against the All Blacks and Australia, and for the Midlands and North against Argentina. An all-embracing tackler with useful line-out ability, he played for England in a 'B' international against France in 1979 and appeared in two England final trials. Interested in astronomy, geology and cycling, he was originally a salesman, but is now a partner in an engineering company.

Apps: 222+1
Points: 56
Scoring: 14 T

FOULKES-ARNOLD, Malcolm Victor

b. Peterborough, Cambridgeshire, 29.11.1957
Educated: Deacon's Grammar School, Peterborough; Leicester Polytechnic
Clubs: Peterborough, Harlequins, Leicester
Debut: 12.9.1979 v Birmingham (H), Won 38-0
Last Game: 12.4.1993 v Wasps (H), Won 14-13

Malcolm Foulkes-Arnold, a lock known as 'Foulksy' or 'Flutter', represented England Students, British Polytechnics, Leicestershire, and Eastern Counties 19 group. He played football and hockey for Cambridgeshire and enjoys squash, tennis, swimming and cricket. He is a chartered architect with his own business, the Foulkes-Arnold-Weston Partnership, and retains an interest in the Tigers in the capacity of under-21 team secretary.

Apps: 259+2
Points: 84
Scoring: 21 T

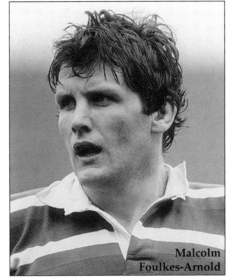

Malcolm Foulkes-Arnold

FRANCIS, David Gwyn

b. Gorseinon, Glamorgan, 2.2 1896
d. Reading, Berkshire, 7.5.1987
Educated: Gowerton Grammar School, University College, Cardiff; Jesus College Oxford
Clubs: Oxford University (Blue 1919), Gorseinon, Loughor, Llanelly, London Welsh, Leicester
Debut: 15.11.1919 v Northampton (A), Drew 6-6
Last Game: 11.2.1922 v Newport (A), Lost 9-24
CAPS: Wales (2) 1919-24

Gwyn Francis, a schoolmaster at Reading School after attaining a degree in modern languages from Jesus College, Oxford, served as a staff sergeant in the Royal Welsh Fusiliers during the First World War. He played in the Welsh pack against the New Zealand Army in 1919, and against Scotland in 1924. He also represented London Counties and Surrey and captained London Welsh in 1924/25. He later became a referee and was President of the Berkshire Rugby Football Union.

Apps: 12
Points: 0

Mike Freer

FREER, Michael Edmund

b. Stoke Albany, near Market Harborough, Northamptonshire, 4.2.1935
Educated: Welland Park School, Market Harborough
Clubs: Kibworth, Leicester
Debut: 21.1.1956 v Rugby (H), Lost 0-3
Last Game: 11.3.1965 v Loughborough Colleges (H), Lost 11-24

Mike Freer, one of a group of talented fly halves at the club in the same period, played for the RAF during his national service with Bomber Command. While he was living in Market Harborough Derek Bircumshaw, the former Tigers forward, persuaded Freer to become a policeman, a vocation that lasted two years and 84 days. His rugby career ended in the game against Loughborough Colleges when he seriously damaged a shoulder, an injury which still troubles him. He runs his own fencing contractors business at Caldecote.

Apps: 203
Points: 66
Scoring: 15 T, 7 DG

GADNEY, Bernard Cecil

b. Oxford, 16.7.1909
Educated: Dragon School, Oxford; Stowe School
Clubs: Richmond, Leicester, Headingley, Barbarians (1932/33)
Debut: 9.11.1929 v Nuneaton (A), Won 4-3
Last Game: 11.4.1939 v Bath (A), Won 28-3 (1T, 3 pts)
CAPS: England (14) 1932-38

Bernard Gadney spent much of his decade in senior rugby wrestling with

Coventry's Jimmy Giles for the England scrum half position. A talented player and captain, Gadney was a big man for his position and gained a reputation for his forceful breaks. Leicester were fortunate to secure his services ahead of Northampton and he made an early impression. The report of a game against Harlequins described how Gadney "electrified the crowd getting away on his own. Three times he was pulled down but each time he got away again and at last, with opponents hanging on to him, he forced his way over the line."

A teacher, he also represented Leicestershire, East Midlands, Oxfordshire and Yorkshire during his distinguished career. He first appeared for the Barbarians in 1932, and became the first Tiger to captain England in 1933/34 when he led the side which won the triple crown for the first time since 1928. He captained the British touring side to Argentina in 1936, with another Leicester player, Doug Prentice, as manager. The team won all ten games on their tour (no Test matches were included).

A good enough footballer to play centre on occasions (where his knack of making openings proved invaluable), he attracted the attention of the two Hull rugby league clubs but preferred to work his way up the teaching ladder and to play union. His first teaching appointment was at the Manor House School in Brackley but he went on to become a headmaster at Malsis School in Yorkshire. During the Second World War, he served in the Royal Naval Volunteer Force. His older brother, Cyril, was an international referee and President of the Rugby Football Union in 1962/63.

Apps: 170
Points: 189
Scoring: 63 T

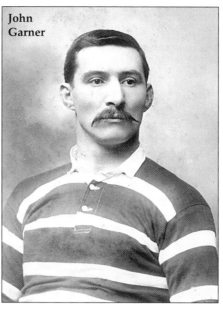
John Garner

GARNER, John William

b. registered in Leicester, June qtr, 1869
d. details not available
Clubs: Belgrave St. Peter's, Leicester
Debut: *6.4.1895 v Sale (H), Won 14-0*
Last Game: *4.10.1902 v Devonport Albion (H), Won 10-7*

John Garner was employed in his father's business, H Garner & Sons, as a shoe clipper. In 1891 he captained Belgrave St Peter's to the final of the Leicestershire Junior Cup competition. In 1894/95 he became the first Belgrave player to win a county cap. A strong forward, Garner appeared in 22 Midland Counties cup ties for Leicester (whom he captained in 1901/02) and was on the losing side only once. This included five consecutive winners' medals between 1898 and 1902.

Apps: 209
Points: 27
Scoring: 3 T, 9 C

Mike Gavins

GAVINS, Michael Neil

b. Leeds, Yorkshire, 14.10.1934
Educated: Roundhay School, Leeds University, Loughborough Colleges
Clubs: Old Roundhegians, Leeds University, Loughborough Colleges, Leicester, Moseley, Middlesbrough
Debut: *31.1.1957 v Royal Air Force (H), Lost 8-18*
Last Game: *28.11.1970 v Moseley (A), Lost 13-16 (2C, 4 pts)*
CAPS: England (1) 1961

The career of Mike Gavins, a full back, was extended when he came out of retirement at the start of the 1970/71 season at the age of 36. Injuries to Robin Money and Richard Cooper had created a crisis which Gavins was able to overcome, reminding spectators of his achievements a decade earlier. He captained Leeds University and the English Universities and represented Leicestershire, Midland Counties and the North Midlands. He established a post-war Leicester record for points scored in the 1958/59 season and broke it the following season. While with Middlesbrough he set a club record of 229 points in the 1967/68 season.

Gavins held various positions as a schoolmaster, including head of the economics department (and coach to the senior and under-16 teams) at Uppingham School, where he has worked since 1968. He also coached the Midlands against Fiji in 1970.

Apps: 121
Points: 592
Scoring: 5 T, 107 C, 119 PG, 2 DG

GILLINGHAM, Nigel Kenneth

b. Guildford, Surrey, 16.1.1953
Educated: Royal Grammar School, Guildford; Loughborough Colleges
Clubs: Richmond, Loughborough Colleges, Leicester
Debut: *2.9.1978 v Bedford (H), Won 37-12*
Last Game: *23.4.1984 v Pontypool (A), Lost 0-19*

Nigel Gillingham, a mobile lock, had one season with Richmond before entering Loughborough Colleges in 1973. Having missed an under-19 schools cap through injury he played for England under-23s; after leaving Loughborough (whom he captained) he joined Leicester and found himself playing alongside Nick Joyce, who shares the same birthday.

Gillingham decided on a career in the RAF and appeared for their representative side as well as for Combined Services (including an appearance against the New Zealanders in 1978). He also took part in the famous Midland Counties (East) win over the 1975 Australians under the Leicester lights. He is now a wing commander at RAF Halton.

Apps: 144+1
Points: 48
Scoring: 12 T

GOODRICH, Alfred

b. registered in Leicester, December qtr, 1874
d. details not available
Clubs: Aylestone, Leicester
Debut: *10.11.1900 v Manchester (H), Won 18-3*
Last Game: *12.4.1909 v Llanelly (A), Lost 3-11*

Alf Goodrich, the brother of Tom, and also a forward appeared in eleven Midland Counties cup ties and was never on the losing side, a record that included three finals in 1904, 1905 and 1909. He was a shire finisher in the hosiery trade.

Apps: 179
Points: 31
Scoring: 9 T, 1 DG

GOODRICH, Thomas William

b. registered in Leicester, December qtr, 1873
d. Leicester, 5.7.1947
Clubs: Old Humberstone, Belgrave, Leicester
Debut: *25.10.1899 v Bedford School (H), Won 29-3 (1T, 3 pts)*
Last Game: *9.3.1910 v Moseley (A), Won 20-0*

Tom Goodrich, a forward like his brother, won all 20 of his Midland Counties cup ties, including five successive finals between 1901 and 1905. He appeared for the Rest of England against Durham, the champion county, at West Hartlepool in 1902, but was as valuable for Leicester when his playing days were over since he became the club trainer. Although Goodrich was employed in the hosiery industry he occupied his position with the club for forty years until the beginning of the 1945/46 season. His sterling work as groundsman was one of the major reasons for Welford Road's good playing surface during this time.

Apps: 205
Points: 24
Scoring: 6 T, 3 C

GREASLEY, George

Clubs: Bakers Thursday, Leicester
Debut: *3.2.1906 v Coventry (A), Lost 3-12*
Last Game: *21.4.1919 v The Army (H), Lost 5-8*

George Greasley, a forward, once an England reserve, was part of Leicester's Midland Counties Cup-winning team in 1909, 1910, 1912 and 1913.

Apps: 174
Points: 84
Scoring: 28 T

GREENLEES, Harry Dickson

b. Pollokshields, Glasgow, 31.7.1903
d. Houghton-on-the-Hill, Leics, 23.5.1969
Educated: Rossall School, Glasgow Academy
Clubs: Glasgow Academicals, Stoneygate, Leicester
Debut: *20.3.1926 v Old Blues (H), Won 21-5*
Last Game: *16.4.1932 v Blackheath (H), Lost 3-5*
CAPS: Scotland (6) 1927-30

Harry Greenlees was a talented fly-half whose career suffered from a string of injuries which prevented him achieving his full potential. That he played six times for Scotland and would have toured with the 1930 British Lions to Australasia (had his uncles given him time off work) indicates his ability.

He was captain of Leicester from 1930-32 but it was not a happy time: in January 1931 he broke his collarbone while playing in a Scottish trial and was unable to play for six weeks. He returned in time to be included on the Easter tour to the West Country but damaged his shoulder in the first game against Bristol, an X-ray at Plymouth Hospital showing he had again suffered the same break.

A scratch golfer and county champion many times he became captain of Leicestershire Golf Club from 1942-44 and finally President in 1950. He married the daughter of J G Grahame (who ran the Leicester Supporters' Club), whose other two daughters married the Meikle brothers, both England internationals. Greenlees was a director of Easi-Fit Shoes which moved from Glasgow to Leicester in the mid-1920s. He became chairman of Grahame Gardner Limited, the school outfitters, and of the sportswear manufacturers, Gymphlex Limited of Horncastle, Lincolnshire.

Apps: 153
Points: 192
Scoring: 32 T, 19 C, 6 PG, 10 DG

GREENWOOD, A. Henry

b. details not available
d. killed in action, Second World War
Clubs: Bedford, Leicester
Debut: *11.9.1926 v Coventry (H), Lost 9-11*
Last Game: *26.11.1932 v Nuneaton (H), Won 12-0*

Henry Greenwood, a forward, first played for Bedford in 1923/24 and was their leading points scorer with 56 in 1925/26. He played for the East Midlands against the Barbarians in both the 1925 and 1926 Mobbs memorial matches.

Apps: 157
Points: 44
Scoring: 12 T, 4 C

Roger Grove

GROVE, Roger Vincent

b. Solihull, Warwickshire, 1.2.1940
Educated: Bristol College of Technology
Clubs: Clevedon, Bristol, Leicester, Moseley
Debut: *1.10.1966 v Coventry (A), Drew 8-8*
Last Game: *25.1.1973 v Royal Navy (H), Won 29-12*

Roger Grove was a prop who captained Leicester in 1971/72; he played for Somerset during his days with Bristol. At one time he was an approved-school instructor and is now a social worker for Cornwall County Council.

Apps: 172
Points: 34
Scoring: 9 T, 2 C, 1 PG

HALL, Brian Philip

b. Newark, Nottinghamshire, 30.12.1946
Educated: Mundella Grammar School, Nottingham
Clubs: Nottingham Moderns, Nottingham, Leicester, Dubai Exiles, Barbarians (1980/81)
Debut: *2.9.1970 v Newport (A), Lost 6-16*
Last Game: *29.4.1984 v South Gulf Select XV (A), Won 44-3*

Brian 'Ossie' Hall joined Leicester from Nottingham. A competent centre, highly rated by his colleagues, he was at times an incisive runner and always a devastating tackler. He played for Midland Counties East against Fiji, for the Midland Counties against the All Blacks, and in the county championship for Notts, Lincs & Derbys and the East Midlands. In 1977/78 he was club captain for Leicester's first John Player Cup final (though injury almost stopped him playing at Twickenham). At one time a production manager with BSS, he is now sales manager with Velan Engineering Co Ltd.

Apps: 308+4
Points: 275
Scoring: 67 T, 2 C, 3 DG

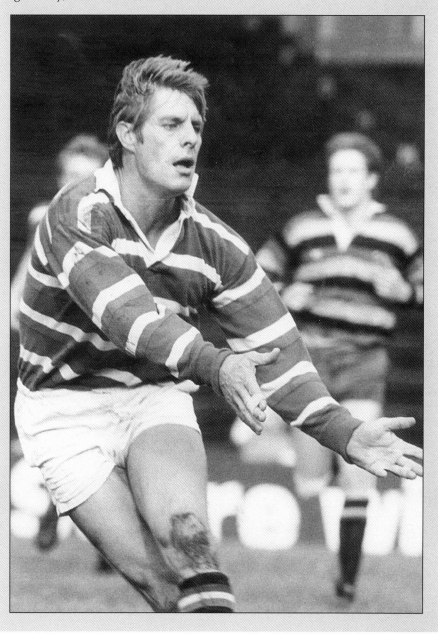

HARE, William Henry

b. Newark, Nottinghamshire, 29.11.1952
Educated: Magnus Grammar School, Newark
Clubs: Newark, Nottingham, Leicester, Barbarians (1973/74 Nottingham)
Debut: 20.10.1976 v Oxford University (H), Won 46-8 (5C, 4PG, 22 pts)
Last Game: 29.4.1989 v Bath (Pilkington Cup Final at Twickenham), Lost 6-10 (2PG, 6 pts)
CAPS: England (25) 1974-84

Over a ten-year period when England's selection methods seemed at times to resemble a blind man with a pin they turned more often than not to 'Dusty' Hare at full back. In consequence, despite being dropped five times, he became his country's most-capped full back and highest points scorer until both marks were overtaken in the 1990s by Jonathan Webb. Even if England under-rated him his popularity was huge in Leicester where crowds appreciated both his points-scoring ability and the breadth his attacking skills gave to the back division.

Hare was raised on the family farm at South Clifton, Newark and carried on the farming tradition. He learnt his rugby at Magnus Grammar School and won his first representative honours at 17 when he played for the Midland Counties East against Fiji at Welford Road on November 7, 1970; he was then playing with Newark but joined Nottingham in 1971, where he won England under-23 honours in 1973 and his first cap a year later. In 1976 he joined Leicester, and was a member of their John Player Cup-winning teams of 1979-81; he withdrew from the side that played in the 1983 final because he did not want to risk his place in the British Lions tour party of that year and Bath denied him the last possible accolade in

an outstanding career when they beat Leicester in the 1989 cup final, Hare's last match.

The high point of Hare's international career was the England grand slam of 1980 which he shared with Paul Dodge, Clive Woodward and Peter Wheeler from Leicester. He toured Japan with England in 1979, Argentina in 1981, Canada and the USA in 1982 and South Africa in 1984; he made six appearances for the Lions in New Zealand in 1983 (though none in the Tests) and was the second highest points scorer with 88.

Hare broke Sam Doble's career points total of 3,651 at the Reddings on April 25, 1981, ironically the home ground of Doble, the former Moseley full back. He went on to a career total of 7,191 points, a mark unlikely to be overtaken. Of those, 240 were scored for England, including the critical late penalty against Wales in 1980 at Twickenham which clinched a 9-8 victory en route to the grand slam; at

Cardiff a year later he could not repeat the performance, leaving Wales the winners, 21-19.

An all-round athlete he played 10 first-class cricket matches for Nottinghamshire between 1971 and 1977 as a middle-order, right-hand batsman and right-arm medium pace bowler. He also represented Nottinghamshire juniors at tennis up to the age of 14. He was awarded an honorary Master of Arts Degree at Leicester University, and his autobiography, "Dusty", was published in 1985. In April 1990 he became Nottingham's director of rugby, but was unable to mastermind a defeat of Leicester when the clubs met in the fourth round of the Pilkington Cup in 1993; later in the year he parted company with Nottingham.

Apps: 393+1
Points: 4,507
Scoring: 87 T, 779 C, 820 PG, 47 DG

HARGRAVE, Ogden James

Clubs: Stoneygate, Leicester
Debut: *17.4.1909 v London Welsh (H), Won 10-0*
Last Game: *2.2.1914 v Pontypool (A), Lost 3-24*

James Hargrave was joined by his younger brother, L Hargrave, for the game against Birkenhead Park on November 11, 1911. He won one Midland Counties Cup-winners' medal, in 1912, and received an England trial. He was a factory manager.

Apps: 110
Points: 163
Scoring: 53 T, 1 DG

'Jez' Harris

HARRIS, Jeremy Charles

b. Kettering, Northamptonshire, 22.2.1965
Educated: Welland Park High School, Robert Smythe College, Market Harborough
Clubs: Vipers, Leicester
Debut: *29.9.1984 v Saracens (H), Won 22-15*

'Jez' Harris, a product of the Leicester youth team, played for Leicestershire schools at under-14 and under-16 levels, and Leicestershire's colts, under-21 and under-23 sides before gaining his senior county cap. He represented Midland colts, was an England colts triallist and has played in the Midlands senior team. Harris has been understudy to a succession of fly halves at Leicester in Les Cusworth, Brian Smith and Gerry Ainscough, but secured a regular place in 1992/93 which he crowned by playing at Twickenham in the Pilkington Cup final, when he dropped a goal in the defeat of Harlequins. He is a narrow-boat builder for Harborough Boats.

Apps: 150+11
Points: 544
Scoring: 18 T, 92 C, 58 PG, 38 DG

Mike Harrison

HARRISON, Michael John

b. Leicester, 23.8.1940
Educated: Wyggeston Boys School, Loughborough Colleges
Clubs: Loughborough Colleges, Leicester
Debut: *6.1.1962 v Bath (A), Lost 5-8*
Last Game: *3.4.1971 v Birkenhead Park (H), Won 23-11*

Mike Harrison had five England trials as a centre, including one for the England XV in his final trial. Captain of the club in the 1964/65 season, he also played for the English Universities. His father (H C) played for the Tigers (once) but regularly for South Leicester, while his brother (D B) played for Old Wyggestonians. Harrison is now vice-principal at Wyggeston and Queen Elizabeth I College.

Apps: 210
Points: 177
Scoring: 58 T, 1 DG

HASELMERE, Edward Ernest

Educated: Murray School, Rugby
Clubs: Rugby, Leicester, Northampton
Debut: *26.12.1918 v 4th Leicestershire Regiment (H), Won 6-5*
Last Game: *8.9.1923 v Plymouth Albion (H), Won 14-5*

Teddy Haselmere first played for the Rugby second XV at half-back, having come through the Rugby schools union. He made his debut for Rugby's first team in 1913/14. After the First World War he played for Leicester, and in his first full season set the club try-scoring record of 59. He gained an England trial in 1920 and played for England against the South in 1921. He returned to Rugby in 1923/24 to play with the famous England international G S Conway's team. The next season he established the Rugby club record for tries in a season with 32, which was not broken until 1987/88 by Eddie Saunders. Haselmere joined Northampton in February 1925, and made 162 appearances, scoring 96 tries, and accumulating 400 points, before finally returning to Rugby in 1930.

Apps: 180
Points: 528
Scoring: 136 T (including a penalty try), 35 C, 6 PG, 8 DG

David Hazell

HAZELL, David St George

b. Taunton, Somerset, 23.4.1931
Educated: Taunton School, Loughborough Colleges
Clubs: Loughborough Colleges, Leicester, Bristol, Barbarians (1954/55)
Debut: *5.9.1953 v Bedford (H), Won 12-6*
Last Game: *23.4.1956 v Northampton (H), Lost 9-16 (2PG, 6 pts)*
CAPS: England (4) 1955

David Hazell propped for Leicestershire, Somerset (whom he captained in 1963/64) and the Western Counties against the All Blacks in the same season, nine years after he won his England caps. He played for Tigers when teaching in Nottingham (subsequently moving to Taunton School, where he was master in charge of rugby and cricket, and joining Bristol). After his last game with Leicester in 1956, he turned out in the traditional end-of-season sevens tournament at Welford Road but damaged his knees so badly that he had to have both cartilages removed, and was out of the game for over twelve months, which finished his international aspirations. He did not play his first game for Bristol until October of the 1957/58 season. During the 1955 Easter tour, Tigers lost at Plymouth despite Hazell's efforts in scoring all his team's 13 points (he scored a total of 33 points in the three games on that tour). He was regularly named in match programmes as Detective Sgt Hazell (D S G being his initials). He played cricket for Somerset colts, and has recently retired from teaching PE and mathematics.

Apps: 81
Points: 265
Scoring: 15 T, 59 C, 33 PG, 1 DG

HENDERSON, Maurice Michael

b. 1914
Educated: Holy Cross Academy, Jordanhill College
Clubs: Jordanhill, Dunfermline, Bedford, Leicester, Barbarians (1936/37 Dunfermline)
Debut: *3.9.1938 v Bedford (H), Lost 0-18*
Last Game: *26.12.1945 v Barbarians (H), Lost 0-3*
CAPS: Scotland (3) 1937

Michael Henderson, a prop forward, was a physical education teacher who gained three international caps for Scotland in 1937. He played for the Barbarians against Leicester in both 1936 and 1937, and captained the East Midlands against the Barbarians at Northampton in 1946. He also appeared for the Midland Counties against the Barbarians at Welford Road in 1940.

Apps: 25
Points: 15
Scoring: 5 T

HESMONDHALGH, William Robert

b. Ambleside, Cumberland, 1869
d. details not available
Clubs: Ambleside, St Helens, Leicester
Debut: *26.11.1892 v Bedford (H), Won 8-0 (1T, 2 pts)*
Last Game: *26.2.1898 v Burton-on-Trent (A), Lost 0-3*

Bob Hesmondhalgh, from Ambleside, made his debut during a visit in November 1892 when he stepped in to play as C J Mason had dropped out of the team. Apparently the newcomer was pleased with the town and the reception he received (especially after scoring a try), and wanted to move to Leicester. In a short while he was a regular member of the team, and a favourite with the crowd; he was often referred to in the local press as 'H——' or 'Clasher' and was reported to be the finest centre seen in Leicester for many a day, good in defence and attack, and a remarkably good tackler; he was the leading try scorer in 1893/94. He represented both Westmoreland and the Midlands Counties. His name went down in the annals of sporting legend when, on April 14, 1894, he was playing for the club in a game against Manchester Free Wanderers only hours after his wedding at St Andrew's Church.

Apps: 101
Points: 129
Scoring: 33 T, 7 C, 1 PG, 4 DG

HIND, Alfred Ernest

b. Preston, Lancashire, 7.4.1878
d. Oadby, Leicester, 21.3.1947
Educated: Uppingham School, Trinity Hall Cambridge
Clubs: Cambridge University (Blue 1900), Leicester, Nottingham
Debut: *7.10.1899 v Exeter (H), Won 11-0*
Last Game: *27.1.1906 v Moseley (A), Won 3-0*
CAPS: England (2) 1905-06

Alfred Hind, a wing, enjoyed something of an annus mirabilis during the 1905/06 season when he played for the club against New Zealand, for the Midland Counties against the same opponents and then won his full cap, adding another appearance against Wales in the new year. He also earned five winners' medals consecutively in the Midland Counties Cup, scoring a hat-trick of tries in the 1905 final.

Hind, a solicitor, whose brother Harold also played for Tigers, won athletics Blues (1899-1901) and ran 100 yards in 9.8 seconds on two occasions. He played cricket for Cambridge University, four times against Oxford between 1898 and 1901, and played one game for Nottinghamshire. He was a lower-order, right-hand batsman, a right-arm medium pace bowler and slip fielder. He went with the 1903 British touring team to South Africa before he was capped by England, but only appeared in the first three tour games.

Apps: 127
Points: 261
Scoring: 81 T, 1 C, 4 DG

HOBBS, A.J.

Clubs: Northampton, Leicester
Debut: *8.9.1906 v Hartlepool Rovers (H), Won 8-0*
Last Game: *23.11.1912 v Moseley (H), Won 24-0*

A J Hobbs, a forward, joined Leicester from Northampton amid accusations of "poaching" from the Northampton fixture secretary in a letter to *The Birmingham Post*. Hobbs played 112 games for the Saints, scoring 18 tries and 54 points, and was part of the Leicester team which won three Midland Counties Cups between 1909 and 1912.

Apps: 195
Points: 78
Scoring: 26 T

HODGSON, John McDonald

b. Gosforth, Northumberland, 13.2.1909
d. 21.4.1970
Educated: Hillbrow School, Rugby; Rugby School
Clubs: Northern (Newcastle), Leicester, Barbarians (1929/30 Northern)
Debut: *28.12.1933 v Waterloo (H), Won 7-6*
Last Game: *14.4.1936 v Exeter (A), Won 24-12 (1C, 2 pts)*
CAPS: England (7) 1932-36, British Isles (2) 1930

Jack Hodgson, known as 'Mac', was a second-row or back-row forward. He learned his rugby at Hillbrow School but later could only make Rugby School's third XV. He joined Northern in 1926, and became, at 19, their youngest captain, leading the side for five of the seven seasons he played for them. He went on to gain representative honours for Northumberland and played for the combined Northumberland/Durham XV against New Zealand in 1935.

A member of the England side that won the international championship in 1932, he was also in the team that won the triple crown in 1934. He went on the British Isles tour to Australia and New Zealand in 1930 (playing in ten games) before being capped by his country, displacing the tour captain, Leicester's Doug Prentice, in the first Test. He joined Tigers while working in London and travelled each weekend to play. A co-ordinating engineer for C A Parsons Turbines in Newcastle, he went to Johannesburg on business in 1936 and then to Turkey, where he also fought during the Second World War. In the services he made a reputation as a useful boxer, to go with his prowess at golf at which he had a handicap of two. He returned to this country shortly before his death. His sister is Margaret Berry, the Great Britain international golfer and wife of the late Tom Berry.

Apps: 37
Points: 52
Scoring: 14 C, 8 PG

HOGARTH, Thomas Bradley

b. registered in Hartlepool, March qtr, 1878
d. 1961
Clubs: Hartlepool Creelers, Hartlepool Rovers, West Hartlepool, Leicester, Gray's Athletic, Durham City
Debut: *14.4.1906 v Newport (A), Lost 0-25*
Last Game: *14.4.1914 v Bath (A), Lost 3-14*
CAPS: England (1) 1906

Tom Hogarth was reputed to have played soccer as an amateur for Huddersfield Town and Southampton. A forward, he scored a try on his club debut and helped Leicester to win three Midland Counties Cups; he appeared for Durham and was capped by England against France. He was a shipyard blacksmith in Hartlepool. He appeared twice for the Tigers along with his brother A (a fellow forward) on the new year tour in 1909.

Apps: 111
Points: 21
Scoring: 7 T

HOPKINS, William Gilbert

b. Lutterworth, Leicestershire, 24.4.1889
d. Leicester, 6.12.1982
Clubs: Leicester, Barbarians (1915)
Debut: *5.9.1908 v Stratford-on-Avon (H), Won 19-3*
Last Game: *21.4.1919 v The Army (H), Lost 5-8*

Gil Hopkins made his debut for the Tigers in 1908 as a prop forward, and held a place in the side until the outbreak of the First World War. When he was 20 he played in the first fixture against the Barbarians, and subsequently played in all six Barbarian fixtures before the War - only once on the losing side. In 1915 he was invited to become a Barbarians member. He played for the Midland Counties in 1912/13 and in 1914 was a member of the championship-winning county side.

Upon his marriage at the age of 30 he is reputed to have promised his wife that he would give up the game. However, as soon as he went down to watch a match

he was talked into playing as two members of the team had cried off late, and ended up playing another half a dozen times. He was the owner of the textiles firm, Yates and Hopkins Ltd, where he worked until his retirement in 1964.

Apps: 216
Points: 42
Scoring: 14 T

Phil Horrocks-Taylor

HORROCKS-TAYLOR, John Philip

b. Halifax, Yorkshire, 27.10.1934
Educated: Heath Grammar School, Halifax; St John's College Cambridge
Clubs: Halifax, Royal Signals, Cambridge University (Blues 1956-57), Wasps, Leicester, Middlesbrough, Barbarians (1957/58 Cambridge University)
Debut: *4.10.1958 v Coventry (A), Lost 9-14*
Last Game: *21.9.1963 v Plymouth Albion (H), Won 13-9*
CAPS: England (9) 1958-64, British Isles (1) 1959

Phil Horrocks-Taylor was one of the most distinguished Yorkshire emigres to have played for Leicester, a compact and shrewd fly-half whose organisation of the back division proved a valuable asset. Like another Yorkshire fly-half after him, Alan Old, he suffered at the hands of the England selectors who had Bev Risman and Richard Sharp to consider, too. He went as a replacement on the British Lions tour of Australasia in 1959 and played in one Test against New Zealand, making four tour appearances in all. He made 61 appearances for Yorkshire, whom he captained. He is a retired company director of Tarmac.

Apps: 92
Points: 48
Scoring: 14 T, 2 DG

HUGHES, Alan Percy

b. Birkenhead, Cheshire, 24.10.1911
d. killed in action, Second World War
Educated: Rossall School
Clubs: Birkenhead Park, Leicester
Debut: *5.9.1931 v Bath (H), Won 6-0*
Last Game: *9.3.1935 v Coventry (A), Lost 0-11*

Alan Hughes represented Cheshire and received an England trial before emigrating to the USA in 1939. His brother, W R, also played full back for Birkenhead Park and opposed Alan in several games. He was described as a "hardworker, seldom in the limelight on the field".

Apps: 113
Points: 9
Scoring: 3 T

John Jackett

JACKETT, Edward John

b. Falmouth, Cornwall, 4.7.1878
d. Middlesbrough, Yorkshire, 11.11.1935
Educated: Falmouth School
Clubs: Falmouth, Leicester, Devonport Albion, Transvaal (South Africa), De Beers (South Africa), Kimberley (South Africa), Dewsbury RL
Debut: *29.12.1904 v Fettes-Lorettonians (H), Lost 0-16*
Last Game: *2.12.1911 v Moseley (A), Won 9-3*
CAPS: England (13) 1905-09, Anglo-Welsh (3) 1908

John Jackett was an outstanding full back whose named is still revered in his native

Cornwall, for whom he made 52 appearances. That tally includes membership (alongside his brother, Dick, who also appeared for Tigers) of the silver-medal winning Cornish side that represented Britain in the 1908 Olympic Games. His England debut came against the 1905 New Zealanders and he was one of only three players to appear in all five internationals that season. He went on the Anglo-Welsh tour of Australia and New Zealand in 1908, playing in 11 games, dropping the only goal and saving a man from drowning in Sydney Harbour.

The son of a Cornish yacht builder John led a somewhat nomadic existence. Much of his boyhood was spent kicking tin cans on Cornish beaches - hence his fame later in life as an accurate touch-kicker - and he tried his hand as a fisherman, then went to South Africa and joined the Cape Mounted Police. He played football for the De Beers team and appeared for Transvaal against the British touring side of 1903. When he returned home he was, briefly, the Cornish cycling champion, and was also a noted oarsman.

Jackett turned professional in 1911 with Dewsbury and was captain when they beat Oldham at Headingley in 1912 to win the Northern Union Cup. He made 73 appearances for them and later became theatre manager at the Dewsbury Empire Palace. He left to manage a greyhound track in Norwich and eventually found his way to Middlesbrough where, shortly before his death, a local physician advised him to move to a healthier part of the country. Despite trying to obtain work elsewhere he was forced to stay and died at the age of 53.

Apps: 183
Points: 108
Scoring: 8 T, 19 C, 9 PG, 4 DG, 1 GM

JACKSON, Frederick Stanley

b. Camborne, Cornwall or Morriston, Wales (see note)
d. Auckland, New Zealand, 16.4.1957
Educated: Camborne School of Mines
Clubs: Plymouth, Leicester
Debut: 30.9.1905 v New Zealand (H), Lost 0-28
Last Game: 21.3.1908 v London Welsh (H), Won 8-5 (1C, 2 pts)
CAPS: Anglo-Welsh (1) 1908

Fred Jackson, a mining engineer, represented Cornwall (alongside Jackett) from 1900 to 1908, captaining the team in

1903/04. He played for Plymouth between 1896 and 1898, and made his Leicester debut against New Zealand in 1905. He was a forward in the 1908 Anglo-Welsh touring side to Australia and New Zealand, and played in the first Test against New Zealand at Dunedin. He made a total of six appearances in New Zealand, scoring 14 points (including the only goal from a mark) but during the tour he was ordered to return home because of doubts over his amateur status. Instead he settled there and played rugby league for New Zealand in 1910. One of his sons, Everard Stanley Jackson, became an All Black, appearing in six Tests between 1936 and 1938 before losing a leg in the Western Desert campaign in the Second World War.

Apps: 77
Points: 129
Scoring: 20 T, 30 C, 3 PG

Note:
F S Jackson's biographical details come from a New Zealand publication previewing the 1908 tour and despite exhaustive research have never been confirmed as correct. The *Cardiff Evening Express* on 4.4.1908 reports "...Jackson, the Leicester forward, is really a Cymro [Welshman] ... having been born of Welsh parents on Morriston." The mystery lives on!

Nick Jackson

JACKSON, Nicholas Adam

b. Nottingham, 11.5.1958
Educated: Nottingham High School, Trent Polytechnic
Clubs: Old Nottinghamians, Leicester, Nottingham Police
Debut: 4.3.1978 v Harlequins (H), Lost 20-22
Last Game: 22.4.1989 v Bath (H) (Courage League), Won 15-12

Nick Jackson, a lock forward, captained his school rugby team at Nottingham HS where the coach was 'Chalkie' White. He played for Nottinghamshire at under-19 and under-23 level, and for Notts, Lincs & Derbys under-23. A useful cricketer, he played for Notts Amateurs, and is also a keen golfer. He appeared in the Leicester side which beat Gosforth in the 1981 John Player Cup final and represented the British Police between 1981-86. He took a course in business studies while at Trent Polytechnic and gave up his career in the police force to join the family business as a beer, wines and spirits wholesaler.

Apps: 98+7
Points: 40
Scoring: 10 T

JACKSON, Walter

b. details not available
d. Edmonton, Canada, April 1924 or 1925
Club: Leicester
Debut: 5.12.1891 v Rugby (H), Won 15-0
Last Game: 15.10.1898 v Rugby (H), Won 44-0

Walter Jackson, a forward, was described as "one of the most reliable men in the team, puts it all in." But a broken collarbone forced him out of the semi-final of the Midland Counties Senior Cup against Moseley in 1894/95 which, with the absence of Banks, considerably weakened Leicester and Moseley won a hollow victory. After this semi-final Moseley refused to renew their fixture with Tigers for eight seasons, unless they were drawn together in the cup. Jackson was a losing finalist in the 1894 Midland Counties Cup, but avenged that defeat with victory in the 1898 final. He served in France during the First World War and then emigrated to Canada.

Apps: 208
Points: 14
Scoring: 4 T, 1 C

JENKINS, John Michael

b. Birmingham, 18.3.1928
d. Brixham, Devon, 4.4.1993
Educated: Oundle School, Clare College Cambridge
Clubs: Cambridge University (Blues 1949 and 1951), Moseley, Leicester
Debut: 20.9.1952 v Plymouth Albion (H), Won 27-6
Last Game: 31.10.1955 v Bective Rangers (H), Lost 6-9

John Jenkins, a lock or back-row forward, captained Cambridge University at Twickenham in 1951. He went on a combined Oxford and Cambridge Universities tour of South Africa before joining Leicester, whom he captained from 1953-55. He became a management consultant in Brixham whose colts he coached. His sons, Rory and Michael, are both rugby players: Rory has won England colts, under-21 and student honours and played for Cambridge in the 1992 university match. Michael plays in New Zealand for the leading Auckland club, Ponsonby.

Apps: 112
Points: 30
Scoring: 10 T

JENKINS, Leighton Hugh

b. New Tredegar, Monmouthshire, 1.7.1931
Educated: Monmouth Training College, Loughborough Colleges
Clubs: Newport, London Welsh, Loughborough Colleges, Leicester, Bath
Debut: 6.9.1958 v Bedford (H), Won 20-11 (1T, 3 pts)
Last Game: 19.12.1959 v Bristol (H), Lost 3-11
CAPS: Wales (5) 1954-56

Leighton Jenkins came to Leicester as a fully-fledged international back-row forward. He played for Leicestershire while at Loughborough Colleges, captained Newport in 1957/58 and joined Tigers after taking up a position at Oakham School. Owing to his teaching duties, he was unable to join Leicester in a visit to Dublin in November 1958, thereby depriving the club of the chance to field international players from all the home countries.

In September 1959 he was given a commission in the RAF as a physical training officer, and was unavailable for the first few games as he had to go on an 11-week refresher course. He had been elected captain for the 1959/60 season but it became obvious that he would not be able to continue with the job so Tom

Bleasdale took his place. As a squadron leader he later represented both the RAF and the Combined Services. He was captain of the RAF between 1962-64 and their fixtures secretary for a number of years.

Apps: 32
Points: 18
Scoring: 6 T

Peter Jerwood

JERWOOD, Harold Peter

b. Oakham, Rutland, 7.6.1916
d. Oakham, Rutland, Leics, 3.2.1993
Educated: Oakham School, Rugby School, Jesus College Cambridge
Clubs: Cambridge University, Leicester, Barbarians (1947/48)
Debut: 3.9.1938 v Bedford (H), Lost 0-18
Last Game: 22.4.1950 v Blackheath (H), Won 14-3 (1T, 3 pts)

Peter Jerwood, a lock or back-row forward, learned his rugby at Oakham School, where his father was the chaplain and a housemaster. He went on tour with Cambridge University to the United States in 1937 and was unlucky not to win a Blue. During the war, he became a major in the Royal Engineers and spent three years in India on Lord Mountbatten's staff. He played for the Midland Counties against the Barbarians in 1940, in a special game in aid of the Army Recreational and Comforts Funds, but had to wait until March 11, 1948, to make his Barbarians debut, against the East Midlands.

He was Leicester's captain from 1947-49, and in 1947/48 earned an England trial. Jerwood also played for

Leicestershire, and was subsequently the County President for three years. He was a sales director with the British United Shoe Machinery Company, a company he worked for all his life.

Apps: 135
Points: 129
Scoring: 13 T, 9 C, 24 PG

JOHNSON, Martin Osborne

b. Solihull, Warwickshire, 9.3.1970
Educated: Welland Park College, Robert Smythe School, Market Harborough
Clubs: Wigston, Leicester, College Old Boys (New Zealand), Barbarians (1991/92)
Debut: 14.2.1989 v Royal Air Force (H), Won 34-12
CAPS: England (1) 1993, British Isles (2) 1993

Martin Johnson, a lock, has played for England at every representative level, schools, colts, under-21, 'A' and seniors. On top of that he spent 18 months playing in New Zealand during 1990/91 and appeared for New Zealand's under-21 team against their Australian counterparts. Three years later he returned to New Zealand as a British Lion.

He played for England schools in 1987/88, England colts the following season, and the under-21s in 1992. He made his England 'B' debut in the 22-18 win over France in Paris in 1992 but a shoulder injury prevented him touring New Zealand with England 'B' that same year. However, he won a full cap when he replaced the injured Wade Dooley 24 hours before the 1993 game with France

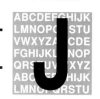

and when Dooley was forced to withdraw from the Lions tour because of the death of his father, Johnson was summoned to replace him. He arrived in New Zealand fresh from England's 'A' tour of Canada and made an instant impact with his dynamic, aggressive style of play, appearing in the last two Tests, as well as two other games on the tour.

A bank officer with the Midland in Market Harborough, Johnson was named as the Whitbread/*Rugby World and Post* most promising player in 1993, shortly after his try-scoring display in the side which won the 1993 Pilkington Cup final.

Apps: 53
Points: 10
Scoring: 2 T

Steve Johnson

JOHNSON, Stephen Robert

b. Leicester, 19.12.1949
Educated: Spencefield School
Clubs: Vipers, Leicester
Debut: *2.10.1976 v Coventry (A), Lost 15-18*
Last Game: *30.4.1983 v Bristol (John Player Cup Final at Twickenham), Lost 22-28*

Steve Johnson was educated at Spencefield School, which produced many fine local players, and following their footsteps he joined Vipers for whom he played for four years. From 1968-1974 he played for the Leicestershire Police and did not join Leicester until he was 25, although he played regularly for the county. On his debut for the club he broke five ribs (the *Leicester Mercury* match report said: "He acquitted himself quite well, but tended to fade in the last 20 minutes.").

A powerful flanker big enough to play lock occasionally, Johnson played for the British Police, the Midlands, and was the first Leicester player to represent England 'B' (in Romania in 1978). He was the club captain from 1981-83 and played in five

John Player Cup finals, three of which were won. A detective inspector in the Leicestershire Constabulary for much of his playing career, he is now superintendent at Melton Mowbray.

Apps: 207
Points: 124
Scoring: 31 T

JONES, Arthur Owen

b. Shelton, Nottinghamshire, 16.8.1872
d. Dunstable, Bedfordshire, 21.12.1914
Educated: Bedford Modern School, Cambridge University
Clubs: Bedford, Blackheath, Burton-on-Trent, Leicester
Debut: *20.4.1895 v Bedford (A), Won 5-3*
Last Game: *26.12.1910 v Birkenhead Park (H), Won 25-5*

Arthur Jones was a brilliant all-round sportsman, excelling in winter as a rugby three-quarter and later a full back, and in the summer at cricket. His greatest fame was achieved at cricket at which he won a blue in 1893, and later captained England in two Test matches on the 1908 MCC tour of Australia. A good batsman, he was renowned as one of the outstanding fielders of his time, unequalled in the slips and was said to have invented the position of gully while at school. He took 466 catches for Nottinghamshire, whom he captained between 1900 and 1914; they won the county championship in 1907. He also played one game of association football for Notts County in 1896 (scoring a hat-trick!).

He was Tigers captain from 1896-99 and again between 1902-1904, and played in six Midland Counties Cup-winning teams. Although he never played international rugby, he did appear for the South versus the North in the England trial of 1896 and he did referee five internationals between 1906-12, including the 1911 game at Stade Colombes in Paris when France achieved their first victory, over Scotland.

He lived in Market Bosworth and worked at Oakham School but suffered from increasingly poor health. Even though he played a few cricket matches for Nottinghamshire in 1914, a few months later he died of tuberculosis, at his brother's home in Dunstable.

Apps: 224
Points: 563
Scoring: 39 T, 113 C, 20 PG, 37 DG, 3 GM

Arthur Jones

Bleddyn Jones

JONES, Bleddyn

b. Brynamman, South Wales, 7.8.1948
Educated: Amman Valley Grammar School, Swansea College of Education
Clubs: Brynamman, Swansea Technical College, Leicester
Debut: 15.11.1969 v Wilmslow (H), Lost 13-23
Last Game: 23.9.1978 v Harlequins (A), Lost 9-21

Bleddyn Jones, a fly-half whose zest for tackling belied his slim frame, is now headmaster at Little Bowden Primary School, although his voice is well known to many in Leicestershire from the regular rugby commentary he does for *BBC Radio Leicester*. While a teacher of general subjects at Humberstone Junior School he had a particular interest in physical education and, with John Duggan and Frank Jones, ran a highly successful club for aspiring gymnasts in the whole county. The same trio were the first organisers of mini-rugby, under the aegis of the Leicestershire RFU.

Jones joined the club after moving to Leicester in 1969, and became a regular first XV player in the second half of the 1969/70 season. A better runner with the ball than he sometimes gave himself credit for, he played for Midlands East against the All Blacks in January 1973, and in Leicester's first John Player Cup final, the 1978 defeat to Gloucester. When he retired, the local press said: "His style on the field and his gentle demeanour off it made him one of the club's most popular players."

Apps: 333
Points: 172
Scoring: 42 T, 1 C, 4 DG

JONES, Charles William

b. Cardiff, Wales, 18.6.1893
d. Birkenhead, Cheshire, 19.1.1960
Clubs: Bridgend, Newport, Harlequins, Leicester, Birkenhead Park
Debut: 16.12.1922 v Bristol (H), Drew 0-0
Last Game: 5.11.1923 v Llanelly (A), Lost 0-23
CAPS: Wales (3) 1920

Charlie Jones served as a company sergeant major in the Welsh Regiment during the First World War. After the war he became the first non-officer to play in the Army side, and also played for his regiment in five Army cup finals (winning four). On leaving the Army, he became a PT instructor at Birkenhead School, and played for Cheshire.

Apps: 29
Points: 3
Scoring: 1 T

Frank Jones

JONES, Francis Horace

b. Shelton, near Newark, Nottinghamshire, 22.2.1874
d. Hemingford Grey, near St Ives, Huntingdonshire, 24.1.1937
Educated: Bedford Grammar School, Emmanuel College Cambridge
Clubs: Cambridge University (Blues 1898-1900), Hinckley, Nuneaton, Leicester
Debut: 2.11.1895 v Rugby (H), Won 33-0 (1T, 3 pts)
Last Game: 27.12.1905 v United Services (H), Won 25-4

Frank Jones was the youngest of eight sons of the Rev. Cartwright Jones, one

brother being A O Jones, the Leicester and Nottinghamshire county cricket captain. Frank, also a wing, was captain of Nuneaton in 1894/95, and joined Leicester the next season; he appeared for the South versus the North in a trial game in Bristol in December 1900. He played in three successive winning Midland Counties Cup finals, scoring three tries in the 1899 final against Nuneaton at Coventry. After previously being a bank clerk in Hinckley, he was ordained in 1900, and was a curate at Blythe, Northumberland before becoming a naval chaplain in 1904. During the First World War he served on the flagship with the North Sea Fleet, and was awarded an OBE in 1918. At the end of the war he became chaplain of the Royal Hospital School, Greenwich, where he met his wife, Edith Sears, who was sister-in-charge of the infirmary. In 1926 he officiated at the Tigers 30th annual service.

Upon his retirement from the navy in 1929 he took up the position of vicar at Ashby-de-la-Zouch parish church but had to retire due to ill health in 1931. However, he became an active member of the St Ives branch of the Royal British Legion, and from time to time assisted in local church services.

Apps: 115
Points: 176
Scoring: 35 T, 32 C, 1 PG, 1 DG

JOYCE, Nicholas James

b. Ashby-de-la-Zouch, Leics, 16.1.1953
Educated: Ashby Boys Grammar School
Clubs: Old Ashbeians, Leicester
Debut: 12.4.1971 v Fylde (A), Won 22-20
Last Game: 7.12.1985 v Gloucester (H) (John Smith's Merit Table A), Lost 9-15

Nick Joyce

Nick Joyce, a lock, is a member of a well-known sporting family which has been the backbone of cricket in Ashby-de-la-Zouch for at least four generations. He joined the police from Ashby Grammar School and played for Old Ashbeians who gave him great encouragement. While at school he played for the under-15 county side and received England trials; when still under 16 he played for the under-19 county schools. He played for Leicestershire colts and the Midland Colts, captaining them in one of their rare victories over the Welsh Youth; he also captained the first England Youth side against Wales. He played for the Midlands under-23, the senior county side, and for the Midlands against Australia in 1981.

Joyce played for Tigers in four John Player Cup finals, winning three in a row from 1979-81. A skilful ball player for such a big man, he was Tigers' main line-out jumper for many years and might have gone further in the game but for the requirements of his job with the Leicestershire constabulary.

Apps: 284+3
Points: 112
Scoring: 28 T

KARDOONI, Aadel

b. Tehran, Iran, 17.5.1968
Educated: Sherborne School, Leicester Polytechnic
Clubs: North Dorset, Wasps, Leicester
Debut: *15.10.1988 v Swansea (A), Lost 16-35*

Aadel Kardooni, a scrum half who won England schools caps at 16 and 18-group level, went on to gain representative honours at student, divisional and England 'B' levels. One of three brothers, he has lived in England since 1976 and his playing career blossomed at school under the guidance of Mike Davis, England's 1980 grand slam coach. He played for the Midlands against South Africa in 1992, having earlier that year toured New Zealand with England 'B', playing in both the "internationals". He has appeared in two Pilkington Cup finals with Leicester, including the victorious 1993 game. Aadel is currently Leisure Centre manager at the Hinckley Island hotel.

Apps: 135
Points: 167
Scoring: 40 T

KEETON, George Haydn

b. Peterborough, Cambridgeshire, 13.10.1878
d. Menton, France, 7.1.1949
Educated: Oakham School, Emmanuel College Cambridge
Clubs: Cambridge University (Blues 1899-1900), Richmond, Leicester
Debut: *12.2.1896 v Bedford School (A), Won 15-0*
Last Game: *31.12.1904 v West Hartlepool (A), Lost 3-6*
CAPS: England (3) 1904

George Keeton, a hooker, played for the Midland Counties and won two Midland Counties Cup-winners' medals with the Tigers. He was a teacher who became a headmaster, his posts including Fettes College and Reading. He is buried in the same cemetery in Menton, France, as William Webb Ellis, founder of the game, and Percy Carpmael, founder of the Barbarians. His three England caps were against each of the other home countries.

Apps: 45
Points: 30
Scoring: 10 T

Aadel Kardooni

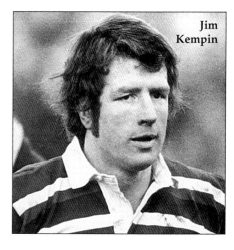

Jim Kempin

KEMPIN, James Stuart

b. Melton Mowbray, Leicestershire, 4.2.1952
Educated: Melton Upper School
Clubs: Melton Mowbray, Leicester
Debut: *23.10.1974 v Oxford University (H), Won 20-13*
Last Game: *28.4.1979 v Moseley (A), Lost 8-14*

Jim Kempin was a hard-tackling flanker who was originally a hooker at school. He captained Melton Mowbray in 1973/74 before moving to Tigers. He is a cousin of Jenny Pitman, the racehorse trainer.

Apps: 107+2
Points: 60
Scoring: 15 T

KENDREW, Douglas Anthony

b. Barnstaple, Devon, 22.7.1910
d. Hayward House Hospice, Nottingham, 28.2.1989
Educated: Uppingham School
Clubs: Woodford, Paignton, City of Derry, Leicester, Barbarians (1929/30 Woodford)
Debut: 15.2.1930 v Bridgwater Albion (H), Won 17-3
Last Game: 18.4.1936 v Blackheath (H), Won 15-6
CAPS: England (10) 1930-36

Major-General Sir Douglas Kendrew, familiarly known as 'Joe', was one of a small band of officers to win the DSO and three bars. Three of his honours were awarded while he was commanding the 6th Battalion, the York and Lancaster Regiment, in North Africa during the Second World War, and the third bar during his year as commander of the 29th Infantry Brigade in the Korean War. He was awarded the CBE in 1944, the CB (Companion of the Order of the Bath) in 1958 and KCMG (Knight Commander of the order of St Michael and St George) in 1963.

His playing career began at school when he was a member of the England under-14 team; he captained English Schools XV against Scotland in 1929. A year later, still 19, he became the youngest man to prop for England and was the youngest member of the British Isles team to tour New Zealand and Australia that summer but did not play in a Test. A strong player, he also had the rare distinction for a front-row forward of kicking goals in international rugby. He captained the Army for two of the five seasons he played for them, as well as representing the Eastern Counties, the Combined Services, and Ulster against New Zealand in 1935 (due to the Leicestershire regiment being stationed in Ulster at the time).

Kendrew was commissioned into the Leicestershire Regiment in 1931 and was an instructor at Sandhurst at the outbreak of the Second World War in 1939. In 1942 he became a brigade major in North Africa and was later appointed to the 6th Battalion, the York and Lancaster Regiment. He was Chief of Staff in Northern Ireland from 1950 to 1952 and then commanded the 29th Infantry Brigade in Korea. His next post

CHURCHMAN'S CIGARETTES

D. A. KENDREW

abroad was as Director of Operations in Cyprus in 1956, during one of the worst periods of the emergency. He led a sweeping campaign against the mountain terrorist gangs and narrowly escaped with his life when terrorists detonated a landmine, missing his car by seconds en route to Government House.

In 1958 he became Director of Infantry at the War Office, and from 1961-63 he was head of British Defence Liaison Staff in Australia. He retired from the Army when he was offered the Governorship of Western Australia, a post he held for 10 years. After retiring from public duties he and Lady Kendrew returned to this country to settle in Northamptonshire as, in his own words, "I don't want to live too far away from the family and I need to be within striking distance to watch the Tigers."

Apps: 30
Points: 17
Scoring: 3 T, 4 C

KENNEY, Stephen

b. Edinburgh, Scotland, 24.8.1956
Educated: Roundhill High School, Longslade Upper School, Charles Keene College, Leicester Polytechnic
Clubs: Leicester, Barbarians (1987/88)
Debut: 10.9.1975 v Nuneaton (H), Won 46-3 (2T, 8 pts)
Last Game: 10.3.1990 v Bristol (A) (Courage League), Won 13-11

Steve Kenney's alliterative partnership at half back with Les Cusworth was one of the distinctive features of Leicester's cup era in the late 1970s and early 1980s. Kenney, a slightly-built scrum half possessed of an exciting break, was the first graduate from the youth team to the senior XV in 1975, when he took over from John Allen.

He was educated at Roundhill and Longslade Upper Schools, with Paul Dodge, both learning their rugby football under the influence of Dave Lyons later the Tigers' youth team coach. Kenney played in the Leicestershire under-15 side when he was only 14, and later captained the county as well as Leicester youth. He was in the England Schools under-15 squad in 1971 and gained his England colts cap in 1975, when he was on the winning side against Wales. He added an England under-23 cap in 1979 and also appeared for the Midlands, and Leicestershire, whom he captained for three years.

A fiery and competitive performer in his younger days he settled into one of the most consistent players at Leicester during the 1980s. He scored the winning try in the 1979 John Player Cup final against Moseley with only two minutes of the game left to play and was part of the team which successfully retained the cup for two more seasons. He is now a sales executive with GPT Communication Systems Ltd.

Apps: 361+4
Points: 276
Scoring: 69 T

KEWNEY, Alfred Lionel

b. registered in Tynemouth, December qtr, 1882
d. Howden, 16.12.1959
Clubs: Rockcliff, Leicester
Debut: *14.4.1906 v Newport (A), Lost 0-25*
Last Game: *2.1.1913 v Manchester (A),*
Won 24-11
CAPS: England (16) 1906-13

Alf Kewney, a forward, represented
Northumberland and was nicknamed
'Kicking Ginger' by the Welsh though it
is doubtful whether that should be
regarded as a compliment. A marine
engineer, he was awarded the OBE for
services during the latter stages of the
First World War, and lived at Barmby
Moor near Pocklington, Yorkshire for
most of his life.

Apps: 27
Points: 3
Scoring: 1 T

Peter
Konig

KONIG, Peter Hans

b. Vienna, Austria, 16.10.1931
Educated: Moat Boys School, Leicester
Clubs: Moat Old Boys, Leicester
Debut: *14.4.1952 v Plymouth Albion (A),*
Won 19-0
Last Game: *23.4.1960 v Rugby (H), Won 9-6*

Peter Konig, a flanker, was a schoolboy
triallist in 1945. An industrious player, he
came out of retirement in December 1966
when he went to watch Leicester play
Blackheath at Welford Road and ended
by filling a vacancy in the Leicester
University XV against the Extras. He was
a wicket-keeper for Leicestershire County
Cricket Club, playing one first-class game
in 1949, in which he made three runs in
his only innings, took one catch and made
one stumping. His son, Martyn, has
represented Great Britain as a slalom
canoeist. Peter is now managing Director
of ICI Seeds UK Ltd.

Apps: 185
Points: 96
Scoring: 32 T

LACEY, Eric Charles

b. Leicester, 14.10.1921
Educated: Wyggeston Grammar School
Clubs: Old Wyggestonians, Leicester
Thursday, Leicester, Barbarians
(1950/51)
Debut: *11.10.1947 v Neath (A), Lost 5-6*
Last Game: *21.2.1959 v Wasps (H),*
Won 22-0

Eric Lacey, a lock forward, played for
Leicestershire and East Midlands XV
against South Africa in the 1951/52
season. He retired in 1955 and became a
member of the selection committee but,
four years later, had to make up the
numbers for the second half of the game
against Wasps as Phil Horrocks-Taylor,
who had been best man at a wedding,
did not turn up. Even so Tigers beat a
Wasps side including five
internationals. Lacey was President of
the Tigers from 1979-81, and has had a
large hand in the growing display of
Tigers memorabilia in the clubhouse.

Apps: 175
Points: 49
Scoring: 15 T, 1 DG

LAWRENCE, Clifford Gwynne Steele

b. Swansea, Wales, 23.6.1927
d. Swansea, Wales, 25.7.1971
Educated: Alderman Newton's School
Clubs: Old Newtonians, Leicester,
Swansea
Debut: *19.3.1949 v Nuneaton (H),*
Won 9-3
Last Game: *18.4.1953 v Sale (A),*
Won 24-19 (2T, 6 pts)

Gwynne Lawrence moved to Leicester
with his family when he was only four
years old. Originally a centre, he moved
to the wing, in which position he
represented Leicestershire and the
Midland Counties against South Africa
in the 1951/52 season. When Steele &
Sons, the family constructional
engineering business, was sold, he
moved to Thyssen's mining engineers
until his untimely death, after a period
of illness, at the age of 44.

Apps: 118
Points: 120
Scoring: 40 T

LAWRENCE, Sidney Frank

Clubs: Moat Road, Leicester
Debut: *1.10.1921 v Headingley (H), Won 14-5*
Last Game: *14.4.1928 v Blackheath (H),*
Lost 8-10 (1T, 3 pts)

Frank Lawrence was a forward, and an
insurance agent who also represented
Leicestershire. He was a member of the
Tigers team which played the touring
Waratahs from New South Wales in
October 1927, the Waratahs went onto
defeat Wales, Ireland and France on that
tour, and were one of the most
accomplished sides ever to emerge from
Australia.

Apps: 135
Points: 33
Scoring: 11 T

LAWRIE, Harry Stephen Balmer

b. registered in Lutterworth, Leics, Sept qtr, 1886
d. Leicester, 15.2.1952
Clubs: Stoneygate, Leicester, Barbarians
(1913/14)
Debut: *30.1.1904 v Swansea (A), Lost 0-17*
Last Game: *2.1.1915 v Barbarians (H),*
Won 21-6 (1C, 2 pts)

Harry Lawrie, Percy's brother, played
mostly as a wing but was equally at home
at fly half, centre, or even full back. He
played against the South Africans for the
Midland Counties in 1912 and was an
England reserve in 1914. He also gained
two winners' medals in the Midland
Counties Cup.

He was the focal point of an incident in
the 1912 game against Harlequins when
the referee, Mr Taylor, sent him off for
rough play. After the match Adrian Stoop,
the Harlequins captain, told reporters that
the referee had made a grave mistake:
Lawrie had not been near the player
alleged to have been kicked and to show
his disapproval of the referee's action,
Stoop had asked Rees - one of his own
players - to leave the field so that the
Tigers should not be at a disadvantage.
Lawrie also turned out for the Barbarians
against Leicester on the occasion when
another Leicester player, Steve Farmer,
also guested for the Barbarians and scored
the winning try.

He was managing director of Lawrie
and Company Limited, underwear
manufacturers of Birstall Street, a
business he founded in 1913.

Apps: 168
Points: 262
Scoring: 29 T, 60 C, 12 PG, 1 DG, 5 GM

LAWRIE, James Ruthven

b. Melrose, Scotland, 11.8.1900
d. Folkestone, Kent, 9.7.1981
Educated: Gala Academy
Clubs: Melrose, Leicester
Debut: 1.9.1923 v Bath (H), Won 6-3
Last Game: 15.4.1926 v Northampton (A), Lost 0-18
CAPS: Scotland (11) 1922-24

'Jock' Lawrie, a flanker, was described by H L V Day as "one of the best line-out forwards I have seen anywhere. He was tall and strong...timing his leap to perfection, many tries we three-quarters owed to his superb line-out work." A commercial traveller, he represented a well known Scottish business house in Leicester.

Apps: 92
Points: 39
Scoring: 13 T

Percy Lawrie

LAWRIE, Percy William

b. Lutterworth, Leicestershire, 26.9.1888
d. Leicester, 27.12.1956
Educated: Wyggeston School
Clubs: Stoneygate, Leicester, Barbarians (1923/24)
Debut: 16.11.1907 v Devonport Albion (A), Lost 0-5
Last Game: 22.4.1924 v Bath (A), Lost 3-28
CAPS: England (2) 1910-11

Percy Lawrie was initially a wing but later changed to centre, and went on to become the club's leading try scorer with 206. He captained Leicester between 1911-14, and 1920-23 during a remarkably long career which might well have brought him more than two England caps but for the First World War. He represented Leicestershire and the Midlands, and appeared (with his brother, Harry) for the Midland Counties against South Africa at Welford Road in November, 1912. In 1910 he became the first of only five Tigers to score three tries in the annual encounter with the Barbarians.

During the war he served as a lieutenant in the Royal Artillery and when cartilage problems forced him to end his senior career in 1924, he rejoined Stoneygate where he had started at the age of 17. Within a year of leaving Leicester he was on the committee and served until 1954 when ill health forced him to retire. Two years later, his death occurred thirty minutes before the start of the 1956 Barbarians match. His son, Gordon, played for the Tigers in 1938.

An accountant, Lawrie had strong views about the game in the 1950s: he believed it was spoiled by three faults: - "the non-application of football brains, lack of straight running and penetration, and the predatory, destructive habits of wing forwards".

Apps: 318
Points: 727
Scoring: 206 T, 23 C, 9 PG, 9 DG

LEYLAND, Roy

b. Astley, Manchester, 6.3.1912
d. Pewsey, Wiltshire, 4.1.1984
Educated: Wigan Grammar School, Liverpool University
Clubs: Wigan Old Boys, Liverpool University, Waterloo, Leicester, Richmond, Barbarians (1934/35)
Debut: 10.9.1934 v Bridgend (H), Won 8-3
Last Game: 29.12.1936 v Manchester (H), Won 9-6 (1T, 3 pts)
CAPS: England (3) 1935

Roy 'Bus' Leyland, a wing or centre, learned his rugby at Wigan Grammar School, where he was also a cricketer and an athlete. He was a member of Lancashire's county championship-winning side of 1934/35 and also played for Hampshire; he played eight times for the Army against the RAF and the Royal Navy while he was in the Education Corps and was the Army representative on the RFU committee. He went on the British Lions tour to South Africa in 1938 but did not play in any of the Tests. A schoolteacher, he served with the BEF in the Second World War and later with the Parachute Regiment, rising to the rank of lieutenant-colonel. He was awarded the OBE in 1957.

Apps: 10
Points: 9
Scoring: 3 T

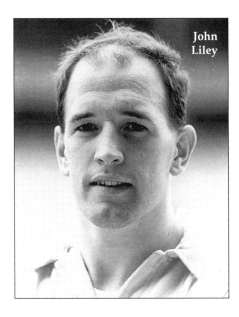
John Liley

LILEY, John Garin

b. Wakefield, Yorkshire, 21.8.1967
Educated: Eastmoor High School, Wakefield
Clubs: Sandal, Wakefield, Leicester
Debut: 8.10.1988 (replacement) v Orrell (H) (Courage League), Lost 15-27

John Liley faced the difficult task of succeeding that Leicester institution at full back, Dusty Hare, yet, by scoring 15 points against Bath in the final game of the 1989/90 season, he took his tally to 439 points in his first season, thus breaking Hare's record by one point.

Liley, who played volleyball as a youngster and appeared in the English Colleges rugby league side against Welsh Colleges in 1986/87, played for Yorkshire colts and under-21, the North under-21, Yorkshire and the Midlands. In 1990 he went on the senior England tour to Argentina and appeared in four games. That same year he played for England 'B' against Namibia at Welford Road, kicking five penalty goals and two conversions in a 31-16 win.

He broke the record for the number of points in a season of the divisional championship with 51 (including 24 in the game against the South-West at Bristol) when the Midlands won the 1991/92 championship. His father and grandfather both played for Wakefield (his father was a selector at the time Les Cusworth played for the Yorkshire club), as does his brother Robert, an England under-21 fly-half. Formerly a swimming pool attendant in Wakefield, he took up a job as a trainee accountant, and now works for the local firm of Power Thompson & Co.

Apps: 128+3
Points: 1,478
Scoring: 51 T, 265 C, 243 PG, 1 DG

W F Lincoln

LINCOLN, W.F.

Clubs: Rugby, Leicester
Debut: *18.4.1896 v Hartlepool Rovers (A), Drew 6-6*
Last Game: *17.4.1900 v Cheltenham (A), Lost 0-3*

W F Lincoln was a forward, who joined Leicester from Rugby in 1896/97, after guesting for them in one game on the north-east tour the previous season. He appeared in eleven Midland Counties Cup ties with the Tigers and was never on the losing side.

Apps: 110
Points: 47
Scoring: 15 T, 1 C

LOVETT, John Thomas

b. Barrow-on-Soar, Leics, March qtr, 1859
d. details not available
Club: Leicester
Debut: *23.10.1880 v Moseley (H), Drew 0-0*
Last Game: *15.2.1890 v Manningham (H), Lost 2-5*

Jack Lovett, a forward was a member of the very first Leicester team which played Moseley in October 1880, and was also one of the founder members of the Loughborough Rugby Football Club in 1895. He was a schoolmaster at a board school.

Apps: 104
Points: 9
Scoring: 9 T

McALPIN, Kenneth

b. 1866
d. Leicester, 16.5.1943
Educated: Mill Hill House School, Bedford School
Clubs: Bedford, Leicester
Debut: *11.10.1884 v Moseley (H), Won 10-0 (2T)*
Last Game: *16.11.1892 v Ashby-de-la-Zouch (H), Won 8-0*

Kenneth McAlpin was part of a famous Leicester footballing family: his father, J W, and younger brothers Colin, Allan, Donal and Jack were noted association and rugby players. He was a forward who played for the Midland Counties and in two Midland Counties Cup finals for Leicester, both lost. He played football at Mill Hill House but turned to rugby at Bedford, though he reverted to the other code when he lived for a time in Germany.

McAlpin served Leicester as Honorary Secretary and President. He played cricket for many years for Leicester Ivanhoe. He was a partner in the legal firm of McAlpin and Halkyard, and was the oldest practising solicitor in Leicester when he died. His other great love, besides rugby, was singing: he was a tenor with the Leicester Philharmonic Society and sang in one hundred consecutive concerts. For forty years he was a member of the choir at St John's Baptist Church. His daughter was Mrs R E Haylock, the well-known Leicestershire tennis player who appeared at Wimbledon.

Apps: 135
Points: 13
Scoring: 13 T

McKECHNIE, Arthur

b. registered in Burnley, Lancashire, June qtr, 1863
d. details not available
Educated: Mellion Street School; Elmfield College, York
Clubs: Horbury, Leicester
Debut: *11.11.1882 v Coventry (A), Drew 0-0*
Last Game: *27.1.1894 v Old Leysians (H), Lost 0-3*

Arthur McKechnie learned his love of football at college where he played under the old "Sheffield" rules. He moved to Wakefield, a rugby stronghold, and played under the rules of the day for several junior teams, most notably Horbury. A splendid full back, he earned a reputation as a safe tackler and a good kicker, cool under pressure. He joined Leicester after taking up a scholastic

appointment at Coalville and became a three-quarter when John Parsons was injured - around the time that the club moved to Belgrave Road. He was the first player to score in the inaugural game at Welford Road when he dropped a goal against Leicestershire. Known as 'Mac', he captained Leicester in 1890/91 and was universally popular with players and public alike.

Apps: 215
Points: 96
Scoring: 19 T, 25 C, 7 DG

Charlie Manson

MANSON, Charles Septimus

b. West Hartlepool, September qtr, 1905
d. Nottingham, 1985
Clubs: Nottingham, Leicester
Debut: *1.9.1928 v Bath (H), Won 17-5*
Last Game: *28.12.1933 v Waterloo (H), Won 7-6*

Charlie Manson was the seventh son of a seventh son, hence Septimus. A full back who represented Notts, Lincs & Derbys, he moved to Nottingham from the north-east due to his involvement in the timber-importing business. He eventually set up his own timber-merchants company, Charles Manson & Sons, which his son Nick still runs.

Apps: 107
Points: 22
Scoring: 9 C, 1 DG

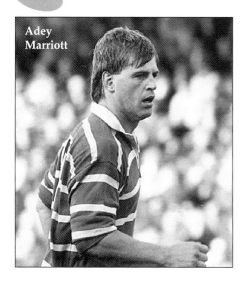

Adey Marriott

MARRIOTT, Adrian Noel

b. Leicester, 9.7.1962
Educated: Stonehill High School, Longslade Upper School
Clubs: Syston, Leicester
Debut: 3.3.1982 (replacement) v Royal Navy (H), Won 17-12
Last Game: 25.4.1992 v Rugby (H) (Courage League), Drew 22-22

Adrian Marriott concentrated on football at school but came to enjoy the challenge of rugby and joined Syston colts as a full back. He played for the county under-18 before joining Tigers youth team and graduated through the Swifts and the Extras before making his debut for the senior team. He changed his position and became an understudy at flanker to Steve Johnson, whose retirement helped Marriott to a regular first-XV place. A qualified farrier/blacksmith, he has his own blacksmith business based in Rothley.

Apps: 114+16
Points: 48
Scoring: 12 T

MARTIN, Colin G.

b. New Zealand, c 1933
Clubs: Westleigh, Leicester, Barbarians (1959/60)
Debut: 29.9.1956 v Newport (A), Lost 3-22 (1PG, 3 pts)
Last Game: 12.4.1966 v Exeter (A), Lost 0-6

It would be hard to overestimate Colin Martin's influence on the club during his playing decade. An engineering graduate from Auckland in New Zealand, he was posted to Europe by the Shell Oil Company while he was recovering from a back injury received in a car accident.

A back-row forward he played initially for Westleigh before bringing his organisational skills to bear on Leicester (whom he captained from 1960-63) and, indeed, the Midland Counties, whom he captained in their 3-3 draw with the 1960 South Africans at Welford Road.

Martin brought far greater shape to Leicester's forward play, in particular the use of the loose forwards among whom he had some distinguished adherents such as David Matthews. His efforts were supplemented behind the scrum by the presence of Phil Horrocks-Taylor and Michael Wade whose efforts ensured a coherent thread throughout the side in an era of generally very sterile play.

Apps: 272
Points: 555
Scoring: 13 T, 126 C, 88 PG

MASSEY, Edward John

b. West Derby, 2.7.1900
d. Woking, Surrey, 30.4.1977
Educated: Ampleforth College
Clubs: Liverpool, Leicester, Barbarians (1922/23 Liverpool)
Debut: 1.1.1923 v Headingley (A), Won 35-0
Last Game: 14.3.1925 v Northampton (H), Won 8-3
CAPS: England (3) 1925

Edward Massey, a scrum half, represented Leicestershire and was a member of the 1925 side that won the county championship; he also made 17 appearances for Lancashire. He broke his collarbone playing for England against Scotland in 1925. He played for the Barbarians against Leicester in December 1922 while still in Liverpool, but joined Tigers after business brought him to Leicester. A farmer, he was also a keen cricketer, being a useful wicket-keeper and batsman. He served with the RASC during the Second World War.

Apps: 31
Points: 18
Scoring: 1 T, 5 PG

MATTHEWS, David Joseph

b. Barrow, Oakham, Rutland, 17.4.1937
Educated: Oakham School
Clubs: Stoneygate, Leicester, Barbarians (1965/66)
Debut: 3.9.1955 v Bedford (H), Lost 11-20
Last Game: 9.3.1974 v Coventry (A), Won 36-16

In his 19-year career David Matthews played 502 times for Leicester, more games than any other player. His consistency as a flanker brought him to the verge of England honours but though he played in trials he could never oust such players as 'Budge' Rogers, the Bedford flanker. A constructive player with a shrewd eye for the game, it was no surprise that the club should turn to him as coach during a time of flux at the end of the 1980s.

Matthews captained Oakham School and did the same for Leicester (between 1965-68) and Leicestershire. In 1960/61, when Leicester established a post-war record of 24 wins, he scored 15 tries - then a post-war record for a forward - and he played for Midland Counties (East) against the Australians in 1966, ironically in the same back row as Rogers. During his time as captain he combined successfully with Colin Martin in the coaching role, both taking a hard-nosed attitude that success had to come before style.

A farmer whose younger brother, Andy, propped for Leicester between 1966-73, Matthews played his 500th game against Northampton on February 23, 1974, leading the team on to the field and being chaired off it. At a dinner given in his honour Matthews received a token of the club's appreciation presented by his old rival, Rogers.

Apps: 502
Points: 451
Scoring: 119 T, 15 C, 20 PG

David Matthews

'Sid' Matthews

MATTHEWS, Joseph William

Clubs: Oadby, Nuneaton, Leicester
Debut: *8.1.1898 v Coventry (A), Won 9-0*
Last Game: *20.4.1908 v Cardiff (A), Lost 11-24*

'Sid' Matthews, a bustling forward, played for the South against the North in the England trial at Welford Road in 1900, and for the Rest of England against an England XV at Weston-super-Mare in 1902. He captained Leicester against the touring All Blacks in 1905, and was captain in two spells from 1904-06 and 1907-09. He played for the Midlands against South Africa in 1906. In 27 Midland Counties Cup ties Matthews was never on the losing side, including seven successive final wins between 1899 and 1905.

Apps: 340
Points: 88
Scoring: 19 T, 14 C, 1 PG

MEIKLE, Graham William Churchill

b. Waterloo, Lancashire, 14.10.1911
d. Whitehaven, June 1981
Educated: St Bees School, Cambridge University
Clubs: Cambridge University, Waterloo, Richmond, Leicester, Barbarians (1933/34 Waterloo)
Debut: *27.12.1933 v Barbarians (H), Won 21-10 (3T, 1DG, 13 pts)*
Last Game: *6.3.1937 v Harlequins (H), Lost 3-11*
CAPS: England (3) 1934

Graham Meikle and his brother, Stephen, both England internationals, played together for Leicester in the 1933 game against the Barbarians, one on each wing (Graham scored three tries and a dropped goal). He played for Lancashire and, on his debut for England against Wales, scored two tries. He also scored in each of his other two internationals (as did his brother on his only international appearance five years earlier). Graham Meikle taught at King Edward's School, Birmingham, then took up a position at Wellington School, Somerset. The two brothers married the Grahame sisters and a third sister married another Tiger, Harry Greenlees.

Apps: 26
Points: 54
Scoring: 14 T, 2 C, 2 DG

MICHIE, Ernest James Stewart

b. 7.11.1933
Educated: Aberdeen Grammar School, Aberdeen University
Clubs: Aberdeen Grammar School FP, Aberdeen University, Leicester, London Scottish, Langholm, Barbarians (1955/56 The Army)
Debut: *7.12.1957 v Waterloo (A), Drew 3-3*
Last Game: *15.3.1958 v Swansea (H), Won 20-8*
CAPS: Scotland (15) 1954-57

Ernie Michie, one of the locks on the British Lions tour of South Africa in 1955 (though he played in none of the Tests), also represented the Army, and went on the Barbarians tour to Canada in 1957.

Apps: 10
Points: 0

MILES, John Henry

b. Grimsby, 1879
d. Sheffield, Yorkshire, 23.1.1953
Educated: Medway Street School
Clubs: Medway Athletic, Stoneygate, Leicester, Northampton
Debut: *9.9.1899 v Handsworth (H), Won 27-0 (3T, 9 pts)*
Last Game: *5.4.1904 v Bristol (A), Drew 0-0*
CAPS: England (1) 1903

Jack Miles, a speedy wing, played for the South against the North in an England trial at Rectory Field, Blackheath in December 1902, and this led to his only cap - thus he can claim the honour of being Leicester's first international. He represented the Midlands and played in

Leicester sides that won the Midland Counties Cup in 1902, 1903 and 1904. He finished his Leicester playing career due to increasing business commitments but subsequently resumed with Northampton. He became a referee and officiated in two internationals in 1913, Ireland-France and France-Wales, and in the Wales-France game the following year. He was a farmer and later a chemist's valuer.

Apps: 93
Points: 225
Scoring: 75 T

Jock Millican

MILLICAN, John Gilbert

b. Edinburgh, Scotland, 21.8.1951
Educated: Berwickshire High School, Edinburgh University, Heriot-Watt University
Clubs: Edinburgh University, Leicester, Boroughmuir, Heriot's FP, Northern, Wilmslow
Debut: *18.1.1975 v Bedford (A), Lost 19-23*
Last Game: *9.10.1976 v Richmond (H), Won 24-12*
CAPS: Scotland (3) 1973

'Jock' Millican gained his three caps as a flanker while a student at Edinburgh University. He played for South of Scotland Schools, for Scottish and British Universities and for Edinburgh and the Anglo-Scots in the district championship. He is a chemical engineer.

Apps: 25
Points: 16
Scoring: 4 T

Robin Money

MONEY, Robin Strang

b. Falkirk, Scotland, 5.9.1945
Educated: Hawick High School, Ardrossan Academy, Harris Academy, Dundee; St Andrew's University, Jordanhill College of PE
Clubs: Jordanhill, Glasgow, Leicester
Debut: *8.10.1968 v Rugby (H), Won 12-11*
Last Game: *8.4.1978 (replacement) v Bristol (A), Lost 0-23*

Robin Money, a full back of considerable flair, with a raking touch-kick and the habit of heading balls into touch if he could not make a safe catch, captained Jordanhill, Leicester and Leicestershire. He moved from Scotland to teach at Wyggeston School, making Anglo-Scots appearances subsequently. However, he left teaching to join the Adidas UK Ltd sportswear company with whom he is now a marketing manager. He plays squash and has a golfing handicap of nine. His father also played club rugby and cricket.

Apps: 255+3
Points: 123
Scoring: 23 T, 12 DG

MOORE, William Kenneth Thomas

b. Leicester, 24.2.1921
Educated: Wyggeston Grammar School
Clubs: Old Wyggestonians, Devonport Services, Leicester, Barbarians (1948/49)
Debut: *8.9.1945 v Cardiff (A), Lost 6-12*
Last Game: *18.4.1953 v Sale (A), Won 24-19*
CAPS: England (7) 1947-50

Bill Moore, an electrical artificer on HMS Defiance during the Second World War before becoming a pilot officer in the Royal Navy, played in two Victory internationals against Scotland. He made his England debut at scrum half against Wales in 1947. He also represented Cornwall and Leicestershire, and captained Tigers from 1950-52. He later became a member of the East Midlands Referees' Society and then the Staffordshire society. Moore studied boot and shoe manufacture after leaving the navy, and became a shoe company sales manager with British United Shoe. He is the grandson of the late W J Foreman the former Tigers half back, and the brother of the 1948 Tiger, Jeff.

Apps: 170
Points: 28
Scoring: 6 T, 2 C, 2 DG

Bill Moore

Mike Mortimer

MORTIMER, Michael Richard

b. Huddersfield, Yorkshire, 31.10.1943
Educated: Teignmouth Grammar School, Devon; St John's College, York
Clubs: St John's College, Stoneygate, Leicester
Debut: 19.3.1971 v Royal Air Force (H), Won 11-6
Last Game: 13.12.1975 v Blackheath (A), Won 13-8

Mike Mortimer moved to Teignmouth when only a few months old and so considers himself a Devonian. He played rugby at St John's College, York, having previously represented Devon Schools at soccer, basketball and athletics. Mortimer, a prop tall enough to play occasionally at lock, played for South Leicester and Stoneygate before joining Leicester midway through the 1969/70 season. He played for Devon and Leicestershire and was twice a replacement for Midland Counties East against representative sides. Once a schoolmaster, he left the profession to become a salesman for Rank Xerox. He has been a member of the Leicestershire Referees' Society since 1982.

Apps: 132
Points: 40
Scoring: 10 T

NEEDHAM, Raymond Ernest

b. Shipley, Yorkshire, 2.11.1949
Educated: Bingley Grammar School, St. Luke's College Exeter
Clubs: Bingley, Leicester
Debut: 5.9.1973 v Nottingham (H), Won 12-9
Last Game: 30.4.1982 v Ballymena (A), Won 21-18

Ray Needham, also known as 'Bingley Bill', propped for Bingley before going to St Luke's College, Exeter, where he spent four years before moving to Leicester. Though overshadowed by Robin Cowling, he was a valuable deputy and played in the club's first John Player Cup final, against Gloucester in 1978; he also played for Yorkshire and Leicestershire. Since retiring, he has worked with the youth team. A teacher specialising in PE and mathematics, Needham is also an accomplished cricketer, having played in the highly-competitive Yorkshire Federation.

Apps: 123+3
Points: 26
Scoring: 5 T, 3 C

Ray Needham

NICHOLAS, Walter Kenneth

b. Newbridge, Monmouthshire, 8.8.1926
Educated: Newbridge Grammar School, Loughborough Colleges
Clubs: Newbridge, Loughborough Colleges, Leicester, Bedford
Debut: 6.3.1948 v Harlequins (H), Won 32-3
Last Game: 5.12.1953 v Waterloo (A), Lost 9-12 (2T, 6 pts)

Ken Nicholas, a fly-half who also played wing or centre, served with the Fleet Air Arm during the Second World War. He represented Leicestershire, Surrey, the Midland Counties and London Counties. He taught geography and PE at Wyggeston Grammar School where he coached Mike Wade, later an England

centre; master and pupil played together for Leicestershire and against each other after Nicholas moved to Bedford, for whom he played from 1954 until 1959 in 82 games scoring 92 points including 12 tries and 9 drop goals. He also appeared in a Scottish international trial, despite his strong Welsh accent. He was a master at Whitgift School in Croydon, Surrey from 1956-91.

Apps: 151
Points: 95
Scoring: 24 T, 1 C, 3 PG, 4 DG

Ken Nicholas

NORMAN, Douglas James

b. Leicester, 12.6.1897
d. Oadby, Leicester, 27.12.1971
Educated: Medway Street School
Clubs: Medway Athletic, Oadby, Leicester, Barbarians (1926/27)
Debut: 17.1.1920 v Headingley (H), Won 54-11 (3C, 6 pts)
Last Game: 18.4.1933 v Bath (A), Lost 8-15
CAPS: England (2) 1932

Doug Norman had to wait until his 35th year before he won the England cap which seemed likely to elude him in the course of a long career retarded by the First World War. He learned his rugby at Medway Street school, under the guidance of James Cooper, the founder of the English Schools Rugby Union. He led the England schoolboys to their first victory over Wales in 1911 and distinguished himself at school as an athlete, swimmer and cricketer.

During the First World War he served in the Royal Artillery in Mesopotamia. When he resumed his rugby career he moved from his original position of full back or wing forward to hooker when the team was short, and soon made that position his own. During the 1920s he was picked to play in several trial games, but seemed doomed to remain a travelling reserve for England. But he was one of those to benefit from the outstanding display by Leicestershire and the East Midlands against the Springboks in November 1931 and though it looked as though an injury sustained in the final trial at Twickenham might deny him his first cap, he made a remarkable recovery from strained neck muscles to play for England against South Africa in January 1932.

He retired from first-class rugby in 1933 after being Leicester's vice captain from 1926-31 and captain in his final season. In the game against Old Blues in September 1932 he did not return for the second half because of a shoulder injury; he had never left the field before, a considerable achievement for one so late in his career. He continued to play local club rugby and during the Second World War, when he served with the Home Guard, Norman helped run the Leicestershire Harlequins. This was a team formed to provide a game for servicemen passing through the county, local players home on leave, and anyone still in the area who wanted to play. This team provided the nucleus for the reformation of the Tigers when hostilities ceased.

In the printing trade, he worked at the College of Art and Technology, and Blackfriars Press Ltd. After the war, he produced and then edited the Midland Counties handbook. He became fixture secretary and then President of the club, as well as President of Oadby RFC and of the Leicestershire Schools Union.

Apps: 453
Points: 131
Scoring: 21 T, 29 C, 2 PG, 1 DG

OBOLENSKY, Alexander

b. St Petersburg, Russia, 17.2.1916
d. Norfolk, 29.3.1940
Educated: Trent College,
Brasenose College Oxford
Clubs: Oxford University (Blues 1935-37),
Chesterfield, Rosslyn Park, Leicester,
Barbarians (1936/37 Oxford University)
Debut: *26.12.1934 v Birkenhead Park (H),
Lost 8-12 (2T, 6 pts)*
Last Game: *28.1.1939 v Richmond (A),
Won 21-13*
CAPS: England (4) 1936

Prince Alexander Obolensky came from a very old Russian family which took its name from the town of Obolensk. The first of his line was made a prince in the 14th

century, and was 11th in descent from Rurik, the founder of the Russian monarchy. Alexander, or 'Obo', came to England as a child after the Russian Revolution and was still a Russian national when he gained his Blue for Oxford. This also provoked some criticism when he was picked to play for England, but in 1936 he became naturalised, and two years later was given a commission as a pilot officer in the RAF Volunteer Reserve. At the outbreak of war he was commissioned into the RAF, and was the first international player to lose his life when his Hawker Hurricane fighter crashed in East Anglia during training.

Obolensky's fame is assured by the try he scored against New Zealand for England in 1936 when he carved a diagonal path from his post on the right wing to score on the left. His spectacular running had already brought him one try in the match, which England won 13-0.

Apps: 17
Points: 36
Scoring: 12 T

ODBERT, Reginald Vere Massey

b. 9.2.1904
d. Killed in action, 18.7.1943
Educated: Blackrock College, Dublin
Clubs: Blackrock College, Leicester,
Nuneaton
Debut: *17.11.1923 v Northampton (H),
Won 13-3*
Last Game: *17.10.1931 v Newport (H),
Drew 8-8*
CAPS: Ireland (1) 1928

Reg Odbert, a centre, represented the RAF and was a group captain in the Second World War. His only international cap was on 28 January, 1928 against France at Ravenhill, Belfast when Ireland won 12-8.

Apps: 13
Points: 3
Scoring: 1 T

OLD, Alan Gerald Bernard

b. Middlesbrough, Yorkshire, 23.9.1945
Educated: Acklam Hall Grammar School,
Middlesbrough; Queen Mary's College,
London; Durham University
Clubs: Middlesbrough, Leicester,
Sheffield, Morpeth, Barbarians (1971/72
Middlesbrough)
Debut: *7.10.1972 v Coventry (A), Lost 6-45*
Last Game: *15.4.1974 v Gosforth (A),
Lost 18-28 (2C, 2PG, 10 pts)*
CAPS: England (16) 1972-78

Alan Old

Though a Tigers player for two seasons while teaching at Worksop Alan Old had so many representative commitments with Yorkshire and England that he made all too few appearances for the club. One of the outstanding fly halves of the 1970s, his worth was never appreciated consistently by the England selectors while the club selectors occasionally tried to compromise when he was available and played both Old and Bleddyn Jones, the regular fly-half, together.

On two occasions Old played international rugby on the same day as Chris, his brother and a Yorkshire fast bowler, played cricket for England - February 2 and 16, 1974. Alan Old was also a tidy cricketer, playing for Durham and once for Warwickshire against Cambridge University in June 1969. He played rugby 74 times for Yorkshire (including with the young Rory Underwood) and appeared for the North-East and the North, as well as England and the British Lions in South Africa in 1974, when he played in four games and scored 59 points until a torn knee cartilage ended his tour. He is now principal at Sir William Turner's Sixth Form College, Redcar.

Apps: 18
Points: 106
Scoring: 3 T, 11 C, 23 PG, 1 DG

O'REILLY, Anthony Joseph Francis Kevin

b. Dublin, Ireland, 7.5.1936
Educated: Belvedere College, University College Dublin
Clubs: Old Belvedere, Leicester, Barbarians (1954/55 Old Belvedere)
Debut: *25.10.1958 v Northampton (H), Lost 3-10*
Last Game: *27.12.1960 v Barbarians (H), Lost 5-14*
CAPS: Ireland (29) 1955-70, British Isles (10) 1955-59

Tony O'Reilly is one of the outstanding personalities to have graced both the rugby world and the business world. He burst onto the international scene in 1955 and was selected as an 18-year-old for the British Lions tour to South Africa where his powerful running on the wing (he also played centre for Ireland) gained him a film-star style following. Four years later he toured Australia and New Zealand with the Lions when he established a series of records unlikely to be beaten: six Test tries, the individual record for most appearances for a wing, and 38 tries for the Lions in all tour matches.

His debut with Leicester was not auspicious as he gave away a penalty try. His international career continued when he returned to Ireland but appeared to have ended in 1963; however, seven years later, having written one of the match articles for the Twickenham programme, he was recalled to Ireland's side to play England when Bill Brown withdrew through an injury. He trained as a solicitor (and is reputed to have turned down the lead role in a remake of the film 'Ben Hur') but has become a businessman of international repute: he was chairman of the Irish Dairy Marketing Board before he was thirty and is now chairman of the H J Heinz Company in Pittsburgh, Pennsylvania. Renowned for his wit, as well as his business wisdom, O'Reilly's company was a sponsor of the 1991 Rugby World Cup. He celebrated his 50th birthday in a quiet manner with a dinner for 450 at his home in Castlemartin, County Kildare.

Apps: 17
Points: 24
Scoring: 8 T

PARSONS, John

b. Leicester, 1861
d. details not available
Educated: Franklin's School
Clubs: Harlequins, Lansdowne, Leicester
Debut: *27.11.1880 v Burton-on-Trent (H), Drew 0-0*
Last Game: *23.3.1889 v Moseley (A) (Midland Counties Cup final), Lost 0-6*

John Parsons was one of only two people to have held every senior post in the club: he was Secretary (and player) in 1880/81, captain from 1886-89 and President from 1891-1901. He played in Leicester's first Midland Counties Cup final and went on to become President of the Leicestershire Rugby Union from 1911-21. A solicitor with Parsons, Wykes and Davis, he played cricket for Leicester Ivanhoe and Leicestershire, became treasurer of Leicestershire County Cricket Club and an Alderman of the City.

Apps: 113
Points: 150
Scoring: 15 T, 48 C, 13 DG

PENNY, Sidney Herbert

b. East End, Finchley, London, 7.10.1875
d. Leicester, 23.5.1965
Educated: St Peter's School
Clubs: Granville, Belgrave St Peter's, Leicester
Debut: *4.1.1896 v Gloucester (A), Lost 12-20*
Last Game: *26.12.1910 v Birkenhead Park (H), Won 25-5*
CAPS: England (1) 1909

Sid Penny, a hooker, held the record for Leicester appearances until 1974 when it was passed by David Matthews. Allegedly one of only two players to have made 500 appearances for the club, Penny also played for the Midland Counties, and was chosen to go on the 1908 Anglo-Welsh tour to New Zealand but he could not afford to take time off work (Sid was actually a clicker at Rawsons Ltd in the boot and shoe trade). However, there was some consolation when the following year he made his only England appearance at the age of 33, against Australia. He was the longest surviving member of the 1898 Midland Counties Cup-winning team before his death at the age of 89. Penny appeared in a record ten winning Midland Counties Cup finals (including eight in succession), and was only once on the losing side in a total of forty cup ties. He retired from work at the age of 85 and when asked if he had any advice for the younger generation said "If you can give young people advice then you're a lucky man, they won't have it".

Apps: 491
Points: 48
Scoring: 16 T

Matt Poole

POOLE, Matthew David

b. Leicester, 6.2.1969
Educated: Roundhill College
Clubs: Syston, Leicester
Debut: *18.10.1988 v Oxford University (H), Won 24-6*

Matt Poole, a lock, is a product of the Leicester Youth team and a member of the inaugural England U-21 side, of which Tony Russ was the assistant coach. Matt reached the ranks of the senior England squad by touring Argentina with them in 1990, but it was a disappointment for him only appearing in three matches. He has also played for Leicestershire at 16 and 18-Group Schools levels and England colts. A member of the 1993 Pilkington Cup winning side, he finished the 1993 South African tour with 99 career appearances.

Apps: 97+2
Points: 35
Scoring: 8 T

PORTER, William Robert

b. Rockingham, Northamptonshire, 1859
d. Leicester, 28.3.1936
Club: Leicester
Debut: *23.10.1880 v Moseley (H), Drew 0-0*
Last Game: *9.4.1892 v Handsworth (A), Won 12-4 (1T, 2 pts)*

William Porter was a stay and corset maker who had a business in Highcross Street, Leicester, and took a yarn agency later in life. One of the original membrs of Leicester Football Club, he appeared in the very first fixture, and started a 55 year association with the club. He became captain in the 1889/90 season, and was part of the team which appeared in Leicester's first Midland Counties Cup final, losing to Moseley at Coventry. He then became a committeeman and later a vice-president, and was also a long standing member of Leicestershire County Cricket Club.

Apps: 169
Points: 11
Scoring: 10

POVOAS, Simon John

b. Leicester, 10.6.1966
Educated: Kibworth High School; Robert Smythe School, Market Harborough
Clubs: Oadby Wyggestonians, Leicester, Barbarians (1989/90)
Debut: *9.9.1986 v Nuneaton (A), Won 49-6*

Simon Povoas started playing rugby at school and represented Leicestershire, East Midlands and Midlands Schools at under-14, under-16 and under-18 levels; he also had under-16 and under-18 England trials. A Leicester youth player, he represented Leicestershire at senior level and joined the England 'B' squad in Paris in 1990 as a replacement for the game against France 'B', a remarkable achievement for a No 8 who has spent so much of his time understudying Dean Richards. However, that season Richards was unable to play because of injury and Povoas came into his own, scoring a club record for a forward of 25 tries in a season. His surname goes back many generations but was originally Portuguese.

Apps: 124+7
Points: 261
Scoring: 64 T

PRATT, Stanley

b. Belgrave, Leicester, 26.12.1922
Educated: Ellis Avenue School
Clubs: Aylestone Athletic, Leicester
Debut: *26.2.1949 v Northampton (A), Drew 9-9*
Last Game: *24.4.1954 v Sale (H), Won 27-14*

Stan Pratt, a hooker, joined the Tigers from Aylestone Athletic (at that time quite a breeding ground for aspiring Tigers). On leaving school he joined Dried Handycrafts in Thornton Lane as an apprentice carpenter. During the war he saw service with the Royal Navy in Russia, Malta, and the Far East. Now retired, he has lived in Adelaide, South Australia since 1973.

Apps: 134
Points: 12
Scoring: 4 T

Simon Povoas

PRENTICE, Frank Douglas

b. registered in Leicester, December qtr, 1898
d. Paddington, London, 3.10.1962
Educated: Wyggeston School
Clubs: Westleigh, Leicester, Barbarians (1926/27)
Debut: *26.11.1923 v Neath (A),*
Lost 6-37 (1T, 3 pts)
Last Game: *18.4.1931 v Blackheath (H),*
Won 25-5 (3C, 1PG, 9 pts)
CAPS: England (3) 1928,
British Isles (2) 1930

Doug Prentice, a back-row forward, served rugby for the best part of fifty years as a player and administrator, both at local and national levels. He led the British Lions teams to New Zealand and Australia in 1930 - with Bill Beaumont, one of only two Englishmen thus far to have captained the Lions - and, after the Second World War, was Secretary of the Rugby Football Union for 15 years.

Prentice played 65 times for Leicestershire, including the county championship-winning team of 1925. He captained Leicester between 1928-30, and in his final match, against Blackheath in 1931, when the referee was Wavell Wakefield. In 1928 he played for the successful England against Scotland, Ireland and France but could not find

LAMBERT & BUTLER'S CIGARETTES

F. D. PRENTICE
LEICESTER & ENGLAND

his best form on the 1930 tour, and had the strength of character to stand down from all but one of the Tests played in New Zealand. He managed the British team to Argentina in 1936 (when Bernard Gadney was captain) and was a national selector from 1932 to 1947; at that stage he became the RFU secretary and continued in that post until ill-health forced him to resign in 1962.

Prentice served with the Royal Artillery in the First World War. He was sent to France and joined the ANZACS, whose native enthusiasm for rugby - they took a ball everywhere - converted him from football. He was badly wounded during the war but his subsequent career indicates how well he recovered. He was a lieutenant-colonel in the RASC during the Second World War and was taken prisoner.

Apps: 239
Points: 575
Scoring: 60 T, 133 C, 43 PG

PRICE, Herbert Leo

b. Sutton, Surrey, 21.6.1899
d. Manchester, 18.7.1943
Educated: Bishop's Stortford College, Corpus Christi College Oxford
Clubs: Oxford University (Blues 1920-21), Leicester, Harlequins, Barbarians (1920/21 Harlequins)
Debut: *23.9.1922 v Nuneaton (H), Won 33-5*
Last Game: *29.11.1924 v Cardiff (H), Drew 3-3*
CAPS: England (4) 1922-23

An all-round athlete, Leo Price made a name for himself by scoring one of the fastest tries in international rugby, against Wales at Twickenham in 1923. After Wavell Wakefield kicked off, Price recovered possession and tried to drop a goal but the wind held the kick and Price, following up, caught it and scored a try without a Welshman having touched the ball.

His versatility caused problems when he was picked to play hockey and rugby for England on the same day, March 18, 1922 (he opted to play against Scotland at Twickenham). A back-row forward Price was, on another occasion, asked to stand by in case Tom Voyce proved unfit for a match at Twickenham; when Voyce was passed fit, Price rushed off to play centre half for England's hockey team in Birmingham. He played 12 times for his country at hockey, having won Blues at that sport in 1920-22 and at water polo (1919-22). He also played two first-class cricket matches for Oxford University between 1920 and 1922 but, though a good right-hand bat and fielder, and a useful left-hand bowler, he missed his Blue.

He played rugby for Leicestershire, made 12 appearances for Surrey, and first appeared for the Barbarians while with Harlequins in 1920/21. During his time with Leicester he was a master at Uppingham School, and subsequently became headmaster at his old school, Bishop Stortford.

Apps: 17
Points: 10
Scoring: 2 T, 1 DG

PULFREY, Peter Graham Smith

b. Grantham, Lincolnshire, 10.9.1938
Educated: Magnus Grammar School, Newark
Clubs: Newark, Leicester
Debut: *15.9.1962 v Plymouth Albion (H), Won 11-6*
Last Game: *27.12.1969 v Barbarians (H), Lost 0-35*

Graham
Pulfrey

Graham Pulfrey, a full back from Newark - which also produced Dusty Hare - played for Notts, Lincs & Derbys, and Leicestershire, and was one of only three Tigers who were selected for the Midland Counties (East) against the touring Springboks at Welford Road in November 1969. Graham is now trade director (Ireland) of Scottish & Newcastle Breweries Ltd. His son, Daniel Robert David, played for the Scottish Schools in 1987/88.

Apps: 173
Points: 74
Scoring: 13 T, 1 C, 6 PG, 5 DG

John
Quick

QUICK, John

b. Sydney, Australia, 12.11.1940
Educated: Sydney Boys High School, Sydney University
Clubs: Randwick, Kibworth, Leicester
Debut: *12.12.1964 v Headingley (A), Won 21-6 (1T, 3 pts)*
Last Game: *20.4.1968 v Llanelli (A), Lost 5-14 (1T, 3 pts)*

John Quick spent three years with Leicester before returning to his native Australia and showed himself to be a powerful and perceptive flanker. He scored a try on his debut and scored three tries against the Barbarians in 1965; he also made 15 appearances for Leicestershire. Quick, a dental surgeon, became a first-grade coach with the Randwick club, which has dominated the Sydney club competition for the past decade. He was coaching advisor to the Japanese national side in 1986 and during their 1987 World Cup campaign, and has coached Australia's under-21 side. His son, Sam, played with Leicester in 1991/92.

Apps: 119
Points: 123
Scoring: 41 T

Stuart Redfern

REDFERN, Stuart Bernard

b. Leicester, 16.6.1961
Educated: South Charnwood High School, King Edward VII Upper School, Coalville
Clubs: Coalville, Leicester
Debut: *16.3.1982 v Loughborough Colleges (H), Won 12-9*
Last Game: *25.4.1992 v Rugby (H) (Courage League), Drew 22-22*

Stuart 'Pebble' Redfern, a loose-head prop and younger brother of Steve, joined Leicester to team up with his brother, starting his playing career in the successful youth team. His representative honours include two England colts caps, two England under-23 caps and an appearance for the Midland Division in the victory over the 1983 All Blacks, though he did not become first-choice prop for the Midlands until the divisional championship of 1986/87. He also played

for an England XV against a Rest of the World XV at Twickenham in 1984, but never gained a full England cap.

He and his brother played together, as props, in the 1983 John Player Cup final against Bristol, though Stuart was never destined to gain a winners' medal; he was on the losing side again in the 1989 final against Bath. A mechanical engineer, he also enjoys football.

Apps: 322+2
Points: 100
Scoring: 25 T

Steve Redfern

REDFERN, Stephen Paul

b. Leicester, 26.10.1957
Educated: Markfield High School, Coalville Grammar School
Clubs: Coalville, Leicester, Sheffield Eagles RL, Leicester Cobblers RL
Debut: *30.10.1976 v Nottingham (A), Won 19-6*
Last Game: *24.11.1984 v Moseley (H), Lost 19-22*
CAPS: England (1) 1984

A prop forward, Steve 'Granite' Redfern joined Leicester youth team from Coalville in 1973, coming into the senior squad in 1976. He made an early entry into representative sides, playing against the England Students for the national under-23 side with whom he toured Canada in 1977, and France and Italy in 1979. In the same year he played for the Midlands against the All Blacks and for England 'B' against France.

A severe neck injury prevented him from playing until December during the 1978/79 season but he appeared in the Midland Counties victory over the touring Wallabies on October 17, 1981. He appeared in five John Player Cup finals for Leicester, including the 1983 final with his brother Stuart (with whom he propped a total of 45 times for Leicester), and emerged with three winners' medals. His one England appearance was as a replacement for Colin White in the 1984 game against Ireland at Twickenham, thereby creating the Leicester record of having seven players in one international team.

He signed professional forms for Sheffield Eagles and made his debut for them at home to Doncaster on December 30 1984. However, he was hampered by injury and retired the following season after only nine appearances, including two as substitute. He played briefly for Leicester's amateur rugby league club before his reinstatement in 1991 as a rugby union coach and administrator.

Apps: 241
Points: 64
Scoring: 16 T

REDMAN, Edward

b. Yorkshire, 1869
d. details not available
Clubs: Yeadon, Guiseley, Manningham, Leicester
Debut: *16.9.1893 v Leicestershire XV (H), Won 26-6 (1T, 3 pts)*
Last Game: *5.11.1900 v Llanelly (A), Won 12-6*

Eddie Redman learned his rugby at the Yeadon and Guiseley clubs, as these were the closest to his home in New Scarborough, Yorkshire. He played in all Yorkshire's games in 1892, and for Yorkshire against the Rest of England in 1892 and 1893. He appeared in an England trial for the North against the South in 1892 and was selected to play for England against Ireland at Manchester on February 6, 1892; but he broke a finger in the Yorkshire-Somerset match and was never given another chance.

When he moved to Leicester he played for the Midland Counties and was noted as one of the best forwards in the Midlands, giving excellent service in the scrummage and being quick about the field. He was captain of the Tigers from 1894-96 and was part of Leicester's first cup-winning team, against Moseley at Coventry for the Midland Counties Cup in 1898. He played cricket for the Leicester South End club and was, for a time, the landlord at the Welford Tavern.

Apps: 143
Points: 39
Scoring: 12 T, 1 PG

RICHARDS, Dean

b. Nuneaton, Warwickshire, 11.7.1963
Educated: St Martin's RC High School, John Cleveland College, Hinckley
Clubs: Roanne (France), Leicester, Barbarians (1982/83)
Debut: *10.4.1982 v Neath (A), Won 25-14*
CAPS: England (34) 1986-92,
British Isles (6) 1989-93

Dean Richards, England's most capped No.8, acquired cult status both for club and country through his singular appearance - socks rolled down, shirt-tail flapping - and singular skills. Not only is he possessed of great mauling strength but his handling and "nose" for the ball compensate for the lack of pace which, in an ideal world, the No 8 should possess. His game was perfectly suited to the set-piece style which dominated English rugby during the late 1980s although one of his finest moments came as a replacement against Scotland in 1992 when he provided a valuable steadying influence at a crucial moment in the second half.

Richards marked his arrival on the international stage by scoring two tries against Ireland in 1986, a feat not achieved by an England player on his debut since Harry Wilkinson against Wales in 1929. He played for England Schools 18 group as a lock forward and following a schools international in France, he returned there instead of going to college,

playing for a junior club, Roanne. When he came home he joined the Leicestershire police (he now works in Hinckley) and in 1982 went into Leicester's first team at the age of 18. He went on to represent Leicestershire, the Midland Division and England under-23 in Romania.

Although he missed much of the 1987 international season through injury he played in all England's games in the 1987 World Cup; in the 1991 World Cup he played in the first three pool games, but Mike Teague was preferred for the knockout stages. In 1989 he was selected to tour Australia with the British Lions and was a dominant force with his sheer strength and presence, playing in all three Tests, and helping the Lions to a 2-1 series victory. He missed all the 1989/90 season with a recurring shoulder injury but toured Australia and Fiji with England in 1991 and played in England's grand slam winning teams of 1991 and 1992.

He captained Leicester for two years (ending 1990/91) and was appointed captain once more for the 1993/94 season. He was again selected in 1993 to tour with the British Lions to New Zealand) and, though overlooked by England during the five nations championship earlier that year, played in all three Tests; he made three other tour appearances, captaining the Lions against Canterbury and scoring a try against Otago.

His father played for Nuneaton and his parents now live in Canada. Richards was the *Leicester Mercury* Sports Personality of the Year in 1987 and was named as the Whitbread/*Rugby World and Post* Player of the Year in May 1991. He holds a somewhat novel record in that when he was a replacement for the Midlands against the All Blacks in 1983 he was only on the field of play for 20 seconds.

Apps: 218
Points: 391
Scoring: 97 T

RICHARDSON, Wayne Philip

b. Leicester, 11.3.1961
Educated: Soar Valley School and Community College
Club: Leicester
Debut: *28.3.1981 v Sale (A), Lost 6-15*

Originally a football player at school, Wayne Richardson was converted by his teacher to rugby and joined Leicester at the age of 14. Taking advice from Robin Cowling he changed from the second row to prop forward and played for Leicestershire schools at under-14 and under-16 levels, as well as appearing for East Midlands and Midlands schools. He was an England schools triallist, played for Midland colts and for the Midlands senior team. He was a replacement for

Wayne Richardson

both the 1981 and 1983 cup finals, and a member of the losing Pilkington Cup final side in 1989. A sales manager for W S Brooks Office Furniture, his other sporting interests are cricket and golf. His brother, Lee, was also a Tiger.

Apps: 219+3
Points: 32
Scoring: 8 T

RINGER, Paul

b. Leeds, Yorkshire, 28.1.1948
Educated: Cardigan Grammar School, Madeley College
Clubs: Cardigan, Leicester, Ebbw Vale, Vichy (France), Llanelli, Cardiff City RL
Debut: *24.3.1973 v Llanelli (H), Won 21-11*
Last Game: *27.12.1974 v Barbarians (H), Lost 4-43*
CAPS: Wales (8) 1978-80

Paul Ringer

Paul Ringer, a flanker, played for Leicester after leaving college and when he returned to Wales he played for their 'B' side and went on to win eight senior caps, as well as appearing for a Welsh XV against Romania in 1979. He was sent off in the 1980 England-Wales match which England won 9-8 on their way to a grand slam. He later switched codes and became the Cardiff rugby league club's first major signing from union; he made his professional debut on August 30, 1981, and went on to win two Welsh RL caps. His brother, Tim, was on the coaching staff at University College of Wales in Aberystwyth and also played for the Tigers. Ringer is employed in the property business.

Apps: 56
Points: 16
Scoring: 4 T

ROBINS, John Denning

b. Cardiff, Wales, 17.5.1926
Clubs: Birkenhead Park, Bradford, Coventry, Sale, London Welsh, Cardiff, Leicester, Barbarians (1950/51 Birkenhead Park)
Debut: *12.12.1959 v Blackheath (H), Won 8-5*
Last Game: *10.2.1962 v Newport (A), Lost 10-22 (2C, 4 pts)*
CAPS: Wales (11) 1950-53, British Isles (5) 1950

John Robins, a prop forward and one of the leading coaches of his time, played two Service internationals for England against Wales in 1945, while playing for the Royal Navy, before winning 11 Welsh caps. He represented two English counties, Cheshire and Yorkshire, and had an England trial in 1948 before opting to play for Wales. A good place kicker, he scored nine conversions and six penalty goals in 16 games (five of them Tests) during the British Isles tour of Australasia in 1950. He returned to Australasia in 1966 as the assistant manager and coach of the Lions - the first time they had taken a coach. A games teacher, Robins was a distinguished coach of Loughborough Colleges, and later at Sheffield University and Cardiff University.

Apps: 27
Points: 115
Scoring: 26 C, 21 PG

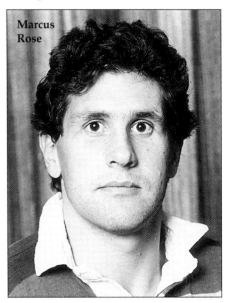
Marcus Rose

ROSE, William Marcus Henderson

b. Loughborough, Leicestershire, 12.1.1957
Educated: Loughborough Grammar School, Durham University, Magdalene College Cambridge
Clubs: Leicester, Cambridge University (Blues 1979-81), Coventry, Harlequins, Barbarians (1982/83 Coventry), French Barbarians
Debut: *20.12.1975 v Bristol (H), Won 17-16 (3PG, 9 pts)*
Last Game: *10.9.1977 v Bath (H), Won 39-26 (2T, 8 pts)*
CAPS: England (10) 1981-87

Marcus Rose burst to prominence in the mid-1970s while still a pupil at Loughborough Grammar School. When Robin Money was injured, Leicester called upon Rose to play full back and he made an immediate impact with his strong attacking style and his goal-kicking. But in 1976 Dusty Hare joined the club and Rose moved on to his university career, later joining Coventry and then Harlequins. He remained one game short of winning his Leicester player's tie which he would have received had not the match with Saracens in September 1976 been cancelled because of the hardness of the pitch.

Rose played for England at schoolboy, student, under-23 and 'B' levels before winning his first cap against Ireland in 1981, when he also scored a try. He played for Leicestershire and the Midlands, and captained Cambridge University against Oxford in 1980. He and Hare alternated as England's full back between 1981-82 but his international career resumed in 1987 and he went to the 1987 World Cup, only to suffer concussion in the first game which ended both his tournament and his England career. He is now a director with the chartered surveyors, RTZ, in London but Welford Road remains his favourite ground.

Apps: 19
Points: 184
.Scoring: 9 T, 29 C, 28 PG, 2 DG

Bob Rowell

ROWELL, Robert Errington

b. Lorbridge, Northumberland, 29.8.1939
Educated: Wymondham College, Norfolk; Hull University, Loughborough Colleges
Clubs: Hull University, Loughborough Colleges, Leicester, Fylde, Waterloo, Barbarians (1976/77)
Debut: 8.3.1962 v Loughborough Colleges (H), Won 16-0 (1T, 3 pts)
Last Game: 29.4.1978 v Northern (H), Won 21-16
CAPS: England (2) 1964-65

Bob Rowell, a lock, played a significant role in the restructuring of the club which occurred in the mid-1970s and, under his captaincy during 1976/77, the successful pattern began to emerge that was to carry the club to their successful cup run. He played for Leicestershire and Lancashire in the county championship, and for

Leicestershire and East Midlands against the 1963 New Zealanders, which contributed towards his two caps, both against Wales in 1964 and 1965. He represented the UAU at athletics and became a teacher before leaving the profession to work in business; he is now self-employed. He was a Midland divisional selector.

Apps: 355
Points: 67
Scoring: 20 T

RUSSELL, John Cannan

b. Helensburgh, Scotland, 6.3.1896
d. Roehampton, 15.8.1956
Educated: Fettes School
Clubs: London Hospitals, Leicester, Barbarians (1919/20 London Hospitals)
Debut: 15.2.1922 v The Army (H), Won 8-3
Last Game: 30.1.1930 v Royal Air Force (H), Won 23-11

John Russell, a scrum half, was educated at Fettes and joined the fledgling RAF during the First World War, becoming a squadron leader very swiftly despite his youth. He was awarded the DSO in 1919 before becoming station commander in Amman, and eventually an Air Commodore in 1939. When he returned home he was offered a place in the London Scottish 'A' team, but preferred to play for Tigers. He captained the RAF team against Leicester in January 1923 and the following season was invited to play in a Scottish trial but could not accept the offer. H L V Day, in his book, "Rugby Union Football", published in 1952, said of Russell: "He was the best scrum half I ever played with - why he was never asked to play for his country is a complete mystery...he had boundless courage and was a devastating tackler, what more could you ask of any scrum half?"

Apps: 141
Points: 33
Scoring: 10 T, 1 GM

RUSSELL, Richard Forbes

b. Bingham, Nottinghamshire, 5.4.1879
d. Lezayre, Isle of Man, 30.5.1960
Educated: St Peter's School, York; Cambridge University
Clubs: Cambridge University, Leicester, Castleford, Cork
Debut: 19.9.1903 v Devonport Albion (A), Lost 0-5
Last Game: 6.9.1913 v Bedford (H), Won 17-8
CAPS: England (1) 1905

Richard 'Tosh' Russell, a forward, played for Yorkshire and won his single cap against New Zealand after a good performance for Leicester against the touring side in 1905. He played for the Midlands against the South Africans the following season, when he was also Leicester captain, and won all seven of his Midland Counties Cup ties for the club, including two finals in 1904 and 1905. Russell was a schoolmaster who taught in Fermoy, County Cork. He was the nephew of Sir Timothy O'Brien, the Middlesex and England cricketer. During the First World War he served as a special constable on the Isle of Man.

Apps: 122
Points: 157
Scoring: 28 T, 26 C, 7 PG

SAMBROOK, Leonard Claude

b. Leicester, 24.11.1895
d. Leicester, 29.8.1957
Educated: Moat Road School
Clubs: Aylestone St James, Leicester
Debut: 12.9.1921 v Burton-on-Trent (A), Won 22-3
Last Game: 3.3.1928 v Harlequins (H), Drew 18-18

Claude Sambrook, a full back whose fielding and kicking of the ball drew more praise than his tackling, played in two international trials in the 1923/24 season and was selected as an England reserve against Scotland at Twickenham on March 15, 1924. It looked as if he would make his debut there when Bristol's Bev Chantrill reported unfit but Chantrill recovered at the last minute to take his place. Sambrook played at Leicester with his brother, Harold Arthur, both appearing in the victorious 1925 Leicestershire team which won the county championship. Claude Sambrook worked in Tom Crumbie's printing business, and later became a commercial traveller; he was also employed at the Ministry of Labour. He retained his involvement with the Tigers after he finished playing by running the line on many occasions until the end of the Second World War.

Apps: 215
Points: 73
Scoring: 24 C, 6 PG, 1 DG, 1 GM

SAUNDERS, Stanley Herbert

b. Leicester, 1.3.1908
Educated: Moat Road School, Alderman Newton's School
Clubs: Aylestone St James, Leicester, Bedford
Debut: *9.3.1929 v Bridgwater Albion (A), Lost 5-6*
Last Game: *13.1.1934 v Rugby (H), Won 12-0*

Stan 'Tubby' Saunders was a good enough forward to receive an England trial at Northampton in the 1928/29 season. However, he had less happy memories of Northampton in 1930, when he collapsed after re-opening a head wound received the previous week; after treatment he carried on. In the same season he conceded the penalty which won the game for the Harlequins although the fog was such that neither team could be seen clearly and it was disputed whether a try had been converted. He got his own back in March 1932 when his last-minute try won the game for Leicester against Harlequins. He was self-employed.

Apps: 131
Points: 63
Scoring: 21 T

SCOTLAND, Kenneth James Forbes

b. Edinburgh, Scotland, 29.8.1936
Educated: Heriot's School Edinburgh, Trinity College Cambridge
Clubs: Heriot's FP, Cambridge University (Blues 1958-60), London Scottish, Ballymena, Leicester, Aberdeenshire, Barbarians (1957/58 Heriot's)
Debut: *9.9.1961 v Bath (H), Lost 11-12 (1C, 1PG, 5 pts)*
Last Game: *8.12.1962 v Blackheath (H), Won 8-6 (1C, 1DG, 5 pts)*
CAPS: Scotland (27) 1957-65, British Isles (5) 1959

Ken Scotland was one of the most talented players to appear at full back for Scotland and he would have thrived had he played a generation later, in the era of the attacking full back. He was at his apogee on the British Lions tour of Australia and New Zealand in 1959, when he showed his versatility by playing in every position behind the scrum save scrum half; he scored 62 points in 21 appearances and New Zealanders were so impressed that he was named one of their five players of the year; the New Zealand Almanack described him as "a potential match winner with his speed, elusiveness and eagerness to attack."

Scotland left George Heriot's school in 1955 after establishing himself as a cricketer and rugby player. In his formative years he lived near the Goldenacre grounds of his school, and spent many hours practising his kicking. His national service was spent in the Royal Corps of Signals and it was his appearances for the Army in the inter-services championship which attracted the interest of the Scottish selectors. In 1957 he made his international debut at Stade Colombes, Paris, and kicked all Scotland's points in a 6-0 victory. The next year he became a double international, playing one first-class cricket match for Scotland as a right-hand batsman (he made a duck in his only innings). On his debut as captain in 1963 he led the Scottish team to another famous victory over France, kicking eight points in the 11-6 away win. That same season Scotland played him twice at fly half.

Although he joined Leicester at the start of the 1961/62 season his first game was against them, since he had earlier agreed to play for Watcyn Thomas' XV in the annual schools union match. He went on to become a great favourite and in two seasons failed to score in only two games.

Apps: 40
Points: 240
Scoring: 4 T, 45 C, 43 PG, 3 DG

SHARRATT, Herbert

b. Hinckley, Leicestershire, 28.5.1892
d. Hinckley, Leicestershire, 29.10.1971
Clubs: Hinckley, Nuneaton, Leicester, Barbarians (1923/24)
Debut: *23.2.1921 v Moseley (A), Drew 11-11*
Last Game: *28.11.1925 v Cardiff (A), Lost 3-9*

'Herb' Sharratt was a member of the team to meet the All Blacks in 1924, and was described at the time as a forward who never had an off day. He played for the Barbarians in the annual Christmas match in 1923 when he was a Leicester player, had an England trial in 1925 and was a member of the Leicestershire team when they became county champions against Gloucestershire at Welford Road. He was the first interlock knitter employed at Atkins Brothers in Hinckley, and was a long-service fireman in the town. In the First World War he served in the Coldstream Guards and was awarded the Military Medal. Sharratt, whose cousin was Bill Brown, was also a keen boxer and wrestler.

Apps: 150
Points: 55
Scoring: 17 T, 1 DG

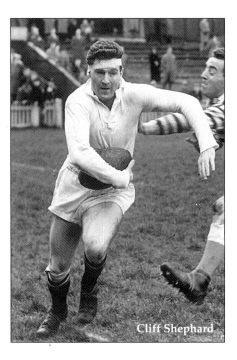
Cliff Shephard

SHEPHARD, Clifford Denis

b. Wigston, Leicester, 21.2.1935
Educated: South Wigston High School
Clubs: Wigston Old Boys, Westleigh, Fylde, Leicester
Debut: *1.10.1955 v Coventry (H), Lost 8-11*
Last Game: *3.10.1964 v Coventry (A), Lost 3-19*

Cliff Shephard, a wing, played in the Leicester schools team and in a final England schools trial. He was captain of the Leicestershire Alliance colts and represented the county and the RAF. He is now retired from his job as a sales representative with Bass Breweries, and is the 1993/4 Leicester Extra First XV team secretary.

Apps: 140
Points: 111
Scoring: 36 T, 1 PG

SIBSON, Harry William

b. Leicester, 15.7.1919
Educated: King Richard's Road Intermediate School
Clubs: Old Ricadians, Aylestonians, Leicester
Debut: *19.4.1947 v Blackheath (H), Won 12-9*
Last Game: *20.11.1954 v Nuneaton (H), Won 11-3*

Harry Sibson, nicknamed 'Darkie', played for Leicester boys under-14 side in 1932/33 and in the second row for Aylestonians. During the Second World War he was a diver in the Royal Engineers and, when he resumed playing, it was as a flanker with Leicester and Leicestershire. He played for Leicestershire and East Midlands against the South Africans in 1951 and was a reserve for an England trial a year earlier. He was a stonemason who set up his own business in Great Central Street after the war making memorial stones. He later became President of the club.

Apps: 183
Points: 78
Scoring: 26 T

Rex Skelton

SKELTON, Rex Patrick

b. Leicester, 10.7.1931
Educated: Wyggeston Grammar School
Clubs: Old Wyggestonians, Leicester
Debut: *28.1.1956 v Rosslyn Park (A), Lost 0-6*
Last Game: *2.5.1970 v New Brighton (H), Won 17-6*

Rex Skelton, a tight-head prop forward, did his national service in the Royal Navy, playing also for Devonport Services, Marine Services and the Royal Navy. He represented Leicestershire and was a reserve for the Midland Counties. He works in the shoe component manufacturing industry.

Apps: 198
Points: 15
Scoring: 5 T

SLOW, Charles Fredrick

b. registered in Northampton, June qtr, 1911
d. Stony Stratford, 15.4.1939
Clubs: Northampton, Leicester, Stony Stratford
Debut: *25.3.1933 v London Welsh (H), Won 31-12*
Last Game: *13.3.1937 v London Welsh (H), Won 9-0*
CAPS: England (1) 1934

For many years the 1931 victory by Leicestershire & East Midlands over the South Africans was known as "Slow's match", after Charlie Slow's virtuoso performance from fly-half during which he scored two tries, set up two more and dropped a goal. It was, though, another three years before he won his only cap, against Scotland. He joined Leicester from Northampton, for whom he played 61 games, scoring 90 points. He served in the RAF volunteer reserve though it was after playing for Stony Stratford against the RAF at Bicester that he was killed in a motor accident on the way home.

Apps: 98
Points: 176
Scoring: 23 T, 4 C, 24 DG, 1 GM

SMALL, Brian Thomas Cartner

b. Liverpool, 6.1.1932
Educated: Kirkham Grammar School, Lancashire; Alderman Newton's, St John's College Cambridge
Clubs: Westleigh, Leicester Thursday, Cambridge University, Leicester, Rosslyn Park
Debut: *27.12.1954 v Birkenhead Park (H), Lost 11-13*
Last Game: *20.4.1963 v Rugby (H), Lost 3-6*

Brian Small, a full back, was a member of the successful county side before joining Tigers. A partner in his own firm of solicitors, he was President of the club in 1989. He is an MBE, and a brother of fellow Tiger Bob.

Apps: 158
Points: 40
Scoring: 3 T, 8 C, 3 PG, 2 DG

SMALL, Robert Wilford

b. Leicester, 29.3.1938
Clubs: Westleigh, Leicester, Rosslyn Park
Debut: *26.12.1957 v Birkenhead Park (H), Lost 8-15*
Last Game: *8.11.1969 v Cambridge University (A), Lost 11-36*

Bob Small, a blind side flank forward, is the younger brother of Brian and is now an importer of textile machinery in Toronto, Canada.

Apps: 119
Points: 66
Scoring: 22 T

SMALLWOOD, Alastair McNaughton

b. Alloa, Scotland, 18.11.1892
d. Uppingham, Rutland, Leics, 10.6.1985
Educated: Royal Grammar School, Newcastle-upon-Tyne; Gonville and Caius College Cambridge
Clubs: Cambridge University (Blue 1919), Gosforth Nomads, Leicester
Debut: *2.10.1920 v Headingley (H), Won 33-3 (1T, 3 pts)*
Last Game: *12.9.1925 v Nuneaton (H), Won 18-0*
CAPS: England (14) 1920-25

Alastair Smallwood, one of the best wings to play for England between the wars, also holds a Leicester record which stands despite the high-scoring of recent seasons: against Manchester in December 1922 he scored seven of the club's ten tries. Since he also kicked a conversion, he scored 23 points from a total of 36 in what was his third match in seven days.

Smallwood began his rugby career at school in Newcastle and went on to represent Northumberland. He played centre for Cambridge in the 1919 university match and joined Tigers after taking up a teaching post at Uppingham, where he coached the school team, who were interested spectators at Welford Road in 1920 when they watched their coach play for his club against his old university. He played for Leicestershire and won the first two of his 14 England caps in the centre in 1920. Indeed, England seemed uncertain of his best position: the following season he played three times on the wing and once at centre, and in 1922 once in each position. But 1923 was his best international season: he shared in a grand slam, scoring tries against Ireland and Scotland and dropping the goal from more than 40 yards against Wales that won the match 7-3.

Alastair Smallwood

He taught general subjects at Uppingham for 32 years, and spent 20 of them as a housemaster until his retirement in 1952. He served as a lieutenant with the 5th Northumberland Fusiliers during the First World War. A bassoonist with Stamford Orchestra, he gained a degree in music from Cambridge University; he was also a noted amateur gardener and a Rutland rural district and county councillor. His grandson, Jeremy Macklin, gained Blues for Cambridge in 1979, 1980 and 1982, and played for Scotland 'B'.

Apps: 64
Points: 151
Scoring: 47 T, 5 C

SMITH, Brian Anthony

b. St George, Australia, 9.9.1966
Educated: Brisbane State High School, Australia; St Anne's College Oxford
Clubs: Wests (Brisbane), Manly (Sydney), Oxford University (Blues 1988-89), Leicester, Barbarians (1990/91), Balmain RL (Australia)
Debut: *1.9.1990 v Bedford(H), Won 57-6 (1T, 4 pts)*
Last Game: *9.3.1991 v Bristol (A) (Courage League), Lost 6-10 (1DG, 3 pts)*
CAPS: Australia (6) 1987, Ireland (9) 1989-91

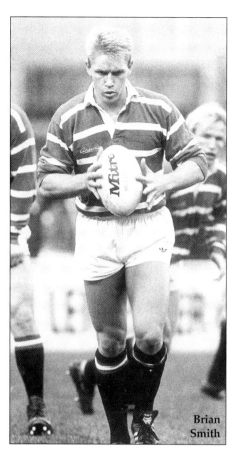

Brian Smith

Brian Smith is one of the rare breed to have been capped for two countries - Australia and Ireland, though there was much controversy over his Irish selection. He played for Australia in every position behind the scrum but his primary role was at half back: he emerged onto the international scene as a scrum half but moved to fly-half, his recognised position during his period in the northern hemisphere.

His father played rugby league, the sport he joined when he signed for Balmain in Sydney in 1991, only seven months before the World Cup in which Ireland hoped he would play a leading role. He played for Australian schools and was called into the senior side that toured New Zealand in 1986; he was a member of Australia's World Cup party of 1987 and toured Argentina. In 1988 he scored 26 points for Australia in the bicentennial celebration game against a World XV, including penalty goals with both feet, but fell out with the national management and came to Oxford University where he won an athletics Blue, specialising in the javelin; he also played representative tennis and athletics. He captained Oxford in the 1989 university match at Twickenham but his time at university was marred by a personality clash over the development of the university rugby club.

Apps: 15
Points: 49
Scoring: 4 T, 9 C, 2 PG, 3 DG

SMITH, Ian Robert

b. Leicester, 26.11.1957
Educated: Wyggeston Grammar School, Milton Keynes College of Education
Clubs: Leicester, Barbarians (1989/90)
Debut: *20.9.1977 v Sheffield (A), Won 47-3*
Last Game: *26.10.1991 v Sale (A), Lost 9-12 (1T, 4 pts)*

Ian Smith, nicknamed 'Dosser' at school because of his alleged tendency to fall asleep during lessons, follows a long line of consistent Leicester flankers who missed international honours but proved assertive thinkers on and off the field. Like David Matthews and Graham Willars, Smith has played for, captained and now coached Leicester. He joined Leicester's first team while still at school and made his first-team debut while only 18. He played for Leicestershire at all age levels - under-14, under-15, under-19 and seniors - and represented the East Midlands and the Midlands at under-15, under-19 and senior levels.

He was included in England's under-19 squad in 1976 and played for England under-23 while his appearances for the Midlands include games against New Zealand in 1978 and the Australian tour parties of 1981 and 1984. He captained Leicester from 1983-85 and played in five John Player Cup finals, on the winning side on three occasions. He retired from first-class rugby at the end of the 1989/90 season, but returned for one game in each of the following two seasons.

A schoolmaster at Uppingham School, where he teaches mathematics and PE, he enjoys all sports. His wife, Sue, represented Britain in the World Games gymnastics and sports acrobatics in 1976.

Apps: 322+9
Points: 268
Scoring: 67 T

SMITH, John Willoughby Dixie

b. Blaby, Leicester, 11.3.1882
d. Harrow-on-the-Hill, Middlesex, 2.10.1959
Clubs: Northampton, Leicester, Nottingham
Debut: *20.1.1902 v Plymouth (A), Lost 3-5*
Last Game: *2.3.1912 v Headingley (H), Lost 12-14*

In the early 1900s Dixie Smith helped foster an excellent spirit between Leicester and Northampton by turning out for the Saints at times when their regular players were injured. (He also played for Nottingham in a game against Leicester in March 1911, arranged when both clubs had found themselves knocked out of the Midland Counties cup.) He played cricket as a right-hand batsman for Leicestershire in two games in 1921, scoring 30 runs in four innings with a top score of 25.

Apps: 132
Points: 81
Scoring: 27 T

Tom Smith

Ron Smith

SMITH, Ronald Hugh

b. Leicester, 5.8.1926
Educated: Wyggeston Boys School, Sutton Bonnington Agricultural College
Clubs: Westleigh, Leicester, Northampton
Debut: *26.11.1949 v Middlesex Hospital (H), Won 6-3*
Last Game: *12.4.1958 v Birkenhead Park (A), Lost 11-13*

Ron Smith played for Westleigh at the unusually early age of 14 and appeared for Leicestershire before joining Tigers as a second row forward. A farmer at Syston, he was also an England triallist in 1955.

Apps: 190
Points: 33
Scoring: 11 T

SMITH, Thomas

b. Leicester, 27.12.1964
Educated: Anstey Martin School, Longslade College
Clubs: Anstey, Vipers, Leicester, Bedford
Debut: *27.4.1984 v Gulf Invitation XV (A), Won 54-3*

Lock forward Tom Smith played for Leicestershire at all levels from under-19 to seniors, and for the Midlands under-23. He gained his players' tie in the game against Fijian Barbarians in November 1986, when the tourists were so impressed with his play they invited him to make a guest appearance against West Hartlepool, though injury prevented him from doing so. He played in the 1989 Pilkington Cup final and, though he moved to Bedford for the 1992/93 season, returned to Leicester in time for the 1993 tour to South Africa. He is a bricklayer, formerly with British Rail but now self-employed. He is also a part-time rugby development coach for Derbyshire.

Apps: 105 1
Points: 69
Scoring: 17 T

178   THE TIGERS TALE

SMITH, Thomas William

b. Rearsby, Leicestershire, 15.8.1883
d. Halton Holegate, Lincolnshire, May 1960
Educated: Wyggeston High School
Clubs: Aylestonians, Leicester,
Broughton Rangers RL
Debut: *17.3.1906 v Birkenhead Park (A),*
Won 3-0
Last Game: *28.3.1908 v Northampton (A),*
Lost 3-11
CAPS: Anglo-Welsh (2) 1908

Tom Smith, a forward, was selected in the
Anglo-Welsh touring party to Australia
and New Zealand in 1908 and played in the
second and third tests (making 12
appearances in all and scoring two tries),
although he never played for England. He
played rugby and cricket for the Leicester
schools from 1894-98 and appeared for the
Midland Counties between 1906-08. A
publican he ran the Wheel Inn at Rearsby
(where he had been born) and later the
Queen's Head in Spilsby, Lincolnshire.

Apps: 58
Points: 12
Scoring: 4 T

STIRLING, Robert Victor

b. Lichfield, Staffordshire, 4.9.1919
d. Halton, 14.1.1991
Educated: Nether Edge Grammar School,
Sheffield
Clubs: Aylestone St James, Leicester,
Wasps, Barbarians (1950/51)
Debut: *4.9.1948 v Bedford (H), Lost 3-21*
Last Game: *4.4.1953 v Bristol (A), Lost 0-6*
CAPS: England (18) 1951-54

Bob Stirling came late to international
rugby at the age of 31 but made up for lost
time by playing 17 successive games at
prop for England, five times as captain
which included the triple crown season of
1953/54. He represented the RAF,
Combined Services, Kent and Notts, Lincs
& Derbys, and played for the Barbarians
against South Africa in 1952 - his third
appearance against the touring side, having
already played for the Combined Services
and England. His popularity at Leicester
can be judged by the reception he received
when he returned to the ground as a touch
judge in the 1955 game against Sale.

He served in the RAF first as a flight
sergeant but rose to wing commander
during the Second World War. He
represented the service as a heavyweight
boxer from 1948-50. After leaving Leicester
he played for Wasps and became a vice
president of the London club. He retired
from the RAF in 1974 but continued to
support services rugby as a selector and
administrator for many years.

Apps: 75
Points: 3
Scoring: 1 T

STURGES, Walter Henry

b. Lutterworth, Leicestershire, 5.10.1869
d. Leicester, 11.2.1952
Educated: Wyggeston School,
Mill Hill House
Clubs: Mill Hill, Leicester
Debut: *6.3.1889 v Bedford (H), Won 4-3*
Last Game: *29.4.1893 v Cardiff Harlequins*
(H), Won 11-7

'Jack' Sturges, better known as an
association footballer at Mill Hill, was a
left wing and a contemporary of Jimmy
Atter, later a star forward with Leicester
Fosse. Sturges was secretary and captain
of Mill Hill House for two years before
joining Leicester in 1888. He became
vice-captain in 1890 and 1891, and was
captain between 1891-93. He played in
every Midland County game in 1890/91
and also played cricket for Leicester
Ivanhoe. When he sat the Law Society
examinations in November 1891 only
one other candidate bettered him out of
260 entrants and he became a solicitor in
January 1892.

Apps: 114
Points: 32
Scoring: 22 T

SWAN, John Spence

b. St Andrew's, Fife, Scotland, 14.7.1930
Educated: Madras College, St Andrew's; St
Andrew's University
Clubs: Madras College Former Pupils, St
Andrew's University, London Scottish,
Coventry, Leicester
Debut: *7.9.1957 v Bedford (H), Won 11-5*
Last Game: *22.4.1959 v Bedford (A), Lost 9-11*
CAPS: Scotland (17) 1953-58

'Ian' Swan (Ian is Gaelic for John) played 16
successive games on Scotland's wing and
would have enjoyed a longer career at
Leicester but for a pre-season training
accident in 1959, when his knee was
damaged so badly in a tackle by David
Senior that he never played rugby again.
His representative honours included
appearances for the North against the
South Africans in 1951 and for the Southern
Counties and Combined Services against
the 1953 New Zealanders. He played for the
Midland Counties against the
Australians in 1957.

Swan studied for a BSc in mathematics
and physics and did his national service as
a mechanical engineer in the REME when
he also represented the Army on the wing.
He joined Leicester from Coventry when he
took a management job at TI at Desford,
and played for two seasons, as captain in
his second season. He now runs a franchise
of Kall-Kwik Printing and has two shops in
Edinburgh.

Apps: 51
Points: 60
Scoring: 20 T

'Ian' Swan

Frank Tarr

TARR, Francis Nathaniel

b. Belper, Derbyshire, 14.8.1887
d. Ypres, 18.7.1915 (killed in action)
Educated: Stoneygate School, Uppingham
School, University College Oxford
Clubs: Oxford University (Blues 1907-09),
Leicester, Headingley, Richmond
Debut: *13.1.1906 v Gloucester (A), Lost 0-20*
Last Game: *27.12.1913 v Jedforest (H),
Won 25-5*
CAPS: England (4) 1909-13

Frank Tarr, a centre, won one of his four
England caps against France at Leicester
in 1909 and scored two tries in a 22-0
victory. He also played for Midland
Counties against the South Africans in
1912 and was on the winning side when
Leicester won the Midland Counties Cup
that year. A solicitor, he was one of the
first international players to join up on the
first day of the First World War and
became a lieutenant in the 4th Battalion,
Leicestershire Regiment, but tragically he
paid the ultimate price.

Apps: 94
Points: 72
Scoring: 24 T

TAYLOR, Frank

b. Leicester, 4.5.1890
d. Leicester, 22.9.1956
Educated: Medway Street School
Clubs: Medway Old Boys,
Medway Athletic, Leicester
Debut: *28.1.1911 v Moseley (H), Won 21-5*
Last Game: *26.4.1924 v Bedford (A),
Won 5-0*
CAPS: England (2) 1920

Frank 'Sos' Taylor, a prop, was told after
being badly wounded serving in the
Leicestershire Regiment during the First
World War that he would never play
rugby again. However, in 1920 he had
recovered so well that he played twice
for England after his thirtieth birthday.
The brother of 'Tim' Taylor, he was one
of six Leicester boys to play in the first
England-Wales schools international in
1904 and went on to represent
Leicestershire and the Midland
Counties. He was in the Leicester side
that won the 1912 and 1913 Midland
Counties Cup finals and Harold Day
said of him, "a grand forward, who
ought to have had more caps. One of the
best line-out forwards I have seen
anywhere."

Apps: 276
Points: 108
Scoring: 36 T

TAYLOR, Frederick Mark

b. Leicester, 18.3.1888
d. Evington, Leicester, 2.3.1966
Educated: Medway Street School
Clubs: Medway Old Boys,
Medway Athletic, Leicester
Debut: *5.10.1907 v Manchester (H),
Won 32-6 (1T, 3 pts)*
Last Game: *28.4.1923 v Newport (H),
Lost 6-7*
CAPS: England (1) 1914

Fred 'Tim' Taylor, a fly-half, represented
Leicestershire and the Midland
Counties. He celebrated his
demobilisation after the First World War
by scoring on his first appearance for
Tigers, against Bedford on December 20,
1919. He was a clerk with a firm of
Leicester solicitors and was involved in
three Midland Counties Cup final wins,
two with his brother 'Sos'.

Apps: 294
Points: 295
Scoring: 97 T, 1 DG

TEBBUTT, Robert Steven

b. Leicester, 14.6.1962
Educated: Anstey Martin High School,
Longslade Upper School,
Hinckley College of FE
Clubs: West Leicester, Leicester,
Northampton
Debut: *16.10.1981 v Northampton (A),
Lost 6-22*
Last Game: *23.3.1991 v Harlequins (H)
(Courage League), Lost 12-15*

Rob Tebbutt, a flanker, joined Leicester's
youth team in 1978 and represented
Leicestershire schools at under-14 and
under-16 levels, as well as playing for
the county colts. He played for England
colts against Wales and France in 1981,
scoring the winning try against the
Welsh, and was a member of the
England under-23 squad. After taking
his City and Guilds exam at Hinckley
College he became a fully qualified
knitting machine mechanic. He left
Leicester for Northampton in 1990,
returned for a season but resumed with
the Saints in 1992. He is now a Sales
Executive with Cavalier Reproductions.

Apps: 153+3
Points: 112
Scoring: 28 T

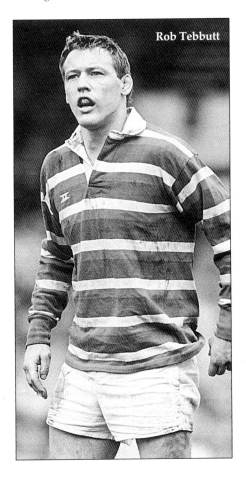

Rob Tebbutt

Haydn Thomas

THORNELOE, Noél Trevor

b. Leicester, 13.7.1898
d. Hove, Sussex, 6.7.1968
Educated: Mill Hill School, London
Clubs: Westleigh, Leicester, Harlequins,
Barbarians (1922/23)
Debut: *1.11.1919 v Royal Navy (H), Won 9-3*
Last Game: *21.4.1930 v Plymouth Albion*
(A), Won 11-9 (1C, 2 pts)

Trevor Thorneloe, a forward, was the
youngest of three brothers, of whom Eric
became the long-serving Leicester secretary
while the third was the father of Peter
Thorneloe. Trevor Thorneloe played at Mill
Hill School in London and joined Westleigh
before beginning his career with Tigers.
When he left to work in London he played
regularly for the Harlequins. He played for
the Barbarians in the 1923 Mobbs memorial
match. He was a lieutenant in the Royal
Naval Air Services during the Second
World War, when he won the Air Force
Cross and was one of the first pilots to be
catapulted off an aircraft carrier. He was a
clothing manufacturer.

Apps: 125
Points: 71
Scoring: 8 T, 19 C, 3 PG

THORNELOE,
Peter Bernard Lulham

b. Leicester, 21.3.1927
Educated: Rugby School
Clubs: US Portsmouth, Leicester
Debut: *29.12.1945 v Swansea (H), Drew 6-6*
Last Game: *14.12.1957 v Blackheath (H),*
Lost 6-13

Peter Thorneloe joined the Royal Navy
after leaving school and played for the
United Services Portsmouth. He
represented Leicestershire and Hampshire.
He is a company director of a Hong Kong-
based clothing manufacturing business. His
father, T B C Thorneloe, was the pre-war
honorary treasurer of Leicestershire County
Cricket Club.

Apps: 221
Points: 33
Scoring: 11 T

THOMAS, Hadyn George

b. Dowlais, Merthyr Tydfil, 7.12.1925
Educated: Merthyr County School,
Loughborough Colleges
Clubs: Loughborough Colleges, Leicester,
Cardiff, Pontypool, Northampton,
Merthyr Tydfil
Debut: *13.10.1945 v Nuneaton (H), Won 8-3*
Last Game: *29.1.1953 v Royal Air Force (H),*
Lost 11-12

Haydn Thomas, a centre, was captain of
Loughborough Colleges (where he later
became Master). After leaving, he
returned to Wales in 1947/48, and played
half a dozen games for Cardiff but he
obtained a post at Humphrey Perkins
School in Barrow-on-Soar which enabled
him to renew his links with Tigers. He
represented Leicestershire and the East
Midlands, the Army and received a Welsh
trial. He became a PE teacher for
Glamorgan County Council.

Apps: 104+1
Points: 117
Scoring: 38 T, 1 DG

THOMPSON, John Sidney

b. Leicester, 7.8.1930
Educated: Moat Road Intermediate School
Clubs: Aylestone Athletic, Leicestershire
Barbarians, Leicester
Debut: *5.2.1955 v London Scottish (A),*
Won 11-9
Last Game: *16.9.1961 v Plymouth Albion*
(H), Lost 9-11

John Thompson, a durable second-row
forward, held the record of 103 consecutive
games for Tigers until overtaken by David
Matthews (after his 100th game Thompson
was presented with a silver tankard by
members of the West Humberstone
Conservative Club). He played for the
Midland Counties against the South
Africans in 1960. His brother, W E
Thompson, also played for Leicester, the
RAF and Combined Services. His nephew,
George Knew, played cricket for
Leicestershire CCC and Leicester Nomads,
and rugby for Oadby Wyggestonians.

Apps: 166
Points: 6
Scoring: 2 T

TOWELL, Allan Clark

b. *Middlesbrough, Yorkshire, June qtr, 1925*
Educated: Middlesbrough College, Loughborough Colleges
Clubs: Middlesbrough, Bedford, Leicester
Debut: *6.9.1947 v Bedford (H), Won 22-3 (1T, 3 pts)*
Last Game: *22.4.1950 v Blackheath (H), Won 14-3*
CAPS: England (2) 1948-51

Allan Towell came to prominence with the RAF in 1946/47, when he played two England trials, and in 1948 he was capped at centre in the final championship match, against France. He was the first Middlesbrough member to appear for England, even though he was playing for Leicester at the time. He captained the club in 1949/50 but then joined Bedford, from where he won his second cap. Towell, a teacher at Dunstable Grammar School, played for Yorkshire, Leicestershire, the East Midlands and the RAF. He captained Bedford in the 1954/55 season, and made 126 appearances for them, scoring 96 points.

Apps: 93
Points: 52
Scoring: 12 T, 5 DG

TRESSLER, Christopher James

b. *Thurmaston, Leicester, 9.1.1961*
Educated: Stonehill High School, Longslade Upper School
Clubs: Belgrave, Syston, Leicester
Debut: *17.9.1980 v Birmingham (H), Won 36-12*
Last Game: *25.4.1992 v Rugby (H) (Courage League), Drew 22-22*

Chris Tressler played centre at school but moved to hooker and joined Leicester when Peter Wheeler was not only club captain but also England's hooker. Tressler played for Leicestershire at under-13, under-19 and senior levels and was picked for the England under-23 squad. He also played cricket for North Leicestershire under-18 and is a keen golfer. Chris is a product manager for Allis Mineral Systems (UK) Ltd.

Apps: 262+2
Points: 56
Scoring: 14 T

TOM, Peter William Gregory

b. *St Germans, Cornwall, 26.7.1940*
Educated: Hinckley Grammar School
Clubs: Hinckley, Leicester
Debut: *2.9.1963 v Torquay (A), Won 18-5*
Last Game: *3.2.1968 v London Scottish (H), Won 19-11*

Peter Tom played lock for Leicestershire and the Midland Counties, and his top honour came with an appearance for the Midland Counties (East) against the touring Wallabies at Welford Road on 22 October, 1966. He is now a group chief executive for Evered Bardon PLC.

Apps: 130
Points: 21
Scoring: 7 T

Chris Tressler

UNDERWOOD, Rory

b. Middlesbrough, Yorkshire, 19.6.1963
Educated: Barnard Castle School, Durham
Clubs: Middlesbrough, Leicester, Barbarians (1983/84)
Debut: *21.9.1983 v Birmingham (H),*
Won 40-3
CAPS: England (60) 1984-93,
British Isles (6) 1989-93

Rory Underwood's list of achievements mounts ever higher: he was the first England player to reach fifty caps, and his number of appearances has yet to be passed; he has scored more international tries than any other Englishman (36 for England at the time of writing and one for the Lions) and stands third in the world rankings behind David Campese and Serge Blanco. His contribution to rugby was recognised in 1992 by the award of the MBE.

Underwood was born to be a wing, blessed not only with natural speed but great strength which has been the envy of several leading athletics coaches. Much of his childhood was spent in Malaysia before he was sent to Barnard Castle School in Durham where he discovered rugby and also shone at cricket and swimming. But he was overlooked at representative schools level before England colts, Durham and Yorkshire uncovered his ability. In 1982 he played for England under-23 and toured in Italy, and later that year for the Northern Division and England 'B'. He played club rugby for Middlesbrough but joined Leicester after moving to Cranwell to begin training as an RAF officer (he has represented the RAF consistently during the inter-services championship).

Underwood made his international debut against Ireland in 1984 and scored the first of his England tries in the following game, against France. He was unable to tour with England in 1984 (South Africa) and 1985 (New Zealand) because of RAF duties but went to Australia and Fiji in 1988 and again in 1991. During England's home game with Fiji in 1989 he scored five tries, equalling the individual record set by Douglas Lambert in 1907 against France.

He played for the British Lions against the Rest of the World in 1986 but had to wait for 1989 for his first Lions tour, to Australia, where he played in the three Tests with eight appearances in all (scoring four tries). In 1993 he toured with the Lions to New Zealand, playing all three Tests and seven games in all, during which he scored three tries, including an outstanding effort in the second Test.

He played in the inaugural World Cup in Australasia in 1987 and was in the England team which reached the 1991 World Cup final; during that tournament he made his fiftieth appearance for England, in the semi-final against Scotland. He shared in the England grand slams of 1991 and 1992, after which he retired from international rugby, only to change his mind at the start of the 1992/93 season when he played in five of England's six internationals - three of them alongside his

brother, Tony. He has never been dropped from an England team since his international career began.

One of the most gifted finishers in the game, his Leicester career has been disrupted by many representative calls but he was delighted to play in the 1993 Pilkington Cup-winning team, thus completing a domestic individual grand slam of playing in sides which have won the club league and cup, the county and divisional championships. He also played in the 1989 cup final when Leicester lost to Bath. He is currently a flight lieutenant in the RAF.

Geoff Cooke, the England team manager, wrote in the foreword to Underwood's autobiography: "Although Rory scored only four tries for England in his first 22 international appearances, he went on to score 31 more in his next 33 games. He became the deadliest finisher in world rugby, and a key component in England's renaissance as a rugby power, and the try he scored against Ireland at Lansdowne Road in 1991 - which gave England the Triple Crown and led them to the Grand Slam - was arguably the most important of all."

Apps: 151
Points: 385
Scoring: 95 T

Rory Underwood -
the Flying Winger!

UNDERWOOD, Tony

b. Ipoh, Malaysia, 17.2.1969
Educated: Barnard Castle School,
Durham; Leicester University;
St Edmund's College Cambridge
Clubs: Cambridge University (Blues
1990-91), Leicester, Barbarians (1989/90)
Debut: *16.1.1988 v Bedford (H), Won 42-9*
CAPS: England (4) 1992-93

Tony Underwood found himself in
direct competition with his older
brother, Rory, when both were
competing for England places against
South Africa in November 1992. In the
event, both played after an injury to Ian
Hunter (Northampton), the first time
that England had fielded brothers in a
full international since 1938 (the
Underwoods had played together for an
England XV against the Barbarians in
1990).

Tony, like his brother Rory, also went
to Barnard Castle School and was in the
school first team by the age of 15. He
played for Durham schools 16 group,
England schools 18 group and English
students whom he represented in the
inaugural student World Cup in France
in 1988. He represented the North and
made the first of several England 'B'
appearances against Fiji in 1989; later
that year he impressed the New
Zealanders with his play against them
for the Barbarians at Twickenham.
However, a broken jaw during a
divisional match at Bristol followed by a
torn knee cartilage hindered his progress
and though he toured Argentina with
England in 1990, he failed to win a cap.

His confidence was lifted by a
sparkling appearance at Twickenham for
Cambridge in 1991, the second of his
university matches, and his consistency
won him a place on the England 'B' tour
to New Zealand in 1992, when his
devastating speed and elusive running
brought him the rare distinction of being
named one of the New Zealand
Almanack's five players of the year. He
made his England debut against Canada
in October that year, scored his first
England try (from his brother's pass)
against South Africa and, though
dropped for the first two championship
matches of 1993, returned for the last
two games and won a place on the
British Lions 1993 tour to New Zealand -
alongside Rory. He scored two tries in
his six appearances. He is a graduate
finance trainee with Lehman Brothers,
an investment bank in London.

Apps: 64
Points: 177
Scoring: 42 T

VALLANCE,
George Philip Colles

b. Manchester, 16.12.1908
Educated: Willaston School, Cheshire
Clubs: Broughton Park, Nottingham,
Leicester, Barbarians (1942/43)
Debut: *1.1.1930 v Manchester (A), Won 9-8*
Last Game: *15.4.1939 v Blackheath (H),
Lost 10-23*

George Vallance, a lock, suffered the
disappointment of being picked by
England (against Wales in 1933 at
Twickenham) but having to withdraw
because he did not consider himself fit
after a bout of influenza. He was not
invited to play again. Vallance played for
Lancashire, then captained Notts, Lincs &
Derbys; he appeared in an England trial in
December 1930. He was seriously ill in
early 1934 and recuperated by going
skiing in Switzerland. On his return he
travelled back to Leicester by train in the
company of the national selectors who
had come to watch him play that
afternoon but on reaching the station he
was greeted by Eric Thorneloe and told he
had not been picked for the game.

Although he suffered cartilage trouble
late in his club career he played for the
Barbarians at Welford Road on Boxing
Day 1942, against J E Thorneloe's XV,
scoring a try in a 21-17 victory, and played
for England Services v Scotland in 1943.
His brother also represented Lancashire.
Vallance was a wholesale photo finisher
for the Rank Organisation.

Apps: 200
Points: 104
Scoring: 27 T, 4 C, 5 PG

Tony Underwood

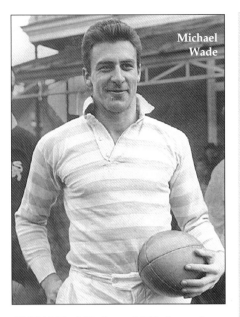

Michael Wade

WADE, Michael Richard

b. Leicester, 13.9.1937
Educated: Wyggeston Grammar School,
Emmanuel College Cambridge
Clubs: Oadby, Old Wyggestonians,
Cambridge University (Blues 1958-61),
Leicester, Barbarians
(1958/59 Cambridge University)
Debut: 24.12.1955 v Bedford (A), Drew 0-0
Last Game: 28.2.1967 v Bath (H), Won 11-3
CAPS: England (3) 1962

Michael Wade, a centre, made an early
impact when he played as a schoolboy for
Leicester over Christmas 1955: within the
space of four days he appeared against
Bedford (who included his master, Ken
Nicholas), Birkenhead Park and the
Barbarians. As he progressed he achieved
the distinguished record of scoring two
tries in his first university match, three
tries on his debut for the Barbarians (at
Newport) and a try in the first minute of
the England-Ireland game of 1962, his
second cap.

Wade represented the RAF and the
Combined Services while doing national
service but continued to play for
Leicester, playing four games in eight
days in October 1957 when required for
Leicester (twice), Leicestershire and his
RAF unit. He captained Cambridge
University to a 9-3 victory over Oxford in
1961, their fifteenth successive win that
season, and he captained Leicester in
1963. Wade represented Leicestershire
and England at all levels, and guested for
the Irish Wolfhounds and Stade Bordelais
University. Business pressure and a
cartilage operation precipitated his
retirement, and in 1970 he moved to the
United States where he is now a
management consultant in Massachusetts.

Apps: 166
Points: 87
Scoring: 27 T, 2 DG

WAKEFIELD, William Wavell

b. Beckenham, Kent, 10.3.1898
d. Kendal, Cumbria, 12.8.1983
Educated: Craig Prep School, Sedbergh
School, Pembroke College Cambridge
Clubs: Cambridge University
(Blues 1921-22), Leicester, Furness,
Harlequins, Barbarians
(1925/26 Harlequins)
Debut: 23.4.1921 v London (H),
Won 20-5 (2T, 6 pts)
Last Game: 26.4.1924 v Bedford (A),
Won 5-0
CAPS: England (31) 1920-27

Wavell Wakefield, as adept at centre as in
his normal back-row position or at lock,
was one of the outstanding players of his
generation. He was also one of the
leading thinkers about the game, credited
with the greater specialisation among the
forwards that developed during the
1920s, during which period he wrote two
instructional and semi-autobiographical
books, *"Rugger"* and *"Rugger - How to
Play it"*. He led England to their 1924
grand slam and his 31 caps represented
an England record for over forty years.
After his playing career ended, his service
as an administrator went hand in hand
with his energetic public life.

Wakefield learned his love of sports at
school where he was captain of the rugby
XV, played in the cricket XI and proved
an outstanding athlete. He left school in
1916 and saw active service during the
First World War in the Royal Naval Air
Service (later the Fleet Air Arm) before
transferring to the Royal Flying Corps.
He was mentioned in despatches, and
rose to the rank of captain. He went up to
Cambridge on an RAF course, gaining a
degree in engineering and leading the
university to a 21-8 victory over Oxford

in 1922. Indeed, he captained all the clubs
he played for: Harlequins in 1920/21
(even though handicapped by a war
wound); the RAF in 1923 to their first
ever victories over the other two services;
Leicester in 1923/24 when his position
with Boots the Chemists, whose head
office was in Nottingham, brought him to
the Midlands; England on 13 occasions;
and Middlesex to their first county
championship in 1929. He held the
England record of 29 consecutive
internationals (1920-26) until overtaken
by John Pullin.

After retiring from the game he became
a referee but though he reached the
international panel, he did not handle an
international game. He represented the
RAF on the RFU committee from 1922-24
and became RFU President in 1950/51.
He was a member of the International
Rugby Football Board from 1954-61. His
many other leisure interests included
skiing (he was chairman of the British Ski
Racing committee) and he was President
of the British Water Ski Federation and
British Sub-Aqua Club.

Wakefield retired from the RAF in 1923
but continued active flying in the reserve
and in 1939 he was appointed director of
the Air Training Corps. From 1935-45 he
was the Conservative MP for Swindon
and was knighted in 1944 "for political
and public services". He subsequently
represented the Marylebone Division
from 1945 to 1963, when he was made the
first Baron Wakefield of Kendal. He
served as a Parliamentary Private
Secretary, and as chairman of the
Parliamentary and Scientific Committee.
He had many business interests in
Cumbria, and was one of the founders of
the Rediffusion Group.

Apps: 29
Points: 30
Scoring: 10 T

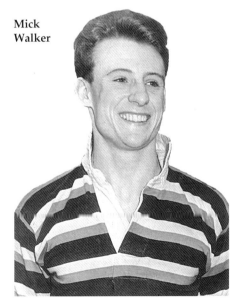

Mick Walker

WALKER, Michael Ronald

b. Leicester, 16.1.1934
Educated: South Wigston School,
Leicester College of Art
Clubs: South Leicester, Nuneaton,
Leicester
Debut: 20.10.1956 v Cheltenham (A),
Lost 0-3
Last Game: 3.12.1966 v Waterloo (A),
Lost 6-10

Mick Walker, a hooker, is a builder and
joiner, played for the county and
Leicestershire Alliance.

Apps: 216
Points: 9
Scoring: 3 T

Billy Wallace

WALLACE, William

Clubs: Percy Park, Leicester
Debut: *13.2.1923 v Racing Club de France (A), Lost 9-19*
Last Game: *30.3.1929 v Bristol (A), Lost 8-14*
CAPS: British Isles (1) 1924

Billy Wallace toured South Africa with the British Isles in 1924 and played in the first Test at Durban but, though he was named reserve wing, never gained an international cap for England.

Apps: 10
Points: 33
Scoring: 11 T

Field Walton

WALTON, Field Laurence Joseph

b. Barnstaple, Devon, 17.4.1940
Educated: Rugby School, Loughborough University
Clubs: Stoneygate, Leicester
Debut: *3.9.1964 v Watcyn Thomas XV (H), Lost 11-12*
Last Game: *27.4.1968 v Manchester (H), Won 13-6 (1T, 3 pts)*

Field Walton, a tough prop forward, represented both Rugby School and Loughborough University. He played for the UAU, English Universities and Leicestershire, and turned out for the Midland Counties (East) against John Thornett's Australian tourists in October 1966. He is now a company director.

Apps: 139
Points: 9
Scoring: 3 T

WARD, George

b. 19.3.1885
d. Leicester, 1963
Clubs: Belgrave, Leicester
Debut: *9.3.1910 v Moseley (A), Won 20-0*
Last Game: *4.1.1926 v Northern (A), Lost 6-8*
CAPS: England (6) 1913-14

George Ward represented Leicestershire and Midland Counties and enjoyed a reputation as the best hooker in Britain during his international career. He won two winners' medals in the Midland Counties Cup, and played in the 3-25 loss for the Midland Counties against Billy Millar's second Springboks at Welford Road in November 1912. George worked for Thorneloe & Clarkson, the clothing manufacturers in Northampton Street.

Apps: 361
Points: 63
Scoring: 21 T

WATKIN, Charles Ernest

b. Leicester, 21.11.1914
d. Leicester, 1.4.1980
Clubs: Aylestone St James, Leicester
Debut: *22.1.1938 v Richmond (H), Won 9-3*
Last Game: *4.9.1948 v Bedford (H), Lost 3-21*

Ernie Watkin, a full back, joined the club from Aylestone St James but the Second World War interrupted his career. He played for Leicestershire and East Midlands against the touring New Zealand Army side in 1946 and against the Australians the following year, when he kicked a penalty and a dropped goal in a 17-11 defeat. Ernie unfortunately died a week before Leicester won the John Player Cup for a second successive time, however, the following year when Leicester won the Cup outright his wife Gwynneth donated the club a splendid presentation case to house the Cup, in honour of her late husband.

Apps: 117
Points: 236
Scoring: 2 T, 64 C, 34 PG

Ernie Watkin

A WHO'S WHO OF CELEBRATED TIGERS

WATSON, Jamie R.

Clubs: Stoneygate, Leicester
Debut: *28.11.1903 v Cambridge University
(A), Lost 0-6*
Last Game: *3.1.1914 v Gloucester (A),
Lost 0-3*

Jamie Watson, a utility back capable of
playing at half-back, five-eighth or centre
was captain of Leicester in the inaugural
fixture against the Barbarians on 29
December 1909, in the middle of his three
seasons as club captain, and was part of
three victorious teams in the Midland
Counties Cup finals of 1909, 1910 and
1913.

Apps: 229
Points: 140
Scoring: 46 T, 1 C

WATTS, William James

b. Llanelly, South Wales, 16.5.1890
d. Roehampton, 16.9.1950
Educated: Llanelly County School,
Carmarthen Training College
Clubs: Llanelly, Leicester, Birkenhead
Park, London Welsh
Debut: *15.4.1914 v Cardiff (A), Lost 6-8*
Last Game: *6.10.1923 v Llanelly (H),
Lost 8-9*
CAPS: Wales (1) 1914

Willie Watts, a centre threequarter
captained Llanelly in 1913/14, when he
won his only cap. A chartered accountant,
he then joined Leicester and returned to
them after the First World War, during
which he was wounded. He later became
President of London Welsh.

Apps: 70
Points: 87
Scoring: 29 T

WELLS, John Martin

b. Driffield, Yorkshire, 12.5.1963
Educated: Magnus Grammar School,
Newark; Loughborough University
Clubs: Loughborough Students, Newark,
Leicester, Barbarians (1988/89)
Debut: *25.9.1982 v Harlequins (A),
Won 29-25 (2T, 8 pts)*

John Wells, a blind-side flanker, came
close to a senior cap in 1988 when he
played in a trial for England against the
Rest, having won international honours at
schoolboy under-16 and under-18,
student, under-23 and 'B' levels. He also
played for an England XV against Italy in

Rovigo in 1990 but in an era of tall
number sixes, his great mauling strength
and support work could not compensate
for a lack of inches.

Wells led the Loughborough Students
side which won the UAU title in 1984 and
played for Notts, Lincs & Derbys. He
represented the victorious Midlands in
every game of the 1986 divisional
championship and toured Spain with
England 'B' in 1989. He captained
Leicester from 1991-93 and led the team

which beat Harlequins in the 1993
Pilkington Cup final.

A partner (with his father) in a farm at
Newark, he trained in sports science and
recreation management and is now
residential care officer at Subton Hall
Boarding School, and a venison retailer.

Apps: 267+4
Points: 178
Scoring: 44 T

John Wells

188   THE TIGERS TALE

WHEELER, Peter John

b. South Norwood, London, 26.11.1948
Educated: John Ruskin Grammar School, Brockley County
Grammar School, South London
Clubs: Old Brockleians, Leicester, Barbarians (1973/74)
Debut: *8.11.1969 v Cambridge University (A), Lost 11-36*
Last Game: *23.10.1985 v Oxford University (A), Won 32-7*
CAPS: England (41) 1975-84,
British Isles (7) 1977-80

Peter Wheeler learned his rugby at Brockley County
Grammar School where, according to his autobiography, "I
had the classical introduction to my position: at the first
games session the master looked me over and said: "Right,
you'll play hooker." He did so to such good effect that he
spent nine years in the England front row and led the
national side in 1983/84. Wheeler was from the classic mould
of tight forwards who are just as effective in the loose: fast
about the field (he scored three tries on his debut for the
Barbarians), he could handle and kick, both for touch and at
goal, and he was part (with Graham Price and Fran Cotton) of
a British Lions front row in New Zealand in 1977 which
demolished the All Blacks.

Wheeler moved to Leicester after joining the
insurance brokers, Hogg Robinson. His early rugby
was with Old Brockleians and he went on to play
for Kent after he had joined Tigers. He represented
Leicestershire between 1970-74 and captained
Leicester between 1973-75; he also led the Midland
Counties (East) against the New Zealanders in
1973 and, subsequently, against Australia in 1975,
and New Zealand in 1978 and 1979. In 1981, when
the Australians opened their tour against the
Midlands, Wheeler captained the side that beat
them and did so again when the New Zealanders
played the Midlands in 1983.

Although he went on England's tour of the Far
East in 1971 he did not win his first cap until
1975 against France, but a serious neck injury in
the next game of that season, against Wales,
checked his career. He recovered to become a
permanent fixture at hooker in succession to
John Pullin (whose record number of caps he
finished one short of). In his first Lions tour, in
1977, he played 13 games including three of the
four Tests after taking over from Bobby
Windsor; he played in all four Tests (11
appearances in all) for the Lions against South
Africa in 1980 and was a leading candidate as
captain for the Lions visit to New Zealand in
1983, but was overlooked in favour of Ciaran
Fitzgerald and Colin Deans.

Wheeler returned to the Far East in 1979
with England and played in the grand slam
team of 1980. His other representative visits
overseas included the Barbarians in Canada
(1976), England in the USA and Canada
(1982) and a five nations party in South
Africa (1983). However, he was not
available for the England visit to Argentina
in 1981, nor for the 1984 tour to South

Africa after his season as England captain during which he
led the side to their first victory over New Zealand since 1936
when another Leicester player, Bernard Gadney, had also
been captain.

A player of forceful personality, with decided views on the
playing and organisation of the game, Wheeler captained
Leicester in their three successive John Player Cup-winning
finals between 1979-81. He continued playing club rugby after
his international career ended and captained the Midlands
against the 1984 Australians, when he was controversially
sent off along with Mark McBain, his opposite number.
Business demands gradually restricted his playing career, but
he was able to help coach the club to win the inaugural
Courage Clubs Championship in 1987/88.

He was awarded an honorary Master of Arts Degree by
Leicester University and serves as a magistrate and member
of the Board of Visitors at Leicester Prison. An insurance
broker, he is now managing director of P & G Bland, who in
1993 were appointed the marketing consultants for Leicester
Football Club.

Apps: 349
Points: 589
Scoring: 66 T (including a penalty try),
61 C, 69 PG

Peter Wheeler

'Chalkie' White

and David Matthews in a different approach to Leicester's preparation during the late 1960s. He coached the club throughout the 1970s, an era ending in the three successive John Player Cup victories of 1979-81.

He became an RFU staff coach and a member of the advisory panel to the RFU coaching sub-committee. Among his representative coaching successes were the Midlands victories over the Australians in 1975 and the Argentinians in 1976. When he moved from Nottingham High School to work for the RFU, he made his home outside Taunton where he covers an area stretching from Land's End to Buckinghamshire.

Apps: 147
Points: 18
Scoring: 6 T

WIENER, Rudolph Alexander Kilgour

b. Cape Town, South Africa, 19.2.1901
d. Thurlestone, Devon, 23.2.1991
Educated: Rondebosch Boys School, University of Cape Town, St Thomas's Hospital
Clubs: St Thomas's Hospital, Harlequins, Coventry, Leicester
Debut: *12.10.1929 v Gloucester (A), Lost 11-20*
Last Game: *17.12.1932 v Waterloo (H), Lost 3-13*

'Doc' Wiener, a forward from South Africa, played for Tigers while working as a doctor at Leicester Royal Infirmary, professional skills which came in useful at times. In September 1930 he had to treat the Plymouth player, W Molls, who had been carried off unconscious and taken to the hospital half an hour after the end of the game. He retired to Thurlestone, Devon in 1984.

Apps: 101
Points: 9
Scoring: 3 T

WHITE, Herbert Victor

b. Carlisle, Cumberland, 16.1.1929
Educated: Creighton Grammar School, Carlisle; Borough Road College, Isleworth; Carnegie College, Leigh
Clubs: Old Creightonians, Penzance-Newlyn, Camborne, Leicester
Debut: *19.10.1957 v Cheltenham (H), Drew 3-3*
Last Game: *30.11.1963 v Cheltenham (H), Won 9-3*

Universally known as 'Chalkie' White, he played scrum half for Tigers but his main contribution to rugby has been as a singularly gifted coach, both with Leicester, successive Midland teams and finally on behalf of the Rugby Football Union whose technical director for the South and South-West Division he became in 1982. White is one of that limited group of men who, though no great player, offered a vision of the game which helped carry teams he prepared to considerable victories and it reflected little credit on the RFU that he was not appointed England coach in the late 1970s.

White was a farmer in Cumberland who went into the Royal Navy and then became a teacher. He represented Cumberland and Westmoreland, Cornwall and Notts, Lincs & Derbys but his playing career ended when he contracted Meniere's disease, which affected his sense of balance. However, he turned an analytical mind to coaching and became involved with Colin Martin

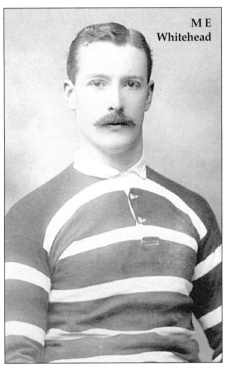

M E Whitehead

WHITEHEAD, M.E.

Clubs: Stoneygate, Leicester
Debut: *23.2.1895 v Burton-on-Trent (A), Lost 6-8 (1T, 3 pts)*
Last Game: *30.11.1901 v Cambridge University (A), Lost 3-21*

M E Whitehead, a forward, gained two winners' medals in the Midland Counties Cup in 1898 and 1900.

Apps: 146
Points: 60
Scoring: 20 T

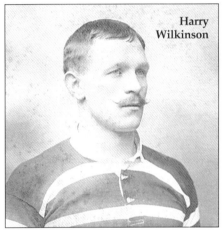

Harry Wilkinson

WILKINSON, Henry

b. May 1876
d. Leicester, 15.5.1953
Clubs: St Matthews, Leicester
Debut: *28.9.1895 v Gloucester (H), Won 6-0*
Last Game: *25.2.1905 v Newport (A), Lost 5-9*

Harry Wilkinson was an extremely fast wing who played in five successive Midland Counties Cup victories from 1898-1902 (he was only once on the losing side in 24 cup ties). He was the older brother of another Tiger, E Wilkinson. He helped run The Model, a lodging house in Brittania Street, and also kept The Sultan public house in Belgrave Gate for some years. During the First World War he worked in munitions.

Apps: 233
Points: 489
Scoring: 153 T, 3 C, 6 DG

WILLARS, Graham George

b. Leicester, 20.11.1939
Educated: Moat Boys School
Clubs: Moat Old Boys, Birstall, Leicester
Debut: *17.10.1959 v Cheltenham (H), Won 23-3*
Last Game: *4.4.1987 (replacement) v Waterloo (A), Won 15-9*

Graham Willars did not play for his school first XV but made up for that with the better part of two decades as a conscientious flanker with Leicester. He joined from Moat Old Boys at the age of 19, encouraged to do so by Doug Norman, and his lengthy playing career included a number of comebacks after nominal retirements. A constructive player, who enjoyed open, running rugby, it was his fate to be playing during the 1960s when rugby was going through one of its more limited phases; however, Willars captained the club in 1972/73 (having previously done so in 1968/69) when it failed by only 12 points to reach his target of 1,000 for the season.

Willars also played for Leicestershire and captained the British Post Office team for seven years. He was the Leicester coach from 1982-87, in succession to 'Chalkie' White, and in 1983 the club reached the John Player Cup final but lost to Bristol - though that season they did score 1,000 points. He became an RFU staff coach in 1986. He was President of Leicester from 1991-93 and is involved with the Old Players' Association, on whose behalf he arranges regular functions. He is a retired telecommunications manager for British Telecom.

Apps: 334+4
Points: 129
Scoring: 38 T

Graham Willars

WILLIAMS, Alexander Kevin

b. Newport, Gwent, 22.8.1956
Educated: St Julian's High School, Newport; Loughborough Colleges
Clubs: Newport, Loughborough Colleges, Leicester
Debut: *12.9.1979 v Birmingham (H), Won 38-0*
Last Game: *20.3.1987 v Loughborough University (H), Won 44-16*

Kevin Williams, a wing, went to Loughborough Colleges in 1975 as a member of Newport but joined Leicester at the end of his four-year teaching course. He played for the Welsh secondary schools from 1973-75 and in the Loughborough VII which won the 1976 Middlesex tournament. He represented the UAU for four years, played for Leicestershire and made two appearances for Wales in 'B' internationals against France and Australia. He toured South Africa in 1981 with the Welsh Academicals; in the same year he played for Leicester in the John Player Cup final win over Gosforth. He runs his own insurance broking business in Leicester - the Williams Partnership in Charles Street.

Apps: 186+5
Points: 256
Scoring: 64 T

WOOD, George William

b. 5.2.1886
d. Leicester, 12.6.1969
Educated: Melbourne Road School
Clubs: Melbourne Road Old Boys,
Leicester, Nuneaton, Barbarians (1915)
Debut: 10.11.1906 v Newport (H), Drew 3-3
Last Game: 9.9.1922 v Plymouth Albion (H),
Lost 6-11
CAPS: England (1) 1914

George 'Pedlar' Wood, a scrum half, won
his only cap in a 10-9 win over Wales in
1914, alongside his club colleague, 'Tim'
Taylor. He played for Leicestershire and
the Midland Counties, whom he helped to
their only county championship title in
1914. A keen tactical student of the game,
he was sent off against Birkenhead Park
that year for adopting what the referee
decided were incorrect scrum tactics. He
played for the Barbarians against the
South African Services team on November
20, 1915, at Richmond in a fund-raising
match to provide comforts for colonial
troops. During his twenty years with
Leicester he won four Midland Counties
Cup winners' medals, and he played on
for a further decade with Nuneaton. He
was a keen cricketer and umpired on
Victoria Park for many years. He was an
inspector with the British United Shoe
Machinery Company until 1959.

Apps: 388
Points: 336
Scoring: 102 T, 15 C

WOOD, Kenneth Berridge

b. registered in Leicester, September qtr, 1885
d. South Africa, c 1960
Clubs: Stoneygate, Leicester
Debut: 13.10.1906 v Bristol (H), Drew 0-0
Last Game: 26.4.1919 v Royal Naval
Division - Plymouth (H), Lost 4-7
CAPS: British Isles (2) 1910

Kenneth Wood, a centre, gained two
winners' medals in the Midland Counties
Cup and was selected for the British Isles
team to South Africa in 1910. He played in
the first and third Test matches, making
nine appearances in all and scoring two
tries, and joins the select band who have
been capped for the British Isles without
playing for their country.

His father W.C. played for the Leicester
Athletic Society team before the Tigers
were founded. Kenneth rose to the rank of
Major in the Army and emigrated to
South Africa where he eventually became
a manager at St Michael's Gold Mine in
Johannesburg.

Apps: 121
Points: 115
Scoring: 33 T, 4 DG

WOODWARD, Clive Ronald

b. Ely, Cambridgeshire, 6.1.1956
Educated: HMS Conway,
Loughborough Colleges
Clubs: Harlequins, Loughborough
Colleges, Leicester, Manly (Australia),
Barbarians (1979/80)
Debut: 1.9.1979 v Bedford (A),
Won 34-12 (1T, 4 pts)
Last Game: 14.9.1985 v Bath (H)
(John Smith's Merit Table A), Lost 15-40
CAPS: England (21) 1980-84,
British Isles (2) 1980

Clive Woodward was one of the most
elusive post-war centres to play for
England, his talents showing to masterful
effect in the deciding grand-slam victory
over Scotland in 1980. His speed also
made him one of the outstanding support
players and he was an ideal foil for Paul
Dodge for club and, 14 times, for country.

He was born into a services family and
was chosen to play
in a Welsh schools
trial but had to
withdraw through
injury. He played
fly-half for England
colts in 1975 and
appeared briefly for
Harlequins before
training as a teacher
at Loughborough
Colleges where he
came under the
influence of Jim
Greenwood, the
former Scotland
and British Lions
No 8 and renowned
as one of the
leading British
coaches.
Woodward
captained the
students in his final
year and played for
England under-23
in 1975-77; he
played his only 'B'
international
against France in
1979 and made his
full England debut
as a replacement
against Ireland in
1980. That year he
also toured with the
British Lions to
South Africa,
playing in the
second and third

Tests, making 11 appearances in all and
scoring 53 points - the second highest total
on the tour. He toured with England to
the USA and Canada in 1982 and with the
Lions to New Zealand in 1983 where he
played seven games.

He played in three John Player Cup
finals for Leicester, in the winning teams
of 1980 and 1981 and the losing team of
1983. He has also represented
Oxfordshire, the Eastern Counties and the
Midlands Division. During the 1980s he
went to work in Australia and played for
the Sydney club, Manly - including an
appearance against the touring Leicester
team in 1987. In 1990 he assisted Oxford
in their preparations for the university
match and has coached Henley. He is now
managing director of Sales Finance Ltd.

Apps: 148
Points: 195
Scoring: 43 T, 4 C, 5 DG

Clive Woodward

WORMLEIGHTON, John Lawrie

b. Leicester, 31.12.1912
d. Leicester, 1.12.1978
Educated: Trent College
Club: Leicester
Debut: 8.10.1932 v Bridgwater Albion (A), Won 11-6
Last Game: 17.4.1937 v Blackheath (H), Won 9-4

Jack Wormleighton, a prop forward, was a nephew of P W Lawrie, and ran Wormleighton & Sons.

Apps: 121
Points: 9
Scoring: 3 T

Mike Yandle

YANDLE, Michael John

b. Hendy, Wales, 28.3.1945
Educated: Llanelli Grammar School, Leeds University
Clubs: Leicester, Swansea, Headingley
Debut: 6.9.1969 v Bedford (A), Lost 5-39
Last Game: 28.4.1973 v Hartlepool Rovers (H), Won 15-7

Mike Yandle, a reliable centre, played for the UAU and Yorkshire. He worked as a textile chemist for the Courtaulds Group when he was with Tigers and, on the same day he was elected club captain for the 1973/74 season, received promotion into senior management at Courtaulds. He was forced to conclude his playing career and Peter Wheeler took over as captain. Yandle now lives in Peru.

Apps: 155
Points: 101
Scoring: 29 T (including a penalty try), 1 DG

YIEND, William

b. registered in Winchcombe, Gloucestershire, September qtr, 1861
d. registered in Cheltenham, 22.1.1939
Clubs: Leicester Victoria, Gloucester, Keighley, Hartlepool Rovers, Leicester, Peterborough, Barbarians (1890 Hartlepool Rovers)
Debut: 19.10.1895 v Guy's Hospital (H), Won 19-0
Last Game: 6.4.1896 v Hartlepool Rovers (H), Won 8-4
CAPS: England (6) 1889-93

William 'Pusher' Yiend, a forward, represented Durham County for ten seasons, only missing one match during that time. He learned his rugby with the Leicester Victoria club before going on to captain Keighley. He was employed as a railway traffic agent and came to play for Leicester when he moved to Peterborough. He played all six of his England games while a member at Hartlepool, whom he captained from 1890-93. He played for both the North and the South in trial matches.

Apps: 10
Points: 6
Scoring: 2 T

YOUNGS, Nicholas Gerald

b. West Runton, Norfolk, 15.12.1959
Educated: Greshams School, Norfolk; Shuttleworth Agricultural College
Clubs: Bedford, Leicester
Debut: 21.11.1981 v Wasps (H), Won 27-18
Last Game: 8.10.1988 (Replaced) v Orrell (H) (Courage League), Lost 15-27
CAPS: England (6) 1983-84

Nick Youngs, a scrum half, played nine times for England schools (four as captain) and five times for England under-23, including their 1979 visit to France, before the first of his England caps against Ireland in 1983. He made 83 appearances for Bedford from 1978-81, scoring 207 points (including 35 tries) and then joined Leicester despite the 236-mile round trip for training from his home in Norfolk. He played in the 1983 John Player Cup final against Bristol and, during the summer, appeared for a Western Province invitation XV while studying farming methods in South Africa. He played in the Midland and England sides that beat the All Blacks in 1983 and returned to South Africa with England the following year, staying on to play club rugby in Durban. He is a farm manager/agricultural salesman and coaches North Walsham. His sister, Lucy, has played hockey for England.

Apps: 145
Points: 284
Scoring: 71 T (including a penalty try)

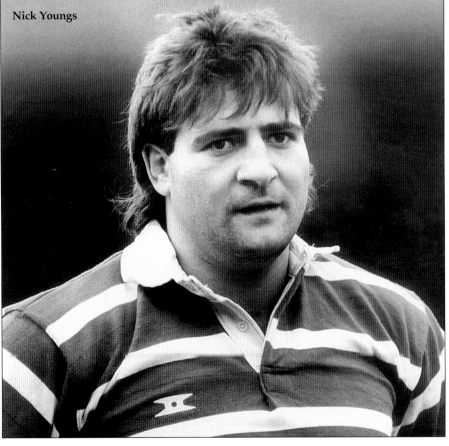

Nick Youngs

TIGER'S INDIVIDUAL CAREER RECORDS

NAME	FROM	TO	APPS	T	C	PG	DG	GM	PTS
Aarvold C.D.	1930/31	only	1	-	-	-	-	-	-
Abel J.R.	1880/81	1886/87	34	-	-	-	-	-	-
Abraham M.	1918/19	only	2	-	-	-	-	-	-
Ackroyd G.	1901/02	only	1	-	-	-	-	-	-
Adams A.M.	1945/46	1947/48	43	14	-	-	-	-	42
Adams C.D.	1921/22	1923/24	4	-	-	-	-	-	-
Adams J.A.	1945/46	only	3	-	-	-	-	-	-
Adams N.	1932/33	1938/39	126	26	-	-	-	-	78
Adcock A.W.	1905/06	only	1	-	-	-	-	-	-
Adcock L.J.	1927/28	1932/33	8	-	-	-	-	-	-
Addison J.H.	1959/60	1960/61	33	-	-	-	-	-	-
Addison -.	1884/85	only	1	-	-	-	-	-	-
Adey G.J.	1966/67	1980/81	381	57	-	-	-	-	215
Afflick V.	1981/82	1986/87	32	4	-	-	-	-	16
Ainscough G.C.	1991/92	only	12	4	14	-	-	-	44
Aitken G.G.	1922/23	only	1	-	-	-	-	-	-
Akers A.	1893/94	1898/99	160	10	1	-	-	-	32
Aldred M.	1898/99	1901/02	52	2	-	-	-	-	6
Aldwinckle J.	1989/90	only	3	-	-	-	-	-	-
Aldwinckle P.J.	1966/67	1969/70	20	6	-	-	-	-	18
Alexander P.C.	1928/29	only	1	-	-	-	-	-	-
Alldridge W.T.	1934/35	1937/38	19	-	-	-	-	-	-
Allen G.R.	1964/65	1967/68	10	-	-	-	-	-	-
Allen J.A.	1960/61	1975/76	457	58	27	17	2	-	297
Allen T.	1958/59	1960/61	31	9	-	-	-	-	27
Allen W.J.	1909/10	1920/21	209	37	25	3	-	-	170
Allen W.M.	1936/37	only	29	2	-	-	-	-	6
Allinson -.	1885/86	only	1	-	-	-	-	-	-
Almey G.A.	1957/58	1963/64	150	31	-	-	-	-	93
Anderson J.D.	1935/36	only	3	-	-	-	-	-	-
Andrews A.	1901/02	1903/04	23	2	-	-	-	-	6
Andrews A.C.	1898/99	1902/03	2	-	-	-	-	-	-
Andrews K.P.	1964/65	1969/70	191	12	-	-	-	-	36
Ansell J.	1910/11	only	2	2	-	-	-	-	6
Anson W.J.	1883/84	1884/85	17	1	-	-	-	-	1
Anstee J.L.	1929/30	only	2	-	-	-	-	-	-
Anthony S.E.A.	1937/38	1938/39	60	6	-	-	-	-	18
Apperley F.	1886/87	only	14	6	-	-	-	-	6
Armstrong A.	1907/08	only	1	-	-	-	-	-	-
Arneil R.J.	1969/70	1970/71	25	4	-	-	-	-	12
Arnold W.R.	1901/02	only	2	-	-	-	-	-	-
Arundell T.	1935/36	only	1	-	-	-	-	-	-
Ash P.	1946/47	1947/48	6	1	-	-	-	-	3
Ash W.N.	1934/35	only	1	-	-	-	-	-	-
Ashley F.M.T.	1947/48	1948/49	8	3	-	-	-	-	9
Ashurst A.D.B.	1951/52	1962/63	112	14	3	3	-	-	57
Ashworth A.	1889/90	only	2	-	-	-	-	-	-
Atkins A.P.	1924/25	only	2	1	-	-	-	-	3
Atkins A.S.	1895/96	1899/00	9	-	-	-	-	-	-
Atkins D.B.	1901/02	1908/09	147	10	-	-	-	-	30
Atkins F.	1912/13	only	2	1	-	-	-	-	3
Atkins G.E.	1912/13	1913/14	5	-	-	-	-	-	-
Atkins H.P.	1896/97	1906/07	186	42	-	-	-	-	126
Atkins J.S.	1923/24	only	1	-	-	-	-	-	-
Atkins -.	1887/88	1888/89	2	-	-	-	-	-	-
Atkinson B.L.	1904/05	1905/06	2	-	-	-	-	-	-
Atterbury J.	1910/11	only	4	1	-	-	-	-	3
Auty J.R.	1929/30	1938/39	19	8	-	-	-	-	24
Avent S.	1983/84	1984/85	4	-	-	-	-	-	-
Babington T.	1929/30	only	16	5	-	-	-	-	15
Back N.A.	1990/91	to date	61	16	-	-	-	-	70
Bacon N.	1928/29	1931/32	2	-	-	-	-	-	-
Baillon L.B.	1933/34	1935/36	10	1	-	-	1	-	7
Baillon R.O.	1934/35	1935/36	2	-	-	-	-	-	-
Bainbridge J.W.	1904/05	1906/07	51	21	-	-	-	-	63
Bainbridge W.	1936/37	1937/38	41	1	3	6	-	-	27
Baines G.P.	1914/15	only	2	-	-	-	-	-	-
Baines S.M.	1890/91	1892/93	21	1	-	-	-	-	1
Baker A.	1922/23	1923/24	2	1	-	-	-	-	3
Baker A.	1952/53	1954/55	30	1	-	2	-	-	9

NAME	FROM	TO	APPS	T	C	PG	DG	GM	PTS
Baker J.L.	1899/00	only	3	-	-	-	-	-	-
Baker P.	1911/12	only	1	-	-	-	-	-	-
Baker P.T.	1954/55	1956/57	38	8	-	-	1	-	27
Ball J.	1889/90	1898/99	46	8	2	-	-	-	19
Ball J.	1934/35	1945/46	5	-	-	-	-	-	-
Ball R.	1938/39	only	1	-	-	-	-	-	-
Bandon -.	1925/26	only	1	1	-	-	-	-	3
Banks G.	1893/94	1897/98	59	5	1	-	-	-	17
Bann E.E.	1967/68	1975/76	163	26	18	18	-	-	188
Barham C.M.	1890/91	1891/92	19	4	-	-	-	-	8
Barker C.C.	1934/35	only	5	1	-	-	1	-	7
Barker F.A.	1902/03	only	1	-	-	-	-	-	-
Barker H.	1938/39	only	2	-	-	-	-	-	-
Barker J.L.	1933/34	1934/35	11	-	-	-	1	-	4
Barker R.G.	1968/69	1979/80	320	158	92	107	2	-	1117
Barker T.H.	1945/46	only	1	-	-	-	-	-	-
Barkes M.	1990/91	1991/92	7	-	-	-	-	-	-
Barlow E.M.	1926/27	1931/32	50	22	-	-	1	-	70
Barnes J.	1900/01	only	1	-	-	-	-	-	-
Barnwell R.C.	1977/78	1982/83	189	95	1	-	-	-	382
Barr R.J.	1928/29	1938/39	241	-	12	6	6	-	66
Barradell H.M.	1887/88	only	6	-	-	-	-	-	-
Barradell J.E.	1887/88	1892/93	21	1	-	-	2	-	7
Barratt M.D.	1954/55	only	1	-	-	-	-	-	-
Barratt T.H.	1947/48	only	2	-	-	-	-	-	-
Barrett A.E.	1919/20	only	8	3	-	-	-	-	9
Barrow C.O.	1889/90	only	3	-	-	-	-	-	-
Barrow E.A.	1948/49	1953/54	90	5	6	6	-	-	45
Barrow J.V.	1909/10	1910/11	7	3	-	-	-	-	9
Barrowcliffe M.	1902/03	1905/0	6 3	1	-	-	-	-	3
Barth W.	1893/94	only	6	1	-	-	-	-	3
Barwick E.F.	1880/81	1882/83	4	-	-	-	-	-	-
Barwick H.J.	1880/81	1882/83	6	-	-	-	-	-	-
Bassett C.T.	1903/04	only	1	-	-	-	-	-	-
Bassett S.R.	1918/19	only	4	-	-	-	-	-	-
Batchelor B.A.	1923/24	only	1	-	-	-	-	-	-
Bateman -.	1906/07	only	1	-	-	-	-	-	-
Bates A.	1913/14	1920/21	61	37	4	-	3	-	131
Bates E.	1931/32	1932/33	36	4	-	-	1	-	16
Bates E.P.R.	1937/38	1938/39	6	-	-	-	-	-	-
Bates G.	1955/56	only	1	-	-	-	-	-	-
Bates I.	1982/83	to date	275	38	-	-	-	-	154
Baxter B.R.	1930/31	1931/32	3	-	-	-	-	-	-
Baxter J.G.	1936/37	only	1	-	-	-	-	-	-
Baxter J.L.	1926/27	only	1	-	-	-	-	-	-
Baynes C.J.	1968/69	1972/73	116	37	-	-	-	-	125
Beamish C.E.St J.	1926/27	1935/36	17	2	-	-	-	-	6
Beamish C.H.	1937/38	1945/46	13	-	-	-	-	-	-
Beamish F.V.	1926/27	1928/29	68	1	-	-	-	-	3
Beamish G.R.	1924/25	1932/33	118	24	1	-	-	-	74
Beasley E.E.	1888/89	only	11	2	-	-	-	-	2
Beasley J.N.	1918/19	only	1	-	-	-	-	-	-
Beason R.	1960/61	1972/73	203	3	-	-	-	-	9
Beattie J.A.	1933/34	only	1	-	-	-	-	-	-
Beaty D.J.	1963/64	1968/69	88	-	-	-	-	-	-
Beaty-Pownall C.C.	1929/30	1931/32	14	2	-	-	-	-	6
Beaver K.	1951/52	only	3	1	-	-	-	-	3
Beaver L.	1904/05	only	3	-	-	-	-	-	-
Beaver W.R.	1920/21	only	3	-	-	-	-	-	-
Beazley N.	1985/86	only	1	-	-	-	-	-	-
Bedggood B.M.	1965/66	1967/68	59	5	4	6	-	-	41
Beevers A.C.	1975/76	1976/77	7	1	-	-	-	-	4
Beith A.E.	1925/26	1926/27	4	-	-	-	-	-	-
Belasco D.G.	1952/53	1953/54	13	-	-	-	1	-	3
Bell E.	1884/85	1889/90	42	2	-	-	-	-	2
Bemrose J.M.	1923/24	only	3	1	-	-	-	-	3
Bennett A.C.	1924/25	only	1	-	-	-	-	-	-
Bennett E.R.	1948/49	1953/54	30	2	-	-	1	-	9
Bennett H.J.	1932/33	1935/36	27	1	-	-	-	-	3
Bennett L.	1902/03	1904/05	10	-	-	-	-	-	-
Bennetts B.B.	1907/08	1910/11	2	-	-	-	-	-	-

NAME	FROM	TO	APPS	T	C	PG	DG	GM	PTS
Benson -.	1885/86	only	2	-	-	-	-	-	-
Berry D.McD.H.	1964/65	1970/71	78	6	-	-	4	-	30
Berry J.H.	1959/60	1968/69	3	-	-	-	-	-	-
Berry J.T.W.	1931/32	1947/48	277	15	-	-	-	-	45
Berry R.T.H.	1965/66	1969/70	27	-	-	-	-	-	-
Betts S.E.	1966/67	1969/70	45	10	-	-	-	-	30
Betts T.	1894/95	only	1	-	-	-	-	-	-
Bevan O.V.	1935/36	only	1	-	-	-	-	-	-
Bevan S.N.	1932/33	1934/35	2	-	-	-	-	-	-
Bevan T.W.	1934/35	1935/36	3	-	-	-	-	-	-
Bevins D.E.	1934/35	1946/47	44	3	5	8	-	-	43
Beynon G.E.	1925/26	only	1	-	-	-	-	-	-
Biggs H.S.	1880/81	only	3	-	-	-	-	-	-
Bignall J.S.W.	1934/35	only	3	-	-	-	-	-	-
Billingham M.F.	1964/65	only	1	-	-	-	-	-	-
Billson J.W.	1887/88	only	1	-	-	-	-	-	-
Bingham W.H.	1907/08	1908/09	8	-	-	-	-	-	-
Birch C.	1907/08	1908/09	10	-	-	-	-	-	-
Bircumshaw D.	1953/54	1956/57	21	4	-	-	-	-	12
Bird D.W.	1960/61	1972/73	285	86	-	-	-	-	258
Bird W.J.	1935/36	only	1	-	-	-	-	-	-
Birkett M.J.	1959/60	1962/63	2	-	-	-	-	-	-
Birkett -.	1885/86	only	4	1	-	-	-	-	1
Bithell L.	1945/46	only	1	-	-	-	-	-	-
Black A.W.	1952/53	1953/54	16	2	-	-	1	-	9
Black D.	1937/38	only	1	-	-	-	-	-	-
Black D.	1980/81	1984/85 57	17	-	-	-	-	68	
Black R.B.	1935/36	only	1	-	-	-	-	-	-
Blackburn W.	1902/03	1904/05	38	1	-	-	1	-	
Blackett G.	1958/59	1959/60	12	2	-	-	4	-	1
Blakiston A.F.	1923/24	only	1	-	-	-	-	-	-
Blandy A.	1945/46	only	2	-	-	-	-	-	-
Bleasdale T.	1949/50	1963/64	340	53	-	-	-	-	159
Bloor A.J.	1918/19	only		1	-	-	-	-	-
Blower W.L.	1918/19	only	4	1	-	-	-	-	3
Bloxham B.C.	1882/83	only	1	-	-	-	-	-	-
Bloxham C.T.	1933/34	only	1	-	-	-	-	-	-
Blunt G.E.	1893/94	only	1	-	-	-	-	-	-
Bodycote -.	1881/82	only	1	-	-	-	-	-	-
Bolesworth A.D.	1936/37	1954/55	330	23	-	-	-	-	69
Bolus A.	1930/31	1931/32	9	3	-	-	-	-	9
Bolus E.	1895/96	1898/99	5	-	-	-	-	-	-
Bolus G.	1905/06	only	1	-	-	-	-	-	-
Bond -.	1907/08	only	1	-	-	-	-	-	-
Bonner F.	1885/86	1890/91	5	1	-	-	-	-	1
Booth E.E.	1908/09	only	5	-	-	-	-	-	-
Booth W.	1918/19	only	1	-	-	-	-	-	-
Bostock H.	1888/89	only	2	-	-	-	-	-	-
Boston F.	1923/24	only	1	-	-	-	-	-	-
Boston N.	1923/24	only	2	-	-	-	-	-	-
Boswell J.S.	1923/24	only	3	-	-	-	-	-	-
Bosworth T.	1880/81	only	1	-	-	-	-	-	-
Botting I.J.	1951/52	1952/53	38	15	-	-	-	-	45
Bottomley W.	1895/96	only	1	-	-	-	-	-	-
Bottrill W.J.H.	1935/36	1938/39	70	20	-	-	-	-	60
Boulter A.	1925/26	only	1	-	-	-	-	-	-
Bourns C.	1906/07	1907/08	15	-	-	-	-	-	-
Bovell-Jones T.P.	1926/27	only	1	-	-	-	-	-	-
Bowell A.E.G.	1914/15	only	1	-	-	-	-	-	-
Bowen H.J.R.	1947/48	only	1	-	1	-	-	-	2
Bowen N.	1930/31	only	1	-	-	-	-	-	-
Bowers B.	1983/84	1985	8	-	-	-	-	-	-
Bowers S.H.	1930/31	1935/36	6	-	-	-	-	-	-
Bowman A.G.	1901/02	1902/03	10	-	-	-	-	-	-
Bown H.	1892/93	only	9	-	1	-	-	-	3
Boyle L.S.	1991	to date	39	8	-	2	-	-	43
Bracewell K.	1974/75	1975/76	29	8	-	-	-	-	32
Brackenbury H.E.	1898/99	only	12	1	1	-	-	-	5
Bradbury A.	1921/22	only	1	1	-	-	-	-	3
Bradford W.H.	1894/95	1895/96	12	-	-	-	-	-	-
Bradley E.G.	1932/33	only	4	2	-	-	-	-	6
Braithwaite E.	1927/28	1928/29	8	-	-	-	-	-	-
Braithwaite J.	1895/96	1906/07	359	67	45	2	15	1	361
Branston K.	1952/53	only	1	-	-	-	-	-	-
Bream J.W.	1910/11	1913/14	101	4	125	22	1	-	332
Brennand J.G.	1945/46	only	3	-	-	-	-	-	-
Brewin J.	1912/13	only	1	-	-	-	-	-	-
Brice A.	1908/09	only	2	-	-	-	-	-	-
Brice A.E.	1880/81	1886/87	21	2	-	-	-	-	2
Bridgewood I.	1979/80	only	1	-	-	-	-	-	-
Brier B.S.	1991/92	to date	8	-	-	-	-	-	-
Brierley B.C.	1945/46	only	3	-	-	-	-	-	-
Briers T.H.	1924/25	1929/30	66	1	-	-	-	-	3
Brittain S.	1907/08	only	2	-	-	-	-	-	-
Britten H.	1910/11	only	1	-	-	-	-	-	-
Broadbent P.	1969/70	only	1	-	-	-	-	-	-
Broadbent S.	1884/85	1885/86	16	-	-	-	-	-	-
Broadhurst J.	1892/93	only	1	1	-	-	-	-	2
Broadley F.R.	1911/12	1914/15	13	8	-	-	-	-	24
Brockbank H.H.	1887/88	1891/92	83	11	35	4	1	-	101
Brodbeck A.F.	1923/24	1927/28	3	-	-	-	-	-	-
Brook D.	1954/55	1956/57	83	16	-	-	-	-	48
Brookes P.G.	1986/87	1990/91	4	-	-	-	-	-	-
Brookhouse R.D.	1954/55	1956/57	11	-	-	-	-	-	-
Brookman F.	1950/51	only	9	-	5	2	4	-	28
Brooks J.	1937/38	only	3	-	-	-	-	-	-
Broome J.	1969/70	only	1	-	-	-	-	-	-
Brown A.	1919/20	only	5	2	-	-	-	-	6
Brown A.E.	1938/39	1946/47	34	3	-	-	-	-	9
Brown F.	1892/93	1894/95	37	-	-	-	1	-	4
"Brown' H.	1889/90	only	8	1	-	-	-	-	1
Brown S.	1922/23	1928/29	4	-	-	-	-	-	-
Brown W.H.	1945/46	1948/49	106	2	-	-	-	-	6
Brownhill M.J.	1965/66	1968/69	73	28	-	-	-	-	84
Brownless G.	1901/02	only	2	-	-	-	-	-	-
Brownson J.M.	1895/96	only	1	1	-	-	-	-	3
Bruce-Lockhart R.B.	1936/37	only	3	1	-	-	-	-	3
Bryan H.	1892/93	1896/97	39	14	17	2	6	-	104
Bryson O.C.	1922/23	1926/27	84	25	-	-	-	-	75
Buchanan J.C.R.	1922/23	1924/25	8	2	-	-	-	-	6
Buckby E.	1992/93	only	2	-	-	-	-	-	-
Buckingham R.A.	1924/25	1934/35	325	117	38	4	1	-	443
Buckle J.	1888/89	1890/91	3	-	-	-	-	-	-
Buckler Wal.	1912/13	1921/22	76	5	-	-	-	-	15
Buckler Wm.	1920/21	only	2	-	-	-	-	-	-
Bull A.G.	1918/19	1919/20	17	2	1	-	-	-	8
Bullus M.J.	1935/36	1938/39	6	-	-	1	-	-	3
Bunney F.M.T.	1928/29	only	2	-	-	-	-	-	-
Burbery J.P.	1907/08	only	1	-	-	-	-	-	-
Burbridge -.	1888/89	only	1	-	-	-	-	-	-
Burch T.	1965/66	only	1	-	-	-	-	-	-
Burdett J.C.	1903/04	1912/13	108	12	-	-	-	-	36
Burdett J.W.	1918/19	only	1	-	-	-	-	-	-
Burford A.J.	1880/81	1884/85	46	-	-	-	-	-	-
Burgess A.H.	1920/21	only	2	-	-	-	-	-	-
Burnell A.P.	1986/87	1987/88	13	2	-	-	-	-	8
Burnhill S.B.	1985/86	1987/88	44	15	-	-	-	-	60
Burrows J.D.	1934/35	only	1	-	-	-	-	-	-
Burrows T.E.	1925/26	1927/28	4	-	-	-	-	-	-
Burton B.C.	1887/88	1888/89	5	-	-	-	-	-	-
Burton C.L.	1918/19	1923/24	14	3	-	-	-	-	9
Burton H.C.	1923/24	only	1	-	-	-	-	-	-
Burton L.S.	1910/11	1913/14	56	5	-	-	-	-	15
Burton L.W.	1925/26	1932/33	41	8	-	-	-	-	24
Burton W.	1893/94	1897/98	8	1	-	-	-	-	3
Burwell T.R.	1974/75	1982/83	120	27	-	-	1	-	111
Bussey W.M.	1963/64	1967/68	121	38	-	-	1	-	117
Butcher E.G.	1919/20	only	5	-	3	-	-	-	6
Butler E.	1893/94	only	1	-	-	-	-	-	-
Butler E.R.	1919/20	only	1	-	-	-	-	-	-
Butler F.G.A.	1894/95	only	9	3	-	-	-	-	9
Butlin A.C.	1895/96	1902/03	252	19	11	1	9	-	118
Buttimore T.J.	1985/86	1990/91	98	15	1	-	-	-	62
Byrne C.J.	1933/34	only	1	-	-	-	-	-	-
Byrne E.J.	1889/90	only	2	-	-	-	-	-	-
Cambridge J.S.	1927/28	only	2	-	-	-	-	-	-
Cameron E.	1903/04	only	1	-	-	-	-	-	-
Campbell D.	1907/08	only	3	-	-	-	-	-	-
Campbell D.A.	1936/37	only	1	-	-	-	-	-	-

NAME	FROM	TO	APPS	T	C	PG	DG	GM	PTS
Campbell J.C.K.	1946/47	only	1	-	-	-	-	-	-
Campbell R.N.	1895/96	1901/02	207	7	-	-	1	-	25
Carey W.H.	1893/94	only	28	1	-	-	-	-	3
Carlisle R.D.	1890/91	1892/93	5	-	-	-	-	-	-
Carr A.W.	1911/12	only	4	-	-	-	-	-	-
Carr W.	1988/89	only	2	-	-	-	-	-	-
Carryer H.P.	1882/83	only	1	-	-	-	-	-	-
Carryer R.	1929/30	1934/35	14	1	-	-	-	-	3
Carter C.D.	1918/19	only	1	-	-	-	-	-	-
Carter H.S.	1922/23	only	1	-	-	-	-	-	-
Cartwright R.	1918/19	only	1	-	-	-	-	-	-
Cary-Elwes A.	1897/98	1899/00	33	4	-	-	-	-	12
Cass J.	1889/90	only	1	-	-	-	-	-	-
Castle R.A.	1923/24	only	1	-	-	-	-	-	-
Cattell G.	1889/90	only	2	-	-	-	-	-	-
Cattell R.H.B.	1889/90	only	2	-	-	-	-	-	-
Cave C.F.	1897/98	only	1	2	-	-	-	-	6
Cave P.	1983/84	only	3	1	-	-	-	-	4
Cavender W.A.	1961/62	only	9	-	-	-	-	-	-
Chamberlain E.W.	1889/90	1892/93	8	-	-	-	-	-	-
Channer M.R.	1945/46	1955/56	127	33	19	35	26	-	327
Chapman A.	1960/61	1969/70	18	5	21	21	2	-	126
Chapman C.	1896/97	only	2	-	-	-	-	-	-
Chapman -.	1901/02	only	1	-	-	-	-	-	-
Charles J.B.	1934/35	1936/37	28	17	-	-	-	-	51
Charles L.	1905/06	only	1	-	-	-	-	-	-
Charles M.R.	1984/85	1987/88	37	15	-	-	-	-	60
Charters F.R.	1891/92	1892/93	5	-	-	-	-	-	-
Chawner F.	1948/49	1963/64	331	23	-	-	-	-	69
Chawner L.	1949/50	1954/55	29	-	-	-	-	-	-
Cherry G.	1957/58	1963/64	66	-	-	-	-	-	-
Cheshire C.	1897/98	only	1	-	-	-	-	-	-
Chettle A.	1888/89	1889/90	14	1	-	-	-	-	1
Chilton K.	1963/64	1966/67	144	26	91	95	2	-	551
Chitham G.	1905/06	only	1	-	-	-	-	-	-
Christie M.G.	1925/26	1931/32	61	10	-	-	-	-	30
Church R.F.	1951/52	only	9	-	-	-	-	-	-
Churchward M.	1972/73	only	2	1	-	-	-	-	4
Clarke C.	1884/85	1895/96	5	-	-	-	-	-	-
Clarke D.C.	1925/26	only	1	-	-	-	-	-	-
Clarke P.S.	1929/30	1930/31	38	3	-	-	-	-	9
Clarke R.A.	1919/20	only	6	2	-	-	-	-	6
Clarke R.J.	1961/62	only	2	-	-	-	-	-	-
Clarke R.W.K.	1933/34	1937/38	27	2	-	-	-	-	6
Clarke T.	1930/31	only	1	-	-	-	-	-	-
Clarke W.J.	1952/53	1953/54	30	1	-	-	1	-	6
Clarke W.V.	1946/47	only	1	-	-	-	-	-	-
Cleaver I.G.	1932/33	only	1	-	-	-	-	-	-
Cleaver L.H.	1930/31	1932/33	4	1	-	-	-	-	3
Cleaver M.J.	1985	1991	12	3	-	-	-	-	12
Clements P.	1968/69	only	2	-	-	-	-	-	-
Clifford L.	1983/84	1986/87	10	1	-	-	-	-	4
Coady R.J.	1965/66	only	27	2	-	-	2	-	12
Coates N.	1918/19	1926/27	203	62	4	-	-	-	194
Coates T.E.	1895/96	only	10	-	-	-	-	-	-
Cockerill R.	1992/93	to date	29	2	-	-	-	-	10
Cohen A.S.	1923/24	only	1	-	-	-	-	-	-
Cole S.A.	1945/46	1946/47	35	2	-	-	-	-	6
Coleman E.G.	1921/22	1932/33	260	18	1	-	-	-	56
Coleman J.G.S.	1880/81	1891/92	140	31	-	-	7	-	52
Coles F.	1906/07	only	2	-	1	1	-	-	5
Coley W.R.	1955/56	only	1	-	-	-	-	-	-
Collier J.	1886/87	only	1	-	-	-	-	-	-
Collington A.P.	1974/75	1985/86	130	22	-	-	-	-	88
Collins B.J.	1961/62	only	1	-	-	-	-	-	-
Collins G.	1987/88	only	1	-	-	-	-	-	-
Collins H.	1895/96	only	1	-	-	-	-	-	-
Collins S.G.	1923/24	only	2	-	-	-	-	-	-
Collis W.J.	1895/96	only	1	-	-	-	-	-	-
Collopy R.J.	1924/25	1925/26	9	-	-	-	-	-	-
Collopy W.P.	1918/19	only	2	-	-	-	-	-	-
Colquhoun J.W.	1926/27	only	1	-	-	-	-	-	-
Colquhoun R.R.	1924/25	only	1	-	-	-	-	-	-
Colston D.W.	1931/32	only	2	-	-	-	-	-	-
Coltman P.D.	1986/87	1988/89	3	-	-	-	-	-	-
Coltman W.	1880/81	1882/83	7	-	-	-	-	-	-
Coltman W.G.	1919/20	only	1	-	-	-	-	-	-
Colver W.	1881/82	1882/83	2	-	-	-	-	-	-
Constable H.E.	1958/59	1959/60	10	1	-	-	-	-	3
Constantine H.A.	1930/31	1933/34	51	9	7	2	-	-	47
Cook T.A.	1883/84	only	1	-	-	-	-	-	-
Cooke A.E.	1889/90	1897/98	158	31	18	6	-	3	163
Cooke J.	1980/81	1981/82	5	2	-	-	-	-	8
Cooke K.H.	1936/37	1939/40	5	3	-	-	-	-	9
Cooke R.C.D.	1892/93	1894/95	41	1	6	-	-	-	18
Cooper R.C.	1960/61	1971/72	50	3	35	21	-	-	143
Coote P.B.	1931/32	1933/34	27	12	13	6	4	-	96
Corby D.	1880/81	1881/82	7	-	-	-	-	-	-
Cornell G.A.	1929/30	only	1	-	-	-	-	-	-
Cotton R.D.	1929/30	only	11	1	-	-	1	-	7
Cotton W.H.V.	1932/33	only	1	-	-	-	-	-	-
Coulter A.J.	1920/21	only	1	-	-	-	-	-	-
Coutts I.D.F.	1953/54	only	1	-	-	-	-	-	-
Coutts W.C.	1965/66	only	3	1	2	-	-	-	7
Coutts-Deacon E.R.	1934/35	only	1	-	-	-	-	-	-
Cowley W.	1888/89	only	1	-	-	-	-	-	-
Cowling R.J.	1974/75	1980/81	184	8	-	-	-	-	32
Cowlishaw W.H.	1889/90	only	1	-	-	-	-	-	-
Cowman R.	1962/63	only	2	1	-	-	-	-	3
Cox H.W.	1923/24	1924/25	5	-	-	-	-	-	-
Craigmile H.W.C.	1921/22	only	8	6	-	-	-	-	18
Cramb R.J.	1945/46	only	6	-	-	-	-	-	-
Cramphorn C.T.	1925/26	1926/27	31	13	-	-	-	-	39
Cramphorn F.L.	1928/29	only	1	-	-	-	-	-	-
Cramphorn J.F.	1926/27	1928/29	22	8	-	-	-	-	24
Crane M.	1956/57	only	2	-	-	-	-	-	-
Crane -.	1881/82	only	1	-	-	-	-	-	-
Craven T.W.	1882/83	only	1	1	-	-	-	-	1
Cressey J.T.	1881/82	1886/87	62	5	-	-	1	-	8
Crick P.C.	1936/37	only	16	-	-	-	-	-	-
Crick T.G.P.	1928/29	only	1	-	-	-	-	-	-
Crisp E.J.	1922/23	only	3	-	-	-	-	-	-
Crofts A.G.J.	1882/83	only	1	-	-	-	-	-	-
Cromar C.P.	1937/38	only	1	-	-	-	-	-	-
Crookes A.	1919/20	only	8	5	-	-	-	-	15
Crosby H.V.	1936/37	only	2	-	-	-	-	-	-
Crosby M.A.	1935/36	only	1	-	-	-	-	-	-
Croson G.	1901/02	only	10	1	-	-	-	-	3
Cross C.W.	1909/10	1923/24	131	19	-	-	-	-	57
Cross F.G.	1882/83	1884/85	10	-	-	-	-	-	-
Crowe M.P.	1932/33	1934/35	72	18	36	9	1	1	160
Crowe P.M.	1934/35	1935/36	5	1	-	-	-	-	3
Crowhurst F.A.	1923/24	only	2	-	-	-	-	-	-
Crowhurst R.A.	1937/38	only	1	-	-	-	-	-	-
Crumbie T.H.	1891/92	1896/97	3	-	-	-	-	-	-
Cullen G.H.	1949/50	1956/57	180	66*	77	57	9	-	550
Cummings K.	1934/35	only	1	-	-	-	-	-	-
Curle C.L.	1914/15	only	2	-	-	-	-	-	-
Currington A.J.	1898/99	only	1	-	-	-	-	-	-
Curry A.	1925/26	only	1	-	-	-	-	-	-
Cusworth L.	1978/79	1989/90	365	66	100	65	96	-	947
Dakin R.W.	1901/02	1905/06	84	23	-	-	-	-	69
Dalby W.A.	1908/09	1913/14	80	26	-	-	-	-	78
Dale W.	1904/05	1907/08	10	-	-	-	-	-	-
Dance F.	1881/82	only	1	-	-	-	-	-	-
Daniells A.E.	1891/92	only	1	1	-	-	-	-	2
Dann E.	1892/93	1895/96	24	1	-	-	-	-	3
Dann W.	1900/01	1908/09	25	1	-	-	-	-	3
Darlington B.	1954/55	only	7	1	-	-	-	-	3
Darnill E.W.	1933/34	1935/36	16	6	-	-	-	-	18
Davey J.	1907/08	only	2	-	-	-	-	-	-
David A.M.	1922/23	only	1	-	-	-	-	-	-
Davidson J.	1985/86	1986/87	30	6	-	-	-	-	24
Davidson W.A.	1962/63	only	3	-	-	-	-	-	-
Davie G.E.	1918/19	only	1	-	-	-	-	-	-
Davies A.J.	1918/19	only	1	-	-	-	-	-	-
Davies J.F.	1945/46	only	18	-	7	5	2	-	37
Davies T.I.	1933/34	only	1	-	-	-	-	-	-
Davis H.S.	1922/23	only	2	-	-	-	-	-	-

NAME	FROM	TO	APPS	T	C	PG	DG	GM	PTS
Davis J.E.	1922/23	1925/26	30	1	-	-	-	-	3
Davis T.	1966/67	only	1	-	-	-	-	-	-
Davis W.J.N.	1895/96	only	1	-	-	-	-	-	-
Dawson J.H.	1968/69	1970/71	75	3	-	-	-	-	9
Dawson-Thomas E.M.	1889/90	1890/91	5	1	-	-	-	-	1
Day G.	1892/93	1893/94	15	-	-	1	-	-	3
Day H.L.V.	1918/19	1928/29	212	108	281	81	4	2	1151
Day J.D.	1945/46	1953/54	76	2	-	-	-	-	6
Deacon H.B.	1948/49	1950/51	29	-	-	-	-	-	-
Deacon J.	1981/82	1982/83	42	1	-	-	-	-	4
Deere A.C.	1938/39	only	1	-	-	-	-	-	-
Delgado G.A.	1934/35	only	9	3	-	-	-	-	9
DeLuca C.	1978/79	only	1	-	-	-	-	-	-
Denner J.	1975/76	only	3	-	3	2	-	-	12
Dennis S.H.	1918/19	1919/20	4	-	-	-	-	-	-
Dermott L.G.	1945/46	1947/48	93	5	-	-	-	-	15
Derry A.	1925/26	only	1	-	-	-	-	-	-
Dexter C.D.	1982/83	1988/89	82	36	-	-	-	-	144
Dickens J.R.	1909/10	only	15	8	-	-	-	-	24
Dickinson C.	1883/84	1884/85	9	-	-	-	-	-	-
Dickinson H.S.	1889/90	only	1	-	-	-	-	-	-
Dingley T.	1982/83	only	7	-	-	-	-	-	-
Dobbs G.C.	1890/91	only	21	13	-	-	-	-	13
Dobson D.D.	1907/08	only	1	-	-	-	-	-	-
Dodge P.W.	1975/76	1992/93	437	93*	33	40	3	-	567
Dodson C.	1911/12	only	1	-	-	-	-	-	-
Dodson I.R.	1980/81	1986/87	62	9	19	13	-	-	113
Doe F.C.	1937/38	1939/40	46	16	-	-	-	-	48
Doherty H.D.	1955/56	only	4	-	-	-	-	-	-
Doore F.R.	1953/54	1956/57	54	3	-	-	-	-	9
Douglas M.S.	1936/37	only	2	-	-	-	-	-	-
Dove S.E.	1912/13	1913/14	12	2	-	-	1	-	10
Downes K.D.	1936/37	1938/39	15	5	4	3	-	-	32
Dowson A.O.	1895/96	only	1	-	-	-	-	-	-
Doyle L.T.	1946/47	1951/52	12	2	-	-	1	-	10
Drake-Lee N.J.	1961/62	1968/69	73	7	-	-	-	-	21
Drake-Lee W.	1990/91	to date	23	6	-	-	-	-	28
Drew A.	1919/20	only	3	-	-	-	-	-	-
Drummond F.C.	1929/30	1935/36	30	9	-	-	-	-	27
Duckering C.	1880/81	only	3	-	-	-	-	-	-
Dudley C.	1922/23	only	1	-	-	-	-	-	-
Duff S.M.	1953/54	only	14	-	2	1	-	-	7
Duffelen M.	1979/80	1980/81	26	-	-	-	-	-	-
Duffin W.	1901/02	only	1	-	-	-	-	-	-
Duggan M.J.	1969/70	1980	302	158*	-	-	-	-	608
Dunkley P.E.	1927/28	1934/35	32	8	1	-	-	-	26
Dunkley -.	1909/10	only	1	-	-	-	-	-	-
Dunmore J.	1889/90	only	2	-	-	-	-	-	-
Dunn J.R.	1945/46	only	2	-	-	-	-	-	-
Duthie J.	1908/09	only	4	-	-	-	-	-	-
Dyke J.C.M.	1907/08	only	2	3	-	-	-	-	9
Dykes J.M.	1926/27	only	20	6	-	-	-	-	18
Dymond M.J.	1961/62	1963/64	25	4	-	-	-	-	12
Dynes E.D.	1924/25	1925/26	27	1	-	-	2	-	11
Eagland D.	1991	to date	5	1	-	-	-	-	5
Earles W.H.	1918/19	only	1	-	-	-	-	-	-
East H.O.	1906/07	only	1	-	-	-	-	-	-
Eathorne R.	1907/08	only	6	-	-	-	-	-	-
Eddison J.H.	1912/13	only	1	-	-	-	-	-	-
Edgell R.A.	1881/82	only	2	1	-	-	-	-	1
Edmiston J.G.	1932/33	only	2	-	-	-	-	-	-
Edmiston J.H.F.	1925/26	1934/35	112	9	8	5	1	-	62
Edmonds J.T.	1891/92	1893/94	51	7	-	-	-	-	14
Edwards A.N.	1963/64	only	2	-	-	-	-	-	-
Edwards B.	1945/46	only	3	1	-	-	-	-	3
Edwards F.G.	1938/39	1947/48	62	30	-	-	-	-	90
Edwards N.	1972/73	1974/75	7	1	-	-	-	-	4
Edwards P.G.	1961/62	1967/68	145	2	-	-	-	-	6
Edwards T.L.	1907/08	only	12	4	-	-	-	-	12
Eking H.C.W.	1928/29	only	1	-	-	-	-	-	-
Elders J.	1953/54	1958/59	144	38	-	3	1	-	126
Elkington T.	1894/95	only	13	-	-	-	-	-	-
Elliott J.J.	1966/67	1970/71	126	20	-	-	-	-	60
Elliott L.	1904/05	1905/06	7	-	-	-	-	-	-

NAME	FROM	TO	APPS	T	C	PG	DG	GM	PTS
Elliott W.	1911/12	1919/20	5	-	-	-	-	-	-
Ellis D.R.	1946/47	1949/50	45	16	-	-	-	-	48
Ellis R.	1964/65	only	2	-	-	-	-	-	-
Ellis S.G.	1919/20	only	1	-	-	-	-	-	-
Ellis W.S.	1909/10	only	22	-	-	-	-	-	-
Ellis-Danvers G.R.	1906/07	only	1	-	-	-	-	-	-
Ellwood L.D.	1907/08	1919/20	53	-	1	-	1	-	6
English -.	1894/95	only	1	-	-	-	-	-	-
Evans B.J.	1981/82	1991/92	265	169	1	-	-	-	678
Evans G.W.	1962/63	1965/66	37	2	-	-	-	-	6
Evans J.	1992/93	only	5	1	-	-	-	-	5
Evans M.	1967/68	1969/70	48	5	34	44	7	-	236
Evans R.	1923/24	only	1	-	-	-	-	-	-
Evans -.	1905/06	only	1	-	-	-	-	-	-
Evans-Evans E.W.	1935/36	only	1	-	-	-	-	-	-
Evers R.D.M.	1934/35	only	1	-	-	-	-	-	-
Everson W.	1895/96	only	1	-	-	-	-	-	-
Ewin B.H.L.	1929/30	only	1	-	-	-	-	-	-
Ewin J.J.M.	1929/30	only	2	3	-	-	-	-	9
Falla G.C.M.	1931/32	only	1	-	-	-	-	-	-
Fallowell R.W.	1933/34	1934/35	7	1	-	-	-	-	3
Farmer E.	1890/91	1891/92	16	-	-	-	-	-	-
Farmer S.	1912/13	1918/19	29	12	-	-	-	-	36
Farmer-Wright I.P.	1947/48	only	1	-	-	-	-	-	-
Farndon W.E.	1924/25	1931/32	183	86	-	-	-	-	258
Farrell J.L.	1930/31	only	1	-	-	-	-	-	-
Faussett C.R.	1907/08	only	3	1	-	-	-	-	3
Ferguson D.J.	1918/19	1919/20	34	-	3	-	-	-	6
Ferguson R.J.C.	1908/09	only	1	2	-	-	-	-	6
Fernie J.	1888/89	only	4	-	-	-	-	-	-
Ferris C.D.	1918/19	only	1	-	-	-	-	-	-
Fforde A.B.	1888/89	only	1	-	-	-	-	-	-
Field A.	1895/96	1896/97	71	20	56	-	-	1	176
Fielding K.J.	1971/72	only	1	-	-	-	-	-	-
Fisher M.W.	1910/11	1913/14	13	2	-	-	-	-	6
Fisher S.H.	1889/90	only	1	-	-	-	-	-	-
Fisk J.W.	1951/52	1952/53	48	-	3	4	1	-	21
Fitchett T.A.	1911/12	only	4	-	-	-	-	-	-
Fitzgerald J.	1908/09	only	1	-	-	-	-	-	-
Fitzgerald R.E.S.	1925/26	only	3	-	-	-	-	-	-
Fletcher D.B.	1957/58	only	2	-	-	-	-	-	-
Fletcher J.	1948/49	only	1	-	-	-	-	-	-
Fletcher T.	1922/23	only	2	-	-	-	-	-	-
Flewitt E.C.A.	1925/26	1930/31	129	73	1	-	-	-	221
Flinn -.	1885/86	only	1	-	-	-	-	-	-
Flint J.	1975/76	only	9	1	13	18	-	-	84
Flint R.	1933/34	only	1	-	-	-	-	-	-
Flower C.A.	1955/56	only	2	-	-	-	-	-	-
Flude M.	1908/09	1910/11	9	2	-	-	-	-	6
Ford A.T.	1946/47	only	2	-	-	-	-	-	-
Ford C.W.	1887/88	1889/90	2	-	-	-	-	-	-
Ford J.G.	1954/55	1957/58	87	2	-	-	-	-	6
Foreman H.	1880/81	only	2	-	-	-	-	-	-
Foreman W.J.	1893/94	1905/06	358	85	4	-	-	-	263
Forfar D.J.	1970/71	1981/82	223	14	-	-	-	-	56
Forrest J.E.	1935/36	only	1	-	-	-	-	-	-
Forrester M.	1937/38	only	1	-	-	-	-	-	-
Foster H.L.	1880/81	1884/85	50	2	4	-	1	-	13
Foulkes-Arnold M.V.	1979/80	1992/93	261	21	-	-	-	-	84
Fowler G.E.	1934/35	1937/38	27	2	-	-	-	-	6
Fox F.	1894/95	only	26	15	32	2	-	-	115
Fox J.B.S.	1934/35	1938/39	58	11	-	-	4	-	49
Foxon A.H.	1901/02	1902/03	10	3	-	-	-	-	9
Francis A.	1922/23	only	1	3	-	-	-	-	9
Francis D.G.	1919/20	1921/22	12	-	-	-	-	-	-
Francks R.H.	1934/35	1935/36	3	-	-	-	-	-	-
Franklin H.W.F.	1927/28	1928/29	28	-	-	-	1	-	4
Freear A.E.	1902/03	1903/04	7	2	-	-	-	-	6
Freeman H.	1894/95	only	1	-	-	-	-	-	-
Freer C.	1914/15	1918/19	2	-	-	-	-	-	-
Freer H.B.	1905/06	only	6	-	-	-	-	-	-
Freer J.W.	1907/08	only	4	-	-	-	-	-	-
Freer M.E.	1955/56	1964/65	203	15	-	-	7	-	66
Freer W.R.	1946/47	1948/49	38	12	-	-	-	-	36

NAME	FROM	TO	APPS	T	C	PG	DG	GM	PTS
Freeston K.	1967/68	only	1	-	-	-	-	-	-
French Ray	1972/73	1987	97	7	-	-	-	-	28
French Roy	1971/72	1976/77	42	2	-	-	-	-	8
Friend G.	1885/86	only	7	1	-	-	-	-	1
Frisby W.L.E.	1925/26	only	3	-	-	-	1	-	4
Frith A.H.	1898/99	1899/00	3	-	-	-	-	-	-
Frowen A.	1922/23	only	1	-	-	-	-	-	-
Fuller C.	1885/86	1887/88	6	-	-	-	-	-	-
Fyfe K.C.	1933/34	only	1	-	-	-	1	-	4
Gabriel T.W.	1921/22	1922/23	2	-	-	-	-	-	-
Gadney B.C.	1929/30	1938/39	170	63	-	-	-	-	189
Gale W.	1894/95	1903/04	41	2	17	-	-	-	40
Gall J.W.	1891/92	only	6	-	-	-	-	-	-
Gamble L.C.	1923/24	1926/27	7	-	-	-	-	-	-
Gardiner A.	1964/65	only	5	-	-	-	-	-	-
Garforth D.J.	1991/92	to date	67	9	-	-	-	-	40
Garner J.W.	1894/95	1902/03	209	3	9	-	-	-	27
Garner W.	1938/39	only	2	-	-	-	-	-	-
Garratt R.	1898/99	only	1	-	-	-	-	-	-
Gaunt J.L.	1947/48	only	5	2	-	-	1	-	10
Gavins D.	1980/81	only	1	-	-	-	-	-	-
Gavins M.N.	1956/57	1970/71	121	5	107	119	2	-	592
Gee G.E.	1951/52	1952/53	11	2	-	-	-	-	6
Geeson F.	1882/83	only	1	-	-	-	-	-	-
George K.C.	1931/32	1932/33	2	-	-	-	-	-	-
George W.G.	1905/06	only	10	-	-	-	-	-	-
Gerald C.	1982/83	1989/90	40	26	-	-	-	-	104
German G.	1889/90	only	1	-	-	-	-	-	-
German G.J.	1921/22	1926/27	66	4	-	-	-	-	12
German H.	1889/90	1893/94	28	5	-	-	-	-	8
Gerrard R.A.	1933/34	only	1	1	-	-	-	-	3
Gerrard R.E.	1935/36	1937/38	35	5	-	-	-	-	15
Gibbons A.	1880/81	only	2	-	-	-	-	-	-
Gibbs J.H.	1884/85	only	1	-	-	-	-	-	-
Gibbs W.J.	1920/21	1924/25	14	4	-	-	-	-	12
Gibson I.M.	1960/61	1964/65	75	14	-	-	-	-	42
Gibson -.	1882/83	only	1	-	-	-	-	-	-
Giddings N.F.F.	1937/38	only	1	-	-	-	-	-	-
Gilbert D.	1897/98	1899/00	12	-	-	-	-	-	-
Gilbert J.	1880/81	1884/85	15	-	-	-	-	-	-
Gilbert R.	1896/97	only	4	-	-	-	-	-	-
Gilbey W.J.	1888/89	1891/92	51	3	-	-	-	-	3
Giles J.L.	1934/35	1935/36	2	-	1	-	-	-	2
Gillespie C.M.	1903/04	only	1	-	-	-	-	-	-
Gillingham N.K.	1978/79	1983/84	145	12	-	-	-	-	48
Gimson C.	1905/06	1911/12	72	10	30	1	-	-	93
Gimson G.	1901/02	only	1	-	-	-	-	-	-
Gissing A.	1987/88	to date	60	16	-	-	-	-	65
Glover D.B.	1926/27	1938/39	10	3	-	-	-	-	9
Glover J.	1964/65	1968/69	6	1	-	-	-	-	3
Goddard E.	1896/97	1900/01	16	4	-	-	1	-	16
Godfrey A.D.	1919/20	1924/25	56	10	-	-	-	-	30
Golder B.	1954/55	only	4	-	-	-	-	-	-
Golding J.	1970/71	only	2	-	-	-	-	-	-
Golding R.	1887/88	1895/96	5	-	-	-	-	-	-
Goodall E.W.	1907/08	only	2	-	-	-	-	-	-
Goode G.E.	1935/36	only	8	-	-	-	-	-	-
Goodman E.L.	1907/08	1910/11	6	1	-	-	-	-	3
Goodman T.E.	1933/34	only	7	-	-	-	-	-	-
Goodrich A.	1900/01	1908/09	179	9	-	-	1	-	31
Goodrich T.	1899/00	1909/10	205	6	3	-	-	-	24
Gordon J.	1957/58	only	1	-	-	-	-	-	-
Gordon T.S.	1885/86	1886/87	9	-	-	-	-	-	-
Gornall W.	1945/46	only	1	1	-	-	-	-	3
Gough F.	1946/47	only	3	-	-	-	-	-	-
Graham A.	1931/32	only	10	-	-	-	-	-	-
Graham-Bryce A.L.	1960/61	only	1	-	-	-	-	-	-
Grant M.	1988/89	to date	51	19	-	-	-	-	76
Grant P.	1989/90	to date	19	2	-	-	-	-	10
Graves W.H.	1927/28	1928/29	16	-	-	-	-	-	-
Gray G.B.	1933/34	only	6	5	-	-	-	-	15
Gray T.	1881/82	only	1	-	-	-	-	-	-
Greasley G.	1905/06	1918/19	174	28	-	-	-	-	84
Greasley H.G.	1933/34	1936/37	23	2	-	-	-	-	6

NAME	FROM	TO	APPS	T	C	PG	DG	GM	PTS
Greaves G.	1932/33	1936/37	87	1	-	-	-	-	3
Green C.	1908/09	only	1	-	-	-	-	-	-
Green D.	1992/93	only	3	-	-	3	1	-	12
Green G.	1900/01	only	1	-	-	-	-	-	-
Greenhow M.	1961/62	1962/63	9	4	-	-	-	-	12
Greenlees H.D.	1925/26	1931/32	153	32	19	6	10	-	192
Greenway H.	1894/95	only	1	-	-	-	-	-	-
Greenwell -.	1887/88	1888/89	3	-	-	-	-	-	-
Greenwood A.H.	1926/27	1932/33	157	12	4	-	-	-	44
Greenwood J.	1892/93	1893/94	12	2	-	-	-	-	4
Greenwood J.E.	1919/20	only	3	-	13	-	-	-	26
Greenwood S.C.	1919/20	1920/21	3	1	-	-	-	-	3
Grewcock D.	1985	to date	31	15	-	-	-	-	66
Grier W.H.	1909/10	only	1	-	-	-	-	-	-
Grierson H.L.	1922/23	only	22	2	-	-	-	-	6
Grieves D.L.	1935/36	only	1	-	-	-	-	-	-
Griffin H.G.	1933/34	only	2	-	-	-	-	-	-
Griffin -.	1887/88	only	1	-	-	-	-	-	-
Griffiths D.	1945/46	only	1	-	-	-	-	-	-
Griffiths H.B.	1959/60	only	1	-	-	-	-	-	-
Griffiths N.	1992/93	only	1	-	-	-	-	-	-
Grimmett -.	1890/91	only	1	-	-	-	-	-	-
Grimsdell A.	1992/93	only	2	-	-	-	-	-	-
Grindall J.	1966/67	only	2	-	-	-	-	-	-
Grocock A.	1975/76	1977/78	10	-	-	-	-	-	-
Grove N.J.	1953/54	only	6	2	-	-	-	-	6
Grove R.V.	1966/67	1972/73	172	9	2	1	-	-	34
Guffick J.M.	1949/50	1953/54	5	1	-	-	-	-	3
Gulliver W.	1907/08	only	5	-	-	-	-	-	-
Gurney -.	1881/82	1882/83	2	-	-	-	-	-	-
Gwynne F.H.X.	1918/19	only	2	-	-	-	-	-	-
Hacker J.H.	1946/47	1951/52	45	3	-	-	-	-	9
Hackney S.T.	1991	to date	45	35	-	-	-	-	154
Haddon E.R.	1935/36	only	1	-	-	-	-	-	-
Haddon N.	1880/81	only	5	-	-	-	-	-	-
Haddon P.A.	1960/61	only	19	1	-	-	-	-	3
Hadfield -.	1888/89	only	1	-	-	-	-	-	-
Hailes B.I.	1956/57	only	2	-	-	-	-	-	-
Haines D.	1953/54	1957/58	43	1	-	-	-	-	3
Haines N.	1968/69	only	2	-	-	-	-	-	-
Hale J.	1890/91	only	1	-	-	-	-	-	-
Hall A.C.	1927/28	1932/33	96	5	-	-	-	-	15
Hall B.P.	1970/71	1984	312	67	2	-	3	-	275
Hall J.	1888/89	only	2	-	-	-	-	-	-
Hall T.	1904/05	1907/08	9	2	-	-	-	-	6
Hall W.	1907/08	1908/09	21	-	-	-	-	-	-
Hall W.	1913/14	only	15	-	-	-	-	-	-
Halliday A.K.	1931/32	only	1	-	-	-	-	-	-
Hamblin L.	1913/14	1918/19	3	-	-	-	-	-	-
Hamilton J.	1990/91	to date	15	2	-	-	-	-	8
Hancock A.S.	1891/92	only	1	-	-	-	-	-	-
Hanna D.A.	1969/70	1970/71	5	-	-	-	-	-	-
Hanney M.	1958/59	1959/60	4	-	-	-	-	-	-
Hardwicke J.T.	1929/30	1934/35	85	40	-	-	-	-	120
Hardyman F.W.	1905/06	1906/07	39	11	-	-	-	-	33
Hare W.H.	1976/77	1988/89	394	87	779	820	47	-	4507
Hargrave L.	1911/12	only	1	1	-	-	-	-	3
Hargrave O.J.	1908/09	1913/14	110	53	-	-	1	-	163
Hargreaves R.	1891/92	only	1	-	-	-	-	-	-
Harlowe A.	1893/94	only	2	1	-	-	-	-	3
Harper-Smith -.	1894/95	only	1	-	-	-	-	-	-
Harris A.W.	1921/22	only	1	-	-	-	-	-	-
Harris C.S.	1933/34	only	9	1	-	-	-	-	3
Harris D.	1968/69	only	6	2	5	5	1	-	34
Harris F.E.	1934/35	only	1	-	-	-	-	-	-
Harris G.A.	1935/36	only	1	-	-	-	-	-	-
Harris G.N.	1933/34	only	31	4	-	-	-	-	12
Harris I.	1955/56	only	3	-	-	-	-	-	-
Harris I.	1992/93	only	2	1	-	-	1	-	8
Harris J.C.	1984/85	to date	161	18	92	58	38	-	544
Harris R.A.	1932/33	only	13	-	1	1	-	-	5
Harris R.A.	1960/61	only	3	-	-	-	-	-	-
Harris R.F.	1945/46	1946/47	27	4	-	-	-	-	12
Harris S.	1992/93	only	1	-	-	-	-	-	-

NAME	FROM	TO	APPS	T	C	PG	DG	GM	PTS
Harrison H.C.	1935/36	only	2	-	-	-	-	-	-
Harrison J.	1945/46	1949/50	16	-	-	-	-	-	-
Harrison J.N.	1933/34	only	1	-	-	-	-	-	-
Harrison M.J.	1961/62	1970/71	210	58	-	-	1	-	177
Harrison S.	1894/95	1896/97	4	-	-	-	-	-	-
Harrison V.J.	1946/47	only	2	-	-	-	-	-	-
Hart J.	1895/96	only	1	-	-	-	-	-	-
Hart T.	1983/84	1984/85	5	-	-	-	-	-	-
Hart T.D.	1880/81	only	5	1	-	-	-	-	1
Hart T.M.	1930/31	only	2	-	-	-	1	-	4
Hart-Davis J.R.	1905/06	only	1	-	-	-	-	-	-
Hartley N.	1977/78	1984/85	8	2	-	-	-	-	8
Harvey J.J.	1948/49	1949/50	21	-	5	11	-	-	43
Harvey R.	1884/85	only	1	-	-	-	-	-	-
Harvey R.B.	1929/30	only	2	-	-	-	-	-	-
Harvey S.G.	1911/12	only	1	-	-	-	-	-	-
Haselmere E.E.	1918/19	1923/24	180	136*	35	6	8	-	528
Hassall K.V.	1938/39	only	1	-	-	-	-	-	-
Havard W.T.	1919/20	only	2	-	-	-	-	-	-
Hawley W.	1901/02	only	16	1	1	-	-	-	5
Hayes -.	1882/83	only	2	-	-	-	-	-	-
Haynes W.	1894/95	only	1	-	-	-	-	-	-
Hayward G.H.	1905/06	1906/07	20	-	-	-	-	-	-
Hazell D.St G.	1953/54	1955/56	81	15	59	33	1	-	265
Hazlerigg A.G.	1976/77	1981/82	98	1	-	-	-	-	4
Heard A.D.	1908/09	1909/10	21	12	-	-	-	-	36
Hegarty C.	1918/19	only	7	1	-	-	-	-	3
Hemingway R.E.	1904/05	only	1	-	-	-	-	-	-
Hemphrey M.J.	1959/60	1962/63	16	-	-	-	-	-	-
Hemsley C.	1975/76	only	3	-	-	-	-	-	-
Henderson C.D.	1932/33	only	2	-	-	-	-	-	-
Henderson M.M.	1938/39	1945/46	25	5	-	-	-	-	15
Henson J.	1891/92	1892/93	2	-	-	-	-	-	-
Herbert D.H.	1930/31	1931/32	15	-	-	-	1	-	4
Herbert G.B.	1935/36	1938/39	66	3	5	5	-	-	34
Herbert P.	1946/47	1952/53	66	8	-	-	-	-	24
Herbert S.F.	1930/31	1938/39	64	18	23	10	-	-	130
Herbert W.J.	1946/47	1949/50	21	-	-	-	1	-	4
Hesmondhalgh W.R.	1892/93	1897/98	101	33	7	1	4	-	129
Hett A.S.	1921/22	1922/23	2	1	-	-	-	-	3
Hewitt E.P.A.	1933/34	only	21	9	-	-	-	-	27
Hicken G.	1893/94	1895/96	3	-	-	-	-	-	-
Hicks W.C.	1919/20	1921/22	92	11	3	-	-	-	39
Higgins A.	1918/19	only	1	-	-	-	-	-	-
Higginson M.A.	1964/65	only	1	-	-	-	-	-	-
Higginson N.L.	1918/19	only	1	-	-	-	-	-	-
Hill D.K.	1961/62	only	1	-	-	-	-	-	-
Hill E.	1880/81	1882/83	2	-	-	-	-	-	-
Hill H.W.	1913/14	1920/21	4	-	-	-	-	-	-
Hill J.	1973/74	1974/75	11	1	-	-	-	-	4
Hill S.B.	1889/90	only	1	-	-	-	-	-	-
Hillicker C.	1972/73	only	2	-	-	-	1	-	3
Hills B.	1897/98	1905/06	46	13	1	-	-	-	41
Hillyer P.	1990/91	1991/92	6	1	-	-	-	-	4
Hincks R.H.	1890/91	only	9	-	-	-	-	-	-
Hind A.E.	1899/00	1905/06	127	81	1	-	4	-	261
Hind H.A.	1901/02	1904/05	88	2	-	-	-	-	6
Hirst H.	1914/15	only	1	-	-	-	-	-	-
Hitch -.	1921/22	only	1	-	-	-	-	-	-
Hitchcock A.E.	1892/93	1894/95	51	16	-	-	-	-	45
Hives R.	1905/06	1907/08	30	1	9	-	-	-	21
Hobbs A.J.	1906/07	1912/13	195	26	-	-	-	-	78
Hodder F.S.	1931/32	1932/33	6	1	-	-	-	-	3
Hodgkinson J.D.	1926/27	1927/28	3	-	-	-	-	-	-
Hodgson J.	1880/81	only	2	-	-	-	-	-	-
Hodgson J.M.	1933/34	1935/36	37	-	14	8	-	-	52
Hogarth A.	1908/09	1910/11	4	-	-	-	-	-	-
Hogarth T.B.	1905/06	1913/14	111	7	-	-	-	-	21
Holden L.	1932/33	only	2	-	-	-	-	-	-
Holden M.S.	1923/24	1926/27	41	14	-	-	3	-	54
Holder -.	1899/00	only	1	-	-	-	-	-	-
Holford G.	1918/19	only	1	-	-	-	-	-	-
Holley E.R.	1973/74	1976/77	39	4	1	1	-	-	21
Holloway N.	1977/78	1978/79	4	-	-	-	-	-	-
Holmes R.W.	1921/22	only	3	-	-	-	-	-	-

NAME	FROM	TO	APPS	T	C	PG	DG	GM	PTS
Holroyd C.A.	1964/65	1968/69	9	-	-	-	-	-	-
Holyoak -.	1881/82	only	1	-	-	-	-	-	-
Homer P.C.H.	1919/20	only	4	-	-	-	-	-	-
Hope P.P.	1919/20	only	2	-	-	-	-	-	-
Hopkin J.	1935/36	only	13	1	-	-	-	-	3
Hopkins A.S.	1959/60	only	1	-	-	-	-	-	-
Hopkins E.	1923/24	only	2	-	-	-	-	-	-
Hopkins E.C.R.	1925/26	1931/32	12	3	-	-	-	-	9
Hopkins G.	1961/62	1962/63	12	-	1	-	-	-	2
Hopkins W.G.	1908/09	1918/19	216	14	-	-	-	-	42
Hopper D.	1987/88	to date	23	2	-	-	-	-	9
Horn J.	1955/56	1956/5714	1	-	-	-	-	-	3
Horner G.	1971/72	1973/74	21	7	-	-	-	-	28
Horner J.W.	1882/83	only	2	-	-	-	-	-	-
Horrocks-Taylor J.P.	1958/59	1963/64	92	14	-	-	2	-	48
Horsley H.M.	1919/20	only	1	-	-	-	-	-	-
Hoskins T.	1956/57	only	1	-	-	-	-	-	-
Hougham J.P.	1913/14	only	3	-	-	-	-	-	-
Howsen D.H.	1931/32	1932/33	10	-	-	-	-	-	-
Hoyle G.	1921/22	only	4	-	-	-	-	-	-
Hoyle T.F.	1886/87	1887/88	10	-	-	-	-	-	-
Hubbard J.	1907/08	1908/09	21	2	-	-	-	-	6
Hudson A.E.	1880/81	only	1	1	-	-	-	-	1
Hudson F.	1882/83	only	3	-	-	-	-	-	-
Hudson G.	1926/27	only	1	-	-	-	-	-	-
Hudson P.E.	1952/53	only	2	-	-	-	-	-	-
Hughes A.P.	1931/32	1934/35	113	3	-	-	-	-	9
Hughes H.P.	1945/46	1947/48	43	-	-	-	-	-	-
Hughes J.K.L.	1951/52	only	5	-	-	-	-	-	-
Hume J.W.G.	1928/29	only	1	-	-	-	-	-	-
Humphries N.G.	1969/70	only	1	-	-	-	-	-	-
Hunt P.B.	1955/56	1958/59	7	1	-	-	-	-	3
Hunt-Davies D.	1923/24	only	1	-	-	-	-	-	-
Hunter I.W.	1947/48	1948/49	10	4	-	-	-	-	12
Hunter S.A.	1911/12	1919/20	36	15	4	1	1	-	60
Huntley N.P.	1949/50	only	6	-	-	-	-	-	-
Hurren B.J.	1930/31	only	1	-	-	-	-	-	-
Huskisson T.F.	1935/36	only	1	-	-	-	-	-	-
Hutt R.J.	1945/46	only	1	-	-	-	-	-	-
Hynd W.H.	1919/20	only	1	-	-	-	-	-	-
Hytch D.	1953/54	only	2	-	-	-	-	-	-
Inchley A.	1894/95	only	1	-	-	-	-	-	-
Inchley A.E.	1920/21	only	3	-	-	-	-	-	-
Ingleby J.	1969/70	1974/75	45	5	62	70	-	-	354
Ireland R.	1905/06	only	3	-	-	-	-	-	-
Jack E.A.	1935/36	only	2	-	-	-	-	-	-
Jackett E.J.	1904/05	1911/12	183	8	19	9	4	1	108
Jackett R.	1904/05	1913/14	59	8	-	-	-	-	24
Jackson A.L.	1890/91	1895/96	24	-	-	-	-	-	-
Jackson F.A.	1894/95	1904/05	72	52	6	-	2	-	176
Jackson F.S.	1905/06	1907/08	77	20	30	3	-	-	129
Jackson G.	1967/68	1972/73	43	16	-	-	-	-	50
Jackson K.	1964/65	only	1	-	-	-	-	-	-
Jackson N.A.	1977/78	1988/89	105	10	-	-	-	-	40
Jackson T.	1904/05	1906/07	36	7	-	-	-	-	21
Jackson W.	1891/92	1898/99	208	4	1	-	-	-	14
Jackson W.A.	1931/32	1945/46	72	16	-	-	-	-	48
Jacomb T.J.	1888/89	1890/91	15	-	-	-	-	-	-
Jagger W.	1895/96	1896/97	4	-	-	-	-	-	-
James H.	1881/82	only	1	-	-	-	-	-	-
Jamieson -.	1895/96	only	3	-	-	-	-	-	-
Jeffery W.G.	1931/32	only	1	-	-	-	-	-	-
Jeffries H.J.F.	1905/06	only	4	-	-	-	-	-	-
Jelley D.	1992/93	to date	3	1	-	-	-	-	5
Jelly J.	1882/83	only	1	-	-	-	-	-	-
Jenkins J.D.	1929/30	only	1	-	-	-	-	-	-
Jenkins J.L.	1922/23	only	2	-	-	-	-	-	-
Jenkins J.M.	1952/53	1955/56	112	10	-	-	-	-	30
Jenkins L.H.	1958/59	1959/60	32	6	-	-	-	-	18
Jenkins O.	1919/20	only	1	-	-	-	-	-	-
Jenkins -.	1896/97	only	1	-	-	-	-	-	-
Jerwood H.P.	1938/39	1949/50	135	13	9	24	-	-	129
Jessop H.G.	1956/57	1959/60	26	5*	-	-	-	-	15

NAME	FROM	TO	APPS	T	C	PG	DG	GM	PTS
John G.A.	1962/63	1967/68	13	-	1	-	-	-	2
Johnson A.	1890/91	only	1	-	-	-	-	-	-
Johnson A.	1991/92	only	1	-	-	-	-	-	-
Johnson C.A.P.	1992/93	to date	8	4	-	-	-	-	20
Johnson E.C.	1892/93	only	1	-	-	-	-	-	-
Johnson M.O.	1988/89	to date	53	2	-	-	-	-	10
Johnson S.R.	1976/77	1982/83	207	31	-	-	-	-	124
Jolliffe C.K.	1937/38	only	1	-	-	-	-	-	-
Jones A.	1901/02	1902/03	7	-	-	-	-	-	-
Jones A.	1958/59	1959/60	50	2	-	-	-	-	6
Jones A.O.	1894/95	1910/11	224	39	113	20	37	3	563
Jones B.	1969/70	1978/79	333	42	1	-	4	-	172
Jones C.W.	1922/23	1923/24	29	1	-	-	-	-	3
Jones D.	1928/29	only	18	3	-	-	-	-	9
Jones D.J.	1912/13	only	2	-	-	-	-	-	-
Jones E.M.	1991/92	only	3	-	-	-	-	-	-
Jones F.	1973/74	1975/76	14	2	-	-	-	-	8
Jones F.H.	1895/96	1905/06	115	35	32	1	1	-	176
Jones G.	1893/94	1895/96	63	16	-	-	-	-	48
Jones G.	1922/23	only	1	2	-	-	-	-	6
Jones I.	1923/24	only	1	-	-	-	-	-	-
Jones J.I.T.	1932/33	only	1	-	-	-	-	-	-
Jones J.M.	1961/62	1962/63	49	2	-	-	-	-	6
Jones K.B.	1964/65	only	2	-	-	-	-	-	-
Jones K.D.	1952/53	only	16	2	-	-	-	-	6
Jones K.J.	1948/49	only	1	-	-	-	-	-	-
Jones R.C.	1920/21	only	1	-	-	-	-	-	-
Jones S.	1925/26	only	2	-	-	-	-	-	-
Jones T.M.	1946/47	1948/49	19	1	-	-	-	-	3
Jones W.	1903/04	only	7	2	-	-	-	-	6
Jones W.H.	1912/13	1913/14	3	-	-	-	-	-	-
Jones W.J.	1912/13	only	1	-	-	-	-	-	-
Jose J.	1905/06	only	1	-	-	-	-	-	-
Joyce H.W.	1891/92	1892/93	11	1	-	-	-	-	2
Joyce N.J.	1970/71	1985/86	287	28	-	-	-	-	112
Joyce R.	1897/98	only	1	1	2	-	1	-	11
Judd W.W.	1883/84	1884/85	13	-	-	-	-	-	-
Kail J.C.	1950/51	only	26	4	-	-	-	-	12
Kardooni A.	1988/89	to date	135	40	-	-	-	-	167
Kaye J.	1934/35	only	1	1	-	-	-	-	3
Keeton G.H.	1895/96	1904/05	45	10	-	-	-	-	30
Kemp G.T.	1929/30	only	1	-	-	-	-	-	-
Kemp T.A.	1936/37	only	1	-	-	-	-	-	-
Kemp -.	1945/46	only	1	-	-	-	-	-	-
Kempin J.S.	1974/75	1978/79	109	15	-	-	-	-	60
Kendall P.	1985	only	2	-	2	-	-	-	4
Kendrew D.A.	1929/30	1935/36	30	3	4	-	-	-	17
Kennewell J.G.	1951/52	1952/53	4	-	-	-	-	-	-
Kenney J.T.	1934/35	only	1	-	-	-	-	-	-
Kenney S.	1975/76	1989/90	365	69	-	-	-	-	276
Kenney W.L.	1923/24	1924/25	15	3	-	-	-	-	9
Kenyon H.J.	1935/36	1938/39	4	-	-	-	1	-	4
Kenyon P.	1895/96	only	1	-	-	-	-	-	-
Kerby W.I.	1929/30	1931/32	12	2	-	-	-	-	6
Kewney A.L.	1905/06	1912/13	27	1	-	-	-	-	3
Key A.M.	1978/79	1991/92	65	13	10	14	-	-	114
Key M.R.	1957/58	1960/61	29	-	9	9	1	-	48
Keywood A.	1898/99	only	1	-	-	-	-	-	-
Kilby G.	1910/11	only	2	1	-	-	-	-	3
Kilford W.A.	1992/93	to date	18	8	10	5	-	-	75
King A.	1912/13	only	1	-	-	-	-	-	-
King A.	1922/23	1924/25	2	-	-	-	-	-	-
King J.	1892/93	1893/94	9	2	-	-	-	-	4
King R.V.	1960/61	only	2	-	-	-	-	-	-
King -.	1885/86	only	2	-	-	-	-	-	-
Kingston C.A.	1889/90	only	1	-	-	-	-	-	-
Kingston H.E.	1901/02	only	2	-	-	-	-	-	-
King-Turner C.J.	1922/23	only	1	-	-	-	-	-	-
Kinton C.	1894/95	1899/00	7	1	-	-	-	-	3
Kirk D.	1973/74	1974/75	10	1	-	-	-	-	4
Kirk L.	1906/07	1908/09	12	6	2	2	-	1	31
Kitchen W.	1908/09	1910/11	6	-	-	-	-	-	-
Kitchener A.	1914/15	only	1	-	-	-	-	-	-
Kitching D.	1988/89	1989/90	8	-	-	-	-	-	-
Knapp E.R.	1938/39	only	5	1	-	-	-	-	3
Knight C.B.	1887/88	1888/89	2	-	-	-	-	-	-
Knight E.M.	1918/19	only	4	-	-	-	-	-	-
'Knott' -.	1888/89	only	1	3	-	-	-	-	3
Knowles M.	1980/81	1981/82	11	3	-	-	-	-	12
Knox H.N.	1927/28	1928/29	8	-	-	-	-	-	-
Konig P.H.	1951/52	1959/60	185	32	-	-	-	-	96
Krych J.	1974/75	1982/83	28	-	-	-	-	-	-
Kyle W.E.	1935/36	only	1	-	-	-	-	-	-
Lacey E.C.	1947/48	1958/59	175	15	-	-	1	-	49
Lacey J.	1971/72	only	1	-	-	-	-	-	-
Laing R.A.	1945/46	only	2	-	-	-	-	-	-
Lakin J.A.	1880/81	1882/83	27	6	-	-	-	-	6
Lakin R.	1891/92	1893/94	6	-	-	-	-	-	-
Lambert J.P.	1938/39	1946/47	5	2	-	-	-	-	6
Lammiman D.A.	1949/50	1950/51	3	-	-	-	-	-	-
Lane P.	1937/38	only	1	-	-	-	-	-	-
Lane R.	1986/87	1987/88	4	2	-	-	-	-	8
Lang J.	1881/82	only	1	-	-	-	-	-	-
Langdon J.	1898/99	only	2	-	-	-	-	-	-
Langley D.	1945/46	only	1	-	-	-	-	-	-
Lashmore G.F.	1927/28	1929/30	4	1	-	-	-	-	3
Lauder R.E.	1933/34	only	1	-	-	-	-	-	-
Laugham -.	1880/81	only	1	-	-	-	-	-	-
Lawrence C.G.S.	1948/49	1952/53	118	40	-	-	-	-	120
Lawrence S.F.	1921/22	1927/28	135	11	-	-	-	-	33
Lawrence T.W.	1889/90	only	6	-	-	-	-	-	-
Lawrence W.	1907/08	only	1	-	-	-	-	-	-
Lawrie G.	1937/38	1938/39	4	-	-	-	-	-	-
Lawrie H.S.B.	1903/04	1914/15	168	29	60	12	1	5	262
Lawrie J.R.	1923/24	1925/26	92	13	-	-	-	-	39
Lawrie P.W.	1907/08	1923/24	318	206	23	9	9	-	727
Lawton A.T.	1924/25	only	1	-	-	1	-	-	3
Lawton T.	1982/83	1983/84	4	-	-	-	-	-	-
Lawton -.	1881/82	only	1	-	-	-	-	-	-
Lea -.	1888/89	only	1	-	-	-	-	-	-
Leader J.	1913/14	only	1	-	-	-	-	-	-
Leakey W.	1885/86	only	6	2	-	-	-	-	2
Leather J.B.	1913/14	only	3	-	-	-	-	-	-
Leather W.M.	1909/10	only	5	-	-	-	-	-	-
Lebens G.A.	1939/40	only	1	-	-	-	-	-	-
Lee G.	1953/54	1954/55	26	8	-	-	-	-	24
Lee J.F.	1899/00	only	1	1	-	-	-	-	3
Lees H.	1938/39	only	1	-	-	-	-	-	-
Leete S.F.	1957/58	1958/59	11	-	1	-	-	-	2
Leggitt R.	1910/11	only	1	-	-	-	-	-	-
Le Good H.J.F.	1934/35	only	3	-	-	-	-	-	-
Le Manco -.	1885/86	only	1	-	1	-	-	-	2
Leslie O.E.H.	1919/20	only	1	-	-	-	-	-	-
Leslie R.E.	1952/53	only	1	-	-	-	-	-	-
Lewis B.A.	1955/56	1956/57	15	2	-	-	-	-	6
Lewis C.G.R.	1931/32	1935/36	53	1	1	1	-	-	8
Lewis D.	1907/08	only	1	-	-	-	-	-	-
Lewis D.W.	1934/35	1935/36	2	-	-	-	-	-	-
Lewis J.	1908/09	1910/11	7	2	-	-	-	-	6
Lewis J.M.C.	1912/13	only	1	-	-	-	-	-	-
Lewis R.	1894/9	only	35	24	17	-	4	-	22
Lewis R.A.	1950/51	only	17	-	-	-	-	-	-
Ley R.G.	1888/89	1893/94	67	5	-	-	-	-	8
Leyland R.	1934/35	1936/37	10	3	-	-	-	-	9
Liley J.G.	1988/89	to date	131	51	265	243	1	-	1478
Lincoln W.F.	1895/96	1899/00	110	15	1	-	-	-	47
Lindsay D.A.	1935/36	only	1	-	-	-	-	-	-
Line E.	1885/86	1889/90	28	-	-	-	-	-	-
Lines F.	1901/02	only	1	-	-	-	-	-	-
Lines S.	1900/01	1904/05	21	-	-	-	-	-	-
Littlewood C.J.	1960/61	only	3	-	-	-	-	-	-
Livingstone S.	1914/15	only	1	-	-	-	-	-	-
Llewellyn B.	1967/68	only	1	-	-	-	-	-	-
Llewellyn J.G.	1928/29	1933/34	39	13	2	-	8	-	75
Lloyd I.	1933/34	only	10	4	-	-	-	-	12
Lloyd-Evans O.	1898/99	only	5	-	1	-	-	-	2
Lockett M.	1968/69	only	2	1	-	-	-	-	3

NAME	FROM	TO	APPS	T	C	PG	DG	GM	PTS
Lockman P.	1903/04	1904/05	7	-	-	-	-	-	-
Lole W.E.	1928/29	only	1	-	-	-	-	-	-
Loveday A.	1884/85	only	1	-	-	-	-	-	-
Lovell W.S.	1889/90	only	1	-	-	-	-	-	-
Lovett J.T.	1880/81	1889/90	104	9	-	-	-	-	9
Lowe C.L.	1921/22	1922/23	3	-	-	-	-	-	-
Loxton S.A.	1933/34	1935/36	70	2	-	-	-	-	6
Lubbock M.G.	1955/56	1960/61	95	7	-	-	-	-	21
Lucas J.	1891/92	only	5	-	-	-	-	-	-
Ludlow W.D.	1889/90	only	2	-	-	-	-	-	-
Lynch M.	1946/47	only	16	2	-	-	-	-	6
Lyons D.	1966/67	only	6	1	-	-	-	-	3
Lyttle V.J.	1936/37	only	1	-	-	-	-	-	-
McAdam A.	1990/91	to date	5	1	-	-	-	-	4
McAlpin D.	1889/90	only	9	-	-	-	-	-	-
McAlpin K.	1884/85	1892/93	135	13	-	-	-	-	13
McArthur D.	1928/29	only	1	-	-	-	-	-	-
Macaulay K.	1881/82	only	4	-	-	-	-	-	-
McConnell R.	1949/50	only	1	-	-	-	-	-	-
McCormack J.T.	1953/54	1956/57	37	5	-	-	-	-	15
McCraith B.	1900/01	1901/02	10	-	-	-	-	-	-
McDonald K.	1985/86	1990/91	19	7	-	-	-	-	28
MacDonald K.R.	1952/53	only	5	-	-	-	-	-	-
Macdonald M.A.	1922/23	only	1	-	-	-	-	-	-
Macey D.	1975/76	only	3	-	-	-	-	-	-
McFarlane N.	1904/05	1906/07	40	5	-	-	-	-	15
McIntyre A.S.	1908/09	1911/12	46	3	-	-	-	-	9
Mackay R.B.	1936/37	1937/38	12	3	-	-	-	-	9
McKechnie A.	1882/83	1893/94	215	19	25	-	7	-	96
McKee J.H.	1937/38	only	1	-	-	-	-	-	-
McKennie -.	1882/83	only	1	-	-	-	-	-	-
McLean J.R.	1933/34	1938/39	39	7	3	1	3	-	42
MacLeod J.N.	1936/37	only	2	1	-	-	-	-	3
McMichael R.D.J.	1976/77	1977/78	7	1	-	-	-	-	4
MacMillan D.	1912/13	1913/14	5	2	-	-	-	-	6
McMurray F.G.	1881/82	only	1	-	-	-	-	-	-
McMurray W.H.	1888/89	1889/90	4	-	-	-	-	-	-
McNichol I.	1929/30	1931/32	6	1	-	-	-	-	3
McSalley O.	1889/90	1891/92	21	1	-	-	-	-	2
McTigue B.J.	1950/51	only	2	-	-	-	-	-	-
Maddocks T.E.	1910/11	1911/12	2	-	-	-	-	-	-
Mainwaring R.	1961/62	only	6	3	-	-	-	-	9
Malone N.G.	1993	only	3	-	2	2	-	-	10
Manley D.P.	1931/32	only	1	-	-	-	-	-	-
Mann A.H.	1892/93	only	1	-	-	-	-	-	-
Mann A.O.	1936/37	only	3	-	-	-	-	-	-
Mann M.M.	1907/08	1908/09	11	2	-	-	-	-	6
Mann P.J.	1986/87	1987/88	23	1	-	-	-	-	4
Mansell J.	1887/88	1889/90	21	2	-	-	-	-	2
Manship D.	1979/80	1981/82	9	-	2	-	-	-	4
Manson C.E.	1928/29	1933/34	107	-	9	-	1	-	22
Manton A.V.	1914/15	1918/19	5	2	-	-	-	-	6
Marques A.C.	1922/23	only	1	1	-	-	-	-	3
Marriott A.N.	1981/82	1991/92	130	12	-	-	-	-	48
Marriott J.	1966/67	only	1	-	-	-	-	-	-
Marris R.W.	1904/05	only	2	-	-	-	-	-	-
Marshall G.G.	1919/20	only	1	-	-	-	-	-	-
Marshall M.	1969/70	1976/77	32	8	-	-	-	-	31
Marshall R.	1949/50	1956/57	87	2	3	1	-	-	15
Marston J.	1882/83	only	1	-	-	-	-	-	-
Martin C.G.	1956/57	1965/66	272	3	126	88	-	-	555
Martin N.	1992/93	only	2	-	-	-	-	-	-
Mason A.	1895/96	only	1	-	-	-	-	-	-
Mason C.J.	1892/93	only	2	-	-	-	-	-	-
Mason H.	1886/87	1890/91	84	11	-	-	-	-	11
Mason -.	1880/81	only	1	-	-	-	-	-	-
Massey E.J.	1922/23	1924/25	31	1	-	5	-	-	18
Massey W.	1881/82	1886/87	3	-	-	-	-	-	-
Matthews A.	1966/67	1972/73	8	-	5	2	-	-	16
Matthews A.D.	1934/35	only	1	-	-	-	-	-	-
Matthews D.J.	1955/56	1973/74	502	119	15	20	-	-	451
Matthews R.D.	1948/49	1956/57	57	14	-	-	-	-	42
Matthews S.	1897/98	1907/08	340	19	14	1	-	-	88
Matts A.	1880/81	only	1	-	-	-	-	-	-
Matts G.A.	1945/46	1949/50	31	-	17	16	3	-	92
Mawbey J.W.	1967/68	1968/69	38	6	-	-	2	-	24
Mawle N.W.R.	1927/28	only	1	-	-	-	-	-	-
Medhurst C.E.H.	1923/24	1924/25	17	-	-	-	1	-	4
Mee G.C.	1900/01	1901/02	2	2	-	-	-	-	6
Meek J.	1891/92	1896/97	32	-	-	-	-	-	-
Meekin J.	1884/85	only	2	-	-	-	-	-	-
Meikle G.W.C.	1933/34	1936/37	26	14	2	-	2	-	4
Meikle S.S.C.	1930/31	1933/34	6	8	1	-	-	-	26
Meldrum A.	1977/78	only	1	-	-	-	-	-	-
Mellor F.	1913/14	1920/21	20	1	2	-	-	-	7
Memory J.	1891/92	1893/94	9	2	-	-	-	-	5
Merriman M.J.P.	1979/80	1981/82	18	3	5	5	-	-	37
Merry E.W.	1901/02	only	3	-	-	-	-	-	-
Metcalfe G.	1890/91	only	2	-	-	-	-	-	-
Michie E.J.S.	1957/58	only	10	-	-	-	-	-	-
Middleton G.	1907/08	1910/11	29	2	-	-	-	-	6
Miles J.H.	1899/00	1903/04	93	75	-	-	-	-	225
Millar C.L.	1930/31	1934/35	5	-	-	-	-	-	-
Millar G.R.	1965/66	1972/73	11	3	-	-	-	-	9
Millard M.L.	1927/28	1928/29	7	-	-	-	-	-	-
Millican J.G.	1974/75	1976/77	25	4	-	-	-	-	16
Mills A.	1907/08	1908/09	48	2	-	-	-	-	6
Mills J.	1889/90	only	1	-	-	-	-	-	-
Milman M.D.	1935/36	only	1	-	-	-	-	-	-
Milne J.W.	1952/53	only	1	-	-	-	-	-	-
Milne K.	1956/57	only	1	-	-	-	-	-	-
Milton J.	1946/47	only	1	-	-	-	-	-	-
Moeller D.	1961/62	only	1	-	-	-	-	-	-
Moller C.B.	1924/25	only	2	-	-	-	-	-	-
Money R.S.	1968/69	1977/78	258	23	-	-	12	-	123
Moon J.H.	1925/26	only	-	-	-	-	-	-	-
Moore A.	1891/92	1893/94	4	1	-	-	-	-	2
Moore C.	1891/92	only	1	-	-	-	-	-	-
Moore J.A.	1948/49	only	2	-	-	-	-	-	-
Moore J.H.	1925/26	only	12	4	-	-	-	-	12
Moore P.J.d'A.	1947/48	only	1	-	-	-	-	-	-
Moore R.L.	1936/37	only	1	-	-	-	-	-	-
Moore S.H.	1927/28	1931/32	13	5	-	-	-	-	15
Moore W.K.T.	1945/46	1952/53	170	6	2	-	2	-	28
Moore -.	1887/88	only	5	-	-	-	-	-	-
Morgan A.	1921/22	only	1	1	-	-	-	-	3
Morgan D.	1963/64	only	3	-	-	-	-	-	-
Morgan E.	1908/09	only	1	-	-	-	-	-	-
Morgan W.R.	1935/36	only	9	2	-	-	-	-	6
Morley D.	1968/69	1971/72	6	-	-	-	-	-	-
Morley E.R.	1885/86	1891/92	97	4	-	-	-	-	4
Morris D.E.	1930/31	1934/35	42	10	-	-	1	-	34
Morris F.	1909/10	only	1	-	-	-	-	-	-
Morris J.	1914/15	only	1	-	-	-	-	-	-
Morris J.P.	1948/49	1951/52	47	2	31	16	4	-	128
Morrison J.	1891/92	only	6	1	-	-	-	-	2
Morrison M.C.	1898/99	1902/03	2	-	-	-	-	-	-
Mortimer M.R.	1970/71	1975/76	132	10	-	-	-	-	40
Morton J.	1922/23	only	1	-	-	-	-	-	-
Morton J.W.	1908/09	only	1	-	-	-	-	-	-
Mosby E.	1896/97	1900/01	73	12	32	1	2	-	111
Mosby -.	1888/89	only	1	-	-	-	-	-	-
Moseby W.G.	1936/37	1945/46	18	4	-	-	-	-	12
Moseley L.G.	1957/58	1958/59	11	1	-	-	-	-	3
Muddimer R.M.	1957/58	only	8	-	-	-	-	-	-
Mullen K.D.	1954/55	only	1	-	-	-	-	-	-
Murgatroyd R.W.	1949/50	1950/51	5	-	-	-	-	-	-
Murmann W.L.	1918/19	only	4	1	-	-	-	-	3
Murphy J.	1988/89	to date	16	1	-	-	-	-	5
Murray A.	1926/27	1928/29	2	-	-	-	-	-	-
Myers E.	1918/19	1924/25	2	-	-	-	-	-	-
Myrtle -.	1885/86	only	1	-	-	-	-	-	-
Nangrave M.	1980/81	only	1	-	-	-	-	-	-
Neal A.E.	1945/46	1948/49	82	1	-	-	-	-	3
Neal O.	1933/34	1934/35	2	-	-	-	-	-	-
Neal -.	1884/85	1890/91	2	-	-	-	-	-	-
Neale A.L.	1918/19	only	2	-	-	-	-	-	-
Needham R.E.	1973/74	1981/82	126	5	3	-	-	-	26

NAME	FROM	TO	APPS	T	C	PG	DG	GM	PTS
Neil M.J.	1957/58	only	4	1	-	-	-	-	3
Neild E.	1888/89	1891/92	14	2	-	-	-	-	2
Nelson J.B.	1926/27	only	2	1	-	-	-	-	3
Nemo C.	1880/81	only	1	-	-	-	-	-	-
Neumann S.	1899/00	1901/02	29	9	-	-	-	-	27
Newman F.C.W.	1913/14	only	1	-	-	-	-	-	-
Newsome S.	1977/78	only	9	-	-	-	-	-	-
Newton M.J.	1976/77	1981/82	26	8	-	-	-	-	32
Nicholas W.K.	1947/48	1953/54	151	24	1	3	4	-	95
Nicholls P.	1970/71	1974/75	57	24	-	-	-	-	85
Nicholson A.	1891/92	only	1	-	-	-	-	-	-
Nicholson C.H.	1894/95	1896/97	21	3	-	-	-	-	9
Nicholson E.S.	1935/36	only	8	-	-	-	-	-	-
Nicol H.St J.	1899/00	only	1	-	-	-	-	-	-
Nixon E.G.	1932/33	only	3	-	-	-	-	-	-
Noble D.T.	1961/62	only	1	-	-	-	-	-	-
Nobleston R.F.	1931/32	only	1	-	-	-	-	-	-
Nobren -.	1889/90	only	1	-	-	-	-	-	-
Nockles R.	1987/88	1988/89	6	-	-	1	-	-	3
Noon F.S.	1885/86	only	2	2	-	-	-	-	2
Norman D.J.	1919/20	1932/33	453	21	29	2	1	-	131
Norman F.H.	1918/19	only	2	-	-	-	-	-	-
Norman F.J.	1932/33	only	3	-	-	-	-	-	-
Norman L.A.	1945/46	only	4	-	-	-	-	-	-
Norman R.A.	1947/48	1948/49	4	-	1	-	1	-	5
Norman W.	1919/20	only	4	-	5	-	-	-	10
Northen A.	1974/75	1975/76	6	-	-	-	-	-	-
Norton D.	1948/49	1949/50	27	2	-	-	-	-	6
Noton J.	1949/50	1953/54	12	-	-	-	-	-	-
Novis A.L.	1927/28	1930/31	3	-	-	-	-	-	-
Nutt A.	1880/81	1888/89	52	12	-	-	-	-	12
Nutt F.	1889/90	1891/92	27	6	-	-	-	-	8
Nutt T.	1888/89	1890/91	11	-	-	-	-	-	-
Oakes C.St C.	1934/35	only	3	1	-	-	-	-	3
Oakley T.P.K.	1932/33	only	1	-	-	-	-	-	-
Obolensky A.	1934/35	1938/39	17	12	-	-	-	-	36
O'Connor J.	1955/56	only	4	1	-	-	-	-	3
O'Connor T.	1954/55	1955/56	34	4	-	-	-	-	12
Odbert R.V.M.	1923/24	1931/32	13	1	-	-	-	-	3
Ogden G.A.	1889/90	only	6	-	-	-	-	-	-
Old A.G.B.	1972/73	1973/74	18	3	11	23	1	-	106
Oldershaw A.	1901/02	only	1	-	-	-	-	-	-
Oldham W.L.	1909/10	only	1	-	-	-	-	-	-
Oliver F.E.	1923/24	only	1	-	-	-	-	-	-
Orchard R.D.	1933/34	1935/36	3	-	-	-	-	-	-
O'Regan T.D.	1964/65	only	4	-	-	-	-	-	-
O'Reilly A.J.F.K.	1958/59	1960/61	17	8	-	-	-	-	24
Orme T.	1898/99	only	2	-	-	-	-	-	-
Orr H.R.	1888/89	only	1	-	-	-	-	-	-
Orton F.	1891/92	1892/93	2	-	-	-	-	-	-
Orton G.W.	1892/93	1894/95	2	-	-	-	-	-	-
Osbourne A.J.	1914/15	1918/19	3	-	-	-	-	-	-
Oscroft A.	1919/20	1920/21	2	-	-	-	-	-	-
Oscroft D.S.	1929/30	1934/35	20	2	-	-	-	-	6
Oscroft P.W.	1897/98	1900/01	49	19	9	1	7	-	106
Owen C.	1969/70	1971/72	38	8	-	-	-	-	25
Owen-Smith H.G.	1933/34	only	1	-	-	-	-	-	-
Oxlade H.W.	1886/87	1889/90	34	5	3	-	1	-	14
Packer H.E.	1932/33	only	1	-	-	-	-	-	-
Page C.A.	1892/93	1903/04	16	5	-	-	-	-	15
Page H.	1918/19	only	4	-	1	-	-	-	2
Page N.C.	1933/34	only	3	-	-	-	-	-	-
Page R.E.	1894/95	1897/98	18	-	-	-	-	-	-
Page S.E.	1892/93	only	4	1	-	-	-	-	2
Pailthorpe R.	1889/90	only	1	-	-	-	-	-	-
Paisley -.	1922/23	only	1	-	-	-	-	-	-
Palfreyman A.J.	1902/03	1903/04	18	-	-	-	-	-	-
Palfreyman H.W.	1909/10	1918/19	4	-	-	-	-	-	-
Palmer A.P.	1928/29	only	3	-	-	-	-	-	-
Palmer G.A.	1920/21	1925/26	12	-	-	-	-	-	-
Palmer J.R.D.	1948/49	only	4	-	-	-	-	-	-
Palmer R.A.	1931/32	1934/35	2	2	-	-	-	-	6
Palmer R.S.	1922/23	1928/29	14	2	1	-	-	-	8

NAME	FROM	TO	APPS	T	C	PG	DG	GM	PTS
Parfitt E.J.	1938/39	1945/46	3	1	-	-	-	-	3
Parker B.	1919/20	only	13	1	-	-	-	-	3
Parker G.W.C.	1925/26	1926/27	27	-	-	-	-	-	-
Parker H.G.	1923/24	only	4	1	-	-	-	-	3
Parker M.G.S.	1924/25	only	2	-	-	-	-	-	-
Parker W.E.	1931/32	1935/36	30	1	-	-	-	-	3
Parkes A.W.	1892/93	only	13	-	-	-	-	-	-
Parkes L.	1975/76	1980	34	7	-	-	-	-	28
Parry J.H.	1881/82	only	2	-	-	-	-	-	-
Parsons A.O.	1902/03	1906/07	44	17	-	-	-	-	51
Parsons J.	1880/81	1888/89	113	15	48	-	13	-	150
Parsons J.	1935/36	1938/39	60	9	-	-	-	-	27
Patchett J.	1891/92	1893/94	36	-	-	-	-	-	-
Patrick T.	1898/99	only	1	-	-	-	-	-	-
Pattinson A.P.	1930/31	only	2	-	-	-	-	-	-
Payne F.W.	1905/06	only	1	-	-	-	-	-	-
Payne J.F.	1932/33	only	3	-	-	1	-	-	3
Pearce C.J.	1884/85	only	2	-	-	-	-	-	-
Pearce H.K.	1908/09	1914/15	13	5	-	-	1	-	19
Pearce S.D.	1939/40	only	1	-	-	-	-	-	-
Peard E.J.	1900/01	only	1	1	-	-	-	-	3
Pearse C.H.	1927/28	1935/36	29	2	-	-	-	-	6
Peddie E.	1888/89	only	2	-	-	-	-	-	-
Peebles J.S.	1935/36	only	1	-	-	-	-	-	-
Pell E.	1947/48	only	1	-	-	-	-	-	-
Pell R.	1983/84	1985/86	20	4	4	2	1	-	33
Pemberton H.J.	1912/13	only	1	1	-	-	-	-	3
Pemberton R.J.	1932/33	only	1	-	-	-	-	-	-
Penny S.H.	1895/96	1910/11	491	16	-	-	-	-	48
Perkins D.	1964/65	1968/69	21	1	-	-	-	-	3
Perry D.G.	1959/60	only	4	-	-	-	-	-	-
Peters D.	1978/79	only	2	-	-	-	-	-	-
Philbrick E.R.	1893/94	only	1	-	-	-	-	-	-
Phillips E.V.	1887/88	only	12	10	-	-	-	-	10
Phillips W.	1934/35	only	2	-	-	-	-	-	-
Phillpotts G.	1928/29	only	1	-	-	-	-	-	-
Phipps E.A.	1891/92	only	1	-	-	-	-	-	-
Phipps G.	1946/47	only	3	1	-	-	-	-	3
Pickard E.H.	1895/96	1896/97	9	6	-	-	-	-	18
Pickering D.	1970/71	1972/73	20	1	-	-	-	-	4
Pickering T.R.	1880/81	only	3	-	-	-	-	-	-
Pierce E.R.	1945/46	only	8	-	-	-	-	-	-
Pilsbury E.	1887/88	1888/89	8	1	-	-	-	-	1
Pilsbury H.	1890/91	1891/92	7	1	-	-	-	-	1
Pole-Kitson J.	1893/94	only	1	-	-	-	-	-	-
Pollard G.E.	1934/35	1937/38	13	-	-	-	-	-	-
Pollard W.	1919/20	1923/24	6	4	-	-	-	-	12
Poole H.	1900/01	only	1	-	-	-	-	-	-
Poole M.D.	1988/89	to date	99	8	-	-	-	-	35
Porter A.T.	1880/81	1888/89	38	4	-	-	1	-	7
Porter G.G.	1888/89	1890/91	8	-	-	-	-	-	-
Porter S.G.	1883/84	1888/89	21	-	-	-	-	-	-
Porter W.R.	1880/81	1891/92	169	10	-	-	-	-	11
Potter A.	1881/82	only	1	-	-	-	-	-	-
Potter A.C.	1935/36	only	1	-	-	-	-	-	-
Potter S.	1992/93	to date	33	8	-	-	-	-	40
Potts J.R.H.	1929/30	1934/35	13	3	-	-	-	-	9
Poulson M.	1979/80	1983/84	43	7	13	26	11	-	165
Povoas S.J.	1985	to date	131	64	-	-	-	-	261
Powell-John -.	1900/01	only	1	-	-	-	-	-	-
Powers J.	1889/90	only	6	-	-	-	-	-	-
Powley H.G.	1955/56	1956/57	3	-	-	-	-	-	-
Pratt S.	1948/49	1953/54	134	4	-	-	-	-	12
Prentice F.D.	1923/24	1930/31	239	60	133	43	-	-	575
Prentice T.H.	1880/81	1881/82	9	-	-	-	-	-	-
Preston J.R.	1936/37	1939/40	23	8	-	-	-	-	24
Preston W.H.	1933/34	only	1	-	-	-	-	-	-
Price H.L.	1922/23	1924/25	17	2	-	-	1	-	10
Price P.G.	1926/27	only	1	-	-	-	-	-	-
Price-Stephens L.	1945/46	only	1	-	-	-	-	-	-
Pugh N.	1953/54	only	3	-	-	-	-	-	-
Pulfrey P.G.S.	1962/63	1969/70	173	13	1	6	5	-	74
Purt A.	1926/27	only	1	-	-	-	-	-	-
Pyart F.	1905/06	only	1	-	-	-	-	-	-
Pym G.	1952/53	1953/54	14	1	-	-	-	-	3

NAME	FROM	TO	APPS	T	C	PG	DG	GM	PTS
Quarry C.H.	1936/37	only	1	-	-	-	-	-	-
Quick J.	1964/65	1967/68	119	41	-	-	-	-	123
Quick S.	1991/92	only	1	-	-	-	-	-	-
Quine D.A.	1947/48	1950/51	27	8	2	4	-	-	40
Radcliffe S.T.A.	1932/33	only	1	-	-	-	-	-	-
Raine A.	1963/64	1968/69	63	4	-	-	-	-	12
Ramsey S.	1898/99	1899/00	3	-	-	-	-	-	-
Randall R.	1923/24	only	1	-	-	-	-	-	-
Randle G.D.O.	1948/49	1952/53	5	-	-	-	-	-	-
Rapsey W.G.	1902/03	1910/11	2	1	-	-	-	-	3
Rathbone J.	1890/91	1892/93	25	13	-	-	-	-	23
Raven E.	1905/06	only	1	-	-	-	-	-	-
Raven J.	1925/26	only	2	-	-	-	-	-	-
Rawes J.	1976/77	only	1	-	-	-	-	-	-
Rawson R.O.	1956/57	1960/61	63	20	2	-	-	-	64
Read C.	1919/20	1920/21	3	1	-	-	-	-	3
Read F.	1912/13	1918/19	12	-	-	-	-	-	-
Read J.	1880/81	only	1	-	-	-	-	-	-
Reading R.	1880/81	only	1	-	-	-	-	-	-
Reay G.H.	1956/57	only	2	-	-	-	-	-	-
Redding A.	1911/12	1913/14	15	-	-	-	-	-	-
Redfern Steve	1976/77	1984/85	241	16	-	-	-	-	64
Redfern Stuart	1981/82	1991/92	324	25	-	-	-	-	100
Redfern W.H.	1950/51	1951/52	12	-	-	-	-	-	-
Redman E.	1893/94	1900/01	143	12	-	1	-	-	39
Reed N.F.	1933/34	only	6	1	-	-	-	-	3
Rees A.	1959/60	only	1	-	-	-	-	-	-
Rees D.	1904/05	only	1	-	-	-	-	-	-
Rees D.E.B.	1947/48	1949/50	76	32	-	-	1	-	99
Rees F.	1911/12	only	1	-	-	-	-	-	-
Rees G.	1945/46	only	4	1	-	-	-	-	3
Rees N.	1925/26	only	1	-	-	-	-	-	-
Reeve J.	1973/74	1976/77	51	18	-	-	-	-	72
Reeve J.S.R.	1930/31	only	1	-	-	-	-	-	-
Reeves D.J.	1922/23	only	1	-	-	-	-	-	-
Reichwald W.M.	1977/78	1978/79	19	2	-	-	1	-	11
Reid M.	1988/89	only	13	1	-	-	-	-	4
Reidy J.P.	1934/35	only	2	-	-	-	-	-	-
Rendle A.R.	1893/94	only	32	-	-	-	-	-	-
Rew A.H.	1932/33	only	1	-	-	-	-	-	-
Reynolds F/O.	1931/32	only	1	-	-	-	-	-	-
Reynolds H.P.	1902/03	1903/04	15	1	-	-	1	-	7
Reynolds T.	1991/92	to date	8	2	-	-	-	-	10
Rhodes J.	1880/81	1881/82	3	-	-	-	-	-	-
Rhodes P.E.F.	1946/47	1948/49	33	3	2	4	1	-	29
Rice E.	1919/20	only	1	-	-	-	-	-	-
Rice W.R.	1894/95	only	25	5	-	-	-	-	15
Richards D.	1981/82	to date	218	97	-	-	-	-	391
Richards F.	1918/19	only	1	-	-	-	-	-	-
Richards K.	1953/54	only	6	2	-	-	-	-	6
Richards W.H.	1936/37	1946/47	47	-	3	1	-	-	9
Richardson L.	1985/86	1989/90	12	2	-	-	-	-	8
Richardson N.D.	1992/93	to date	14	6	-	-	-	-	30
Richardson W.P.	1980/81	to date	222	8	-	-	-	-	32
Riddle C.B.	1922/23	only	1	-	-	-	-	-	-
Ridgway T.G.	1935/36	1939/40	95	1	-	-	-	-	3
Ridsdale -.	1904/05	only	2	-	-	-	-	-	-
Rigby -.	1883/84	only	1	-	-	-	-	-	-
Rigney B.	1958/59	1959/60	3	-	-	-	-	-	-
Riley P.	1961/62	1971/72	34	4	-	-	-	-	12
Riley T.A.	1938/39	only	1	-	-	-	-	-	-
Ring B.D.	1959/60	1960/61	35	4	-	1	-	-	15
Ringer P.	1972/73	1974/75	56	4	-	-	-	-	16
Ringer T.	1973/74	1974/75	7	-	-	-	-	-	-
Ringrose R.O.	1913/14	1919/20	12	5	-	-	-	-	15
Robb G.	1984/85	1985	3	2	-	-	-	-	8
Roberts A.D.T.	1923/24	only	2	-	-	-	-	-	-
Roberts H.	1986/87	1990/91	54	7	-	-	-	-	28
Roberts H.S.	1918/19	only	1	2	-	-	-	-	6
Roberts S.C.	1908/09	only	1	1	-	-	-	-	3
Roberts T.	1982/83	only	5	-	-	-	-	-	-
Roberts W.K.	1893/94	only	1	-	-	-	-	-	-
Robertson J.	1888/89	only	2	-	-	-	-	-	-
Robins J.D.	1959/60	1961/62	27	-	26	21	-	-	115

NAME	FROM	TO	APPS	T	C	PG	DG	GM	PTS
Robinson B.V.	1934/35	only	1	-	-	-	-	-	-
Robinson F.	1910/11	only	1	-	-	-	-	-	-
Robinson H.H.	1910/11	only	18	-	-	-	-	-	-
Robinson M.A.	1933/34	1936/37	96	3	-	-	-	-	9
Robinson R.	1923/24	only	1	-	-	-	-	-	-
Robinson T.	1880/81	1889/90	3	-	-	-	-	-	-
Robinson W.	1901/02	1903/04	46	1	-	-	-	-	3
Robson R.	1992/93	only	1	-	-	-	-	-	-
Rocyn-Jones D.N.	1925/26	only	1	-	-	-	-	-	-
Roderick J.	1938/39	only	6	1	-	-	-	-	3
Roderick W.B.N.	1924/25	only	17	-	-	-	-	-	-
Rogers A.V.	1935/36	1937/38	32	3	-	-	-	-	9
Rogers F.A.	1889/90	only	3	-	-	-	-	-	-
Rogers G.	1945/46	only	1	-	-	-	-	-	-
Rogers J.G.	1935/36	only	1	-	-	-	-	-	-
Rose W.M.H.	1975/76	1977/78	19	9	29	28	2	-	184
Rotherham H.	1885/86	only	1	-	-	-	-	-	-
Round C.L.	1949/50	only	4	-	-	-	-	-	-
Rowe A.J.	1937/38	1938/39	2	-	-	-	-	-	-
Rowell R.E.	1961/62	1977/78	355	20	-	-	-	-	67
Rowlands A.	1919/20	only	6	4	-	-	-	-	12
Rowntree G.C.	1990/91	to date	61	5	-	-	-	-	22
Roxburgh A.	1922/23	1923/24	23	1	-	-	-	-	3
Roxburgh W.	1924/25	only	3	1	-	-	-	-	3
Roy S.	1984/85	only	5	1	-	-	-	-	4
Royce R.	1971/72	only	2	-	-	-	-	-	-
Royer A.R.	1991/92	only	1	-	-	-	-	-	-
Russell J.C.	1921/22	1929/30	141	10	-	-	-	1	33
Russell R.F.	1903/04	1913/14	122	28	26	7	-	-	157
Ryan D.R.	1991/92	only	2	-	-	-	-	-	-
Ryan M.	1967/68	only	1	-	-	-	-	-	-
Ryley D.W.R.	1926/27	1927/28	16	1	-	-	-	-	3
Ryley R.J.	1946/47	1947/48	33	16	-	-	1	-	52
Salmon G.H.	1913/14	only	3	-	-	-	-	-	-
Salmon H.W.	1880/81	1887/88	89	1	-	-	-	-	1
Salmon P.G.	1885/86	1888/89	3	-	-	-	-	-	-
Sambrook H.A.	1924/25	1925/26	34	3	-	-	-	1	12
Sambrook L.C.	1921/22	1927/28	215	-	24	6	1	1	73
Sanderson G.	1904/05	only	1	-	-	-	-	-	-
Sanderson G.A.	1904/05	only	1	-	-	-	-	-	-
Sandford P.	1989/90	to date	60	35	-	-	-	-	152
Sargeant J.	1938/39	only	1	-	-	-	-	-	-
Sarson F.	1896/97	only	1	-	-	-	-	-	-
Saunders E.	1966/67	only	7	-	-	-	1	-	3
Saunders S.H.	1928/29	1933/34	131	21	-	-	-	-	63
Sayer M.F.	1962/63	1968/69	56	13	-	-	-	-	39
Scattergood I.M.S.	1965/66	only	3	1	-	-	-	-	3
Scholes F.S.	1918/19	only	1	-	-	-	-	-	-
Scotland K.J.F.	1961/62	1962/63	40	4	45	43	3	-	240
Scott A.F.	1906/07	1909/10	11	6	-	-	-	-	18
Scott F.C.	1933/34	only	1	-	-	-	-	-	-
Scott H.	1918/19	only	2	-	-	-	-	-	-
Scott J.R.	1947/48	only	5	-	-	-	-	-	-
Scott M.S.	1898/99	1911/12	68	4	4	-	-	-	20
Scott P.G.	1923/24	1926/27	41	9	-	-	-	-	27
Seager J.C.	1919/20	1922/23	3	-	-	-	-	-	-
Seale -.	1881/82	only	1	-	-	-	-	-	-
Selkirk I.	1948/49	only	4	-	-	-	-	-	-
Sellers J.W.	1882/83	only	1	-	-	-	-	-	-
Sellicks D.	1957/58	only	3	-	-	-	-	-	-
Senior D.	1959/60	1962/63	84	58	-	-	1	-	177
Sewell A.	1892/93	only	28	2	-	-	-	-	4
Sharp J.R.	1936/37	1937/38	31	-	-	-	-	-	-
Sharpe G.	1911/12	only	12	-	-	-	-	-	-
Sharpe P.	1933/34	only	1	-	-	-	-	-	-
Sharratt H.	1920/21	1925/26	150	17	-	-	1	-	55
Shaw D.M.	1970/71	1972/73	57	2	-	-	-	-	8
Shaw F.H.	1904/05	1906/07	3	-	-	-	-	-	-
Shaw I.	1935/36	only	2	-	-	-	-	-	-
Sheen F.	1880/81	1881/82	9	1	-	-	-	-	1
Sheffield J.E.	1884/85	1885/86	5	-	-	-	-	-	-
Sheffield W.A.	1880/81	1887/88	98	18	-	-	-	-	18
Shelton B.	1880/81	only	1	-	-	-	-	-	-
Shentall J.	1924/25	only	1	-	-	-	-	-	-

NAME	FROM	TO	APPS	T	C	PG	DG	GM	PTS
Shephard C.D.	1955/56	1964/65	140	36	-	1	-	-	111
Shepherd J.K.	1950/51	only	1	-	-	-	-	-	-
Shepherd W.V.	1933/34	1935/36	49	25	1	1	-	-	80
Sheppard W.S.	1889/90	only	4	-	-	-	-	-	-
Sheppard -.	1882/83	only	1	-	-	-	-	-	-
Shingler G.	1906/07	1908/09	2	-	-	-	-	-	-
Shipton G.L.	1926/27	1929/30	8	1	1	-	-	-	5
Shuttlewood J.	1952/53	1953/54	36	9	-	-	-	-	27
Sibson A.F.	1932/33	1933/34	2	-	-	-	-	-	-
Sibson H.W.	1946/47	1954/55	183	26	-	-	-	-	78
Siggins G.B.	1957/58	only	1	-	-	-	-	-	-
Simcoe J.	1896/97	only	1	-	-	-	-	-	-
Sime W.A.	1931/32	1937/38	7	1	-	-	-	-	3
Simmonds S.C.	1947/48	only	1	-	-	-	-	-	-
Simpson A.	1908/09	only	2	-	-	-	-	-	-
Simpson F.	1888/89	1892/93	7	-	,	-	-	-	-
Simpson F.R.	1904/05	only	2	-	-	-	-	-	-
Simpson H.J.	1891/92	1895/96	91	9	-	-	-	-	24
Simpson J.	1904/05	only	1	2	-	-	-	-	6
Simpson R.B.Y.	1919/20	1923/24	16	5	-	-	-	-	15
Simpson T.M.	1947/48	only	1	-	-	-	-	-	-
Sinclair F.O.	1924/25	only	5	-	-	-	-	-	-
Skelton R.P.	1955/56	1969/70	198	5	-	-	-	-	15
Skelton -.	1897/98	only	1	-	-	-	-	-	-
Skinner-Jones -.	1889/90	only	1	-	-	-	-	-	-
Slack D.G.	1920/21	only	1	-	-	-	-	-	-
Sleigh R.	1966/67	1969/70	71	33	-	-	1	-	102
Slow C.F.	1932/33	1936/37	98	23	4	-	24	1	176
Sly P.	1985		2	-	-	-	-	-	-
Small B.T.C.	1954/55	1962/63	158	3	8	3	2	-	40
Small R.W.	1957/58	1969/70	119	22	-	-	-	-	66
Smalley H.	1901/02	1904/05	3	-	-	-	-	-	-
Smallwood A.M.	1920/21	1925/26	64	47	5	-	-	-	151
Smith A.	1924/25	only	1	-	-	-	-	-	-
Smith A.J.	1903/04	1904/05	2	-	-	-	-	-	-
Smith B.A.	1990/91	only	15	4	9	2	3	-	49
Smith B.A.F.	1954/55	1959/60	53	19	-	-	1	-	60
Smith D.H.	1952/53	only	2	-	-	-	-	-	-
Smith G.	1978/79	1985/86	4	-	-	-	-	-	-
Smith G.D.P.	1888/89	only	10	-	-	-	-	-	-
Smith H.	1923/24	only	1	-	-	-	-	-	-
Smith H.W.	1945/46	only	2	-	-	-	-	-	-
Smith I.R.	1977/78	1991/92	331	67	-	-	-	-	268
Smith J.	1885/86	only	1	-	-	-	-	-	-
'Smith' J.B.	1889/90	only	1	-	-	-	-	-	-
Smith J.W.D.	1901/02	1911/12	132	27	-	-	-	-	81
Smith K.T.	1961/62	1962/63	8	3	-	-	-	-	9
Smith L.A.	1931/32	only	1	-	-	-	-	-	-
Smith L.W.	1947/48	only	1	-	-	-	-	-	-
Smith P.D.	1979/80	only	1	-	-	-	-	-	-
Smith R.	1938/39	1948/49	4	-	-	-	-	-	-
Smith R.H.	1949/50	1957/58	190	11	-	-	-	-	33
Smith R.S.	1967/68	1969/70	23	4	-	-	-	-	12
Smith S.A.	1918/19	1931/32	80	10	-	-	-	-	30
Smith T.	1881/82	only	1	-	-	-	-	-	-
Smith T.	1984	to date	166	17	-	-	-	-	69
Smith T.W.	1905/06	1907/08	58	4	-	-	-	-	12
Smith W.	1904/05	only	1	-	-	-	-	-	-
Smith W.A.	1935/36	only	4	-	8	2	-	-	22
Smith W.M.	1881/82	1888/89	56	5	-	-	-	-	5
Smitten P.	1911/12	1921/22	16	2	-	-	1	-	10
Snaith -.	1922/23	only	1	-	-	-	-	-	-
Snowden R.S.	1886/87	1892/93	67	10	-	-	-	-	11
Sobey D.	1973/74	only	4	-	-	-	-	-	-
Solomons S.J.	1973/74	1980/81	11	-	-	-	-	-	-
Somerville H.R.	1905/06	only	1	-	-	-	-	-	-
Souster F.C.	1920/21	1921/22	13	2	-	-	-	-	6
Spence T.	1967/68	1969/70	46	19	-	-	-	-	57
Spicer I.	1910/11	1919/20	15	1	-	-	-	-	3
Sproul D.L.	1952/53	only	1	-	-	-	-	-	-
Squibbs R.A.	1936/37	1938/39	38	9	4	3	1	-	48
Squirrell W.E.	1924/25	1928/29	8	-	-	-	-	-	-
Stafford C.	1905/06	1906/07	25	-	-	-	-	-	-
Stagg E.	1923/24	only	1	-	-	-	-	-	-
Staines L.	1880/81	1881/82	5	-	-	-	-	-	-
Standerwick D.C.	1959/60	only	1	-	-	-	-	-	-
Stanley C.G.J.	1932/33	1933/34	6	-	-	-	-	-	-
Stannard H.	1888/89	only	2	-	-	-	-	-	-
Stanyon H.	1887/88	only	1	-	-	-	-	-	-
Stanyon-Jacques K.A.	1932/33	1937/38	5	2	-	-	-	-	6
Stapleford J.R.	1946/47	1947/48	8	2	-	-	-	-	6
Stapleton J.W.	1937/38	1939/40	32	1	-	-	-	-	3
Starkey N.E.	1934/35	only	3	-	-	-	-	-	-
Steadman W.	1988/89	only	3	-	-	-	-	-	-
Steinitz J.J.	1894/95	only	2	1	-	-	-	-	3
Stenson S.	1922/23	only	1	-	-	-	-	-	-
Stephens J.T.	1923/24	only	1	-	-	-	-	-	-
Stephens R.J.	1928/29	only	3	1	-	-	-	-	3
Stephens R.P.	1926/27	only	1	-	-	-	-	-	-
Steptoe K.	1977/78	1985/86	15	2	-	-	-	-	8
Stevens J.	1954/55	1956/57	66	1	-	-	-	-	3
Stevenson L.W.	1936/37	only	1	-	-	-	-	-	-
Stewart I.G.H.	1954/55	only	3	-	-	-	-	-	-
Stewart K.	1963/64	1964/65	14	1	-	-	-	-	3
Stewart W.	1891/92	1892/93	25	1	-	-	-	-	2
Stimpson K.	1945/46	only	6	3	-	-	-	-	9
Stirling R.V.	1948/49	1952/53	75	1	-	-	-	-	3
Stocks F.W.	1894/95	only	1	-	-	-	-	-	-
Stokes L.J.	1945/46	1946/47	26	-	-	-	-	-	-
Stone P.H.	1979/80	1981/82	9	-	-	-	-	-	-
Storer D.	1957/58	only	3	-	-	-	-	-	-
Storey K.	1913/14	only	1	-	-	-	-	-	-
Storrs H.H.	1921/22	1923/24	9	5	-	-	-	-	15
Straker H.	1899/00	only	4	-	-	-	-	-	-
Strang -.	1928/29	only	1	-	-	-	-	-	-
Stratton L.	1984/85	1985/86	4	-	-	-	-	-	-
Streather W.J.	1923/24	1924/25	8	-	-	-	-	-	-
Strickland P.	1977/78	1978/79	3	-	-	-	-	-	-
Sturges W.H.	1888/89	1892/93	114	22	-	-	-	-	32
Sturgess H.	1919/20	only	1	-	-	-	-	-	-
Sturrock T.	1904/05	only	1	-	-	-	-	-	-
Sturtridge G.S.	1936/37	only	1	1	-	-	-	-	3
Sulley A.	1887/88	1892/93	6	6	3	-	-	-	13
Sulley W.	1881/82	only	2	-	-	-	-	-	-
Sutcliffe J.	1913/14	only	4	-	-	-	-	-	-
Sutton N.	1903/04	1904/05	32	10	-	-	1	-	34
Swain A.E.	1903/04	1906/07	66	2	-	-	-	-	6
Swain M.	1895/96	1903/04	5	2	-	-	-	-	6
Swain P.	1904/05	1905/06	2	-	-	-	-	-	-
Swain R.P.	1893/94	1897/98	97	13	-	-	-	-	39
Swan J.S.	1957/58	1958/59	51	20	-	-	-	-	60
Swanwick L.	1954/55	only	2	-	-	-	-	-	-
Sweatman E.A.	1926/27	1930/31	19	3	-	-	-	-	9
Swift -.	1892/93	only	1	-	-	-	-	-	-
Sykes W.	1891/92	only	5	-	-	-	-	-	-
Symington J.W.	1880/81	1883/84	49	5	-	-	1	-	8
Symington K.W.	1928/29	only	4	1	-	-	-	-	3
Symonds F.B.	1954/55	1958/59	6	3	-	-	-	-	9
Tahany M.P.	1945/46	1947/48	33	3	-	1	-	-	12
Tarr F.N.	1905/06	1913/14	94	24	-	-	-	-	72
Tassell C.	1974/75	only	1	-	-	-	-	-	-
Tate C.B.	1925/26	only	7	1	-	-	-	-	3
Tate J.R.	1951/52	1952/53	4	-	-	-	-	-	-
Tatham L.	1957/58	1962/63	89	14	1	2	5	-	65
Taylor F.	1910/11	1923/24	276	36	-	-	-	-	108
Taylor F.M.	1907/08	1922/23	294	97	-	-	1	-	295
Taylor G.C.	1922/23	1923/24	3	1	-	-	-	-	3
Taylor G.W.	1880/81	1881/82	6	-	-	-	-	-	-
Taylor J.A.S.	1936/37	1939/40	37	4	2	-	8	-	48
Taylor J.E.	1954/55	1958/59	49	12	-	-	-	-	36
Tearle A.	1921/22	only	1	-	-	-	-	-	-
Tebbutt J.L.	1926/27	only	1	-	-	-	-	-	-
Tebbutt R.S.	1981/82	1990/91	156	28	-	-	-	-	112
Terrington H.L.	1947/48	1949/50	31	2	2	1	3	-	22
Thacker T.A.	1987/88	to date	47	5	-	-	-	-	20
Thomas A.	1897/98	only	1	-	-	-	-	-	-
Thomas A.L.	1910/11	1911/12	6	2	-	-	-	-	6
Thomas D.G.	1982	only	2	-	-	-	-	-	-
Thomas D.J.	1923/24	1924/25	6	-	-	-	-	-	-

NAME	FROM	TO	APPS	T	C	PG	DG	GM	PTS
Thomas D.W.	1892/93	only	1	-	-	-	-	-	-
Thomas G.	1936/37	1937/38	8	3	-	-	-	-	9
Thomas G.M.	1919/20	1920/21	19	5	-	-	-	1	18
Thomas H.G.	1945/46	1952/53	105	38	-	-	1	-	117
Thomas M.	1973/74	1974/75	7	2	-	-	-	-	8
Thomas S.	1923/24	only	1	-	-	-	-	-	-
Thomas -.	1896/97	only	1	-	-	-	-	-	-
Thomas -.	1908/09	only	1	-	-	-	-	-	-
Thompson A.C.	1895/96	only	1	1	-	-	-	-	3
Thompson C.F.	1892/93	only	1	-	-	-	-	-	-
Thompson C.H.B.	1904/05	only	1	-	-	-	-	-	-
Thompson J.	1907/08	only	2	-	-	-	-	-	-
Thompson J.D.	1911/12	1912/13	3	-	-	-	-	-	-
Thompson J.S.	1954/55	1961/62	166	2	-	-	-	-	6
Thompson W.E.	1898/99	1900/01	17	1	-	-	-	-	3
Thompson W.E.	1946/47	1949/50	16	1	-	-	-	-	3
Thompson W.S.	1926/27	1932/33	13	-	-	-	-	-	-
Thorneloe J.E.	1919/20	only	7	-	-	-	-	-	-
Thorneloe N.T.	1919/20	1929/30	125	8	19	3	-	-	71
Thorneloe P.B.L.	1945/46	1957/58	221	11	-	-	-	-	33
Thornley P.T.	1987/88	1988/89	28	8	-	-	-	-	32
Thornton D.L.	1932/33	only	1	-	-	-	-	-	-
Thornton J.A.C.	1919/20	1920/21	2	1	-	-	-	-	3
Thorpe H.C.	1892/93	only	1	-	-	-	-	-	-
Timlock C.	1898/99	1903/04	4	-	-	-	-	-	-
Timms G.E.	1912/13	1913/14	25	10	-	-	-	-	30
Timson R.C.	1948/49	only	5	-	-	-	-	-	-
Timson -.	1907/08	only	1	-	-	-	-	-	-
Tindall N.J.	1932/33	1933/34	5	3	-	-	-	-	9
Toach R.	1929/30	only	1	-	-	-	-	-	-
Todman D.I.	1928/29	only	1	-	-	-	-	-	-
Toft H.B.	1934/35	only	1	-	-	-	-	-	-
Tom P.W.G.	1963/64	1967/68	130	7	-	-	-	-	21
Tomalin I.	1977/78	only	1	-	-	-	-	-	-
Tomlin F.M.	1933/34	only	5	-	-	-	-	-	-
Toone A.	1955/56	only	1	-	-	-	-	-	-
Toone F.C.	1891/92	1892/93	22	5	-	-	-	-	10
Toone H.	1903/04	only	5	-	-	-	-	-	-
Toone W.G.	1935/36	only	4	-	-	-	-	-	-
Topham H.G.	1885/86	only	3	-	-	-	-	-	-
Touhey J.	1892/93	1893/94	48	7	-	-	-	-	19
Towell A.C.	1947/48	1949/50	93	12	-	-	5	-	52
Towns S.	1992/93	only	1	-	-	-	-	-	-
Townsend J.W.	1929/30	only	3	-	-	-	-	-	-
Townsend N.	1933/34	1935/36	6	1	-	-	-	-	3
Traders F.B.	1928/29	only	1	-	-	-	-	-	-
Trebley J.	1880/81	only	1	-	-	-	-	-	-
Treharne G.J.	1937/38	1938/39	12	6	-	-	-	-	18
Tressler C.J.	1980/81	1991/92	264	14	-	-	-	-	56
Truman D.	1970/71	1972/73	14	1	-	-	-	-	4
Tucker G.R.	1948/49	1949/50	5	1	-	-	-	-	3
Tucker R.	1966/67	only	1	-	-	-	-	-	-
Tudor R.E.	1945/46	1949/50	73						
Turnbull F.	1921/22	only	1	-	-	-	-	-	-
Turnbull W.	1928/29	only	1	-	-	-	-	-	-
Turner A.	1880/81	1890/9	25	1	-	-	-	-	1
Turner J.A.	1957/58	only	5	-	-	-	-	-	-
Turney F.H.R.	1923/24	1927/28	3	-	-	-	-	-	-
Twigg J.	1912/13	1913/14	37	2	-	-	-	-	6
Tyler E.	1882/83	1884/85	7	-	-	-	-	-	-
Tyler F.	1891/92	only	1	-	-	-	-	-	-
Tyler H.P.	1927/28	1929/30	12	2	-	-	-	-	6
Underwood D.E.	1905/06	only	21	5	-	-	1	-	19
Underwood R.	1983/84	to date	151	95	-	-	-	-	385
Underwood T.	1987/88	to date	64	42	-	-	-	-	177
Ungoed-Thomas L.	1930/31	only	8	2	-	-	-	-	6
Upex M.	1990/91	only	3	-	-	-	-	-	-
Usher H.N.	1921/22	only	10						
Usher R.H.C.	1921/22	1923/24	69	5	-	-	-	-	15
Vallance G.P.C.	1929/30	1938/39	200	27	4	5	-	-	104
Varnish H.L.	1937/38	only	1	-	-	-	-	-	-
Vears G.	1918/19	1921/22	85	6	-	-	-	-	18

NAME	FROM	TO	APPS	T	C	PG	DG	GM	PTS
Venables P.F.R.	1930/31	only	7	-	-	-	-	-	-
Vesty A.B.	1946/47	only	1	-	-	-	-	-	-
Vesty P.N.	1971/72	1975/76	47	-	-	-	-	-	-
Vine E.R.	1935/36	only	1	-	-	-	-	-	-
Vity E.	1893/94	1894/95	32	5	-	-	-	-	15
Voakes W.J.	1898/99	1902/03	9	2	-	-	-	-	6
Voce J.	1886/87	only	5	1	-	-	-	-	1
Voss J.	1902/03	1906/07	3	-	-	-	-	-	-
Wackett E.C.	1923/24	only	1	-	-	-	-	-	-
Waddell D.A.	1912/13	only	11	2	-	-	-	-	6
Waddingham D.	1980/81	1985	23	-	-	-	-	-	-
Wade M.R.	1955/56	1966/67	166	27	-	-	2	-	87
Wade S.C.	1937/38	1938/39	4	-	-	-	-	-	-
Wainwright C.Y.	1880/81	1883/84	30	1	-	-	-	-	1
Waite K.A.	1937/38	only	1	-	-	-	-	-	-
Wakefield W.W.	1920/21	1923/24	29	10	-	-	-	-	30
Waldock C.H.M.	1923/24	1925/26	7	1	-	-	-	-	3
Wale A.	1880/81	1885/86	68	6	-	-	1	-	9
Wale H.	1907/08	only	1	-	-	-	-	-	-
Wales C.B.	1922/23	1925/26	3	-	-	-	-	-	-
Walker D.F.	1933/34	only	4	-	-	-	-	-	-
Walker G.F.	1895/96	1896/97	4	1	-	-	-	-	3
Walker J.B.	1894/95	only	1	-	-	-	-	-	-
Walker J.G.	1880/81	1881/82	5	-	-	-	-	-	-
Walker M.R.	1956/57	1966/67	216	3	-	-	-	-	9
Walker S.G.	1934/35	1935/36	8	3	-	-	-	-	9
Walker T.M.	1983/84	1984/85	8	1	-	-	-	-	4
Wallace W.	1922/23	1928/29	10	11	-	-	-	-	33
Wallace -.	1889/90	only	1	-	1	-	-	-	2
Walley T.A.	1973/74	1979/80	30	2	-	-	-	-	8
Walsh J.	1888/89	only	1	-	-	-	-	-	-
Walton E.J.	1901/02	only	1	-	-	-	-	-	-
Walton F.L.J.	1964/65	1967/68	139	3	-	-	-	-	9
Ward A.	1952/53	only	2	-	-	-	-	-	-
Ward E.	1905/06	only	1	-	-	-	-	-	-
Ward E.	1920/21	only	5	-	-	-	-	-	-
Ward G.	1893/94	only	1	-	-	-	-	-	-
Ward G.	1902/03	only	1	-	-	-	-	-	-
Ward G.	1909/10	1925/26	361	21	-	-	-	-	63
Ward L.F.	1889/90	1891/92	70	15	27	1	-	1	102
Ward P.E.	1928/29	1938/39	43	1	-	-	-	-	3
Ward R.E.H.	1928/29	only	1	-	-	-	-	-	-
Ward W.	1913/14	1919/20	2	-	-	-	-	-	-
Wardrop D.	1922/23	only	2	1	-	-	-	-	3
Wareham R.A.	1990/91	to date	9	-	-	-	-	-	-
Warner E.J.	1945/46	only	2	-	-	-	-	-	-
Warner P.A.	1934/35	only	1	-	-	-	-	-	-
Warner R.H.	1880/81	1883/84	10	1	-	-	-	-	1
Warren W.	1882/83	only	1	-	-	-	-	-	-
Warwood A.M.	1988/89	1991/92	27	4	-	-	-	-	16
Watchorn R.C.	1900/01	1909/10	65	4	-	-	-	-	12
Waterfield W.	1928/29	only	2	-	-	-	-	-	-
Waterman S.L.	1911/12	only	1	-	-	-	-	-	-
Waters J.A.	1933/34	only	1	-	-	-	-	-	-
Watkin C.E.	1937/38	1948/49	117	2	64	34	-	-	236
Watkins J.	1911/12	only	1	-	-	-	-	-	-
Watkiss T.	1959/60	only	1	-	-	-	-	-	-
Watney H.B.	1922/23	only	1	-	-	-	-	-	-
Watson J.R.	1903/04	1913/14	229	46	1	-	-	-	140
Watson R.	1899/00	only	3	-	-	-	-	-	-
Watson R.	1970/71	1975/76	70	5	-	-	-	-	20
Watson W.	1911/12	only	1	-	-	-	-	-	-
Watson W.H.	1884/85	only	1	-	-	-	-	-	-
Watt J.	1973/74	only	2	-	-	-	-	-	-
Watts C.E.	1891/92	1896/97	44	11	-	-	1	-	33
Watts L.	1927/28	only	2	-	-	-	-	-	-
Watts W.A.	1889/90	1893/94	52	11	1	-	1	-	28
Watts W.E.	1880/81	1881/82	5	1	-	-	-	-	1
Watts W.J.	1913/14	1923/24	70	29	-	-	-	-	87
Wayte A.P.	1923/24	only	1	-	-	-	-	-	-
Webb D.	1976/77	only	1	-	-	-	-	-	-
Weighill R.H.G.	1950/51	only	8	-	-	-	-	-	-
Weinberg G.	1972/73	only	6	3	-	-	-	-	12
Wells F.S.	1923/24	1925/26	13	4	-	-	-	-	12

NAME	FROM	TO	APPS	T	C	PG	DG	GM	PTS
Wells J.M.	1982/83	to date	271	44	-	-	-	-	178
Wemyss A.	1925/26	only	1	-	-	-	-	-	-
West D.E.	1988/89	1989/90	4	1	-	-	-	-	4
West F.	1930/31	only	1	-	-	-	-	-	-
Weston C.J.	1946/47	only	1	-	-	-	-	-	-
Weston T.A.	1906/07	only	1	-	-	-	-	-	-
Wetherell C.W.S.	1898/99	only	1	-	-	-	-	-	-
Wetton R.H.	1923/24	only	2	-	-	-	-	-	-
Wheeler F.E.	1880/81	only	1	-	-	-	-	-	-
Wheeler P.J.	1969/70	1985/86	349	66*	61	69	-	-	589
Wheeler W.A.	1880/81	1889/90	26	-	4	-	-	-	8
Whetstone E.D.	1896/97	1901/02	61	5	-	-	-	-	15
Whibley D.F.	1970/71	1972/73	45	3	71	75	-	-	379
Whitcombe M.	1981/82	1985/86	68	8	-	-	-	-	32
White A.	1910/11	only	2	-	-	-	-	-	-
White G.A.	1938/39	only	3	-	3	-	-	-	6
White G.R.	1929/30	1930/31	19	7	-	-	-	-	21
White H.V.	1957/58	1963/64	147	6	-	-	-	-	18
White J.C.	1961/62	1965/66	2	-	4	2	-	-	14
White J.H.	1959/60	only	1	-	-	-	-	-	-
White J.R.	1974/75	1980	73	15	-	-	-	-	60
White R.	1988/8	only	3	-	-	-	-	-	-
White T.	1992/93	only	1	-	-	-	-	-	-
White -.	1888/89	only	1	-	-	-	-	-	-
Whitehall A.	1968/69	only	2	-	-	-	-	-	-
Whitehead A.D.	1880/81	1884/85	33	2	-	-	-	-	2
Whitehead M.E.	1894/95	1901/02	146	20	-	-	-	-	60
Whitehurst J.B.H.	1891/92	only	8	-	-	-	-	-	-
Whitestone R.	1899/00	only	1	-	-	-	-	-	-
Whitley H.	1925/26	only	1	1	-	-	-	-	3
Wickson J.	1920/21	1923/24	16	3	-	-	-	-	9
Wiener R.A.K.	1929/30	1932/33	101	3	-	-	-	-	9
Wigley B.T.	1959/60	only	14	4	-	-	-	-	12
Wigley D.L.	1991	to date	14	4	-	-	-	-	18
Wigley S.T.	1990/91	to date	4	2	-	-	-	-	8
Wigley V.	1969/70	1970/71	4	-	-	-	-	-	-
Wilby W.	1891/92	only	2	-	-	-	-	-	-
Wilcock J.H.	1888/89	1889/90	5	2	-	-	-	-	2
Wilcock S.H.	1957/58	only	1	-	-	-	-	-	-
Wilford K.R.	1978/79	1979/80	5	-	-	-	-	-	-
Wilkes T.R.	1889/90	only	4	-	-	-	-	-	-
Wilkie I.A.	1963/64	1964/65	8	1	-	-	-	-	3
Wilkins G.M.C.	1918/19	1923/24	4	1	-	-	-	-	3
Wilkins W.C.	1921/22	1923/24	50	20	-	-	-	-	60
Wilkinson B.	1885/86	1889/90	42	7	-	-	-	-	7
Wilkinson E.	1900/01	1902/03	12	2	-	-	-	-	6
Wilkinson H.	1895/96	1904/05	233	153	3	-	6	-	489
Wilkinson H.C.	1892/93	1893/94	37	6	-	-	-	-	16
Wilkinson J.	1908/09	1913/14	19	1	2	1	-	-	10
Wilkinson J.	1919/20	1921/22	97	-	70	7	2	-	169
Wilkinson J.S.	1886/87	1888/89	18	1	-	-	-	-	1
Willars G.G.	1959/60	1986/87	338	38	-	-	-	-	129
Willcox J.	1918/19	only	1	-	-	-	-	-	-
Willcox M.J.	1963/64	1964/65	4	-	-	-	-	-	-
Willcox R.J.	1935/36	1936/37	41	6	-	-	-	-	18
Willey W.J.	1888/89	only	12	3	-	-	-	-	3
Williams A.	1938/39	only	2	-	-	-	-	-	-
Williams A.K.	1979/80	1986/87	191	64	-	-	-	-	256
Williams C.H.	1929/30	1935/36	19	3	-	-	-	-	9
Williams D.	1892/93	only	19	4	-	-	-	-	8
Williams D.	1979/80	1982/83	17	8	-	-	-	-	32
Williams E.	1935/36	only	3	-	-	-	-	-	-
Williams F.L.	1936/37	only	1	-	-	-	-	-	-
Williams G.	1957/58	only	7	3	-	-	-	-	9
Williams G.	1983/84	only	2	-	-	-	-	-	-
Williams G.E.S.	1929/30	1931/32	7	2	-	-	-	-	6
Williams G.F.	1935/36	only	1	-	-	-	-	-	-
Williams I.	1924/25	only	1	-	-	-	-	-	-
Williams J.R.	1950/51	only	1	-	-	-	-	-	-
Williams R.	1972/73	only	1	-	-	-	-	-	-
Williamson W.	1889/90	only	5	-	-	-	-	-	-
Willis K.B.	1938/39	only	3	-	-	-	-	-	-
Wills S.R.	1989/90	to date	24	8	11	13	-	-	93
Wilson G.	1913/14	only	25	-	-	-	-	-	-
Wilson T.W.	1906/07	1907/08	5	2	-	-	-	-	6
Wilson W.C.	1908/09	1910/11	5	1	-	-	-	-	3
Wolfe S.G.	1913/14	only	10	-	-	-	-	-	-
Wood F.E.	1920/21	1929/30	69	26	-	1	1	-	85
Wood G.H.	1928/29	1930/31	6	2	-	-	-	-	6
Wood G.W.	1906/07	1922/23	388	102	15	-	-	-	336
Wood J.	1985	only	1	-	-	-	-	-	-
Wood K.B.	1906/07	1918/19	121	33	-	-	4	-	115
Woodford F.	1896/97	only	1	-	-	-	-	-	-
Woodford G.H.	1903/04	only	2	-	-	-	-	-	-
Woodhead L.	1920/21	only	1	-	-	-	-	-	-
Woodward A.	1901/02	only	3	-	-	-	-	-	-
Woodward C.R.	1979/80	1985/86	148	43	4	-	5	-	195
Woodyatt A.W.	1894/95	1898/99	22	7	3	-	-	-	27
Woolerton J.	1908/09	only	1	-	-	-	-	-	-
Wooller G.	1936/37	only	2	-	-	-	-	-	-
Woolley J.	1918/19	only	6	-	-	-	-	-	-
Woolley J.	1957/58	1958/59	5	-	-	-	-	-	-
Wormleighton J.L.	1932/33	1936/37	121	3	-	-	-	-	9
Worsley -.	1905/06	only	2	1	-	-	-	-	3
Worthington C.E.	1880/81	1885/86	14	-	-	-	-	-	-
Wotherspoon W.L.	1889/90	1890/91	18	-	-	-	-	-	-
Wrench M.J.B.	1961/62	only	5	-	-	-	-	-	-
Wright A.	1905/06	only	5	-	-	-	-	-	-
Wright A.E.	1887/88	only	5	-	-	-	-	-	-
Wright D.	1990/91	only	3	2	-	-	-	-	8
Wright F.	1922/23	only	38	11	-	-	-	-	33
Wright G.	1922/23	only	1	-	-	-	-	-	-
Wright L.	1907/08	only	3	-	-	-	-	-	-
Wright R.E.	1933/34	only	1	-	-	-	-	-	-
Wright S.R.	1889/90	only	3	-	-	-	-	-	-
Wright S.T.H.	1949/50	only	5	-	-	-	-	-	-
Wright S.W.	1895/96	only	2	-	-	-	-	-	-
Wykes E.C.	1894/95	1903/04	21	-	-	-	-	-	-
Wykes S.R.	1889/90	1891/92	25	1	-	-	-	-	1
Wyman A.A.	1934/35	only	1	-	-	-	-	-	-
Wyness J.	1966/67	only	1	-	-	-	-	-	-
Wynne C.H.L.	1913/14	1923/24	7	7	-	-	-	-	21
Wynne E.	1913/14	only	7	1	-	-	-	-	3
Wynne O.	1890/91	1892/93	34	-	-	-	1	-	3
Yandle M.J.	1969/70	1972/73	155	29*	-	-	1	-	101
Yarnall A.L.	1926/27	only	2	-	1	-	-	-	2
Yeld G.G.	1900/01	1908/09	69	1	20	3	-	-	52
Yeomans S.C.	1897/98	1898/99	7	-	-	-	-	-	-
Yiend W.	1895/96	only	10	2	-	-	-	-	6
York N.A.	1933/34	1938/39	46	2	26	16	-	1	109
Yorke J.	1889/90	1892/93	70	5	-	-	-	-	7
Young A.J.	1892/93	only	1	-	-	-	-	-	-
Young J.	1972/73	only	1	1	-	-	-	-	4
Young L.	1880/81	1884/85	37	6	-	-	-	-	6
Young W.G.	1937/38	1938/39	38	13	-	-	2	-	47
Younger G.D.	1924/25	only	1	-	-	-	-	-	-
Youngs N.G.	1981/82	1988/89	145	71*	-	-	-	-	284

OFFICERS OF THE CLUB

PRESIDENTS

1880-1881	W A Wheeler		1965-1968	D J Norman
1881-1891	E S Burnaby		1968-1971	H P Hughes
1891-1901	J Parsons		1971-1974	J T W Berry
1901-1912	J Collier		1974-1977	R J Willcox
1912-1924	H W Salmon		1977-1979	K R Kinder
1924-1926	K McAlpin		1979-1981	E C Lacey
1926-1931	Sir Samuel Faire		1981-1983	H W Sibson
1931-1939	Sir Frederick Oliver		1983-1985	P Herbert
1939-1945	A Lovell		1985-1987	R Beason
1945-1951	W N Bradshaw		1987-1989	K P Andrews
1951-1957	C W Cross		1989-1991	B T C Small
1957-1959	J E Thorneloe		1991-1993	G G Willars
1959-1962	R L Bedingfield		1993-	J T Thomas
1962-1965	R J Barr			

HONORARY SECRETARIES

1880-1881	J A Lakin		1895-1928	T H Crumbie
1880-1881	J Parsons		1928-1957	J E Thorneloe
1881-1890	H W Salmon		1957-1962	R J Barr
1890-1891	G R Wykes		1962-1966	R E Gerrard
1891-1893	K McAlpin		1966-1982	J D Day
1893-1894	J H Harcock		1982-	J A Allen
1894-1895	T W Pettifor			

CLUB CAPTAINS

1880-1881	A E Brice		1949-1950	A C Towell
	Resigned due to illness in September 1881		1950-1952	W K T Moore
1881-1882	A T Porter		1952-1953	A D Bolesworth
1882-1883	L Young		1953-1955	J M Jenkins
1883-1885	J G S Coleman		1955-1956	J Elders
1885-1886	W A Sheffield		1956-1958	T Bleasdale
1886-1889	J Parsons		1958-1959	J S Swan
	resigned at Christmas 1889		1959-1960	T Bleasdale
1889	R S Snowden			*(J M Jenkins was originally appointed)*
1889-1890	W R Porter		1960-1963	C G Martin
1890-1891	A McKechnie		1963-1964	M R Wade
1891-1893	W H Sturges			*Injury forced his replacement in Nov 1964*
1893-1894	A E Cooke		1964-1965	M J Harrison
1894-1896	E Redman		1965-1968	D J Matthews
1896-1899	A O Jones		1968-1969	G G Willars
1899-1901	W J Foreman		1969-1970	K P Andrews
1901-1902	J W Garner		1970-1971	J A Allen
1902-1904	A O Jones		1971-1972	R V Grove
1904-1906	S Matthews		1972-1973	G G Willars
1906-1907	R F Russell		1973-1975	P J Wheeler
1907-1908	S Matthews			*(M J Yandle was originally appointed)*
1908-1911	J R Watson		1975-1976	R S Money
1911-1914	P W Lawrie		1976-1977	R E Rowell
1918-1920	W J Allen		1977-1978	B P Hall
1920-1923	P W Lawrie		1978-1981	P J Wheeler
1923-1924	W W Wakefield		1981-1983	S R Johnson
1924-1928	H L V Day		1983-1985	I R Smith
1928-1930	F D Prentice		1985-1987	L Cusworth
1930-1932	H D Greenlees		1987-1989	P W Dodge
1932-1933	D J Norman		1989	D Richards
1933-1934	R A Buckingham			*Injury forced his replacement in Sept 1989*
1934-1936	B C Gadney		1989-1990	L Cusworth
1936-1938	R J Barr		1990-1991	D Richards
1938-1947	J T W Berry		1991-1993	J M Wells
1947-1949	H P Jerwood		1993-	D Richards

ABCDEFGHIJK
LMNOPQRSTU
VWXYZABCDE
FGHIJKLMNOP
QRSTUVWXYZ
ABCDEFGHIJK
LMNOPQRSTU

EARLY MEMORABILIA

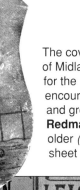

The cover of Tigers' Souvenir Brochure to celebrate the trio of Midland Counties Cup victories *(top left)*, and a 2/6d ticket for the 1903 Final *(top right)*. Two early beer-mats offer encouragement, one from 1892 with Tigers in scarlet, white and green stripes, while the other, featuring **Edward Redman** was issued by the Bedford Hotel in 1895. Even older *(below)* from the days before Welford Road, is a team sheet from 1890 when Leicester played in claret and grey.

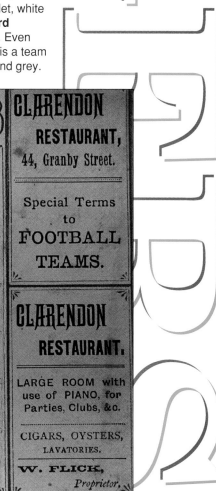

TIGERS

The magnificent scroll *(above)* was presented to **Sid Penney** in 1910 to mark his retirement from the game and as a tribute to his completion of '500' first team games.

Below are **Tom Smith's** representative caps which include the 1908 Anglo-Welsh tour to New Zealand *(left)*, the Midland Counties season 1906/07 *(right)* and Leicester Football Club season 1906/07 *(centre)*.

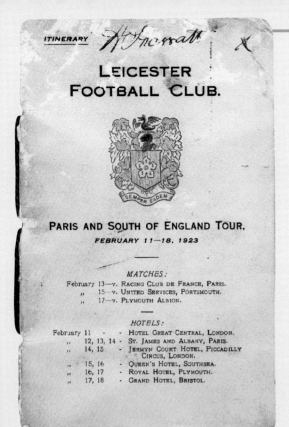

TIGERS' ON TOUR

(Below) is the tour map and itinerary for 1925 which is magnificently preserved in **George Ward's** leather-bound booklet, while *(left)* is **Herb Sharatt's** 1923 tour card for Paris and the South of England.

More recent is **Peter Thorneloe's** 1956 card *(below)* for the Easter tour to the West Country.

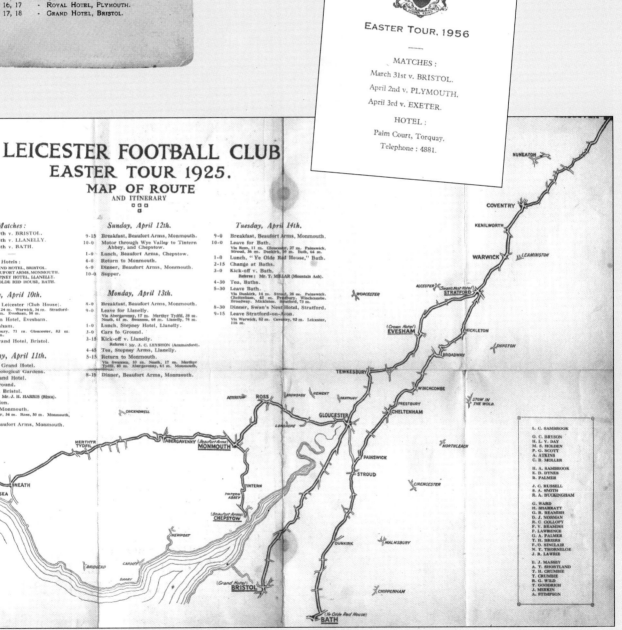

TIGERS' TRIBUTES & CELEBRATIONS

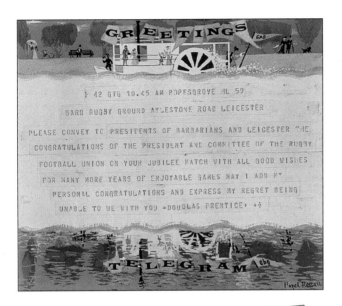

(Above) is the scroll presented in 1912 to one of Tigers' founder members **Joseph Collier** to mark his retirement as President of the Club.

(Top left) is a telegram from **Doug Prentice** on the occasion of the Jubilee Barbarians match in 1959.

(Left) is the cover of the souvenir menu published when Tigers celebrated their 75th Anniversary in 1955 with a dinner at the Bell Hotel, Leicester.

FAMOUS TIGERS PLAYERS APPEARED ON VARIOUS CIGARETTE CARDS DURING THE 1920'S AND 1930'S.

(Left) is a caricature of Leicester's Scottish international fly-half **Harry Greenlees**, while *(below left)* is England international **'Joe' Kendrew** who went on to a distinguished military career.

Also pictured in Leicester colours is scrum-half **Bernard Gadney** who in 1933/34 became the first Tiger to captain England.

CHURCHMAN'S CIGARETTES

D A KENDREW

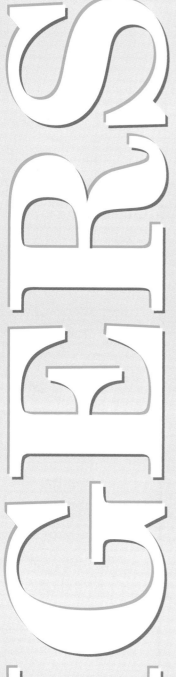

Pictured *(above)* is the first Supporters' Club membership card issued for 1948/49 to George Goodwin and *(below)* **Peter Thorneloe's** Old Player's Season Ticket for 1950-51.

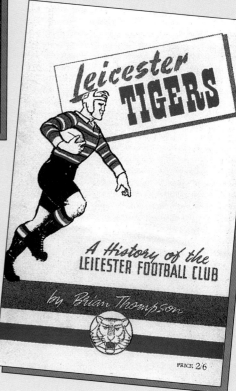

"Leicester Tigers - A History of the Leicester Football Club" was a readable little book written by former *Leicester Mercury* rugby correspondent Brian Thompson.

(Below) is a special first day cover posted at Welford Road to mark the Tigers' Centenary in 1980.

JOHN PLAYER CUP
WINNERS 1979

LEICESTER 15
MOSELEY 12

Steve Johnson in line-out action *(top)* during Tigers' spectacular 43-7 away win over Wasps in the semi-final when Leicester ran in no less than eight tries.

More semi-final action *(above)* as five Tigers combine to squash a Wasp!

At Twickenham, Tigers, seen *(left)* in more line-out action, beat Moseley 15-12 in the final to lift the trophy.

JOHN PLAYER CUP WINNERS 1980

TIGERS RETAINED THE TROPHY THE FOLLOWING YEAR WITH A CUP RUN THAT BEGAN WITH A 16-7 HOME WIN OVER ORRELL.

John Duggan is seen *(above)* lending support to a Leicester attack while *(left)* is more action from the same match.

Tigers marched on to Twickenham and *(below)* **Peter Wheeler** hoists the trophy.

LEICESTER 21 v LONDON IRISH 9

JOHN PLAYER CUP WINNERS 1981

Tigers completed a remarkable treble of Cup victories with another triumph at Twickenham, this time over Gosforth who succumbed to tries by **Steve Kenney**, **Tim Barnwell** and **'Dusty' Hare**. The three pictures here all depict action from the final.

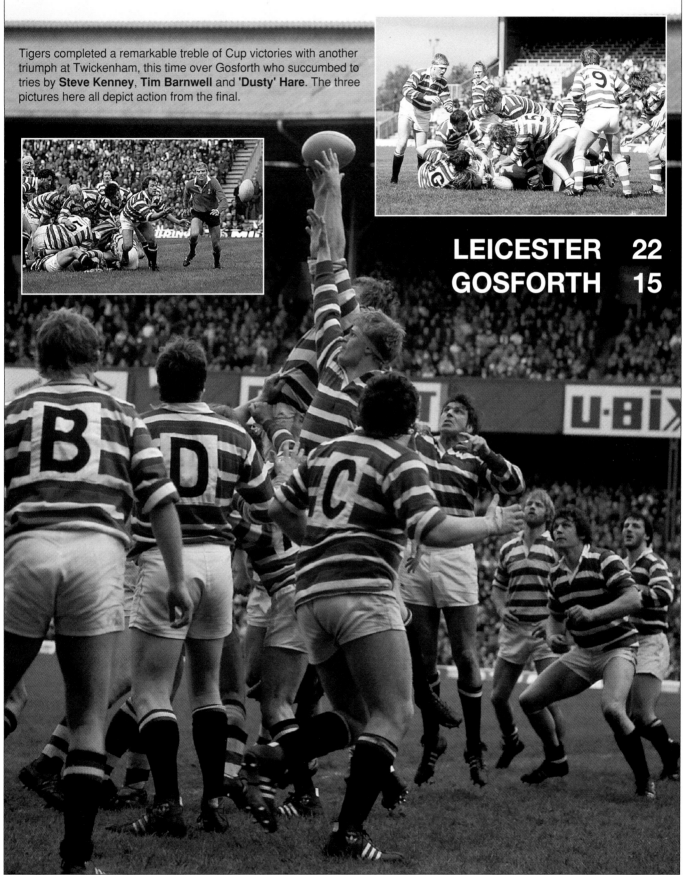

LEICESTER   22
GOSFORTH   15

PILKINGTON CUP WINNERS 1993

LEICESTER 23
HARLEQUINS 16

Tigers fourth Cup success progressed in crushing style with a 76-0 demolition of Exeter at Welford Road in the quarter-final. Here though **Rory Underwood** *(left)* is halted during another attacking wave. The semi-final brought a quite superb 28-6 win over Northampton. **Ian Bates** is pictured breaking clear, while *(below)* the team take a well-earned interval breather after their sensational first-half display had destroyed the Saints' challenge.

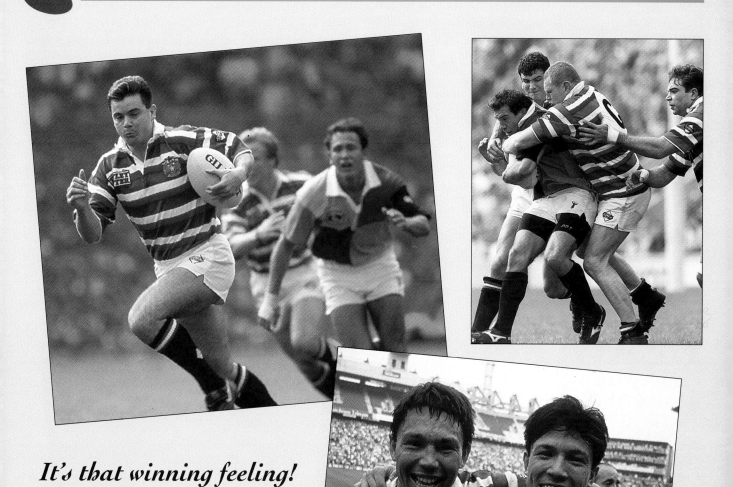

It's that winning feeling!

More scenes from the 1993 Pilkington Cup victory as **Stuart Potter** *(above)* races clear to score Leicester's first try, while a Harlequins challenge *(above right)* is halted in its tracks. It's a day of delight for Tigers' England pair **Rory** and **Tony Underwood** *(right)* and a proud moment *(below)* for the team and skipper **John Wells.**

LEAGUE CHAMPIONS 1988

Tigers were the first winners of the new Courage Clubs Championship which was clinched with a 39-15 home win over Waterloo. (*Above and right*) is action from that match, while (*right*) skipper **Paul Dodge** shows off the trophy and (*below*) is the champions line-up on the day.

NEAR MISSES!

It has not all been glory in the Cup. In 1983 Tigers lost out 22-28 to Bristol in a titanic John Player Cup final. *(Above)* is action from the game as **Les Cusworth** races free while lock **Nigel Gillingham** is in the thick of the fray.

The 1989 Pilkington Cup final brought further disappointment. **'Dusty' Hare** *(left)* finished his last match with two penalties but a wry runners'-up smile, while *(below)* **Aadel Kardooni** looks for an opening during Bath's 6-10 victory.

LEICESTER

v

BARBARIANS

TIGERS' MATCHES WITH THE BARBARIANS WILL ALWAYS HOLD A SPECIAL PLACE IN THE CLUB'S CHRISTMAS HOLIDAY CALENDAR.

There have been many memorable games and thrilling moments for the big crowds down the years, but Leicester's 41-14 success in December 1992 was certainly one for the fans to savour.

Action from that match sees **Dean Richards** *(above)* driving through, while *(left)*, **Tony Underwood** breaks clear to score one of Tigers' six tries on the day.

TIGERS' FUTURE BURNING BRIGHT?

LEICESTER'S HOPES OF FURTHER SUCCESS IN THE YEARS AHEAD LOOK PROMISING AS A NEW TEAM DEVELOPS AROUND SEVERAL KEY PLAYERS.

Two of these are England internationals **Martin Johnson** and **Tony Underwood**. A dynamic and aggressive lock forward, **Johnson** *(above)* broke into the international scene during 1993 and was also called onto the British Lions summer tour to New Zealand, while **Underwood**, who also toured with the Lions in 1993, has a devastating turn of speed and looks set to follow in the fleet and elusive footsteps of his illustrious brother Rory.

TIGERS FUTURE

Few of the leading current players fill both the Club and its growing band of supporters with as much optimism for the future as talented fair-haired flanker **Neil Back** *(right)* who surely will earn England international recognition in the immediate future.

Tigers' current front-row forwards *(below)* are affectionately known as 'The Crazy Gang'. **Darren Garforth** *(left)*, **Richard Cockerill** and **Graham Rowntree** are the trio who make-up a young and aggressive front-line who possess a genuine touch of 'steel'.

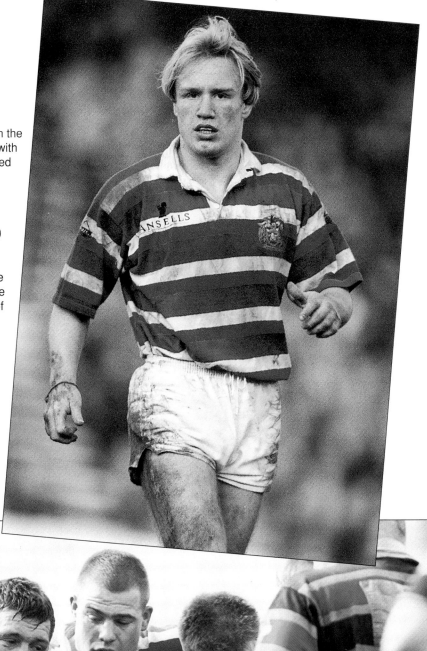

NOTES ON THE CHARTS
THE EVOLUTION OF THE LAWS AND SCORING

According to tradition rugby football was first played at Rugby School in November 1823 when William Webb Ellis (later the Reverend) picked the ball up and ran with it during a game of football. The origins prior to this could well have dated as far back as the Romans, who had a war game called 'Harpastum', (derived from the Greek word meaning to 'seize') where two opposing teams tried to carry a ball up to lines marked at each end of a playing area, and then throw it over these lines to register a score. Mauling and driving play certainly formed part of this game.

After Webb Ellis's exploits the handling code of football evolved, and was known to have been played at Cambridge University by 1839, having been introduced there by Old Rugbeians. On 28th August 1845 the Sixth Form sanctioned 37 Laws of Football played at Rugby School, extracts of this follow:
20. All matches are drawn after five days, but after three if no goal has been kicked.
25. No strangers, in any match, may have a place kick at goal.
26. No hacking with the heel, or above the knee, is fair. ('Hacking' was considered a very good thing, although officially forbidden. "It promoted running scrummages which were the beauty of the game" and "developed the passive virtues by teaching those who play to keep their tempers sometimes under trying circumstances.")
28. No player may wear projecting nails or iron plates on the heels or soles of his shoes or boots.
29. No player may take the ball out of the Close.

In those early days the playing pitch was 200 yards long by 100 yards wide and the in-goal area was limitless. Players were known to dodge in and out amongst the spectators in an attempt to ground the ball. Some of the original terms that are still in use today are offside, knock-on, touch and goal line. The word 'try' also originated here when a touch-down allowed you a try (or attempt) at goal. Goals were the only method of scoring, therefore if the kick failed no score was registered, not even for the try.

On 26th January 1871, 32 representatives from 20 clubs met at Pall Mall Restaurant in central London and formed the Rugby Football Union. The founder members were Blackheath, Richmond, Wellington College, Guy's Hospital, Harlequins, King's College, St Paul's School, Civil Service, Marlborough Nomads, Queen's House, West Kent, Wimbledon Hornets, Gipsies, Clapham Rovers, Law, Flamingoes, Lausanne, Addison, Mohicans and Belsize Park. The Wasps should have been there but did not turn up!

In June of that year the RFU approved 59 rules of rugby football, which was the foundation of the game as we know it today. Matches were to be decided on a majority of goals, that is any successful kick except a punt, either directly from the field of play, or after obtaining a 'try at goal'. Up until as recently as 1957 the conversion had to be taken with the aid of a 'placer', another member of the team who lay on the ground and held or 'placed' the ball for the goal-kicker to take the kick.

The refereeing of games was done initially by the playing captains of each team, and later by a non-playing umpire from each team. A referee was first seen in 1885/86, in addition to the umpires, who eventually became touch judges. The Rugby Union's "Regulations for the guidance of Umpires and Referees" was adopted in October 1886 when referees were provided with whistles and umpires with sticks, later to become flags.

In 1876 the methods of scoring were amended, results were now decided by a majority of goals and tries, and in some games by a complicated affair known as 'minors'. (Minors being rather like 'near misses' such as touch in goal, dead balls, missed drop goals etc.) Scoring by points was not introduced until 1886/87, a try being worth one point, a conversion two and a dropped goal three.

Since their introduction in 1886/87 the scoring values have evolved as follows:

	Try	Conv	Drop Goal	Pen Goal	Mark
	(T)	(C)	(DG)	(PG)	(GM)
1886/87 to 1888/89	1	2	3	Void	3
1889/90 to 1890/91	1	2	3	2	3
1891/92 to 1892/93	2	3	4	3	4
1893/94 to 1904/05	3	2	4	3	4
1905/06 to 1947/48	3	2	4	3	3
1948/49 to 1970/71	3	2	3	3	3
1971/72 to 1976/77	4	2	3	3	3
1977/78 to 1991/92	4	2	3	3	Void
1992/93 to date	5	2	3	3	Void

Note: Throughout the individual records and the biographical section I have retrospectively applied the scoring values introduced in 1886/87, to games played before that date for comparison purposes.

The penalty goal was not introduced until 1889, initially just as a 'free kick' for offside, and even then you could drop kick the ball between the posts to register the points. A player was allowed to call for a 'fair catch' or 'mark' virtually anywhere on the field. Hence, if you were within range anyone from your team could then take a place kick to attempt to score 'a goal from a mark'. This scoring method however, ceased to exist when the Free Kick clause was introduced in 1977/78. Another early method of scoring was a Field Goal, which was achieved by fly kicking a rolling or stationary ball from the ground between the posts, this was abolished in 1905.

THE RESULTS CHART

Leicester's games for each season are listed in chronological sequence the game numbers cross-referring to the appearance chart. Cancelled games are also shown with a reason for the cancellation if possible. The opponents name is shown in capitals for a home fixture, and is followed where applicable by the tournament details in brackets.

Cup Competitions and round number
MCC - Midland Counties Cup
RFU - RFU Knockout Cup
JPC - John Player Cup
PC - Pilkington Cup
Round numbers also include
P-Preliminary, R-Replay, QF-Quarter Final,
SF-Semi Final, F-Final)

League Competitions
MMT - Midland Merit Table
JSA - John Smith's National Merit Table A
CL - Courage League - Division One

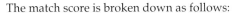

The match score is broken down as follows:

G   - Converted try (traditionally known as a goal)
T   - Unconverted try
D   - Drop goal (an asterisk in this column indicates that a
      Goal from a Mark is included in the total)
P   - Penalty goal

All Leicester's individual scorers are then named with the type of score following in brackets:

T   - Try (an asterisk denotes a Penalty try is included)
C   - Conversion
D   - Drop Goal
P   - Penalty Goal
M   - Goal from a mark.

THE APPEARANCE CHARTS AND TEAM FORMATIONS

The appearance charts denote the team lineups for every game, corresponding with the game number on the results chart. It indicates which position each player played in that game, as follows:

FB	- Full-back	3Q	- Threequarter
W	- Wing threequarter	FE	- Five-eighth
C	- Centre threequarter	HB	- Half-back
FH	- Fly-half	F	- Forward
SH	- Scrum-half	WF	- Wing-forward
P	- Prop forward	BR	- Back-row forward
H	- Hooker	r1	- Replacement 1
L	- Lock forward	r2	- Replacement 2
FL	- Flanker		
8	- Number eight		

Modern day terminology for names of positions has been used throughout to avoid confusion, even though the players may have been described differently during their playing days. For instance, a 1950s wing-forward would be described as he is known today, a flanker, even though that term was quite unknown at the time.

15 players a-side was first standardised in 1875. By 1880, 2 full-backs, 2 threequarters, 2 half-backs, and 9 forwards was the usual formation, and the initial one which Leicester adopted. From 1881/2 one of the full-backs moved into the three-quarter line and this formation remained for two seasons, when following the lead of Cardiff Leicester adopted a fourth threequarter. This configuration was first used against South Warwickshire Rovers in December 1883, and became the norm by the end of the 1889/90 season. It is only from then that wing and centre threequarters are denoted by 'W' and 'C', prior to this I have used '3Q' to describe those positions.

Up until the turn of the century the half-backs had a dual role; sharing the scrum-half and outside or fly-half duties, and were sometimes known as left or right halves. In these instances I have used 'HB' to describe both positions.

In the late 1890s the New Zealanders introduced another back formation which they still use today, comprising of three threequarters with an extra man permanently stationed between the centre threequarter and the fly-half. This extra man became known as the five-eighth, or later the second five-eighth (with the fly-half being labelled as the first five-eighth). Leicester experimented with this formation for the first six games of the 1906/7 season, twelve months after testing out a variation of this theme by having just one five-eighth replace the fly-half. This lineup also included a wing-forward or 'rover' so in these games I have used 'FE' to denote the five-eighth position, and 'WF' for the wing-forward player.

Initially Leicester employed nine forwards, and on three occasions ten, but more usually it was eight, a combination they have used since 1893/94. However, between December 1919 and April 1927 only seven forwards were used, when the 2-3-2 diamond scrum was adopted. The extra man was initially utilised as an additional centre-threequarter, and from 1924/25 as one of a pair of five-eighths. From 1927/28 team lineups reverted back to eight forwards and have remained so ever since.

Specialisation has not always existed therefore it is only since the last war that the prop/hooker/prop/lock/lock/flanker/number-eight/flanker formation so familiar today is given with any certainty. Before then scrummages were carried out on a 'first-up, first-down' free-for-all basis, in these cases 'F' has been used to denote all the forwards.

In 1922 the scrummaging laws were changed to outlaw the 'rover' or wing forward, and prescribe that front rows had to contain no more than three players, subsequently this became the forerunner of the modern 3-4-1 scrum pattern (always favoured in South Africa). The front-row forward evolved into the hooker or prop; the back or side-row forwards ultimately became flankers; number 8's and second-row men became, much more precisely, lock-forwards.

From 1976/77 onwards, replacements for injured players are recorded only if they actually played for any part of the match in question. On the charts the first replacement is designated 'r1' and the player he replaced is shown with an *. The second replacement (if applicable) is 'r2', the player he replaced marked with ^.

On the right of the appearance table are a further three columns: 'APPS'-for the total number of appearances; 'T'-for the total number of tries (an asterisk means a Penalty try is included); and 'PTS'-for the total number of points scored that season. Names of players who have made only a few appearances in a season are to be found listed alphabetically at the base of the appearances table showing position, game number in brackets, and if applicable tries scored (T) and points total in square brackets.

NO	DATE		OPPONENTS	V	RES	FOR					AGAINST					SCORERS
						G	T	D	P	PTS	G	T	D	P	PTS	
1	Oct	23	MOSELEY	H	Drew	-	-	-	-	0	-	-	-	-	0	
2		30	LEICESTER VICTORIA	H	Won	2	4	-	-	10	-	-	-	-	0	Unknown(6T,2C)
3	Nov	6	NORTHAMPTON	H	Drew	-	-	-	-	0	-	-	-	-	0	
4		13	Rushden	A	Lost	-	-	-	-	0	2	4	-	-	10	
5		20	COVENTRY	H	Won	-	2	-	-	2	-	-	-	-	0	A.T.Porter(T) Young(T)
6		27	BURTON-ON-TRENT	H	Drew	-	-	-	-	0	-	-	-	-	0	
7	Dec	4	Bedford Rovers	A	Won	1	-	-	-	3	-	1	-	-	1	Foster(C) Hart(T)
8		11	Moseley	A	Won	1	1	-	-	4	-	-	-	-	0	Unknown(2T,C)
9		18	Market Harborough	A	Won	1	3	-	-	6	-	-	-	-	0	W.A.Wheeler(C) Young(T) Hudson(T) Sheen(T) Lovett(T)
10	Jan	1	Rugby Rovers	A	Drew	-	-	-	-	0	-	-	-	-	0	
11		8	RUSHDEN	H	Won	1	1	-	-	4	-	-	-	-	0	W.A.Wheeler(C) A.T.Porter(T) Coleman(T)
12	Feb	5	BURTON ANGLESEY RVRS	H	Won	1	1	-	-	4	-	-	-	-	0	W.A.Wheeler(C) Watts(T) Lovett(T)
13		19	NUNEATON	H	Won	-	1	1	-	4	-	1	-	-	1	Coleman(D) Brice(T)
14		26	Kettering	A	Drew	1	-	-	-	3	-	-	1	-	3	W.A.Wheeler(C) Lovett(T)
15	Mar	5	RUGBY ROVERS	H	Won	-	-	1	-	3	-	-	-	-	0	Parsons(D)
16		12	KETTERING	H	Lost	-	-	-	-	0	-	1	-	-	1	
17		26	Moseley	A	Lost	-	-	-	-	0	4	2	-	-	14	

INDIVIDUAL APPEARANCES 1880-1881

NAME	1	2	3	4	5	6	7	8	9	10	11	12	13	14	15	16	17	TOTAL	T	PTS
H.L.Foster	FB	-	FB	FB	FB	FB	FB	-	-	-	-	-	FB	FB	FB	FB	FB	11	-	2
W.A.Wheeler	FB	3Q	-	3Q	FB	FB	FB	-	FB	-	FB	3Q	F	HB	HB	HB	HB	14	-	8
David Corby	-	FB	-	-	-	-	-	-	FB	-	FB	-	F	-	FB	F	-	6	-	-
Sherrard Coleman	-	FB	FB	3Q	-	-	3Q	-	-	3Q	-	-	3Q	3Q	3Q	3Q	3Q	10	1	4
R.H.Warner	-	-	FB	-	-	-	-	-	-	-	FB	-	F	-	-	-	-	3	-	-
H.Foreman	-	-	-	-	-	-	-	FB	-	3Q	-	-	-	-	-	-	-	2	-	-
T.D.Hart	3Q	3Q	-	-	3Q	HB	-	-	HB	-	-	-	-	-	-	-	-	5	1	2
Arthur Porter	3Q	-	-	3Q	3Q	3Q	-	-	3Q	3Q	-	-	-	-	-	-	-	6	2	2
J.A.Lakin	-	-	3Q	-	3Q	-	3Q	-	-	-	-	-	3Q	3Q	HB	-	3Q	7	-	-
J.G.Walker	-	-	3Q	-	-	HB	-	-	FB	-	HB	-	-	-	-	-	-	4	-	-
A.Wale	-	-	-	3Q	-	-	-	3Q	HB	3Q	-	3Q	-	3Q	3Q	-	-	7	-	-
T.H.Prentice	-	-	-	-	-	-	3Q	-	3Q	-	3Q	-	-	-	3Q	-	-	4	-	-
A.E.Brice	HB	-	F	HB	F	F	F	-	F	-	-	-	HB	HB	-	HB	HB	11	1	1
L.Young	HB	HB	HB	HB	HB	HB	HB	-	HB	-	HB	-	-	-	-	-	-	9	2	2
C.Duckering	-	HB	-	-	HB	-	-	-	HB	-	-	-	-	-	-	-	-	3	-	-
H.S.Biggs	F	-	-	-	-	-	-	-	-	-	-	-	FB	-	-	-	FB	3	-	-
A.J.Burford	F	-	-	F	-	-	-	-	F	F	-	-	-	-	-	F	-	5	-	-
J.Gilbert	F	-	F	-	F	-	-	-	F	-	-	-	-	-	-	-	-	4	-	-
Jack Lovett	F	-	-	F	F	-	-	-	F	-	F	-	F	-	F	-	F	7	3	3
Thomas Pickering	F	-	-	F	-	-	-	-	-	-	-	-	-	-	-	-	F	3	-	-
W.R.Porter	F	-	-	-	-	-	-	-	-	-	F	F	-	-	-	-	F	5	-	-
F.Sheen	F	-	F	F	-	F	F	-	F	F	F	-	-	-	-	-	-	8	1	1
A.Turner	F	-	F	F	-	F	F	-	-	F	-	F	F	F	F	F	-	11	-	-
C.E.Worthington	F	-	-	-	-	F	-	-	-	-	-	-	-	-	-	-	F	3	-	-
Henry Barwick	-	F	-	F	-	-	-	-	F	-	-	-	-	-	-	-	-	3	-	-
A.Gibbons	-	F	-	-	-	-	-	-	-	FB	-	-	-	-	-	-	-	2	-	-
J.Hodgson	-	F	-	-	-	-	-	-	-	-	-	-	F	-	-	-	-	2	-	-
J.Rhodes	-	F	-	-	-	-	-	-	F	-	-	-	-	-	-	-	-	2	-	-
Hedley Salmon	-	F	F	F	-	F	F	-	-	-	-	-	F	F	F	F	F	11	-	-
N.Haddon	-	-	-	-	F	-	F	-	F	F	F	-	-	-	-	-	-	5	-	-
W.A.Sheffield	-	-	F	F	-	-	-	-	F	-	F	-	F	F	F	F	F	10	-	-
J.W.Symington	-	-	F	F	F	F	F	-	-	-	-	-	F	F	-	F	-	9	-	-
A.D.Whitehead	-	-	F	F	-	-	-	-	-	-	F	-	F	-	F	-	-	5	-	-
W.F.Watts	-	-	-	F	-	-	-	-	-	F	-	F	-	-	-	-	-	3	1	1
Guy Taylor	-	-	-	-	F	-	-	-	3Q	-	-	-	HB	-	-	3Q	-	4	-	-
John Parsons	-	-	-	-	-	F	F	-	-	-	F	-	F	F	F	F	-	7	-	3
W.Coltman	-	-	-	-	-	-	-	-	-	F	-	F	-	F	-	-	F	4	-	-
C.Y.Wainwright	-	-	-	-	-	-	-	-	-	F	-	-	F	-	-	-	-	2	-	-

1 game: J.R.Abel F(2), E.F.Barwick HB(12), T.Bosworth F(12), Edwin Hill F(12), A.E.Hudson F(9)[1T-1], -.Laugham F(10), -.Mason HB(10), A.Matts F(2), C.Nemo F(15), Ally Nutt F(2), John Read F(15), R.Reading F(9), T.Robinson HB(2), B.Shelton F(2), L.Staines F(10), J.Trebley F(14), F.E.Wheeler F(12)

LEICESTER FOOTBALL CLUB 1880-81 (no named individuals can be positively identified on this very early photograph)

NO	DATE		OPPONENTS	V	RES	FOR				PTS	AGAINST				PTS	SCORERS
						G	T	D	P		G	T	D	P		
1	Oct	8	Moseley	A	Lost	-	-	-	-	0	3	4	-	-	13	
2		15	BURTON-ON-TRENT	H	Lost	-	-	-	-	0	3	2	-	-	11	
3		22	Edgbaston Crusaders (MCC1)	A	Lost	-	-	-	-	0	1	2	-	-	5	
4		29	RUGBY	H	Lost	-	-	-	-	0	1	-	-	-	3	
5	Nov	5	Kettering	A	Drew	-	-	-	-	0	-	-	-	-	0	
6		12	COVENTRY	H	Won	1	-	-	-	3	-	-	-	-	0	Foster(C) Lakin(T)
7		19	Nuneaton	A	Won	1	1	-	-	4	-	-	-	-	0	Young(T) Parsons(C) W.M.Smith(T)
8		26	LEAMINGTON	H	Won	1	1	-	-	4	-	-	-	-	0	Parsons(C) Lakin(T) Sheffield(T)
	Dec	3	Handsworth	A		Cancelled										
9		10	EDGBASTON CRUSADERS	H	Won	-	2	-	-	2	-	-	-	-	0	Sheffield(T) Edgell(T)
10		17	Rugby Rovers	A	Won	-	1	-	-	1	-	-	-	-	0	Parsons(T)
		24	NARBOROUGH	H		Cancelled										
11	Jan	7	Rugby	A	Lost	-	-	-	-	0	3	5	-	-	14	
12		21	Rugby Rovers	A	Lost	-	1	-	-	1	-	-	1	-	3	Lakin(T)
13		28	KETTERING	H	Won	-	1	1	-	4	-	-	-	-	0	Symington(D) Whitehead(T)
14	Feb	4	Coventry	A	Lost	1	1	-	-	4	1	2	-	-	5	Wale(D) Sheffield(T)
15		11	Edgbaston Crusaders	A	Won	-	2	-	-	2	-	-	-	-	0	Lakin(T) Cressey(T)
16		18	RUSHDEN	H	Drew	-	-	-	-	0	-	-	-	-	0	
17		25	MOSELEY	H	Lost	-	-	-	-	0	-	3	-	-	3	
18	Mar	4	Burton-on-Trent	A	Won	-	4	-	-	4	-	-	-	-	0	Wale(T) Symington(2T) Sheffield(T)
19		18	Rushden	A	Won	1	1	-	-	4	1	-	-	-	3	Parsons(C) Lakin(T) Brice(T)

INDIVIDUAL APPEARANCES 1881-1882

NAME	1	2	3	4	5	6	7	8	9	10	11	12	13	14	15	16	17	18	19	20	21	22	23	24	25	26	27	28	29	30	31	32	33	34	35	36	37	38	39	40	41	42	43	44	45	46	TOTAL	T	PTS
J.R.Abel	FB	-	-	-	-	3Q	-	-	-	-	-	-	-	-	-	-	-	-	-																												2	-	-
John Parsons	FB	-	F	F	-	-	F	3Q	F	HB	-	F	F	-	F	-	F	3Q	3Q																												13	1	7
H.L.Foster	-	-	FB	FB	FB	FB	-	-	3Q	3Q	-	3Q	FB	-	3Q	-	3Q	-	-																												10	-	2
W.A.Wheeler	-	-	-	-	-	-	-	-	-	-	-	-	-	-	FB	-	FB	-	-																												2	-	-
W.Sulley	3Q	-	-	-	-	-	-	-	-	3Q	-	-	-	-	-	-	-	-	-																												2	-	-
T.H.Prentice	-	3Q	-	3Q	-	-	3Q	3Q	-	-	FB	-	-	-	-	-	-	-	-																												5	-	-
K.Macaulay	-	-	3Q	3Q	3Q	3Q	-	-	-	-	-	-	-	-	-	-	-	-	-																												4	-	-
Arthur Porter	-	-	3Q	-	3Q	-	-	-	-	-	-	-	-	-	-	-	-	-	-																												2	-	-
Sherrard Coleman	-	-	-	3Q	-	-	-	-	-	-	3Q	3Q	-	3Q	-	3Q	3Q	3Q	-																												7	-	-
J.Gilbert	-	-	-	-	3Q	-	FB	FB	FB	FB	-	FB	-	-	F	-	FB	FB	-																												9	-	-
A.Wale	-	-	-	-	-	-	3Q	3Q	3Q	3Q	3Q	3Q	3Q	3Q	-	3Q	3Q	3Q	-																												12	1	4
J.A.Lakin	HB	HB	HB	HB	HB	HB	HB	HB	HB	-	HB	-	HB	HB	-	HB	HB	HB	-																												16	5	5
L.Young	-	-	HB	HB	-	HB	HB	HB	HB	-	-	HB	HB	-	HB	-	HB	HB	HB																												12	1	1
Guy Taylor	-	-	-	HB	-	-	-	-	HB	-	-	-	-	-	-	-	-	-	-																												2	-	-
A.J.Burford	F	F	-	F	F	F	F	-	F	F	F	-	-	F	F	-	F	-	-																												14	-	-
J.T.Cressey	F	-	F	F	F	-	-	F	-	-	-	F	-	F	-	F	F	F	-																												10	1	1
J.H.Parry	F	-	-	-	-	-	-	-	F	-	-	-	-	-	-	-	-	-	-																												2	-	-
W.R.Porter	F	-	F	F	-	F	F	F	F	-	F	-	-	F	-	F	-	F	-																												11	-	-
Hedley Salmon	F	F	-	-	-	-	-	-	F	F	F	F	-	-	F	-	F	F	F																												10	-	-
W.F.Watts	F	-	-	F	-	-	-	-	-	-	-	-	-	-	-	-	-	-	-																												2	-	-
A.D.Whitehead	F	-	-	F	-	F	-	F	-	-	-	F	F	-	-	F	F	-	-																												8	1	1
C.E.Worthington	F	F	F	-	F	-	-	F	-	-	F	-	-	-	-	-	-	F	-																												7	-	-
Henry Barwick	-	-	F	-	-	F	-	-	-	-	-	-	-	-	-	-	-	-	-																												2	-	-
W.Coltman	-	-	F	F	-	-	-	-	-	-	-	-	-	-	-	-	-	-	-																												2	-	-
W.A.Sheffield	-	-	F	F	F	F	F	F	F	F	F	F	F	F	-	F	F	F	-																												16	4	4
L.Staines	-	-	-	-	F	F	-	F	-	F	-	-	-	-	-	-	-	-	-																												4	-	-
J.W.Symington	-	-	F	F	-	F	F	F	F	-	F	F	-	F	F	F	-	-	-																												12	2	5
C.Y.Wainwright	-	-	-	F	F	F	F	F	F	F	-	-	-	F	F	F	-	-	-																												10	-	-
Ally Nutt	-	-	-	-	F	-	-	-	F	-	F	-	-	F	-	-	-	-	-																												3	-	-
W.M.Smith	-	-	-	-	-	F	-	F	F	-	-	-	-	-	-	-	-	-	-																												3	1	1
A.N.Other	-	-	-	-	-	-	-	F	-	F	-	-	F	-	-	-	-	-	-																												2	-	-
R.A.Edgell	-	-	-	-	-	-	F	-	-	-	-	-	-	F	-	-	-	-	-																												2	1	1
A.E.Brice	-	-	-	-	-	-	-	-	F	-	-	-	F	-	-	-	-	-	F																												2	1	1
A.Turner	-	-	-	-	-	-	-	-	-	F	F	-	-	-	-	-	F	-	-																												3	-	-
Jack Lovett	-	-	-	-	-	-	-	-	-	-	F	-	F	-	-	-	-	-	-																												2	-	-

1 game: -.Bodycote HB(11), W.Colver F(10), David Corby F(5), -.Crane 3Q(11), F.Dance 3Q(6), T.Gray F(11), -.Gurney F(11), -.Holyoak F(11), H.James F(1), J.Lang F(7), -.Lawton F(18), F.G.McMurray 3Q(9), William Massey F(18), A.Potter F(6), J.Rhodes F(6),-.Seale F(10), F.Sheen 3Q(13), T.Smith 3Q(1), J.G.Walker HB(1), R.H.Warner FB(11)

NO	DATE		OPPONENTS	V	RES	FOR					AGAINST					SCORERS
						G	T	D	P	PTS	G	T	D	P	PTS	
1	Oct	7	KETTERING	H	Won	1	1	-	-	4	-	-	-	-	0	Parsons(C) Young(T) Lakin(T)
2		21	BEDFORD GRAMMAR SCH.	H	Won	-	2	-	-	2	-	-	-	-	0	Wale(T) Sheffield(T)
3		28	Moseley (MCC2)	A	Lost	-	-	-	-	0	2	1	-	-	7	
4	Nov	4	EDGBASTON CRUSADERS	H	Won	1	1	1	-	7	-	-	-	-	0	Parsons(D) Warner(T) Unknown(T,C)
5		11	Coventry	A	Drew	-	-	-	-	0	-	-	-	-	0	
6		18	RUGBY	H	Lost	-	-	-	-	0	1	-	1	-	6	
7		25	LEICESTER VICTORIA	H	Won	-	4	-	-	4	-	-	-	-	0	Craven(T) Unknown(3T)
8	Dec	2	BURTON-ON-TRENT	H	Won	-	3	1	-	6	1	1	-	-	4	Parsons(D) Nutt(T) Unknown(2T)
9		9	Stamford	A	Won	4	2	1	-	17	-	1	-	-	1	Young(T) Parsons(T,4C) Sheffield(T) Cressey(T,D) Symington(T) Turner(T)
		16	RUSHDEN	H		Cancelled										
10	Jan	13	NORTHAMPTON	H	Lost	-	-	-	-	0	1	2	-	-	5	
11		20	COVENTRY	H	Won	-	3	-	-	3	-	-	-	-	0	Smith(T) Cressey(T) Sheffield(T)
12		27	RUSHDEN	H	Drew	-	1	-	-	1	-	1	-	-	1	Unknown(T)
	Feb	3	EDGBASTON CRUSADERS	H		Cancelled										
13		10	Bedford Grammar Sch.	A	Won	-	1	-	-	1	-	-	-	-	0	Young(T)
14		24	Rushden	A	Lost	-	-	-	-	0	-	1	-	-	1	
	Mar	3	Northampton	A		Cancelled										
		17	MOSELEY	H		Cancelled										

INDIVIDUAL APPEARANCES 1882-1883

NAME	1	2	3	4	5	6	7	8	9	10	11	12	13	14	15	16	17	18	19	20	21	22	23	24	25	26	27	28	29	30	31	32	33	34	35	36	37	38	39	40	41	42	43	44	45	46	TOTAL	T	PTS
H.L.Foster	FB	3Q	3Q	3Q	-	3Q	-	FB	-	HB	3Q	-	FB	-																																	9	-	-
R.H.Warner	-	FB	-	F	-	FB																																									3	1	1
Sherrard Coleman	-	-	FB	-	-	-	-	-	-	FB	-	-	3Q																																		3	-	-
J.R.Abel	-	-	FB	-	-	3Q	-	FB	-	-	-	-	F																																		4	-	-
Arthur McKechnie	-	-	-	-	FB	-	FB	-	-	-	-	-	-																																		2	-	-
John Parsons	3Q	3Q	3Q	3Q	3Q	3Q	-	3Q	3Q	-	3Q	-	3Q	3Q																																	11	1	17
A.Wale	3Q	3Q	3Q	3Q	3Q	-	-	3Q	-	-	3Q	-	3Q	FB																																	9	1	1
E.Tyler	-	-	-	-	3Q	F	-	F	HB	-	-	F	F	-																																	6	-	-
-.Hayes	-	-	-	-	-	-	3Q	-	-	F	-	-	-	-																																	2	-	-
J.W.Horner	-	-	-	-	-	-	3Q	-	-	HB	-	-	-	-																																	2	-	-
J.A.Lakin	HB	HB	HB	-	-	-	3Q	-	-	-	-	-	-	-																																	4	1	1
L.Young	HB	HB	HB	HB	HB	HB	-	HB	3Q	-	-	3Q	3Q	-																																	10	3	3
A.J.Burford	F	F	F	F	-	F	-	F	-	F	F	-	F	-																																	9	-	-
J.T.Cressey	F	F	F	F	F	-	F	F	-	F	F	-																																			10	2	5
Ally Nutt	F	-	F	HB	HB	HB	-	HB	-	HB	-	HB	HB	HB																																	10	1	1
Hedley Salmon	F	F	F	F	F	-	F	F	-	F	-	-																																			11	-	-
W.A.Sheffield	F	F	F	F	F	F	-	F	HB	-	F	-	HB	HB																																	11	3	3
J.W.Symington	F	F	F	F	F	-	F	F	-	F	-	-	F																																		10	1	1
A.Turner	F	F	F	F	F	F	-	F	-	F	F	-	F	F																																	10	1	1
W.R.Porter	-	F	F	F	F	F	F	F	F	-	-	-	F	F																																	10	-	-
C.E.Worthington	-	-	F	-	-	-	-	-	F	-	-	-	-	-																																	2	-	-
C.Y.Wainwright	-	-	-	F	F	F	F	-	F	-	F	-	F	-																																	6	-	-
E.F.Barwick	-	-	-	-	-	-	F	HB	-	-	3Q	-	-	-																																	3	-	-
W.M.Smith	-	-	-	-	-	-	F	-	-	F	F	-	F	F																																	5	1	1
F.Hudson	-	-	-	-	-	-	-	-	-	F	-	F	F	F																																	3	-	-

1 game: Henry Barwick 3Q(10), B.C.Bloxham FB(9), H.P.Carryer 3Q(1), W.Coltman F(7), W.Colver F(7), T.W.Craven F(7)[1T-1], A.G.J.Crofts F(7), F.G.Cross F(10), Fred Geeson F(7), -.Gibson F(7), J.Gilbert F(1), -.Gurney F(7), Edwin Hill HB(7), J.Jelly F(10),-.Kenny F(10), Jack Lovett F(2), -.McKennie F(10), J.Marston F(7), William Massey F(10), J.W.Sellers F(8), -.Sheppard HB(11), W.Warren F(1)

NO	DATE		OPPONENTS	V	RES	FOR					AGAINST					SCORERS
						G	T	D	P	PTS	G	T	D	P	PTS	
1	Oct	6	Moseley	A	Lost	-	-	-	-	0	3	2	-	-	11	
2		13	RUGBY	H	Won	1	2	-	-	5	-	-	-	-	0	Parsons(C) Sheffield(T) Nutt(T) Lovett(T)
3		20	Stafford (MCC)	A	Won	2	6	-	-	12	-	-	-	-	0	Parsons(2C) Nutt(5T) Symington(T) Anson(T) Cressey(T)
4		27	Rushden (MCC2)	A	Drew	-	-	-	-	0	-	-	-	-	0	
5	Nov	3	BURTON-ON-TRENT	H	Won	1	1	2	-	10	-	-	-	-	0	Parsons(C,D) Nutt(T) Coleman(D) Sheffield(T)
6		10	Kettering	A	Lost	-	1	-	-	1	1	1	-	-	4	Lovett(T)
		17	BEDFORD ROVERS	H		Cancelled Rain										
7		24	Bedford Grammar Sch.	A	Won	1	-	-	-	3	-	1	-	-	1	Foster(C) Wainwright(T)
8	Dec	1	COVENTRY	H	Won	-	1	-	-	1	-	-	-	-	0	Parsons(T)
9		8	DERBY WANDERERS	H	Won	1	2	-	-	5	-	1	-	-	1	Nutt(T) Coleman(T) Sheffield(T) Foster(C)
10		15	Rugby	A	Won	1	-	-	-	3	-	1	-	-	1	Parsons(C) Lovett(T)
11		29	S.WARWICKSHIRE RVRS.	H	Won	1	-	1	-	6	1	-	-	-	3	Parsons(C,D) Coleman(T)
12	Jan	12	RUSHDEN (MCCR)	H	Drew	-	1	-	-	1	-	1	-	-	1	Wale(T)
13		19	Coventry	A	Lost	-	-	-	-	0	2	3	-	-	9	
14		26	Bedford Rovers	A	Won	-	1	-	-	1	-	-	-	-	0	Sheffield(T)
	Feb	2	Coventry	A		Cancelled										
15		9	KETTERING	H	Won	1	-	-	-	3	-	-	-	-	0	Parsons(C) Coleman(T)
16		16	Rushden (MCCR)	A	Won	-	1	-	-	1	-	-	-	-	0	Lovett(T)
17		23	Burton-on-Trent	A	Drew	-	1	-	-	1	-	1	-	-	1	Symington(T)
18	Mar	1	BEDFORD GRAMMAR SCH.	H	Lost	1	-	-	-	3	1	1	-	-	4	McKechnie(C) Whitehead(T)
19		15	Moseley (MCC4)	A	Lost	-	1	-	-	1	1	-	-	-	3	Foster(T)
20		22	S.Warwickshire Rvrs.	A	Won	-	1	1	-	4	-	-	-	-	0	Foster(D) Lovett(T)
21		29	Derby Wanderers	A	Won	2	3	1	-	12	-	1	-	-	1	McKechnie(2C) Coleman(2T,D) Foster(T) Sheffield(T) Lovett(T)

INDIVIDUAL APPEARANCES 1883-1884

NAME	1	2	3	4	5	6	7	8	9	10	11	12	13	14	15	16	17	18	19	20	21	22	23	24	25	26	27	28	29	30	31	32	33	34	35	36	37	38	39	40	41	42	43	44	45	46	TOTAL	T	PTS
R.H.Warner	FB	-	-	-	F	FB	-	-	-	-	-	-	-	-	-	-	-	-	-	-	-																										3	-	-
A.Wale	-	FB	FB	FB	FB	3Q	3Q	3Q	3Q	3Q	3Q	3Q	3Q	3Q	3Q	3Q	-	3Q	3Q	3Q	3Q																										19	1	1
Arthur McKechnie	-	-	-	-	-	-	FB	FB	FB	FB	-	FB	FB	FB	FB	FB	FB	-	FB	FB	FB																										14	-	6
Sherrard Coleman	3Q	3Q	3Q	3Q	3Q	3Q	3Q	3Q	3Q	-	3Q	3Q	3Q	3Q	3Q	-	3Q	3Q	3Q	3Q	3Q																										19	5	11
John Parsons	3Q	3Q	3Q	3Q	3Q	-	3Q	-	3Q	3Q	3Q	-	-	3Q	3Q	-	3Q	3Q	-	-	-																										13	1	21
H.L.Foster	-	-	-	-	-	-	3Q	HB	HB	-	-	-	HB	HB	HB	HB	HB	HB	HB	HB	HB																										12	2	9
Arthur Porter	-	-	-	-	-	-	-	-	-	-	-	-	-	-	3Q	3Q	-	3Q	3Q	-	3Q																										5	-	-
Ally Nutt	HB	HB	HB	3Q	3Q	3Q	HB	-	3Q	3Q	3Q	HB	-	-	-	-	-	-	-	-	-																										11	8	8
L.Young	HB	3Q	3Q	HB	-	-	-	-	-	HB	-	-	-	-	-	-	-	-	-	-	-																										5	-	-
C.Dickinson	-	-	-	-	-	-	-	-	-	HB	F	-	-	F	F	3Q	-	F	-	-	-																										6	-	-
J.R.Abel	F	-	F	-	-	F	F	F	F	F	F	F	-	-	F	-	-	-	-	-	F																										11	-	-
J.T.Cressey	F	F	F	F	F	F	F	-	F	F	-	F	F	F	F	F	F	F	F	F	F																										19	1	1
F.G.Cross	F	-	-	-	-	-	F	-	-	-	F	3Q	-	-	-	-	-	-	F	F	-																										6	-	-
Jack Lovett	F	F	F	F	F	F	F	F	F	-	F	F	F	F	F	F	F	F	F	F	F																										20	6	6
W.R.Porter	F	F	F	F	F	F	F	F	F	F	F	F	F	F	F	-	F	-	F	F	-																										19	-	-
Hedley Salmon	F	F	F	F	F	-	F	F	-	F	F	F	F	F	F	-	-	F	F	-	-																										17	-	-
W.A.Sheffield	F	HB	HB	HB	HB	HB	HB	HB	HB	HB	HB	HB	HB	HB	HB	HB	HB	HB	HB	HB	HB																										21	5	5
C.Y.Wainwright	F	F	F	F	F	F	F	F	F	F	F	F	-	-	-	-	-	-	-	-	-																										12	1	1
A.D.Whitehead	F	F	F	F	F	F	F	F	F	-	F	-	-	F	-	F	F	F	F	-	-																										15	1	1
W.J.Anson	-	F	F	F	F	F	F	-	F	F	F	F	-	-	F	F	F	F	F	F	-																										16	1	1
J.W.Symington	-	F	F	F	HB	HB	F	F	F	F	F	F	-	-	F	F	F	F	F	F	F																										18	2	2
W.W.Judd	-	-	-	F	-	F	-	-	F	-	FB	-	F	F	-	-	F	F	-	F	-																										10	-	-
A.J.Burford	-	-	-	-	F	F	-	-	-	F	-	F	F	F	F	F	F	-	F	-	-																										10	-	-
S.G.Porter	-	-	-	-	-	-	-	-	F	-	F	F	-	-	F	-	-	F	-	-	F																										5	-	-
A.E.Brice	-	-	-	-	-	-	-	-	-	-	-	-	F	-	-	-	-	-	F	-	-																										2	-	-

1 game: T.A.Cook 3Q(1), Rev. Rigby 3Q(13)

NO	DATE		OPPONENTS	V	RES	FOR					AGAINST					SCORERS
						G	T	D	P	PTS	G	T	D	P	PTS	
1	Oct	11	MOSELEY	H	Won	2	1	1	-	10	-	-	-	-	0	Coleman(T,D) Parsons(2C) McAlpin(2T)
2		18	Moseley Woodstock (MCC1)	A	Won	1	-	-	-	3	-	1	-	-	1	Coleman(T) Parsons(C)
3		25	BURTON-ON-TRENT (MCC2)	H	Won	-	-	2	-	6	-	1	-	-	1	Parsons(D) Coleman(D)
4	Nov	1	Derbyshire	A	Lost	-	1	-	-	1	-	2	-	-	2	Wale(T)
5		8	NOTTINGHAM	H	Won	1	2	-	-	5	-	-	-	-	0	Parsons(C) Wale(T) Coleman(T) W.A.Sheffield(T)
6		15	RUSHDEN	H	Lost	-	1	-	-	1	1	-	-	-	3	W.A.Sheffield(T)
7		22	Bedford Grammar Sch.	A	Won	-	-	2	-	6	-	-	-	-	0	Parsons(D) Coleman(D)
8		29	Coventry	A	Lost	-	1	-	-	1	1	1	-	-	4	W.A.Sheffield(T)
	Dec	6	BURTON-ON-TRENT	H		Cancelled										
9		13	Rugby	A	Lost	-	-	-	-	0	-	1	-	-	1	
10		20	Nottingham	A	Lost	-	-	-	-	0	-	1	-	-	1	
11		27	BEDFORD SWIFTS	H	Won	1	-	-	-	3	-	-	-	-	0	Wale(T) Parsons(C)
	Jan	10	DERBYSHIRE	H		Cancelled										
12		17	RUGBY	H	Won	-	1	1	-	4	-	-	-	-	0	A.T.Porter(T) Coleman(D)
13	Feb	14	Burton-on-Trent	A	Won	1	-	-	-	3	-	1	-	-	1	McKechnie(C) W.A.Sheffield(T)
14		21	BEDFORD GRAMMAR SCH.	H	Lost	-	-	-	-	0	-	-	1	-	3	
15		28	Rushden	A	Drew	-	-	-	-	0	-	-	-	-	0	
16	Mar	7	Moseley	A	Lost	-	-	-	-	0	-	3	-	-	3	
17		14	LEICESTER PAST	H	Lost	-	1	-	-	1	2	-	-	-	6	Unknown(T)
18		21	Moseley (MCC1)	A	Lost	-	-	-	-	0	2	2	-	-	8	

INDIVIDUAL APPEARANCES 1884-1885

NAME	1	2	3	4	5	6	7	8	9	10	11	12	13	14	15	16	17	18	19	20	21	22	23	24	25	26	27	28	29	30	31	32	33	34	35	36	37	38	39	40	41	42	43	44	45	46	TOTAL	T	PTS
Arthur McKechnie	FB	FB	FB	FB	FB	FB	FB	FB	FB	FB	-	FB	FB	FB	3Q	HB	-	FB																													16	-	2
J.E.Sheffield	-	-	-	-	-	-	-	-	-	-	FB	-	-	-	FB	3Q																															3		
Sherrard Coleman	3Q	3Q	3Q	-	3Q	3Q	3Q	3Q	3Q	3Q	3Q	HB	3Q	3Q	-	-	-	3Q																													14	3	15
C.Dickinson	3Q	3Q	F	-	-	-	-	-	-	-	-	-	-	-	-	-	-	-																													3	-	-
John Parsons	3Q	3Q	3Q	-	3Q	3Q	3Q	3Q	3Q	3Q	3Q	3Q	-	3Q	-	-	-	3Q																													13	-	16
A.Wale	3Q	3Q	3Q	3Q	3Q	3Q	-	3Q	3Q	3Q	3Q	3Q	3Q	HB	3Q	3Q	-	3Q																													16	3	3
Arthur Porter	-	-	3Q	-	-	-	-	-	-	-	-	-	3Q	3Q	3Q	3Q	-	3Q																													7	1	1
H.L.Foster	HB	HB	HB	-	-	-	3Q	HB	HB	-	-	-	HB	-	-	-	-	HB																													8	-	-
W.A.Sheffield	HB	HB	HB	HB	HB	HB	HB	HB	HB	HB	HB	HB	HB	HB	HB	HB	-	HB																													17	4	4
Ally Nutt	-	-	-	-	-	-	-	-	-	HB	F	-	-	-	-	-	-	-																													2	-	-
J.R.Abel	F	-	-	F	F	F	F	F	F	-	-	-	-	-	-	F	-	-																													8	-	-
A.E.Brice	F	-	-	-	-	F	-	-	F	-	-	-	-	-	-	-	-	-																													3	-	-
A.J.Burford	F	F	F	F	F	F	F	F	F	-	-	-	-	-	-	-	-	-																													8	-	-
J.T.Cressey	-	-	F	F	F	F	F	F	F	F	-	F	-	-	F	F	-	F																													13	-	-
Jack Lovett	F	F	F	F	F	F	F	F	F	F	F	F	-	F	-	-	-	F																													17	-	-
Kenneth McAlpin	F	F	F	F	F	F	HB	-	F	F	F	F	F	F	F	F	-	F																													16	2	2
W.R.Porter	F	-	F	F	-	F	F	-	F	F	F	F	F	F	F	-	F	-	F																												14	-	-
Hedley Salmon	F	F	F	F	HB	HB	F	F	F	F	F	F	F	F	F	-	F	-																													17	-	-
F.G.Cross	-	F	-	3Q	-	F	F	-	-	-	-	-	-	-	-	-	-	-																													3	-	-
W.W.Judd	-	F	-	3Q	-	-	F	-	-	-	-	-	-	-	-	-	-	-																													3	-	-
A.D.Whitehead	-	-	F	-	-	-	-	-	-	-	F	-	F	-	F	-	F	-																													5	-	-
S.G.Porter	-	-	-	F	F	-	F	-	-	F	F	F	F	F	F	F	-	-																													10	-	-
S.Broadbent	-	-	-	-	F	F	-	-	F	-	F	F	F	F	F	F	-	F																													10	-	-
C.J.Pearce	-	-	-	-	-	-	-	F	F	-	-	-	-	-	-	-	-	-																													2	-	-
J.Meekin	-	-	-	-	-	-	-	-	-	F	-	HB	-	-	-	-	-	-																													2	-	-
W.M.Smith	-	-	-	-	-	-	-	-	-	F	F	F	F	F	F	F	F	-	F																												9	-	-

1 game: - .Addison 3Q(8), W.J.Anson F(14), Dickie Bell F(15), C.Clarke FB(16), J.H.Gibbs F(10), J.Gilbert F(11), R.Harvey F(5), A.Loveday F(4), -.Neal F(8), E.Tyler HB(15), W.H.Watson 3Q(4), W.A.Wheeler 3Q(4), L.Young HB(4)

NO	DATE		OPPONENTS	V	RES	FOR					AGAINST					SCORERS
						G	T	D	P	PTS	G	T	D	P	PTS	
1	Oct	10	MOSELEY WOODSTOCK	H	Won	2	1	-	-	7	-	-	-	-	0	Parsons(2C) Noon(2T) McAlpin(T)
2		24	RUSHDEN	H	Won	1	1	-	-	4	-	1	-	-	1	Unknown(2T,C)
3		31	BURTON-ON-TRENT	H	Won	-	2	1	-	5	-	-	-	-	0	Parsons(T,D) Wilkinson(T)
4	Nov	7	Rugby	A	Lost	-	-	-	-	0	2	1	1	-	10	
5		14	COVENTRY	H	Won	-	1	-	-	1	-	-	-	-	0	Leakey(T)
6		21	Bedford Grammar Sch.	A	Won	-	1	-	-	1	-	-	-	-	0	Leakey(T)
7		28	NOTTINGHAM	H	Won	1	-	-	-	3	-	-	-	-	0	McKechnie(C) Parsons(T)
	Dec	12	BEDFORD GRAMMAR SCH.	H		Cancelled Frost										
8		26	MOSELEY	H	Lost	-	-	-	-	0	1	1	1	-	7	
9	Jan	16	Nottingham	A	Drew	-	-	-	-	0	-	-	-	-	0	
		23	KETTERING	H		Cancelled Frost										
10		30	Burton-on-Trent	A	Lost	1	-	-	-	3	2	2	-	-	8	Le Manco(C) Birkett(T)
11	Feb	6	BEDFORD SWIFTS	H	Won	-	4	-	-	4	-	-	-	-	0	W.A.Sheffield(T) Unknown(3T)
12		20	RUGBY	H	Won	-	1	-	-	1	-	-	-	-	0	Friend(T)
13		27	Rushden	A	Drew	-	1	-	-	1	-	1	-	-	1	Coleman(T)
	Mar	6	LEICESTER PAST	H		Cancelled Frost										
		13	Coventry (MCC2)	A		Cancelled Snow										
14		20	Coventry (MCC2)	A	Lost	-	-	-	-	0	1	-	1*	-	6	

INDIVIDUAL APPEARANCES 1885-1886

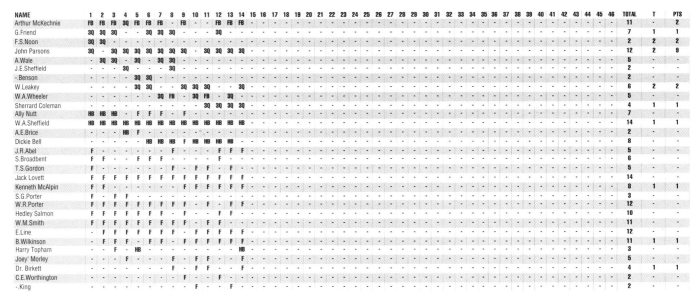

NAME	1	2	3	4	5	6	7	8	9	10	11	12	13	14	15	16	17	18	19	20	21	22	23	24	25	26	27	28	29	30	31	32	33	34	35	36	37	38	39	40	41	42	43	44	45	46	TOTAL	T	PTS
Arthur McKechnie	FB	FB	FB	3Q	FB	FB	FB	-	FB	-	-	FB	FB	FB	-	-	-	-	-	-	-	-	-	-	-	-	-	-	-	-	-	-	-	-	-	-	-	-	-	-	-	-	-	-	-	-	11	-	2
G.Friend	3Q	3Q	3Q	-	-	3Q	3Q	3Q	-	-	-	3Q	-	-	-	-	-	-	-	-	-	-	-	-	-	-	-	-	-	-	-	-	-	-	-	-	-	-	-	-	-	-	-	-	-	-	7	1	1
F.S.Noon	3Q	3Q	-	-	-	-	-	-	-	-	-	-	-	-	-	-	-	-	-	-	-	-	-	-	-	-	-	-	-	-	-	-	-	-	-	-	-	-	-	-	-	-	-	-	-	-	2	2	2
John Parsons	3Q	-	3Q	3Q	3Q	3Q	3Q	3Q	3Q	-	3Q	3Q	3Q	3Q	-	-	-	-	-	-	-	-	-	-	-	-	-	-	-	-	-	-	-	-	-	-	-	-	-	-	-	-	-	-	-	-	12	2	9
A.Wale	-	3Q	3Q	-	3Q	-	3Q	3Q	-	-	-	-	-	-	-	-	-	-	-	-	-	-	-	-	-	-	-	-	-	-	-	-	-	-	-	-	-	-	-	-	-	-	-	-	-	-	5	-	-
J.E.Sheffield	-	-	-	3Q	-	-	-	3Q	-	-	-	-	-	-	-	-	-	-	-	-	-	-	-	-	-	-	-	-	-	-	-	-	-	-	-	-	-	-	-	-	-	-	-	-	-	-	2	-	-
-.Benson	-	-	-	3Q	3Q	-	-	-	-	-	-	-	-	-	-	-	-	-	-	-	-	-	-	-	-	-	-	-	-	-	-	-	-	-	-	-	-	-	-	-	-	-	-	-	-	-	2	-	-
W.Leakey	-	-	-	3Q	3Q	-	-	3Q	3Q	3Q	-	-	3Q	-	-	-	-	-	-	-	-	-	-	-	-	-	-	-	-	-	-	-	-	-	-	-	-	-	-	-	-	-	-	-	-	-	6	2	2
W.A.Wheeler	-	-	-	-	-	-	3Q	FB	-	3Q	FB	-	3Q	-	-	-	-	-	-	-	-	-	-	-	-	-	-	-	-	-	-	-	-	-	-	-	-	-	-	-	-	-	-	-	-	-	5	-	-
Sherrard Coleman	-	-	-	-	-	-	-	-	-	3Q	3Q	3Q	3Q	-	-	-	-	-	-	-	-	-	-	-	-	-	-	-	-	-	-	-	-	-	-	-	-	-	-	-	-	-	-	-	-	-	4	1	1
Ally Nutt	HB	HB	HB	-	F	F	F	-	F	-	-	-	-	-	-	-	-	-	-	-	-	-	-	-	-	-	-	-	-	-	-	-	-	-	-	-	-	-	-	-	-	-	-	-	-	-	7	-	-
W.A.Sheffield	HB	HB	HB	HB	HB	HB	HB	HB	HB	HB	HB	HB	HB	HB	-	-	-	-	-	-	-	-	-	-	-	-	-	-	-	-	-	-	-	-	-	-	-	-	-	-	-	-	-	-	-	-	14	1	1
A.E.Brice	-	-	-	HB	F	-	-	-	-	-	-	-	-	-	-	-	-	-	-	-	-	-	-	-	-	-	-	-	-	-	-	-	-	-	-	-	-	-	-	-	-	-	-	-	-	-	2	-	-
Dickie Bell	-	-	-	-	-	HB	HB	HB	F	HB	HB	HB	HB	-	-	-	-	-	-	-	-	-	-	-	-	-	-	-	-	-	-	-	-	-	-	-	-	-	-	-	-	-	-	-	-	-	8	-	-
J.R.Abel	F	-	-	-	-	-	-	F	-	-	-	F	F	F	-	-	-	-	-	-	-	-	-	-	-	-	-	-	-	-	-	-	-	-	-	-	-	-	-	-	-	-	-	-	-	-	5	-	-
S.Broadbent	F	F	-	-	F	F	F	-	-	-	-	F	-	-	-	-	-	-	-	-	-	-	-	-	-	-	-	-	-	-	-	-	-	-	-	-	-	-	-	-	-	-	-	-	-	-	6	-	-
T.S.Gordon	F	-	-	-	-	-	-	-	F	-	F	F	-	-	-	-	-	-	-	-	-	-	-	-	-	-	-	-	-	-	-	-	-	-	-	-	-	-	-	-	-	-	-	-	-	-	5	-	-
Jack Lovett	F	F	F	F	F	F	F	F	F	F	F	F	F	F	-	-	-	-	-	-	-	-	-	-	-	-	-	-	-	-	-	-	-	-	-	-	-	-	-	-	-	-	-	-	-	-	14	-	-
Kenneth McAlpin	F	F	-	-	-	-	-	F	F	F	F	F	F	F	-	-	-	-	-	-	-	-	-	-	-	-	-	-	-	-	-	-	-	-	-	-	-	-	-	-	-	-	-	-	-	-	8	1	1
S.G.Porter	F	-	F	F	-	-	-	-	-	-	-	-	-	-	-	-	-	-	-	-	-	-	-	-	-	-	-	-	-	-	-	-	-	-	-	-	-	-	-	-	-	-	-	-	-	-	3	-	-
W.R.Porter	F	F	F	F	F	F	F	F	F	-	F	-	F	F	-	-	-	-	-	-	-	-	-	-	-	-	-	-	-	-	-	-	-	-	-	-	-	-	-	-	-	-	-	-	-	-	12	-	-
Hedley Salmon	F	F	F	F	F	F	F	F	-	F	-	-	F	F	-	-	-	-	-	-	-	-	-	-	-	-	-	-	-	-	-	-	-	-	-	-	-	-	-	-	-	-	-	-	-	-	10	-	-
W.M.Smith	F	F	F	F	F	F	F	F	-	F	F	-	F	F	-	-	-	-	-	-	-	-	-	-	-	-	-	-	-	-	-	-	-	-	-	-	-	-	-	-	-	-	-	-	-	-	11	-	-
E.Line	-	F	F	F	F	F	F	F	-	F	F	F	F	F	-	-	-	-	-	-	-	-	-	-	-	-	-	-	-	-	-	-	-	-	-	-	-	-	-	-	-	-	-	-	-	-	12	-	-
B.Wilkinson	-	F	F	F	-	F	F	-	F	F	F	F	F	F	-	-	-	-	-	-	-	-	-	-	-	-	-	-	-	-	-	-	-	-	-	-	-	-	-	-	-	-	-	-	-	-	11	1	1
Harry Topham	-	-	F	-	HB	-	-	-	-	-	-	HB	-	-	-	-	-	-	-	-	-	-	-	-	-	-	-	-	-	-	-	-	-	-	-	-	-	-	-	-	-	-	-	-	-	-	3	-	-
Joey' Morley	-	-	-	F	-	-	-	F	F	-	F	F	-	-	F	-	-	-	-	-	-	-	-	-	-	-	-	-	-	-	-	-	-	-	-	-	-	-	-	-	-	-	-	-	-	-	5	-	-
Dr. Birkett	-	-	-	-	-	-	F	-	F	F	-	F	-	-	-	-	-	-	-	-	-	-	-	-	-	-	-	-	-	-	-	-	-	-	-	-	-	-	-	-	-	-	-	-	-	-	4	1	1
C.E.Worthington	-	-	-	-	-	-	-	F	-	-	-	F	-	-	-	-	-	-	-	-	-	-	-	-	-	-	-	-	-	-	-	-	-	-	-	-	-	-	-	-	-	-	-	-	-	-	2	-	-
-.King	-	-	-	-	-	-	-	-	F	-	-	F	-	-	-	-	-	-	-	-	-	-	-	-	-	-	-	-	-	-	-	-	-	-	-	-	-	-	-	-	-	-	-	-	-	-	2	-	-

1 game: -.Allinson F(4), F.Bonner F(10), -.Flinn 3Q(14), Charles Fuller F(2), -.Le Manco 3Q(10)[2], -.Myrtle FB(10), Hugh Rotherham HB(9), P.G.Salmon FB(4), J.Smith 3Q(9)

NO	DATE		OPPONENTS	V	RES	FOR					AGAINST					SCORERS
						G	T	D	P	PTS	G	T	D	P	PTS	
1	Oct	9	20 OF TOWN & DIST.	H	Won	2	2	1	-	11	-	-	-	-	0	McKechnie(2C) Coleman(2T) Parsons(D) Smith(T) Morley(T)
2		16	Moseley Woodstock	A	Won	5	2	-	-	17	-	-	-	-	0	Parsons(5C) Coleman(T) Apperley(T) Snowden(2T) Mason(2T) Bonner(T)
3		23	MOSELEY	H	Lost	-	-	-	-	0	1	1	-	-	4	
4		30	Rushden	A	Won	4	-	1	-	15	1	-	-	-	3	McKechnie(D) Apperley(T) Parsons(4C) Coleman(2T) Voce(T)
5	Nov	6	KETTERING	H	Won	1	1	-	-	4	-	-	-	-	0	Parsons(C) Apperley(T) McKechnie(T)
6		20	Coventry	A	Drew	-	-	-	-	0	-	-	-	-	0	
7		27	BEDFORD	H	Won	2	4	-	-	10	-	-	-	-	0	McKechnie(C) Apperley(2T) Parsons(C) Cressey(T) Porter(T) B.Wilkinson(2T)
	Dec	4	RUGBY	H		Cancelled Frost										
8		11	RUSHDEN	H	Won	-	2	-	-	2	-	1	-	-	1	Coleman(T) Sheffield(T)
		28	RUSHDEN	H		Cancelled Frost										
	Jan	1	Old Edwardians	A		Cancelled Fog										
		8	BURTON-ON-TRENT	H		Cancelled Snow										
9		22	COVENTRY	H	Drew	1	-	-	-	3	1	-	-	-	3	Parsons(C) McAlpin(T)
10		29	Kettering	A	Drew	-	-	-	-	0	-	-	-	-	0	
	Feb	5	OLD EDWARDIANS	H		Cancelled										
11		12	Bedford	A	Drew	-	-	-	-	0	-	-	-	-	0	
12		19	Moseley	A	Lost	-	-	-	-	0	4	3	-	-	15	
13		26	Rugby	A	Drew	-	-	-	-	0	-	-	-	-	0	
14	Mar	5	MOSELEY WOODSTOCK	H	Won	1	5	1	-	11	-	-	-	-	0	Parsons(T,C,D) Coleman(T) Snowden(3T) J.S.Wilkinson(T)
15		12	Rugby (MCCSF)	A	Lost	-	-	-	-	0	1	-	-	-	3	
		19	BEDFORD GRAMMAR SCH.	H		Cancelled										
16		26	NOTTINGHAM	H	Won	3	3	1	-	15	-	-	-	-	0	McKechnie(3C) Parsons(T,D) Coleman(T) Snowden(T) Porter(T) Mason(T) Morley(T)
17	Apr	2	Nottingham	A	Lost	-	1	-	-	1	1	3	-	-	6	Apperley(T)

INDIVIDUAL APPEARANCES 1886-1887

NAME	1	2	3	4	5	6	7	8	9	10	11	12	13	14	15	16	17	18	19	20	21	22	23	24	25	26	27	28	29	30	31	32	33	34	35	36	37	38	39	40	41	42	43	44	45	46	TOTAL	T	PTS
Arthur McKechnie	FB	FB	FB	FB	3Q	HB	FB	3Q	-	F	-	-	3Q	FB	3Q	FB	FB																														14	1	16
T.F.Hoyle	-	-	-	-	FB	FB	-	FB	FB	FB	-	FB	-	-	-	-	-																														6		-
Sherrard Coleman	3Q	3Q	3Q	3Q	-	3Q	3Q	3Q	3Q	3Q	-	3Q	3Q	3Q	3Q	3Q	3Q																														14	8	8
H.W.Oxlade	3Q	-	-	-	-	-	-	-	HB	3Q	HB	-	HB	-	-	-	-																														5		-
John Parsons	3Q	3Q	3Q	3Q	3Q	3Q	3Q	3Q	3Q	3Q	-	3Q	3Q	3Q	3Q	3Q	3Q																														16	2	37
Fred Apperley	-	3Q	3Q	3Q	3Q	3Q	3Q	3Q	3Q	-	3Q	-	3Q	3Q	3Q	3Q	-																														14	6	6
W.A.Wheeler	-	-	-	-	-	-	-	-	-	-	-	-	3Q	-	FB	-	-																														2		-
W.A.Sheffield	HB	HB	HB	HB	-	-	HB	-	-	HB	-	-	HB	-	-	-	-																														7	1	1
Dickie Snowden	HB	HB	HB	HB	HB	HB	HB	HB	HB	HB	HB	HB	HB	HB	HB	HB	HB																														16	6	6
F.Bonner	F	F	F	-	-	-	-	-	-	-	-	-	-	-	-	-	-																														3	1	1
J.T.Cressey	F	F	F	F	F	F	F	F	F	F	F	-	-	-	-	-	-																														10	1	1
E.Line	F	-	-	F	F	F	F	F	F	F	F	-	F	F	-	F	-																														11	-	-
Jack Lovett	F	F	F	-	F	-	-	-	F	-	-	-	F	-	F	F	-																														8		-
Henry Mason	F	F	F	F	F	F	F	F	F	F	F	-	F	F	F	F	-																														15	3	3
Joey Morley	F	F	F	F	F	F	F	F	F	F	-	F	F	-	F	F	-																														14	2	2
W.R.Porter	F	F	F	-	F	F	F	-	-	F	-	F	F	-	F	F	-																														11	2	2
W.M.Smith	F	F	F	F	-	-	-	-	-	-	-	-	-	-	-	-	-																														4	1	1
B.Wilkinson	F	F	F	-	F	F	F	F	F	-	-	F	F	-	F	-	-																														11	2	2
Kenneth McAlpin	-	F	F	F	-	F	HB	F	HB	F	-	F	HB	-	F	-	-																														11	1	1
T.S.Gordon	-	-	-	F	F	-	-	-	-	-	-	F	F	-	-	-	-																														4		-
J.Voce	-	-	-	-	F	HB	F	F	F	-	-	-	-	-	-	-	-																														5	1	1
J.S.Wilkinson	-	-	-	F	-	-	-	-	-	F	3Q	-	-	F	-	-	-																														4	1	1
J.R.Abel	-	-	-	-	-	-	F	F	-	F	-	-	-	-	-	-	-																														3		
Hedley Salmon	-	-	-	-	-	F	F	F	F	-	F	F	F	F	-	-	-																														8	-	-

1 game: A.N.Other F(12), Dickie Bell FB(11), A.E.Brice F(5), Joseph Collier FB(13), William Massey F(12)

LEICESTER FOOTBALL CLUB 1886-87
Back: E.R. Morley, W.A. Wheeler, E. Line, J. Collier (Umpire), B. Wilkinson, Dr.H. Mason, W.A. Sheffield.
Middle: K. McAlpin, H.W. Salmon, J. Parsons (Capt), W.R. Porter, R.S. Snowden.
Front: F. Apperley, A. McKechnie, J.T. Lovett, J.G.S. Coleman.

NO	DATE		OPPONENTS	V	RES	FOR					AGAINST					SCORERS
						G	T	D	P	PTS	G	T	D	P	PTS	
1	Oct	1	Coventry	A	Drew	-	-	-	-	0	-	-	-	-	0	
2		'8	KETTERING	H	Won	-	-	1	-	3	-	-	-	-	0	Oxlade(D)
3		15	Bedford	A	Lost	-	-	-	-	0	2	2	-	-	8	
4		22	Moseley	A	Lost	-	-	-	-	0	1	1	1	-	7	
5		29	BEDFORD GRAMMAR SCH.	H	Won	2	1	-	-	7	-	-	-	-	0	Parsons(C) Coleman(2T) Oxlade(T) Unknown(C)
6	Nov	12	Kettering	A	Won	2	1	-	-	10	1	-	-	-	3	Parsons(T,2C,D) Coleman(T) Snowden(T)
		19	COVENTRY	H		Cancelled Frost										
7		26	Peterborough & Dist.	A	Won	3	4	-	-	13	-	-	-	-	0	Phillips(2T) Coleman(2T) Oxlade(T,3C) B.Wilkinson(T) Mason(T)
8	Dec	3	RUGBY	H	Won	2	-	-	-	6	-	-	-	-	0	Parsons(T,2C) Oxlade(T)
9		10	NORTHAMPTON UNITY	H	Won	3	5	1	-	17	-	-	-	-	0	Parsons(3T,3C,D) Coleman(T) Phillips(2T) Oxlade(T) McAlpin(T)
10		17	BURTON-ON-TRENT	H	Lost	-	-	-	-	0	1	2	-	-	5	
11		24	RUSHDEN	H	Won	2	3	-	-	9	-	1	-	-	1	Sulley(T,2C) Phillips(T) Pilsbury(T) Brockbank(T) Salmon(T)
12		31	NOTTINGHAM	H	Won	1	1	-	-	4	-	-	-	-	0	Parsons(C) Brockbank(2T)
13	Jan	7	Burton-on-Trent	A	Lost	-	-	-	-	0	-	1	-	-	1	
14		14	NOTTINGHAM	H	Won	1	5	-	-	8	-	-	-	-	0	Phillips(2T) Parsons(2T) Brockbank(C) Smith(T) B.Wilkinson(T)
15		21	Rugby	A	Lost	-	-	-	-	0	1	2	-	-	5	
		28	Burton-on-Trent	A		Cancelled Frost										
16	Feb	4	MOSELEY	H	Drew	-	-	-	-	0	-	-	-	-	0	
17		11	Bedford Grammar Sch.	A	Won	2	1	-	-	7	1	-	-	-	3	Parsons(2C) Phillips(T) Porter(T) Smith(T)
		18	Bedford	A		Cancelled Snow										
		25	Northampton Unity	A		Cancelled Snow										
18	Mar	3	NORTHAMPTON	H	Won	-	4	-	-	4	-	-	-	-	0	Phillips(2T) Coleman(T) Morley(T)
19		10	Manningham	A	Lost	1	1	-	-	4	1	1	1	1	10	McKechnie(C) Parsons(T) Oxlade(T)
		17	STOKE-ON-TRENT (MCC3)	H		Cancelled										
20		24	BURTON-ON-TRENT (MCCSF)	H	Drew	-	-	-	-	0	-	-	-	-	0	
21		31	Northampton	A	Lost	-	-	-	-	0	1	1	-	-	4	

INDIVIDUAL APPEARANCES 1887-1888

NAME	1	2	3	4	5	6	7	8	9	10	11	12	13	14	15	16	17	18	19	20	21	TOTAL	T	PTS
Arthur McKechnie	FB	FB	-	3Q	3Q	3Q	-	FB	FB	FB	-	-	FB	FB	FB	FB	FB	FB	FB	FB	-	16	-	2
Joe Barradell	-	-	-	-	-	-	-	-	-	-	-	FB	-	-	-	3Q	-	-	-	-	-	2	-	-
Sherrard Coleman	3Q	3Q	3Q	3Q	3Q	3Q	3Q	3Q	3Q	3Q	3Q	-	-	-	-	3Q	3Q	3Q	-	-	-	16	7	7
John Parsons	3Q	3Q	3Q	3Q	3Q	3Q	3Q	3Q	3Q	HB	3Q	3Q	3Q	3Q	3Q	HB	3Q	3Q	3Q	-	-	21	8	36
E.Pilsbury	3Q	3Q	-	-	-	-	-	-	-	HB	HB	3Q	-	-	-	-	3Q	-	-	-	-	6	1	1
T.F.Hoyle	-	-	3Q	FB	FB	FB	-	-	-	-	-	-	-	-	-	-	-	-	-	-	-	4	-	-
E.V.Phillips	-	-	-	-	-	-	3Q	3Q	3Q	3Q	3Q	3Q	-	-	3Q	3Q	3Q	3Q	3Q	3Q	-	12	10	10
Bob Golding	-	-	-	-	-	-	-	-	-	3Q	-	-	3Q	-	-	-	-	-	-	-	-	2	-	-
J.Mansell	-	-	-	-	-	-	-	-	-	-	-	-	-	-	-	3Q	-	3Q	-	-	-	2	-	-
H.W.Oxlade	HB	HB	HB	HB	HB	HB	HB	HB	HB	HB	-	HB	HB	HB	HB	HB	HB	HB	HB	-	-	18	5	14
Dickie Snowden	HB	HB	HB	HB	HB	HB	HB	HB	HB	-	-	HB	HB	-	HB	HB	-	HB	HB	-	-	16	1	1
Harry Brockbank	F	-	F	F	F	F	-	F	F	F	F	F	F	3Q	-	F	F	F	F	-	-	17	3	5
E.Line	F	F	F	F	-	-	-	-	-	-	-	-	-	-	-	-	-	-	-	-	-	4	-	-
Henry Mason	F	F	F	F	F	F	F	F	F	F	F	F	F	F	-	F	F	F	F	-	-	19	1	1
Kenneth McAlpin	F	F	F	3Q	F	F	-	F	F	F	F	F	F	F	HB	F	F	F	F	-	-	19	1	1
Joey' Morley	F	F	F	F	F	F	-	F	F	F	F	F	F	F	F	F	F	F	F	-	-	19	1	1
-.Moore	F	F	F	F	F	-	-	-	-	-	-	-	-	-	-	-	-	-	-	-	-	5	-	-
Hedley Salmon	F	F	-	-	-	F	-	-	F	F	-	-	-	-	-	-	-	-	-	-	-	5	1	1
Mamma' Wright	F	F	F	-	-	-	-	-	-	3Q	-	-	F	-	-	-	-	-	-	-	-	5	-	-
Jack Lovett	-	F	F	F	F	F	-	F	F	F	F	F	F	F	F	F	F	F	-	-	-	18	-	-
W.R.Porter	-	F	F	-	F	F	-	F	F	F	F	F	F	F	F	F	F	F	-	-	-	16	1	1
W.M.Smith	-	-	-	F	F	-	F	F	F	F	F	F	F	F	F	F	F	F	-	-	-	15	2	2
J.S.Wilkinson	-	-	-	-	-	F	-	F	F	F	-	-	-	F	F	-	F	F	F	-	-	9	-	-
B.Wilkinson	-	-	-	-	-	-	F	-	-	-	-	F	-	-	F	-	F	F	-	-	-	5	2	2
W.A.Sheffield	-	-	-	-	-	-	-	-	-	F	F	-	-	-	-	-	-	-	-	-	-	2	-	-
H.M.Barradell	-	-	-	-	-	-	-	-	F	F	F	F	F	-	-	F	-	-	-	-	-	6	-	-
Charles Fuller	-	-	-	-	-	-	-	-	-	F	F	F	F	F	-	-	-	-	-	-	-	5	-	-

1 game: -.Atkins F(6), J.W.Billson F(21), B.C.Burton F(4), C.W.Ford 3Q(5), -.Greenwell 3Q(1), -.Griffin 3Q(7), C.B.Knight HB(12), H.Stanyon FB(3), A.Sulley 3Q(11)[1T-5], W.A.Wheeler FB(11)

LEICESTER FOOTBALL CLUB 'A' TEAM 1887-88
Back: H.W. Oxlade, F. Bonner, A. Nutt, J.R. Abel, C.B. Knight, Mr.J.W. Symington (Referee), T.F. Hoyle, A.W. Howard, W. Coltman, W. Massey.
Middle: C.W. Ford, H. Stanyon, E. Bell (Capt), B.C. Burton.
Front: P.G. Salmon, A.R. Kaye.

NO	DATE		OPPONENTS	V	RES	FOR					AGAINST					SCORERS
						G	T	D	P	PTS	G	T	D	P	PTS	
1	Sep	29	COLTS TOWN & COUNTRY	H	Won	2	1	-	-	7	-	-	-	-	0	Parsons(2C) Mason(T) McAlpin(T) Brockbank(T)
2	Oct	6	SWINTON	H	Lost	-	1	-	-	1	2	5	-	-	11	Brockbank(T)
3		13	COVENTRY	H	Drew	-	1	-	-	1	-	1	-	-	1	Snowden(T)
4		17	Bedford	A	Drew	-	1	-	-	1	-	1	-	-	1	McAlpin(T)
5		20	Manningham	A	Lost	-	-	-	-	0	2	3	-	-	9	
6		27	Edgbaston Crusaders	A	Drew	-	2	-	-	2	-	2	-	-	2	Mansell(T) Coleman(T)
7	Nov	3	RUGBY	H	Drew	-	-	-	-	0	-	-	-	-	0	
8		10	Old Edwardians	A	Lost	-	1	-	-	1	1	1	-	-	4	B.Wilkinson(T)
9		17	MOSELEY	H	Lost	1	1	-	-	4	1	2	-	-	5	Gilbey(T) Brockbank(C) Morley(T)
10		24	Coventry	A	Drew	-	-	-	-	0	-	-	-	-	0	
11	Dec	1	BEDFORD GRAMMAR SCH.	H	Lost	-	1	-	-	1	1	1	-	-	4	Beasley(T)
12		8	Burton-on-Trent	A	Lost	-	-	-	-	0	1	2	-	-	5	
13		15	BEDFORD	H	Drew	-	3	-	-	3	1	-	-	-	3	Brockbank(T) Willey(2T)
14		22	Rugby	A	Lost	-	1	-	-	1	1	1	-	-	4	Wilcock(T)
15		26	RUSHDEN	H	Won	2	4	-	-	10	-	-	-	-	0	Wilcock(T) Gilbey(T) Brockbank(2C) Mason(2T) Beasley(T) Coleman(T)
16		29	NOTTINGHAM	H	Won	3	1	1	-	13	-	-	-	-	0	A.Nutt(2T) McKechnie(T) Brockbank(3C,D) Coleman(T)
	Jan	5	Kettering	A				Cancelled Frost								
17		12	BURTON-ON-TRENT	H	Won	1	1	1	-	7	-	-	-	-	0	McKechnie(D) Coleman(2T) Brockbank(C)
18		19	KETTERING	H	Drew	-	1	-	1	4	-	1	-	1	4	Willey(T) Brockbank(P)
19		26	Moseley	A	Lost	-	-	-	-	0	2	1	1	-	10	
20	Feb	2	Bedford	A	Lost	-	1	-	-	1	1	-	-	-	3	Bell(T)
21		5	MANNINGHAM	H	Lost	-	-	-	-	0	-	4	-	-	4	
22		9	EDGBASTON CRUSADERS	H	Won	-	3	-	-	3	-	1	-	-	1	McKechnie(T) Ley(T) Bell(T)
23		16	Swinton	A	Lost	-	-	-	-	0	1	7	-	-	10	
24		18	Oldham	A	Lost	-	-	-	-	0	-	3	-	-	3	
25		23	OLD EDWARDIANS	H	Won	1	2	-	-	5	-	1	1	-	4	Snowden(T) Brockbank(C) McAlpin(T) Mason(T)
26		28	LEICESTER SWIFTS	H	Won	2	7	-	-	13	-	-	-	-	0	Chettle(T) McKechnie(2T,2C) A.Nutt(T) W.R.Porter(T) McAlpin(3T) Mansell(T)
27	Mar	2	MOSELEY HARLEQUINS (MCC1)	H	Won	-	2	-	-	2	-	-	-	-	0	McKechnie(T) Brockbank(T)
28		6	BEDFORD	H	Won	-	4	-	-	4	1	-	-	-	3	'Knott'(3T) McAlpin(T)
29		9	Rugby (MCC2)	A	Won	1	-	1	-	6	-	2	1	-	5	McKechnie(D) A.T.Porter(T) Brockbank(C)
30		16	STRATFORD-UPON-AVON (MCCSF)	H	Won	-	1	1	-	4	1	-	-	-	3	A.T.Porter(D) B.Wilkinson(T)
31		23	Moseley (MCCF)	A	Lost	-	-	-	-	0	1	-	1	-	6	
32		30	CARDIFF HARLEQUINS	H	Lost	-	-	-	-	0	1	2	-	-	5	
	Apr	6	BEDFORD GRAMMAR SCH.	H				Cancelled									
33		13	18 of TOWN & DIST.	H	Lost	-	-	-	-	0	-	2	-	-	2	

INDIVIDUAL APPEARANCES 1888-1889

NAME	1	2	3	4	5	6	7	8	9	10	11	12	13	14	15	16	17	18	19	20	21	22	23	24	25	26	27	28	29	30	31	32	33	34	35	36	37	38	39	40	41	42	43	44	45	46	TOTAL	T	PTS
Arthur McKechnie	FB	FB	FB	-	FB	FB	FB	FB	FB	-	3Q	3Q	3Q	3Q	3Q	3Q	3Q	3Q	3Q	3Q	3Q	3Q	-	3Q	3Q	3Q	3Q	3Q	3Q	3Q																	30	5	15
A.Chettle	-	-	-	-	-	-	-	-	-	-	-	-	-	-	-	-	-	-	-	-	-	-	FB	FB	-	FB	-	3Q	FB	-	FB	-	-														6	1	1
Tom Nutt	-	-	-	-	-	-	-	-	-	-	-	-	-	-	-	-	-	-	-	-	-	FB	-	-	-	F	FB	-	F																		4	-	-
Sherrard Coleman	3Q	-	3Q	FB	3Q	3Q	-	3Q	-	F	F	3Q	-	F	F	F	F	F	F	F	F	F	-	-	F	-	F	F	F	3Q	F	F	-														25	5	5
John Parsons	3Q	3Q	3Q	3Q	3Q	3Q	-	-	-	-	-	-	-	-	-	-	-	-	-	-	-	-	-	-	-	FB	-	-	-																		7	-	4
E.Pilsbury	3Q	3Q	-	-	-	-	-	-	-	-	-	-	-	-	-	-	-	-	-	-	-	-	-	-	-	-	-	-	-																		2	-	-
J.Fernie	-	3Q	-	3Q	-	-	-	-	3Q	-	-	-	-	-	-	-	-	-	-	-	-	-	-	-	-	-	-	-	-	3Q																	4	-	-
J.Mansell	-	-	3Q	-	3Q	3Q	3Q	3Q	3Q	F	FB	FB	FB	-	-	-	-	-	FB	FB	F	FB	-	-	-	-	F	F	F	-	3Q																	18	2	2
Arthur Porter	-	-	-	-	-	-	-	-	-	3Q	3Q	3Q	3Q	3Q	3Q	3Q	3Q	3Q	3Q	3Q	3Q	3Q	3Q	-	3Q	3Q	3Q																				18	1	4
J.H.Wilcock	-	-	-	-	-	-	-	-	-	-	-	-	3Q	3Q	-	-	-	-	-	-	-	-	-	-	-	-	-	-	-																		2	2	2
J.Robertson	-	-	-	-	-	-	-	-	-	-	-	-	-	-	-	-	-	-	-	-	3Q	3Q	-	-	-	-	-	-	-																		2	-	-
H.W.Oxlade	HB	HB	HB	-	3Q	HB	HB	HB	-	-	-	-	-	-	-	-	-	-	HB	-	-	-	-	-	-	-	-	-	-																		8	-	-
Dickie Snowden	HB	HB	HB	HB	HB	HB	3Q	3Q	3Q	3Q	HB	HB	HB	-	-	HB	HB	HB	HB	HB	HB	HB	-	3Q	HB	HB	HB	F																			26	2	2
Robert Ley	-	-	-	HB	HB	-	HB	-	HB	HB	HB	-	HB	HB	-	-	HB	HB	-	HB	HB	-	HB	HB	-	HB	HB	HB	HB	-																	20	1	1
W.J.Gilbey	-	-	-	-	-	-	-	-	HB	HB	-	HB	3Q	F	HB	HB	F	-	F	F	F	F	HB	HB	HB	F	-	HB	-	HB	HB	HB	HB	-													22	2	2
E.Peddie	-	-	-	-	-	-	-	-	-	-	-	-	-	-	-	-	-	-	-	-	-	-	-	-	-	-	HB	-	-	-	-	-	HB														2	-	-
Harry Brockbank	F	-	F	-	F	-	F	F	F	F	F	F	F	F	-	F	F	F	F	F	F	F	-	F	F	F	F	-	F	FB	F	F	F	F	FB												29	4	28
B.C.Burton	F	F	F	-	F	-	-	F	-	-	-	-	-	-	-	-	-	-	-	-	-	-	-	-	-	-	-	-	-																		4	-	-
-.Greenwell	F	-	-	F	-	-	F	-	-	-	-	-	-	-	-	-	-	-	-	-	-	-	-	-	-	-	-	-	-																		2	-	-
Jack Lovett	F	-	-	-	-	-	-	-	-	-	F	F	F	F	F	-	-	F	-	-	F	-	-	F	-	-	-	-	F																		9	-	-
Henry Mason	F	F	-	-	F	F	F	F	F	3Q	3Q	F	F	-	F	F	-	-	F	F	-	-	-	F	F	-	-	F	F	-	F	F	F	-													23	4	4
Kenneth McAlpin	F	F	F	F	F	3Q	HB	3Q	3Q	HB	F	F	-	F	F	F	F	F	F	F	F	F	F	F	F	F	F	F	F	F	F	-															32	7	7
'Joey' Morley	F	F	F	F	F	F	F	F	F	F	F	F	F	F	F	-	F	F	-	F	F	F	F	F	F	F	F	F	F	F	-																30	1	1
W.R.Porter	F	F	F	F	F	F	F	F	-	-	F	F	F	-	F	F	F	F	F	F	F	F	F	F	F	F	F	F	F	-																	29	1	1
G.D.P.Smith	F	F	-	F	F	F	F	F	F	-	F	-	F	-	-	-	-	-	-	-	-	-	-	-	-	-	-	-	-																		10	-	-
W.M.Smith	-	-	-	F	-	F	F	F	F	-	-	-	-	-	-	-	-	-	-	-	-	-	-	-	-	-	-	-	-																		9	-	-
Ally Nutt	-	F	F	-	-	-	-	-	F	-	3Q	-	-	HB	3Q	3Q	3Q	3Q	-	3Q	-	-	3Q	3Q	3Q	3Q	-	3Q	3Q	3Q	3Q	-																18	3	3
B.Wilkinson	-	-	F	F	F	F	F	F	F	F	F	-	-	-	-	-	-	-	-	-	-	-	-	-	-	-	-	F	F	F	-																	13	2	2
S.G.Porter	-	-	-	F	-	F	-	F	-	-	-	-	-	-	-	-	-	-	-	-	-	-	-	-	-	-	-	-	-																		3	-	-
Fred Simpson	-	-	-	-	-	-	F	-	F	-	-	-	-	-	-	-	-	-	-	-	-	-	-	-	-	-	-	-	-																		2	-	-
J.S.Wilkinson	-	-	-	F	F	-	-	-	-	-	-	-	-	-	-	-	-	-	-	-	-	-	-	-	-	-	F	F	-	F	-																	5	-	-
E.E.Beasley	-	-	-	-	F	F	F	F	F	F	-	F	F	F	F	F	-	-	-	-	-	-	-	-	-	-	-	-	-																		11	2	2
P.G.Salmon	-	-	-	-	-	-	-	F	F	-	-	-	-	-	-	-	-	-	-	-	-	-	-	-	-	-	-	-	-																		2	-	-
H.Bostock	-	-	-	-	-	-	-	F	F	-	-	-	-	-	-	-	-	-	-	-	-	-	-	-	-	-	-	-	-																		2	-	-
W.J.Willey	-	-	-	-	-	-	-	-	F	F	F	-	F	F	F	-	F	F	-	-	-	-	-	-	-	-	F	-	F	-																	12	3	3
Dickie Bell	-	-	-	-	-	-	-	-	F	F	HB	-	-	-	F	F	F	F	F	F	F	F	F	-	F	-	F	F	F	F																	15	2	2
Sgt.T.J.Jacomb	-	-	-	-	-	-	-	F	-	FB	FB	-	-	F	FB	-	-	F	-	-	FB	F	-	-	-	F	-	-	-																		9	-	-
J.Hall	-	-	-	-	-	-	-	-	-	-	-	-	-	-	-	-	-	-	-	F	F	-	-	-	-	-	-	-	-																		2	-	-
H.Stannard	-	-	-	-	-	-	-	-	-	-	-	-	-	-	-	-	-	-	F	F	-	-	-	-	-	-	-	-	-																		2	-	-

1 game: A.N.Other F(20), -.Atkins F(12), J.Buckle F(28), -.Burbridge F(25), W.Cowley F(10), A.B.Fforde 3Q(4), -.Hadfield F(21), C.B.Knight FB(15), -."Knott' 3Q(28)[3T-3], -.Lea FB(14), W.H.McMurray F(14), -.Mosby FB(18), E.Neild 3Q(32), Herbert Orr 3Q(21), George Porter F(20), Jack Sturges F(28), J.Walsh HB(24), -.White F(11)

NO	DATE		OPPONENTS	V	RES	FOR					AGAINST					SCORERS
						G	T	D	P	PTS	G	T	D	P	PTS	
1	Sep	28	Stratford-upon-Avon	A	Lost	-	-	-	-	0	1	4	-	-	7	
2	Oct	5	OLD EDWARDIANS	H	Lost	-	-	-	1	2	2	1	-	-	7	Brockbank(P)
3		12	RUGBY	H	Won	-	1	1	-	4	-	-	-	-	0	McKechnie(D) Sturges(T)
4		19	Oldham	A	Lost	-	-	-	-	0	2	4	-	-	10	
5		26	BEDFORD GRAMMAR SCH.	H	Lost	1	-	-	-	3	1	1	-	-	4	McKechnie(C) W.R.Porter(T)
6	Nov	2	MOSSLEY	H	Lost	1	-	-	-	3	-	4	-	-	4	McKechnie(C) Mason(T)
7		9	Moseley	A	Lost	-	-	-	-	0	2	1	-	-	7	
8		16	OLDHAM	H	Lost	-	-	-	-	0	-	3	1	-	6	
9		23	Swinton	A	Lost	-	-	-	-	0	2	4	-	1	12	
10		30	NORTHAMPTON	H	Won	1	-	-	-	3	-	-	-	-	0	McKechnie(C) Neild(T)
	Dec	7	Rugby	A	Cancelled											
11		14	COVENTRY	H	Drew	1	-	-	-	3	1	-	-	-	3	McKechnie(C) Ball(T)
12		21	STRATFORD-UPON-AVON	H	Lost	-	-	-	-	0	-	2	-	-	2	
13		26	MANCHESTER FREE WAND	H	Won	3	6	-	-	15	-	-	-	-	0	Ball(C) McKechnie(T,C) Sulley(4T,C) Gilbey(T) H.German(T) Sturges(T) 'Brown'(T)
14		28	Coventry	A	Lost	-	-	-	-	0	-	3	-	-	3	
	Jan	4	SWINTON	H	Cancelled Frost											
		11	Mossley	A	Cancelled											
15		18	LEAMINGTON	H	Won	-	3	-	-	3	-	-	-	-	0	McKechnie(2T) W.R.Porter(T)
16		20	SWINTON	H	Lost	-	-	-	-	0	1	3	-	-	6	
17		25	Manningham	A	Lost	-	-	-	-	0	1	3	-	-	6	
18	Feb	1	BURTON-ON-TRENT	H	Lost	-	1	-	-	1	2	2	-	-	8	Neild(T)
19		5	Rugby	A	Lost	-	-	-	-	0	4	3	-	-	15	
		6	Bedford Grammar Sch.	A	Cancelled											
20		8	MOSELEY	H	Lost	-	1	-	-	1	1	2	-	-	5	McKechnie(T)
21		15	MANNINGHAM	H	Lost	-	2	-	-	2	1	2	-	-	5	Ball(T) McKechnie(T)
22		22	Old Edwardians	A	Lost	-	-	-	-	0	2	3	-	-	9	
23	Mar	1	Stratford-upon-Avon (MCC1)	A	Lost	-	-	-	-	0	4	1	-	-	13	
24		5	ASHBY-DE-LA-ZOUCH	H	Won	1	2	-	-	5	-	1	-	-	1	Wallace(C) McKechnie(2T) Coleman(T)
25		29	Burton-on-Trent	A	Drew	-	-	-	-	0	-	-	-	-	0	
26	Apr	7	Cardiff	A	Lost	-	-	-	-	0	-	2	-	-	2	
27		8	Newport	A	Lost	-	1	-	-	1	2	3	-	-	9	H.German(T)

INDIVIDUAL APPEARANCES 1889-1890

NAME	1	2	3	4	5	6	7	8	9	10	11	12	13	14	15	16	17	18	19	20	21	22	23	24	25	26	27	28	TOTAL	T	PTS
W.L.Wotherspoon	FB	-	-	-	FB	-	FB	-	-	FB	-	-	-	-	-	-	-	-	-	-	-	-	-	-	-	FB	-	-	5		
Donal McAlpin	-	-	-	-	-	-	-	-	-	-	-	-	-	FB	FB	FB	FB	FB	FB	FB	FB	FB	-	-	-	-	-	-	9		
J.Ball	W	-	-	C	-	-	-	-	-	W	W	C	FB	W	-	-	W	C	W	W	W	W	W	-	-	-	-	-	14	2	4
A.Chettle	W	FB	FB	FB	-	W	W	FB	FB	-	-	-	-	-	-	-	-	-	-	-	-	-	-	-	-	-	-	-	8		
H.W.Oxlade	-	W	W	-	-	HB	-	-	-	-	-	-	-	-	-	-	-	-	-	-	-	-	-	-	-	-	-	-	3		
W.S.Sheppard	-	-	-	W	-	F	-	-	-	-	-	-	-	-	-	-	-	F	F	-	-	-	-	-	-	-	-	-	4		
F.Nutt	-	-	-	-	W	-	-	-	-	-	-	-	-	-	-	-	-	-	-	-	-	-	-	-	C	C	-	FB	4		
G.A.Ogden	-	-	-	-	-	-	-	W	-	HB	HB	HB	HB	-	FB	-	-	-	-	-	-	-	-	-	-	-	-	-	6		
Harry German	-	-	-	-	-	-	-	W	-	-	F	-	-	-	-	-	C	-	-	-	-	F	F	F	-	-	-	-	6	2	2
A.Sulley	-	-	-	-	-	-	-	-	-	-	-	-	W	-	W	-	-	-	-	-	-	-	-	-	-	-	-	-	2	4	6
Tom Nutt	-	-	-	-	-	-	-	-	-	-	-	-	-	-	W	F	-	-	C	W	-	C	-	-	-	-	-	-	5		
E.J.Byrne	-	-	-	-	-	-	-	-	-	-	-	-	-	-	-	-	-	-	-	-	-	-	-	-	W	W	-	-	2		
F.A.Rogers	-	-	-	-	-	-	-	-	-	-	-	-	-	-	-	-	-	-	-	-	-	-	-	-	W	C	W	-	3		
G.Cattell	-	-	-	-	-	-	-	-	-	-	-	-	-	-	-	-	-	-	-	-	-	-	-	-	-	W	C	-	2		
W.Williamson	C	W	W	W	W	-	-	-	-	-	-	-	-	-	-	-	-	-	-	-	-	-	-	-	-	-	-	-	5		
J.H.Wilcock	-	C	-	-	-	-	-	-	-	-	-	-	W	-	-	-	-	-	W	-	-	-	-	-	-	-	-	-	3		
Arthur McKechnie	-	-	C	C	C	C	C	W	C	W	W	FB	W	W	C	C	C	W	-	W	C	C	W	W	-	FB	W	-	23	7	20
E.M.Dawson-Thomas	-	-	-	-	-	-	-	C	W	-	FB	-	-	-	-	-	-	-	-	-	-	-	-	-	-	-	-	-	3		
Abel Ashworth	-	-	-	-	-	-	-	-	-	-	-	-	-	-	-	-	-	-	-	-	-	-	-	-	C	C	-	-	2		
Dickie Bell	HB	HB	-	HB	HB	HB	HB	F	F*	F	F	F	-	HB	-	F	F	-	F	-	F	F	-	-	-	-	-	-	17		
W.J.Gilbey	-	-	HB	-	HB	-	HB	HB	-	F	F	F	HB	HB	-	-	HB	HB	-	HB	-	-	-	-	-	-	-	-	12	1	1
Robert Ley	-	-	HB	-	-	-	-	-	-	-	-	HB	-	-	-	-	-	-	-	-	-	-	-	-	-	-	-	-	2		
Joe Barradell	-	-	-	-	-	-	-	-	-	-	-	-	-	HB	-	-	-	-	-	HB	-	HB	HB	-	-	-	-	-	4		
E.W.Chamberlain	-	-	-	-	-	-	-	-	-	-	-	-	-	-	HB	HB	HB	HB	HB	HB	HB	-	-	-	-	-	-	-	7		
J.Dunmore	-	-	-	-	-	-	-	-	-	-	-	-	-	-	-	-	-	-	-	-	HB	-	-	F	-	-	-	-	2		
Dick Cattell	-	-	-	-	-	-	-	-	-	-	-	-	-	-	-	-	-	-	-	-	-	-	-	-	-	HB	HB	-	2		
Sherrard Coleman	F	F	F	F	F	W	C	-	F	C	C	W	C	C	W	F	W	F	W	F	W	F	F	F	F	-	-	-	26	1	1
Sgt.T.J.Jacomb	F	F	-	-	F	-	-	F	-	F	-	-	-	-	-	-	-	-	-	-	F	-	-	F	-	-	-	-	5		
Kenneth McAlpin	F	F	-	F	F	F	F	F	F	F	F	F	F	F	F	F	F	F	-	F	F	F	F	F	F	-	-	-	25		
Joey' Morley	F	F	F	F	F	F	-	F	-	F	F	F	F	-	-	-	-	F	-	F	F	F	F	-	-	-	-	-	18		
W.R.Porter	F	F	F	F	F	F	F	F	-	F	F	F	F	F	F	F	F	F	F	F	F	F	F	F	F	F	-	-	26	2	2
Jack Sturges	F	-	F	F	F	F	F	F	F	F	F	F	F	F	F	F	F	F	F	F	F	F	F	F	F	F	F	-	26	2	2
Harry Brockbank	-	F	-	F	-	-	-	-	-	-	-	-	-	-	-	-	-	-	-	-	-	-	-	-	-	-	-	-	2		2
T.W.Lawrence	-	F	-	F	-	-	-	F	F	-	-	-	-	-	-	-	-	-	F	F	-	-	-	-	-	-	-	-	6		
Leonard Ward	-	F	F	-	F	F	F	F	F	F	F	-	F	-	F	F	-	F	F	F	F	-	F	F	F	-	-	-	21		
C.O.Barrow	-	-	F	F	F	F	-	-	-	-	-	-	-	-	-	-	-	-	-	-	-	-	-	-	-	-	-	-	3		
Henry Mason	-	-	F	-	F	F	F	F	-	-	-	-	-	-	-	-	-	-	-	-	F	-	-	-	-	-	-	-	5	1	1
E.Neild	-	-	F	-	-	-	-	-	HB	HB	HB	HB	HB	-	HB	HB	HB	HB	-	-	-	-	-	-	HB	HB	-	-	12	2	2
John Powers	-	-	F	-	F	F	F	F	-	-	-	F	F	-	-	-	-	-	-	-	-	-	-	-	-	-	-	-	6		
Jack Lovett	-	-	-	-	F	F	F	F	-	-	-	F	-	F	F	-	-	F	-	-	-	-	-	-	-	-	-	-	8		
George Porter	-	-	-	-	F	-	F	F	F	F	-	F	-	-	-	-	-	-	-	-	-	-	-	-	F	-	-	-	6		
Dr.H. 'Brown'	-	-	-	-	F	F	F	F	-	F	-	F	F	-	F	-	F	-	-	-	F	-	F	-	-	-	-	-	8	1	1
Sam Wright	-	-	-	-	-	-	-	-	-	F	-	F	-	F	-	F	-	F	-	-	-	-	-	-	-	-	-	-	3		
W.H.McMurray	-	-	-	-	-	-	-	-	-	F	F	-	F	-	-	-	-	-	-	-	-	-	-	-	-	-	-	-	3		
O.McSalley	-	-	-	-	-	-	-	-	-	-	-	-	-	-	-	-	-	-	-	-	-	-	-	-	HB	-	-	-	2		
Jack Yorke	-	-	-	-	-	-	-	-	-	-	-	F	-	-	-	-	-	-	-	-	F	-	-	-	-	-	-	-	2		
T.R.Wilkes	-	-	-	-	-	-	-	-	-	-	-	-	F	-	F	F	-	F	-	-	F	-	F	-	-	-	-	-	4		
T.Robinson	-	-	-	-	-	-	-	-	-	-	-	-	-	-	-	-	-	F	-	F	-	-	-	-	-	-	-	-	2		
W.D.Ludlow	-	-	-	-	-	-	-	-	-	-	-	-	-	-	-	-	-	-	-	-	-	-	-	-	-	F	F	-	2		
B.Wilkinson	-	-	-	-	-	-	-	-	-	-	-	-	-	-	-	-	-	-	-	-	-	-	-	-	-	F	F	-	2		

1 game: J.Buckle F(19), J.Cass F(17), Ted Cooke HB(1), W.H.Cowlishaw F(1), H.S.Dickinson F(18), S.H.Fisher F(16), C.W.Ford F(24), G.German F(19), S.B.Hill F(11), C.A.Kingston W(16), E.Line F(8), W.S.Lovell F(19), J.Mansell F(2), J.Mills F(19), -.Nobren F(24), R.Pailthorpe HB(16), -.Skinner-Jones W(8), J.B."Smith' F(16), Dickie Snowden HB(4), -.Wallace FB(24)[2], Willie Watts W(24), W.A.Wheeler FB(6), Sid Wykes F(25)

NO	DATE		OPPONENTS	V	RES	FOR					AGAINST					SCORERS
						G	T	D	P	PTS	G	T	D	P	PTS	
1	Oct	4	MOSELEY	H	Won	2	1	-	1	9	-	-	2	-	6	F.Nutt(T) Pilsbury(T) Brockbank(2C,P) Ward(T)
2		8	ASHBY-DE-LA-ZOUCH	H	Won	1	2	1	-	8	-	-	-	-	0	McKechnie(C) Rathbone(T) Barradell(D) McAlpin(T) Sturges(T)
3		11	Old Edwardians	A	Drew	-	1	-	-	1	-	1	-	-	1	Ward(T)
4		18	LEICESTER CRUSADERS	H	Won	2	2	-	1	10	-	1	-	-	1	McKechnie(T) Sturges(3T) Brockbank(2C,P)
5		25	EDGBASTON CRUSADERS	H	Won	2	2	1	-	11	-	-	-	-	0	McKechnie(D) F.Nutt(2T) Sturges(T) Brockbank(2C) Dobbs(T)
6	Nov	1	BEDFORD GRAMMAR SCH.	H	Won	1	-	1*	-	6	-	-	-	-	3	Ward(C,M) Dobbs(T)
7		8	Bedford	A	Won	2	1	-	-	7	2	-	-	-	6	Dobbs(2T) Ward(T) Brockbank(2C)
8		15	LEICESTERSHIRE XV	H	Won	1	2	1	-	8	-	1	-	-	1	McKechnie(T) F.Nutt(T) Barradell(D) Wykes(T) Brockbank(C)
9		22	SALE	H	Won	1	-	-	-	3	-	1	-	-	1	McKechnie(T) Brockbank(C)
		29	LEAMINGTON	H		Cancelled										
10	Dec	6	Rugby	A	Won	1	5	-	-	8	-	-	-	-	0	Dawson-Thomas(T) McKechnie(T,C) Sturges(T) Ward(3T)
		13	Coventry	A		Cancelled Frost										
		20	NORTHAMPTON	H		Cancelled Frost										
		26	OLD DENSTONIANS	H		CancelledFrost										
		27	RUGBY	H		Cancelled Frost										
	Jan	3	COVENTRY	H		Cancelled Frost										
		10	Northampton	A		Cancelled Frost										
		17	Edgbaston Crusaders	A		Cancelled										
11		24	BEDFORD	H	Won	1	3	-	-	6	-	-	-	-	0	Sturges(T) Brockbank(C) Dobbs(3T)
12		31	HANDSWORTH	H	Won	1	2	-	-	5	-	1	-	-	1	Sturges(T) Mason(2T) Brockbank(C)
13	Feb	7	WOLVERTON	H	Won	2	2	-	-	8	-	-	-	-	0	McKechnie(T) Baines(T) Barradell(T) Dobbs(T) Brockbank(2C)
14		9	RUGBY	H	Won	-	2	-	-	2	-	-	-	-	0	Yorke(T) Brockbank(T)
15		14	Bedford Grammar Sch.	A	Won	4	-	-	-	12	1	1	-	-	4	Ley(T) Sturges(T) Dobbs(T) W.R.Porter(T) Brockbank(4C)
16		21	OLD EDWARDIANS	H	Lost	-	1	-	-	1	-	-	1	-	3	W.R.Porter(T)
17		28	Moseley	A	Lost	-	-	-	-	0	3	2	-	-	11	
18	Mar	7	BROMSGROVE (MCC1)	H	Won	4	2	-	-	14	-	-	-	-	0	Ward(4C) Dobbs(4T) Yorke(2T)
		9	SWINTON	H		Cancelled										
		11	Ashby-de-la-Zouch	A		Cancelled										
19		14	HANDSWORTH (MCC2)	H	Won	-	-	-	1	2	-	1	-	-	1	Ward(P)
20		16	SWINTON	H	Lost	-	-	-	-	0	3	1	-	-	10	
21		21	OLD EDWARDIANS (MCCSF)	H	Won	1	1	1	-	7	-	1	1	-	4	Rathbone(T) Wynne(D) Ward(T) Brockbank(C)
22		28	MOSSLEY	H	Won	1	2	-	-	5	1	-	-	-	3	Watts(T) Ward(T,C) Sturges(T)
23		30	KIRKSTALL	H	Drew	-	-	-	-	0	-	-	-	-	0	
24		31	PENYGRAIG	H	Lost	1	1	-	-	4	2	2	-	-	8	Rathbone(T) Brockbank(C) W.R.Porter(T)
25	Apr	4	Coventry (MCCF)	A	Lost	-	-	-	-	0	2	2	-	-	8	

INDIVIDUAL APPEARANCES 1890-1891

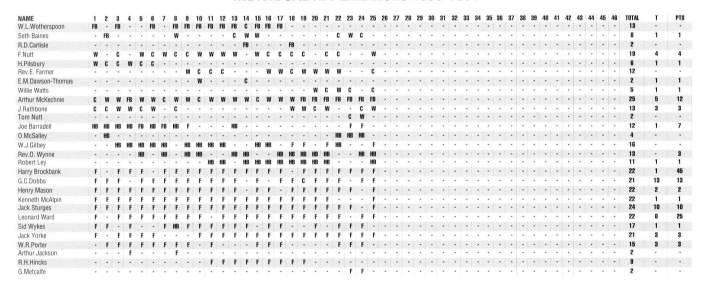

NAME	1	2	3	4	5	6	7	8	9	10	11	12	13	14	15	16	17	18	19	20	21	22	23	24	25	26	27	28	29	30	31	32	33	34	35	36	37	38	39	40	41	42	43	44	45	46	TOTAL	T	PTS
W.L.Wotherspoon	FB	-	FB	-	-	FB	-	FB	FB	FB	FB	FB	FB	C	FB	FB	FB	-	-	-	-	-	-	-	-	-	-	-	-	-	-	-	-	-	-	-	-	-	-	-	-	-	-	-	-	-	13	-	-
Seth Baines	-	FB	-	-	-	-	W	-	-	-	-	C	W	W	-	-	-	-	-	-	C	W	C	-	-	-	-	-	-	-	-	-	-	-	-	-	-	-	-	-	-	-	-	-	-	-	8	1	1
R.D.Carlisle	-	-	-	-	-	-	-	-	-	-	FB	FB	-	-	FB	-	-	FB	-	-	-	-	-	-	-	-	-	-	-	-	-	-	-	-	-	-	-	-	-	-	-	-	-	-	-	-	2	-	-
F.Nutt	W	-	C	-	W	C	W	C	C	W	W	W	W	-	W	C	C	C	C	-	C	C	-	-	W	-	-	-	-	-	-	-	-	-	-	-	-	-	-	-	-	-	-	-	-	-	19	4	4
H.Pilsbury	W	C	C	W	C	C	-	-	-	-	-	-	-	-	-	-	-	-	-	-	-	-	-	-	-	-	-	-	-	-	-	-	-	-	-	-	-	-	-	-	-	-	-	-	-	-	6	1	1
Rev.E. Farmer	-	-	-	-	-	-	-	W	C	C	C	-	-	-	-	W	W	C	W	W	W	W	-	-	C	-	-	-	-	-	-	-	-	-	-	-	-	-	-	-	-	-	-	-	-	-	12	-	-
E.M.Dawson-Thomas	-	-	-	-	-	-	-	-	W	-	-	C	-	-	-	-	-	-	-	-	-	-	-	-	-	-	-	-	-	-	-	-	-	-	-	-	-	-	-	-	-	-	-	-	-	-	2	1	1
Willie Watts	-	-	-	-	-	-	-	-	-	-	-	-	-	-	-	-	-	-	-	-	-	W	C	W	C	-	C	-	-	-	-	-	-	-	-	-	-	-	-	-	-	-	-	-	-	-	5	1	1
Arthur McKechnie	C	W	W	FB	W	W	C	W	W	C	W	W	W	W	C	W	W	W	FB	FB	FB	FB	FB	FB	FB	FB	-	-	-	-	-	-	-	-	-	-	-	-	-	-	-	-	-	-	-	-	25	5	12
J.Rathbone	C	C	W	W	C	W	-	C	-	-	-	-	-	-	-	-	-	-	W	W	C	W	-	-	C	W	-	-	-	-	-	-	-	-	-	-	-	-	-	-	-	-	-	-	-	-	13	3	3
Tom Nutt	-	-	-	-	-	-	-	-	-	-	-	-	-	-	-	-	-	-	-	-	-	-	C	W	-	-	-	-	-	-	-	-	-	-	-	-	-	-	-	-	-	-	-	-	-	-	2	-	-
Joe Barradell	HB	HB	HB	HB	HB	FB	HB	FB	HB	F	-	-	HB	-	-	-	-	-	-	-	-	-	F	F	-	-	-	-	-	-	-	-	-	-	-	-	-	-	-	-	-	-	-	-	-	-	12	1	7
O.McSalley	-	HB	-	-	-	-	-	-	-	-	-	-	-	-	-	-	-	-	-	-	HB	HB	HB	-	-	-	-	-	-	-	-	-	-	-	-	-	-	-	-	-	-	-	-	-	-	-	4	-	-
W.J.Gilbey	-	-	-	HB	HB	HB	HB	HB	-	HB	HB	HB	HB	-	HB	HB	-	F	F	-	F	HB	-	-	-	F	-	-	-	-	-	-	-	-	-	-	-	-	-	-	-	-	-	-	-	-	16	-	-
Rev.O. Wynne	-	-	-	-	-	HB	-	HB	-	-	HB	HB	-	-	HB	HB	-	HB	HB	HB	HB	HB	HB	-	-	HB	HB	-	-	-	-	-	-	-	-	-	-	-	-	-	-	-	-	-	-	-	13	-	3
Robert Ley	-	-	-	-	-	-	-	-	-	-	-	-	HB	HB	HB	HB	HB	HB	HB	HB	HB	HB	HB	-	-	HB	-	-	-	-	-	-	-	-	-	-	-	-	-	-	-	-	-	-	-	-	11	1	1
Harry Brockbank	F	-	F	-	F	F	-	F	F	F	F	F	F	F	F	F	F	F	-	-	F	F	F	F	-	F	F	F	F	-	-	-	-	-	-	-	-	-	-	-	-	-	-	-	-	-	22	1	45
G.C.Dobbs	F	F	F	-	-	F	F	F	F	F	F	F	F	-	F	-	F	-	F	F	C	F	F	F	-	F	F	-	-	-	-	-	-	-	-	-	-	-	-	-	-	-	-	-	-	-	21	13	13
Henry Mason	F	F	F	F	F	F	F	F	F	F	F	F	F	F	-	F	F	-	F	F	F	F	F	F	-	F	-	-	-	-	-	-	-	-	-	-	-	-	-	-	-	-	-	-	-	-	22	2	2
Kenneth McAlpin	F	F	F	F	F	F	F	F	F	F	F	F	F	F	F	F	F	F	F	F	F	F	F	-	-	F	-	-	-	-	-	-	-	-	-	-	-	-	-	-	-	-	-	-	-	-	22	1	1
Jack Sturges	F	-	F	F	F	F	F	F	F	F	F	F	F	F	F	F	F	F	F	F	F	F	F	F	-	F	F	-	-	-	-	-	-	-	-	-	-	-	-	-	-	-	-	-	-	-	24	10	10
Leonard Ward	F	-	F	F	F	F	F	F	F	F	F	F	F	F	F	F	F	F	F	F	F	F	F	-	-	F	F	-	-	-	-	-	-	-	-	-	-	-	-	-	-	-	-	-	-	-	22	8	25
Sid Wykes	F	F	-	F	-	-	F	HB	F	F	F	F	F	F	-	F	F	-	-	-	F	F	F	-	-	-	-	-	-	-	-	-	-	-	-	-	-	-	-	-	-	-	-	-	-	-	17	1	1
Jack Yorke	F	-	F	F	F	F	-	-	F	F	F	F	F	F	F	F	F	F	F	F	F	F	F	F	-	F	F	F	-	-	-	-	-	-	-	-	-	-	-	-	-	-	-	-	-	-	21	3	3
W.R.Porter	-	F	F	F	F	F	F	F	F	-	F	-	-	F	F	F	-	-	-	-	F	F	F	-	-	-	-	-	-	-	-	-	-	-	-	-	-	-	-	-	-	-	-	-	-	-	15	3	3
Arthur Jackson	-	-	-	F	-	-	F	-	-	-	-	-	-	-	-	-	-	-	-	-	-	-	-	-	-	-	-	-	-	-	-	-	-	-	-	-	-	-	-	-	-	-	-	-	-	-	2	-	-
R.H.Hincks	-	-	-	-	-	-	-	-	-	F	F	F	F	F	F	F	F	F	F	-	-	-	-	-	-	-	-	-	-	-	-	-	-	-	-	-	-	-	-	-	-	-	-	-	-	-	9	-	-
G.Metcalfe	-	-	-	-	-	-	-	-	-	-	-	-	-	-	-	-	-	-	-	-	-	-	F	F	-	-	-	-	-	-	-	-	-	-	-	-	-	-	-	-	-	-	-	-	-	-	2	-	-

1 game: Rev.C.M. Barham W(23), F.Bonner F(2), J.Buckle F(6), Ted Cooke W(24), -.Grimmett C(4), J.Hale F(14), Sgt.T.J. Jacomb F(2), A.Johnson W(7), -.Neal W(2), George Porter F(7), Dickie Snowden HB(23), A.Sulley C(20), A.Turner HB(1)

NO	DATE		OPPONENTS	V	RES	FOR					AGAINST					SCORERS
						G	T	D	P	PTS	G	T	D	P	PTS	
1	Oct	3	WOLVERTON	H	Won	7	3	-	-	41	-	-	-	-	0	W.A.Watts(T) Barham(T) Nutt(2T) Sturges(2T) Ward(T,7C) Edmonds(2T) Stewart(T)
2		10	Old Edwardians	A	Won	-	2	-	-	4	-	-	-	-	0	Sturges(T) Brockbank(T)
3		14	Bedford Grammar Sch.	A	Lost	1	1	-	-	7	2	1	-	-	12	Sulley(T) Sturges(T) Ward(C)
4		17	EDGBASTON CRUSADERS	H	Won	4	4	-	-	28	-	-	-	-	0	Barham(2T) W.A.Watts(T) Ball(T) Sturges(T) Ward(T) Brockbank(2T,4C)
5		24	MOSELEY	H	Lost	-	-	-	-	0	-	1	-	-	2	
		28	Ashby-de-la-Zouch	A		Cancelled										
6		31	GLOUCESTER	H	Lost	-	-	-	-	0	3	-	-	-	15	
7	Nov	7	BURTON-ON-TRENT	H	Lost	-	-	-	-	0	-	1	-	-	2	
8		14	COVENTRY	H	Won	1	-	-	-	5	-	-	-	-	0	Ward(T) Brockbank(C)
9		21	Bedford	A	Drew	-	-	-	-	0	-	-	-	-	0	
10		28	Ashby-de-la-Zouch	A	Won	1	-	-	-	5	-	-	-	-	0	Barham(T) Ward(C)
11	Dec	5	RUGBY	H	Won	1	5	-	-	15	-	-	-	-	0	McKechnie(C) W.A.Watts(T) Ball(2T) Morrison(T) Yorke(T) Edmonds(T)
12		12	Burton-on-Trent	A	Lost	-	-	-	-	0	-	1	-	-	2	
		19	LEICESTERSHIRE XV	H		Cancelled Frost										
		21	WEST HARTLEPOOL	H		Cancelled Frost										
13		26	LEICESTER SWIFTS	H	Won	-	2	-	-	4	-	-	-	-	0	Memory(T) Daniells(T)
		28	PENYGRAIG	H		Cancelled										
14	Jan	2	Gloucester	A	Lost	-	-	-	-	0	-	3	-	-	6	
15		9	Coventry	A	Lost	-	-	-	-	0	1	1	-	-	7	
		16	BEDFORD	H		Cancelled Frost										
16		23	Rugby	A	Drew	-	-	-	-	0	-	-	-	-	0	
17		30	BEDFORD GRAMMAR SCH.	H	Lost	-	-	-	-	0	1	-	-	-	5	
18	Feb	6	OLD EDWARDIANS	H	Lost	-	-	-	-	0	-	1	-	-	2	
19		13	Blackheath	A	Lost	-	-	-	-	0	5	6	-	-	37	
20		20	HANDSWORTH	H	Won	-	1	-	-	2	-	-	-	-	0	Rathbone(T)
21		27	STOURBRIDGE	H	Won	3	1	-	-	17	-	-	-	-	0	W.A.Watts(T) German(2T) Ward(T,3C)
22	Mar	2	ASHBY-DE-LA-ZOUCH	H	Won	3	3	-	-	21	-	-	-	-	0	Rathbone(4T) Snowden(T) Sturges(T) Ward(3C)
23		5	STRATFORD-UPON-AVON	H	Won	2	1	-	-	12	1	1	-	-	7	Sturges(T) Ward(T,2C) Joyce(T)
24		12	LEICESTER SWIFTS (MCC2)	H	Won	2	1	-	-	12	-	-	-	-	0	Rathbone(2T) Ward(T,2C)
25		14	SWINTON	H	Lost	-	-	-	-	0	1	4	-	-	13	
26		19	Old Edwardians (MCC3)	A	Lost	-	-	-	-	0	3	3	-	-	21	
27		26	EDGBASTON CRUSADERS	H	Won	1	4	-	-	13	-	-	-	-	0	McKechnie(T) Rathbone(2T) W.A.Watts(C) McSalley(T) Simpson(T)
	Apr	2	Moseley	A		Cancelled										
28		9	Handsworth	A	Won	2	1	-	-	12	-	-	1	-	4	Ward(T,2C) Edmonds(T) Porter(T)
29		15	Dukinfield	A	Won	1	-	-	-	5	-	2	-	-	4	McKechnie(C) German(T)
30		16	St Helens	A	Lost	-	-	-	-	0	-	3	-	-	6	
31		18	Walkden	A	Lost	-	-	-	-	0	-	4	1	-	12	

INDIVIDUAL APPEARANCES 1891-1892

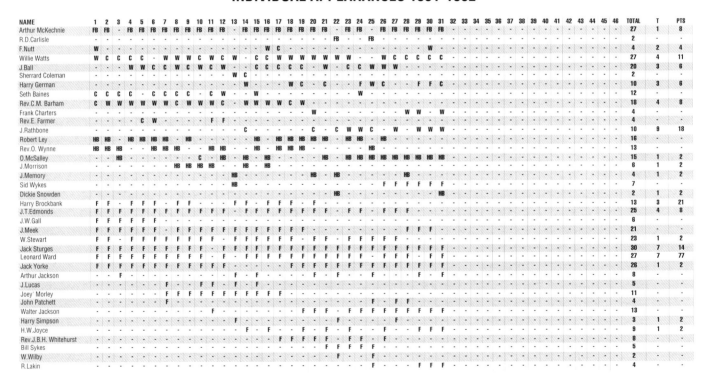

1 game: Tom Crumbie W(28), A.E.Daniells F(13)[1T-2], W.J.Gilbey HB(5), A.S.Hancock FB(13), R.Hargreaves F(22), J.Henson C(22), Kenneth McAlpin F(12), C.Moore W(2), Arthur Moore HB(27), E.Neild HB(30), A.Nicholson F(3), Fred Orton HB(10), E.A.Phipps W(22), H.Pilsbury FB(3), W.R.Porter F(28)[1T-2], A.Sulley W(3)[1T-2], Freddy Toone HB(29), Frank Tyler HB(4), Charlie Watts C(13)

LEICESTER FOOTBALL CLUB 1891-92
Back: J. Collier (Touch Judge), Rev L.F. Ward, Rev J.B.H. Whitehurst, A. McKechnie, Rev C.M. Barham, H.W. Joyce, H. German,
W. Jackson, J.T. Edmonds, Rev O. Wynne, K. McAlpin (Hon.Sec).
Front: J. Meek, Rev R.G. Ley, W.A. Watts, W.H. Sturges (Capt), J. Ball, J. Yorke.

LEICESTER FOOTBALL CLUB 1892-93
Back: J. Collier (Touch Judge), J. Touhey, Rev H.C. Wilkinson, A. Sewell, R.C.D. Cooke, W.R. Hesmondhalgh, K. McAlpin (Hon.Sec)
Middle: J. Yorke, W. Jackson, J. Patchett, W.H. Sturges (Capt), A.E. Cooke, J.T. Edmonds.
Front: H. Bryan, F.C. Toone, A. McKechnie, Rev R.G. Ley.

1892-1893

NO	DATE		OPPONENTS	V	RES	FOR G	FOR T	FOR D	FOR P	PTS	AGAINST G	AGAINST T	AGAINST D	AGAINST P	PTS	SCORERS
1	Sep	10	LEICESTERSHIRE XV	H	Won	1	4	1	-	17	-	-	-	-	0	McKechnie(D) W.A.Watts(T) Rathbone(T) Toone(T) A.E.Cooke(T,C) Sewell(T)
2		17	MANCHESTER FREE WAND	H	Lost	-	-	-	-	0	1	-	-	-	5	
3		24	S.NORTHAMPTONSHIRE	H	Won	6	3	-	1	39	-	-	-	-	0	W.A.Watts(2T) Bryan(T) Ley(2T) Toone(2T) Sturges(T) Yorke(T) A.E.Cooke(3C,P) R.C.D.Cooke(3C)
4	Oct	1	Rugby	A	Won	-	5	2	-	18	-	-	-	-	0	W.A.Watts(T,D) Ball(2T) Bryan(T,D) A.E.Cooke(T)
5		8	OLD EDWARDIANS	H	Drew	-	1	-	-	2	-	1	-	-	2	W.A.Watts(T)
6		15	PENDLETON	H	Lost	-	1	-	-	2	1	-	1	-	9	Edmonds(T)
7		22	Moseley	A	Lost	-	-	-	-	0	3	6	-	-	27	
8		29	Burton-on-Trent	A	Drew	-	1	-	-	2	-	1	-	-	2	Edmonds(T)
9	Nov	5	BEDFORD GRAMMAR SCH.	H	Lost	-	1	-	-	2	4	3	-	-	26	Ley(T)
10		12	Coventry	A	Lost	-	1	-	-	2	2	1	-	-	12	W.A.Watts(T)
11		14	SALFORD	H	Lost	-	-	-	-	0	-	3	-	-	6	
12		16	ASHBY-DE-LA-ZOUCH	H	Won	-	4	-	-	8	-	-	-	-	0	Williams(4T)
13		19	GLOUCESTER	H	Lost	-	-	-	-	0	2	3	-	-	16	
14		26	BEDFORD	H	Won	-	2	1	-	8	-	-	-	-	0	Bryan(D) Hesmondhalgh(T) Greenwood(T)
15	Dec	3	KIRKSTALL	H	Won	2	1	-	-	12	1	-	-	-	5	McKechnie(C) S.E.Page(T) Bown(C) Hesmondhalgh(T) Sewell(T)
		10	Bedford	A		Cancelled Frost										
16		17	SALE	H	Won	1	1	-	-	7	-	-	-	-	0	Bryan(T,C) Greenwood(T)
17		24	COVENTRY	H	Drew	1	-	-	-	5	1	-	-	-	5	Bryan(C) King(T)
18		26	SWINTON	H	Lost	-	-	-	-	0	2	-	-	-	10	
		31	Stourbridge			Cancelled Frost										
	Jan	7	Old Edwardians	A		Cancelled Frost										
19		14	BURTON-ON-TRENT	H	Drew	-	1	-	-	2	-	1	-	-	2	King(T)
20		21	GUY'S HOSPITAL	H	Drew	1	1	1	-	11	1	3	-	-	11	Bryan(C) Hesmondhalgh(D) Sturges(2T)
21		28	RUGBY	H	Lost	-	1	1	-	6	3	1	-	1	20	Hesmondhalgh(D) Toone(T)
22	Feb	4	ST THOMAS' HOSPITAL	H	Lost	-	-	1*	-	4	1	1	-	-	7	A.E.Cooke(M)
23		8	Bedford Grammar Sch.	A	Lost	-	2	-	-	4	1	1	-	-	7	Bryan(T) Hitchcock(T)
24		11	OLD MERCHANT TAYLORS	H	Lost	-	-	-	-	0	-	1	-	-	2	
25		18	Gloucester	A	Lost	-	-	-	-	0	2	1	-	-	12	
26		23	ST BARTHOLOMEW'S HOS	H	Won	1	2	-	-	9	-	2	-	-	4	Moore(T) Edmonds(T) A.E.Cooke(C) Touhey(T)
27		25	MOSELEY	H	Won	-	1	1	-	6	-	-	1	-	4	Bryan(D) Toone(T)
28	Mar	1	Ashby-de-la-Zouch	A	Won	-	2	-	-	4	-	-	-	-	0	C.E.Watts(T) Hitchcock(T)
29		4	COVENTRY EXCELSIOR (MCC1)	H	Won	1	5	-	1	18	-	-	-	-	0	Bryan(2T,P) Hesmondhalgh(T) Wilkinson(2T) A.E.Cooke(T,C)
30		11	COVENTRY (MCC2)	H	Lost	-	-	-	-	0	2	1	-	-	12	
31		18	HANDSWORTH	H	Won	1	-	2	1	16	-	-	-	-	0	Bryan(C,2D) A.E.Cooke(P) H.J.Simpson(T)
32	Apr	3	BROUGHTON RANGERS	H	Won	1	-	-	-	5	-	-	-	-	0	Hitchcock(T) A.E.Cooke(C)
33		4	YORK	H	Won	-	1	1	-	6	-	-	1	-	4	McKechnie(D) H.J.Simpson(T)
34		15	KENT WANDERERS	H	Won	-	3	-	1	9	1	-	-	-	5	Day(P) C.E.Watts(2T) Touhey(T)
35		22	MANNINGHAM	H	Lost	-	1	-	-	2	1	5	1	-	19	A.E.Cooke(T)
36		29	CARDIFF HARLEQUINS	H	Won	1	1	1*	-	11	1	1	-	-	7	Broadhurst(T) C.E.Watts(T) A.E.Cooke(C,M)

INDIVIDUAL APPEARANCES 1892-1893

NAME	1	2	3	4	5	6	7	8	9	10	11	12	13	14	15	16	17	18	19	20	21	22	23	24	25	26	27	28	29	30	31	32	33	34	35	36	37	38	39	40	41	42	43	44	45	46	TOTAL	T	PTS
Arthur McKechnie	FB	-	FB	FB	FB	FB	C	FB	FB	FB	-	-	FB	FB	FB	FB	FB	FB	FB	FB	FB	FB	-	FB	-	-	FB	-	FB	FB	FB	FB	FB	-	-	FB	-	-	-	-	-	-	-	-	-	-	27	-	11
Frank Brown	-	-	-	-	-	-	-	-	-	-	-	-	-	-	-	-	-	-	-	-	-	-	FB	-	-	FB	-	-	-	-	-	-	-	-	-	-	-	-	-	-	-	-	-	-	-	-	2	-	-
C.A.Page	W	W	-	-	-	-	-	-	-	-	-	-	-	-	-	-	-	-	-	-	-	-	-	-	-	-	-	-	-	-	-	-	-	-	-	-	-	-	-	-	-	-	-	-	-	-	2	-	-
Willie Watts	W	W	W	W	W	W	-	-	W	W	W	-	W	HB	HB	HB	-	-	W	-	-	W	-	-	-	W	-	-	-	-	-	-	-	-	-	-	-	-	-	-	-	-	-	-	-	-	16	6	16
Hugh Bryan	-	-	W	W	W	W	-	C	-	-	-	-	C	W	-	W	W	W	-	W	W	-	W	W	-	-	W	-	W	W	W	-	-	-	-	-	-	-	-	-	-	-	-	-	-	-	18	6	47
Bob Hesmondhalgh	-	-	-	-	-	-	-	-	-	-	-	-	-	W	W	W	C	C	C	C	C	C	C	C	W	C	C	C	C	C	-	C	W	W	W	W	-	-	-	-	-	-	-	-	-	-	22	3	14
Rev.H.C. Wilkinson	-	-	-	-	-	-	-	-	-	-	-	-	-	-	-	-	W	W	-	-	W	W	-	-	-	-	W	-	W	W	W	-	-	-	C	C	-	-	-	-	-	-	-	-	-	-	10	2	4
G.Day	-	-	-	-	-	-	-	-	-	-	-	-	-	-	-	-	-	-	-	-	-	-	-	W	-	-	-	-	-	-	-	C	C	FB	FB	-	-	-	-	-	-	-	-	-	-	-	5	-	3
J.Ball	C	FB	C	C	C	C	W	W	-	-	-	W	-	-	-	-	-	-	-	-	-	-	-	-	-	-	-	-	-	-	-	-	-	-	-	-	-	-	-	-	-	-	-	-	-	-	9	2	4
J.Rathbone	C	C	-	-	-	-	-	-	-	-	-	-	-	-	-	-	-	-	-	-	-	-	-	-	-	-	-	-	-	-	-	-	-	-	-	-	-	-	-	-	-	-	-	-	-	-	2	1	2
S.E.Page	-	-	-	-	-	-	-	-	C	W	-	-	W	-	W	-	-	-	-	-	-	-	-	-	-	-	-	-	-	-	-	-	-	-	-	-	-	-	-	-	-	-	-	-	-	-	4	1	2
C.J.Mason	-	-	-	-	-	-	-	-	-	C	C	-	-	-	-	-	-	-	-	-	-	-	-	-	-	-	-	-	-	-	-	-	-	-	-	-	-	-	-	-	-	-	-	-	-	-	2	-	-
Robert Ley	HB	-	HB	-	HB	-	HB	HB	W	-	HB	-	-	-	-	HB	HB	-	-	-	-	-	-	-	-	-	HB	-	HB	HB	HB	-	-	HB	-	-	-	-	-	-	-	-	-	-	-	-	14	3	6
Freddy Toone	HB	HB	HB	HB	HB	HB	HB	HB	HB	HB	-	-	HB	HB	-	-	-	HB	-	HB	HB	HB	-	HB	HB	-	HB	-	HB	HB	-	-	-	-	-	-	-	-	-	-	-	-	-	-	-	-	21	5	10
J.Memory	-	HB	-	HB	-	-	-	-	HB	-	-	-	-	-	-	-	-	-	-	-	-	-	-	-	-	-	-	-	-	-	-	-	-	-	-	-	-	-	-	-	-	-	-	-	-	-	3	-	-
Rev.O. Wynne	-	-	-	-	-	HB	-	-	-	HB	HB	-	HB	-	-	-	HB	HB	-	-	HB	HB	-	-	-	-	-	-	-	-	-	-	-	-	-	-	-	-	-	-	-	-	-	-	-	-	8	-	-
Arthur Moore	-	-	-	-	-	-	-	-	-	-	-	-	-	-	HB	-	-	-	-	-	-	-	-	-	-	HB	-	-	-	-	-	-	-	-	-	-	-	-	-	-	-	-	-	-	-	-	2	1	2
Joe Barradell	-	-	-	-	-	-	-	-	-	-	-	-	-	-	-	-	-	-	HB	-	-	-	-	HB	-	-	-	HB	-	-	-	-	-	-	-	-	-	-	-	-	-	-	-	-	-	-	3	-	-
Dickie Snowden	-	-	-	-	-	-	-	-	-	-	-	-	-	-	-	-	-	-	HB	HB	-	-	-	-	HB	HB	-	-	-	-	-	HB	-	-	-	-	-	-	-	-	-	-	-	-	-	-	5	-	-
H.Bown	F	-	-	-	-	-	-	-	-	-	W	-	-	C	C	C	F	C	F	-	-	-	HB	-	-	-	-	-	-	-	-	-	-	-	-	-	-	-	-	-	-	-	-	-	-	-	9	-	3
Ted Cooke	F	F	F	F	F	F	F	F	F	F	F	F	F	F	F	F	F	F	F	F	F	F	-	F	F	F	F	F	F	F	F	F	F	F	F	F	-	-	-	-	-	-	-	-	-	-	35	4	46
H.W.Joyce	F	F	-	-	-	-	-	-	-	-	-	-	-	-	-	-	-	-	-	-	-	-	-	-	-	-	-	-	-	-	-	-	-	-	-	-	-	-	-	-	-	-	-	-	-	-	2	-	-
John Patchett	F	F	F	F	F	F	F	F	F	F	F	-	F	F	F	F	-	F	F	F	F	F	-	-	W	F	F	-	F	F	F	-	F	F	F	F	-	-	-	-	-	-	-	-	-	-	30	-	-
A.Sewell	F	F	F	F	F	F	F	F	F	F	F	-	F	F	F	F	F	F	F	F	-	F	F	F	F	F	F	F	F	F	-	-	-	-	-	-	-	-	-	-	-	-	-	-	-	-	28	2	4
W.Stewart	F	F	-	-	-	-	-	-	-	-	-	-	-	-	-	-	-	-	-	-	-	-	-	-	-	-	-	-	-	-	-	-	-	-	-	-	-	-	-	-	-	-	-	-	-	-	2	-	-
Jack Sturges	F	-	F	F	F	F	F	F	F	F	F	-	F	F	F	F	F	F	F	F	F	F	F	F	F	F	F	-	F	F	F	F	F	F	F	F	-	-	-	-	-	-	-	-	-	-	33	3	6
Jack Yorke	F	F	F	F	F	F	-	-	-	-	-	-	-	-	-	-	-	-	-	-	-	F	F	F	F	F	F	F	F	F	F	F	F	F	F	F	-	-	-	-	-	-	-	-	-	-	21	1	2
Rupert Cooke	-	F	F	F	F	F	F	F	F	F	F	F	F	F	F	F	F	F	F	F	F	F	-	F	F	F	F	F	F	F	F	F	F	F	F	F	-	-	-	-	-	-	-	-	-	-	34	-	9
J.T.Edmonds	-	F	-	F	F	F	F	F	F	F	F	F	F	F	F	F	F	-	F	F	F	F	-	F	-	F	F	-	F	F	F	-	-	-	-	-	-	-	-	-	-	-	-	-	-	-	25	3	6
Rev.A.W. Parkes	-	F	F	F	F	F	F	F	-	F	F	F	F	F	-	-	-	-	-	-	-	-	-	-	-	-	-	-	F	-	-	-	-	-	-	-	-	-	-	-	-	-	-	-	-	-	13	-	-
Walter Jackson	-	-	F	-	-	-	F	F	F	F	F	F	F	F	F	F	-	-	-	-	F	F	F	F	F	F	F	F	F	F	F	F	-	F	F	F	-	-	-	-	-	-	-	-	-	-	26	-	-
D.Williams	-	-	F	F	F	F	F	F	F	F	F	F	F	-	F	F	F	F	-	F	F	F	-	-	F	-	-	-	-	-	-	-	-	-	-	-	-	-	-	-	-	-	-	-	-	-	19	4	8
A.E.Hitchcock	-	-	-	-	-	-	-	-	F	-	-	F	-	-	-	-	-	-	-	-	-	-	W	-	C	W	-	W	-	-	-	W	W	W	W	W	-	-	-	-	-	-	-	-	-	-	11	3	6
Fred Simpson	-	-	-	-	-	-	-	-	-	-	-	F	-	-	-	-	-	-	-	-	-	-	F	-	-	-	-	F	-	-	-	-	F	-	-	-	-	-	-	-	-	-	-	-	-	-	4	-	-
Harry Simpson	-	-	-	-	-	-	-	-	-	-	-	F	-	-	-	-	-	-	-	-	-	-	-	-	-	-	-	F	-	-	F	F	HB	HB	HB	HB	-	-	-	-	-	-	-	-	-	-	8	2	4
J.Greenwood	-	-	-	-	-	-	-	-	-	-	-	-	-	F	F	F	F	F	-	F	F	-	-	-	-	-	-	-	-	-	-	F	F	-	-	F	-	-	-	-	-	-	-	-	-	-	10	2	4
Jabez King	-	-	-	-	-	-	-	-	-	-	-	-	-	-	-	-	F	F	W	W	-	-	-	-	-	-	-	-	-	-	-	-	-	-	F	-	-	-	-	-	-	-	-	-	-	-	5	2	4
E.Dann	-	-	-	-	-	-	-	-	-	-	-	-	-	-	-	-	-	-	F	F	F	-	F	F	-	-	-	-	-	-	-	-	-	F	-	-	-	-	-	-	-	-	-	-	-	-	6	-	-
J.Meek	-	-	-	-	-	-	-	-	-	-	-	-	-	-	-	-	-	-	F	-	-	-	-	-	-	-	-	F	-	-	-	-	-	-	-	-	-	-	-	-	-	-	-	-	-	-	2	-	-
Charlie Watts	-	-	-	-	-	-	-	-	-	-	-	-	-	-	-	-	-	-	-	-	-	-	F	-	-	-	-	W	-	-	HB	HB	HB	C	HB	HB	-	-	-	-	-	-	-	-	-	-	8	4	8
Arthur Jackson	-	-	-	-	-	-	-	-	-	-	-	-	-	-	-	-	-	-	-	-	-	-	-	F	-	-	-	-	-	-	-	-	F	F	F	-	-	-	-	-	-	-	-	-	-	-	4	-	-
James Touhey	-	-	-	-	-	-	-	-	-	-	-	-	-	-	-	-	-	-	-	-	-	-	-	-	F	F	F	F	-	F	F	F	F	F	F	F	-	-	-	-	-	-	-	-	-	-	11	2	4

1 game: Seth Baines FB(11), Jack Broadhurst C(36)[1T-2], R.D.Carlisle FB(25), E.W.Chamberlain FB(12), Frank Charters C(31), Tom Crumbie W(12), Harry German W(8), J.Henson C(12), Ellis Johnson HB(12), Kenneth McAlpin HB(12), A.H.Mann W(7), George Orton FB(28), Fred Orton HB(28), A.Sulley W(32), -.Swift FB(7), D.W.Thomas C(25), C.F.Thompson HB(23), H.C.Thorpe F(23), A.J.Young F(23)

NO	DATE		OPPONENTS	V	RES	FOR G	FOR T	FOR D	FOR P	PTS	AGAINST G	AGAINST T	AGAINST D	AGAINST P	PTS	SCORERS
1	Sep	16	LEICESTERSHIRE XV	H	Won	4	2	-	-	26	-	2	-	-	6	C.E.Watts(T) Hitchcock(2T) Memory(T) Redman(T) A.E.Cooke(T,C) R.C.D.Cooke(3C)
2		23	LEICESTER CRUSADERS	H	Won	4	1	-	-	23	-	-	-	-	0	Hesmondhalgh(T) Hitchcock(2T) A.E.Cooke(T,4C) W.Jackson(T)
3		30	KENT WANDERERS	H	Lost	-	1	-	1	6	2	-	1	-	14	C.E.Watts(T) A.E.Cooke(P)
4	Oct	2	SWINTON	H	Drew	-	-	-	-	0	-	-	-	-	0	
5		7	GLOUCESTER	H	Lost	-	1	-	-	3	1	1	-	-	8	C.E.Watts(T)
6		14	COVENTRY	H	Lost	-	-	-	-	0	-	1	-	-	3	
7		21	MOSELEY	H	Won	-	2	-	-	6	1	-	-	-	5	Hesmondhalgh(T) C.E.Watts(T)
8		25	Bedford Grammar Sch.	A	Won	1	2	-	-	11	-	-	1	-	4	Hitchcock(T) Hesmondhalgh(T,C) Touhey(T)
9		28	BURTON-ON-TRENT	H	Won	-	1	1*	-	7	1	-	-	-	5	Simpson(T) A.E.Cooke(M)
10	Nov	4	EDGBASTON CRUSADERS	H	Won	1	2	-	-	11	-	-	1	-	4	Hitchcock(T) Foreman(T) Banks(C) Touhey(T)
11		11	Coventry	A	Lost	-	-	-	-	0	1	1	-	-	8	
12		18	RUGBY	H	Won	-	1	-	-	3	-	-	-	-	0	Hitchcock(T)
13		25	Rugby	A	Won	1	-	-	1	8	-	-	1*	1	7	McKechnie(C) C.E.Watts(T) A.E.Cooke(P)
	Dec	2	Old Edwardians	A		Cancelled Frost										
14		9	Moseley	A	Drew	-	-	-	-	0	-	-	-	-	0	
15		16	SALE	H	Won	-	2	1	-	10	-	-	-	-	0	C.E.Watts(T,D) Hesmondhalgh(T)
16		23	Bedford	A	Lost	-	2	-	-	6	1	1	-	-	8	Foreman(T) A.E.Cooke(T)
17		26	PENYGRAIG	H	Won	2	1	-	-	13	-	1	-	-	3	Wilkinson(T) Hesmondhalgh(T) Bryan(T,2C)
18		27	PONTEFRACT	H	Won	3	2	-	-	21	-	1	-	-	3	Wilkinson(T) C.E.Watts(T) Bryan(T,3C) A.E.Cooke(T) Banks(T)
19		30	BEDFORD	H	Lost	-	-	-	1	3	-	1	1	-	7	Bryan(P)
20	Jan	1	BECTIVE RANGERS	H	Won	1	-	-	-	5	-	-	-	-	0	Bryan(C) Touhey(T)
		6	Gloucester	A		Cancelled Frost										
21		13	Burton-on-Trent	A	Won	1	-	-	-	5	-	1	-	-	3	Bryan(T,C)
22		20	ST THOMAS' HOSPITAL	H	Drew	-	-	-	-	0	-	-	-	-	0	
23		27	OLD LEYSIANS	H	Lost	-	-	-	-	0	-	1	-	-	3	
24	Feb	3	HANDSWORTH	H	Won	2	3	-	-	19	-	-	-	-	0	Hesmondhalgh(T,C) Foreman(2T,C) Carey(T) Harlowe(T)
25		10	GUY'S HOSPITAL	H	Lost	-	-	-	-	0	3	-	-	-	15	
26		12	ST BARTHOLOMEW'S HOS	H	Won	3	1	-	-	18	-	-	-	-	0	Hesmondhalgh(T,2C) Foreman(2T,C) A.E.Cooke(T)
27		17	OLD EDWARDIANS	H	Won	1	-	-	-	5	-	-	-	-	0	Hesmondhalgh(C) Hitchcock(T)
28		24	BEDFORD GRAMMAR SCH.	H	Won	-	1	-	-	3	-	-	-	-	0	Akers(T)
29	Mar	3	CROYDON	H	Won	-	1	-	-	3	-	-	-	-	0	Foreman(T)
30		10	AMBLESIDE	H	Won	2	2	-	-	16	1	-	-	-	5	Wilkinson(T) Hesmondhalgh(T,C) Foreman(C) A.E.Cooke(T) Touhey(T)
31		17	STONEYGATE (MCC3)	H	Won	1	7	-	-	26	-	-	-	-	0	Wilkinson(T) Hesmondhalgh(3T) Hitchcock(2T) W.Jackson(T,C) Touhey(T)
32		24	Rugby (MCCSF)	A	Won	-	2	-	-	6	1	-	-	-	5	Vity(T) Banks(T)
33		26	BROUGHTON RANGERS	H	Lost	-	1	-	-	3	2	2	-	-	16	Hesmondhalgh(T)
34		27	EAST SHEEN	H	Lost	-	1	-	-	3	1	-	-	-	5	Barth(T)
35		31	Coventry (MCCF)	A	Lost	-	-	-	-	0	1	2	-	-	11	
36	Apr	7	OLD MERCHANT TAYLORS	H	Won	1	-	-	-	5	-	1	-	-	3	A.E.Cooke(T,C)
37		14	MANCHESTER FREE WAND	H	Won	1	-	1	-	9	-	-	-	-	0	Brown(D) A.E.Cooke(T,C)

INDIVIDUAL APPEARANCES 1893-1894

NAME	1	2	3	4	5	6	7	8	9	10	11	12	13	14	15	16	17	18	19	20	21	22	23	24	25	26	27	28	29	30	31	32	33	34	35	36	37	38	39	40	41	42	43	44	45	46	TOTAL	T	PTS
Frank Brown	FB	-	-	FB	FB	FB	FB	FB	FB	FB	FB	FB	-	-	-	FB	FB	-	-	-	FB	-	-	FB	-	FB	-	-	FB	-	-	-	-	FB	-	FB	FB	-	-	-	-	-	-	-	-	-	19	-	4
Arthur McKechnie	-	FB	FB	-	-	-	-	-	-	-	-	-	FB	FB	FB	-	-	-	FB	FB	W	FB	FB	-	-	-	-	-	-	-	-	-	-	-	-	-	-	-	-	-	-	-	-	-	-	-	10	-	2
A.E.Hitchcock	W	C	W	W	W	C	C	C	C	C	C	C	C	C	W	W	-	-	-	-	W	W	C	C	W	W	W	C	C	W	W	C	-	-	-	C	W	-	-	-	-	-	-	-	-	-	30	10	30
Charlie Watts	W	HB	HB	W	C	F	W	W	W	W	W	W	W	W	C	C	C	C	C	C	C	C	C	W	-	-	-	-	-	C	C	W	C	C	C	-	-	-	-	-	-	-	-	-	-	-	30	7	25
G.Day	-	W	W	-	-	-	-	-	-	-	-	-	-	-	-	-	-	-	-	-	-	-	-	-	FB	-	FB	FB	-	FB	FB	FB	FB	-	FB	-	-	-	-	-	-	-	-	-	-	-	10	-	-
Rev.H.C. Wilkinson	-	-	-	-	-	W	W	W	W	W	W	W	W	-	W	-	W	W	W	W	-	W	W	-	W	W	W	W	W	W	W	-	W	W	W	W	W	-	-	-	-	-	-	-	-	-	27	4	12
Hugh Bryan	-	-	-	-	-	-	-	-	-	-	-	-	-	-	-	W	W	W	W	W	C	-	-	-	-	-	-	-	-	-	-	W	-	-	W	-	-	-	-	-	-	-	-	-	-	-	8	3	26
Bob Hesmondhalgh	C	W	C	C	W	C	C	C	C	C	C	C	C	W	C	-	C	C	C	-	-	-	W	W	C	C	C	W	W	C	C	C	C	C	C	W	C	-	-	-	-	-	-	-	-	-	33	12	48
Willie Watts	-	-	-	C	C	-	-	-	-	-	-	-	-	-	-	C	-	-	-	-	-	-	-	-	-	-	-	-	-	-	-	-	-	-	-	-	-	-	-	-	-	-	-	-	-	-	3	-	-
W.Barth	-	-	-	-	-	-	-	-	-	-	-	-	-	-	-	-	-	-	-	-	-	-	-	-	-	-	C	C	C	-	-	-	W	W	-	C	-	-	-	-	-	-	-	-	-	-	6	1	3
J.Memory	HB	HB	-	-	-	-	-	-	-	-	-	-	-	-	-	-	-	-	-	-	-	-	-	-	-	-	-	-	-	-	-	-	-	-	-	-	-	-	-	-	-	-	-	-	-	-	2	1	3
Harry Simpson	HB	-	HB	HB	HB	HB	HB	HB	HB	HB	HB	HB	HB	-	HB	HB	HB	HB	HB	F	HB	-	HB	HB	HB	HB	HB	-	HB	HB	HB	HB	HB	-	HB	HB	HB	-	-	-	-	-	-	-	-	-	32	1	3
Robert Ley	-	-	-	HB	-	-	-	-	-	-	-	-	-	-	-	-	-	HB	-	-	-	-	-	-	-	-	-	-	-	-	-	-	HB	HB	-	-	-	-	-	-	-	-	-	-	-	-	4	-	-
Billy Foreman	-	-	-	-	HB	HB	HB	HB	HB	HB	HB	HB	HB	HB	HB	HB	-	-	HB	HB	HB	HB	HB	HB	HB	HB	HB	HB	HB	HB	HB	HB	-	HB	HB	HB	HB	-	-	-	-	-	-	-	-	-	30	7	27
George Banks	F	F	F	F	-	F	F	F	F	F	F	F	F	F	F	F	F	F	F	F	F	F	F	F	-	-	-	-	-	-	F	F	F	-	F	F	F	-	-	-	-	-	-	-	-	-	29	2	8
Rupert Cooke	F	F	F	F	F	-	-	-	-	-	-	-	-	-	-	-	-	-	-	-	-	-	-	-	-	-	-	-	-	-	-	-	-	-	-	-	-	-	-	-	-	-	-	-	-	-	5	-	6
Ted Cooke	F	F	F	F	F	F	F	-	F	F	F	F	F	F	F	F	F	F	F	F	F	F	F	F	F	F	F	F	F	F	F	F	F	-	F	F	F	-	-	-	-	-	-	-	-	-	35	8	48
J.Greenwood	F	-	F	-	-	-	-	-	-	-	-	-	-	-	-	-	-	-	-	-	-	-	-	-	-	-	-	-	-	-	-	-	-	-	-	-	-	-	-	-	-	-	-	-	-	-	2	-	-
Walter Jackson	F	F	F	F	F	F	F	F	F	F	F	F	F	F	F	F	F	F	F	F	F	-	F	F	F	F	F	F	F	F	F	F	F	F	F	F	F	-	-	-	-	-	-	-	-	-	36	2	8
Jabez King	F	F	-	-	-	W	-	-	-	-	-	-	-	F	-	-	-	-	-	-	-	-	-	-	-	-	-	-	-	-	-	-	-	-	-	-	-	-	-	-	-	-	-	-	-	-	4	-	-
Dr.A.R. Rendle	F	F	F	F	F	F	F	F	F	F	F	F	F	F	F	F	F	F	F	F	-	F	-	-	-	-	F	F	F	F	F	F	F	F	F	F	F	-	-	-	-	-	-	-	-	-	32	-	-
Eddie Redman	F	F	F	F	F	F	F	F	F	F	-	F	F	HB	F	-	-	-	-	-	-	-	-	-	-	-	-	-	-	-	-	-	-	-	-	-	-	-	-	-	-	-	-	-	-	-	14	1	3
James Touhey	F	F	F	F	F	F	F	F	F	F	F	F	F	F	F	F	F	F	F	F	F	F	F	F	F	F	F	F	F	F	F	F	F	F	F	F	F	-	-	-	-	-	-	-	-	-	37	5	15
W.H.Carey	-	-	F	F	F	F	F	F	F	F	F	F	-	-	F	F	F	F	F	-	-	F	F	F	F	-	F	F	F	F	F	-	F	-	F	F	F	-	-	-	-	-	-	-	-	-	28	1	3
Arthur Jackson	-	-	-	-	F	-	-	-	-	-	-	-	-	F	-	-	-	-	-	F	F	-	-	-	-	F	-	-	-	-	-	F	-	-	-	-	-	-	-	-	-	-	-	-	-	-	6	-	-
E.Dann	-	-	-	-	-	-	-	F	-	-	-	-	-	-	-	-	-	-	-	F	F	F	-	F	-	-	-	-	-	-	-	-	F	-	-	-	-	-	-	-	-	-	-	-	-	-	6	-	-
J.Meek	-	-	-	-	-	-	-	F	F	F	-	-	F	-	-	-	-	-	-	-	-	-	-	-	-	F	-	-	-	-	-	-	-	-	-	-	-	-	-	-	-	-	-	-	-	-	5	-	-
Harry German	-	-	-	-	-	-	-	-	-	-	F	F	-	F	F	F	F	F	F	-	F	HB	F	-	-	-	-	-	-	-	-	-	-	-	-	-	-	-	-	-	-	-	-	-	-	-	11	-	-
John Patchett	-	-	-	-	-	-	-	-	-	-	F	-	-	-	-	-	-	-	-	-	-	-	-	-	-	-	-	-	-	-	-	-	-	F	-	-	-	-	-	-	-	-	-	-	-	-	2	-	-
Arthur Akers	-	-	-	-	-	-	-	-	-	-	-	-	F	F	-	F	F	F	F	F	F	F	F	F	F	F	F	F	F	F	F	F	-	-	F	-	-	-	-	-	-	-	-	-	-	-	20	1	3
R.Lakin	-	-	-	-	-	-	-	-	-	-	-	-	-	-	-	-	-	-	-	-	-	F	-	-	-	-	-	-	-	-	-	-	-	F	-	-	-	-	-	-	-	-	-	-	-	-	2	-	-
E.Vity	-	-	-	-	-	-	-	-	-	-	-	-	-	-	-	-	-	-	-	-	-	-	F	F	F	F	F	F	F	F	F	F	F	-	F	F	F	-	-	-	-	-	-	-	-	-	14	1	3
A.Harlowe	-	-	-	-	-	-	-	-	-	-	-	-	-	-	-	-	-	-	-	-	-	-	-	F	F	-	-	-	-	-	-	-	-	-	-	-	-	-	-	-	-	-	-	-	-	-	2	1	3
Paddy Swain	-	-	-	-	-	-	-	-	-	-	-	-	-	-	-	-	-	-	-	-	-	-	-	-	F	F	F	F	F	-	-	-	-	F	-	F	F	-	-	-	-	-	-	-	-	-	8	-	-
Bob Golding	-	-	-	-	-	-	-	-	-	-	-	-	-	-	-	-	-	-	-	-	-	-	-	-	-	-	-	-	-	F	-	-	-	F	-	-	-	-	-	-	-	-	-	-	-	-	2	-	-

1 game: G.E.Blunt FB(18), W.Burton F(25), E.Butler C(37), J.T.Edmonds F(2), George Hicken HB(28), George Jones F(26), Arthur Moore HB(17), E.R.Philbrick F(34), Jack Pole-Kitson F(22), W.K.Roberts HB(20), G.Ward F(7)

LEICESTER FOOTBALL CLUB 1893-94
Back: J. Collier (Touch Judge), G. Day, J. Touhey, Rev H.C. Wilkinson, Dr.A.R. Rendle, W.R. Hesmondhalgh, Mr. Cave, J. Parsons (President).
Middle: W. Jackson, E. Vity, A.E. Cooke (Capt), W.J. Foreman, A. Akers, H.J. Simpson.
Front: W.H. Carey, C.E. Watts, A.E. Hitchcock, G. Banks.

LEICESTER FOOTBALL CLUB 1894-95
Back: J. Collier (Touch Judge), T.W. Pettifor (Hon.Sec), R.P. Swain, E. Vity, G. Banks, G. Jones, A. Akers, H.W. Salmon, R.S. Snowden.
Middle: J. Parsons (President), A.E. Hitchcock, W. Jackson, E. Redman (Capt), W.R. Hesmondhalgh, E. Dann, A.E. Cooke.
Front: F. Brown, F.A. Jackson, H.J. Simpson, W.J. Foreman, R. Lewis.

NO	DATE	OPPONENTS	V	RES	FOR					AGAINST					SCORERS
					G	T	D	P	PTS	G	T	D	P	PTS	
1	Sep 1	Huddersfield	A	Lost	-	1	-	-	3	-	1	1	-	7	Vity(T)
2	8	BURFIELD RANGERS	H	Won	10	7	-	-	71	-	-	-	-	0	Bryan(C) Lewis(3T,6C) Fox(2T) Foreman(2T) Simpson(T) Redman(T) G.Jones(3T) A.E.Cooke(T,3C) W.Jackson(T) Steinitz(T) Vity(T) Hitchcock(T)
3	15	LEICESTERSHIRE XV	H	Won	5	2	-	-	31	1	-	-	-	5	Bryan(T) Lewis(T,5C) Hesmondhalgh(2T) Fox(2T)
4	22	Northampton	A	Won	1	2	-	-	11	-	-	-	-	0	Hesmondhalgh(2T) Lewis(C) Foreman(T)
5	29	MANCHESTER FREE WAND	H	Won	4	6	-	-	38	-	-	-	-	0	Hitchcock(2T) Hesmondhalgh(2T) Lewis(4T,C) Fox(3C) Simpson(T) Banks(T)
6	Oct 6	OLD EDWARDIANS	H	Won	-	-	-	-	0	-	1	-	-	3	
7	13	BURTON-ON-TRENT	H	Won	3	4	-	-	27	-	-	-	-	0	Hesmondhalgh(T) Fox(2T,3C) Foreman(T) Simpson(T) A.E.Cooke(T) W.Jackson(T)
8	20	Coventry	A	Lost	-	-	-	-	0	-	-	-	1	3	
9	27	Rugby	A	Lost	-	-	-	-	0	1	-	-	-	5	
10	Nov 3	GUY'S HOSPITAL	H	Won	-	2	-	-	6	-	-	-	-	0	A.E.Cooke(T) Swain(T)
11	10	BEDFORD GRAMMAR SCH.	H	Won	-	2	-	-	6	1	-	-	-	5	F.A.Jackson(T) Simpson(T)
12	17	MOSELEY	H	Won	2	-	-	-	10	-	-	-	-	0	Fox(2C) Lewis(T) Simpson(T)
13	24	SWINTON	H	Won	3	-	-	-	15	-	1	-	-	3	Lewis(T) Fox(3C) A.E.Cooke(T) G.Jones(T)
14	27	HALIFAX	H	Lost	-	-	-	-	0	1	1	-	-	8	
15	Dec 1	ST THOMAS' HOSPITAL	H	Won	3	2	-	-	21	-	-	-	-	0	Fox(3C) Lewis(T) F.A.Jackson(T) A.E.Cooke(T) Vity(T) Swain(T)
16	8	ST BARTHOLOMEW'S HOS	H	Won	-	2	-	-	6	-	1	-	-	3	Foreman(T) A.E.Cooke(T)
17	15	Gloucester	A	Drew	-	-	-	-	0	-	-	-	-	0	
18	22	BEDFORD	H	Won	1	3	-	-	14	-	1	-	-	3	Fox(2T,C) Lewis(T) G.Jones(T)
19	26	PONTYPRIDD	H	Won	1	4	1	1	24	-	-	-	-	0	Butler(T) Bryan(T) Hesmondhalgh(T) Lewis(D) Fox(T,C,P) Vity(T)
20	27	MIDDLESEX WANDERERS	H	Won	-	2	1	-	10	-	-	-	-	0	Bryan(D) Banks(T) G.Jones(T)
21	29	EDGBASTON CRUSADERS	H	Won	1	2	-	-	11	-	-	-	-	0	Bryan(C) Fox(T) Redman(T) Rice(T)
22	Jan 3	BECTIVE RANGERS	H	Drew	-	-	1	-	4	-	-	-	-	0	Lewis(D)
	5	Handsworth	A		Cancelled Frost										
	12	Bedford	A		CancelledFrost										
23	19	Moseley	A	Won	-	3	-	-	9	-	-	-	-	0	Fox(T) A.E.Cooke(2T)
24	26	COVENTRY	H	Won	1	-	-	-	5	-	-	-	-	0	F.A.Jackson(T) Fox(C)
25	Feb 2	OLD EDWARDIANS	H	Lost	2	2	-	-	16	-	-	-	-	0	F.A.Jackson(T) Hesmondhalgh(T) Fox(T,2C) A.E.Cooke(T)
	9	RUGBY	H		Cancelled Refused										
	13	Bedford Grammar Sch.	A		Cancelled Frost										
26	16	GLOUCESTER	H	Won	1	-	1	-	9	-	-	-	-	0	Lewis(D) Fox(C) Nicholson(T)
27	23	Burton-on-Trent	A	Lost	-	1	-	1	6	1	1	-	-	8	Fox(P) Whitehead(T)
28	26	HUDDERSFIELD	H	Drew	-	-	-	-	0	-	-	-	-	0	
29	Mar 2	WORCESTER (MCC1)	H	Won	8	3	1	-	53	-	-	-	-	0	Fox(T,6C) Lewis(6T) Hesmondhalgh(T,D) F.A.Jackson(T,2C) Rice(2T)
30	9	LEICESTER CRUSADERS (MCC2)	H	Won	4	3	1	-	33	-	-	-	-	0	Fox(T,4C) Hesmondhalgh(2T,D) Lewis(3T) R.C.D.Cooke(T)
31	16	Nuneaton (MCC3)	A	Won	2	3	-	-	19	-	-	-	-	0	F.A.Jackson(2T) Lewis(T) Fox(T,2C) Hesmondhalgh(T)
32	23	Moseley (MCCSF)	A	Lost	-	-	-	-	0	-	1	2*	-	11	
33	30	LEEDS	H	Lost	-	-	-	-	0	1	1	-	-	8	
34	Apr 6	SALE	H	Won	1	3	-	-	14	-	-	-	-	0	Lewis(C) F.A.Jackson(3T) Swain(T)
35	13	NORTHAMPTON	H	Won	1	4	1	-	21	-	1	1*	-	7	Bryan(2T,C) Lewis(T,D) Swain(T) A.E.Cooke(T) G.Jones(T)
36	15	PENARTH	H	Lost	-	-	-	-	0	2	1	-	-	13	
37	16	KIRKSTALL	H	Won	4	8	-	1	47	-	-	-	-	0	Swain(T) Lewis(T,3C) Hesmondhalgh(2T,C,P) Butler(2T) Foreman(T) G.Jones(2T) A.E.Cooke(T) Rice(2T)
38	20	Bedford	A	Won	1	-	-	-	5	-	1	-	-	3	F.A.Jackson(C) Whitehead(T)

INDIVIDUAL APPEARANCES 1894-1895

NAME	1	2	3	4	5	6	7	8	9	10	11	12	13	14	15	16	17	18	19	20	21	22	23	24	25	26	27	28	29	30	31	32	33	34	35	36	37	38	39	40	41	42	43	44	45	46	TOTAL	T	PTS
Frank Brown	FB	FB	FB	-	-	-	FB	FB	FB	FB	FB	FB	FB	FB	FB	FB	FB	FB	-	-	-	FB	-	-	-	-	-	-	-	-	-	-	-	-	-	-	-	-	-	-	-	-	-	-	-	-	16	-	-
F.G.A.Butler	-	-	-	-	FB	-	-	-	-	-	-	-	-	-	-	-	-	-	FB	-	FB	-	-	-	-	-	-	-	-	-	-	C	W	-	C	C	W	W	-	-	-	-	-	-	-	-	9	3	9
T.Elkington	-	-	-	-	-	-	-	-	-	-	-	-	-	-	-	-	-	-	-	-	-	-	-	FB	FB	FB	FB	FB	FB	FB	FB	FB	FB	FB	FB	FB	-	-	-	-	-	-	-	-	-	-	13	-	-
Hugh Bryan	W	W	W	-	-	-	-	-	-	-	-	-	-	-	-	-	-	-	W	W	W	W	-	-	-	-	-	-	-	-	-	-	-	-	W	W	-	-	-	-	-	-	-	-	-	-	9	4	22
F.Fox	W	W	W	W	W	W	W	W	-	-	-	W	W	W	W	-	W	W	W	W	W	W	W	W	W	W	W	-	W	W	C	-	-	-	-	-	-	-	-	-	-	-	-	-	-	-	26	15	115
Archie Woodyatt	-	-	-	-	-	-	-	-	-	-	-	-	W	-	-	W	-	-	-	-	-	-	-	-	-	C	-	C	-	-	-	-	-	-	-	-	-	-	-	-	-	-	-	-	-	-	4	-	-
Bob Hesmondhalgh	C	C	C	C	C	FB	C	C	C	C	C	C	C	C	-	-	C	C	C	C	C	C	C	C	C	C	C	-	C	C	W	W	C	C	C	W	C	C	-	-	-	-	-	-	-	-	35	15	58
Bobby Lewis	C	C	C	C	C	C	C	C	C	C	C	C	C	C	C	C	C	C	C	-	C	C	C	C	C	W	-	C	C	C	C	C	-	C	W	C	C	W	-	-	-	-	-	-	-	-	35	24	122
Frank Jackson	-	-	-	-	-	C	W	W	W	W	W	W	-	W	W	C	W	W	-	-	-	-	W	W	W	-	-	W	W	W	W	W	W	W	-	-	-	C	-	-	-	-	-	-	-	-	23	10	36
Shirley Harrison	-	-	-	-	-	-	-	-	-	-	-	-	-	-	-	-	-	-	-	-	-	-	-	-	-	-	C	-	-	-	-	-	-	-	-	-	-	F	-	-	-	-	-	-	-	-	2	-	-
Billy Foreman	HB	HB	HB	HB	HB	HB	HB	HB	HB	HB	HB	HB	HB	HB	HB	HB	HB	HB	HB	HB	HB	HB	HB	HB	HB	HB	HB	HB	HB	-	HB	HB	HB	HB	HB	HB	HB	HB	-	-	-	-	-	-	-	-	37	6	18
Harry Simpson	HB	HB	HB	HB	HB	HB	HB	HB	HB	HB	HB	HB	HB	HB	HB	HB	HB	HB	HB	-	HB	HB	HB	HB	-	HB	-	-	HB	HB	HB	HB	-	HB	HB	-	-	HB	-	-	-	-	-	-	-	-	31	5	15
E.C.Wykes	-	-	-	-	-	-	-	-	-	-	-	-	-	-	-	-	-	-	-	-	-	-	-	-	HB	-	HB	-	-	-	-	-	-	-	-	HB	HB	-	-	-	-	-	-	-	-	-	4	-	-
Arthur Akers	F	-	-	F	F	F	-	-	F	F	F	F	F	F	F	F	F	F	F	F	F	-	F	F	F	F	F	F	-	F	F	F	-	-	-	F	F	-	-	-	-	-	-	-	-	-	28	-	-
George Banks	F	-	F	F	F	F	F	F	F	F	-	F	F	F	F	F	F	-	F	F	F	F	F	F	F	F	F	-	-	F	F	F	-	-	-	-	-	-	-	-	-	-	-	-	-	-	27	2	6
Walter Jackson	F	F	F	F	F	F	F	F	-	F	F	F	F	F	F	F	F	F	F	F	F	F	F	F	F	-	F	F	F	F	F	F	-	-	-	-	-	-	-	-	-	-	-	-	-	-	30	2	6
Arthur Jackson	F	-	-	-	-	-	-	-	-	-	-	-	-	-	-	-	-	-	-	-	-	F	-	-	-	-	-	-	-	-	-	F	-	-	-	-	-	-	-	-	-	-	-	-	-	-	3	-	-
George Jones	F	F	F	F	F	F	F	F	-	F	F	F	F	F	F	F	F	F	-	F	F	F	F	F	F	F	F	-	-	-	-	-	F	F	F	F	F	F	-	-	-	-	-	-	-	-	31	9	27
Eddie Redman	F	F	F	F	F	F	F	F	F	F	F	F	F	F	C	-	-	F	F	C	F	F	F	F	F	F	W	F	F	F	F	F	F	W	F	F	F	F	-	-	-	-	-	-	-	-	36	2	6
Paddy Swain	F	F	F	F	F	F	F	F	F	F	F	F	F	-	F	F	F	F	F	F	-	F	F	F	F	F	F	W	F	HB	F	F	F	F	F	F	W	F	-	-	-	-	-	-	-	-	36	5	15
E.Vity	F	F	-	F	F	F	F	F	F	-	F	F	F	F	F	F	F	F	F	-	F	-	-	-	-	-	-	-	-	-	-	-	-	-	-	-	-	-	-	-	-	-	-	-	-	-	18	4	12
Ted Cooke	-	F	F	F	F	F	F	F	F	F	F	F	F	F	F	F	F	F	F	F	F	F	F	F	F	-	-	-	-	F	F	F	F	F	F	F	F	F	-	-	-	-	-	-	-	-	33	11	39
A.E.Hitchcock	-	F	F	W	W	W	-	-	W	W	W	-	-	-	-	W	-	-	-	-	-	-	-	-	-	-	-	-	-	-	-	-	C	-	-	-	-	-	-	-	-	-	-	-	-	-	10	3	9
J.J.Steinitz	-	F	F	-	-	-	-	-	-	-	-	-	-	-	-	-	-	-	-	-	-	-	-	-	-	-	-	-	-	-	-	-	-	-	-	-	-	-	-	-	-	-	-	-	-	-	2	1	3
E.Dann	-	-	-	-	-	-	F	F	-	F	F	-	-	-	-	-	-	-	-	F	-	-	-	-	-	-	-	F	-	-	-	-	F	F	F	F	-	-	-	-	-	-	-	-	-	-	10	-	-
R.E.Page	-	-	-	-	-	-	-	-	F	-	-	-	-	-	-	-	-	-	-	-	-	-	-	-	-	-	-	F	-	-	-	-	F	-	-	-	F	-	-	-	-	-	-	-	-	-	4	-	-
Tuffie' Rice	-	-	-	-	-	-	-	-	-	-	-	-	-	F	F	F	F	F	F	F	F	F	F	F	F	F	F	F	F	F	F	F	F	F	F	F	F	F	-	-	-	-	-	-	-	-	25	5	15
W.Burton	-	-	-	-	-	-	-	-	-	-	-	-	-	-	-	-	-	-	-	-	-	-	-	-	-	F	-	F	-	-	-	-	-	-	-	-	-	-	-	-	-	-	-	-	-	-	2	-	-
Dr.C.H. Nicholson	-	-	-	-	-	-	-	-	-	-	-	-	-	-	-	-	-	-	-	-	-	-	-	-	-	F	F	F	-	-	-	-	F	F	F	F	-	-	-	-	-	-	-	-	-	-	7	1	3
M.E.Whitehead	-	-	-	-	-	-	-	-	-	-	-	-	-	-	-	-	-	-	-	-	-	-	-	-	-	-	F	-	-	-	-	-	-	-	-	-	-	F	-	-	-	-	-	-	-	-	2	2	6
Rupert Cooke	-	-	-	-	-	-	-	-	-	-	-	-	-	-	-	-	-	-	-	-	-	-	-	-	-	-	-	-	-	F	F	-	-	-	-	-	-	-	-	-	-	-	-	-	-	-	2	1	3
W.H.Bradford	-	-	-	-	-	-	-	-	-	-	-	-	-	-	-	-	-	-	-	-	-	-	-	-	-	-	-	-	-	-	-	-	-	F	F	-	F	F	-	-	-	-	-	-	-	-	4	-	-

1 game: T.Betts F(30), -.English HB(28), H.Freeman F(29), W.Gale FB(37), John Garner F(34), H.Greenway HB(20), -.Harper-Smith F(9), W.Haynes FB(20), George Hicken HB(33), A.Inchley FB(4), Arthur Jones FB(38), C.Kinton F(29), J.Meek F(37), George Orton F(29), Francis Stocks FB(23), J.B.Walker F(29)

NO	DATE		OPPONENTS	V	RES	FOR G	FOR T	FOR D	FOR P	FOR PTS	AGAINST G	AGAINST T	AGAINST D	AGAINST P	AGAINST PTS	SCORERS
1	Sep	21	NUNEATON	H	Won	3	3	-	-	24	-	-	-	-	0	Field(2C) Thompson(T) F.A.Jackson(4T,C) Campbell(T)
2		28	GLOUCESTER	H	Won	-	2	-	-	6	-	-	-	-	0	Hesmondhalgh(T) Nicholson(T)
3	Oct	5	NORTHAMPTON	H	Won	-	-	-	1	3	-	-	-	-	0	Cooke(P)
4		12	Bedford	A	Lost	-	1	-	-	3	1	1	-	-	8	Nicholson(T)
5		19	GUY'S HOSPITAL	H	Won	2	3	-	-	19	-	-	-	-	0	Field(2C) F.A.Jackson(T) Woodyatt(T) Foreman(2T) Cooke(T)
6		26	Burton-on-Trent	A	Won	-	4	-	1	15	-	-	-	-	0	Woodyatt(T) Hesmondhalgh(T) G.Jones(T) Cooke(T,P)
7	Nov	2	RUGBY	H	Won	3	6	-	-	33	-	-	-	-	0	Field(T,C) F.H.Jones(T) Hesmondhalgh(T) F.A.Jackson(3T,2C) Foreman(T) Cooke(T) Dann(T)
8		9	COVENTRY	H	Lost	-	-	-	-	0	-	1	-	-	3	
9		16	Old Edwardians	A	Drew	-	-	-	-	0	-	-	-	-	0	
10		23	Swinton	A	Lost	-	-	-	-	0	-	3	1	-	13	
11		30	BEDFORD	H	Won	2	1	-	-	13	-	-	-	-	0	Field(2T,2C) Whitehead(T)
12	Dec	7	BEDFORD GRAMMAR SCH.	H	Won	-	3	-	-	9	-	1	-	-	3	A.O.Jones(T) F.H.Jones(T) G.Jones(T)
13		14	SWINTON	H	Lost	-	-	-	-	0	-	1	-	1	6	
14		21	Northampton	A	Lost	1	1	-	-	8	1	1	-	1	11	Field(C) Butlin(T) Whitehead(T)
15		26	SALFORD	H	Drew	-	-	-	-	0	-	-	-	-	0	
16		27	LEICESTERSHIRE XV	H	Won	5	5	-	-	40	-	1	-	-	3	Foreman(T,C) A.O.Jones(5T,C) Bryan(T,3C) Pickard(T) G.Jones(T) Cooke(T)
17		28	HARLEQUINS	H	Lost	-	-	-	-	0	-	2	-	-	6	
18	Jan	1	BECTIVE RANGERS	H	Drew	-	-	-	-	0	-	-	-	-	0	
19		4	Gloucester	A	Lost	1	-	1*	1	12	1	5	-	-	20	Field(T,C,M) Redman(P)
20		11	ST THOMAS' HOSPITAL	H	Won	2	2	-	-	16	-	-	-	-	0	F.A.Jackson(T) F.H.Jones(C) Field(T,C) Akers(2T)
21		18	BRIDGWATER	H	Won	5	5	1	-	44	-	1	-	-	3	A.O.Jones(D) F.A.Jackson(3T) Field(5C) Butlin(3T) Redman(T) G.Jones(3T)
22		20	ST BARTHOLOMEW'S HOS	H	Won	7	3	-	-	44	-	-	-	-	0	Butlin(T) Field(7C) Pickard(T) F.A.Jackson(6T) Whitehead(T) Yiend(T)
23		25	Coventry	A	Drew	-	-	-	-	0	-	-	-	-	0	
24	Feb	1	SALE	H	Won	1	-	-	-	5	-	-	-	-	0	Field(C) Foreman(T)
25		8	Rugby	A	Won	-	1	-	-	3	-	-	-	-	0	Yiend(T)
26		12	Bedford Grammar Sch.	A	Won	-	5	-	-	15	-	-	-	-	0	Wilkinson(T) F.H.Jones(T) Foreman(2T) Burton(T)
27		15	OLD EDWARDIANS	H	Drew	-	1	-	-	3	-	-	-	1	3	Whitehead(T)
28		22	BURTON-ON-TRENT	H	Won	3	1	-	-	18	-	-	-	-	0	Field(3C) Pickard(3T) Foreman(T)
29		29	CROYDON	H	Won	1	-	1	-	9	-	-	-	-	0	Butlin(D) Field(C) Akers(T)
30	Mar	7	WOLVERHAMPTON (MCC1)	H	Won	7	1	-	-	38	-	-	-	-	0	Butlin(T) Field(T,7C) F.A.Jackson(2T) Foreman(T) Whitehead(T) Cooke(T) Akers(T)
31		14	LEICESTER CRUSADERS (MCC2)	H	Won	1	3	1	-	18	-	-	-	-	0	F.A.Jackson(T,D) Field(T,C) Butlin(T) G.Jones(T)
32		21	Moseley (MCC3)	A	Lost	-	-	-	-	0	-	-	-	1	3	
33		28	Northampton	A	Lost	-	-	1	-	4	1	-	-	-	5	Butlin(D)
34	Apr	4	WORTLEY	H	Won	2	2	-	-	16	1	-	-	-	5	Pickard(T) Field(2C) Ball(T) Campbell(2T)
35		6	HARTLEPOOL ROVERS	H	Won	1	1	-	-	8	-	-	1	-	4	Butlin(T) Field(C) Wilkinson(T)
36		7	CHELTENHAM	H	Won	-	1	-	-	3	-	-	-	-	0	Foreman(T)
37		11	Devonport Albion	A	Lost	-	1	-	-	3	1	2	-	-	11	F.A.Jackson(T)
38		13	Bridgwater	A	Won	-	1	-	-	3	-	-	-	-	0	Butlin(T)
39		18	Hartlepool Rovers	A	Drew	-	2	-	-	6	-	2	-	-	6	Brownson(T) Wilkinson(T)

INDIVIDUAL APPEARANCES 1895-1896

NAME	1	2	3	4	5	6	7	8	9	10	11	12	13	14	15	16	17	18	19	20	21	22	23	24	25	26	27	28	29	30	31	32	33	34	35	36	37	38	39	40	41	42	43	44	45	46	TOTAL	T	PTS
Arthur Jones	FB	FB	FB	-	FB	-	FB	FB	FB	W	FB	FB	FB	FB	FB	W	C	W	FB	FB	FB	FB	FB	FB	-	FB	FB	-	FB	FB	FB	FB	FB	-	-	-	FB	-	-	-	-	-	-	-	-	-	30	6	24
W.Gale	-	-	-	FB	-	-	-	-	-	FB	-	-	-	-	-	-	-	-	-	-	-	-	-	-	-	-	-	-	-	-	-	-	-	-	-	FB	-	FB	-	-	-	-	-	-	-	-	4	-	-
John Garner	-	-	-	-	-	FB	-	-	-	F	-	-	F	F	-	F	-	-	F	-	-	-	-	-	-	-	-	-	-	-	-	-	-	-	-	-	F	F	-	-	-	-	-	-	-	-	8	-	-
Archie Field	W	W	W	W	W	W	W	W	W	C	C	C	C	C	-	-	-	C	C	C	C	C	C	C	W	C	C	W	C	C	C	C	C	C	C	C	C	C	W	-	-	-	-	-	-	-	36	7	101
Frank Jackson	W	W	W	-	C	W	W	W	W	-	W	W	W	-	-	-	-	-	-	W	W	W	W	W	W	-	W	-	-	W	W	W	-	-	-	-	W	-	-	-	-	-	-	-	-	-	22	22	76
Archie Woodyatt	-	-	-	-	W	C	-	-	-	C	-	-	-	-	-	-	-	-	-	-	-	-	-	-	-	-	-	-	-	-	-	-	-	-	-	-	-	-	C	-	-	-	-	-	-	-	4	2	6
Alf Butlin	-	-	-	-	-	-	-	-	-	W	-	-	-	C	W	-	FB	FB	W	-	W	W	W	W	FB	W	W	FB	W	W	W	W	W	FB	FB	W	W	W	-	-	-	-	-	-	-	-	24	9	35
Shirley Atkins	-	-	-	-	-	-	-	-	-	-	W	-	W	W	-	W	-	-	-	-	-	-	-	-	-	-	-	-	-	-	-	-	-	-	-	-	-	-	-	-	-	-	-	-	-	-	4	-	-
Bob Hesmondhalgh	C	C	C	C	C	C	C	C	C	-	-	W	-	-	-	-	-	-	-	-	-	-	-	-	-	-	-	-	-	-	-	-	-	-	-	-	-	-	-	-	-	-	-	-	-	-	10	3	9
Harry Wilkinson	-	C	-	-	-	-	-	-	-	-	-	-	-	-	C	-	W	W	W	W	-	-	-	-	C	W	-	-	-	-	-	-	-	W	C	W	-	W	W	-	-	-	-	-	-	-	13	3	9
J.Ball	-	-	-	C	-	-	-	-	-	-	-	-	-	-	-	-	-	-	-	-	-	-	-	-	-	-	-	-	-	-	-	-	-	W	-	-	-	-	-	-	-	-	-	-	-	-	2	1	3
Frank Jones	-	-	-	-	-	-	C	C	C	-	C	C	C	SH	W	-	-	-	-	C	C	-	C	C	-	C	C	C	C	C	C	C	C	-	W	-	-	-	-	-	-	-	-	-	-	-	21	3	11
Dr. Jamieson	-	-	-	-	-	-	-	-	-	-	-	-	-	-	C	F	F	-	-	-	-	-	-	-	-	-	-	-	-	-	-	-	-	-	-	-	-	-	-	-	-	-	-	-	-	-	3	-	-
Hugh Bryan	-	-	-	-	-	-	-	-	-	-	-	-	-	-	-	C	W	-	-	-	-	-	-	-	-	-	-	-	-	-	-	-	-	-	-	-	-	-	-	-	-	-	-	-	-	-	2	1	9
E.H.Pickard	-	-	-	-	-	-	-	-	-	-	-	-	-	-	-	C	-	-	-	-	-	C	-	-	-	-	-	C	-	-	-	-	W	C	-	C	C	C	-	-	-	-	-	-	-	-	8	6	18
S.W.Wright	-	-	-	-	-	-	-	-	-	-	-	-	-	-	-	-	-	C	C	-	-	-	-	-	-	-	-	-	-	-	-	-	-	-	-	-	-	-	-	-	-	-	-	-	-	-	2	-	-
Billy Foreman	FH	FH	FH	W	FH	FH	FH	FH	FH	FH	FH	FH	FH	FH	FH	FB	-	-	-	FH	FH	FH	FH	FH	FH	FH	FH	SH	FH	FH	-	FH	-	FH	FH	FH	FH	FH	FH	-	-	-	-	-	-	-	34	10	32
Charlie Watts	-	-	-	-	-	-	-	-	-	-	-	-	-	-	-	FH	-	-	-	-	-	-	-	-	-	-	-	W	-	-	-	-	SH	-	-	-	-	-	-	-	-	-	-	-	-	-	3	-	-
Harry Simpson	SH	SH	SH	-	SH	-	-	SH	-	-	SH	SH	SH	-	-	-	-	-	-	-	-	-	SH	SH	SH	-	SH	FH	SH	SH	SH	SH	-	-	-	-	-	-	-	-	-	-	-	-	-	-	17	-	-
Jacky Braithwaite	-	-	-	SH	-	-	-	-	-	-	-	-	-	-	-	-	-	-	SH	SH	SH	-	-	-	-	SH	-	-	-	-	-	-	-	-	-	-	-	SH	SH	-	-	-	-	-	-	-	7	-	-
C.Clarke	-	-	-	-	-	-	-	-	-	-	-	-	-	-	-	-	-	-	-	-	-	-	-	-	-	-	-	-	-	-	-	-	-	SH	SH	SH	SH	-	-	-	-	-	-	-	-	-	4	-	-
W.H.Bradford	F	F	F	F	-	-	-	-	-	-	-	-	-	F	-	-	-	-	F	-	-	-	F	-	-	F	-	-	-	-	-	-	-	-	-	-	-	-	-	-	-	-	-	-	-	-	8	-	-
Bob Campbell	F	F	F	F	F	F	F	F	F	F	F	F	F	F	F	F	F	F	-	F	F	F	F	F	F	-	F	F	F	F	F	F	F	F	F	F	F	F	F	-	-	-	-	-	-	-	37	3	9
Ted Cooke	F	F	F	F	F	F	F	F	F	-	F	-	F	-	F	F	F	F	F	F	F	F	F	F	F	-	F	F	F	F	F	F	F	F	F	F	F	F	F	-	-	-	-	-	-	-	35	5	21
Walter Jackson	F	F	F	F	F	F	F	F	F	F	F	F	F	F	F	F	-	F	F	F	F	F	F	F	F	F	F	F	F	F	F	F	F	F	F	-	F	F	F	-	-	-	-	-	-	-	37	-	-
George Jones	F	F	F	F	F	F	F	F	F	F	F	F	F	F	F	F	F	F	F	F	F	F	-	-	-	-	-	-	-	F	F	F	F	F	F	F	-	F	F	-	-	-	-	-	-	-	31	7	21
Eddie Redman	F	-	-	-	-	F	F	F	F	F	F	F	F	F	F	SH	F	F	F	F	F	F	F	F	C	F	F	F	F	F	FH	F	F	F	F	F	F	F	F	-	-	-	-	-	-	-	35	1	6
Paddy Swain	F	F	F	FH	F	SH	SH	F	SH	SH	-	-	-	-	-	-	FH	-	-	-	-	SH	-	-	-	-	-	-	-	-	-	-	-	-	-	-	-	-	-	-	-	-	-	-	-	-	12	-	-
M.E.Whitehead	F	F	F	-	F	F	F	F	F	F	F	F	-	F	F	-	F	F	-	F	F	F	F	F	F	F	F	F	F	F	F	F	F	F	F	F	F	-	-	-	-	-	-	-	-	-	33	5	15
Dr.C.H. Nicholson	-	F	F	F	F	-	-	-	-	-	-	-	-	-	SH	-	C	FH	FH	-	-	-	-	-	-	-	-	-	-	-	-	-	-	-	-	-	-	-	-	-	-	-	-	-	-	-	8	2	6
Arthur Akers	-	-	-	F	-	F	F	-	F	F	F	F	F	F	F	-	F	F	F	F	F	F	F	F	F	-	F	F	F	F	F	F	F	F	F	F	F	F	-	-	-	-	-	-	-	-	31	4	12
William Yiend	-	-	-	-	F	-	-	F	-	-	-	F	-	-	-	-	F	-	-	-	-	F	-	-	F	-	-	-	-	-	-	F	F	F	F	-	-	-	-	-	-	-	-	-	-	-	10	2	6
T.E.Coates	-	-	-	-	-	F	-	-	F	-	F	F	F	-	-	-	-	-	-	-	-	-	-	F	F	-	F	F	F	-	-	-	-	-	-	-	-	-	-	-	-	-	-	-	-	-	10	-	-
E.Dann	-	-	-	-	-	-	F	-	-	F	-	-	-	-	-	-	-	-	-	-	-	-	-	-	-	-	-	-	-	-	-	-	-	-	-	-	-	-	-	-	-	-	-	-	-	-	2	1	3
W.Burton	-	-	-	-	-	-	-	-	-	-	-	-	-	-	-	-	-	F	-	-	-	-	-	-	-	F	-	-	-	-	-	-	-	-	-	-	-	-	-	-	-	-	-	-	-	-	2	1	3
Sid Penny	-	-	-	-	-	-	-	-	-	-	-	-	-	-	-	-	-	-	F	F	F	-	F	F	F	F	F	-	-	-	-	-	-	-	-	F	F	F	-	-	-	-	-	-	-	-	11	-	-
George Banks	-	-	-	-	-	-	-	-	-	-	-	-	-	-	-	-	-	-	-	-	-	-	-	-	-	-	-	-	F	-	F	-	-	-	-	-	-	-	-	-	-	-	-	-	-	-	2	-	-
George Walker	-	-	-	-	-	-	-	-	-	-	-	-	-	-	-	-	-	-	-	-	-	-	-	-	-	-	-	-	-	F	F	-	-	-	-	-	-	-	-	-	-	-	-	-	-	-	2	-	-

1 game: E.Bolus F(28), W.Bottomley F(36), Monty Brownson C(39)[1T-3], Harry Collins F(26), W.J.Collis FB(39), William Davis F(15), Aubrey Dowson W(29), W.Everson W(14), Bob Golding F(39), Shirley Harrison F(16), J.Hart F(4), George Hicken FH(33), Arthur Jackson F(16), W.Jagger W(35), George Keeton F(26), P.Kenyon F(39), W.F.Lincoln F(39), A.Mason C(3), M.Swain SH(17), A.C.Thompson C(1)[1T-3], E.C.Wykes SH(18)

LEICESTER FOOTBALL CLUB 1895-96
Back: W.A. Wheeler, R.P. Swain, A.E. Cooke, G. Jones, W. Yiend, Dr.C.H. Nicholson, A.W. Woodyatt, R.S. Snowden,
W.H. Swingler (Hon.Tres), T.H. Crumbie (Hon.Sec).
Middle: H.W. Salmon, W. Jackson, E. Redman (Capt), R.N. Campbell, W.R. Hesmondhalgh, A.O. Jones, J. Parsons (President).
Front: M.E. Whitehead, H.J. Simpson, W.J. Foreman, F.A. Jackson, A. Field.

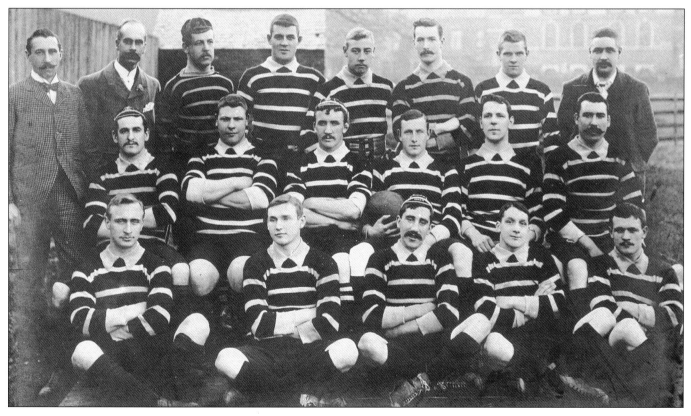

LEICESTER FOOTBALL CLUB 1896-97
Back: J. Parsons (President), T.W. Pettifor (Hon.Tres), Dr.C.H. Nicholson, E. Redman, F.A. Jackson, M.E. Whitehead,
S.H. Penny, T.H. Crumbie (Hon.Sec).
Middle: W.J. Foreman, A. Akers, R.N. Campbell, A.O. Jones (Capt), W. Jackson, A.E. Cooke.
Front: R.P. Swain, F.H. Jones, A.C. Butlin, A. Field, H. Wilkinson.

NO	DATE		OPPONENTS	V	RES	FOR					AGAINST					SCORERS
						G	T	D	P	PTS	G	T	D	P	PTS	
1	Sep	19	CHELTENHAM	H	Won	1	1	-	-	8	-	-	-	-	0	Field(T,C) Foreman(T)
2		26	NORTHAMPTON	H	Won	1	2	-	-	11	-	1	-	-	3	Field(T,C) Wilkinson(T) Foreman(T)
3	Oct	3	Coventry	A	Lost	-	-	-	-	0	-	2	-	-	6	
4		10	BURTON-ON-TRENT	H	Drew	-	-	-	-	0	-	-	-	-	0	
5		17	RUGBY	H	Won	4	1	-	-	23	-	-	-	-	0	Field(T,4C) Foreman(T) Redman(2T) Cooke(T)
6		24	Swansea	A	Lost	1	-	-	-	5	1	1	-	-	8	Field(T,C)
7		26	Llanelli	A	Lost	-	-	-	-	0	1	3	-	-	14	
8		27	Mountain Ash	A	Lost	-	-	-	-	0	1	2	-	-	11	
9		31	Old Edwardians	A	Won	1	1	-	-	8	-	1	-	-	3	Wilkinson(T) Field(C) Akers(T)
10	Nov	7	BEDFORD GRAMMAR SCH.	H	Won	1	3	-	-	14	-	-	-	-	0	Butlin(T) Field(T,C) F.H.Jones(T) Wilkinson(T)
11		14	LANCASTER	H	Won	-	1	-	-	3	-	-	-	-	0	
12		21	COVENTRY	H	Won	2	3	-	-	19	-	-	-	-	0	A.O.Jones(2C) Wilkinson(2T) Field(T) Foreman(T) Braithwaite(T)
13		28	MANCHESTER	H	Won	3	3	-	-	24	-	1	-	-	3	A.O.Jones(C) Field(2C) Wilkinson(2T) Foreman(2T) Braithwaite(T) Lincoln(T)
	Dec	3	Nuneaton	A			Cancelled Frost										
14		5	COVENTRY	H	Won	-	1	-	-	3	-	-	-	-	0	Wilkinson(T)
15		12	HAMPSTEAD	H	Won	1	1	-	-	8	-	-	-	-	0	A.O.Jones(T,C) Mosby(T)
16		14	JESUS COLLEGE,OXFORD	H	Won	-	4	1	-	16	-	-	-	-	0	A.O.Jones(D) Walker(T) Wilkinson(T) Penny(T) Lincoln(T)
17		19	Bedford	A	Won	2	1	-	-	13	-	-	-	-	0	A.O.Jones(2C) Field(2T) Wilkinson(T)
18		26	ASPATRIA	H	Drew	-	-	-	1	3	-	1	-	-	3	A.O.Jones(P)
19		28	HARLEQUINS	H	Drew	-	-	-	-	0	-	-	-	-	0	
20		29	MOUNTAIN ASH	H	Won	-	1	-	-	3	-	-	-	-	0	A.O.Jones(T)
21	Jan	2	Burton-on-Trent	A	Lost	-	1	-	-	3	-	-	1	-	4	Braithwaite(T)
22		9	ST THOMAS' HOSPITAL	H	Won	3	2	-	-	21	-	-	-	-	0	Butlin(T) Field(T,3C) Wilkinson(2T) Foreman(T)
		16	RUGBY	H			Cancelled Snow										
23		23	BEDFORD	H	Won	-	1	2	-	11	1	-	-	-	5	A.O.Jones(2D) Foreman(T)
24		30	ALTRINCHAM	H	Won	-	2	-	-	6	-	-	-	-	0	F.A.Jackson(T) F.H.Jones(T)
25	Feb	6	SWANSEA	H	Won	1	-	-	-	5	-	-	-	-	0	A.O.Jones(C) Whitehead(T)
26		13	OLD EDWARDIANS	H	Won	2	1	-	-	13	-	-	-	-	0	A.O.Jones(2C) Whitehead(2T) Swain(T)
27		17	Bedford Grammar Sch.	A	Won	2	3	-	-	19	-	2	-	1	9	A.O.Jones(C) Butlin(2T) F.H.Jones(T) Field(C) Foreman(2T)
28		20	GUY'S HOSPITAL	H	Won	1	4	-	-	17	-	1	-	-	3	Swain(T) Field(T) F.H.Jones(C) Braithwaite(T) Redman(2T)
29		27	Manchester	A	Drew	1	-	-	-	5	1	-	-	-	5	F.H.Jones(T) Field(C)
30	Mar	6	LITTLEBOROUGH	H	Won	4	4	-	-	32	-	-	-	-	0	Wilkinson(2T) Field(2T) F.H.Jones(4C) Swain(2T) Foreman(T) Cooke(T)
31		13	Rugby (MCC2)	A	Won	3	5	-	-	30	-	-	-	-	0	A.O.Jones(C) Butlin(T) Field(2C) F.H.Jones(3T) Wilkinson(2T) Foreman(T) Redman(T)
32		20	Coventry (MCC3)	A	Won	-	2	-	-	6	-	1	-	-	3	Butlin(T) Wilkinson(T)
33		27	OLD EDWARDIANS (MCCSF)	H	Lost	-	-	-	-	0	-	1	-	-	3	
34	Apr	3	NUNEATON	H	Won	-	3	-	-	9	-	-	-	-	0	F.H.Jones(T) Wilkinson(2T)
35		5	LLANELLI	H	Drew	-	-	-	-	0	-	-	-	-	0	
36		10	Northampton	A	Lost	1	2	-	-	11	3	-	-	-	15	Wilkinson(T) F.H.Jones(C) Atkins(T) Foreman(T)
37		17	SALE	H	Won	-	2	-	-	6	-	-	-	-	0	Swain(T) Akers(T)
38		19	PORTSMOUTH	H	Won	1	3	-	-	14	1	-	-	-	5	Atkins(2T) Field(T) F.H.Jones(C) Wilkinson(T)
39		20	PENYGRAIG	H	Won	-	1	1	-	7	-	-	-	-	0	Butlin(T) Braithwaite(D)

INDIVIDUAL APPEARANCES 1896-1897

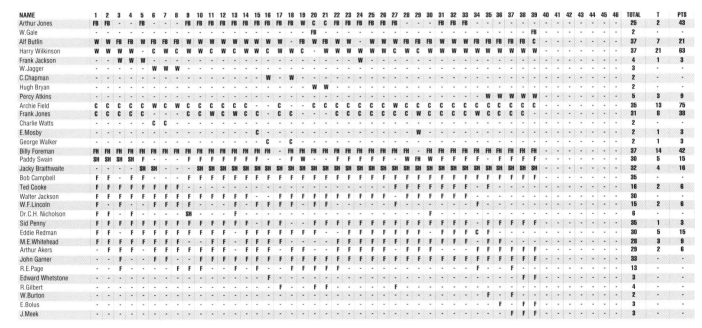

1 game: Tom Crumbie F(21), E.Goddard C(8), Shirley Harrison F(36), -.Jenkins SH(8), George Keeton F(19), E.H.Pickard C(19), F.Sarson F(34), J.Simcoe FH(17), -.Thomas SH(7), F.Woodford F(19)

NO	DATE		OPPONENTS	V	RES	FOR					AGAINST					SCORERS
						G	T	D	P	PTS	G	T	D	P	PTS	
1	Sep	4	LEICESTERSHIRE XV	H	Won	3	4	1	-	31	-	-	-	-	0	F.H.Jones(C) Wilkinson(3T) Joyce(T,2C,D) Foreman(T) Cooke(T) Lincoln(T)
2		11	NUNEATON	H	Won	2	4	-	-	22	1	-	-	1	8	Oscroft(T) F.H.Jones(2T,C) Foreman(2T) Braithwaite(T,C)
3		18	CHELTENHAM	H	Won	4	3	-	-	29	-	-	-	-	0	A.O.Jones(2C) Oscroft(2T,C) Atkins(T) F.H.Jones(C) Foreman(T) Braithwaite(T) Redman(2T)
4		25	HANDSWORTH	H	Won	1	3	-	1	17	-	-	1	-	4	A.O.Jones(P) Swain(T) F.H.Jones(T) Butlin(C) Foreman(2T)
5	Oct	2	LLANELLI	H	Won	2	1	-	-	13	-	-	-	-	0	F.A.Jackson(T) A.O.Jones(2T,2C)
6		4	BRISTOL	H	Won	-	3	-	-	9	1	-	-	-	5	F.A.Jackson(T) Atkins(T) Foreman(T)
7		9	BURTON-ON-TRENT	H	Won	2	4	-	-	22	-	-	-	1	3	A.O.Jones(2C) Wilkinson(2T) Foreman(T) Whitehead(T) Penny(T) Swain(T)
8		16	RUGBY	H	Won	4	1	-	-	23	-	-	-	-	0	Mosby(T) A.O.Jones(T,4C) Braithwaite(T) Whitehead(T) Lincoln(T)
9		23	COVENTRY	H	Won	-	1	1	-	7	-	1	-	-	3	A.O.Jones(D) Akers(T)
10		30	OLD EDWARDIANS	H	Won	2	3	-	-	19	-	-	-	-	0	F.H.Jones(2C) Atkins(2T) Mosby(T) Wilkinson(2T)
11	Nov	6	NORTHAMPTON	H	Won	2	-	-	-	10	-	-	-	-	0	A.O.Jones(T,2C) Foreman(T)
12		13	BEDFORD GRAMMAR SCH.	H	Won	1	8	-	-	29	-	-	-	-	0	Wilkinson(3T) F.H.Jones(C) A.O.Jones(3T) Braithwaite(T) Redman(T) Swain(T)
13		20	Northampton	A	Lost	1	1	-	-	8	2	2	-	-	16	Atkins(T) A.O.Jones(C) Foreman(T)
14		27	SWANSEA	H	Lost	-	-	-	-	0	-	1	-	-	3	
15	Dec	4	Rugby	A	Won	-	4	-	-	12	-	-	-	-	0	Butlin(T) Wilkinson(2T) Lincoln(T)
16		11	Manchester	A	Won	-	1	-	-	3	-	-	-	-	0	F.H.Jones(T)
17		18	BEDFORD	H	Won	1	3	-	-	14	-	-	-	-	0	Mosby(T,C) Wilkinson(2T) Keeton(T)
18		24	OLNEY	H	Won	4	-	-	-	20	-	1	-	-	3	Oscroft(T) F.H.Jones(2T) A.O.Jones(T,4C)
19		27	MOUNTAIN ASH	H	Won	2	-	1	-	14	1	-	-	-	5	A.O.Jones(2C) Oscroft(D) F.A.Jackson(T) Braithwaite(T)
20		28	HARLEQUINS	H	Won	-	1	1	-	7	-	1	-	-	3	A.O.Jones(D) Braithwaite(T)
21	Jan	1	Bedford	A	Lost	-	-	-	-	0	-	1	-	-	3	
22		8	Coventry	A	Won	1	-	1	-	9	-	-	-	-	0	Mosby(T) A.O.Jones(C,D)
23		15	SALE	H	Won	1	5	-	-	20	-	-	-	-	0	A.O.Jones(T,C) Wilkinson(2T) Penny(T) Akers(2T)
24		22	COVENTRY	H	Won	1	-	1	-	9	-	-	-	-	0	Mosby(T,C) A.O.Jones(D)
25		29	MANCHESTER	H	Won	2	2	-	-	16	-	-	-	1	3	A.O.Jones(2C) Wilkinson(2T) Hills(T) Campbell(T)
26	Feb	5	GUY'S HOSPITAL	H	Won	2	-	-	-	10	-	-	-	-	0	F.H.Jones(T) A.O.Jones(2C) Banks(T)
27		8	Bedford Grammar Sch.	A	Won	1	2	-	-	11	-	-	-	-	0	Butlin(C) Cave(2T) Whitehead(T)
28		12	Old Edwardians	A	Won	-	1	1*	-	7	-	-	-	-	0	A.O.Jones(M) Lincoln(T)
29		19	ST BARTHOLOMEW'S HOS	H	Won	2	2	-	-	16	-	-	-	-	0	Atkins(T) Braithwaite(2C) Keeton(T) Cary-Elwes(2T)
30		26	Burton-on-Trent	A	Lost	-	-	-	-	0	-	1	-	-	3	
31	Mar	5	RUGBY (MCC1)	H	Won	2	7	-	-	31	-	-	-	-	0	F.A.Jackson(2T) Atkins(T) Wilkinson(3T) A.O.Jones(T,2C) Cary-Elwes(T) Keeton(T)
32		12	BURTON-ON-TRENT (MCC2)	H	Won	1	3	-	1	17	-	-	-	-	0	F.A.Jackson(3T) A.O.Jones(T,C,P)
33		19	Coventry (MCCSF)	A	Won	1	-	1	1	12	1	-	-	-	5	A.O.Jones(C,D,P) Wilkinson(T)
34	Apr	6	Moseley (MCCF)	A	Won	1	-	-	-	5	-	-	-	1	3	Oscroft(T) F.H.Jones(C)
35		9	Swansea	A	Lost	-	-	-	-	0	1	4	-	-	17	
36		11	Llanelli	A	Lost	-	-	-	-	0	1	-	-	-	5	
37		12	Bristol	A	Won	2	-	1	-	14	2	-	-	-	10	Wilkinson(T) Oscroft(2C,D) Foreman(T)
38		16	Northampton	A	Lost	-	1	-	-	3	1	1	-	-	8	Wilkinson(T)

INDIVIDUAL APPEARANCES 1897-1898

NAME	1	2	3	4	5	6	7	8	9	10	11	12	13	14	15	16	17	18	19	20	21	22	23	24	25	26	27	28	29	30	31	32	33	34	35	36	37	38	39	40	41	42	43	44	45	46	TOTAL	T	PTS
Alf Butlin	FB	-	W	W	FB	FB	FB	FB	FB	FB	FB	FB	FB	FB	W	C	FB	FB	-	FB	FB	FB	FB	FB	FB	FB	FB	FB	FB	FB	FB	FB	FB	FB	FB	FB	FB	FB	-	-	-	-	-	-	-	-	36	1	7
Arthur Jones	-	-	FB	FB	C	-	C	C	C	-	C	C	C	C	-	-	C	SH	FB	C	C	C	C	C	C	C	C	-	C	-	-	FH	C	C	-	-	-	-	-	-	-	-	-	-	-	-	24	11	124
W.Gale	-	-	-	-	-	-	-	-	-	-	-	-	-	-	FB	FB	-	-	-	-	-	-	-	-	-	-	-	-	-	-	-	-	-	-	-	-	-	-	-	-	-	-	-	-	-	-	2	-	-
Percy Atkins	W	C	C	C	C	W	W	W	W	C	W	-	W	W	C	-	C	W	-	-	-	C	C	C	-	-	-	W	C	C	-	-	C	-	W	W	W	-	-	-	-	-	-	-	-	-	26	7	21
Percy Oscroft	-	W	W	-	-	-	-	-	-	C	-	-	-	-	-	-	C	C	-	-	-	-	-	-	-	-	-	C	-	W	C	C	-	C	C	-	-	-	-	-	-	-	-	-	-	-	11	5	29
Frank Jackson	-	-	-	-	W	W	-	-	-	-	-	-	-	-	-	-	-	-	W	C	W	-	-	-	-	-	-	W	-	W	W	-	-	-	-	-	-	-	-	-	-	-	-	-	-	-	8	8	24
Sammy Matthews	-	-	-	-	-	-	-	-	-	-	-	-	-	-	-	-	-	-	W	-	-	W	W	W	C	C	C	-	-	-	-	-	-	-	-	-	-	-	-	-	-	-	-	-	-	-	7	-	-
Archie Woodyatt	-	-	-	-	-	-	-	-	-	-	-	-	-	-	-	-	-	-	-	-	-	-	-	-	-	-	-	W	-	-	-	-	C	C	-	-	-	-	-	-	-	-	-	-	-	-	3	-	-
Frank Jones	C	C	C	C	W	-	-	-	C	W	-	C	-	C	-	C	-	C	C	W	C	-	-	-	C	C	-	-	C	C	W	W	-	-	-	-	-	-	-	-	-	-	-	-	-	-	20	7	35
Harry Wilkinson	C	W	-	-	-	C	W	-	W	W	W	W	-	W	C	W	W	W	W	-	W	-	W	W	C	W	C	W	C	W	W	W	W	W	W	W	W	W	-	-	-	-	-	-	-	-	31	24	72
E.Mosby	-	-	-	-	-	-	-	W	W	-	W	-	W	W	W	-	W	-	W	W	W	W	-	-	-	-	-	C	C	C	-	-	-	-	-	-	-	-	-	-	-	-	-	-	-	-	16	5	19
Billy Foreman	FH	FH	FH	FH	FH	FH	FH	FH	FH	FH	FH	FH	FH	-	FH	FH	FH	FH	FH	FH	FH	FH	FH	FH	FH	-	-	-	FH	SH	FH	FH	FH	FH	FH	-	-	-	-	-	-	-	-	-	-	-	34	11	33
Bertie Hills	-	-	-	-	-	-	-	-	-	-	-	-	FH	-	-	-	-	-	-	-	-	-	SH	-	-	FH	-	-	-	-	-	-	-	-	SH	-	-	-	-	-	-	-	-	-	-	-	4	1	3
Jacky Braithwaite	SH	SH	SH	SH	SH	SH	SH	SH	SH	SH	SH	SH	SH	SH	SH	SH	SH	SH	-	SH	SH	SH	SH	SH	SH	-	SH	SH	SH	SH	SH	SH	-	SH	SH	SH	SH	SH	-	-	-	-	-	-	-	-	34	6	24
Bob Campbell	F	-	F	-	F	F	F	F	F	-	F	F	F	F	F	F	F	F	F	-	-	F	F	-	-	-	F	F	F	F	F	F	F	F	F	F	F	F	-	-	-	-	-	-	-	-	34	1	3
Rev.A. Cary-Elwes	F	F	F	F	F	F	F	-	F	F	F	F	F	F	F	F	F	-	F	F	-	F	F	F	-	F	F	F	F	F	-	-	-	-	-	-	-	-	-	-	-	-	-	-	-	-	27	3	9
Ted Cooke	F	F	-	-	-	-	-	-	-	-	-	-	-	-	-	-	-	-	-	-	-	-	-	-	-	-	-	-	-	-	-	-	-	-	-	-	-	-	-	-	-	-	-	-	-	-	2	1	3
John Garner	-	F	F	-	F	F	F	F	F	F	F	F	F	F	F	F	F	F	F	F	F	F	F	F	F	F	F	F	F	F	F	F	F	F	F	F	F	F	-	-	-	-	-	-	-	-	37	-	-
Walter Jackson	F	F	-	F	-	F	F	F	F	F	F	F	F	F	F	F	F	F	F	F	-	F	F	F	-	-	F	F	-	-	F	F	-	-	F	F	-	F	-	-	-	-	-	-	-	-	29	-	-
W.F.Lincoln	F	-	-	-	-	-	F	F	F	-	F	-	F	F	-	F	F	F	F	F	F	F	F	-	-	-	FH	F	-	-	F	F	-	F	F	-	-	-	-	-	-	-	-	-	-	-	19	4	12
Sid Penny	F	F	F	F	F	F	F	F	F	F	F	F	F	F	-	F	F	F	F	F	-	F	F	-	F	F	-	F	F	F	F	F	F	F	F	F	F	F	-	-	-	-	-	-	-	-	34	2	6
Paddy Swain	-	F	F	W	F	C	F	F	-	F	F	C	F	-	-	-	-	-	-	-	-	-	-	-	-	-	-	-	-	-	-	-	-	-	-	-	-	-	-	-	-	-	-	-	-	-	11	3	9
M.E.Whitehead	-	-	F	F	F	F	F	F	F	F	-	F	F	F	F	F	F	-	F	F	F	-	F	F	F	F	F	F	-	-	F	F	-	F	F	F	F	F	-	-	-	-	-	-	-	-	31	3	9
Eddie Redman	-	-	F	F	F	-	F	-	-	F	F	F	F	F	-	F	F	F	-	F	F	F	F	F	F	F	-	-	-	F	F	F	-	F	-	F	-	F	-	-	-	-	-	-	-	-	26	3	9
Arthur Akers	-	-	-	F	F	F	F	F	F	F	F	-	-	-	F	F	-	-	F	F	-	-	-	F	F	F	F	F	F	F	F	-	F	-	F	F	F	F	-	-	-	-	-	-	-	-	24	3	9
George Keeton	-	-	-	-	-	-	F	-	-	-	-	-	-	-	-	-	F	F	-	-	F	F	-	-	-	F	F	-	F	-	F	-	F	-	F	F	F	F	-	-	-	-	-	-	-	-	14	3	9
S.C.Yeomans	-	-	-	-	-	-	-	-	-	-	F	-	-	-	-	-	-	F	F	-	-	-	-	-	-	-	-	-	-	-	-	-	-	-	-	-	-	-	-	-	-	-	-	-	-	-	3	-	-
Edward Whetstone	-	-	-	-	-	-	-	-	-	-	-	-	-	-	-	-	-	-	F	-	-	F	F	-	-	F	F	-	-	-	F	-	-	-	F	-	-	-	-	-	-	-	-	-	-	-	9	-	-
D.Gilbert	-	-	-	-	-	-	-	-	-	-	-	-	-	-	-	-	-	-	-	-	F	-	F	-	-	-	-	F	-	-	-	F	-	-	-	-	-	-	-	-	-	-	-	-	-	-	3	-	-

1 game: George Banks F(26)[1T-3], W.Burton F(3), C.F.Cave W(27)[2T-6], C.Cheshire W(8), Bob Hesmondhalgh W(30), Ralph Joyce W(1)[1T-11], R.E.Page F(1), -.Skelton F(20), A.Thomas FB(2), E.C.Wykes FH(29)

LEICESTER FOOTBALL CLUB 1897-98
Back: J. Parsons (President), W. Burton, E. Redman, Rev A. Cary-Elwes, R.P. Swain, T.H. Crumbie (Hon.Sec), H.N. Stroud (Hon.Tres).
Middle: W.J. Foreman, J.W. Garner, P.W. Oscroft, A.O. Jones (Capt), R.N. Campbell, S.H. Penny.
Front: H.P. Atkins, J. Braithwaite, F.H. Jones, A.C. Butlin, M.E. Whitehead.

LEICESTER FOOTBALL CLUB 1898-99
Back: J. Collier (Touch Judge), J. Parsons (President), T.H. Crumbie (Hon.Sec), H.N. Stroud (Hon.Tres).
Middle: H. Wilkinson, F.H. Jones, W.E. Thompson, W.F. Lincoln, A.W. Woodyatt.
Front: A. Akers, S.H. Penny, A.O. Jones (Capt), W.J. Foreman, S. Matthews, J.W. Garner.
Seated: R.N. Campbell, M.S. Scott, A.C. Butlin, J. Braithwaite.

NO	DATE	OPPONENTS	V	RES	FOR					AGAINST					SCORERS
					G	T	D	P	PTS	G	T	D	P	PTS	
1	Sep 3	NUNEATON	H	Won	2	1	1*	-	17	-	1	-	-	3	Oscroft(T) F.H.Jones(T,2C) Foreman(T) Braithwaite(M)
2	10	TREHERBERT	H	Won	-	2	-	-	6	-	1	-	-	3	A.O.Jones(T) Oscroft(T)
3	17	HANDSWORTH	H	Won	3	4	2	-	35	-	1	-	-	3	Wilkinson(2T) A.O.Jones(T,3C,2D) F.H.Jones(T) H.P.Atkins(T) Penny(T) Keeton(T)
4	24	DEVONPORT ALBION	H	Won	2	-	-	-	10	-	-	1	-	4	F.H.Jones(2T,2C)
5	Oct 1	LLANELLI	H	Lost	-	-	1	-	4	2	-	-	-	10	A.O.Jones(D)
6	8	MANCHESTER	H	Won	3	5	2	-	38	-	-	-	-	0	Wilkinson(T,D) F.H.Jones(2T,C) A.O.Jones(T,D) Foreman(T) Braithwaite(2C) Keeton(T) Whitehead(2T)
7	12	BEDFORD GRAMMAR SCH.	H	Won	-	7	1	-	25	-	1	-	-	3	Wilkinson(3T) Goddard(D) Braithwaite(2T) Penny(T) Cary-Elwes(T)
8	15	RUGBY	H	Won	5	4	1	1	44	-	-	-	-	0	Wilkinson(2T,D) H.P.Atkins(2T) A.O.Jones(T,5C,P) Goddard(T) Foreman(T) Braithwaite(T) Whitehead(T)
9	22	Richmond	A	Lost	-	1	-	-	3	1	-	-	-	5	Wilkinson(T)
10	29	OLD EDWARDIANS	H	Won	2	-	2	-	18	1	-	-	-	5	A.O.Jones(T,2C,2D) Lincoln(T)
11	Nov 5	NORTHAMPTON	H	Won	-	1	-	1	6	-	1	-	-	3	Wilkinson(T) A.O.Jones(P)
12	12	Coventry	A	Lost	-	1	-	-	3	1	-	-	-	5	Braithwaite(T)
13	19	Swansea	A	Lost	-	-	-	-	0	2	1	1	1	20	
14	21	Treherbert	A	Won	1	-	-	-	5	-	1	-	-	3	A.O.Jones(C) Braithwaite(T)
15	26	LANSDOWNE	H	Drew	1	-	-	-	5	1	-	-	-	5	A.O.Jones(C) Mosby(T)
16	Dec 3	Northampton	A	Won	-	-	1	-	4	-	-	-	-	0	A.O.Jones(D)
17	10	Burton-on-Trent	A	Won	3	4	-	-	27	-	1	-	-	3	F.A.Jackson(T) Mosby(3C) Wilkinson(2T) Foreman(T) Braithwaite(3T)
18	17	Manchester	A	Lost	-	-	-	-	0	-	-	1	-	4	
19	24	SALE	H	Won	1	5	-	-	20	-	1	-	-	3	Wilkinson(T) F.H.Jones(T,C) F.A.Jackson(2T) A.O.Jones(2T)
20	26	LLWYNYPIA	H	Drew	-	-	-	-	0	-	-	-	-	0	
21	27	HARLEQUINS	H	Won	-	3	-	-	9	-	1	-	-	3	Wilkinson(2T) Penny(T)
22	31	CARDIFF	H	Lost	-	-	-	1	3	1	1	-	-	8	F.H.Jones(P)
23	Jan 2	EDINBURGH ROYAL H.S.	H	Lost	1	-	-	-	5	-	2	-	-	6	F.H.Jones(C) Foreman(T)
24	7	Devonport Albion	A	Lost	-	1	1*	-	7	2	-	-	-	10	A.O.Jones(M) Foreman(T)
25	9	Exeter	A	Won	-	1	-	-	3	-	-	-	-	0	F.H.Jones(T)
26	14	RICHMOND	H	Won	1	5	-	-	20	-	1	-	-	3	Wilkinson(3T) F.H.Jones(T,C) Page(2T)
27	21	EXETER	H	Drew	-	-	-	-	0	-	-	-	-	0	
28	28	COVENTRY	H	Won	-	3	-	-	9	1	1	-	-	8	Woodyatt(2T) Braithwaite(T)
29	Feb 4	BURTON-ON-TRENT	H	Won	3	1	-	1	21	-	-	1	-	4	Wilkinson(T) Woodyatt(3C) A.O.Jones(T,P) Mosby(T) Whitehead(T)
30	8	Bedford Grammar Sch.	A	Won	2	1	1	-	17	-	-	-	-	0	Wilkinson(2T) A.O.Jones(2C,D) Woodyatt(T)
31	11	Old Edwardians	A	Won	-	2	-	-	6	-	-	-	1	3	Wilkinson(T) Whitehead(T)
32	14	Nuneaton	A	Won	1	1	-	-	8	-	1	-	-	3	A.O.Jones(C) F.A.Jackson(T) Foreman(T)
33	18	SWANSEA	H	Lost	-	-	-	2	6	2	-	1	-	14	A.O.Jones(2P)
34	25	NORTHAMPTON	H	Won	4	-	1	-	24	1	-	-	-	5	Wilkinson(T) Mosby(4C,D) F.A.Jackson(T) Matthews(T) Lincoln(T)
35	Mar 4	Gloucester	A	Lost	-	1	-	-	3	-	2	-	-	6	Wilkinson(T)
36	11	BELGRAVE ST PETER'S (MCC2)	H	Won	9	5	2	-	68	-	1	-	-	3	Wilkinson(4T,C) F.H.Jones(C) Oscroft(2T,C) F.A.Jackson(2T,D) A.O.Jones(2T,D) Lloyd-Evans(C) Campbell(T) Garner(C) Akers(C) Lincoln(T,C) Scott(T) Brackenbury(T,C) Ball(C)
37	18	FIVE WAYS OLD EDW. (MCC3)	H	Won	7	2	-	-	41	-	1	1	-	7	Wilkinson(4T) F.H.Jones(3C) A.O.Jones(4C) F.A.Jackson(3T) Thompson(T) Scott(T)
38	25	MOSELEY (MCCSF)	H	Drew	-	-	-	-	0	-	-	-	-	0	
39	29	Moseley (MCCSF)	A	Won	1	1	-	-	8	-	1	-	-	3	A.O.Jones(C) F.H.Jones(T) Woodyatt(T)
40	Apr 1	Nuneaton (MCCF)	A	Won	1	5	-	-	20	-	1	-	-	3	Wilkinson(2T) F.H.Jones(3T,C) Woodyatt(T)
41	3	PONTYPRIDD	H	Lost	-	-	-	-	0	-	1	-	-	3	
42	4	CARLISLE	H	Won	-	2	-	-	6	-	-	-	-	0	Wilkinson(2T)
43	8	Cardiff	A	Lost	-	-	-	-	0	2	3	-	-	19	
44	15	GLOUCESTER	H	Won	-	2	-	-	6	-	-	1	-	4	Mosby(T) Wilkinson(T)

INDIVIDUAL APPEARANCES 1898-1899

NAME	1	2	3	4	5	6	7	8	9	10	11	12	13	14	15	16	17	18	19	20	21	22	23	24	25	26	27	28	29	30	31	32	33	34	35	36	37	38	39	40	41	42	43	44	45	46	TOTAL	T	PTS
Alf Butlin	FB	W	FB	FB	FB	FB	FB	FB	FB	FB	FB	FB	FB	FB	FB	FB	FB	FB	FB	W	W	FB	FB	FB	FB	FB	FB	FB	FB	FB	FB	FB	FB	FB	FB	FB	FB	FB	FB	FB	FB	FB	FB	FB	-	-	44	-	-
Arthur Jones	-	FB	C	C	C	C	C	C	C	C	C	C	C	C	W	C	-	C	FH	FB	FB	C	C	C	-	C	C	C	C	C	C	W	C	-	-	FH	C	C	C	C	-	-	-	-	-	-	35	10	125
Percy Atkins	W	W	W	-	W	-	C	C	C	-	-	-	-	-	C	-	C	-	-	-	-	-	-	-	-	-	-	-	-	-	-	-	-	-	-	-	-	-	-	-	-	-	C	-	-	-	10	3	9
Harry Wilkinson	-	-	W	W	W	W	W	W	W	-	W	W	W	W	-	W	W	W	W	W	W	W	W	W	W	W	W	W	W	W	W	C	W	W	W	W	W	W	W	W	W	W	C	W	-	-	40	37	121
E.Goddard	-	-	-	-	-	W	W	W	W	W	-	W	-	-	-	-	-	-	-	-	-	-	-	-	-	-	-	-	-	-	-	-	-	-	-	-	-	-	-	-	-	W	-	-	-	-	7	1	7
Archie Woodyatt	-	-	-	-	-	-	-	-	-	W	-	-	W	-	-	-	-	W	-	-	-	-	-	-	-	-	-	C	C	W	-	-	W	-	-	-	-	W	W	W	-	-	W	-	-	-	11	5	21
Frank Jackson	-	-	-	-	-	-	-	-	-	-	-	-	-	-	-	-	W	-	W	-	-	-	-	-	-	-	-	-	-	-	-	C	-	W	W	W	W	-	-	-	-	-	-	-	-	-	7	10	34
C.A.Page	-	-	-	-	-	-	-	-	-	-	-	-	-	-	-	-	-	-	-	-	-	-	W	-	W	W	W	W	-	-	-	W	-	-	-	-	-	-	-	-	-	-	-	-	-	-	6	2	6
Frank Jones	C	C	C	C	C	C	-	-	-	-	-	-	-	-	-	-	-	-	C	C	C	C	C	C	C	C	-	-	-	-	-	-	-	-	-	C	C	C	C	C	C	C	-	C	-	-	22	13	68
Percy Oscroft	C	C	-	W	-	-	-	-	-	-	W	-	-	-	-	C	-	-	C	C	C	-	-	-	-	-	-	-	-	-	-	-	C	C	C	C	-	-	-	-	-	-	-	W	-	-	13	4	14
E.Mosby	-	-	-	-	-	-	-	-	-	C	C	C	C	C	C	W	C	C	-	-	-	-	-	W	C	-	C	-	W	-	C	-	-	C	C	-	-	-	-	-	C	C	-	C	-	-	19	3	27
Billy Foreman	FH	FH	FH	FH	FH	FH	-	FH	FH	FH	FH	FH	FH	FH	FH	FH	FH	-	-	FH	FH	FH	FH	FH	FH	FH	-	FH	FH	FH	FH	FH	FH	FH	FH	-	-	FH	FH	FH	FH	FH	-	FH	-	-	37	7	21
Owen Lloyd-Evans	-	-	-	-	-	-	FH	-	-	-	-	-	-	-	-	-	-	FH	-	-	-	-	SH	-	-	-	-	-	-	-	-	-	-	-	-	SH	SH	-	-	-	-	-	-	-	-	-	5	-	2
Jacky Braithwaite	SH	SH	SH	SH	SH	SH	SH	SH	SH	SH	SH	SH	SH	SH	SH	SH	SH	SH	SH	SH	SH	SH	-	SH	SH	SH	SH	SH	-	SH	SH	SH	SH	SH	SH	-	FH	SH	SH	SH	SH	SH	SH	SH	-	-	41	9	35
Bob Campbell	F	F	F	F	F	F	F	F	F	F	F	F	F	F	F	F	F	F	F	F	F	F	-	-	-	F	F	F	F	F	F	F	F	F	F	F	F	F	F	F	F	F	F	F	-	-	41	1	3
D.Gilbert	F	-	-	-	-	-	-	-	-	-	-	-	-	-	-	-	-	-	-	-	-	-	-	-	-	-	-	F	F	-	-	F	-	-	-	-	-	-	-	-	-	-	-	F	-	-	5	-	-
W.F.Lincoln	F	F	F	F	F	F	F	F	F	F	F	F	F	F	W	F	F	F	F	F	F	W	F	F	F	F	F	F	F	F	F	F	F	F	F	F	F	F	F	W	F	F	F	F	-	-	44	3	11
Sammy Matthews	F	-	F	F	F	F	F	F	F	F	F	F	F	-	-	-	F	-	F	F	F	F	F	F	F	F	F	F	F	-	F	-	F	F	F	F	F	F	F	F	F	-	-	F	-	-	35	1	3
Sid Penny	F	F	F	F	F	F	F	F	F	F	F	-	F	F	F	F	F	F	F	F	F	F	F	F	F	F	F	F	F	-	F	F	F	F	F	-	-	F	F	F	F	F	F	F	-	-	40	3	9
Arthur Akers	-	F	-	-	F	-	-	-	-	-	F	-	F	F	F	F	F	F	-	F	F	F	F	F	F	-	F	-	-	-	-	-	F	F	F	F	F	F	F	F	F	F	F	F	-	-	28	-	2
Walter Jackson	-	F	F	F	F	F	F	F	-	-	-	-	-	-	-	-	-	-	-	-	-	-	-	-	-	-	-	-	-	-	-	-	-	-	-	-	-	-	-	-	-	-	-	-	-	-	7	-	-
George Keeton	-	F	F	F	F	F	-	-	-	-	-	-	-	-	-	-	-	-	F	F	F	F	F	-	-	F	-	-	-	-	-	-	-	-	-	-	F	-	-	-	F	-	-	-	-	-	13	2	6
Edward Whetstone	-	F	F	F	-	-	-	-	-	-	-	-	-	-	-	-	-	-	-	-	-	-	-	-	-	-	-	-	F	-	-	-	-	-	-	-	-	-	-	-	-	F	-	-	-	-	5	-	-
M.E.Whitehead	-	-	F	F	F	F	-	F	F	F	F	F	F	F	F	F	-	F	-	-	-	-	-	-	-	-	F	F	F	F	F	-	F	F	F	-	-	F	F	-	-	-	-	-	-	-	24	5	15
Rev.A.Cary-Elwes	-	-	-	-	-	F	F	F	F	-	-	F	-	-	-	-	-	-	-	-	-	-	-	-	-	-	-	-	-	-	-	-	-	-	-	-	-	-	-	-	-	-	-	-	-	-	5	1	3
Shirley Atkins	-	-	-	-	-	-	F	F	F	F	-	-	-	-	-	-	-	-	-	-	-	-	-	-	-	-	-	-	-	-	-	-	-	-	-	-	-	-	-	-	-	-	-	-	-	-	4	-	-
W.E.Thompson	-	-	-	-	-	-	F	-	-	-	-	-	-	-	-	-	-	-	F	-	F	F	F	F	F	F	-	-	-	-	-	-	-	-	-	-	F	-	-	F	F	-	F	-	-	-	12	1	3
John Garner	-	-	-	-	-	-	-	-	F	F	F	F	F	F	F	F	F	F	F	F	F	F	F	F	F	F	F	F	F	F	F	-	F	F	F	F	F	F	F	F	F	F	F	F	-	-	35	-	2
H.E.Brackenbury	-	-	-	-	-	-	-	-	-	F	F	F	F	F	F	F	F	F	-	-	-	-	-	-	-	-	-	-	-	F	F	-	-	-	-	F	-	-	-	-	-	-	-	-	-	-	12	1	5
S.C.Yeomans	-	-	-	-	-	-	-	-	-	-	-	-	-	F	F	-	F	-	-	F	-	-	-	-	-	-	-	-	-	-	-	-	-	-	-	-	-	-	-	-	-	-	-	-	-	-	4	-	-
C.Kinton	-	-	-	-	-	-	-	-	-	-	-	-	-	-	F	F	-	F	-	-	-	-	-	-	-	-	-	-	-	-	-	-	-	-	-	-	-	-	-	-	-	F	-	F	-	-	5	-	-
M.Aldred	-	-	-	-	-	-	-	-	-	-	-	-	-	-	-	-	-	-	F	-	-	-	F	F	F	F	F	F	-	-	-	-	-	-	-	-	-	-	-	-	-	-	-	-	-	-	7	-	-
Lt.M.S.Scott	-	-	-	-	-	-	-	-	-	-	-	-	-	-	-	-	-	-	-	-	-	-	-	-	-	-	-	-	-	-	F	F	F	F	F	F	F	F	F	F	F	F	F	-	-	-	13	2	6

2 games: Arthur Frith W(14,43), W.Gale W(1,31), J.Langdon F(30,32), T.Orme F(30,32), S.Ramsey F(24,25)
1 game: Arthur Andrews FH(43), J.Ball F(36)[2], E.Bolus F(2), A.J.Currington F(43), R.Garratt F(30), Bertie Hills FH(27), -.Keywood F(32), Mark Morrison F(22), T.Patrick F(1), Eddie Redman F(1), C.Timlock F(12), W.J.Voakes SH(29), C.W.S.Wetherell C(30)

NO	DATE		OPPONENTS	V	RES	FOR					AGAINST					SCORERS
						G	T	D	P	PTS	G	T	D	P	PTS	
1	Sep	2	NUNEATON	H	Won	2	1	1	-	17	-	1	-	-	3	Oscroft(T,2C,D) Campbell(T) Kinton(T)
2		9	HANDSWORTH	H	Won	3	4	-	-	27	-	-	-	-	0	Wilkinson(2T,C) Gale(C) Miles(3T) Braithwaite(T,C) H.P.Atkins(T)
3		16	PERCY PARK	H	Won	2	1	-	-	13	-	-	-	-	0	Wilkinson(2T) Mosby(2C) Lincoln(T)
4		23	ABERAVON	H	Won	2	1	1	1	20	-	2	-	-	6	A.O.Jones(D) Wilkinson(T) Mosby(2C,P) Penny(T) Aldred(T)
5		30	DEVONPORT ALBION	H	Drew	-	-	-	-	0	-	-	-	-	0	
6	Oct	7	EXETER	H	Won	1	1	-	1	11	-	-	-	-	0	A.O.Jones(C,P) Wilkinson(T) F.H.Jones(T)
7		14	COVENTRY	H	Won	3	2	-	-	21	-	-	-	-	0	Wilkinson(T) Oscroft(T,C) F.H.Jones(T) Foreman(2T) Braithwaite(2C)
8		21	RICHMOND	H	Won	1	2	1	-	15	-	-	-	-	0	A.O.Jones(C,D) Wilkinson(2T) Oscroft(T)
9		25	BEDFORD GRAMMAR SCH.	H	Won	1	8	-	-	29	-	-	-	1	3	Gale(T) Mosby(C) Miles(2T) Swain(2T) Voakes(T) Penny(T) Lee(T) Goodrich(T)
10		28	OLD EDWARDIANS	H	Won	4	2	1	-	30	-	-	-	-	0	A.O.Jones(C) Wilkinson(T) Oscroft(2T,D) Mosby(T,3C) Butlin(2T)
11	Nov	4	NORTHAMPTON	H	Won	-	-	1	-	4	-	-	-	-	0	Oscroft(D)
12		8	Cambridge University	A	Lost	-	-	-	-	0	2	3	-	-	19	
13		11	KEIGHLEY	H	Won	1	1	1*	-	12	-	3	-	-	9	A.O.Jones(M) Wilkinson(T) Mosby(C) Hind(T)
		18	LLANELLI	H		Cancelled Fog										
14		25	SWANSEA	H	Lost	-	-	-	-	0	1	-	-	-	5	
15	Dec	2	Northampton	A	Drew	-	1	-	-	3	-	1	-	-	3	Foreman(T)
16		9	Coventry	A	Won	1	1	-	-	8	1	-	-	-	5	Oscroft(2T) Mosby(C)
		16	BURTON-ON-TRENT	H		Cancelled Frost										
17		23	Cardiff	A	Lost	-	-	-	-	0	2	4	1	-	26	
18		26	LLWYNYPIA	H	Won	-	3	-	-	9	-	1	-	-	3	Wilkinson(2T) Lincoln(T)
19		27	HARLEQUINS	H	Won	1	4	2	-	25	1	1	-	-	8	Wilkinson(2T) A.O.Jones(T) F.H.Jones(C,D) Hind(T) Braithwaite(T,D)
20		30	Exeter	A	Won	1	2	-	-	11	-	1	-	-	3	Wilkinson(T) Mosby(C) Foreman(2T)
21	Jan	1	Devonport Albion	A	Lost	-	-	-	-	0	3	1	1*	-	22	
22		6	BRISTOL	H	Won	1	-	1	-	9	-	-	-	-	0	Butlin(D) Mosby(C) Braithwaite(T)
23		13	Richmond	A	Won	-	3	-	-	9	-	1	-	-	3	Wilkinson(2T) Miles(T)
24		20	Burton-on-Trent	A	Won	2	3	1	-	23	-	-	-	-	0	Wilkinson(2T,D) Mosby(2C) Miles(3T)
25		27	GLOUCESTER	H	Lost	-	1	-	-	3	-	2	1	-	10	Wilkinson(T)
	Feb	3	CARDIFF	H		Cancelled Snow										
		10	Old Edwardians	A		Cancelled										
26		17	TREHERBERT	H	Won	-	-	2	-	8	-	-	-	-	0	A.O.Jones(2D)
27		24	Gloucester	A	Drew	-	-	-	-	0	-	-	-	-	0	
		27	Nuneaton	A		Cancelled										
28	Mar	3	MANCHESTER	H	Won	3	4	1	-	31	1	-	-	-	5	Butlin(C) Wilkinson(T) Oscroft(T,D) Goddard(T) Foreman(T) Whitehead(T) Scott(2C) Lincoln(T) Whetstone(T)
29		10	Five Ways Old Edw. (MCC2)	A	Won	3	3	1	-	28	-	-	-	-	0	Wilkinson(2T) Oscroft(T,D) A.O.Jones(C) Goddard(T) Braithwaite(T) Scott(2C) Lincoln(T)
30		17	Coventry (MCC3)	A	Won	1	1	-	-	8	-	-	-	1	3	Wilkinson(T) A.O.Jones(C) Braithwaite(T)
31		24	RUGBY (MCCSF)	H	Won	2	2	-	1	19	-	-	-	-	0	Wilkinson(T) Oscroft(T) F.H.Jones(C) A.O.Jones(C,P) Foreman(T) Scott(T)
32		31	Moseley (MCCF)	A	Won	2	1	-	-	13	-	-	1	-	4	F.H.Jones(2T,C) A.O.Jones(C) Foreman(T)
33	Apr	7	NUNEATON	H	Won	3	5	-	-	30	-	-	1	-	4	Wilkinson(T) H.P.Atkins(T) Gale(3C) Lincoln(2T) Braithwaite(2T) Voakes(T) Whitehead(T)
34		14	Swansea	A	Lost	1	-	-	-	5	3	-	-	-	15	Wilkinson(T) Mosby(C)
35		16	Llanelli	A	Lost	-	-	-	-	0	1	1	-	-	8	
36		17	Cheltenham	A	Lost	-	-	-	-	0	-	1	-	-	3	

INDIVIDUAL APPEARANCES 1899-1900

NAME	1	2	3	4	5	6	7	8	9	10	11	12	13	14	15	16	17	18	19	20	21	22	23	24	25	26	27	28	29	30	31	32	33	34	35	36	37	38	39	40	41	42	43	44	45	46	TOTAL	T	PTS
W.Gale	FB	C	C	C	-	-	-	-	C	-	-	C	-	-	-	-	-	C	-	-	-	-	-	-	-	-	-	-	-	-	-	-	C	-	-	-											8	1	11
Arthur Jones	-	-	FB	FB	FB	FB	FB	FB	FB	FB	FB	FB	FB	FB	FB	FB	C	-	FB	-	C	C	C	C	C	C	C	W	W	W																	28	1	43
Alf Butlin	W	FB	W	W	W	-	F	W	W	W	W	-	F	F	F	F	F	F	FB	FB	W	FB	FB	FB	FB	FB	FB	FB	FB	FB	FB	-	FB														33	2	12
Harry Wilkinson	W	W	W	W	W	W	W	-	W	W	W	W	W	W	W	W	W	W	W	W	W	W	W	W	W	W	W	W	W	W	W	W	W	W	W	W											35	28	90
Jack Miles	-	W	-	-	-	-	-	-	W	-	-	-	-	W	-	-	-	-	-	-	W	W	W	W	-	C	-																				8	9	27
Ernest Hind	-	-	-	-	-	W	W	-	-	-	W	W	-	W	W	W	W	W	-																												9	2	6
Frank Jackson	-	-	-	-	-	-	-	-	-	-	-	-	W	-	-	-	-	-	-	-	-	-	-	-	W																						2		
E.Goddard	-	-	-	-	-	-	-	-	-	-	-	-	-	-	-	-	-	-	-	-	-	-	-	-	-	-	-	W	W	W																	3	2	6
S.Neumann	-	-	-	-	-	-	-	-	-	-	-	-	-	-	-	-	-	-	-	-	-	-	-	-	-	-	-	-	-	-	-	-	W	W	W												3		
Percy Atkins	C	F	F	F	-	F	F	F	F	-	F	F	F	F	F	F	-	F	F	F	F	F	-	F	F	F	-	-	-	-	-	C	-	F	F												25	2	6
Percy Oscroft	C	-	-	C	C	C	C	C	-	C	C	C	-	C	C	C	C	C	-	-	C	C	-	C	C	C	C	-	-	C	C	C	-	-	-												21	10	56
E.Mosby	-	C	C	C	-	C	C	C	-	C	C	C	-	-	C	C	C	-	-	C	C	C	-	-	C	C	C	-																			18	1	36
Frank Jones	-	-	-	C	C	C	-	-	-	-	-	-	-	-	-	-	-	C	-	C	C	C	C	C	-	-	-	-	C	C	C	-															12	4	22
Billy Foreman	FH	FH	FH	FH	FH	FH	FH	-	-	FH	FH	FH	FH	FH	FH	FH	FH	FH	FH	FH	FH	FH	FH	FH	-	FH	FH	FH	FH	-	FH	FH	FH														33	8	24
Jacky Braithwaite	SH	SH	SH	SH	SH	SH	SH	SH	-	SH	SH	SH	-	SH	SH	SH	SH	SH	SH	SH	SH	SH	SH	SH	SH	SH	SH	SH	FH	SH	SH	-	SH	C													34	7	31
W.J.Voakes	-	-	-	-	-	-	-	-	SH	FH	-	SH	-	-	-	-	-	-	-	-	-	-	-	-	-	-	-	-	-	-	-	-	SH	C													5	2	6
M.Aldred	F	-	F	-	F	F	F	-	-	F	-	-	F	-	-	F	F	-	F	-	-	F	F	-	-	-	-	-	-	-	-	F	F	-													15	1	3
Bob Campbell	F	-	F	F	F	-	-	F	F	-	F	F	F	F	F	-	-	F	F	F	F	F	F	F	F	F	F	-	F	F	F	F	-														29	1	3
John Garner	F	-	F	F	F	F	F	F	-	F	F	-	-	-	-	-	-	-	-	-	-	-	-	F	F	F	F	F	F	F	F	F	F	-													22		
D.Gilbert	F	F	-	-	-	-	-	F	F	-	-	-	-	-	-	-	-	-	-	-	-	-	-	-	-	-	-	-	-	-	-	-	-														4		
Sammy Matthews	F	-	F	-	F	F	F	F	-	F	F	F	F	F	F	-	-	F	F	F	F	F	-	-	F	F	-	-	F	F	-	F	F	F	F	F	F										32		
Sid Penny	F	F	F	F	F	-	F	F	-	F	F	F	-	F	F	F	F	F	F	F	F	F	F	F	F	-	F	F	F	F	F	-	-														29	2	6
C.Timlock	F	-	-	-	-	-	-	F	-	-	-	-	-	-	-	-	-	-	-	-	-	-	-	-	-	-	-	-	-	-	-	-	-														2		
W.F.Lincoln	-	F	F	F	-	F	F	F	F	-	F	F	F	F	F	F	F	F	-	F	F	F	F	F	-	-	F	F	F	F	F	F	W	F	FB	F											31	6	18
W.E.Thompson	-	F	F	F	F	-	-	-	-	-	-	-	-	-	-	-	-	-	-	-	-	-	-	-	-	-	-	-	-	-	-	-	-														4		
Lt.M.S.Scott	-	-	-	F	F	F	F	-	F	F	F	F	F	F	-	F	F	F	F	F	F	-	F	F	F	F	F	F	F	F	F	F	F	F													29	1	11
M.E.Whitehead	-	-	-	F	F	-	F	-	F	-	-	F	F	F	F	F	-	F	F	F	F	-	F	F	F	F	F	F	F	F	F	F	F	-													23	2	6
Tom Goodrich	-	-	-	-	-	-	-	-	F	-	-	-	-	-	F	F	F	-	F	-	F	-	F	F	F	F																					11	1	3
J.L.Baker	-	-	-	-	-	-	-	-	-	-	-	F	-	F	-	-	-	-	-	F	-	-	-	-	F																						3		
Edward Whetstone	-	-	-	-	-	-	-	-	-	-	-	-	-	F	F	-	-	-	-	F	F	F	F	F	F	-	F	F																			11	1	3
H.Straker	-	-	-	-	-	-	-	-	-	-	-	-	-	-	-	-	-	-	-	-	-	-	F	F	F	F																					4		
R.Watson	-	-	-	-	-	-	-	-	-	-	-	-	-	-	-	-	-	-	-	-	-	-	-	F	F	F	F																				3		

1 game: Shirley Atkins F(19), Rev.A. Cary-Elwes F(9), Arthur Frith C(12), -.Holder F(9), George Keeton F(7), C.Kinton F(1)[1T-3], J.F.Lee F(9)[1T-3], H.S.Nicol C(35), S.Ramsey F(17), M.Swain FH(9)[2T-6], R.Whitestone F(34)

NO	DATE		OPPONENTS	V	RES	FOR					AGAINST					SCORERS
						G	T	D	P	PTS	G	T	D	P	PTS	
1	Sep	1	NUNEATON	H	Won	2	2	1	-	20	-	-	-	-	0	H.Wilkinson(T) Neumann(2T) Gale(2C) Foreman(T) Campbell(D)
2		8	PORTSMOUTH	H	Won	2	2	-	-	16	-	1	-	-	3	H.Wilkinson(2T) Gale(2C) Hind(T) Atkins(T)
3		15	HANDSWORTH	H	Won	6	9	1	-	61	-	-	-	-	0	Butlin(C,D) H.Wilkinson(T,C) Neumann(T) Mee(T) Hind(4T) Foreman(3T) Braithwaite(2T) Garner(4C) Atkins(2T) T.Goodrich(T)
4		22	PLYMOUTH	H	Won	1	-	-	-	5	-	-	-	-	0	H.Wilkinson(T) Garner(C)
5		29	EXETER	H	Won	1	6	-	-	23	-	-	-	-	0	H.Wilkinson(4T) Neumann(T) F.H.Jones(C) Foreman(T) Braithwaite(T)
6	Oct	6	DEVONPORT ALBION	H	Lost	-	-	-	-	0	-	2	-	-	6	
7		13	NORTHAMPTON	H	Drew	-	-	-	-	0	-	-	-	-	0	
8		20	LLANELLI	H	Won	-	-	1	-	4	-	1	-	-	3	Butlin(D)
9		27	OLD EDWARDIANS	H	Won	2	-	-	-	10	-	-	-	-	0	Mosby(2C) Foreman(T) Whetstone(T)
10	Nov	3	Cardiff	A	Lost	-	-	-	-	0	1	1	-	-	8	
11		5	Llanelli	A	Won	1	1	1	-	12	-	2	-	-	6	A.O.Jones(D) Mosby(T,C) T.Goodrich(T)
12		10	MANCHESTER	H	Won	1	3	1	-	18	-	1	-	-	3	H.Wilkinson(T) Mosby(C) A.O.Jones(D) Jackson(T) Braithwaite(T) Garner(T)
13		17	Swansea	A	Lost	-	-	1	-	4	2	2	-	-	16	Mosby(D)
14		24	Coventry	A	Lost	1	1	-	-	8	-	1	1	1	10	Mosby(C) Goddard(T) Matthews(T)
15	Dec	1	CAMBRIDGE UNIVERSITY	H	Won	1	1	-	-	8	-	-	-	-	0	Mosby(C) Foreman(2T)
16		8	Northampton	A	Won	-	-	1	-	4	-	-	-	-	0	Braithwaite(D)
17		15	BURTON-ON-TRENT	H	Won	2	2	1	-	20	1	1	-	-	8	H.Wilkinson(3T) Neumann(T) Mosby(2C) Braithwaite(D)
18		22	Newport	A	Lost	-	-	-	-	0	1	2	-	-	11	
19		24	LENNOX	H	Won	-	1	1	-	7	-	-	-	-	0	Foreman(T) Braithwaite(D)
20		26	LLWYNYPIA	H	Won	2	4	-	-	22	-	-	-	-	0	H.Wilkinson(T) Oscroft(2C) Foreman(T) Braithwaite(T) Matthews(T) Atkins(T) Whetstone(T)
21		27	EDINBURGH ROYAL H.S.	H	Won	-	2	-	1	9	-	1	-	-	3	Butlin(P) Hind(2T)
22		29	Devonport Albion	A	Lost	-	-	-	-	0	1	1	-	-	8	
23		31	Exeter	A	Won	3	-	-	2	21	-	-	-	-	0	Hind(T) Peard(T) A.O.Jones(3C,2P) Campbell(T)
24	Jan	5	CHELTENHAM	H	Won	4	1	-	-	23	1	2	-	-	11	H.Wilkinson(T) A.O.Jones(2T,4C) Hind(2T)
		12	Richmond	A		Cancelled Fog										
25		19	GLOUCESTER	H	Lost	-	-	-	-	0	1	-	-	-	5	
26	Feb	9	CARDIFF	H	Won	-	-	1	-	4	-	1	-	-	3	H.Wilkinson(D)
27		16	COVENTRY	H	Won	-	4	-	-	12	-	-	-	-	0	H.Wilkinson(2T) Mosby(T) E.Wilkinson(T)
		20	Bedford Grammar Sch.	A		Cancelled										
28		23	SWANSEA	H	Drew	-	-	-	-	0	-	-	-	-	0	
29	Mar	2	Burton-on-Trent	A	Won	1	2	-	-	11	-	-	-	-	0	H.Wilkinson(T) A.O.Jones(C) Foreman(2T)
30		9	BURTON-ON-TRENT (MCC2)	H	Won	3	2	-	-	21	-	-	-	-	0	H.Wilkinson(4T) A.O.Jones(3C) Neumann(T)
31		16	STONEYGATE (MCC3)	H	Won	2	9	1	-	41	-	-	-	-	0	H.Wilkinson(T) A.O.Jones(2C,D) Atkins(T) Neumann(2T) Braithwaite(T) Aldred(T) Whetstone(T) Yeld(T)
32		23	NUNEATON (MCCSF)	H	Won	2	3	2	1	30	1	-	1*	-	9	Butlin(D) H.Wilkinson(T) A.O.Jones(T,2C,D,P) Braithwaite(2T) Atkins(T)
33		30	Moseley (MCCF)	A	Won	1	1	-	-	8	-	1	-	-	3	H.Wilkinson(T) A.O.Jones(C) Foreman(T)
34	Apr	6	Gloucester	A	Lost	-	-	-	-	0	-	2	-	-	6	
35		8	Bristol	A	Lost	-	1	-	-	3	-	2	1	-	10	Atkins(T)
36		9	Plymouth	A	Lost	-	1	-	-	3	1	2	-	-	11	A.O.Jones(T)
37		13	NEWPORT	H	Lost	-	-	-	1	3	-	1	1	-	7	Oscroft(P)

INDIVIDUAL APPEARANCES 1900-1901

NAME	1	2	3	4	5	6	7	8	9	10	11	12	13	14	15	16	17	18	19	20	21	22	23	24	25	26	27	28	29	30	31	32	33	34	35	36	37	38	39	40	41	42	43	44	45	46	TOTAL	T	PTS
Alf Butlin	FB	FB	FB	FB	FB	FB	FB	FB	FB	FB	FB	FB	FB	FB	FB	FB	FB	FB	FB	FB	FB	FB	FB	FB	FB	FB	FB	FB	FB	FB	FB	FB	FB	FB	FB	FB	FB	-	-	-	-	-	-	-	-	-	37	-	17
Harry Wilkinson	W	W	W	W	W	W	W	W	-	W	W	W	W	W	W	W	W	W	W	W	-	W	-	W	W	W	W	W	W	W	W	W	C	W	-	W	-	-	-	-	-	-	-	-	-	-	33	28	90
Ernest Hind	-	W	W	W	W	W	W	W	-	-	-	-	-	-	-	-	-	-	W	W	W	W	W	W	-	-	-	-	-	-	-	W	-	-	-	W	-	-	-	-	-	-	-	-	-	-	14	10	30
E.C.Wykes	-	-	-	-	-	-	-	W	SH	-	-	FH	-	-	-	-	FH	-	-	-	-	-	-	-	-	-	-	-	-	-	-	-	-	-	-	-	-	-	-	-	-	-	-	-	-	-	4	-	-
Frank Jackson	-	-	-	-	-	-	-	W	W	-	W	-	-	-	-	-	W	-	-	-	-	-	-	-	-	-	-	-	-	-	-	-	-	-	-	-	-	-	-	-	-	-	-	-	-	-	4	1	3
E.Wilkinson	-	-	-	-	-	-	-	W	-	-	-	-	-	-	-	-	-	-	C	-	-	-	-	-	W	W	W	C	-	-	-	-	-	-	-	-	-	-	-	-	-	-	-	-	-	-	8	1	3
E.Goddard	-	-	-	-	-	-	-	-	-	W	W	-	-	-	-	W	-	-	C	-	-	C	-	-	W	-	-	-	-	-	-	-	-	-	-	-	-	-	-	-	-	-	-	-	-	-	5	1	3
W.Gale	C	C	-	-	-	-	-	-	-	-	-	-	-	-	-	-	-	-	-	-	-	-	-	-	-	-	-	-	-	-	-	-	-	-	-	-	-	-	-	-	-	-	-	-	-	-	2	-	8
S.Neumann	C	C	C	C	C	-	C	C	C	-	-	-	-	W	W	C	-	-	W	C	-	C	-	C	C	-	-	-	W	W	W	W	-	C	W	-	C	-	-	-	-	-	-	-	-	-	22	8	24
E.Mosby	-	-	-	C	-	-	-	C	C	C	C	C	C	C	C	C	C	-	-	C	-	-	C	-	-	C	C	C	C	-	-	C	-	-	-	-	-	-	-	-	-	-	-	-	-	-	18	2	26
Frank Jones	-	-	-	-	C	C	C	-	-	-	-	-	-	-	-	-	-	-	C	C	-	-	-	-	-	-	-	-	-	-	-	-	-	-	-	-	-	-	-	-	-	-	-	-	-	-	5	-	2
Arthur Jones	-	-	-	-	-	-	-	-	C	C	C	C	C	C	C	C	-	-	-	-	C	C	-	C	C	-	C	C	C	C	C	C	C	-	-	C	-	-	-	-	-	-	-	-	-	-	18	4	69
Percy Oscroft	-	-	-	-	-	-	-	-	-	-	-	-	-	-	-	-	-	-	C	C	-	-	-	-	-	-	-	-	-	-	-	-	C	-	-	-	C	-	-	-	-	-	-	-	-	-	4	-	7
Billy Foreman	FH	FH	FH	FH	FH	FH	FH	FH	-	FH	FH	FH	FH	FH	FH	-	FH	FH	FH	FH	FH	FH	FH	FH	FH	FH	FH	-	-	-	-	-	-	-	-	-	-	-	-	-	-	-	-	-	-	-	35	13	39
Jacky Braithwaite	SH	SH	SH	SH	SH	SH	SH	SH	-	SH	SH	SH	SH	SH	SH	SH	SH	SH	SH	SH	SH	SH	SH	SH	SH	SH	SH	SH	SH	SH	SH	SH	SH	SH	SH	SH	-	-	-	-	-	-	-	-	-	-	36	8	36
M.Aldred	F	F	F	F	F	-	F	F	F	-	F	F	-	F	F	F	F	F	-	-	-	F	F	F	F	F	F	F	F	-	F	F	F	F	F	F	F	-	-	-	-	-	-	-	-	-	29	1	3
Percy Atkins	F	F	F	-	F	C	F	F	F	-	-	-	-	-	C	-	F	F	-	-	F	F	F	F	F	F	F	C	C	F	-	-	C	C	F	-	-	-	-	-	-	-	-	-	-	-	23	7	21
Bob Campbell	F	F	F	F	F	-	F	-	F	F	F	F	F	F	F	F	F	-	F	-	F	F	F	F	F	-	F	F	F	F	-	-	-	-	-	-	-	-	-	-	-	-	-	-	-	-	29	1	7
John Garner	F	F	F	F	F	F	F	F	F	F	F	F	F	F	F	F	F	-	F	F	F	F	F	F	F	F	F	F	F	F	F	F	F	F	F	F	F	-	-	-	-	-	-	-	-	-	37	1	13
Tom Goodrich	F	F	F	F	F	F	F	F	W	F	F	-	F	F	F	F	F	-	F	-	F	-	F	F	F	F	F	F	F	F	F	F	F	F	F	F	-	-	-	-	-	-	-	-	-	-	34	2	6
Sammy Matthews	F	F	F	F	F	F	F	F	F	F	F	F	F	F	F	-	F	F	F	F	F	-	F	F	-	F	F	-	F	-	-	F	-	-	F	-	-	-	-	-	-	-	-	-	-	-	30	2	6
Sid Penny	F	F	F	F	F	F	F	F	F	F	F	F	F	F	F	F	F	-	F	F	F	F	F	F	F	F	F	F	F	F	F	-	F	F	F	-	F	-	-	-	-	-	-	-	-	-	36	-	-
Edward Whetstone	F	F	F	F	F	F	F	-	F	F	-	-	F	F	F	F	F	F	-	F	-	F	F	-	F	F	F	-	F	F	F	F	F	F	F	F	-	-	-	-	-	-	-	-	-	-	30	3	9
George Yeld	-	-	-	F	F	F	F	F	F	F	-	F	F	F	-	F	F	-	-	-	-	-	F	-	-	-	-	F	-	-	F	F	F	F	F	W	F	F	-	-	-	-	-	-	-	-	22	1	3
S.Lines	-	-	-	-	-	-	-	-	-	F	F	-	-	-	F	-	-	-	F	F	F	F	-	F	-	-	F	-	-	-	-	-	-	-	F	-	-	-	-	-	-	-	-	-	-	-	10	-	-
Alf Goodrich	-	-	-	-	-	-	-	-	-	-	F	-	-	-	-	-	F	F	-	-	-	-	-	-	-	-	-	-	-	-	-	-	-	-	-	-	-	-	-	-	-	-	-	-	-	-	3	-	-
B.McCraith	-	-	-	-	-	-	-	-	-	-	-	-	-	-	-	F	F	-	F	F	F	F	-	-	-	-	-	-	-	F	F	F	-	-	-	-	-	-	-	-	-	-	-	-	-	-	9	-	-
M.E.Whitehead	-	-	-	-	-	-	-	-	-	-	-	-	-	-	-	-	-	-	-	-	-	-	-	-	-	-	-	-	F	-	-	-	-	-	F	F	-	F	-	-	-	-	-	-	-	-	4	-	-
R.C.Watchorn	-	-	-	-	-	-	-	-	-	-	-	-	-	-	-	-	-	-	-	-	-	-	-	-	-	-	-	-	-	-	-	-	-	F	F	-	-	-	-	-	-	-	-	-	-	-	2	-	-

1 game: J.Barnes W(34), W.Dann F(19), -.Green F(31), Bertie Hills W(36), G.C.Mee C(3)[1T-3], Jack Miles W(1), E.J.Peard C(23)[1T-3], Howard Poole F(11), -.Powell-John W(23), Eddie Redman F(11), W.E.Thompson F(6)

LEICESTER FOOTBALL CLUB 1900-01
Back: H.N. Stroud (Hon.Tres), B. McCraith, G.G. Yeld, A.O. Jones, A.E. Hind, M. Aldred, H.P. Atkins, P.W. Oscroft, T.H. Crumbie (Hon.Sec).
Middle: J. Collier (Touch Judge), A.C. Butlin, S.H. Penny, H. Wilkinson, W.J. Foreman (Capt), J.W. Garner, S. Matthews, J. Parsons (President).
Front: T. Goodrich, S. Neumann, J. Braithwaite, R.N. Campbell.

LEICESTER FOOTBALL CLUB 1901-02
Back: T.H. Crumbie (Hon.Sec), D.B. Atkins, H.P. Atkins, H. Wilkinson, G.H. Keeton, A. Andrews, G. Croson, H.N. Stroud (Hon.Tres).
Middle: J. Collier (President), J.H. Miles, S.H. Penny, A.E. Hind, J.W. Garner (Capt), S. Matthews, W.J. Foreman, T. Goodrich.
Front: W. Robinson, A.C. Butlin, W. Hawley, J. Braithwaite.

NO	DATE	OPPONENTS	V	RES	FOR G	FOR T	FOR D	FOR P	FOR PTS	AGAINST G	AGAINST T	AGAINST D	AGAINST P	AGAINST PTS	SCORERS
1	Sep 7	NUNEATON	H	Won	3	4	-	-	27	-	1	-	-	3	Miles(3T) H.P.Atkins(T) Braithwaite(T) Garner(3C) Whetstone(T) Matthews(T)
2	14	CASTLEFORD	H	Won	-	2	1	-	10	-	1	-	-	3	Miles(2T) Braithwaite(D)
3	21	BRISTOL	H	Lost	-	1	-	-	3	-	2	-	-	6	Miles(T)
4	28	DEVONPORT ALBION	H	Lost	-	-	-	1	3	2	1	-	-	13	Braithwaite(P)
5	Oct 5	EXETER	H	Won	-	3	1	-	13	-	-	-	-	0	H.Wilkinson(T) Foreman(T) Braithwaite(D) Penny(T)
6	12	COVENTRY	H	Won	3	2	-	-	21	-	-	-	-	0	H.Wilkinson(T) E.Wilkinson(T) Dakin(T) Braithwaite(T) Yeld(3C) Watchorn(T)
7	19	LLANELLI	H	Won	-	1	1	-	7	-	-	-	1	3	H.Wilkinson(T) Braithwaite(D)
8	26	PLYMOUTH	H	Drew	-	1	-	-	3	-	1	-	-	3	A.E.Hind(T)
9	Nov 2	BURTON-ON-TRENT	H	Won	2	3	1	-	23	-	-	-	-	0	Neumann(T) Braithwaite(D) Matthews(T) Goodrich(T) Yeld(2C) Foxon(2T)
10	9	OLD EDWARDIANS	H	Won	1	7	1	-	30	1	-	-	-	5	H.Wilkinson(T) Miles(T) A.E.Hind(2T) Braithwaite(T,D) Penny(T) Watchorn(T) Gale(T,C)
	16	SWANSEA	H		Cancelled Frost										
11	23	Northampton	A	Won	1	2	-	-	11	-	2	-	-	6	H.Wilkinson(T) A.E.Hind(2T) Yeld(C)
12	30	Cambridge University	A	Lost	-	-	-	1	3	1	2	1	2	21	Yeld(P)
13	Dec 7	RUGBY	H	Won	3	3	-	-	24	-	1	-	-	3	Miles(2T) Dakin(T) Mee(T) Hills(2T) Yeld(3C)
	14	Old Edwardians	A		Cancelled Snow										
	21	NEWPORT	H		Cancelled Frost										
14	26	LLWYNYPIA	H	Won	1	1	-	-	8	-	-	-	-	0	Dakin(T) A.E.Hind(T) Gale(C)
15	27	WEST HARTLEPOOL	H	Lost	-	-	-	-	0	1	1	1	-	12	
16	28	OLD MERCHANT TAYLORS	H	Lost	-	-	-	-	0	-	1	-	-	3	
17	Jan 4	Swansea	A	Lost	-	-	-	-	0	1	2	-	-	11	
18	6	Llanelli	A	Drew	-	-	-	-	0	-	-	-	-	0	
	11	Richmond			Cancelled										
19	18	Devonport Albion	A	Lost	-	-	-	-	0	2	1	-	-	13	
20	20	Plymouth	A	Lost	-	1	-	-	3	1	-	-	-	5	Smith(T)
21	21	Exeter	A	Drew	-	-	-	-	0	-	-	-	-	0	
22	25	Gloucester	A	Won	-	-	-	1	3	-	-	-	-	0	Yeld(P)
23	Feb 1	PERCY PARK	H	Won	-	2	2	-	14	1	-	-	-	5	A.E.Hind(T,D) Braithwaite(D) Garner(T)
	15	Coventry	A		Cancelled										
24	22	NORTHAMPTON	H	Won	1	3	-	-	14	-	-	-	-	0	Butlin(C) H.Wilkinson(T) Miles(2T) H.P.Atkins(T)
25	Mar 1	GLOUCESTER	H	Won	-	2	-	-	6	-	-	-	-	0	Miles(T) Braithwaite(T)
26	8	Nuneaton (MCC2)	A	Won	2	-	1	-	14	-	-	-	-	0	Butlin(2C) H.Wilkinson(D) Miles(2T)
27	15	CAMP HILL OLD EDW. (MCC3)	H	Won	2	5	-	-	25	-	-	-	-	0	Butlin(C) A.E.Hind(T) Hawley(C) Miles(T) Foreman(T) Braithwaite(T) H.P.Atkins(2T) Croson(T)
28	22	BURTON-ON-TRENT (MCCSF)	H	Won	1	3	1	-	18	-	1	-	-	3	Butlin(C) H.P.Atkins(T) Miles(2T) Braithwaite(T,D)
29	29	Moseley (MCCF)	A	Won	1	-	-	-	5	-	-	-	-	0	Butlin(C) A.E.Hind(T)
30	31	Cardiff	A	Lost	-	1	-	-	3	1	1	-	-	8	Miles(T)
31	Apr 1	Bristol	A	Lost	-	-	-	-	0	1	1	-	-	8	
32	5	Newport	A	Lost	-	3	-	-	9	1	2	-	-	11	Hawley(T) Keeton(2T)
33	12	CARDIFF	H	Won	-	-	1	-	4	-	-	-	1	3	H.Wilkinson(D)
34	17	MIDLANDS XV	H	Won	1	3	-	-	14	-	1	-	-	3	H.Wilkinson(T) Miles(2T) Braithwaite(C) H.P.Atkins(T)
35	19	Nuneaton	A	Won	1	3	-	-	14	-	-	-	-	0	Butlin(C) Garner(T) Matthews(2T) Robinson(T)

INDIVIDUAL APPEARANCES 1901-1902

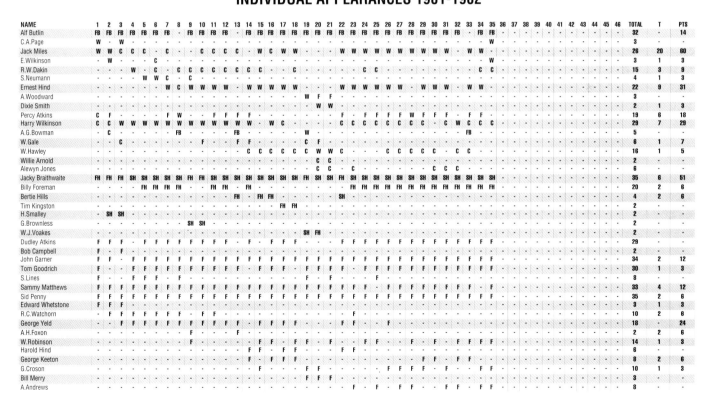

NAME	1	2	3	4	5	6	7	8	9	10	11	12	13	14	15	16	17	18	19	20	21	22	23	24	25	26	27	28	29	30	31	32	33	34	35	36	37	38	39	40	41	42	43	44	45	46	TOTAL	T	PTS
Alf Butlin	FB	FB	FB	FB	FB	FB	FB	-	FB	FB	FB	FB	-	FB	FB	FB	FB	FB	FB	FB	FB	FB	FB	FB	FB	FB	FB	FB	FB	FB	FB	FB	-	FB	FB	-	-	-	-	-	-	-	-	-	-	-	32	-	14
C.A.Page	W	-	W	-	-	-	-	-	-	-	-	-	-	-	-	-	-	-	-	-	-	-	-	-	-	-	-	-	-	-	-	-	-	-	W	-	-	-	-	-	-	-	-	-	-	-	3	-	-
Jack Miles	W	W	C	C	C	-	C	-	-	C	C	C	C	-	W	C	W	W	-	-	-	W	W	W	W	W	W	W	W	W	W	-	W	W	-	-	-	-	-	-	-	-	-	-	-	-	26	20	60
E.Wilkinson	-	W	-	-	-	C	-	-	-	-	-	-	-	-	-	-	-	-	-	-	-	-	-	-	-	-	-	-	-	-	-	-	-	-	W	-	-	-	-	-	-	-	-	-	-	-	3	1	3
R.W.Dakin	-	-	-	W	-	C	-	C	C	C	C	C	C	C	C	-	-	C	-	-	-	-	-	C	C	-	-	-	-	-	-	-	-	C	C	-	-	-	-	-	-	-	-	-	-	-	15	3	9
S.Neumann	-	-	-	-	W	W	C	-	C	-	-	-	-	-	-	-	-	-	-	-	-	-	-	-	-	-	-	-	-	-	-	-	-	-	-	-	-	-	-	-	-	-	-	-	-	-	4	1	3
Ernest Hind	-	-	-	-	-	-	W	C	W	W	W	W	-	W	W	W	W	W	-	-	-	W	W	W	W	W	W	-	W	W	W	-	W	W	-	-	-	-	-	-	-	-	-	-	-	-	22	9	31
A.Woodward	-	-	-	-	-	-	-	-	-	-	-	-	-	-	-	-	-	-	W	F	F	-	-	-	-	-	-	-	-	-	-	-	-	-	-	-	-	-	-	-	-	-	-	-	-	-	3	-	-
Dixie Smith	-	-	-	-	-	-	-	-	-	-	-	-	-	-	-	-	-	-	-	W	W	-	-	-	-	-	-	-	-	-	-	-	-	-	-	-	-	-	-	-	-	-	-	-	-	-	2	1	3
Percy Atkins	C	F	-	-	-	-	F	W	-	-	F	F	F	F	-	-	-	-	-	-	-	F	-	F	F	F	F	W	F	F	F	-	F	F	-	-	-	-	-	-	-	-	-	-	-	-	19	6	18
Harry Wilkinson	C	C	W	W	W	W	W	W	W	W	W	W	W	W	-	W	C	-	-	-	-	C	C	C	C	C	C	C	C	-	C	W	C	C	C	-	-	-	-	-	-	-	-	-	-	-	29	7	29
A.G.Bowman	-	C	-	-	-	-	-	FB	-	-	-	-	FB	-	-	-	-	-	W	-	-	-	-	-	-	-	-	-	-	-	-	-	FB	-	-	-	-	-	-	-	-	-	-	-	-	-	5	-	-
W.Gale	-	-	C	-	-	-	-	-	-	F	-	-	F	F	-	-	-	-	C	F	-	-	-	-	-	-	-	-	-	-	-	-	-	-	-	-	-	-	-	-	-	-	-	-	-	-	6	1	7
W.Hawley	-	-	-	-	-	-	-	-	-	-	-	-	-	C	C	C	C	C	C	W	W	C	-	-	-	C	C	C	C	C	-	C	C	-	-	-	-	-	-	-	-	-	-	-	-	-	16	1	5
Willie Arnold	-	-	-	-	-	-	-	-	-	-	-	-	-	-	-	-	-	-	-	C	C	-	-	-	-	-	-	-	-	-	-	-	-	-	-	-	-	-	-	-	-	-	-	-	-	-	2	-	-
Alewyn Jones	-	-	-	-	-	-	-	-	-	-	-	-	-	-	-	-	-	-	-	C	C	-	C	-	-	-	-	-	-	C	C	C	-	-	-	-	-	-	-	-	-	-	-	-	-	-	6	-	-
Jacky Braithwaite	FH	FH	FH	SH	SH	SH	SH	SH	FH	FH	SH	SH	SH	SH	SH	SH	SH	SH	FH	SH	SH	FH	SH	SH	SH	SH	SH	SH	SH	SH	SH	SH	SH	SH	SH	-	-	-	-	-	-	-	-	-	-	-	35	6	51
Billy Foreman	-	-	-	-	FH	FH	FH	FH	-	-	FH	FH	-	FH	-	-	-	-	-	-	-	-	FH	FH	FH	FH	FH	FH	FH	FH	FH	FH	FH	FH	FH	-	-	-	-	-	-	-	-	-	-	-	20	2	6
Bertie Hills	-	-	-	-	-	-	-	-	-	-	-	-	FH	-	FH	FH	-	-	-	-	-	SH	-	-	-	-	-	-	-	-	-	-	-	-	-	-	-	-	-	-	-	-	-	-	-	-	4	2	6
Tim Kingston	-	-	-	-	-	-	-	-	-	-	-	-	-	-	-	-	FH	FH	-	-	-	-	-	-	-	-	-	-	-	-	-	-	-	-	-	-	-	-	-	-	-	-	-	-	-	-	2	-	-
H.Smalley	-	SH	SH	-	-	-	-	-	-	-	-	-	-	-	-	-	-	-	-	-	-	-	-	-	-	-	-	-	-	-	-	-	-	-	-	-	-	-	-	-	-	-	-	-	-	-	2	-	-
G.Brownless	-	-	-	-	-	-	-	-	SH	SH	-	-	-	-	-	-	-	-	-	-	-	-	-	-	-	-	-	-	-	-	-	-	-	-	-	-	-	-	-	-	-	-	-	-	-	-	2	-	-
W.J.Voakes	-	-	-	-	-	-	-	-	-	-	-	-	-	-	-	-	-	-	SH	FH	-	-	-	-	-	-	-	-	-	-	-	-	-	-	-	-	-	-	-	-	-	-	-	-	-	-	2	-	-
Dudley Atkins	F	F	F	-	F	F	F	F	F	F	F	F	-	F	-	F	F	F	-	-	-	F	F	F	F	F	F	F	F	F	F	F	F	F	F	-	-	-	-	-	-	-	-	-	-	-	29	-	-
Bob Campbell	F	-	F	-	-	-	-	-	-	-	-	-	-	-	-	-	-	-	-	-	-	-	-	-	-	-	-	-	-	-	-	-	-	-	-	-	-	-	-	-	-	-	-	-	-	-	2	-	-
John Garner	F	F	-	F	F	F	F	F	F	F	F	F	F	F	F	F	F	F	F	F	F	F	F	F	F	F	F	F	F	F	F	F	F	F	F	-	-	-	-	-	-	-	-	-	-	-	34	2	12
Tom Goodrich	F	-	-	F	F	F	F	F	F	F	F	F	F	-	F	F	F	-	F	F	F	F	-	F	F	F	F	F	F	F	F	F	F	F	F	-	-	-	-	-	-	-	-	-	-	-	30	1	3
S.Lines	F	-	-	F	F	F	-	F	-	-	-	-	-	-	-	-	-	-	F	-	F	-	-	-	F	-	-	-	-	-	-	-	-	-	-	-	-	-	-	-	-	-	-	-	-	-	8	-	-
Sammy Matthews	F	F	F	F	F	F	F	F	F	F	F	F	F	F	F	F	F	F	F	F	F	F	F	F	-	F	F	F	F	F	F	F	F	-	F	-	-	-	-	-	-	-	-	-	-	-	33	4	12
Sid Penny	F	F	F	F	F	F	F	F	F	F	F	F	F	F	F	F	F	F	F	F	F	F	F	F	F	F	F	F	F	F	F	F	F	F	F	-	-	-	-	-	-	-	-	-	-	-	35	2	6
Edward Whetstone	F	F	F	-	-	-	-	-	-	-	-	-	-	-	-	-	-	-	-	-	-	-	-	-	-	-	-	-	-	-	-	-	-	-	-	-	-	-	-	-	-	-	-	-	-	-	3	1	3
R.C.Watchorn	-	F	F	F	F	F	F	F	-	F	F	-	-	-	-	-	-	-	-	-	-	-	F	-	-	-	-	-	-	-	-	-	-	-	-	-	-	-	-	-	-	-	-	-	-	-	10	2	6
George Yeld	-	-	F	F	F	F	F	F	F	F	F	F	F	-	F	F	F	F	-	-	-	F	F	-	-	F	-	-	-	-	-	-	-	-	-	-	-	-	-	-	-	-	-	-	-	-	18	-	24
A.H.Foxon	-	-	-	-	-	-	-	-	F	-	-	-	F	-	-	-	-	-	-	-	-	-	-	-	-	-	-	-	-	-	-	-	-	-	-	-	-	-	-	-	-	-	-	-	-	-	2	2	6
W.Robinson	-	-	-	-	-	-	-	-	F	-	-	-	-	-	F	F	-	F	F	-	F	-	-	F	F	-	-	F	-	F	-	F	F	F	F	-	-	-	-	-	-	-	-	-	-	-	14	1	3
Harold Hind	-	-	-	-	-	-	-	-	-	-	-	-	-	F	F	-	F	F	-	-	-	F	F	-	-	-	-	-	-	-	-	-	-	-	-	-	-	-	-	-	-	-	-	-	-	-	6	-	-
George Keeton	-	-	-	-	-	-	-	-	-	-	-	-	-	F	-	F	F	F	-	-	-	-	-	-	-	-	-	-	F	F	-	F	F	-	-	-	-	-	-	-	-	-	-	-	-	-	8	2	6
G.Croson	-	-	-	-	-	-	-	-	-	-	-	-	-	-	F	-	-	-	F	F	-	-	-	-	-	F	F	F	F	-	F	-	-	F	F	-	-	-	-	-	-	-	-	-	-	-	10	1	3
Bill Merry	-	-	-	-	-	-	-	-	-	-	-	-	-	-	-	-	-	-	F	F	F	-	-	-	-	-	-	-	-	-	-	-	-	-	-	-	-	-	-	-	-	-	-	-	-	-	3	-	-
A.Andrews	-	-	-	-	-	-	-	-	-	-	-	-	-	-	-	-	-	-	-	-	-	-	F	-	F	-	F	F	-	-	F	F	-	F	F	-	-	-	-	-	-	-	-	-	-	-	8	-	-

1 game: G.Ackroyd C(5), M.Aldred F(2), -.Chapman W(32), W.Duffin FH(21), G.Gimson F(24), Frank Jackson C(4), F.Lines F(4), B.McCraith F(3), G.C.Mee W(13)[1T-3], A.Oldershaw SH(1), Ernest Walton FH(4), M.E.Whitehead F(12)

NO	DATE		OPPONENTS	V	RES	FOR					AGAINST					SCORERS
						G	T	D	P	PTS	G	T	D	P	PTS	
1	Sep	13	EXETER	H	Won	1	4	1	-	21	-	-	-	-	0	Butlin(D) A.E.Hind(2T) Dakin(T) Miles(T) Braithwaite(C) D.B.Atkins(T)
2		20	BRISTOL	H	Won	-	1	1	-	7	-	-	-	-	0	Butlin(D) Braithwaite(T)
3		27	PLYMOUTH	H	Won	-	4	-	-	12	-	-	-	-	0	A.E.Hind(T) Miles(2T) Matthews(T)
4	Oct	4	DEVONPORT ALBION	H	Won	-	1	1	1	10	-	-	1	1	7	A.O.Jones(T,D,P)
5		11	RICHMOND	H	Won	3	1	-	-	18	-	1	-	-	3	Miles(2T) A.E.Hind(2T) Matthews(3C)
6		18	LONDON WELSH	H	Won	-	2	1	1	13	-	-	-	-	0	A.E.Hind(T) A.O.Jones(D,P) Scott(T)
7		25	LLANELLI	H	Won	1	2	1	-	15	-	1	-	-	3	A.E.Hind(T) Reynolds(D) Miles(T) Dakin(T) Matthews(C)
8	Nov	1	Newport	A	Lost	-	-	-	-	0	-	2	-	-	6	
9		3	Llanelli	A	Lost	-	1	-	-	3	-	3	1	1	16	A.E.Hind(T)
10		8	Moseley	A	Won	1	4	-	-	17	-	2	1	-	10	Miles(2T) A.O.Jones(C) A.E.Hind(T) Foreman(T) D.B.Atkins(T)
11		15	NORTHAMPTON	H	Won	2	1	-	-	13	-	-	-	-	0	Barrowcliffe(T) A.O.Jones(2C) A.E.Hind(T) Matthews(T)
12		22	CASTLEFORD	H	Won	3	-	1	-	19	-	-	-	-	0	A.E.Hind(T) A.O.Jones(3C,D) Miles(T) Watchorn(T)
13		29	CAMBRIDGE UNIVERSITY	H	Won	-	2	-	-	6	-	-	-	-	0	Miles(T) Matthews(T)
14	Dec	6	COVENTRY	H	Won	1	2	-	-	11	-	-	-	-	0	Page(T) Miles(T) T.Goodrich(C) Foxon(T)
15		13	Northampton	A	Won	1	1	1	-	12	-	2	-	-	6	Butlin(D) Matthews(C) D.B.Atkins(T) Watchorn(T)
16		20	Cardiff	A	Lost	-	-	-	-	0	-	2	-	-	6	
17		26	EDINBURGH ROYAL H.S.	H	Won	2	-	-	-	10	-	-	-	-	0	Gale(2C) Miles(T) Braithwaite(T)
18		27	BECTIVE RANGERS	H	Won	5	4	-	-	37	-	-	-	-	0	Gale(4C) Miles(2T) Dakin(2T) A.E.Hind(T) Foreman(2T) Braithwaite(2T,C)
19	Jan	3	Devonport Albion	A	Lost	-	1	-	-	3	-	3	-	-	9	Dakin(T)
20		5	London Welsh	A	Won	1	2	1	-	15	1	-	-	-	5	Gale(C) Page(T) Dakin(T) Braithwaite(T) A.Goodrich(D)
21		10	GLOUCESTER	H	Won	-	2	-	-	6	-	1	-	-	3	Page(T) A.E.Hind(T)
		17	NEWPORT	H			Cancelled Frost										
22		24	CARDIFF	H	Lost	1	-	-	-	5	1	3	-	-	14	Braithwaite(C) Matthews(T)
23		31	Swansea	A	Lost	1	-	-	-	5	3	3	-	-	24	Reynolds(T) Matthews(C)
24	Feb	7	OLD EDWARDIANS	H	Won	-	7	1	-	25	-	-	-	-	0	A.E.Hind(2T,D) Miles(T) Foreman(2T) Braithwaite(T) D.B.Atkins(T)
25		14	MOSELEY	H	Won	1	4	-	-	17	-	-	-	-	0	A.E.Hind(3T) Miles(T) Matthews(C) T.Goodrich(T)
26		21	Coventry	A	Won	-	3	-	-	9	-	1	-	-	3	A.O.Jones(T) Miles(2T)
27		28	SWANSEA	H	Lost	-	1	-	-	3	1	1	-	-	8	Dakin(T)
28	Mar	7	Gloucester	A	Won	-	3	-	-	9	1	-	-	-	5	A.E.Hind(T) Dakin(T) Braithwaite(T)
29		14	STRATFORD-UPON-AVON (MCC1)	H	Won	3	7	-	1	39	-	-	-	-	0	A.E.Hind(5T,C) A.O.Jones(C,P) Miles(T) Braithwaite(2T,C) H.P.Atkins(2T)
30		21	BELGRAVE (MCC2)	H	Won	7	5	1	-	54	-	-	-	-	0	A.E.Hind(6T) A.O.Jones(T,2C,D) Dakin(3T) Braithwaite(T,4C) Matthews(C) H.P.Atkins(T)
31		28	NUNEATON (MCCSF)	H	Won	5	7	-	1	49	1	2	-	-	11	A.E.Hind(5T) A.O.Jones(T) Dakin(T) Miles(4T) Braithwaite(T,5C,P)
32	Apr	4	Rugby (MCCF)	A	Won	3	1	-	-	18	-	-	-	-	0	A.E.Hind(2T) A.O.Jones(3C) Dakin(T) Miles(T)
33		11	Exeter	A	Drew	-	-	-	-	0	-	-	-	-	0	
34		13	Plymouth	A	Lost	-	-	-	-	0	1	2	1	-	15	
35		14	Bristol	A	Won	-	2	-	-	6	-	-	-	-	0	Miles(T) Rapsey(T)
36		18	NEWPORT	H	Lost	-	-	-	-	0	1	4	-	-	17	

INDIVIDUAL APPEARANCES 1902-1903

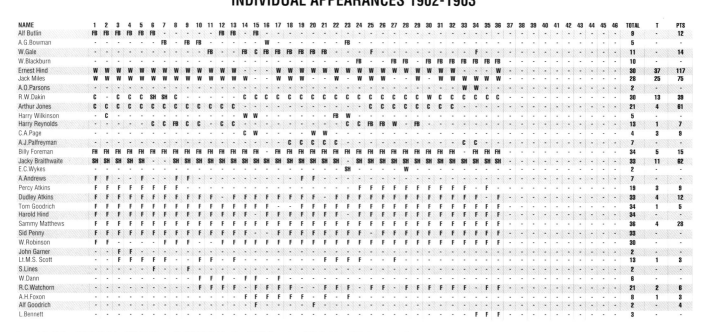

1 game: Arthur Andrews FH(33), F.A.Barker C(17), Matt Barrowcliffe C(11)[1T-3], Arthur Freear W(35), Alewyn Jones C(16), Frank Jones C(36), George Keeton F(16), Mark Morrison F(18), W.G.Rapsey C(35)[1T-3], W.J.Voakes FH(16), J.Voss W(16), George Ward F(2), E.Wilkinson C(30)

LEICESTER FOOTBALL CLUB 1902-03
Back: T.H. Crumbie (Hon.Sec), H.A. Hind, H.P. Atkins, R.C. Watchorn, L. Bennett, D.B. Atkins, Rev F.H. Jones, H.N. Stroud (Hon.Tres).
Middle: J. Collier (President), J.H. Miles, S.H. Penny, W.J. Foreman, A.O. Jones (Capt), A.E. Hind, S. Matthews, T. Goodrich.
Front: W. Robinson, J. Braithwaite, R.W. Dakin, W. Blackburn.

LEICESTER FOOTBALL CLUB 'A' TEAM 1903-04
Back: C. Cheshire (Hon.Sec), A.G. Bowman, B. Hills, W. Dann, S. Lines, W.J. Foreman, W. Gale.
Middle: A. Keywood, H. Beesley, W.J. Voakes, C.A. Page (Capt), R. Hives, J.W. Ofield, W. Beesley.
Front: H. Toone, G. Green, L. Beaver, M. Barrowcliffe, C. Matthews.

NO	DATE		OPPONENTS	V	RES	FOR					AGAINST					SCORERS
						G	T	D	P	PTS	G	T	D	P	PTS	
1	Sep	12	HARTLEPOOL ROVERS	H	Won	1	2	-	-	11	-	-	1*	-	4	Miles(T) Freear(T) Braithwaite(T) T.Goodrich(C)
2		19	Devonport Albion	A	Lost	-	-	-	-	0	1	-	-	-	5	
3		21	Plymouth	A	Lost	1	1	-	-	8	-	4	-	-	12	Dakin(T) Freear(T) T.Goodrich(C)
4		22	Exeter	A	Lost	-	1	-	-	3	-	2	-	-	6	Russell(T)
5		26	WEST HARTLEPOOL	H	Lost	-	1	1	-	7	1	1	-	-	8	Blackburn(D) Miles(T)
6	Oct	3	PLYMOUTH	H	Drew	1	1	-	-	8	1	1	-	-	8	Miles(T) A.O.Jones(C) Russell(T)
7		10	OLD EDWARDIANS	H	Won	2	3	-	1	22	-	2	-	-	6	Miles(3T) Dakin(T) Braithwaite(2C) Matthews(T) Russell(P)
8		17	BRISTOL	H	Won	2	1	-	-	13	1	-	1	-	9	Miles(T) Foreman(T) Braithwaite(C) H.P.Atkins(T) Russell(C)
9		24	MOSELEY	H	Won	1	-	1	1	12	-	-	-	-	0	Sutton(T) A.O.Jones(C,D,P)
10		31	CARDIFF	H	Lost	-	-	-	-	0	3	2	-	1	24	
11	Nov	7	LONDON WELSH	H	Lost	-	-	-	-	0	1	2	-	-	11	
12		14	NORTHAMPTON	H	Won	2	-	1	-	14	-	1	-	-	3	A.O.Jones(C) J.W.D.Smith(T) A.E.Hind(T,D) Russell(C)
13		21	SWANSEA	H	Lost	-	-	-	-	0	1	2	-	-	11	
14		28	Cambridge University	A	Lost	-	-	-	-	0	-	2	-	-	6	
15	Dec	5	COVENTRY	H	Won	1	3	-	-	14	1	-	-	-	5	A.O.Jones(C) Miles(T) Sutton(T) J.W.D.Smith(T) Foreman(T)
16		12	EXETER	H	Won	-	1	-	-	3	-	-	-	-	0	Miles(T)
17		17	OXFORD UNIVERSITY	H	Lost	-	-	-	-	0	-	2	-	-	6	
18		19	NEWPORT	H	Lost	-	-	-	-	0	-	1	1	-	7	
19		26	TREHERBERT	H	Won	1	3	1	-	18	-	1	-	-	3	W.Jones(T) A.E.Hind(T,D) H.P.Atkins(T) D.B.Atkins(T) Russell(C)
20		28	CHELTENHAM	H	Won	3	2	-	-	21	-	-	-	-	0	A.O.Jones(2C) Miles(3T) A.E.Hind(2T) Russell(C)
21		29	Northampton	A	Won	1	3	-	-	14	1	-	-	-	5	A.O.Jones(C) Sutton(2T) A.E.Hind(2T)
22	Jan	1	West Hartlepool	A	Drew	-	-	-	-	0	-	-	-	-	0	
23		2	Hartlepool Rovers	A	Lost	-	1	-	-	3	1	3	-	-	14	Keeton(T)
24		4	Castleford	A	Won	2	2	-	-	16	1	-	-	-	5	W.Jones(T) Russell(T,2C) Andrews(2T)
25		16	Gloucester	A	Lost	-	-	-	-	0	3	2	-	-	21	
26		23	DEVONPORT ALBION	H	Lost	-	-	-	-	0	2	1	-	-	13	
27		30	Swansea	A	Lost	-	-	-	-	0	1	3	-	1	17	
28	Feb	6	HARLEQUINS	H	Won	1	1	-	-	8	-	-	-	-	0	A.E.Hind(T) Russell(T,C)
29		13	Moseley	A	Won	-	2	-	-	6	1	-	-	-	5	Miles(T) Sutton(T)
30		20	CASTLEFORD	H	Won	2	5	-	1	28	1	-	-	-	5	Miles(2T) Sutton(2T) A.E.Hind(3T) Russell(2C,P)
31		27	Richmond	A	Lost	-	-	-	-	0	1	1	-	-	8	
32	Mar	5	GLOUCESTER	H	Won	-	1	-	-	3	-	-	-	-	0	Braithwaite(T)
33		12	NOTTINGHAM (MCC1)	H	Won	1	7	1	-	30	-	1	-	-	3	Miles(3T) Sutton(T) A.O.Jones(D) Hills(T) Braithwaite(2T,C) D.B.Atkins(T)
34		19	FIVE WAYS OLD EDW. (MCC2)	H	Won	1	4	3	-	29	-	1	-	-	3	Sutton(T,D) A.O.Jones(D) Dakin(2T) Hills(T) Braithwaite(C,D) A.Goodrich(T)
35		26	NUNEATON (MCCSF)	H	Won	-	7	1	-	25	-	-	-	-	0	Miles(3T) A.O.Jones(D) Dakin(3T) Hills(T)
36	Apr	2	Moseley (MCCF)	A	Won	2	1	-	-	13	-	-	-	1	3	Sutton(T) A.O.Jones(2C) D.B.Atkins(T) Russell(T)
37		4	Newport	A	Lost	-	1	-	-	3	2	4	-	-	22	A.E.Swain(T)
38		5	Bristol	A	Drew	-	-	-	-	0	-	-	-	-	0	
39		9	Cardiff	A	Lost	-	2	-	-	6	1	5	1	-	24	Blackburn(T) T.Goodrich(T)

INDIVIDUAL APPEARANCES 1903-1904

NAME	1	2	3	4	5	6	7	8	9	10	11	12	13	14	15	16	17	18	19	20	21	22	23	24	25	26	27	28	29	30	31	32	33	34	35	36	37	38	39	40	41	42	43	44	45	46	TOTAL	T	PTS
W.Blackburn	FB	FB	FB	FB	FB																												FB	FB	FB	FB			C								10	1	7
A.J.Palfreyman							FB	FB	FB	FB				C	C	C		C	C						C	C																					11		
Danny Woodford														FB												FB																					2		
Harry Lawrie																							FB	FB	FB	FB	FB	FB									FB										7		
Peter Lockman																																					FB	FB									2		
Arthur Freear	W	W	W	W	W													C																													6	2	6
Jack Miles	W	W	W	W	W	W	W	W		W			W		W	W	W	W	W	W	W	W			W	W		W	W	W	W	W	W	W	W	W	W									30	21	63
Ernest Hind								W			W	W		W	W	W	W	W	W	W	W	W	W	W	W	W	W	W	W	W					W												20	10	38
R.W.Dakin	C	C	C	C	C	W	C			C	C	W												C		C	C					W	W	W			W										17	7	21
Norman Sutton	C	C			C	C	C	C	C	C	C	C	C	C		C	C	C	C		C	C	C	C		C		C	C	C	C	C	C	C	C	C										31	10	34
Harry Reynolds			C	C																																											2		
Arthur Jones					C	C			C		C	FB	FB		FB	FB	FB		FB	FB				C	C	C	C		C	C	C	C							C								20		37
H.Toone								C	W	W	W																						C														5		
Pussy' Jones																					C	C	C	C	C	C												C									7	2	6
Billy Foreman	FH	FH	FH	FH				FH	FH	FH		FH			FH	FH	FH	FH	FH	FH	FH	FH	FH	FH		FH	FH	FH	FH	FH	FH				FH												25	2	6
Bertie Hills																																FH	FH	FH	FH	FH	C	FH	FH								8	3	9
Jacky Braithwaite	SH	SH	SH		SH	SH	SH	SH	SH	SH	SH	SH			SH		SH				SH	SH	SH	SH	SH	SH	SH	SH	SH	SH	SH	SH	SH	SH	SH	SH	SH										30	4	26
Dixie Smith				SH	FH	FH	FH			C	FH	W	FH	W	W		SH	SH	SH		SH	SH	SH					W	W	W	FB	W				W	W										18	2	6
E.C.Wykes													SH	SH	SH		SH	SH	SH		FB	FB	FB																								9		
M.Swain																			SH	SH					FH																						3		
Percy Atkins	F		F	F	F	F	F	F		F	F	F	F			F	F	F	F	F	F																										17	2	6
Dudley Atkins	F	F	F	F	F	F	F	F	F		F		F	F	F	F	F	F	F	F	F	F				F	F	F		F	F	F	F	F	F	F	F	F	F								32	3	9
Tom Goodrich	F	F	F	F	F	F	F	F	F		FB	F	F	F	F	F	F	F	F		F			F		F	F		F	F	F	F	F	F	F	F	F	F	F								33	1	7
Harold Hind	F	F				F	F			F	F	F	F	F	F	F	F	F	F	F	F	F	F	F	F	F	F	F	F	F	F	F	F	F	F	F	F	F	F								33		
Sammy Matthews	F	F	F		F	F	F	F	F	F	F	F	F	F	F	F	F	F	F	F	F	F	F	F	F	F	F	F	F	F	F	F	F	F	F	F	F	F	F								38	1	3
Sid Penny	F					F			F				F	F	F	F	F	F	F	F	F	F	F	F	F	F	F	F	F	F	F	F	F	F	F	F	F	F	F								29		
A.E.Swain	F	F	F	F	F		F		F	F	F	F	F	F	F	F	F	F	F	F				F	F	F	F		F	F	F	F	F	F	F	F	F	F	F								32	1	3
R.C.Watchorn	F	F	F			F	F				F			F	F								F	F	F										F												13		
W.Robinson		F		F																																											2		
Tosh' Russell		F	F	F	F	F	F	F	F	F		F	F			F	F				F	F	F	F	F	F	F	F	F		F		F	F	F	F	F										29	5	39
W.Gale			F	F															FB																												3		
Alf Goodrich						F	F	F	F			F	F			F		F	F					F	F	F	F	F	F	F	F		F	F	F	F	F	F	F								27	1	3
Lt.M.S.Scott					F	F	F	F	F	F	F																					F		F													9		
A.Andrews																							F	F	F				F	F							F		F								8	2	6
George Keeton																							F	F		F																					3	1	3
L.Bennett																																					F	C									3		

1 game: Matt Barrowcliffe W(8), C.T.Bassett F(24), Jimmy Burdett F(15), E.Cameron FB(6), C.M.Gillespie W(7), C.A.Page W(11), A.O.Parsons W(39), A.J.Smith F(39), C.Timlock F(17), Jamie Watson FH(14), Harry Wilkinson C(27)

NO	DATE		OPPONENTS	V	RES	FOR					AGAINST					SCORERS
						G	T	D	P	PTS	G	T	D	P	PTS	
1	Sep	10	HARTLEPOOL ROVERS	H	Won	1	1	-	-	8	-	1	-	-	3	J.W.D.Smith(T) Hills(T) Yeld(C)
2		17	PLYMOUTH	H	Won	-	3	-	-	9	-	-	-	-	0	Parsons(T) Braithwaite(T) A.E.Swain(T)
3		24	WEST HARTLEPOOL	H	Won	1	2	-	-	11	-	-	1	-	4	McFarlane(T) Braithwaite(C) Matthews(T) Russell(T)
4	Oct	1	DEVONPORT ALBION	H	Lost	-	1	-	-	3	1	2	-	-	11	T.Jackson(T)
5		8	BIRKENHEAD PARK	H	Won	2	2	-	-	16	1	1	-	-	8	McFarlane(T) H.P.Atkins(T) Parsons(T) Hills(T) Braithwaite(2C)
6		15	BRISTOL	H	Won	1	2	-	-	11	1	-	-	-	5	Parsons(T) Braithwaite(T) H.P.Atkins(T) Yeld(C)
7		22	Moseley	A	Won	-	1	-	-	3	-	-	-	-	0	J.W.D.Smith(T)
8		29	RICHMOND	H	Won	2	1	-	-	13	-	2	-	-	6	Parsons(T) H.P.Atkins(2T) Yeld(2C)
9	Nov	5	Oxford University	A	Lost	-	-	-	1	3	-	-	1	-	4	Yeld(P)
10		12	COVENTRY	H	Won	3	1	-	-	18	-	-	-	-	0	McFarlane(T) J.W.D.Smith(2T) H.A.Hind(T) Russell(3C)
11		19	Swansea	A	Drew	1	1	-	-	8	1	1	-	-	8	Braithwaite(T) Yeld(C) A.Goodrich(T)
		26	CAMBRIDGE UNIVERSITY	H		Cancelled Frost										
12	Dec	3	Northampton	A	Drew	-	-	-	-	0	-	-	-	-	0	
13		10	LONDON SCOTTISH	H	Won	1	1	-	-	8	-	1	-	-	3	Parsons(T) H.A.Hind(T) Russell(C)
14		17	NORTHAMPTON	H	Won	1	1	-	-	8	-	-	-	-	0	A.E.Hind(T) Parsons(T) Russell(C)
		24	OLD MERCHANT TAYLORS	H		Cancelled Frost										
15		26	EDINBURGH ROYAL H.S.	H	Drew	-	1	-	1	6	-	2	-	-	6	Braithwaite(T) Russell(P)
16		27	RUGBY	H	Won	1	10	-	-	35	1	2	1	-	15	J.Simpson(2T) Wilkinson(2T) A.E.Hind(T) Braithwaite(T) Keeton(2T) A.Goodrich(T) Russell(2T,C)
17		29	FETTES-LORETTONIANS	H	Lost	-	-	-	-	0	2	2	-	-	16	
18		31	West Hartlepool	A	Lost	-	1	-	-	3	-	2	-	-	6	Parsons(T)
19	Jan	2	Hartlepool Rovers	A	Won	2	1	-	-	13	-	1	-	-	3	Wilkinson(T) Braithwaite(2C) Russell(2T)
20		7	CARDIFF	H	Lost	1	1	-	-	8	2	2	-	-	16	Wilkinson(T) Braithwaite(C) Russell(T)
21		14	Coventry	A	Won	2	3	-	-	19	1	2	-	-	11	Parsons(2T) Bainbridge(2T) Hills(T) Braithwaite(C) Matthews(C)
		21	NEWPORT	H		Cancelled Frost										
22		28	GLOUCESTER	H	Won	-	2	-	-	6	-	1	-	-	3	Parsons(T) A.Goodrich(T)
23	Feb	4	Harlequins	A	Won	-	3	-	-	9	-	-	-	-	0	Wilkinson(T) Bainbridge(T) Braithwaite(T)
24		11	MOSELEY	H	Drew	1	1	-	-	8	1	-	-	1	8	Jones(C) Parsons(T) Matthews(T)
25		18	SWANSEA	H	Drew	-	-	-	-	0	-	-	-	-	0	
26		25	Newport	A	Lost	1	-	-	-	5	-	3	-	-	9	Braithwaite(T) Matthews(C)
27	Mar	4	Devonport Albion	A	Lost	-	-	-	-	0	2	1	-	-	13	
28		11	Coventry (MCC2)	A	Won	1	4	-	-	17	-	-	-	-	0	Bainbridge(3T) E.J.Jackett(T) Braithwaite(T) Matthews(C)
29		18	FIVE WAYS OLD EDW. (MCC3)	H	Won	4	1	-	1	26	-	1	-	1	6	A.E.Hind(T) Bainbridge(2T) E.J.Jackett(T) Russell(T,4C,P)
30		25	RUGBY (MCCSF)	H	Won	1	6	-	-	23	-	-	-	-	0	Parsons(T) A.E.Hind(T) Hills(2T,C) Braithwaite(T) Russell(T) T.Jackson(T)
31	Apr	1	Nottingham (MCCF)	A	Won	3	4	1	-	31	-	-	-	-	0	Jones(C) A.E.Hind(3T) E.J.Jackett(C) Parsons(3T) Hills(T) Braithwaite(D) Matthews(C)
32		8	Cardiff	A	Lost	-	-	-	-	0	-	2	-	-	6	
33		15	OLD EDWARDIANS	H	Won	1	4	-	-	17	1	-	-	-	5	A.E.Hind(T) Bainbridge(T) Hills(T) Braithwaite(C) Matthews(T) T.Jackson(T)
34		22	Gloucester	A	Lost	-	-	-	-	0	1	1	-	-	9	
35		24	Plymouth	A	Drew	1	-	-	-	5	1	-	-	-	5	Parsons(T) Matthews(C)
36		25	Bristol	A	Lost	-	-	-	-	0	1	-	-	-	5	
37		29	NEWPORT	H	Won	2	1	-	-	13	-	-	1	-	4	Parsons(T) Russell(T,2C) Dann(T)

INDIVIDUAL APPEARANCES 1904-1905

NAME	1	2	3	4	5	6	7	8	9	10	11	12	13	14	15	16	17	18	19	20	21	22	23	24	25	26	27	28	29	30	31	32	33	34	35	36	37	38	39	40	41	42	43	44	45	46	TOTAL	T	PTS
W.Blackburn	FB	FB	FB	FB	FB	FB	FB	FB	FB	FB	-	FB	FB	FB	-	-	FB	FB	-	FB	FB	FB																									18	-	-
L.Elliott															FB	FB																															2	-	-
Arthur Jones																						FB	FB	FB	-	Jones		FB	-	FB	FB																8	-	4
Peter Lockman																													FB	-	FB	FB	FB	FB													5	-	-
Dixie Smith	W	C	C	-	-	C	C	C	C	C	C	C	SH	C	-	-	-	-	-	C								FB	-	-	FB	-	W	-	-	-											16	4	12
Dr.N McFarlane	W	W	W	W	W	W	W	-	W	W	W	-	C	C	C	-	W	W	W											W																	17	3	9
A.O.Parsons	-	W	W	W	W	W	W	W	W	W	W	-	W	W	-	W	W	W	W	W	W	W	W	W	W	W	W	W	W	W	-	W	W	W	W	-											34	17	51
F.R.Simpson										W				-			W																														2	-	-
Ernest Hind													W	W	W	W				-	-	-	C	W	C	W	W	-	W	W	W	W	-	W	W	-	W	W								17	8	24
R.W.Marris																																W	W														2	-	-
R.W.Dakin	-	C	C	C	C	C	C	C	C	-	C	W	C	-	C	C	C	C	-	FH	F	W						F	F	-	F	F	-	F	-												18	-	-
Percy Atkins	-	-	-	-	C	F	F	F	-	C	-	F	-	F	F	-	F	-					-						F	-	F	-	F	-													15	4	12
Harry Wilkinson															-	C	C	C	C	C	W	-	C	W	-	FB																					9	5	15
James Bainbridge																					-	C	C	C	C	C	C	C	C	C	C	C	C	C	C	C	-										17	9	27
Bertie Hills	FH	FH	-	FH	FH	FH	FH	FH	FH	FH	FH	FH	FH	-	-	-	FH	FH	-				FH	-				FH	FH	FH	FH	-	FH	FH	-												24	7	23
John Jackett															-	FH	FH	FH	-	-	FH	FH	FH	C	C	-	C	C	C	C	C	-	C	C	C	-											17	2	8
-.Ridsdale																												-	FH	FH	FH	FH															2	-	-
Jacky Braithwaite	SH	SH	SH	SH	SH	SH	SH	SH	SH	-	-	SH	SH	-	SH	SH	SH	SH	SH	SH	SH	SH	SH	SH	SH	SH	SH	SH	SH	SH	SH	SH	SH	SH	SH	SH	SH										35	9	47
Jamie Watson									-	SH															-	-	FH	-	-	-	FH															3	-	-
Jimmy Burdett	F																							-				F																			2	-	-
W.Dann	F	-	-	-	-	-	F					F	-	-	F	-	F	F			-		F	-	F	-				-	-	F	F	F	-	F	F										12	1	3
Alf Goodrich	F	F	F	F	-	F	F	F	F	F	F	F	F	F	F	F	F	F	-	F	F	F	F	F	F	F	F	F	F	F	F	F	F	F	F	F	-										36	3	9
Harold Hind	F	F	F	F	F	-	F	-	F	F	F	F	F	-	F	F	F	-	-	F	F																										15	2	6
Sammy Matthews	F	F	F	F	F	-	F	F	F	F	F	F	F	-	F	F	F	F	-	F	F	F	F	F	F	F	F	F	F	F	F	F	F	F	F	F	F										37	3	19
Tosh' Russell	F	-	F	F	-	F	F	F	F	F	F	-	F	F	-	F	F	F	F	F	F	F	F	-	F	-	-	F	F	F	-	-	F	F	F	F	-										29	9	57
A.E.Swain	F	F	F	F	F	F	F	F	F	F	F	F	F	F	-	-	-	-	F	F	F	F	F	F	-	F	F	F	-																		25	1	3
George Yeld	F	F	-	F	F	F	F	F	F	F	-	F	F	-	F	F	F	F	F	F	F	F	-	F	F	-	F	-																			19	-	13
Tom Goodrich	-	F	-	F	F	F	F	-	F	-	-	F	F	F	-	F	F	F	F	F	F	F	F	F	F	F	F	F	F	F	F	-	F	-	F	-	F										32	-	-
Sid Penny	-	F	F	F	-	F	F	F	F	-	F	F	F	F	F	F	-	-	-	F	F	F	F	F	F	F	F	F	F	F	F	F	F	F	-	F	-										30	-	-
Tom Jackson	-	-	F	F	F	-																								F	F	F	F	F	F	F	F										11	3	9
Dudley Atkins	-	-	-	-	-	-	-	-	F	-	F	-	-	-	-	-	-	-	-	F	F	F	F	F	F	F	F	F	F	-	F	F	F	-	F	-											16	-	-
George Keeton														F	F	F																															3	2	6
L.Beaver																								F	-				-	F	-	F															3	-	-
L.Bennett																																	F	-	F	-	F	F									4	-	-
Richard Jackett																																			-	F	F										2	-	-

1 game: B.L.Atkinson FB(11), W.Dale FB(27), Billy Foreman FH(16), T.Hall C(33), Ralph Hemingway F(22), Frank Jackson W(8), S.Lines F(26), Danny Rees C(1), Jerry Sanderson FB(19), George Sanderson F(19), Lt.M.S. Scott F(10), F.H.Shaw C(21), J.Simpson W(16)[2T-6], H.Smalley FH(15), W.Smith F(32), A.J.Smith F(32), T.Sturrock C(19), Norman Sutton C(1), Percy Swain C(27), Dr.C.H.B. Thompson C(4)

LEICESTER FOOTBALL CLUB 1904-05
Back: T.H. Crumbie (Hon.Sec), D.B. Atkins, L. Bennett, A.O. Parsons, R.F. Russell, H.P. Atkins, T. Goodrich.
Middle: J. Collier (President), B. Hills, E.J. Jackett, A.E. Hind, S. Matthews (Capt), J. Braithwaite, S.H. Penny, F. St.Clair Pain (Hon.Tres).
Front: A. Goodrich, P. Lockman, J.W. Bainbridge, W. Dann.

LEICESTER FOOTBALL CLUB 1906-07
Back: F. St.Clair Pain (Hon.Tres), J. Braithwaite, A. Goodrich, C. Bourns, C. Stafford, D.B. Atkins, R. Hives, T.H. Crumbie (Hon.Sec).
Middle: J. Collier (President), S.H. Penny, J.R. Watson, F.S. Jackson, A.J. Hobbs, T.W. Smith, F.W. Hardyman.
Front: G.W. Wood, T. Jackson, E.J. Jackett, K.B. Wood, A.F. Scott.
Inset: S. Matthews (Capt 1905-06), R.F. Russell (Capt 1906-07).

NO	DATE		OPPONENTS	V	RES	FOR					AGAINST					SCORERS
						G	T	D	P	PTS	G	T	D	P	PTS	
1	Sep	9	HARTLEPOOL ROVERS	H	Won	1	1	-	-	8	-	1	-	-	3	Bainbridge(2T) Braithwaite(C)
2		16	WEST HARTLEPOOL	H	Won	2	2	-	-	16	-	-	-	1	3	Bainbridge(T) Braithwaite(C) Matthews(T) H.P.Atkins(T) D.B.Atkins(T) Yeld(C)
3		23	PLYMOUTH	H	Drew	-	-	-	-	0	-	-	-	-	0	
4		30	NEW ZEALAND	H	Lost	-	-	-	-	0	5	1	-	-	28	
5	Oct	7	Devonport Albion	A	Drew	-	1	-	-	3	-	1	-	-	3	H.P.Atkins(T)
6		9	Plymouth	A	Drew	-	-	-	-	0	-	-	-	-	0	
7		10	United Services	A	Lost	-	1	-	-	3	-	-	-	1	6	Hardyman(T)
8		14	BRISTOL	H	Drew	1	1	-	1	11	1	2	-	-	11	Bainbridge(T) Braithwaite(C) Russell(T,P)
9		21	MOSELEY	H	Won	2	2	-	-	16	1	-	-	1	8	Hind(T) Bainbridge(T) Braithwaite(T,2C) A.Goodrich(T)
10	Nov	4	OXFORD UNIVERSITY	H	Won	-	2	1	-	10	1	1	-	-	8	Hind(T) A.O.Jones(D) H.P.Atkins(T)
11		11	SWANSEA	H	Lost	-	-	-	-	0	-	-	-	1	3	
12		18	NORTHAMPTON	H	Lost	-	1	-	-	3	-	2	1	-	10	D.B.Atkins(T)
13		25	LLANELLI	H	Won	-	2	-	-	6	-	-	-	-	0	Hind(2T)
14	Dec	2	Northampton	A	Lost	-	-	-	-	0	1	1	-	-	8	
15		9	London Scottish	A	Lost	-	1	1	-	7	2	1	1	-	17	Underwood(D) Braithwaite(T)
16		16	Richmond	A	Won	1	-	-	-	5	-	1	-	-	3	A.O.Jones(C) Bainbridge(T)
17		23	COVENTRY	H	Won	-	2	-	-	6	1	-	-	-	5	A.O.Jones(T) H.P.Atkins(T)
18		26	BIRKENHEAD PARK	H	Won	-	3	-	1	12	1	-	-	-	5	Hind(T) A.O.Jones(P) Russell(T) D.B.Atkins(T)
19		27	UNITED SERVICES	H	Won	3	2	1	-	25	-	-	1	-	4	Watson(2T) A.O.Jones(3C,D) Russell(2T) Gimson(T)
20		28	FETTES-LORETTONIANS	H	Lost	-	-	-	-	0	-	1	-	-	3	
21		30	West Hartlepool	A	Won	1	1	-	1	11	-	1	-	-	3	Worsley(T) Braithwaite(C) Matthews(T) Russell(P)
22	Jan	1	Hartlepool Rovers	A	Lost	-	-	-	-	0	1	1	-	-	8	
23		6	Rugby	A	Won	1	1	1	-	12	1	1	-	-	8	Bainbridge(T) A.O.Jones(C,D) H.P.Atkins(T)
24		13	Gloucester	A	Lost	-	-	-	-	0	1	5	-	-	20	
25		20	DEVONPORT ALBION	H	Won	1	2	-	-	11	1	-	1	-	9	Tarr(T) Underwood(T) Braithwaite(T) Matthews(C)
26		27	Moseley	A	Won	-	1	-	-	3	-	-	-	-	0	Underwood(T)
27	Feb	3	Coventry	A	Lost	-	-	-	1	3	1	1	1*	-	12	E.J.Jackett(P)
		10	HARLEQUINS	H		Cancelled										
28		17	Swansea	A	Lost	-	-	-	-	0	1	5	-	-	20	
29		24	NEWPORT	H	Lost	-	-	-	-	0	1	1	-	-	8	
30	Mar	3	CARDIFF	H	Drew	-	1	-	-	3	-	1	-	-	3	Bainbridge(T)
31		10	HEADINGLEY	H	Won	-	1	1	-	7	-	-	1	-	4	Underwood(T) Braithwaite(D)
32		17	Birkenhead Park	A	Won	-	1	-	-	3	-	-	-	-	0	Russell(T)
33		24	BEDFORD	H	Won	2	1	-	-	13	1	-	-	-	5	Underwood(T) Bainbridge(T) Braithwaite(2C) Penny(T)
34	Apr	7	OLD EDWARDIANS	H	Won	1	3	-	-	14	-	-	-	-	0	Underwood(T) Bainbridge(T) McFarlane(2T) Braithwaite(C)
35		14	Newport	A	Lost	-	-	-	-	0	2	5	-	-	25	
36		16	Cardiff	A	Lost	-	-	-	-	0	2	1	-	-	13	
37		17	Bristol	A	Drew	-	-	-	-	0	-	-	-	-	0	

INDIVIDUAL APPEARANCES 1905-1906

NAME	TOTAL	T	PTS
Dudley Atkins	19	3	9
Arthur Jones	13	1	28
W.Dale	5	-	-
L.Elliott	5	-	-
G.H.Hayward	6	-	-
Ernest Hind	15	5	15
A.O.Parsons	6	-	-
D.E.Underwood	21	5	19
Fred Hardyman	9	1	3
Frank Jones	3	-	-
James Bainbridge	27	10	30
Dr.N McFarlane	21	2	6
John Jackett	26	-	3
R.W.Dakin	4	-	-
Lt.Worsley	2	1	3
Frank Tarr	4	1	3
Jamie Watson	28	2	6
Bertie Hills	4	-	-
A.Wright	5	-	-
Jacky Braithwaite	33	3	31
H.J.F.Jeffries	4	-	-
Percy Atkins	23	5	15
Alf Goodrich	35	1	3
Tom Goodrich	20	-	-
Sammy Matthews	34	2	8
Sid Penny	36	1	3
Tosh' Russell	27	5	21
C.Stafford	2	-	-
George Yeld	3	-	2
Fred Jackson	26	-	-
W.Dann	5	-	-
Richard Jackett	3	-	-
R.Hives	18	-	-
R.Ireland	3	-	-
Horace Freer	6	-	-
R.C.Watchorn	3	-	-
Chris Gimson	4	1	3
Tom Jackson	5	-	-
Lt.M.S.Scott	2	-	-
W.G.George	10	-	-
George Greasley	5	-	-
Tom Smith	5	-	-
Tom Hogarth	3	-	-
Lionel Kewney	3	-	-

1 game: A.W.Adcock FB(15), B.L.Atkinson FB(14), Matt Barrowcliffe FH(27), G.Bolus F(27), L.Charles W(27), G.Chitham W(28), Cpt. Evans F(10), Billy Foreman SH(27), J.R.Hart-Davis C(20), J.Jose W(28), F.W.Payne FH(14), F.Pyart F(24), E.Raven F(28), H.R.Somerville FH(32), Percy Swain FH(24), E.Ward W(30).

1906-1907

NO	DATE	OPPONENTS	V	RES	FOR G	FOR T	FOR D	FOR P	FOR PTS	AGAINST G	AGAINST T	AGAINST D	AGAINST P	AGAINST PTS	SCORERS
1	Sep 8	HARTLEPOOL ROVERS	H	Won	1	1	-	-	8	-	-	-	-	0	Coles(C) Bainbridge(T) Russell(T)
2	15	WEST HARTLEPOOL	H	Won	-	2	-	1	9	-	1	-	-	3	Coles(P) Hardyman(T) Russell(T)
3	22	PLYMOUTH	H	Won	1	2	-	1	14	-	-	-	-	0	Jones(C,P) Hardyman(T) Bainbridge(T) A.Goodrich(T)
4	Oct 6	DEVONPORT ALBION	H	Lost	-	-	-	-	0	1	1	-	-	8	
5	13	BRISTOL	H	Drew	-	-	-	-	0	-	-	-	-	0	
6	20	Moseley	A	Won	-	1	-	-	3	-	-	-	-	0	Watson(T)
7	27	RICHMOND	H	Won	1	2	-	-	11	-	-	-	-	0	Watson(T) Braithwaite(C) Smith(T) Greasley(T)
8	Nov 3	Oxford University	A	Lost	-	2	-	-	6	1	2	-	-	11	Russell(T) Hardyman(T)
9	10	NEWPORT	H	Drew	-	1	-	-	3	-	1	-	-	3	Hardyman(T)
10	17	Swansea	A	Lost	-	-	-	-	0	1	1	-	-	8	
11	24	LLANELLI	H	Lost	-	-	-	1	3	1	-	-	-	5	Matthews(P)
12	Dec 1	Northampton	A	Drew	-	1	-	-	3	-	1	-	-	3	Watson(T)
13	8	LONDON SCOTTISH	H	Lost	-	1	-	-	3	1	1	-	-	8	K.B.Wood(T)
14	15	HEADINGLEY	H	Won	-	4	-	-	12	-	1	-	-	3	Hall(T) Hardyman(T) F.S.Jackson(T) Hives(T)
15	22	Coventry	A	Drew	-	-	-	-	0	-	-	-	-	0	
16	24	EDINBURGH ROYAL H.S.	H	Won	4	2	-	-	26	-	-	-	-	0	T.Jackson(T) G.W.Wood(2T) Matthews(2T) R.Jackett(T) Hives(4C)
	26	BIRKENHEAD PARK	H		Cancelled Snow										
17	27	FETTES-LORETTONIANS	H	Drew	-	1	-	-	3	-	1	-	-	3	Russell(T)
	29	West Hartlepool	A		Cancelled Snow										
	31	Hartlepool Rovers	A		Cancelled Snow										
	Jan 1	Headingley	A		Cancelled Snow										
18	5	HARLEQUINS	H	Won	-	3	-	-	9	-	-	-	-	0	T.Jackson(T) Hardyman(T) F.S.Jackson(T)
19	12	PERCY PARK	H	Won	5	4	-	-	37	-	2	-	-	6	Hardyman(4T) K.B.Wood(T) T.Jackson(T) Russell(T) F.S.Jackson(2T) Hives(5C)
20	19	COVENTRY	H	Won	-	3	-	-	9	-	-	-	1	3	Scott(T) K.B.Wood(T) Watson(T)
	26	MOSELEY	H		Cancelled Frost										
	Feb 2	Bedford	A		Cancelled Frost										
	9	CARDIFF	H		Cancelled Frost										
21	16	SWANSEA	H	Won	-	2	-	2	12	-	-	-	1	3	E.J.Jackett(2P) Hobbs(T) F.S.Jackson(T)
22	23	Newport	A	Lost	-	-	-	-	0	1	3	-	-	14	
23	Mar 2	GLOUCESTER	H	Won	1	4	-	-	17	1	-	-	-	5	Scott(2T) K.B.Wood(2T) G.W.Wood(T) Russell(C)
24	9	NORTHAMPTON	H	Won	1	2	-	-	11	-	-	-	-	0	Scott(2T) K.B.Wood(T) G.W.Wood(C)
25	16	Birkenhead Park	A	Won	2	1	-	-	13	-	1	-	-	3	G.W.Wood(2C) Hobbs(T) Smith(2T)
26	23	LONDON WELSH	H	Lost	-	1	-	-	3	1	-	-	-	5	G.W.Wood(T)
27	30	Llanelli	A	Lost	-	1	-	-	3	-	2	-	-	6	Kirk(T)
28	Apr 1	Cardiff	A	Lost	-	-	-	-	0	-	2	-	1	9	
29	2	Bristol	A	Lost	1	-	-	-	5	-	2	1	1	13	Tarr(T) F.S.Jackson(C)
30	6	Devonport Albion	A	Lost	-	-	-	-	0	-	3	-	-	9	
31	8	Plymouth	A	Lost	1	-	-	1	8	-	3	-	-	9	K.B.Wood(T) F.S.Jackson(C,P)
32	13	OLD EDWARDIANS	H	Won	2	2	-	1	19	-	-	-	-	0	E.J.Jackett(T) K.B.Wood(2T) T.Jackson(T) Kirk(P) F.S.Jackson(2C)
33	20	LONDON	H	Won	2	3	-	-	19	-	2	-	-	6	Wilson(T) Russell(2T,C) Smith(T) F.S.Jackson(T,C)

INDIVIDUAL APPEARANCES 1906-1907

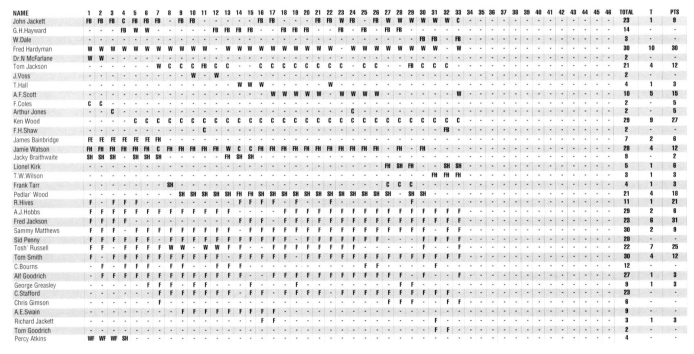

NAME	1	2	3	4	5	6	7	8	9	10	11	12	13	14	15	16	17	18	19	20	21	22	23	24	25	26	27	28	29	30	31	32	33	34	35	36	37	38	39	40	41	42	43	44	45	46	TOTAL	T	PTS
John Jackett	FB	FB	FB	C	FB	FB	FB	-	FB	FB	-	-	-	-	-	FB	FB	-	-	-	FB	FB	W	FB	-	FB	W	W	W	W	W	W	C	-	-	-	-	-	-	-	-	-	-	-	-	-	23	1	9
G.H.Hayward	-	-	-	FB	W	W	-	-	-	-	-	FB	FB	FB	FB	-	-	FB	FB	FB	-	-	FB	-	FB	-	FB	FB	-	-	-	-	-	-	-	-	-	-	-	-	-	-	-	-	-	-	14	-	-
W.Dale	-	-	-	-	-	-	-	-	-	-	-	-	-	-	-	-	-	-	-	-	-	-	-	-	-	-	-	-	-	FB	FB	-	FB	-	-	-	-	-	-	-	-	-	-	-	-	-	3	-	-
Fred Hardyman	W	W	W	W	W	W	W	W	W	W	W	-	W	W	W	W	W	W	W	W	W	W	-	W	W	W	W	W	W	W	W	-	W	-	-	-	-	-	-	-	-	-	-	-	-	-	30	10	30
Dr.N McFarlane	W	W	-	-	-	-	-	-	-	-	-	-	-	-	-	-	-	-	-	-	-	-	-	-	-	-	-	-	-	-	-	-	-	-	-	-	-	-	-	-	-	-	-	-	-	-	2	-	-
Tom Jackson	-	-	-	-	-	-	W	C	C	C	FB	C	C	-	-	C	C	C	C	C	C	C	C	-	C	C	-	-	FB	C	C	C	-	-	-	-	-	-	-	-	-	-	-	-	-	-	21	4	12
J.Voss	-	-	-	-	-	-	-	-	-	W	-	W	-	-	-	-	-	-	-	-	-	-	-	-	-	-	-	-	-	-	-	-	-	-	-	-	-	-	-	-	-	-	-	-	-	-	2	-	-
T.Hall	-	-	-	-	-	-	-	-	-	-	-	-	-	W	W	W	-	-	-	-	-	W	-	-	-	-	-	-	-	-	-	-	-	-	-	-	-	-	-	-	-	-	-	-	-	-	4	1	3
A.F.Scott	-	-	-	-	-	-	-	-	-	-	-	-	-	-	-	-	W	W	W	W	W	-	W	W	W	W	-	-	-	-	-	-	W	-	-	-	-	-	-	-	-	-	-	-	-	-	10	5	15
F.Coles	C	C	-	-	-	-	-	-	-	-	-	-	-	-	-	-	-	-	-	-	-	-	-	-	-	-	-	-	-	-	-	-	-	-	-	-	-	-	-	-	-	-	-	-	-	-	2	-	5
Arthur Jones	-	-	C	-	-	-	-	-	-	-	-	-	-	-	-	-	-	-	-	-	-	-	-	C	-	-	-	-	-	-	-	-	-	-	-	-	-	-	-	-	-	-	-	-	-	-	2	-	5
Ken Wood	-	-	-	-	C	C	C	C	C	C	C	C	C	C	C	C	C	C	C	C	C	C	C	C	C	C	C	C	C	C	C	C	C	-	-	-	-	-	-	-	-	-	-	-	-	-	29	9	27
F.H.Shaw	-	-	-	-	-	-	-	-	-	-	C	-	-	-	-	-	-	-	-	-	-	-	-	-	-	-	-	-	-	-	-	FB	-	-	-	-	-	-	-	-	-	-	-	-	-	-	2	-	-
James Bainbridge	FE	FE	FE	FE	FE	FE	FH	-	-	-	-	-	-	-	-	-	-	-	-	-	-	-	-	-	-	-	-	-	-	-	-	-	-	-	-	-	-	-	-	-	-	-	-	-	-	-	7	2	6
Jamie Watson	FH	FH	FH	FH	FH	FH	C	FH	FH	FH	FH	FH	W	C	C	FH	FH	FH	FH	FH	FH	FH	FH	FH	FH	FH	-	FH	-	FH	-	-	-	-	-	-	-	-	-	-	-	-	-	-	-	-	28	4	12
Jacky Braithwaite	SH	SH	SH	-	SH	SH	SH	-	-	-	-	-	FH	SH	SH	-	-	-	-	-	-	-	-	-	-	-	-	-	-	-	-	-	-	-	-	-	-	-	-	-	-	-	-	-	-	-	9	-	2
Lionel Kirk	-	-	-	-	-	-	-	-	-	-	-	-	-	-	-	-	-	-	-	-	-	-	-	-	-	-	FH	SH	FH	-	-	SH	SH	-	-	-	-	-	-	-	-	-	-	-	-	-	5	1	6
T.W.Wilson	-	-	-	-	-	-	-	-	-	-	-	-	-	-	-	-	-	-	-	-	-	-	-	-	-	-	-	-	-	-	FH	FH	FH	-	-	-	-	-	-	-	-	-	-	-	-	-	3	1	3
Frank Tarr	-	-	-	-	-	-	-	SH	-	-	-	-	-	-	-	-	-	-	-	-	-	-	-	-	-	-	C	C	C	-	-	-	-	-	-	-	-	-	-	-	-	-	-	-	-	-	4	1	3
Pedlar' Wood	-	-	-	-	-	-	-	-	SH	SH	SH	SH	SH	FH	FH	SH	SH	SH	SH	SH	SH	SH	SH	SH	SH	SH	SH	-	SH	SH	-	-	-	-	-	-	-	-	-	-	-	-	-	-	-	-	21	4	18
R.Hives	F	-	F	F	F	-	-	-	-	-	-	-	-	F	F	F	F	-	F	-	-	F	-	-	-	-	-	-	F	-	-	-	-	-	-	-	-	-	-	-	-	-	-	-	-	-	11	1	21
A.J.Hobbs	F	F	F	F	F	F	F	F	F	F	F	F	F	-	-	-	-	F	F	F	F	F	F	F	F	F	F	F	F	F	F	F	F	-	-	-	-	-	-	-	-	-	-	-	-	-	29	2	6
Fred Jackson	F	F	F	F	-	-	-	-	-	-	-	-	-	F	F	F	-	F	F	F	F	F	F	F	F	F	F	F	F	F	F	F	F	-	-	-	-	-	-	-	-	-	-	-	-	-	23	6	31
Sammy Matthews	F	F	F	-	F	F	F	F	F	F	F	F	F	-	F	F	F	F	F	F	F	F	F	F	F	F	F	F	F	F	-	F	F	-	-	-	-	-	-	-	-	-	-	-	-	-	30	2	9
Sid Penny	F	F	F	F	F	F	-	F	F	F	F	F	F	F	F	F	F	F	-	F	F	F	F	F	F	F	-	-	-	F	F	F	F	-	-	-	-	-	-	-	-	-	-	-	-	-	28	-	-
Tosh' Russell	F	F	-	F	F	F	F	W	W	-	W	W	F	F	-	-	F	F	F	F	F	F	F	F	-	-	-	-	-	F	-	-	F	-	-	-	-	-	-	-	-	-	-	-	-	-	22	7	25
Tom Smith	F	-	F	F	F	F	F	F	F	F	F	F	-	F	F	F	F	F	-	F	F	F	F	F	F	F	F	F	F	F	F	F	F	-	-	-	-	-	-	-	-	-	-	-	-	-	30	4	12
C.Bourns	-	F	-	F	F	F	-	F	F	-	-	F	F	F	-	-	-	-	-	-	-	-	-	-	F	F	-	-	-	-	F	-	-	-	-	-	-	-	-	-	-	-	-	-	-	-	12	-	-
Alf Goodrich	-	F	F	F	F	F	F	F	F	F	F	F	F	F	-	-	F	F	F	F	F	F	F	F	F	F	F	F	-	F	-	-	F	-	-	-	-	-	-	-	-	-	-	-	-	-	27	1	3
George Greasley	-	-	-	-	-	F	F	F	-	F	F	-	-	-	F	-	-	-	F	-	-	-	-	-	-	-	-	F	F	-	-	-	-	-	-	-	-	-	-	-	-	-	-	-	-	-	9	1	3
C.Stafford	-	-	-	-	-	-	F	F	F	F	F	F	F	-	F	F	-	F	F	F	F	-	F	F	F	F	F	F	F	F	F	F	-	-	-	-	-	-	-	-	-	-	-	-	-	-	23	-	-
Chris Gimson	-	-	-	-	-	-	F	-	-	-	-	-	-	-	-	-	-	-	-	-	-	-	-	-	-	-	F	F	F	-	-	F	F	-	-	-	-	-	-	-	-	-	-	-	-	-	6	-	-
A.E.Swain	-	-	-	-	-	-	-	-	F	F	F	F	F	F	F	F	F	-	-	-	-	-	-	-	-	-	-	-	-	-	-	-	-	-	-	-	-	-	-	-	-	-	-	-	-	-	9	-	-
Richard Jackett	-	-	-	-	-	-	-	-	-	-	-	-	-	-	-	F	F	-	-	-	-	-	-	-	-	-	-	-	-	-	F	-	-	-	-	-	-	-	-	-	-	-	-	-	-	-	3	1	3
Tom Goodrich	-	-	-	-	-	-	-	-	-	-	-	-	-	-	-	-	-	-	-	-	-	-	-	-	-	-	-	-	-	-	F	F	-	-	-	-	-	-	-	-	-	-	-	-	-	-	2	-	-
Percy Atkins	WF	WF	WF	SH	-	-	-	-	-	-	-	-	-	-	-	-	-	-	-	-	-	-	-	-	-	-	-	-	-	-	-	-	-	-	-	-	-	-	-	-	-	-	-	-	-	-	4	-	-

1 game: -.Bateman SH(31), H.O.East FB(8), G.R.Ellis-Danvers W(3), A.O.Parsons W(4), George Shingler W(32), T.A.Weston F(27)

NO	DATE	OPPONENTS	V	RES	FOR G	FOR T	FOR D	FOR P	FOR PTS	AGAINST G	AGAINST T	AGAINST D	AGAINST P	AGAINST PTS	SCORERS
1	Sep 14	HARTLEPOOL ROVERS	H	Won	2	2	-	1	19	1	-	-	-	5	Tarr(2T) Wilson(T) Hobbs(T) Jackson(2C,P)
2	21	WEST HARTLEPOOL	H	Won	4	8	1	-	48	1	-	-	-	5	E.J.Jackett(D) K.B.Wood(2T) Watson(3T) Faussett(T) G.W.Wood(T,2C) Russell(T) Gimson(T) Jackson(3T,2C)
3	28	PLYMOUTH	H	Lost	-	-	-	-	0	-	1	-	-	3	
4	Oct 5	MANCHESTER	H	Won	4	4	-	-	32	-	2	-	-	6	Watson(T) K.B.Wood(T) Taylor(T) Russell(2C) A.Goodrich(T) Jackson(T,2C) Hobbs(T) Gimson(2T)
5	12	BRISTOL	H	Won	1	1	-	1	11	-	2	1	-	10	G.W.Wood(T) Russell(P) Jackson(T,C)
6	19	MOSELEY	H	Won	1	4	-	-	17	-	-	-	-	0	K.B.Wood(T) Watson(T) Russell(T) Jackson(T,C) Hobbs(T)
7	26	Richmond	A	Lost	-	1	-	1	6	-	2	1	-	10	E.J.Jackett(P) A.Goodrich(T)
8	Nov 2	OXFORD UNIVERSITY	H	Lost	-	2	-	-	6	3	3	-	1	27	Mann(T) Watson(T)
9	9	SWANSEA	H	Lost	-	-	-	-	0	1	-	-	-	5	
10	16	Devonport Albion	A	Lost	-	-	-	-	0	1	-	-	-	5	
11	18	Plymouth	A	Lost	-	-	-	-	0	-	4	-	-	12	
12	23	LLANELLI	H	Drew	1	-	-	-	5	1	-	-	-	5	K.B.Wood(T) Jackson(C)
13	30	PENARTH	H	Drew	-	1	-	-	3	-	1	-	-	3	Penny(T)
14	Dec 7	London Scottish	A	Lost	-	-	-	-	0	6	3	-	-	39	
15	14	Gloucester	A	Lost	-	2	-	-	6	1	-	-	1	8	G.W.Wood(2T)
16	21	COVENTRY	H	Won	-	2	-	-	6	-	-	-	-	0	P.W.Lawrie(T) G.W.Wood(T)
17	26	FETTES-LORETTONIANS	H	Won	3	2	-	-	21	1	1	-	-	8	H.S.B.Lawrie(T) Watson(T) Jackson(3C) Hobbs(2T) Gimson(T)
18	27	BECTIVE RANGERS	H	Won	-	3	-	-	9	-	-	-	-	0	T.Hall(T) G.W.Wood(T) Penny(T)
19	28	BIRKENHEAD PARK	H	Won	1	2	-	-	11	1	-	-	-	5	Jackson(3T) Gimson(C)
20	Jan 1	West Hartlepool	A	Won	1	3	-	-	14	-	-	1	1	7	Dyke(2T) Goodman(T) E.J.Jackett(T) Jackson(C)
21	2	Hartlepool Rovers	A	Lost	-	1	-	-	3	-	-	1	-	4	Dyke(T)
	4	Harlequins	A		Cancelled										
	11	CARDIFF	H		Cancelled Snow										
22	18	BEDFORD	H	Won	3	7	1	-	40	-	-	-	-	0	E.J.Jackett(T) P.W.Lawrie(T) J.W.D.Smith(T) K.B.Wood(D) Watson(2T,C) G.W.Wood(T) Jackson(3T,2C) Hobbs(T)
23	25	Moseley	A	Lost	-	-	-	-	0	-	-	-	1	3	
24	Feb 1	NORTHAMPTON	H	Won	2	1	-	-	13	-	1	-	-	3	J.W.D.Smith(T) P.W.Lawrie(T) Jackson(2C) Hobbs(T)
25	8	GLOUCESTER	H	Won	1	2	-	-	11	-	-	-	-	0	J.W.D.Smith(2T) Jackson(T,C)
26	15	Swansea	A	Lost	-	-	-	-	0	1	1	-	1	11	
27	22	NEWPORT	H	Drew	1	-	-	-	5	1	-	-	-	5	Jackson(T,C)
28	29	Coventry	A	Won	1	-	-	-	5	-	-	-	1	3	Jackson(C) Hobbs(T)
29	Mar 7	DEVONPORT ALBION	H	Won	2	1	-	1	16	-	-	-	-	0	Edwards(T) J.W.D.Smith(T) G.W.Wood(T) Jackson(2C,P)
30	14	Birkenhead Park	A	Won	2	1	-	-	13	-	-	1	-	4	Edwards(2T) K.B.Wood(T) Jackson(2C)
31	21	LONDON WELSH	H	Won	1	1	-	-	8	1	-	-	-	5	J.W.D.Smith(T) Kirk(T) Jackson(C)
32	28	Northampton	A	Lost	-	1	-	-	3	1	2	-	-	11	Edwards(T)
	Apr 4	Headingley	A		Cancelled										
33	11	Newport	A	Lost	-	-	1	-	4	2	4	-	-	22	K.B.Wood(D)
34	18	Llanelli	A	Drew	-	-	-	-	0	-	-	-	-	0	
35	20	Cardiff	A	Lost	1	2	-	-	11	3	3	-	-	24	P.W.Lawrie(T) Kirk(T) Gimson(C) Mills(T)
36	21	Bristol	A	Won	-	1	-	-	3	-	-	-	-	0	Kirk(T)

INDIVIDUAL APPEARANCES 1907-1908

NAME	1	2	3	4	5	6	7	8	9	10	11	12	13	14	15	16	17	18	19	20	21	22	23	24	25	26	27	28	29	30	31	32	33	34	35	36	37	38	39	40	41	42	43	44	45	46	TOTAL	T	PTS
John Jackett	-	FB	FB	FB	FB	W	C	-	FB	FB	FB	FB	FB	-	FB	FB	FB	FB	FB	W	W	FB	-	FB	FB	C	C	C	FB	FB	FB	-	-	-	-	-	-	-	-	-	-	-	-	-	-	-	27	2	13
Dixie Smith	-	-	-	-	-	FB	FB	FB	C	FH	FH	FH	C	FB	C	C	C	C	C	-	-	C	FB	C	C	C	C	C	C	C	W	-	C	W	W	-	-	-	-	-	-	-	-	-	-	-	27	6	18
R.Eathorne	-	-	-	-	-	-	-	-	-	-	-	-	-	-	-	-	-	-	-	FB	FB	-	-	-	-	FB	FB	FB	-	-	-	FB	-	-	-	-	-	-	-	-	-	-	-	-	-	-	6	-	-
C.Birch	-	-	-	-	-	-	-	-	-	-	-	-	-	-	-	-	-	-	-	-	-	-	-	-	-	-	-	-	-	-	-	-	FB	FB	-	-	-	-	-	-	-	-	-	-	-	-	2	-	-
Dan Ellwood	-	-	-	-	-	-	-	-	-	-	-	-	-	-	-	-	-	-	-	-	-	-	-	-	-	-	-	-	-	-	-	-	-	-	FB	FB	-	-	-	-	-	-	-	-	-	-	2	-	-
Frank Tarr	W	W	W	-	-	-	-	-	-	-	-	-	-	-	-	-	-	-	-	C	C	-	-	-	-	-	-	-	-	-	C	C	-	-	-	-	-	-	-	-	-	-	-	-	-	-	7	2	6
C.R.Faussett	-	W	W	W	-	-	-	-	-	-	-	-	-	-	-	-	-	-	-	-	-	-	-	-	-	-	-	-	-	-	-	-	-	-	-	-	-	-	-	-	-	-	-	-	-	-	3	1	3
W.Gulliver	-	-	-	-	W	W	W	-	-	-	-	-	W	W	-	-	-	-	-	-	-	-	-	-	-	-	-	-	-	-	-	-	-	-	-	-	-	-	-	-	-	-	-	-	-	-	5	-	-
Maurice Mann	-	-	-	-	-	-	-	W	W	W	W	W	-	-	W	W	W	-	-	-	-	-	C	-	-	-	-	-	-	-	-	-	-	-	-	-	-	-	-	-	-	-	-	-	-	-	9	1	3
T.L.Edwards	-	-	-	-	-	-	-	-	W	-	-	W	W	W	-	-	-	-	W	-	-	-	-	-	W	W	W	W	W	W	-	W	-	-	-	-	-	-	-	-	-	-	-	-	-	-	12	4	12
Harry Lawrie	-	-	-	-	-	-	-	-	-	-	-	-	-	-	-	-	W	W	-	-	-	-	-	-	-	-	-	-	-	-	-	-	-	-	-	-	-	-	-	-	-	-	-	-	-	-	2	1	3
T.Hall	-	-	-	-	-	-	-	-	-	-	-	-	-	-	-	-	-	W	W	-	-	W	W	-	-	-	-	-	-	-	-	-	-	-	-	-	-	-	-	-	-	-	-	-	-	-	4	1	3
John Dyke	-	-	-	-	-	-	-	-	-	-	-	-	-	-	-	-	-	-	-	W	W	-	-	-	-	-	-	-	-	-	-	-	-	-	-	-	-	-	-	-	-	-	-	-	-	-	2	3	9
D.Campbell	-	-	-	-	-	-	-	-	-	-	-	-	-	-	-	-	-	-	-	-	-	-	-	-	-	-	-	-	-	-	-	-	W	F	-	F	-	-	-	-	-	-	-	-	-	-	3	-	-
Jamie Watson	C	C	C	C	C	C	W	C	FH	-	-	-	FH	FH	FH	FH	FH	FH	FH	-	-	FH	FH	FH	FH	FH	FH	FH	FH	FH	W	FH	FH	-	C	C	-	-	-	-	-	-	-	-	-	-	30	9	29
Ken Wood	C	C	C	C	C	C	C	C	C	C	C	C	-	C	C	C	C	C	C	-	-	C	C	W	C	-	-	-	C	C	C	C	C	C	C	C	-	-	-	-	-	-	-	-	-	-	30	6	26
Percy Lawrie	-	-	-	-	-	-	-	-	-	C	C	C	C	C	W	W	-	-	-	-	-	W	W	C	W	W	W	W	W	-	-	-	W	W	W	W	-	-	-	-	-	-	-	-	-	-	19	4	12
E.L.Goodman	-	-	-	-	-	-	-	-	-	-	-	-	-	-	-	-	-	-	-	C	C	-	-	-	-	-	-	-	-	-	-	-	-	C	-	-	-	-	-	-	-	-	-	-	-	-	3	1	3
T.W.Wilson	FH	FH	-	-	-	-	-	-	-	-	-	-	-	-	-	-	-	-	-	-	-	-	-	-	-	-	-	-	-	-	-	-	-	-	-	-	-	-	-	-	-	-	-	-	-	-	2	1	3
Tim' Taylor	-	-	-	FH	FH	-	-	-	-	-	-	-	-	-	-	-	-	-	-	-	-	-	-	-	-	-	-	-	-	-	-	-	-	-	-	-	-	-	-	-	-	-	-	-	-	-	2	1	3
E.W.Goodall	-	-	-	-	-	FH	-	FH	-	-	-	-	-	-	-	-	-	-	-	-	-	-	-	-	-	-	-	-	-	-	-	-	-	-	-	-	-	-	-	-	-	-	-	-	-	-	2	-	-
Maffer' Davey	-	-	-	-	-	-	-	-	-	-	-	-	-	-	-	-	-	-	-	FH	FH	-	-	-	-	-	-	-	-	-	-	-	-	-	-	-	-	-	-	-	-	-	-	-	-	-	2	-	-
J.Thompson	-	-	-	-	-	-	-	-	-	-	-	-	-	-	-	-	-	-	-	-	-	-	-	-	-	-	-	-	-	-	-	-	-	-	FH	FH	-	-	-	-	-	-	-	-	-	-	2	-	-
Pedlar' Wood	SH	SH	SH	SH	SH	SH	SH	SH	SH	SH	SH	SH	SH	SH	SH	SH	SH	SH	SH	SH	SH	SH	SH	SH	SH	SH	SH	SH	SH	SH	FH	SH	SH	FH	-	SH	-	-	-	-	-	-	-	-	-	-	35	8	28
Lionel Kirk	-	-	-	-	-	-	-	-	-	-	-	-	-	-	-	-	-	-	-	-	-	-	-	-	-	-	-	-	-	-	SH	W	-	SH	SH	W	-	-	-	-	-	-	-	-	-	-	5	3	9
Dudley Atkins	F	-	-	-	-	-	F	F	F	F	F	-	-	F	F	F	F	F	-	-	-	-	-	-	-	-	-	F	F	F	F	F	-	-	-	-	-	-	-	-	-	-	-	-	-	-	16	-	-
Alf Goodrich	F	F	F	F	F	F	F	F	-	-	-	F	-	-	-	-	-	-	-	-	-	F	-	F	F	F	F	F	F	F	F	F	-	F	-	F	-	-	-	-	-	-	-	-	-	-	21	2	6
W.Hall	F	F	F	F	F	F	F	F	F	F	F	F	-	F	-	-	-	F	-	F	F	-	F	-	-	-	-	-	-	-	-	-	F	-	-	-	-	-	-	-	-	-	-	-	-	-	18	-	-
A.J.Hobbs	F	F	F	F	F	F	-	F	F	F	F	F	F	-	F	-	F	-	F	F	F	F	F	F	F	F	-	F	F	F	-	F	F	F	F	F	-	-	-	-	-	-	-	-	-	-	30	8	24
Fred Jackson	F	F	F	F	F	F	F	F	F	F	F	F	F	-	F	F	F	F	F	F	F	F	-	F	F	-	F	F	F	F	F	-	-	-	-	-	-	-	-	-	-	-	-	-	-	-	28	14	98
Sid Penny	F	F	F	F	F	F	F	F	F	F	F	F	F	F	F	F	F	F	F	F	F	F	F	F	F	F	F	F	-	F	F	F	F	F	F	F	-	-	-	-	-	-	-	-	-	-	35	2	6
Tosh' Russell	F	F	F	F	F	F	-	F	F	W	-	F	F	-	-	-	-	-	-	-	-	-	-	-	-	-	-	-	-	-	-	-	-	-	-	-	-	-	-	-	-	-	-	-	-	-	11	2	13
Tom Smith	F	F	F	W	-	-	-	-	-	-	-	-	F	F	F	F	F	-	F	F	F	F	F	F	F	F	F	F	F	F	F	F	-	-	-	-	-	-	-	-	-	-	-	-	-	-	23	-	-
Chris Gimson	-	F	F	F	F	-	-	-	-	-	-	-	-	-	-	F	F	F	F	F	F	-	-	-	-	-	-	-	-	-	-	F	F	F	F	F	-	-	-	-	-	-	-	-	-	-	15	4	16
C.Bourns	-	-	-	F	F	F	-	-	-	-	-	-	-	-	-	-	-	-	-	-	-	-	-	-	-	-	-	-	-	-	-	-	-	-	-	-	-	-	-	-	-	-	-	-	-	-	3	-	-
A.Mills	-	-	-	-	-	F	-	-	-	-	-	-	-	-	F	F	-	F	F	-	-	F	F	F	F	-	F	F	F	F	F	-	-	-	F	-	-	-	-	-	-	-	-	-	-	-	15	1	3
Sammy Matthews	-	-	-	-	-	-	F	F	F	F	F	F	F	F	F	F	F	F	-	F	F	F	F	F	F	F	F	F	F	F	F	F	F	F	F	-	-	-	-	-	-	-	-	-	-	-	28	-	-
L.Wright	-	-	-	-	-	-	F	-	F	-	-	-	-	-	-	-	-	-	-	-	-	-	F	-	-	-	-	-	-	-	-	-	-	-	-	-	-	-	-	-	-	-	-	-	-	-	3	-	-
Richard Jackett	-	-	-	-	-	-	-	-	-	F	F	-	-	-	-	-	F	F	F	F	F	-	-	-	-	F	-	-	-	-	-	-	-	-	-	-	-	-	-	-	-	-	-	-	-	-	8	-	-
J.W.Freer	-	-	-	-	-	-	-	-	-	-	-	F	F	-	F	-	-	-	-	-	-	-	-	-	-	-	-	-	-	-	-	-	F	-	-	-	-	-	-	-	-	-	-	-	-	-	4	-	-
J.Hubbard	-	-	-	-	-	-	-	-	-	-	-	-	F	F	-	-	-	-	-	-	-	F	F	F	-	-	F	-	F	-	-	-	-	-	-	-	-	-	-	-	-	-	-	-	-	-	7	-	-
R.C.Watchorn	-	-	-	-	-	-	-	-	-	-	-	-	-	F	-	F	-	-	F	-	-	-	-	-	-	-	-	-	-	W	-	F	-	-	-	-	-	-	-	-	-	-	-	-	-	-	5	-	-
W.H.Bingham	-	-	-	-	-	-	-	-	-	-	-	-	-	-	-	-	-	-	-	-	-	-	-	-	F	F	F	-	-	-	F	-	F	-	-	-	-	-	-	-	-	-	-	-	-	-	5	-	-
Tom Hogarth	-	-	-	-	-	-	-	-	-	-	-	-	-	-	-	-	-	-	-	-	-	-	-	-	-	F	-	-	-	-	-	-	-	F	F	F	-	-	-	-	-	-	-	-	-	-	4	-	-
Lionel Kewney	-	-	-	-	-	-	-	-	-	-	-	-	-	-	-	-	-	-	-	-	-	-	-	-	-	-	-	-	-	-	-	-	-	F	F	F	-	-	-	-	-	-	-	-	-	-	3	-	-
S.Brittain	-	-	-	-	-	-	-	-	-	-	-	-	-	-	-	-	-	-	-	-	-	-	-	-	-	-	-	-	-	-	-	-	-	-	F	F	-	-	-	-	-	-	-	-	-	-	2	-	-

1 game: A.Armstrong F(14), Barrie Bennetts W(11), -.Bond FH(7), Rev.J.P. Burbery W(5), W.Dale FB(1), Denys Dobson F(11), Tom Goodrich F(10), R.Hives W(1), W.Lawrence W(24), D.Lewis W(8), G.Middleton F(33), -.Timson F(7), H.Wale FH(3)

1908-1909

NO	DATE		OPPONENTS	V	RES	FOR G	FOR T	FOR D	FOR P	FOR PTS	AGAINST G	AGAINST T	AGAINST D	AGAINST P	AGAINST PTS	SCORERS
1	Sep	5	STRATFORD-UPON-AVON	H	Won	2	2	1*	-	19	-	1	-	-	3	P.W.Lawrie(3T) Kirk(T,C,M) G.W.Wood(C)
2		12	HARTLEPOOL ROVERS	H	Won	1	3	-	1	17	-	-	-	-	0	Smith(T) K.B.Wood(T) P.W.Lawrie(T) Kirk(T,C,P)
3		19	NEATH	H	Lost	1	-	-	-	5	1	1	-	-	8	G.W.Wood(T,C)
4		26	HEADINGLEY	H	Won	2	2	1	-	20	-	-	-	2	6	P.W.Lawrie(2T) K.B.Wood(T,D) G.W.Wood(T,2C)
5	Oct	1	1ST LEICESTERS.REGT.	H	Won	4	6	-	-	38	-	-	-	-	0	P.W.Lawrie(2T,C) K.B.Wood(2T) Watson(T) Smith(3T) Taylor(T) G.W.Wood(T,3C)
6		3	DEVONPORT ALBION	H	Won	-	2	-	-	6	-	1	-	-	3	Taylor(T) P.W.Lawrie(T)
7		10	BRISTOL	H	Won	2	1	-	-	13	-	-	-	-	0	Smith(T) Hobbs(T) Yeld(2C) Mills(T)
8		14	Birkenhead Park	A	Won	-	3	-	-	9	-	1	-	1	6	K.B.Wood(T) P.W.Lawrie(2T)
9		17	Northampton	A	Lost	-	1	-	-	3	1	2	-	-	11	P.W.Lawrie(T)
10		24	RICHMOND	H	Won	3	5	-	-	30	1	2	-	-	11	Ferguson(2T) H.S.B.Lawrie(2T) Watson(T) Hobbs(T) Yeld(3C) Hopkins(2T)
11		31	CARDIFF	H	Won	-	1	1	-	7	-	-	-	-	0	E.J.Jackett(D) H.S.B.Lawrie(T)
12	Nov	7	NEWPORT	H	Won	-	2	1	-	10	1	-	-	-	5	P.W.Lawrie(T) H.S.B.Lawrie(D) Hubbard(T)
13		14	Swansea	A	Lost	-	-	-	-	0	1	3	-	-	14	
14		16	Neath	A	Lost	-	-	-	-	0	2	-	-	1	13	
15		21	LLANELLI	H	Won	-	1	1	1	10	-	1	-	-	3	E.J.Jackett(D,P) G.W.Wood(T)
16		28	LONDON SCOTTISH	H	Won	4	5	1	-	39	-	-	1	-	4	P.W.Lawrie(T) K.B.Wood(D) Smith(T) H.S.B.Lawrie(3T,2C) Watson(2T) G.W.Wood(T,2C) Hopkins(T)
17	Dec	5	Manchester	A	Won	1	4	-	-	17	-	3	-	1	12	P.W.Lawrie(C) Mann(T) Roberts(T) G.W.Wood(2T) Hobbs(T)
18		12	Gloucester	A	Lost	-	1	-	-	3	2	1	-	-	13	G.W.Wood(T)
19		19	Coventry	A	Lost	-	-	-	-	0	-	3	1*	-	12	
20		26	BIRKENHEAD PARK	H	Won	3	1	-	-	18	-	2	-	-	6	H.S.B.Lawrie(3C) P.W.Lawrie(2T) K.B.Wood(T) Smith(T)
21		28	PENARTH	H	Won	1	1	-	-	8	-	2	-	-	6	P.W.Lawrie(T) H.S.B.Lawrie(C) Hobbs(T)
		31	FETTES-LORETTONIANS	H	Cancelled											
22	Jan	1	Headingley	A	Lost	-	-	-	-	0	-	1	-	1	6	
23		2	Hartlepool Rovers	A	Lost	1	1	-	-	8	-	2	1	-	10	E.J.Jackett(C) Smith(T) P.W.Lawrie(T)
24		9	Bedford	A	Won	1	1	-	-	8	1	-	-	-	5	H.S.B.Lawrie(C) Lewis(T) Hubbard(T)
25		16	MOSELEY	H	Won	2	4	1*	-	25	1	-	-	-	5	Lewis(T) H.S.B.Lawrie(T,2C,M) P.W.Lawrie(2T) Goodrich(T) Greasley(T)
26		23	Moseley	A	Won	2	1	-	-	13	-	2	-	-	6	H.S.B.Lawrie(2C) Flude(T) G.W.Wood(T) Greasley(T)
27	Feb	4	Richmond	A	Won	2	1	-	-	13	-	-	-	-	0	P.W.Lawrie(T) K.B.Wood(T) Heard(T) H.S.B.Lawrie(2C)
28		6	COVENTRY	H	Lost	-	-	-	-	0	-	-	1	1	7	
29		13	SWANSEA	H	Won	-	1	-	-	3	-	-	-	-	0	G.W.Wood(T)
30		20	Newport	A	Lost	1	-	-	-	5	1	-	1	-	9	K.B.Wood(T) H.S.B.Lawrie(C)
31		27	GLOUCESTER	H	Won	2	3	1	-	23	-	1	2	-	11	E.J.Jackett(2C) P.W.Lawrie(D) Penny(T) T.B.Hogarth(T) Middleton(T) Hopkins(T) McIntyre(T)
32	Mar	6	Devonport Albion	A	Lost	-	-	-	-	0	1	1	1	-	12	
33		13	HARLEQUINS	H	Lost	-	1	2*	1	13	4	-	-	-	20	E.J.Jackett(D) H.S.B.Lawrie(T,2P)
34		20	STONEYGATE (MCC4)	H	Won	3	3	-	-	24	-	-	-	1	3	H.S.B.Lawrie(2C) P.W.Lawrie(2T) Watson(3T) Gimson(T,C)
35		27	STRATFORD-UPON-AVON (MCCSF)	H	Won	1	4	-	-	17	1	1	-	-	8	K.B.Wood(T) Watson(T) G.W.Wood(T) Penny(T) Greasley(T) Gimson(C)
36	Apr	3	Coventry (MCCF)	A	Won	1	1	-	-	8	-	1	-	-	3	P.W.Lawrie(2T) Gimson(C)
37		10	Cardiff	A	Drew	1	1	-	-	8	1	1	-	-	8	P.W.Lawrie(T) Gimson(T,C)
38		12	Llanelli	A	Lost	-	1	-	-	3	1	2	-	-	11	Smith(T)
39		13	Bristol	A	Won	-	1	-	-	3	-	-	-	-	0	P.W.Lawrie(T)
40		17	LONDON WELSH	H	Won	2	-	-	-	10	-	-	-	-	0	G.W.Wood(T) Greasley(T) Gimson(2C)
41		24	NORTHAMPTON	H	Won	2	2	-	-	16	-	-	-	-	0	P.W.Lawrie(T) E.J.Jackett(C) G.W.Wood(T) Hobbs(T) Greasley(T) Russell(C)

INDIVIDUAL APPEARANCES 1908-1909

NAME	1	2	3	4	5	6	7	8	9	10	11	12	13	14	15	16	17	18	19	20	21	22	23	24	25	26	27	28	29	30	31	32	33	34	35	36	37	38	39	40	41	42	43	44	45	46	TOTAL	T	PTS
C.Birch	FB	FB	FB	-	FB	FB	-	-	-	-	-	FB	-	-	-	-	FB	FB	-	-	-	-	-	-	-	-	-	-	-	-	-	-	-	-	-	-	-	-	-	-	-	-	-	-	-	-	8	-	-
John Jackett	-	-	-	-	-	-	FB	FB	FB	-	FB	-	FB	FB	FB	FB	-	-	FB	FH	FB	C	W	-	-	FB	-	FB	-	FB	FB	FB	FB	-	-	FB	C	-	C	C	C	-	-	-	-	-	24	-	23
W.Kitchen	-	-	-	-	-	-	-	-	-	-	-	-	-	-	-	-	-	-	-	-	-	FB	FB	FB	FB	-	-	-	-	-	-	-	-	-	FB	-	-	-	-	-	-	-	-	-	-	-	5	-	-
Dan Ellwood	-	-	-	-	-	-	-	-	-	-	-	-	-	-	-	-	-	-	-	-	-	-	-	-	-	-	-	-	-	-	-	-	-	-	-	-	FB	FB	FB	FB	FB	-	-	-	-	-	5	-	-
Percy Lawrie	W	W	W	W	W	W	W	W	W	W	W	W	W	W	W	W	W	W	C	W	W	W	W	W	W	-	W	W	W	W	C	W	W	W	-	W	W	W	W	W	W	-	-	-	-	-	39	28	92
Dixie Smith	-	W	W	FB	W	C	C	C	C	FB	C	C	C	C	C	C	C	C	FH	C	C	-	C	C	C	C	FB	C	W	C	-	C	W	C	C	C	C	C	C	-	-	-	-	-	-	-	36	9	27
Harry Lawrie	-	-	-	-	-	-	-	W	W	W	W	W	W	W	W	W	-	FH	-	FB	FH	-	-	C	C	W	FH	W	FB	FH	-	W	C	FB	-	-	-	-	-	-	-	-	-	-	-	-	22	8	69
Arthur McIntyre	-	-	-	-	-	-	-	-	-	-	-	-	-	-	-	-	-	W	W	-	-	-	-	F	-	-	F	F	F	F	F	F	F	W	W	F	F	-	F	F	-	-	-	-	-	-	16	1	3
J.Lewis	-	-	-	-	-	-	-	-	-	-	-	-	-	-	-	-	-	-	W	W	-	W	-	W	W	W	-	-	-	-	-	-	-	-	-	-	-	-	-	-	-	-	-	-	-	-	6	2	6
A.D.Heard	-	-	-	-	-	-	-	-	-	-	-	-	-	-	-	-	-	-	-	-	-	-	-	-	-	-	W	-	-	-	-	-	-	-	-	-	W	W	W	-	-	-	-	-	-	-	4	1	3
H.K.Pearce	-	-	-	-	-	-	-	-	-	-	-	-	-	-	-	-	-	-	-	-	-	-	-	-	-	-	-	-	-	W	W	-	-	-	-	-	-	C	-	-	-	-	-	-	-	-	3	-	-
Jamie Watson	C	C	C	C	C	FH	FH	FH	FH	FH	FH	FH	FH	FH	FH	FH	FH	-	-	-	-	-	-	-	FH	FH	-	FH	FH	-	FH	FH	FH	FH	FH	FH	FH	FH	FH	-	FH	-	-	-	-	-	31	8	24
Ken Wood	C	C	C	C	C	C	C	C	C	C	C	C	C	C	C	C	-	C	C	C	C	C	C	-	-	-	C	C	C	C	C	-	-	C	C	C	-	-	-	-	-	-	-	-	-	-	30	9	35
Ernest Booth	-	-	-	-	-	-	-	-	-	-	-	-	-	-	-	-	-	-	-	-	-	-	-	-	-	-	C	-	C	-	W	C	C	-	-	-	-	-	-	-	-	-	-	-	-	-	5	-	-
Tim' Taylor	-	-	FH	FH	FH	W	-	-	-	-	-	-	-	-	-	-	-	-	-	-	-	-	-	-	-	-	-	-	-	-	-	-	-	-	-	-	-	-	-	-	-	-	-	-	-	-	4	2	6
Pedlar' Wood	SH	SH	SH	SH	SH	SH	SH	SH	SH	SH	SH	SH	SH	SH	SH	SH	SH	SH	SH	SH	SH	SH	SH	SH	SH	SH	SH	SH	SH	SH	SH	SH	SH	SH	SH	SH	SH	SH	SH	SH	SH	-	-	-	-	-	41	13	57
Chris Gimson	F	-	F	-	-	-	-	-	-	-	-	-	-	-	-	-	-	-	F	F	F	-	-	-	-	-	-	-	F	-	-	-	-	F	F	W	F	F	-	F	-	-	-	-	-	-	12	2	18
Alf Goodrich	F	F	F	-	F	F	F	F	F	F	F	F	F	F	F	F	F	-	-	-	-	-	-	-	F	F	F	F	F	F	-	F	F	F	F	F	-	F	-	-	-	-	-	-	-	-	28	1	3
W.Hall	F	-	-	F	F	-	-	-	-	-	-	-	-	-	-	-	-	-	-	-	-	-	-	-	-	-	-	-	-	-	-	-	-	-	-	-	-	-	-	-	-	-	-	-	-	-	3	-	-
Gil Hopkins	F	F	-	F	-	-	-	-	-	F	F	F	-	-	-	F	F	-	F	-	F	-	-	F	F	F	-	-	F	F	F	F	F	F	F	F	F	-	F	F	F	-	-	-	-	-	25	4	12
A.J.Hobbs	F	F	F	F	F	F	F	F	F	F	F	F	F	F	F	F	F	F	-	F	F	F	F	F	F	F	-	-	-	-	-	-	-	F	F	F	F	F	F	F	F	-	-	-	-	-	33	5	15
A.Mills	F	F	F	F	-	F	F	-	F	F	F	F	F	-	F	F	F	F	F	F	F	F	F	F	F	F	F	F	-	F	F	F	F	F	F	F	-	-	F	-	-	-	-	-	-	-	33	1	3
Sid Penny	F	F	F	F	F	F	F	F	F	F	F	F	F	F	F	F	-	F	F	F	F	F	F	-	F	F	F	F	F	F	F	F	F	F	F	F	F	F	-	F	F	-	-	-	-	-	38	2	6
R.C.Watchorn	F	F	-	F	F	-	-	F	-	-	-	-	-	-	-	-	-	-	-	-	-	-	-	-	-	-	-	-	-	-	-	-	-	-	-	-	-	-	-	-	-	-	-	-	-	-	5	-	-
George Greasley	-	F	F	F	F	F	F	-	-	-	-	-	-	-	-	-	F	F	F	F	F	-	F	F	F	F	F	F	F	F	F	F	F	F	F	F	F	-	F	F	F	-	-	-	-	-	29	5	15
Tom Hogarth	-	F	-	-	-	F	-	F	F	-	-	-	F	F	F	F	-	F	F	F	F	F	F	-	F	F	F	F	F	F	-	-	-	F	F	F	F	F	F	F	F	-	-	-	-	-	28	1	3
W.H.Bingham	-	-	F	-	F	-	-	-	-	-	-	-	-	-	-	-	F	-	-	-	-	-	-	-	-	-	-	-	-	-	-	-	-	-	-	-	-	-	-	-	-	-	-	-	-	-	3	-	-
J.Hubbard	-	-	F	F	F	F	F	F	F	F	-	F	F	F	F	F	-	-	-	-	-	-	-	F	-	-	-	-	-	-	-	-	-	-	-	-	-	-	-	-	-	-	-	-	-	-	14	2	6
Lionel Kewney	-	-	-	-	-	F	F	-	F	-	F	-	-	-	F	-	-	F	-	F	-	-	-	-	-	-	F	-	-	-	-	-	-	-	-	-	-	F	F	-	F	-	-	-	-	-	11	-	-
George Yeld	-	-	-	-	-	-	F	F	F	F	F	F	F	-	-	-	-	-	-	-	-	-	-	-	-	-	-	-	-	-	-	-	-	-	-	-	-	-	-	-	-	-	-	-	-	-	7	-	10
G.Middleton	-	-	-	-	-	-	-	-	-	-	-	F	-	F	-	F	F	F	F	-	F	F	F	F	F	-	F	-	F	F	F	F	F	F	-	-	-	-	-	-	-	-	-	-	-	-	18	1	3
Richard Jackett	-	-	-	-	-	-	-	-	-	-	-	-	F	F	F	-	-	-	-	-	-	-	-	-	-	-	F	F	-	-	-	-	-	-	-	-	-	-	-	-	-	-	-	-	-	-	5	-	-
Tosh' Russell	-	-	-	-	-	-	-	-	-	-	-	-	-	-	-	-	-	-	-	F	W	-	-	-	-	-	-	-	-	-	-	-	-	-	-	-	-	-	-	-	F	-	-	-	-	-	3	-	2
James Duthie	-	-	-	-	-	-	-	-	-	-	-	-	-	-	-	-	-	-	-	-	-	F	F	-	-	-	-	-	-	-	-	-	-	-	-	-	F	F	-	-	-	-	-	-	-	-	4	-	-
Jimmy Burdett	-	-	-	-	-	-	-	-	-	-	-	-	-	-	-	-	-	-	-	-	-	-	-	F	-	-	-	-	-	-	F	F	F	-	-	-	-	F	F	F	F	-	-	-	-	-	8	-	-

2 games: Dudley Atkins F(10,11), Alfred Brice FH(22,23), M.Flude C(26)W(40)[1T-3], A.Hogarth F(22,23), Lionel Kirk W(1)FH(2)[2T-16], Maurice Mann W(7)C(17)[1T-3], A.Simpson F(17,18)

1 game: W.A.Dalby F(19), W.Dann F(22), R.J.C.Ferguson C(10)[2T-6], J.Fitzgerald FH(1), E.L.Goodman W(41), C.Green F(8), James Hargrave FH(40), Eddie Morgan F(14), J.W.Morton W(4), S.C.Roberts W(17)[1T-3], George Shingler W(35), Sgt.Thomas F(26), J.Wilkinson C(40), W.C.Wilson C(41), J.Woolerton FH(24)

LEICESTER FOOTBALL CLUB 1908-09

Back: R.F. Russell, J.C. Burdett, Lt.W.C. Wilson, K.B. Wood, H.S.B. Lawrie, A. Goodrich, G. Middleton, A. Mills.

Middle: T.H. Crumbie (Hon.Sec), T.B. Hogarth, A.J. Hobbs, S.H. Penny, J.R. Watson (Capt), W.G. Hopkins, E.L. Goodman, F. St.Clair Pain (Hon.Tres), J. Collier (President).

Front: P.W. Lawrie, E.J. Jackett, G. Greasley, G.W. Wood, A.L. Kewney, L.D. Ellwood.

Inset: J.W.D. Smith, Lt.A.S. McIntyre.

1909-1910

NO	DATE		OPPONENTS	V	RES	FOR					AGAINST					SCORERS
						G	T	D	P	PTS	G	T	D	P	PTS	
1	Sep	4	STRATFORD-UPON-AVON	H	Won	5	6	-	-	43	-	-	-	-	0	P.W.Lawrie(2T) K.B.Wood(3T) Smith(T) Heard(T) Watson(T) G.W.Wood(T) Hobbs(T) H.S.B.Lawrie(5C) Hopkins(T)
2		11	HARTLEPOOL ROVERS	H	Won	4	2	-	1	29	-	1	-	-	3	P.W.Lawrie(3T) Heard(2T) G.W.Wood(T) Gimson(4C,P)
3		18	NEATH	H	Won	2	1	-	-	13	1	-	-	-	5	K.B.Wood(T) Tarr(T) Heard(T) H.S.B.Lawrie(2C)
4		25	MANCHESTER	H	Won	2	3	-	1	22	1	-	-	-	5	P.W.Lawrie(T) Heard(2T) G.W.Wood(T) Hobbs(T) H.S.B.Lawrie(2C,P)
5	Oct	2	HEADINGLEY	H	Won	4	4	-	-	32	-	2	-	-	6	P.W.Lawrie(4T) Watson(T) G.W.Wood(T) Hobbs(T) H.S.B.Lawrie(T,4C)
6		9	BRISTOL	H	Won	-	3	-	1	12	1	1	-	-	8	P.W.Lawrie(T) H.S.B.Lawrie(P)
7		16	NORTHAMPTON	H	Lost	-	-	-	1	3	1	2	-	-	11	H.S.B.Lawrie(P)
8		23	Richmond	A	Lost	-	-	-	-	0	-	1	-	-	3	
9		30	Devonport Albion	A	Lost	-	1	-	-	3	1	-	-	-	5	P.W.Lawrie(T)
10	Nov	6	CARDIFF	H	Drew	-	1	-	-	3	-	1	-	-	3	Flude(T)
11		13	SWANSEA	H	Drew	-	-	-	-	0	-	-	-	-	0	
12		20	Newport	A	Lost	-	1	-	-	3	4	1	-	-	23	P.W.Lawrie(T)
13		27	Birkenhead Park	A	Won	-	1	-	-	3	-	-	-	-	0	Smith(T)
14	Dec	4	Stratford-upon-Avon	A	Won	1	-	-	-	5	-	-	-	-	0	Taylor(T) H.S.B.Lawrie(C)
15		11	Northampton	A	Won	1	-	1*	-	8	-	1	-	-	3	H.S.B.Lawrie(C,M) K.B.Wood(T)
16		18	COVENTRY	H	Won	1	2	-	-	11	-	-	-	-	0	Heard(T) K.B.Wood(T) Dickens(T) H.S.B.Lawrie(C)
17		24	CINDERFORD	H	Won	1	4	-	-	17	-	2	-	-	6	Dickens(T) Heard(3T) G.W.Wood(T) Gimson(C)
18		27	BIRKENHEAD PARK	H	Won	1	3	-	-	14	-	1	-	1	6	Smith(T) Watson(2T) H.S.B.Lawrie(C) Greasley(T)
19		28	PENARTH	H	Won	-	4	-	-	12	-	2	-	-	6	E.J.Jackett(T) G.W.Wood(2T) Allen(T)
20		29	BARBARIANS	H	Drew	-	3	-	-	9	-	3	-	-	9	G.W.Wood(T) Greasley(T) Burdett(T)
21		31	Headingley	A	Won	1	4	-	-	17	-	1	-	-	3	Dickens(T) Wilson(T) G.W.Wood(T) Gimson(C) Greasley(2T)
22	Jan	1	Hartlepool Rovers	A	Won	2	-	-	1	13	1	1	-	-	8	E.J.Jackett(2C,P) Barrow(T) Hargrave(T)
23		8	London Welsh	A	Won	2	2	-	-	16	-	1	-	1	6	Watson(T) Dickens(T) Hargrave(T) G.W.Wood(T) H.S.B.Lawrie(2C)
24		15	GLOUCESTER	H	Drew	-	-	-	-	0	-	-	-	-	0	
		22	Moseley	A		Cancelled Frost										
		29	BEDFORD	H		Cancelled Frost										
25	Feb	5	Coventry	A	Won	-	1	-	-	3	-	-	-	-	0	P.W.Lawrie(T)
26		12	Swansea	A	Lost	-	-	-	-	0	1	-	1	-	9	
27		14	Neath	A	Lost	-	-	-	-	0	1	2	-	-	11	
28		19	NEWPORT	H	Lost	1	-	-	-	5	-	2	-	-	6	Dickens(T) H.S.B.Lawrie(C)
29		26	MOSELEY	H	Won	2	2	-	-	16	-	-	-	-	0	E.J.Jackett(2C) P.W.Lawrie(2T) Watson(T) Taylor(T)
30	Mar	5	DEVONPORT ALBION	H	Lost	-	-	-	1	3	1	1	-	-	8	H.S.B.Lawrie(P)
31		9	Moseley	A	Won	1	5	-	-	20	-	-	-	-	0	E.J.Jackett(C) Heard(T) Watson(2T) P.W.Lawrie(T) Penny(T) Hobbs(T)
32		12	Harlequins	A	Won	-	1	-	-	3	-	-	-	-	0	P.W.Lawrie(T)
33		19	NUNEATON (MCC4)	H	Won	4	5	-	-	35	1	-	-	-	5	E.J.Jackett(2C) Scott(T) Dickens(3T) Taylor(3T) G.W.Wood(2T) H.S.B.Lawrie(2C)
34		26	Burton-on-Trent (MCCSF)	A	Won	5	3	-	-	34	1	-	-	1	8	P.W.Lawrie(T) K.B.Wood(T) Taylor(T) G.W.Wood(2T) Hobbs(T) H.S.B.Lawrie(5C) Burdett(T) Hogarth(T)
35		28	Cardiff	A	Drew	2	-	-	-	10	2	-	-	-	10	E.J.Jackett(2C) K.B.Wood(2T)
36		29	Bristol	A	Lost	1	-	-	-	5	3	-	-	-	15	P.W.Lawrie(T) E.J.Jackett(C)
37	Apr	2	Coventry (MCCF)	A	Won	1	-	1*	-	8	-	1	-	1	6	E.J.Jackett(C,M) G.W.Wood(T)
38		9	LONDON WELSH	H	Won	1	2	-	-	11	-	1	-	-	3	E.J.Jackett(C) Smith(T) Watson(T) Cross(T)
39		16	Gloucester	A	Lost	-	-	-	-	0	1	3	-	-	14	

INDIVIDUAL APPEARANCES 1909-1910

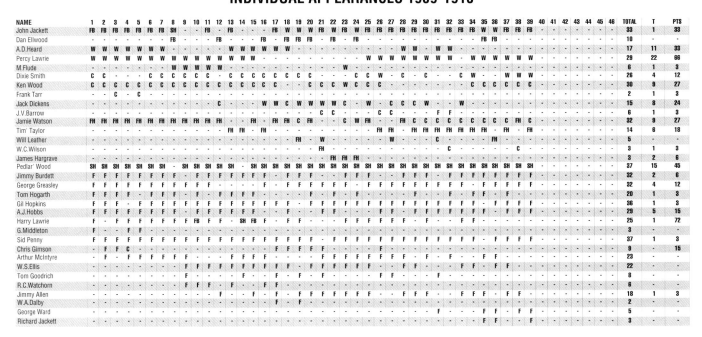

NAME	TOTAL	T	PTS
John Jackett	33	1	33
Dan Ellwood	10	-	-
A.D.Heard	17	11	33
Percy Lawrie	29	22	66
M.Flude	6	1	3
Dixie Smith	26	4	12
Ken Wood	30	9	27
Frank Tarr	2	1	3
Jack Dickens	15	8	24
J.V.Barrow	6	1	3
Jamie Watson	32	9	27
Tim Taylor	14	6	18
Will Leather	5	-	-
W.C.Wilson	3	1	3
James Hargrave	3	2	6
Pedlar Wood	37	15	45
Jimmy Burdett	32	2	6
George Greasley	32	4	12
Tom Hogarth	20	1	3
Gil Hopkins	36	1	3
A.J.Hobbs	29	5	15
Harry Lawrie	25	1	72
G.Middleton	3	-	-
Sid Penny	37	1	3
Chris Gimson	9	-	15
Arthur McIntyre	23	-	-
W.S.Ellis	22	-	-
Tom Goodrich	8	-	-
R.C.Watchorn	6	-	-
Jimmy Allen	18	1	3
W.A.Dalby	2	-	-
George Ward	5	-	-
Richard Jackett	3	-	-

1 game: Charlie Cross F(38)[1T-3], -.Dunkley FB(14), W.H.Grier F(27), F.Morris F(31), W.L.Oldham F(39), H.W.Palfreyman FB(9), A.F.Scott W(33)[1T-3]

NO	DATE		OPPONENTS	V	RES	FOR					AGAINST					SCORERS
						G	T	D	P	PTS	G	T	D	P	PTS	
1	Sep	3	HARTLEPOOL ROVERS	H	Won	2	4	1*	-	25	-	-	-	-	0	P.W.Lawrie(3T) Smith(T) Wood(T) Allen(T) H.S.B.Lawrie(2C,M)
2		10	PLYMOUTH	H	Won	1	1	-	-	8	-	-	1	-	4	P.W.Lawrie(2T) H.S.B.Lawrie(C)
3		17	NEATH	H	Won	-	-	1*	-	3	-	-	-	-	0	H.S.B.Lawrie(M)
4		24	LLANELLI	H	Lost	1	1	1	-	12	2	2	-	-	16	F.M.Taylor(D) Wood(T) H.S.B.Lawrie(C) Allen(T)
5	Oct	1	DEVONPORT ALBION	H	Won	-	3	-	-	9	-	-	-	2	6	P.W.Lawrie(T) Watson(T) H.S.B.Lawrie(T)
6		6	Birkenhead Park	A	Won	2	7	-	1	34	-	2	-	-	6	P.W.Lawrie(2T,C,P) Watson(T) Barrow(2T) Wood(2T,C) R.Jackett(2T)
7		8	BRISTOL	H	Won	1	3	-	2	20	1	1	-	-	8	P.W.Lawrie(T) Hargrave(2T) F.M.Taylor(T) H.S.B.Lawrie(C,2P)
8		15	Northampton	A	Won	1	2	-	1	14	-	1	-	-	3	E.J.Jackett(C,P) P.W.Lawrie(T) Hargrave(T) T.B.Hogarth(T)
9		22	NEWPORT	H	Lost	-	-	-	2	6	1	-	-	1	8	E.J.Jackett(2P)
10		29	CARDIFF	H	Lost	-	-	-	-	0	-	2	-	-	6	
11	Nov	5	CINDERFORD	H	Drew	-	1	-	-	3	-	1	-	-	3	P.W.Lawrie(T)
12		12	Swansea	A	Lost	1	-	-	-	5	-	2	-	-	6	E.J.Jackett(C) Burdett(T)
13		14	Neath	A	Lost	-	1	-	-	3	3	1	-	-	18	Kilby(T)
14		19	COVENTRY	H	Won	2	3	-	2	25	-	1	-	-	3	P.W.Lawrie(T) Watson(T) F.M.Taylor(T) Wood(T) Burdett(T) H.S.B.Lawrie(2C,2P)
15		26	LONDON WELSH	H	Won	1	6	-	2	29	-	1	1	-	7	P.W.Lawrie(T,C,P) Watson(T) Hargrave(T) F.M.Taylor(T) Wood(T) H.S.B.Lawrie(P) Allen(2T)
16	Dec	3	Bedford	A	Won	-	2	-	-	6	-	-	-	1	3	P.W.Lawrie(T) Burdett(T)
17		10	NORTHAMPTON	H	Drew	-	-	-	-	0	-	-	-	-	0	
18		17	Coventry	A	Drew	-	1	-	-	3	-	-	-	1	3	P.W.Lawrie(T)
19		24	HEADINGLEY	H	Won	2	3	-	-	19	1	1	-	-	8	Wilkinson(T) Watson(T) P.W.Lawrie(T) F.M.Taylor(T) Wood(T) Gimson(2C)
20		26	BIRKENHEAD PARK	H	Won	2	4	-	1	25	1	-	-	-	5	P.W.Lawrie(3T,C,P) Watson(T) Hopkins(T) Gimson(C) Atterbury(T)
21		27	KENDAL	H	Won	3	5	-	1	33	-	-	-	-	0	Wilkinson(2C,P) Pearce(T) Tarr(T) P.W.Lawrie(T,C) F.M.Taylor(T) T.B.Hogarth(T) Hobbs(T) Cross(T) Middleton(T)
22		28	BARBARIANS	H	Won	4	3	-	-	29	-	1	-	-	3	P.W.Lawrie(3T,C) Tarr(T) Wood(T) R.Jackett(T) Gimson(3C) Greasley(T)
23		30	Headingley	A	Lost	-	-	1	-	4	-	1	1	-	7	P.W.Lawrie(D)
24		31	Hartlepool Rovers	A	Lost	-	-	1	1	7	-	2	-	1	9	P.W.Lawrie(P) Pearce(D)
25	Jan	2	Manchester	A	Won	-	4	-	-	12	-	2	-	-	6	P.W.Lawrie(T) F.M.Taylor(2T) Wood(T)
26		7	London Welsh	A	Won	-	3	-	-	9	1	1	-	-	8	Watson(T) Pearce(T) Gimson(T)
27		14	GLOUCESTER	H	Won	-	1	-	-	3	-	-	-	-	0	Greasley(T)
28		21	Moseley	A	Won	-	7	-	-	21	-	1	-	-	3	Ansell(2T) Hargrave(T) F.M.Taylor(2T) Wood(T) Hobbs(T)
29		28	MOSELEY	H	Won	-	6	-	1	21	1	-	-	-	5	E.J.Jackett(2T) Bream(P) Hargrave(T) Fisher(T) H.S.B.Lawrie(T) Greasley(T)
30	Feb	4	Blackheath	A	Drew	-	3	-	-	9	1	-	1	-	9	Hargrave(T) Hopkins(T) Allen(T)
31		11	SWANSEA	H	Lost	-	-	-	-	0	-	1	-	-	3	
32		18	Newport	A	Lost	-	1	-	-	3	1	3	-	-	14	Gimson(T)
33		25	RICHMOND	H	Won	3	6	-	-	33	-	-	-	-	0	P.W.Lawrie(2T) Watson(T) Hargrave(T) F.M.Taylor(T) Burdett(T) Gimson(3C) Allen(2T) H.S.B.Lawrie(T)
34	Mar	4	Devonport Albion	A	Lost	-	-	-	-	0	-	3	-	-	9	
35		6	Plymouth	A	Drew	-	2	-	-	6	-	2	-	-	6	Allen(T) H.S.B.Lawrie(T)
36		11	HARLEQUINS	H	Won	1	2	-	-	11	1	1	-	-	8	F.M.Taylor(T) Wood(T) Gimson(C) Hobbs(T)
37		18	Coventry (MCC4)	A	Lost	-	1	-	1	6	3	2	-	-	21	Pearce(T) H.S.B.Lawrie(P)
38		25	NOTTINGHAM	H	Won	5	8	-	-	49	-	-	-	-	0	Hargrave(2T) Bream(T) Watson(T) P.W.Lawrie(3T) F.M.Taylor(T) Wood(3T) Burdett(T) Gimson(5C) Hobbs(T)
39	Apr	8	Cardiff	A	Lost	-	1	-	-	3	2	2	-	-	16	F.M.Taylor(T)
40		15	Gloucester	A	Drew	1	-	-	-	5	1	-	-	-	5	P.W.Lawrie(T) H.S.B.Lawrie(C)
41		17	Llanelli	A	Lost	-	1	-	-	3	-	1	1*	-	6	Wood(T)
42		18	Bristol	A	Won	4	1	-	-	23	1	-	-	-	5	P.W.Lawrie(T,C) Thomas(2T) F.M.Taylor(T) H.S.B.Lawrie(2C) Gimson(T,C)

INDIVIDUAL APPEARANCES 1910-1911

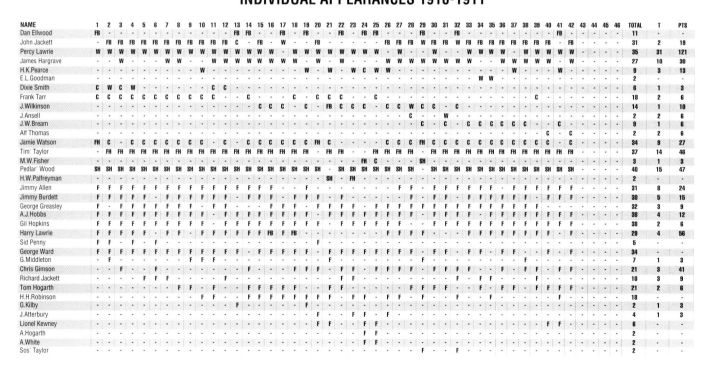

NAME	1	2	3	4	5	6	7	8	9	10	11	12	13	14	15	16	17	18	19	20	21	22	23	24	25	26	27	28	29	30	31	32	33	34	35	36	37	38	39	40	41	42	43	44	45	46	TOTAL	T	PTS
Dan Ellwood	FB	-	-	-	-	-	-	-	-	-	-	FB	FB	-	FB	-	-	FB	-	FB	-	-	FB	-	FB	-	-	-	-	-	FB	-	-	FB	-	-	-	-	-	-	FB	-	-	-	-	-	11	-	-
John Jackett	-	FB	FB	FB	FB	FB	FB	FB	FB	FB	FB	-	C	-	FB	-	W	-	FB	-	-	-	-	-	-	FB	FB	FB	FB	-	FB	FB	W	FB	FB	FB	FB	FB	-	FB	-	FB	-	-	-	-	31	2	19
Percy Lawrie	W	W	W	W	W	W	W	W	W	W	W	W	W	W	W	W	-	W	W	W	W	W	W	W	W	W	-	-	W	-	-	W	-	-	W	W	W	-	W	W	W	W	-	-	-	-	35	31	121
James Hargrave	-	-	W	-	-	W	W	-	W	W	W	W	W	W	W	W	-	-	-	W	-	W	-	-	W	-	-	W	W	W	W	W	W	W	W	W	-	W	W	-	-	-	-	-	-	-	27	10	30
H.K.Pearce	-	-	-	-	-	-	-	-	-	W	-	-	-	-	-	-	-	-	W	-	W	-	W	C	W	W	-	-	-	-	-	-	-	-	-	-	W	-	-	W	-	-	-	-	-	-	9	3	13
E.L.Goodman	-	-	-	-	-	-	-	-	-	-	-	-	-	-	-	-	-	-	-	-	-	-	-	-	-	-	-	-	-	-	-	-	W	W	-	-	-	-	-	-	-	-	-	-	-	-	2	-	-
Dixie Smith	C	W	C	W	-	-	-	-	-	C	C	-	-	-	-	-	-	-	-	-	-	-	-	-	-	-	-	-	-	-	-	-	-	-	-	-	-	-	-	-	-	-	-	-	-	-	6	1	3
Frank Tarr	C	C	C	C	C	C	C	C	C	C	C	-	-	C	-	-	C	-	C	C	C	C	-	C	-	-	-	-	-	-	-	-	C	-	-	-	-	-	-	-	-	-	-	-	-	-	18	2	6
J.Wilkinson	-	-	-	-	-	-	-	-	-	-	-	-	C	C	C	-	C	-	FB	C	C	C	-	C	C	W	C	C	-	C	-	-	-	-	-	-	-	-	-	-	-	-	-	-	-	-	14	1	10
J.Ansell	-	-	-	-	-	-	-	-	-	-	-	-	-	-	-	-	-	-	-	-	-	-	-	-	-	-	C	-	W	-	-	-	-	-	-	-	-	-	-	-	-	-	-	-	-	-	2	2	6
J.W.Bream	-	-	-	-	-	-	-	-	-	-	-	-	-	-	-	-	-	-	-	-	-	-	C	-	C	-	C	C	C	C	-	C	-	-	-	-	-	-	-	-	-	-	-	-	-	-	9	1	6
Alf Thomas	-	-	-	-	-	-	-	-	-	-	-	-	-	-	-	-	-	-	-	-	-	-	-	-	-	-	-	-	-	-	-	-	-	-	-	-	-	-	C	-	C	-	-	-	-	-	2	2	6
Jamie Watson	FH	C	-	C	C	C	C	C	C	C	-	C	-	C	C	C	C	C	C	FH	C	-	-	C	C	C	FH	-	C	C	C	C	C	C	C	C	C	C	-	C	-	-	-	-	-	-	34	9	27
Tim' Taylor	-	FH	FH	FH	FH	FH	FH	FH	FH	FH	FH	FH	FH	FH	FH	FH	FH	-	FH	FH	-	FH	FH	-	FH	FH	FH	FH	-	FH	FH	FH	FH	FH	FH	FH	FH	FH	FH	FH	-	-	-	-	-	-	37	14	46
M.W.Fisher	-	-	-	-	-	-	-	-	-	-	-	-	-	-	-	-	-	-	-	-	-	FH	C	-	-	-	-	-	SH	-	-	-	-	-	-	-	-	-	-	-	-	-	-	-	-	-	3	1	3
Pedlar' Wood	SH	SH	SH	SH	SH	SH	SH	SH	SH	SH	SH	SH	SH	SH	SH	SH	SH	-	SH	-	SH	SH	SH	SH	SH	SH	-	SH	SH	SH	SH	SH	SH	SH	SH	SH	SH	SH	SH	SH	-	-	-	-	-	-	40	15	47
H.W.Palfreyman	-	-	-	-	-	-	-	-	-	-	-	-	-	-	-	-	-	-	-	SH	-	FH	-	-	-	-	-	-	-	-	-	-	-	-	-	-	-	-	-	-	-	-	-	-	-	-	2	-	-
Jimmy Allen	F	-	F	F	F	F	F	F	F	F	F	F	F	F	F	F	F	-	F	-	-	-	-	-	-	-	-	-	F	F	-	-	F	-	F	F	F	F	-	F	F	F	F	F	-	-	31	8	24
Jimmy Burdett	F	F	F	F	F	-	F	-	F	-	F	F	F	F	F	-	F	F	-	F	-	F	-	-	F	-	F	F	-	-	F	-	F	-	-	F	-	F	F	-	F	F	F	-	-	-	30	5	15
George Greasley	F	-	F	F	F	F	F	F	-	F	-	F	-	-	-	F	F	-	F	F	-	F	F	F	F	-	-	F	F	F	F	F	F	F	F	-	F	F	F	-	-	-	-	-	-	-	32	3	9
A.J.Hobbs	F	F	F	F	F	F	-	F	F	-	F	F	-	F	F	F	F	F	-	F	-	F	F	F	F	F	-	-	F	F	F	-	F	F	F	F	F	F	F	F	-	-	-	-	-	-	38	4	12
Gil Hopkins	F	F	F	F	F	F	F	F	-	F	F	-	-	F	F	F	F	F	F	F	-	F	F	-	-	F	-	F	F	F	F	-	F	F	F	F	F	F	F	F	-	F	-	-	-	-	38	2	6
Harry Lawrie	F	F	F	F	-	F	-	F	F	-	-	F	F	F	F	FB	F	FB	-	-	-	-	-	-	F	F	F	-	-	-	F	F	F	F	-	F	F	F	F	F	F	-	-	-	-	-	29	4	56
Sid Penny	F	F	-	F	-	F	-	F	-	-	-	-	-	-	-	-	-	-	F	-	-	-	-	-	-	-	-	-	-	-	-	-	-	-	-	-	-	-	-	-	-	-	-	-	-	-	5	-	-
George Ward	F	F	F	F	F	F	F	F	F	F	F	F	F	F	F	F	-	F	-	F	-	F	F	F	F	F	F	F	-	F	F	F	F	F	-	-	F	-	F	F	-	-	-	-	-	-	34	-	-
G.Middleton	-	F	-	-	-	-	-	-	-	F	F	F	F	-	-	-	-	-	-	F	-	-	-	F	-	-	-	-	-	-	-	-	-	-	-	-	-	-	-	-	-	-	-	-	-	-	7	1	3
Chris Gimson	-	-	F	-	F	-	-	-	-	-	-	-	-	F	F	-	F	-	F	F	F	F	-	F	F	F	-	F	F	F	F	F	F	F	F	F	F	F	F	F	-	-	-	-	-	-	21	3	41
Richard Jackett	-	-	-	F	F	F	F	-	-	-	-	-	F	-	-	-	-	-	-	F	-	-	F	F	-	-	-	-	-	-	-	-	-	F	-	-	-	-	-	-	-	-	-	-	-	-	10	3	9
Tom Hogarth	-	-	F	F	F	-	-	-	-	-	F	-	F	F	F	F	F	-	F	F	-	F	-	F	F	F	-	F	-	F	F	F	F	F	F	-	F	F	F	F	-	-	-	-	-	-	21	2	6
H.H.Robinson	-	-	-	-	-	-	-	-	-	F	F	-	-	F	F	F	F	F	-	-	-	-	F	F	-	F	-	F	-	F	F	F	-	F	-	F	-	F	F	-	-	-	-	-	-	-	18	-	-
G.Kilby	-	-	-	-	-	-	-	-	-	-	-	F	F	-	-	-	-	-	-	-	-	-	-	-	-	-	-	-	-	-	-	-	-	-	-	-	-	-	-	-	-	-	-	-	-	-	2	1	3
J.Atterbury	-	-	-	-	-	-	-	-	-	-	-	-	-	-	-	-	-	-	-	F	-	-	F	-	-	F	F	-	-	-	-	-	-	-	-	-	-	-	-	-	-	-	-	-	-	-	4	1	3
Lionel Kewney	-	-	-	-	-	-	-	-	-	-	-	-	-	-	-	-	-	-	-	-	F	F	-	F	F	F	-	-	-	-	-	-	-	-	-	-	F	F	-	-	-	-	-	-	-	-	6	-	-
A.Hogarth	-	-	-	-	-	-	-	-	-	-	-	-	-	-	-	-	-	-	-	-	-	-	-	-	F	F	-	-	-	-	-	-	-	-	-	-	-	-	-	-	-	-	-	-	-	-	2	-	-
A.White	-	-	-	-	-	-	-	-	-	-	-	-	-	-	-	-	-	-	-	-	-	-	-	-	F	F	-	-	-	-	-	-	-	-	-	-	-	-	-	-	-	-	-	-	-	-	2	-	-
Sos' Taylor	-	-	-	-	-	-	-	-	-	-	-	-	-	-	-	-	-	-	-	-	-	-	-	-	-	-	-	-	-	-	-	-	-	-	-	F	-	-	-	-	-	-	-	-	-	-	2	-	-

1 game: J.V.Barrow W(6)[2T-6], Barrie Bennetts C(23), H.Britten W(9), L.S.Burton F(29), Charlie Cross F(21)[1T-3], M.Flude W(5), Arthur Jones C(20), W.Kitchen FB(23), R.Leggitt F(13), J.Lewis W(24), Arthur McIntyre F(17), T.E.Maddocks C(41), W.G.Rapsey Q(13), Frank Robinson F(13), I.Spicer F(29), W.C.Wilson W(1)

NO	DATE		OPPONENTS	V	RES	FOR					AGAINST					SCORERS
						G	T	D	P	PTS	G	T	D	P	PTS	
1	Sep	2	BEDFORD	H	Won	2	4	-	-	22	-	1	-	-	3	P.W.Lawrie(T) J.R.Watson(T) Bream(2C) O.J.Hargrave(2T) F.M.Taylor(T) Wood(T)
2		9	PLYMOUTH	H	Won	2	-	-	1	13	-	-	1	-	4	Bream(2C,P) Wood(T) Allen(T)
3		16	NEATH	H	Drew	-	1	-	-	3	-	1	-	-	3	O.J.Hargrave(T)
4		23	LLANELLI	H	Won	2	-	1*	-	13	-	-	-	-	0	P.W.Lawrie(T) J.R.Watson(T) H.S.B.Lawrie(2C,M)
5		30	Devonport Albion	A	Lost	-	-	-	-	0	2	2	-	-	16	
6	Oct	2	Plymouth	A	Lost	-	1	-	-	3	1	1	-	1	11	F.M.Taylor(T)
7		7	COVENTRY	H	Won	2	4	-	-	22	-	-	-	-	0	P.W.Lawrie(T) J.R.Watson(T) Bream(2C) O.J.Hargrave(T) F.M.Taylor(2T) H.S.B.Lawrie(T)
8		14	NORTHAMPTON	H	Won	2	2	-	-	16	-	1	-	-	3	P.W.Lawrie(T) F.M.Taylor(2T) Greasley(T) H.S.B.Lawrie(2C)
9		21	Newport	A	Lost	-	-	-	-	0	1	-	-	-	5	
10		28	MANCHESTER	H	Won	2	2	-	1	19	-	-	-	-	0	P.W.Lawrie(T) Bream(2C,P) Burdett(T) Hopkins(T) Hogarth(T)
11	Nov	4	SWANSEA	H	Lost	1	-	-	1	8	2	2	-	-	16	Bream(C,P) Hopkins(T)
12		11	Birkenhead Park	A	Won	2	2	-	-	16	-	3	-	-	9	L.Hargrave(T) Bream(2C) O.J.Hargrave(2T) F.M.Taylor(T)
13		18	Coventry	A	Won	-	-	1	-	4	-	-	-	-	0	Ellwood(D)
14		25	CARDIFF	H	Lost	1	-	-	-	5	-	1	-	1	6	Bream(C) Hobbs(T)
15	Dec	2	Moseley	A	Won	-	3	-	-	9	-	1	-	-	3	Broadley(2T) O.J.Hargrave(T)
16		9	Northampton	A	Won	1	1	-	-	8	-	1	-	-	3	Bream(C) O.J.Hargrave(T) Greasley(T)
17		16	BRISTOL	H	Won	1	1	-	-	8	-	1	-	-	3	Bream(C) O.J.Hargrave(T) Burdett(T)
18		23	CINDERFORD	H	Won	1	4	1	-	21	1	-	-	-	5	P.W.Lawrie(3T) Bream(C) Smitten(D) Hopkins(T) Hobbs(T)
19		26	BIRKENHEAD PARK	H	Won	-	7	-	-	21	1	-	-	-	5	Bream(C) P.W.Lawrie(2T) Wood(T) Ward(T) F.Taylor(T)
20		27	GLASGOW UNIVERSITY	H	Won	4	2	-	-	26	-	1	-	-	3	O.J.Hargrave(T) Broadley(3T) Allen(T,4C) Greasley(T)
21		28	BARBARIANS	H	Won	2	1	-	-	13	-	2	-	-	6	Burdett(T) Allen(2C) R.Jackett(T) Hopkins(T)
22		30	Headingley	A	Drew	-	1	-	1	6	-	2	-	-	6	Bream(P) Greasley(T)
23	Jan	6	LONDON WELSH	H	Won	1	1	-	-	8	-	-	-	-	0	Bream(C) P.W.Lawrie(T) O.J.Hargrave(T)
24		13	GLOUCESTER	H	Lost	-	-	-	-	0	-	1	1	-	7	
25		20	DEVONPORT ALBION	H	Lost	-	-	-	-	0	-	2	-	-	6	
26		27	MOSELEY	H	Won	2	7	-	-	31	-	1	-	-	3	Bream(C) P.W.Lawrie(3T) Tarr(2T) J.R.Watson(T) O.J.Hargrave(2T) Allen(C) Hopkins(T)
	Feb	3	Gloucester	A		Cancelled Frost										
27		10	Swansea	A	Lost	-	1	-	-	3	4	4	-	-	32	P.W.Lawrie(T)
28		12	Neath	A	Lost	-	1	-	-	3	1	3	-	-	14	O.J.Hargrave(T)
29		17	NEWPORT	H	Lost	-	1	-	-	3	1	1	-	-	8	Greasley(T)
30		24	Richmond	A	Lost	-	1	-	-	3	2	-	-	1	13	Greasley(T)
31	Mar	2	HEADINGLEY	H	Lost	-	4	-	-	12	1	3	-	-	14	O.J.Hargrave(T) Wood(2T) H.S.B.Lawrie(T)
32		9	Harlequins	A	Lost	-	2	-	-	6	3	1	-	-	18	P.W.Lawrie(T) Greasley(T)
33		16	Rugby (MCC4)	A	Won	3	3	-	-	24	1	-	-	-	5	Bream(3C) P.W.Lawrie(2T) O.J.Hargrave(2T) F.M.Taylor(T) Burdett(T)
34		23	NEWBOLD-ON-AVON (MCCSF)	H	Won	7	10	-	-	65	-	-	-	-	0	Bream(7C) P.W.Lawrie(4T) Tarr(T) H.S.B.Lawrie(3T) O.J.Hargrave(3T) F.M.Taylor(3T) McIntyre(2T) F.Taylor(T)
35		30	Coventry (MCCF)	A	Won	2	1	-	1	16	-	-	-	-	0	Bream(2C,P) P.W.Lawrie(T) Hogarth(T) Greasley(T)
36	Apr	6	Llanelli	A	Lost	2	-	-	-	10	1	3	-	1	17	Bream(2C) Hogarth(T) H.S.B.Lawrie(T)
37		8	Cardiff	A	Lost	-	-	-	-	0	1	1	-	1	11	
38		9	Bristol	A	Lost	-	1	-	1	6	1	1	-	-	8	Bream(P) Burdett(T)
39		13	BLACKHEATH	H	Won	1	5	-	1	23	-	-	1	-	4	Bream(C,P) P.W.Lawrie(T) Tarr(2T) O.J.Hargrave(T) Greasley(T) Dalby(T)

INDIVIDUAL APPEARANCES 1911-1912

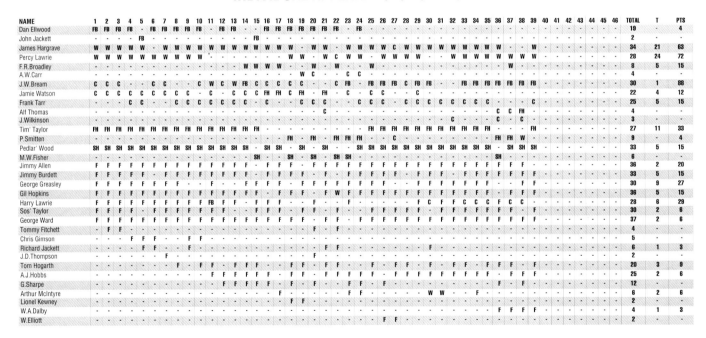

1 game: P.Baker FB(32), C.Dodson F(20), L.Hargrave W(12)[1T-3], S.G.Harvey W(6), S.A.Hunter C(39), T.E.Maddocks W(27), A.Redding F(28), Fred Rees FB(28), Lt.M.S.Scott F(1), Dixie Smith FB(31), S.L.Waterman C(17), J.Watkins F(28), W.Watson C(31)

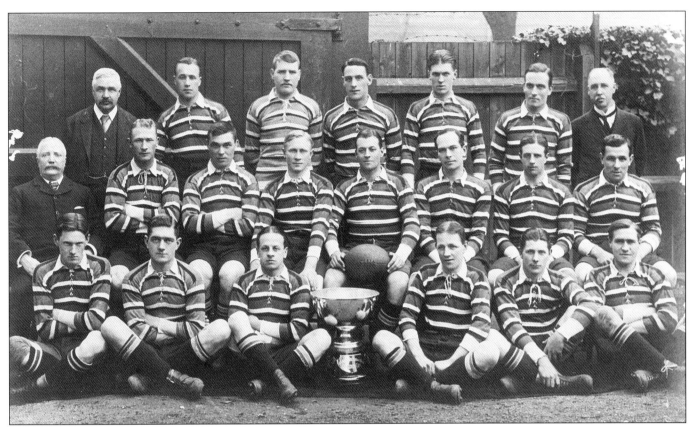

LEICESTER FOOTBALL CLUB 1911-12
Back: T.H. Crumbie (Hon.Sec), W.G. Hopkins, T.B. Hogarth, G. Ward, J.W. Bream, H.S.B. Lawrie, J. Collier (President).
Middle: F. St.Clair Pain (Hon.Tres), W.A. Dalby, A.J. Hobbs, J.R. Watson, P.W. Lawrie (Capt), J.C. Burdett, F.N. Tarr, W.J. Allen.
Front: S.A. Hunter, F. Taylor, F.M. Taylor, G.W. Wood, O.J. Hargrave, G. Greasley.

LEICESTER FOOTBALL CLUB 1913-14
Back: T.H. Crumbie (Hon.Sec), F. Taylor, L.S. Burton, E. Wynne, Dr.G. Wilson, H.S.B. Lawrie, O.J. Hargrave.
Middle: F. St.Clair Pain (Hon.Tres), W.J. Allen, W.A. Dalby, W.G. Hopkins, P.W. Lawrie (Capt), G. Ward, S.A. Hunter, H.W. Salmon (President).
Front: J.W. Bream, S. Farmer, G.W. Wood, C.H.L. Wynne, F. Mellor, F.M. Taylor, F.N. Tarr.

1912-1913

NO	DATE	OPPONENTS	V	RES	FOR					AGAINST					SCORERS
					G	T	D	P	PTS	G	T	D	P	PTS	
1	Sep 7	HEADINGLEY	H	Won	3	1	-	-	18	-	-	-	-	0	Bream(3C) P.W.Lawrie(T) F.M.Taylor(T) Wood(T) F.Taylor(T)
2	14	BRIDGEND	H	Won	2	5	1	1	32	-	1	-	-	3	Bream(2C,P) P.W.Lawrie(T,D) Hunter(2T) H.S.B.Lawrie(T) Allen(2T) Dalby(T)
3	21	NEATH	H	Won	-	3	1	-	13	-	2	-	-	6	P.W.Lawrie(2T) Hunter(D) Dalby(T)
4	28	DEVONPORT ALBION	H	Won	-	1	-	1	6	-	-	-	-	0	Bream(P) P.W.Lawrie(T)
5	Oct 5	ABERAVON	H	Won	3	1	-	-	18	-	-	-	-	0	Bream(3C) P.W.Lawrie(T) Allen(2T) Greasley(T)
6	12	Northampton	A	Won	1	1	1	-	12	1	-	-	-	5	Bream(C) P.W.Lawrie(D) Hunter(T) Hargrave(T)
7	19	NEWPORT	H	Won	-	2	-	-	6	-	-	-	-	0	Hargrave(T) F.M.Taylor(T)
8	26	LLANELLI	H	Won	4	1	-	1	26	-	1	-	-	3	Bream(4C,P) P.W.Lawrie(T) Tarr(T) F.M.Taylor(T) Greasley(2T)
9	Nov 2	Swansea	A	Lost	2	1	-	-	13	4	1	-	1	26	Hunter(2C) F.M.Taylor(T) Wood(T) H.S.B.Lawrie(T)
10	4	Aberavon	A	Lost	-	-	-	1	3	-	3	1	-	13	Hunter(P)
11	13	Oxford University	A	Lost	1	3	-	-	14	4	2	-	-	26	P.W.Lawrie(C) Wood(T) H.S.B.Lawrie(T) Dalby(2T)
12	16	Coventry	A	Won	2	2	-	-	16	-	-	-	-	0	P.W.Lawrie(T) Hunter(2T,C) F.M.Taylor(T) H.S.B.Lawrie(C)
13	23	MOSELEY	H	Won	3	2	-	1	24	-	-	-	-	0	Bream(3C,P) Hunter(T) Tarr(T) Ward(T) Waddell(2T)
14	30	CARDIFF	H	Drew	-	-	-	1	3	-	1	-	-	3	Bream(P)
15	Dec 7	NORTHAMPTON	H	Won	3	1	-	-	18	1	-	-	-	5	Bream(3C) Farmer(T) H.S.B.Lawrie(T) Dalby(T) Allen(T)
16	14	Headingley	A	Won	7	2	-	-	41	-	-	-	-	0	Bream(7C) Farmer(T) Tarr(2T) Hunter(T) Hargrave(T) F.M.Taylor(T) Dalby(2T) Ward(T)
17	21	Blackheath	A	Won	3	4	-	-	27	1	2	-	1	14	Bream(3C) Watson(T) Tarr(T) Farmer(2T) F.M.Taylor(T) Jackett(T) Allen(T)
18	26	BIRKENHEAD PARK	H	Won	4	2	-	-	26	-	2	-	-	6	Bream(4C) P.W.Lawrie(T) Tarr(2T) Wood(T) Kewney(T) Greasley(T)
19	27	CINDERFORD	H	Won	-	4	-	-	12	-	1	-	-	3	P.W.Lawrie(T) Tarr(T) Jackett(T) Ward(T)
20	28	SALE	H	Won	1	2	1	-	15	-	1	-	-	3	Bream(C) P.W.Lawrie(2T,D) Allen(T)
21	30	BARBARIANS	H	Won	-	4	-	1	15	1	1	-	1	11	Bream(P) P.W.Lawrie(2T) Hargrave(T) Wood(T)
22	Jan 2	Manchester	A	Won	1	5	1	-	24	1	2	-	-	11	Bream(C) P.W.Lawrie(2T,D) Pemberton(T) Wood(T) Dalby(T) Burton(T)
23	4	GLOUCESTER	H	Lost	1	-	-	1	8	-	3	1	-	13	Bream(C,P) Allen(T)
24	11	COVENTRY	H	Won	-	2	-	-	6	-	1	-	-	3	P.W.Lawrie(T) Farmer(T)
25	18	Bedford	A	Won	4	2	-	-	26	-	1	-	2	9	Bream(4C) Farmer(T) Broadley(2T) F.M.Taylor(T) F.Taylor(T) Burton(T)
26	25	Moseley	A	Won	4	1	-	-	23	-	1	-	-	3	Bream(4C) P.W.Lawrie(T) Farmer(T) Wood(2T) H.S.B.Lawrie(T)
27	Feb 1	Gloucester	A	Lost	-	1	-	-	3	1	1	-	1	11	P.W.Lawrie(T)
28	8	SWANSEA	H	Drew	-	-	-	-	0	-	-	-	-	0	
29	15	Newport	A	Lost	1	-	-	-	5	2	2	-	-	16	Bream(C) F.M.Taylor(T)
30	22	RICHMOND	H	Won	2	5	-	-	25	1	1	-	-	8	Bream(2C) P.W.Lawrie(2T) Tarr(T) Hunter(T) Hargrave(T) Greasley(T) F.Taylor(T)
31	Mar 1	Devonport Albion	A	Drew	-	1	-	-	3	-	1	-	-	3	P.W.Lawrie(T)
32	8	HARLEQUINS	H	Won	1	4	-	-	17	-	1	-	-	3	Bream(C) Wood(T) H.S.B.Lawrie(T) Dalby(T) Allen(T) F.Taylor(T)
33	15	Stratford-upon-Avon (MCC4)	A	Won	3	7	-	-	36	1	1	-	1	11	Bream(3C) Farmer(T) Hunter(3T) Hargrave(2T) F.M.Taylor(T) Dalby(2T) Burton(T)
34	22	Llanelli	A	Lost	-	-	-	-	0	1	1	-	-	8	
35	24	Neath	A	Lost	-	-	-	-	0	2	6	-	1	31	
36	25	Bristol	A	Won	-	2	-	-	6	-	-	-	-	0	Hargrave(T) F.Atkins(T)
37	29	Coventry (MCCSF)	A	Won	-	3	-	-	9	-	-	-	-	0	P.W.Lawrie(3T)
38	Apr 5	BELGRAVE PREMIER WKS (MCCF)	H	Won	3	8	-	-	39	1	1	-	-	8	Bream(C) P.W.Lawrie(2T,C) Hunter(2T,C) Farmer(2T) F.M.Taylor(T) Dalby(3T) Greasley(T)
39	12	Birkenhead Park	A	Won	2	1	-	-	13	-	-	-	-	0	Bream(2C) P.W.Lawrie(T) MacMillan(T) Wood(T)
40	19	Cardiff	A	Lost	2	-	-	-	10	1	3	-	-	14	Bream(2C) MacMillan(T) Timms(T)
41	26	LONDON	H	Won	2	5	-	-	25	2	-	-	-	10	Bream(2C) Tarr(T) Wood(2T) Allen(T) Twigg(T) Dalby(2T)

INDIVIDUAL APPEARANCES 1912-1913

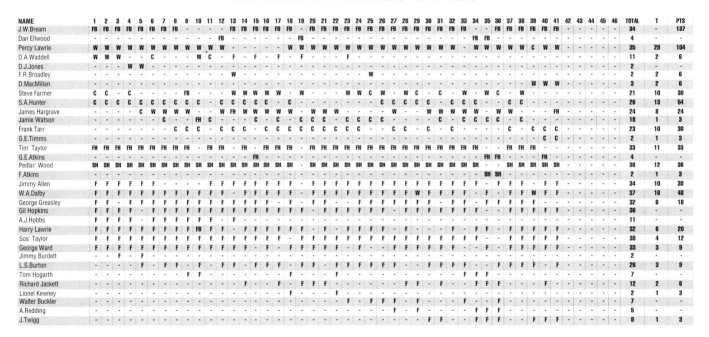

NAME	1	2	3	4	5	6	7	8	9	10	11	12	13	14	15	16	17	18	19	20	21	22	23	24	25	26	27	28	29	30	31	32	33	34	35	36	37	38	39	40	41	42	43	44	45	46	TOTAL	T	PTS
J.W.Bream	FB	FB	FB	FB	FB	FB	FB	FB	-	-	-	-	FB	FB	FB	FB	FB	FB	-	FB	FB	FB	FB	FB	FB	FB	FB	FB	FB	FB	FB	FB	FB	-	-	FB	FB	FB	FB	FB	FB	-	-	-	-	-	34	-	137
Dan Ellwood	-	-	-	-	-	-	-	-	-	-	-	FB	-	-	-	-	-	-	FB	-	-	-	-	-	-	-	-	-	-	-	-	-	-	FB	FB	-	-	-	-	-	-	-	-	-	-	-	4	-	-
Percy Lawrie	W	W	W	W	W	W	W	W	W	W	W	W	-	-	-	-	-	W	W	W	W	W	W	W	W	W	W	W	W	W	W	W	-	W	W	W	W	W	C	W	W	-	-	-	-	-	35	28	104
D.A.Waddell	W	W	W	-	-	C	-	-	-	W	C	-	F	-	F	-	F	-	F	-	-	-	F	-	-	-	-	-	-	-	-	-	-	-	-	-	-	-	-	-	-	-	-	-	-	-	11	2	6
D.J.Jones	-	-	-	W	W	-	-	-	-	-	-	-	-	-	-	-	-	-	-	-	-	-	-	-	-	-	-	-	-	-	-	-	-	-	-	-	-	-	-	-	-	-	-	-	-	-	2	-	-
F.R.Broadley	-	-	-	-	-	-	-	-	-	-	-	-	W	-	-	-	-	-	-	-	-	-	-	-	W	-	-	-	-	-	-	-	-	-	-	-	-	-	-	-	-	-	-	-	-	-	2	2	6
D.MacMillan	-	-	-	-	-	-	-	-	-	-	-	-	-	-	-	-	-	-	-	-	-	-	-	-	-	-	-	-	-	-	-	-	-	-	-	-	-	-	W	W	W	-	-	-	-	-	3	2	6
Steve Farmer	C	C	-	C	-	-	-	-	FB	-	-	-	W	W	W	W	W	-	W	-	-	-	W	W	C	W	-	W	C	-	C	-	W	-	W	C	-	W	-	-	-	-	-	-	-	-	21	10	30
S.A.Hunter	C	C	C	C	C	C	C	C	C	C	-	C	C	C	C	C	-	C	-	-	-	-	-	-	-	C	C	C	C	C	-	C	C	C	-	-	C	C	-	-	-	-	-	-	-	-	26	13	54
James Hargrave	-	-	-	-	C	W	W	W	W	-	-	W	FH	W	W	W	W	W	-	W	W	W	-	-	-	-	W	-	-	W	W	W	W	W	-	W	W	-	-	-	FH	-	-	-	-	-	24	8	24
Jamie Watson	-	-	-	-	-	-	C	-	-	FH	C	-	-	-	C	-	C	-	C	C	C	-	C	C	C	C	-	-	-	-	C	-	C	C	C	C	-	C	-	-	-	-	-	-	-	-	18	1	3
Frank Tarr	-	-	-	-	-	-	-	C	C	C	-	C	C	C	-	C	C	C	C	C	C	C	C	C	-	-	C	C	-	C	-	C	-	-	-	-	C	-	C	C	C	-	-	-	-	-	23	10	30
G.E.Timms	-	-	-	-	-	-	-	-	-	-	-	-	-	-	-	-	-	-	-	-	-	-	-	-	-	-	-	-	-	-	-	-	-	-	-	-	-	-	-	C	C	-	-	-	-	-	2	1	3
Tim' Taylor	FH	FH	FH	FH	FH	FH	FH	FH	FH	-	FH	FH	-	FH	-	FH	FH	FH	-	FH	FH	FH	FH	FH	FH	FH	FH	FH	FH	FH	FH	FH	FH	FH	-	-	FH	FH	FH	-	-	-	-	-	-	-	33	11	33
G.E.Atkins	-	-	-	-	-	-	-	-	-	-	-	-	-	-	FH	-	-	-	-	-	-	-	-	-	-	-	-	-	-	-	-	-	-	-	FH	FH	-	-	-	FH	-	-	-	-	-	-	4	-	-
Pedlar' Wood	SH	SH	SH	SH	SH	SH	SH	SH	SH	SH	SH	SH	SH	SH	SH	SH	SH	SH	-	SH	SH	SH	SH	SH	SH	SH	SH	SH	SH	SH	SH	SH	SH	SH	-	-	SH	SH	SH	SH	SH	-	-	-	-	-	38	12	36
F.Atkins	-	-	-	-	-	-	-	-	-	-	-	-	-	-	-	-	-	-	-	-	-	-	-	-	-	-	-	-	-	-	-	-	-	-	SH	SH	-	-	-	-	-	-	-	-	-	-	2	1	3
Jimmy Allen	F	F	F	F	F	F	-	-	-	-	F	F	F	F	F	F	F	F	-	F	F	F	F	F	F	F	F	F	F	F	F	F	F	F	-	F	F	F	-	F	F	-	-	-	-	-	34	10	30
W.A.Dalby	F	F	F	F	F	F	F	F	F	F	F	F	-	F	F	F	F	F	-	F	F	F	F	F	F	F	F	F	W	F	F	F	F	-	F	-	F	F	W	F	F	-	-	-	-	-	37	16	48
George Greasley	F	F	-	F	F	F	F	F	F	F	F	F	F	F	F	F	-	F	-	F	F	-	-	F	F	F	F	F	F	F	-	F	F	-	F	F	F	F	F	-	-	-	-	-	-	-	32	6	18
Gil Hopkins	F	F	F	F	-	F	F	F	F	F	F	F	F	F	F	F	F	F	F	-	F	F	F	F	F	F	F	-	F	F	F	F	F	F	-	-	F	F	F	F	F	-	-	-	-	-	36	-	-
A.J.Hobbs	F	F	F	F	-	F	F	F	F	F	F	-	F	-	-	-	-	-	-	-	-	-	-	-	-	-	-	-	-	-	-	-	-	-	-	-	-	-	-	-	-	-	-	-	-	-	11	-	-
Harry Lawrie	F	F	F	F	F	F	F	F	F	FB	F	F	-	F	F	F	F	F	F	-	F	-	F	F	F	F	-	F	-	-	-	F	-	F	F	-	F	F	F	F	F	-	-	-	-	-	32	6	20
Sos' Taylor	F	F	F	F	F	F	F	F	F	F	F	F	F	F	F	F	F	-	F	F	F	F	F	F	F	F	F	F	F	F	F	F	F	F	-	-	F	F	F	F	F	-	-	-	-	-	38	4	12
George Ward	F	F	F	F	F	F	F	F	F	F	F	F	F	F	-	F	-	F	F	F	F	F	-	F	-	-	F	F	F	F	F	F	-	-	F	-	F	F	F	F	F	-	-	-	-	-	33	3	9
Jimmy Burdett	-	-	F	-	F	-	-	-	-	-	-	-	-	-	-	-	-	-	-	-	-	-	-	-	-	-	-	-	-	-	-	-	-	-	-	-	-	-	-	-	-	-	-	-	-	-	2	-	-
L.S.Burton	-	-	-	-	F	-	F	F	-	F	-	F	F	-	F	F	F	-	F	F	-	F	F	F	F	F	F	-	-	F	F	F	F	-	-	F	F	F	F	-	F	-	-	-	-	-	26	3	9
Tom Hogarth	-	-	-	-	-	-	-	-	F	F	-	-	-	-	-	-	-	F	-	-	-	F	-	-	-	-	-	-	-	-	-	-	F	F	F	-	-	-	-	-	-	-	-	-	-	-	7	-	-
Richard Jackett	-	-	-	-	-	-	-	-	-	-	-	-	-	F	-	-	F	-	F	F	F	-	-	-	-	-	-	F	F	-	F	-	-	F	F	F	-	-	-	F	-	-	-	-	-	-	12	2	6
Lionel Kewney	-	-	-	-	-	-	-	-	-	-	-	-	-	-	-	-	-	F	-	-	-	F	-	-	-	-	-	-	-	-	-	-	-	-	-	-	-	-	-	-	-	-	-	-	-	-	2	1	3
Walter Buckler	-	-	-	-	-	-	-	-	-	-	-	-	-	-	-	-	-	-	-	-	-	-	F	-	F	F	F	-	F	-	-	-	F	-	-	F	-	-	-	-	-	-	-	-	-	-	7	-	-
A.Redding	-	-	-	-	-	-	-	-	-	-	-	-	-	-	-	-	-	-	-	-	-	-	-	-	-	-	F	-	F	-	-	-	-	F	F	F	-	-	-	-	-	-	-	-	-	-	5	-	-
J.Twigg	-	-	-	-	-	-	-	-	-	-	-	-	-	-	-	-	-	-	-	-	-	-	-	-	-	-	-	-	-	F	F	-	-	F	F	F	-	-	F	F	F	-	-	-	-	-	8	1	3

1 game: J.Brewin F(39), S.E.Dove C(35), John Eddison F(20), M.W.Fisher SH(19), W.H.Jones F(36), W.J.Jones W(11), Arthur King FH(19), Clem Lewis C(3), H.J.Pemberton C(22)[1T-3], F.Read FB(11), J.D.Thompson F(19)

NO	DATE		OPPONENTS	V	RES	FOR					AGAINST					SCORERS
						G	T	D	P	PTS	G	T	D	P	PTS	
1	Sep	6	BEDFORD	H	Won	1	4	-	-	17	1	1	-	-	8	Bream(T,C) Hargrave(T) F.M.Taylor(T) Burton(2T)
2		13	BATH	H	Won	2	3	-	-	19	1	-	-	-	5	Bream(2C) Hunter(T) Timms(T) Hargrave(T) Allen(T) F.Taylor(T)
3		20	PONTYPOOL	H	Lost	-	1	-	-	3	-	-	2	-	8	Hargrave(T)
4		27	Devonport Albion	A	Drew	1	1	-	-	8	1	1	-	-	8	Bream(C) Farmer(T) Wood(T)
5	Oct	4	HEADINGLEY	H	Won	1	4	-	-	17	-	2	-	-	6	Bream(C) P.W.Lawrie(2T) Tarr(T) F.M.Taylor(T) Dalby(T)
6		11	NORTHAMPTON	H	Won	3	2	-	-	21	-	1	-	-	3	Bream(3C) Timms(T) Hopkins(T) G.Ward(2T) Dalby(T)
7		18	COVENTRY	H	Won	1	2	-	1	14	-	1	-	1	6	Bream(C,P) Timms(2T) F.Taylor(T)
8		25	Newport	A	Lost	1	1	-	-	8	1	2	-	-	11	Bream(C) H.S.B.Lawrie(T) Hopkins(T)
9	Nov	1	LLANELLI	H	Won	4	-	-	1	23	-	-	-	-	0	Bream(4C,P) Timms(T) F.M.Taylor(T) Wood(T) Dalby(T)
10		8	SWANSEA	H	Won	-	2	-	-	6	-	1	-	-	3	P.W.Lawrie(T) Hargrave(T)
11		13	OXFORD UNIVERSITY	H	Won	-	2	-	2	12	-	3	-	-	9	Bream(2P) F.M.Taylor(T) Wood(T)
12		15	Northampton	A	Won	4	1	1	-	27	-	1	-	-	3	Bream(4C) P.W.Lawrie(2T) Timms(T) Hargrave(D) F.M.Taylor(2T)
13		22	ABERAVON	H	Drew	-	1	-	-	3	-	1	-	-	3	Dove(T)
14		29	Moseley	A	Won	2	-	-	-	10	-	-	-	-	0	Bream(2C) Timms(T) F.M.Taylor(T)
15	Dec	6	CARDIFF	H	Won	-	2	1	-	10	-	1	-	-	3	P.W.Lawrie(T) Dove(D) Dalby(T)
16		13	Headingley	A	Won	-	6	-	1	21	-	2	-	-	6	Bream(P) P.W.Lawrie(2T) Tarr(T) Hargrave(3T)
17		20	BLACKHEATH	H	Lost	1	1	-	-	8	2	-	-	-	10	Ellwood(C) Timms(T) F.M.Taylor(T)
18		26	BIRKENHEAD PARK	H	Won	4	2	-	-	26	1	1	-	-	8	Bream(T,4C) C.H.L.Wynne(T) Hargrave(2T) F.M.Taylor(T) Dalby(T)
19		27	JEDFOREST	H	Won	3	2	1	-	25	1	-	-	-	5	Bream(3C,D) Broadley(T) C.H.L.Wynne(3T) Allen(T)
		29	BARBARIANS	H		Cancelled Snow										
20	Jan	3	Gloucester	A	Lost	-	-	-	-	0	-	1	-	-	3	
21		10	MANCHESTER	H	Won	3	2	-	-	21	-	2	-	-	6	Mellor(C) C.H.L.Wynne(T) P.W.Lawrie(T) Hargrave(2T) Fisher(T) H.S.B.Lawrie(C) Allen(C)
22		17	Coventry	A	Won	-	1	-	-	3	-	-	-	-	0	Dalby(T)
23		24	DEVONPORT ALBION	H	Won	-	3	-	-	9	-	-	-	1	3	P.W.Lawrie(T) Hargrave(T) H.S.B.Lawrie(T)
24		31	Swansea	A	Lost	-	-	-	-	0	2	1	-	-	13	
25	Feb	2	Pontypool	A	Lost	-	1	-	-	3	-	8	-	-	24	Allen(T)
26		7	MOSELEY	H	Won	2	2	-	-	16	-	-	-	1	3	Bream(2C) P.W.Lawrie(T) Timms(T) Mellor(T) Twigg(T)
27		14	NEWPORT	H	Won	2	1	-	-	13	1	1	-	-	8	Bream(2C) P.W.Lawrie(T) F.M.Taylor(T) Dalby(T)
28		21	Richmond	A	Drew	-	-	-	-	0	-	-	-	-	0	
29		23	BARBARIANS	H	Lost	-	1	-	-	3	1	-	-	-	5	Dalby(T)
30		28	BRISTOL	H	Won	1	1	-	-	8	-	1	-	-	3	Bream(C) P.W.Lawrie(2T)
31	Mar	7	Harlequins	A	Lost	-	1	-	-	3	-	5	-	-	15	Wood(T)
32		14	GLOUCESTER	H	Lost	-	-	-	1	3	-	2	-	-	6	P.W.Lawrie(P)
33		21	Newbold-on-Avon (MCC4)	A	Won	3	2	-	2	27	-	-	-	-	0	Bream(3C,2P) P.W.Lawrie(T) Hunter(T) E.Wynne(T) H.S.B.Lawrie(T) Dalby(T)
34	Apr	4	COVENTRY (MCCSF)	H	Lost	-	-	-	-	0	1	1	-	-	8	
35		11	Llanelli	A	Lost	1	-	-	-	5	-	5	-	-	15	Mellor(C) F.M.Taylor(T)
36		13	Penarth	A	Lost	-	3	-	-	9	1	5	-	-	20	Dove(T) Jackett(T) F.Taylor(T)
37		14	Bath	A	Lost	-	1	-	-	3	1	3	-	-	14	Allen(T)
38		15	Cardiff	A	Lost	-	2	-	-	6	1	1	-	-	8	C.H.L.Wynne(2T)
39		18	Birkenhead Park	A	Lost	-	-	-	-	0	2	1	1	2	23	

INDIVIDUAL APPEARANCES 1913-1914

NAME	1	2	3	4	5	6	7	8	9	10	11	12	13	14	15	16	17	18	19	20	21	22	23	24	25	26	27	28	29	30	31	32	33	34	35	36	37	38	39	40	41	42	43	44	45	46	TOTAL	T	PTS
J.W.Bream	FB	FB	FB	FB	FB	FB	FB	FB	FB	FB	FB	FB	FB	FB	FB	FB	-	FB	FB	C	-	-	FB	C	C	FB	FB	FB	FB	FB	-	-	FB	-	-	-	-	-	-	-	-	-	-	-	-	-	28	2	101
Fred Mellor	-	-	-	-	-	-	-	-	-	-	-	-	-	-	-	-	-	-	-	FB	FB	FB	-	FB	FB	W	-	W	W	W	-	W	W	W	FB	FB	-	FB	FB	-	-	-	-	-	-	-	16	1	7
J.P.Hougham	-	-	-	-	-	-	-	-	-	-	-	-	-	-	-	-	-	-	-	-	-	-	-	-	-	-	-	-	-	-	FB	FB	-	FB	-	-	-	-	-	-	-	-	-	-	-	-	3	-	-
D.MacMillan	W	-	-	-	-	-	-	-	W	-	-	-	-	-	-	-	-	-	-	-	-	-	-	-	-	-	-	-	-	-	-	-	-	-	-	-	-	-	-	-	-	-	-	-	-	-	2	-	-
G.E.Timms	W	C	C	C	C	C	C	-	C	C	C	C	C	C	C	C	C	-	C	-	-	-	-	-	-	C	C	C	C	-	C	C	-	-	-	-	-	-	-	-	-	-	-	-	-	-	23	9	27
S.A.Hunter	-	W	W	-	-	-	-	-	-	-	-	-	-	-	-	-	-	-	-	-	-	-	-	-	-	C	W	C	-	C	-	-	C	C	-	-	-	-	-	-	-	-	-	-	-	-	8	2	6
Percy Lawrie	-	-	-	-	W	W	W	W	W	W	W	W	W	W	W	W	-	-	-	-	C	W	W	W	W	W	W	W	W	W	W	W	W	-	-	-	W	-	W	-	-	-	-	-	-	-	27	15	48
F.R.Broadley	-	-	-	-	-	-	-	-	-	-	-	-	-	-	-	-	W	-	W	-	-	-	-	-	-	-	-	-	-	-	-	-	-	-	-	-	-	-	-	-	-	-	-	-	-	-	2	1	3
C.H.L.Wynne	-	-	-	-	-	-	-	-	-	-	-	-	-	-	-	-	-	W	W	-	W	W	-	-	-	-	-	-	-	-	-	-	-	-	-	-	-	W	W	-	-	-	-	-	-	-	6	7	21
Robert Ringrose	-	-	-	-	-	-	-	-	-	-	-	-	-	-	-	-	-	-	-	-	-	-	-	-	-	-	-	-	-	-	-	-	-	-	W	W	C	W	-	-	-	-	-	-	-	-	4	-	-
J.Sutcliffe	-	-	-	-	-	-	-	-	-	-	-	-	-	-	-	-	-	-	-	-	-	-	-	-	-	-	-	-	-	-	-	-	-	-	W	W	FB	-	F	-	-	-	-	-	-	-	4	-	-
L.Hamblin	-	-	-	-	-	-	-	-	-	-	-	-	-	-	-	-	-	-	-	-	-	-	-	-	-	-	-	-	-	-	-	-	-	-	-	-	W	C	-	-	-	-	-	-	-	-	2	-	-
Steve Farmer	C	-	-	W	-	C	-	-	-	-	-	-	-	C	W	-	-	-	-	-	-	-	-	-	-	-	-	-	-	C	C	-	-	-	-	-	-	-	-	-	-	-	-	-	-	-	7	1	3
James Hargrave	C	W	W	W	W	W	W	C	-	W	W	W	W	W	-	W	W	W	-	-	FH	FH	W	C	C	-	-	-	-	-	-	-	-	-	-	-	-	-	-	-	-	-	-	-	-	-	21	12	40
Frank Tarr	-	C	C	-	C	-	C	C	C	C	C	-	-	-	-	C	-	C	C	-	-	-	-	-	-	-	-	-	-	-	-	-	-	-	-	-	-	-	-	-	-	-	-	-	-	-	11	2	6
S.E.Dove	-	-	-	C	-	-	-	-	-	-	-	C	C	-	C	-	C	C	-	-	-	C	C	-	-	-	-	-	-	-	W	-	-	-	-	C	C	-	-	-	-	-	-	-	-	-	11	2	10
E.Wynne	-	-	-	-	-	-	-	-	-	-	-	-	-	-	-	-	-	-	-	-	C	C	C	-	-	-	C	-	-	-	-	-	C	C	-	-	-	-	C	-	-	-	-	-	-	-	7	1	3
Alf Bates	-	-	-	-	-	-	-	-	-	-	-	-	-	-	-	-	-	-	-	-	-	-	-	-	-	-	-	-	-	-	-	-	-	-	C	-	SH	-	-	-	-	-	-	-	-	-	2	-	-
Gordon Salmon	-	-	-	-	-	-	-	-	-	-	-	-	-	-	-	-	-	-	-	-	-	-	-	-	-	-	-	-	-	-	-	-	-	-	-	C	FH	-	C	-	-	-	-	-	-	-	3	-	-
Tim' Taylor	FH	FH	FH	FH	FH	FH	FH	FH	FH	FH	FH	FH	FH	FH	FH	FH	FH	FH	-	-	-	-	FH	FH	FH	FH	FH	FH	FH	FH	FH	FH	FH	FH	FH	FH	-	FH	FH	-	-	-	-	-	-	-	34	11	33
Jamie Watson	-	-	-	-	-	-	-	-	-	-	-	-	-	-	-	-	-	-	FH	FH	-	-	-	-	-	-	-	-	-	-	-	-	-	-	-	-	-	-	-	-	-	-	-	-	-	-	2	-	-
Pedlar' Wood	SH	SH	SH	SH	SH	SH	SH	SH	SH	SH	SH	SH	SH	SH	SH	SH	SH	SH	-	-	-	-	SH	SH	SH	SH	SH	SH	SH	SH	SH	SH	SH	SH	SH	SH	-	SH	SH	-	-	-	-	-	-	-	34	4	12
M.W.Fisher	-	-	-	-	-	-	-	-	-	-	-	-	-	-	-	-	-	-	-	SH	SH	SH	-	-	-	-	-	-	-	-	-	-	-	-	-	-	-	-	-	-	-	-	-	-	-	-	3	1	3
Jimmy Allen	F	F	F	-	-	-	F	F	F	F	F	F	F	F	-	F	F	-	F	-	F	F	F	F	F	F	F	F	F	F	F	F	F	F	F	-	F	F	-	-	-	-	-	-	-	-	31	4	14
L.S.Burton	F	F	F	-	F	-	-	F	F	-	F	-	F	F	-	F	-	F	F	F	F	F	F	F	F	F	F	F	F	-	F	F	F	F	-	F	F	-	F	-	-	-	-	-	-	-	29	2	6
W.A.Dalby	F	F	F	F	F	F	F	W	F	F	F	-	F	F	F	F	F	F	-	C	W	F	F	W	W	F	F	F	F	F	F	C	F	W	F	F	-	F	F	-	-	-	-	-	-	-	36	9	27
Harry Lawrie	F	-	F	F	F	F	F	F	F	F	F	F	-	F	-	F	-	F	-	-	F	-	F	F	-	-	-	-	-	F	F	F	F	F	-	-	-	-	-	-	-	-	-	-	-	-	22	3	11
Sos' Taylor	F	F	F	F	F	F	F	F	-	F	F	F	F	F	F	F	F	F	-	F	F	-	-	-	-	-	-	-	-	-	-	F	F	F	-	F	F	-	F	-	-	-	-	-	-	-	25	3	9
George Ward	F	F	F	F	F	F	F	F	F	-	-	F	F	F	-	F	F	F	-	-	F	-	-	F	F	F	-	F	F	F	-	-	-	F	F	-	-	F	-	-	-	-	-	-	-	-	25	2	6
Gil Hopkins	-	F	F	F	F	F	F	F	F	F	F	F	F	F	F	F	F	F	F	-	F	F	F	F	F	F	F	F	F	F	F	F	F	F	-	F	F	F	F	-	-	-	-	-	-	-	36	2	6
W.H.Jones	-	F	-	-	-	-	-	-	-	-	-	-	-	-	-	-	-	-	-	-	-	-	-	-	-	-	-	-	-	-	-	-	-	-	-	-	-	-	F	-	-	-	-	-	-	-	2	-	-
J.Twigg	-	F	F	F	F	F	-	F	F	F	F	F	F	F	F	F	F	-	F	F	F	F	F	F	F	F	F	F	F	F	F	F	-	-	-	-	-	-	-	-	-	-	-	-	-	-	29	1	3
W.Hall	-	-	-	F	F	F	F	F	-	F	-	F	F	-	F	-	F	-	F	F	-	F	F	-	F	-	-	-	-	-	-	-	-	-	-	-	-	-	-	-	-	-	-	-	-	-	15	-	-
Richard Jackett	-	-	-	F	-	-	-	-	-	-	-	-	-	-	-	-	-	-	F	F	-	-	-	-	-	-	F	-	-	-	-	-	-	-	F	F	-	F	-	-	-	-	-	-	-	-	7	1	3
G.Wilson	-	-	-	-	-	F	F	-	F	F	F	F	-	-	F	-	F	F	-	F	F	F	F	F	F	F	F	F	F	F	F	F	F	F	-	-	F	-	-	-	-	-	-	-	-	-	25	-	-
Tom Hogarth	-	-	-	-	-	-	-	-	-	-	-	-	-	-	F	-	-	F	F	F	-	-	-	-	-	-	-	-	-	-	-	-	F	F	-	F	F	-	-	-	-	-	-	-	-	-	8	-	-
A.Redding	-	-	-	-	-	-	-	-	-	-	-	-	-	-	F	-	-	-	F	F	-	F	-	F	F	-	-	-	-	-	-	-	-	-	F	-	-	F	F	-	-	-	-	-	-	-	9	-	-
S.G.Wolfe	-	-	-	-	-	-	-	-	-	-	-	-	-	-	-	-	-	-	-	-	-	-	-	-	-	F	F	F	-	F	F	F	-	-	F	-	F	F	F	-	-	-	-	-	-	-	10	-	-
Jim Leather	-	-	-	-	-	-	-	-	-	-	-	-	-	-	-	-	-	-	-	-	-	-	-	-	-	-	-	-	F	-	-	-	-	-	F	F	-	-	-	-	-	-	-	-	-	-	3	-	-
H.W.Hill	-	-	-	-	-	-	-	-	-	-	-	-	-	-	-	-	-	-	-	-	-	-	-	-	-	-	-	-	-	-	-	-	-	-	F	F	-	F	-	-	-	-	-	-	-	-	3	-	-

1 game: G.E.Atkins SH(19), Dan Ellwood FB(17)[2], George Greasley F(1), J.Leader F(37), Fred Newman C(29), 'Tosh' Russell F(1), K.Storey C(35), W.Ward W(20), Willy Watts C(38), J.Wilkinson W(20)

1918-1919

NO	DATE		OPPONENTS	V	RES	FOR					AGAINST					SCORERS
						G	T	D	P	PTS	G	T	D	P	PTS	
1	Dec	26	4TH LEICESTERS.REGT.	H	Won	-	2	-	-	6	1	-	-	-	5	Lawrie(2T)
2		27	3RD LEICESTERS.REGT.	H	Won	1	1	-	-	8	-	1	-	-	3	Manton(T) Lawrie(T) Bull(C)
	Jan	4	N.ZEALAND SERVICES	H		Cancelled Snow										
3		11	N.ZEALAND SERVICES	H	Lost	-	-	-	-	0	-	5	1	-	19	
4		18	MACHINE GUN CORPS	H	Won	3	4	-	-	27	1	-	-	-	5	Murmann(T) Farmer(T) Day(2T,3C) G.W.Wood(2T) Allen(T)
5		25	NEW ZEALAND M.G.C.	H	Won	2	1	-	1	16	1	-	-	-	5	Allen(2T,2C,P) Bull(T)
6	Feb	1	COVENTRY	H	Won	3	2	-	-	21	-	-	1*	-	3	Day(3T,3C) Allen(T) Vears(T)
7		8	GLOUCESTER	H	Won	1	1	1	1	15	-	-	-	-	0	Day(C,D,P) Taylor(T) Bull(T)
8		15	BEDFORD & DISTRICT	H	Won	7	12	-	-	71	-	-	-	-	0	Haselmere(5T) Coates(3T) Roberts(2T) Day(4T,3C) Bates(3T) G.W.Wood(T) Allen(4C) Hegarty(T)
9		22	AUSTRALIAN FORCES	H	Lost	-	2	-	-	6	1	-	-	1	8	Smitten(T) Watts(T)
10	Mar	1	YORKSHIRE	H	Won	2	3	-	-	19	-	-	-	-	0	Haselmere(3T,2C) Lawrie(T) Bates(T)
11		22	COVENTRY	H	Won	3	4	-	-	27	-	-	-	-	0	Lawrie(T) Watts(T) Haselmere(C) Bates(3T) Allen(2C) Taylor(T) Blower(T)
12		29	MOSELEY	H	Won	3	2	-	-	21	-	2	-	-	6	Lawrie(T) Watts(T) Haselmere(3C) Bates(2T) G.W.Wood(T)
13	Apr	3	SOUTH AFRICAN FORCES	H	Lost	-	-	1	-	4	-	2	-	-	6	Bates(D)
14		5	CARDIFF	H	Lost	-	1	-	-	3	-	1	1	1	10	Lawrie(T)
15		10	CANADIAN FORCES	H	Won	2	3	-	-	19	-	1	-	-	3	Page(C) Wilkins(T) Lawrie(2T) Watts(T) Haselmere(C) Bates(T)
16		19	ROYAL AIR FORCE	H	Lost	1	1	-	-	8	2	4	-	-	22	Haselmere(T) Allen(T,C)
17		21	THE ARMY	H	Lost	-	1	-	-	5	1	1	-	-	8	Haselmere(C) Ward(T)
18		22	ENGLAND M.G.C.	H	Won	6	3	-	-	39	1	2	-	-	11	Watts(T) Haselmere(3T,3C) Bates(2T) Smitten(T) Allen(3C) Vears(T) Buckler(T)
19		26	ROYAL NAVAL DIVISION	H	Lost	-	-	1	-	4	-	1	1	-	7	Bates(D)

INDIVIDUAL APPEARANCES 1918-1919

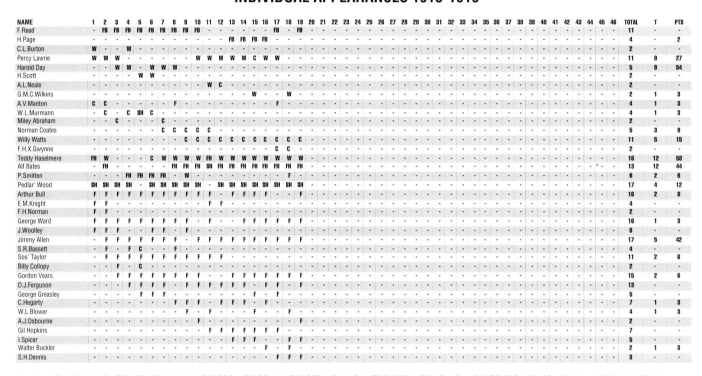

NAME	1	2	3	4	5	6	7	8	9	10	11	12	13	14	15	16	17	18	19	TOTAL	T	PTS
F.Read	-	FB	FB	FB	FB	FB	FB	FB	FB	FB	-	-	-	-	-	-	FB	-	FB	11	-	-
H.Page	-	-	-	-	-	-	-	-	-	-	-	FB	FB	FB	FB	-	-	-	-	4	-	2
C.L.Burton	W	-	-	W	-	-	-	-	-	-	-	-	-	-	-	-	-	-	-	2	-	-
Percy Lawrie	W	W	W	-	-	-	-	-	-	W	W	W	W	W	C	W	W	-	-	11	9	27
Harold Day	-	-	W	W	-	W	W	W	W	-	-	-	-	-	-	-	-	-	-	5	9	54
H.Scott	-	-	-	W	W	-	-	-	-	-	-	-	-	-	-	-	-	-	-	2	-	-
A.L.Neale	-	-	-	-	-	-	-	-	-	W	C	-	-	-	-	-	-	-	-	2	-	-
G.M.C.Wilkins	-	-	-	-	-	-	-	-	-	-	-	-	-	W	-	-	-	W	-	2	1	3
A.V.Manton	C	C	-	-	-	-	F	-	-	-	-	-	-	-	-	-	F	-	-	4	1	3
W.L.Murmann	-	C	-	C	SH	C	-	-	-	-	-	-	-	-	-	-	-	-	-	4	1	3
Miley Abraham	-	-	C	-	-	-	C	-	-	-	-	-	-	-	-	-	-	-	-	2	-	-
Norman Coates	-	-	-	-	-	-	-	C	C	C	C	C	-	-	-	-	-	-	-	5	3	9
Willy Watts	-	-	-	-	-	-	-	-	-	C	C	C	C	C	C	C	C	C	C	11	5	15
F.H.X.Gwynne	-	-	-	-	-	-	-	-	-	-	-	-	-	-	-	-	C	C	-	2	-	-
Teddy Haselmere	FH	W	-	-	-	C	W	W	W	FH	W	W	W	W	W	W	W	W	W	16	12	58
Alf Bates	-	FH	-	-	-	-	-	FH	FH	FH	SH	FH	FH	FH	FH	FH	FH	FH	FH	13	12	44
P.Smitten	-	-	-	FH	FH	FH	FH	-	W	-	-	-	-	-	-	-	-	-	-	6	2	6
Pedlar' Wood	SH	SH	SH	SH	-	SH	SH	SH	SH	SH	-	SH	SH	SH	SH	SH	SH	SH	-	16	4	12
Arthur Bull	F	F	F	F	F	F	F	F	F	F	F	F	-	F	F	F	F	-	F	16	2	8
E.M.Knight	F	F	-	-	-	-	-	-	-	F	F	-	-	-	-	-	-	-	-	4	-	-
F.H.Norman	F	F	-	-	-	-	-	-	-	-	-	-	-	-	-	-	-	-	-	2	-	-
George Ward	F	F	F	F	F	F	F	F	F	F	-	F	-	F	F	F	F	F	-	16	1	3
J.Woolley	F	F	F	-	-	F	-	F	-	-	-	-	-	-	-	-	-	-	-	6	-	-
Jimmy Allen	-	F	F	F	F	F	F	F	F	-	F	F	F	F	F	F	F	F	-	17	5	42
S.R.Bassett	-	F	-	F	C	-	F	-	-	-	-	-	-	-	-	-	-	-	-	4	-	-
Sos' Taylor	-	F	F	F	F	F	F	F	F	F	F	-	-	-	-	-	-	-	-	11	2	6
Billy Collopy	-	-	F	-	C	-	-	-	-	-	-	-	-	-	-	-	-	-	-	2	-	-
Gordon Vears	-	-	F	F	F	F	F	F	F	F	-	-	F	F	F	F	F	F	-	15	2	6
D.J.Ferguson	-	-	-	F	F	F	F	-	-	F	F	F	F	F	F	-	F	F	-	13	-	-
George Greasley	-	-	-	-	-	F	F	F	-	-	-	-	-	F	-	F	-	-	-	5	-	-
C.Hegarty	-	-	-	-	-	-	-	F	F	F	-	-	F	F	F	-	F	-	-	7	1	3
W.L.Blower	-	-	-	-	-	-	-	-	F	-	F	-	-	-	-	-	-	-	-	4	1	3
A.J.Osbourne	-	-	-	-	-	-	-	-	F	-	-	-	-	-	-	-	F	-	-	2	-	-
Gil Hopkins	-	-	-	-	-	-	-	-	-	-	F	F	F	F	F	F	F	-	-	7	-	-
I.Spicer	-	-	-	-	-	-	-	-	-	-	-	-	F	F	F	-	-	-	-	5	-	-
Walter Buckler	-	-	-	-	-	-	-	-	-	-	-	-	-	-	-	F	-	F	-	2	1	3
S.H.Dennis	-	-	-	-	-	-	-	-	-	-	-	-	-	-	F	F	F	-	-	3	-	-

1 game: Joseph Beasley C(14), A.J.Bloor F(12), W.Booth F(4), John Burdett C(16), C.D.Carter C(3), R.Cartwright F(12), G.E.Davie F(1), A.J.Davies FB(18), W.H.Earles FB(11), Steve Farmer C(4)[1T-3], C.D.Ferris F(3), C.Freer C(1), L.Hamblin C(13), A.Higgins FB(12), N.L.Higginson F(1), Gwyn Holford F(13), Eddie Myers FH(3), H.W.Palfreyman FB(1), F.Richards F(5), Robert Ringrose W(19), H.S.Roberts C(8)[2T-6], F.S.Scholes F(1), Stuart Smith F(10), J.Willcox W(5), Ken Wood C(19)

NO	DATE		OPPONENTS	V	RES	FOR					AGAINST					SCORERS
						G	T	D	P	PTS	G	T	D	P	PTS	
1	Sep	6	BATH	H	Lost	-	1	-	-	3	2	2	-	-	16	Haselmere(T)
2		13	ROYAL NAVY	H	Won	4	2	-	2	32	-	-	-	-	0	Haselmere(2T,3C,P) Bates(T) Wood(T) Allen(T,C,P) Hicks(T)
3		20	COVENTRY	H	Won	6	3	-	-	39	-	1	-	-	3	Watts(T) Coates(T) Haselmere(2T,6C) Bates(2T) Wood(T) Hicks(T) Parker(T)
4		27	PLYMOUTH ALBION	H	Won	1	1	-	1	11	1	-	-	-	5	Haselmere(T,P) Allen(C) F.Taylor(T)
5	Oct	4	BURTON-ON-TRENT	H	Won	9	3	1	-	58	-	-	-	-	0	Haselmere(5T,6C,D) Coates(2T) Watts(T) Bates(T) G.Ward(T) Ferguson(3C) Brown(T) Spicer(T)
6		11	LLANELLI	H	Lost	-	2	-	-	6	-	3	-	-	9	Watts(T) Clarke(T)
7		18	BRISTOL	H	Won	-	5	-	3	24	2	1	-	1	16	Haselmere(2T,2P) Coates(T) Clarke(T) Allen(P) Brown(T)
8		25	NEWPORT	H	Lost	-	-	-	-	0	1	2	-	-	11	
9	Nov	1	ROYAL NAVY	H	Won	-	3	-	-	9	-	1	-	-	3	Haselmere(2T) Coates(T)
10		8	Swansea	A	Lost	-	2	-	-	6	-	2	1	-	10	Coates(T) Bates(T)
11		10	Llanelli	A	Lost	1	-	-	-	5	1	1	-	-	8	Haselmere(T,C)
12		12	Oxford University	A	Lost	1	-	-	1	8	2	2	-	-	16	Haselmere(T,C,P)
13		15	Northampton	A	Drew	-	2	-	-	6	-	1	-	1	6	Haselmere(T) Bates(T)
14		22	THE ARMY	H	Won	2	3	-	-	19	-	-	2	-	8	Haselmere(3T,2C) F.Taylor(T) Vears(T)
15		29	CARDIFF	H	Lost	-	-	-	-	0	-	1	-	-	3	
16	Dec	6	Moseley	A	Won	1	6	-	-	23	1	-	-	-	5	Haselmere(2T,C) Watts(2T) Ringrose(T) F.M.Taylor(T) Allen(T)
17		13	Blackheath	A	Lost	-	-	-	-	0	1	-	-	-	5	
18		20	BEDFORD	H	Won	3	8	1	-	43	-	-	-	-	0	Haselmere(3T,D) Watts(3T) Coates(T,2C) Crookes(2T) F.M.Taylor(T) Bates(C) Vears(T)
19		26	BIRKENHEAD PARK	H	Won	1	6	-	-	23	-	-	-	-	0	Wilkinson(C) Crookes(T) Ringrose(T) Haselmere(3T) F.M.Taylor(2T)
20		27	ROYAL AIR FORCE	H	Won	2	4	-	-	22	1	-	-	-	5	Haselmere(T) Ringrose(2T) Butcher(2C) Bates(2T) Wood(T)
21		29	BARBARIANS	H	Won	1	4	-	-	17	-	2	-	-	6	Crookes(T) Butcher(C) Haselmere(T) Bates(T) Wood(T) Hicks(T)
22	Jan	1	Manchester	A	Won	3	5	-	-	30	1	1	-	-	8	Haselmere(4T) Watts(T) Coates(T) F.M.Taylor(T) Bates(T,3C)
23		3	GLOUCESTER	H	Won	1	3	-	-	14	-	3	-	-	9	F.M.Taylor(2T) Bates(T) Wood(T) Hicks(C)
24		10	Coventry	A	Won	-	4	-	-	12	-	-	-	-	0	Coates(2T) Crookes(T) F.M.Taylor(T)
25		17	HEADINGLEY	H	Won	6	7	-	1	54	1	1	-	1	11	Wilkinson(P) Haselmere(5T,C) Coates(2T) F.M.Taylor(T) Ringrose(T) Wood(T) Bates(T) G.Ward(T) Hicks(T) W.Norman(2C) D.J.Norman(3C)
26		24	The Army	A	Won	2	4	-	-	22	-	1	-	-	3	Rowlands(2T) Bates(3T) Allen(T) W.Norman(2C)
27		31	SWANSEA	H	Lost	-	3	-	-	9	1	1	-	1	11	Haselmere(T) Watts(T) Rowlands(T)
28	Feb	7	MOSELEY	H	Won	2	4	-	-	22	-	1	-	1	6	Rowlands(T) Barrett(T) Bates(2T) Wood(T) F.Taylor(T) J.E.Greenwood(2C)
29		14	Newport	A	Lost	1	-	-	-	5	5	4	-	-	37	Bates(T) W.Norman(C)
30		21	RICHMOND	H	Won	10	4	-	-	62	-	1	-	-	3	Haselmere(4T) Watts(2T) Coates(3T) F.M.Taylor(2T) Bates(T) Wood(T) J.E.Greenwood(10C) Hicks(T)
31		28	Cardiff	A	Won	2	2	-	-	16	-	1	-	-	3	Wilkinson(2C) F.M.Taylor(T) Wood(T) Bates(T) D.J.Norman(T)
32	Mar	6	HARLEQUINS	H	Won	1	5	-	-	20	-	-	-	-	0	Haselmere(T) F.M.Taylor(T) Read(T) J.E.Greenwood(C) G.Ward(3T)
33		13	Gloucester	A	Won	-	1	-	-	3	-	-	-	-	0	D.J.Norman(T)
34		20	NORTHAMPTON	H	Won	3	1	-	-	18	-	-	-	-	0	Haselmere(2T) Coates(T) F.M.Taylor(T) Allen(3C)
35		27	LONDON	H	Won	-	4	-	1	15	-	2	-	-	6	Coates(T) Wood(T) F.Taylor(T) Cross(T) D.J.Norman(P)
36	Apr	3	Bristol	A	Lost	-	3	-	-	9	2	1	-	-	13	Haselmere(T) Watts(2T)
37		5	Plymouth Albion	A	Lost	1	-	-	1	8	2	-	-	1	13	Wilkinson(C,P) Barrett(T)
38		6	Bath	A	Lost	1	1	-	-	8	1	1	2	-	16	Wilkinson(C) Haselmere(T) Coates(T)
39		10	OLD MERCHANT TAYLORS	H	Won	4	3	-	-	29	1	1	-	-	8	Wilkinson(4C) Haselmere(4T) Coates(T) F.M.Taylor(T) Barrett(T)
40		17	Birkenhead Park	A	Won	-	7	-	-	21	-	2	-	-	6	Haselmere(T) Coates(T) Thomas(2T) Bates(T) Allen(T) Hicks(T)
41		24	Northampton	A	Won	2	5	-	-	25	-	2	-	-	6	Wilkinson(2C) Haselmere(4T) Watts(T) Wood(T) Vears(T)

INDIVIDUAL APPEARANCES 1919-1920

NAME	TOTAL	T	PTS
J.Wilkinson	33		28
Teddy Haselmere	40	59	242
Eric Thorneloe	7		
A.Brown	5	2	6
R.A.Clarke	6	2	6
E.G.Butcher	5		6
Philip Hope	2		
A.Crookes	8	5	15
A.E.Barrett	8	3	9
Willy Watts	30	15	45
Norman Coates	29	20	64
R.B.Y.Simpson	2		
A.Rowlands	6	4	12
Robert Ringrose	7	5	15
G.M.Thomas	5	2	6
Tim' Taylor	26	15	45
Alf Bates	40	21	71
Pedlar' Wood	39	11	33
D.J.Ferguson	21		6
W.C.Hicks	34	6	20
Gordon Vears	36	3	9
George Ward	37	5	15
Jimmy Allen	35	4	28
A.Drew	3		
B.Parker	13	1	3
I.Spicer	9	1	3
Sos' Taylor	30	4	12
Trevor Thorneloe	17		
Bill Havard	2		
Gwyn Francis	11		
W.Elliott	3		
Charlie Cross	20	1	3
P.C.H.Homer	4		
Doug Norman	9	2	15
W.Norman	4		10
John Greenwood	3		26

1 game: Arthur Bull F(12), E.R.Butler F(36), W.G.Coltman W(7), Harold Day W(27), S.H.Dennis F(1), S.G.Ellis F(1), Dan Ellwood FB(2), A.D.Godfrey FH(4), S.C.Greenwood F(16), H.M.Horsley W(14), S.A.Hunter FB(3), W.H.Hynd F(20), Oswald Jenkins C(31), O.E.H. Leslie C(21), G.G.Marshall FB(21), Fred Mellor FB(1), A.Oscroft SH(18), W.Pollard W(23), C.Read C(32)[1T-3], E.Rice F(1), J.C.Seager C(1), Stuart Smith F(14), H.Sturgess F(1), John Thornton W(25), W.Ward W(1)

LEICESTER FOOTBALL CLUB 1919-20

Back: T. Thorpe (Hon.Tres), F. Taylor, G. Ward, W.C. Hicks, G. Vears, N. Coates, W.J. Watts, P.W. Lawrie.
Middle: H.W. Salmon (President), A.E. Barrett, D.G. Francis, J. Wilkinson, W.J. Allen (Capt), C.W. Cross, G.M. Thomas, T.H. Crumbie (Hon.Sec).
Front: D.J. Norman, E.E. Haselmere, A. Bates, G.W. Wood, F.M. Taylor.

NO	DATE		OPPONENTS	V	RES	FOR G	FOR T	FOR D	FOR P	FOR PTS	AGAINST G	AGAINST T	AGAINST D	AGAINST P	AGAINST PTS	SCORERS
1	Sep	4	BATH	H	Won	6	1	1	-	37	-	2	-	-	6	Wilkinson(6C) Haselmere(T) Coates(T) Thomas(T) Watts(T) G.W.Wood(T) Bates(D) F.Taylor(T) Hicks(T)
2		11	PLYMOUTH ALBION	H	Won	-	3	-	-	9	-	1	-	-	3	Lawrie(2T) Cross(T)
3		18	UNITED SERVICES	H	Won	4	4	-	-	32	-	1	1	-	7	Wilkinson(4C) Lawrie(T) Thomas(T) Haselmere(2T) G.Ward(2T) Wal.Buckler(2T)
4		22	Rugby	A	Won	2	4	-	-	22	-	2	-	-	6	Wilkinson(2C) Haselmere(2T) Coates(T) Watts(T) G.W.Wood(T) Bates(T)
5		25	BRADFORD	H	Won	4	3	1	-	33	2	-	-	-	10	Wilkinson(4C) Haselmere(D) Coates(T) Thomas(T) Lawrie(2T) Day(2T) Cross(T)
6	Oct	2	HEADINGLEY	H	Won	3	5	-	1	33	-	1	-	-	3	Wilkinson(2C) Haselmere(2T,C,P) Smallwood(T) Day(T) Bates(3T) Hicks(T)
7		9	LLANELLI	H	Won	1	4	1*	1	23	-	1	-	-	3	Wilkinson(P) Haselmere(3T) Thomas(M) Day(C) F.M.Taylor(T) F.Taylor(T)
8		16	BRISTOL	H	Won	4	1	-	-	23	-	4	-	-	12	Wilkinson(4C) Smallwood(T) Lawrie(T) Thornton(T) F.M.Taylor(T) G.Ward(T)
9		23	Newport	A	Lost	-	-	-	1	3	2	4	-	-	22	Wilkinson(P)
10		30	ABERAVON	H	Won	1	1	1*	-	11	-	1	-	1	6	Wilkinson(C) Day(T,M) F.Taylor(T)
11	Nov	6	OXFORD UNIVERSITY	H	Won	1	2	-	-	11	1	-	1	-	9	Wilkinson(C) Lawrie(T) Haselmere(2T)
12		13	CAMBRIDGE UNIVERSITY	H	Lost	1	2	-	-	11	1	2	-	1	14	Smallwood(T) Lawrie(T) Day(C) G.W.Wood(T)
13		20	THE ARMY	H	Won	2	3	-	-	19	1	1	1	-	12	Wilkinson(2C) Haselmere(T) Watts(2T) Lawrie(T) Vears(T)
14		27	Cardiff	A	Lost	1	1	-	-	8	1	2	-	-	11	Day(T,C) G.W.Wood(T)
15	Dec	4	MOSELEY	H	Won	3	6	-	-	33	1	-	-	-	5	F.E.Wood(T) Lawrie(T) Day(3T,3C) Cross(T) Coates(3T)
16		11	BLACKHEATH	H	Won	-	1	-	1	6	1	-	-	-	5	Day(P) Coates(T)
17		24	Coventry	A	Won	-	2	-	-	6	-	-	-	-	0	Haselmere(T) Watts(T)
18		27	BIRKENHEAD PARK	H	Won	3	2	-	-	21	1	2	-	1	14	Wilkinson(3C) Haselmere(3T) Lawrie(T) Norman(T)
19		28	ROYAL AIR FORCE	H	Won	5	1	-	-	28	2	2	-	-	16	Wilkinson(5C) Haselmere(T) Lawrie(2T) Norman(T) Wal.Buckler(T) Wickson(T)
20		29	BARBARIANS	H	Won	1	1	-	-	8	-	2	-	-	6	Wilkinson(C) F.M.Taylor(2T)
21	Jan	1	MANCHESTER	H	Won	4	5	-	1	38	-	3	-	-	9	Wilkinson(4C,P) Lawrie(T) Simpson(T) Haselmere(3T) G.W.Wood(T) Watts(T) Coates(T) Wickson(T)
22		8	Gloucester	A	Lost	-	1	-	-	3	1	1	1	-	12	Coates(T)
23		15	Bradford	A	Won	3	3	-	-	24	4	-	-	-	20	Day(T,3C) Lawrie(2T) G.W.Wood(T) F.M.Taylor(T) Coates(T)
24		17	Headingley	A	Won	1	3	-	-	14	-	-	-	-	0	Haselmere(T) Simpson(T) Day(C) Smallwood(2T)
25		22	COVENTRY	H	Won	-	1	-	-	3	-	-	-	-	0	Norman(T)
26		29	Llanelli	A	Lost	-	1	-	-	3	-	3	1	-	13	Lawrie(T)
27	Feb	5	Richmond	A	Won	2	1	-	-	13	-	1	-	-	3	Haselmere(2T) Lawrie(2C) Coates(T)
28		12	NEWPORT	H	Drew	-	-	-	1	3	-	1	-	-	3	Day(P)
29		23	Moseley	A	Drew	1	1	-	1	11	1	2	-	-	11	Wilkinson(C) Haselmere(2T) Lawrie(P)
30		26	CARDIFF	H	Won	1	3	-	-	14	1	-	1	-	9	Haselmere(T) Smallwood(T) Day(C) F.Taylor(T) Coates(T)
31	Mar	5	Harlequins	A	Lost	-	1	-	-	3	1	2	-	-	11	Watts(T)
32		12	LONDON WELSH	H	Won	3	3	-	-	24	1	-	-	1	8	Wilkinson(C) Haselmere(T) Day(2T,2C) Lawrie(2T) Allen(T)
33		19	Northampton	A	Lost	-	-	-	-	0	-	3	-	1	12	
34		26	Bristol	A	Won	2	-	-	-	10	-	1	1	-	7	Day(2C) G.W.Wood(T) Norman(T)
35		28	Plymouth Albion	A	Lost	1	-	-	-	5	-	5	-	-	15	Day(T,C)
36		29	Bath	A	Won	2	1	1	1	20	1	3	-	-	14	Haselmere(T) Day(2C,D,P) Lawrie(T) Allen(T)
37	Apr	2	GLOUCESTER	H	Won	-	1	-	-	3	-	-	-	-	0	F.Taylor(T)
38		9	NORTHAMPTON	H	Won	4	2	1	-	30	-	-	-	-	0	Wilkinson(4C) Souster(T) Lawrie(2T,D) Haselmere(T) G.Ward(2T)
39		12	Nuneaton	A	Won	2	3	-	-	19	-	-	-	1	3	Wilkinson(2C) Lawrie(2T) Gibbs(T) F.Taylor(T) Greenwood(T)
40		16	Birkenhead Park	A	Won	-	1	-	-	3	-	-	-	-	0	Lawrie(T)
41		23	LONDON	H	Won	1	4	-	1	20	1	-	-	-	5	Haselmere(T) Day(2T,C,P) Wakefield(2T)

INDIVIDUAL APPEARANCES 1920-1921

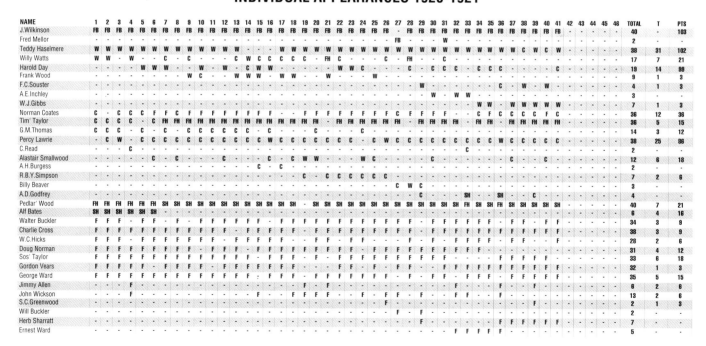

NAME	1	2	3	4	5	6	7	8	9	10	11	12	13	14	15	16	17	18	19	20	21	22	23	24	25	26	27	28	29	30	31	32	33	34	35	36	37	38	39	40	41	42	43	44	45	46	TOTAL	T	PTS
J.Wilkinson	FB	FB	FB	FB	FB	FB	FB	FB	FB	FB	FB	FB	FB	FB	FB	FB	FB	FB	FB	FB	FB	FB	FB	FB	FB	FB	-	FB	FB	FB	FB	FB	FB	FB	FB	FB	FB	FB	FB	FB	FB	-	-	-	-	-	40	-	103
Fred Mellor	-	-	-	-	-	-	-	-	-	-	-	-	-	-	-	-	-	-	-	-	-	-	-	-	-	-	FB	-	-	-	W	-	-	-	-	-	-	-	-	-	-	-	-	-	-	-	2	-	-
Teddy Haselmere	W	W	W	W	W	W	W	W	W	W	W	W	W	-	-	-	W	W	W	W	W	W	W	W	W	W	W	W	W	W	W	W	W	W	W	W	W	C	W	C	W	-	-	-	-	-	38	31	102
Willy Watts	W	W	-	W	-	-	C	-	C	-	-	-	C	W	C	C	C	C	C	-	FH	C	-	-	-	C	-	FH	-	-	C	-	-	-	-	-	-	-	-	-	-	-	-	-	-	-	17	7	21
Harold Day	-	-	-	-	W	W	W	-	-	W	-	W	-	C	W	W	-	-	-	-	-	W	W	C	-	-	-	C	-	C	C	C	-	C	C	C	-	-	-	-	C	-	-	-	-	-	19	14	99
Frank Wood	-	-	-	-	-	-	-	-	W	C	-	-	W	W	W	-	W	W	-	-	W	-	-	-	W	-	-	-	-	-	-	-	-	-	-	-	-	-	-	-	-	-	-	-	-	-	9	1	3
F.C.Souster	-	-	-	-	-	-	-	-	-	-	-	-	-	-	-	-	-	-	-	-	-	-	-	-	-	-	-	-	W	-	-	-	-	-	-	C	-	W	-	W	-	-	-	-	-	-	4	1	3
A.E.Inchley	-	-	-	-	-	-	-	-	-	-	-	-	-	-	-	-	-	-	-	-	-	-	-	-	-	-	-	-	-	W	-	W	W	-	-	-	-	-	-	-	-	-	-	-	-	-	3	-	-
W.J.Gibbs	-	-	-	-	-	-	-	-	-	-	-	-	-	-	-	-	-	-	-	-	-	-	-	-	-	-	-	-	-	-	-	-	-	W	W	-	W	W	W	W	W	-	-	-	-	-	7	1	3
Norman Coates	C	-	C	C	C	F	F	C	F	F	F	F	F	F	F	F	-	-	F	F	F	F	F	F	F	F	C	F	F	F	F	-	-	C	F	C	C	C	C	F	C	-	-	-	-	-	36	12	36
Tim' Taylor	C	C	C	C	-	C	FH	FH	FH	FH	FH	FH	FH	FH	FH	FH	FH	FH	FH	FH	-	FH	FH	FH	FH	FH	FH	-	FH	FH	FH	FH	-	FH	FH	-	FH	FH	FH	FH	FH	-	-	-	-	-	36	5	15
G.M.Thomas	C	C	C	-	C	-	C	-	C	C	C	C	C	C	-	C	-	-	-	C	-	-	-	C	-	-	-	-	-	-	-	-	-	-	-	-	-	-	-	-	-	-	-	-	-	-	14	3	12
Percy Lawrie	-	C	W	-	C	C	C	C	C	C	C	C	C	C	C	W	C	C	C	C	C	C	C	-	C	W	C	C	C	C	C	C	C	C	C	W	C	C	C	C	C	-	-	-	-	-	38	25	86
C.Read	-	-	-	C	-	-	-	-	-	-	-	-	-	-	-	-	-	-	-	-	-	-	-	-	-	-	-	-	-	-	-	-	C	-	-	-	-	-	-	-	-	-	-	-	-	-	2	-	-
Alastair Smallwood	-	-	-	-	-	C	-	C	-	-	-	-	C	-	-	C	-	C	W	W	-	-	-	W	C	-	-	-	-	C	-	-	-	-	-	-	C	-	-	C	-	-	-	-	-	-	12	6	18
A.H.Burgess	-	-	-	-	-	-	-	-	-	-	-	-	-	-	C	-	C	-	-	-	-	-	-	-	-	-	-	-	-	-	-	-	-	-	-	-	-	-	-	-	-	-	-	-	-	-	2	-	-
R.B.Y.Simpson	-	-	-	-	-	-	-	-	-	-	-	-	-	-	-	-	-	-	C	-	C	C	C	C	C	C	-	-	-	-	-	-	-	-	-	-	-	-	-	-	-	-	-	-	-	-	7	2	6
Billy Beaver	-	-	-	-	-	-	-	-	-	-	-	-	-	-	-	-	-	-	-	-	-	-	-	-	-	-	C	W	C	-	-	-	-	-	-	-	-	-	-	-	-	-	-	-	-	-	3	-	-
A.D.Godfrey	-	-	-	-	-	-	-	-	-	-	-	-	-	-	-	-	-	-	-	-	-	-	-	-	-	-	-	-	C	-	-	-	SH	-	-	SH	-	-	C	-	-	-	-	-	-	-	4	-	-
Pedlar' Wood	FH	FH	FH	FH	FH	FH	SH	SH	SH	SH	SH	SH	SH	SH	SH	SH	SH	SH	-	SH	SH	SH	SH	SH	SH	SH	SH	SH	SH	SH	SH	SH	FH	SH	SH	FH	SH	SH	SH	SH	SH	-	-	-	-	-	40	7	21
Alf Bates	SH	SH	SH	SH	SH	SH	-	-	-	-	-	-	-	-	-	-	-	-	-	-	-	-	-	-	-	-	-	-	-	-	-	-	-	-	-	-	-	-	-	-	-	-	-	-	-	-	6	4	16
Walter Buckler	F	F	F	-	F	F	-	F	-	F	F	F	F	F	F	-	F	F	F	F	F	F	F	F	F	F	F	F	-	F	F	F	F	F	F	-	F	F	-	F	F	-	-	-	-	-	34	3	9
Charlie Cross	F	F	F	F	F	F	F	F	F	F	F	F	-	F	F	F	F	F	F	-	F	F	F	F	F	F	F	F	-	F	F	F	F	F	F	F	F	F	F	F	F	-	-	-	-	-	38	3	9
W.C.Hicks	F	F	F	-	F	F	F	F	F	F	F	-	F	F	F	F	F	-	-	F	F	-	F	F	-	-	-	F	-	F	-	F	F	F	F	-	F	F	-	-	F	-	-	-	-	-	28	2	6
Doug Norman	F	F	F	F	F	F	F	F	F	-	F	F	F	-	F	F	F	F	F	F	F	F	F	-	F	F	F	F	F	F	F	F	F	F	-	-	-	-	-	-	-	-	-	-	-	-	31	4	12
Sos' Taylor	F	F	F	F	F	F	F	F	F	F	F	F	F	F	-	F	F	F	-	F	-	F	F	F	F	F	F	F	F	F	F	-	-	-	-	F	F	F	F	F	-	-	-	-	-	-	33	6	18
Gordon Vears	F	F	F	F	F	-	F	F	F	F	-	F	F	F	F	F	F	F	-	-	-	F	F	-	F	-	F	F	-	-	F	F	F	F	F	F	F	F	F	F	F	-	-	-	-	-	32	1	3
George Ward	F	F	F	F	F	F	F	F	F	F	F	F	F	F	-	F	F	F	-	F	F	F	F	F	F	F	-	F	-	F	F	-	F	F	F	-	F	F	F	F	F	-	-	-	-	-	35	5	15
Jimmy Allen	-	-	-	F	-	-	-	-	-	-	-	-	-	-	-	-	-	-	F	-	F	-	-	-	-	-	-	-	-	-	-	F	-	-	-	F	-	-	F	-	-	-	-	-	-	-	6	2	6
John Wickson	-	-	-	F	-	-	-	-	-	-	-	-	-	-	F	-	-	F	F	F	F	-	-	F	-	F	F	-	F	-	-	F	F	-	-	F	-	-	-	-	-	-	-	-	-	-	13	2	6
S.C.Greenwood	-	-	-	-	-	-	-	-	-	-	-	-	-	-	-	-	-	-	-	-	-	-	-	-	-	F	-	-	-	-	-	-	-	-	-	-	-	-	F	-	-	-	-	-	-	-	2	1	3
Will Buckler	-	-	-	-	-	-	-	-	-	-	-	-	-	-	-	-	-	-	-	-	-	-	-	-	-	-	F	-	F	-	-	-	-	-	-	-	-	-	-	-	-	-	-	-	-	-	2	-	-
Herb Sharratt	-	-	-	-	-	-	-	-	-	-	-	-	-	-	-	-	-	-	-	-	-	-	-	-	-	-	-	-	F	-	-	-	-	-	-	F	F	F	F	F	F	-	-	-	-	-	7	-	-
Ernest Ward	-	-	-	-	-	-	-	-	-	-	-	-	-	-	-	-	-	-	-	-	-	-	-	-	-	-	-	-	-	-	-	F	F	F	F	F	-	-	-	-	-	-	-	-	-	-	5	-	-

1 game: C.L.Burton W(11), A.J.Coulter F(19), H.W.Hill F(19), R.C.Jones C(35), A.Oscroft SH(19), Arthur Palmer F(29), D.G.Slack W(27), John Thornton W(8)[1T-3], Wavell Wakefield F(41)[2T-6], L.Woodhead C(11)

1921-1922

NO	DATE		OPPONENTS	V	RES	FOR					AGAINST					SCORERS
						G	T	D	P	PTS	G	T	D	P	PTS	
1	Sep	3	BATH	H	Won	-	3	1	-	13	-	2	-	-	6	Day(T,D) Watts(T) Coates(T)
2		10	PLYMOUTH ALBION	H	Lost	-	-	1	-	4	1	-	-	-	5	Haselmere(D)
3		12	Burton-on-Trent	A	Won	2	4	-	-	22	-	-	-	1	3	Haselmere(4T) Day(T,2C) Souster(T)
4		17	UNITED SERVICES	H	Won	-	1	-	1	6	1	-	-	-	5	Wilkinson(P) Lawrie(T)
5		24	BRADFORD	H	Won	2	2	-	-	16	1	2	1	-	15	Day(2C) Lawrie(2T) Smallwood(T) Sharratt(T)
6		28	Sheffield	A	Won	1	4	-	-	17	-	2	-	-	6	Wilkinson(C) Gibbs(2T) Lawrie(T) Godfrey(T) Coates(T)
7	Oct	1	HEADINGLEY	H	Won	1	3	-	-	14	1	-	-	-	5	Wilkinson(C) Godfrey(T) Lawrie(2T) Gibbs(T)
8		8	LLANELLI	H	Won	-	1	-	1	6	-	1	-	-	3	Day(P) Lawrie(T)
9		15	ABERAVON	H	Won	2	2	-	1	19	-	2	-	-	6	Craigmile(2T) Day(T,2C,P) Haselmere(T)
10		22	NORTHAMPTON	H	Won	4	3	-	-	29	-	-	1	-	4	Wilkinson(2C) Day(2T,2C) Godfrey(T) Lawrie(T) Coates(T) Norman(T) Sharratt(T)
11		27	Cambridge University	A	Won	2	1	-	-	13	1	2	-	-	11	Day(2C) Lawrie(T) Smallwood(T) Coates(T)
12		29	NEWPORT	H	Lost	-	1	-	1	6	2	-	-	-	10	Day(P) Norman(T)
13	Nov	5	SWANSEA	H	Lost	-	-	-	1	3	1	-	-	-	5	Day(P)
		12	LANSDOWNE	H		Cancelled Fog										
14		16	Oxford University	A	Lost	1	-	-	-	5	-	3	-	1	12	Day(C) German(T)
15		19	COVENTRY	H	Won	2	6	-	-	28	-	-	-	-	0	Wilkinson(C) Haselmere(2T) Day(T) Godfrey(T) Coates(C) Wilkins(T) F.M.Taylor(T) F.Taylor(2T)
16		26	CARDIFF	H	Won	-	2	-	1	9	-	1	-	-	3	Day(P) Coates(2T)
17	Dec	3	Moseley	A	Won	-	4	-	-	12	-	-	-	-	0	Wilkins(T) F.M.Taylor(T) Godfrey(2T)
18		10	Blackheath	A	Drew	-	2	-	-	6	-	2	-	-	6	Wilkins(T) Norman(T)
19		17	BRISTOL	H	Lost	1	2	-	-	11	2	-	1	-	14	Sambrook(C) Coates(T) F.M.Taylor(T) Sharratt(T)
20		24	ROYAL AIR FORCE	H	Won	-	1	-	1	6	1	-	-	-	5	Wilkinson(P) Wilkins(T)
21		26	BIRKENHEAD PARK	H	Won	1	2	-	-	11	-	2	-	-	6	Sambrook(C) Haselmere(T) Watts(T) Buckler(T)
22		27	BARBARIANS	H	Won	3	3	1	-	28	2	-	-	-	10	Wilkinson(D) Wilkins(T) Day(T,3C) Coates(T) Cross(T) Hicks(T) R.H.C.Usher(T)
23		31	WAKEFIELD	H	Won	4	2	1	-	30	-	-	-	-	0	Wilkinson(4C,D) Haselmere(T) Smallwood(3T) Wilkins(T) Cross(T)
24	Jan	2	Manchester	A	Won	3	2	-	-	21	1	-	-	-	5	Wilkinson(3C) Haselmere(T) Smallwood(T) Cross(T) Lawrence(T) R.H.C.Usher(T)
25		7	GLOUCESTER	H	Lost	-	3	-	-	9	2	-	-	-	10	Pollard(T) Wilkins(T) Cross(T)
26		14	Swansea	A	Won	2	1	-	-	13	-	1	-	2	9	Day(2T,2C) F.Taylor(T)
27		16	Llanelli	A	Lost	-	1	-	-	3	-	3	1	-	13	Wilkins(T)
28		21	PILL HARRIERS	H	Won	3	2	-	1	24	-	-	-	-	0	Sambrook(3C,P) Craigmile(3T) Godfrey(T) Lawrence(T)
29		28	Coventry	A	Won	4	1	-	-	23	1	-	-	-	5	Haselmere(T) Day(T,4C) Craigmile(T) Coates(T) Norman(T)
30	Feb	4	RICHMOND	H	Won	-	2	-	-	6	1	-	-	-	5	Coates(T) Lawrence(T)
31		11	Newport	A	Lost	-	3	-	-	9	1	3	1	2	24	Haselmere(T) Coates(T) Norman(T)
32		15	THE ARMY	H	Won	1	1	-	-	8	-	1	-	-	3	Sambrook(C) Wilkins(T) Bradbury(T)
33		18	MOSELEY	H	Won	1	7	-	-	26	-	1	-	-	3	Coates(C) Godfrey(T) Haselmere(3T) F.M.Taylor(T) Wood(T) F.Taylor(T) Cross(T)
34		25	Cardiff	A	Drew	-	1	-	-	3	-	1	-	-	3	Morgan(T)
35	Mar	4	HARLEQUINS	H	Won	1	1	-	-	8	-	-	-	-	0	Haselmere(T) Smallwood(T) Hicks(C)
36		11	LONDON WELSH	H	Won	3	3	-	-	24	1	-	-	-	5	Wilkins(T) Godfrey(T) Hett(T) Haselmere(2C) F.M.Taylor(T) Wood(T) Lawrence(T) Thorneloe(C)
37		18	Northampton	A	Won	1	2	-	-	11	-	-	1	1	7	Sambrook(C) Coates(T) Haselmere(T) Cross(T)
38		25	Gloucester	A	Lost	-	1	-	-	3	1	3	-	1	17	F.M.Taylor(T)
39		27	Bradford	A	Won	1	4	-	-	17	-	2	-	-	6	Haselmere(T) Coates(T) Day(C) Wilkins(T) F.M.Taylor(T) Cross(T)
40	Apr	1	LONDON	H	Won	3	6	-	-	33	-	1	-	-	3	Haselmere(T) Day(2T,2C) Smallwood(T,C) Wilkins(T) Hicks(2T) Cross(2T)
41		8	Birkenhead Park	A	Lost	1	-	-	-	5	3	-	-	-	15	F.M.Taylor(T) Hicks(C)
42		15	Bristol	A	Drew	-	-	-	-	0	-	-	-	-	0	
43		17	Plymouth Albion	A	Drew	-	-	-	-	0	-	-	-	-	0	
44		18	Bath	A	Lost	-	-	-	-	0	1	1	-	-	8	

INDIVIDUAL APPEARANCES 1921-1922

NAME	1	2	3	4	5	6	7	8	9	10	11	12	13	14	15	16	17	18	19	20	21	22	23	24	25	26	27	28	29	30	31	32	33	34	35	36	37	38	39	40	41	42	43	44	45	46	TOTAL	T	PTS
J.Wilkinson	FB	FB	FB	FB	-	FB	FB	FB	FB	FB	FB	FB	FB	FB	FB	FB	FB	FB	-	FB	-	FB	FB	FB	FB	FB	FB	-	-	-	-	-	-	-	-	-	-	-	-	-	-	-	-	-	-	-	24	-	38
Teddy Haselmere	W	W	W	C	W	-	-	-	W	W	W	W	W	C	W	W	W	W	W	W	W	W	W	W	W	-	-	W	W	W	W	C	W	W	W	W	W	W	W	W	W	W	W	W	-	-	39	19	65
F.C.Souster	W	W	W	W	-	W	W	W	C	-	-	-	W	-	-	-	-	-	-	-	-	-	-	-	-	-	-	-	-	-	-	-	-	-	-	-	-	-	-	-	-	-	-	-	-	-	9	1	3
W.J.Gibbs	-	-	-	W	-	W	W	-	-	-	-	-	-	W	-	-	-	-	-	-	-	-	-	-	-	-	-	-	-	-	-	-	-	-	-	-	-	-	-	-	-	-	-	-	-	-	4	3	9
H.W.C.Craigmile	-	-	-	-	W	-	C	W	W	W	-	W	-	-	-	-	-	-	-	-	-	-	-	-	-	-	-	C	C	-	-	-	-	-	-	-	-	-	-	-	-	-	-	-	-	-	8	6	18
W.C.Wilkins	-	-	-	-	-	-	-	-	-	-	-	-	-	W	W	W	C	W	W	W	W	W	W	W	W	W	W	-	W	W	W	W	-	-	W	W	W	-	W	W	W	-	-	-	-	-	24	12	36
R.W.Holmes	-	-	-	-	-	-	-	-	-	-	-	-	-	-	-	-	-	-	-	-	-	-	-	-	-	-	-	W	-	-	-	-	W	W	-	-	-	-	-	-	-	-	-	-	-	-	3	-	-
Harold Day	C	C	C	-	C	-	-	C	C	C	C	C	C	C	C	C	-	-	-	-	-	C	-	-	-	C	C	-	C	C	-	-	-	-	-	-	-	C	C	C	-	C	-	-	-	-	22	12	101
Percy Lawrie	C	C	-	C	C	C	C	C	-	C	C	C	-	-	-	-	-	-	-	-	-	-	-	-	-	-	-	-	-	-	-	-	-	-	-	-	-	-	-	-	-	-	-	-	-	-	10	9	27
Willy Watts	C	C	C	C	-	-	-	-	-	-	-	-	-	-	-	-	W	-	-	-	C	-	-	-	-	C	W	-	-	-	-	-	-	-	-	-	-	-	-	-	-	-	C	C	-	-	10	2	6
Claude Sambrook	-	-	C	-	FB	-	-	-	-	-	-	-	-	-	-	-	-	-	FB	-	FB	-	-	-	-	-	-	FB	FB	FB	FB	FB	FB	FB	FB	FB	FB	FB	FB	FB	FB	FB	FB	FB	-	-	21	-	17
Alastair Smallwood	-	-	-	-	C	-	-	-	-	-	W	-	-	-	-	-	-	-	-	C	C	C	C	C	-	-	-	-	-	C	-	-	-	-	C	-	-	-	-	C	-	C	C	C	-	-	13	8	26
G.Hoyle	-	-	-	-	-	-	-	-	-	-	-	-	C	-	-	-	C	C	C	-	-	-	-	-	-	-	-	-	-	-	-	-	-	-	-	-	-	-	-	-	-	-	-	-	-	-	4	-	-
H.N.Usher	-	-	-	-	-	-	-	-	-	-	-	-	-	-	-	-	-	-	-	-	-	-	C	C	C	-	C	C	C	C	-	C	C	-	-	-	C	-	-	-	-	-	-	-	-	-	10	-	-
H.H.Storrs	-	-	-	-	-	-	-	-	-	-	-	-	-	-	-	-	-	-	-	-	-	-	-	-	-	-	-	-	-	-	-	-	-	-	-	-	-	-	-	-	-	C	C	W	-	-	3	-	-
Tim' Taylor	FH	-	-	FH	FH	FH	FH	FH	FH	FH	FH	FH	FH	FH	FH	FH	FH	FH	FH	FH	FH	FH	FH	FH	FH	FH	FH	FH	FH	FH	FH	FH	FH	FH	FH	FH	FH	FH	FH	FH	FH	FH	FH	-	-	-	41	8	24
A.D.Godfrey	-	FH	FH	-	SH	SH	C	C	C	C	C	C	SH	C	C	C	SH	C	C	C	C	C	C	C	-	-	-	SH	SH	SH	C	-	C	C	C	C	C	C	C	-	C	-	W	FH	-	-	36	9	27
Pedlar' Wood	SH	SH	SH	SH	-	-	SH	-	-	-	-	-	-	-	-	-	-	SH	-	-	-	-	-	SH	-	-	-	-	-	-	SH	-	SH	-	-	SH	-	-	-	-	-	-	-	-	-	-	10	2	6
Guy German	-	-	-	-	-	-	-	SH	SH	SH	SH	SH	-	SH	SH	-	-	-	SH	SH	SH	SH	SH	-	SH	SH	SH	-	-	-	-	-	-	-	-	-	SH	-	-	-	SH	-	-	-	-	-	17	1	3
John Russell	-	-	-	-	-	-	-	-	-	-	-	-	-	-	-	-	-	-	-	-	-	-	-	-	-	-	-	-	-	-	-	SH	-	SH	SH	-	-	SH	SH	SH	C	SH	SH	SH	-	-	10	-	-
Walter Buckler	F	F	-	F	-	-	-	-	-	-	-	-	F	F	F	F	F	F	F	F	F	-	F	F	F	F	F	F	F	F	F	F	F	F	F	F	F	F	F	F	F	F	-	F	-	-	33	1	3
Norman Coates	F	F	F	F	F	F	F	F	F	F	F	F	C	-	C	C	C	C	C	-	F	F	F	-	C	C	C	C	F	F	C	C	C	C	C	C	C	W	C	C	C	W	-	C	-	-	40	13	43
Charlie Cross	F	F	F	F	F	F	F	F	F	F	-	F	F	-	-	F	F	F	-	F	F	F	F	F	F	F	F	F	F	F	F	-	F	-	-	F	F	F	F	F	F	F	F	F	-	-	37	9	27
W.C.Hicks	F	F	F	F	F	F	F	F	F	F	F	F	F	F	F	F	F	F	-	-	-	F	F	-	-	F	-	-	-	-	F	F	-	F	F	-	-	F	F	F	F	F	-	-	-	-	30	3	13
Herb Sharratt	F	-	F	F	F	F	F	F	F	F	F	F	F	F	F	-	F	-	F	F	-	-	-	-	-	-	-	F	-	-	-	F	F	-	-	F	F	-	-	-	-	-	-	-	-	-	22	3	9
Sos' Taylor	F	F	-	-	-	-	-	-	-	-	-	-	-	F	F	F	F	F	F	F	F	F	F	F	F	F	F	F	F	F	F	F	F	F	F	F	F	F	F	F	F	F	F	F	-	-	33	4	12
George Ward	F	F	F	F	-	-	F	F	F	F	F	F	F	F	F	F	F	F	F	F	F	F	-	F	F	F	F	F	F	F	-	-	F	F	F	F	-	F	F	F	F	F	F	F	-	-	38	-	-
Doug Norman	-	F	F	F	F	F	F	F	F	F	F	F	F	F	F	F	-	F	F	F	F	F	F	F	F	-	F	F	F	F	F	F	F	F	F	-	-	-	F	F	F	-	F	F	-	-	37	5	15
Frank Lawrence	-	-	-	-	-	-	F	F	F	F	F	F	F	F	F	F	F	F	F	F	-	-	-	F	F	F	F	F	F	F	F	F	F	F	F	F	F	F	-	-	-	-	F	F	-	-	31	4	12
Trevor Thorneloe	-	-	-	-	-	-	-	-	-	-	-	-	-	-	-	-	-	-	F	-	-	-	-	-	F	-	-	-	-	-	-	F	-	-	-	F	F	-	-	-	-	-	-	-	-	-	5	-	2
Bob Usher	-	-	-	-	-	-	-	-	-	-	-	-	-	-	-	-	-	-	-	-	-	F	F	F	-	F	F	-	-	-	F	-	-	F	F	-	F	F	F	F	F	F	F	F	-	-	16	2	6

2 games: Cyril Adams F(38,43), W.Pollard C(25)W(26)[1T-3], Gordon Vears F(3,5), John Wickson F(5,6)
1 game: A.Bradbury W(32)[1T-3], Ernie Coleman F(11), Gwyn Francis F(31), T.W.Gabriel C(20), A.W.Harris F(21), A.S.Hett C(36)[1T-3], Col. Hitch F(6), C.L.Lowe F(42), Arthur Morgan C(34)[1T-3], P.Smitten C(6), A.Tearle F(6), F.Turnbull SH(16)

LEICESTER FOOTBALL CLUB 1921-22

Back: T.H. Crumbie (Hon.Sec), A.D. Godfrey, G.J. German, N.T. Thorneloe, H.N. Usher, W.C. Hicks, H. Sharratt, S.F. Lawrence, J. Wilkinson, A.M. Smallwood.

Middle: T. Thorpe (Hon.Tres), F. Taylor, D.J. Norman, G. Ward, P.W. Lawrie (Capt), H.L.V. Day, N. Coates, C.W. Cross, R.H.C. Usher.

Front: J.C. Russell, W.C. Wilkins, F.M. Taylor, E.E. Haselmere, L.C. Sambrook, W. Buckler.

1922-1923

NO	DATE		OPPONENTS	V	RES	FOR G	FOR T	FOR D	FOR P	FOR PTS	AGAINST G	AGAINST T	AGAINST D	AGAINST P	AGAINST PTS	SCORERS
1	Sep	2	BATH	H	Won	1	1	2	-	16	1	1	-	-	8	Storrs(T) Day(T,C,D) Norman(D)
2		9	PLYMOUTH ALBION	H	Lost	-	-	-	2	6	1	2	-	-	11	Sambrook(2P)
3		16	NEATH	H	Won	-	1	-	1	6	-	1	-	-	3	Storrs(T) Day(P)
4		20	Rugby B.T.H.	A	Won	2	3	-	-	19	-	-	-	-	0	Coates(T) Haselmere(T) Lawrie(T,2C) F.M.Taylor(T) Buchanan(T)
5		23	NUNEATON	H	Won	4	2	1	1	33	1	-	-	-	5	Storrs(T) Haselmere(D) Day(T,4C,P) F.Wright(T) Coates(T) Cross(T) Buchanan(T)
6		30	HEADINGLEY	H	Won	5	5	-	2	46	1	-	-	-	5	Sambrook(C) Storrs(T) Smallwood(2T) Day(2T,4C,2P) F.Wright(T) Russell(T) F.Taylor(T) Coates(T) Grierson(T)
7	Oct	7	LLANELLI	H	Lost	-	1	-	-	3	-	-	1	-	4	F.M.Taylor(T)
8		11	Moseley	A	Won	2	3	-	-	19	-	2	-	-	6	Lawrie(2C) Haselmere(2T) Marques(T) German(T) Norman(T)
9		14	ABERAVON	H	Won	-	1	-	-	3	-	-	-	-	0	F.Wright(T)
10		21	Newport	A	Lost	-	-	-	1	3	1	4	-	-	17	Day(P)
11		28	OXFORD UNIVERSITY	H	Won	5	1	-	-	28	-	-	-	-	0	Day(5C) Coates(T) F.Wright(T) F.M.Taylor(2T) F.Taylor(2T)
12	Nov	4	SWANSEA	H	Won	1	1	-	-	8	-	-	-	-	0	Haselmere(T) Day(C) F.Wright(T)
13		11	CAMBRIDGE UNIVERSITY	H	Won	1	2	1	-	15	-	1	-	1	6	Day(2T,C) Haselmere(D) F.M.Taylor(T)
14		18	Northampton	A	Won	3	1	1*	-	21	-	1	-	-	3	Sambrook(M) Day(T,3C) Bryson(2T) F.M.Taylor(T)
15		25	CARDIFF	H	Lost	-	-	-	1	3	-	1	1	-	7	Day(P)
16	Dec	2	Harlequins	A	Won	2	-	-	-	10	-	1	-	1	6	Sambrook(2C) F.Wright(T) Sharratt(T)
17		9	BLACKHEATH	H	Won	-	2	-	1	9	-	1	-	-	3	Day(2T,P)
18		16	BRISTOL	H	Drew	-	-	-	-	0	-	-	-	-	0	
19		23	Coventry	A	Won	1	3	-	-	14	-	-	-	-	0	Sambrook(C) Haselmere(T) F.M.Taylor(T) Coates(2T)
20		26	BIRKENHEAD PARK	H	Won	1	2	-	-	11	1	-	-	-	5	Smallwood(T,C) Russell(T) Sharratt(T)
21		27	BARBARIANS	H	Drew	-	1	-	-	3	-	1	-	-	3	F.Taylor(T)
22		28	RACING CLUB FRANCE	H	Won	-	-	1	-	4	-	-	-	-	0	Haselmere(D)
23		30	MANCHESTER	H	Won	3	7	-	-	36	-	-	-	-	0	Sambrook(2C) Smallwood(7T,C) Haselmere(2T) Sharratt(T)
24	Jan	1	Headingley	A	Won	4	5	-	-	35	-	-	-	-	0	Sambrook(C) Francis(3T) G.Jones(2T) F.Wright(T) Baker(T) Cross(T) Sharratt(T) Thorneloe(3C)
25		6	ROYAL AIR FORCE	H	Won	2	-	1	-	14	-	1	-	-	3	Sambrook(2C) Haselmere(D) F.M.Taylor(T) C.W.Jones(T)
26		13	Swansea	A	Won	-	2	-	-	6	-	-	1	-	4	Haselmere(T) Usher(T)
27		20	LONDON IRISH	H	Won	2	3	-	1	22	-	-	-	1	3	Sambrook(2C,P) Wardrop(T) Roxburgh(T) F.Wright(T) F.Taylor(T) J.E.Davis(T)
28		27	COVENTRY	H	Won	2	2	-	2	22	1	-	-	-	5	Day(2C,2P) F.Wright(2T) F.Taylor(T) Sharratt(T)
29	Feb	3	Richmond	A	Won	2	1	-	-	13	1	-	-	-	5	Haselmere(T) Coates(T) Sharratt(T) Thorneloe(2C)
30		13	Racing Club France	A	Lost	-	3	-	-	9	2	3	-	-	19	Wallace(T) F.M.Taylor(T) Cross(T)
31		15	United Services	A	Drew	-	-	-	1	3	-	-	-	1	3	Thorneloe(P)
32		17	Plymouth Albion	A	Lost	1	-	-	-	5	-	5	-	-	15	Sambrook(C) F.M.Taylor(T)
33		24	Cardiff	A	Lost	-	-	-	-	0	3	3	-	-	24	
34	Mar	3	HARLEQUINS	H	Won	1	2	-	-	11	-	-	1	-	4	Smallwood(T,C) F.M.Taylor(T) Ward(T)
35		10	NORTHAMPTON	H	Won	1	3	-	-	14	1	2	-	-	11	Haselmere(T) Day(T,C) F.Wright(T) F.Taylor(T)
36		17	LONDON WELSH	H	Won	4	2	1	1	33	1	-	-	1	8	Sambrook(D) Day(T,4C,P) Pollard(2T) F.Taylor(2T) Grierson(T)
37		31	Bristol	A	Won	-	1	-	-	3	-	-	-	-	0	Haselmere(T)
38	Apr	2	Llanelli	A	Lost	-	-	-	-	0	-	5	1	-	19	
39		3	Aberavon	A	Drew	1	1	-	-	8	1	1	-	-	8	Sambrook(C) Haselmere(2T)
40		4	Bath	A	Lost	-	-	-	1	3	2	1	1	-	17	Day(P)
41		7	LONDON SCOTTISH	H	Won	3	4	-	1	30	1	1	1	-	12	Day(T,3C,P) Price(T) Burton(T) F.M.Taylor(T) Cross(T) Thorneloe(2T)
42		9	Nuneaton	A	Won	-	4	-	-	12	-	1	-	-	3	Haselmere(2T) Pollard(T) Lawrie(T)
43		18	Birkenhead Park	A	Drew	-	2	-	-	6	-	2	-	-	6	Coates(T) Ward(T)
44		21	LONDON	H	Won	1	2	-	-	11	-	2	1	-	10	Lawrie(C) Bryson(T) Burton(T) F.M.Taylor(T)
45		28	NEWPORT	H	Lost	-	-	-	2	6	-	-	1	1	7	Day(2P)

INDIVIDUAL APPEARANCES 1922-1923

NAME	1	2	3	4	5	6	7	8	9	10	11	12	13	14	15	16	17	18	19	20	21	22	23	24	25	26	27	28	29	30	31	32	33	34	35	36	37	38	39	40	41	42	43	44	45	46	TOTAL	T	PTS
Claude Sambrook	FB	FB	FB	-	FB	FB	FB	-	-	-	FB	FB	FB	FB	FB	FB	FB	FB	FB	FB	FB	FB	FB	FB	FB	FB	FB	-	FB	FB	FB	FB	FB	FB	FB	FB	FB	FB	FB	FB	FB	FB	-	FB	FB	-	39	-	42
E.J.Crisp	-	-	-	FB	-	-	-	-	FB	FB	-	-	-	-	-	-	-	-	-	-	-	-	-	-	-	-	-	-	-	-	-	-	-	-	-	-	-	-	-	-	-	-	-	-	-	-	3	-	-
Teddy Haselmere	W	W	C	C	C	C	W	W	W	C	W	W	C	W	W	C	C	C	W	C	C	W	C	W	C	W	W	W	W	C	W	C	W	W	W	W	W	W	W	W	W	W	C	W	W	-	45	15	61
F.Wright	W	W	W	W	W	W	W	W	W	W	W	W	W	W	W	W	W	W	C	-	W	W	W	W	W	W	W	W	W	W	-	W	W	W	W	-	W	W	W	-	-	W	W	-	-	-	38	11	33
W.C.Wilkins	-	-	-	-	-	-	-	-	-	-	-	-	-	-	-	W	W	W	W	W	W	-	-	-	-	-	-	-	-	-	-	-	-	-	-	-	-	-	-	-	-	-	-	-	-	-	6	-	-
C.L.Burton	-	-	-	-	-	-	-	-	-	-	-	-	-	-	-	-	-	-	-	-	-	-	-	-	-	-	-	-	-	-	-	-	-	-	-	-	-	-	-	W	W	-	W	W	W	-	5	2	6
Norman Coates	C	C	F	C	F	F	F	C	C	C	C	C	-	C	F	C	F	-	F	C	-	C	-	-	-	-	-	F	C	C	-	C	C	-	-	C	C	C	C	C	-	C	C	C	C	-	33	8	24
Harold Day	C	-	C	-	C	C	C	-	C	C	C	C	C	C	C	-	C	-	-	-	-	-	-	-	-	-	-	FB	-	-	-	-	-	-	C	C	C	-	-	C	C	-	-	-	C	-	20	12	140
H.H.Storrs	C	-	W	-	W	W	-	-	-	-	-	-	-	-	-	-	-	-	-	-	-	-	-	-	-	-	-	-	-	-	-	-	-	-	-	-	-	-	-	-	-	-	-	-	-	-	4	4	12
Alastair Smallwood	-	-	C	-	-	C	-	-	C	-	-	-	W	-	C	-	-	-	-	W	C	C	C	-	-	-	-	C	-	-	-	-	-	C	C	-	-	-	-	-	-	-	-	-	-	-	12	11	39
Percy Lawrie	-	-	-	C	C	-	-	FB	-	-	-	-	-	-	-	-	-	C	-	-	-	-	-	-	-	-	-	-	-	-	-	-	-	-	-	-	-	-	-	C	C	C	-	C	C	-	9	2	16
O.C.Bryson	-	-	-	-	-	-	C	-	-	W	C	C	C	C	C	C	C	C	C	-	-	-	-	-	-	C	C	C	-	-	C	-	-	C	-	-	-	-	-	-	-	-	-	C	-	-	17	3	9
Andy Roxburgh	-	-	-	-	-	-	-	-	-	-	-	-	-	-	-	-	-	-	C	C	C	C	C	-	C	C	C	C	C	C	C	C	-	C	C	C	C	-	-	-	SH	SH	FH	-	-	-	20	1	3
A.D.Godfrey	FH	C	-	-	-	-	C	C	-	-	-	-	-	-	-	-	-	-	-	-	-	-	-	-	-	-	-	-	-	-	-	-	-	-	-	-	-	-	-	-	-	-	-	-	-	-	4	-	-
Tim' Taylor	-	-	FH	FH	FH	FH	FH	FH	FH	FH	FH	FH	FH	FH	FH	FH	FH	FH	FH	FH	FH	-	FH	FH	FH	FH	FH	FH	FH	FH	FH	FH	FH	FH	FH	FH	FH	-	-	-	FH	FH	-	FH	FH	-	38	13	39
John Russell	SH	-	-	-	SH	SH	SH	-	SH	SH	SH	SH	SH	SH	SH	SH	SH	SH	SH	SH	SH	-	-	-	-	SH	-	-	-	-	-	SH	-	-	-	SH	SH	-	C	SH	-	-	-	-	-	-	24	2	6
Edward Massey	-	-	-	-	-	-	-	-	-	-	-	-	-	-	-	-	-	-	-	-	-	-	-	SH	-	-	-	-	-	-	-	-	-	-	-	-	-	-	-	-	-	-	-	SH	SH	-	3	-	-
John Buchanan	F	F	F	F	F	-	-	-	-	-	-	-	-	-	-	-	-	-	-	-	-	-	-	-	-	-	-	-	-	-	-	-	-	-	-	-	-	-	-	F	-	-	-	-	F	-	7	2	6
Frank Lawrence	F	F	-	F	-	-	F	F	F	F	F	F	-	F	F	F	F	F	-	F	-	-	F	F	F	F	-	-	-	F	-	F	-	F	F	F	F	-	F	-	F	F	-	-	-	-	28	-	-
Doug Norman	F	F	F	F	-	F	F	F	F	F	F	F	F	-	-	F	-	F	F	F	F	F	-	-	F	F	F	F	F	-	F	F	F	F	F	F	F	F	F	-	-	F	F	F	-	-	35	1	7
Sos' Taylor	F	F	F	F	F	F	F	F	F	F	F	F	F	F	F	F	F	-	F	-	F	F	F	F	F	F	F	F	F	F	F	F	F	F	F	F	F	F	-	F	F	-	F	F	F	-	41	9	27
Bob Usher	F	F	-	-	F	-	F	-	F	F	F	F	F	F	F	-	F	F	F	-	F	F	-	-	-	F	-	F	-	-	F	-	-	-	-	-	-	-	-	F	F	-	F	F	F	-	24	1	3
George Ward	F	F	F	F	F	-	-	-	-	-	-	F	F	F	F	F	F	F	F	F	-	F	-	-	-	F	F	-	F	F	-	F	F	F	F	-	-	-	-	-	F	F	F	F	F	-	28	2	6
Guy German	-	F	SH	SH	-	-	-	SH	-	-	-	-	-	-	-	-	-	-	-	-	-	-	-	-	-	-	-	-	SH	-	-	-	SH	SH	SH	-	-	SH	SH	-	-	-	SH	-	-	-	11	1	3
Charlie Cross	-	-	F	-	F	F	F	F	F	F	F	F	F	F	F	F	F	-	F	F	-	F	F	F	F	-	F	F	F	F	-	-	F	F	F	-	F	F	F	-	F	-	-	F	-	-	32	4	12
Henry Grierson	-	-	F	F	-	F	F	F	F	F	F	-	F	F	-	F	-	F	F	-	F	-	F	-	-	-	-	F	F	-	F	-	-	-	-	F	-	F	F	-	F	-	-	-	-	-	22	2	6
Leo Price	-	-	-	-	F	F	-	-	-	-	F	-	F	-	-	-	F	-	-	-	F	FH	-	-	-	-	-	-	-	-	-	-	-	-	-	-	-	-	-	-	C	-	-	-	-	-	8	1	3
Herb Sharratt	-	-	-	-	-	F	-	F	F	F	-	F	-	F	F	F	-	F	-	F	F	F	F	F	F	F	F	F	F	F	F	F	F	F	F	F	F	F	F	F	-	F	F	F	F	-	34	6	18
Trevor Thorneloe	-	-	-	-	-	-	-	F	-	-	-	-	-	-	-	-	-	-	-	-	-	-	-	F	F	-	-	-	F	F	F	F	F	-	F	F	F	-	F	F	F	F	-	-	F	-	16	2	19
Charlie Jones	-	-	-	-	-	-	-	-	-	-	-	-	-	-	-	-	-	F	-	F	F	F	-	F	F	F	-	-	-	F	F	F	F	F	-	F	F	F	F	-	-	F	F	F	F	-	20	1	3
John Davis	-	-	-	-	-	-	-	-	-	-	-	-	-	-	-	-	-	-	-	-	-	-	F	-	-	-	F	-	-	-	-	-	-	-	-	-	-	-	-	-	-	F	F	-	-	-	4	1	3

2 games: Stan Brown SH(27,28), H.S.Davis W(23,25), T.Fletcher C(38,39), Lew Jenkins F(38,40), C.L.Lowe F(20,23), W.Pollard W(36)C(42)[3T-9], J.C.Seager SH(30,31), C.B.Wales FH(38,39), D.Wardrop C(26,27)[1T-3]

1 game: Cyril Adams F(40), G.G.Aitken FH(40), Ambrose Baker F(24)[1T-3], H.S.Carter SH(23), A.M.David C(33), C.Dudley W(32), A.Francis C(24)[3T-9], A.Frowen FH(2), T.W.Gabriel C(2), A.S.Hett C(24), G.Jones C(24)[2T-6], A.King C(29), Charles King-Turner C(33), M.A.Macdonald W(4), A.C.Marques C(8)[1T-3], John Morton FB(43), -.Paisley C(38), Ron Palmer C(43), D.J.Reeves F(1), C.B.Riddle W(31), Sgt. Snaith C(31), S.Stenson SH(25), G.C.Taylor C(25), William Wallace W(30)[1T-3], H.B.Watney F(4), "Pedlar' Wood SH(2) G.Wright F(27)

1923-1924

NO	DATE	OPPONENTS	V	RES	FOR G	T	D	P	PTS	AGAINST G	T	D	P	PTS	SCORERS
1	Sep 1	BATH	H	Won	-	-	-	2	6	-	1	-	-	3	P.W.Lawrie(2P)
2	8	PLYMOUTH ALBION	H	Won	2	-	1	-	14	1	-	-	-	5	P.W.Lawrie(T,2C,D) Bryson(T)
3	15	NEATH	H	Won	1	-	-	1	8	-	1	-	-	3	Day(C,P) Wakefield(T)
4	17	Headingley	A	Won	3	3	-	-	24	1	-	1	-	9	Day(3C) Wakefield(T) Bryson(3T) Wallace(T) Bemrose(T)
5	22	CROSS KEYS	H	Lost	-	2	-	-	6	1	1	-	-	8	Storrs(T) Price(T)
6	29	ABERAVON	H	Lost	-	-	-	-	0	1	1	-	-	8	
7	Oct 6	LLANELLI	H	Lost	1	-	-	1	8	-	1	1*	1	9	P.W.Lawrie(C,P) G.C.Taylor(T)
8	13	MOSELEY	H	Won	-	1	-	2	9	1	1	-	-	8	Day(2P) Wakefield(T)
9	20	NEWPORT	H	Won	-	1	1	-	7	1	-	-	-	5	P.W.Lawrie(T) Price(D)
10	27	NUNEATON	H	Drew	-	-	-	-	0	-	-	-	-	0	
11	31	Oxford University	A	Lost	1	2	-	-	11	1	6	-	-	23	Bryson(2T) P.W.Lawrie(C) Godfrey(T)
12	Nov 3	Swansea	A	Drew	1	-	-	-	5	1	-	-	-	5	Day(T,C)
13	5	Llanelli	A	Lost	-	-	-	-	0	2	3	1	-	23	
14	10	Cambridge University	A	Won	1	2	-	1	14	1	2	-	-	11	Sambrook(C,P) Smallwood(2T) Russell(T)
15	17	NORTHAMPTON	H	Won	2	1	-	-	13	-	1	-	-	3	Day(2T,2C) J.R.Lawrie(T)
16	24	Cardiff	A	Lost	-	-	-	1	3	-	3	-	-	9	Day(P)
17	26	Neath	A	Lost	-	2	-	-	6	2	9	-	-	37	Wickson(T) Prentice(T)
18	Dec 1	Harlequins	A	Lost	1	-	-	1	8	2	-	-	-	10	Day(C,P) Norman(T)
19	8	Blackheath	A	Won	2	-	1	-	14	-	1	1	-	7	Bryson(T) Day(2C) Holden(T) Medhurst(D)
20	15	BRISTOL	H	Won	1	-	-	2	11	-	-	-	-	0	Day(C,2P) W.C.Wilkins(T)
21	22	Coventry	A	Drew	-	-	-	-	0	-	-	-	-	0	
22	26	BIRKENHEAD PARK	H	Won	1	4	-	-	17	-	-	-	1	3	Simpson(2T) Day(T,C) Wakefield(T) Prentice(T)
23	27	BARBARIANS	H	Lost	-	-	-	1	3	1	-	-	-	5	Day(P)
24	29	RACING CLUB FRANCE	H	Won	3	-	-	3	24	1	-	-	-	5	Day(T,3C,3P) German(T) Wakefield(T)
25	Jan 1	Manchester	A	Won	2	4	-	-	22	1	1	-	-	8	Coates(T) Day(2T,2C) German(T) F.Taylor(T) Prentice(T)
26	5	UNITED SERVICES	H	Won	2	3	-	1	22	1	-	-	-	5	P.W.Lawrie(T) Day(2C,P) Simpson(T) J.R.Lawrie(T) Usher(T) Prentice(T)
27	12	SWANSEA	H	Lost	-	-	-	-	0	-	3	-	-	9	
28	19	ROYAL AIR FORCE	H	Lost	-	2	-	-	6	1	-	1	-	9	Day(T) Thorneloe(T)
29	26	THE ARMY	H	Lost	2	1	-	-	13	-	3	-	2	15	P.W.Lawrie(2T) Day(2C) W.C.Wilkins(T)
30	Feb 2	RICHMOND	H	Won	4	2	-	1	29	1	2	-	-	11	Parker(T) Day(2T,4C,P) Smallwood(T) F.Taylor(T) Prentice(T)
31	9	Newport	A	Lost	1	-	-	1	8	-	6	1	-	22	Prentice(T) Thorneloe(C,P)
32	16	CARDIFF	H	Won	2	1	-	-	13	-	-	-	-	0	Day(2C) W.C.Wilkins(T) Smallwood(T) Usher(T)
33	23	COVENTRY	H	Won	1	2	-	1	14	-	2	-	-	6	P.W.Lawrie(T) Day(C,P) W.C.Wilkins(T) Sharratt(T)
34	Mar 1	HARLEQUINS	H	Won	1	2	-	1	14	1	-	-	-	5	Bryson(T) Day(C,P) W.C.Wilkins(T) Prentice(T)
35	4	Racing Club France	A	Lost	-	-	-	1	3	2	4	-	-	22	Day(P)
36	8	Northampton	A	Lost	2	-	-	2	16	2	2	-	1	19	Coates(T) Day(2C,2P) Smallwood(T)
37	15	LONDON WELSH	H	Won	-	4	-	-	12	1	-	-	-	5	Kenney(T) P.W.Lawrie(T) Day(T) W.C.Wilkins(T)
38	22	OLD BLUES	H	Lost	-	4	-	-	12	3	1	-	-	18	Smallwood(3T) W.C.Wilkins(T)
39	29	ROYAL AIR FORCE	H	Won	2	-	-	-	10	-	2	-	-	6	Day(2C) Wakefield(2T)
40	31	Nuneaton	A	Won	3	2	-	-	21	1	-	-	-	5	Bryson(T) P.W.Lawrie(T) Coates(2T) Day(3C) Russell(T)
41	Apr 5	RICHMOND	H	Lost	1	2	-	1	14	2	1	1	-	17	Smallwood(T) Day(C,P) W.C.Wilkins(T) Wakefield(T)
42	12	Birkenhead Park	A	Won	2	-	1	-	14	-	2	-	-	6	P.W.Lawrie(T,D) Day(T,2C)
43	19	Bristol	A	Lost	-	-	-	-	0	1	2	-	-	11	
44	21	Plymouth Albion	A	Won	5	3	-	-	34	-	4	-	-	12	Day(T,5C) Coates(T) Wallace(4T) J.R.Lawrie(2T)
45	22	Bath	A	Lost	-	1	-	-	3	5	1	-	-	28	Sharratt(T)
46	26	Bedford	A	Won	1	-	-	-	5	-	-	-	-	0	Day(C) C.L.Burton(T)

INDIVIDUAL APPEARANCES 1923-1924

NAME	1	2	3	4	5	6	7	8	9	10	11	12	13	14	15	16	17	18	19	20	21	22	23	24	25	26	27	28	29	30	31	32	33	34	35	36	37	38	39	40	41	42	43	44	45	46	TOTAL	T	PTS
Claude Sambrook	FB	FB	FB	FB	FB	FB	FB	FB	FB	FB	FB	FB	-	FB	FB	FB	FB	-	FB	-	FB	FB	FB	FB	FB	FB	FB	FB	FB	FB	FB	FB	FB	FB	FB	FB	-	-	FB	FB	FB	FB	FB	FB	FB	FB	41	-	5
C.L.Burton	W	W	W	-	-	-	-	-	-	-	W	-	-	-	-	-	-	-	-	-	-	-	-	-	-	-	-	-	-	-	-	-	-	-	W	-	-	-	-	-	-	-	-	-	-	W	6	1	3
Alastair Smallwood	-	-	W	-	-	-	-	-	W	-	-	-	-	W	-	-	-	-	-	-	-	-	W	W	-	-	-	-	-	FH	-	FH	-	FH	-	FH	-	C	-	-	C	W	W	W	-	-	14	9	27
William Wallace	-	-	-	W	-	-	-	-	-	-	-	-	-	-	-	-	-	-	-	-	-	-	-	-	-	-	-	-	-	-	-	-	-	-	-	-	-	-	-	-	-	-	W	W	W	-	4	5	15
Leo Price	-	-	-	-	W	-	-	C	FH	-	-	-	-	FH	-	-	-	-	-	-	-	-	-	-	-	-	-	-	FH	-	-	-	-	-	-	-	-	-	-	-	-	-	-	-	-	-	5	1	7
D.J.Thomas	-	-	-	-	-	-	W	-	-	-	-	-	-	-	-	-	-	-	-	-	W	W	-	-	W	-	W	-	-	-	-	-	-	-	-	-	-	-	-	-	-	-	-	-	-	-	5	-	-
Frank Lawrence	-	-	-	-	-	-	-	-	-	W	F	-	-	-	-	-	-	-	-	-	-	-	-	-	-	-	-	-	-	F	W	-	F	-	-	-	F	-	-	F	-	-	-	-	-	-	7	-	-
W.C.Wilkins	-	-	-	-	-	-	-	-	-	-	-	-	W	-	W	C	W	W	-	W	C	-	-	W	-	-	-	-	C	W	W	W	W	W	C	-	W	W	W	W	W	-	-	-	-	-	20	8	24
C.E.H.Medhurst	-	-	-	-	-	-	-	-	-	-	-	-	-	-	W	W	FH	FH	FH	FH	-	-	-	FH	-	FH	FH	FH	-	-	-	-	-	-	-	-	FH	FH	-	-	FH	FH	-	-	C	C	16	-	4
M.S.Holden	-	-	-	-	-	-	-	-	-	-	-	-	-	-	-	W	C	FB	W	FB	-	W	-	-	-	W	W	-	-	-	-	-	-	-	-	-	-	-	-	-	-	-	-	-	-	-	8	1	3
R.B.Y.Simpson	-	-	-	-	-	-	-	-	-	-	-	-	-	-	-	-	-	-	-	W	C	C	C	C	C	W	-	-	-	-	-	-	-	-	-	-	-	-	-	-	-	-	-	-	-	-	7	3	9
H.G.Parker	-	-	-	-	-	-	-	-	-	-	-	-	-	-	-	-	-	-	-	-	-	-	-	-	-	-	-	W	W	W	C	-	-	-	-	-	-	-	-	-	-	-	-	-	-	-	4	1	3
Bill Kenney	-	-	-	-	-	-	-	-	-	-	-	-	-	-	-	-	-	-	-	-	-	-	-	-	-	-	-	-	-	-	-	-	-	-	-	-	W	W	W	-	-	W	-	-	W	-	5	1	3
O.C.Bryson	C	C	C	C	C	C	-	W	W	-	W	-	-	W	-	-	-	W	W	-	W	-	-	-	-	-	C	-	-	-	-	-	-	W	-	-	-	-	-	W	W	-	-	-	-	-	17	9	27
Percy Lawrie	C	C	C	C	C	-	C	C	C	C	C	-	-	C	C	C	-	C	C	C	FH	C	C	C	W	C	-	C	W	C	C	C	C	C	-	W	C	-	C	C	C	C	-	-	C	-	36	9	52
Norman Coates	-	C	FH	FH	FH	FH	C	FH	C	C	C	C	-	C	-	-	-	C	C	C	-	FH	-	-	C	C	C	C	C	C	C	C	C	C	SH	C	-	-	C	C	-	C	C	C	-	-	33	5	15
Harold Day	-	-	C	W	-	-	-	C	C	C	-	C	-	-	C	C	-	C	C	C	C	C	W	C	C	C	C	C	C	C	-	C	C	C	C	C	C	C	C	C	C	C	C	C	-	C	35	13	186
A.D.Godfrey	-	-	-	-	-	-	-	-	-	-	C	FH	FH	C	C	-	-	-	-	-	-	-	-	-	FH	-	-	-	-	-	-	-	FH	-	C	C	C	-	-	-	-	-	-	-	-	-	10	1	3
H.W.Cox	-	-	-	-	-	-	-	-	-	-	-	-	-	-	-	-	-	-	-	-	-	-	-	-	-	-	-	-	-	-	-	-	-	-	-	-	-	-	-	-	-	-	FH	FH	SH	FH	4	-	-
Guy German	SH	SH	SH	SH	-	SH	-	F	F	-	-	-	-	-	-	-	-	SH	SH	SH	F	-	-	SH	F	F	F	-	SH	SH	SH	SH	-	SH	F	SH	F	-	FH	F	SH	SH	SH	SH	-	F	30	2	6
John Russell	-	-	-	-	SH	C	SH	SH	SH	-	-	SH	-	SH	-	-	-	-	-	-	SH	SH	-	-	SH	SH	SH	-	-	-	-	-	-	-	-	-	-	-	-	SH	-	-	-	-	-	-	13	2	6
Stuart Smith	-	-	-	-	-	-	-	-	-	-	-	-	-	-	-	-	-	-	-	-	-	-	-	-	-	-	-	SH	-	-	FH	W	SH	-	-	-	SH	SH	SH	-	-	-	-	-	-	-	7	-	-
Charlie Jones	F	F	-	F	F	F	-	F	-	-	F	C	C	-	-	-	-	-	-	-	-	-	-	-	-	-	-	-	-	-	-	-	-	-	-	-	-	-	-	-	-	-	-	-	-	-	9	-	-
Jock Lawrie	F	F	F	-	-	F	F	F	F	F	-	F	-	F	F	F	-	F	-	F	F	F	F	F	-	F	F	-	F	-	F	F	-	F	-	F	-	-	F	F	F	F	F	F	-	F	32	4	12
Doug Norman	F	-	F	F	F	-	-	F	F	F	F	F	F	F	-	F	F	F	F	F	-	F	F	-	-	-	-	F	F	F	F	-	F	-	F	F	-	-	F	-	-	-	-	-	-	-	26	1	3
Herb Sharratt	F	F	-	F	F	F	-	-	-	-	F	F	F	F	F	F	F	F	F	-	F	F	-	F	F	F	F	-	F	F	F	F	F	F	F	F	F	-	F	F	F	F	F	F	F	F	37	2	6
Sos' Taylor	F	F	F	-	-	-	F	F	F	F	F	-	-	-	F	F	F	-	F	F	-	-	F	F	F	F	-	F	F	F	F	F	F	F	-	F	F	-	F	F	F	F	F	-	F	F	33	2	6
George Ward	F	F	F	F	F	F	F	F	F	F	-	F	F	F	F	F	F	F	F	-	F	-	F	F	F	-	F	F	F	-	F	F	F	F	F	F	F	-	F	F	F	-	F	F	-	-	37	-	-
John Davis	-	F	-	F	F	F	F	-	-	F	-	F	F	F	F	-	-	F	F	F	F	-	F	F	-	-	-	F	-	-	-	-	-	-	-	-	-	-	-	-	-	-	-	-	-	-	17	-	-
Bob Usher	-	F	F	-	F	-	F	-	F	F	F	F	-	F	F	F	-	F	F	F	F	F	F	F	F	F	F	-	-	-	-	F	-	F	-	-	-	F	-	-	F	F	F	F	F	-	29	2	6
Trevor Thorneloe	-	-	F	F	-	F	F	-	-	-	-	-	-	-	-	-	-	-	-	F	F	-	F	-	F	F	F	F	-	F	F	-	F	-	F	-	-	-	-	-	-	-	-	-	-	-	15	1	8
Wavell Wakefield	-	-	F	C	F	C	F	F	F	F	-	-	-	F	F	F	-	-	F	-	-	F	F	F	-	-	F	-	F	F	-	F	-	F	-	F	-	F	F	-	F	F	F	C	-	C	28	8	24
Doug Prentice	-	-	-	-	-	-	-	-	-	-	-	-	-	-	-	-	F	F	-	F	-	F	-	-	F	F	-	F	F	F	F	F	F	F	F	F	F	-	F	F	F	F	F	F	F	F	24	7	21

3 games: J.M.Bemrose F(4,6,38)[1T-3], J.S.Boswell SH(15,16,17), Edward Massey SH(11,23,46), Reg Odbert FH(15,16)W(17), Andy Roxburgh FH(1,2,10), W.J.Streather F(42,44,45)

2 games: Norman Boston F(37,38), S.G.Collins F(38,46), F.A.Crowhurst F(12,13), L.C.Gamble FB(37,38), Teddy Haselmere W(1,2), E.Hopkins W(12,13), A.D.T.Roberts F(44,45), P.G.Scott C(38,43), H.H.Storrs W(5,6)[1T-3], G.C.Taylor FH(7,11)[1T-3], F.S.Wells W(10,12), R.H.Wetton W(33,36), G.M.C.Wilkins C(5)W(6)

1 game: Cyril Adams F(45), J.S.Atkins F(28), Ambrose Baker F(13), B.A.Batchelor F(1), Arthur Blakiston F(46), F.Boston F(38), A.F.Brodbeck FH(40), H.C.Burton W(35), R.A.Castle W(8), A.S.Cohen F(35), Charlie Cross F(22), R.Evans C(17), W.J.Gibbs W(46), D.Hunt-Davies C(13), Ivor Jones FB(13), F.E.Oliver SH(10), Ron Palmer C(17), Arthur Palmer F(17), W.Pollard W(7), R.Randall F(13), R.Robinson FH(23), H.Smith C(13), E.Stagg F(45), J.T.Stephens F(11), S.Thomas SH(13), F.H.R.Turney C(1), F/O.E.C. Wackett F(38), C.H.M.Waldock FH(45), Willy Watts C(7), A.P.Wayte FH(35), John Wickson F(17)[1T-3], C.H.L.Wynne W(28)

LEICESTER FOOTBALL CLUB 1924-25

Back: T.H. Crumbie (Hon.Sec), E.D. Dynes, J.C. Russell, J.E. Davis, N. Coates, G.A. Palmer, P.G. Scott, S.F. Lawrence, E.J. Massey, S.A. Smith, F.O. Sinclair.

Middle: T. Th'orpe (Hon.Tres), G.R. Beamish, D.J. Norman, H. Sharratt, G. Ward, H.L.V. Day (Capt), J.R. Lawrie, F.D. Prentice, N.T. Thorneloe, O.C. Bryson, K. McAlpin (President).

Front: R.A. Buckingham, H.A. Sambrook, G.J. German, R.S. Palmer, A.M. Smallwood, L.C. Sambrook, M.S. Holden.

1924-1925

NO	DATE	OPPONENTS	V	RES	FOR G	FOR T	FOR D	FOR P	FOR PTS	AGAINST G	AGAINST T	AGAINST D	AGAINST P	AGAINST PTS	SCORERS
1	Sep 6	BATH	H	Won	1	2	-	1	14	1	2	-	-	11	Smallwood(2T) Day(C,P) Norman(T)
2	10	Rugby B.T.H.	A	Won	3	3	-	-	24	-	-	-	-	0	Day(3T,3C) Roxburgh(T) Lawrie(T) Lawrence(T)
3	13	NUNEATON	H	Won	1	1	-	2	14	1	-	1	-	9	Bryson(T) Smallwood(C) Kenney(T) Massey(2P)
4	20	PLYMOUTH ALBION	H	Lost	-	1	-	2	9	1	2	-	-	11	Bryson(T) Massey(2P)
5	27	CROSS KEYS	H	Won	1	1	-	-	8	-	-	-	-	0	L.C.Sambrook(C) Holden(T) Lawrie(T)
6	Oct 4	NEW ZEALAND	H	Lost	-	-	-	-	0	3	3	-	1	27	
7	11	LLANELLI	H	Won	-	2	-	-	6	-	-	-	1	3	Holden(T) Day(T)
8	18	Newport	A	Lost	-	1	-	2	9	3	6	-	-	33	L.C.Sambrook(P) Massey(P) Norman(T)
9	25	OXFORD UNIVERSITY	H	Lost	-	-	2*	1	10	1	2	-	-	11	Day(P,M) Dynes(D)
10	29	Moseley	A	Won	-	5	-	-	15	1	-	-	-	5	Buckingham(2T) H.A.Sambrook(T) R.S.Palmer(T) Thorneloe(T)
11	Nov 1	UNITED SERVICES	H	Won	-	2	1*	-	9	-	-	-	-	0	Day(T) Massey(T) Russell(M)
12	8	CAMBRIDGE UNIVERSITY	H	Won	6	3	-	-	39	-	1	-	-	3	Day(T,6C) Smallwood(4T) Holden(T) Kenney(T) Scott(T) Prentice(T)
13	15	SWANSEA	H	Lost	-	-	-	1	3	3	1	-	-	18	Day(P)
14	22	Northampton	A	Won	-	2	-	-	6	-	1	-	-	3	Scott(T) H.A.Sambrook(T)
15	29	CARDIFF	H	Drew	-	-	-	1	3	-	1	-	-	3	Day(P)
16	Dec 6	Harlequins	A	Won	1	4	-	-	17	1	2	-	-	11	Bryson(T) Day(T,C) Scott(T) Coates(T) Sharratt(T)
17	13	Blackheath	A	Won	-	3	-	-	9	-	-	-	-	0	Buckingham(T) Day(2T)
18	20	BRISTOL	H	Won	1	5	-	1	23	-	2	-	-	6	L.C.Sambrook(C) Bryson(T) Smallwood(3T) Buckingham(T) Lawton(P) Prentice(T)
19	26	BIRKENHEAD PARK	H	Won	2	1	-	-	13	1	2	-	-	11	Holden(T) Day(T,2C) Buckingham(T)
20	27	HERIOTONIANS	H	Won	3	1	1	-	22	-	-	-	-	0	Smallwood(T) Day(T,3C) Holden(T) Dynes(D) Prentice(T)
21	29	BARBARIANS	H	Won	2	2	-	-	16	-	2	-	-	6	Smallwood(T) Day(2C) Lawrie(T) Prentice(2T)
22	Jan 3	MANCHESTER	H	Won	2	1	-	-	13	1	-	-	-	5	Day(2C) Holden(T) Buckingham(T) Lawrie(T)
23	10	Swansea	A	Lost	1	-	-	1	8	1	2	-	1	14	Day(T,C,P)
24	17	Coventry	A	Won	-	3	-	-	9	-	1	-	-	3	Holden(T) Scott(T) Buckingham(T)
25	24	THE ARMY	H	Won	4	1	-	-	23	-	-	-	-	0	Smallwood(T) Day(4C) Holden(T) Sharratt(T) Prentice(2T)
26	31	Richmond	A	Won	2	1	-	-	13	-	-	1	-	4	Day(T,2C) Holden(T) Dynes(T)
27	Feb 7	Plymouth Albion	A	Won	1	2	-	-	11	-	1	-	-	3	Wells(T) Holden(T) Sharratt(T) Thorneloe(C)
28	14	NEWPORT	H	Drew	-	2	-	-	6	-	2	-	-	6	Wells(T) Buckingham(T)
29	21	Cardiff	A	Lost	-	2	-	-	6	1	2	-	1	14	Holden(T) Lawrie(T)
30	28	COVENTRY	H	Won	-	1	-	-	3	-	-	-	-	0	Day(T)
31	Mar 7	HARLEQUINS	H	Won	5	-	-	-	25	1	1	1*	-	11	Smallwood(T) Day(T,5C) Beamish(T) Sharratt(2T)
32	14	NORTHAMPTON	H	Won	1	-	-	1	8	-	1	-	-	3	Day(C,P) Sharratt(T)
33	21	OLD BLUES	H	Won	2	2	-	-	16	1	3	-	-	14	Day(2C) Waldock(T) R.S.Palmer(T) Buckingham(T) S.A.Smith(T)
34	23	United Services	A	Lost	-	-	-	-	0	-	1	-	-	3	
35	Apr 4	BLACKHEATH	H	Won	2	2	-	-	16	2	1	-	-	13	Day(2C) Bryson(2T) H.A.Sambrook(T) Buckingham(T)
36	7	Nuneaton	A	Won	3	-	1	-	19	2	1	-	-	13	Day(3C) Scott(2T) Sharratt(D) Prentice(T)
37	11	Bristol	A	Lost	2	-	-	-	10	1	1	-	2	14	Day(2C) Buckingham(T) Beamish(T)
38	13	Llanelli	A	Lost	-	1	-	-	3	1	3	-	-	14	Beamish(T)
39	14	Bath	A	Drew	-	2	1	-	10	-	2	1	-	10	Bryson(T) Atkins(T) Buckingham(D)
40	18	Birkenhead Park	A	Won	1	1	-	1	11	1	-	-	-	5	Day(2T,C,P)

INDIVIDUAL APPEARANCES 1924-1925

NAME	1	2	3	4	5	6	7	8	9	10	11	12	13	14	15	16	17	18	19	20	21	22	23	24	25	26	27	28	29	30	31	32	33	34	35	36	37	38	39	40	41	42	43	44	45	46	TOTAL	T	PTS
Claude Sambrook	FB	FB	FB	FB	FB	FB	-	FB	-	FB	FB	-	-	FB	-	FB	FB	FB	FB	FB	FB	FB	FB	FB	FB	FB	FB	FB	FB	FB	FB	FB	FB	FB	FB	FB	FB	FB	FB	FB	-	-	-	-	-	-	35	-	7
O.C.Bryson	W	-	W	W	W	W	-	-	W	FE	W	-	W	-	C	W	-	W	-	-	-	-	-	-	-	-	-	-	-	W	W	-	W	-	W	-	W	W	C	W	-	-	-	-	-	-	20	7	21
Bill Kenney	W	-	W	W	W	-	FB	W	W	W	W	W	-	-	-	-	-	-	-	-	-	-	-	-	-	-	-	-	-	-	-	-	-	-	-	-	-	-	-	-	-	-	-	-	-	-	10	2	6
W.J.Gibbs	-	-	-	-	-	-	-	-	-	-	-	-	-	-	-	-	-	-	W	-	W	-	-	-	-	-	-	-	-	-	-	-	-	-	-	-	-	-	-	-	-	-	-	-	-	-	2	-	-
F.S.Wells	-	-	-	-	-	-	-	-	-	-	-	-	-	-	-	-	-	-	-	-	-	W	W	-	-	W	W	W	W	-	-	W	-	-	-	-	-	-	-	-	-	-	-	-	-	-	7	2	6
C.B.Moller	-	-	-	-	-	-	-	-	-	-	-	-	-	-	-	-	-	-	-	-	-	-	-	-	-	-	-	-	-	-	-	-	-	-	-	W	-	-	W	-	-	-	-	-	-	-	2	-	-
Alf Atkins	-	-	-	-	-	-	-	-	-	-	-	-	-	-	-	-	-	-	-	-	-	-	-	-	-	-	-	-	-	-	-	-	-	-	-	-	W	-	W	-	-	-	-	-	-	-	2	1	3
Harold Day	C	C	-	-	-	-	W	-	FB	-	C	FB	FB	C	FB	C	C	-	C	C	C	C	C	C	C	C	-	-	C	C	C	C	C	-	C	C	C	C	-	C	-	-	-	-	-	-	29	17	161
Harold Sambrook	C	-	FE	-	-	-	FE	-	FE	W	FE	-	FE	FE	FE	FE	FE	FE	-	-	-	FE	FE	FE	FE	FE	FE	FE	FE	FE	-	FE	-	-	FE	-	FE	FE	-	-	-	-	-	-	-	-	25	3	9
Alastair Smallwood	C	-	C	-	-	FE	-	-	-	-	-	W	-	-	W	-	-	C	-	W	W	-	-	-	W	-	-	-	-	W	W	-	-	-	W	-	-	-	-	-	-	-	-	-	-	-	12	13	41
Ralph Buckingham	-	C	-	-	-	-	-	-	-	C	-	-	-	-	-	-	W	W	FE	FE	FE	FE	FH	FH	FH	FH	FH	C	FE	FE	FE	FH	FH	FH	FH	FH	FH	FH	FH	FH	-	-	-	-	-	-	26	11	37
P.G.Scott	-	-	-	C	FE	W	W	C	-	-	-	FE	C	W	FE	W	W	-	-	FE	FE	-	-	W	-	-	-	-	-	-	-	-	W	W	-	FE	FE	W	-	-	-	-	-	-	-	-	19	6	18
M.S.Holden	-	-	-	-	C	C	C	-	C	-	-	C	W	W	W	-	-	-	W	W	-	W	W	W	W	W	W	W	W	-	FE	-	-	-	FE	-	-	-	FE	FE	-	-	-	-	-	-	22	11	33
Leo Price	-	-	-	FE	-	FE	-	-	F	-	-	-	-	-	F	-	-	-	-	-	-	-	-	-	-	-	-	-	-	-	-	-	-	-	-	-	-	-	-	-	-	-	-	-	-	-	4	-	-
Ernie Dynes	-	-	-	-	FE	-	FE	C	FE	FE	FE	FE	FE	FE	FH	FE	FE	FE	FH	FH	FH	FH	-	-	FE	FE	-	FE	-	-	-	FE	-	-	-	-	-	FE	FE	FE	-	-	-	-	-	-	24	1	11
W.Roxburgh	-	FH	FE	FE	-	-	-	-	-	-	-	-	-	-	-	-	-	-	-	-	-	-	-	-	-	-	-	-	-	-	-	-	-	-	-	-	-	-	-	-	-	-	-	-	-	-	3	1	3
Norman Coates	-	-	-	FH	-	-	-	-	-	F	F	F	SH	-	-	F	F	F	F	F	F	F	F	F	-	-	-	-	-	-	-	-	-	-	-	-	-	-	-	-	-	-	-	-	-	-	14	1	3
Ron Palmer	-	-	-	-	-	-	-	-	-	FH	-	-	-	-	-	-	-	-	FE	-	-	-	FE	FE	-	-	-	FH	-	-	-	-	FE	FE	-	FE	-	-	-	-	-	-	-	-	-	-	8	2	6
Stuart Smith	-	-	-	-	-	-	-	-	-	-	-	-	-	-	-	FH	FH	-	-	-	-	-	-	-	-	-	-	-	FH	-	-	-	SH	SH	-	SH	-	-	SH	-	-	-	-	-	-	-	7	1	3
Edward Massey	SH	-	FH	SH	FH	FH	FH	FH	FH	SH	FH	FH	FH	FH	SH	-	SH	-	-	SH	SH	-	SH	-	SH	SH	SH	-	SH	FH	SH	SH	-	-	-	-	-	-	-	-	-	-	-	-	-	-	25	1	18
John Russell	-	-	SH	-	SH	SH	SH	SH	SH	-	SH	SH	-	-	-	-	-	SH	SH	-	-	SH	-	SH	-	-	-	SH	-	SH	-	-	-	-	-	-	SH	SH	-	SH	-	-	-	-	-	-	17	-	3
C.H.M.Waldock	-	-	-	-	-	-	-	-	-	-	-	-	-	SH	-	SH	-	-	-	-	-	-	-	-	-	-	-	-	-	-	-	-	FE	FE	-	-	-	-	-	-	-	-	-	-	-	-	4	1	3
John Davis	F	F	F	-	F	F	-	-	-	-	-	-	-	-	-	-	-	-	-	-	-	-	-	-	-	-	-	-	-	-	-	-	-	-	-	-	-	-	-	-	-	-	-	-	-	-	5	-	-
Jock Lawrie	F	F	F	F	F	F	F	-	F	-	-	F	F	F	F	F	F	F	-	-	F	F	-	-	-	F	F	F	F	F	F	W	F	-	F	F	F	-	-	-	-	-	-	-	-	-	28	5	15
Doug Norman	F	F	F	F	F	-	F	F	F	F	F	-	F	F	F	F	F	F	-	F	F	F	F	F	F	F	F	F	F	F	F	F	F	F	F	-	F	F	F	F	-	-	-	-	-	-	36	2	6
Doug Prentice	F	-	-	F	F	F	F	F	F	F	F	F	F	F	F	-	F	F	F	F	F	F	F	-	F	F	F	F	F	F	F	F	-	F	F	F	-	-	-	-	-	-	-	-	-	-	31	8	24
Herb Sharratt	F	-	F	F	F	F	F	F	F	F	F	F	F	F	F	F	F	F	F	F	F	F	F	F	F	F	F	F	F	F	F	F	-	F	F	F	F	F	F	F	-	-	-	-	-	-	38	6	22
W.J.Streather	F	F	F	-	-	-	-	-	-	-	-	-	-	-	-	-	-	-	F	F	-	-	-	-	-	-	-	-	-	-	-	-	-	-	-	-	-	-	-	-	-	-	-	-	-	-	5	-	-
George Ward	F	F	-	F	-	F	-	F	-	-	F	-	F	-	-	-	-	-	F	-	-	-	-	F	F	F	F	F	F	F	F	F	-	F	F	F	F	-	F	F	-	-	-	-	-	-	23	-	-
Frank Lawrence	-	F	F	F	-	-	F	F	F	F	F	F	-	F	-	F	-	-	-	F	-	-	F	F	F	F	F	F	-	-	-	F	-	F	-	-	-	-	F	-	-	-	-	-	-	-	21	1	3
Malcolm Parker	-	F	F	-	-	-	-	-	-	-	-	-	-	-	-	-	-	-	-	-	-	-	-	-	-	-	-	-	-	-	-	-	-	-	-	-	-	-	-	-	-	-	-	-	-	-	2	-	-
Trevor Thorneloe	-	-	-	F	F	-	F	-	-	F	F	F	F	F	F	F	F	F	F	-	-	F	-	F	F	F	F	F	F	F	F	F	F	-	F	-	-	-	F	F	-	-	-	-	-	-	27	1	5
W.B.N.Roderick	-	-	-	-	F	F	F	F	F	F	-	F	F	F	F	F	F	F	F	-	F	F	F	-	-	-	-	-	-	-	-	-	-	-	-	-	-	-	-	-	-	-	-	-	-	-	17	-	-
George Beamish	-	-	-	-	-	-	-	-	-	-	-	-	-	-	-	-	-	-	-	F	F	-	F	-	-	-	-	-	-	-	F	-	F	-	F	F	F	F	-	F	-	-	-	-	-	-	10	3	9
Harry Briers	-	-	-	-	-	-	-	-	-	-	-	-	-	-	-	-	-	-	-	-	-	-	-	F	F	-	-	-	-	-	-	-	F	-	-	-	-	F	-	-	-	-	-	-	-	-	4	-	-
Arthur Palmer	-	-	-	-	-	-	-	-	-	-	-	-	-	-	-	-	-	-	-	-	-	-	-	-	-	-	-	-	F	F	-	F	F	F	-	F	-	F	F	F	-	-	-	-	-	-	9	-	-
F.O.Sinclair	-	-	-	-	-	-	-	-	-	-	-	-	-	-	-	-	-	-	-	-	-	-	-	-	-	-	-	-	-	-	-	-	F	F	-	F	F	F	-	-	-	-	-	-	-	-	5	-	-
Dick Collopy	-	-	-	-	-	-	-	-	-	-	-	-	-	-	-	-	-	-	-	-	-	-	-	-	-	-	-	-	-	-	-	-	-	-	-	-	F	F	F	-	-	-	-	-	-	-	3	-	-

1 game: A.C.Bennett C(34), A.F.Brodbeck SH(2), John Buchanan F(6), Ernie Coleman F(40), R.R.Colquhoun W(8), H.W.Cox W(2), Ewart Farndon W(40), Guy German SH(35), A.D.Godfrey C(2), A.King W(36), Tom Lawton FH(18)[3], C.E.H.Medhurst FH(1), Eddie Myers FH(31), J.Shentall W(34), A.Smith C(27), W.E.Squirrell FE(27), D.J.Thomas W(2), Ivor Williams F(8), G.D.Younger F(8)

1925-1926

NO	DATE	OPPONENTS	V	RES	FOR G	FOR T	FOR D	FOR P	PTS	AGAINST G	AGAINST T	AGAINST D	AGAINST P	PTS	SCORERS
1	Sep 5	BATH	H	Won	2	2	1	1	23	1	1	-	-	8	Farndon(T) Holden(T,D) Smith(2T) Thorneloe(2C,P)
2	12	NUNEATON	H	Won	1	3	1	-	18	-	-	-	-	0	Farndon(T) Holden(T,D) Norman(T) Thorneloe(T,C)
3	19	PLYMOUTH ALBION	H	Drew	-	-	1*	1	6	-	2	-	-	6	Day(P) H.A.Sambrook(M)
4	23	Percy Park	A	Drew	1	-	-	-	5	1	-	-	-	5	Scott(T) Thorneloe(C)
5	26	BRIDGWATER	H	Won	2	2	-	1	19	-	1	-	1	6	Day(2C,P) Wells(2T) Ward(T) Coleman(T)
6	Oct 1	Nuneaton	A	Lost	1	-	-	-	5	2	1	-	-	13	Farndon(T) Thorneloe(C)
7	3	NORTHERN	H	Won	2	2	1	-	20	-	1	-	-	3	Bryson(2T) Day(2C) Holden(D) Thorneloe(T) Coleman(T)
8	10	COVENTRY	H	Won	1	-	-	1	8	-	2	-	-	6	Day(C,P) Coleman(T)
9	17	NEWPORT	H	Won	-	1	-	1	6	1	-	-	-	5	Day(P) Prentice(T)
10	24	Moseley	A	Lost	1	-	-	1	8	1	2	-	-	11	Day(C,P) Smith(T)
11	31	NORTHAMPTON	H	Won	1	1	-	1	11	1	-	-	-	5	Moore(T) Day(C,P) Bryson(T)
12	Nov 7	CAMBRIDGE UNIVERSITY	H	Drew	-	1	-	-	3	-	1	-	-	3	Scott(T)
13	12	Oxford University	A	Lost	-	1	-	-	3	3	4	-	-	27	Coleman(T)
14	14	Swansea	A	Lost	-	-	-	1	3	1	3	-	1	17	Day(P)
15	21	UNITED SERVICES	H	Won	-	1	-	1	6	-	-	-	-	0	Day(P) Moore(T)
16	28	Cardiff	A	Lost	-	1	-	-	3	-	2	-	1	9	Prentice(T)
17	Dec 5	Harlequins	A	Won	1	1	-	1	11	-	2	-	1	9	Day(C,P) Scott(T) Lawrie(T)
18	12	Blackheath	A	Won	2	-	-	-	10	-	1	1	-	7	Day(2C) Buckingham(2T)
19	19	BRISTOL	H	Won	-	3	-	1	12	1	-	-	-	5	Tate(T) Day(T,P) Lawrie(T)
20	26	BIRKENHEAD PARK	H	Won	2	2	-	-	16	-	-	-	1	3	Flewitt(2T) Day(2C) Bryson(T) Buckingham(T)
21	28	BARBARIANS	H	Won	1	3	-	-	14	-	3	-	-	9	Flewitt(T) Day(T,C) Farndon(2T)
22	Jan 1	Manchester	A	Lost	2	-	-	-	10	-	2	-	2	12	Day(T,2C) Buckingham(T)
23	2	Heriotonians	A	Lost	1	-	-	-	5	1	1	-	-	8	Day(C) Buckingham(T)
24	4	Northern	A	Lost	-	2	-	-	6	1	-	-	1	8	Farndon(T) Buckingham(T)
25	9	SWANSEA	H	Drew	1	-	-	1	8	1	-	1*	-	8	Day(C,P) Buckingham(T)
26	16	ROYAL AIR FORCE	H	Won	3	2	-	-	21	-	1	-	-	3	Farndon(T) Day(T,3C) Buckingham(2T) Thorneloe(T)
27	23	THE ARMY	H	Won	1	1	-	-	8	1	-	-	-	5	Moore(2T) Day(C)
28	30	RICHMOND	H	Won	3	1	-	-	18	-	-	-	-	0	Farndon(2T) Day(T,3C) Whitley(T)
29	Feb 6	LONDON SCOTTISH	H	Won	2	4	-	-	22	1	1	-	1	11	Cramphorn(T) Flewitt(T) Day(2T,2C) Burton(T) Coleman(T)
30	13	Newport	A	Lost	1	1	-	1	11	1	3	-	-	14	Flewitt(T) Day(C,P) Buckingham(T)
31	20	CARDIFF	H	Won	1	-	-	1	8	-	1	-	-	3	Day(C,P) Buckingham(T)
32	27	Coventry	A	Lost	1	1	-	-	8	1	4	1	-	21	Farndon(T) Day(C) Buckingham(T)
33	Mar 6	HARLEQUINS	H	Lost	2	-	-	-	10	1	2	-	-	11	Cramphorn(T) Day(T,2C)
	13	Northampton	A		Cancelled										
34	20	OLD BLUES	H	Won	3	2	-	-	21	1	-	-	-	5	Farndon(T) Cramphorn(T) Buckingham(T) Thorneloe(T,3C) Lawrie(T)
35	27	United Services	A	Won	3	1	1	2	28	3	2	-	-	21	Frisby(D) Cramphorn(T) Day(T,3C,2P) Greenlees(T) Prentice(T)
36	Apr 3	Bristol	A	Lost	-	2	-	-	6	2	-	-	1	13	Bandon(T) Day(T)
37	5	Plymouth Albion	A	Lost	2	-	-	1	13	1	2	-	1	14	Cramphorn(T) Day(2C,P) Lawrie(T)
38	6	Bath	A	Won	2	1	-	-	13	-	1	-	1	6	Hopkins(T) Flewitt(T) Day(2C) Bryson(T)
39	10	Birkenhead Park	A	Lost	2	2	-	-	16	2	4	-	2	28	Farndon(2T) Flewitt(2T) Prentice(C) Thorneloe(C)
40	15	Northampton	A	Lost	-	-	-	-	0	-	5	-	1	18	
41	17	BLACKHEATH	H	Won	1	3	-	-	14	-	1	-	-	3	Bryson(T) Day(C) Buckingham(T) Norman(T) Christie(T)

INDIVIDUAL APPEARANCES 1925-1926

NAME	1	2	3	4	5	6	7	8	9	10	11	12	13	14	15	16	17	18	19	20	21	22	23	24	25	26	27	28	29	30	31	32	33	34	35	36	37	38	39	40	41	42	43	44	45	46	TOTAL	T	PTS
Claude Sambrook	FB	FB	FB	FB	FB	FB	FB	FB	FB	FB	FB	FB	FB	FB	FB	FB	FB	FB	FB	FB	FB	FB	-	-	FB	FB	FB	FB	FB	FB	FB	FB	-	-	-	-	-	-	-	-	FB	-	-	-	-	-	31	-	-
Frank Lawrence	-	-	-	-	-	-	-	-	-	-	-	-	-	-	-	-	-	-	-	-	-	-	FB	F	-	-	-	F	-	-	-	-	-	-	-	-	-	-	-	-	F	-	-	-	-	-	4	-	-
Wally Frisby	-	-	-	-	-	-	-	-	-	-	-	-	-	-	-	-	-	-	-	-	-	-	-	FB	-	-	-	-	-	-	-	-	-	-	FB	-	-	-	FB	-	-	-	-	-	-	-	3	-	4
L.C.Gamble	-	-	-	-	-	-	-	-	-	-	-	-	-	-	-	-	-	-	-	-	-	-	-	-	-	-	-	-	-	-	-	-	-	-	-	FB	FB	FB	-	FB	-	-	-	-	-	-	4	-	-
O.C.Bryson	W	W	-	-	-	-	W	W	W	-	FE	FE	FE	-	FE	FE	W	-	C	FE	FE	W	FE	FE	W	-	-	-	-	-	FE	FE	-	FE	-	-	-	FE	-	FE	W	-	-	-	-	-	24	6	18
Ewart Farndon	W	W	-	W	W	FE	-	W	W	W	W	W	W	W	W	W	-	W	W	W	W	W	W	W	W	W	W	W	-	W	W	W	W	W	W	-	W	W	W	W	-	-	-	-	-	-	35	13	39
P.G.Scott	-	-	W	C	FE	-	FE	FE	FE	FE	FE	FE	FE	-	FE	FE	W	-	-	-	-	-	-	-	-	-	-	-	-	-	-	-	-	FE	-	FE	FE	-	FE	FE	FE	-	-	-	-	-	19	3	9
F.S.Wells	-	-	W	W	W	W	-	-	-	-	-	-	-	-	-	-	-	-	-	-	-	-	-	-	-	-	-	-	-	-	-	-	-	-	-	-	-	-	-	-	-	-	-	-	-	-	4	2	6
S.Jones	-	-	-	-	-	W	-	-	-	-	-	-	-	-	-	W	-	-	-	-	-	-	-	-	-	-	-	-	-	-	-	-	-	-	-	-	-	-	-	-	-	-	-	-	-	-	2	-	-
J.H.Moore	-	-	-	-	-	-	W	-	-	-	W	W	W	C	W	-	C	W	W	-	-	-	-	-	-	-	W	W	-	-	-	-	W	-	-	-	-	-	-	-	-	-	-	-	-	-	12	4	12
Ted Flewitt	-	-	-	-	-	-	-	-	-	-	-	-	-	-	-	-	-	-	-	W	W	-	W	FE	FE	FE	FE	FE	W	W	W	W	FE	W	W	W	W	W	W	W	W	-	-	-	-	-	21	8	24
M.S.Holden	C	FE	-	-	-	-	FE	FE	FE	FE	-	-	-	W	-	-	-	-	-	-	-	-	-	-	-	C	C	-	-	-	-	-	-	-	-	-	-	-	-	-	-	-	-	-	-	-	9	2	18
Harold Day	-	-	C	-	C	-	C	C	C	C	C	C	-	C	C	C	C	C	FH	C	C	C	C	-	FE	FE	FE	FE	FE	FE	FE	FE	FE	-	FE	FE	FE	FE	-	-	FE	-	-	-	-	-	32	10	156
E.C.R.Hopkins	-	-	-	-	-	-	-	-	-	-	-	-	-	-	-	-	-	-	-	-	-	-	-	-	C	-	-	-	-	-	-	-	-	-	-	C	-	C	FE	-	C	-	-	-	-	-	5	1	3
Charlie Cramphorn	-	-	-	-	-	-	-	-	-	-	-	-	-	-	-	-	-	-	-	-	-	-	-	-	-	-	-	C	C	C	-	C	C	C	C	-	C	-	-	-	-	-	-	-	-	-	8	5	15
Ernie Dynes	FE	FH	-	-	-	FE	-	-	-	-	-	-	-	-	-	-	-	-	-	-	-	-	-	-	-	-	-	-	-	-	-	-	-	-	-	-	-	-	-	-	-	-	-	-	-	-	3	-	-
Harold Sambrook	FE	FE	C	FE	FE	-	-	-	FH	FH	-	-	-	-	-	-	-	-	-	-	-	-	-	-	-	-	-	-	FE	FE	-	-	-	-	-	-	-	-	-	-	-	-	-	-	-	-	9	-	3
R.E.S.Fitzgerald	-	-	-	-	-	-	-	-	-	-	-	-	-	-	-	-	-	FE	FE	-	-	FE	-	-	-	-	-	-	-	-	-	-	-	-	-	-	-	-	-	-	-	-	-	-	-	-	3	-	-
C.B.Tate	-	-	-	-	-	-	-	-	-	-	-	-	-	-	-	-	-	FE	FE	FE	FE	FE	FE	W	-	-	-	-	-	-	-	-	-	-	-	-	-	-	-	-	-	-	-	-	-	-	7	1	3
Ralph Buckingham	FH	-	-	FH	FH	FH	FH	FH	-	-	FH	FH	FH	FH	FH	FH	FH	FH	-	FH	FH	FH	FH	C	FH	FH	FH	FH	FH	FH	FH	FH	FH	FH	FE	FH	FH	FH	FH	FH	FH	-	-	-	-	-	36	14	42
C.H.M.Waldock	-	-	FH	FE	-	-	-	-	-	-	-	-	-	-	-	-	-	-	-	-	-	-	-	-	-	-	-	-	-	-	-	-	-	-	-	-	-	-	-	-	-	-	-	-	-	-	2	-	-
Stuart Smith	SH	SH	SH	SH	SH	SH	SH	SH	SH	SH	SH	SH	SH	SH	-	-	-	-	-	-	-	-	-	-	-	-	-	-	-	-	-	-	-	-	-	-	-	-	-	-	-	-	-	-	-	-	14	3	9
John Russell	-	-	-	-	-	-	-	-	-	-	-	-	-	-	SH	-	SH	SH	SH	-	SH	SH	SH	FH	-	-	-	-	-	-	SH	-	-	-	-	SH	-	SH	-	-	-	-	-	-	-	-	11	-	-
J.Raven	-	-	-	-	-	-	-	-	-	-	-	-	-	-	-	SH	-	-	-	-	-	-	-	-	-	-	SH	-	-	-	-	-	-	-	-	-	-	-	-	-	-	-	-	-	-	-	2	-	-
Langley Burton	-	-	-	-	-	-	-	-	-	-	-	-	-	-	-	-	-	-	-	SH	-	-	-	SH	SH	SH	-	-	SH	SH	-	SH	SH	-	-	-	-	-	SH	-	-	-	-	-	-	-	9	1	3
Harry Greenlees	-	-	-	-	-	-	-	-	-	-	-	-	-	-	-	-	-	-	-	-	-	-	-	-	-	-	-	-	-	-	-	-	-	SH	SH	-	SH	-	-	SH	SH	-	-	-	-	-	5	1	3
George Beamish	F	-	F	F	F	-	F	F	-	-	F	F	-	F	F	-	-	-	-	-	-	-	-	-	-	-	-	-	-	-	-	-	-	-	-	-	-	-	-	-	-	-	-	-	-	-	10	-	-
Ernie Coleman	F	F	F	F	F	F	F	F	F	F	F	F	F	F	F	F	F	F	F	-	F	F	F	F	F	F	F	F	F	F	F	F	F	-	F	F	F	F	F	F	F	-	-	-	-	-	39	5	15
Jock Lawrie	F	F	F	-	F	-	-	-	F	F	F	F	-	F	F	F	F	F	F	F	F	F	-	F	-	F	F	F	F	F	F	F	F	F	F	F	F	-	F	F	-	-	-	-	-	-	32	4	12
Doug Norman	F	F	F	F	F	F	F	-	F	F	F	F	F	F	F	F	F	F	F	F	F	F	F	F	F	F	F	F	F	F	F	F	F	F	F	F	F	F	F	F	F	-	-	-	-	-	40	2	6
Herb Sharratt	F	F	F	-	F	F	F	F	F	F	F	F	-	-	-	F	-	-	-	-	-	-	-	-	-	-	-	-	-	-	-	-	-	-	-	-	-	-	-	-	-	-	-	-	-	-	12	-	-
Trevor Thorneloe	F	F	F	F	F	F	F	F	F	-	-	-	F	F	F	F	F	F	F	F	F	F	-	F	F	F	F	F	F	F	F	F	F	F	F	-	-	F	F	F	F	-	-	-	-	-	35	4	33
George Ward	F	F	F	F	F	F	F	F	-	-	-	-	-	-	-	-	-	F	-	-	-	-	F	F	-	-	-	-	-	-	-	-	-	-	-	-	-	-	-	-	-	-	-	-	-	-	11	1	3
John Davis	-	F	-	F	-	F	-	-	-	-	-	-	-	-	-	-	-	-	-	-	-	-	-	-	-	-	-	-	-	-	-	-	F	-	-	-	-	-	-	-	-	-	-	-	-	-	4	-	-
Dick Collopy	-	-	F	F	-	C	F	F	-	F	-	-	-	-	-	-	-	-	-	-	-	-	-	-	-	-	-	-	-	-	-	-	-	-	-	-	-	-	-	-	-	-	-	-	-	-	6	-	-
Doug Prentice	-	-	-	-	-	-	-	F	F	F	F	F	F	F	F	F	F	F	F	F	F	F	F	F	F	F	F	F	-	F	F	F	F	F	F	F	F	F	F	F	F	-	-	-	-	-	[illegible]	[illegible]	11
G.W.C.Parker	-	-	-	-	-	-	-	-	F	F	F	F	F	-	F	-	F	-	F	F	F	-	-	-	F	F	F	-	F	F	F	F	F	F	F	F	F	F	-	-	-	-	-	-	-	-	23	-	-
Harry Briers	-	-	-	-	-	-	-	-	-	-	-	-	F	F	-	F	F	F	F	F	-	F	F	F	F	F	F	F	F	-	F	F	-	-	-	-	F	-	F	-	-	-	-	-	-	-	19	-	-
Guy German	-	-	-	-	-	-	-	-	-	-	-	-	F	-	-	-	F	-	-	-	-	F	-	-	-	-	-	-	-	-	-	-	-	-	-	-	-	-	-	-	-	-	-	-	-	-	3	-	-
William Beith	-	-	-	-	-	-	-	-	-	-	-	-	-	-	-	-	-	-	-	F	F	F	-	-	-	-	-	-	-	-	-	-	-	-	-	-	-	-	-	-	-	-	-	-	-	-	3	-	-
Norman Coates	-	-	-	-	-	-	-	-	-	-	-	-	-	-	-	-	-	-	-	-	-	-	-	-	-	-	-	-	-	F	F	-	-	F	-	F	-	F	-	C	-	-	-	-	-	-	6	-	-
Harry Edmiston	-	-	-	-	-	-	-	-	-	-	-	-	-	-	-	-	-	-	-	-	-	-	-	-	-	-	-	-	-	-	-	-	-	F	F	F	F	F	F	F	F	-	-	-	-	-	8	-	-
Mog' Christie	-	-	-	-	-	-	-	-	-	-	-	-	-	-	-	-	-	-	-	-	-	-	-	-	-	-	-	-	-	-	-	-	-	-	-	-	-	-	-	F	F	-	-	-	-	-	2	1	3

1 game: Lord Bandon W(36)[1T-3], Eddie Beynon W(29), Len Boulter W(10), T.E.Burrows C(31), D.C.Clarke FH(35), A.Curry FB(33), A.Derry W(26), J.H.Moon F(14), Arthur Palmer F(6), Noel Rees C(39), Nathan Rocyn-Jones FB(34), Alastair Smallwood C(2), C.B.Wales C(13), Jock Wemyss F(23), Herbert Whitley SH(28)[1T-3]

LEICESTER FOOTBALL CLUB 1926-27

Back: R.A. Buckingham, L.C. Sambrook, N. Coates, A.H. Greenwood, T.H. Briers, M.G. Christie, D.W.R. Ryley, S.F. Lawrence, E.M. Barlow, L.W. Burton.

Middle: T.H. Crumbie (Hon.Sec), T. Thorpe (Hon.Tres), W.E. Farndon, F.D. Prentice, H.L.V. Day (Capt), D.J. Norman, F.E. Wood, E.G. Coleman, Sir Samuel Faire (President).

Front: J.C. Russell, H.D. Greenlees, W.S. Thompson, E.C.A. Flewitt, J.H.F. Edmiston, F.V. Beamish.

1926-1927

NO	DATE	OPPONENTS	V	RES	FOR G	FOR T	FOR D	FOR P	FOR PTS	AGAINST G	AGAINST T	AGAINST D	AGAINST P	AGAINST PTS	SCORERS
1	Sep 4	BATH	H	Won	1	2	-	1	14	-	-	-	-	0	Flewitt(T) Day(C,P) Farndon(T) Russell(T)
2	11	COVENTRY	H	Lost	-	3	-	-	9	1	2	-	-	11	Flewitt(2T) Buckingham(T)
3	15	Rugby B.T.H.	A	Won	3	4	-	-	27	1	-	-	-	5	Shipton(T,C) Barlow(T) Flewitt(T) Buckingham(3T) Christie(T) Greenwood(2C)
4	18	PLYMOUTH ALBION	H	Won	5	1	-	1	31	-	1	1	-	7	Flewitt(T) Day(2T,5C,P) Buckingham(2T) Prentice(T)
5	25	LONDON WELSH	H	Won	1	-	-	1	8	-	-	-	-	0	Day(T,C,P)
6	Oct 2	NORTHERN	H	Won	4	7	-	-	41	-	1	1	-	7	Farndon(T) C.T.Cramphorn(T) Flewitt(3T) Day(2T,C) Buckingham(T) Greenlees(T) Burton(T) Prentice(3C) Coleman(T)
7	9	BECTIVE RANGERS	H	Won	3	3	-	-	24	-	1	-	-	3	C.T.Cramphorn(T) Flewitt(2T) Day(T,3C) Buckingham(2T)
8	16	Newport	A	Won	2	2	-	1	19	2	1	1	-	17	Farndon(T) Flewitt(T) Day(T,2C,P) Greenlees(T)
9	23	MOSELEY	H	Won	6	4	-	-	42	-	-	-	-	0	C.T.Cramphorn(2T) Flewitt(C) Day(5C) Buckingham(T) Greenlees(2T) Russell(T) Dykes(4T)
10	27	Cambridge University	A	Lost	-	-	-	-	0	3	1	-	-	18	
11	30	Northampton	A	Lost	-	3	-	-	9	3	1	-	-	18	Farndon(T) Flewitt(T) Prentice(T)
12	Nov 6	UNITED SERVICES	H	Won	3	-	-	-	15	1	-	-	-	5	Day(3C) Buckingham(3T)
13	13	OXFORD UNIVERSITY	H	Won	-	2	-	-	6	-	1	-	-	3	Farndon(T) Prentice(T)
14	20	SWANSEA	H	Lost	1	1	-	1	11	2	2	-	-	16	Farndon(T) Greenlees(T) Prentice(C,P)
15	27	MAORIS	H	Lost	2	-	-	1	13	1	2	1	-	15	Farndon(T) Prentice(T,2C,P)
16	29	CARDIFF	H	Won	1	-	-	1	8	-	1	1	-	7	Prentice(C,P) Dykes(T)
17	Dec 4	Harlequins	A	Lost	-	1	-	-	3	1	-	-	-	5	Farndon(T)
18	11	Blackheath	A	Lost	-	1	-	1	6	3	1	-	-	18	Prentice(P) Dykes(T)
19	18	BRISTOL	H	Won	1	2	-	-	11	-	1	-	-	3	C.T.Cramphorn(2T) Flewitt(T) Day(C)
20	24	Coventry	A	Lost	-	1	-	-	3	1	2	-	-	11	Prentice(T)
21	27	BIRKENHEAD PARK	H	Won	2	3	-	-	19	1	2	-	-	11	C.T.Cramphorn(T) Hopkins(T) Buckingham(3T) Prentice(2C)
22	28	BARBARIANS	H	Won	2	1	-	-	13	1	1	-	-	8	Farndon(T) Flewitt(T) Greenlees(T) Prentice(2C)
23	Jan 1	MANCHESTER	H	Won	1	2	-	-	11	1	1	-	-	8	Farndon(T) C.T.Cramphorn(T) Sweatman(T) Prentice(C)
24	8	Swansea	A	Lost	-	1	-	-	3	-	-	2	-	8	Buckingham(T)
25	15	GLOUCESTER	H	Won	1	1	-	1	11	-	1	-	-	3	Sweatman(T) Russell(T) Prentice(C,P)
26	22	PERCY PARK	H	Won	3	1	-	1	21	-	-	1	-	4	Farndon(T) Wood(T) Buckingham(2T) Prentice(3C,P)
27	26	ROYAL AIR FORCE	H	Won	1	1	-	1	11	-	1	-	-	3	Flewitt(T) Barlow(T) Prentice(C,P)
28	29	Richmond	A	Lost	-	2	-	-	6	2	-	-	1	13	Buckingham(T) Nelson(T)
29	Feb 5	London Scottish	A	Lost	1	-	-	-	5	3	1	-	-	18	Yarnall(C) Glover(T)
30	12	NEWPORT	H	Lost	1	1	-	-	8	1	1	1	-	12	Buckingham(T) Day(C) Edmiston(T)
31	19	Bath	A	Lost	1	-	-	1	8	3	1	-	-	18	Flewitt(T) Day(C,P)
32	26	Cardiff	A	Lost	-	1	-	-	3	1	1	-	-	8	Glover(T)
33	Mar 5	HARLEQUINS	H	Won	1	2	-	-	11	-	1	-	-	3	Day(2T,C) Edmiston(T)
34	19	Birkenhead Park	A	Lost	-	1	-	1	6	-	2	-	1	9	Flewitt(T) Day(P)
35	26	OLD MERCHANT TAYLORS	H	Won	1	2	-	2	17	-	-	-	-	0	Flewitt(2T) Day(C,2P) Greenlees(T)
36	Apr 2	Gloucester	A	Lost	-	1	-	-	3	1	-	1	1	12	Barlow(T)
37	9	BLACKHEATH	H	Won	2	1	-	-	13	-	1	-	-	3	Farndon(2T) Wood(T) Day(2C)
38	16	Bristol	A	Lost	-	2	-	-	6	2	3	1	1	26	Wood(T) Edmiston(T)
39	18	Plymouth Albion	A	Won	3	1	-	-	18	-	1	-	-	3	Day(3C) Flewitt(3T) Greenlees(T)
40	19	Bridgwater	A	Won	2	6	-	-	28	1	-	1	-	9	Barlow(T) Wood(T) Wallace(3T) Day(T,2C) Coleman(T) Greenwood(T)
41	30	NORTHAMPTON	H	Drew	1	-	-	-	5	1	-	-	-	5	Day(C) Edmiston(T)

INDIVIDUAL APPEARANCES 1926-1927

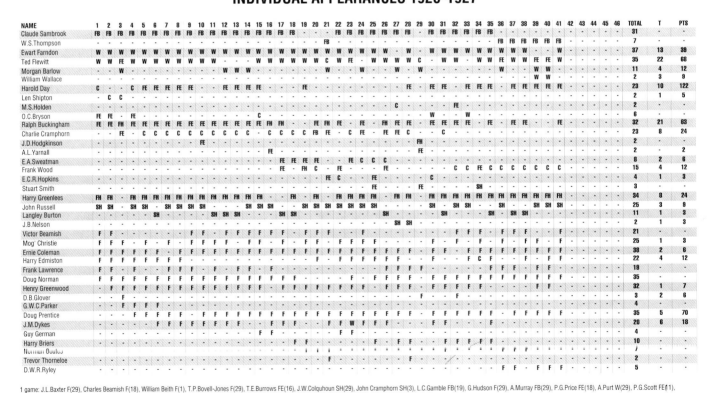

NAME	1	2	3	4	5	6	7	8	9	10	11	12	13	14	15	16	17	18	19	20	21	22	23	24	25	26	27	28	29	30	31	32	33	34	35	36	37	38	39	40	41	42	43	44	45	46	TOTAL	T	PTS
Claude Sambrook	FB	FB	FB	FB	FB	FB	FB	FB	FB	FB	FB	FB	FB	FB	FB	FB	FB	FB	-	-	-	FB	FB	FB	FB	FB	FB	FB	-	FB	FB	FB	FB	FB	FB	-	-	-	-	-	-	-	-	-	-	-	31	-	-
W.S.Thompson	-	-	-	-	-	-	-	-	-	-	-	-	-	-	-	-	-	-	-	-	FB	-	-	-	-	-	-	-	-	-	-	-	-	-	-	FB	FB	FB	FB	FB	FB	-	-	-	-	-	7	-	-
Ewart Farndon	W	W	W	W	W	W	W	W	W	W	W	W	W	W	W	W	W	W	W	W	W	W	W	W	W	W	-	W	-	W	W	W	W	W	W	W	W	W	-	-	W	-	-	-	-	-	37	13	39
Ted Flewitt	W	W	FE	W	W	W	W	W	W	W	W	-	-	-	W	W	W	W	W	W	C	W	FE	-	W	W	W	W	C	-	W	W	-	W	W	FE	W	W	FE	FE	W	-	-	-	-	-	35	22	68
Morgan Barlow	-	-	W	-	-	-	-	-	-	-	-	W	W	W	-	-	-	-	-	-	W	-	-	W	-	-	W	-	W	-	-	-	-	-	-	W	-	-	W	W	-	-	-	-	-	-	11	4	12
William Wallace	-	-	-	-	-	-	-	-	-	-	-	-	-	-	-	-	-	-	-	-	-	-	-	-	-	-	-	-	-	-	-	-	-	-	-	-	-	-	W	W	-	-	-	-	-	-	2	3	9
Harold Day	C	-	-	C	FE	FE	FE	FE	FE	-	-	FE	FE	FE	FE	-	-	-	FE	-	-	-	-	-	-	-	-	FE	-	FE	FE	-	FE	FE	FE	-	FE	FE	FE	FE	FE	-	-	-	-	-	23	10	122
Len Shipton	-	C	C	-	-	-	-	-	-	-	-	-	-	-	-	-	-	-	-	-	-	-	-	-	-	-	-	-	-	-	-	-	-	-	-	-	-	-	-	-	-	-	-	-	-	-	2	1	5
M.S.Holden	-	-	-	-	-	-	-	-	-	-	-	-	-	-	-	-	-	-	-	-	-	-	-	-	-	-	C	-	-	-	-	FE	-	-	-	-	-	-	-	-	-	-	-	-	-	-	2	-	-
O.C.Bryson	FE	FE	-	FE	-	-	-	-	-	-	-	-	-	-	C	-	-	-	-	-	-	-	-	-	-	-	-	-	-	W	-	-	W	-	-	-	-	-	-	-	-	-	-	-	-	-	6	-	-
Ralph Buckingham	FE	FE	FH	FE	FE	FE	FE	FE	FE	FE	FE	FE	FE	FE	FE	FH	FH	-	-	FE	FH	FE	-	FE	-	FH	FE	FE	-	FE	FE	FE	FE	-	FE	-	FE	FE	-	-	FE	-	-	-	-	-	32	21	63
Charlie Cramphorn	-	-	FE	-	C	C	C	C	C	C	C	C	C	C	-	C	C	C	C	FB	FE	-	C	FE	-	FE	FE	C	-	-	C	-	-	-	-	-	-	-	-	-	-	-	-	-	-	-	23	8	24
J.D.Hodgkinson	-	-	-	-	-	-	-	-	-	FE	-	-	-	-	-	-	-	-	-	-	-	-	-	-	-	-	-	-	FH	-	-	-	-	-	-	-	-	-	-	-	-	-	-	-	-	-	2	-	-
A.L.Yarnall	-	-	-	-	-	-	-	-	-	-	-	-	-	-	-	FE	-	-	-	-	-	-	-	-	-	-	-	-	FE	-	-	-	-	-	-	-	-	-	-	-	-	-	-	-	-	-	2	-	2
E.A.Sweatman	-	-	-	-	-	-	-	-	-	-	-	-	-	-	-	-	FE	FE	FE	FE	-	-	FE	C	C	C	-	-	-	-	-	-	-	-	-	-	-	-	-	-	-	-	-	-	-	-	8	2	6
Frank Wood	-	-	-	-	-	-	-	-	-	-	-	-	-	-	-	-	FE	-	FH	C	-	FE	-	-	-	FE	-	-	-	-	-	C	C	FE	C	C	C	C	C	C	C	-	-	-	-	-	15	4	12
E.C.R.Hopkins	-	-	-	-	-	-	-	-	-	-	-	-	-	-	-	-	-	-	-	-	FE	C	-	-	FE	-	-	-	-	C	-	-	-	-	-	-	-	-	-	-	-	-	-	-	-	-	4	1	3
Stuart Smith	-	-	-	-	-	-	-	-	-	-	-	-	-	-	-	-	-	-	-	-	-	-	-	-	FE	-	-	-	FE	-	-	-	-	SH	-	-	-	-	-	-	-	-	-	-	-	-	3	-	-
Harry Greenlees	FH	FH	-	FH	FH	FH	FH	FH	FH	FH	FH	FH	FH	FH	FH	-	-	FH	-	FH	-	FH	FH	FH	FH	-	FH	FH	-	FH	FH	FH	FH	FH	FH	FH	FH	FH	FH	FH	FH	-	-	-	-	-	34	8	24
John Russell	SH	SH	-	SH	SH	-	SH	SH	SH	SH	-	-	-	SH	SH	SH	-	-	SH	SH	SH	SH	SH	SH	SH	-	-	-	-	SH	-	SH	SH	-	-	SH	-	-	SH	SH	SH	-	-	-	-	-	25	3	9
Langley Burton	-	-	-	-	-	SH	-	-	-	-	SH	SH	SH	-	-	-	SH	SH	-	-	-	-	-	-	-	SH	-	-	-	-	SH	-	-	-	SH	-	SH	SH	-	-	-	-	-	-	-	-	11	1	3
J.B.Nelson	-	-	-	-	-	-	-	-	-	-	-	-	-	-	-	-	-	-	-	-	-	-	-	-	-	-	SH	SH	-	-	-	-	-	-	-	-	-	-	-	-	-	-	-	-	-	-	2	1	3
Victor Beamish	F	F	-	-	-	-	-	-	F	F	-	F	F	F	F	F	F	-	F	F	F	-	-	F	-	-	-	-	-	-	-	F	F	F	-	F	F	F	-	-	F	-	-	-	-	-	21	-	-
Mog' Christie	F	F	F	-	F	-	F	-	F	F	F	F	-	F	F	-	F	-	F	F	-	F	F	F	F	-	-	-	-	F	-	F	-	F	-	F	-	F	F	-	F	-	-	-	-	-	25	1	3
Ernie Coleman	F	F	F	F	F	F	-	F	F	F	F	F	F	F	F	F	F	F	F	F	F	F	F	F	F	F	F	F	-	F	F	-	F	F	F	F	F	F	F	F	F	-	-	-	-	-	38	2	6
Harry Edmiston	F	F	F	F	F	F	F	F	-	-	-	-	-	-	-	-	-	-	-	F	-	F	F	F	F	F	F	-	-	F	-	-	F	C	F	-	-	F	-	F	F	-	-	-	-	-	22	4	12
Frank Lawrence	F	F	-	F	-	-	F	F	F	-	F	-	F	F	-	F	-	-	-	-	-	-	-	-	-	F	F	F	F	-	-	-	-	-	F	F	F	-	F	F	-	-	-	-	-	-	19	-	-
Doug Norman	F	F	F	F	F	F	F	F	F	F	F	F	F	F	F	F	F	F	-	-	-	-	F	-	F	F	F	F	-	F	F	F	F	F	F	F	F	F	F	F	F	-	-	-	-	-	35	-	-
Henry Greenwood	-	F	F	F	F	F	F	F	F	F	F	F	F	F	F	-	F	F	F	F	F	F	F	F	-	F	F	F	-	F	F	F	F	F	-	-	-	-	F	F	-	-	-	-	-	-	32	1	7
D.B.Glover	-	-	F	-	-	-	-	-	-	-	-	-	-	-	-	-	-	-	-	-	-	-	-	-	-	-	-	-	F	-	-	F	-	-	-	-	-	-	-	-	-	-	-	-	-	-	3	2	6
G.W.C.Parker	-	-	F	F	F	F	-	-	-	-	-	-	-	-	-	-	-	-	-	-	-	-	-	-	-	-	-	-	-	-	-	-	-	-	-	-	-	-	-	-	-	-	-	-	-	-	4	-	-
Doug Prentice	-	-	-	F	F	F	F	F	-	F	F	F	F	F	F	F	F	F	F	F	F	F	F	F	F	F	F	F	-	F	F	F	F	F	F	-	F	F	F	F	F	-	-	-	-	-	35	5	70
J.M.Dykes	-	-	-	-	-	F	F	F	F	F	F	F	F	-	-	F	F	F	-	-	F	F	W	F	F	F	-	-	-	F	F	-	-	-	F	-	-	-	-	-	-	-	-	-	-	-	20	6	18
Guy German	-	-	-	-	-	-	-	-	-	-	-	-	-	-	F	F	-	-	-	-	-	F	F	-	-	-	-	-	-	-	-	-	-	-	-	-	-	-	-	-	-	-	-	-	-	-	4	-	-
Harry Briers	-	-	-	-	-	-	-	-	-	-	-	-	-	-	-	-	-	F	F	-	-	-	-	-	F	-	F	F	-	-	F	F	F	F	F	-	-	-	-	-	-	-	-	-	-	-	10	-	-
[illegible]	-	-	-	-	-	-	-	-	-	-	-	-	-	-	-	-	-	-	F	F	F	-	-	-	-	-	-	-	-	-	F	-	-	-	-	F	F	F	-	-	-	-	-	-	-	-	7	-	-
Trevor Thorneloe	-	-	-	-	-	-	-	-	-	-	-	-	-	-	-	-	-	-	-	-	F	-	-	-	-	-	-	F	-	-	-	-	-	-	-	-	-	-	-	-	-	-	-	-	-	-	2	-	-
D.W.R.Ryley	-	-	-	-	-	-	-	-	-	-	-	-	-	-	-	-	-	-	-	-	-	-	-	-	-	-	-	-	-	-	-	-	-	-	-	F	F	-	F	F	F	-	-	-	-	-	5	-	-

1 game: J.L.Baxter F(29), Charles Beamish F(18), William Beith F(1), T.P.Bovell-Jones F(29), T.E.Burrows FE(16), J.W.Colquhoun SH(29), John Cramphorn SH(3), L.C.Gamble FB(19), G.Hudson F(29), A.Murray FB(29), P.G.Price FE(18), A.Purt W(29), P.G.Scott FE(11), R.P.Stephens F(29), J.L.Tebbutt F(29), F.H.R.Turney FE(36)

					FOR					AGAINST					
NO	DATE	OPPONENTS	V	RES	G	T	D	P	PTS	G	T	D	P	PTS	SCORERS
1	Sep 3	BATH	H	Won	6	1	-	-	33	-	-	-	-	0	Farndon(2T) Wood(2T) Day(T,6C) Flewitt(T) Buckingham(T)
2	10	HARTLEPOOL ROVERS	H	Won	5	5	-	-	40	1	1	-	-	8	Farndon(3T) Day(T,5C) Flewitt(T) Buckingham(2T) Prentice(T) Christie(2T)
3	17	NUNEATON	H	Won	2	-	-	1	13	1	-	-	-	5	Day(2C,P) G.R.Beamish(T) Ryley(T)
4	24	PLYMOUTH ALBION	H	Won	1	3	-	-	14	1	1	-	-	8	Farndon(T) Day(C) Flewitt(T) Christie(2T)
5	Oct 1	United Services	A	Won	-	-	-	1	3	-	-	-	-	0	Day(P)
6	8	OLD BLUES	H	Won	3	1	-	-	18	1	1	1*	-	11	Day(T,3C) Flewitt(T) Prentice(T) G.R.Beamish(T)
7	15	NEWPORT	H	Lost	1	-	-	-	5	1	1	-	-	8	Farndon(T) Day(C)
8	22	Moseley	A	Won	3	4	-	-	27	-	-	-	-	0	Farndon(T) Wood(2T) Day(2T,2C) Flewitt(T) Greenlees(T) Prentice(C)
9	Nov 5	CAMBRIDGE UNIVERSITY	H	Drew	2	-	1	-	14	1	3	-	-	14	Buckingham(T) Greenlees(D) Prentice(T,2C)
10	10	OXFORD UNIVERSITY	H	Won	1	3	-	-	14	-	1	-	-	3	Farndon(T) Buckingham(T) Greenlees(T) Prentice(T,C)
11	12	NORTHAMPTON	H	Drew	-	-	-	1	3	-	1	-	-	3	Day(P)
12	19	Swansea	A	Lost	-	1	-	-	3	-	2	-	-	6	G.R.Beamish(T)
13	26	CARDIFF	H	Won	1	2	1	-	15	-	-	1	1	7	Buckingham(T) Day(C) Wood(2T,D)
14	Dec 3	Harlequins	A	Lost	-	-	-	-	0	-	1	-	-	3	
15	10	Blackheath	A	Lost	-	1	-	-	3	3	2	-	-	21	G.R.Beamish(T)
	17	BRISTOL	H		Cancelled Frost										
16	24	BRIDGWATER	H	Won	4	2	-	1	29	-	-	-	-	0	Farndon(3T) Day(4C,P) F.V.Beamish(T) Christie(T) Lawrence(T)
17	26	BIRKENHEAD PARK	H	Won	4	4	-	-	32	-	-	-	-	0	Wood(2T) Day(T,4C) Farndon(2T) Smith(T) Hall(T) Briers(T)
18	27	BARBARIANS	H	Won	2	2	-	-	16	2	1	-	-	13	Day(2T,2C) Sweatman(T) Prentice(T)
	31	Coventry	A		Cancelled Frost										
	Jan 2	Manchester	A		Cancelled Frost										
19	3	Hartlepool Rovers	A	Won	1	3	-	2	20	-	-	-	-	0	Christie(T) Wood(T) Smith(T) Prentice(T,C,2P)
20	7	SWANSEA	H	Won	1	1	-	1	11	-	-	-	-	0	Prentice(C,P) Christie(T) Lawrence(T)
21	14	Gloucester	A	Lost	-	-	-	1	3	-	2	-	-	6	Day(P)
22	21	LONDON WELSH	H	Won	2	4	-	-	22	-	-	-	-	0	Wood(T) Day(2C) Smith(T) Prentice(T) Lawrence(T) Dunkley(2T)
23	25	ROYAL AIR FORCE	H	Won	2	2	-	-	16	1	2	-	-	11	Barlow(3T) Wood(T) Prentice(2C)
	28	RICHMOND	H		Cancelled										
24	Feb 4	LONDON SCOTTISH	H	Won	4	3	-	1	32	-	1	-	-	3	Wood(T) Tyler(T) Buckingham(T) Prentice(2T,4C,P) Coleman(T) Dunkley(T)
25	11	Newport	A	Lost	-	1	-	-	3	1	1	-	1	11	Barlow(T)
26	18	COVENTRY	H	Won	2	4	-	1	25	2	2	-	-	16	Barlow(T) Buckingham(T) Smith(T) Prentice(2C,P) Coleman(T) Lawrence(T) Dunkley(T)
27	25	Cardiff	A	Lost	1	1	-	-	8	2	5	-	-	25	Sambrook(C) Coleman(T) Lawrence(T)
28	Mar 3	HARLEQUINS	H	Drew	3	-	-	1	18	3	1	-	-	18	Wood(2T) Prentice(3C,P) Christie(T)
29	10	Northampton	A	Lost	-	1	-	-	3	-	2	-	-	6	Coleman(T)
30	17	PENARTH	H	Won	-	-	-	1	3	-	-	-	-	0	Day(P)
31	24	OLD MERCHANT TAYLORS	H	Won	2	5	-	-	25	-	-	-	-	0	Barlow(2T) Buckingham(2T) Wood(2T) Tyler(T) Prentice(C) Norman(C)
32	31	GLOUCESTER	H	Won	1	2	1	1	18	-	2	-	-	6	Franklin(D) Day(T,C,P) Prentice(2T)
33	Apr 7	Bristol	A	Lost	1	2	-	-	11	1	3	-	-	14	Wallace(2T) Wood(T) Prentice(C)
34	9	Plymouth Albion	A	Drew	3	-	-	-	15	1	1	1	1	15	Wood(T) Greenlees(T) Prentice(T,3C)
35	10	Bath	A	Lost	-	1	-	-	3	1	2	-	-	11	Prentice(T)
36	14	BLACKHEATH	H	Lost	1	1	-	-	8	-	2	1	-	10	Farndon(T) Prentice(C) Lawrence(T)
37	19	RICHMOND	H	Lost	1	-	-	-	5	-	3	-	-	9	Wood(T) Thorneloe(C)
38	21	Birkenhead Park	A	Lost	2	-	-	-	10	-	3	1	1	16	Day(T,2C) Edmiston(T)
39	25	Coventry	A	Lost	1	-	-	-	5	-	5	-	-	15	Greenlees(T) Prentice(C)

INDIVIDUAL APPEARANCES 1927-1928

NAME	1	2	3	4	5	6	7	8	9	10	11	12	13	14	15	16	17	18	19	20	21	22	23	24	25	26	27	28	29	30	31	32	33	34	35	36	37	38	39	40	41	42	43	44	45	46	TOTAL	T	PTS
Claude Sambrook	FB	FB	FB	FB	FB	FB	FB	-	-	-	FB	FB	-	-	FB	-	FB	-	-	-	-	FB	FB	FB	FB	-	FB	FB	-	-	-	-	-	-	-	-	-	-	-	-	-	-	-	-	-	-	17	-	2
Henry Franklin	-	-	-	-	-	-	-	-	FB	-	-	-	FB	FB	-	FB	-	FB	FB	FB	FB	-	-	-	-	FB	-	-	FB	FB	FB	FB	FB	FB	FB	FB	FB	FB	FB	-	-	-	-	-	-	-	20	-	4
Ewart Farndon	W	W	-	W	W	W	W	W	W	W	W	W	-	-	W	W	W	W	-	W	W	-	-	-	-	-	-	-	-	-	-	-	-	-	W	W	-	W	-	-	-	-	-	-	-	-	20	15	45
Ted Flewitt	W	W	W	W	-	W	W	W	-	-	-	-	-	-	-	-	-	-	-	-	-	-	-	-	-	-	-	-	-	-	-	-	-	-	-	-	C	-	W	-	-	-	-	-	-	-	9	5	15
E.A.Sweatman	-	-	-	-	-	-	-	-	-	W	-	-	-	-	-	W	-	W	-	C	-	-	-	W	-	-	-	-	C	-	-	-	-	-	-	-	-	-	-	-	-	-	-	-	-	-	6	1	3
Morgan Barlow	-	-	-	-	-	-	-	-	-	-	-	-	-	-	-	-	W	-	W	W	-	W	C	W	W	W	W	W	W	W	W	-	-	W	W	W	W	W	-	-	-	-	-	-	-	-	18	7	21
L.J.Adcock	-	-	-	-	-	-	-	-	-	-	-	-	-	-	-	-	-	-	-	-	-	W	W	-	-	-	-	W	-	W	-	-	-	-	-	-	W	-	-	-	-	-	-	-	-	-	5	-	-
Harold Day	C	C	C	C	C	C	C	C	-	-	C	C	C	C	C	C	C	C	-	-	C	FH	-	-	-	-	-	-	-	C	-	C	-	-	-	-	-	C	-	-	-	-	-	-	-	-	21	10	123
Frank Wood	C	C	W	-	W	C	C	C	C	C	W	W	W	W	C	C	C	-	C	C	W	C	W	C	FH	W	C	C	W	C	C	W	W	C	C	C	C	C	C	-	-	-	-	-	-	-	37	19	61
Len Shipton	-	-	-	-	-	-	-	-	-	-	-	-	-	C	-	-	-	-	-	-	-	-	-	-	W	-	W	-	-	-	-	-	-	-	-	-	-	-	-	-	-	-	-	-	-	-	3	-	-
H.P.Tyler	-	-	-	-	-	-	-	-	-	-	-	-	-	-	-	-	-	-	C	-	-	C	-	C	C	C	C	C	-	-	W	W	C	-	-	-	-	-	-	-	-	-	-	-	-	-	10	2	6
Ralph Buckingham	FH	FH	C	C	C	FH	-	FH	C	C	C	C	C	-	-	FH	FH	C	FH	-	C	-	C	FH	-	C	-	FH	FH	-	C	C	C	C	-	C	-	-	-	-	-	-	-	-	-	-	27	10	30
W.E.Squirrell	-	-	-	-	-	-	-	-	-	-	-	-	-	-	-	-	-	-	-	-	-	-	FH	-	-	-	-	-	-	FH	-	-	-	-	-	-	-	SH	-	-	-	-	-	-	-	-	3	-	-
Harry Greenlees	SH	SH	FH	FH	FH	-	FH	SH	FH	FH	FH	FH	FH	FH	-	-	-	FH	-	FH	FH	-	-	-	-	FH	FH	-	-	-	FH	FH	FH	FH	FH	FH	-	FH	FH	-	-	-	-	-	-	-	26	4	16
John Russell	-	-	SH	SH	SH	SH	SH	-	-	-	-	-	-	-	-	-	-	SH	-	SH	SH	-	-	SH	-	-	SH	-	SH	-	-	SH	SH	SH	-	-	-	-	-	-	-	-	-	-	-	-	14	-	-
Stuart Smith	-	-	-	-	-	-	-	-	SH	SH	SH	SH	SH	SH	SH	SH	SH	-	SH	-	-	SH	SH	-	SH	SH	-	SH	C	SH	SH	-	-	-	SH	SH	-	-	SH	-	-	-	-	-	-	-	21	4	12
George Beamish	P	P	P	P	P	P	P	P	-	-	-	L	L	P	P	P	P	P	L	P	-	-	-	-	-	L	-	-	-	L	-	L	L	L	P	L	-	-	-	-	-	-	-	-	-	-	24	4	12
Doug Prentice	P	P	P	P	P	P	P	P	P	P	P	P	P	P	P	P	P	P	P	P	P	P	P	P	-	P	-	P	P	-	P	P	P	P	P	P	-	-	P	-	-	-	-	-	-	-	34	13	105
Doug Norman	H	H	H	H	H	H	H	H	H	H	H	H	H	H	H	H	H	H	H	H	H	H	H	H	P	H	P	H	H	P	H	H	H	H	H	H	P	P	-	-	-	-	-	-	-	-	38	-	2
Ernie Coleman	L	L	L	L	L	L	L	L	P	P	P	P	P	L	L	L	L	L	P	-	P	P	P	P	H	P	H	P	P	H	P	P	P	P	-	P	H	H	H	-	-	-	-	-	-	-	37	4	12
D.W.R.Ryley	L	L	L	L	L	L	L	L	L	L	L	-	-	-	-	-	-	-	-	-	-	-	-	-	-	-	-	-	-	-	-	-	-	-	-	-	-	-	-	-	-	-	-	-	-	-	11	1	3
Victor Beamish	BR	BR	BR	BR	BR	BR	BR	BR	BR	BR	BR	BR	L	L	L	L	BR	BR	-	L	-	-	-	BR	L	L	-	-	L	P	-	L	BR	BR	-	-	-	-	-	-	-	-	-	-	-	-	27	1	3
Mog' Christie	BR	BR	BR	BR	BR	BR	BR	-	L	L	-	L	W	BR	BR	BR	-	BR	W	L	L	-	-	-	-	-	-	L	-	-	-	BR	L	L	L	L	-	-	-	-	-	-	-	-	-	-	24	8	24
Harry Edmiston	BR	BR	BR	BR	BR	BR	-	-	-	-	-	-	-	-	-	-	-	L	L	BR	L	L	-	-	-	-	-	-	-	BR	L	BR	-	BR	L	-	P	L	L	-	-	-	-	-	-	-	19	1	3
Harry Briers	-	-	-	-	-	-	BR	BR	BR	BR	BR	BR	BR	-	-	BR	BR	-	BR	-	BR	BR	BR	L	L	BR	L	BR	BR	-	BR	-	-	-	BR	-	L	BR	BR	-	-	-	-	-	-	-	24	1	3
Frank Lawrence	-	-	-	-	-	-	-	BR	BR	BR	BR	BR	BR	BR	BR	BR	BR	BR	BR	BR	BR	L	L	L	P	BR	P	L	L	BR	L	-	-	-	-	BR	-	-	-	-	-	-	-	-	-	-	25	6	18
A.C.Hall	-	-	-	-	-	-	-	-	-	-	L	-	BR	BR	BR	-	L	-	BR	BR	BR	-	-	-	-	-	L	-	-	-	-	-	BR	BR	BR	-	L	L	P	-	-	-	-	-	-	-	15	1	3
Phil Dunkley	-	-	-	-	-	-	-	-	-	-	-	-	-	-	-	-	-	-	-	-	-	BR	-	BR	-	BR	-	BR	BR	-	BR	BR	-	-	-	BR	-	P	-	-	-	-	-	-	-	-	9	4	12
M.L.Millard	-	-	-	-	-	-	-	-	-	-	-	-	-	-	-	-	-	-	-	-	-	BR	BR	-	BR	-	-	-	-	L	-	-	-	-	-	-	-	-	-	-	-	-	-	-	-	-	4	-	-
E.Braithwaite	-	-	-	-	-	-	-	-	-	-	-	-	-	-	-	-	-	-	-	-	-	-	BR	BR	BR	-	-	-	-	-	-	-	-	-	-	-	-	-	-	-	-	-	-	-	-	-	3	-	-
W.H.Graves	-	-	-	-	-	-	-	-	-	-	-	-	-	-	-	-	-	-	-	-	-	-	-	-	-	-	BR	-	-	-	BR	-	-	-	-	-	BR	-	BR	-	-	-	-	-	-	-	4	-	-
H.N.Knox	-	-	-	-	-	-	-	-	-	-	-	-	-	-	-	-	-	-	-	-	-	-	-	-	-	-	-	BR	BR	BR	-	-	BR	-	BR	BR	-	-	L	-	-	-	-	-	-	-	7	-	-

2 games: T.E.Burrows W(14,15), J.S.Cambridge BR(38,39), G.F.Lashmore BR(25,27), Shirley Moore W(9,39), Ron Palmer FH(37)C(39), W.S.Thompson FB(8,10), William Wallace W(33,34)[2T-6], L.Watts L(23)BR(27)
1 game: A.F.Brodbeck SH(37), J.D.Hodgkinson FH(15), N.W.R.Mawle BR(37), Tony Novis C(35), C.H.Pearse BR(38), Trevor Thorneloe BR(37)[2], F.H.R.Turney C(25)

LEICESTER FOOTBALL CLUB 1927-28
(Winners of the first Leicestershire seven-a-side Charity Competition)
Back: J.E. Thorneloe (Hon.Sec), F.E. Wood, A.C. Hall, E.G. Coleman.
Front: D.J. Norman, F.D. Prentice (Capt), H.D. Greenlees, W.E. Farndon.

LEICESTER FOOTBALL CLUB 1928-29
Back: A.H. Greenwood, T.H. Briers, C.S. Manson, P.E. Dunkley, W.H. Graves, F.E. Wood, J.F. Cramphorn, E.M. Barlow,
J.H.F. Edmiston, J.E. Thorneloe (Hon.Sec).
Middle: E.G. Coleman, G.R. Beamish, D.J. Norman, F.D. Prentice (Capt), R.A. Buckingham, H.D. Greenlees, W.E. Farndon.
Front: S.H. Saunders, R.J. Barr, E.C.A. Flewitt, A.C. Hall, L.W. Burton.

NO	DATE		OPPONENTS	V	RES	FOR G	FOR T	FOR D	FOR P	PTS	AGAINST G	AGAINST T	AGAINST D	AGAINST P	PTS	SCORERS
1	Sep	1	BATH	H	Won	1	4	-	-	17	1	-	-	-	5	Flewitt(3T) F.E.Wood(T) Prentice(T) Norman(C)
2		8	OLD BLUES	H	Won	3	4	-	-	27	3	-	-	-	15	F.E.Wood(T) Buckingham(2T) Farndon(T) Greenlees(T) Prentice(3C) Edmiston(T) Hall(T)
3		15	PLYMOUTH ALBION	H	Lost	-	-	-	1	3	1	-	-	-	5	Prentice(P)
4		22	NUNEATON	H	Won	2	-	-	-	10	-	1	-	-	3	Flewitt(T) Farndon(T) Prentice(2C)
5		29	MOSELEY	H	Won	2	2	-	-	16	-	-	-	-	0	Flewitt(3T) Greenlees(T) Prentice(2C)
6	Oct	6	ROSSLYN PARK	H	Won	2	5	-	-	25	-	3	-	-	9	Buckingham(2T) Flewitt(3T) Prentice(2T,2C)
7		13	COVENTRY	H	Drew	-	1	-	2	9	-	1	-	2	9	Prentice(2P) Jones(T)
8		20	Newport	A	Lost	1	-	-	-	5	-	1	-	2	9	Flewitt(T) Prentice(C)
9		27	Northampton	A	Lost	1	-	-	1	8	1	2	-	-	11	Flewitt(T) Prentice(C,P)
10	Nov	3	Cambridge University	A	Lost	-	-	-	1	3	1	4	-	1	20	Prentice(P)
11		10	CARDIFF	H	Won	1	1	-	-	8	1	-	-	-	5	Farndon(T) Prentice(T,C)
12		17	SWANSEA	H	Won	-	2	-	1	9	1	-	-	-	5	Prentice(T,P) Jones(T)
13		24	BEDFORD	H	Won	3	4	-	-	27	-	3	-	-	9	Flewitt(2T) Symington(T) Day(T,C) Farndon(T) Buckingham(T) Burton(T) Prentice(2C)
14		29	Oxford University	A	Lost	-	1	-	-	3	2	-	-	-	10	Barlow(T)
15	Dec	1	Harlequins	A	Lost	1	-	-	-	5	1	4	-	-	17	Jones(T) Dunkley(C)
16		8	Blackheath	A	Lost	1	1	-	-	8	4	2	-	1	29	Prentice(C) Dunkley(T) Greenwood(T)
17		15	BRISTOL	H	Lost	-	1	-	-	3	1	1	-	-	8	Prentice(T)
18		22	Nuneaton	A	Won	2	4	-	-	22	-	-	-	-	0	Farndon(2T) J.F.Cramphorn(T) Flewitt(T) Barlow(2T) Prentice(2C)
19		26	BIRKENHEAD PARK	H	Lost	2	-	-	1	13	4	1	1	-	27	Prentice(T,2C,P) Greenwood(T)
20		27	BARBARIANS	H	Lost	1	1	-	-	8	3	3	-	-	24	Odbert(T) Prentice(C) Edmiston(T)
21		29	MANCHESTER	H	Lost	1	1	1	-	12	2	2	-	-	16	J.F.Cramphorn(2T) Barlow(D) Edmiston(C)
	Jan	5	Swansea	A		Cancelled Frost										
22		12	Gloucester	A	Lost	-	1	-	-	3	1	1	-	1	11	J.F.Cramphorn(T)
23		19	LONDON WELSH	H	Won	2	1	-	-	13	-	1	-	-	3	J.F.Cramphorn(T) Day(2C) Greenlees(T) Greenwood(T)
24		24	ROYAL AIR FORCE	H	Lost	-	2	-	-	6	1	1	-	-	8	J.F.Cramphorn(T) G.H.Wood(T)
25		26	Richmond	A	Lost	-	1	-	-	3	1	1	1	-	12	Flewitt(T)
26	Feb	2	London Scottish	A	Won	5	1	-	-	28	-	1	-	-	3	Farndon(T) Greenlees(2T) Russell(T) Prentice(T,5C) Coleman(T)
27		9	NEWPORT	H	Won	-	1	-	-	3	-	-	-	-	0	Buckingham(T)
		16	Coventry	A		Cancelled Frost										
28		23	NORTHAMPTON	H	Lost	1	1	-	-	8	-	1	1	1	10	R.S.Palmer(C) Buckingham(T) Russell(T)
	Mar	2	HARLEQUINS	H		Cancelled Frost										
29		9	Bridgwater	A	Lost	1	-	-	-	5	-	2	-	-	6	Farndon(T) Prentice(C)
30		16	Cardiff	A	Lost	1	-	-	-	5	1	1	-	-	8	Buckingham(T) Prentice(C)
31		18	Swansea	A	Lost	2	-	-	2	16	3	1	-	2	24	J.F.Cramphorn(T) Prentice(T,2C,2P)
32		23	GLOUCESTER	H	Won	-	2	-	2	12	-	-	-	1	3	Buckingham(T) Russell(T) Prentice(2P)
33		30	Bristol	A	Lost	1	1	-	-	8	1	3	-	-	14	Farndon(T) Prentice(C) Stephens(T)
34	Apr	1	Plymouth Albion	A	Won	2	2	-	-	16	1	-	-	-	5	Flewitt(T) J.F.Cramphorn(T) Prentice(T,2C) Dunkley(T)
35		2	Bath	A	Won	2	2	-	-	16	-	1	-	2	9	Farndon(2T) Greenlees(T) Prentice(T,2C)
36		6	Birkenhead Park	A	Lost	-	-	-	-	0	-	1	-	-	3	
37		13	BLACKHEATH	H	Won	-	6	-	-	18	2	1	-	-	13	Farndon(T) Barlow(T) Burton(T) Hall(T) Greenwood(T) Dunkley(T)
38		15	Coventry	A	Lost	-	-	-	-	0	1	1	1	-	12	

INDIVIDUAL APPEARANCES 1928-1929

NAME	1	2	3	4	5	6	7	8	9	10	11	12	13	14	15	16	17	18	19	20	21	22	23	24	25	26	27	28	29	30	31	32	33	34	35	36	37	38	39	40	41	42	43	44	45	46	TOTAL	T	PTS
Charlie Manson	FB	FB	-	FB	-	-	-	FB	-	W	-	FB	-	-	FB	FB	FB	FB	-	FB	FB	FB	FB	FB	FB	-	FB	FB	FB	-	-	FB	-	-	-	-	-	-	-	-	-	-	-	-	-	-	20	-	-
Henry Franklin	-	-	FB	-	FB	FB	FB	-	FB	-	-	-	FB	FB	-	-	-	-	FB	-	-	-	-	-	-	-	-	-	-	-	-	-	-	-	-	-	-	-	-	-	-	-	-	-	-	-	8	-	-
Bobby Barr	-	-	-	-	-	-	-	-	-	FB	-	-	-	-	-	-	-	-	-	-	-	-	-	-	-	FB	-	-	-	FB	FB	-	FB	FB	FB	FB	FB	FB	-	-	-	-	-	-	-	-	10	-	-
Ewart Farndon	W	W	W	W	W	W	W	W	W	W	W	W	W	W	W	W	W	W	W	W	W	-	-	-	W	W	W	W	W	W	W	W	W	-	W	W	W	W	-	-	-	-	-	-	-	-	34	12	36
Ted Flewitt	W	W	W	W	W	W	W	W	W	-	W	W	W	-	-	W	-	C	-	-	-	-	-	-	W	-	-	-	-	W	C	W	C	W	W	C	C	W	-	-	-	-	-	-	-	-	24	17	51
Morgan Barlow	-	-	-	-	-	-	-	-	-	-	-	-	-	W	-	-	-	W	W	W	W	W	-	-	-	-	-	-	-	-	-	-	-	-	-	-	W	-	-	-	-	-	-	-	-	-	7	4	16
G.H.Wood	-	-	-	-	-	-	-	-	-	-	-	-	-	-	-	-	-	-	-	-	-	W	W	W	-	W	-	-	-	-	-	-	-	-	-	-	-	-	-	-	-	-	-	-	-	-	4	1	3
Ralph Buckingham	C	C	C	FH	C	C	C	FH	C	C	C	C	FH	-	-	C	-	FH	FH	C	-	C	-	C	C	C	C	C	C	C	FH	C	-	-	-	C	C	FH	-	-	-	-	-	-	-	-	30	9	27
Frank Wood	C	C	C	C	-	-	C	-	-	-	-	-	-	-	-	-	-	-	-	-	-	-	-	-	-	-	-	-	-	-	-	-	-	-	-	-	-	-	-	-	-	-	-	-	-	-	5	2	6
John Cramphorn	-	-	-	C	C	C	-	C	-	-	-	-	-	-	W	C	C	C	-	-	C	C	C	W	-	C	C	W	W	C	C	C	-	W	C	-	-	-	-	-	-	-	-	-	-	-	21	8	24
Harold Day	-	-	-	-	-	-	-	-	C	-	-	C	C	-	-	-	-	-	-	-	-	-	C	-	C	-	-	-	-	-	-	-	-	-	-	-	-	-	-	-	-	-	-	-	-	-	5	1	9
K.W.Symington	-	-	-	-	-	-	-	-	-	C	C	-	C	-	-	-	W	-	-	-	-	-	-	-	-	-	-	-	-	-	-	-	-	-	-	-	-	-	-	-	-	-	-	-	-	-	4	1	3
Stuart Smith	-	-	-	-	-	-	-	-	-	-	-	-	-	C	C	-	C	SH	-	-	SH	SH	SH	-	-	-	-	-	-	-	-	-	-	-	-	-	-	-	-	-	-	-	-	-	-	-	7	-	-
Ron Palmer	-	-	-	-	-	-	-	-	-	-	-	-	-	-	-	-	-	-	-	-	-	-	-	-	-	-	-	C	-	-	-	-	-	-	-	-	-	C	-	-	-	-	-	-	-	-	2	-	2
Harry Greenlees	FH	FH	FH	SH	FH	FH	FH	-	FH	FH	FH	FH	-	-	-	-	-	-	-	-	-	-	W	FH	FH	FH	FH	-	FH	-	-	FH	-	FH	FH	FH	FH	-	-	-	-	-	-	-	-	-	22	6	18
W.E.Squirrell	-	-	-	-	-	-	-	-	-	-	-	-	-	-	FH	-	FH	-	C	-	-	FH	-	-	-	-	-	-	-	-	-	-	-	-	-	-	-	-	-	-	-	-	-	-	-	-	4	-	-
Reg Odbert	-	-	-	-	-	-	-	-	-	-	-	-	-	-	-	-	-	-	-	FH	FH	-	FH	-	-	-	-	FH	C	-	-	-	C	C	-	-	-	-	-	-	-	-	-	-	-	-	7	1	3
W.Waterfield	-	-	-	-	-	-	-	-	-	-	-	-	-	-	-	-	-	-	-	-	-	-	-	-	-	-	-	-	-	FH	W	-	-	-	-	-	-	-	-	-	-	-	-	-	-	-	2	-	-
J.G.Llewellyn	-	-	-	-	-	-	-	-	-	-	-	-	-	-	-	-	-	-	-	-	-	-	-	-	-	-	-	-	-	-	-	-	FH	C	C	-	-	C	-	-	-	-	-	-	-	-	4	-	-
John Russell	SH	SH	SH	-	-	-	-	SH	SH	SH	SH	SH	-	-	SH	SH	SH	-	SH	-	-	-	-	-	SH	SH	SH	SH	SH	-	-	SH	SH	SH	SH	SH	-	SH	-	-	-	-	-	-	-	-	23	3	9
Langley Burton	-	-	-	-	SH	SH	SH	C	-	-	-	-	SH	-	-	-	-	-	-	-	-	-	-	-	-	-	-	-	-	-	-	-	-	-	-	-	SH	-	-	-	-	-	-	-	-	-	6	2	6
F.M.T.Bunney	-	-	-	-	-	-	-	-	-	-	-	-	-	-	-	-	-	-	-	SH	-	-	-	SH	-	-	-	-	-	-	-	-	-	-	-	-	-	-	-	-	-	-	-	-	-	-	2	-	-
Stan Brown	-	-	-	-	-	-	-	-	-	-	-	-	-	-	-	-	-	-	-	-	-	-	-	-	-	-	-	-	-	SH	SH	-	-	-	-	-	-	-	-	-	-	-	-	-	-	-	2	-	-
Ernie Coleman	P	P	P	P	-	P	P	P	P	P	P	P	P	H	-	P	P	P	P	P	H	H	P	-	P	P	P	-	P	P	H	P	-	H	L	L	P	P	-	-	-	-	-	-	-	-	33	1	3
Doug Prentice	P	P	P	P	P	P	P	P	P	P	P	P	P	-	-	P	P	P	P	P	-	P	P	P	P	P	P	-	P	P	P	P	P	P	P	P	-	-	-	-	-	-	-	-	-	-	32	11	134
Doug Norman	H	H	H	H	H	H	H	H	H	H	H	H	H	P	P	H	H	H	H	H	P	-	H	H	H	H	H	P	H	H	-	H	H	L	H	H	P	H	-	-	-	-	-	-	-	-	36	-	2
George Beamish	L	-	L	-	P	-	L	-	L	-	L	L	-	P	H	L	-	-	-	-	-	P	L	-	-	L	-	-	-	-	-	-	P	L	P	P	H	-	-	-	-	-	-	-	-	-	18	-	-
Victor Beamish	L	L	L	L	L	L	L	L	L	-	L	-	L	L	P	-	L	-	-	L	P	-	L	-	L	L	-	L	-	-	-	-	-	-	-	-	-	-	-	-	-	-	-	-	-	-	20	-	-
E.Braithwaite	-	-	-	-	-	-	-	-	-	-	-	L	BR	BR	BR	-	-	-	-	-	-	-	-	-	BR	-	-	-	-	-	-	-	-	-	-	-	-	-	-	-	-	-	-	-	-	-	5	-	-
Harry Edmiston	BR	L	BR	L	L	BR	-	-	-	-	-	-	-	-	-	-	BR	-	C	BR	BR	BR	-	L	-	BR	-	-	-	-	-	-	-	BR	-	BR	BR	L	-	-	-	-	-	-	-	-	17	2	8
Henry Greenwood	BR	BR	BR	BR	BR	-	-	-	BR	-	BR	BR	BR	BR	BR	BR	BR	BR	L	BR	-	-	BR	-	BR	BR	L	H	L	L	L	BR	BR	BR	L	-	L	P	-	-	-	-	-	-	-	-	30	4	12
A.C.Hall	BR	BR	BR	BR	BR	BR	BR	BR	-	-	-	-	BR	-	BR	BR	BR	BR	L	BR	L	L	BR	-	BR	BR	BR	P	BR	-	-	L	L	BR	-	L	L	-	-	-	-	-	-	-	-	-	28	2	6
W.H.Graves	-	BR	-	-	-	-	-	BR	-	BR	-	-	-	-	-	-	-	L	BR	-	BR	-	-	-	-	-	-	BR	BR	BR	-	BR	-	-	BR	-	-	BR	-	-	-	-	-	-	-	-	12	-	-
D.Jones	-	-	-	BR	BR	L	BR	BR	BR	L	BR	BR	L	L	L	BR	L	-	-	-	-	-	-	-	-	-	L	L	-	BR	P	-	-	-	-	-	-	-	-	-	-	-	-	-	-	-	18	3	9
Phil Dunkley	-	-	-	-	-	BR	BR	L	BR	L	-	BR	-	-	L	L	-	-	BR	L	-	L	-	-	L	-	BR	-	L	L	-	L	L	P	-	-	BR	L	-	-	-	-	-	-	-	-	20	3	11
Harry Briers	-	-	-	-	-	-	-	-	-	BR	-	-	-	-	-	-	-	L	-	-	-	BR	-	-	-	-	BR	BR	-	-	BR	-	-	-	-	BR	-	-	-	-	-	-	-	-	-	-	7	-	-
M.L.Millard	-	-	-	-	-	-	-	-	-	-	BR	-	-	-	-	-	-	-	-	-	L	-	BR	-	-	-	-	-	-	-	-	-	-	-	-	-	-	-	-	-	-	-	-	-	-	-	3	-	-
Trevor Thorneloe	-	-	-	-	-	-	-	-	-	-	-	-	-	BR	-	-	-	-	BR	-	-	-	-	L	-	-	-	-	-	-	-	-	-	-	-	-	-	-	-	-	-	-	-	-	-	-	3	-	-
Phil Palmer	-	-	-	-	-	-	-	-	-	-	-	-	-	-	-	-	-	-	-	-	-	BR	-	BR	-	-	-	BR	-	-	-	-	-	-	-	-	-	-	-	-	-	-	-	-	-	-	3	-	-
Stan Saunders	-	-	-	-	-	-	-	-	-	-	-	-	-	-	-	-	-	-	-	-	-	-	-	-	-	-	-	-	BR	BR	L	BR	BR	-	BR	BR	BR	BR	-	-	-	-	-	-	-	-	9	-	-
R.J.Stephens	-	-	-	-	-	-	-	-	-	-	-	-	-	-	-	-	-	-	-	-	-	-	-	-	-	-	-	-	-	-	-	-	BR	-	BR	-	-	BR	-	-	-	-	-	-	-	-	3	1	3

1 game: L.J.Adcock W(27), P.C.Alexander C(14), N.Bacon C(21), Frank Cramphorn C(15), T.G.P.Crick BR(21), H.C.W.Eking P(24), J.W.G.Hume C(24), H.N.Knox SH(14), W.E.Lole FH(14), D.McArthur BR(31), A.Murray FB(11), Tony Novis C(20), G.Phillpotts FH(16), Dr. Strang BR(10), D.I.Todman BR(24), F.B.Traders BR(31), W.Turnbull BR(18), William Wallace W(33), Percy Ward BR(24), R.E.H.Ward W(36)

					FOR					AGAINST					
NO	DATE	OPPONENTS	V	RES	G	T	D	P	PTS	G	T	D	P	PTS	SCORERS
1	Sep 7	BATH	H	Won	2	2	-	1	19	-	2	-	-	6	Llewellyn(2T) Prentice(2C,P) Hall(T) Greenwood(T)
2	14	PLYMOUTH ALBION	H	Won	1	1	1	-	12	-	2	-	-	6	Flewitt(T) Greenlees(T,D) Prentice(C)
3	21	OLD BLUES	H	Won	2	5	-	1	28	1	-	-	-	5	Farndon(2T) Babington(2T) Greenlees(T) Burton(T) Prentice(T,P) Norman(2C)
4	28	NUNEATON	H	Won	3	2	-	1	24	1	-	-	1	8	Farndon(2T) Babington(T) Flewitt(T) Burton(T) Prentice(3C,P)
5	Oct 5	COVENTRY	H	Lost	-	-	-	2	6	1	1	-	1	11	Prentice(2P)
6	12	Gloucester	A	Lost	1	1	-	1	11	2	2	1	-	20	Farndon(T) Burton(T) Prentice(C,P)
7	19	NEWPORT	H	Won	1	-	1	1	12	-	-	-	2	6	Llewellyn(D) Babington(T) Prentice(C,P)
8	26	NORTHAMPTON	H	Won	2	-	-	-	10	-	1	-	-	3	Prentice(2C) Beamish(2T)
9	Nov 2	CAMBRIDGE UNIVERSITY	H	Drew	1	3	-	-	14	1	2	-	1	14	Farndon(2T) Babington(T) Greenlees(T) Prentice(C)
10	9	Nuneaton	A	Won	-	-	1	-	4	-	1	-	-	3	Llewellyn(D)
11	16	Swansea	A	Lost	1	1	-	-	8	-	2	-	2	12	Prentice(C) Beamish(2T)
12	23	Moseley	A	Won	2	2	1	-	20	-	1	-	-	3	Flewitt(2T) Llewellyn(T,D) Coleman(T) Prentice(2C)
13	30	OXFORD UNIVERSITY	H	Won	-	2	-	-	6	-	1	-	-	3	Prentice(T) G.E.S.Williams(T)
14	Dec 7	Harlequins	A	Drew	1	1	-	-	8	1	1	-	-	8	Farndon(T) Gadney(T) Prentice(C)
15	14	Blackheath	A	Lost	-	1	-	1	6	2	-	-	1	13	Prentice(T,P)
16	21	BRISTOL	H	Won	-	2	-	1	9	1	-	-	-	5	Potts(T) Flewitt(T) Prentice(P)
17	26	BARBARIANS	H	Lost	1	2	-	1	14	3	1	-	1	21	Potts(T) Llewellyn(T) Prentice(C,P) C.H.Williams(T)
18	27	WATERLOO	H	Won	1	2	1	2	21	2	1	-	-	13	Potts(T) Llewellyn(D) Prentice(C,2P) Beamish(2T)
19	28	BIRKENHEAD PARK	H	Won	2	2	-	-	16	1	1	-	-	8	Flewitt(2T) Prentice(T,2C) Lashmore(T)
20	Jan 1	Manchester	A	Won	-	3	-	-	9	1	1	-	-	8	J.J.M.Ewin(3T)
21	4	SWANSEA	H	Lost	-	1	-	1	6	1	2	-	-	11	Wood(P) Flewitt(T)
22	11	ROSSLYN PARK	H	Won	1	4	-	-	17	1	2	-	-	11	Llewellyn(3T) Flewitt(T) Gadney(T) Prentice(C)
23	18	LONDON WELSH	H	Lost	-	1	-	1	6	1	-	1	-	9	Flewitt(T) Prentice(P)
24	25	RICHMOND	H	Lost	1	-	-	-	5	-	2	-	-	6	Flewitt(T) Norman(C)
25	30	ROYAL AIR FORCE	H	Won	1	6	-	-	23	1	2	-	-	11	Farndon(3T) Flewitt(3T) Beamish(T,C)
26	Feb 1	LONDON SCOTTISH	H	Won	2	-	-	-	10	-	2	-	-	6	Flewitt(T) Norman(T,2C)
27	8	Newport	A	Lost	1	-	-	-	5	2	4	-	-	22	Norman(C) C.H.Williams(T)
28	15	BRIDGWATER	H	Won	1	4	-	-	17	-	1	-	-	3	Farndon(2T) Flewitt(T) Gadney(T) Norman(C) Drummond(T)
29	22	Northampton	A	Won	3	1	-	-	18	-	-	-	1	3	Farndon(T) Beaty-Pownall(T) Flewitt(T) Gadney(T) Prentice(3C)
30	Mar 1	HARLEQUINS	H	Lost	2	1	-	-	13	3	-	-	-	15	Farndon(T) Gadney(2T) Prentice(2C)
31	8	BEDFORD	H	Won	2	2	1	-	20	-	1	-	-	3	Manson(D) Gadney(T) Norman(2C) Kendrew(T) Coleman(T) C.H.Williams(T)
32	15	PERCY PARK	H	Won	2	7	-	-	31	-	1	-	-	3	Cotton(T) Farndon(3T) Buckingham(2T) Gadney(T) Norman(C) Wiener(T) Coleman(C) Clarke(T)
33	22	Coventry	A	Won	1	2	-	-	11	-	1	-	1	6	Buckingham(T) Carryer(T) Prentice(T,C)
34	29	GLOUCESTER	H	Won	-	4	1	-	16	1	-	-	-	5	Flewitt(T) Cotton(D) Greenlees(T) Gadney(T) Saunders(T)
35	Apr 5	Birkenhead Park	A	Drew	1	1	-	-	8	1	1	-	-	8	Buckingham(T) Greenlees(T) Norman(C)
36	12	BLACKHEATH	H	Won	2	4	-	-	22	1	-	1	-	9	Flewitt(T) Farndon(2T) Greenlees(C) Gadney(T) Norman(C) Saunders(T) Hall(T)
37	19	Bristol	A	Won	-	3	-	-	9	-	1	-	-	3	Farndon(T) Buckingham(T) Flewitt(T)
38	21	Plymouth Albion	A	Won	1	2	-	-	11	-	2	-	1	9	Farndon(T) Flewitt(T) Greenwood(T) Thorneloe(C)
39	22	Bath	A	Won	-	2	-	-	6	-	-	-	1	3	Farndon(T) Kerby(T)

INDIVIDUAL APPEARANCES 1929-1930

NAME	1	2	3	4	5	6	7	8	9	10	11	12	13	14	15	16	17	18	19	20	21	22	23	24	25	26	27	28	29	30	31	32	33	34	35	36	37	38	39	40	41	42	43	44	45	46	TOTAL	T	PTS
Charlie Manson	FB	FB	-	FB	FB	FB	FB	FB	FB	FB	FB	FB	FB	FB	FB	FB	FB	FB	-	-	FB	FB	FB	FB	FB	FB	FB	FB	FB	FB	FB	FB	FB	FB	FB	FB	FB	FB	-	-	-	-	-	-	-	-	35	-	4
W.S.Thompson	-	-	-	-	-	-	-	-	-	-	-	-	-	-	-	-	-	-	FB	-	-	-	-	C	-	-	C	-	-	-	-	-	-	-	-	-	-	-	-	-	-	-	-	-	-	-	3	-	-
Len Shipton	-	-	-	-	-	-	-	-	-	-	-	-	-	-	-	-	-	-	-	FB	-	-	-	-	-	-	FH	FH	-	-	-	-	-	-	-	-	-	-	-	-	-	-	-	-	-	-	3	-	-
Ewart Farndon	W	W	W	W	W	W	-	-	W	W	W	W	W	W	W	W	W	W	W	-	W	-	W	W	W	W	W	W	W	W	W	W	W	W	-	W	W	W	C	-	-	-	-	-	-	-	34	23	69
Ted Flewitt	-	W	W	W	W	W	W	W	C	C	W	W	W	W	W	W	W	W	W	-	W	W	W	W	W	W	W	W	W	W	-	-	W	W	W	W	C	C	W	-	-	-	-	-	-	-	35	21	63
Jeff Hardwicke	-	-	-	-	-	-	W	-	W	W	-	-	-	-	-	-	-	-	-	-	-	-	-	-	-	-	-	-	-	-	-	W	-	-	W	-	-	-	-	-	-	-	-	-	-	-	5	-	-
J.J.M.Ewin	-	-	-	-	-	-	-	-	-	-	-	-	-	-	-	-	-	-	-	W	-	-	-	-	-	-	-	-	-	-	W	-	-	-	-	-	-	-	-	-	-	-	-	-	-	-	2	3	9
C.C.Beaty-Pownall	-	-	-	-	-	-	-	-	-	-	-	-	-	-	-	-	-	-	-	W	-	-	-	-	C	C	-	-	C	-	-	-	-	-	-	C	-	-	-	-	-	-	-	-	-	-	5	1	3
G.R.White	-	-	-	-	-	-	-	-	-	-	-	-	-	-	-	-	-	-	-	-	-	-	-	-	-	-	-	-	-	-	-	-	-	-	-	-	W	W	W	-	-	-	-	-	-	-	3	-	-
Ralph Buckingham	C	C	C	C	FH	C	-	C	-	-	-	-	C	-	-	-	C	-	-	-	-	-	-	-	-	-	-	-	-	-	-	FH	C	C	C	C	C	C	C	-	-	-	-	-	-	-	17	5	15
J.G.Llewellyn	C	-	-	-	-	-	C	C	-	FH	C	FH	FH	FH	FH	FH	FH	FH	FH	-	-	C	-	-	-	-	-	-	-	-	-	-	-	-	-	-	-	-	-	-	-	-	-	-	-	-	14	7	37
T.Babington	-	C	C	C	C	-	C	-	C	-	C	C	C	C	C	C	-	-	-	-	-	-	C	FH	-	FH	C	-	-	-	-	-	-	-	-	-	-	-	-	-	-	-	-	-	-	-	16	5	15
Frank Wood	-	-	-	-	C	C	-	-	-	-	-	-	-	-	-	-	-	-	-	-	C	-	-	-	-	-	-	-	-	-	-	-	-	-	-	-	-	-	-	-	-	-	-	-	-	-	3	-	3
R.D.Cotton	-	-	-	-	-	-	-	-	-	C	-	-	-	C	-	-	-	-	C	C	-	W	-	-	-	-	-	C	C	C	-	C	-	C	C	-	-	-	-	-	-	-	-	-	-	-	11	1	7
Donald Oscroft	-	-	-	-	-	-	-	-	-	-	-	-	-	-	-	-	-	C	-	-	-	-	-	C	-	-	-	-	-	-	-	-	-	-	-	-	-	-	-	-	-	-	-	-	-	-	2	-	-
H.P.Tyler	-	-	-	-	-	-	-	-	-	-	-	-	-	-	-	-	-	-	-	-	-	-	-	-	C	C	-	-	-	-	-	-	-	-	-	-	-	-	-	-	-	-	-	-	-	-	2	-	-
Rupert Carryer	-	-	-	-	-	-	-	-	-	-	-	-	-	-	-	-	-	-	-	-	-	-	-	-	-	-	-	-	-	-	-	C	C	-	-	-	-	-	FB	-	-	-	-	-	-	-	3	1	3
Harry Greenlees	FH	FH	FH	FH	-	-	FH	FH	FH	-	FH	-	-	-	-	-	-	-	-	-	-	FH	-	-	-	-	-	-	-	C	FH	-	FH	FH	FH	FH	FH	FH	FH	-	-	-	-	-	-	-	18	5	21
J.R.H.Potts	-	-	-	-	-	FH	-	W	-	-	-	C	-	-	C	C	C	C	C	FH	-	C	-	-	-	-	-	FH	FH	-	-	-	-	-	-	-	-	-	-	-	-	-	-	-	-	-	12	3	9
Langley Burton	SH	SH	SH	SH	SH	SH	SH	SH	SH	-	-	-	-	-	-	-	-	-	-	-	-	-	-	-	-	-	-	-	-	-	C	-	-	-	-	-	-	-	-	-	-	-	-	-	-	-	10	3	9
Bernard Gadney	-	-	-	-	-	-	-	-	-	SH	SH	SH	SH	SH	SH	SH	SH	-	SH	C	SH	SH	C	SH	-	SH	SH	SH	SH	SH	SH	SH	SH	SH	SH	SH	SH	SH	SH	-	-	-	-	-	-	-	28	10	30
John Russell	-	-	-	-	-	-	-	-	-	-	-	-	-	-	-	-	-	SH	-	SH	-	-	SH	-	SH	-	-	-	-	-	-	-	-	-	-	-	-	-	-	-	-	-	-	-	-	-	4	-	-
Ernie Coleman	P	P	P	BR	BR	BR	BR	BR	L	BR	BR	P	BR	BR	L	P	BR	BR	L	L	P	L	BR	L	BR	L	L	L	L	BR	L	L	BR	BR	L	L	L	P	P	-	-	-	-	-	-	-	39	2	8
Doug Prentice	P	P	P	P	P	P	P	P	P	P	P	L	P	P	P	P	P	P	P	-	-	P	P	-	-	-	-	P	P	P	-	-	P	P	-	-	-	-	-	-	-	-	-	-	-	-	26	5	106
Joe' Kendrew	-	-	-	-	-	-	-	-	-	-	-	-	-	-	-	-	-	-	-	-	-	-	-	-	-	-	-	P	-	-	H	-	P	L	-	-	-	-	-	-	-	-	-	-	-	-	4	1	3
Doug Norman	H	H	H	H	H	H	H	H	H	H	H	BR	H	H	H	-	H	H	H	P	-	H	H	P	P	P	P	H	H	H	P	P	H	H	P	P	P	P	P	-	-	-	-	-	-	-	37	1	27
Henry Greenwood	L	BR	BR	BR	L	BR	BR	BR	BR	-	-	H	L	BR	BR	L	L	BR	BR	-	L	BR	BR	L	-	L	L	BR	BR	BR	BR	L	BR	-	-	L	L	L	L	-	-	-	-	-	-	-	33	2	6
A.C.Hall	L	L	L	L	P	L	-	L	L	L	L	P	-	L	BR	BR	-	L	-	L	-	BR	-	-	-	-	-	-	-	-	-	BR	-	-	BR	BR	BR	BR	BR	-	-	-	-	-	-	-	23	2	6
George Beamish	-	L	L	P	-	P	P	P	-	P	P	BR	P	P	-	-	P	P	P	-	-	-	-	-	H	-	-	-	-	P	-	-	-	P	-	-	-	-	-	-	-	-	-	-	-	-	17	7	23
Harry Briers	-	-	-	-	-	-	L	-	BR	-	-	-	-	-	-	-	-	-	-	-	-	-	-	-	-	-	-	-	-	-	-	-	-	-	-	-	-	-	-	-	-	-	-	-	-	-	2	-	-
Harry Edmiston	BR	BR	-	-	-	-	-	-	-	-	-	-	-	-	-	-	-	-	-	-	-	-	-	-	-	-	-	-	-	-	-	-	-	-	-	-	-	-	-	-	-	-	-	-	-	-	2	-	-
Stan Saunders	BR	BR	BR	L	L	L	L	L	P	L	L	BR	L	-	P	H	L	-	BR	H	H	P	L	H	P	H	H	-	P	L	L	P	L	BR	L	P	P	H	H	-	-	-	-	-	-	-	36	2	6
J.W.Townsend	BR	-	-	-	BR	-	-	-	-	-	-	-	-	-	-	-	-	-	-	-	BR	-	-	-	-	-	-	-	-	-	-	-	-	-	-	-	-	-	-	-	-	-	-	-	-	-	3	-	-
C.H.Williams	-	-	BR	BR	BR	-	-	-	-	-	-	-	-	-	-	BR	BR	-	-	BR	-	BR	-	BR	BR	BR	BR	-	BR	-	BR	BR	BR	-	BR	BR	BR	-	-	-	-	-	-	-	-	-	18	3	9
Dr.R.A.K. Wiener	-	-	-	-	-	BR	BR	BR	BR	BR	BR	L	BR	L	L	L	BR	L	L	P	P	L	L	P	L	P	P	L	L	L	P	H	L	L	P	H	H	-	-	-	-	-	-	-	-	-	32	1	3
G.E.S.Williams	-	-	-	-	-	-	-	-	-	BR	BR	-	BR	BR	BR	-	-	-	-	-	-	-	-	-	-	-	-	-	-	-	-	-	-	-	-	-	-	-	-	-	-	-	-	-	-	-	5	1	3
Trevor Thorneloe	-	-	-	-	-	-	-	-	-	-	-	-	-	-	-	BR	-	-	-	-	L	-	-	-	L	-	-	-	-	-	-	-	-	-	-	-	-	BR	-	-	-	-	-	-	-	-	4	-	2
G.F.Lashmore	-	-	-	-	-	-	-	-	-	-	-	-	-	-	-	-	-	-	BR	BR	-	-	-	-	-	-	-	-	-	-	-	-	-	-	-	-	-	-	-	-	-	-	-	-	-	-	2	1	3
J.L.Anstee	-	-	-	-	-	-	-	-	-	-	-	-	-	-	-	-	-	-	-	-	-	-	-	-	-	BR	-	-	-	-	-	-	-	-	H	-	-	-	-	-	-	-	-	-	-	-	2	-	-
Fred Drummond	-	-	-	-	-	-	-	-	-	-	-	-	-	-	-	-	-	-	-	-	BR	-	BR	BR	-	-	BR	BR	-	-	-	-	-	-	-	-	-	-	-	-	-	-	-	-	-	-	5	1	3
R.B.Harvey	-	-	-	-	-	-	-	-	-	-	-	-	-	-	-	-	-	-	-	-	BR	-	P	-	-	-	-	-	-	-	-	-	-	-	-	-	-	-	-	-	-	-	-	-	-	-	2	-	-
Percy Clarke	-	-	-	-	-	-	-	-	-	-	-	-	-	-	-	-	-	-	-	-	-	-	-	BR	BR	BR	BR	BR	BR	BR	BR	BR	-	BR	BR	BR	BR	L	L	-	-	-	-	-	-	-	15	1	3
W.I.Kerby	-	-	-	-	-	-	-	-	-	-	-	-	-	-	-	-	-	-	-	-	-	-	-	-	-	-	-	-	-	-	-	-	-	-	-	-	-	BR	BR	-	-	-	-	-	-	-	2	1	3

1 game: Dick Auty FH(25), Bobby Barr FB(3), George Cornell C(21), Phil Dunkley BR(18), B.H.L.Ewin C(31), J.D.Jenkins FH(23), G.T.Kemp BR(39), I.McNichol FH(21), Stuart Smith C(28), R.Toach W(1), George Vallance BR(20)

LEICESTER FOOTBALL CLUB 1929-30
Back: N. Coates (Touch Judge), A.C. Hall, R.A.K. Wiener, C.S. Manson, C.H. Williams, R.D. Cotton, B.C. Gadney,
W.N. Bradshaw (Hon.Tres), J.E. Thorneloe (Hon.Sec).
Middle: A.H. Greenwood, G.R. Beamish, H.D. Greenlees, F.D. Prentice (Capt), D.J. Norman, R.A. Buckingham, E.G. Coleman.
Front: S.H. Saunders, W.E. Farndon, D.A. Kendrew, P.S. Clarke, E.C.A. Flewitt.

LEICESTER FOOTBALL CLUB 1930-31
Back: N. Coates (Touch Judge), B.C. Gadney, C.S. Manson, H.A. Constantine, A.H. Greenwood, P.S. Clarke, A. Bolus, S.A. Smith,
E.M. Barlow, W.N. Bradshaw (Hon.Tres), J.E. Thorneloe (Hon.Sec).
Middle: R.A.K. Wiener, E.G. Coleman, D.J. Norman, H.D. Greenlees (Capt), F.D. Prentice, R.A. Buckingham, G.R. Beamish.
Front: J.G. Llewelyn, D.E. Morris, R.J. Barr, G.P.C. Vallance, I. McNichol, J.T. Hardwicke, S.H. Saunders.

1930-1931

NO	DATE		OPPONENTS	V	RES	FOR G	FOR T	FOR D	FOR P	PTS	AGAINST G	AGAINST T	AGAINST D	AGAINST P	PTS	SCORERS
1	Sep	6	BATH	H	Drew	-	1	-	-	3	-	1	-	-	3	Llewellyn(T)
2		13	OLD BLUES	H	Won	1	4	-	1	20	-	-	-	-	0	Buckingham(T) Llewellyn(2T) Farndon(T) Greenlees(P) Norman(C) Kerby(T)
3		20	PLYMOUTH ALBION	H	Won	2	2	1	-	20	-	2	-	1	9	Farndon(T) White(T) Greenlees(T,2C,D) Saunders(T)
4		27	NUNEATON	H	Won	1	4	-	1	20	-	-	-	-	0	Buckingham(T) White(2T) Greenlees(P) Saunders(T) P.S.Clarke(T) Greenwood(C)
5	Oct	4	Coventry	A	Lost	1	1	-	-	8	1	4	1	-	21	Farndon(2T) Greenlees(C)
6		11	GLOUCESTER	H	Won	3	4	-	-	27	1	1	-	-	8	Manson(3C) Farndon(2T) Buckingham(3T) White(T) Gadney(T)
7		18	Newport	A	Lost	-	-	1	-	4	4	-	-	-	20	Greenlees(D)
8		25	Northampton	A	Won	-	1	-	1	6	-	1	-	-	3	Farndon(T) Greenlees(P)
9	Nov	1	OLD MERCHANT TAYLORS	H	Lost	-	1	-	-	3	1	1	-	-	8	Greenlees(T)
10		5	Oxford University	A	Won	2	2	-	-	16	-	2	-	1	9	Manson(C) Buckingham(T) Auty(2T) Smith(T) Constantine(C)
11		8	Cambridge University	A	Lost	-	2	-	-	6	5	1	-	-	28	Farndon(T) Beamish(T)
12		15	SWANSEA	H	Drew	-	-	-	-	0	-	-	-	-	0	
13		22	MOSELEY	H	Won	-	4	-	-	12	-	2	-	-	6	Buckingham(T) White(T) Greenlees(T) Saunders(T)
14		29	WATERLOO	H	Won	3	2	-	-	21	1	-	-	-	5	Greenlees(2T) Buckingham(T) Prentice(3C) Saunders(T) Constantine(T)
15	Dec	6	Harlequins	A	Lost	1	2	-	-	11	2	-	-	1	13	Buckingham(T) White(T) Prentice(C) Saunders(T)
16		13	Blackheath	A	Won	-	-	1	-	4	-	1	-	-	3	Llewellyn(D)
17		20	BRISTOL	H	Won	1	1	-	1	11	-	-	-	-	0	Farndon(T) Prentice(T,C,P)
18		26	BARBARIANS	H	Lost	-	1	-	1	6	2	1	-	-	13	Buckingham(T) Prentice(P)
19		27	BIRKENHEAD PARK	H	Won	3	1	1	1	25	1	-	1	-	9	Farndon(T) Hopkins(T) Llewellyn(C,D) Smith(T) Prentice(2C,P) Wiener(T)
20		29	MANCHESTER	H	Won	-	3	1	1	16	-	1	-	-	3	Llewellyn(D) Wood(T) Norman(T) Prentice(P) Saunders(T)
21	Jan	3	Swansea	A	Lost	-	-	-	-	0	1	2	-	2	17	
		10	ROSSLYN PARK	H		Cancelled Frost										
22		17	LONDON WELSH	H	Won	1	3	-	-	14	1	1	-	-	8	Buckingham(T) Gadney(T) Norman(T) Prentice(C) Vallance(T)
23		24	Richmond	A	Won	1	2	-	-	11	-	2	-	-	6	Ungoed-Thomas(T) White(T) Buckingham(T) Prentice(C)
24		29	ROYAL AIR FORCE	H	Won	2	5	-	-	25	-	2	-	-	6	Moore(2T) Hardwicke(T) Llewellyn(T) Prentice(2C) Saunders(2T) P.S.Clarke(T)
25		31	Percy Park	A	Won	-	2	-	-	6	1	-	-	-	5	Hardwicke(T) Gadney(T)
26	Feb	7	London Scottish	A	Drew	1	1	-	-	8	1	1	-	-	8	Llewellyn(T) Prentice(T,C)
27		14	NEWPORT	H	Lost	1	-	-	-	5	1	-	1	-	9	Norman(C) Saunders(T)
28		21	Bath	A	Lost	-	2	-	1	9	2	3	-	-	19	Hardwicke(T) Prentice(P) Coleman(T)
29		28	NORTHAMPTON	H	Drew	-	2	1	-	10	2	-	-	-	10	Hardwicke(T) Hart(D) Gadney(T)
30	Mar	7	HARLEQUINS	H	Won	5	1	1	-	32	-	-	-	1	3	Buckingham(2T) Greenlees(T,D) Prentice(T,5C) Wiener(T) Vallance(T)
31		14	BEDFORD	H	Won	4	1	-	-	23	-	-	-	-	0	Hardwicke(T) Ungoed-Thomas(T) Gadney(T) Prentice(2T,4C)
32		21	COVENTRY	H	Won	-	2	1	1	13	-	-	-	-	0	Greenlees(D,P) Gadney(T) Constantine(T)
33		28	Gloucester	A	Lost	1	1	-	-	8	2	2	-	-	16	Prentice(C) Coleman(T) Vallance(T)
34	Apr	4	Bristol	A	Won	2	1	-	-	13	1	1	-	-	8	Hardwicke(T) Auty(T) Prentice(T,2C)
35		6	Plymouth Albion	A	Won	3	2	-	-	21	2	1	-	-	13	Barlow(T) Hardwicke(T) Gadney(T) Prentice(T,3C) Saunders(T)
36		7	Bridgwater	A	Won	2	9	-	-	37	-	-	-	-	0	Barlow(T) Bolus(3T) Buckingham(T,C) Hardwicke(T) Llewellyn(T) Gadney(3T) Norman(C) Cleaver(T)
37		11	Birkenhead Park	A	Lost	1	1	-	-	8	-	3	-	-	9	Gadney(T) Prentice(T,C)
38		16	ENGLAND XV	H	Lost	-	1	-	-	3	3	-	-	-	15	Meikle(T)
39		18	BLACKHEATH	H	Won	3	1	1	1	25	1	-	-	-	5	McNichol(T) Morris(T) Llewellyn(D) Gadney(T) Prentice(3C,P) Constantine(T)

INDIVIDUAL APPEARANCES 1930-1931

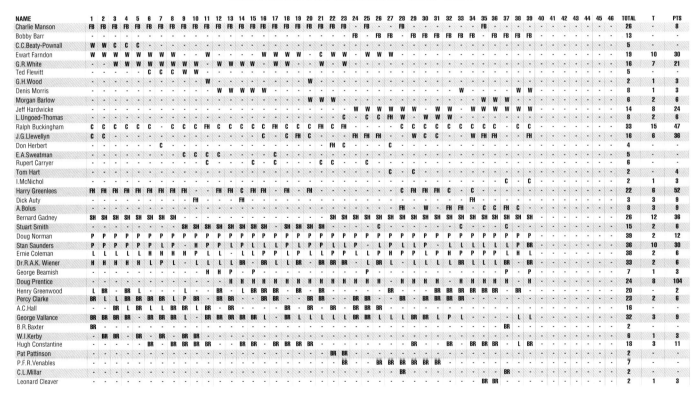

NAME	1	2	3	4	5	6	7	8	9	10	11	12	13	14	15	16	17	18	19	20	21	22	23	24	25	26	27	28	29	30	31	32	33	34	35	36	37	38	39	40	41	42	43	44	45	46	TOTAL	T	PTS
Charlie Manson	FB	FB	FB	FB	FB	FB	FB	FB	FB	FB	FB	FB	FB	FB	FB	FB	FB	FB	FB	FB	FB	FB	FB	-	FB	-	-	FB	-	-	-	-	-	-	FB	-	-	-	-	-	-	-	-	-	-	-	26	-	8
Bobby Barr	-	-	-	-	-	-	-	-	-	-	-	-	-	-	-	-	-	-	-	-	-	-	-	FB	-	FB	FB	-	FB	FB	FB	FB	FB	FB	-	FB	FB	FB	FB	-	-	-	-	-	-	-	13	-	-
C.C.Beaty-Pownall	W	W	C	C	C	-	-	-	-	-	-	-	-	-	-	-	-	-	-	-	-	-	-	-	-	-	-	-	-	-	-	-	-	-	-	-	-	-	-	-	-	-	-	-	-	-	5	-	-
Ewart Farndon	W	W	W	W	W	W	W	W	-	-	W	-	-	-	-	W	W	W	W	-	C	W	W	-	W	W	W	-	-	-	-	-	-	-	-	-	-	-	-	-	-	-	-	-	-	-	19	10	30
G.R.White	-	-	W	W	W	W	W	W	W	W	-	W	W	W	W	-	W	W	-	-	W	-	W	-	-	-	-	-	-	-	-	-	-	-	-	-	-	-	-	-	-	-	-	-	-	-	16	7	21
Ted Flewitt	-	-	-	-	-	C	C	C	W	W	-	-	-	-	-	-	-	-	-	-	-	-	-	-	-	-	-	-	-	-	-	-	-	-	-	-	-	-	-	-	-	-	-	-	-	-	5	-	-
G.H.Wood	-	-	-	-	-	-	-	-	-	-	W	-	-	-	-	-	-	-	-	W	-	-	-	-	-	-	-	-	-	-	-	-	-	-	-	-	-	-	-	-	-	-	-	-	-	-	2	1	3
Denis Morris	-	-	-	-	-	-	-	-	-	-	-	W	W	W	W	W	-	-	-	-	-	-	-	-	-	-	-	-	-	-	-	-	W	-	-	-	-	W	W	-	-	-	-	-	-	-	8	1	3
Morgan Barlow	-	-	-	-	-	-	-	-	-	-	-	-	-	-	-	-	-	-	-	W	W	W	-	-	-	-	-	-	-	-	-	-	-	-	W	W	W	-	-	-	-	-	-	-	-	-	6	2	6
Jeff Hardwicke	-	-	-	-	-	-	-	-	-	-	-	-	-	-	-	-	-	-	-	-	-	-	-	W	W	W	W	W	W	-	W	W	-	W	W	W	W	W	W	-	-	-	-	-	-	-	14	8	24
L.Ungoed-Thomas	-	-	-	-	-	-	-	-	-	-	-	-	-	-	-	-	-	-	-	-	-	-	C	-	C	C	FH	W	-	W	W	W	-	-	-	-	-	-	-	-	-	-	-	-	-	-	8	2	6
Ralph Buckingham	C	C	C	C	C	C	-	C	C	C	FH	C	C	C	C	C	FH	C	C	C	FH	C	FH	-	-	-	-	C	C	C	C	C	C	C	C	C	-	C	C	-	-	-	-	-	-	-	33	15	47
J.G.Llewellyn	C	C	-	-	-	-	-	-	-	-	-	-	-	-	-	C	-	C	FH	C	-	-	-	FH	FH	FH	-	-	W	C	C	-	-	W	FH	FH	-	-	FH	-	-	-	-	-	-	-	16	6	36
Don Herbert	-	-	-	-	-	-	C	-	-	-	-	-	-	-	-	-	-	-	-	-	-	FH	C	-	-	-	C	-	-	-	-	-	-	-	-	-	-	-	-	-	-	-	-	-	-	-	4	-	-
E.A.Sweatman	-	-	-	-	-	-	-	-	C	C	C	C	-	-	-	-	C	-	-	-	-	-	-	-	-	-	-	-	-	-	-	-	-	-	-	-	-	-	-	-	-	-	-	-	-	-	5	-	-
Rupert Carryer	-	-	-	-	-	-	-	-	-	-	C	-	-	-	C	-	C	-	-	-	C	C	-	-	C	-	-	-	-	-	-	-	-	-	-	-	-	-	-	-	-	-	-	-	-	-	6	-	-
Tom Hart	-	-	-	-	-	-	-	-	-	-	-	-	-	-	-	-	-	-	-	-	-	-	-	-	-	-	C	-	C	-	-	-	-	-	-	-	-	-	-	-	-	-	-	-	-	-	2	-	4
I.McNichol	-	-	-	-	-	-	-	-	-	-	-	-	-	-	-	-	-	-	-	-	-	-	-	-	-	-	-	-	-	-	-	-	-	-	-	-	C	-	C	-	-	-	-	-	-	-	2	1	3
Harry Greenlees	FH	FH	FH	FH	FH	FH	FH	FH	FH	-	-	FH	FH	C	FH	FH	-	FH	-	FH	-	-	-	-	-	-	-	C	FH	FH	FH	C	-	C	-	-	-	-	-	-	-	-	-	-	-	-	22	6	52
Dick Auty	-	-	-	-	-	-	-	-	-	FH	-	-	-	FH	-	-	-	-	-	-	-	-	-	-	-	-	-	-	-	-	-	-	-	FH	-	-	-	-	-	-	-	-	-	-	-	-	3	3	9
A.Bolus	-	-	-	-	-	-	-	-	-	-	-	-	-	-	-	-	-	-	-	-	-	-	-	-	-	-	-	FH	-	W	-	FH	FH	-	C	C	FH	C	-	-	-	-	-	-	-	-	8	3	9
Bernard Gadney	SH	SH	SH	SH	SH	SH	SH	SH	-	-	-	-	-	-	-	-	-	-	-	-	-	SH	SH	SH	SH	SH	SH	SH	SH	SH	SH	SH	SH	SH	SH	SH	SH	SH	SH	-	-	-	-	-	-	-	26	12	36
Stuart Smith	-	-	-	-	-	-	-	-	SH	SH	SH	SH	SH	SH	SH	SH	-	SH	SH	SH	SH	-	-	-	-	C	-	-	-	-	-	-	C	-	-	-	C	-	-	-	-	-	-	-	-	-	15	2	6
Doug Norman	P	P	P	P	P	P	P	P	P	P	P	P	P	P	P	P	P	P	P	P	P	P	P	P	P	P	P	P	P	P	P	P	P	P	P	P	P	P	P	-	-	-	-	-	-	-	39	2	12
Stan Saunders	P	P	P	P	P	P	L	P	-	H	P	P	L	P	L	L	L	P	L	P	P	L	L	P	-	L	P	L	L	P	-	L	L	L	L	L	L	P	BR	-	-	-	-	-	-	-	36	10	30
Ernie Coleman	L	L	L	L	L	H	H	H	H	P	L	L	-	L	L	P	P	L	P	L	L	P	P	L	L	P	H	P	P	L	P	H	P	P	P	P	L	H	L	-	-	-	-	-	-	-	38	2	6
Dr.R.A.K. Wiener	H	H	H	H	H	L	P	L	-	L	L	L	L	BR	-	BR	L	L	BR	-	BR	BR	BR	-	L	BR	L	-	L	L	L	L	BR	L	L	L	BR	-	BR	-	-	-	-	-	-	-	33	2	6
George Beamish	-	-	-	-	-	-	-	-	-	-	H	H	P	-	P	-	-	-	-	-	-	-	-	-	P	-	-	-	-	-	-	-	-	-	-	-	P	-	P	-	-	-	-	-	-	-	7	1	3
Doug Prentice	-	-	-	-	-	-	-	-	-	-	-	-	H	H	H	H	H	H	H	H	H	H	H	H	H	H	-	H	H	H	H	-	H	H	H	H	H	-	H	-	-	-	-	-	-	-	24	8	104
Henry Greenwood	L	BR	-	BR	L	-	-	-	L	-	-	BR	-	L	BR	BR	BR	-	BR	-	BR	-	-	-	-	-	BR	-	-	-	BR	BR	BR	BR	BR	BR	-	BR	-	-	-	-	-	-	-	-	20	-	2
Percy Clarke	BR	L	L	BR	BR	BR	BR	L	P	BR	-	BR	BR	-	-	BR	BR	-	-	BR	BR	-	-	BR	BR	-	-	BR	-	BR	BR	BR	BR	-	-	-	-	-	-	-	-	-	-	-	-	-	23	2	6
A.C.Hall	-	-	BR	L	BR	L	L	BR	BR	L	BR	-	BR	-	-	-	-	BR	-	BR	-	BR	-	BR	BR	BR	-	-	-	-	-	-	-	-	-	-	-	-	-	-	-	-	-	-	-	-	16	-	-
George Vallance	BR	BR	BR	BR	-	BR	BR	BR	L	-	BR	BR	BR	BR	BR	L	-	BR	L	L	L	L	L	BR	BR	L	L	L	BR	BR	L	P	L	-	-	-	-	L	L	-	-	-	-	-	-	-	32	3	9
B.R.Baxter	BR	-	-	-	-	-	-	-	-	-	-	-	-	-	-	-	-	-	-	-	-	-	-	-	-	-	-	-	-	-	-	-	-	-	-	-	BR	-	-	-	-	-	-	-	-	-	2	-	-
W.I.Kerby	-	BR	BR	-	BR	-	BR	-	BR	BR	-	-	-	-	-	-	-	-	-	-	-	-	-	-	-	-	-	-	-	-	-	-	-	-	-	-	-	-	-	-	-	-	-	-	-	-	6	1	3
Hugh Constantine	-	-	-	-	-	BR	-	BR	BR	BR	BR	-	-	BR	BR	-	BR	BR	BR	BR	-	-	-	-	-	-	-	-	BR	-	-	BR	-	BR	BR	BR	-	L	BR	-	-	-	-	-	-	-	18	3	11
Pat Pattinson	-	-	-	-	-	-	-	-	-	-	-	-	-	-	-	-	-	-	-	-	-	BR	BR	-	-	-	-	-	-	-	-	-	-	-	-	-	-	-	-	-	-	-	-	-	-	-	2	-	-
P.F.R.Venables	-	-	-	-	-	-	-	-	-	-	-	-	-	-	-	-	-	-	-	-	-	-	BR	-	-	BR	BR	BR	BR	BR	BR	-	-	-	-	-	-	-	-	-	-	-	-	-	-	-	7	-	-
C.L.Millar	-	-	-	-	-	-	-	-	-	-	-	-	-	-	-	-	-	-	-	-	-	-	-	-	-	-	-	BR	-	-	-	-	-	-	-	-	BR	-	-	-	-	-	-	-	-	-	2	-	-
Leonard Cleaver	-	-	-	-	-	-	-	-	-	-	-	-	-	-	-	-	-	-	-	-	-	-	-	-	-	-	-	-	-	-	-	-	-	-	BR	BR	-	-	-	-	-	-	-	-	-	-	2	1	3

1 game: Carl Aarvold C(24), N.Bowen C(13), Sid Bowers SH(17), Tom Clarke BR(27), Jimmy Farrell L(24), Frank Herbert W(33), E.C.R.Hopkins C(19)[1T-3], B.J.Hurren BR(34), Stephen Meikle FH(38)[1T-3], Shirley Moore W(24)[2T-6], Tony Novis C(24), James ReeveW(19), F.West BR(38), G.E.S.Williams BR(38)

NO	DATE		OPPONENTS	V	RES	FOR G	FOR T	FOR D	FOR P	PTS	AGAINST G	AGAINST T	AGAINST D	AGAINST P	PTS	SCORERS
1	Sep	5	BATH	H	Won	-	2	-	-	6	-	-	-	-	0	Gadney(2T)
2		12	OLD BLUES	H	Won	2	2	-	-	16	-	-	-	-	0	Barr(2C) Hardwicke(T) Barlow(T) Gadney(2T)
3		19	PLYMOUTH ALBION	H	Won	1	1	-	-	8	-	-	-	-	0	Buckingham(T) Gadney(T) Norman(C)
4		26	NUNEATON	H	Won	3	2	1	-	25	-	-	-	-	0	Barr(C) Hardwicke(T) D.H.Herbert(D) Barlow(T) Gadney(T) Norman(2C) Vallance(T) Constantine(T)
5	Oct	3	COVENTRY	H	Won	-	3	-	-	9	-	-	-	-	0	Hardwicke(T) Barlow(2T)
6		10	Gloucester	A	Lost	-	2	-	-	6	1	-	1	1	12	Hardwicke(T) Gadney(T)
7		17	NEWPORT	H	Drew	1	1	-	-	8	1	-	-	1	8	Barr(C) Buckingham(T) Beamish(T)
8		24	NORTHAMPTON	H	Won	-	3	1	-	13	2	-	-	-	10	Coote(T) Greenlees(D) Beamish(T) Vallance(T)
9		31	CAMBRIDGE UNIVERSITY	H	Lost	-	1	-	1	6	4	1	-	1	26	Hardwicke(T) Greenlees(P)
10	Nov	5	OXFORD UNIVERSITY	H	Lost	1	-	-	-	5	2	-	-	-	10	Greenlees(C) Morris(T)
11		7	OLD MERCHANT TAYLORS	H	Won	1	5	-	-	20	1	1	-	-	8	Hardwicke(2T) Morris(2T) Norman(C) Coleman(T) Greenwood(T)
12		21	Swansea	A	Lost	-	-	-	-	0	1	1	-	1	11	
13		28	MOSELEY	H	Won	1	3	-	1	17	1	-	-	-	5	Hardwicke(T) Morris(T) Barlow(T) Norman(C,P) Coleman(T)
14	Dec	5	HARLEQUINS	H	Won	1	2	-	-	11	-	-	-	-	0	Hardwicke(T) Coote(2T) Greenlees(C)
15		12	Blackheath	A	Won	1	2	-	1	14	1	1	-	-	8	Barr(P) Buckingham(T) Coote(T) Greenlees(T,C)
		19	BRISTOL	H		Cancelled Fog										
16		26	BIRKENHEAD PARK	H	Drew	2	-	-	-	10	2	-	-	-	10	Coote(T) Greenlees(2C) Vallance(T)
17		28	BARBARIANS	H	Lost	2	1	-	-	13	1	3	-	-	14	Greenlees(T,2C) Gadney(T) Constantine(T)
18		29	WATERLOO	H	Drew	1	2	-	-	11	1	1	-	1	11	Greenlees(C) Greenwood(2T) Williams(T)
	Jan	1	Manchester	A		Cancelled Frost										
19		2	SWANSEA	H	Drew	-	1	-	-	3	-	1	-	-	3	Greenwood(T)
20		9	ROSSLYN PARK	H	Won	1	3	-	-	14	1	-	-	-	5	Hardwicke(2T) Greenlees(C) Gadney(2T)
21		16	LONDON WELSH	H	Lost	-	-	-	1	3	-	3	-	-	9	Greenlees(P)
22		23	RICHMOND	H	Lost	-	-	-	-	0	2	1	-	-	13	
23		28	ROYAL AIR FORCE	H	Won	1	2	-	1	14	-	1	-	-	3	Barr(C,P) S.F.Herbert(T) Auty(T) Vallance(T)
24		30	Moseley	A	Won	-	3	-	-	9	-	-	-	-	0	S.F.Herbert(T) Greenwood(T) Beamish(T)
25	Feb	6	LONDON SCOTTISH	H	Lost	-	1	-	1	6	3	3	-	-	24	Barr(P) Vallance(T)
26		13	Newport	A	Lost	-	-	-	-	0	1	2	1	2	21	
27		20	GLOUCESTER	H	Won	-	1	1	-	7	1	-	-	-	5	Hardwicke(T) Greenlees(D)
28		27	Northampton	A	Lost	-	-	-	-	0	1	3	1	-	18	
29	Mar	5	HARLEQUINS	H	Won	-	3	1	-	13	1	2	-	-	11	Moore(T) Greenlees(D) Berry(T) Saunders(T)
30		12	BEDFORD	H	Won	1	2	1	1	18	-	2	1	-	10	Hardwicke(T) Greenlees(D) Moore(T) Norman(T) Vallance(C,P)
31		19	Coventry	A	Lost	2	-	-	-	10	6	1	-	-	33	Moore(T) Greenlees(C) Kendrew(C) Berry(T)
32		26	Bristol	A	Lost	-	-	-	2	6	2	-	-	1	13	Coote(2P)
33		28	Plymouth Albion	A	Won	3	-	-	1	18	1	1	-	-	8	Beaty-Pownall(T) Hodder(T) Coote(P) Greenlees(3C) Beamish(T)
34		29	Bath	A	Lost	-	3	-	-	9	1	2	-	-	11	Hardwicke(T) Beamish(2T)
35	Apr	2	BRIDGWATER	H	Won	3	5	-	-	30	1	-	-	-	5	Barr(C) Hardwicke(T) Buckingham(T) Morris(2T) Bates(T) Gadney(T) Greenwood(C) Vallance(C) Pearse(T) Saunders(T)
36		4	NUNEATON	H	Drew	-	1	-	-	3	-	1	-	-	3	Palmer(T)
37		9	Birkenhead Park	A	Drew	2	1	-	-	13	2	1	-	-	13	Buckingham(T) Greenlees(2C) Vallance(T) Constantine(T)
38		16	BLACKHEATH	H	Lost	-	1	-	-	3	1	-	-	-	5	Gadney(T)

INDIVIDUAL APPEARANCES 1931-1932

NAME	1	2	3	4	5	6	7	8	9	10	11	12	13	14	15	16	17	18	19	20	21	22	23	24	25	26	27	28	29	30	31	32	33	34	35	36	37	38	39	40	41	42	43	44	45	46	TOTAL	T	PTS
Bobby Barr	FB	FB	FB	FB	FB	FB	FB	FB	FB	FB	FB	FB	-	-	FB	FB	-	-	-	-	-	FB	FB	-	FB	-	FB	-	FB	FB	-	FB	-	FB	FB	FB	FB	FB	-	-	-	-	-	-	-	-	26	-	21
Charlie Manson	-	-	-	-	-	-	-	-	-	-	-	-	FB	FB	-	-	FB	-	FB	FB	FB	-	-	FB	-	FB	-	FB	-	-	FB	-	FB	-	-	-	-	-	-	-	-	-	-	-	-	-	11	-	-
Jeff Hardwicke	W	W	W	W	W	W	W	W	W	W	W	W	W	W	W	W	W	W	-	W	W	W	W	W	W	W	W	W	W	W	W	W	W	W	W	-	-	W	-	-	-	-	-	-	-	-	35	15	45
Ewart Farndon	W	-	-	-	-	-	-	-	-	-	W	W	-	-	-	-	-	-	-	-	-	-	-	-	-	-	-	-	-	-	-	-	-	-	-	-	-	-	-	-	-	-	-	-	-	-	3	-	-
Morgan Barlow	-	W	W	W	W	W	W	-	-	-	-	-	W	-	-	-	-	-	W	-	-	-	-	-	-	-	-	-	-	-	-	-	-	-	-	-	-	-	-	-	-	-	-	-	-	-	8	5	15
Denis Morris	-	-	-	-	-	-	-	-	W	W	C	C	C	C	W	-	W	-	-	C	C	C	C	C	C	C	C	C	C	-	-	-	-	W	W	-	-	W	-	-	-	-	-	-	-	-	21	6	18
Frank Herbert	-	-	-	-	-	-	-	-	-	-	-	-	-	W	-	-	-	W	W	-	W	W	W	W	W	-	-	-	-	-	-	-	-	-	-	W	W	-	-	-	-	-	-	-	-	-	10	2	6
I.McNichol	-	-	-	-	-	-	-	-	-	-	-	-	-	-	-	W	-	C	C	-	-	-	-	-	-	-	-	-	-	-	-	-	-	-	-	-	-	-	-	-	-	-	-	-	-	-	3	-	-
Shirley Moore	-	-	-	-	-	-	-	-	-	-	-	-	-	-	-	-	-	-	-	-	-	-	-	-	-	W	W	W	W	W	W	W	W	-	-	W	W	-	-	-	-	-	-	-	-	-	10	3	9
Ralph Buckingham	C	C	C	C	C	-	C	C	C	C	FH	FH	FH	FH	C	C	C	FB	FH	C	C	-	C	FH	FH	-	-	-	-	-	-	-	-	-	C	C	C	C	-	-	-	-	-	-	-	-	27	5	15
Don Herbert	-	C	C	C	C	C	-	C	C	-	C	C	C	-	-	-	-	-	-	-	-	C	-	-	-	-	-	-	-	-	-	-	-	-	-	-	-	-	-	-	-	-	-	-	-	-	11	-	4
Paddy Coote	-	-	-	-	-	C	-	W	-	-	-	-	-	C	C	C	C	-	C	-	-	-	-	-	-	-	-	-	-	-	-	C	FH	-	-	-	-	-	-	-	-	-	-	-	-	-	9	5	24
E.C.R.Hopkins	-	-	-	-	-	-	C	-	-	-	-	-	-	-	-	-	-	C	-	-	-	-	-	-	-	-	-	-	-	-	-	-	-	-	-	-	-	-	-	-	-	-	-	-	-	-	2	-	-
Francis Hodder	-	-	-	-	-	-	-	-	-	-	-	-	-	-	-	-	-	-	-	-	-	-	-	C	-	-	-	C	-	-	-	C	C	C	-	-	-	-	-	-	-	-	-	-	-	-	5	1	3
C.C.Beaty-Pownall	-	-	-	-	-	-	-	-	-	-	-	-	-	-	-	-	-	-	-	-	-	-	-	-	-	-	-	-	-	C	C	-	C	C	-	-	-	-	-	-	-	-	-	-	-	-	4	1	3
Wilf Jackson	-	-	-	-	-	-	-	-	-	-	-	-	-	-	-	-	-	-	-	-	-	-	-	-	-	-	-	-	-	-	C	-	-	-	-	-	C	-	-	-	-	-	-	-	-	-	2	-	-
Harry Greenlees	FH	FH	FH	-	FH	-	-	FH	FH	C	-	-	-	SH	FH	FH	FH	FH	-	FH	FH	FH	-	-	-	-	FH	FH	FH	C	SH	FH	SH	SH	C	-	SH	C	-	-	-	-	-	-	-	-	26	2	58
Reg Odbert	-	-	-	FH	-	FH	FH	-	-	-	-	-	-	-	-	-	-	-	-	-	-	-	-	-	-	-	-	-	-	-	-	-	-	-	-	-	-	-	-	-	-	-	-	-	-	-	3	-	-
Dick Auty	-	-	-	-	-	-	-	-	-	FH	-	-	-	-	-	-	-	-	-	-	-	-	FH	-	-	-	-	-	-	-	-	-	-	-	-	-	-	-	-	-	-	-	-	-	-	-	2	1	3
E.Bates	-	-	-	-	-	-	-	-	-	-	-	-	-	-	-	-	-	-	-	-	-	-	-	-	-	-	-	-	C	FH	FH	-	-	-	FH	FH	FH	FH	-	-	-	-	-	-	-	-	7	1	3
Bernard Gadney	SH	SH	SH	SH	SH	SH	-	-	SH	-	SH	SH	-	-	SH	SH	SH	SH	-	SH	-	SH	SH	SH	SH	-	SH	-	SH	-	-	-	-	-	SH	-	-	SH	-	-	-	-	-	-	-	-	22	12	36
Stuart Smith	-	-	-	-	-	-	SH	SH	-	SH	-	-	-	-	-	-	-	-	-	-	-	-	-	-	-	-	-	-	-	-	-	-	-	-	-	-	-	-	-	-	-	-	-	-	-	-	3	-	-
D.H.Howsen	-	-	-	-	-	-	-	-	-	-	-	-	-	-	-	-	-	-	SH	-	SH	-	-	-	-	-	-	-	-	-	-	-	-	-	-	-	-	-	-	-	-	-	-	-	-	-	2	-	-
D.W.Colston	-	-	-	-	-	-	-	-	-	-	-	-	-	-	-	-	-	-	-	-	-	-	-	-	-	SH	-	SH	-	-	-	-	-	-	-	-	-	-	-	-	-	-	-	-	-	-	2	-	-
Doug Norman	P	P	P	P	P	P	P	P	P	P	P	P	P	-	P	-	-	-	-	-	-	H	H	H	H	H	H	H	H	H	-	H	H	H	H	H	H	H	-	-	-	-	-	-	-	-	30	1	16
Ernie Coleman	P	-	-	-	-	-	-	BR	BR	L	L	BR	BR	H	P	H	H	H	P	H	P	P	BR	-	BR	BR	BR	-	-	-	-	-	-	-	BR	-	-	-	-	-	-	-	-	-	-	-	21	2	6
C.L.Millar	-	-	-	-	-	-	-	-	-	-	-	-	-	-	-	-	-	-	-	P	H	-	-	-	-	-	-	-	-	-	-	-	-	-	-	-	-	-	-	-	-	-	-	-	-	-	2	-	-
Henry Greenwood	-	BR	BR	BR	BR	L	L	BR	L	-	BR	L	P	-	L	P	P	P	H	-	P	P	P	P	P	P	P	L	P	P	P	P	P	L	P	-	P	P	-	-	-	-	-	-	-	-	33	5	17
A.C.Hall	BR	BR	-	-	-	-	-	-	-	-	-	-	-	-	-	-	-	-	-	-	-	-	P	-	P	P	P	P	P	P	P	P	P	P	-	-	-	-	-	-	-	-	-	-	-	-	13	-	-
George Beamish	H	H	H	H	H	H	H	H	-	-	-	H	-	P	-	-	BR	BR	-	-	-	-	-	BR	-	-	-	-	-	-	-	BR	BR	BR	-	-	-	BR	-	-	-	-	-	-	-	-	17	6	18
Stan Saunders	L	L	L	L	L	-	-	L	P	P	P	L	L	L	BR	BR	BR	-	BR	BR	L	-	-	-	-	-	-	-	BR	BR	BR	-	BR	BR	BR	L	BR	-	-	-	-	-	-	-	-	-	26	2	6
George Vallance	L	P	P	P	P	P	P	P	H	H	H	P	H	P	H	L	L	L	L	L	-	L	L	L	L	L	L	-	L	L	-	-	-	-	P	P	L	L	-	-	-	-	-	-	-	-	32	6	25
Dr.R.A.K. Wiener	BR	L	L	L	L	L	L	L	L	L	L	BR	L	L	L	L	P	L	L	L	L	L	L	L	-	L	L	L	-	-	-	L	-	P	L	P	L	L	-	-	-	-	-	-	-	-	33	-	-
Cyril Lewis	-	-	-	-	-	-	-	-	-	-	-	-	-	-	-	-	-	-	-	-	-	-	-	-	-	-	-	-	-	-	-	L	L	-	-	-	-	-	-	-	-	-	-	-	-	-	2	-	-
Alan Hughes	BR	BR	BR	BR	BR	BR	BR	-	BR	-	BR	-	-	BR	-	P	-	-	P	P	BR	-	-	P	L	BR	BR	BR	L	L	BR	-	L	-	-	-	P	P	-	-	-	-	-	-	-	-	25	-	-
Hugh Constantine	-	-	BR	BR	-	BR	BR	-	-	BR	-	-	BR	BR	BR	-	L	-	-	-	-	-	-	-	-	-	-	BR	-	-	-	BR	BR	-	-	L	BR	BR	-	-	-	-	-	-	-	-	15	3	9
Mog' Christie	-	-	-	-	BR	BR	BR	BR	BR	BR	BR	BR	BR	-	-	-	-	-	-	-	-	-	-	BR	-	-	-	-	-	-	-	-	-	-	-	-	-	-	-	-	-	-	-	-	-	-	10	-	-
W.I.Kerby	-	-	-	-	-	-	-	-	-	BR	-	-	-	-	-	-	-	-	-	-	-	BR	BR	-	BR	-	-	-	-	-	-	-	-	-	-	-	-	-	-	-	-	-	-	-	-	-	4	-	-
Bill Parker	-	-	-	-	-	-	-	-	-	-	-	-	-	BR	-	BR	-	BR	BR	BR	BR	BR	-	-	-	-	-	-	-	-	-	-	-	-	-	-	-	-	-	-	-	-	-	-	-	-	7	-	-
Alistair Graham	-	-	-	-	-	-	-	-	-	-	-	-	-	-	BR	BR	BR	-	BR	BR	BR	BR	-	BR	BR	BR	-	-	-	-	-	-	-	-	-	-	-	-	-	-	-	-	-	-	-	-	10	-	-
C.H.Pearse	-	-	-	-	-	-	-	-	-	-	-	-	-	-	-	-	-	-	-	-	-	-	BR	-	-	-	BR	BR	BR	BR	L	BR	-	L	L	BR	-	-	-	-	-	-	-	-	-	-	10	1	3
Tom Berry	-	-	-	-	-	-	-	-	-	-	-	-	-	-	-	-	-	-	-	-	-	-	-	-	-	-	-	-	BR	BR	L	-	-	BR	BR	BR	BR	BR	-	-	-	-	-	-	-	-	8	2	6

1 game: N.Bacon C(27), B.R.Baxter BR(31), A.Bolus C(1), Sid Bowers SH(13), Langley Burton C(25), G.C.M.Falla P(18), K.C.George BR(36), A.K.Halliday SH(36), Bill Jeffery SH(30), "Joe' Kendrew H(31)[2], Dennis Manley W(20), R.F.Nobleston SH(32), Donald Oscroft C(26), R.A.Palmer C(36)[1T-3], F/O.Reynolds P(28), Arnold Sime FH(34), L.A.Smith FH(26), G.E.S.Williams BR(18)[1T-3]

LEICESTER FOOTBALL CLUB 1931-32
Back: N. Coates (Touch Judge), E.G. Coleman, A.H. Greenwood, D.E. Morris, H.A. Constantine, C.S. Manson, J.T. Hardwicke, G.P.C. Vallance, W.N. Bradshaw (Hon.Tres), J.E. Thorneloe (Hon.Sec).
Middle: B.C. Gadney, R.A. Buckingham, D.J. Norman, H.D. Greenlees (Capt), G.R. Beamish, R.J. Barr, R.A.K. Wiener.
Front: J.T.W. Berry, A.P. Hughes, E. Bates, S.H. Saunders, S.H. Moore, C.H. Pearse.

LEICESTER FOOTBALL CLUB 1932-33
Back: W.N. Bradshaw (Hon.Tres), S.H. Saunders, D.E. Morris, D.S. Oscroft, C.H. Pearse, C.G.R. Lewis, J.L. Wormleighton, E. Bates, J.E. Thorneloe (Hon.Sec).
Middle: A.P. Hughes, B.C. Gadney, R.A. Buckingham, D.J. Norman (Capt), G.R. Beamish, P.B. Coote, J.H.F. Edmiston.
Front: W.A. Jackson, R.A. Harris, J.T.W. Berry, J.T. Hardwicke, C.F. Slow, G. Greaves.
Inset: M.P. Crowe, G.P.C. Vallance.

NO	DATE		OPPONENTS	V	RES	FOR G	FOR T	FOR D	FOR P	FOR PTS	AGAINST G	AGAINST T	AGAINST D	AGAINST P	AGAINST PTS	SCORERS
1	Sep	3	BEDFORD	H	Won	-	2	1	-	10	1	-	-	-	5	Hardwicke(T) Buckingham(T) Morris(D)
2		10	OLD BLUES	H	Won	1	2	-	-	11	1	-	-	-	5	Buckingham(T) Bates(T) Vallance(T,C)
3		17	PLYMOUTH ALBION	H	Won	-	3	1	-	13	1	1	-	-	8	Hardwicke(T) Coote(T,D) Lewis(T)
4		24	BRISTOL	H	Won	-	-	-	1	3	-	-	-	-	0	Payne(P)
5	Oct	1	COVENTRY	H	Won	2	2	-	-	16	-	-	1	-	4	Coote(2T,2C) Morris(T) Gadney(T)
6		8	Bridgwater	A	Won	1	1	-	1	11	-	-	-	2	6	Manson(C) Crowe(T) Jackson(T) Vallance(P)
7		15	Newport	A	Won	2	-	-	-	10	-	1	-	1	6	Hardwicke(2T) Coote(2C)
8		17	BECTIVE RANGERS	H	Won	4	1	1*	-	26	-	-	-	-	0	Hardwicke(T) Coote(3C) Crowe(M) Meikle(2T) Kendrew(C) Vallance(2T)
9		22	Northampton	A	Won	1	-	1	-	9	-	2	-	-	6	Coote(C,D) Bates(T)
10		29	GLOUCESTER	H	Won	-	1	-	1	6	-	1	-	-	3	Coote(P) Buckingham(T)
11	Nov	5	MOSELEY	H	Won	3	5	1	1	37	-	-	1	1	7	Manson(C) Coote(T,C,D) Crowe(T) Bradley(T) Meikle(T,C) Kendrew(2T) Edmiston(T,P) Constantine(T)
12		9	Oxford University	A	Won	3	2	-	-	21	1	-	-	-	5	Coote(3C) Meikle(4T) Auty(T)
13		12	Cambridge University	A	Lost	-	1	-	-	3	1	1	-	-	8	Edmiston(T)
14		19	OLD MERCHANT TAYLORS	H	Lost	1	-	-	-	5	4	1	1	-	27	Hardwicke(T) Vallance(C)
15		26	NUNEATON	H	Won	-	2	-	2	12	-	-	-	-	0	Bradley(T) Vallance(2P) Constantine(T)
16	Dec	3	Harlequins	A	Won	2	4	-	-	22	2	1	-	-	13	Hardwicke(2T) Buckingham(T) Crowe(T,2C) Tindall(T) Beamish(T)
17		10	Blackheath	A	Lost	1	2	-	-	11	1	2	-	1	14	Tindall(T) Hughes(T) Edmiston(C) Constantine(T)
18		17	WATERLOO	H	Lost	-	1	-	-	3	2	1	-	-	13	Saunders(T)
19		24	Bedford	A	Lost	2	-	-	-	10	2	1	-	-	13	Stanyon-Jacques(T) Saunders(T) Edmiston(2C)
20		26	BIRKENHEAD PARK	H	Won	1	3	-	-	14	1	-	-	-	5	Hardwicke(T) Coote(T,C) Crowe(T) Buckingham(T)
21		27	BARBARIANS	H	Lost	-	2	1	-	10	2	3	-	1	22	Burton(T) Edmiston(D) Dunkley(T)
22		28	MANCHESTER	H	Won	-	2	-	1	9	1	1	-	-	8	Greaves(T) Berry(T) Edmiston(P)
23		31	Swansea	A	Lost	-	-	-	-	0	1	2	-	-	11	
24	Jan	7	ROSSLYN PARK	H	Won	-	1	-	-	3	-	-	-	-	0	Buckingham(T)
25		21	BATH	H	Won	1	1	-	1	11	-	-	-	-	0	Crowe(T,C,P) Buckingham(T)
		26	ROYAL AIR FORCE	H		Cancelled Frost										
		28	Richmond	A		Cancelled Frost										
26	Feb	4	London Scottish	A	Lost	1	2	-	-	11	2	1	-	-	13	Hardwicke(2T) Bates(T) Edmiston(C)
27		11	NEWPORT	H	Lost	-	-	1	1	7	2	-	-	-	10	Crowe(P) Bates(D)
28		18	Gloucester	A	Won	1	2	-	-	11	-	2	-	1	9	Hardwicke(T) Oscroft(T) Crowe(C) Buckingham(T)
		25	SWANSEA	H		Cancelled Snow										
29	Mar	4	HARLEQUINS	H	Lost	1	2	-	-	11	3	1	-	-	18	Crowe(T) Buckingham(T) Edmiston(C) Saunders(T)
30		11	NORTHAMPTON	H	Lost	-	1	-	-	3	1	3	1	1	21	Oscroft(T)
31		18	Coventry	A	Lost	-	-	-	-	0	1	-	-	-	5	
32		25	LONDON WELSH	H	Won	5	2	-	-	31	1	1	1	-	12	Crowe(5C) Buckingham(2T) Vallance(T) Adams(T) Saunders(3T)
33	Apr	1	Birkenhead Park	A	Won	1	3	1	-	18	1	2	-	-	11	Buckingham(2T) Slow(D) D.J.Norman(C) Saunders(T) Berry(T)
34		8	BLACKHEATH	H	Lost	1	2	-	-	11	3	1	-	-	18	Buckingham(2T) Slow(T) D.J.Norman(C)
35		15	Bristol	A	Won	1	1	1	-	12	-	-	1	-	4	Crowe(T) Slow(D) D.J.Norman(C) Beamish(T)
36		17	Plymouth Albion	A	Won	1	2	-	-	11	-	2	-	-	6	Crowe(T) Jackson(T) D.J.Norman(C) Beamish(T)
37		18	Bath	A	Lost	1	-	-	1	8	3	-	-	-	15	Harris(C,P) Buckingham(T)

INDIVIDUAL APPEARANCES 1932-1933

NAME	1	2	3	4	5	6	7	8	9	10	11	12	13	14	15	16	17	18	19	20	21	22	23	24	25	26	27	28	29	30	31	32	33	34	35	36	37	38	39	40	41	42	43	44	45	46	TOTAL	T	PTS
Bobby Barr	FB	FB	FB	FB	FB	-	-	FB	FB	FB	-	FB	FB	-	-	-	FB	FB	FB	-	-	-	-	-	-	-	-	-	-	-	-	-	-	-	-	-	-	-	-	-	-	-	-	-	-	-	13	-	-
Charlie Manson	-	-	-	-	-	FB	-	-	-	-	FB	-	-	FB	-	-	-	-	-	-	-	-	-	-	-	-	-	-	-	-	-	-	-	-	-	-	-	-	-	-	-	-	-	-	-	-	3	-	4
R.A.Harris	-	-	-	-	-	-	-	-	-	-	-	-	-	-	-	-	-	-	-	-	-	FB	-	FB	FB	FB	FB	FB	FB	FB	FB	-	-	FB	FB	FB	FB	-	-	-	-	-	-	-	-	-	13	-	5
Jeff Hardwicke	W	W	W	-	W	-	W	W	W	-	-	-	-	W	-	W	W	W	-	W	W	W	-	W	W	W	W	W	W	W	W	W	-	W	W	-	W	-	-	-	-	-	-	-	-	-	26	12	36
Denis Morris	W	W	-	W	W	-	W	-	-	W	-	-	W	W	-	-	-	-	-	-	-	-	-	-	-	-	-	-	-	-	-	-	-	-	-	-	-	-	-	-	-	-	-	-	-	-	8	1	7
E.G.Bradley	-	-	-	-	-	W	-	-	-	-	W	-	-	-	W	-	-	-	W	-	-	-	-	-	-	-	-	-	-	-	-	-	-	-	-	-	-	-	-	-	-	-	-	-	-	-	4	2	6
Frank Herbert	-	-	-	-	-	W	-	-	-	-	-	-	-	-	-	-	-	-	W	-	-	W	-	-	-	W	-	-	-	-	-	-	W	-	-	-	-	-	-	-	-	-	-	-	-	-	5	-	-
N.J.Tindall	-	-	-	-	-	-	-	-	-	-	-	-	-	-	W	W	W	W	-	-	-	-	-	-	-	-	-	-	-	-	-	-	-	-	-	-	-	-	-	-	-	-	-	-	-	-	4	2	6
Ralph Buckingham	C	C	C	W	-	-	FH	-	W	W	-	-	W	C	-	C	C	C	C	W	W	C	C	W	W	C	W	W	W	C	W	W	W	W	W	W	W	-	-	-	-	-	-	-	-	-	31	16	48
J.F.Payne	-	C	C	C	-	-	-	-	-	-	-	-	-	-	-	-	-	-	-	-	-	-	-	-	-	-	-	-	-	-	-	-	-	-	-	-	-	-	-	-	-	-	-	-	-	-	3	-	3
Paddy Coote	-	-	W	C	C	-	C	C	C	C	C	C	C	-	-	-	-	-	-	C	C	-	-	-	-	-	-	-	-	-	-	-	-	C	-	-	-	-	-	-	-	-	-	-	-	-	13	5	56
Morgan Crowe	-	-	-	-	C	C	C	C	C	C	C	C	C	C	FH	C	C	-	C	C	C	-	-	C	C	-	C	C	C	-	C	C	-	-	C	C	-	-	-	-	-	-	-	-	-	-	25	8	51
Wilf Jackson	-	-	-	-	-	C	-	-	-	-	-	-	-	-	-	-	-	-	-	-	-	-	C	-	-	-	-	-	-	W	-	C	C	C	C	C	C	-	-	-	-	-	-	-	-	-	9	2	6
Donald Oscroft	-	-	-	-	-	-	-	-	-	-	-	-	-	-	-	-	-	C	-	-	-	C	W	C	C	C	C	C	C	C	C	-	C	-	-	-	C	-	-	-	-	-	-	-	-	-	13	2	6
E.Bates	FH	FH	FH	FH	FH	-	-	FH	FH	FH	-	W	-	FH	-	FH	FH	FH	FH	FH	-	FH	FH	FH	FH	FH	FH	FH	FH	FH	FH	FB	FB	-	-	W	FH	-	-	-	-	-	-	-	-	-	29	3	13
Stephen Meikle	-	-	-	-	-	-	-	W	-	-	FH	W	FH	-	-	-	-	-	-	-	-	-	-	-	-	-	-	-	-	-	-	-	-	-	-	-	-	-	-	-	-	-	-	-	-	-	4	7	23
Charlie Slow	-	-	-	-	-	-	-	-	-	-	-	-	-	-	-	-	-	-	-	-	-	-	-	-	-	-	-	-	-	-	-	FH	FH	FH	FH	FH	-	-	-	-	-	-	-	-	-	-	5	1	11
Bernard Gadney	SH	SH	SH	SH	SH	-	-	-	SH	SH	-	SH	-	-	-	-	-	-	-	-	-	-	-	SH	-	SH	-	-	SH	SH	-	SH	SH	SH	SH	SH	SH	-	-	-	-	-	-	-	-	-	18	1	3
D.H.Howsen	-	-	-	-	-	SH	SH	SH	-	-	-	-	SH	-	SH	SH	SH	SH	-	-	-	-	-	-	-	-	-	-	-	-	-	-	-	-	-	-	-	-	-	-	-	-	-	-	-	-	8	-	-
Langley Burton	-	-	-	-	-	-	-	-	-	-	SH	-	-	SH	-	-	-	-	-	SH	SH	-	-	-	-	-	-	-	-	-	-	-	-	-	-	-	-	-	-	-	-	-	-	-	-	-	4	1	3
Sid Bowers	-	-	-	-	-	-	-	-	-	-	-	-	-	-	-	-	-	-	-	-	-	-	SH	-	-	-	-	SH	-	-	SH	-	-	-	-	-	-	-	-	-	-	-	-	-	-	-	3	-	-
Henry Greenwood	P	H	P	P	-	-	P	P	P	P	-	-	-	-	P	-	-	-	-	-	-	-	-	-	-	-	-	-	-	-	-	-	-	-	-	-	-	-	-	-	-	-	-	-	-	-	9	-	-
Stan Saunders	P	P	-	-	-	-	-	-	-	-	BR	-	-	-	-	BR	BR	BR	L	BR	-	BR	BR	-	-	BR	-	BR	BR	BR	BR	BR	BR	-	-	-	-	-	-	-	-	-	-	-	-	-	17	7	21
Alan Hughes	L	L	P	H	P	-	P	P	P	-	-	P	P	P	-	P	P	P	-	P	P	-	P	P	P	P	P	P	P	-	P	P	P	P	P	-	-	-	-	-	-	-	-	-	-	-	28	1	3
George Greaves	-	-	-	P	P	-	L	L	L	L	-	L	-	P	-	P	-	P	P	-	-	P	P	P	-	P	P	P	P	P	-	-	-	P	P	P	P	-	-	-	-	-	-	-	-	-	23	1	3
Jack Wormleighton	-	-	-	-	-	P	-	-	-	-	P	-	-	-	-	-	P	-	P	P	-	P	-	-	P	-	-	-	-	P	P	P	P	-	-	-	-	-	-	-	-	-	-	-	-	-	11	-	-
Doug Norman	H	P	-	-	-	-	-	-	-	H	-	H	H	H	-	H	H	H	H	H	H	-	H	H	H	H	-	-	-	H	H	H	H	H	H	H	H	-	-	-	-	-	-	-	-	-	24	-	8
Harold Bennett	-	-	-	-	-	H	H	-	-	-	H	-	-	-	H	-	-	-	-	-	-	H	-	-	-	-	H	H	H	-	-	-	-	-	-	-	P	-	-	-	-	-	-	-	-	-	9	-	-
Ernie Coleman	-	-	-	-	H	-	-	-	-	L	L	-	L	L	-	L	L	L	L	L	-	-	L	L	-	-	-	-	-	L	-	-	-	-	-	-	-	-	-	-	-	-	-	-	-	-	13	-	-
Joe' Kendrew	-	-	-	-	-	-	-	H	H	P	P	P	P	-	P	-	-	-	-	-	-	-	-	-	-	-	-	-	-	-	-	-	-	-	-	-	-	-	-	-	-	-	-	-	-	-	7	2	8
George Vallance	L	L	L	L	L	L	-	L	L	-	-	-	L	L	L	-	-	-	-	-	-	-	-	-	L	L	L	L	L	-	L	L	L	L	L	L	-	-	-	-	-	-	-	-	-	-	22	4	25
Cyril Lewis	-	-	L	L	L	-	L	-	-	BR	L	L	-	-	L	-	-	-	-	-	L	-	-	-	-	-	L	-	-	-	L	-	L	L	L	L	L	-	-	-	-	-	-	-	-	-	16	1	3
Dr.R.A.K. Wiener	-	-	-	-	-	-	-	-	-	-	-	-	-	-	-	L	L	L	-	-	-	-	-	-	-	-	-	-	-	-	-	-	-	-	-	-	-	-	-	-	-	-	-	-	-	-	3	-	-
E.G.Nixon	-	-	-	-	-	-	-	-	-	-	-	-	-	-	-	-	-	-	-	L	L	L	-	-	-	-	-	-	-	-	-	-	-	-	-	-	-	-	-	-	-	-	-	-	-	-	3	-	-
Tom Berry	BR	BR	BR	-	BR	-	BR	BR	BR	-	-	-	BR	-	-	-	-	BR	BR	BR	-	BR	L	L	L	L	BR	L	L	L	BR	L	BR	BR	BR	BR	BR	-	-	-	-	-	-	-	-	-	27	2	6
Harry Edmiston	BR	BR	BR	BR	BR	L	BR	-	BR	BR	BR	BR	BR	BR	-	-	BR	BR	BR	BR	BR	BR	BR	BR	BR	BR	BR	BR	BR	BR	-	BR	-	BR	-	BR	-	-	-	-	-	-	-	-	-	-	30	2	26
C.H.Pearse	BR	BR	-	BR	-	-	-	BR	-	BR	-	BR	-	BR	BR	-	-	-	-	-	-	-	BR	BR	-	-	BR	BR	BR	-	-	-	-	-	-	-	-	-	-	-	-	-	-	-	-	-	13	-	-
George Beamish	-	-	BR	BR	BR	-	BR	BR	BR	-	-	BR	BR	BR	-	BR	-	-	-	-	BR	-	-	-	-	-	-	-	-	-	BR	-	-	BR	BR	BR	-	-	-	-	-	-	-	-	-	-	15	3	9
Hugh Constantine	-	-	-	-	-	BR	-	-	-	-	BR	-	-	-	BR	-	BR	-	-	-	-	-	-	-	-	-	-	-	-	-	-	-	-	-	-	-	-	-	-	-	-	-	-	-	-	-	4	3	9
F.J.Norman	-	-	-	-	-	-	-	-	-	-	-	-	-	-	BR	-	-	-	-	-	-	-	-	BR	BR	-	-	-	-	-	-	-	-	-	-	-	-	-	-	-	-	-	-	-	-	-	3	-	-
Newton Adams	-	-	-	-	-	-	-	-	-	-	-	-	-	-	-	-	-	-	-	-	-	-	-	-	-	-	-	-	-	BR	-	BR	BR	-	-	-	BR	-	-	-	-	-	-	-	-	-	4	1	3

2 games: L.J.Adcock W(11,23), Dick Auty FH(12,21)[1T-3], Leonard Cleaver P(36)L(37), J.G.Edmiston SH(25,27), C.D.Henderson BR(19)L(22), L.Holden FB(16,20), Bill Parker BR(25,26)
1 game: Spencer Bevan FB(7), I.G.Cleaver BR(16), W.H.V.Cotton FB(23), Phil Dunkley BR(21)[1T-3], K.C.George BR(6), A.C.Hall P(6), Francis Hodder C(15), J.I.T.Jones FH(6), Keith Oakley BR(37), H.E.Packer C(1), Reg Pemberton H(3), Stephen Radcliffe FB(21), Henry Rew P(21), A.F.Sibson C(15), Arnold Sime SH(22), C.G.J.Stanley BR(35), K.A.Stanyon-Jacques SH(19)[1T-3], W.S.Thompson FB(15), D.L.Thornton BR(6)

1933-1934

NO	DATE		OPPONENTS	V	RES	FOR G	FOR T	FOR D	FOR P	FOR PTS	AGAINST G	AGAINST T	AGAINST D	AGAINST P	AGAINST PTS	SCORERS
1	Sep	2	BEDFORD	H	Won	2	3	1	1	26	2	-	-	1	13	Hardwicke(T) Jackson(T) Crowe(2C,P) Buckingham(T) Slow(T,D) Gadney(T)
2		9	OLD BLUES	H	Won	3	5	-	1	33	-	-	-	-	0	Manson(2C) Crowe(C) Jackson(T) Hardwicke(2T) Gadney(4T) Vallance(P) Adams(T)
3		16	PLYMOUTH ALBION	H	Won	-	5	-	-	15	-	-	1	-	4	Jackson(T) Darnill(T) Gadney(T) Bennett(T) Drummond(T)
4		23	GLOUCESTER	H	Lost	-	-	1	-	4	2	-	2	-	18	Slow(D)
5		30	LONDON WELSH	H	Won	3	2	1	-	25	1	-	1	-	9	Crowe(2T,3C) Jackson(T) Darnill(T) Slow(D) Vallance(T)
6	Oct	7	Coventry	A	Drew	1	-	-	-	5	1	-	-	-	5	Crowe(C) Slow(T)
7		14	BRIDGWATER	H	Won	3	1	1	-	22	1	-	-	-	5	Shepherd(T) Lloyd(T) Slow(T,D) Vallance(T) Constantine(2C) Edmiston(C)
8		19	BECTIVE RANGERS	H	Lost	-	-	-	1	3	1	3	-	-	14	Edmiston(P)
9		21	NEWPORT	H	Lost	-	-	-	1	3	1	-	1	-	9	Edmiston(P)
10		28	NORTHAMPTON	H	Won	2	-	-	-	10	-	1	-	-	3	Crowe(2C) Slow(T) Gadney(T)
11	Nov	4	Moseley	A	Lost	-	-	-	1	3	2	2	-	-	16	Edmiston(P)
12		9	OXFORD UNIVERSITY	H	Won	1	1	1	-	12	1	1	-	-	8	Buckingham(T) Crowe(C) Coote(D) Slow(T)
13		11	CAMBRIDGE UNIVERSITY	H	Won	2	-	-	1	13	2	-	-	-	10	Crowe(2C) Coote(2T,P)
14		18	Swansea	A	Lost	-	1	-	1	6	1	1	-	-	8	Hewitt(T) Coote(P)
15		25	Nuneaton	A	Lost	2	-	-	1	13	2	3	-	-	19	Manson(C) Lloyd(2T) Llewellyn(C) Constantine(P)
16	Dec	2	Harlequins	A	Won	-	-	1	-	4	-	-	-	-	0	Crowe(D)
17		9	Blackheath	A	Lost	1	3	-	-	14	2	1	1	-	17	Lloyd(T) Hewitt(T) Gadney(T) G.N.Harris(T) Constantine(C)
18		16	BRISTOL	H	Won	-	1	1	1	10	-	2	-	-	6	Barr(D) Buckingham(T) Crowe(P)
19		23	Bedford	A	Lost	2	-	-	-	10	1	4	-	1	20	Crowe(2C) Darnill(T) Buckingham(T)
20		26	BIRKENHEAD PARK	H	Won	1	-	-	-	5	-	1	-	-	3	Crowe(C) Slow(T)
21		27	BARBARIANS	H	Won	1	4	1	-	21	-	2	1	-	10	Crowe(T,C) Gerrard(T) G.W.C.Meikle(3T,D)
22		28	WATERLOO	H	Won	-	1	1	-	7	-	1	1*	-	6	Jackson(T) Fyfe(D)
23		30	ROSSLYN PARK	H	Won	1	2	-	-	11	1	-	-	-	5	Jackson(T) Gray(T) Constantine(C) Drummond(T)
24	Jan	1	Manchester	A	Won	-	4	-	-	12	-	1	-	-	3	Gray(3T) Drummond(T)
25		6	SWANSEA	H	Lost	-	-	-	-	0	-	1	-	-	3	
26		13	RUGBY	H	Won	-	4	-	-	12	-	-	-	-	0	Darnill(3T) Hewitt(T)
27		20	BATH	H	Won	-	4	-	-	12	1	1	-	-	8	Hewitt(2T) Reed(T) Adams(T)
28		27	RICHMOND	H	Won	2	3	1	1	26	-	1	-	-	3	Buckingham(T) Slow(D) Gadney(T) Adams(T) G.N.Harris(T) Constantine(2C,P) C.S.Harris(T)
29	Feb	1	ROYAL AIR FORCE	H	Won	-	7	-	-	21	1	2	-	-	11	Jackson(T) Tindall(T) Sime(T) Slow(2T) Berry(T) G.N.Harris(T)
30		3	LONDON SCOTTISH	H	Lost	1	-	-	-	5	-	2	-	-	6	Crowe(C) Robinson(T)
31		10	Newport	A	Lost	-	1	-	-	3	3	-	-	-	15	Parker(T)
32		17	Gloucester	A	Lost	-	-	1	1	7	5	2	1	-	35	Crowe(P) Slow(D)
33		24	Northampton	A	Lost	1	-	-	1	8	1	1	-	2	14	Crowe(C,P) Adams(T)
34	Mar	3	HARLEQUINS	H	Won	1	1	1	1	15	-	-	-	-	0	Buckingham(T) Crowe(T,C,P) Slow(D)
35		10	GUY'S HOSPITAL	H	Won	2	3	-	-	19	-	-	-	-	0	Hewitt(3T) McLean(2C) Wormleighton(T) Robinson(T)
36		17	Bath	A	Lost	-	-	-	-	0	1	1	-	-	8	
37		24	COVENTRY	H	Lost	-	-	-	1	3	2	-	1	-	14	Crowe(P)
38		31	Bristol	A	Won	1	-	-	-	5	-	-	-	1	3	Crowe(T,C)
39	Apr	2	Plymouth Albion	A	Lost	-	2	1	-	10	1	2	-	-	11	McLean(T,D) G.N.Harris(T)
40		3	Exeter	A	Won	-	1	3	-	15	2	-	-	-	10	Barr(D) Jackson(T) Slow(2D)
41		7	Birkenhead Park	A	Won	2	1	-	-	13	1	-	-	-	5	Gray(T) Crowe(T,C) Hughes(T) Edmiston(C)
42		14	BLACKHEATH	H	Lost	1	2	-	-	11	1	3	-	-	14	Jackson(T) Crowe(C) Gadney(T) Adams(T)
43		21	OLD MERCHANT TAYLORS	H	Won	-	2	-	1	9	-	-	-	1	3	Hewitt(T) Crowe(P) Gadney(T)

INDIVIDUAL APPEARANCES 1933-1934

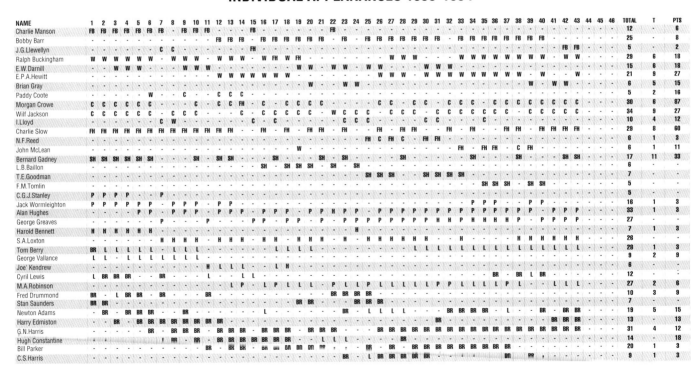

NAME	1	2	3	4	5	6	7	8	9	10	11	12	13	14	15	16	17	18	19	20	21	22	23	24	25	26	27	28	29	30	31	32	33	34	35	36	37	38	39	40	41	42	43	44	45	46	TOTAL	T	PTS
Charlie Manson	FB	FB	FB	FB	FB	FB	FB	-	FB	FB	FB	-	-	-	FB	-	-	-	-	-	-	FB	-	-	-	-	-	-	-	-	-	-	-	-	-	-	-	-	-	-	-	-	-	-	-	-	12	-	6
Bobby Barr	-	-	-	-	-	-	-	-	-	-	-	FB	FB	FB	-	FB	FB	FB	FB	FB	FB	-	FB	-	FB	FB	FB	FB	FB	FB	FB	-	FB	FB	FB	FB	FB	FB	FB	FB	-	-	-	-	-	-	25	-	8
J.G.Llewellyn	-	-	-	-	-	-	C	C	-	-	-	-	-	-	FH	-	-	-	-	-	-	-	-	-	-	-	-	-	-	-	-	-	-	-	-	-	-	-	-	-	-	FB	FB	-	-	-	5	-	2
Ralph Buckingham	W	W	W	W	W	W	-	W	W	W	-	W	W	W	-	W	FH	W	FH	-	-	-	-	-	-	-	W	W	W	-	-	-	W	W	W	W	W	W	W	W	-	W	W	-	-	-	29	6	18
E.W.Darnill	-	-	W	W	W	-	-	-	W	W	W	-	-	-	-	-	-	-	W	W	-	W	W	-	W	W	-	-	-	W	W	W	-	-	-	-	-	-	-	-	-	-	-	-	-	-	15	6	18
E.P.A.Hewitt	-	-	-	-	-	-	-	-	-	-	-	W	W	W	W	W	W	W	-	-	-	-	-	-	-	W	W	W	-	W	W	W	W	W	W	W	W	W	-	W	-	-	W	-	-	-	21	9	27
Brian Gray	-	-	-	-	-	-	-	-	-	-	-	-	-	-	-	-	-	-	-	W	-	-	W	W	-	-	-	-	-	-	-	-	-	-	-	-	-	-	W	-	W	W	-	-	-	-	6	5	15
Paddy Coote	-	-	-	-	-	W	-	-	C	-	-	C	C	C	-	-	-	-	-	-	-	-	-	-	-	-	-	-	-	-	-	-	-	-	-	-	-	-	-	-	-	-	-	-	-	-	5	2	16
Morgan Crowe	C	C	C	C	C	C	-	-	-	C	-	C	C	FH	-	C	-	C	C	C	C	-	-	-	-	C	C	-	C	C	-	C	C	C	-	C	C	C	C	C	C	C	C	-	-	-	30	6	87
Wilf Jackson	C	C	C	C	C	C	-	C	C	C	-	-	-	C	-	C	C	C	C	C	-	W	C	C	C	-	C	C	C	-	C	C	C	C	C	C	C	-	C	C	C	C	C	-	-	-	34	9	27
I.Lloyd	-	-	-	-	-	-	C	W	-	-	-	-	-	-	C	-	C	-	-	-	-	-	C	C	C	-	-	-	-	C	C	-	-	-	C	-	-	-	-	-	-	-	-	-	-	-	10	4	12
Charlie Slow	FH	FH	FH	FH	FH	FH	FH	FH	FH	FH	FH	FH	FH	-	-	FH	-	FH	-	FH	FH	-	FH	-	-	FH	-	FH	FH	-	-	FH	-	FH	-	-	FH	FH	-	FH	FH	FH	FH	-	-	-	29	8	60
N.F.Reed	-	-	-	-	-	-	-	-	-	-	-	-	-	-	-	-	-	-	-	-	-	-	-	-	FH	C	FH	C	-	FH	FH	-	-	-	-	-	-	-	-	-	-	-	-	-	-	-	6	1	3
John McLean	-	-	-	-	-	-	-	-	-	-	-	-	-	-	-	-	-	-	W	-	-	-	-	-	-	-	-	-	-	-	-	-	FH	-	FH	FH	-	C	FH	-	-	-	-	-	-	-	6	1	11
Bernard Gadney	SH	SH	SH	SH	SH	SH	-	-	-	SH	-	SH	SH	-	-	-	SH	-	-	-	SH	-	SH	-	-	-	-	SH	-	-	-	-	-	SH	-	-	-	SH	-	-	-	SH	SH	-	-	-	17	11	33
L.B.Baillon	-	-	-	-	-	-	-	-	-	-	-	-	-	-	-	SH	-	SH	SH	SH	-	SH	-	SH	-	-	-	-	-	-	-	-	-	-	-	-	-	-	-	-	-	-	-	-	-	-	6	-	-
T.E.Goodman	-	-	-	-	-	-	-	-	-	-	-	-	-	-	-	-	-	-	-	-	-	-	-	-	SH	SH	SH	-	-	SH	SH	SH	SH	-	-	-	-	-	-	-	-	-	-	-	-	-	7	-	-
F.M.Tomlin	-	-	-	-	-	-	-	-	-	-	-	-	-	-	-	-	-	-	-	-	-	-	-	-	-	-	-	-	-	-	-	-	-	-	SH	SH	SH	-	SH	SH	-	-	-	-	-	-	5	-	-
C.G.J.Stanley	P	P	P	P	-	-	P	-	-	-	-	-	-	-	-	-	-	-	-	-	-	-	-	-	-	-	-	-	-	-	-	-	-	-	-	-	-	-	-	-	-	-	-	-	-	-	5	-	-
Jack Wormleighton	P	P	P	P	P	P	-	P	P	P	-	P	P	-	-	-	-	-	-	-	-	-	-	-	-	-	-	-	-	-	-	-	-	P	P	P	-	-	P	P	-	-	-	-	-	-	16	1	3
Alan Hughes	-	-	-	-	P	P	-	P	P	P	-	P	P	P	-	P	P	P	-	P	P	H	P	P	-	P	P	P	P	P	P	P	P	P	P	P	P	P	P	-	P	P	P	-	-	-	33	1	3
George Greaves	-	-	-	-	-	-	P	-	-	-	P	-	-	-	P	P	-	P	P	-	P	-	P	P	P	P	P	P	P	P	H	H	P	H	H	H	H	P	-	P	P	P	P	-	-	-	27	-	-
Harold Bennett	H	H	H	H	H	H	-	-	-	-	-	-	-	-	-	-	-	-	-	-	-	-	-	H	-	-	-	-	-	-	-	-	-	-	-	-	-	-	-	-	-	-	-	-	-	-	7	1	3
S.A.Loxton	-	-	-	-	-	-	H	H	H	H	-	H	H	H	-	H	H	-	H	H	H	-	H	-	H	H	H	H	H	H	-	-	H	-	-	-	-	H	H	H	H	H	H	-	-	-	26	-	-
Tom Berry	BR	L	L	L	L	L	-	L	L	L	-	-	-	-	-	-	L	L	L	L	-	-	-	-	-	-	-	-	L	L	L	L	L	L	L	L	L	L	L	L	L	L	L	-	-	-	28	1	3
George Vallance	L	L	-	L	L	L	L	L	L	L	-	-	-	-	-	-	-	-	-	-	-	-	-	-	-	-	-	-	-	-	-	-	-	-	-	-	-	-	-	-	-	-	-	-	-	-	9	2	9
Joe' Kendrew	-	-	-	-	-	-	-	-	-	-	H	L	L	L	-	-	L	H	-	-	-	-	-	-	-	-	-	-	-	-	-	-	-	-	-	-	-	-	-	-	-	-	-	-	-	-	6	-	-
Cyril Lewis	L	BR	BR	BR	-	-	BR	-	-	-	L	-	-	L	L	-	-	-	-	-	-	-	-	-	-	-	-	-	-	-	-	-	-	-	-	BR	-	BR	L	BR	-	-	-	-	-	-	12	-	-
M.A.Robinson	-	-	-	-	-	-	-	-	-	-	-	-	L	P	-	L	P	L	L	L	-	P	L	L	P	L	L	L	L	L	P	P	L	L	L	L	P	L	-	-	L	L	L	-	-	-	27	2	6
Fred Drummond	BR	-	L	BR	BR	-	BR	-	-	-	BR	-	-	-	-	-	-	-	-	-	-	BR	BR	BR	BR	-	-	-	-	-	-	-	-	-	-	-	-	-	-	-	-	-	-	-	-	-	10	3	9
Stan Saunders	BR	BR	-	-	-	-	-	-	-	-	-	-	-	-	-	-	-	-	BR	BR	-	-	-	BR	BR	BR	-	-	-	-	-	-	-	-	-	-	-	-	-	-	-	-	-	-	-	-	7	-	-
Newton Adams	-	BR	-	BR	BR	BR	-	-	BR	-	-	-	-	-	-	L	-	-	-	-	-	-	BR	-	L	L	L	L	-	-	-	BR	BR	BR	BR	-	L	-	-	BR	-	BR	BR	-	-	-	19	5	15
Harry Edmiston	-	-	BR	-	BR	BR	BR	BR	BR	BR	BR	BR	-	-	-	-	-	-	-	-	-	-	-	-	-	-	-	-	-	-	BR	-	-	-	-	-	-	-	-	-	BR	BR	BR	-	-	-	13	-	13
G.N.Harris	-	-	-	-	-	BR	-	BR	BR	BR	-	BR	BR	BR	-	BR	BR	BR	-	BR	BR	BR	-	-	-	BR	BR	BR	BR	BR	BR	BR	BR	BR	BR	BR	BR	BR	BR	BR	BR	BR	BR	-	-	-	31	4	12
Hugh Constantine	-	-	-	-	-	-	[illegible]	BR	-	BR	-	BR	BR	BR	BR	BR	BR	BR	-	-	L	L	L	-	-	-	-	BR	-	-	-	-	-	-	-	-	-	-	-	-	-	-	-	-	-	-	14	-	18
Bill Parker	-	-	-	-	-	-	-	-	-	-	BR	-	BR	BR	-	BR	BR	BR	BR	BR	BR	-	-	-	BR	-	BR	-	BR	BR	BR	BR	BR	BR	BR	BR	BR	-	-	-	-	-	-	-	-	-	20	1	3
C.S.Harris	-	-	-	-	-	-	-	-	-	-	-	-	-	-	-	-	-	-	-	-	-	-	BR	-	L	BR	BR	BR	BR	BR	-	-	-	-	-	-	BR	-	BR	-	-	-	-	-	-	-	9	1	3

4 games: Charles Beamish P(19,20)L(21,32), Frank Herbert W(7,11,15,25), Jack Hodgson BR(22,38,39)L(40), David Walker SH(9,11,14,15)
3 games: Jeff Hardwicke W(1,2,17)[3T-9], Norman Page FB(24,32,41)
2 games: H.G.Griffin L(11,15), Arnold Sime SH(8,29)[1T-3], Norman York L(12,24)
1 game: J.L.Barker SH(41), John Beattie L(22), Charles Bloxham BR(19), C.J.Byrne P(11), R.W.K.Clarke FH(24), T.I.Davies C(11), Bob Fallowell BR(21), R.Flint H(15), Ken Fyfe C(22)[4], Ron Gerrard C(21)[1T-3], Harry Greasley BR(24), John Harrison W(24), RE.Lauder FH(22), Graham Meikle W(21)[3T-13], Stephen Meikle W(21), Denis Morris W(41), O.Neal P(15), Roger Orchard C(11), 'Tuppy' Owen-Smith C(22), C.H.Pearse BR(3), W.H.Preston L(31), F.C.Scott BR(15), P.Sharpe BR(15), W.V.Shepherd W(7)[1T-3], A.F.Sibson C(15), K.A.Stanyon-Jacques SH(7), N.J.Tindall W(29)[1T-3], Noel Townsend BR(41), John Waters P(22), R.E.Wright FB(8)

LEICESTER FOOTBALL CLUB 1933-34
Back: W.N. Bradshaw (Hon.Tres), J.G. Llewelyn, G. Greaves, W.E. Parker, N. Adams, W.A. Jackson, G.N. Harris, J.E. Thorneloe (Hon.Sec).
Middle: C.F. Slow, J.T.W. Berry, B.C. Gadney, R.A. Buckingham (Capt), M.P. Crowe, J.H.F. Edmiston, A.P. Hughes.
Front: J.L. Wormleighton, S.A. Loxton, M.A. Robinson, E.P.A. Hewitt.

LEICESTER FOOTBALL CLUB 1934-35
Back: A.P. Hughes, W.A. Jackson, N. Adams, H.G. Greasley, J.McD. Hodgson, J.B. Charles, W.V. Shepherd, C.F. Slow, J.E. Thorneloe (Hon.Sec).
Middle: C.G.R. Lewis, M.P. Crowe, R.A. Buckingham, B.C. Gadney (Capt), R.J. Barr, J.T.W. Berry, G.P.C. Vallance.
Front: S.A. Loxton, J.L. Wormleighton, G.A. Delgado, M.A. Robinson.

NO	DATE		OPPONENTS	V	RES	FOR					AGAINST					SCORERS
						G	T	D	P	PTS	G	T	D	P	PTS	
1	Sep	1	BEDFORD	H	Won	-	1	2*	-	10	1	-	-	1	8	Jackson(T) Slow(D,M)
2		8	PENARTH	H	Won	4	7	-	-	41	-	-	-	-	0	Buckingham(2C) McLean(T) Shepherd(4T,C) Slow(T) Hughes(T) C.G.R.Lewis(C) Adams(3T) Drummond(T)
3		10	BRIDGEND	H	Won	1	1	-	-	8	-	1	-	-	3	Shepherd(T) Giles(C) Berry(T)
4		15	PLYMOUTH ALBION	H	Won	2	2	1	-	20	-	-	-	-	0	Buckingham(T) M.P.Crowe(2C) McLean(D) Loxton(T) Drummond(2T)
5		22	Bedford	A	Won	-	3	-	-	9	1	-	-	-	5	Jackson(T) Leyland(T) Gadney(T)
6		27	LLANELLI	H	Won	-	2	-	-	6	-	-	-	1	3	Palmer(T) Hardwicke(T)
7		29	WATERLOO	H	Won	2	5	1	-	29	1	-	-	-	5	Shepherd(3T) M.P.Crowe(T) Buckingham(2C) Hardwicke(T) McLean(D) Adams(T) Drummond(T)
8	Oct	6	COVENTRY	H	Won	2	-	-	-	10	-	1	-	-	3	M.P.Crowe(T,C) Meikle(T) McLean(T)
9		8	BECTIVE RANGERS	H	Won	1	1	-	1	11	-	2	-	-	6	M.P.Crowe(C) Shepherd(T) McLean(P) Gadney(T)
10		13	Bridgwater	A	Drew	-	-	-	-	0	-	-	-	-	0	
11		20	Newport	A	Lost	2	1	-	-	13	3	3	-	-	24	Shepherd(T) Buckingham(C) McLean(C) Adams(T) Fallowell(T)
12		27	Northampton	A	Lost	-	1	-	-	3	1	2	-	-	11	Buckingham(T)
13	Nov	3	MOSELEY	H	Won	-	2	-	1	9	1	1	-	-	8	Morris(T) C.G.R.Lewis(P) Oakes(T)
14		7	Oxford University	A	Won	1	1	-	1	11	-	-	-	-	0	Buckingham(C,P) Leyland(T) Jackson(T)
15		10	Cambridge University	A	Lost	-	-	1	-	4	3	2	-	1	24	Slow(D)
16		17	Rugby	A	Won	1	1	-	-	8	-	2	-	-	6	Meikle(T) Slow(T) Kendrew(C)
17		24	NUNEATON	H	Lost	-	3	-	-	9	-	2	1	-	10	C.C.Barker(T) Meikle(T) Pearse(T)
18	Dec	1	Harlequins	A	Lost	-	-	1	-	4	2	-	-	-	10	J.L.Barker(D)
19		8	Blackheath	A	Won	2	-	-	1	13	-	1	-	1	6	Buckingham(2C,P) Adams(2T)
20		15	BRISTOL	H	Won	1	-	1	1	12	1	1	-	-	8	Shepherd(T) Buckingham(C,P) Slow(D)
21		22	LONDON WELSH	H	Won	-	-	2	-	8	-	-	-	-	0	C.C.Barker(D) Fox(D)
22		26	BIRKENHEAD PARK	H	Lost	1	1	-	-	8	1	1	1	-	12	Buckingham(C) Obolensky(2T)
23		27	BARBARIANS	H	Lost	1	-	-	-	5	-	2	-	-	6	Buckingham(C) Berry(T)
24		28	MANCHESTER	H	Won	-	1	-	-	3	-	-	-	-	0	Drummond(T)
25		29	GLOUCESTER	H	Won	3	4	-	-	27	-	-	-	-	0	Buckingham(3C) Shepherd(T) Jackson(2T) Kaye(T) Gadney(2T) Vallance(T)
26	Jan	5	SWANSEA	A	Lost	-	1	-	-	3	1	-	-	-	5	Adams(T)
27		12	OLD MERCHANT TAYLORS	H	Won	1	4	-	-	17	-	-	-	-	0	Fox(T) Buckingham(T,C) McLean(T) Vallance(T) Adams(T)
28		19	Bath	A	Lost	-	-	-	-	0	-	4	-	-	12	
29		24	ROYAL AIR FORCE	H	Lost	-	-	-	-	0	-	-	1	-	4	
30		26	Richmond	A	Won	1	2	-	-	11	-	-	1	-	4	Fox(T) Buckingham(C) Morris(T) Greasley(T)
31	Feb	2	London Scottish	A	Won	1	-	1	-	9	-	1	-	-	3	Buckingham(C) Slow(D) Adams(T)
32		9	NEWPORT	H	Drew	-	-	-	-	0	-	-	-	-	0	
33		16	Swansea	A	Lost	-	-	-	-	0	-	-	-	1	3	
34		23	NORTHAMPTON	H	Won	2	1	-	-	13	1	1	-	-	8	Buckingham(2C) Shepherd(2T) Auty(T)
35	Mar	2	HARLEQUINS	H	Drew	1	-	-	-	5	1	-	-	-	5	Buckingham(C) Vallance(T)
36		9	Coventry	A	Lost	-	-	-	-	0	1	2	-	-	11	
37		16	ROSSLYN PARK	H	Won	4	-	-	-	20	2	-	-	-	10	Buckingham(4C) Charles(T) L.B.Baillon(T) M.A.Robinson(T) Greasley(T)
38		23	Gloucester	A	Lost	-	-	-	-	0	3	3	2	-	32	
39		30	BATH	A	Won	1	2	-	-	11	-	1	-	1	6	Buckingham(C) Charles(2T) Vallance(T)
40	Apr	6	Birkenhead Park	A	Won	3	2	-	1	24	-	1	-	-	6	Buckingham(T,3C,P) Charles(3T) Gadney(T)
41		13	BLACKHEATH	H	Won	6	3	-	-	39	1	1	-	-	8	Delgado(T) Buckingham(T,6C) M.P.Crowe(T) Charles(T) Slow(2T) Gadney(T) Loxton(T) Wormleighton(T)
42		20	Bristol	A	Lost	-	2	-	-	6	1	2	-	-	11	P.M.Crowe(T) Obolensky(T)
43		22	Plymouth Albion	A	Drew	-	1	-	-	3	-	1	-	-	3	Obolensky(T)
44		23	Exeter	A	Won	6	4	-	-	42	-	-	-	-	0	Buckingham(3C) M.P.Crowe(T,C) Walker(3T) Delgado(2T) Slow(T,C) Gadney(3T) Hodgson(C)

INDIVIDUAL APPEARANCES 1934-1935

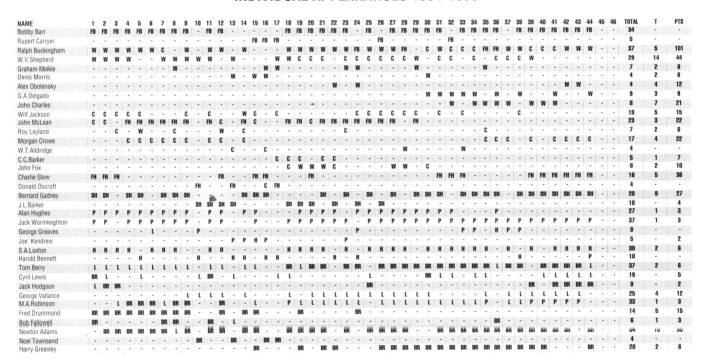

3 games: Charles Beamish BR(18,20,25), J.S.W.Bignall P(10,13,16), Phil Crowe C(40,42,43)[1T-3], H.J.F.Le Good C(10,13)W(15), C.St C.Oakes BR(13,16)L(17)[1T-3], C.H.Pearse L(4)BR(16,17)[1T-3], N.E.Starkey BR(10,13,17)
2 games: Dick Auty FH(30,34)[1T-3], L.B.Baillon FH(37,38)[1T-3], Eric Bevins SH(32,37), G.E.Fowler BR(24,29), Jeff Hardwicke W(6,7)[2T-6], W.Phillips L(33,36), J.P.Reidy BR(22,23)
1 game: W.N.Ash P(17), R.O.Baillon FB(14), Jack Ball SH(17), Spencer Bevan FB(10), T.W.Bevan FB(13), J.D.Burrows FB(37), E.R.Coutts-Deacon BR(43), K.Cummings W(26), Phil Dunkley BR(22), Harry Edmiston BR(10), Denis Evers SH(28), R.H.Francks C(10), Jimmy Giles SH(3)[2], F.E.Harris L(39), J.Kaye W(25)[1T-3], J.T.Kenney P(17), D.W.Lewis SH(6), Austin Matthews BR(14), C.L.Millar H(40), O.Neal L(16), R.A.Palmer C(6)[1T-3], G.E.Pollard W(40), J.R.H.Potts C(29), B.V.Robinson W(10), H.B.Toft H(29), S.G.Walker C(44)[3T-9], P.A.Warner L(16), A.A.Wyman H(9), Norman York P(3)

NO	DATE		OPPONENTS	V	RES	FOR G	FOR T	FOR D	FOR P	FOR PTS	AGAINST G	AGAINST T	AGAINST D	AGAINST P	AGAINST PTS	SCORERS
1	Sep	7	BEDFORD	H	Won	4	1	1	1	30	1	2	-	-	11	Charles(2T) Smith(4C,P) Obolensky(T) Slow(D) Gadney(T) Vallance(T)
2		14	PENARTH	H	Won	4	5	-	1	38	-	-	-	-	0	Charles(T) Fox(T) Smith(4C,P) Obolensky(T) Slow(T) Vallance(2T) Adams(T) Beamish(2T)
3		21	PLYMOUTH ALBION	H	Won	-	3	1	-	13	-	1	-	-	3	Shepherd(3T) Slow(D)
4		28	WATERLOO	H	Won	2	1	1	3	26	1	-	1	-	9	Barr(D) Obolensky(T) Shepherd(T) Slow(T) Hodgson(2C,3P)
5	Oct	5	Coventry	A	Lost	1	-	-	2	11	-	3	-	1	12	Obolensky(T) Hodgson(C,2P)
6		12	BRIDGWATER	H	Lost	2	-	-	-	10	-	3	2	-	17	Shepherd(T) Hodgson(2C) Townsend(T)
7		19	NEWPORT	H	Lost	-	1	-	-	3	-	1	1	-	7	Charles(T)
8		26	NORTHAMPTON	H	Won	-	2	2	-	14	-	-	-	-	0	Fox(D) Shepherd(T) Slow(D) Berry(T)
9	Nov	2	Moseley	A	Won	3	-	-	-	15	-	-	-	1	3	Shepherd(T) Morgan(T) Slow(3C) Willcox(T)
10		9	CAMBRIDGE UNIVERSITY	H	Lost	-	2	-	1	9	3	2	-	-	21	Charles(T) Shepherd(T,P)
11		14	OXFORD UNIVERSITY	H	Lost	-	-	1	-	4	2	2	-	-	16	Fox(D)
12		23	Nuneaton	A	Won	1	-	-	-	5	-	-	-	1	3	Shepherd(T) Hodgson(C)
13		30	BRISTOL	H	Lost	-	1	-	-	3	2	1	-	-	13	Gadney(T)
14	Dec	7	Harlequins	A	Lost	1	-	-	-	5	1	2	-	-	11	Willcox(T) Hodgson(C)
15		14	Blackheath	A	Lost	1	-	-	-	5	-	2	-	-	6	Shepherd(T) Kendrew(C)
		21	Bedford	A		Cancelled Frost										
16		26	BIRKENHEAD PARK	H	Won	-	1	1	1	10	-	1	1	-	7	Barr(P) Slow(D) Adams(T)
17		27	BARBARIANS	H	Drew	-	-	-	-	0	-	-	-	-	0	
18		28	ROSSLYN PARK	H	Drew	-	-	-	-	0	-	-	-	-	0	
19	Jan	1	Manchester	A	Lost	1	-	-	-	5	-	2	-	-	6	Auty(T) Hodgson(C)
20		4	SWANSEA	H	Won	-	1	-	1	6	1	-	-	-	5	Morgan(T) Hodgson(P)
21		11	GLOUCESTER	H	Lost	-	1	-	1	6	2	2	-	-	16	Hopkin(T) Hodgson(P)
22		18	Bath	A	Lost	-	-	-	-	0	1	3	-	-	14	
		25	RICHMOND	H		Cancelled King died										
23		30	ROYAL AIR FORCE	H	Won	1	-	-	-	5	-	1	-	-	3	Fox(T) Hodgson(C)
24	Feb	1	LONDON SCOTTISH	H	Drew	-	1	-	-	3	-	1	-	-	3	Gadney(T)
25		8	Newport	A	Lost	-	-	-	-	0	2	1	1	1	20	
26		15	Swansea	A	Lost	-	-	-	-	0	1	4	1	1	24	
27		22	Northampton	A	Lost	-	-	-	-	0	-	2	-	-	6	
28		29	OLD MERCHANT TAYLORS	H	Won	-	1	-	1	6	-	1	-	-	3	Bottrill(T) York(P)
29	Mar	7	HARLEQUINS	H	Lost	1	2	-	-	11	1	3	-	-	14	Meikle(T) Bottrill(2T) Hodgson(C)
30		14	Gloucester	A	Lost	-	-	1	1	7	3	1	-	1	21	L.B.Baillon(D) York(P)
31		21	BATH	H	Won	1	-	-	-	5	-	-	-	-	0	Hodgson(C) Willcox(T)
32		28	COVENTRY	H	Lost	1	-	-	1	8	2	3	-	-	19	Slow(T) York(C,P)
33	Apr	2	Bedford	A	Won	-	-	1	1	7	-	2	-	-	6	Slow(D) Hodgson(P)
34		4	Birkenhead Park	A	Lost	-	1	-	-	3	2	-	-	-	10	Charles(T)
35		11	Bristol	A	Lost	-	1	1*	-	6	2	1	-	-	13	York(M) Willcox(T)
36		13	Plymouth Albion	A	Lost	1	1	-	-	8	-	3	-	-	9	Gadney(T) Vallance(T) Hodgson(C)
37		14	Exeter	A	Won	3	3	-	-	24	-	3	-	1	12	Charles(3T) Bottrill(T) Slow(T) G.B.Herbert(2C) Hodgson(C) Adams(T)
38		18	BLACKHEATH	H	Won	1	1	1	1	15	-	2	-	-	6	Slow(T,D) York(C,P) Willcox(T)
39		25	COMBINED LOCAL XV	H	Won	-	2	1	1	13	-	1	-	-	3	Fox(T) Adams(T) Hodgson(P) Hopkin(D)

INDIVIDUAL APPEARANCES 1935-1936

NAME	1	2	3	4	5	6	7	8	9	10	11	12	13	14	15	16	17	18	19	20	21	22	23	24	25	26	27	28	29	30	31	32	33	34	35	36	37	38	39	40	41	42	43	44	45	46	TOTAL	T	PTS
Bobby Barr	FB	FB	FB	FB	FB	-	FB	FB	FB	FB	-	-	FB	FB	FB	FB	FB	FB	FB	-	FB	FB	FB	FB	FB	FB	FB	FB	FB	FB	FB	FB	FB	FB	FB	FB	-	-	-	-	-	-	-	-	-	-	32	-	7
John Charles	W	W	W	-	-	-	W	W	W	W	-	-	FH	-	W	-	-	-	-	-	-	-	-	W	C	-	C	W	W	-	W	W	-	W	-	W	W	-	-	-	-	-	-	-	-	-	19	9	27
Alex Obolensky	W	W	-	W	W	-	-	-	-	-	-	-	-	-	-	-	W	-	-	-	-	-	-	-	-	-	-	-	-	-	-	-	-	-	-	-	-	-	-	-	-	-	-	-	-	-	5	4	12
W.V.Shepherd	-	-	W	W	-	W	W	W	C	C	W	C	W	W	W	W	W	W	-	W	W	W	-	-	-	-	W	-	-	-	-	-	-	-	-	-	-	-	-	-	-	-	-	-	-	-	19	10	33
Graham Meikle	-	-	-	-	W	-	-	-	-	-	-	-	-	-	-	-	-	C	-	-	-	-	-	-	-	-	-	-	C	-	-	-	-	-	-	-	-	-	-	-	-	-	-	-	-	-	3	1	3
W.R.Morgan	-	-	-	-	-	-	-	-	W	W	-	W	W	W	-	-	-	-	-	W	-	-	W	W	W	-	-	-	-	-	-	-	-	-	-	-	-	-	-	-	-	-	-	-	-	-	9	2	6
W.T.Alldridge	-	-	-	-	-	-	-	-	-	-	-	-	-	-	-	-	-	-	W	-	-	-	-	-	-	-	-	-	-	W	-	-	-	C	-	-	-	-	-	-	-	-	-	-	-	-	3	-	-
Guy Toone	-	-	-	-	-	-	-	-	-	-	-	-	-	-	-	-	-	-	-	-	-	-	-	-	W	W	-	-	-	W	-	-	W	-	-	-	-	-	-	-	-	-	-	-	-	-	4	-	-
Bill Bottrill	-	-	-	-	-	-	-	-	-	-	-	-	-	-	-	-	-	-	-	-	-	-	-	-	-	W	W	W	W	-	W	W	-	W	W	W	W	-	-	-	-	-	-	-	-	-	10	4	12
John Fox	C	C	C	-	-	-	C	C	C	C	C	-	C	-	-	W	-	-	-	C	-	W	W	C	-	-	-	C	-	-	-	-	-	-	W	-	C	-	-	-	-	-	-	-	-	-	17	2	14
Walter Smith	C	C	C	-	-	-	-	-	-	-	-	-	-	-	C	-	-	-	-	-	-	-	-	-	-	-	-	-	-	-	-	-	-	-	-	-	-	-	-	-	-	-	-	-	-	-	4	-	22
Ronnie Gerrard	-	-	-	C	C	-	C	C	-	-	-	-	-	-	-	-	-	-	-	-	-	C	-	C	C	C	-	-	-	-	-	-	-	-	-	-	-	-	-	-	-	-	-	-	-	-	8	-	-
S.G.Walker	-	-	-	C	C	-	-	-	-	-	-	C	C	FH	-	-	-	-	-	-	-	C	-	-	-	-	-	-	-	FH	-	-	-	-	-	-	-	-	-	-	-	-	-	-	-	-	7	-	-
G.E.Goode	-	-	-	-	-	-	-	-	-	-	-	-	-	-	-	-	-	-	-	-	-	-	-	-	-	-	-	C	C	C	C	C	-	C	C	-	-	C	-	-	-	-	-	-	-	-	8	-	-
Charlie Slow	FH	FH	FH	FH	FH	FH	FH	FH	FH	FH	-	-	-	-	-	FH	C	FH	C	FH	-	FH	-	FH	FH	FH	FH	-	-	-	FH	C	C	-	C	-	FH	FH	-	-	-	-	-	-	-	-	26	5	45
J.D.Anderson	-	-	-	-	-	-	-	-	-	-	-	FH	-	-	-	-	-	C	W	-	-	-	-	-	-	-	-	-	-	-	-	-	-	-	-	-	-	-	-	-	-	-	-	-	-	-	3	-	-
A.V.Rogers	-	-	-	-	-	-	-	-	-	-	-	-	-	-	FH	C	-	-	-	C	C	-	-	-	-	C	C	FH	FH	-	C	FH	FH	FH	FH	FH	FB	-	-	-	-	-	-	-	-	-	15	-	-
Dick Auty	-	-	-	-	-	-	-	-	-	-	-	-	-	-	-	-	FH	-	FH	-	-	-	FH	-	-	-	-	-	-	-	-	-	-	-	-	-	-	-	-	-	-	-	-	-	-	-	3	1	3
Bernard Gadney	SH	SH	SH	SH	SH	-	SH	SH	-	SH	-	-	SH	-	-	-	SH	-	-	-	-	-	-	SH	-	-	SH	-	SH	-	-	SH	-	SH	SH	C	-	-	-	-	-	-	-	-	-	-	17	4	12
Jim Parsons	-	-	-	-	-	-	-	-	-	-	-	-	-	-	-	SH	-	-	-	SH	-	SH	-	-	SH	SH	-	SH	-	SH	SH	-	SH	-	-	SH	SH	SH	-	-	-	-	-	-	-	-	12	-	-
E.Williams	-	-	-	-	-	-	-	-	-	-	-	-	-	-	-	-	-	SH	SH	-	-	-	SH	-	-	-	-	-	-	-	-	-	-	-	-	-	-	-	-	-	-	-	-	-	-	-	3	-	-
M.A.Robinson	P	P	P	P	L	-	L	P	L	L	-	L	L	P	L	L	L	L	L	P	-	H	P	H	H	H	H	H	H	H	H	H	P	H	P	-	P	L	-	-	-	-	-	-	-	-	34	-	-
Jack Wormleighton	P	P	P	P	P	-	P	-	P	L	P	P	P	-	P	P	P	P	-	P	P	P	P	P	P	-	P	P	P	P	P	P	-	-	-	-	-	-	-	-	-	-	-	-	-	-	27	-	-
George Greaves	-	-	-	-	-	P	-	P	P	P	-	-	P	P	-	P	P	-	P	-	-	-	-	-	-	-	-	-	-	P	-	-	-	P	-	P	P	P	-	-	-	-	-	-	-	-	14	-	-
Geoff Herbert	-	-	-	-	-	P	-	-	-	-	-	-	-	-	-	-	-	-	P	-	-	L	-	L	L	P	L	L	L	-	-	-	-	-	-	-	L	-	-	-	-	-	-	-	-	-	10	-	4
Joe' Kendrew	-	-	-	-	-	-	-	-	-	-	-	P	-	-	P	-	-	P	-	-	-	-	-	-	-	-	-	-	-	-	-	-	-	-	H	H	H	H	-	-	-	-	-	-	-	-	7	-	2
Norman York	-	-	-	-	-	-	-	-	-	-	-	-	-	-	-	-	-	-	-	-	-	P	-	P	P	P	P	P	P	L	P	P	P	P	P	P	-	P	-	-	-	-	-	-	-	-	15	-	19
S.A.Loxton	H	H	H	H	P	-	P	-	-	P	-	H	H	H	H	L	-	H	-	H	-	-	-	-	-	-	-	-	-	-	-	-	-	-	-	-	-	-	-	-	-	-	-	-	-	-	14	-	-
Edward Nicholson	-	-	-	-	H	H	H	H	H	H	-	-	-	-	-	-	H	-	-	-	H	-	-	-	-	-	-	-	-	-	-	-	-	-	-	-	-	-	-	-	-	-	-	-	-	-	8	-	-
George Ridgway	-	-	-	-	-	-	-	-	-	-	-	-	-	-	-	H	-	-	-	-	-	-	H	-	-	-	-	-	-	-	-	-	H	-	-	-	-	-	-	-	-	-	-	-	-	-	3	-	-
Cyril Lewis	L	-	-	-	-	-	-	L	-	-	-	-	-	L	L	-	-	-	-	-	-	-	-	-	-	-	-	-	-	-	-	-	-	-	-	-	-	-	-	-	-	-	-	-	-	-	4	-	-
George Vallance	L	L	-	L	-	L	L	L	-	-	L	-	-	L	-	-	-	-	-	-	L	L	L	-	-	-	-	-	-	L	L	L	L	L	L	L	-	L	-	-	-	-	-	-	-	-	19	4	12
Tom Berry	-	-	L	L	L	-	BR	BR	BR	BR	BR	BR	L	BR	BR	BR	L	BR	BR	BR	BR	-	L	L	L	L	L	L	L	BR	L	L	BR	-	L	L	L	BR	-	-	-	-	-	-	-	-	33	1	3
Newton Adams	BR	BR	BR	BR	BR	-	BR	BR	-	-	-	BR	BR	-	BR	BR	BR	L	-	L	BR	BR	BR	BR	BR	L	BR	BR	BR	-	-	BR	-	L	BR	BR	BR	-	-	-	-	-	-	-	-	-	28	3	9
Charles Beamish	BR	BR	-	BR	BR	-	-	-	-	BR	-	L	-	-	-	BR	-	-	-	-	L	-	-	BR	-	-	-	-	-	-	-	-	-	-	-	-	-	-	-	-	-	-	-	-	-	-	9	2	6
Jack Hodgson	BR	BR	BR	BR	BR	BR	BR	-	-	-	BR	BR	-	BR	-	-	BR	BR	BR	BR	BR	-	BR	-	-	BR	-	-	BR	-	BR	-	BR	BR	BR	BR	BR	-	-	-	-	-	-	-	-	-	24	-	50
John Hopkin	-	-	-	-	-	-	-	-	BR	-	-	-	-	-	-	-	-	-	-	L	P	BR	-	BR	BR	BR	BR	BR	-	BR	BR	-	-	BR	-	-	-	BR	-	-	-	-	-	-	-	-	13	1	3
Rodney Willcox	-	-	-	-	-	-	-	-	BR	BR	BR	-	BR	BR	-	-	-	BR	BR	BR	-	BR	BR	-	BR	BR	BR	BR	BR	BR	BR	BR	BR	BR	BR	BR	BR	BR	-	-	-	-	-	-	-	-	24	5	15

2 games: L.B.Baillon C(14,30)[4], Jack Ball SH(9,12), T.W.Bevan FB(12,38), Phil Crowe C(36,37), R.H.Francks C(6)W(38), H.C.Harrison C(6,21), E.A.Jack L(2,3), Wilf Jackson C(23)W(33), Roger Orchard C(16,19), I.Shaw FB(6,20), Arnold Sime SH(11,15)
1 game: T.Arundell FH(21), R.O.Baillon FB(11), Harold Bennett H(19), Owen Bevan P(11), W.J.Bird H(11), R.B.Black L(6), Sid Bowers SH(6), Maurice Bullus BR(17), M.A.Crosby W(11), E.W.Darnill W(12), Fred Drummond BR(3), E.W.Evans-Evans L(11), James ForrestW(18), Jimmy Giles SH(21), Harry Greasley BR(8), D.L.Grieves C(38), E.R.Haddon L(19), G.A.Harris W(21), Frank Herbert W(6), Tom Huskisson L(33), Harry Kenyon C(11), W.E.Kyle W(38), D.W.Lewis SH(14), Roy Leyland C(17), D.A.Lindsay L(9), M.D.Milman C(23), Bill Parker BR(6), C.H.Pearse BR(13), J.S.Peebles C(14), A.C.Potter C(33), J.G.Rogers C(15), Noel Townsend BR(6)[1T-3], Reg Vine BR(32), G.F.Williams FH(11), C.H.Williams BR(15)

LEICESTER FOOTBALL CLUB 1935-36
Back: B.W. Tolton (Referee), R.J. Barr, N.A. York, T.W. Bevan, G.E. Goode, J. Hopkin, R.J. Willcox, W.N. Bradshaw (Hon.Tres).
Middle: A.V. Rogers, N. Adams, M.A. Robinson, J.T.W. Berry, B.C. Gadney (Capt), J.McD. Hodgson, G.P.C. Vallance, J.B. Charles, J.B.S. Fox.
Front: W.J.H. Bottrill, J. Parsons.

LEICESTER FOOTBALL CLUB 1936-37
Back: J.E. Thorneloe (Hon.Sec), W.J.H. Bottrill, J.R. Preston, P.C. Crick, A. Obolensky, W. Bainbridge, R.J. Willcox, T.G. Ridgway, J.G. Grahame (Jt.Hon.Tres), W.N. Bradshaw (Jt.Hon.Tres).
Middle: A.V. Rogers, J.L. Wormleighton, N. Adams, R.J. Barr (Capt), J.T.W. Berry, G.P.C. Vallance, J. Parsons.
Front: R.A. Squibbs, W.G. Moseby, J.R. Sharp, K.H. Cooke.

NO	DATE		OPPONENTS	V	RES	FOR G	FOR T	FOR D	FOR P	FOR PTS	AGAINST G	AGAINST T	AGAINST D	AGAINST P	AGAINST PTS	SCORERS
1	Sep	5	BEDFORD	H	Lost	-	3	-	1	12	1	3	1	-	18	Charles(T) Gerrard(T) Willcox(T) York(P)
2		12	WATERLOO	H	Won	2	-	-	1	13	-	2	-	-	6	York(2C,P) Vallance(T) Adams(T)
3		19	PLYMOUTH ALBION	H	Won	4	-	-	-	20	1	-	-	-	5	Gerrard(2T) Bottrill(T) Parsons(T) York(4C)
4		26	NORTHAMPTON	H	Won	2	3	-	1	22	-	-	-	1	3	Barr(C) Bottrill(T) Slow(2T) Parsons(T) York(C,P) Adams(T)
5	Oct	3	Coventry	A	Lost	-	-	-	1	3	1	4	-	-	17	York(P)
6		10	HEADINGLEY	H	Drew	1	-	-	1	8	1	1	-	-	8	York(T,C,P)
7		17	Newport	A	Drew	3	1	-	-	18	-	6	-	-	18	Parsons(T) Meikle(T) Bottrill(T) York(3C) Adams(T)
8		24	Northampton	A	Lost	-	1	-	-	3	-	3	-	1	12	Parsons(T)
9		31	OLD MERCHANT TAYLORS	H	Won	-	5	1	1	22	-	1	-	-	3	Mackay(T) Meikle(2T) Taylor(D) Wormleighton(T) York(T,P)
10	Nov	4	Oxford University	A	Won	2	1	-	1	16	-	3	1	-	13	Bottrill(T) Gadney(2T) York(2C,P)
11		7	GLOUCESTER	H	Won	-	1	1	-	7	-	1	-	-	3	Barr(D) Parsons(T)
12		14	Cambridge University	A	Lost	-	2	-	-	6	1	1	-	-	8	Meikle(2T)
13		21	NUNEATON	H	Won	3	4	-	-	27	-	-	-	1	3	Meikle(3T) Taylor(T) Bottrill(2T) Gadney(T) York(3C)
14		28	BATH	H	Won	-	1	2	-	11	-	-	-	-	0	Barr(D) Meikle(D) Allen(T)
15	Dec	5	Harlequins	A	Lost	1	-	-	-	5	3	2	-	1	24	MacLeod(T) York(C)
16		12	Blackheath	A	Lost	1	1	1	-	12	2	1	-	-	13	Slow(T,D) York(C) Vallance(T)
17		19	Bedford	A	Lost	-	-	-	1	3	1	1	-	-	8	York(P)
18		26	BIRKENHEAD PARK	H	Lost	-	-	-	-	0	1	1	-	-	8	
19		28	BARBARIANS	H	Lost	1	-	-	-	5	4	-	-	-	20	York(C) Adams(T)
20		29	MANCHESTER	H	Won	-	1	-	2	9	-	2	-	-	6	Leyland(T) York(2P)
21	Jan	2	Swansea	A	Lost	-	1	-	-	3	-	2	1	-	10	Preston(T)
22		9	Gloucester	A	Lost	1	1	1	-	12	1	3	-	-	14	Preston(T) Taylor(T,D) York(C)
23		16	MOSELEY	H	Won	-	1	-	-	3	-	-	-	-	0	Preston(T)
24		23	Richmond	A	Won	1	1	1	-	12	1	1	-	1	11	Taylor(C) Slow(T,D) Berry(T)
25		28	ROYAL AIR FORCE	H	Lost	-	-	1	-	4	2	2	-	-	16	Taylor(D)
26		30	COVENTRY	H	Lost	-	1	-	-	3	1	1	1	-	12	Taylor(T)
27	Feb	6	London Scottish	A	Lost	-	-	-	-	0	2	2	-	-	16	
28		13	NEWPORT	H	Lost	-	-	-	-	0	2	4	-	-	22	
29		20	SWANSEA	H	Lost	1	-	-	-	5	2	2	1	1	23	Meikle(C) Sturtridge(T)
30		27	NORTHAMPTON	H	Lost	-	-	1	-	4	1	1	-	1	11	Slow(D)
31	Mar	6	HARLEQUINS	H	Lost	-	1	-	-	3	1	1	-	1	11	Mackay(T)
32		13	LONDON WELSH	H	Won	-	3	-	-	9	-	-	-	-	0	Bottrill(T) Obolensky(T) Allen(T)
33		20	Coventry	A	Lost	1	1	-	1	11	3	1	-	2	24	Mackay(T) Gerrard(T) York(C,P)
34		27	Bristol	A	Lost	-	-	-	-	0	1	2	-	-	11	
35		29	Plymouth Albion	A	Lost	-	1	-	-	3	-	2	1	-	10	Auty(T)
36		30	Bath	A	Lost	2	1	-	-	13	1	-	3	-	17	Squibbs(T) Obolensky(T) Bruce-Lockhart(T) York(2C)
37	Apr	3	Birkenhead Park	A	Lost	1	1	-	1	11	3	1	-	1	21	Squibbs(T) Cooke(T) York(C,P)
38		10	BRISTOL	H	Won	1	2	-	-	11	-	1	-	-	3	Barr(C) Rogers(T) Preston(2T)
39		17	BLACKHEATH	H	Won	-	3	-	-	9	-	-	1	-	4	Cooke(T) Obolensky(T) Moseby(T)

INDIVIDUAL APPEARANCES 1936-1937

NAME	1	2	3	4	5	6	7	8	9	10	11	12	13	14	15	16	17	18	19	20	21	22	23	24	25	26	27	28	29	30	31	32	33	34	35	36	37	38	39	40	41	42	43	44	45	46	TOTAL	T	PTS
Bobby Barr	FB	FB	FB	FB	FB	FB	-	FB	FB	FB	FB	FB	FB	FB	-	FB	FB	FB	FB	FB	FB	FB	FB	FB	FB	FB	FB	FB	FB	FB	FB	FB	FB	FB	FB	FB	FB	FB	FB	-	-	-	-	-	-	-	37	-	12
Bill Bottrill	W	W	W	W	W	W	W	W	W	W	W	W	W	W	W	-	W	W	W	W	-	W	W	W	-	W	W	W	W	W	W	W	W	-	-	-	-	-	-	-	-	-	-	-	-	-	30	7	21
John Fox	-	W	W	W	W	W	-	-	-	-	-	-	-	-	-	-	-	-	-	-	-	-	-	-	-	-	-	-	-	-	-	-	-	-	-	-	-	-	-	-	-	-	-	-	-	-	5	-	-
R.B.Mackay	-	-	-	-	-	-	-	-	W	W	W	W	W	-	-	-	-	-	-	-	-	-	-	-	-	W	W	-	W	W	W	-	W	-	-	-	-	-	-	-	-	-	-	-	-	-	11	3	9
J.N.MacLeod	-	-	-	-	-	-	-	-	-	-	-	-	-	W	W	-	-	-	-	-	-	-	-	-	-	-	-	-	-	-	-	-	-	-	-	-	-	-	-	-	-	-	-	-	-	-	2	1	3
Ken Cooke	-	-	-	-	-	-	-	-	-	-	-	-	-	-	-	-	-	W	-	-	-	-	-	-	-	-	-	-	-	-	-	-	-	-	-	-	W	W	W	-	-	-	-	-	-	-	4	2	6
G.E.Pollard	-	-	-	-	-	-	-	-	-	-	-	-	-	-	-	-	-	-	-	W	W	-	W	-	-	-	-	-	-	-	-	-	-	-	-	-	-	-	-	-	-	-	-	-	-	-	3	-	-
Dick Auty	-	-	-	-	-	-	-	-	-	FH	-	-	-	-	-	FH	-	-	-	-	-	-	-	-	-	-	-	-	-	-	-	-	-	W	W	W	-	-	-	-	-	-	-	-	-	-	5	1	3
Alex Obolensky	-	-	-	-	-	-	-	-	-	-	-	-	-	-	-	-	-	-	-	-	-	W	-	-	-	-	-	-	-	-	-	W	-	-	-	W	-	-	W	-	-	-	-	-	-	-	4	3	9
Ronnie Gerrard	C	C	C	C	C	C	C	W	C	C	-	-	-	-	FB	W	W	-	-	-	-	-	-	-	W	-	-	W	-	-	-	-	C	-	-	-	C	-	-	-	-	-	-	-	-	-	17	4	12
W.T.Alldridge	-	-	C	-	-	-	-	C	-	-	-	-	-	-	-	-	-	-	-	-	-	-	C	W	W	-	-	C	-	-	-	-	-	-	-	-	-	-	-	-	-	-	-	-	-	-	6	-	-
Graham Meikle	-	-	-	C	C	C	C	C	C	-	C	C	C	C	-	-	C	-	-	-	-	-	-	-	-	-	-	C	C	C	FH	-	-	-	-	-	-	-	-	-	-	-	-	-	-	-	15	8	30
Harry Kenyon	-	-	-	-	-	-	-	-	-	C	-	-	-	-	-	-	-	-	-	-	-	-	-	-	C	-	-	-	-	-	-	-	-	-	-	-	-	-	-	-	-	-	-	-	-	-	2	-	-
James Taylor	-	-	-	-	-	FH	FH	FH	FH	-	C	C	C	C	C	C	C	C	C	C	C	C	-	C	FH	C	C	FH	C	-	-	-	-	-	-	-	-	-	-	-	-	-	-	-	-	-	22	3	23
Gordon Wooller	-	-	-	-	-	-	-	-	-	-	-	-	-	-	C	-	-	-	-	-	-	-	-	-	C	-	-	-	-	-	-	-	-	-	-	-	-	-	-	-	-	-	-	-	-	-	2	-	-
J.R.Preston	-	-	-	-	-	-	-	-	-	-	-	-	-	-	-	-	-	C	-	-	W	C	C	C	-	C	C	-	-	-	-	C	C	W	W	-	W	W	-	-	-	-	-	-	-	-	13	5	15
Roy Leyland	-	-	-	-	-	-	-	-	-	-	-	-	-	-	-	-	-	-	C	C	-	-	-	-	-	-	-	-	-	-	-	-	-	-	-	-	-	-	-	-	-	-	-	-	-	-	2	1	3
Gwyn Thomas	-	-	-	-	-	-	-	-	-	-	-	-	-	-	-	-	-	-	-	-	C	-	-	-	-	-	-	-	-	-	-	-	-	C	-	C	-	-	-	-	-	-	-	-	-	-	3	-	-
R.A.Squibbs	-	-	-	-	-	-	-	-	-	-	-	-	-	-	-	-	-	-	-	-	-	-	-	-	-	-	-	-	-	C	C	C	-	-	C	C	C	C	C	-	-	-	-	-	-	-	8	2	6
A.V.Rogers	-	-	-	-	-	-	-	-	-	-	-	-	-	-	-	-	-	-	-	-	-	-	-	-	-	-	-	-	-	-	-	-	-	-	-	-	-	C	C	-	-	-	-	-	-	-	2	1	3
Charlie Slow	FH	FH	FH	FH	FH	-	-	-	-	-	FH	FH	FH	FH	FH	C	FH	FH	FH	FH	FH	-	FH	FH	-	FH	FH	-	-	FH	-	FH	-	-	-	-	-	-	-	-	-	-	-	-	-	-	22	4	24
M.S.Douglas	-	-	-	-	-	-	-	-	-	-	-	-	-	-	-	-	-	-	-	-	-	-	-	-	-	-	-	-	-	-	-	-	FH	-	-	-	FH	-	-	-	-	-	-	-	-	-	2	-	-
Rab Bruce-Lockhart	-	-	-	-	-	-	-	-	-	-	-	-	-	-	-	-	-	-	-	-	-	-	-	-	-	-	-	-	-	-	-	-	-	FH	FH	FH	-	-	-	-	-	-	-	-	-	-	3	1	3
W.G.Moseby	-	-	-	-	-	-	-	-	-	-	-	-	-	-	-	-	-	-	-	-	-	-	-	-	-	-	-	-	-	-	-	-	-	-	C	-	-	FH	FH	-	-	-	-	-	-	-	3	1	3
Jim Parsons	SH	SH	SH	SH	SH	SH	W	SH	-	-	SH	-	-	-	SH	W	SH	-	SH	SH	SH	-	-	-	SH	SH	-	-	-	-	-	-	SH	SH	SH	SH	SH	SH	SH	-	-	-	-	-	-	-	24	5	15
Bernard Gadney	-	-	-	-	-	-	SH	-	SH	SH	-	SH	SH	SH	-	SH	-	SH	-	-	-	SH	-	-	-	-	-	-	-	-	SH	SH	-	-	-	-	-	-	-	-	-	-	-	-	-	-	11	3	9
A.O.Mann	-	-	-	-	-	-	-	-	-	-	-	-	-	-	-	-	-	-	-	-	-	-	-	SH	-	-	SH	SH	-	-	-	-	-	-	-	-	-	-	-	-	-	-	-	-	-	-	3	-	-
George Greaves	-	P	P	P	P	P	P	P	P	P	P	-	P	-	-	P	-	P	P	-	-	-	-	-	-	-	-	P	-	-	-	-	-	-	-	-	-	-	-	-	-	-	-	-	-	-	15	-	-
Jack Wormleighton	P	P	P	P	P	P	-	-	P	-	P	P	P	P	P	P	P	P	P	P	-	-	P	P	P	P	P	-	P	P	P	P	-	-	P	P	-	P	P	-	-	-	-	-	-	-	30	1	3
Percy Ward	-	H	-	-	L	-	P	P	-	-	-	P	-	P	P	-	P	-	-	P	-	P	P	P	P	P	P	P	P	P	P	-	-	-	-	-	-	-	-	-	-	-	-	-	-	-	19	-	-
J.R.Sharp	-	-	-	-	-	-	-	-	-	-	-	-	-	-	-	-	-	-	-	-	P	P	L	L	-	L	L	L	-	-	L	P	P	P	P	L	P	P	P	-	-	-	-	-	-	-	16	-	-
George Ridgway	H	-	H	H	H	-	H	H	H	H	H	H	H	H	H	H	H	H	H	H	H	H	-	H	-	H	H	H	H	H	H	H	H	H	H	H	H	H	H	-	-	-	-	-	-	-	35	-	-
Viv Crosby	-	-	-	-	-	H	-	-	-	-	-	-	-	-	-	-	-	-	-	-	-	-	-	-	H	-	-	-	-	-	-	-	-	-	-	-	-	-	-	-	-	-	-	-	-	-	2	-	-
M.A.Robinson	-	-	-	-	-	-	-	-	-	-	-	-	-	-	-	-	-	-	-	-	-	-	H	-	-	-	-	-	-	-	L	-	-	-	-	-	-	-	-	-	-	-	-	-	-	-	2	-	-
George Vallance	L	L	L	-	-	L	L	-	L	L	L	L	L	L	L	L	L	L	L	L	L	-	-	-	L	L	L	-	L	L	-	L	L	L	L	-	L	L	L	-	-	-	-	-	-	-	30	2	6
Norman York	L	L	L	L	L	L	L	L	L	L	L	L	L	L	L	L	L	L	L	L	P	L	-	-	-	-	-	-	-	-	-	L	P	P	-	P	P	-	-	-	-	-	-	-	-	-	27	2	90
Bill Bainbridge	-	-	-	-	-	-	-	-	-	-	-	-	-	-	-	-	-	-	-	-	-	-	-	-	-	-	-	-	-	-	-	-	-	-	-	-	L	L	L	-	-	-	-	-	-	-	3	-	-
Newton Adams	BR	BR	BR	BR	BR	BR	BR	BR	BR	BR	BR	BR	BR	-	-	BR	-	BR	BR	-	-	BR	BR	BR	BR	-	-	-	-	-	-	BR	BR	BR	BR	BR	BR	BR	BR	-	-	-	-	-	-	-	28	4	12
W.M.Allen	BR	BR	-	L	-	BR	-	L	BR	-	BR	BR	BR	BR	BR	-	BR	BR	BR	BR	L	L	L	L	L	BR	BR	L	L	L	-	BR	L	L	L	-	-	-	-	-	-	-	-	-	-	-	29	2	6
Tom Berry	P	BR	BR	BR	-	-	BR	BR	-	-	BR	BR	BR	BR	BR	BR	BR	BR	BR	-	-	BR	BR	BR	BR	BR	-	BR	BR	BR	BR	BR	BR	BR	BR	L	BR	BR	BR	-	-	-	-	-	-	-	32	1	3
Rodney Willcox	C	C	BR	BR	BR	BR	BR	BR	BR	BR	-	-	-	BR	BR	BR	BR	-	-	BR	BR	-	-	-	-	-	-	BR	-	-	-	-	-	-	-	-	-	-	-	-	-	-	-	-	-	-	17	1	3
Harry Richards	-	-	-	-	BR	-	-	-	-	-	-	-	-	-	-	-	-	-	-	-	BR	-	-	-	-	-	BR	-	-	BR	-	-	-	-	-	-	-	-	-	-	-	-	-	-	-	-	4	-	-
Maurice Bullus	-	-	-	-	-	-	-	-	-	BR	-	-	-	-	-	-	-	-	-	-	-	-	-	-	-	-	-	-	-	-	-	-	-	BR	BR	BR	-	-	-	-	-	-	-	-	-	-	4	-	-
P.C.Crick	-	-	-	-	-	-	-	-	-	-	-	-	-	-	-	-	-	-	-	BR	BR	-	BR	BR	BR	BR	BR	BR	BR	BR	BR	-	BR	-	-	BR	BR	BR	BR	-	-	-	-	-	-	-	16	-	-

1 game: Jack Ball SH(23), J.G.Baxter BR(31), Denis Bolesworth P(10), David Campbell BR(22), John Charles W(1)[1T-3], Keith Downes C(31), Harry Greasley BR(1), Tom Kemp FH(22), Vic Lyttle W(19), R.L.Moore BR(29), C.H.Quarry SH(29), K.A.Stanyon-Jacques SH(30), L.W.Stevenson FB(7), Gordon Sturtridge FH(29)[1T-3], Frank Williams C(34)

NO	DATE		OPPONENTS	V	RES	FOR					AGAINST					SCORERS
						G	T	D	P	PTS	G	T	D	P	PTS	
1	Sep	4	BEDFORD	H	Lost	-	2	-	2	12	3	1	-	-	18	Bainbridge(2P) Fowler(2T)
2		11	SALE	H	Won	1	1	-	1	11	1	1	-	-	8	Thomas(T) Parsons(T) Bainbridge(C,P)
3		18	PLYMOUTH ALBION	H	Won	2	1	-	1	16	-	2	-	-	6	Thomas(2T) Moseby(T) Bainbridge(2C,P)
4		25	WATERLOO	H	Lost	-	2	-	-	6	3	1	-	-	18	Adams(2T)
5	Oct	2	COVENTRY	H	Lost	-	-	1	-	4	1	5	-	1	23	Taylor(D)
6		9	Northampton	A	Lost	-	2	-	-	6	2	2	-	-	16	Fox(T) Squibbs(T)
7		16	NEWPORT	H	Won	1	-	1	-	12	-	1	-	-	3	Barr(C,D,P) Fox(T)
8		21	OXFORD UNIVERSITY	H	Lost	1	1	-	1	11	2	-	1	-	14	Barr(C,P) Squibbs(T) Anthony(T)
9		23	NORTHAMPTON	H	Won	2	-	-	-	10	-	1	-	-	3	Barr(2C) Taylor(T) Moseby(T)
10		30	ROSSLYN PARK	H	Lost	-	1	-	2	9	2	-	-	-	10	Rogers(T) G.B.Herbert(P) Bainbridge(P)
11	Nov	6	Gloucester	A	Lost	-	2	-	1	9	1	2	-	1	14	
12		13	CAMBRIDGE UNIVERSITY	H	Won	2	2	-	1	19	1	2	-	2	17	S.F.Herbert(T,2C) Gerrard(T) Fox(T) G.B.Herbert(P) Bolesworth(T)
13		20	Nuneaton	A	Won	1	-	-	1	8	-	-	-	-	0	S.F.Herbert(C) Fox(T) G.B.Herbert(P)
14		27	BRISTOL	H	Drew	-	-	-	1	3	-	1	-	-	3	S.F.Herbert(P)
15	Dec	4	Harlequins	A	Won	1	1	-	1	11	1	1	-	-	8	S.F.Herbert(T) Bevins(T) G.B.Herbert(C,P)
16		11	Blackheath	A	Won	1	2	-	-	11	-	3	-	-	9	S.F.Herbert(T) Clarke(T) Bevins(T) G.B.Herbert(C)
17		18	Bedford	A	Lost	-	-	-	-	0	-	1	-	-	3	
18		27	BIRKENHEAD PARK	H	Won	-	2	1	2	16	1	2	-	-	11	S.F.Herbert(T,P) Taylor(D) Bainbridge(P) Berry(T)
19		28	BARBARIANS	H	Lost	-	-	-	-	0	5	3	-	-	34	
20	Jan	1	SWANSEA	H	Won	1	1	-	-	8	1	-	-	-	5	S.F.Herbert(T,C) Preston(T)
21		8	GLOUCESTER	H	Drew	-	2	-	-	6	-	1	-	1	6	S.F.Herbert(T) Clarke(T)
22		15	Headingley	A	Lost	1	-	-	-	5	1	2	-	-	11	S.F.Herbert(T) G.B.Herbert(C)
23		22	RICHMOND	H	Won	-	3	-	-	9	-	-	-	1	3	Young(T) Obolensky(T) Bainbridge(T)
24		27	ROYAL AIR FORCE	H	Lost	-	1	-	-	3	1	-	-	-	5	Young(T)
25		29	Coventry	A	Lost	-	-	-	3	9	2	6	-	-	28	Bevins(3P)
26	Feb	5	LONDON SCOTTISH	H	Won	1	1	-	1	11	-	1	-	-	3	Rogers(T) Bevins(C,P) Doe(T)
27		12	Newport	A	Lost	-	-	-	-	0	1	2	-	1	14	
28		19	Swansea	A	Lost	1	-	-	-	8	3	2	-	-	21	Bevins(C,P) Doe(T)
29		26	Northampton	A	Lost	-	-	-	1	3	-	3	-	1	12	Bevins(P)
30	Mar	5	HARLEQUINS	H	Lost	-	1	-	1	6	1	2	-	-	11	Bevins(P) Doe(T)
31		12	LONDON WELSH	H	Won	2	-	-	1	13	-	-	-	-	5	Young(T) Bevins(2C,P) Anthony(T)
32		19	BATH	H	Won	1	5	-	-	20	-	1	-	-	3	S.F.Herbert(T) Young(2T) Preston(T) Bevins(C) Glover(T) Anthony(T)
33		26	COVENTRY	H	Lost	-	-	-	2	6	3	1	-	1	21	S.F.Herbert(2P)
34	Apr	2	Birkenhead Park	A	Lost	-	2	-	-	6	1	2	-	1	14	S.F.Herbert(T) Stanyon-Jacques(T)
35		9	BLACKHEATH	H	Won	2	2	-	-	16	-	-	-	-	0	S.F.Herbert(2C) Doe(4T)
36		16	Bristol	A	Lost	1	1	-	1	11	1	3	-	-	14	S.F.Herbert(T,C,P) Stapleton(T)
37		18	Plymouth Albion	A	Lost	-	2	1	-	10	2	1	-	-	13	S.F.Herbert(T) Fox(D) Doe(T)
38		19	Bath	A	Won	3	2	-	2	27	-	-	-	-	0	Fox(T) Young(T) S.F.Herbert(T,3C,2P) G.B.Herbert(T) Doe(T)

INDIVIDUAL APPEARANCES 1937-1938

NAME	TOTAL	T	PTS
Bobby Barr	26	-	18
Ernie Watkin	12	-	-
John Fox	25	5	19
G.E.Pollard	9	-	-
Bill Bottrill	3	-	-
Ronnie Gerrard	10	1	3
Frank Herbert	21	12	77
Sidney Wade	3	-	-
J.R.Preston	7	2	6
Alex Obolensky	3	1	3
J.Brooks	3	-	-
R.A.Squibbs	10	2	6
Gwyn Thomas	5	3	9
A.V.Rogers	15	2	6
Wilfred Young	16	6	18
W.T.Alldridge	6	-	-
Gordon Lawrie	2	-	-
W.G.Moseby	14	3	9
James Taylor	7	1	11
R.W.K.Clarke	26	2	6
Jim Parsons	7	1	3
Eric Bevins	24	2	40
K.A.Stanyon-Jacques	2	1	3
J.R.Sharp	15	-	-
Percy Ward	20	1	3
Denis Bolesworth	29	1	3
Geoff Herbert	27	1	24
Jim Stapleton	9	1	3
George Ridgway	34	-	-
Bill Bainbridge	38	1	27
G.E.Fowler	25	2	6
George Vallance	15	-	-
D.B.Glover	6	1	3
Eric Bates	3	-	-
Newton Adams	9	2	6
S.E.A.Anthony	31	3	9
Tom Berry	24	1	3
Fred Doe	13	9	27
Cecil Beamish	2	-	-

1 game: Don Black BR(27), Charles Cromar H(11), R.A.Crowhurst C(30), Michael Forrester C(36), N.F.F.Giddings C(24), C.K.Jolliffe SH(33), P.Lane SH(6), R.B.Mackay W(5), J.H.McKee P(37), A.J.Rowe C(28), Arnold Sime SH(8), G.J.Treharne W(22), H.L.Varnish P(8), Ken Waite SH(24)

LEICESTER FOOTBALL CLUB 1937-38
Back: C.E. Watkin, J.A.S. Taylor, G.P.C. Vallance, W. Bainbridge, A.D. Bolesworth, G.B. Herbert, F.C. Doe, D.B. Glover, J.W. Stapleton, J.E. Thorneloe (Hon.Sec).
Middle: G.E. Fowler, J.B.S. Fox, J.T.W. Berry, R.J. Barr (Capt), T.G. Ridgway, S.F. Herbert, S.E.A. Anthony.
Front: R.W.K. Clarke, J.R. Preston, D.E. Bevins, G. Lawrie.

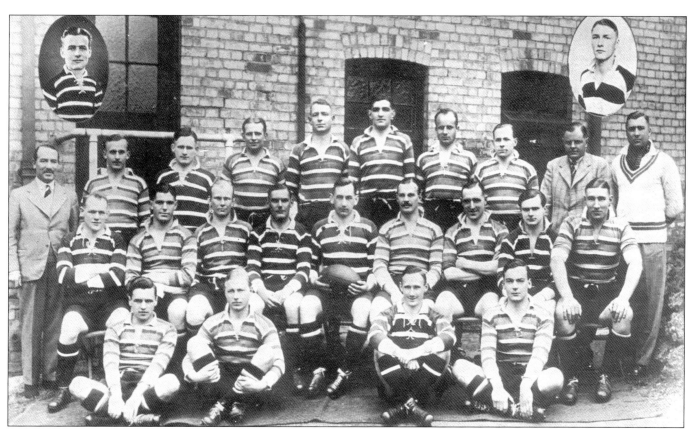

LEICESTER FOOTBALL CLUB 1938-39
Back: J.E. Thorneloe (Hon.Sec), R.A. Squibbs, T.G. Ridgway, J.W. Stapleton, F.C. Doe, H.P. Jerwood, W.H. Richards, W.J.H. Bottrill, R.L. Bedingfield (Hon.Tres), R.A. Buckingham (Touch Judge).
Middle: M.M. Henderson, G.B. Herbert, S.E.A. Anthony, S.F. Herbert, J.T.W. Berry (Capt), R.J. Barr, G.P.C. Vallance, J. Parsons, A.D. Bolesworth.
Front: G.J. Treharne, J.B.S. Fox, D.E. Bevins, J.A.S. Taylor.
Inset: W.G. Young, F.G. Edwards.

1938-1939

NO	DATE	OPPONENTS	V	RES	FOR G	FOR T	FOR D	FOR P	FOR PTS	AGAINST G	AGAINST T	AGAINST D	AGAINST P	AGAINST PTS	SCORERS
1	Sep 3	BEDFORD	H	Lost	-	-	-	-	0	3	1	-	-	18	
2	10	HEADINGLEY	H	Drew	-	-	-	1	3	-	1	-	-	3	Jerwood(P)
3	17	PLYMOUTH ALBION	H	Won	2	-	-	-	10	-	2	-	-	6	Watkin(2C) Preston(T) Bottrill(T)
4	24	WATERLOO	H	Lost	-	1	-	-	3	3	1	-	-	18	Doe(T)
5	Oct 1	Coventry	A	Lost	-	-	-	1	3	1	-	-	-	5	S.F.Herbert(P)
6	8	NORTHAMPTON	H	Won	1	1	-	-	8	-	-	-	1	3	Bottrill(T) Bevins(T) Jerwood(C)
7	15	Newport	A	Lost	1	1	-	-	8	1	1	-	1	11	S.F.Herbert(C) Bottrill(T) Anthony(T)
8	22	NEATH	H	Won	1	3	-	2	20	-	1	1	2	13	S.F.Herbert(T) Squibbs(T,C) Jerwood(2P) Henderson(2T)
9	29	OLD MERCHANT TAYLORS	H	Won	-	5	-	-	15	1	-	-	-	5	S.F.Herbert(T) Young(2T) Squibbs(T) McLean(T)
10	Nov 5	GLOUCESTER	H	Lost	2	-	-	1	13	2	1	1	-	17	S.F.Herbert(2C) Bolesworth(T) Jerwood(P) Adams(T)
11	9	Oxford University	A	Won	2	-	1	1	17	-	1	-	-	3	S.F.Herbert(2C) McLean(2T) Kenyon(D) Bullus(P)
12	12	Cambridge University	A	Lost	2	2	-	2	22	2	2	-	4	28	Watkin(P) S.F.Herbert(T,2C,P) Young(T) Berry(T) Doe(T)
13	19	COVENTRY	H	Won	-	1	-	1	6	-	-	-	-	0	Squibbs(P) Vallance(T)
14	26	BRISTOL	H	Won	1	3	-	-	14	-	2	-	-	6	S.F.Herbert(C) Young(2T) Edwards(T) Berry(T)
15	Dec 3	Harlequins	A	Lost	1	-	-	2	11	4	-	-	-	20	S.F.Herbert(C,P) Knapp(T) Jerwood(P)
16	10	Blackheath	A	Lost	1	1	-	-	8	2	4	-	-	22	S.F.Herbert(C) Ridgway(T) Doe(T)
17	17	ROSSLYN PARK	H	Won	1	2	-	1	14	1	-	-	-	5	S.F.Herbert(C) Squibbs(T) Fox(T) Parsons(T) Jerwood(P)
	24	Bedford	A		Cancelled Frost										
18	26	BIRKENHEAD PARK	H	Won	-	2	-	-	6	-	-	-	1	3	Downes(T) Edwards(T)
19	27	BARBARIANS	H	Won	1	1	-	-	8	-	2	-	-	6	S.F.Herbert(C) Edwards(2T)
20	31	Northampton	A	Won	1	-	-	-	5	-	1	-	-	3	S.F.Herbert(C) Bottrill(T)
	Jan 7	Swansea	A		Cancelled										
21	14	Gloucester	A	Lost	-	-	-	1	3	1	1	-	-	8	Jerwood(P)
22	21	NUNEATON	H	Won	1	3	-	-	14	-	1	-	-	3	S.F.Herbert(T) Downes(2T) Squibbs(T) Jerwood(C)
	26	ROYAL AIR FORCE	H		Cancelled										
23	28	Richmond	A	Won	3	2	-	-	21	-	3	1	-	13	Edwards(2T) White(3C) Doe(T) Anthony(T) Berry(T)
24	Feb 4	London Scottish	A	Lost	1	1	-	-	8	1	2	-	2	17	Edwards(T) Bottrill(T) Jerwood(C)
25	11	NEWPORT	H	Lost	1	-	1	-	9	4	1	-	-	23	Taylor(D) Jerwood(C) Henderson(T)
26	18	SWANSEA	H	Won	-	1	-	2	9	1	-	-	-	5	Squibbs(2P) Doe(T)
27	25	NORTHAMPTON	H	Drew	1	3	-	-	14	1	2	-	1	14	Bottrill(T) Squibbs(C) Treharne(T) Parsons(T) Henderson(T)
28	Mar 4	HARLEQUINS	H	Won	-	3	1	-	13	-	1	-	-	3	Squibbs(T) Young(D) Parsons(T) Doe(T)
29	11	BATH	H	Won	1	3	-	1	17	-	-	-	1	3	Squibbs(C) Edwards(T) Treharne(T) Jerwood(P) Vallance(T) Roderick(T)
30	18	LONDON WELSH	H	Won	-	2	-	2	12	-	-	-	2	6	Bottrill(T) Downes(2P) Treharne(T)
31	25	Coventry	A	Won	1	4	-	1	20	1	3	-	-	14	Bottrill(T) Downes(T,C,P) Edwards(T) Treharne(T) Young(T)
32	Apr 1	Birkenhead Park	A	Drew	-	1	-	-	3	-	-	-	1	3	G.B.Herbert(T)
33	8	Bristol	A	Lost	2	-	-	-	10	3	1	-	-	18	Squibbs(C) Treharne(T) Jerwood(C) Henderson(T)
34	10	Plymouth Albion	A	Won	-	2	1	-	10	-	1	-	-	3	Bottrill(T) Young(T,D)
35	11	Bath	A	Won	3	3	1	-	28	-	1	-	-	3	Downes(T,3C) Squibbs(D) Treharne(T) Gadney(T) Bolesworth(T) G.B.Herbert(T) Anthony(T)
36	15	BLACKHEATH	H	Lost	-	1	1	1	10	4	1	-	-	23	Fox(T) Taylor(D) Jerwood(P)

INDIVIDUAL APPEARANCES 1938-1939

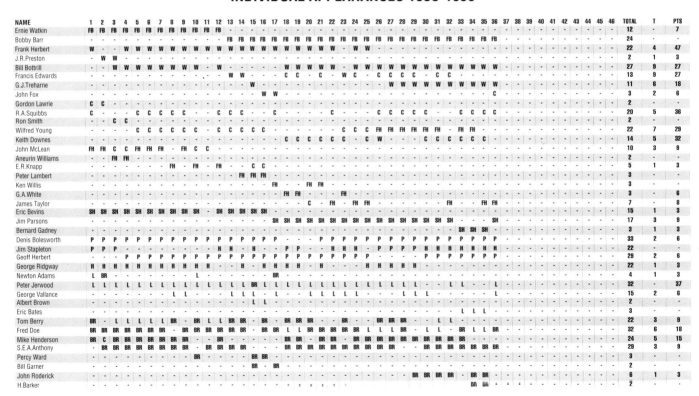

NAME	1	2	3	4	5	6	7	8	9	10	11	12	13	14	15	16	17	18	19	20	21	22	23	24	25	26	27	28	29	30	31	32	33	34	35	36	37	38	39	40	41	42	43	44	45	46	TOTAL	T	PTS
Ernie Watkin	FB	FB	FB	FB	FB	FB	FB	FB	FB	FB	FB	FB	-	-	-	-	-	-	-	-	-	-	-	-	-	-	-	-	-	-	-	-	-	-	-	-	-	-	-	-	-	-	-	-	-	-	12	-	7
Bobby Barr	-	-	-	-	-	-	-	-	-	-	-	-	FB	FB	FB	FB	FB	FB	FB	FB	FB	FB	FB	FB	FB	FB	FB	FB	FB	FB	FB	FB	FB	FB	FB	FB	-	-	-	-	-	-	-	-	-	-	24	-	-
Frank Herbert	W	-	-	W	W	W	W	W	W	W	W	W	W	W	W	W	W	W	W	W	W	W	-	W	W	-	-	-	-	-	-	-	-	-	-	-	-	-	-	-	-	-	-	-	-	-	22	4	47
J.R.Preston	-	W	W	-	-	-	-	-	-	-	-	-	-	-	-	-	-	-	-	-	-	-	-	-	-	-	-	-	-	-	-	-	-	-	-	-	-	-	-	-	-	-	-	-	-	-	2	1	3
Bill Bottrill	-	-	W	W	W	W	W	W	W	W	-	W	-	-	-	-	-	W	W	W	W	W	-	W	W	W	W	W	W	W	W	W	W	W	W	W	-	-	-	-	-	-	-	-	-	-	27	9	27
Francis Edwards	-	-	-	-	-	-	-	-	-	-	-	-	W	W	-	-	-	C	C	-	C	-	W	C	-	C	C	C	C	-	C	C	-	-	-	-	-	-	-	-	-	-	-	-	-	-	13	9	27
G.J.Treharne	-	-	-	-	-	-	-	-	-	-	-	-	-	-	W	-	-	-	-	-	-	-	-	-	-	-	W	W	W	W	W	W	W	W	W	W	-	-	-	-	-	-	-	-	-	-	11	6	18
John Fox	-	-	-	-	-	-	-	-	-	-	-	-	-	-	-	W	W	-	-	-	-	-	-	-	-	-	-	-	-	-	-	-	-	-	-	C	-	-	-	-	-	-	-	-	-	-	3	2	6
Gordon Lawrie	C	C	-	-	-	-	-	-	-	-	-	-	-	-	-	-	-	-	-	-	-	-	-	-	-	-	-	-	-	-	-	-	-	-	-	-	-	-	-	-	-	-	-	-	-	-	2	-	-
R.A.Squibbs	C	-	-	-	C	C	C	C	C	-	-	C	C	C	-	-	C	-	-	-	-	C	-	-	-	C	C	C	C	C	-	-	C	C	C	C	-	-	-	-	-	-	-	-	-	-	20	5	36
Ron Smith	-	-	C	C	-	-	-	-	-	-	-	-	-	-	-	-	-	-	-	-	-	-	-	-	-	-	-	-	-	-	-	-	-	-	-	-	-	-	-	-	-	-	-	-	-	-	2	-	-
Wilfred Young	-	-	-	-	C	C	C	C	C	C	-	C	C	C	C	C	-	-	-	-	-	-	C	C	C	FH	FH	FH	FH	FH	FH	-	FH	FH	-	-	-	-	-	-	-	-	-	-	-	-	22	7	29
Keith Downes	-	-	-	-	-	-	-	-	-	-	-	-	-	-	-	-	-	C	C	C	C	C	C	-	C	W	-	-	-	C	C	C	C	C	C	-	-	-	-	-	-	-	-	-	-	-	14	5	32
John McLean	FH	FH	C	C	FH	FH	FH	-	FH	C	C	-	-	-	-	-	-	-	-	-	-	-	-	-	-	-	-	-	-	-	-	-	-	-	-	-	-	-	-	-	-	-	-	-	-	-	10	3	9
Aneurin Williams	-	-	FH	FH	-	-	-	-	-	-	-	-	-	-	-	-	-	-	-	-	-	-	-	-	-	-	-	-	-	-	-	-	-	-	-	-	-	-	-	-	-	-	-	-	-	-	2	-	-
E.R.Knapp	-	-	-	-	-	-	-	FH	-	FH	-	FH	-	-	C	C	-	-	-	-	-	-	-	-	-	-	-	-	-	-	-	-	-	-	-	-	-	-	-	-	-	-	-	-	-	-	5	1	3
Peter Lambert	-	-	-	-	-	-	-	-	-	-	-	-	-	FH	FH	FH	-	-	-	-	-	-	-	-	-	-	-	-	-	-	-	-	-	-	-	-	-	-	-	-	-	-	-	-	-	-	3	-	-
Ken Willis	-	-	-	-	-	-	-	-	-	-	-	-	-	-	-	-	FH	-	-	FH	FH	-	-	-	-	-	-	-	-	-	-	-	-	-	-	-	-	-	-	-	-	-	-	-	-	-	3	-	-
G.A.White	-	-	-	-	-	-	-	-	-	-	-	-	-	-	-	-	-	FH	FH	-	-	-	FH	-	-	-	-	-	-	-	-	-	-	-	-	-	-	-	-	-	-	-	-	-	-	-	3	-	6
James Taylor	-	-	-	-	-	-	-	-	-	-	-	-	-	-	-	-	-	-	-	C	-	FH	-	FH	FH	-	-	-	-	-	-	FH	-	-	FH	FH	-	-	-	-	-	-	-	-	-	-	7	-	8
Eric Bevins	SH	SH	SH	SH	SH	SH	SH	SH	SH	SH	-	SH	SH	SH	SH	SH	-	-	-	-	-	-	-	-	-	-	-	-	-	-	-	-	-	-	-	-	-	-	-	-	-	-	-	-	-	-	15	1	3
Jim Parsons	-	-	-	-	-	-	-	-	-	-	-	-	-	-	-	-	SH	SH	SH	SH	SH	SH	SH	SH	SH	SH	SH	SH	SH	SH	SH	SH	-	-	-	SH	-	-	-	-	-	-	-	-	-	-	17	3	9
Bernard Gadney	-	-	-	-	-	-	-	-	-	-	-	-	-	-	-	-	-	-	-	-	-	-	-	-	-	-	-	-	-	-	-	-	SH	SH	SH	-	-	-	-	-	-	-	-	-	-	-	3	1	3
Denis Bolesworth	P	P	P	P	P	P	P	P	P	P	P	P	P	P	P	P	P	-	-	-	P	P	P	P	P	P	P	P	P	P	P	P	P	P	P	P	-	-	-	-	-	-	-	-	-	-	33	2	6
Jim Stapleton	P	P	P	-	-	-	-	-	-	-	-	H	H	-	H	-	-	P	P	-	-	H	H	H	-	P	P	P	P	H	H	H	H	H	H	H	-	-	-	-	-	-	-	-	-	-	22	-	-
Geoff Herbert	-	-	-	P	P	P	P	P	P	P	P	P	P	P	P	P	P	P	P	P	P	P	P	P	P	-	-	-	-	P	P	P	P	P	P	P	-	-	-	-	-	-	-	-	-	-	29	2	6
George Ridgway	H	H	H	H	H	H	H	H	H	H	H	-	-	H	-	H	H	H	H	-	H	-	-	-	H	H	H	H	H	-	-	-	-	-	-	-	-	-	-	-	-	-	-	-	-	-	22	1	3
Newton Adams	L	BR	-	-	-	-	-	-	-	L	-	-	-	-	-	-	BR	-	-	-	-	-	-	-	-	-	-	-	-	-	-	-	-	-	-	-	-	-	-	-	-	-	-	-	-	-	4	1	3
Peter Jerwood	L	L	L	L	L	L	L	L	L	L	L	L	L	L	BR	L	L	L	L	L	L	L	L	L	L	L	L	L	L	-	-	L	L	-	-	L	-	-	-	-	-	-	-	-	-	-	32	-	37
George Vallance	-	-	-	-	-	-	-	L	L	-	-	-	L	L	L	-	L	-	-	L	L	L	L	L	-	-	-	L	L	L	-	-	-	-	-	L	-	-	-	-	-	-	-	-	-	-	15	2	6
Albert Brown	-	-	-	-	-	-	-	-	-	-	-	-	-	-	L	L	-	-	-	-	-	-	-	-	-	-	-	-	-	-	-	-	-	-	-	-	-	-	-	-	-	-	-	-	-	-	2	-	-
Eric Bates	-	-	-	-	-	-	-	-	-	-	-	-	-	-	-	-	-	-	-	-	-	-	-	-	-	-	-	-	-	-	-	-	L	L	L	-	-	-	-	-	-	-	-	-	-	-	3	-	-
Tom Berry	BR	-	L	L	L	L	L	BR	-	BR	L	L	BR	BR	-	BR	-	BR	BR	BR	-	-	BR	-	-	BR	BR	BR	-	-	L	L	-	-	-	-	-	-	-	-	-	-	-	-	-	-	22	3	9
Fred Doe	BR	BR	BR	BR	BR	BR	BR	-	BR	BR	BR	BR	BR	BR	-	BR	BR	L	L	BR	BR	BR	BR	BR	L	L	L	BR	-	L	L	-	BR	L	L	BR	-	-	-	-	-	-	-	-	-	-	32	6	18
Mike Henderson	BR	C	BR	BR	BR	BR	BR	BR	BR	-	-	BR	-	-	-	-	-	BR	BR	-	BR	BR	-	BR	BR	BR	BR	BR	BR	BR	BR	BR	BR	-	-	-	-	-	-	-	-	-	-	-	-	-	24	5	15
S.E.A.Anthony	-	BR	BR	BR	BR	BR	BR	BR	BR	-	BR	BR	BR	BR	-	-	-	BR	BR	BR	BR	BR	BR	BR	BR	BR	BR	-	-	BR	BR	BR	BR	BR	BR	BR	-	-	-	-	-	-	-	-	-	-	29	3	9
Percy Ward	-	-	-	-	-	-	-	-	-	BR	-	-	-	-	BR	BR	-	-	-	-	-	-	-	-	-	-	-	-	-	-	-	-	-	-	-	-	-	-	-	-	-	-	-	-	-	-	3	-	-
Bill Garner	-	-	-	-	-	-	-	-	-	-	-	-	-	-	BR	-	BR	-	-	-	-	-	-	-	-	-	-	-	-	-	-	-	-	-	-	-	-	-	-	-	-	-	-	-	-	-	2	-	-
John Roderick	-	-	-	-	-	-	-	-	-	-	-	-	-	-	-	-	-	-	-	-	-	-	-	-	-	-	-	-	BR	BR	BR	BR	-	BR	BR	-	-	-	-	-	-	-	-	-	-	-	6	1	3
H.Barker	-	-	-	-	-	-	-	-	-	-	-	-	-	-	-	-	-	-	-	-	-	-	-	-	-	-	-	-	-	-	-	-	-	BR	BR	-	-	-	-	-	-	-	-	-	-	-	2	-	-

1 game: Dick Auty FH(11), Ron Ball FH(13), Maurice Bullus BR(11)[3], A.C.Deere C(17), D.B.Glover L(2), K.V.Hassall BR(29), Harry Kenyon C(11)[4], Harry Lees P(20), Alex Obolensky W(23), Ted Parfitt SH(11), Harry Richards BR(36), T.A.Riley W(1), A.J.RoweBR(25), J.Sargeant W(2), Sidney Wade W(11), Norman York H(20)

NO	DATE		OPPONENTS	V	RES	G	T	D	P	PTS	G	T	D	P	PTS	SCORERS
1	Sep	8	Cardiff	A	Lost	-	1	-	1	6	-	4	-	-	12	A.M.Adams(T) Richards(P)
		15	PLYMOUTH ALBION	H		Cancelled										
2		22	WATERLOO	H	Lost	-	-	-	2	6	-	-	-	-	11	Watkin(2P)
		29	OLD MERCHANT TAYLORS	H		Cancelled										
3	Oct	6	COVENTRY	H	Lost	-	1	-	-	3	2	-	-	1	13	Gornall(T)
4		13	NUNEATON	H	Won	1	1	-	-	8	-	-	-	1	3	B.Edwards(T) A.M.Adams(T) Richards(C)
5		20	NEWPORT	H	Lost	-	1	-	1	6	1	1	-	-	8	Watkin(P) Bolesworth(T)
6		27	Northampton	A	Lost	-	-	-	-	0	1	-	-	-	5	
7	Nov	3	Gloucester	A	Lost	-	-	-	-	0	3	2	-	2	27	
8		10	CAMBRIDGE UNIVERSITY	H	Won	-	2	-	-	6	-	1	-	-	3	Parfitt(T) A.E.Brown(T)
9		17	RUGBY	H	Won	-	3	-	-	9	-	1	-	-	3	Rees(T) Thomas(T) Harris(T)
10		24	BATH	H	Won	-	2	-	1	9	-	1	-	-	3	Watkin(P) Thomas(T) A.E.Brown(T)
11	Dec	1	Harlequins	A	Lost	-	-	1	-	4	3	-	-	-	15	Davies(D)
12		8	Guy's Hospital	A	Lost	1	-	-	-	5	-	1	-	1	6	Harris(T) Richards(C)
13		15	BRISTOL	H	Lost	-	-	-	-	0	1	1	-	-	8	
14		22	Bedford	A	Lost	-	1	-	-	3	-	2	-	-	6	W.Brown(T)
15		26	BARBARIANS	H	Lost	-	-	-	-	0	-	1	-	-	3	
16		27	N.ZEALAND SERVICES	H	Lost	-	-	-	1	3	2	3	-	-	19	Tahany(P)
17		29	SWANSEA	H	Drew	-	-	-	2	6	-	2	-	-	6	Watkin(P) Davies(P)
18	Jan	5	CARDIFF	H	Won	1	1	1	-	12	1	-	-	1	8	F.G.Edwards(T) A.M.Adams(T) Davies(C,D)
19		12	GLOUCESTER	H	Lost	1	1	-	1	11	1	-	1	1	12	Watkin(P) A.M.Adams(T) F.G.Edwards(T) Davies(C)
		19	Nuneaton	A		Cancelled										
20		26	RICHMOND/BLACKHEATH	H	Won	1	3	-	-	14	-	1	-	1	6	A.M.Adams(T) F.G.Edwards(T) Davies(C) Dermott(T) Berry(T)
21	Feb	2	LONDON SCOTTISH	H	Won	1	2	-	1	14	-	1	-	-	5	Thomas(T) F.G.Edwards(2T) Davies(C,P)
22		9	Newport	A	Lost	1	-	-	-	5	1	2	1	-	15	Stimpson(T) Davies(C)
23		16	Swansea	A	Lost	-	1	-	1	6	2	1	-	2	19	Harris(T) Davies(P)
24		23	NORTHAMPTON	H	Won	-	2	-	-	6	-	-	-	-	0	Harris(T) Cole(T)
25	Mar	2	HARLEQUINS	H	Drew	1	-	-	1	8	1	1	-	-	8	Davies(C,P) Day(T)
26		9	Coventry	A	Lost	1	-	-	-	5	-	1	-	-	3	Thomas(T) Davies(C)
27		16	BEDFORD	H	Won	2	-	-	-	10	-	2	-	1	9	Watkin(C) Channer(T) F.G.Edwards(T) Richards(C)
28		23	ROSSLYN PARK	H	Won	-	-	1	2	10	-	-	-	-	0	Matts(D,2P)
29		30	Rugby	A	Won	1	1	-	-	8	-	1	-	1	6	Matts(C) Stimpson(T) Watkin(T)
30	Apr	6	MIDDLESEX HOSPITAL	H	Won	1	4	-	1	20	1	2	-	-	11	Matts(C) Stimpson(T) A.M.Adams(T) F.G.Edwards(2T) Davies(P) Berry(T)
31		13	Waterloo	A	Won	1	1	-	-	8	-	2	-	-	6	Matts(C) Channer(T) Day(T)
32		20	Bristol	A	Won	-	2	-	1	9	-	1	-	1	6	Watkin(P) Thomas(T) F.G.Edwards(T)
33		22	Exeter	A	Lost	1	-	-	-	5	1	1	-	-	8	Watkin(C) A.M.Adams(T)
34		23	Bath	A	Won	1	3	-	1	17	1	-	-	-	5	Watkin(P) Channer(3T,C) A.E.Brown(T)

INDIVIDUAL APPEARANCES 1945-1946

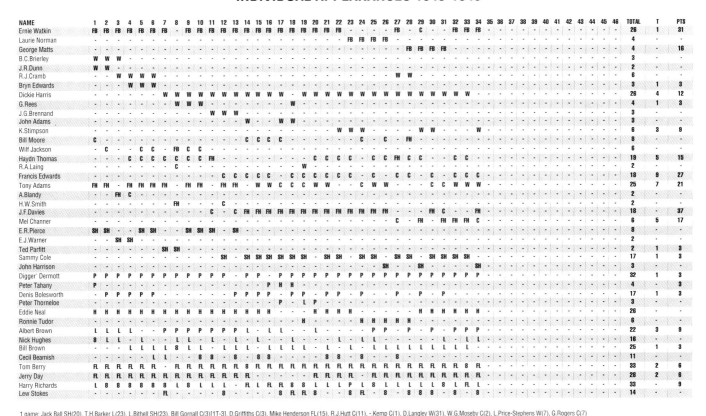

1 game: Jack Ball SH(20), T.H.Barker L(23), L.Bithell SH(23), Bill Gornall C(3)[1T-3], D.Griffiths C(3), Mike Henderson FL(15), R.J.Hutt C(11), -.Kemp C(1), D.Langley W(31), W.G.Moseby C(2), L.Price-Stephens W(7), G.Rogers C(7)

LEICESTER FOOTBALL CLUB 1945-46
Back: W.N. Bradshaw (President), D.J. Norman, A.M. Adams, G.A. Matts, A.E. Brown, W.H. Brown, H.P. Hughes, R.L. Bedingfield (Hon.Tres), J.E. Thorneloe (Hon.Sec).
Middle: S.A. Cole, W.H. Richards, F.G. Edwards, J.T.W. Berry (Capt), L.G. Dermott, J.D. Day, A.E. Neal.
Front: K. Stimpson, R.F. Harris, L.J. Stokes, J.F. Davies.
Inset: W.K.T. Moore, C.H. Beamish, A.D. Bolesworth, C.E. Watkin, H.G. Thomas, M.R. Channer.

LEICESTER FOOTBALL CLUB 1946-47
Back: D.J. Norman ('A' Team Sec.), H.W. Sibson, W.H. Brown, R.J. Ryley, P.E.F. Rhodes, M. Lynch, R.L. Bedingfield (Hon.Tres), J.E. Thorneloe (Hon.Sec).
Middle: A.E. Neal, C.E. Watkin, A.D. Bolesworth, J.T.W. Berry (Capt), F.G. Edwards, H.P. Jerwood, L.G. Dermott.
Front: W.R. Freer, W.J. Herbert. **Inset:** S.A. Cole, H.P. Hughes, W.K.T. Moore, M.R. Channer.

NO	DATE		OPPONENTS	V	RES	FOR G	T	D	P	PTS	AGAINST G	T	D	P	PTS	SCORERS
1	Sep	7	BEDFORD	H	Won	-	4	-	-	12	-	-	-	-	0	Phipps(T) Channer(3T)
2		14	BATH	H	Won	-	1	-	1	6	-	-	1*	-	3	Watkin(P) Adams(T)
3		21	PLYMOUTH ALBION	H	Won	-	4	-	-	12	-	-	1	-	4	Channer(2T) Rhodes(T) Adams(T)
4		25	Nuneaton	A	Won	1	-	-	2	11	-	-	-	-	0	Watkin(C,2P) Freer(T)
5		28	WATERLOO	H	Lost	2	1	-	2	19	5	2	-	1	34	Watkin(2C,2P) Ellis(T) Edwards(T) Cole(T)
6	Oct	3	Rugby	A	Won	-	2	1	-	10	-	2	-	-	6	Lambert(T) Edwards(T) Doyle(D)
7		5	Coventry	A	Lost	-	-	-	1	3	1	2	-	2	17	Watkin(P)
8		12	NEATH	H	Drew	-	1	-	1	6	-	1	-	1	6	Watkin(P) Lambert(T)
9		19	Newport	A	Lost	-	1	-	1	6	1	2	-	1	14	Watkin(P) Neal(T)
10		26	NORTHAMPTON	H	Lost	1	-	-	-	5	-	-	1	1	7	Watkin(C) Freer(T)
11		30	Oxford University	A	Lost	-	-	-	1	3	1	1	1	1	15	Rhodes(P)
12	Nov	2	GLOUCESTER	H	Won	2	2	-	-	16	-	-	-	1	3	Watkin(2C) Ryley(2T) Edwards(T) Channer(T)
13		9	Cambridge University	A	Won	-	-	-	1	3	-	-	-	-	0	Watkin(P)
14		16	CARDIFF	H	Lost	1	1	-	-	8	2	2	-	1	19	Rhodes(C) Jerwood(T) P.Herbert(T)
15		23	GUY'S HOSPITAL	H	Won	4	2	-	-	26	1	-	-	-	5	Watkin(4C) Ryley(T) Rhodes(T) Edwards(T) Freer(T) Dermott(T) P.Herbert(T)
16		30	SWANSEA	H	Won	1	1	-	1	11	-	2	-	-	6	Watkin(C) Rhodes(P) Ryley(T) Channer(T)
17	Dec	7	Harlequins	A	Won	-	1	1	-	7	-	-	-	-	0	Channer(D) Jerwood(T)
18		14	Blackheath	A	Won	-	2	1	-	10	-	2	-	-	6	Channer(T,D) Thomas(T)
		21	BRISTOL	H		Cancelled Frost										
19		26	BIRKENHEAD PARK	H	Won	5	1	1	-	32	1	-	-	-	5	Watkin(5C) Freer(3T) Ryley(T) Channer(2T,D)
20		27	BARBARIANS	H	Lost	-	1	-	-	3	1	1	-	-	8	Edwards(T)
21		28	RUGBY	H	Won	3	2	-	1	24	-	1	-	-	3	Watkin(3C,P) Thomas(4T) Edwards(T)
22	Jan	4	HEADINGLEY	H	Won	1	5	-	-	20	2	1	-	-	13	Stapleford(2T) Rhodes(C) Edwards(T) Channer(T) Jerwood(T) Lynch(T)
23		11	Gloucester	A	Lost	-	-	-	1	3	-	1	1	1	10	Watkin(C) Edwards(T)
24		18	NUNEATON	H	Won	3	1	1	-	22	-	-	-	-	0	Watkin(3C) Freer(T) Rhodes(D) Ryley(T) Bolesworth(T) Lynch(T)
		25	Richmond	A		Cancelled Frost/snow										
		30	ROYAL AIR FORCE	H		Cancelled Frost/snow										
	Feb	1	London Scottish	A		Cancelled Frost/snow										
		8	NEWPORT	H		Cancelled Frost/snow										
		15	Swansea	A		Cancelled Frost/snow										
		22	Northampton	A		Cancelled Frost/snow										
	Mar	1	HARLEQUINS	H		Cancelled Frost/snow										
		8	COVENTRY	H		Cancelled Frost/snow										
25		15	Cardiff	A	Lost	1	-	-	-	5	1	3	-	1	17	Watkin(C) Rhodes(T)
26		22	Bedford	A	Won	-	3	-	-	9	-	-	-	-	0	Freer(T) Ryley(T) Hacker(T)
27		29	ROSSLYN PARK	H	Won	3	1	-	-	18	-	3	-	-	9	Watkin(3C) Freer(T) Edwards(3T)
28	Apr	5	Bristol	A	Lost	-	-	-	-	0	-	2	-	-	6	
29		7	Plymouth Albion	A	Lost	-	-	-	1	3	1	-	-	1	8	Watkin(P)
30		8	Bath	A	Lost	1	1	-	-	8	1	1	1	-	12	Watkin(C) Thomas(T) Channer(T)
31		12	Birkenhead Park	A	Lost	-	2	-	-	6	2	-	-	1	13	Freer(T) Ryley(T)
32		19	BLACKHEATH	H	Won	1	1	1	-	12	-	1	-	2	9	Watkin(C) Edwards(T) Ryley(T,D)

INDIVIDUAL APPEARANCES 1946-1947

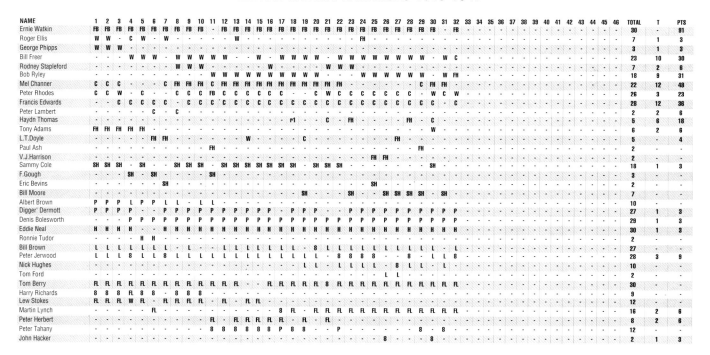

NAME	1	2	3	4	5	6	7	8	9	10	11	12	13	14	15	16	17	18	19	20	21	22	23	24	25	26	27	28	29	30	31	32	33	34	35	36	37	38	39	40	41	42	43	44	45	46	TOTAL	T	PTS
Ernie Watkin	FB	FB	FB	FB	FB	FB	FB	FB	FB	FB	-	FB	FB	FB	FB	FB	FB	FB	FB	FB	FB	FB	FB	FB	FB	FB	FB	FB	FB	FB	FB	-	FB														30	-	91
Roger Ellis	W	W	-	C	W	-	W	-	-	-	-	-	W	-	-	-	-	-	-	-	-	-	-	FH																							7	1	3
George Phipps	W	W	W	-	-	-	-	-	-	-	-	-	-	-	-	-	-	-	-	-	-	-	-	-																							3	1	3
Bill Freer	-	-	-	W	W	W	-	W	W	W	W	W	-	-	W	-	W	W	W	W	-	W	W	W	W	W	W	W	W	W	-	W	C														23	10	30
Rodney Stapleford	-	-	-	-	-	-	-	W	W	W	-	-	-	-	W	-	-	-	W	W	W	-	-	-																							7	2	6
Bob Ryley	-	-	-	-	-	-	-	-	-	W	W	W	W	W	W	W	W	W	W	W	-	-	W	W	W	W	W	W	-	W	FH																18	9	31
Mel Channer	C	C	C	-	-	-	C	FH	FH	FH	C	FH	FH	FH	FH	FH	FH	FH	FH	FH	FH	FH	-	-	C	FH	FH																				22	12	48
Peter Rhodes	C	C	W	-	C	-	C	-	C	C	C	FB	C	C	C	C	C	C	-	C	W	C	C	C	C	C	C	C	-	W	C	W															26	3	23
Francis Edwards	-	-	C	C	C	C	C	-	C	C	C	C	C	C	C	C	C	C	C	C	C	C	C	C	C	C	C	C	C	C	-	C															28	12	36
Peter Lambert	-	-	-	-	-	C	-	C	-	-	-	-	-	-	-	-	-	-	-	-	-	-	-	-																							2	2	6
Haydn Thomas	-	-	-	-	-	-	-	-	-	-	-	-	-	-	-	-	-	p1	-	-	C	-	FH	-	-	-	FH	-	C																		5	6	18
Tony Adams	FH	FH	FH	FH	FH	-	-	-	-	-	-	-	-	-	-	-	-	-	-	-	-	-	-	-	-	-	-	-	-	W																	6	2	6
L.T.Doyle	-	-	-	-	-	FH	FH	-	-	-	-	-	-	-	-	-	W	-	-	-	C	-	-	-	-	-	FH																				5	-	4
Paul Ash	-	-	-	-	-	-	-	-	-	-	FH	-	-	-	-	-	-	-	-	-	-	-	-	-	-	-	-	FH																			2	-	-
V.J.Harrison	-	-	-	-	-	-	-	-	-	-	-	-	-	-	-	-	-	-	-	-	-	-	FH	FH																							2	-	-
Sammy Cole	SH	SH	SH	-	SH	-	-	SH	SH	SH	-	SH	SH	SH	SH	SH	SH	SH	-	SH	SH	SH	-	-	-	-	SH																				18	1	3
F.Gough	-	-	-	-	SH	-	SH	-	-	-	SH	-	-	-	-	-	-	-	-	-	-	-	-	-																							3	-	-
Eric Bevins	-	-	-	-	-	-	-	SH	-	-	-	-	-	-	-	-	-	-	-	-	-	-	-	SH																							2	-	-
Bill Moore	-	-	-	-	-	-	-	-	-	-	-	-	-	-	-	-	-	-	SH	-	-	-	SH	-	-	SH	SH	SH	SH	-	SH																7	-	-
Albert Brown	P	P	P	-	L	P	P	-	L	L	-	L	L																																		10	-	-
Digger' Dermott	P	P	P	P	-	-	P	P	P	P	P	P	P	P	-	-	P	P	-	P	P	P	P	P	P	P	P	P	-	P																	27	1	3
Denis Bolesworth	-	-	-	P	P	P	P	P	P	P	P	P	P	P	P	P	P	P	-	P	P	P	P	P	P	P	P	P	P	P	P																29	1	3
Eddie Neal	H	H	H	H	-	-	-	H	H	H	H	H	H	H	H	H	H	H	H	H	H	H	H	H	H	H	H	H	H	H	H	H															30	1	3
Ronnie Tudor	-	-	-	-	H	H	H	-	-	-	-	-	-	-	-	-	-	-	-	-	-	-	-	-																							2	-	-
Bill Brown	L	L	L	L	L	L	L	-	L	-	-	L	L	L	L	L	L	L	L	-	-	-	-	-	-	-	-	-	-	-	-	-															27	-	-
Peter Jerwood	L	L	L	8	L	L	L	8	L	L	L	L	L	L	L	L	L	L	L	L	-	8	8	8	8	-	-	8	-	L	L	8															28	3	9
Nick Hughes	-	-	-	-	-	-	-	-	-	-	-	-	-	-	-	-	L	L	-	L	L	L	L	-	8	L	L	L	-	L																	10	-	-
Tom Ford	-	-	-	-	-	-	-	-	-	-	-	-	-	-	-	-	-	-	-	-	-	-	-	-	-	-	L	L																			2	-	-
Tom Berry	FL	FL	FL	FL	FL	FL	FL	FL	FL	FL	FL	FL	FL	-	-	FL	FL	FL	FL	FL	FL	8	FL	FL	FL	FL	FL	FL	FL	FL	FL	FL															30	-	-
Harry Richards	8	8	8	FL	8	8	-	8	8	8	-																																				9	-	-
Lew Stokes	FL	FL	FL	W	FL	-	FL	FL	FL	8	-	FL	-	FL	FL																																12	-	-
Martin Lynch	-	-	-	-	FL	-	-	-	-	-	-	-	-	-	-	8	FL	-	FL	FL	FL	FL	FL	FL	FL	FL	FL	FL	FL	FL	FL	FL															16	2	6
Peter Herbert	-	-	-	-	-	-	-	-	-	-	FL	-	FL	FL	FL	FL	FL	-	FL	-	FL																										8	2	6
Peter Tahany	-	-	-	-	-	-	-	8	8	8	8	8	8	8	P	8	8	-	P	-	-	-	8	-	8																						12	-	-
John Hacker	-	-	-	-	-	-	-	-	-	-	-	-	-	-	-	-	-	8	-	-	8																										2	1	3

1 game: J.C.K.Campbell C*(18), W.V.Clarke W(6), Dickie Harris W(7), Bill Herbert SH(32), Trevor Jones C(31), George Matts FB(31), J.Milton L(21), Harry Sibson L(32), Bill Thompson P(21), Bernard Vesty W(32), C.J.Weston SH(24)

NO	DATE		OPPONENTS	V	RES	FOR G	T	D	P	PTS	AGAINST G	T	D	P	PTS	SCORERS
1	Sep	6	BEDFORD	H	Won	2	4	-	-	22	-	1	-	-	3	Watkin(2C) Adams(T) Towell(T) Ryley(T) Dermott(T) Jerwood(2T)
2		13	BATH	H	Won	2	3	3	-	31	-	-	2	1	11	Adams(T) Rees(2T) Channer(C,3D) Dermott(T) Tahany(T) Jerwood(C)
3		20	PLYMOUTH ALBION	H	Won	-	4	-	-	12	-	1	-	-	3	Freer(T) Adams(T) Rees(T) Ryley(T)
4		27	Waterloo	A	Lost	-	1	-	1	6	4	1	-	-	23	Watkin(P) Ryley(T)
5	Oct	4	COVENTRY	H	Lost	1	2	-	1	14	1	1	2	1	19	Adams(2T) Channer(C,P) Jerwood(T)
6		11	Neath	A	Lost	1	-	-	-	5	-	1	-	1	6	Watkin(C) Thomas(T)
7		18	NEWPORT	H	Lost	-	-	1	2	10	2	1	2	-	21	Watkin(2P) Gaunt(D)
8		25	Northampton	A	Lost	-	-	-	-	0	1	1	-	1	11	
9		29	OXFORD UNIVERSITY	H	Lost	-	-	1	2	10	-	4	1	-	16	Watkin(2P) W.J.Herbert(D)
10	Nov	1	Gloucester	A	Lost	-	2	-	-	6	2	1	1	1	20	Ellis(2T)
11		8	CAMBRIDGE UNIVERSITY	H	Lost	2	-	-	-	10	1	1	-	-	11	Watkin(C) Ashley(T) Ash(T)
12		15	Cardiff	A	Lost	1	-	-	-	5	7	4	-	1	50	Bowen(C) P.Herbert(T)
13		22	Swansea	A	Drew	-	1	-	-	3	-	1	-	-	3	Sibson(T)
14		29	CARDIFF	H	Lost	-	-	1	-	4	1	1	-	-	8	Towell(D)
15	Dec	6	Harlequins	A	Won	1	2	-	-	11	1	-	-	-	5	Watkin(C) Rees(2T) Ashley(T)
16		13	MIDDLESEX HOSPITAL	H	Won	1	3	-	-	14	-	1	-	-	3	Watkin(C) Freer(T) Towell(2T) W.K.T.Moore(T)
17		20	BRISTOL	H	Lost	2	-	-	1	13	2	1	-	1	16	Watkin(C) Towell(2T) Jerwood(C,P)
18		26	BARBARIANS	H	Lost	2	-	-	-	10	3	-	-	-	15	Watkin(2C) Towell(T) Jerwood(T)
19		27	BIRKENHEAD PARK	H	Won	2	2	-	1	19	1	1	-	-	8	Norman(C) Quine(T) Gaunt(2T) Jerwood(T,C,P)
20	Jan	3	Headingley	A	Lost	-	-	-	1	3	-	1	1	1	7	Jerwood(P)
21		10	GLOUCESTER	H	Lost	-	1	-	1	6	2	1	-	-	13	Towell(T) Jerwood(P)
22		17	Nuneaton	A	Won	1	1	-	2	14	-	-	-	-	0	Watkin(C,2P) Ryley(T) Quine(T)
23		24	RICHMOND	H	Won	3	3	-	-	24	1	-	-	1	8	Watkin(3C) Jones(T) Quine(2T) Ryley(2T) Jerwood(T)
24		29	ROYAL AIR FORCE	H	Won	1	2	-	-	11	-	-	-	-	0	Watkin(C) Ryley(T) Bolesworth(T) Dermott(T)
25		31	Blackheath	A	Won	3	-	1	1	22	1	1	-	1	11	Watkin(3C,P) W.K.T.Moore(T) Lacey(T,D) Jerwood(T)
26	Feb	7	LONDON SCOTTISH	H	Lost	1	-	-	-	5	1	3	-	-	14	Watkin(C) Bolesworth(T)
27		14	Newport	A	Lost	-	1	-	1	6	4	3	-	1	32	Watkin(P) Tahany(T)
28		21	SWANSEA	H	Lost	-	1	-	-	3	1	-	-	-	5	Tahany(T)
29		28	NORTHAMPTON	H	Won	1	2	-	1	14	-	-	1	1	7	Watkin(C,P) Ellis(T) Rees(2T)
30	Mar	6	HARLEQUINS	H	Won	4	1	-	3	32	-	-	-	1	3	Watkin(4C,2P) Ellis(T) Rees(T) W.K.T.Moore(T) Sibson(T) Jerwood(T,P)
31		13	Coventry	A	Won	1	-	-	-	5	-	-	-	-	0	Watkin(C) P.Herbert(T)
32		20	Rugby	A	Won	1	-	-	-	5	-	-	-	-	0	Watkin(C) Terrington(T)
33		27	Bristol	A	Lost	1	3	-	-	14	2	1	1	1	20	Watkin(C) Hunter(2T) Rees(T) Channer(T)
34		29	Plymouth Albion	A	Lost	-	1	1	1	10	1	2	-	1	14	Watkin(P) Hunter(T) Channer(D)
35		30	Bath	A	Won	2	2	-	-	16	-	1	-	-	3	Watkin(2C) Nicholas(T) Ellis(T) Channer(T) Bolesworth(T)
36	Apr	3	Bedford	A	Lost	-	-	-	-	0	-	1	-	1	6	
37		10	Birkenhead Park	A	Won	1	2	-	1	14	-	2	-	1	9	Watkin(C,P) Ellis(2T) Bolesworth(T)
38		17	BLACKHEATH	H	Won	-	2	-	-	6	1	-	-	-	5	Rees(2T)

INDIVIDUAL APPEARANCES 1947-1948

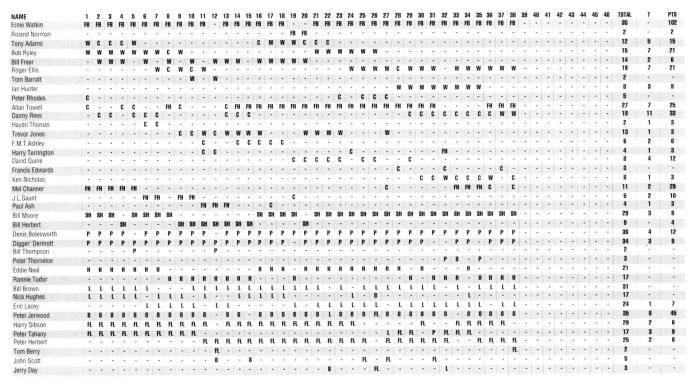

1 game: H.J.R.Bowen FB(12)(2), I.P.Farmer-Wright G(24), George Matts W(28), P.J.d'A.Moore P(19), F.Pell W(8), S.C.Simmonds G(18), T.M.Simpson L(36), J.W.Smith L(20), Ron Smith C(37), Rodney Stapleford W(15)

LEICESTER FOOTBALL CLUB 1947-48
Back: J.E. Thorneloe (Hon.Sec), R.L. Bedingfield (Hon.Tres), H.W. Sibson, D.A. Quine, D.R. Ellis, H.P. Hughes, E.C. Lacey, P. Herbert,
W.H. Brown, D.E.B. Rees, A.C. Towell, W.K. Nicholas, W.N. Bradshaw (President), R.J. Barr (Team Hon.Sec).
Front: R.E. Tudor, W.K.T. Moore, L.G. Dermott, J.T.W. Berry, H.P. Jerwood (Capt), C.E. Watkin, A.D. Bolesworth, M.R. Channer, A.E. Neal.

LEICESTER FOOTBALL CLUB 1948-49
Back: W.N. Bradshaw (President), R.L. Bedingfield (Hon.Tres), W.H. Brown, R.V. Stirling, D.E.B. Rees, P.B.L. Thorneloe, E.R. Bennett,
H.W. Sibson, R.J. Barr (Team Hon.Sec), J.E. Thorneloe (Hon.Sec), F. Read (Touch Judge).
Middle: R.E. Tudor, A.D. Bolesworth, E.C. Lacey, A.C. Towell, H.P. Jerwood (Capt), W.K.T. Moore, D.R. Ellis, W.K. Nicholas, G.A. Matts.
Front: G.R. Tucker, C.G.S. Lawrence, E.A. Barrow, J.J. Harvey, I. Selkirk.
Inset: P. Herbert, D. Norton.

NO	DATE	OPPONENTS	V	RES	FOR G	FOR T	FOR D	FOR P	FOR PTS	AGAINST G	AGAINST T	AGAINST D	AGAINST P	AGAINST PTS	SCORERS
1	Sep 4	BEDFORD	H	Lost	-	-	-	1	3	3	1	-	1	21	Rhodes(P)
2	11	BATH	H	Won	-	4	-	1	15	-	1	-	-	3	Rhodes(P) Ellis(2T) Rees(2T)
3	18	PLYMOUTH ALBION	H	Won	2	2	-	1	19	-	-	-	-	0	Matts(2C,P) Quine(T) Nicholas(T) Towell(T) Sibson(T)
4	25	WATERLOO	H	Won	1	3	-	1	17	1	1	-	-	8	Matts(C,P) Ellis(T) Quine(T) Rees(T) Towell(T)
5	Oct 2	Coventry	A	Lost	-	3	-	-	9	-	3	1	1	15	Ellis(T) Rees(T) Towell(T)
6	9	RICHMOND	H	Won	1	1	1	1	14	-	-	-	2	6	Matts(C,D) Ashley(T) Nicholas(P) Rees(T)
7	16	Newport	A	Lost	-	1	-	-	3	2	2	1	1	22	Rees(T)
8	23	NORTHAMPTON	H	Lost	-	-	1	1	6	1	1	-	-	8	Matts(P) Towell(D)
9	27	Oxford University	A	Lost	-	1	-	-	3	3	-	-	-	15	Nicholas(T)
10	30	ST MARY'S HOSPITAL	H	Lost	-	-	-	1	3	1	-	-	1	8	Nicholas(P)
11	Nov 6	Gloucester	A	Lost	2	1	1	-	16	3	1	-	-	18	Matts(2C) Hunter(T) Norman(D) Bolesworth(T) Herbert(T)
12	13	Cambridge University	A	Lost	1	-	-	-	5	1	4	1	2	26	Matts(C) Ellis(T)
13	20	CARDIFF	H	Lost	-	-	-	-	0	-	-	-	2	6	
14	27	MIDDLESEX HOSPITAL	H	Won	1	2	2	1	20	-	2	-	-	6	Nicholas(C,P) Rees(D) Terrington(D) Bolesworth(T) Stirling(T) Sibson(T)
15	Dec 4	Harlequins	A	Lost	-	1	-	-	3	1	-	-	-	5	Rees(T)
16	11	Blackheath	A	Won	2	-	-	-	10	-	1	-	-	3	Harvey(2C) Ellis(T) Rees(T)
17	18	BRISTOL	H	Lost	-	1	-	1	6	3	2	-	-	21	Harvey(P) Lacey(T)
18	27	BIRKENHEAD PARK	H	Lost	-	1	-	2	9	2	2	-	-	16	Ellis(T) Jerwood(2P)
19	28	BARBARIANS	H	Won	-	2	-	1	9	1	1	-	-	8	Lacey(T) Jerwood(T,P)
20	Jan 1	HEADINGLEY	H	Won	-	1	-	1	6	-	-	-	1	3	Nicholas(T) Jerwood(P)
21	8	GLOUCESTER	H	Won	-	1	-	1	6	-	-	-	1	3	Bennett(T) Jerwood(P)
22	15	Bedford	A	Lost	-	-	-	-	0	-	-	-	1	3	
23	22	Cardiff	A	Lost	-	-	-	2	6	2	4	-	-	22	Harvey(2P)
24	27	ROYAL AIR FORCE	H	Won	-	2	-	2	12	1	-	-	-	5	Harvey(2P) Towell(T) Rees(T)
25	29	ROSSLYN PARK	H	Lost	-	1	1	-	6	-	3	-	-	9	Towell(D) Barrow(T)
	Feb 5	London Scottish	A		Cancelled Frost										
26	12	NEWPORT	H	Lost	-	-	-	1	3	2	3	-	1	22	Jerwood(P)
27	19	SWANSEA	H	Won	1	2	-	1	14	-	-	1	-	3	Matts(P) Rees(T) Norton(T) Herbert(T) Jerwood(C)
28	26	Northampton	A	Drew	-	-	1	2	9	-	1	1	1	9	Matts(2P) Towell(D)
29	Mar 5	HARLEQUINS	H	Won	-	1	-	1	6	-	-	-	-	0	Matts(P) Towell(T)
30	12	COVENTRY	H	Lost	-	-	-	-	0	-	2	-	-	6	
31	19	NUNEATON	H	Won	-	1	-	2	9	-	-	-	1	3	Rees(T) Jerwood(2P)
32	26	Swansea	A	Lost	-	1	3	-	12	-	4	1	-	15	Thomas(T) Towell(D) W.K.T.Moore(2D)
33	Apr 2	Birkenhead Park	A	Lost	-	2	-	-	6	1	2	-	-	11	Lawrence(T) Norton(T)
34	9	BLACKHEATH	H	Won	4	1	-	-	23	-	1	-	1	6	Matts(4C) Ellis(T) Lawrence(T) Nicholas(T) Tucker(T) Lacey(T)
35	16	Bristol	A	Lost	-	1	-	2	9	1	2	1	1	17	Matts(P) Nicholas(T) Jerwood(P)
36	18	Plymouth Albion	A	Won	2	1	-	-	13	1	-	1	1	11	Matts(2C) Rees(T) W.K.T.Moore(T) Lacey(T)
37	19	Bath	A	Won	1	1	-	-	8	-	1	-	-	3	Matts(C) Bennett(T) Brown(T)

INDIVIDUAL APPEARANCES 1948-1949

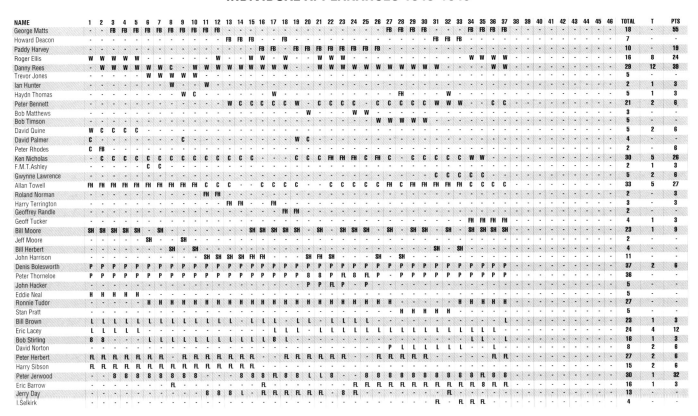

NAME	1	2	3	4	5	6	7	8	9	10	11	12	13	14	15	16	17	18	19	20	21	22	23	24	25	26	27	28	29	30	31	32	33	34	35	36	37	38	39	40	41	42	43	44	45	46	TOTAL	T	PTS
George Matts	-	-	FB	FB	FB	FB	FB	FB	FB	FB	FB	FB	-	-	-	-	-	-	-	-	-	-	-	-	-	-	FB	FB	FB	FB	-	-	-	FB	FB	FB	FB	-	-	-	-	-	-	-	-	-	18	-	55
Howard Deacon	-	-	-	-	-	-	-	-	-	-	-	-	FB	FB	FB	-	-	FB	-	-	-	-	-	-	-	-	-	-	-	-	FB	FB	FB	-	-	-	-	-	-	-	-	-	-	-	-	-	7	-	-
Paddy Harvey	-	-	-	-	-	-	-	-	-	-	-	-	-	-	-	FB	FB	-	FB	FB	FB	FB	FB	FB	FB	FB	-	-	-	-	-	-	-	-	-	-	-	-	-	-	-	-	-	-	-	-	10	-	19
Roger Ellis	W	W	W	W	W	-	-	-	-	-	-	W	-	-	W	W	-	W	-	-	W	W	W	-	-	-	-	-	-	-	-	-	-	W	W	W	W	-	-	-	-	-	-	-	-	-	16	8	24
Danny Rees	-	W	W	W	W	W	W	C	-	W	W	W	W	W	W	W	W	W	-	-	W	W	W	W	W	W	W	W	W	W	W	-	-	-	-	W	W	-	-	-	-	-	-	-	-	-	29	12	39
Trevor Jones	-	-	-	-	-	W	W	W	W	W	-	-	-	-	-	-	-	-	-	-	-	-	-	-	-	-	-	-	-	-	-	-	-	-	-	-	-	-	-	-	-	-	-	-	-	-	5	-	-
Ian Hunter	-	-	-	-	-	-	-	W	-	-	W	-	-	-	-	-	-	-	-	-	-	-	-	-	-	-	-	-	-	-	-	-	-	-	-	-	-	-	-	-	-	-	-	-	-	-	2	1	3
Haydn Thomas	-	-	-	-	-	-	-	-	W	C	-	-	-	-	-	-	W	-	-	-	-	-	-	-	-	-	-	FH	-	-	-	W	-	-	-	-	-	-	-	-	-	-	-	-	-	-	5	1	3
Peter Bennett	-	-	-	-	-	-	-	-	-	-	-	-	W	C	C	C	C	C	W	-	C	C	C	C	-	C	C	C	C	C	W	W	W	-	-	C	C	-	-	-	-	-	-	-	-	-	21	2	6
Bob Matthews	-	-	-	-	-	-	-	-	-	-	-	-	-	-	-	-	-	-	-	W	-	-	-	W	W	-	-	-	-	-	-	-	-	-	-	-	-	-	-	-	-	-	-	-	-	-	3	-	-
Bob Timson	-	-	-	-	-	-	-	-	-	-	-	-	-	-	-	-	-	-	-	-	-	-	-	-	-	W	W	W	W	W	-	-	-	-	-	-	-	-	-	-	-	-	-	-	-	-	5	-	-
David Quine	W	C	C	C	C	-	-	-	-	-	-	-	-	-	-	-	-	-	-	-	-	-	-	-	-	-	-	-	-	-	-	-	-	-	-	-	-	-	-	-	-	-	-	-	-	-	5	2	6
David Palmer	C	-	-	-	-	-	-	-	C	-	-	-	-	-	-	-	-	-	W	C	-	-	-	-	-	-	-	-	-	-	-	-	-	-	-	-	-	-	-	-	-	-	-	-	-	-	4	-	-
Peter Rhodes	C	FB	-	-	-	-	-	-	-	-	-	-	-	-	-	-	-	-	-	-	-	-	-	-	-	-	-	-	-	-	-	-	-	-	-	-	-	-	-	-	-	-	-	-	-	-	2	-	6
Ken Nicholas	-	C	C	C	C	C	C	C	C	C	C	C	C	C	C	-	-	-	C	C	C	FH	FH	FH	C	FH	C	-	C	C	C	C	C	W	W	-	-	-	-	-	-	-	-	-	-	-	30	5	26
F.M.T.Ashley	-	-	-	-	-	C	C	-	-	-	-	-	-	-	-	-	-	-	-	-	-	-	-	-	-	-	-	-	-	-	-	-	-	-	-	-	-	-	-	-	-	-	-	-	-	-	2	1	3
Gwynne Lawrence	-	-	-	-	-	-	-	-	-	-	-	-	-	-	-	-	-	-	-	-	-	-	-	-	-	-	-	-	-	-	C	C	C	C	C	-	-	-	-	-	-	-	-	-	-	-	5	2	6
Allan Towell	FH	FH	FH	FH	FH	FH	FH	FH	FH	FH	C	C	C	-	-	C	C	C	C	-	-	C	C	C	C	C	FH	C	FH	FH	FH	FH	FH	C	C	C	C	-	-	-	-	-	-	-	-	-	33	5	27
Roland Norman	-	-	-	-	-	-	-	-	-	-	FH	FH	-	-	-	-	-	-	-	-	-	-	-	-	-	-	-	-	-	-	-	-	-	-	-	-	-	-	-	-	-	-	-	-	-	-	2	-	3
Harry Terrington	-	-	-	-	-	-	-	-	-	-	-	-	FH	FH	-	-	FH	-	-	-	-	-	-	-	-	-	-	-	-	-	-	-	-	-	-	-	-	-	-	-	-	-	-	-	-	-	3	-	3
Geoffrey Randle	-	-	-	-	-	-	-	-	-	-	-	-	-	-	-	-	-	FH	FH	-	-	-	-	-	-	-	-	-	-	-	-	-	-	-	-	-	-	-	-	-	-	-	-	-	-	-	2	-	-
Geoff Tucker	-	-	-	-	-	-	-	-	-	-	-	-	-	-	-	-	-	-	-	-	-	-	-	-	-	-	-	-	-	-	-	-	-	FH	FH	FH	FH	-	-	-	-	-	-	-	-	-	4	1	3
Bill Moore	SH	SH	SH	SH	SH	-	SH	-	-	-	-	-	-	-	SH	SH	SH	SH	SH	-	SH	-	SH	SH	SH	-	SH	-	SH	SH	-	SH	-	SH	SH	SH	SH	-	-	-	-	-	-	-	-	-	23	1	9
Jeff Moore	-	-	-	-	-	SH	-	-	SH	-	-	-	-	-	-	-	-	-	-	-	-	-	-	-	-	-	-	-	-	-	-	-	-	-	-	-	-	-	-	-	-	-	-	-	-	-	2	-	-
Bill Herbert	-	-	-	-	-	-	-	SH	-	SH	-	-	-	-	-	-	-	-	-	-	-	-	-	-	-	-	-	-	-	-	SH	-	SH	-	-	-	-	-	-	-	-	-	-	-	-	-	4	-	-
John Harrison	-	-	-	-	-	-	-	-	-	-	SH	SH	SH	SH	FH	FH	-	-	-	SH	FH	SH	-	-	-	SH	-	SH	-	-	-	-	-	-	-	-	-	-	-	-	-	-	-	-	-	-	11	-	-
Denis Bolesworth	P	P	P	P	P	P	P	P	P	P	P	P	P	P	P	P	P	P	P	P	P	P	P	P	P	P	P	P	P	P	P	P	P	P	P	P	P	-	-	-	-	-	-	-	-	-	37	2	6
Peter Thorneloe	P	P	P	P	P	P	P	P	P	P	P	P	P	P	P	P	P	P	P	8	8	P	FL	8	FL	P	-	P	P	P	P	P	P	P	P	P	P	-	-	-	-	-	-	-	-	-	36	-	-
John Hacker	-	-	-	-	-	-	-	-	-	-	-	-	-	-	-	-	-	-	-	P	P	FL	P	-	P	-	-	-	-	-	-	-	-	-	-	-	-	-	-	-	-	-	-	-	-	-	5	-	-
Eddie Neal	H	H	H	H	H	-	-	-	-	-	-	-	-	-	-	-	-	-	-	-	-	-	-	-	-	-	-	-	-	-	-	-	-	-	-	-	-	-	-	-	-	-	-	-	-	-	5	-	-
Ronnie Tudor	-	-	-	-	-	H	H	H	H	H	H	H	H	H	H	H	H	H	H	H	H	H	H	H	H	H	H	-	-	-	-	-	H	H	H	H	H	-	-	-	-	-	-	-	-	-	27	-	-
Stan Pratt	-	-	-	-	-	-	-	-	-	-	-	-	-	-	-	-	-	-	-	-	-	-	-	-	-	-	-	H	H	H	H	H	-	-	-	-	-	-	-	-	-	-	-	-	-	-	5	-	-
Bill Brown	L	L	L	L	L	L	L	L	L	L	L	L	L	-	L	L	L	-	L	L	-	L	L	L	L	-	-	-	-	-	-	-	-	-	-	-	L	-	-	-	-	-	-	-	-	-	23	1	3
Eric Lacey	L	L	L	L	L	-	-	-	-	-	-	-	-	-	-	-	L	L	L	-	L	L	L	L	L	L	L	L	L	L	L	L	L	L	L	L	-	-	-	-	-	-	-	-	-	-	24	4	12
Bob Stirling	8	8	-	-	-	L	L	L	L	L	L	L	L	L	L	L	8	L	-	-	-	-	-	-	-	-	-	-	-	-	-	-	-	L	L	-	L	-	-	-	-	-	-	-	-	-	18	1	3
David Norton	-	-	-	-	-	-	-	-	-	-	-	-	-	-	-	-	-	-	-	-	-	-	-	-	-	-	P	L	L	L	L	L	L	-	-	L	-	-	-	-	-	-	-	-	-	-	8	2	6
Peter Herbert	FL	FL	FL	FL	FL	FL	FL	-	FL	FL	FL	FL	FL	FL	FL	-	-	FL	FL	FL	FL	FL	FL	-	-	FL	FL	FL	FL	FL	-	-	-	-	-	FL	FL	-	-	-	-	-	-	-	-	-	27	2	6
Harry Sibson	FL	FL	FL	FL	FL	FL	FL	FL	FL	FL	FL	FL	FL	FL	FL	-	-	-	-	-	-	-	-	-	-	-	-	-	-	-	-	-	-	-	-	-	-	-	-	-	-	-	-	-	-	-	15	2	6
Peter Jerwood	-	-	8	8	8	8	8	8	8	8	-	-	-	8	8	8	FL	8	8	L	L	8	-	-	8	8	8	8	8	8	8	8	8	8	FL	8	8	-	-	-	-	-	-	-	-	-	30	1	32
Eric Barrow	-	-	-	-	-	-	-	FL	-	-	-	-	-	-	-	FL	-	-	-	-	-	-	-	FL	FL	FL	FL	FL	FL	FL	FL	FL	FL	FL	8	FL	FL	-	-	-	-	-	-	-	-	-	16	1	3
Jerry Day	-	-	-	-	-	-	-	-	-	-	8	8	8	L	-	FL	FL	FL	FL	FL	FL	-	8	FL	-	-	-	-	-	-	-	FL	-	-	-	-	-	-	-	-	-	-	-	-	-	-	13	-	-
I.Selkirk	-	-	-	-	-	-	-	-	-	-	-	-	-	-	-	-	-	-	-	-	-	-	-	-	-	-	-	-	-	-	FL	-	FL	FL	FL	-	-	-	-	-	-	-	-	-	-	-	4	-	-

1 game: Frank Chawner L(27), L.T.Doyle FH(20), J.Fletcher L(26), Bill Freer W(33), Ken Jones W(14), Jim Morris FH(25), Ron Smith W(20), Bill Thompson P(24), Ernie Watkin FB(1)

NO	DATE		OPPONENTS	V	RES	FOR					AGAINST					SCORERS
						G	T	D	P	PTS	G	T	D	P	PTS	
1	Sep	3	BEDFORD	H	Lost	-	-	1	1	6	2	2	-	-	16	Matts(D,P)
2		10	BATH	H	Won	-	2	1	-	9	-	-	-	-	0	Nicholas(T,D) P.Herbert(T)
3		17	PLYMOUTH ALBION	H	Lost	-	-	-	1	3	-	-	-	1	5	Matts(P)
4		24	Waterloo	A	Lost	2	-	-	1	13	2	-	-	2	16	Matts(P) Nicholas(T) Moore(2C) P.Herbert(T)
5		26	CARDIFF	H	Lost	-	1	1	-	6	1	2	-	-	11	Rees(T) Bennett(D)
6	Oct	1	COVENTRY	H	Lost	-	-	-	1	3	-	1	-	1	6	Harvey(P)
7		8	Richmond	A	Won	-	4	-	-	12	1	-	-	1	8	Rees(T) Lawrence(T) Nicholas(T) Lacey(T)
8		15	NEWPORT	H	Won	2	1	-	-	13	1	-	-	1	8	Harvey(2C) Rees(T) Thomas(T) Barrow(T)
9		22	Northampton	A	Lost	-	-	-	1	3	1	-	1	2	14	Harvey(P)
10		27	OXFORD UNIVERSITY	H	Lost	-	-	-	-	0	2	3	1	-	22	
11		29	Swansea	A	Lost	-	1	1	-	6	1	2	1	-	14	Nicholas(D) Thorneloe(T)
12	Nov	5	Gloucester	A	Lost	-	-	-	2	6	3	1	-	-	18	Harvey(2P)
13		12	CAMBRIDGE UNIVERSITY	H	Won	1	2	-	-	11	-	1	-	-	3	Harvey(C) Rees(T) Lawrence(T) Sibson(T)
14		19	NEATH	H	Lost	-	-	-	1	3	1	-	-	1	8	Harvey(P)
15		26	MIDDLESEX HOSPITAL	H	Won	-	-	1	1	6	-	1	-	-	3	Harvey(P) Terrington(D)
16	Dec	3	Harlequins	A	Lost	-	1	-	-	3	1	2	-	1	14	Sibson(T)
17		10	Blackheath	A	Won	1	1	-	1	11	-	1	-	1	6	Terrington(T) Nicholas(T) Morris(C,P)
18		17	BRISTOL	H	Won	1	-	-	-	5	-	1	-	-	3	Thomas(T) Morris(C)
19		24	Rugby	A	Lost	-	-	-	1	3	2	1	1	-	16	Morris(P)
20		26	BIRKENHEAD PARK	H	Lost	-	-	-	-	0	1	-	-	-	5	
21		27	BARBARIANS	H	Lost	-	-	-	-	0	4	1	-	2	29	
22		31	Bath	A	Won	1	1	-	1	11	1	-	-	-	5	Quine(C,P) Cullen(T) Sibson(T)
23	Jan	7	CARDIFF	H	Drew	-	-	-	1	3	-	1	-	-	3	Quine(P)
24		14	GLOUCESTER	H	Won	-	1	1	-	6	-	1	-	-	3	Rees(T) Terrington(D)
25		21	Headingley	A	Lost	-	-	-	1	3	-	-	-	1	5	Terrington(P)
		26	ROYAL AIR FORCE	H		Cancelled Frost											
		28	Rosslyn Park	A		Cancelled Frost											
26	Feb	4	LONDON SCOTTISH	H	Won	2	2	-	-	16	-	1	-	-	3	Rees(T) Morris(T,2C) Lacey(T) Thorneloe(T)
27		11	Newport	A	Lost	-	-	-	1	3	2	-	-	1	13	Morris(P)
28		18	RUGBY	H	Won	-	2	-	1	9	-	2	-	-	6	Morris(P) Rees(2T)
29		25	NORTHAMPTON	H	Lost	-	1	-	-	3	-	2	1	-	9	Bolesworth(T)
30	Mar	4	HARLEQUINS	H	Lost	-	1	-	2	9	1	1	-	1	11	Matts(2P) Guffick(T)
31		11	Coventry	A	Lost	-	-	-	1	3	-	3	-	-	9	Matts(P)
32		18	Nuneaton	A	Lost	-	1	-	-	3	1	-	-	-	5	Rees(T)
33		25	SWANSEA	H	Lost	1	-	-	1	8	2	3	1	1	25	Nicholas(T) Quine(C,P)
34	Apr	1	Birkenhead Park	A	Lost	-	1	-	1	6	2	1	-	-	13	Quine(P) Thomas(T)
35		8	Bristol	A	Lost	-	1	-	-	3	1	4	-	1	20	Thomas(T)
36		10	Plymouth Albion	A	Won	3	2	-	1	24	-	-	-	1	3	Cullen(2T,2C,P) Thomas(2T) Terrington(C) Bleasdale(T)
37		11	Exeter	A	Won	1	1	-	-	8	-	2	-	-	6	Cullen(C) Thompson(T) Bleasdale(T)
38		15	NUNEATON	H	Won	2	-	1	1	16	1	1	-	-	8	Cullen(2T,C,D,P) Terrington(C)
39		22	BLACKHEATH	H	Won	1	2	-	1	14	-	-	-	1	3	Quine(T) Cullen(C,P) Smith(T) Jerwood(T)

INDIVIDUAL APPEARANCES 1949-1950

1 game: J.M.Guffick FH(30)[1T-3], Roy McConnell W(34), Bob Matthews W(12), Geoff Tucker FH(18)

LEICESTER FOOTBALL CLUB 1949-50
Back: R.L. Bedingfield (Hon.Tres), W.N. Bradshaw (President), H.G. Thomas, D. Norton, T. Bleasdale, R.H. Smith, W.E. Thompson,
R. Marshall, H.B. Deacon, R.J. Barr (Team Hon.Sec), F. Read (Touch Judge).
Middle: W.K. Nicholas, H.P. Jerwood, W.K.T. Moore, A.C. Towell (Capt), A.D. Bolesworth, H.W. Sibson, P.B.L. Thorneloe.
Front: H.L. Terrington, G.H. Cullen, R.E. Tudor, S. Pratt. **Inset:** E.C. Lacey.

LEICESTER FOOTBALL CLUB 1950-51
Back: J.E. Thorneloe (Hon. Sec), R.J. Barr (Team Hon.Sec), H.P. Jerwood, J.C. Kail, G.H. Cullen, J.H. Hacker, R.A. Lewis,
F. Chawner, C.G.S. Lawrence, W.N. Bradshaw (President), R.L. Bedingfield (Hon.Tres).
Middle: T. Bleasdale, W.K. Nicholas, E.C. Lacey, A.D. Bolesworth, W.K.T. Moore (Capt), R.V. Stirling, H.W. Sibson, H.G. Thomas, S. Pratt.
Front: R.D. Matthews, R. Marshall.

NO	DATE		OPPONENTS	V	RES	FOR					AGAINST					SCORERS
						G	T	D	P	PTS	G	T	D	P	PTS	
1	Sep	2	BEDFORD	H	Lost	1	1	1	-	11	1	2	-	1	14	Brookman(C,D) Cullen(T) Hacker(T)
2		9	BATH	H	Won	1	1	-	-	8	-	1	-	1	6	Quine(T) Cullen(T,C)
3		16	PLYMOUTH ALBION	H	Won	3	3	3	-	33	-	1	2	-	9	Lawrence(T) Bolesworth(T) Lacey(T) Brookman(3C,D) Cullen(T,2D) Sibson(T) Nicholas(T)
4		23	WATERLOO	H	Won	1	1	2	-	14	-	-	-	-	0	Lawrence(T) Brookman(C,2D) Cullen(T)
5		30	CARDIFF	H	Lost	-	-	-	-	0	-	1	-	-	3	
6	Oct	7	Coventry	A	Lost	-	-	-	-	0	-	2	-	1	9	
7		14	RICHMOND	H	Won	2	3	1	4	34	1	-	-	2	11	Lacey(2T) Cullen(T,2C,4P) Sibson(T) Hacker(T) Nicholas(D)
8		21	Newport	A	Lost	-	-	1	1	6	2	-	1	2	19	Cullen(D,P)
9		25	Oxford University	A	Drew	-	-	-	2	6	-	2	-	-	6	Brookman(2P)
10		28	NORTHAMPTON	H	Won	4	2	-	-	26	1	-	-	1	8	Lawrence(2T) Bolesworth(T) Cullen(2C) Thomas(T) Sibson(T) Morris(2C) Nicholas(T)
11	Nov	4	GLOUCESTER	H	Won	2	2	-	1	19	1	2	-	1	14	Lacey(T) Cullen(2T,P) Sibson(T) Morris(2C)
12		11	Cambridge University	A	Won	1	-	1	-	8	-	1	-	1	6	Cullen(D) Thomas(T) Morris(C)
13		18	Cardiff	A	Lost	-	-	-	2	6	1	2	-	2	17	Morris(2P)
14		25	MIDDLESEX HOSPITAL	H	Won	2	4	-	-	22	1	-	-	-	5	Lawrence(3T) Thomas(2T) Morris(2C) Nicholas(T)
15	Dec	2	Harlequins	A	Lost	2	-	-	-	10	2	2	-	-	16	Thomas(T) Morris(2C) Matthews(T)
16		9	Blackheath	A	Won	1	4	-	1	20	-	1	1	1	9	Lawrence(T) Thomas(T) Sibson(T) Morris(C,P) Pratt(T) Moore(T)
		16	BRISTOL	H		Cancelled Frost										
		23	RUGBY	H		Cancelled Frost										
17		26	BIRKENHEAD PARK	H	Won	1	3	-	-	14	1	2	-	-	11	Lacey(T) Cullen(2T) Sibson(T) Morris(C)
18		27	BARBARIANS	H	Drew	2	1	-	-	13	2	1	-	-	13	Lawrence(T) Thomas(T) Sibson(T) Morris(2C)
19		30	HEADINGLEY	H	Won	4	-	-	2	26	1	2	-	-	11	Bolesworth(T) Cullen(T,2P) Thomas(T) Morris(4C) Nicholas(T)
20	Jan	6	Nuneaton	A	Won	-	1	-	-	3	-	-	-	-	0	Kail(T)
21		13	Gloucester	A	Won	1	-	-	-	8	-	1	-	-	3	Thomas(T) Morris(C,P)
22		20	Bedford	A	Won	-	2	1	2	15	1	-	-	2	11	Lawrence(T) Thomas(T) Morris(D,2P)
23		25	ROYAL AIR FORCE	H	Won	3	-	2	-	21	-	1	-	-	3	Lawrence(T) Cullen(T,D) Sibson(T) Morris(3C,D)
24		27	ROSSLYN PARK	H	Lost	1	-	-	1	8	-	1	1	2	12	Thomas(T) Morris(C,P)
25	Feb	3	London Scottish	A	Won	1	2	-	1	14	-	-	-	-	0	Lawrence(2T) Thomas(T) Morris(C,P)
26		10	NEWPORT	H	Lost	-	-	-	-	0	2	1	-	1	16	
27		17	Bath	A	Won	-	5	-	-	15	-	1	-	-	3	Cullen(T) Thomas(2T) Sibson(T) Nicholas(T)
28		24	Northampton	A	Won	1	3	-	-	14	1	-	-	-	5	Cullen(2T,C) Thomas(2T)
29	Mar	3	HARLEQUINS	H	Won	1	-	-	1	8	-	-	-	1	3	Cullen(C,P) Kail(T)
30		10	COVENTRY	H	Lost	1	-	-	-	5	2	-	-	1	13	Cullen(C) Kail(T)
31		17	SWANSEA	H	Lost	-	1	-	-	3	1	1	-	-	8	Sibson(T)
32		24	Bristol	A	Won	1	1	-	1	11	-	-	-	1	3	Cullen(C,P) Kail(T) Morris(T)
33		26	Plymouth Albion	A	Lost	-	1	-	-	3	-	1	-	1	6	Barrow(T)
34		27	Exeter	A	Won	1	-	-	-	5	-	-	-	-	0	Cullen(T,C)
35		31	Bedford	A	Lost	-	-	-	-	0	-	-	-	1	3	
36	Apr	7	Birkenhead Park	A	Won	2	1	-	-	13	-	-	-	1	3	Cullen(T,2C) Sibson(T) Matthews(T)
37		14	Swansea	A	Lost	-	-	-	2	6	2	2	1	-	19	Cullen(2P)
38		21	BLACKHEATH	H	Won	1	2	1	-	14	-	,1	-	-	3	Cullen(C,D) Pratt(T) Bleasdale(T) Nicholas(T)

INDIVIDUAL APPEARANCES 1950-1951

NAME	1	2	3	4	5	6	7	8	9	10	11	12	13	14	15	16	17	18	19	20	21	22	23	24	25	26	27	28	29	30	31	32	33	34	35	36	37	38	39	40	41	42	43	44	45	46	TOTAL	T	PTS
Rae Marshall	FB	FB	FB	-	-	-	-	-	-	-	-	-	-	-	FB	FB	FB	FB	FB	FB	-	-	-	-	-	-	-	-	-	-	-	-	-	-	-	-	-	-	-	-	-	-	-	-	-	-	12	-	-
R.A.Lewis	-	-	-	FB	FB	FB	FB	FB	FB	FB	FB	FB	-	-	-	-	-	-	-	FB	FB	FB	FB	FB	FB	FB	-	-	-	-	-	-	-	-	-	-	-	-	-	-	-	-	-	-	-	-	17	-	-
Howard Deacon	-	-	-	-	-	-	-	-	-	-	-	-	-	-	-	-	-	-	-	-	-	-	-	-	-	-	FB	FB	FB	FB	FB	FB	FB	FB	FB	-	-	-	-	-	-	-	-	-	-	-	9	-	-
Ken Nicholas	W	W	W	W	W	W	W	W	W	W	W	W	W	W	-	W	W	W	W	W	W	W	W	W	W	W	W	W	W	W	W	W	W	W	W	-	-	-	-	-	-	-	-	-	-	-	37	6	21
Gwynne Lawrence	-	W	W	W	W	W	W	W	-	W	W	W	W	W	C	W	W	W	W	W	W	W	W	W	W	C	C	C	W	-	-	W	C	C	C	-	-	-	-	-	-	-	-	-	-	-	32	13	39
Bob Matthews	-	-	-	-	-	-	-	-	-	-	-	-	-	W	-	-	-	-	-	-	-	-	-	-	-	-	W	-	W	-	W	W	-	W	W	W	-	-	-	-	-	-	-	-	-	-	8	2	6
George Cullen	C	C	C	C	C	C	C	C	C	C	C	C	-	C	-	C	C	C	C	C	C	C	C	C	C	C	W	W	C	C	C	C	C	C	C	FH	FH	FH	-	-	-	-	-	-	-	-	36	16	128
David Quine	C	C	C	C	-	-	-	-	-	-	-	-	-	-	-	-	-	-	-	-	-	-	-	-	-	-	-	W	-	-	-	-	-	-	-	-	-	-	-	-	-	-	-	-	-	-	5	1	3
Haydn Thomas	-	-	-	C	C	C	C	C	C	C	C	C	C	C	C	C	C	C	C	C	C	C	C	C	C	C	C	C	-	C	C	C	C	C	C	C	C	C	-	-	-	-	-	-	-	-	33	16	48
Franklyn Brookman	FH	FH	FH	FH	FH	FH	FH	FH	W	-	-	-	-	-	-	-	-	-	-	-	-	-	-	-	-	-	-	-	-	-	-	-	-	-	-	-	-	-	-	-	-	-	-	-	-	-	9	-	28
Jim Morris	-	-	-	-	-	-	-	-	-	FH	FH	FH	C	FH	FH	FH	FH	FH	FH	FH	FH	FH	FH	FH	FH	FH	FH	FH	FH	FH	FH	FH	FH	FH	FH	-	-	-	-	-	-	-	-	-	-	-	26	1	79
Roy Murgatroyd	SH	-	-	-	-	-	-	-	-	-	-	-	-	-	-	-	-	-	-	SH	SH	-	-	-	-	-	-	-	-	-	-	-	-	-	-	-	-	-	-	-	-	-	-	-	-	-	3	-	-
John Noton	-	SH	SH	-	-	-	-	-	-	-	-	-	-	-	-	-	-	-	-	-	-	-	-	-	-	-	SH	SH	SH	-	-	-	-	-	-	-	-	-	-	-	-	-	-	-	-	-	5	-	-
Bill Moore	-	-	-	SH	SH	SH	SH	SH	SH	SH	SH	SH	SH	SH	-	SH	SH	SH	SH	-	-	-	-	SH	SH	SH	-	-	SH	SH	SH	SH	SH	-	-	-	SH	SH	-	-	-	-	-	-	-	-	27	1	3
John McTigue	-	-	-	-	-	-	-	-	-	-	-	-	-	SH	-	-	-	-	SH	-	-	-	-	-	-	-	-	-	-	-	-	-	-	-	-	-	-	-	-	-	-	-	-	-	-	-	2	-	-
Denis Bolesworth	P	P	P	P	P	P	P	P	P	P	P	P	P	P	P	P	P	P	P	P	P	P	P	P	P	P	P	P	P	P	P	P	P	P	P	P	P	-	-	-	-	-	-	-	-	-	38	3	9
John Hacker	P	P	P	P	P	P	P	P	P	P	P	P	P	P	P	P	P	P	P	P	P	P	P	P	P	P	P	P	-	P	P	P	-	P	-	-	-	-	-	-	-	-	-	-	-	-	35	2	6
Stan Pratt	H	H	H	H	H	H	H	H	-	H	H	H	-	H	H	H	H	H	H	H	H	H	H	H	H	H	H	-	-	-	H	H	-	H	H	-	-	-	-	-	-	-	-	-	-	-	32	2	6
Len Chawner	-	-	-	-	-	-	-	-	-	H	-	-	-	H	-	-	-	-	-	-	-	-	-	-	-	-	-	H	H	H	-	-	-	-	-	-	-	-	-	-	-	-	-	-	-	-	6	-	-
Eric Lacey	L	L	L	L	L	L	L	L	-	L	L	L	L	L	L	L	L	L	L	-	L	L	L	L	L	L	L	L	L	L	L	L	-	L	-	L	L	L	-	-	-	-	-	-	-	-	34	5	15
Bob Stirling	L	L	L	L	L	L	L	L	-	L	-	L	L	-	L	L	-	L	L	L	L	-	-	L	-	-	-	-	P	L	-	P	-	P	-	-	-	-	-	-	-	-	-	-	-	-	20	-	-
Frank Chawner	-	-	-	-	-	-	-	L	-	L	L	-	L	-	-	-	-	L	L	-	-	-	L	L	L	L	L	L	L	L	L	L	-	L	L	-	-	-	-	-	-	-	-	-	-	-	19	-	-
Ron Smith	-	-	-	-	-	-	-	L	-	-	-	-	-	-	-	-	-	-	-	-	-	-	-	-	-	-	-	-	-	-	L	-	-	-	-	-	-	-	-	-	-	-	-	-	-	-	2	-	-
Jerry Day	8	FL	FL	FL	FL	-	-	-	-	-	-	-	-	-	-	-	-	-	-	-	-	-	-	-	-	-	-	-	-	-	-	-	-	-	-	-	-	-	-	-	-	-	-	-	-	-	5	-	-
Colin Kail	FL	-	-	-	-	-	-	-	-	-	-	-	FL	FL	FL	FL	FL	FL	FL	FL	FL	FL	FL	FL	FL	FL	FL	FL	FL	FL	FL	FL	FL	FL	FL	FL	FL	FL	-	-	-	-	-	-	-	-	26	4	12
Harry Sibson	FL	FL	FL	FL	FL	FL	FL	FL	FL	FL	FL	FL	8	FL	FL	FL	FL	FL	FL	FL	FL	FL	FL	FL	FL	FL	FL	FL	FL	FL	FL	FL	FL	FL	FL	FL	FL	FL	-	-	-	-	-	-	-	-	38	11	33
Bob Weighill	-	8	8	8	8	8	8	-	8	-	-	-	-	-	-	-	-	-	-	-	-	-	-	-	-	-	-	-	-	-	-	-	-	-	-	-	-	-	-	-	-	-	-	-	-	-	8	-	-
Tom Bleasdale	-	-	-	-	-	-	-	FL	FL	FL	FL	FL	FL	FL	8	8	8	8	8	8	L	8	8	8	8	8	8	8	8	8	8	8	-	-	-	8	8	8	-	-	-	-	-	-	-	-	30	1	3
Eric Barrow	-	-	-	-	-	-	-	-	8	-	8	8	FL	-	-	-	-	-	-	8	-	L	L	L	-	-	-	-	-	-	-	-	8	8	8	-	-	-	-	-	-	-	-	-	-	-	11	1	3

1 game: J.M.Guffick FH(9), David Lammiman W(1), W.H.Redfern W(15), J.K.Shepherd SH(24), J.R.Williams FH(13)

NO	DATE		OPPONENTS	V	RES	FOR					AGAINST					SCORERS
						G	T	D	P	PTS	G	T	D	P	PTS	
1	Sep	1	BEDFORD	H	Lost	-	-	-	1	3	-	-	1	1	6	Morris(P)
2		8	BATH	H	Won	-	-	-	2	6	-	-	-	1	3	Morris(2P)
3		15	PLYMOUTH ALBION	H	Won	1	3	-	-	14	-	2	-	1	9	Nicholas(T) Morris(C) Bolesworth(T) Lacey(T) Bleasdale(T)
4		22	Waterloo	A	Won	-	2	-	-	6	1	-	-	-	5	F.Chawner(T) Bleasdale(T)
5		29	MOSELEY	H	Won	1	2	1	1	17	-	1	-	-	3	Cullen(T) Lawrence(T) Morris(C,D,P) Bolesworth(T)
6	Oct	6	COVENTRY	H	Lost	2	-	1	-	13	4	-	-	-	20	Morris(2C,D) Sibson(T) Bleasdale(T)
7		13	Richmond	A	Won	4	-	-	1	23	1	-	-	-	5	Thomas(T) Cullen(4C,P) Bleasdale(3T)
8		20	NEWPORT	H	Lost	-	1	-	-	3	2	1	-	1	16	Doyle(T)
9		25	OXFORD UNIVERSITY	H	Lost	2	1	-	1	16	1	2	1	2	20	Lawrence(T) Cullen(2C,P) Bleasdale(2T)
10		27	Northampton	A	Lost	1	1	-	1	11	2	1	-	-	13	Nicholas(T) Cullen(T,C,P)
11	Nov	3	Gloucester	A	Lost	1	-	-	1	8	2	2	-	-	16	Cullen(T,C,P)
12		10	CAMBRIDGE UNIVERSITY	H	Lost	-	1	-	1	6	1	1	-	-	8	Lawrence(T) Cullen(P)
13		17	MIDDLESEX HOSPITAL	H	Won	2	4	-	2	28	1	-	-	1	8	Cullen(T,2C,2P) Channer(T) Pratt(T) Bleasdale(T) Ashurst(2T)
		24	Neath	A		Cancelled Rain										
14	Dec	1	Harlequins	A	Lost	-	-	-	1	3	-	1	-	2	9	Fisk(P)
15		8	BLACKHEATH	H	Lost	-	1	-	-	3	-	2	-	-	6	Bleasdale(T)
16		15	BRISTOL	H	Won	1	-	1	-	8	1	-	-	-	5	Fisk(C) Channer(D) Ashurst(T)
17		22	Rugby	A	Drew	-	1	1	-	6	-	2	-	-	6	Channer(D) Bleasdale(T)
18		26	BIRKENHEAD PARK	H	Lost	-	-	-	1	3	-	1	-	1	6	Cullen(P)
19		27	BARBARIANS	H	Won	2	1	-	-	13	1	1	-	-	8	Thomas(T) Cullen(2C) Smith(T) Sibson(T)
20	Jan	5	Bath	A	Won	-	2	-	-	6	-	-	-	-	0	Lawrence(T) Cullen(T)
21		12	GLOUCESTER	H	Won	-	1	1	1	9	1	-	-	-	5	Fisk(D) Cullen(P) Lawrence(T)
22		19	Bedford	A	Lost	-	1	-	-	3	1	-	-	-	5	Bolesworth(T)
23		24	ROYAL AIR FORCE	H	Drew	1	-	1	-	8	1	-	-	1	8	Thomas(D) Barrow(C) Bleasdale(T)
		26	Headingley	A		Cancelled Snow										
	Feb	2	LONDON SCOTTISH	H		Cancelled Frost										
		9	Newport	A		Cancelled Funeral										
24		16	Moseley	A	Won	1	1	-	-	8	-	-	-	-	0	Cullen(C) Moore(T) Bolesworth(T)
25		23	NORTHAMPTON	H	Lost	-	1	-	-	3	1	-	-	-	5	Cullen(T)
26	Mar	1	HARLEQUINS	H	Lost	-	1	-	3	12	2	2	-	2	22	Cullen(2P) Beaver(T) Barrow(P)
27		8	Coventry	A	Lost	-	-	1	1	6	2	-	-	1	13	Cullen(D,P)
28		15	SWANSEA	H	Won	1	-	-	1	8	-	-	-	-	0	Botting(T) Cullen(C) Barrow(P)
29		22	NUNEATON	H	Won	2	2	-	2	22	1	-	1	1	11	Botting(T) Cullen(T,2C,2P) Lawrence(T) Doyle(T)
30		29	Cardiff	A	Lost	1	-	1	-	8	1	1	-	2	14	Cullen(T,C) Channer(D)
31	Apr	5	Birkenhead Park	A	Lost	-	-	-	-	0	2	-	-	-	10	
32		12	Bristol	A	Won	2	2	1	-	19	-	1	1	2	12	Matthews(T) Thomas(T) Cullen(2C) Channer(T,D) Bleasdale(T)
33		14	Plymouth Albion	A	Won	2	3	-	-	19	-	-	-	-	0	Lawrence(2T) Cullen(2C) Gee(T) Botting(2T)
34		15	Exeter	A	Lost	-	-	-	-	0	1	2	-	-	11	
35		19	SALE	H	Won	2	5	-	-	25	-	-	-	1	3	Botting(2T) Gee(T) Cullen(T,2C) Lawrence(2T) Sibson(T)

INDIVIDUAL APPEARANCES 1951-1952

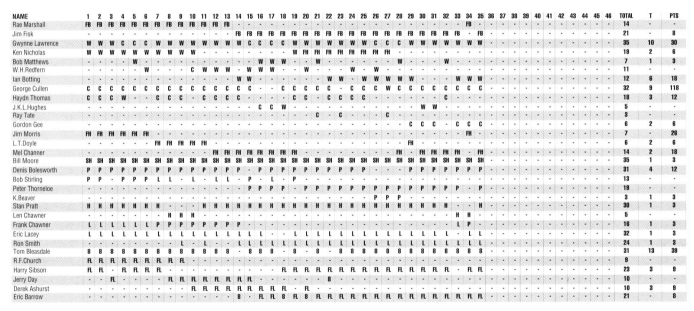

1 game: John Hacker P(3), J.G.Kennewell L(18), Peter Konig FL(33)

LEICESTER FOOTBALL CLUB 1951-52
Back: J.E. Thorneloe (Hon.Sec), W.N. Bradshaw (President), J.W. Fisk, R. Marshall, P.B.L. Thorneloe, R.H. Smith, I.J. Botting, C.G.S. Lawrence,
W.K. Nicholas, R.L. Bedingfield (Hon.Tres), R.J. Barr (Team Hon.Sec).
Middle: H.W. Sibson, G.H. Cullen, M.R. Channer, A.D. Bolesworth, W.K.T. Moore (Capt), T. Bleasdale, E.C. Lacey, S. Pratt, E.A. Barrow.
Front: G.E. Gee, W.H. Redfern. **Inset:** H.G. Thomas, R.V. Stirling.

LEICESTER FOOTBALL CLUB 1952-53
Back: J.E. Thorneloe (Hon.Sec), C.W. Cross (President), S. Pratt, L. Chawner, I.J. Botting, J.M. Jenkins, T. Bleasdale, R.H. Smith,
P.H. Konig, H.W. Sibson, R.L. Bedingfield (Hon.Tres), H.P. Jerwood, R.J. Barr (Team Hon.Sec).
Middle: W.K. Nicholas, E.A. Barrow, W.K.T. Moore, A.D. Bolesworth (Capt), C.G.S. Lawrence, P.B.L. Thorneloe, G.H. Cullen.
Front: W.J. Clarke, J.W. Fisk.

1952-1953

NO	DATE		OPPONENTS	V	RES	FOR G	FOR T	FOR D	FOR P	FOR PTS	AGAINST G	AGAINST T	AGAINST D	AGAINST P	AGAINST PTS	SCORERS
1	Sep	6	BEDFORD	H	Won	2	1	-	1	16	2	-	-	-	10	Cullen(2C,P) Matthews(T) F.Chawner(T) Bleasdale(T)
2		13	BATH	H	Won	-	2	-	1	9	-	-	-	1	3	Botting(T) Channer(P) Konig(T)
3		20	PLYMOUTH ALBION	H	Won	3	3	1	-	27	-	1	-	1	6	Cullen(T,C) Channer(D) Jones(T) Bolesworth(T) F.Chawner(T) Barrow(2C) Konig(2T)
4		23	CARDIFF	H	Lost	-	-	-	2	6	-	2	-	1	9	Channer(P) Barrow(P)
5		27	WATERLOO	H	Won	-	2	-	3	15	1	2	-	1	14	Cullen(2P) Lawrence(T) Channer(P) Jenkins(T)
6	Oct	4	Coventry	A	Won	1	2	-	3	20	1	-	-	1	8	Cullen(C,2P) Lawrence(T) Channer(P) R.H.Smith(T) Barrow(T)
7		18	Nuneaton	A	Lost	-	-	-	2	6	-	2	-	1	9	Fisk(P) Barrow(P)
8		22	Oxford University	A	Drew	-	2	-	-	6	-	2	-	-	6	Botting(T) Konig(T)
9		25	Northampton	A	Lost	-	-	-	-	0	1	1	-	1	11	
10	Nov	1	GLOUCESTER	H	Lost	-	1	-	-	3	-	2	-	-	6	Jenkins(T)
11		8	Cambridge University	A	Lost	-	-	-	-	0	1	-	1	-	8	
12		15	RUGBY	H	Won	1	-	-	1	8	-	2	-	-	6	Channer(C,P) Sibson(T)
13		22	NUNEATON	H	Drew	-	1	-	-	3	-	1	-	-	3	Shuttlewood(T)
		29	Rugby	A		Cancelled Frost										
	Dec	6	Harlequins	A		Cancelled Frost										
14		13	Blackheath	A	Lost	1	1	-	-	8	3	-	-	-	15	Cullen(C) R.H.Smith(T) Barrow(T)
15		20	BRISTOL	H	Won	-	-	1	1	6	1	-	-	-	5	Channer(D,P)
16		26	BARBARIANS	H	Lost	-	1	1	1	9	2	2	-	2	22	Lawrence(T) Channer(D,P)
		27	BIRKENHEAD PARK	H		Cancelled Fog										
17	Jan	3	Bath	A	*Won	1	1	-	-	8	1	-	-	-	5	Cullen(C) Lawrence(T) Konig(T)
18		10	Gloucester	A	Lost	-	2	-	-	6	2	-	-	-	10	R.H.Smith(T) Jenkins(T)
19		17	MIDDLESEX HOSPITAL	H	Won	-	2	-	1	9	-	1	-	-	3	Botting(T) Shuttlewood(T) Cullen(P)
20		24	Bedford	A	Won	3	-	-	1	18	-	1	-	-	3	Botting(T) Cullen(3C,P) Lawrence(T) Jones(T)
21		29	ROYAL AIR FORCE	H	Lost	1	-	-	2	11	-	2	1	1	12	Fisk(C,2P) Bolesworth(T)
22		31	ROSSLYN PARK	H	Won	-	3	-	-	9	-	-	-	2	6	Lawrence(2T) Bleasdale(T)
23	Feb	7	London Scottish	A	Lost	-	1	2	-	9	2	1	-	-	13	Channer(D) Cullen(T,D)
24		14	NEWPORT	H	Lost	-	-	-	1	3	1	1	1	1	14	Cullen(P)
25		21	Moseley	A	Lost	-	2	-	1	9	1	2	-	1	14	Botting(T) Cullen(P) Lawrence(T)
26		28	NORTHAMPTON	H	Lost	-	3	-	-	9	2	-	-	-	10	Botting(T) Cullen(T) Lawrence(T)
27	Mar	7	HARLEQUINS	H	Drew	-	2	-	-	6	-	1	-	1	6	Botting(T) Nicholas(T)
28		14	COVENTRY	H	Lost	2	-	-	-	10	2	-	-	2	16	Cullen(T) Jenkins(T) Barrow(2C)
29		21	Swansea	A	Lost	-	1	-	-	3	1	1	-	-	8	Lawrence(T)
30		28	HEADINGLEY	H	Won	-	3	-	1	12	1	-	-	1	8	Botting(T) Cullen(T) Jenkins(T) Barrow(P)
31	Apr	4	Bristol	A	Lost	-	-	-	-	0	-	-	-	2	6	
32		6	Plymouth Albion	A	Won	1	1	-	-	8	1	-	-	-	5	Botting(T) Barrow(C) Jenkins(T)
33		7	Exeter	A	Won	2	1	-	-	13	1	-	-	-	5	Cullen(2T,2C) F.Chawner(T)
34		11	Birkenhead Park	A	Lost	1	1	-	-	8	2	3	1	-	22	Fisk(C) Lawrence(T) R.H.Smith(T)
35		18	Sale	A	Won	-	7	-	1	24	2	1	-	2	19	Nicholas(T) Cullen(3T) Lawrence(2T) Barrow(P) Konig(T)

INDIVIDUAL APPEARANCES 1952-1953

NAME	1	2	3	4	5	6	7	8	9	10	11	12	13	14	15	16	17	18	19	20	21	22	23	24	25	26	27	28	29	30	31	32	33	34	35	36	37	38	39	40	41	42	43	44	45	46	TOTAL	T	PTS
Jim Fisk	FB	FB	FB	FB	FB	FB	FB	FB	FB	FB	FB	FB	-	FB	-	-	-	-	-	FB	FB	FB	FB	FB	FB	FB	FB	FB	-	FB	FB	FB	FB	FB	-	-	-	-	-	-	-	-	-	-	-	-	27	-	13
Rae Marshall	-	-	-	-	-	-	-	-	-	-	-	-	FB	-	FB	FB	FB	FB	-	-	-	-	-	-	-	-	-	-	FB	-	-	-	-	-	FB	-	-	-	-	-	-	-	-	-	-	-	7	-	-
Bob Matthews	W	-	-	-	W	-	W	-	-	-	-	-	-	-	-	-	-	-	-	-	-	-	-	-	-	-	-	-	-	-	-	-	-	-	-	-	-	-	-	-	-	-	-	-	-	-	3	1	3
Ken Nicholas	W	-	-	-	-	-	-	-	-	-	-	-	-	-	-	-	-	-	-	-	-	-	-	C	C	C	C	C	W	C	W	-	FH	C	C	-	-	-	-	-	-	-	-	-	-	-	12	2	6
Ian Botting	-	W	W	W	-	W	-	W	W	-	W	W	W	-	W	W	W	W	W	W	W	W	W	W	W	W	W	W	-	W	-	W	W	-	-	-	-	-	-	-	-	-	-	-	-	-	26	9	27
David Belasco	-	-	-	-	-	-	-	-	-	W	-	-	-	W	-	-	-	-	-	-	-	-	-	-	-	-	-	-	-	-	-	-	W	W	W	-	-	-	-	-	-	-	-	-	-	-	5	-	-
A.Ward	-	-	-	-	-	-	-	-	-	-	-	W	W	-	-	-	-	-	-	-	-	-	-	-	-	-	-	-	-	-	-	-	-	-	-	-	-	-	-	-	-	-	-	-	-	-	2	-	-
George Cullen	C	C	C	-	C	C	-	-	C	C	FH	-	-	C	C	C	C	C	C	C	-	C	C	C	C	C	C	C	C	C	C	C	C	-	C	-	-	-	-	-	-	-	-	-	-	-	28	10	82
Gwynne Lawrence	C	W	W	W	W	W	W	W	W	W	W	-	-	W	W	W	W	W	W	W	W	W	W	W	W	W	W	W	W	W	W	W	C	W	W	-	-	-	-	-	-	-	-	-	-	-	33	13	39
Gordon Gee	-	C	C	C	C	-	C	-	-	-	-	-	-	-	-	-	-	-	-	-	-	-	-	-	-	-	-	-	-	-	-	-	-	-	-	-	-	-	-	-	-	-	-	-	-	-	5	-	-
Keith MacDonald	-	-	-	C	-	C	-	-	-	C	C	C	-	-	-	-	-	-	-	-	-	-	-	-	-	-	-	-	-	-	-	-	-	-	-	-	-	-	-	-	-	-	-	-	-	-	5	-	-
J.M.Guffick	-	-	-	-	-	-	-	-	C	FH	-	-	-	-	-	-	-	-	-	-	-	-	-	-	-	-	-	-	-	-	-	-	-	-	-	-	-	-	-	-	-	-	-	-	-	-	2	-	-
D.H.Smith	-	-	-	-	-	-	-	-	-	-	C	-	C	-	-	-	-	-	-	-	-	-	-	-	-	-	-	-	-	-	-	-	-	-	-	-	-	-	-	-	-	-	-	-	-	-	2	-	-
John Shuttlewood	-	-	-	-	-	-	-	-	-	-	-	C	C	C	-	-	C	C	C	C	C	-	-	-	-	-	-	-	C	-	C	-	-	C	-	-	-	-	-	-	-	-	-	-	-	-	11	2	6
Mel Channer	FH	FH	FH	FH	FH	FH	-	FH	FH	-	-	FH	-	-	C	FH	-	-	FB	-	-	C	C	-	-	-	-	-	-	-	FH	C	-	-	-	-	-	-	-	-	-	-	-	-	-	-	16	-	35
G.Pym	-	-	-	-	-	-	-	-	-	-	-	-	FH	FH	-	-	-	-	-	-	-	-	-	-	FH	-	-	-	-	-	-	-	-	-	-	-	-	-	-	-	-	-	-	-	-	-	3	-	-
W.J.Clarke	-	-	-	-	-	-	-	-	-	-	-	-	-	-	FH	-	FH	FH	FH	FH	FH	FH	FH	FH	-	FH	FH	FH	FH	FH	-	FH	-	FH	FH	-	-	-	-	-	-	-	-	-	-	-	17	-	-
K.D.Jones	SH	SH	SH	SH	SH	-	SH	-	SH	SH	SH	-	-	SH	SH	-	SH	-	-	SH	SH	SH	SH	-	-	-	-	-	-	-	-	-	-	-	-	-	-	-	-	-	-	-	-	-	-	-	16	2	6
John Noton	-	-	-	-	-	SH	-	SH	-	-	-	-	-	-	-	-	-	-	-	-	-	-	-	-	-	-	-	-	-	-	-	-	-	-	-	-	-	-	-	-	-	-	-	-	-	-	2	-	-
Bill Moore	-	-	-	-	-	-	-	-	-	-	-	SH	SH	-	-	SH	-	SH	SH	-	-	-	-	SH	SH	SH	SH	SH	-	SH	-	-	SH	SH	SH	-	-	-	-	-	-	-	-	-	-	-	14	-	-
Gus Black	-	-	-	-	-	-	-	-	-	-	-	-	-	-	-	-	-	-	-	-	-	-	-	-	-	-	-	-	SH	-	SH	SH	-	-	-	-	-	-	-	-	-	-	-	-	-	-	3	-	-
Denis Bolesworth	P	P	P	P	P	P	P	P	P	P	P	-	-	P	P	P	P	P	P	P	P	P	P	P	P	P	P	P	P	P	P	P	P	P	P	-	-	-	-	-	-	-	-	-	-	-	33	2	6
Bob Stirling	P	P	P	-	-	P	-	P	L	-	L	P	-	-	-	L	-	-	-	P	P	P	P	-	-	-	-	-	-	-	P	-	-	-	-	-	-	-	-	-	-	-	-	-	-	-	14	-	-
Peter Thorneloe	-	-	-	P	P	-	-	-	P	P	P	-	-	P	P	P	P	P	P	-	-	-	-	P	P	P	P	P	P	P	-	P	P	L	-	-	-	-	-	-	-	-	-	-	-	-	21	-	-
Peter Hudson	-	-	-	-	-	-	-	-	-	-	-	P	P	-	-	-	-	-	-	-	-	-	-	-	-	-	-	-	-	-	-	-	-	-	-	-	-	-	-	-	-	-	-	-	-	-	2	-	-
Stan Pratt	H	H	H	H	H	H	H	H	-	H	H	-	-	H	H	H	H	H	-	-	-	H	H	H	H	H	H	H	H	H	H	H	-	H	H	-	-	-	-	-	-	-	-	-	-	-	28	-	-
Len Chawner	-	-	-	-	-	-	-	-	H	-	-	H	H	-	-	-	-	-	H	H	H	-	-	-	-	-	-	-	-	-	-	-	H	-	-	-	-	-	-	-	-	-	-	-	-	-	7	-	-
Frank Chawner	L	L	L	L	L	L	P	L	-	L	L	-	-	L	-	-	-	-	L	-	-	-	-	L	-	L	L	-	L	L	L	L	L	P	P	-	-	-	-	-	-	-	-	-	-	-	22	3	9
Ron Smith	L	L	L	L	L	L	L	L	L	L	-	-	-	L	L	L	L	L	L	L	-	L	L	L	L	L	L	L	L	-	-	L	L	L	L	-	-	-	-	-	-	-	-	-	-	-	29	4	12
Jerry Day	-	-	-	-	-	-	-	-	-	-	-	L	P	-	-	-	-	-	-	-	-	-	-	-	-	-	-	-	-	-	-	-	-	-	-	-	-	-	-	-	-	-	-	-	-	-	2	-	-
J.G.Kennewell	-	-	-	-	-	-	-	-	-	-	-	L	L	-	-	-	-	-	-	-	L	-	-	-	-	-	-	-	-	-	-	-	-	-	-	-	-	-	-	-	-	-	-	-	-	-	3	-	-
Eric Barrow	FL	FL	FL	FL	FL	FL	FL	FL	FL	FL	FL	-	-	FL	8	FL	8	8	8	-	-	-	-	FL	FL	FL	FL	FL	FL	FL	FL	FL	FL	FL	FL	-	-	-	-	-	-	-	-	-	-	-	29	2	28
Tom Bleasdale	8	8	-	-	-	-	8	-	8	-	-	-	-	-	-	-	-	-	-	L	L	L	8	FL	8	FL	FL	FL	FL	8	8	FL	FL	FL	8	-	-	-	-	-	-	-	-	-	-	-	20	2	6
Peter Konig	FL	FL	FL	FL	FL	FL	FL	FL	FL	FL	FL	-	-	FL	FL	FL	FL	FL	FL	FL	FL	FL	FL	-	FL	-	8	8	-	FL	FL	-	-	-	FL	-	-	-	-	-	-	-	-	-	-	-	27	6	18
John Jenkins	-	-	8	8	8	8	L	8	-	8	8	8	8	8	L	8	L	L	-	8	8	8	L	8	L	8	-	L	8	L	L	8	8	8	L	-	-	-	-	-	-	-	-	-	-	-	30	6	18
Harry Sibson	-	-	-	-	-	-	-	-	-	-	-	FL	FL	-	FL	-	FL	FL	FL	FL	FL	FL	FL	-	-	-	-	-	-	-	-	-	-	-	-	-	-	-	-	-	-	-	-	-	-	-	10	1	3

1 game: Alan Baker L(13), Keith Branston FH(7), Peter Herbert FL(12), R.E.Leslie C(8), J.W.Milne FL(13), Geoffrey Randle C(16), Don Sproul C(8), Ray Tate C(7), Haydn Thomas C(21)

NO	DATE		OPPONENTS	V	RES	FOR G	T	D	P	PTS	AGAINST G	T	D	P	PTS	SCORERS
1	Sep	5	BEDFORD	H	Won	-	3	1	-	12	-	1	-	1	6	Shuttlewood(2T) Channer(T,D)
2		12	BATH	H	Won	3	2	-	1	24	-	1	-	1	6	Elders(T) Cullen(T,2C,P) Channer(T) Hazell(C) Jenkins(T) Konig(T)
3		19	PLYMOUTH ALBION	H	Won	2	3	1	1	25	-	-	-	1	3	Duff(P) Elders(T) Shuttlewood(T) Channer(D) Hazell(T,2C) Sibson(2T)
4		21	CARDIFF	H	Lost	-	-	1	-	3	-	3	-	1	12	Channer(D)
5		26	Harlequins	A	Won	-	2	-	1	9	-	-	1	1	6	Cullen(P) Shuttlewood(T) Bleasdale(T)
6	Oct	3	COVENTRY	H	Won	1	-	1	2	14	-	-	-	1	3	Cullen(C,P) Channer(T,D) Baker(P)
7		10	Cheltenham	A	Lost	-	-	-	-	0	1	-	-	-	5	
8		15	LOUGHBOROUGH COLLEGE	H	Won	-	3	2	-	15	-	1	-	2	9	Pym(T) Nicholas(D) Black(D) Pratt(T) Bleasdale(T)
9		17	MOSELEY	H	Lost	-	1	-	-	3	-	1	1	-	6	Bleasdale(T)
10		21	OXFORD UNIVERSITY	H	Won	2	1	-	-	13	-	-	-	3	9	Duff(2C) Nicholas(T) Grove(2T)
11		24	NORTHAMPTON	H	Won	-	1	2	1	12	1	-	-	1	8	Cullen(P) Belasco(D) Channer(D) Black(T)
12		31	RUGBY	H	Won	-	3	-	2	15	-	2	-	-	6	Channer(2P) Smith(T) Lacey(T) Sibson(T)
13	Nov	7	GLOUCESTER	H	Won	2	1	-	-	13	1	1	-	-	8	Elders(T) Clarke(T) Hazell(2C) Bleasdale(T)
14		14	CAMBRIDGE UNIVERSITY	H	Won	1	2	-	2	17	1	3	-	-	14	Elders(2T) Black(T) Hazell(C,2P)
15		21	Nuneaton	A	Lost	1	-	-	2	11	1	-	-	4	17	Marshall(C) Lee(T) Channer(2P)
16	Dec	5	Waterloo	A	Lost	-	3	-	-	9	-	1	-	3	12	Nicholas(2T) Bolesworth(T)
17		12	BLACKHEATH	H	Won	2	1	-	2	19	-	3	-	-	9	Shuttlewood(2T) Hazell(T,2C,2P)
18		19	BRISTOL	H	Won	1	1	-	-	8	-	1	1	-	6	Channer(C) Hazell(2T)
19		26	BIRKENHEAD PARK	H	Won	2	1	-	-	13	1	1	-	-	8	Hazell(T,2C) Bleasdale(T) Ashurst(T)
20		28	BARBARIANS	H	Lost	1	1	-	1	11	6	3	-	-	39	Hazell(T,C,P) Ashurst(T)
21	Jan	2	Bath	A	Drew	-	-	-	1	3	-	1	-	-	3	Baker(P)
22		9	Gloucester	A	Lost	-	-	-	-	0	2	3	-	-	19	
23		16	Headingley	A	Lost	-	1	-	-	3	-	2	-	2	12	Thorneloe(T)
24		23	Bedford	A	Lost	1	-	-	-	5	2	3	1	-	22	Elders(T) Hazell(C)
		30	Rosslyn Park	A		CancelledFrost										
	Feb	4	ROYAL AIR FORCE	H		CancelledFrost										
		6	LONDON SCOTTISH	H		CancelledFrost										
25		13	Newport	A	Lost	-	1	-	-	3	1	5	-	-	20	Jenkins(T)
26		20	MIDDLESEX HOSPITAL	H	Won	-	3	-	1	12	-	1	-	-	3	Marshall(P) Lee(2T) Sibson(T)
27		27	Northampton	A	Lost	1	-	-	-	5	2	3	-	-	19	Hazell(C) Thorneloe(T)
28	Mar	6	HARLEQUINS	H	Won	-	4	-	-	12	-	-	-	1	3	Marshall(T) Doore(T) Thorneloe(T) Jenkins(T)
29		13	Coventry	A	Won	2	-	-	-	10	1	-	1	-	8	Richards(T) Hazell(2C) Konig(T)
30		20	SWANSEA	H	Drew	-	-	-	2	6	-	2	-	-	6	Hazell(2P)
31		27	LOUGHBOROUGH COLLEGE	H	Won	2	3	1	-	22	-	-	-	-	0	Lee(T) Clarke(D) Matthews(T) Haines(T) Hazell(2C) Lacey(T) Konig(T)
32	Apr	3	Birkenhead Park	A	Won	1	2	-	1	14	-	3	-	-	9	Elders(T) Matthews(T) Hazell(C,P) Konig(T)
33		10	NUNEATON	H	Won	2	1	-	-	13	-	1	-	-	3	Shuttlewood(T) Hazell(T,2C) Smith(T)
34		17	Bristol	A	Lost	-	1	-	-	3	3	-	1	-	18	Richards(T)
35		19	Plymouth Albion	A	Won	3	1	-	-	18	-	1	-	-	3	Hazell(3C) Bolesworth(T) Konig(3T)
36		20	Exeter	A	Lost	1	-	-	-	5	-	2	-	1	9	Konig(T) Hazell(C)
37		24	SALE	H	Won	3	3	1	-	27	1	1	-	2	14	Matthews(T) Elders(T) Channer(2T,D) Hazell(T,3C) Smith(T)

INDIVIDUAL APPEARANCES 1953-1954

NAME	1	2	3	4	5	6	7	8	9	10	11	12	13	14	15	16	17	18	19	20	21	22	23	24	25	26	27	28	29	30	31	32	33	34	35	36	37	38	39	40	41	42	43	44	45	46	TOTAL	T	PTS
S.M.Duff	FB	FB	FB	FB	-	FB	FB	FB	FB	FB	FB	FB	FB	FB	-	-	-	-	-	-	-	C	-	-	-	-	-	-	-	-	-	-	-	-	-	-	-	-	-	-	-	-	-	-	-	-	14	-	7
Rae Marshall	-	-	-	-	FB	-	-	-	-	-	-	-	-	-	FB	FB	FB	FB	FB	FB	FB	FB	FB	FB	FB	FB	FB	FB	FB	FB	FB	FB	FB	FB	FB	FB	FB	-	-	-	-	-	-	-	-	-	24	1	8
Ken Nicholas	W	W	W	W	-	-	W	W	W	W	W	W	W	-	-	W	-	-	-	-	-	-	-	-	-	-	-	-	-	-	-	-	-	-	-	-	-	-	-	-	-	-	-	-	-	-	12	3	12
John Shuttlewood	W	W	W	W	W	W	W	W	-	-	-	W	W	W	W	W	W	W	W	W	W	W	W	-	-	-	W	-	-	-	-	-	W	C	W	-	W	-	-	-	-	-	-	-	-	-	25	7	21
David Belasco	-	-	-	-	W	W	-	-	W	W	W	-	-	W	-	-	-	-	-	-	-	-	-	-	W	-	-	-	-	-	-	-	-	-	-	W	-	-	-	-	-	-	-	-	-	-	8	-	3
Geoffrey Lee	-	-	-	-	-	-	-	-	-	-	-	-	-	-	W	-	-	W	W	W	W	-	W	W	-	W	-	W	W	W	W	W	-	-	-	-	-	-	-	-	-	-	-	-	-	-	13	4	12
Bob Matthews	-	-	-	-	-	-	-	-	-	-	-	-	-	-	-	-	W	-	-	-	-	-	-	-	W	W	-	-	-	-	W	W	W	W	W	-	W	-	-	-	-	-	-	-	-	-	9	3	9
Ken Richards	-	-	-	-	-	-	-	-	-	-	-	-	-	-	-	-	-	-	-	-	-	-	-	-	-	-	W	W	W	W	-	-	-	W	-	W	-	-	-	-	-	-	-	-	-	-	6	2	6
George Cullen	C	C	C	C	C	C	-	-	C	-	C	-	C	-	-	-	C	-	-	-	-	-	-	-	-	-	-	-	-	-	-	-	-	-	-	-	-	-	-	-	-	-	-	-	-	-	10	1	21
John Elders	C	C	C	C	C	C	-	C	C	C	C	-	C	C	-	-	C	C	C	C	C	C	C	C	C	C	C	C	C	C	C	C	C	-	C	-	C	-	-	-	-	-	-	-	-	-	31	8	24
Dennis Haines	-	-	-	-	-	-	C	-	-	-	-	C	-	C	C	C	FH	C	C	C	C	FH	C	-	C	-	FH	FH	FH	FH	FH	FH	FH	FH	FH	FH	FH	-	-	-	-	-	-	-	-	-	24	1	3
G.Pym	-	-	-	-	-	-	C	C	-	-	-	C	-	-	C	C	-	-	-	-	-	-	-	C	FH	C	C	C	-	C	-	-	-	-	-	-	-	-	-	-	-	-	-	-	-	-	11	1	3
Mel Channer	FH	FH	FH	FH	FH	FH	FH	FH	FH	-	FH	FH	-	FH	FH	FH	-	FH	-	FH	-	-	-	W	-	-	-	-	C	-	-	-	-	-	-	-	C	-	-	-	-	-	-	-	-	-	19	5	47
W.J.Clarke	-	-	-	-	-	-	-	-	-	FH	-	-	FH	-	-	-	-	-	FH	-	FH	SH	FH	FH	-	-	-	-	-	-	C	C	C	C	C	C	-	-	-	-	-	-	-	-	-	-	13	1	6
Gus Black	SH	SH	SH	SH	SH	SH	SH	SH	-	-	SH	SH	-	SH	-	-	-	SH	-	SH	-	-	-	-	-	-	-	-	-	-	-	-	-	-	-	-	-	-	-	-	-	-	-	-	-	-	13	2	9
Norman Grove	-	-	-	-	-	-	-	-	SH	SH	-	-	SH	-	-	-	SH	-	SH	-	-	-	-	SH	-	-	-	-	-	-	-	-	-	-	-	-	-	-	-	-	-	-	-	-	-	-	6	2	6
John Noton	-	-	-	-	-	-	-	-	-	-	-	-	-	-	SH	SH	-	-	-	-	SH	-	-	-	-	-	-	-	-	-	-	-	-	-	-	-	-	-	-	-	-	-	-	-	-	-	3	-	-
D.Hytch	-	-	-	-	-	-	-	-	-	-	-	-	-	-	-	-	-	-	-	-	-	-	SH	-	-	-	-	-	-	-	-	-	SH	-	-	-	-	-	-	-	-	-	-	-	-	-	2	-	-
Freddy Doore	-	-	-	-	-	-	-	-	-	-	-	-	-	-	-	-	-	-	-	-	-	-	-	-	SH	SH	SH	SH	SH	SH	SH	SH	-	SH	SH	-	-	-	-	-	-	-	-	-	-	-	10	1	3
David Hazell	P	P	P	P	P	P	-	P	P	-	P	-	P	P	-	-	P	P	P	P	P	P	-	P	P	-	P	P	P	P	P	P	P	P	P	P	P	-	-	-	-	-	-	-	-	-	30	8	102
Peter Thorneloe	P	P	P	-	-	-	P	P	P	P	P	-	P	-	-	-	P	P	P	P	-	P	P	P	P	P	P	P	P	P	P	P	P	P	-	P	-	-	-	-	-	-	-	-	-	-	27	3	9
Denis Bolesworth	-	-	-	P	P	P	-	-	-	P	-	P	-	P	P	P	-	-	-	-	-	-	-	-	-	-	-	-	-	-	-	-	-	-	P	-	P	-	-	-	-	-	-	-	-	-	10	2	6
Frank Chawner	-	-	-	-	-	-	P	-	-	-	-	P	-	-	P	P	-	-	-	-	P	-	P	-	L	P	-	-	-	-	-	-	-	-	-	-	-	-	-	-	-	-	-	-	-	-	8	-	-
Stan Pratt	H	H	H	H	H	H	-	H	H	H	H	-	H	-	-	-	H	H	H	H	H	H	H	H	-	H	H	H	H	H	H	H	-	H	H	H	H	-	-	-	-	-	-	-	-	-	30	1	3
N.Pugh	-	-	-	-	-	-	H	-	-	-	-	H	-	-	H	-	-	-	-	-	-	-	-	-	-	-	-	-	-	-	-	-	-	-	-	-	-	-	-	-	-	-	-	-	-	-	3	-	-
Len Chawner	-	-	-	-	-	-	-	-	-	-	-	-	-	H	-	H	-	-	-	-	-	-	-	-	H	-	-	-	-	-	-	-	H	-	-	-	-	-	-	-	-	-	-	-	-	-	4	-	-
John Jenkins	L	L	-	8	L	8	-	L	8	8	8	-	8	8	-	-	L	L	L	L	8	8	8	8	8	8	L	L	L	-	-	L	L	L	8	L	L	-	-	-	-	-	-	-	-	-	30	3	9
Eric Lacey	L	L	L	L	-	-	L	-	-	-	-	L	-	-	L	L	-	-	-	-	-	-	-	-	-	L	-	-	L	L	L	L	L	L	L	-	L	-	-	-	-	-	-	-	-	-	17	2	6
Alan Baker	-	-	L	L	L	L	-	L	L	L	L	-	L	L	-	L	L	L	L	L	L	L	L	L	-	-	L	L	-	-	-	-	-	-	L	L	-	-	-	-	-	-	-	-	-	-	23	-	6
Ron Smith	-	-	-	-	-	L	-	-	L	L	L	L	L	L	L	8	-	-	-	-	L	L	L	L	L	L	8	8	8	L	L	8	8	8	-	8	8	-	-	-	-	-	-	-	-	-	25	3	9
Jerry Day	-	-	-	-	-	-	L	-	-	-	-	8	-	-	8	-	-	-	-	-	-	-	-	-	-	-	-	-	-	-	-	-	-	-	-	-	-	-	-	-	-	-	-	-	-	-	3	-	-
Eric Barrow	8	8	8	FL	-	-	8	-	-	-	-	-	-	-	-	-	-	-	-	-	-	-	-	-	-	-	-	-	-	-	-	-	-	-	-	-	-	-	-	-	-	-	-	-	-	-	5	-	-
Tom Bleasdale	FL	FL	-	-	8	-	-	8	FL	FL	FL	-	FL	FL	-	-	8	8	8	8	-	-	-	-	-	-	-	-	-	-	-	-	-	-	-	-	-	-	-	-	-	-	-	-	-	-	13	5	15
Peter Konig	FL	FL	FL	FL	FL	FL	-	FL	-	-	-	-	-	-	FL	FL	FL	-	-	-	-	-	-	-	FL	FL	FL	FL	FL	FL	FL	FL	FL	FL	FL	SH	SH	-	-	-	-	-	-	-	-	-	23	8	24
Harry Sibson	-	-	FL	-	FL	FL	FL	FL	FL	FL	FL	FL	FL	FL	FL	FL	FL	FL	FL	FL	FL	FL	FL	FL	FL	FL	-	-	-	-	-	-	-	-	-	FL	FL	-	-	-	-	-	-	-	-	-	25	4	12
Derek Ashurst	-	-	-	-	-	-	FL	-	-	-	-	FL	-	-	-	-	-	FL	FL	FL	FL	W	FL	FL	-	-	FL	FL	FL	FL	FL	FL	FL	FL	FL	FL	FL	-	-	-	-	-	-	-	-	-	20	2	6
Derek Bircumshaw	-	-	-	-	-	-	-	-	-	-	-	-	-	-	-	-	-	-	-	-	-	-	-	-	-	-	-	-	-	8	8	-	-	-	-	-	-	-	-	-	-	-	-	-	-	-	2	-	-

1 game: Peter Bennett C(36), Ian Coutts C(10), J.M.Guffick FH(26), John McCormack FL(22)

Photo Tale

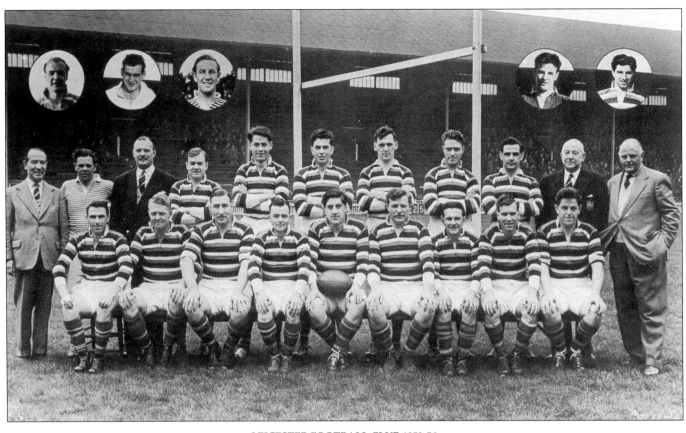

LEICESTER FOOTBALL CLUB 1953-54
Back: J.E. Thorneloe (Hon.Sec), G.A. Walker (Referee), R.J. Barr (Team Hon.Sec), D. Haines, J. Shuttlewood, P.H. Konig, J. Elders,
A.D.B. Ashurst, R.D. Matthews, C.W. Cross (President), R.L. Bedingfield (Hon.Tres).
Front: H.W. Sibson, R.H. Smith, A.D. Bolesworth, M.R. Channer, J.M. Jenkins (Capt), E.C. Lacey, S. Pratt, R. Marshall, D.St.G. Hazell.
Inset: A. Baker, A.W. Black, P.B.L. Thorneloe, T. Bleasdale, G.H. Cullen.

LEICESTER FOOTBALL CLUB 1954-55
Back: J.E. Thorneloe (Hon.Sec), R.J. Barr (Team Hon.Sec), J. Stevens, A.D.B. Ashurst, P.H. Konig, J.G. Ford, B.T.C. Small, J.E. Taylor,
D. Brook, C.W. Cross (President), R.L. Bedingfield (Hon.Tres).
Middle: R. Marshall, F. Chawner, R.H. Smith, J.M. Jenkins (Capt), J. Elders, T. Bleasdale, P.B.L. Thorneloe.
Front: F.R. Doore, G. Lee.

1954-1955

NO	DATE		OPPONENTS	V	RES	FOR					AGAINST					SCORERS
						G	T	D	P	PTS	G	T	D	P	PTS	
1	Sep	4	BEDFORD	H	Won	1	3	-	1	17	1	1	-	-	8	Lee(T) Taylor(T) Brook(T) Hazell(C,P) Konig(T)
2		11	BATH	H	Won	1	-	-	-	5	-	-	-	1	3	Hazell(C) Konig(T)
3		18	PLYMOUTH ALBION	H	Won	2	1	-	2	19	1	2	-	-	11	Taylor(2T) Cullen(T) Channer(C,2P) Hazell(C)
4		20	CARDIFF	H	Lost	1	-	-	2	11	1	-	-	3	14	Channer(C,2P) A.Baker(T)
5		25	Harlequins	A	Lost	2	-	-	2	16	2	3	-	3	28	Channer(T,2C,2P) Bleasdale(T)
6	Oct	2	Coventry	A	Lost	1	-	-	3	14	4	2	-	1	29	Channer(C,3P) Smith(T)
7		6	LOUGHBOROUGH COLLEGE	H	Won	2	-	-	3	19	-	-	-	1	3	Taylor(T) Channer(2C,3P) Konig(T)
8		9	Cheltenham	A	Won	1	2	-	-	11	-	2	1	-	9	Darlington(T) Cullen(T) Channer(T,C)
9		16	NORTHAMPTON	H	Lost	1	-	-	-	5	-	3	-	-	9	Doore(T) Hazell(C)
10		20	Oxford University	A	Lost	-	-	-	-	0	3	-	-	1	18	
11		23	MOSELEY	H	Won	-	2	-	1	9	1	-	1	-	8	Matthews(T) Channer(P) Doore(T)
12		30	Rugby	A	Won	2	-	-	-	10	-	-	-	1	3	Elders(T) Brook(T) Hazell(2C)
13	Nov	6	GLOUCESTER	H	Won	-	3	-	1	12	-	1	-	1	6	Hazell(P) Thorneloe(T) McCormack(2T)
14		13	Cambridge University	A	Lost	-	-	1	1	6	-	3	-	1	12	Channer(D) Hazell(P)
15		20	NUNEATON	H	Won	1	1	-	1	11	-	1	-	-	3	Matthews(T) Channer(C,P) O'Connor(T)
16		27	OLD BLUES	H	Won	2	1	-	-	13	-	1	-	1	6	Symonds(2T) Cullen(2C) Bircumshaw(T)
17	Dec	4	WATERLOO	H	Won	1	2	-	-	11	1	1	-	-	8	Cullen(2T) Channer(C) F.Chawner(T)
18		11	Blackheath	A	Lost	-	2	-	1	9	1	1	1	-	11	Taylor(T) Symonds(T) Channer(P)
19		18	BRISTOL	H	Lost	1	2	-	-	11	1	3	-	1	17	Marshall(C) Brook(T) Elders(T) Konig(T)
20		27	BIRKENHEAD PARK	H	Lost	1	1	-	1	11	2	-	-	1	13	Lee(T) Channer(T) Hazell(C,P)
21		28	BARBARIANS	H	Lost	2	-	-	1	13	2	3	-	1	22	Elders(T) Channer(T) Hazell(2C,P)
22	Jan	1	Bath	A	Won	-	4	-	-	12	-	1	-	1	6	Cullen(3T) Bircumshaw(T)
23		8	Gloucester	A	Lost	-	3	-	-	9	1	1	-	1	11	Lee(T) Cullen(T) Konig(T)
		15	HEADINGLEY	H		Cancelled Snow										
24		22	Bedford	A	Won	-	2	-	1	9	-	-	-	-	0	Small(P) Cullen(T) Bircumshaw(T)
25		27	ROYAL AIR FORCE	H	Won	-	2	-	1	9	1	1	-	-	8	Brook(2T) Channer(P)
26		29	ROSSLYN PARK	H	Won	2	1	-	2	19	-	1	-	3	12	Taylor(T) Elders(T) Hazell(2C,2P) F.Chawner(T)
27	Feb	5	London Scottish	A	Won	1	1	-	1	11	-	1	-	2	9	Taylor(T) Lee(T) Channer(C,P)
28		12	NEWPORT	H	Lost	-	-	-	1	3	-	3	-	-	9	Channer(P)
		19	BRITISH POLICE	H		Cancelled Snow										
		26	Northampton	A		Cancelled Snow										
29	Mar	5	HARLEQUINS	H	Lost	1	-	-	1	8	1	3	-	-	14	Brook(T) Hazell(C,P)
30		12	COVENTRY	H	Drew	1	2	-	-	11	1	2	-	-	11	Small(C) Brook(T) O'Connor(T) Stevens(T)
31		19	Swansea	A	Won	1	1	-	-	8	1	-	-	-	5	Marshall(C) Elders(T) Thorneloe(T)
32		26	Cardiff	A	Lost	-	2	-	1	9	4	3	-	1	32	Cullen(T) Hazell(T,P)
33	Apr	2	Birkenhead Park	A	Drew	-	-	-	-	0	-	-	-	-	0	
34		9	Bristol	A	Won	2	1	-	2	19	-	3	-	1	12	Elders(T) Cullen(T) Brook(T) Hazell(2C,2P)
35		11	Plymouth Albion	A	Lost	2	-	-	1	13	-	2	-	3	15	Hazell(2T,2C,P)
36		12	Exeter	A	Won	5	2	-	-	31	-	-	-	-	0	Elders(3T) Taylor(T) Brook(2T) Hazell(5C) Bleasdale(T)
37		16	LLANELLI	H	Lost	-	3	1	1	15	3	-	1	-	18	Elders(D) Cullen(T) Hazell(P) Ashurst(2T)
38		18	Northampton	A	Won	1	1	-	-	8	-	2	-	-	6	Taylor(T) Cullen(T) Hazell(C)
39		23	Moseley	A	Lost	2	-	-	-	10	1	3	-	-	14	Taylor(T) Brook(T) Hazell(2C)
40		30	SALE	H	Won	1	-	-	4	17	3	-	-	-	15	Small(C) Cullen(4P) Konig(T)

INDIVIDUAL APPEARANCES 1954-1955

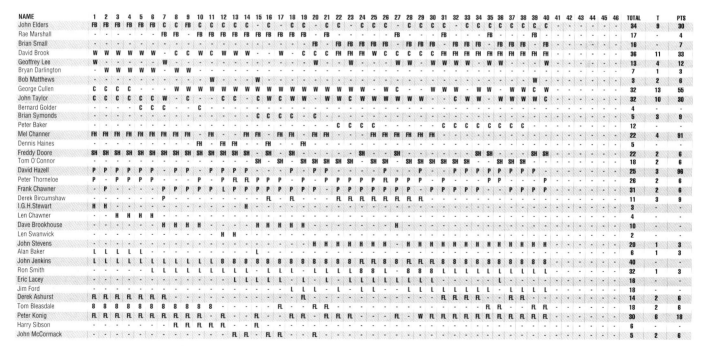

NAME	1	2	3	4	5	6	7	8	9	10	11	12	13	14	15	16	17	18	19	20	21	22	23	24	25	26	27	28	29	30	31	32	33	34	35	36	37	38	39	40	41	42	43	44	45	46	TOTAL	T	PTS
John Elders	FB	FB	FB	FB	FB	FB	C	C	FB	C	C	C	C	C	-	C	-	C	C	-	C	C	-	C	C	C	-	C	C	C	C	-	C	C	C	C	C	C	C	C	-	-	-	-	-	-	34	9	30
Rae Marshall	-	-	-	-	-	-	FB	FB	-	FB	FB	FB	FB	FB	FB	FB	FB	FB	FB	-	FB	-	-	-	-	-	FB	-	-	-	FB	-	-	-	FB	-	-	-	FB	-	-	-	-	-	-	-	17	-	4
Brian Small	-	-	-	-	-	-	-	-	-	-	-	-	-	-	-	-	-	-	-	FB	-	FB	FB	FB	FB	FB	-	FB	FB	FB	-	FB	FB	FB	-	FB	FB	FB	-	FB	-	-	-	-	-	-	16	-	7
David Brook	W	W	W	W	W	W	-	C	C	W	C	W	W	W	-	-	W	-	C	C	C	FH	FH	FH	W	C	C	C	C	C	FH	FH	FH	FH	FH	FH	FH	FH	FH	FH	-	-	-	-	-	-	36	11	33
Geoffrey Lee	W	-	-	-	-	-	W	-	-	-	-	-	-	-	-	-	-	-	-	W	-	-	W	-	-	-	W	W	-	W	W	W	W	-	W	W	-	-	-	W	-	-	-	-	-	-	13	4	12
Bryan Darlington	-	W	W	W	W	W	-	W	W	-	-	-	-	-	-	-	-	-	-	-	-	-	-	-	-	-	-	-	-	-	-	-	-	-	-	-	-	-	-	-	-	-	-	-	-	-	7	1	3
Bob Matthews	-	-	-	-	-	-	-	-	-	-	W	-	-	-	W	-	-	-	-	-	-	-	-	-	-	-	-	-	-	-	-	-	-	-	-	-	-	-	W	-	-	-	-	-	-	-	3	2	6
George Cullen	C	C	C	C	-	-	-	W	W	W	W	W	W	W	W	W	W	W	W	W	W	W	W	W	-	W	C	-	-	W	W	W	-	W	W	-	W	W	C	W	-	-	-	-	-	-	32	13	55
John Taylor	C	C	C	C	C	C	W	-	C	-	-	C	C	-	C	W	C	W	W	-	W	W	C	W	W	W	W	W	W	-	-	C	W	W	-	W	W	W	W	C	-	-	-	-	-	-	32	10	30
Bernard Golder	-	-	-	-	C	C	C	-	-	C	-	-	-	-	-	-	-	-	-	-	-	-	-	-	-	-	-	-	-	-	-	-	-	-	-	-	-	-	-	-	-	-	-	-	-	-	4	-	-
Brian Symonds	-	-	-	-	-	-	-	-	-	-	-	-	-	-	C	C	C	C	-	C	-	-	-	-	-	-	-	-	-	-	-	-	-	-	-	-	-	-	-	-	-	-	-	-	-	-	5	3	9
Peter Baker	-	-	-	-	-	-	-	-	-	-	-	-	-	-	-	-	-	-	-	-	-	C	C	C	C	-	-	-	-	-	C	C	C	C	C	C	C	C	-	-	-	-	-	-	-	-	12	-	-
Mel Channer	FH	FH	FH	FH	FH	FH	FH	FH	FH	-	FH	-	-	FH	FH	-	FH	FH	-	FH	FH	-	-	-	FH	FH	FH	FH	FH	FH	-	-	-	-	-	-	-	-	-	-	-	-	-	-	-	-	22	4	91
Dennis Haines	-	-	-	-	-	-	-	-	-	FH	-	FH	FH	-	-	FH	-	-	FH	-	-	-	-	-	-	-	-	-	-	-	-	-	-	-	-	-	-	-	-	-	-	-	-	-	-	-	5	-	-
Freddy Doore	SH	SH	SH	SH	SH	SH	SH	SH	SH	SH	SH	SH	SH	SH	-	SH	-	SH	-	-	-	-	-	SH	-	-	SH	-	-	-	-	-	-	SH	SH	-	-	-	SH	SH	-	-	-	-	-	-	22	2	6
Tom O'Connor	-	-	-	-	-	-	-	-	-	-	-	-	-	-	SH	-	SH	-	SH	SH	SH	SH	SH	-	SH	SH	-	SH	SH	SH	SH	SH	SH	-	-	SH	SH	SH	-	-	-	-	-	-	-	-	18	2	6
David Hazell	P	P	P	P	P	P	-	P	P	-	P	P	P	P	-	-	-	P	-	P	P	-	-	-	-	P	-	-	P	-	-	P	P	P	P	P	P	P	P	-	-	-	-	-	-	-	25	3	96
Peter Thorneloe	P	-	P	P	P	P	-	-	-	P	-	P	FL	FL	P	P	P	-	P	-	P	P	P	P	P	FL	P	P	P	-	P	-	-	-	P	P	-	-	-	P	-	-	-	-	-	-	26	2	6
Frank Chawner	-	P	-	-	-	-	P	P	P	P	P	L	P	P	P	P	P	P	P	P	-	P	P	P	P	P	P	P	P	-	P	P	P	P	-	-	P	P	P	P	-	-	-	-	-	-	31	2	6
Derek Bircumshaw	-	-	-	-	-	-	P	-	-	-	-	-	-	-	-	FL	-	FL	-	-	-	FL	FL	FL	FL	FL	FL	FL	FL	-	-	-	-	-	-	-	-	-	-	-	-	-	-	-	-	-	11	3	9
I.G.H.Stewart	H	H	-	-	-	-	-	-	-	-	-	-	-	H	-	-	-	-	-	-	-	-	-	-	-	-	-	-	-	-	-	-	-	-	-	-	-	-	-	-	-	-	-	-	-	-	3	-	-
Len Chawner	-	-	H	H	H	H	-	-	-	-	-	-	-	-	-	-	-	-	-	-	-	-	-	-	-	-	-	-	-	-	-	-	-	-	-	-	-	-	-	-	-	-	-	-	-	-	4	-	-
Dave Brookhouse	-	-	-	-	-	-	H	H	H	H	-	-	-	-	H	H	H	H	H	-	-	-	-	-	-	-	H	-	-	-	-	-	-	-	-	-	-	-	-	-	-	-	-	-	-	-	10	-	-
Len Swanwick	-	-	-	-	-	-	-	-	-	-	-	H	H	-	-	-	-	-	-	-	-	-	-	-	-	-	-	-	-	-	-	-	-	-	-	-	-	-	-	-	-	-	-	-	-	-	2	-	-
John Stevens	-	-	-	-	-	-	-	-	-	-	-	-	-	-	-	-	-	-	-	H	H	H	H	H	H	H	-	H	H	H	H	H	H	H	H	H	H	H	H	H	-	-	-	-	-	-	20	1	3
Alan Baker	L	L	L	L	L	-	-	-	-	-	-	-	-	-	L	-	-	-	-	-	-	-	-	-	-	-	-	-	-	-	-	-	-	-	-	-	-	-	-	-	-	-	-	-	-	-	6	1	3
John Jenkins	L	L	L	L	L	L	L	L	L	L	L	8	8	8	8	8	8	8	8	8	8	8	8	FL	FL	8	8	FL	FL	FL	8	8	8	8	8	8	8	8	8	8	-	-	-	-	-	-	40	-	-
Ron Smith	-	-	-	-	-	L	L	L	L	L	L	L	L	L	-	L	L	L	-	L	L	L	L	8	8	L	-	8	8	8	L	L	L	L	L	L	L	L	L	L	-	-	-	-	-	-	32	1	3
Eric Lacey	-	-	-	-	-	-	-	-	-	-	-	-	L	L	L	L	L	-	L	-	L	-	L	L	L	L	L	L	L	L	-	-	-	-	-	L	-	-	-	-	-	-	-	-	-	-	16	-	-
Jim Ford	-	-	-	-	-	-	-	-	-	-	-	-	-	-	-	-	-	L	L	L	-	L	-	L	L	-	-	L	L	L	L	L	L	L	L	-	L	L	L	L	-	-	-	-	-	-	18	-	-
Derek Ashurst	FL	FL	FL	FL	FL	FL	FL	-	-	-	-	-	-	-	-	-	-	-	FL	-	-	-	-	-	-	-	-	-	-	-	FL	FL	FL	FL	-	-	FL	FL	-	-	-	-	-	-	-	-	14	2	6
Tom Bleasdale	8	8	8	8	8	8	8	8	8	8	8	-	-	-	-	-	FL	-	-	FL	FL	-	-	-	-	-	-	-	-	-	-	-	-	-	FL	FL	-	-	FL	FL	-	-	-	-	-	-	18	2	6
Peter Konig	FL	FL	FL	FL	FL	FL	FL	FL	FL	FL	-	FL	-	-	FL	-	-	FL	FL	-	FL	FL	FL	-	-	-	FL	-	W	FL	FL	FL	FL	FL	FL	FL	FL	FL	FL	FL	-	-	-	-	-	-	30	6	18
Harry Sibson	-	-	-	-	-	-	-	FL	FL	FL	FL	FL	-	-	FL	-	-	-	-	-	-	-	-	-	-	-	-	-	-	-	-	-	-	-	-	-	-	-	-	-	-	-	-	-	-	-	6	-	-
John McCormack	-	-	-	-	-	-	-	-	-	-	-	-	FL	FL	-	FL	FL	-	-	FL	-	-	-	-	-	-	-	-	-	-	-	-	-	-	-	-	-	-	-	-	-	-	-	-	-	-	5	2	6

1 game: M.D.Barratt FL(11), Denis Bolesworth P(30), Karl Mullen H(11), Brian Smith C(14), John Thompson L(27)

NO	DATE		OPPONENTS	V	RES	FOR					AGAINST					SCORERS
						G	T	D	P	PTS	G	T	D	P	PTS	
1	Sep	3	BEDFORD	H	Lost	1	-	-	2	11	1	1	3	1	20	Cullen(C,P) Channer(P) T.O'Connor(T)
2		10	BATH	H	Won	3	2	1	-	24	1	1	1	-	11	Elders(T) Cullen(T,2C) Channer(2T,C,D) Ashurst(T)
3		17	PLYMOUTH ALBION	H	Won	4	1	-	-	23	-	1	1	-	6	Taylor(T) Elders(T) Cullen(T,4C) Hazell(T) Ashurst(T)
4		19	CARDIFF	H	Won	-	1	-	1	6	-	-	-	1	3	Cullen(T) Channer(P)
5		24	Harlequins	A	Lost	-	1	-	1	6	2	-	-	-	10	Cullen(T,P)
6	Oct	1	COVENTRY	H	Lost	1	-	-	1	8	1	2	-	-	11	Channer(C) Hazell(P) Chawner(T)
7		5	LOUGHBOROUGH COLLEGE	H	Won	1	1	-	1	11	-	2	-	-	6	Hunt(T) Hazell(C,P) Ashurst(T)
8		8	CHELTENHAM	H	Won	2	2	1	2	25	-	-	1	-	3	Cullen(2C,2P) Channer(T,D) Bleasdale(T) Jenkins(T) McCormack(T)
9		15	MOSELEY	H	Won	2	1	-	1	16		-	1	-	3	Elders(T) Cullen(2T,2C,P)
10		19	OXFORD UNIVERSITY	H	Lost	-	-	-	1	3	-	2	-	-	6	Shephard(P)
11		22	Northampton	A	Lost	2	-	-	-	10	2	3	-	-	19	J.O'Connor(T) Hazell(2C) Thorneloe(T)
12		29	OLD BLUES	H	Won	1	1	-	-	8	-	-	-	-	0	Elders(2T) Cullen(C)
13		31	BECTIVE RANGERS	H	Lost	-	-	1	1	6	-	3	-	-	9	Cullen(P) Channer(D)
14	Nov	5	Gloucester	A	Lost	1	1	-	1	11	2	2	-	2	22	Elders(T) Cullen(C,P) Bleasdale(T)
15		12	CAMBRIDGE UNIVERSITY	H	Lost	1	1	-	2	14	-	6	-	1	21	Elders(T) Cullen(C,2P) McCormack(T)
16		19	Nuneaton	A	Lost	-	1	-	1	6	-	-	-	3	9	Lewis(T) Channer(P)
17		26	Moseley	A	Won	2	-	-	1	13	-	3	-	-	9	Marshall(T) Cullen(T,2C,P)
18	Dec	3	Waterloo	A	Lost	-	1	-	1	6	2	-	-	1	13	R.D.Matthews(T) Channer(P)
19		10	BLACKHEATH	H	Won	-	1	1	-	6	-	1	-	-	3	Cullen(T) Channer(D)
20		17	BRISTOL	H	Lost	1	-	-	1	8	2	1	-	1	16	Channer(C,P) Ford(T)
21		24	Bedford	A	Drew	-	-	-	-	0	-	-	-	-	0	
22		26	BIRKENHEAD PARK	H	Won	1	4	-	-	17	1	-	-	-	5	Brook(T) Wade(T) R.D.Matthews(T) Hazell(T,C) Bleasdale(T)
23		27	BARBARIANS	H	Lost	-	1	-	-	3	-	3	-	1	12	Konig(T)
24		31	Headingley	A	Won	1	1	-	-	8	-	-	-	-	5	Cullen(T,C) Ashurst(T)
25	Jan	2	Northern	A	Won	1	2	-	-	11	1	1	-	-	8	Cullen(T,C) Channer(T) McCormack(T)
26		7	Bath	A	Lost	-	-	-	-	0	1	2	-	-	11	
27		14	GLOUCESTER	H	Won	-	-	1	2	9	1	-	-	-	5	Small(D) Hazell(2P)
28		21	RUGBY	H	Lost	-	-	-	-	0	-	1	-	-	3	
29		28	Rosslyn Park	A	Lost	-	-	-	-	0	-	2	-	-	6	
	Feb	2	ROYAL AIR FORCE	H		Cancelled										
		4	LONDON SCOTTISH	H		Cancelled Frost										
30		11	Newport	A	Lost	-	-	-	1	3	2	-	-	-	10	Hazell(D)
		18	WASPS	H		Cancelled Frost										
		25	NORTHAMPTON	H		Cancelled Frost										
31	Mar	3	HARLEQUINS	H	Lost	1	-	-	3	14	-	3	1	1	15	Lubbock(T) Hazell(C,3P)
32		10	Coventry	A	Lost	-	-	-	-	0	-	1	-	-	3	
33		17	SWANSEA	H	Drew	-	2	-	1	9	-	-	1	2	9	Lubbock(T) Hazell(P) Thorneloe(T)
34		24	LOUGHBOROUGH COLLEGE	H	Won	-	2	-	-	6	1	-	-	-	5	R.D.Matthews(T) Chawner(T)
35		31	Bristol	A	Lost	-	-	-	-	0	1	3	-	-	14	
36	Apr	2	Plymouth Albion	A	Won	1	1	-	1	11	-	-	-	3	9	Brook(T) Hazell(T,C,P)
37		3	Exeter	A	Won	1	4	-	2	23	-	1	-	3	12	Small(C) Elders(T) Cullen(T,P) Hazell(T,P) Bleasdale(T) Konig(T)
38		7	Birkenhead Park	A	Won	1	-	1	-	8	-	-	-	2	6	Elders(T) Wade(D) Hazell(C)
39		14	Llanelli	A	Lost	1	4	-	1	20	3	3	-	-	24	Small(C,P) Brook(T) Wade(T) T.O'Connor(T) Thorneloe(T) Chawner(T)
40		21	Cardiff	A	Lost	1	-	-	-	5	1	5	-	-	20	R.D.Matthews(T) Hazell(C)
41		23	NORTHAMPTON	H	Lost	-	1	-	2	9	2	1	-	1	16	Hazell(2P) Thompson(T)

INDIVIDUAL APPEARANCES 1955-1956

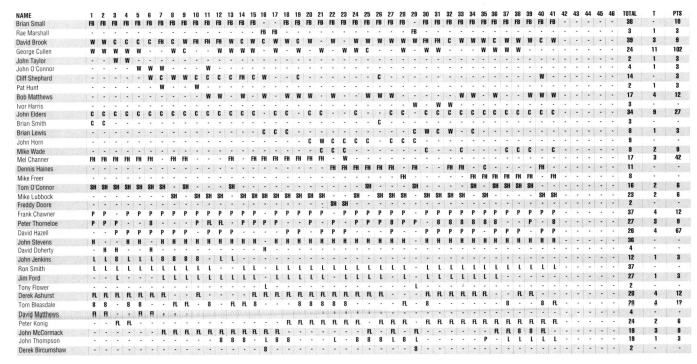

NAME	TOTAL	T	PTS
Brian Small	38	-	10
Rae Marshall	3	1	3
David Brook	39	3	9
George Cullen	24	11	102
John Taylor	2	1	3
John O'Connor	4	1	3
Cliff Shephard	14	-	3
Pat Hunt	2	1	3
Bob Matthews	17	4	12
Ivor Harris	3	-	-
John Elders	34	9	27
Brian Smith	3	-	-
Brian Lewis	9	1	3
John Horn	9	-	-
Mike Wade	9	2	9
Mel Channer	17	3	42
Dennis Haines	11	-	-
Mike Freer	8	-	-
Tom O'Connor	16	2	6
Mike Lubbock	23	2	6
Freddy Doore	2	-	-
Frank Chawner	37	4	12
Peter Thorneloe	27	3	9
David Hazell	26	4	67
John Stevens	36	-	-
David Doherty	4	-	-
John Jenkins	12	1	3
Ron Smith	37	-	-
Jim Ford	27	1	3
Tony Flower	2	-	-
Derek Ashurst	28	4	12
Tom Bleasdale	20	4	12
David Matthews	4	-	-
Peter Konig	24	2	6
John McCormack	19	3	9
John Thompson	19	1	3
Derek Bircumshaw	2	-	-

1 game: G.Bates H(29), Roger Coley W(10), Harry Powley FL(29), Rex Skelton P(29), A.Toone P(16)

LEICESTER FOOTBALL CLUB 1955-56
Back: R.J. Barr (Team Hon.Sec), J. Stevens, J.T. McCormack, M.G. Lubbock, J.G. Ford, B.T.C. Small, D. Brook, J.E. Thorneloe (Hon.Sec).
Middle: R.L. Bedingfield (Hon.Tres), F. Chawner, D.St.G. Hazell, T. Bleasdale, J. Elders (Capt), R.H. Smith,
P.B.L. Thorneloe, P.H. Konig, C.W. Cross (President).
Front: M.E. Freer, J.S. Thompson, M.R. Wade, R.D. Matthews.

LEICESTER FOOTBALL CLUB 1956-57
Back: J.E. Thorneloe (Hon.Sec), R.J. Barr (Team Hon.Sec), M.E. Freer, R.P. Skelton, R. Marshall, R.O. Rawson, B.A.F. Smith, M.R. Wade,
G.H. Cullen, C.W. Cross (President), R.L. Bedingfield (Hon.Tres).
Middle: M.G. Lubbock, J.G. Ford, F. Chawner, J. Elders, T. Bleasdale (Capt), P.B.L. Thorneloe, J.S. Thompson, P.H. Konig, B.T.C. Small.
Front: M.R. Walker, J.T. McCormack. Inset: J. Elders.

1956-1957

NO	DATE		OPPONENTS	V	RES	FOR G	FOR T	FOR D	FOR P	FOR PTS	AGAINST G	AGAINST T	AGAINST D	AGAINST P	AGAINST PTS	SCORERS
1	Sep	1	BEDFORD	H	Lost	1	1	-	-	8	1	1	-	1	11	Small(C) Smith(2T)
2		8	ROMANIA	H	Drew	-	-	-	2	6	-	-	2	-	6	Ashurst(2P)
3		15	PLYMOUTH ALBION	H	Won	3	-	1	-	18	-	-	-	-	0	Baker(D) Smith(T) R.D.Matthews(T) Chawner(T) Ashurst(3C)
4		17	CARDIFF	H	Lost	-	2	-	1	9	3	-	-	1	18	Brook(T) Elders(T) Ashurst(P)
5		22	Harlequins	A	Lost	1	2	-	-	11	2	6	1	1	34	Small(C) Smith(3T)
6		29	Newport	A	Lost	-	-	-	1	3	2	1	-	3	22	Martin(P)
7	Oct	6	Coventry	A	Lost	2	-	-	1	13	1	4	-	-	17	Brook(T) Skelton(T) Martin(2C,P)
8		13	RICHMOND	H	Won	2	1	-	2	19	1	1	-	-	8	Baker(2T) Thorneloe(T) Martin(2C,2P)
9		20	Cheltenham	A	Lost	-	-	-	-	0	-	1	-	-	3	
10		24	Oxford University	A	Lost	-	-	-	-	0	-	3	-	-	9	
11		27	NORTHAMPTON	H	Drew	-	2	-	1	9	-	-	-	3	9	Baker(T) Rawson(T) Martin(P)
12	Nov	3	GLOUCESTER	H	Won	1	3	-	-	14	1	-	-	1	8	Baker(T) Rawson(T) Skelton(T) Martin(C) Konig(T)
13		10	CAMBRIDGE UNIVERSITY	H	Drew	-	-	-	1	3	-	1	-	-	3	Martin(P)
14		17	Lansdowne	A	Lost	2	1	-	1	16	1	1	-	3	17	Elders(T) Wade(T) Walker(T) Martin(2C,P)
15		18	Old Belvedere	A	Lost	-	-	-	1	3	1	5	-	1	23	Martin(P)
16		24	OLD BLUES	H	Won	1	2	-	-	11	1	-	-	1	8	Elders(T) Wade(T) Martin(C) Konig(T)
17	Dec	1	WATERLOO	H	Lost	-	1	-	-	3	1	-	-	2	11	Baker(T)
18		8	Blackheath	A	Won	1	1	-	-	8	-	-	1	1	6	Baker(T) Martin(C) Konig(T)
19		15	BRISTOL	H	Lost	-	-	-	2	6	1	1	-	1	11	Elders(P) Martin(P)
20		22	Rugby	A	Drew	1	2	-	-	11	1	1	-	1	11	Lewis(T) Rawson(T,C) Bleasdale(T)
21		26	BIRKENHEAD PARK	H	Won	-	1	-	-	3	-	-	-	-	0	Rawson(T)
22		27	BARBARIANS	H	Lost	-	-	-	2	6	1	6	-	-	23	Martin(2P)
23		29	HEADINGLEY	H	Lost	-	-	-	-	0	-	1	-	-	3	
24	Jan	5	Bath	A	Drew	-	1	-	-	3	-	-	-	1	3	Ford(T)
25		12	Gloucester	A	Won	-	2	-	-	6	-	-	-	-	0	Horn(T) Rawson(T)
26		19	Bedford	A	Drew	-	-	-	1	3	-	-	1	-	3	Martin(P)
27		26	ROSSLYN PARK	H	Won	1	1	-	-	8	-	-	-	-	0	Baker(T) Chawner(T) Martin(C)
28		31	ROYAL AIR FORCE	H	Lost	1	-	-	1	8	-	6	-	-	18	Shephard(T) Martin(C,P)
29	Feb	2	London Scottish	A	Lost	1	-	-	-	5	4	-	-	1	23	Gavins(C) Baker(T)
30		9	NEWPORT	H	Won	2	1	-	-	13	-	1	-	-	3	Elders(T) Martin(2C) Bleasdale(T) Konig(T)
31		16	BRITISH POLICE	H	Won	2	2	-	-	16	1	-	-	1	8	Rawson(T) Martin(2C) Bleasdale(T) Konig(2T)
32		23	Northampton	A	Won	2	1	-	-	13	-	1	-	1	6	Rawson(2T) Thompson(T) Martin(2C)
33	Mar	2	HARLEQUINS	H	Won	1	1	-	-	8	-	1	-	-	3	Martin(C) Bleasdale(2T)
34		9	COVENTRY	H	Won	2	-	-	-	10	-	1	-	-	3	Wade(T) Rawson(T) Martin(2C)
35		14	LOUGHBOROUGH COLLEGE	H	Won	1	-	-	1	8	-	-	-	2	6	Small(C) Elders(P) Bircumshaw(T)
36		16	Swansea	A	Lost	-	1	-	1	6	1	2	-	-	11	Chawner(T) Martin(P)
37		23	NUNEATON	H	Won	-	1	-	3	12	1	-	1*	-	8	Elders(T) Martin(3P)
38		30	SALE	H	Won	2	3	-	2	25	1	-	-	2	11	Smith(T) Elders(T) Wade(T) Rawson(T) Martin(T,2C,2P)
39	Apr	6	Birkenhead Park	A	Lost	1	1	-	-	8	2	1	-	-	13	Gavins(T,C) Konig(T)
40		13	LLANELLI	H	Won	2	2	-	1	19	-	-	-	1	3	Elders(P) Cullen(2C) Rawson(2T) Chawner(T) Bleasdale(T)
41		20	Bristol	A	Lost	1	1	-	-	8	1	1	-	1	11	Smith(T) Lubbock(T) Martin(C)
42		22	Plymouth Albion	A	Won	2	2	-	-	16	1	-	-	2	11	Gavins(2C) Smith(T) Elders(T) Cullen(T) Bleasdale(T)
43		23	Exeter	A	Lost	2	-	-	-	10	1	1	-	2	14	Shephard(T) Elders(T) Martin(2C)

INDIVIDUAL APPEARANCES 1956-1957

NAME	1	2	3	4	5	6	7	8	9	10	11	12	13	14	15	16	17	18	19	20	21	22	23	24	25	26	27	28	29	30	31	32	33	34	35	36	37	38	39	40	41	42	43	44	45	46	TOTAL	T	PTS
Brian Small	FB	FB	FB	FB	FB	FB	FB	FB	-	FB	FB	FB	FB	FB	FB	FB	FB	FB	FB	FB	FB	FB	FB	FB	FB	FB	FB	-	-	FB	FB	FB	FB	FB	FB	FB	FB	-	-	-	-	-	FB	-	-	-	35	-	6
Rae Marshall	-	-	-	-	-	-	-	-	FB	-	-	-	-	-	-	-	-	-	-	-	-	-	-	-	-	-	-	-	-	-	-	-	-	-	-	-	-	-	-	FB	-	-	-	-	-	-	2	-	-
Mike Gavins	-	-	-	-	-	-	-	-	-	-	-	-	-	-	-	-	-	-	-	-	-	-	-	-	-	-	-	FB	FB	-	-	-	-	-	-	-	-	FB	FB	-	FB	FB	-	-	-	-	6	1	11
David Brook	W	-	-	W	-	W	W	-	-	W	-	-	-	-	W	-	-	-	-	-	C	-	C	-	-	-	-	-	-	-	-	-	-	-	-	-	-	-	-	-	-	-	-	-	-	-	8	2	6
Bob Matthews	W	W	W	W	W	W	-	-	-	-	-	-	-	-	-	-	-	-	-	-	-	-	-	-	-	-	-	-	-	-	-	-	-	-	-	-	-	-	-	-	-	-	-	-	-	-	6	1	3
Peter Baker	-	W	W	-	W	C	-	W	W	-	W	W	W	W	W	W	W	W	-	-	-	W	W	W	W	W	W	-	W	W	W	W	-	W	-	-	W	-	-	-	-	-	-	-	-	-	26	8	27
Dick Rawson	-	-	-	-	-	-	-	W	-	W	W	W	W	W	-	W	W	W	W	W	W	W	W	W	W	W	W	-	-	W	W	W	W	W	W	W	W	W	W	W	W	-	-	-	-	-	30	12	38
Cliff Shephard	-	-	-	-	-	-	-	-	-	-	-	-	-	-	-	-	-	-	-	-	-	-	-	-	-	-	-	W	W	-	-	C	W	-	W	-	-	-	-	-	-	W	W	-	-	-	7	2	6
John Elders	C	C	C	C	C	C	C	C	-	C	C	C	C	C	C	C	-	C	C	C	C	C	-	C	C	-	C	-	-	C	C	C	C	C	C	C	C	C	C	C	C	C	C	-	-	-	37	8	33
Brian Smith	C	C	C	C	C	-	W	-	-	-	-	-	C	-	-	-	-	-	-	-	-	-	-	-	-	-	-	-	-	-	-	-	-	-	-	-	-	W	W	W	W	W	-	-	-	-	12	9	27
Mike Wade	-	-	-	-	-	-	C	C	C	C	C	C	-	C	C	C	C	C	C	C	-	C	-	C	-	C	-	C	C	C	C	-	-	C	-	C	C	C	C	-	-	-	-	-	-	-	25	4	12
George Reay	-	-	-	-	-	-	-	-	C	FH	-	-	-	-	-	-	-	-	-	-	-	-	-	-	-	-	-	-	-	-	-	-	-	-	-	-	-	-	-	-	-	-	-	-	-	-	2	-	-
Brian Lewis	-	-	-	-	-	-	-	-	-	-	-	-	-	-	-	-	C	-	W	W	W	-	C	-	-	-	-	W	-	-	-	-	-	-	C	-	-	-	-	-	-	-	-	-	-	-	7	1	3
John Horn	-	-	-	-	-	-	-	-	-	-	-	-	-	-	-	-	-	-	-	-	-	-	-	-	C	C	C	C	C	-	-	-	-	-	-	-	-	-	-	-	-	-	-	-	-	-	5	1	3
George Cullen	-	-	-	-	-	-	-	-	-	-	-	-	-	-	-	-	-	-	-	-	-	-	-	-	-	-	-	-	-	-	-	-	C	-	-	W	-	-	-	C	C	C	C	-	-	-	6	1	7
Mike Freer	FH	FH	FH	FH	FH	FH	-	-	FH	-	FH	FH	FH	FH	FH	FH	FH	FH	FH	FH	FH	FH	FH	FH	FH	FH	FH	FH	FH	FH	FH	FH	FH	FH	FH	FH	FH	FH	FH	FH	FH	FH	FH	-	-	-	40	-	-
Dennis Haines	-	-	-	-	-	-	FH	FH	-	-	-	-	-	-	-	-	-	-	-	-	-	-	-	-	-	-	-	-	-	-	-	-	-	-	-	-	-	-	-	-	-	-	-	-	-	-	2	-	-
Mike Lubbock	SH	SH	-	-	-	-	-	-	-	-	-	-	-	-	-	-	-	-	-	-	SH	SH	SH	SH	SH	SH	SH	SH	-	SH	SH	-	SH	-	SH	SH	SH	SH	SH	SH	SH	SH	-	-	-	-	21	1	3
Freddy Doore	-	-	SH	SH	SH	-	SH	SH	SH	SH	SH	SH	SH	SH	SH	SH	SH	SH	SH	SH	-	-	-	-	-	-	-	-	SH	-	-	-	-	SH	-	-	-	-	-	-	-	-	SH	-	-	-	20	-	-
Mike Crane	-	-	-	-	-	SH	-	-	-	-	-	-	-	-	-	-	-	-	-	-	-	-	-	-	-	-	-	-	-	-	-	SH	-	-	-	-	-	-	-	-	-	-	-	-	-	-	2	-	-
Frank Chawner	P	P	P	P	P	P	P	P	-	P	P	P	P	P	P	P	P	P	P	P	P	P	P	P	P	-	P	-	-	P	P	P	P	P	P	P	P	P	P	P	P	P	P	-	-	-	39	4	12
Rex Skelton	P	-	-	-	-	P	P	P	P	P	-	P	P	P	-	P	P	P	P	P	P	P	P	P	P	P	P	P	-	-	-	-	-	-	-	-	-	-	-	-	-	-	-	-	-	-	22	2	6
John Stevens	H	H	H	H	H	H	H	H	-	-	-	-	-	-	H	-	-	-	-	-	-	-	-	-	-	-	-	H	-	-	-	-	-	-	-	-	-	-	-	-	-	-	-	-	-	-	10	-	-
Mick Walker	-	-	-	-	-	-	-	-	H	H	H	H	H	H	-	H	H	H	H	H	H	H	H	H	H	H	H	-	-	H	H	H	H	H	H	H	H	H	H	H	H	H	-	-	-	-	31	1	3
Jim Ford	L	L	L	L	L	L	L	L	-	-	L	L	L	L	L	L	L	L	L	L	L	L	L	L	L	L	L	-	-	L	L	L	L	L	L	L	-	L	L	L	L	L	-	-	-	-	37	1	3
John Thompson	L	P	P	P	P	L	L	L	L	L	L	L	L	L	L	L	L	L	L	L	L	L	L	L	L	L	L	L	L	L	L	L	L	L	L	L	L	L	L	L	L	L	L	-	-	-	43	1	3
Ron Smith	-	L	L	L	L	-	-	-	-	-	-	-	-	-	-	-	-	-	-	-	-	-	-	-	-	-	-	-	-	-	-	-	-	-	-	-	-	-	-	-	-	-	-	-	-	-	4	-	-
Harry Powley	-	-	-	-	-	-	-	-	L	L	-	-	-	-	-	-	-	-	-	-	-	-	-	-	-	-	-	-	-	-	-	-	-	-	-	-	-	-	-	-	-	-	-	-	-	-	2	-	-
Brian Hailes	-	-	-	-	-	-	-	-	-	-	-	-	-	-	-	-	-	-	-	-	-	-	-	-	-	-	-	L	L	-	-	-	-	-	-	-	-	-	-	-	-	-	-	-	-	-	2	-	-
Peter Konig	FL	FL	FL	FL	FL	-	FL	FL	FL	FL	FL	FL	FL	FL	FL	FL	FL	FL	FL	FL	FL	FL	FL	FL	FL	FL	FL	FL	FL	FL	FL	FL	FL	FL	FL	FL	FL	FL	FL	FL	FL	-	-	-	-	-	40	7	21
David Matthews	FL	-	-	-	-	FL	-	-	FL	-	-	-	-	-	-	-	-	-	-	-	-	-	-	-	-	-	-	-	-	-	-	-	-	-	-	-	-	-	-	-	-	FL	8	-	-	-	5	-	-
John McCormack	8	8	8	8	8	-	-	-	-	-	-	-	-	-	-	-	-	-	-	-	FL	-	-	-	-	-	-	-	FL	-	-	-	-	-	FL	-	-	-	FL	FL	-	FL	FL	-	-	-	12	-	-
Derek Ashurst	-	FL	FL	FL	FL	FL	-	-	-	-	-	-	-	-	-	-	-	-	-	-	-	-	-	-	-	-	-	-	-	-	-	-	-	-	-	-	-	-	-	-	-	-	-	-	-	-	5	-	15
Colin Martin	-	-	-	-	-	8	8	8	-	8	8	8	FL	FL	FL	FL	-	FL	FL	-	FL	FL	FL	-	FL	FL	FL	FL	-	FL	FL	FL	FL	FL	-	FL	FL	FL	-	-	FL	-	FL	-	-	-	29	1	110
Peter Thorneloe	-	-	-	-	-	-	FL	FL	P	FL	FL	-	-	-	P	-	FL	-	-	-	-	-	-	FL	-	-	-	P	P	P	P	P	P	P	-	P	P	P	-	P	P	P	P	-	-	-	22	1	3
Derek Bircumshaw	-	-	-	-	-	-	-	-	8	-	-	-	-	-	-	-	-	-	-	-	-	-	-	-	-	-	-	P	P	-	-	-	-	-	P	-	L	-	P	-	-	-	-	-	-	-	6	1	3
Tom Bleasdale	-	-	-	-	-	-	-	-	-	-	-	FL	8	8	8	8	8	8	8	8	8	8	8	8	8	8	8	8	8	8	8	8	8	8	8	8	8	8	8	8	8	8	L	-	-	-	32	7	21

1 game: Dave Brookhouse H(29), Tom Hoskins H(43), Pat Hunt W(9), Harry Jessop W(43), Ken Milne P(11)

NO	DATE		OPPONENTS	V	RES	FOR G	T	D	P	PTS	AGAINST G	T	D	P	PTS	SCORERS
1	Sep	7	BEDFORD	H	Won	1	1	-	1	11	1	-	-	-	5	B.A.F.Smith(T) Skelton(T) Martin(C,P)
2		14	BATH	H	Won	4	-	-	2	26	-	-	1	-	3	B.A.F.Smith(T) Wade(2T) Martin(4C,2P) Bleasdale(T)
3		21	PLYMOUTH ALBION	H	Won	2	2	-	1	19	1	-	-	3	14	Swan(T) B.A.F.Smith(T) Rawson(T) Walker(T) Martin(2C,P)
4		28	Harlequins	A	Lost	-	1	-	1	6	2	2	-	1	19	Swan(T) Martin(P)
5	Oct	5	COVENTRY	H	Won	2	1	-	1	16	-	-	-	1	3	Swan(2T) Wade(T) Martin(2C,P)
6		12	Richmond	A	Lost	-	-	1	-	3	2	6	-	-	28	Key(D)
7		19	CHELTENHAM	H	Drew	-	-	-	1	3	-	-	1	-	3	Martin(P)
8		23	OXFORD UNIVERSITY	H	Lost	-	-	-	1	3	2	2	-	-	16	Martin(P)
9		26	Northampton	A	Drew	-	-	-	1	3	-	1	-	-	3	Martin(P)
10	Nov	2	Gloucester	A	Lost	1	1	-	-	8	-	3	-	1	12	Swan(2T) Martin(C)
11		9	Cambridge University	A	Lost	-	1	-	-	3	3	3	1	1	30	Swan(T)
12		16	OLD BLUES	H	Won	1	1	-	-	8	-	1	-	-	3	Rawson(T) White(T) Martin(C)
13		23	Moseley	A	Won	2	1	-	1	16	1	1	-	-	8	Swan(T) R.H.Smith(T) Martin(2C,P) Bleasdale(T)
14		30	NEWPORT	H	Lost	1	-	-	1	8	-	1	-	2	9	B.A.F.Smith(T) Martin(C,P)
15	Dec	7	Waterloo	A	Drew	-	-	-	1	3	-	-	-	1	3	Martin(P)
16		14	BLACKHEATH	H	Lost	-	1	-	-	6	2	-	-	-	13	Wade(T) Martin(P)
17		21	Bristol	A	Lost	-	-	-	2	6	-	3	-	1	12	Gavins(2P)
18		26	BIRKENHEAD PARK	H	Lost	1	1	-	-	8	3	-	-	-	15	Leete(C) Moseley(T) Matthews(T)
19		27	BARBARIANS	H	Lost	-	-	-	2	6	2	5	-	-	25	Martin(2P)
20		28	Rugby	A	Won	-	2	-	-	6	-	1	-	-	3	Elders(T) Wade(T)
21	Jan	4	Bath	A	Drew	1	1	-	-	8	1	-	-	1	8	Elders(T) Almey(T) Martin(C)
22		11	GLOUCESTER	H	Lost	-	-	-	-	0	1	2	-	-	11	
23		18	Bedford	A	Drew	-	-	-	-	6	-	2	-	-	6	B.T.C.Small(P) Shephard(T)
		25	ROSSLYN PARK	H				Cancelled Frost									
24		30	ROYAL AIR FORCE	H	Won	1	1	-	1	11	-	1	-	2	9	Key(C,P) B.T.C.Small(T) Williams(T)
25	Feb	1	LONDON SCOTTISH	H	Drew	-	1	-	1	6	-	2	-	-	6	Key(P) Shephard(T)
		8	Newport	A				Cancelled Snow									
26		15	Wasps	A	Lost	-	1	-	-	3	-	2	-	1	9	Matthews(T)
27		22	NORTHAMPTON	H	Lost	1	-	-	1	8	1	2	-	-	11	Key(C,P) Lubbock(T)
28	Mar	1	HARLEQUINS	H	Won	-	3	-	-	9	-	-	-	-	0	B.A.F.Smith(T) Williams(T) Bleasdale(T)
29		8	LEICESTERSHIRE XV	H	Won	-	1	-	1	6	-	-	-	-	0	Swan(T) Tatham(P)
30		13	LOUGHBOROUGH COLLEGE	H	Lost	-	-	-	1	3	-	1	-	1	6	Tatham(P)
31		15	SWANSEA	H	Won	1	2	1	2	20	1	1	-	-	8	Key(C,2P) Swan(T) Williams(T) Tatham(T,D)
32		22	Nuneaton	A	Lost	1	-	-	-	5	2	-	-	1	13	Key(C) Bleasdale(T)
33		29	HEADINGLEY	H	Lost	-	1	-	1	6	2	1	-	-	13	Key(P) Shephard(T)
34	Apr	5	Bristol	A	Won	1	-	-	-	5	-	1	-	-	3	Key(C) Swan(T)
35		7	Plymouth Albion	A	Won	2	1	-	1	16	-	1	-	2	9	Neil(T) Gavins(T,2C,P) Lubbock(T)
36		8	Exeter	A	Won	3	1	1	-	21	-	1	-	1	6	Gavins(3C) Elders(T) Freer(T,D) Chawner(T) Bleasdale(T)
37		12	Birkenhead Park	A	Lost	1	2	-	-	11	2	1	-	-	13	Wade(T) Swan(T) Bleasdale(T) Matthews(C)
38		19	Llanelli	A	Lost	1	2	-	-	11	3	4	1	1	33	Key(C) Taylor(T) Shephard(T) Bleasdale(T)
39		23	Coventry	A	Lost	1	-	-	2	11	2	-	-	2	16	Gavins(C,2P) Swan(T)

INDIVIDUAL APPEARANCES 1957-1958

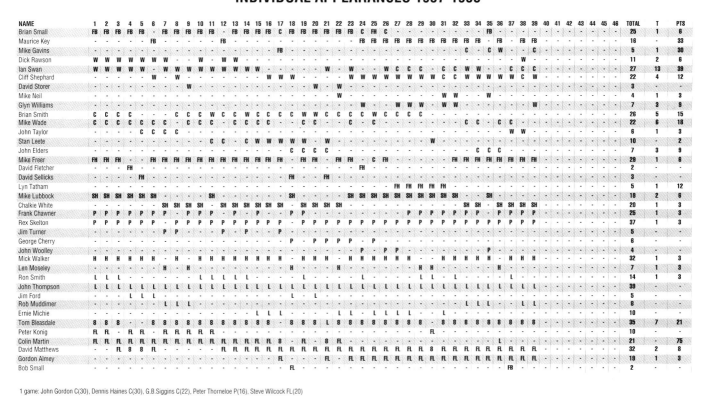

NAME	TOTAL	T	PTS
Brian Small	25	1	6
Maurice Key	16	-	33
Mike Gavins	5	1	30
Dick Rawson	11	2	6
Ian Swan	27	13	39
Cliff Shephard	22	4	12
David Storer	3	-	-
Mike Neil	4	1	3
Glyn Williams	7	3	9
Brian Smith	26	5	15
Mike Wade	22	6	18
John Taylor	6	1	3
Stan Leete	10	-	2
John Elders	7	3	9
Mike Freer	29	1	6
David Fletcher	2	-	-
David Sellicks	3	-	-
Lyn Tatham	5	1	12
Mike Lubbock	19	2	6
Chalkie White	20	1	3
Frank Chawner	25	1	3
Rex Skelton	37	1	3
Jim Turner	5	-	-
George Cherry	6	-	-
John Woolley	4	-	-
Mick Walker	32	1	3
Len Moseley	7	1	3
Ron Smith	14	1	3
John Thompson	39	-	-
Jim Ford	5	-	-
Rob Muddimer	8	-	-
Ernie Michie	10	-	-
Tom Bleasdale	35	7	21
Peter Konig	10	-	-
Colin Martin	21	-	75
David Matthews	32	2	8
Gordon Almey	19	1	3
Bob Small	2	-	-

1 game: John Gordon C(30), Dennis Haines C(30), G.B.Siggins C(22), Peter Thorneloe P(16), Steve Wilcock FL(20)

LEICESTER FOOTBALL CLUB 1957-58
Back: R.J. Barr (Hon.Sec), C.D. Shephard, R.P. Skelton, C.G. Martin, B.A.F. Smith, E.J.S. Michie, G.A. Almey, H.V. White, M.R. Key,
R.L. Bedingfield (Hon.Tres).
Front: M.G. Lubbock, M.R. Walker, J.S. Swan, B.T.C. Small, T. Bleasdale (Capt), F. Chawner, J.S. Thompson, D.J. Matthews, M.E. Freer.

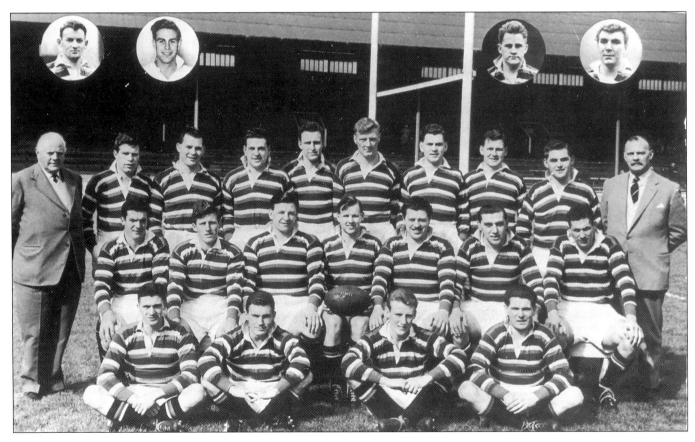

LEICESTER FOOTBALL CLUB 1958-59
Back: R.L. Bedingfield (Hon.Tres), G.A. Almey, R.P. Skelton, T. Allen, J.P. Horrocks-Taylor, L.H. Jenkins, H.G. Jessop, M.N. Gavins,
M.G. Lubbock, R.J. Barr (Hon.Sec).
Middle: D.J. Matthews, M.E. Freer, T. Bleasdale, J.S. Swan (Capt), F. Chawner, J.S. Thompson, C.G. Martin.
Front: H.V. White, C.D. Shephard, M.R. Walker, M.R. Key. **Inset:** G. Blackett, R.O. Rawson, A. Jones, A.J.F.K. O'Reilly.

NO	DATE		OPPONENTS	V	RES	FOR					AGAINST					SCORERS
						G	T	D	P	PTS	G	T	D	P	PTS	
1	Sep	6	BEDFORD	H	Won	1	2	-	3	20	1	1	-	1	11	Bleasdale(T) Gavins(C,3P) Jenkins(T) Jessop(T)
2		13	BATH	H	Won	2	3	-	2	25	-	1	-	1	6	Bleasdale(T) Gavins(2C,2P) Jenkins(T) Matthews(T) Shephard(2T)
3		15	WATCYN THOMAS XV	H	Won	3	1	-	-	18	-	1	-	-	3	Bleasdale(T) Freer(T) Gavins(3C) Jenkins(T) Walker(T)
4		20	PLYMOUTH ALBION	H	Won	3	-	-	1	18	1	-	-	-	5	Almey(T) Bleasdale(T) Gavins(3C,P) White(T)
5		27	Harlequins	A	Drew	1	-	-	2	11	1	2	-	-	11	Gavins(C,2P) Jessop(T)
6	Oct	4	Coventry	A	Lost	-	1	-	2	9	1	2	1	-	14	Gavins(2P) Jenkins(T)
7		11	RICHMOND	H	Won	-	1	-	1	6	-	-	-	1	3	Gavins(P) Swan(T)
8		18	Cheltenham	A	Lost	-	1	-	-	3	1	-	-	-	5	Almey(T)
9		22	Oxford University	A	Lost	1	1	-	-	8	1	1	-	1	11	Constable(T) Gavins(C) Horrocks-Taylor(T)
10		25	NORTHAMPTON	H	Lost	-	-	-	1	3	2	-	-	-	10	Gavins(P)
11	Nov	1	GLOUCESTER	H	Lost	-	1	-	1	6	-	2	-	2	12	Chawner(T) Gavins(P)
12		8	CAMBRIDGE UNIVERSITY	H	Won	1	1	-	-	8	-	-	-	1	3	Gavins(T,C) Swan(T)
13		15	Bective Rangers	A	Lost	1	1	-	1	11	2	2	-	-	16	Gavins(C,P) Swan(T) White(T)
14		16	Old Belvedere	A	Lost	-	1	-	-	3	1	3	-	-	14	Horrocks-Taylor(T)
15		22	Moseley	A	Drew	-	-	1	1	6	-	-	-	2	6	Freer(D) Gavins(P)
16		29	Newport	A	Lost	-	-	-	-	0	4	1	1	1	29	
17	Dec	6	WATERLOO	H	Won	2	1	-	-	13	1	-	-	2	11	Almey(T) Gavins(2C) Martin(T) Rawson(T)
18		13	Blackheath	A	Lost	-	-	-	-	0	-	1	-	-	3	
19		20	BRISTOL	H	Won	1	4	-	-	17	-	1	-	1	6	Gavins(C) Jenkins(T) Lubbock(T) Rawson(T) Swan(2T)
20		26	BARBARIANS	H	Won	-	3	-	-	9	-	1	-	-	3	Jenkins(T) Matthews(T) Shephard(T)
21		27	BIRKENHEAD PARK	H	Drew	1	1	-	-	8	1	1	-	-	8	Elders(T) Gavins(C) Jones(T)
	Jan	3	Bath	A		Cancelled Frost										
		10	Gloucester	A		Cancelled Frost										
		17	Bedford	A		Cancelled Frost										
22		24	ROSSLYN PARK	H	Won	1	1	-	-	8	-	2	-	-	6	Almey(T) Gavins(C) Swan(T)
23		31	Headingley	A	Won	-	1	-	1	6	-	-	-	1	3	Gavins(P) Swan(T)
24	Feb	7	London Scottish	A	Won	3	1	-	1	21	-	-	-	1	3	Bleasdale(T) Gavins(3C,P) O'Reilly(T) Shephard(T) Tatham(T)
25		14	NEWPORT	H	Lost	-	-	1	-	3	2	1	-	2	19	Blackett(D)
26		21	WASPS	H	Won	2	2	1	-	22	-	-	-	-	0	Blackett(T,D) Gavins(2C,P) Lubbock(T) O'Reilly(2T)
27		28	Northampton	A	Lost	2	-	-	1	13	2	3	-	-	22	Almey(T) Gavins(2C,P) Martin(T)
28	Mar	7	HARLEQUINS	H	Won	-	1	-	2	9	-	1	-	1	6	Gavins(2P) Horrocks-Taylor(T)
29		12	LOUGHBOROUGH COLLEGE	H	Won	-	2	-	1	9	-	1	-	1	6	Almey(2T) Gavins(P)
30		14	COVENTRY	H	Won	2	1	-	1	13	1	1	-	1	11	Almey(T) Gavins(2C) Horrocks-Taylor(T) Wade(T)
31		21	Bradford	A	Drew	1	-	-	1	8	1	-	-	1	8	Gavins(C,P) Wade(T)
32		28	Bristol	A	Lost	-	2	1	-	9	1	2	-	2	17	Allen(T) Freer(D) Shephard(T)
33		30	Plymouth Albion	A	Won	1	2	-	-	11	-	-	1	1	6	Almey(T) Allen(T) Martin(C) Shephard(T)
34		31	Exeter	A	Drew	-	-	-	1	3	-	-	-	1	3	Martin(P)
35	Apr	4	Birkenhead Park	A	Lost	-	-	1	1	6	2	-	-	-	10	Horrocks-Taylor(D) Key(P)
36		11	NUNEATON	H	Won	2	1	-	1	16	-	1	-	-	3	Allen(T) Bleasdale(T) Horrocks-Taylor(T) Key(2C,P)
37		18	LLANELLI	H	Won	1	2	-	4	23	-	2	-	1	9	Almey(T) Allen(T) Gavins(C,4P) Shephard(T)
38		22	Bedford	A	Lost	-	2	-	1	9	1	1	1	-	11	Gavins(P) Horrocks-Taylor(T) Shephard(T)

INDIVIDUAL APPEARANCES 1958-1959

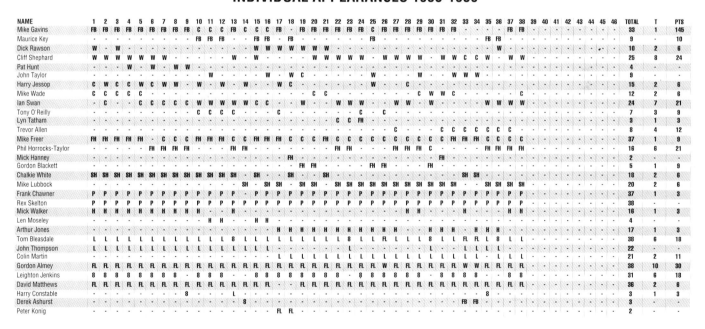

1 game: John Elders C(21)[1T-3], Eric Lacey L(26), Stan Leete W(9), Brian Rigney H(14), Brian Small FB(14), Brian Symonds C(17), John Woolley P(14)

1959-1960

NO	DATE	OPPONENTS	V	RES	FOR G	FOR T	FOR D	FOR P	FOR PTS	AGAINST G	AGAINST T	AGAINST D	AGAINST P	AGAINST PTS	SCORERS
1	Sep 5	BEDFORD	H	Lost	1	1	-	1	11	1	1	1	3	20	Gavins(C,P) Shephard(T) Wigley(T)
2	12	BATH	H	Won	-	1	1	2	12	1	1	-	1	11	Gavins(2P) Rawson(T) Tatham(D)
3	16	WATCYN THOMAS XV	H	Won	1	1	1	4	23	2	1	-	1	16	Gavins(C,4P) Smith(T) Blackett(D) Ashurst(T)
4	19	PLYMOUTH ALBION	H	Won	2	1	-	4	25	1	2	-	-	11	Gavins(2C,4P) Shephard(2T) Blackett(T)
5	26	Harlequins	A	Lost	1	1	-	1	11	3	-	-	1	18	Gavins(C,P) Wigley(T) Bleasdale(T)
6	Oct 3	COVENTRY	H	Won	3	1	-	1	21	2	1	-	-	13	Gavins(3C,P) Smith(T) Senior(T) H.V.White(T) Almey(T)
7	10	Richmond	A	Lost	-	-	-	1	3	1	1	-	1	11	Gavins(P)
8	17	CHELTENHAM	H	Won	1	4	-	2	23	-	1	-	-	3	Gavins(C,2P) Jessop(T) Smith(2T) Senior(T) Matthews(T)
9	21	OXFORD UNIVERSITY	H	Lost	-	1	-	-	3	-	1	-	1	6	Senior(T)
10	24	Northampton	A	Lost	1	2	1	-	14	1	3	-	1	17	Gavins(T,C) Smith(T,D) Senior(T)
11	31	NUNEATON	H	Won	1	4	-	4	29	-	-	-	2	6	Gavins(C,4P) Wigley(T) Jessop(T) Senior(3T)
12	Nov 7	Gloucester	A	Lost	2	1	-	-	13	-	5	-	1	18	Gavins(2C) Wigley(T) Senior(T) Jones(T)
13	14	Cambridge University	A	Lost	-	-	-	-	0	1	2	-	2	17	
14	21	Llanelli	A	Won	1	-	1	-	8	-	1	-	-	3	Gavins(C,D) Konig(T)
15	28	MOSELEY	H	Drew	-	-	-	2	6	-	1	-	1	6	Gavins(2P)
16	Dec 5	Waterloo	A	Won	1	1	-	-	8	-	-	-	-	0	Gavins(C) Senior(2T)
17	12	BLACKHEATH	H	Won	1	-	-	1	8	1	-	-	-	5	Gavins(C,P) O'Reilly(T)
18	19	BRISTOL	H	Lost	-	-	1	-	3	1	1	1	-	11	Blackett(D)
19	26	BIRKENHEAD PARK	H	Lost	-	-	-	1	3	6	2	-	-	36	Robins(P)
20	28	BARBARIANS	H	Lost	-	1	-	2	9	1	3	-	1	17	Gavins(2P) Martin(T)
21	Jan 2	Bath	A	Drew	-	-	-	-	0	-	-	-	-	0	
22	9	GLOUCESTER	H	Won	-	1	-	1	6	-	-	-	1	3	Gavins(P) Senior(T)
	16	Bedford	A		Cancelled										
23	23	Rosslyn Park	A	Drew	-	-	-	-	0	-	-	-	-	0	
24	28	ROYAL AIR FORCE	H	Lost	-	-	-	2	6	1	1	-	1	11	Gavins(2P)
25	30	HEADINGLEY	H	Won	-	2	-	1	9	-	-	-	2	6	Gavins(P) Horrocks-Taylor(T) Senior(T)
26	Feb 6	LONDON SCOTTISH	H	Won	-	4	-	1	15	-	-	-	1	3	Gavins(P) Freer(T) Ring(T) Senior(2T)
27	13	Newport	A	Lost	-	-	2	1	9	2	3	-	-	19	Gavins(P) Freer(2D)
28	20	Wasps	A	Won	-	-	-	1	3	-	-	-	-	0	Gavins(P)
29	27	NORTHAMPTON	H	Drew	-	1	-	1	6	-	1	-	1	6	Gavins(P) Tatham(T)
30	Mar 5	HARLEQUINS	H	Won	2	1	1	-	16	-	-	-	2	6	Gavins(C,D) Rawson(T) Robins(C) Almey(2T)
31	12	LEICESTERSHIRE XV	H	Won	1	1	-	1	11	-	-	-	1	3	Ring(T) Robins(C,P) Konig(T)
32	19	BRADFORD	H	Won	3	3	-	2	30	-	1	-	1	6	Gavins(C,P) Freer(T) O'Reilly(T) Senior(2T) Robins(2C,P) Martin(T) Almey(T)
33	26	LOUGHBOROUGH COLLEGE	H	Won	3	-	-	1	18	-	-	-	-	0	Gavins(T) Robins(3C,P) Martin(T) Almey(T)
34	Apr 2	Birkenhead Park	A	Won	2	-	-	2	16	-	1	-	-	3	Senior(2T) Robins(2C,2P)
35	9	NEWPORT	H	Won	1	-	-	4	17	1	-	1	1	11	Robins(C,4P) Konig(T)
36	16	Bristol	A	Lost	-	1	-	1	6	-	4	1	2	21	Gavins(P) Senior(T)
37	18	Plymouth Albion	A	Won	1	5	-	-	20	-	-	2	1	9	Rawson(T,C) O'Reilly(2T) Senior(3T)
38	19	Exeter	A	Won	-	3	-	-	9	-	-	-	-	0	Rawson(T) O'Reilly(T) Horrocks-Taylor(T)
39	23	RUGBY	H	Won	-	2	-	1	9	-	-	-	2	6	Allen(T) Jessop(T) Martin(P)
40	27	Bedford	A	Lost	-	1	-	2	9	1	3	-	1	17	Senior(T) Robins(2P)

INDIVIDUAL APPEARANCES 1959-1960

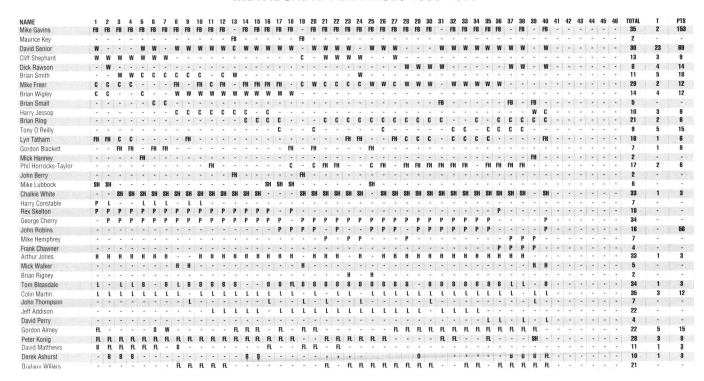

NAME	1	2	3	4	5	6	7	8	9	10	11	12	13	14	15	16	17	18	19	20	21	22	23	24	25	26	27	28	29	30	31	32	33	34	35	36	37	38	39	40	41	42	43	44	45	46	TOTAL	T	PTS
Mike Gavins	FB	FB	FB	FB	FB	FB	FB	FB	FB	FB	FB	FB	-	FB	FB	FB	FB	FB	-	FB	FB	FB	FB	FB	FB	FB	FB	FB	FB	FB	-	FB	FB	FB	FB	FB	-	FB	-	FB	-	-	-	-	-	-	35	2	153
Maurice Key	-	-	-	-	-	-	-	-	-	-	-	-	FB	-	-	-	-	-	FB	-	-	-	-	-	-	-	-	-	-	-	-	-	-	-	-	-	-	-	-	-	-	-	-	-	-	-	2	-	-
David Senior	W	-	-	-	W	W	-	W	W	W	W	W	C	W	W	W	W	W	-	W	W	W	W	-	W	W	W	-	-	-	W	W	W	W	W	W	W	W	-	W	-	-	-	-	-	-	30	23	69
Cliff Shephard	W	W	W	W	W	W	W	-	-	-	-	-	-	-	-	-	-	-	C	-	W	W	W	W	-	-	W	-	-	-	-	-	-	-	-	-	-	-	-	-	-	-	-	-	-	-	13	3	9
Dick Rawson	-	W	-	-	-	-	-	-	-	-	-	-	-	-	-	-	-	-	-	-	-	-	-	-	-	-	-	W	W	W	W	-	-	-	-	-	W	W	-	W	-	-	-	-	-	-	8	4	14
Brian Smith	-	-	W	W	C	C	C	C	C	C	-	C	W	-	-	-	-	-	-	-	-	-	-	W	-	-	-	-	-	-	-	-	-	-	-	-	-	-	-	-	-	-	-	-	-	-	11	5	18
Mike Freer	C	C	C	C	-	-	-	FH	-	FH	C	FH	-	FH	FH	FH	FH	-	C	W	C	C	C	C	W	W	C	W	W	W	-	W	W	W	W	W	-	-	-	-	-	-	-	-	-	-	29	2	12
Brian Wigley	C	C	-	-	C	-	-	W	W	W	W	W	W	W	W	W	W	W	-	-	-	-	-	-	-	-	-	-	-	-	-	-	-	-	-	-	-	-	-	-	-	-	-	-	-	-	14	4	12
Brian Small	-	-	-	-	-	C	C	-	-	-	-	-	-	-	-	-	-	-	-	-	-	-	-	-	-	-	-	-	-	-	FB	-	-	-	-	-	FB	-	FB	-	-	-	-	-	-	-	5	-	-
Harry Jessop	-	-	-	-	-	-	-	C	C	C	C	C	C	C	-	C	-	-	-	-	-	-	-	-	-	-	-	-	-	-	-	-	-	-	-	-	-	-	W	C	-	-	-	-	-	-	10	3	9
Brian Ring	-	-	-	-	-	-	-	-	-	-	-	-	-	C	C	C	C	-	-	-	C	C	C	C	C	C	C	C	C	C	C	-	-	C	-	C	C	C	C	C	-	-	-	-	-	-	21	2	6
Tony O'Reilly	-	-	-	-	-	-	-	-	-	-	-	-	-	-	-	-	C	-	-	C	-	-	-	-	-	C	-	-	-	-	-	C	C	-	C	C	C	C	-	-	-	-	-	-	-	-	9	5	15
Lyn Tatham	FH	FH	C	C	-	-	-	-	FH	-	-	-	-	-	-	-	-	-	-	-	-	-	FH	FH	-	-	FH	C	C	C	-	C	C	C	C	-	-	-	-	FH	-	-	-	-	-	-	16	1	6
Gordon Blackett	-	-	FH	FH	-	FH	FH	-	-	-	-	-	-	-	-	-	-	FH	-	FH	-	-	-	-	FH	-	-	-	-	-	-	-	-	-	-	-	-	-	-	-	-	-	-	-	-	-	7	1	9
Mick Hanney	-	-	-	-	FH	-	-	-	-	-	-	-	-	-	-	-	-	-	-	-	-	-	-	-	-	-	-	-	-	-	-	-	-	-	-	-	-	-	FH	-	-	-	-	-	-	-	2	-	-
Phil Horrocks-Taylor	-	-	-	-	-	-	-	-	-	-	FH	-	-	-	-	-	-	C	-	C	FH	FH	-	-	C	FH	-	FH	FH	FH	FH	FH	FH	-	FH	FH	FH	FH	-	-	-	-	-	-	-	-	17	2	6
John Berry	-	-	-	-	-	-	-	-	-	-	-	-	FH	-	-	-	-	-	FH	-	-	-	-	-	-	-	-	-	-	-	-	-	-	-	-	-	-	-	-	-	-	-	-	-	-	-	2	-	-
Mike Lubbock	SH	SH	-	-	-	-	-	-	-	-	-	-	-	-	-	SH	SH	SH	-	-	-	-	-	-	SH	-	-	-	-	-	-	-	-	-	-	-	-	-	-	-	-	-	-	-	-	-	6	-	-
Chalkie White	-	-	SH	SH	SH	SH	SH	SH	SH	SH	SH	SH	SH	SH	SH	-	-	-	SH	SH	SH	SH	SH	SH	-	SH	SH	SH	SH	SH	SH	SH	SH	SH	SH	SH	SH	SH	-	SH	-	-	-	-	-	-	33	1	3
Harry Constable	P	L	-	-	L	L	L	-	L	L	-	-	-	-	-	-	-	-	-	-	-	-	-	-	-	-	-	-	-	-	-	-	-	-	-	-	-	-	-	-	-	-	-	-	-	-	7	-	-
Rex Skelton	P	P	P	P	P	P	P	P	P	P	P	P	P	P	P	P	-	P	-	-	-	-	-	-	-	-	-	-	-	-	-	-	-	-	-	P	-	-	-	-	-	-	-	-	-	-	18	-	-
George Cherry	-	P	P	P	P	P	P	P	P	P	P	P	P	P	P	P	P	-	P	P	P	P	P	P	P	P	P	P	P	P	P	P	P	P	P	-	-	-	-	P	-	-	-	-	-	-	34	-	-
John Robins	-	-	-	-	-	-	-	-	-	-	-	-	-	-	-	-	P	P	P	P	-	P	-	-	P	P	P	-	P	P	P	P	P	P	P	-	-	-	-	P	-	-	-	-	-	-	16	-	56
Mike Hemphrey	-	-	-	-	-	-	-	-	-	-	-	-	-	-	-	-	-	-	-	-	P	-	P	P	-	-	-	P	-	-	-	-	-	-	-	-	P	P	P	-	-	-	-	-	-	-	7	-	-
Frank Chawner	-	-	-	-	-	-	-	-	-	-	-	-	-	-	-	-	-	-	-	-	-	-	-	-	-	-	-	-	-	-	-	-	-	-	-	P	P	P	P	-	-	-	-	-	-	-	4	-	-
Arthur Jones	H	H	H	H	H	H	H	-	-	H	H	H	H	H	H	H	H	H	-	H	H	H	-	H	-	H	H	H	H	H	H	H	H	H	H	H	H	H	-	-	-	-	-	-	-	-	33	1	3
Mick Walker	-	-	-	-	-	-	-	H	H	-	-	-	-	-	-	-	-	-	H	-	-	-	-	-	-	-	-	-	-	-	-	-	-	-	-	-	-	-	H	H	-	-	-	-	-	-	5	-	-
Brian Rigney	-	-	-	-	-	-	-	-	-	-	-	-	-	-	-	-	-	-	-	-	-	-	H	-	H	-	-	-	-	-	-	-	-	-	-	-	-	-	-	-	-	-	-	-	-	-	2	-	-
Tom Bleasdale	L	-	L	L	8	-	8	L	8	8	8	8	8	-	-	8	8	FL	8	8	8	8	8	8	8	8	8	8	-	8	8	8	8	8	8	8	L	L	-	8	-	-	-	-	-	-	34	1	3
Colin Martin	L	L	L	L	L	L	L	L	-	L	L	L	L	L	L	L	L	L	-	L	-	L	L	-	L	L	L	L	L	L	L	L	L	L	L	L	L	-	L	L	-	-	-	-	-	-	35	3	12
John Thompson	-	-	-	-	-	-	-	-	L	-	-	-	-	-	-	L	-	-	L	-	L	-	-	L	-	-	-	-	-	L	-	-	-	-	-	-	-	-	L	-	-	-	-	-	-	-	7	-	-
Jeff Addison	-	-	-	-	-	-	-	-	-	-	L	L	L	L	L	-	L	L	L	L	L	L	L	L	L	L	L	L	L	-	L	L	L	L	-	-	-	-	-	-	-	-	-	-	-	-	22	-	-
David Perry	-	-	-	-	-	-	-	-	-	-	-	-	-	-	-	-	-	-	-	-	-	-	-	-	-	-	-	-	-	-	-	-	-	-	L	L	-	L	-	L	-	-	-	-	-	-	4	-	-
Gordon Almey	FL	-	-	-	-	8	W	-	-	-	-	-	FL	FL	FL	-	FL	-	FL	FL	-	-	-	-	-	-	FL	FL	FL	FL	FL	FL	FL	FL	FL	FL	FL	FL	FL	-	-	-	-	-	-	-	22	5	15
Peter Konig	FL	FL	FL	FL	FL	FL	FL	FL	FL	FL	FL	FL	FL	FL	FL	FL	FL	FL	-	-	FL	FL	FL	FL	FL	FL	-	-	-	-	FL	FL	-	-	FL	-	-	-	SH	-	-	-	-	-	-	-	28	3	9
David Matthews	8	FL	FL	FL	FL	FL	-	8	-	-	-	-	-	-	-	FL	-	-	FL	FL	-	FL	-	-	-	-	-	-	-	-	-	-	-	-	-	-	-	-	-	-	-	-	-	-	-	-	11	1	3
Derek Ashurst	-	8	8	8	-	-	-	-	-	-	-	-	-	8	8	-	-	-	-	-	-	-	-	-	-	-	-	-	0	-	-	-	-	-	-	-	8	8	8	FL	-	-	-	-	-	-	10	1	3
Graham Willars	-	-	-	-	-	-	-	FL	FL	FL	FL	FL	-	-	-	-	-	-	-	-	FL	-	FL	FL	FL	FL	FL	FL	FL	FL	-	-	FL	FL	-	FL	FL	FL	FL	FL	-	-	-	-	-	-	21	-	-

1 game: Trevor Allen W(39)[1T-3], Martin Birkett W(19), H.B.Griffiths C(15), Alan Hopkins W(19), Leighton Jenkins 8(18), Alan Rees FH(34), D.C.Standerwick C(39), Mike Wade C(18), Trevor Watkiss C(31), John White FL(7)

LEICESTER FOOTBALL CLUB 1959-60
Back: R.E. Gerrard (Hon.Tres), G.A. Almey, P.H. Konig, G.G. Willars, D.G. Perry, G. Cherry, J.H. Addison,
A.D. Bolesworth (Team Hon.Sec), R.L. Bedingfield (President).
Middle: D. Senior, A.J.F.K. O'Reilly, C.G. Martin, T. Bleasdale (Capt), M.N. Gavins, J.P. Horrocks-Taylor, J.D. Robins.
Front: M.E. Freer, H.V. White, A. Jones.

LEICESTER FOOTBALL CLUB 1960-61
Back: R.J. Barr (Hon.Sec), T. Allen, D.J. Matthews, J.S. Thompson, R. Beason, R.P. Skelton, L. Tatham,
A.D. Bolesworth (Team Hon.Sec), R.L. Bedingfield (President).
Middle: I.M. Gibson, G.A. Almey, J.P. Horrocks-Taylor, C.G. Martin (Capt), M.R. Walker, T. Bleasdale, M.N. Gavins.
Front: C.D. Shephard, H.V. White.

1960-1961

NO	DATE	OPPONENTS	V	RES	FOR G	FOR T	FOR D	FOR P	FOR PTS	AGAINST G	AGAINST T	AGAINST D	AGAINST P	AGAINST PTS	SCORERS
1	Sep 3	BEDFORD	H	Drew	-	1	-	2	9	-	2	-	1	9	Gavins(2P) Bird(T)
2	7	WATCYN THOMAS XV	H	Lost	-	1	-	3	12	2	2	-	1	19	Gavins(3P) Ashurst(T)
3	10	Bath	A	Won	2	3	-	-	19	1	-	-	2	11	Gavins(2C) Tatham(T) Senior(3T) Horrocks-Taylor(T)
4	17	PLYMOUTH ALBION	H	Won	3	4	-	1	30	-	-	-	1	3	Gavins(3C,P) Ring(T) Senior(3T) Horrocks-Taylor(T) Bleasdale(T) Matthews(T)
5	24	Harlequins	A	Lost	-	-	-	-	0	-	2	-	-	6	
6	Oct 1	Coventry	A	Lost	-	-	-	1	3	2	1	-	1	16	Key(P)
7	8	RICHMOND	H	Won	-	-	-	2	6	-	1	-	-	3	Gavins(2P)
8	15	Cheltenham	A	Lost	1	1	-	-	8	1	2	-	-	11	Key(C) B.T.C.Small(T) Senior(T)
9	19	Oxford University	A	Won	3	2	1	-	24	-	-	1	-	3	Bird(T) Tatham(T) Ring(D) White(T) Martin(3C) Ashurst(T) Matthews(T)
10	22	NORTHAMPTON	H	Lost	-	-	-	-	0	-	2	-	1	9	
	29	Nuneaton	A		Cancelled Rain										
11	Nov 5	Gloucester	A	Lost	1	1	-	-	8	1	2	-	-	11	B.T.C.Small(C) Freer(T) Ring(T)
12	12	CAMBRIDGE UNIVERSITY	H	Lost	-	-	-	2	6	1	4	-	1	20	Martin(2P)
13	19	Newport	A	Lost	1	1	-	-	8	-	2	-	2	12	Skelton(T) Martin(C) Matthews(T)
14	26	Moseley	A	Won	3	-	1	-	18	2	1	-	-	13	Gavins(C) Freer(T) Tatham(T,D) Martin(2C) Matthews(T)
15	Dec 3	WATERLOO	H	Won	1	-	-	-	5	-	-	-	-	0	Shephard(T) Martin(C)
16	10	Blackheath	A	Lost	-	-	-	-	0	1	-	-	-	5	
17	17	BRISTOL	H	Won	-	1	1	2	12	-	-	1	2	9	Wade(D) Haddon(T) Martin(2P)
18	24	Rugby	A	Won	5	2	-	-	31	-	1	-	-	3	Gavins(5C) Shephard(2T) Wade(T) Senior(T) Martin(T) Almey(T) Willars(T)
19	26	BIRKENHEAD PARK	H	Drew	-	1	-	-	3	-	1	-	-	3	Shephard(T)
20	27	BARBARIANS	H	Lost	1	-	-	-	5	1	3	-	-	14	Gavins(C) Freer(T)
21	31	Headingley	A	Lost	-	-	-	2	6	1	-	-	2	11	Gavins(2P)
22	Jan 7	BATH	H	Won	2	-	-	2	16	-	1	-	-	3	Gavins(2C,2P) Senior(2T)
23	14	GLOUCESTER	H	Won	3	1	-	1	21	-	1	-	-	3	Freer(T) Senior(T) Horrocks-Taylor(T) Robins(3C,P) Martin(T)
24	21	Bedford	A	Won	-	2	-	-	6	-	-	-	-	0	Freer(T) Almey(T)
25	26	ROYAL AIR FORCE	H	Lost	-	1	-	1	6	1	2	-	-	11	Cooper(P) Almey(T)
26	28	ROSSLYN PARK	H	Won	2	1	-	-	13	-	-	-	-	0	Gavins(2C) Shephard(T) Freer(T) Allen(T)
27	Feb 4	London Scottish	A	Lost	-	1	-	-	3	1	4	-	-	17	Martin(T)
28	11	NEWPORT	H	Won	1	2	-	3	20	1	1	-	-	8	Shephard(T) Robins(C,3P) Matthews(2T)
29	18	WASPS	H	Won	1	-	-	3	14	1	-	-	1	8	Allen(T) Robins(C,3P)
30	25	Northampton	A	Lost	-	-	1	-	3	1	-	-	1	8	Tatham(D)
31	Mar 4	HARLEQUINS	H	Won	4	3	-	-	29	-	2	-	-	6	Shephard(2T) Freer(T) Senior(T) Robins(4C) Almey(T) Bleasdale(T) Matthews(T)
32	9	LOUGHBOROUGH COLLEGE	H	Won	1	1	-	2	14	1	1	-	-	8	Gavins(C,2P) B.T.C.Small(T) Bleasdale(T)
33	11	COVENTRY	H	Lost	-	-	1	-	3	-	-	1	3	12	B.T.C.Small(D)
34	18	Bradford	A	Won	1	-	-	3	14	-	1	-	1	6	Gavins(C,3P) Matthews(T)
35	25	LLANELLI	H	Won	4	-	1	1	26	-	1	-	1	6	Freer(T) Senior(T) Horrocks-Taylor(D) Robins(4C,P) Matthews(2T)
36	Apr 1	Bristol	A	Lost	1	-	-	-	5	1	2	-	1	14	White(T) Martin(C)
37	3	Plymouth Albion	A	Won	-	1	-	-	3	-	-	-	-	0	Matthews(T)
38	4	Exeter	A	Won	1	2	-	-	11	-	1	-	1	6	Gavins(C) Senior(2T) Matthews(T)
39	8	BIRKENHEAD PARK	H	Won	4	-	-	2	26	-	1	-	1	6	Gavins(4C,2P) Shephard(3T) Matthews(T)
40	15	LIVERPOOL	H	Won	1	1	-	1	11	-	1	-	2	9	Gavins(C,P) Freer(T) Matthews(T)
41	19	Nuneaton	A	Won	1	1	-	1	11	-	-	-	-	0	Gavins(C,P) Allen(2T)
42	22	NORTHERN	H	Won	2	1	-	3	22	-	-	-	3	9	Gavins(2C,3P) Shephard(3T)

INDIVIDUAL APPEARANCES 1960-1961

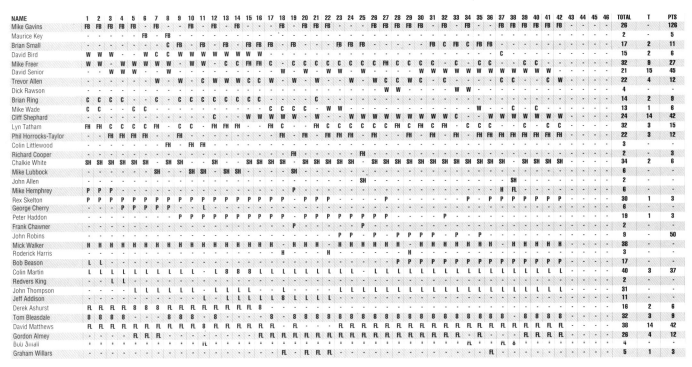

NAME	1	2	3	4	5	6	7	8	9	10	11	12	13	14	15	16	17	18	19	20	21	22	23	24	25	26	27	28	29	30	31	32	33	34	35	36	37	38	39	40	41	42	43	44	45	46	TOTAL	T	PTS
Mike Gavins	FB	FB	FB	FB	FB	-	FB	-	-	FB	-	FB	-	FB	-	-	-	FB	-	FB	FB	FB	-	-	-	FB	FB	FB	FB	FB	-	FB	-	FB	-	-	FB	FB	FB	FB	FB	FB	-	-	-	-	26	-	126
Maurice Key	-	-	-	-	-	FB	-	FB	-	-	-	-	-	-	-	-	-	-	-	-	-	-	-	-	-	-	-	-	-	-	-	-	-	-	-	-	-	-	-	-	-	-	-	-	-	-	2	-	5
Brian Small	-	-	-	-	-	-	-	C	FB	-	FB	-	FB	-	FB	FB	FB	-	FB	-	-	-	FB	FB	FB	-	-	-	-	-	FB	C	FB	C	FB	FB	-	-	-	-	-	-	-	-	-	-	17	2	11
David Bird	W	W	W	-	-	W	C	C	W	W	W	W	W	W	W	W	-	-	-	-	-	-	-	-	-	-	-	-	-	-	-	-	-	-	-	-	C	-	-	-	-	-	-	-	-	-	15	2	6
Mike Freer	W	W	-	W	W	W	W	W	-	W	W	-	C	C	FH	FH	C	-	C	C	C	C	C	C	C	C	FH	C	C	C	C	-	C	-	C	C	-	-	C	C	-	-	-	-	-	-	32	9	27
David Senior	-	-	W	W	W	-	-	W	-	-	-	-	-	-	-	-	-	W	-	W	-	W	W	-	W	-	-	-	-	W	W	W	W	W	W	W	W	W	W	W	W	-	-	-	-	-	21	15	45
Trevor Allen	-	-	-	-	-	-	W	-	W	-	C	W	W	W	C	C	W	-	W	-	W	-	-	W	-	W	C	C	W	C	-	C	-	-	-	-	C	C	-	-	C	W	-	-	-	-	22	4	12
Dick Rawson	-	-	-	-	-	-	-	-	-	-	-	-	-	-	-	-	-	-	-	-	-	-	-	-	-	-	W	W	-	-	-	-	W	W	-	-	-	-	-	-	-	-	-	-	-	-	4	-	-
Brian Ring	C	C	C	C	-	-	C	-	C	C	C	C	C	C	C	C	-	-	-	-	C	-	-	-	-	-	-	-	-	-	-	-	-	-	-	-	-	-	-	-	-	-	-	-	-	-	14	2	9
Mike Wade	C	C	-	-	C	C	-	-	-	-	-	-	-	-	-	-	C	C	C	C	-	W	W	-	-	-	-	-	-	-	-	-	-	-	W	-	-	C	-	C	-	-	-	-	-	-	13	1	6
Cliff Shephard	-	-	-	-	-	-	-	-	-	-	-	C	-	-	W	W	W	W	W	-	W	-	-	W	W	W	W	W	W	W	W	W	C	-	-	W	W	W	W	W	W	W	-	-	-	-	24	14	42
Lyn Tatham	FH	FH	C	C	C	C	FH	-	C	C	-	FH	FH	FH	-	-	FH	C	-	-	FH	C	C	C	C	C	C	FH	C	FH	C	FH	-	C	C	C	-	-	C	-	C	C	-	-	-	-	32	3	15
Phil Horrocks-Taylor	-	-	FH	FH	FH	FH	-	-	FH	-	-	-	-	-	-	-	-	FH	-	FH	-	FH	FH	FH	-	FH	-	-	FH	-	FH	-	FH	-	FH	FH	FH	FH	FH	FH	FH	FH	-	-	-	-	22	3	12
Colin Littlewood	-	-	-	-	-	-	-	FH	-	FH	FH	-	-	-	-	-	-	-	-	-	-	-	-	-	-	-	-	-	-	-	-	-	-	-	-	-	-	-	-	-	-	-	-	-	-	-	3	-	-
Richard Cooper	-	-	-	-	-	-	-	-	-	-	-	-	-	-	-	-	-	-	FH	-	-	-	-	-	FH	-	-	-	-	-	-	-	-	-	-	-	-	-	-	-	-	-	-	-	-	-	2	-	3
Chalkie White	SH	SH	SH	SH	SH	SH	-	SH	SH	-	-	SH	-	-	SH	SH	SH	SH	-	SH	SH	SH	SH	SH	-	SH	SH	SH	SH	SH	SH	SH	SH	SH	SH	SH	SH	-	SH	SH	SH	SH	-	-	-	-	34	2	6
Mike Lubbock	-	-	-	-	-	-	SH	-	-	SH	SH	-	SH	SH	-	-	-	-	SH	-	-	-	-	-	-	-	-	-	-	-	-	-	-	-	-	-	-	-	-	-	-	-	-	-	-	-	6	-	-
John Allen	-	-	-	-	-	-	-	-	-	-	-	-	-	-	-	-	-	-	-	-	-	-	-	-	SH	-	-	-	-	-	-	-	-	-	-	-	-	SH	-	-	-	-	-	-	-	-	2	-	-
Mike Hemphrey	P	P	P	-	-	-	-	-	-	-	-	-	-	-	-	-	-	-	P	-	-	-	-	-	-	-	-	-	-	-	-	-	-	-	-	-	H	FL	-	-	-	-	-	-	-	-	6	-	-
Rex Skelton	P	P	P	P	P	P	P	P	P	P	P	P	P	P	P	P	P	P	-	P	P	P	-	-	-	-	P	-	-	-	-	-	-	P	-	P	P	P	P	P	P	P	-	-	-	-	30	1	3
George Cherry	-	-	-	P	P	P	P	P	-	-	L	-	-	-	-	-	-	-	-	-	-	-	-	-	-	-	-	-	-	-	-	-	-	-	-	-	-	-	-	-	-	-	-	-	-	-	6	-	-
Peter Haddon	-	-	-	-	-	-	-	-	P	P	P	P	P	P	P	P	P	P	-	P	P	P	P	P	P	P	P	-	-	-	-	P	-	-	-	-	-	-	-	-	-	-	-	-	-	-	19	1	3
Frank Chawner	-	-	-	-	-	-	-	-	-	-	-	-	-	-	-	-	-	-	P	-	-	-	-	-	P	-	-	-	-	-	-	-	-	-	-	-	-	-	-	-	-	-	-	-	-	-	2	-	-
John Robins	-	-	-	-	-	-	-	-	-	-	-	-	-	-	-	-	-	-	-	-	-	-	P	P	-	P	-	P	P	P	P	-	P	-	P	-	-	-	-	-	-	-	-	-	-	-	9	-	50
Mick Walker	H	H	H	H	H	H	H	H	H	H	H	H	H	H	H	H	H	-	H	H	H	-	H	H	H	H	H	H	-	H	H	H	H	H	H	H	-	H	H	H	H	H	-	-	-	-	38	-	-
Roderick Harris	-	-	-	-	-	-	-	-	-	-	-	-	-	-	-	-	-	H	-	-	-	H	-	-	-	-	-	-	H	-	-	-	-	-	-	-	-	-	-	-	-	-	-	-	-	-	3	-	-
Bob Beason	L	L	-	-	-	-	-	-	-	-	-	-	-	-	-	-	-	-	-	-	-	-	-	-	-	-	-	P	P	P	P	P	P	P	P	P	P	P	P	P	P	P	-	-	-	-	17	-	-
Colin Martin	L	L	L	L	L	L	L	L	L	L	-	L	8	8	8	L	L	L	L	L	L	L	L	L	-	L	L	L	L	L	L	L	L	L	L	L	L	L	L	L	L	L	-	-	-	-	40	3	37
Redvers King	-	-	L	L	-	-	-	-	-	-	-	-	-	-	-	-	-	-	-	-	-	-	-	-	-	-	-	-	-	-	-	-	-	-	-	-	-	-	-	-	-	-	-	-	-	-	2	-	-
John Thompson	-	-	-	-	L	L	L	L	L	L	-	L	L	L	L	-	-	L	-	-	-	-	L	L	L	L	L	L	L	L	L	L	L	L	L	L	L	L	L	L	L	L	-	-	-	-	31	-	-
Jeff Addison	-	-	-	-	-	-	-	-	-	-	L	-	L	L	L	L	L	8	L	L	L	L	-	-	-	-	-	-	-	-	-	-	-	-	-	-	-	-	-	-	-	-	-	-	-	-	11	-	-
Derek Ashurst	FL	FL	FL	FL	8	8	8	FL	FL	FL	FL	FL	FL	FL	FL	8	-	-	-	-	-	-	-	-	-	-	-	-	-	-	-	-	-	-	-	-	-	-	-	-	-	-	-	-	-	-	16	2	6
Tom Bleasdale	8	8	8	8	-	-	-	8	8	8	-	8	-	-	-	-	8	-	8	8	8	8	8	8	8	8	8	8	8	8	8	8	8	8	8	8	8	-	8	8	8	8	-	-	-	-	32	3	9
David Matthews	FL	FL	FL	FL	FL	FL	FL	FL	FL	FL	8	FL	FL	FL	FL	FL	FL	-	FL	-	-	-	FL	FL	FL	FL	FL	FL	FL	FL	FL	FL	FL	FL	FL	FL	FL	FL	FL	FL	FL	FL	-	-	-	-	38	14	42
Gordon Almey	-	-	-	-	FL	FL	FL	-	-	-	-	-	-	-	-	FL	FL	FL	FL	FL	FL	FL	FL	FL	FL	FL	FL	FL	FL	FL	FL	FL	FL	-	FL	-	-	-	FL	FL	FL	FL	-	-	-	-	26	4	12
Bob Small	-	-	-	-	-	-	-	-	-	-	FL	-	-	-	-	-	-	-	-	-	-	-	-	-	-	-	-	-	-	-	-	-	-	FL	-	-	FL	8	-	-	-	-	-	-	-	-	4	-	-
Graham Willars	-	-	-	-	-	-	-	-	-	-	-	-	-	-	-	-	-	FL	-	FL	FL	FL	-	-	-	-	-	-	-	-	-	-	-	-	-	FL	-	-	-	-	-	-	-	-	-	-	5	1	3

1 game: Arthur Chapman FH(34), Ian Gibson C(42), Alastair Graham-Bryce L(25), Tony O'Reilly W(20)

NO	DATE		OPPONENTS	V	RES	FOR G	FOR T	FOR D	FOR P	FOR PTS	AGAINST G	AGAINST T	AGAINST D	AGAINST P	AGAINST PTS	SCORERS
1	Sep	2	Bedford	A	Lost	2	-	-	1	13	3	2	-	-	21	Gavins(2C,P) Freer(T) Tatham(T)
2		6	WATCYN THOMAS XV	H	Won	1	3	-	1	17	2	-	-	-	10	Gavins(C,P) Shephard(T) Senior(2T) Matthews(T)
3		9	BATH	H	Lost	1	1	-	1	11	-	-	-	4	12	Scotland(C,P) Senior(T) Almey(T)
4		16	PLYMOUTH ALBION	H	Lost	-	1	-	2	9	1	-	1	1	11	Scotland(2P) Shephard(T)
5		23	Harlequins	A	Won	2	-	-	1	13	-	1	-	1	6	Scotland(2C,P) Shephard(T) Allen(T)
6		27	RUGBY	H	Won	2	1	1	3	25	-	1	-	1	6	Scotland(2C,D,3P) Shephard(T) Tatham(T) Edwards(T)
7		30	NEWPORT	H	Lost	-	-	-	1	3	-	3	-	-	9	Scotland(P)
8	Oct	7	COVENTRY	H	Lost	-	-	-	2	6	2	-	1	2	19	Scotland(2P)
9		14	Richmond	A	Lost	-	-	-	1	3	3	1	1	1	24	Scotland(P)
10		21	CHELTENHAM	H	Won	-	2	-	2	12	-	-	1	-	3	Scotland(2P) Bird(T) Horrocks-Taylor(T)
11		25	OXFORD UNIVERSITY	H	Won	1	-	-	3	14	1	1	-	1	11	Mainwaring(T) Scotland(C,3P)
12		28	Northampton	A	Lost	2	-	-	1	13	4	1	1	1	29	Bird(T) Martin(2C,P) Matthews(T)
13	Nov	4	Gloucester	A	Lost	1	-	-	2	11	4	1	-	1	26	Bird(T) Scotland(C,2P)
14		11	Cambridge University	A	Lost	-	1	-	-	3	1	2	-	-	11	Mainwaring(T)
15		18	LEICESTERSHIRE XV	H	Won	2	-	-	-	10	-	-	2	-	6	Mainwaring(T) Scotland(2C) Almey(T)
16		25	MOSELEY	H	Won	4	-	-	1	23	-	-	2*	1	9	Scotland(4C,P) Greenhow(T) Skelton(T) Matthews(2T)
17	Dec	2	Waterloo	A	Lost	-	1	-	-	3	1	-	-	-	5	Matthews(T)
18		9	Blackheath	A	Lost	-	1	-	1	6	1	1	-	1	11	Scotland(P) Greenhow(T)
19		16	BRISTOL	H	Won	1	1	-	-	8	-	2	-	-	6	Hopkins(C) Bird(T) Dymond(T)
20		23	London Irish	A	Won	-	1	-	1	6	-	-	1	-	3	Martin(P) Matthews(T)
		26	BIRKENHEAD PARK	H	Cancelled Frost											
		27	BARBARIANS	H	Cancelled Frost											
		30	HEADINGLEY	H	Cancelled Frost											
21	Jan	6	Bath	A	Lost	1	-	-	-	5	1	1	-	-	8	Tatham(T) Martin(C)
22		13	GLOUCESTER	H	Won	2	1	-	1	16	-	1	-	-	3	Wade(T) Senior(T) Chawner(T) Martin(2C,P)
23		20	BEDFORD	H	Won	2	2	-	1	19	-	-	-	-	0	Bird(T) Tatham(T) Senior(2T) Scotland(P) Martin(2C)
24		27	Rosslyn Park	A	Lost	1	1	-	-	8	1	2	-	1	14	Tatham(2T) Martin(C)
25	Feb	3	LONDON SCOTTISH	H	Won	1	3	1	1	20	-	-	-	-	0	Bird(T) Wade(T) Tatham(D) Robins(C,P) Jones(T) Almey(T)
26		10	Newport	A	Lost	2	-	-	-	10	2	4	-	-	22	Greenhow(T) Robins(2C) Matthews(T)
27		17	Wasps	A	Drew	-	1	-	1	6	-	1	-	1	6	Scotland(P) Greenhow(T)
28		24	NORTHAMPTON	H	Won	1	-	-	-	5	-	-	-	-	0	Shephard(T) Martin(C)
	Mar	3	HARLEQUINS	H	Cancelled Snow											
29		8	LOUGHBOROUGH COLLEGE	H	Won	2	1	1	-	16	-	-	-	-	0	Freer(T,D) Rowell(T) Martin(T,2C)
30		13	Coventry	A	Lost	1	-	-	-	5	2	-	-	-	10	Almey(T) Martin(C)
31		17	ROYAL AIR FORCE	H	Won	1	1	-	2	14	2	-	-	-	10	Senior(T) Martin(C,2P) Matthews(T)
32		24	BRADFORD	H	Won	4	3	-	1	32	1	-	-	-	5	Scotland(C) Bird(3T) Gibson(T) Senior(3T) Martin(3C,P)
33		29	BARBARIANS	H	Lost	-	-	-	1	3	1	-	-	-	5	Scotland(P)
34		31	Llanelli	A	Lost	-	1	-	-	3	-	4	-	-	12	Scotland(T)
35	Apr	5	NUNEATON	H	Won	2	1	1	1	19	-	-	-	1	3	Scotland(C) Senior(3T,D) Martin(C,P)
36		7	Birkenhead Park	A	Won	5	-	-	3	34	-	-	-	1	3	Scotland(5C,3P) Wade(T) Tatham(2T) Drake-Lee(T) Matthews(T)
37		9	MAESTEG	H	Won	2	-	-	1	13	1	2	-	-	11	Scotland(T,C,P) Senior(T) Martin(C)
38		14	Liverpool	A	Won	-	-	-	2	6	-	1	-	-	3	Scotland(2P)
39		21	Bristol	A	Drew	1	-	-	2	11	1	1	-	1	11	Martin(C,2P) Matthews(T)
40		23	Plymouth Albion	A	Won	1	2	-	-	11	-	-	-	2	6	Bird(T) Senior(T) R.W.Small(T) Martin(C)
41		24	Exeter	A	Won	5	1	-	1	31	1	-	-	3	14	Bird(T) Wade(3T) Senior(T) Martin(5C,P) Matthews(T)

INDIVIDUAL APPEARANCES 1961-1962

NAME	1	2	3	4	5	6	7	8	9	10	11	12	13	14	15	16	17	18	19	20	21	22	23	24	25	26	27	28	29	30	31	32	33	34	35	36	37	38	39	40	41	42	43	44	45	46	TOTAL	T	PTS
Mike Gavins	FB	FB	-	-	-	-	-	-	-	-	-	-	-	-	-	-	-	-	-	-	-	-	-	-	-	-	-	-	-	-	-	-	-	-	-	-	-	-	-	-	-	-	-	-	-	-	2	-	12
Ken Scotland	-	-	FB	FB	FB	FB	FB	FB	FB	FB	FH	-	FH	FH	FH	FB	FH	FB	-	-	-	-	FH	-	-	-	FB	-	-	-	-	FB	FB	FB	FB	FB	FB	FB	-	-	-	-	-	-	-	-	24	2	138
Brian Small	-	-	-	-	-	-	-	-	-	-	FB	FB	FB	FB	-	-	-	-	C	-	FB	FB	-	FB	-	-	-	-	FB	-	-	-	-	-	-	-	-	-	-	-	-	-	-	-	-	-	9	-	-
Gareth Hopkins	-	-	-	-	-	-	-	-	-	-	-	-	-	-	FB	-	FB	-	FB	-	-	-	FB	-	FB	FB	-	-	-	FB	FB	-	-	-	-	-	-	-	FB	FB	FB	-	-	-	-	-	11	-	2
Mike Hemphrey	-	-	-	-	-	-	-	-	-	-	-	-	-	-	-	-	-	-	-	FB	-	-	-	-	-	-	-	-	-	-	-	-	-	-	-	-	-	-	-	-	P	-	-	-	-	-	2	-	-
David Senior	W	W	W	W	W	W	W	-	-	-	-	-	-	-	-	-	-	-	-	-	-	W	W	W	W	-	-	-	-	-	W	W	W	-	W	-	W	-	W	W	W	-	-	-	-	-	19	16	51
Cliff Shephard	W	W	-	W	W	W	W	W	W	W	W	W	W	W	W	-	-	W	-	W	W	-	-	-	-	W	W	W	W	W	-	-	-	-	-	W	-	W	-	-	-	-	-	-	-	-	24	5	15
David Bird	-	-	-	-	-	-	-	W	W	C	C	W	W	C	-	W	C	W	W	W	W	W	W	W	W	W	W	W	W	W	W	W	W	W	W	W	-	W	W	W	W	-	-	-	-	-	32	11	33
Dick Mainwaring	-	-	-	-	-	-	-	-	-	W	W	-	-	W	W	W	W	-	-	-	-	-	-	-	-	-	-	-	-	-	-	-	-	-	-	-	-	-	-	-	-	-	-	-	-	-	6	3	9
Roger Clarke	-	-	-	-	-	-	-	-	-	-	-	-	-	-	-	-	W	-	-	-	-	-	-	-	-	-	-	-	-	-	-	-	-	W	-	-	-	-	-	-	-	-	-	-	-	-	2	-	-
Mike Freer	C	-	-	C	-	-	-	C	C	-	-	C	C	-	-	-	-	-	W	C	-	C	C	-	-	-	-	-	C	-	-	-	-	-	-	-	-	C	-	-	-	-	-	-	-	-	12	2	9
Malcolm Greenhow	C	-	-	-	-	-	-	-	-	-	-	-	-	-	C	C	-	C	-	-	-	-	-	-	-	C	C	-	C	-	-	-	-	-	-	-	-	-	-	C	-	-	-	-	-	-	8	4	12
Ian Gibson	-	-	C	-	C	-	-	-	-	-	C	C	-	-	C	C	C	C	C	-	C	-	-	-	-	-	-	-	-	-	C	C	-	-	C	C	C	-	C	-	C	-	-	-	-	-	17	1	3
Mike Wade	-	C	W	-	C	C	C	C	-	-	-	-	-	-	-	-	-	-	-	C	-	C	-	C	C	-	-	-	-	C	C	C	C	-	C	C	W	-	C	C	C	-	-	-	-	-	20	6	18
Mike Harrison	-	-	-	-	-	-	-	-	-	-	-	-	-	-	-	-	-	-	-	-	C	-	-	-	-	-	-	C	-	-	-	-	-	-	-	-	-	C	-	-	-	-	-	-	-	-	3	-	-
Ken Smith	-	-	-	-	-	-	-	-	-	-	-	-	-	-	-	-	-	-	-	-	-	-	-	-	-	C	C	C	-	-	-	-	-	-	-	-	-	-	-	-	-	-	-	-	-	-	3	-	-
Lyn Tatham	FH	C	C	C	-	C	C	FH	FH	C	-	FH	C	C	-	FH	-	FH	FH	-	FH	FH	C	C	C	FH	FH	FH	-	C	-	-	C	C	FH	FH	C	-	-	-	-	-	-	-	-	-	29	8	27
Phil Horrocks-Taylor	-	FH	FH	FH	FH	FH	FH	-	-	FH	-	-	-	-	-	-	-	-	-	-	-	-	-	FH	FH	-	-	-	FH	FH	-	FH	FH	FH	-	-	FH	FH	FH	FH	-	-	-	-	-	-	18	1	3
Richard Cooper	-	-	-	-	-	-	-	-	-	-	-	-	-	-	-	-	-	-	-	FH	-	-	-	-	-	-	-	-	-	-	-	-	-	C	-	-	-	-	-	-	FH	-	-	-	-	-	3	-	-
Chalkie White	SH	SH	SH	-	-	-	-	-	-	-	-	-	-	-	-	-	-	-	-	SH	SH	SH	SH	SH	SH	SH	SH	SH	SH	SH	-	SH	SH	SH	SH	SH	SH	SH	SH	-	SH	-	-	-	-	-	23	-	-
John Allen	-	-	-	SH	SH	SH	SH	SH	SH	SH	SH	SH	SH	SH	-	-	SH	-	-	-	-	-	-	-	-	-	-	-	-	-	-	-	-	-	-	-	-	-	-	SH	-	-	-	-	-	-	13	1	3
Mike Dymond	-	-	-	-	-	-	-	-	-	-	-	-	-	-	SH	SH	-	SH	SH	-	-	-	-	-	-	-	-	-	-	-	SH	-	-	-	-	-	-	-	-	-	-	-	-	-	-	-	5	1	3
Bob Beason	P	P	P	P	-	-	-	-	-	-	-	-	-	-	-	-	-	-	-	-	-	-	-	-	-	-	-	-	-	-	-	-	-	-	-	-	-	-	-	-	-	-	-	-	-	-	4	-	-
George Cherry	P	P	P	P	P	P	P	P	P	-	-	-	-	-	-	-	-	-	-	-	-	-	-	-	-	-	-	P	P	P	P	-	-	-	-	-	-	-	-	P	-	-	-	-	-	-	14	-	-
Mark Wrench	-	-	-	-	P	P	P	P	P	-	-	-	-	-	-	-	-	-	-	-	-	-	-	-	-	-	-	-	-	-	-	-	-	-	-	-	-	-	-	-	-	-	-	-	-	-	5	-	-
Frank Chawner	-	-	-	-	-	-	-	-	-	P	P	P	P	P	P	P	P	P	P	P	P	P	P	P	P	P	P	P	P	P	P	P	P	P	P	P	P	P	P	P	P	-	-	-	-	-	32	1	3
Rex Skelton	-	-	-	-	-	-	-	-	-	P	P	P	P	P	P	P	P	P	P	P	-	-	P	P	-	-	P	-	-	-	-	-	-	-	-	-	-	-	-	-	-	-	-	-	-	-	14	1	3
Nick Drake-Lee	-	-	-	-	-	-	-	-	-	-	-	-	-	-	-	-	-	-	-	-	P	P	-	-	-	-	-	-	-	-	-	P	P	P	P	P	P	P	P	-	-	-	-	-	-	-	10	1	3
John Robins	-	-	-	-	-	-	-	-	-	-	-	-	-	-	-	-	-	-	-	-	-	-	-	-	P	P	-	-	-	-	-	-	-	-	-	-	-	-	-	-	-	-	-	-	-	-	2	-	9
Mick Walker	H	H	H	-	-	-	-	-	-	-	-	-	-	-	-	-	-	-	-	-	-	-	H	-	H	H	H	-	H	H	H	H	H	H	-	H	H	H	H	-	H	-	-	-	-	-	18	-	-
Peter Edwards	-	-	-	H	H	H	H	H	H	H	H	H	H	H	H	H	H	H	H	H	H	H	-	H	-	-	-	H	-	-	-	-	-	-	-	-	-	-	-	H	-	-	-	-	-	-	22	1	3
Colin Martin	L	L	L	L	L	L	L	L	L	L	L	L	L	L	L	L	L	L	L	L	L	L	8	8	8	8	8	8	8	8	8	8	8	8	8	8	8	8	8	8	8	-	-	-	-	-	41	1	83
John Thompson	L	L	L	L	-	-	-	-	-	-	-	-	-	-	-	-	-	-	-	-	-	-	-	-	-	-	-	-	-	-	-	-	-	-	-	-	-	-	-	-	-	-	-	-	-	-	4	-	-
Mike Jones	-	-	-	-	L	L	-	L	L	L	-	L	L	L	L	L	L	L	L	L	L	L	L	L	L	L	L	L	-	L	-	L	L	L	L	L	L	-	L	L	-	-	-	-	-	-	31	1	3
Peter Riley	-	-	-	-	-	-	-	-	-	-	L	-	-	-	-	-	-	-	-	-	-	-	L	L	L	L	L	L	L	L	L	-	-	-	-	-	-	L	-	-	L	-	-	-	-	-	12	-	-
Bob Rowell	-	-	-	-	-	-	-	-	-	-	-	-	-	-	-	-	-	-	-	-	-	-	-	-	-	-	-	-	L	-	L	L	L	L	L	L	L	L	L	L	L	-	-	-	-	-	12	1	3
Gordon Almey	FL	FL	FL	FL	-	-	-	-	-	-	-	-	-	FL	FL	FL	FL	FL	FL	-	FL	-	-	FL	FL	-	FL	FL	FL	FL	-	FL	FL	-	FL	-	FL	-	FL	-	-	-	-	-	-	-	22	4	12
Tom Bleasdale	8	8	8	8	8	8	8	8	8	8	8	8	8	8	8	8	8	8	8	8	8	8	-	-	-	-	-	-	-	-	-	-	-	-	-	-	-	-	-	-	-	-	-	-	-	-	22	-	-
David Matthews	FL	FL	FL	FL	FL	FL	FL	FL	C	FL	FL	FL	FL	FL	FL	FL	FL	FL	FL	FL	FL	FL	FL	FL	FL	FL	FL	FL	FL	FL	FL	FL	FL	FL	FL	FL	FL	FL	FL	FL	FL	-	-	-	-	-	41	11	33
Tony Cavender	-	-	-	-	FL	FL	FL	FL	FL	FL	FL	FL	FL	-	-	-	-	-	-	-	-	-	-	-	-	-	-	-	-	-	-	-	-	-	-	-	-	-	-	-	-	-	-	-	-	-	9	-	-
Derek Ashurst	-	-	-	-	-	-	-	-	-	-	-	-	-	-	-	-	-	-	-	FL	-	FL	-	-	-	FL	-	-	-	-	-	-	-	FL	-	-	-	-	-	-	-	-	-	-	-	-	4	-	-
Bob Small	-	-	-	-	-	-	-	-	-	-	-	-	-	-	-	-	-	-	-	-	-	-	FL	-	-	-	-	-	-	-	FL	-	-	-	-	FL	-	FL	-	FL	FL	-	-	-	-	-	6	1	3

1 game: Brian Collins H(35), D.K.Hill FH(31), David Moeller FL(9), David Noble L(7), John White FB(28)

LEICESTER FOOTBALL CLUB 1961-62
Back: R.J. Barr (Hon.Sec), A.D. Bolesworth (Team Hon.Sec), J.A. Allen, G. Hopkins, C.D. Shephard, J.M. Jones,
R.E. Rowell, P. Riley, B.T.C. Small, D.W. Bird, G. Cherry, R.L. Bedingfield (President).
Middle: M.R. Walker, M.R. Wade, J.P. Horrocks-Taylor, C.G. Martin (Capt), K.J.F. Scotland, F. Chawner, G.A. Almey, D. Senior.
Front: D.J. Matthews, L. Tatham, I.M. Gibson, H.V. White, N.J. Drake-Lee.

LEICESTER FOOTBALL CLUB 1962-63
Back: R.J. Barr (President), G.W. Evans, R.C. Cooper, R.P. Skelton, I.M. Gibson, R.E. Rowell, R. Beason,
R.W. Small, A.D. Bolesworth (Team Hon.Sec).
Middle: M.R. Wade, G.A. Almey, D.J. Matthews, C.G. Martin (Capt), M.R. Walker, F. Chawner, J.P. Horrocks-Taylor.
Front: C.D. Shephard, D.W. Bird, M.J. Dymond. **Inset:** P. Riley, H.V. White.

					FOR					AGAINST					
NO	DATE	OPPONENTS	V	RES	G	T	D	P	PTS	G	T	D	P	PTS	SCORERS
1	Sep 1	BEDFORD	H	Won	3	1	-	-	18	2	-	-	1	13	Scotland(3C) Wade(T) Bird(T) Dymond(T) R.W.Small(T)
2	5	WATCYN THOMAS XV	H	Won	3	-	-	2	21	-	1	-	-	3	Scotland(3C,2P) Bird(2T) Gibson(T)
3	8	Bath	A	Won	3	2	-	-	21	1	-	-	-	5	Scotland(T,3C) Gibson(T) Senior(T) Chawner(T) Matthews(T)
4	12	Sheffield	A	Won	2	1	-	2	19	-	-	-	-	0	Scotland(2C,2P) Riley(2T) Matthews(T)
5	15	PLYMOUTH ALBION	H	Won	1	2	-	-	11	-	-	-	2	6	Bird(T) Harrison(T) Tatham(C) Chawner(T)
6	22	Harlequins	A	Lost	1	1	-	-	8	-	2	-	2	12	Scotland(C) Drake-Lee(T) Matthews(T)
7	29	Swansea	A	Won	4	-	-	3	29	-	1	-	1	6	Scotland(4C,3P) Gibson(T) Horrocks-Taylor(2T) Drake-Lee(T)
8	Oct 6	Coventry	A	Lost	-	1	-	2	9	2	1	-	1	16	Scotland(2P) Drake-Lee(T)
9	13	RICHMOND	H	Won	3	2	-	-	21	-	1	-	-	3	Scotland(T,3C) Smith(2T) R.W.Small(T) Matthews(T)
10	20	Cheltenham	A	Drew	-	-	-	-	0	-	-	-	-	0	
11	24	Oxford University	A	Lost	-	-	-	-	0	-	-	-	4	12	
12	27	NORTHAMPTON	H	Won	-	2	-	2	12	-	1	1	1	9	Scotland(2P) Smith(T) Jones(T)
13	Nov 3	Gloucester	A	Won	1	1	-	-	8	-	2	-	-	6	Bird(T) Scotland(C) Chawner(T)
14	10	CAMBRIDGE UNIVERSITY	H	Won	-	-	1	1	6	-	-	-	-	0	Scotland(D,P)
15	17	Newport	A	Lost	-	1	-	-	3	-	4	-	-	12	Dymond(T)
16	24	Moseley	A	Won	1	1	-	1	11	-	1	-	2	9	Scotland(C,P) Martin(T) Matthews(T)
17	Dec 1	WATERLOO	H	Won	2	3	-	1	22	-	1	-	-	3	Gibson(T) Senior(T) Scotland(2C,P) Chawner(T) R.W.Small(T) Matthews(T)
18	8	BLACKHEATH	H	Won	1	-	1	-	8	-	-	2	-	6	Scotland(C,D) R.W.Small(T)
19	15	BRISTOL	H	Won	1	-	-	1	8	-	1	-	1	6	Martin(C,P) Matthews(T)
	22	LONDON IRISH	H		Cancelled Fog										
	26	BIRKENHEAD PARK	H		Cancelled Frost										
	27	BARBARIANS	H		Cancelled Frost										
	29	Headingley	A		Cancelled Frost										
	Jan 5	BATH	H		Cancelled Frost										
	12	GLOUCESTER	H		Cancelled Frost										
	19	Bedford	A		Cancelled Frost										
	26	ROSSLYN PARK	H		Cancelled Frost										
	Feb 2	London Scottish	A		Cancelled Frost										
	9	NEWPORT	H		Cancelled Frost										
	16	WASPS	H		Cancelled Frost										
	23	Nottingham	A		Cancelled Frost										
20	Mar 2	Harlequins	A	Won	3	-	-	-	15	1	1	-	-	8	Bird(T) Gibson(T) Rowell(T) Martin(3C)
	7	LOUGHBOROUGH COLLEGE	H		Cancelled Frost										
21	9	COVENTRY	H	Lost	-	-	-	1	3	3	2	-	-	21	Martin(P)
22	16	ROYAL AIR FORCE	H	Won	-	1	-	2	9	-	-	-	-	0	R.W.Small(T) Martin(2P)
23	23	Saracens	A	Won	2	3	-	2	25	-	2	-	-	6	Bird(T) Gibson(T) Senior(T) R.W.Small(T) Martin(2C,2P) Matthews(T)
24	28	BARBARIANS	H	Won	2	2	-	-	16	-	3	-	-	9	Bird(T) Wade(T) Dymond(T) Martin(2C) Matthews(T)
25	30	LLANELLI	H	Won	-	1	-	1	6	-	1	-	-	3	Senior(T) Cooper(P)
26	Apr 4	Nuneaton	A	Won	1	1	-	-	8	-	1	-	-	3	Chawner(T) Riley(T) Martin(C)
27	6	Birkenhead Park	A	Won	-	1	-	1	6	-	-	1	-	3	Martin(P) Matthews(T)
28	13	Bristol	A	Lost	1	-	-	1	8	2	6	1	-	31	Sayer(T) Martin(C,P)
29	15	Plymouth Albion	A	Lost	-	-	-	-	0	1	2	-	1	14	
30	16	Exeter	A	Lost	-	3	-	-	9	-	3	1	-	12	Bird(T) Gibson(T) Matthews(T)
31	20	RUGBY	A	Lost	-	1	-	-	3	-	-	-	2	6	Cowman(T)

INDIVIDUAL APPEARANCES 1962-1963

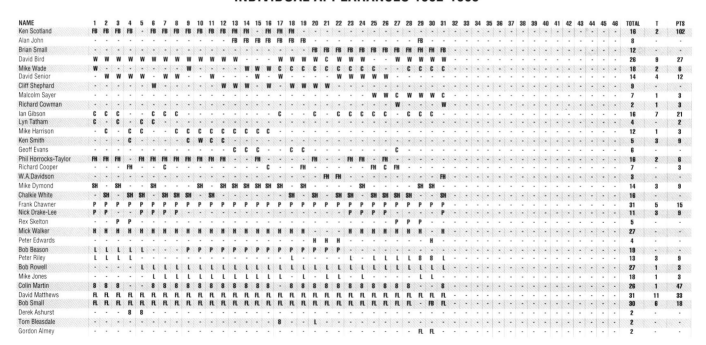

NAME	1	2	3	4	5	6	7	8	9	10	11	12	13	14	15	16	17	18	19	20	21	22	23	24	25	26	27	28	29	30	31	32	33	34	35	36	37	38	39	40	41	42	43	44	45	46	TOTAL	T	PTS
Ken Scotland	FB	FB	FB	FB	-	FB	FB	FB	FB	FB	FB	FB	FH	FH	-	FH	FH	FH	-	-	-	-	-	-	-	-	-	-	-	-	-	-	-	-	-	-	-	-	-	-	-	-	-	-	-	-	16	2	102
Alan John	-	-	-	-	-	-	-	-	-	-	-	-	FB	FB	FB	FB	FB	FB	FB	-	-	-	-	-	-	-	-	-	FB	-	-	-	-	-	-	-	-	-	-	-	-	-	-	-	-	-	8	-	-
Brian Small	-	-	-	-	-	-	-	-	-	-	-	-	-	-	-	-	-	-	-	FB	FB	FB	FB	FB	FB	FB	FB	FH	FH	FH	FB	-	-	-	-	-	-	-	-	-	-	-	-	-	-	-	12	-	-
David Bird	W	W	W	W	W	W	W	W	W	W	W	W	W	-	-	-	W	W	W	W	C	W	W	W	-	-	W	W	W	W	W	-	-	-	-	-	-	-	-	-	-	-	-	-	-	-	26	9	27
Mike Wade	W	-	-	-	-	-	-	-	W	-	-	-	-	W	W	W	C	C	C	C	C	C	C	C	C	-	-	C	C	C	C	-	-	-	-	-	-	-	-	-	-	-	-	-	-	-	18	2	6
David Senior	-	W	W	W	W	-	W	W	-	-	W	-	-	-	W	-	W	-	-	-	-	W	W	W	W	W	-	-	-	-	-	-	-	-	-	-	-	-	-	-	-	-	-	-	-	-	14	4	12
Cliff Shephard	-	-	-	-	-	W	-	-	-	-	-	W	W	W	-	W	-	W	W	W	W	-	-	-	-	-	-	-	-	-	-	-	-	-	-	-	-	-	-	-	-	-	-	-	-	-	9	-	-
Malcolm Sayer	-	-	-	-	-	-	-	-	-	-	-	-	-	-	-	-	-	-	-	-	-	-	-	-	W	W	C	W	W	W	C	-	-	-	-	-	-	-	-	-	-	-	-	-	-	-	7	1	3
Richard Cowman	-	-	-	-	-	-	-	-	-	-	-	-	-	-	-	-	-	-	-	-	-	-	-	-	-	-	W	-	-	-	W	-	-	-	-	-	-	-	-	-	-	-	-	-	-	-	2	1	3
Ian Gibson	C	C	C	-	-	C	C	C	-	-	-	-	-	-	-	-	C	-	-	C	-	C	C	C	C	C	-	C	C	C	-	-	-	-	-	-	-	-	-	-	-	-	-	-	-	-	16	7	21
Lyn Tatham	C	-	C	-	C	C	-	-	-	-	-	-	-	-	-	-	-	-	-	-	-	-	-	-	-	-	-	-	-	-	-	-	-	-	-	-	-	-	-	-	-	-	-	-	-	-	4	-	2
Mike Harrison	-	C	-	C	C	-	-	C	C	C	C	C	C	C	C	C	-	-	-	-	-	-	-	-	-	-	-	-	-	-	-	-	-	-	-	-	-	-	-	-	-	-	-	-	-	-	12	1	3
Ken Smith	-	-	-	C	-	-	-	-	C	W	C	C	-	-	-	-	-	-	-	-	-	-	-	-	-	-	-	-	-	-	-	-	-	-	-	-	-	-	-	-	-	-	-	-	-	-	5	3	9
Geoff Evans	-	-	-	-	-	-	-	-	-	-	-	-	C	C	C	-	-	C	C	-	-	-	-	-	-	-	C	-	-	-	-	-	-	-	-	-	-	-	-	-	-	-	-	-	-	-	6	-	-
Phil Horrocks-Taylor	FH	FH	FH	-	FH	FH	FH	FH	FH	FH	FH	FH	-	-	FH	-	-	-	-	FH	-	-	FH	FH	-	FH	-	-	-	-	-	-	-	-	-	-	-	-	-	-	-	-	-	-	-	-	16	2	6
Richard Cooper	-	-	-	FH	-	-	C	-	-	-	-	-	-	-	-	C	-	-	FH	-	-	-	-	-	FH	C	FH	-	-	-	-	-	-	-	-	-	-	-	-	-	-	-	-	-	-	-	7	-	3
W.A.Davidson	-	-	-	-	-	-	-	-	-	-	-	-	-	-	-	-	-	-	-	-	FH	FH	-	-	-	-	-	-	-	-	FH	-	-	-	-	-	-	-	-	-	-	-	-	-	-	-	3	-	-
Mike Dymond	SH	-	SH	-	-	SH	-	-	-	SH	-	SH	SH	SH	SH	SH	SH	-	SH	-	-	-	-	SH	-	-	-	-	SH	SH	-	-	-	-	-	-	-	-	-	-	-	-	-	-	-	-	14	3	9
Chalkie White	-	SH	-	SH	SH	-	SH	SH	SH	-	SH	-	-	-	-	-	-	SH	-	SH	-	SH	SH	-	SH	SH	SH	SH	-	-	SH	-	-	-	-	-	-	-	-	-	-	-	-	-	-	-	16	-	-
Frank Chawner	P	P	P	P	P	P	P	P	P	P	P	P	P	P	P	P	P	P	P	P	P	P	P	P	P	P	P	P	P	P	P	-	-	-	-	-	-	-	-	-	-	-	-	-	-	-	31	5	15
Nick Drake-Lee	P	P	-	-	P	P	P	P	-	-	-	-	-	-	-	-	-	-	-	-	-	-	P	P	P	P	-	-	-	-	P	-	-	-	-	-	-	-	-	-	-	-	-	-	-	-	11	3	9
Rex Skelton	-	-	P	P	-	-	-	-	-	-	-	-	-	-	-	-	-	-	-	-	-	-	-	-	-	-	P	P	P	-	-	-	-	-	-	-	-	-	-	-	-	-	-	-	-	-	5	-	-
Mick Walker	H	H	H	H	H	H	H	H	H	H	H	H	H	H	H	H	H	H	H	-	-	-	H	H	H	H	H	H	H	-	H	-	-	-	-	-	-	-	-	-	-	-	-	-	-	-	27	-	-
Peter Edwards	-	-	-	-	-	-	-	-	-	-	-	-	-	-	-	-	-	-	-	H	H	H	-	-	-	-	-	-	-	H	-	-	-	-	-	-	-	-	-	-	-	-	-	-	-	-	4	-	-
Bob Beason	L	L	L	L	L	-	-	-	P	P	P	P	P	P	P	P	P	P	P	P	P	P	-	-	-	-	-	-	-	-	-	-	-	-	-	-	-	-	-	-	-	-	-	-	-	-	19	-	-
Peter Riley	L	L	L	L	-	-	-	-	-	-	-	-	-	-	-	-	-	L	-	-	-	-	L	-	L	L	L	L	8	8	L	-	-	-	-	-	-	-	-	-	-	-	-	-	-	-	13	3	9
Bob Rowell	-	-	-	-	L	L	L	L	L	L	L	L	L	L	L	L	L	L	L	L	L	L	L	L	L	L	L	L	L	L	L	-	-	-	-	-	-	-	-	-	-	-	-	-	-	-	27	1	3
Mike Jones	-	-	-	-	-	L	L	L	L	L	L	L	L	L	L	L	L	-	L	-	L	L	-	L	-	-	-	-	L	L	-	-	-	-	-	-	-	-	-	-	-	-	-	-	-	-	18	1	3
Colin Martin	8	8	8	-	-	8	8	8	8	8	8	8	8	8	8	8	-	8	8	8	8	8	8	8	8	8	8	8	-	-	8	-	-	-	-	-	-	-	-	-	-	-	-	-	-	-	26	1	47
David Matthews	FL	FL	FL	FL	FL	FL	FL	FL	FL	FL	FL	FL	FL	FL	FL	FL	FL	FL	FL	FL	FL	FL	FL	FL	FL	FL	FL	FL	FL	FL	FL	-	-	-	-	-	-	-	-	-	-	-	-	-	-	-	31	11	33
Bob Small	FL	FL	FL	FL	FL	FL	FL	FL	FL	FL	FL	FL	FL	FL	FL	FL	FL	FL	FL	FL	FL	FL	FL	FL	FL	FL	FL	FL	-	FB	FL	-	-	-	-	-	-	-	-	-	-	-	-	-	-	-	30	6	18
Derek Ashurst	-	-	-	8	8	-	-	-	-	-	-	-	-	-	-	-	-	-	-	-	-	-	-	-	-	-	-	-	-	-	-	-	-	-	-	-	-	-	-	-	-	-	-	-	-	-	2	-	-
Tom Bleasdale	-	-	-	-	-	-	-	-	-	-	-	-	-	-	-	-	8	-	-	L	-	-	-	-	-	-	-	-	-	-	-	-	-	-	-	-	-	-	-	-	-	-	-	-	-	-	2	-	-
Gordon Almey	-	-	-	-	-	-	-	-	-	-	-	-	-	-	-	-	-	-	-	-	-	-	-	-	-	-	-	-	FL	FL	-	-	-	-	-	-	-	-	-	-	-	-	-	-	-	-	2	-	-

1 game: John Allen SH(21), Martin Birkett W(21), Malcolm Greenhow C(10), Mike Hemphrey P(30), Gareth Hopkins FB(28), Graham Pulfrey FB(5)

NO	DATE		OPPONENTS	V	RES	FOR					AGAINST					SCORERS
						G	T	D	P	PTS	G	T	D	P	PTS	
1	Sep	2	Torquay Athletic	A	Won	3	1	-	-	18	1	-	-	-	5	Chilton(3C) Cooper(T) Rowell(T) Almey(T) Matthews(T)
2		7	BEDFORD	H	Won	-	2	-	1	9	-	-	-	-	0	Gibson(T) Chawner(T) Martin(P)
3		11	WATCYN THOMAS XV	H	Won	-	3	-	1	12	1	-	-	-	5	Chilton(P) Bird(T) Bussey(T) Matthews(T)
4		14	BATH	H	Won	2	3	-	1	22	-	-	-	1	3	Chilton(2C) Gibson(T) Bussey(T) Almey(T) Martin(P) Matthews(2T)
5		21	PLYMOUTH ALBION	H	Won	2	1	-	-	13	-	2	1	-	9	Chilton(2C) Gibson(T) Bussey(T) Rowell(T)
6		28	Harlequins	A	Lost	-	2	-	-	6	2	-	-	1	13	Gibson(T) Allen(T)
7	Oct	5	COVENTRY	H	Lost	-	-	-	-	0	1	-	1	-	8	
8		12	Richmond	A	Won	1	-	-	2	11	1	1	-	-	8	Chilton(C,2P) Wade(T)
9		19	HEADINGLEY	H	Won	-	2	-	1	9	-	1	-	-	3	Chilton(P) Harrison(T) Almey(T)
10		26	Northampton	A	Won	1	-	-	2	11	-	-	-	-	0	Chilton(C,2P) Harrison(T)
11		30	OXFORD UNIVERSITY	H	Lost	-	-	-	-	0	2	2	-	-	16	
12	Nov	2	GLOUCESTER	H	Lost	-	1	-	-	3	-	3	-	-	9	Bird(T)
13		9	Cambridge University	A	Drew	-	1	-	2	9	-	1	-	2	9	Chilton(2P) Matthews(T)
14		16	Rugby	A	Lost	1	2	-	-	11	1	1	-	4	20	Bird(T) Harrison(2T) Martin(C)
15		23	MOSELEY	H	Won	1	2	-	2	17	-	1	-	3	12	Chilton(C,2P) Bussey(2T) Wade(T)
16		30	CHELTENHAM	H	Won	-	2	-	1	9	-	1	-	-	3	Chilton(P) Bird(T) Sayer(T)
17	Dec	7	Waterloo	A	Won	4	1	-	2	29	2	-	-	-	10	Bird(T) Sayer(2T) Bussey(2T) Martin(4C,2P)
18		14	BLACKHEATH	H	Won	1	-	-	1	8	-	1	-	-	3	Almey(T) Martin(C,P)
		21	BRISTOL	H		Cancelled										
19		26	BARBARIANS	H	Lost	-	-	-	2	6	2	1	-	-	13	Martin(2P)
20	Jan	4	Bath	A	Lost	-	-	-	-	0	1	2	-	-	11	
21		11	Gloucester	A	Won	1	2	-	-	11	-	-	-	-	0	Bird(T) Sayer(T) Almey(T) Martin(C)
		18	Bedford	A		Cancelled Frost										
22		25	Rosslyn Park	A	Won	1	3	-	-	14	1	1	-	-	8	Chilton(T) Harrison(T) Allen(T) Almey(T) Martin(C)
23	Feb	1	LONDON SCOTTISH	H	Won	1	-	-	-	5	-	-	-	1	3	Harrison(T) Martin(C)
24		8	Birkenhead Park	A	Won	1	1	1	2	17	1	-	-	1	8	Pulfrey(D) Bird(T) Chilton(T,C,2P)
25		15	Wasps	A	Won	6	-	-	-	30	-	1	-	-	3	Chilton(6C) Harrison(T) Bussey(2T) Rowell(T) Matthews(2T)
26		22	NORTHAMPTON	H	Won	3	2	-	2	27	-	1	-	-	3	Chilton(2T,3C,2P) Bird(2T) Harrison(T)
27		29	Llanelli	A	Lost	-	-	-	2	6	2	-	-	-	10	Chilton(2P)
28	Mar	7	HARLEQUINS	H	Lost	-	-	-	-	0	-	1	-	1	6	
29		12	LOUGHBOROUGH COLLEGE	H	Won	-	-	1	3	12	-	-	1	-	3	Chilton(3P) Freer(D)
30		14	THE ARMY	H	Won	1	2	-	1	14	-	1	-	-	3	Chilton(C,P) Bussey(T) Wade(T) Almey(T)
31		21	ROYAL AIR FORCE	H	Won	3	2	-	2	27	-	-	-	1	3	Chilton(T,2P) Bird(T) Harrison(2T) Gibson(T) Martin(3C)
32		28	Bristol	A	Won	2	2	-	-	16	-	2	-	1	9	Bird(3T) Rowell(T) Martin(2C)
33		30	Plymouth Albion	A	Drew	1	-	-	-	5	1	-	-	-	5	John(C) Harrison(T)
34	Apr	1	Exeter	A	Won	2	-	-	2	16	-	1	-	1	6	Small(T) Martin(2C,2P) Matthews(T)
35		4	SWANSEA	H	Lost	-	1	-	-	6	1	-	1	1	11	Bird(T) Martin(C)
36		8	NUNEATON	H	Won	2	4	-	-	22	1	1	-	-	8	Chilton(T) Harrison(T) Allen(T) P.G.Edwards(T) Matthews(T) Martin(2C) Willars(T)
37		11	Newport	A	Drew	1	1	-	-	8	1	-	-	1	8	Bussey(T) Wade(T) Martin(C)
38		15	London Irish	A	Won	2	1	-	-	13	1	-	-	2	11	Beason(T) Martin(2C) Matthews(2T)
39		18	SARACENS	H	Won	-	3	-	-	9	-	1	-	-	3	Chilton(T) Gibson(T) Bussey(T)
40		22	Coventry	A	Lost	-	-	-	2	6	1	1	-	2	14	Martin(2P)
41		29	Bedford	A	Lost	1	-	-	1	8	1	2	-	-	11	Chilton(T) Martin(C,P)

INDIVIDUAL APPEARANCES 1963-1964

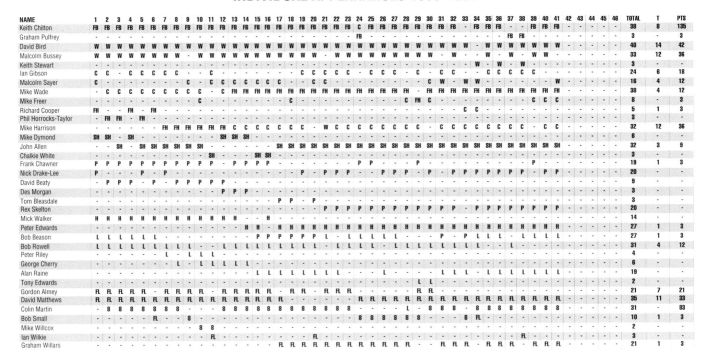

1 game: Geoff Evans C(3), Alan John FB(33)[2], Cliff Shephard W(9), Peter Tom 8(1)

LEICESTER FOOTBALL CLUB 1963-64

Back: R.J. Barr (President), M.E. Freer, M.R. Walker, M.F. Sayer, R. Beason, A. Raine, R.E. Rowell, G.G. Willars, G.A. Almey, M.J. Harrison, W.M. Bussey, A.D. Bolesworth (Team Hon.Sec.) R.E. Gerrard (Hon.Sec.)

Middle: I.M. Gibson, F. Chawner, R.P. Skelton, C.G. Martin, M.R. Wade (Capt), D.J. Matthews, K. Chilton, D.W. Bird.

Front: J.A. Allen, P.G. Edwards.

NO	DATE		OPPONENTS	V	RES	FOR					AGAINST					SCORERS
						G	T	D	P	PTS	G	T	D	P	PTS	
1	Sep	3	WATCYN THOMAS XV	H	Lost	1	2	-	-	11	-	4	-	-	12	Chilton(T) Rowell(T) Martin(C) Matthews(T)
2		5	BEDFORD	H	Won	-	1	-	2	9	-	1	-	1	6	Rowell(T) Martin(2P)
3		12	Bath	A	Won	5	1	-	1	31	1	1	-	-	8	Bird(2T) Bussey(2T) Cooper(T) Martin(5C,P) Willars(T)
4		19	PLYMOUTH ALBION	H	Won	2	-	-	1	13	-	-	-	-	0	Chilton(C,P) Harrison(T) Matthews(T,C)
5		26	Harlequins	A	Lost	-	1	-	-	3	2	3	-	-	19	Willars(T)
6	Oct	3	Coventry	A	Lost	-	-	-	1	3	2	2	-	1	19	Pulfrey(P)
7		8	MIDLANDS XV	H	Won	5	1	-	1	31	-	-	-	-	8	Stewart(T) Harrison(3T) Evans(T) Willars(T) Martin(5C,P)
8		10	RICHMOND	H	Lost	-	-	-	1	3	3	3	-	1	27	Martin(P)
9		17	Cheltenham	A	Won	1	-	-	1	8	-	-	-	-	0	Martin(T,C,P)
10		21	Oxford University	A	Lost	-	-	-	2	6	2	2	-	-	16	Chilton(2P)
11		24	Swansea	A	Lost	-	-	-	-	0	2	2	1	-	19	
12		31	NUNEATON	H	Won	2	2	-	1	19	1	-	-	-	5	Chilton(T) Harrison(2T) Perkins(T) Martin(2C,P)
13	Nov	1	Old Belvedere	A	Lost	1	1	1	1	14	2	2	-	-	16	Chilton(T,C,D,P) J.A.Allen(T)
14		7	Gloucester	A	Lost	-	2	-	1	9	2	3	1	-	22	Chilton(P) Drake-Lee(T) Matthews(T)
15		14	CAMBRIDGE UNIVERSITY	H	Won	1	-	-	2	11	-	-	-	-	0	Drake-Lee(T) Martin(C,2P)
16		21	Rugby	A	Lost	-	-	-	-	0	1	2	-	1	14	
17		28	Moseley	A	Won	-	-	-	2	6	-	-	-	1	3	Chilton(2P)
18	Dec	5	WATERLOO	H	Won	2	3	-	1	22	-	-	-	2	6	Chilton(2C,P) J.A.Allen(2T) Drake-Lee(T) Raine(T) Matthews(T)
19		12	Headingley	A	Won	3	1	-	1	21	-	1	-	1	6	Chilton(3C,P) Harrison(3T) Quick(T)
20		19	BRISTOL	H	Lost	-	1	-	2	9	1	2	1	-	14	Chilton(2P) Raine(T)
		26	BIRKENHEAD PARK	H		Cancelled										
21		28	BARBARIANS	H	Won	-	2	-	2	12	1	1	-	1	11	Bird(T) Martin(2P) Matthews(T)
22	Jan	2	BATH	H	Won	1	2	-	-	11	1	1	-	-	8	Chilton(C) Bussey(T) Beason(T) Raine(T)
23		9	GLOUCESTER	H	Won	3	2	-	-	21	-	-	-	-	0	Chilton(2T,3C) J.A.Allen(T) Matthews(T) Quick(T)
24		16	Bedford	A	Won	2	2	1	1	22	-	1	-	-	3	Chilton(2C,D,P) Harrison(T) Bussey(T) Matthews(T) Wilkie(T)
'25		23	ROSSLYN PARK	H	Won	2	-	-	1	13	1	-	-	-	5	Chilton(2C,P) Evans(T) Martin(T)
		30	LLANELLI	H		Cancelled										
26	Feb	6	London Scottish	A	Won	1	2	-	-	11	-	1	1	-	6	Bussey(T) Rowell(T) Martin(C) Matthews(T)
27		13	NEWPORT	H	Lost	2	-	-	-	10	3	3	1	1	30	Chilton(2C) Bussey(T) Matthews(T)
28		20	WASPS	H	Lost	-	-	-	3	9	-	4	-	-	12	Chilton(3P)
29		27	Northampton	A	Lost	1	-	-	1	8	-	2	2	2	18	Chilton(C,P) Harrison(T)
30	Mar	6	HARLEQUINS	H	Lost	1	1	1	-	11	2	-	-	1	13	Chilton(C) Bussey(T,D) Willars(T)
31		11	LOUGHBOROUGH COLLEGE	H	Lost	1	-	-	2	11	3	2	-	1	24	Chilton(2P) Bussey(T)
32		13	NEWBRIDGE	H	Lost	-	1	-	1	6	3	-	-	-	15	Chilton(P) Willars(T)
33		19	ROYAL AIR FORCE	H	Drew	-	-	-	-	0	-	-	-	-	0	
34		27	Saracens	A	Drew	-	-	-	1	3	-	1	-	-	3	Chilton(P)
35		31	NORTHAMPTON	H	Won	1	-	-	3	14	-	1	-	-	3	Bird(T) Martin(C,3P)
36	Apr	3	Birkenhead Park	A	Won	1	3	-	1	17	2	1	-	-	13	Pulfrey(P) Bird(2T) Glover(T) Willars(T) Martin(C)
37		10	Newport	A	Lost	-	-	-	1	3	-	2	-	3	15	Martin(P)
38		17	Bristol	A	Lost	-	-	-	1	3	1	-	-	-	18	Martin(P)
39		19	Plymouth Albion	A	Won	-	2	-	-	6	-	-	-	-	0	Bird(T) Willars(T)
40		20	Exeter	A	Lost	-	-	-	1	3	1	1	-	1	11	Martin(P)
41		24	Northern	A	Won	2	2	-	-	16	-	-	-	1	3	Bird(2T) Chilton(T) Martin(2C) Matthews(T)

INDIVIDUAL APPEARANCES 1964-1965

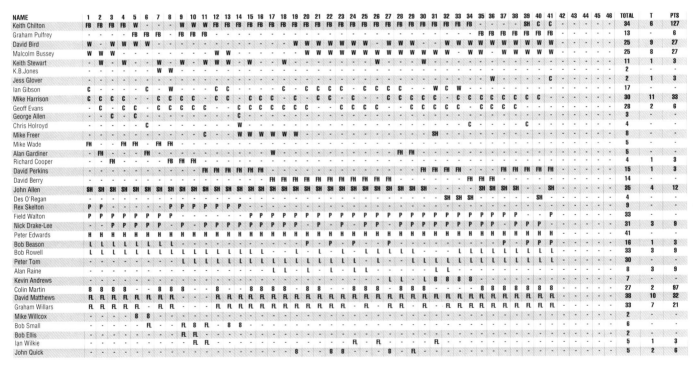

NAME	TOTAL	T	PTS
Keith Chilton	34	6	127
Graham Pulfrey	13	-	6
David Bird	25	9	27
Malcolm Bussey	25	8	27
Keith Stewart	11	1	3
K.B.Jones	2	-	-
Jess Glover	2	1	3
Ian Gibson	17	-	-
Mike Harrison	30	11	33
Geoff Evans	28	2	6
George Allen	3	-	-
Chris Holroyd	4	-	-
Mike Freer	8	-	-
Mike Wade	5	-	-
Alan Gardiner	5	-	-
Richard Cooper	4	1	3
David Perkins	15	1	3
David Berry	14	-	-
John Allen	35	4	12
Des O'Regan	4	-	-
Rex Skelton	9	-	-
Field Walton	33	-	-
Nick Drake-Lee	31	3	9
Peter Edwards	41	-	-
Bob Beason	16	1	3
Bob Rowell	33	3	9
Peter Tom	30	-	-
Alan Raine	8	3	9
Kevin Andrews	7	-	-
Colin Martin	27	2	97
David Matthews	38	10	32
Graham Willars	33	7	21
Mike Willcox	2	-	-
Bob Small	6	-	-
Bob Ellis	2	-	-
Ian Wilkie	5	1	3
John Quick	5	2	6

1 game: David Beaty P(10), M.F.Billingham 8(11), M.A.Higginson W(16), Keith Jackson W(10), Cliff Shephard W(6)

					FOR					AGAINST					
NO	DATE	OPPONENTS	V	RES	G	T	D	P	PTS	G	T	D	P	PTS	SCORERS
1	Sep 4	Bedford	A	Lost	-	1	-	1	6	1	1	-	1	11	Chilton(P) Bird(T)
2	8	WATCYN THOMAS XV	H	Won	1	-	-	-	5	-	-	-	-	0	Chilton(C) Harrison(T)
3	11	BATH	H	Won	-	2	-	1	9	-	-	-	1	3	Chilton(P) Harrison(T) J.A.Allen(T)
4	15	LEICESTERSHIRE XV	H	Won	4	3	-	2	35	1	-	-	1	8	White(4C,2P) Bussey(2T) Harrison(2T) Bird(T) J.A.Allen(T) Quick(T)
5	18	PLYMOUTH ALBION	H	Won	1	1	-	2	14	-	-	1	-	3	Chilton(T,C,2P) Quick(T)
6	25	Harlequins	A	Won	1	-	-	1	8	-	1	-	-	3	Chilton(C,P) Quick(T)
7	29	Nuneaton	A	Won	2	-	-	1	13	-	-	-	-	0	Pulfrey(C) Chilton(T,C,P) Matthews(T)
8	Oct 2	COVENTRY	H	Drew	1	-	-	-	5	1	-	-	-	5	Chilton(T,C)
9	9	Richmond	A	Lost	-	-	-	1	3	2	1	-	-	13	Pulfrey(P)
10	16	CHELTENHAM	H	Won	3	5	-	1	33	1	-	-	-	5	Harrison(T) Chilton(T,3C,P) Bussey(T) Bedggood(T) Matthews(T) Quick(2T) Small(T)
11	20	OXFORD UNIVERSITY	H	Won	1	2	-	1	14	1	1	-	1	11	Pulfrey(T) Chilton(C) Bussey(T) Bedggood(T,P)
12	23	NOTTINGHAM	H	Won	1	2	-	1	14	-	-	-	-	0	Bird(T) Chilton(C,P) Small(2T)
13	30	SWANSEA	H	Won	-	1	-	2	9	1	-	-	1	8	Chilton(P) Bedggood(P) J.A.Allen(T)
14	31	Old Belvedere	A	Lost	-	1	-	1	6	-	2	-	2	12	Pulfrey(P) Tom(T)
15	Nov 6	Gloucester	A	Won	-	1	-	-	3	-	-	-	-	0	Quick(T)
16	13	Cambridge University	A	Won	2	3	-	-	19	-	-	-	1	3	Chilton(2C) Harrison(T) Bussey(T) J.A.Allen(T) Small(T) Matthews(T)
17	20	LONDON IRISH	H	Won	5	2	-	4	43	-	-	1	-	3	Bird(T) Chilton(5C,4P) Bussey(T) Small(T) Quick(2T) Matthews(2T)
18	27	MOSELEY	H	Won	-	3	-	-	9	-	1	-	1	6	Quick(T) Matthews(2T)
19	Dec 4	Waterloo	A	Won	2	1	-	2	19	-	-	-	-	0	Chilton(T,2C,2P) Rowell(2T)
20	11	Blackheath	A	Won	-	1	-	1	6	-	-	-	1	3	Pulfrey(P) Harrison(T)
21	18	BRISTOL	H	Lost	-	2	-	1	9	1	2	-	-	11	Harrison(T) Chilton(T,P)
22	28	BARBARIANS	H	Won	1	2	-	1	14	2	-	-	-	10	Chilton(C,P) Quick(3T)
23	Jan 1	Bath	A	Won	-	3	-	-	9	-	1	-	-	3	Bedggood(T) Bussey(T) Small(T)
24	8	GLOUCESTER	H	Lost	-	-	-	-	0	-	1	-	-	3	
	15	BEDFORD	H		Cancelled Frost										
	22	Rosslyn Park	A		Cancelled Frost										
25	29	Llanelli	A	Lost	-	1	-	-	3	1	2	-	1	14	Scattergood(T)
26	Feb 5	LONDON SCOTTISH	H	Won	-	2	-	1	9	-	1	-	-	3	Harrison(T) Chilton(P) Bussey(T)
	12	NEWPORT	H		CancelledFrost										
27	16	BEDFORD	H	Won	-	3	-	-	9	1	-	-	-	5	Bussey(T) Coady(T) Quick(T)
28	19	Wasps	A	Won	1	-	-	-	5	-	-	-	1	3	Chilton(T,C)
29	26	NORTHAMPTON	H	Won	2	2	-	-	16	1	-	-	2	11	Bird(T) Harrison(T) Chilton(2C) Bussey(T) Walton(T)
30	Mar 5	HARLEQUINS	H	Won	1	1	-	2	14	-	-	-	1	3	Harrison(T) Chilton(C,2P) Bussey(T)
31	10	LOUGHBOROUGH COLLEGE	H	Won	3	4	-	2	33	-	-	-	1	3	Bird(2T) Chilton(3C,2P) Bussey(T) Coady(T) J.A.Allen(T) Small(T) Penalty Try
32	12	Coventry	A	Lost	1	-	1	1	11	2	1	-	-	13	Chilton(C,P) Coady(D) Matthews(T)
33	15	Moseley	A	Lost	-	-	-	1	3	-	1	-	1	6	Chilton(P)
34	18	ROYAL AIR FORCE	H	Won	2	2	-	-	16	2	-	-	-	10	Coutts(T,2C) J.A.Allen(2T) Willars(T)
35	24	Northampton	A	Won	-	3	-	-	9	-	1	-	-	3	Brownhill(T) Harrison(T) Chilton(T)
36	26	HEADINGLEY	H	Lost	1	-	-	-	5	2	-	-	-	10	Chilton(C) Tom(T)
37	29	FYLDE	H	Won	2	4	1	-	25	-	-	-	2	6	Pulfrey(D) Bird(T) Chilton(T,2C) Quick(2T) Small(2T)
	Apr 2	Birkenhead Park	A		Cancelled										
38	9	Bristol	A	Lost	-	-	-	-	0	3	-	-	-	15	
39	11	Plymouth Albion	A	Lost	-	-	-	-	0	-	4	-	1	15	
40	12	Exeter	A	Lost	-	-	-	-	0	-	1	1	-	6	
41	16	SARACENS	H	Won	1	-	-	3	14	1	1	-	-	8	Chilton(C,3P) Willars(T)
42	23	Newport	A	Lost	-	-	-	-	0	1	1	-	-	8	
43	27	RUGBY	H	Won	2	1	-	-	13	-	-	-	-	0	Chilton(2C) Bussey(T) Willars(T) Small(T)
44	29	Newbridge	A	Won	1	1	1	1	14	-	1	-	-	3	Chilton(C,P) Coady(D) Willars(T) Small(T)

INDIVIDUAL APPEARANCES 1965-1966

NAME	1	2	3	4	5	6	7	8	9	10	11	12	13	14	15	16	17	18	19	20	21	22	23	24	25	26	27	28	29	30	31	32	33	34	35	36	37	38	39	40	41	42	43	44	45	46	TOTAL	T	PTS
Keith Chilton	FB	FB	FB	-	FB	C	C	C	C	C	C	C	C	C	C	C	C	C	C	-	C	C	C	C	-	C	C	C	C	C	C	C	C	C	C	C	C	C	C	-	C	C	C	C	-	-	40	9	181
Graham Pulfrey	-	-	-	-	-	FB	FB	FB	FB	FB	FB	FB	FB	FB	FB	FB	FB	FB	FB	FB	FB	FB	FB	FB	FB	FB	FB	FB	FB	FB	FB	FB	FB	FB	FB	FB	FB	FB	FB	FB	FB	FB	FB	FB	-	-	39	1	17
David Bird	W	W	W	W	W	W	W	W	W	W	W	W	W	W	W	W	W	W	W	W	W	W	W	W	W	W	W	W	W	W	W	W	W	-	-	-	W	W	W	W	W	W	W	W	-	-	41	8	24
Malcolm Bussey	W	W	W	W	W	W	W	W	W	W	W	W	W	W	W	W	W	W	W	W	W	W	W	W	-	W	W	W	W	W	W	W	W	W	W	W	W	-	W	W	W	W	W	-	-	-	41	13	39
Mike Brownhill	-	-	-	-	-	-	-	-	-	-	-	-	-	-	-	-	-	-	-	-	-	-	-	-	-	-	-	-	-	-	-	-	-	W	W	W	-	W	-	-	-	-	-	W	-	-	5	1	3
George Allen	C	C	C	-	-	-	-	-	-	-	-	-	-	-	-	-	-	-	-	-	-	-	-	-	-	-	-	-	-	-	-	-	-	-	-	-	-	-	-	-	-	-	-	-	-	-	3	-	-
Mike Harrison	C	C	C	C	C	C	-	C	C	C	C	C	C	C	-	C	C	C	C	C	C	C	-	C	-	C	C	C	C	C	C	C	-	C	C	C	-	C	C	C	-	-	-	-	-	-	34	12	36
Geoff Evans	-	-	-	-	-	-	-	-	-	-	-	-	-	-	C	-	-	-	-	-	-	-	-	-	C	-	-	-	-	-	-	-	-	-	-	-	-	-	-	-	-	-	-	-	-	-	2	-	-
Malcolm Sayer	-	-	-	-	-	-	-	-	-	-	-	-	-	-	-	-	-	-	-	-	-	-	-	-	-	-	-	-	-	-	-	-	-	-	-	-	-	-	-	-	-	-	C	C	-	-	2	-	-
Bev Bedggood	-	FH	FH	C	C	-	-	-	-	FH	FH	FH	FH	FH	FH	FH	-	-	-	C	-	-	C	-	C	-	-	-	-	-	-	-	C	-	-	-	C	-	-	C	C	C	-	-	-	-	19	3	15
David Berry	-	-	-	FH	-	-	C	-	-	-	-	-	-	-	-	-	-	-	-	-	-	-	-	-	FH	-	-	-	-	-	-	-	FH	-	-	-	FH	-	-	-	-	-	-	-	-	-	5	-	-
Rod Coady	-	-	-	-	FH	FH	FH	FH	FH	-	-	-	-	-	-	-	FH	FH	FH	FH	FH	FH	FH	FH	-	FH	FH	FH	FH	FH	FH	FH	-	-	-	-	-	FH	FH	FH	FH	FH	FH	FH	-	-	27	2	12
Bill Coutts	-	-	-	-	-	-	-	-	-	-	-	-	-	-	-	-	-	-	-	-	-	-	-	-	-	-	-	-	-	-	-	-	-	FH	FH	FH	-	-	-	-	-	-	-	-	-	-	3	1	7
John Allen	SH	SH	SH	SH	SH	SH	SH	SH	SH	SH	SH	SH	SH	SH	SH	SH	SH	SH	SH	SH	-	SH	-	SH	-	SH	SH	SH	SH	SH	SH	SH	SH	SH	SH	SH	SH	SH	SH	SH	SH	SH	SH	SH	-	-	41	7	21
Guy Millar	-	-	-	-	-	-	-	-	-	-	-	-	-	-	-	-	-	-	-	-	SH	-	SH	-	SH	-	-	-	-	-	-	-	-	-	-	-	-	-	-	-	-	-	-	-	-	-	3	-	-
Bob Beason	P	P	P	-	P	-	-	-	-	-	P	-	-	-	-	-	-	-	P	-	P	-	P	-	-	-	-	-	P	P	P	P	P	P	P	P	-	P	P	P	P	P	P	P	-	-	23	-	-
David Beaty	P	P	P	P	P	P	P	P	P	P	-	P	P	P	P	P	P	P	-	P	-	P	-	P	-	P	P	P	-	-	-	-	-	-	-	-	P	-	-	-	-	-	-	-	-	-	24	-	-
Field Walton	-	-	-	P	-	P	P	P	P	P	P	P	P	P	P	P	P	P	P	P	P	P	P	P	P	P	P	P	P	P	P	P	P	P	P	P	P	P	P	P	P	P	P	P	-	-	40	1	3
Peter Edwards	H	H	H	H	-	-	-	-	-	-	-	-	-	-	-	-	-	-	-	-	-	-	-	-	H	H	H	H	H	H	H	H	H	H	H	H	-	H	H	H	H	H	H	H	-	-	23	-	-
Mick Walker	-	-	-	-	H	H	H	H	H	H	H	H	H	H	H	H	H	H	H	H	H	H	H	H	-	-	-	-	-	-	-	-	-	-	-	-	H	-	-	-	-	-	-	-	-	-	21	-	-
Kevin Andrews	L	L	L	-	L	L	L	L	L	L	L	L	L	L	L	L	L	-	-	L	-	L	-	-	L	L	L	L	L	L	L	L	L	L	L	L	L	-	-	-	L	L	L	L	-	-	35	-	-
Peter Tom	L	L	L	L	L	L	L	L	L	L	L	L	L	L	L	L	L	L	L	L	L	L	L	L	-	L	L	L	L	L	L	L	L	L	L	L	L	L	L	L	L	L	L	L	-	-	43	2	6
Alan Raine	-	-	-	L	-	-	-	-	-	-	-	-	-	-	-	-	-	-	-	-	-	-	-	-	L	-	-	-	-	-	-	-	-	-	-	-	-	-	-	-	-	-	-	-	-	-	2	-	-
Bob Rowell	-	-	-	-	-	-	-	-	-	-	-	-	-	-	-	-	-	L	L	-	L	-	L	L	-	-	-	-	-	-	-	-	-	-	-	-	-	L	L	-	-	-	-	-	-	-	7	2	6
David Matthews	FL	FL	FL	FL	FL	FL	FL	FL	FL	FL	FL	FL	FL	FL	FL	FL	FL	FL	-	FL	-	FL	FL	FL	-	FL	FL	FL	FL	FL	FL	FL	FL	-	-	-	-	FL	-	-	-	-	-	-	-	-	31	8	24
John Quick	8	8	8	8	8	8	8	8	8	8	8	8	8	8	8	8	8	8	8	8	8	8	8	8	-	8	8	8	8	8	8	8	8	8	8	8	8	8	8	8	8	8	8	8	-	-	43	15	45
Graham Willars	FL	-	-	-	-	-	-	-	-	-	-	-	-	-	-	-	-	-	-	-	-	-	-	-	-	-	-	-	-	-	-	-	-	FL	FL	FL	FL	-	FL	FL	FL	FL	FL	FL	-	-	11	4	12
Bob Small	-	FL	FL	FL	FL	FL	FL	-	-	FL	FL	FL	FL	FL	FL	FL	FL	FL	FL	FL	FL	FL	FL	FL	FL	FL	FL	FL	FL	FL	FL	FL	FL	FL	FL	FL	FL	FL	FL	FL	FL	FL	FL	FL	-	-	41	11	33
Richard Berry	-	-	-	-	-	-	-	FL	FL	-	-	-	-	-	-	-	-	-	-	-	-	-	-	-	8	-	-	-	-	-	-	-	-	-	-	-	-	-	-	-	-	-	-	-	-	-	3	-	-
Ian Scattergood	-	-	-	-	-	-	-	-	-	-	-	-	-	-	-	-	-	-	FL	-	FL	-	-	-	FL	-	-	-	-	-	-	-	-	-	-	-	-	-	-	-	-	-	-	-	-	-	3	1	3

1 game: Tom Burch W(25), Richard Cooper FH(1), Colin Martin L(40), Rex Skelton P(25), John White FB(4)[14]

LEICESTER FOOTBALL CLUB 1965-66
Back: J.D. Day (Team Hon.Sec), C.G. Martin, J. Quick, R. Beason, B.M. Bedggood, M.J. Harrison, M.R. Walker, P.W.G. Tom,
D.J. Beaty, M.F. Sayer, F.L.J. Walton, P.G.S. Pulfrey, D.J. Norman (President), R.E. Gerrard (Hon.Sec).
Middle: R.W. Small, K. Chilton, D.J. Matthews (Capt), K.P. Andrews, J.A. Allen, G.G. Willars.
Front: D.W. Bird, W.M. Bussey, R.J. Coady, P.G. Edwards.

LEICESTER FOOTBALL CLUB 1966-67
Back: A.S. Thorpe (Hon.Tres), D.J. Norman (President), W.M. Bussey, M.R. Walker, R.V. Grove, F.L.J. Walton, R. Beason, B.M. Bedggood,
P.W.G. Tom, P.G.S. Pulfrey, M.J. Brownhill, D.McD.H. Berry, J.D. Day (Hon.Sec).
Middle: R. Sleigh, G.G. Willars, K. Chilton, K.P. Andrews, D.J. Matthews (Capt), M.J. Harrison, J. Quick, J.A. Allen, P.G. Edwards.
Front: J.J. Elliott, P.J. Aldwinckle.

NO	DATE	OPPONENTS	V	RES	FOR G	FOR T	FOR D	FOR P	FOR PTS	AGAINST G	AGAINST T	AGAINST D	AGAINST P	AGAINST PTS	SCORERS
1	Sep 1	WATCYN THOMAS XV	H	Won	3	2	-	-	21	-	-	1	2	9	Pulfrey(T) Bird(2T) Chilton(2T) Cooper(C) J.A.Allen(2C)
2	3	BEDFORD	H	Won	1	1	-	2	14	-	-	-	1	3	Chilton(P) Bussey(T) J.A.Allen(T,C,P)
3	10	Bath	A	Lost	1	-	-	1	8	1	2	-	1	14	Harrison(T) Chilton(P) J.A.Allen(C)
4	13	NUNEATON	H	Won	2	3	-	1	22	-	-	1	1	6	Pulfrey(T) Brownhill(3T) Chilton(C,P) Bussey(T) J.A.Allen(C)
5	17	PLYMOUTH ALBION	H	Drew	-	-	-	2	6	-	1	-	1	6	Chilton(2P)
6	19	IRISH WOLFHOUNDS	H	Lost	-	-	-	1	3	3	-	-	-	15	J.A.Allen(P)
7	24	Harlequins	A	Lost	1	-	-	-	5	1	1	-	-	8	Brownhill(T) J.A.Allen(C)
8	Oct 1	Coventry	A	Drew	1	1	-	-	8	1	1	-	-	8	Bussey(T) J.A.Allen(C) Tom(T)
9	8	RICHMOND	H	Won	2	2	1	1	22	-	-	-	1	3	Pulfrey(D) Sleigh(T) Bedggood(C) Bussey(T) J.A.Allen(T,C,P) D.J.Matthews(T)
10	15	NORTHAMPTON	H	Won	1	2	-	2	17	-	-	-	3	9	Pulfrey(T) Brownhill(T) Chilton(C,2P) J.A.Allen(T)
11	19	OXFORD UNIVERSITY	H	Won	-	-	-	3	9	-	1	-	-	3	Bedggood(2P) Grove(P)
12	22	Cheltenham	A	Won	1	1	-	1	11	-	-	-	-	0	Brownhill(T) Sleigh(T) A.Matthews(C,P)
13	28	Swansea	A	Lost	-	-	-	-	0	1	1	-	1	11	
14	Nov 5	Gloucester	A	Won	-	-	-	1	3	-	-	-	-	0	Chilton(P)
15	12	CAMBRIDGE UNIVERSITY	H	Won	-	-	-	2	6	-	-	-	-	0	Chilton(2P)
16	19	NEWPORT	H	Won	2	-	1	1	16	-	1	1	-	6	Chilton(2C,P) Sleigh(D) Quick(2T)
17	26	Moseley	A	Won	2	1	-	-	13	-	-	-	-	0	Harrison(T) Chilton(T,C) J.A.Allen(C) Quick(T)
18	Dec 3	Waterloo	A	Lost	-	1	1	-	6	2	-	-	-	10	D.McD.H.Berry(D) Willars(T)
19	10	BLACKHEATH	H	Won	-	-	1	-	3	-	-	-	-	0	Saunders(D)
20	17	BRISTOL	H	Won	2	5	-	-	25	-	2	2	-	12	Chilton(2C) Lyons(T) Sleigh(T) J.A.Allen(T) Tom(T) Quick(2T) D.J.Matthews(T)
21	24	London Irish	A	Won	-	-	-	1	3	-	-	-	-	0	Chilton(P)
22	27	BARBARIANS	H	Won	1	3	-	-	14	-	1	-	-	3	Brownhill(T) Harrison(T) Bird(T) J.A.Allen(C) Andrews(T)
23	31	Headingley	A	Lost	-	-	-	2	6	-	1	-	2	9	Chilton(2P)
	Jan 7	BATH	H		Cancelled										
24	14	GLOUCESTER	H	Won	-	2	-	1	9	-	-	-	1	3	Brownhill(T) Chilton(P) J.A.Allen(T)
25	21	Bedford	A	Lost	-	2	-	1	9	1	-	1	2	14	Brownhill(2T) Chilton(P)
26	28	ROSSLYN PARK	H	Won	2	2	-	1	19	-	-	-	-	0	Brownhill(T) Chilton(2C,P) Andrews(T) Quick(T) D.J.Matthews(T)
27	Feb 4	London Scottish	A	Lost	2	-	-	-	10	1	3	1	-	17	Brownhill(T) Millar(T) A.Matthews(2C)
28	11	Newport	A	Lost	-	-	-	2	6	1	1	1	3	20	Chilton(2P)
29	18	WASPS	H	Won	-	1	-	1	6	-	1	-	-	3	Chilton(P) Quick(T)
30	24	Northampton	A	Won	1	-	-	1	8	-	-	-	1	3	J.A.Allen(T,P) Grove(C)
31	28	BATH	H	Won	1	1	-	1	11	-	1	-	-	3	Bedggood(T) J.A.Allen(C,P) Raine(T)
32	Mar 4	HARLEQUINS	H	Won	1	3	-	-	14	-	-	-	-	0	Brownhill(T) Chilton(C) Andrews(T) Quick(2T)
33	8	LOUGHBOROUGH COLLEGE	H	Won	1	2	1	-	14	-	1	-	1	6	Harrison(T) Bussey(T) D.McD.H.Berry(D) J.A.Allen(C) Andrews(T)
34	11	COVENTRY	H	Lost	1	-	-	-	5	-	1	-	1	6	J.A.Allen(C) D.J.Matthews(T)
35	17	ROYAL AIR FORCE	H	Won	4	5	-	-	35	-	1	-	2	9	Brownhill(2T) Harrison(2T) Bedggood(C) Chilton(3C) Millar(T) Elliott(2T) Tom(T) Quick(T)
36	25	Bristol	A	Lost	-	-	-	-	0	1	3	-	1	17	
37	27	Plymouth Albion	A	Won	2	1	-	1	16	-	-	-	1	3	Sleigh(2T) J.A.Allen(2C,P) Quick(T)
38	28	Exeter	A	Won	-	3	-	1	12	1	-	-	1	8	D.McD.H.Berry(2T) J.A.Allen(P) Small(T)
39	Apr 1	BIRKENHEAD PARK	H	Won	1	2	-	1	14	-	-	1	1	6	Chilton(C,P) Sleigh(T) Elliott(2T)
40	8	LLANELLI	H	Won	1	2	-	2	17	1	1	-	-	8	Pulfrey(P) Sleigh(2T) J.A.Allen(C,P) Andrews(T)
41	11	MOSELEY	H	Won	-	1	-	-	3	-	-	-	-	0	Quick(T)
42	15	Saracens	A	Won	1	1	-	1	11	-	1	-	-	3	Chilton(C,P) Sleigh(T) D.J.Matthews(T)
43	18	SALE	H	Won	1	3	1	1	20	-	1	-	-	3	Pulfrey(T) Bedggood(T) D.McD.H.Berry(D) Aldwinckle(T) A.Matthews(C,P) D.J.Matthews(T)
44	22	ABERAVON	H	Won	-	2	-	1	9	-	-	-	-	0	Chilton(P) Grove(T) Walton(T)
45	26	RUGBY	H	Won	1	1	-	1	11	-	1	-	-	3	Brownhill(T) Bedggood(C,P) Elliott(T)
46	29	FYLDE	H	Won	-	2	-	1	9	1	-	-	1	8	Brownhill(T) Aldwinckle(T) D.J.Matthews(P)

INDIVIDUAL APPEARANCES 1966-1967

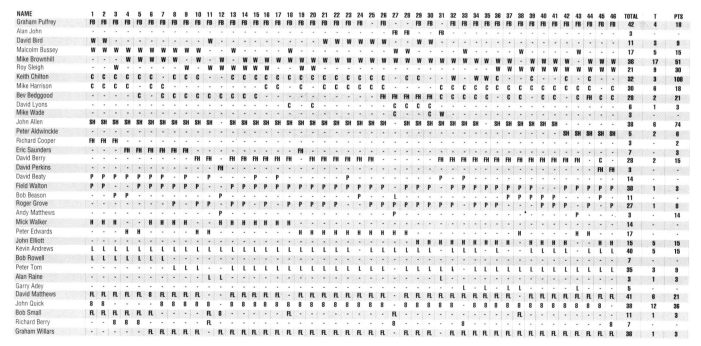

NAME	1	2	3	4	5	6	7	8	9	10	11	12	13	14	15	16	17	18	19	20	21	22	23
Graham Pulfrey	FB	FB	FB	FB	FB	FB	FB	FB	FB	FB	FB	FB	FB	FB	FB	FB	FB	FB	FB	FB	FB	FB	FB
Alan John	-	-	-	-	-	-	-	-	-	-	-	-	-	-	-	-	-	-	-	-	-	-	-
David Bird	W	W	-	-	-	-	-	-	-	-	W	-	-	-	-	-	-	-	-	-	W	W	W
Malcolm Bussey	W	W	W	W	W	W	W	W	W	W	-	-	W	-	-	-	-	W	-	-	-	-	-
Mike Brownhill	-	-	-	W	W	W	W	W	-	W	-	W	-	W	W	W	W	W	W	W	W	W	W
Roy Sleigh	-	-	W	-	-	-	-	-	W	-	W	W	W	W	W	W	-	-	W	W	-	-	-
Keith Chilton	C	C	C	C	C	C	-	C	C	C	-	-	C	C	C	C	C	C	C	C	C	C	C
Mike Harrison	C	C	C	C	-	C	C	-	-	-	-	-	-	-	-	C	C	-	C	-	C	C	C
Bev Bedggood	-	-	-	-	C	-	C	C	C	C	C	C	C	C	C	-	-	-	-	-	-	-	-
David Lyons	-	-	-	-	-	-	-	-	-	-	-	-	-	-	-	-	-	C	-	C	-	-	-
Mike Wade	-	-	-	-	-	-	-	-	-	-	-	-	-	-	-	-	-	-	-	-	-	-	-
John Allen	SH	SH	SH	SH	SH	SH	SH	SH	SH	SH	SH	-	SH	SH	SH	SH	SH	SH	SH	SH	SH	SH	SH
Peter Aldwinckle	-	-	-	-	-	-	-	-	-	-	-	-	-	-	-	-	-	-	-	-	-	-	-
Richard Cooper	FH	FH	FH	-	-	-	-	-	-	-	-	-	-	-	-	-	-	-	-	-	-	-	-
Eric Saunders	-	-	-	FH	FH	FH	FH	FH	FH	-	-	-	-	-	-	-	-	-	FH	-	-	-	-
David Berry	-	-	-	-	-	-	-	-	-	FH	FH	-	FH	FH	FH	FH	FH	FH	-	FH	FH	FH	FH
David Perkins	-	-	-	-	-	-	-	-	-	-	-	FH	-	-	-	-	-	-	-	-	-	-	-
David Beaty	P	P	P	P	P	P	P	-	P	-	P	-	-	-	P	-	P	-	-	-	-	-	P
Field Walton	P	P	-	-	P	P	P	P	P	P	-	-	P	P	P	P	P	P	P	P	P	P	P
Bob Beason	-	-	P	P	-	-	-	-	-	-	-	P	-	-	-	-	-	-	-	-	-	-	-
Roger Grove	-	-	-	-	-	-	-	P	-	P	P	-	P	P	-	P	-	P	P	P	P	P	-
Andy Matthews	-	-	-	-	-	-	-	-	-	-	-	P	-	-	-	-	-	-	-	-	-	-	-
Mick Walker	H	H	H	-	-	H	H	H	H	-	-	H	H	H	H	H	H	H	-	-	-	-	-
Peter Edwards	-	-	-	H	H	-	-	-	-	H	H	-	-	-	-	-	-	-	H	H	H	H	H
John Elliott	-	-	-	-	-	-	-	-	-	-	-	-	-	-	-	-	-	-	-	-	-	-	-
Kevin Andrews	L	L	L	L	L	L	L	L	L	L	L	L	L	L	L	L	L	L	L	L	L	L	L
Bob Rowell	L	L	L	L	L	L	L	-	-	-	-	-	-	-	-	-	-	-	-	-	-	-	-
Peter Tom	-	-	-	-	-	-	-	L	L	L	-	-	L	L	L	L	L	L	L	L	L	L	L
Alan Raine	-	-	-	-	-	-	-	-	-	-	L	L	-	-	-	-	-	-	-	-	-	-	-
Garry Adey	-	-	-	-	-	-	-	-	-	-	-	-	-	-	-	-	-	-	-	-	-	-	-
David Matthews	FL	FL	FL	FL	FL	8	FL	FL	FL	FL	-	-	FL	FL	FL	FL	FL	-	FL	FL	FL	FL	FL
John Quick	8	8	-	-	-	-	8	8	8	8	8	-	8	8	8	8	8	8	8	8	8	8	8
Bob Small	FL	FL	FL	FL	FL	FL	-	-	-	-	FL	8	-	-	-	-	-	FL	-	-	-	-	-
Richard Berry	-	-	8	8	8	-	-	-	-	-	FL	-	-	-	-	-	-	-	-	-	-	-	-
Graham Willars	-	-	-	-	-	FL	FL	FL	FL	FL	-	FL	FL	FL	FL	FL	FL	FL	FL	FL	FL	FL	FL

NAME	24	25	26	27	28	29	30	31	32	33	34	35	36	37	38	39	40	41	42	43	44	45	46	TOTAL	T	PTS
Graham Pulfrey	FB	-	FB	-	-	FB	FB	-	FB	FB	FB	FB	FB	FB	FB	FB	FB	FB	FB	FB	FB	FB	FB	42	4	18
Alan John	-	-	-	FB	FB	-	-	FB	-	-	-	-	-	-	-	-	-	-	-	-	-	-	-	3	-	-
David Bird	W	W	W	-	-	W	W	-	-	-	-	-	-	-	-	-	-	-	-	-	-	-	-	11	3	9
Malcolm Bussey	-	-	-	W	W	-	-	-	-	W	-	-	-	-	W	-	-	-	-	W	-	-	-	17	5	15
Mike Brownhill	W	W	W	W	W	W	W	W	W	W	W	W	W	W	-	W	W	W	W	-	W	W	W	38	17	51
Roy Sleigh	-	-	-	-	-	-	-	-	-	-	-	-	W	W	W	W	W	W	W	W	W	W	W	21	9	30
Keith Chilton	C	C	C	-	C	C	-	-	W	-	W	W	C	-	-	C	-	-	C	-	C	-	-	32	3	108
Mike Harrison	C	C	C	-	-	-	-	C	C	C	C	C	C	C	C	C	C	C	C	C	C	-	C	30	6	18
Bev Bedggood	-	-	FH	FH	FH	FH	FH	C	C	C	C	C	-	C	C	-	C	C	-	C	FH	C	C	28	2	21
David Lyons	-	-	-	C	C	C	C	-	-	-	-	-	-	-	-	-	-	-	-	-	-	-	-	6	1	3
Mike Wade	-	-	-	C	-	-	C	W	-	-	-	-	-	-	-	-	-	-	-	-	-	-	-	3	-	-
John Allen	SH	SH	SH	-	SH	SH	SH	SH	SH	SH	SH	-	SH	SH	SH	SH	SH	SH	-	-	-	-	-	38	6	74
Peter Aldwinckle	-	-	-	-	-	-	-	-	-	-	-	-	-	-	-	-	-	-	SH	SH	SH	SH	SH	5	2	6
Richard Cooper	-	-	-	-	-	-	-	-	-	-	-	-	-	-	-	-	-	-	-	-	-	-	-	3	-	2
Eric Saunders	-	-	-	-	-	-	-	-	-	-	-	-	-	-	-	-	-	-	-	-	-	-	-	7	-	3
David Berry	FH	FH	-	-	-	-	-	FH	FH	FH	FH	FH	FH	FH	FH	FH	FH	FH	FH	FH	-	C	-	28	2	15
David Perkins	-	-	-	-	-	-	-	-	-	-	-	-	-	-	-	-	-	-	-	-	-	FH	FH	3	-	-
David Beaty	-	-	-	-	-	-	-	P	-	P	-	-	-	-	-	-	-	-	-	-	-	-	-	14	-	-
Field Walton	P	P	P	-	P	P	P	-	P	P	P	P	P	P	P	P	-	-	P	P	P	P	P	38	1	3
Bob Beason	P	-	-	L	-	-	-	-	-	-	-	-	-	P	P	P	P	P	-	-	-	P	-	11	-	-
Roger Grove	-	P	P	P	P	P	P	P	P	-	P	P	P	-	-	-	P	P	P	-	P	-	P	27	1	8
Andy Matthews	-	-	-	P	-	-	-	-	-	-	-	-	-	-	-	-	-	-	-	P	-	-	-	3	-	14
Mick Walker	-	-	-	-	-	-	-	-	-	-	-	-	-	-	-	-	-	-	-	-	-	-	-	14	-	-
Peter Edwards	H	H	H	H	H	-	-	-	-	-	-	-	-	-	H	-	-	-	-	H	H	-	-	17	-	-
John Elliott	-	-	-	-	-	H	H	H	H	H	H	H	H	H	-	H	H	H	H	-	-	H	H	15	5	15
Kevin Andrews	-	L	L	L	L	L	L	-	L	L	L	-	L	-	-	L	L	L	L	-	L	L	L	40	5	15
Bob Rowell	-	-	-	-	-	-	-	-	-	-	-	-	-	-	-	-	-	-	-	-	-	-	-	7	-	-
Peter Tom	L	L	L	-	L	L	L	L	L	-	L	L	L	L	L	L	L	L	L	L	L	L	L	35	3	9
Alan Raine	-	-	-	-	-	-	-	L	-	-	-	-	-	-	-	-	-	-	-	-	-	-	-	3	1	3
Garry Adey	-	-	-	-	-	-	-	-	-	L	-	L	-	L	L	-	-	-	-	L	-	-	-	5	-	-
David Matthews	FL	FL	FL	-	FL	FL	FL	FL	FL	FL	FL	FL	FL	FL	-	FL	FL	FL	FL	FL	FL	FL	FL	41	6	21
John Quick	8	8	8	-	8	8	8	8	8	-	8	8	8	8	8	8	8	8	8	8	8	8	-	38	12	36
Bob Small	-	-	-	FL	-	-	-	-	-	-	-	-	-	-	FL	-	-	-	-	-	-	-	-	11	1	3
Richard Berry	-	-	-	8	-	-	-	-	-	8	-	-	-	-	-	-	-	-	-	-	-	-	8	7	-	-
Graham Willars	FL	FL	FL	-	FL	FL	FL	-	FL	FL	FL	FL	FL	FL	FL	FL	FL	FL	FL	FL	FL	FL	FL	38	1	3

2 games: George Allen C(11,12), Joe Grindall FL(12,27), Guy Millar SH(27,35)[2T-6]
1 game: Steve Betts FL(31), Terry Davis W(17), J.Marriott L(24), R.Tucker SH(12), Jim Wyness FB(25)

1967-1968

NO	DATE		OPPONENTS	V	RES	FOR					AGAINST					SCORERS
						G	T	D	P	PTS	G	T	D	P	PTS	
1	Sep	2	Bedford	A	Won	3	-	-	3	24	1	-	-	1	8	J.A.Allen(3C,P) Grove(T) Quick(2T) D.J.Matthews(2P)
2		7	WATCYN THOMAS XV	H	Won	2	1	-	-	13	-	-	-	-	0	Sleigh(T) J.A.Allen(C) Beason(T) D.J.Matthews(T,C)
3		9	BATH	H	Won	1	2	-	2	17	1	-	-	1	8	Pulfrey(T) Harrison(T) J.A.Allen(C,2P) Willars(T)
4		16	PLYMOUTH ALBION	H	Won	1	1	1	2	17	1	-	-	-	5	Harrison(D) D.McD.H.Berry(T) J.A.Allen(C,2P) Willars(T)
5		23	Harlequins	A	Won	1	1	-	-	8	-	-	1	-	3	J.A.Allen(T) Quick(T) D.J.Matthews(C)
6		30	SARACENS	H	Won	-	4	-	-	12	1	-	-	-	5	Pulfrey(T) Brownhill(T) Tom(T) Willars(T)
7	Oct	4	NUNEATON	H	Won	1	2	-	2	17	1	-	1	-	8	Grove(T,C) Tom(T) D.J.Matthews(T,2P)
8		7	COVENTRY	H	Drew	-	2	-	-	6	-	1	-	1	6	Sleigh(2T)
9		14	Richmond	A	Lost	-	-	-	-	0	2	1	-	-	13	
10		21	Northampton	A	Lost	-	1	-	-	3	-	2	-	2	12	Brownhill(T)
11		25	Oxford University	A	Lost	-	-	-	-	0	-	1	-	-	3	
12		28	CHELTENHAM	H	Won	1	-	-	1	8	1	2	-	-	11	Bedggood(C,P) D.J.Matthews(T)
13	Nov	4	GLOUCESTER	H	Won	-	2	-	1	9	-	1	-	1	6	Jackson(T) Quick(T) D.J.Matthews(P)
14		11	Cambridge University	A	Lost	1	3	-	-	14	2	1	2	-	19	Sayer(T) J.A.Allen(C) Quick(3T)
15		18	Rugby	A	Drew	-	-	-	1	3	-	-	1	-	3	D.J.Matthews(P)
16		25	MOSELEY	H	Won	1	2	-	-	11	-	2	-	1	9	Bird(2T) Harrison(T) D.J.Matthews(C)
17	Dec	2	Waterloo	A	Won	1	2	-	-	11	-	1	-	-	3	Bird(T) Sleigh(2T) A.Matthews(C)
		9	Blackheath	A		Cancelled Frost										
18		16	BRISTOL	H	Won	1	2	-	2	17	-	3	-	1	12	Harrison(2T) Quick(T) D.J.Matthews(C,2P)
19		23	LONDON IRISH	H	Won	1	3	-	1	17	-	-	-	-	0	Bird(2T) D.McD.H.Berry(T) J.A.Allen(T) D.J.Matthews(C,P)
20		27	BARBARIANS	H	Lost	-	1	-	1	6	-	2	-	3	15	Pulfrey(T) D.J.Matthews(P)
21		30	Newport	A	Lost	1	-	-	-	5	2	-	-	-	10	Quick(T) D.J.Matthews(C)
22	Jan	6	Bath	A	Drew	1	1	-	1	11	1	1	-	1	11	Sayer(T) D.McD.H.Berry(T) D.J.Matthews(C,P)
		13	Gloucester	A		Cancelled Snow										
23		19	BEDFORD	H	Drew	-	1	-	-	3	-	1	-	-	3	D.J.Matthews(T)
24		27	Rosslyn Park	A	Lost	1	2	-	1	14	2	-	1	1	16	Bird(T) Sayer(T) J.A.Allen(T) D.J.Matthews(C,P)
25	Feb	3	LONDON SCOTTISH	H	Won	2	-	1	2	19	1	-	-	2	11	Pulfrey(T) Evans(2C,2P) Sleigh(T) D.McD.H.Berry(D)
26		10	NEWPORT	H	Lost	1	1	-	-	8	-	4	-	-	12	Bird(2T) Evans(C)
27		17	Wasps	A	Won	2	1	1	-	19	-	2	-	1	9	Sleigh(2T) Evans(2C,D,P) Quick(T)
28		20	Moseley	A	Won	1	3	-	-	14	1	1	-	-	8	Pulfrey(T) Sleigh(T) Evans(C) J.A.Allen(T) Grove(T)
29		24	NORTHAMPTON	H	Won	-	2	-	1	9	-	-	-	2	6	Harrison(T) Sleigh(T) Evans(P)
30	Mar	2	HARLEQUINS	H	Lost	1	-	-	-	5	2	-	-	-	10	Evans(C) D.J.Matthews(T)
31		7	LOUGHBOROUGH COLLEGE	H	Won	4	3	-	1	32	-	-	-	3	9	Bird(T) Sayer(T) Evans(4C,P) Aldwinckle(3T) Betts(T) Quick(T)
		9	Coventry	A		Cancelled										
32		15	ROYAL AIR FORCE	H	Won	1	7	-	1	29	1	-	-	1	8	Bird(T) Harrison(2T) Sleigh(2T) Evans(P) Elliott(T) D.J.Matthews(2T,C)
33		19	LEICS. PRESIDENTS XV	H	Won	1	1	-	2	14	1	1	-	-	8	Pulfrey(T) Evans(C,2P) Smith(T)
34		23	SWANSEA	H	Won	1	-	-	4	17	1	-	-	1	8	Bird(T) Evans(C,4P)
35		30	Aberavon	A	Lost	1	1	-	-	8	2	1	-	-	13	Brownhill(T) D.J.Matthews(C) Betts(T)
36	Apr	6	HEADINGLEY	H	Won	1	-	-	2	11	-	1	-	1	6	Sayer(T) D.J.Matthews(C,2P)
37		13	Bristol	A	Lost	-	-	-	-	0	-	2	1	-	9	
38		15	Plymouth Albion	A	Won	3	2	1	1	27	-	1	-	-	3	Brownhill(T) D.McD.H.Berry(T) Bird(2T) Evans(2C,D,P) J.A.Allen(C) Betts(T)
39		16	Stroud	A	Lost	1	1	-	-	8	-	-	1	2	9	Pulfrey(T) Evans(C) Betts(T)
40		20	Llanelli	A	Lost	1	-	-	-	5	1	2	-	1	14	Cooper(C) Quick(T)
41		27	MANCHESTER	H	Won	2	-	-	1	13	-	1	1	-	6	Cooper(2C,P) Walton(T) Penalty Try

INDIVIDUAL APPEARANCES 1967-1968

NAME	TOTAL	T	PTS
Graham Pulfrey	39	7	21
Mike Brownhill	17	4	12
Roy Sleigh	29	12	36
Malcolm Bussey	5		
Jess Glover	2		
Graham Jackson	3	1	3
David Bird	26	13	39
Bev Bedggood	12		5
Mike Harrison	30	7	24
Chris Holroyd	3		
Malcolm Sayer	21	5	15
Mike Evans	15		77
John Mawbey	9		
Trevor Spence	2		
David Berry	25	4	15
George Allen	2		
Richard Cooper	2		9
John Allen	31	4	43
Peter Aldwinckle	10	3	9
Bob Beason	16	1	3
Roger Grove	34	3	11
Field Walton	28	1	3
Andy Matthews	3		2
John Elliott	29	1	3
Peter Edwards	11		
Kevin Andrews	29		
Peter Tom	21	2	6
Garry Adey	12		
Alan Raine	19		
David Matthews	36	7	85
John Quick	33	12	36
Graham Willars	31	3	9
Richard Berry	4		
Steve Betts	14	4	12
Bob Smith	0		

Position codes across games 1–46: Pulfrey (FB), Brownhill/Sleigh/Bussey/Glover/Jackson/Bird (W), Bedggood/Harrison/Holroyd/Sayer/Mawbey/Spence (C), Evans/D.Berry/G.Allen/Cooper (FH), J.Allen/Aldwinckle (SH), Beason/Grove/Walton/A.Matthews (P), Elliott/Edwards (H), Andrews/Tom/Adey/Raine (L), D.Matthews/Willars/Betts/Smith (FL), Quick/R.Berry (8).

1 game: Eric Bann L(41), David Beaty P(3), Keith Freeston FH(17), Alan John FB(4), Brian Llewellyn 8(28), David Perkins FH(3), Mike Ryan FB(10)

LEICESTER FOOTBALL CLUB 1967-68

Back: D.J. Norman (President), A.S. Thorpe (Hon.Tres), J.W. Mawby, R.V. Grove, S.E. Betts, R.W. Small, E.E. Bann, R.C. Cooper, M.F. Sayer, P.G.S. Pulfrey, H.V. White (Coach), J.D. Day (Hon.Sec).
Middle: D.W. Bird, F.L.J. Walton, M.J. Harrison, D.J. Matthews (Capt), K.P. Andrews, J.A. Allen, A. Raine.
Front: D.McD.H. Berry, M.J. Brownhill, P.J. Aldwinckle, J.J. Elliott.

1968-1969

NO	DATE		OPPONENTS	V	RES	FOR					AGAINST					SCORERS
						G	T	D	P	PTS	G	T	D	P	PTS	
1	Sep	5	WATCYN THOMAS XV	H	Won	2	3	1	1	25	1	3	-	-	14	Lockett(T) Harris(2C,D,P) Andrews(T) Smith(2T) Matthews(T)
2		7	BEDFORD	H	Won	2	2	-	-	16	3	-	-	-	15	Harris(T,2C) Sleigh(T) Matthews(2T)
3		14	Bath	A	Won	-	1	1	2	12	-	1	1	-	6	Harris(2P) Evans(D) Andrews(T)
4		17	NUNEATON	H	Lost	-	3	-	1	12	2	3	-	-	19	Mawbey(T) Evans(P) Matthews(2T)
5		21	PLYMOUTH ALBION	H	Won	3	3	1	2	33	1	-	-	1	8	Mawbey(D) Harris(C,2P) Bird(2T) Evans(2T,2C) Matthews(2T)
6		28	Harlequins	A	Drew	-	-	-	3	9	-	-	-	3	9	Evans(3P)
7	Oct	5	Coventry	A	Lost	-	2	1	1	12	1	2	-	2	17	Sleigh(2T) Evans(D,P)
8		8	RUGBY	H	Won	-	1	-	3	12	1	-	-	2	11	Jackson(T) Evans(3P)
9		12	RICHMOND	H	Won	2	2	-	4	28	2	1	-	2	19	Sleigh(T) Mawbey(2T) Jackson(T) Cooper(2C,4P)
10		19	NORTHAMPTON	H	Drew	1	-	-	4	17	1	1	1	2	17	Barker(T) Evans(C,4P)
11		23	OXFORD UNIVERSITY	H	Won	3	2	-	1	24	1	-	-	1	8	Sleigh(2T) Sayer(T) Jackson(2T) Evans(3C,P)
12		26	Swansea	A	Won	1	1	-	2	14	-	1	1	1	9	Evans(T,C,2P) Allen(T)
13	Nov	2	Gloucester	A	Lost	-	-	-	1	3	-	1	-	2	9	Evans(P)
14		9	CAMBRIDGE UNIVERSITY	H	Won	-	2	-	1	9	-	2	-	-	6	Sleigh(2T) Evans(P)
15		16	Newport	A	Lost	-	-	-	-	0	3	1	-	-	18	
16		23	Moseley	A	Lost	-	1	-	-	3	2	1	-	1	16	Smith(T)
17		30	OLD BELVEDERE	H	Won	3	1	-	-	18	1	-	-	-	5	Mawbey(T) Sayer(T) Cooper(3C) Matthews(2T)
18	Dec	7	WATERLOO	H	Lost	1	-	-	1	8	-	-	1	3	12	Harris(T) Cooper(C,P)
19		14	BLACKHEATH	H	Won	1	3	-	-	17	-	-	-	-	0	Sayer(T) Mawbey(T) Evans(T,C,P) Andrews(T)
20		21	BRISTOL	H	Won	1	3	1	1	20	-	-	-	1	3	Money(T) Mawbey(T,D) Evans(C,P) Matthews(T) Betts(T)
		27	BARBARIANS	H		Cancelled											
21	Jan	4	BATH	H	Won	1	1	2	-	14	2	1	-	-	13	Evans(C,2D) Grove(T) Matthews(T)
22		11	GLOUCESTER	H	Won	-	1	1	2	12	1	-	-	1	8	Evans(D,2P) Allen(T)
		18	Bedford	A		Cancelled											
23		25	ROSSLYN PARK	H	Won	-	3	-	2	15	1	1	-	1	11	Bird(T) Spence(T) Elliott(T) Bann(2P)
24	Feb	1	London Scottish	A	Won	1	2	-	1	14	-	1	-	-	3	Bird(T) Spence(T) Bann(C,P) Matthews(T)
		8	NEWPORT	H		Cancelled Frost											
		15	WASPS	H		Cancelled Snow											
		18	MOSELEY	H		Cancelled Frost											
		22	Northampton	A		Cancelled Snow											
25		27	BARBARIANS	H	Lost	1	2	-	-	11	2	2	-	1	19	Allen(T) Grove(T) Bann(C) Matthews(T)
26	Mar	1	HARLEQUINS	H	Lost	-	-	-	1	3	1	2	-	-	11	Bann(P)
27		5	LOUGHBOROUGH COLLEGE	H	Won	-	4	-	4	24	-	1	-	2	9	Spence(T) Sleigh(T) Evans(3P) Grove(T) Elliott(T) Bann(P)
28		8	COVENTRY	H	Lost	-	1	-	-	6	1	3	1	1	20	Evans(P) Allen(T)
29		13	ROYAL AIR FORCE	H	Won	4	3	-	-	29	-	-	-	-	0	Sleigh(2T) Evans(T,C) Allen(T) Andrews(T) Bann(3C) Willars(T) Matthews(T)
30		19	COVENTRY	H	Won	-	4	-	-	15	-	-	-	2	6	Harrison(T) Evans(P) Bann(T) Matthews(2T)
31		22	Headingley	A	Lost	-	-	-	-	0	2	3	-	1	22	
32		26	Gloucester	A	Won	-	-	-	2	6	-	-	-	-	0	Evans(2P)
33		29	BRADFORD	H	Won	3	2	-	1	24	2	-	-	-	10	Bird(T) Harrison(T) Spence(2T) Evans(3C,P) Baynes(T)
34	Apr	5	Bristol	A	Drew	1	1	-	1	11	1	1	-	-	11	Bird(T) Evans(C,P) Matthews(T)
35		7	Plymouth Albion	A	Won	-	2	-	2	12	-	-	-	3	9	Brownhill(T) Bird(T) Cooper(2P)
36		8	Stroud	A	Won	6	5	-	-	45	-	-	-	2	6	Brownhill(T) Harrison(T) Barker(T) Spence(T) Cooper(6C) Allen(2T) Bann(T) Baynes(T) Matthews(T) Betts(2T)
37		12	BIRKENHEAD PARK	H	Won	2	4	-	1	25	1	-	1	-	8	Bird(3T) Cooper(2C,P) Allen(T) Elliott(T) Matthews(T)
38		16	MOSELEY	H	Lost	3	1	-	2	24	1	4	1	2	26	Harrison(T) Brownhill(T) Cooper(C,2P) Bann(2C) Matthews(T) Baynes(T)
39		19	LLANELLI	H	Drew	-	-	-	3	9	-	2	-	1	9	Matthews(3P)
40		22	Moseley	A	Lost	-	-	-	-	0	1	1	-	1	11	
41		26	HARTLEPOOL ROVERS	H	Won	1	2	-	2	17	1	1	-	-	8	Barker(2T) Brownhill(T) Cooper(C,2P)
42		30	CHELTENHAM	H	Won	4	5	1	1	41	3	-	-	-	15	Pulfrey(D) Spence(2T) Brownhill(2T) Cooper(4C,P) Baynes(T) Adey(3T) Matthews(T)
43	May	3	BROUGHTON PARK	H	Won	1	1	-	-	8	1	-	-	-	5	Barker(T) Cooper(C) Allen(T)

INDIVIDUAL APPEARANCES 1968-1969

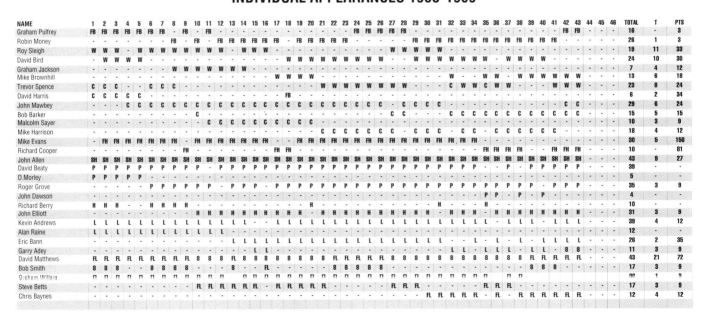

NAME	TOTAL	T	PTS
Graham Pulfrey	16		3
Robin Money	26	1	3
Roy Sleigh	19	11	33
David Bird	24	10	30
Graham Jackson	7	4	12
Mike Brownhill	13	6	18
Trevor Spence	23	8	24
David Harris	6	2	34
John Mawbey	29	6	24
Bob Barker	15	5	15
Malcolm Sayer	10	3	9
Mike Harrison	18	4	12
Mike Evans	30	5	150
Richard Cooper	10		81
John Allen	43	9	27
David Beaty	39		
D.Morley	5		
Roger Grove	35	3	9
John Dawson	4		
Richard Berry	10		
John Elliott	31	3	9
Kevin Andrews	39	4	12
Alan Raine	12		
Eric Bann	26	2	35
Garry Adey	11	3	9
David Matthews	43	21	72
Bob Smith	17	3	9
Graham Willars	00	1	0
Steve Betts	17	3	9
Chris Baynes	12	4	12

2 games: Bob Beason P(11,12), Pete Clements 8(4,5), Jess Glover W(6,7), N.Haines W(13,17), Chris Holroyd W(15,16), Mike Lockett W(1,4)[1T-3], David Perkins FH(39,40), Alan Whitehall H(4,5)
1 game: John Berry C(9), David Berry FH(1), Nick Drake-Lee P(16)

NO	DATE		OPPONENTS	V	RES	FOR					AGAINST					SCORERS
						G	T	D	P	PTS	G	T	D	P	PTS	
1	Sep	6	Bedford	A	Lost	1	-	-	-	5	6	2	-	1	39	Sleigh(T) Evans(C)
2		10	LEICESTER & DISTRICT	H	Won	3	2	-	2	27	-	1	-	2	9	Spence(T) Chapman(T,3C,2P) Allen(T) Elliott(T) Small(T)
3		13	BATH	H	Won	1	1	-	2	14	1	-	-	2	11	Spence(T) Barker(T) Chapman(C,2P)
4		15	IRISH WOLFHOUNDS	H	Won	3	1	1	4	33	3	1	-	1	21	Spence(T) Jackson(T) Chapman(T,3C,D,4P) Betts(T)
5		20	GOSFORTH	H	Won	6	5	-	1	48	-	-	-	2	6	Pulfrey(T) Spence(2T) Barker(T) Yandle(2T) Jackson(2T) Chapman(T,6C,P) Owen(T) Dawson(T)
6		23	Nuneaton	A	Won	2	2	-	1	19	-	1	-	2	9	Spence(3T) Evans(2C,P) Betts(T)
7		27	Harlequins	A	Lost	1	-	-	2	11	-	2	-	4	17	Chapman(2C,2P) Elliott(T)
8		30	Fylde	A	Won	1	1	-	3	17	2	1	-	1	16	Barker(T) Cooper(C,3P) Adey(T)
9	Oct	2	MOSELEY	H	Won	-	3	-	1	12	-	-	-	1	3	Chapman(P) Grove(T) Adey(T) Betts(T)
10		4	COVENTRY	H	Lost	1	-	-	2	11	1	-	-	3	14	Chapman(T,C,2P)
11		11	Richmond	A	Lost	2	2	-	1	19	2	3	-	1	22	Chapman(2C,P) Elliott(T) Owen(T) Baynes(2T)
12		18	Northampton	A	Lost	1	1	-	-	8	4	2	-	1	29	Chapman(T,C) Rowell(T)
13		22	Oxford University	A	Lost	-	-	-	-	0	4	-	-	1	23	
14		25	SWANSEA	H	Drew	-	-	-	3	9	-	1	-	2	9	Chapman(3P)
15	Nov	1	GLOUCESTER	H	Won	-	3	1	1	15	-	2	1	1	12	Bird(T) Spence(T) Chapman(D,P) Small(T)
16		8	Cambridge University	A	Lost	1	2	-	-	11	3	7	-	-	36	Spence(T) Chapman(C) Millar(T) Owen(T)
17		15	WILMSLOW	H	Lost	2	-	-	1	13	1	4	-	2	23	Bann(C) Matthews(T,C,P) Arneil(T)
18		19	COMBINED SERVICES	H	Drew	-	2	-	-	6	-	1	-	1	6	Jones(T) Matthews(T)
19		22	MOSELEY	H	Lost	1	2	-	1	14	1	2	1	1	17	Jackson(T) Chapman(C,P) Bann(T) Willars(T)
		29	Saracens	A		Cancelled Snow										
20	Dec	6	WATERLOO	H	Won	2	2	-	1	19	-	-	-	1	3	Cooper(C) Spence(T) Chapman(C,P) Aldwinckle(T) Bann(T) Matthews(T)
21		13	Blackheath	A	Won	3	1	1	-	21	1	2	-	-	11	Pulfrey(D) Cooper(3C) Jackson(T) Elliott(T) Dawson(T) Matthews(T)
22		20	Bristol	A	Lost	-	-	-	-	0	1	3	1	1	20	
23		27	BARBARIANS	H	Lost	-	-	-	-	0	4	5	-	-	35	
24	Jan	3	Bath	A	Lost	-	2	-	1	9	2	-	1	-	13	Barker(P) Baynes(T) Willars(T)
25		10	Gloucester	A	Won	1	-	-	1	8	-	2	-	-	6	Barker(T,C,P)
26		17	BEDFORD	H	Won	-	1	-	1	6	1	-	-	-	5	Barker(P) Baynes(T)
27		24	Rosslyn Park	A	Won	-	1	-	-	3	-	-	-	-	0	Bird(T)
28		30	HEADINGLEY	H	Lost	-	-	-	4	12	2	-	1	1	16	Barker(4P)
29	Feb	4	Cheltenham	A	Drew	-	2	-	-	6	-	1	-	1	6	Bird(T) Elliott(T)
		6	LONDON SCOTTISH	H		Cancelled Frost										
		14	Newport	A		Cancelled Frost										
		18	Moseley	A		Cancelled Frost										
30		21	Wasps	A	Won	1	1	-	1	11	1	-	-	-	5	Barker(C,P) Baynes(T) Adey(T)
31		27	NORTHAMPTON	H	Won	1	3	-	-	14	-	1	1	1	9	Barker(C) Bird(T) Jones(T) Allen(T) Adey(T)
	Mar	4	GLOUCESTER	H		Cancelled Snow										
		7	HARLEQUINS	H		Cancelled Snow										
32		11	LOUGHBOROUGH COLLEGE	H	Won	3	3	-	1	27	-	1	-	-	3	Barker(T,3C,P) Harrison(T) Duggan(T) Jones(T) Allen(T) Adey(T)
33		14	Coventry	A	Lost	-	1	1	-	6	-	1	1	1	9	Money(D) Andrews(T)
34		18	ROYAL NAVY	H	Won	3	2	-	2	27	-	-	-	2	6	Barker(3C,2P) Allen(3T) Andrews(2T)
35		20	ROYAL AIR FORCE	H	Won	2	-	1	1	16	2	-	-	1	13	Duggan(T) Yandle(T) Barker(2C,P) Allen(D)
36		28	LIVERPOOL	H	Won	1	1	-	1	11	-	-	-	-	0	Money(T) Barker(C,P) Matthews(T)
37		30	FYLDE	H	Won	1	3	1	1	20	-	1	-	3	12	Barker(C,P) Harrison(T) Jones(D) Elliott(2T) Matthews(T)
38		31	MANCHESTER	H	Won	2	2	-	1	19	-	-	-	-	0	Barker(T,2C,P) Harrison(T) Jackson(T) Matthews(T)
39	Apr	4	Birkenhead Park	A	Won	4	6	-	1	41	-	1	-	-	3	Money(T) Duggan(3T) Barker(T,4C,P) Yandle(T) Jackson(2T) Riley(T) Arneil(T)
40		11	NEWPORT	H	Won	2	-	-	1	13	-	-	-	1	3	Barker(2C,P) Harrison(T) Rowell(T)
41		18	Llanelli	A	Lost	1	-	1	1	11	5	3	1	2	43	Money(D) Barker(C,P) Marshall(T)
42		23	Coventry	A	Won	1	2	-	-	11	-	1	-	1	6	Barker(C) Yandle(T) Jones(T) Baynes(T)
43		25	HALIFAX	H	Won	2	5	1	1	31	1	1	-	-	8	Money(D) Barker(2T,2C,P) Harrison(T) Duggan(T) Jones(T) Allen(T) Matthews(T)
44	May	2	NEW BRIGHTON	H	Won	1	1	-	3	17	-	1	-	1	6	Barker(C,3P) Duggan(T) Elliott(T)

INDIVIDUAL APPEARANCES 1969-1970

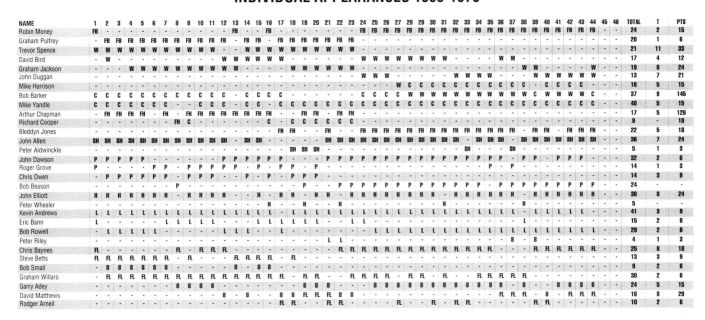

NAME	TOTAL	T	PTS
Robin Money	24	2	15
Graham Pulfrey	20	1	6
Trevor Spence	21	11	33
David Bird	17	4	12
Graham Jackson	19	8	24
John Duggan	13	7	21
Mike Harrison	16	5	15
Bob Barker	37	9	145
Mike Yandle	40	5	15
Arthur Chapman	17	5	126
Richard Cooper	9	-	19
Bleddyn Jones	22	5	18
John Allen	36	7	24
Peter Aldwinckle	5	1	3
John Dawson	32	2	6
Roger Grove	14	1	3
Chris Owen	14	3	9
Bob Beason	24	-	-
John Elliott	36	8	24
Peter Wheeler	5	-	-
Kevin Andrews	41	3	9
Eric Bann	15	2	8
Bob Rowell	29	2	6
Peter Riley	4	1	3
Chris Baynes	25	6	18
Steve Betts	13	3	9
Bob Small	9	2	6
Graham Willars	30	2	6
Garry Adey	24	5	15
David Matthews	16	8	29
Rodger Arneil	10	2	6

3 games: Richard Berry H(8,13,14), Mike Evans FH(1,6)C(13)[9], Guy Millar SH(13,16,17)[1T-3], Rex Skelton P(21,40,44)
2 games: John Ingleby FH(38,41), Roy Sleigh W(1,3)[1T-3]
1 game: Peter Broadbent 8(24), John Broome C(8), Dave Hanna L(44), Nick Humphries P(8), Mike Marshall FL(41)[1T-3], Bob Smith 8(1), Viv Wigley C(13)

LEICESTER FOOTBALL CLUB 1968-69
Back: A.S. Thorpe (Hon.Tres), Dr.H.P. Hughes (President), E.E. Bann, D.J. Beaty, R.S. Smith, C.J. Baynes, P.G.S. Pulfrey,
R.G. Barker, G.J. Adey, D.J. Matthews, R. Sleigh, H.V. White (Coach), J.D. Day (Hon.Sec).
Middle: S.E. Betts, M.J. Harrison, M. Evans, K.P. Andrews, G.G. Willars (Capt), J.A. Allen, J.J. Elliott, R.V. Grove, J.W. Mawby, M.J. Brownhill.
Front: D.W. Bird, R.S. Money, T. Spence, R.C. Cooper.

LEICESTER FOOTBALL CLUB 1969-70
Back: H.V. White (Coach), Dr.H.P. Hughes (President), D.W. Bird, T. Spence, G. Jackson, G.J. Adey, P.G.S. Pulfrey, R.J. Arneil,
G.G. Willars, C.J. Baynes, J.D. Day (Hon.Sec), H.W. Sibson (Team Hon.Sec).
Middle: R.G. Barker, R.P. Skelton, D.J. Matthews, M.J. Harrison, K.P. Andrews (Capt), J.A. Allen, J.J. Elliott, R. Beason, R.E. Rowell.
Front: B. Jones, M.J. Duggan, R.S. Money, M.J. Yandle.

NO	DATE		OPPONENTS	V	RES	FOR G	FOR T	FOR D	FOR P	FOR PTS	AGAINST G	AGAINST T	AGAINST D	AGAINST P	AGAINST PTS	SCORERS
1	Sep	2	Newport	A	Lost	-	-	-	2	6	2	1	-	1	16	Gavins(2P)
2		5	BEDFORD	H	Won	1	-	-	3	14	1	-	-	-	5	Gavins(C,3P) Jones(T)
3		9	LEICESTER & DISTRICT	H	Won	5	6	-	-	43	2	-	-	2	16	Gavins(5C) Duggan(3T) Yandle(T) Hall(T) Jackson(T) Baynes(3T) Adey(T) Willars(T)
4		12	Bath	A	Lost	-	2	-	1	9	1	2	-	-	11	Gavins(P) Barker(T) Yandle(T)
5		15	Burton-on-Trent	A	Won	2	2	-	2	22	-	-	-	2	6	Cooper(2C,2P) Duggan(T) Barker(2T) Owen(T)
6		19	HARROGATE	H	Won	6	1	-	2	39	1	-	-	1	8	Gavins(6C,2P) Duggan(2T) Yandle(T) Hall(T) Baynes(2T) Willars(T)
7		26	Harlequins	A	Won	1	2	-	3	20	1	2	-	2	17	Gavins(C,3P) Barker(T) Jones(T) Adey(T)
8	Oct	3	Coventry	A	Lost	1	-	-	3	14	-	4	1	1	18	Gavins(C,3P) Duggan(T)
9		10	NORTH OF IRELAND	H	Won	1	1	-	2	14	-	-	-	1	3	Gavins(C,2P) Yandle(T) Elliott(T)
10		17	NORTHAMPTON	H	Drew	-	1	-	1	6	-	1	1	-	6	Gavins(P) Hall(T)
11		21	OXFORD UNIVERSITY	H	Lost	-	2	-	1	9	1	2	-	1	14	Gavins(P) Barker(T) Adey(T)
12		24	Swansea	A	Lost	-	-	-	1	3	3	2	-	-	21	Whibley(P)
13		31	SARACENS	H	Won	-	1	-	2	9	-	-	-	1	3	Gavins(2P) Elliott(T)
14	Nov	7	Gloucester	A	Lost	-	-	1	4	15	2	2	-	3	25	Whibley(4P) Jones(D)
15		14	CAMBRIDGE UNIVERSITY	H	Won	3	2	-	1	24	1	2	-	-	11	Gavins(3C,P) Barker(T) Yandle(T) Jones(T) Elliott(T) Arneil(T)
16		21	NEWPORT	H	Lost	-	-	-	4	12	2	1	-	1	16	Gavins(4P)
17		28	Moseley	A	Lost	2	1	-	-	13	2	-	-	2	16	Gavins(2C) Yandle(2T) Bann(T)
18	Dec	5	WATERLOO	H	Won	5	3	-	2	40	-	-	-	1	3	Duggan(2T) Hall(T) Barker(5C,2P) Allen(2T) Owen(T) Matthews(2T)
19		12	BLACKHEATH	H	Won	1	3	1	2	23	-	1	-	1	6	Money(D) Yandle(T) Barker(2T,C,2P) Jones(T)
20		19	Bristol	A	Lost	-	-	-	-	0	2	-	-	-	10	
21		26	BARBARIANS	H	Lost	-	2	-	-	6	3	1	-	-	18	Jones(T) Allen(T)
	Jan	2	BATH	H		Cancelled										
22		9	GLOUCESTER	H	Won	1	1	-	3	17	-	1	-	4	15	Allen(T) Wheeler(P) Bann(C,2P) Baynes(T)
23		15	Cardiff	A	Lost	1	-	-	1	8	-	1	-	3	12	Wheeler(C,P) Baynes(T)
24		23	ROSSLYN PARK	H	Won	2	1	-	1	16	-	1	-	2	9	Wheeler(T,2C,P) Owen(2T)
25		30	Headingley	A	Lost	-	-	-	-	0	1	1	-	-	8	
26	Feb	6	London Scottish	A	Lost	-	3	-	-	9	2	1	1	-	16	Nicholls(T) Barker(T) Wheeler(T)
27		13	Newport	A	Lost	1	1	-	-	8	3	3	1	-	27	Hall(T) Wheeler(C) Matthews(T)
28		17	Moseley	A	Lost	-	-	-	-	0	1	-	-	2	11	
29		20	WASPS	H	Won	1	3	-	1	17	-	-	-	1	3	Duggan(3T) Yandle(T) Wheeler(C,P)
30		26	Northampton	A	Lost	1	1	-	-	8	-	1	1	1	9	Duggan(T) Bann(C) Baynes(T)
31	Mar	2	LOUGHBOROUGH COLLEGE	H	Drew	-	1	-	3	12	-	2	-	2	12	Nicholls(T) Bann(3P)
32		6	HARLEQUINS	H	Won	1	2	-	-	11	-	2	-	-	6	Bird(T) Wheeler(C) Baynes(T) Adey(T)
33		13	COVENTRY	H	Lost	1	-	-	2	11	-	4	-	1	15	Bird(T) Bann(C,2P)
34		19	ROYAL AIR FORCE	H	Won	1	1	-	1	11	-	1	-	1	6	Yandle(T) Nicholls(T) Bann(C,P)
35		24	Nuneaton	A	Lost	-	-	-	1	3	1	1	-	-	8	Wheeler(P)
36		27	LLANELLI	H	Won	-	2	-	2	12	-	1	-	-	3	Nicholls(T) Wheeler(T,2P)
37		31	RUGBY	H	Won	3	2	-	-	21	-	1	-	1	6	Barker(2T) Yandle(T) Allen(T) Wheeler(3C) Dawson(T)
38	Apr	3	BIRKENHEAD PARK	H	Won	1	5	-	1	23	1	1	-	1	11	Barker(T) Yandle(T) Nicholls(2T) Wheeler(P) Bann(C) Baynes(T) Adey(T)
39		10	Liverpool	A	Lost	1	-	-	1	8	1	1	-	2	14	Wheeler(C,P) Willars(T)
40		12	Fylde	A	Won	2	1	-	3	22	1	2	-	3	20	Nicholls(T) Grove(T) Wheeler(2C,3P) Baynes(T)
41		13	Manchester	A	Won	1	1	-	3	17	-	1	-	2	9	Nicholls(T) Wheeler(T,C,3P)
42		17	RICHMOND	H	Won	3	4	-	2	33	1	-	-	1	8	Duggan(2T) Hall(T) Wheeler(3C,2P) Bann(T) Baynes(2T) Arneil(T)
43		24	SALE	H	Won	-	-	-	1	3	-	-	-	-	0	Wheeler(P)
44		28	Bedford	A	Lost	1	1	-	1	11	-	2	1	1	12	Money(T) Yandle(T) Wheeler(C,P)
45	May	1	New Brighton	A	Won	4	3	1	-	32	-	1	-	1	6	Money(T) Duggan(2T) Bird(T) Nicholls(3T) Jones(D) Wheeler(4C)

INDIVIDUAL APPEARANCES 1970-1971

NAME	1	2	3	4	5	6	7	8	9	10	11	12	13	14	15	16	17	18	19	20	21	22	23
Mike Gavins	FB	FB	FB	FB	-	FB	FB	FB	FB	FB	FB	-	FB	-	FB	FB	FB	-	-	-	-	-	-
Dave Whibley	-	-	-	-	-	-	-	-	-	-	-	FB	-	FB	-	-	-	-	-	-	-	-	-
Robin Money	-	-	-	-	-	-	-	-	-	-	-	-	-	-	-	-	-	FB	FB	FB	FB	FB	FB
John Duggan	W	W	W	-	W	W	W	W	W	W	W	W	W	-	-	W	W	W	W	W	W	W	W
Graham Jackson	W	W	W	W	-	-	-	-	-	-	-	-	-	W	-	-	-	-	-	-	-	W	W
Bob Barker	-	-	-	W	W	W	W	W	W	W	C	W	C	C	W	W	W	W	W	W	W	-	C
David Bird	-	-	-	-	-	-	-	-	-	-	W	-	W	W	W	-	-	-	-	-	-	-	-
Peter Nicholls	-	-	-	-	-	-	-	-	-	-	-	-	-	-	-	-	-	-	-	-	-	-	-
Brian Hall	C	C	C	C	C	C	C	C	C	C	C	C	-	-	C	C	C	C	C	C	C	C	-
Mike Yandle	C	C	C	C	C	C	C	C	C	C	-	C	C	-	C	C	C	C	C	C	C	C	C
Viv Wigley	-	-	-	-	-	-	-	-	-	-	-	-	-	C	-	-	-	-	-	-	-	-	-
Mike Harrison	-	-	-	-	-	-	-	-	-	-	-	-	-	-	-	-	-	-	-	-	-	-	-
Bleddyn Jones	FH	FH	-	FH	FH	FH	FH	FH	FH	FH	FH	FH	FH	FH	FH	FH	FH	FH	FH	FH	FH	FH	FH
Richard Cooper	-	-	FH	-	FB	-	-	-	-	-	-	-	-	-	-	-	-	-	-	-	-	-	-
David Berry	-	-	-	-	-	-	-	-	-	-	-	-	-	-	-	-	-	-	-	-	-	-	-
John Allen	SH	SH	SH	SH	SH	SH	SH	SH	SH	SH	SH	SH	SH	SH	SH	SH	SH	SH	SH	SH	SH	SH	SH
Bob Beason	P	P	P	P	-	-	-	-	P	P	P	P	P	P	P	P	P	-	-	-	-	-	-
John Dawson	P	P	P	P	P	P	P	P	P	P	P	P	P	P	P	P	P	P	P	P	P	P	P
Chris Owen	-	-	-	-	P	P	P	P	-	-	-	-	-	8	-	-	-	P	P	P	P	P	P
Mike Mortimer	-	-	-	-	-	-	-	-	-	-	-	-	-	-	-	-	-	-	-	-	-	-	-
Roger Grove	-	-	-	-	-	-	-	-	-	-	-	-	-	-	-	-	-	-	-	-	-	-	-
Peter Wheeler	H	H	H	H	-	-	-	-	-	-	-	-	-	H	-	-	-	-	-	-	H	H	H
John Elliott	-	-	-	-	H	H	H	H	H	H	H	H	H	-	H	H	H	H	H	H	-	-	-
David Pickering	-	-	-	-	-	-	-	-	-	-	-	-	-	-	-	-	-	-	-	-	-	-	-
Eric Bann	L	L	-	L	-	-	-	-	-	L	L	L	L	-	L	L	L	L	L	L	L	L	-
Dave Shaw	L	L	L	L	L	L	L	L	L	L	L	L	L	L	L	L	L	-	-	L	L	L	L
Bob Watson	-	-	L	-	L	-	-	-	-	-	-	-	-	L	-	-	-	-	-	-	-	-	L
Dave Hanna	-	-	-	-	-	L	L	L	L	-	-	-	-	-	-	-	-	-	-	-	-	-	-
J.Golding	-	-	-	-	-	-	-	-	-	-	-	-	-	-	-	-	-	L	L	-	-	-	-
Bob Rowell	-	-	-	-	-	-	-	-	-	-	-	-	-	-	-	-	-	-	-	-	-	-	-
Nick Joyce	-	-	-	-	-	-	-	-	-	-	-	-	-	-	-	-	-	-	-	-	-	-	-
Garry Adey	8	8	8	8	8	8	8	8	8	8	8	8	8	-	-	-	-	-	-	-	-	-	-
Chris Baynes	FL	FL	FL	FL	FL	FL	FL	FL	FL	FL	FL	FL	-	-	FL	FL	FL	FL	FL	FL	FL	FL	FL
Graham Willars	FL	FL	FL	FL	FL	FL	-	FL	-	-	-	FL	-	FL	-	-	-	-	-	FL	-	FL	FL
Rodger Arneil	-	-	-	-	-	-	FL	-	-	-	-	-	FL	FL	FL	FL	FL	FL	FL	-	FL	-	-
David Matthews	-	-	-	-	-	-	-	-	FL	FL	FL	-	FL	-	8	8	8	8	8	8	8	8	8

NAME	24	25	26	27	28	29	30	31	32	33	34	35	36	37	38	39	40	41	42	43	44	45	46	TOTAL	T	PTS
Mike Gavins	-	-	-	-	-	-	-	-	-	-	-	-	-	-	-	-	-	-	-	-	-	-	-	14	-	115
Dave Whibley	-	-	-	-	FB	-	-	-	-	-	-	-	-	-	-	-	-	-	-	-	-	-	-	3	-	15
Robin Money	FB	FB	FB	FB	-	FB	FB	FB	FB	FB	FB	FB	FB	FB	FB	FB	FB	FB	FB	FB	FB	FB	-	27	2	9
John Duggan	W	-	-	W	-	W	W	W	W	W	-	-	-	-	-	-	W	W	W	W	W	W	-	33	17	51
Graham Jackson	W	W	W	-	-	-	-	-	-	-	-	-	-	-	-	-	-	-	-	-	-	-	-	10	1	3
Bob Barker	C	C	C	C	W	-	-	-	-	-	W	W	W	W	W	W	-	-	-	-	-	-	-	30	12	60
David Bird	-	-	-	-	C	C	C	C	C	C	-	C	-	-	-	-	-	C	C	C	C	C	-	16	3	9
Peter Nicholls	-	-	W	W	W	W	W	W	W	W	W	W	W	W	W	W	W	W	W	W	W	W	-	20	11	33
Brian Hall	-	W	C	C	C	-	-	-	-	-	-	-	-	-	-	-	-	-	C	-	-	-	-	25	6	18
Mike Yandle	C	C	-	-	-	C	C	C	C	C	C	-	C	C	C	C	C	C	-	C	C	C	-	38	13	39
Viv Wigley	-	-	-	-	-	-	-	-	-	-	-	-	-	-	-	C	C	-	-	-	-	-	-	3	-	-
Mike Harrison	-	-	-	-	-	-	-	-	-	-	C	C	C	C	C	-	-	-	-	-	-	-	-	5	-	-
Bleddyn Jones	FH	FH	FH	FH	FH	FH	-	-	-	-	FH	FH	-	FH	FH	FH	FH	FH	FH	FH	FH	FH	-	39	5	21
Richard Cooper	-	-	-	-	-	-	-	-	-	-	-	-	-	-	-	-	-	-	-	-	-	-	-	2	-	10
David Berry	-	-	-	-	-	-	FH	FH	FH	FH	-	-	FH	-	-	-	-	-	-	-	-	-	-	5	-	-
John Allen	SH	SH	SH	SH	SH	SH	SH	SH	SH	SH	SH	SH	SH	SH	SH	SH	SH	-	SH	SH	SH	SH	-	44	5	15
Bob Beason	P	P	P	-	-	-	P	P	P	P	-	-	-	-	-	-	-	-	P	P	P	P	-	24	-	-
John Dawson	-	-	-	P	P	P	P	P	P	P	P	P	P	P	P	P	P	P	-	-	P	-	-	39	1	3
Chris Owen	P	P	P	P	P	P	-	-	-	-	-	-	-	-	-	-	-	-	-	-	-	-	-	17	4	12
Mike Mortimer	-	-	-	-	-	-	-	-	-	-	P	P	P	-	-	-	-	-	-	-	-	-	-	3	-	-
Roger Grove	-	-	-	-	-	-	-	-	-	-	-	-	-	P	P	P	P	P	P	P	-	P	-	8	1	3
Peter Wheeler	H	H	H	H	H	H	-	-	H	H	H	H	H	H	H	H	H	H	H	H	H	H	-	28	4	111
John Elliott	-	-	-	-	-	-	-	-	-	-	-	-	-	-	-	-	-	-	-	-	-	-	-	15	3	9
David Pickering	-	-	-	-	-	-	H	H	-	-	-	-	-	-	-	-	-	-	-	-	-	-	-	2	-	-
Eric Bann	L	L	L	-	-	-	L	L	L	L	L	L	L	L	L	-	-	-	L	L	L	-	-	30	2	40
Dave Shaw	L	L	L	L	L	L	-	-	-	-	L	-	-	-	-	L	L	L	L	L	-	-	-	33	-	-
Bob Watson	-	-	-	L	-	L	-	-	-	-	-	-	-	-	-	-	-	-	-	-	-	-	-	6	-	-
Dave Hanna	-	-	-	-	-	-	-	-	-	-	-	-	-	-	-	-	-	-	-	-	-	-	-	4	-	-
J.Golding	-	-	-	-	-	-	-	-	-	-	-	-	-	-	-	-	-	-	-	-	-	-	-	2	-	-
Bob Rowell	-	-	-	-	L	-	L	L	L	L	-	L	L	L	L	L	-	L	-	-	-	-	-	11	-	-
Nick Joyce	-	-	-	-	-	-	-	-	-	-	-	-	-	-	-	-	L	-	-	-	L	L	-	3	-	-
Garry Adey	-	-	8	8	8	8	8	8	8	8	8	8	8	8	8	8	8	8	8	8	8	L	-	33	5	15
Chris Baynes	FL	FL	FL	-	FL	-	FL	FL	FL	FL	FL	FL	FL	FL	FL	FL	FL	FL	FL	FL	FL	FL	-	41	13	39
Graham Willars	-	-	-	-	-	-	-	-	-	-	-	-	-	-	-	FL	FL	-	-	-	FL	FL	-	16	3	9
Rodger Arneil	FL	FL	-	FL	-	FL	-	-	-	-	-	-	-	-	-	-	-	-	FL	FL	-	-	-	15	2	6
David Matthews	8	8	FL	FL	FL	FL	FL	FL	FL	FL	FL	FL	FL	FL	FL	-	-	-	-	-	-	8	-	29	3	9

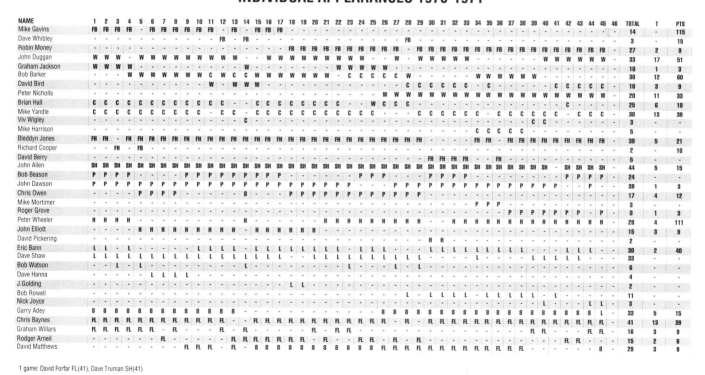

1 game: David Forfar FL(41), Dave Truman SH(41)

1971-1972

NO	DATE	OPPONENTS	V	RES	FOR G	FOR T	FOR D	FOR P	FOR PTS	AGAINST G	AGAINST T	AGAINST D	AGAINST P	AGAINST PTS	SCORERS
1	Sep 4	Bedford	A	Lost	2	1	-	-	16	3	2	-	3	35	Duggan(2T) Wheeler(2C) Matthews(T)
2	8	LEICESTER & DISTRICT	H	Won	1	1	1	1	16	-	1	-	3	13	Money(T,D) Truman(T) Wheeler(C,P)
3	11	BATH	H	Won	3	1	-	-	22	-	1	-	2	10	Yandle(T) Nicholls(T) Bann(T,3C) Baynes(T)
4	15	NUNEATON	H	Won	1	-	-	2	12	-	-	-	2	6	Duggan(T) Bann(C,2P)
5	18	Liverpool	A	Lost	-	2	-	-	8	2	-	-	2	18	Nicholls(T) Allen(T)
6	25	Harlequins	A	Lost	1	-	-	1	9	3	1	-	2	28	Nicholls(T) Matthews(C,P)
7	Oct 2	COVENTRY	H	Lost	-	1	-	2	10	3	1	-	1	25	Duggan(T) Bann(2P)
8	9	Richmond	A	Lost	-	-	-	4	12	2	-	-	2	18	Whibley(4P)
9	16	Northampton	A	Lost	-	1	-	-	4	1	-	-	2	12	Nicholls(T)
10	20	Oxford University	A	Won	1	2	-	1	17	-	1	-	2	10	Whibley(C,P) Nicholls(T) Hall(T) Duggan(T)
11	23	SWANSEA	H	Drew	-	1	-	1	7	-	1	-	1	7	Whibley(P) Duggan(T)
12	30	Rugby	A	Drew	-	-	-	4	12	1	-	-	2	12	Whibley(4P)
13	Nov 6	GLOUCESTER	H	Won	3	1	-	3	31	-	-	-	3	9	Whibley(3C,3P) Barker(T) Owen(T) Baynes(T) Willars(T)
14	13	Cambridge University	A	Won	2	-	1	3	24	-	-	1	2	9	Whibley(2C,3P) Yandle(T) Hall(D) Barker(T)
15	20	NEW BRIGHTON	H	Won	3	2	-	1	29	-	1	-	1	7	Whibley(3C,P) Barker(T) Jones(T) Baynes(2T) Willars(T)
16	21	Nottingham (RFU1)	A	Lost	-	-	-	1	3	-	1	1	1	10	Whibley(P)
17	27	MOSELEY	H	Won	-	2	-	1	11	1	-	-	1	9	Whibley(P) Adey(T) Willars(T)
18	Dec 4	Waterloo	A	Won	4	1	-	1	31	1	-	-	-	6	Whibley(4C,P) Barker(2T) Yandle(T) Horner(2T)
19	11	Blackheath	A	Won	-	3	-	1	15	1	1	-	1	13	Money(T) Barker(T,P) Baynes(T)
20	18	BRISTOL	H	Won	1	6	-	3	39	1	1	-	1	13	Money(T) Barker(T,C,3P) Hall(2T) Horner(T) Jones(T) Baynes(T)
21	28	BARBARIANS	H	Won	1	2	-	2	20	1	2	-	-	14	Whibley(C,2P) Barker(3T)
22	Jan 1	Bath	A	Lost	-	3	-	1	15	1	2	1	-	17	Money(T) Barker(P) Horner(T) Adey(T)
23	8	Bridgend	A	Lost	-	3	-	-	12	1	2	1	1	20	Barker(T) Wheeler(T) Adey(T)
24	16	BEDFORD	H	Lost	1	1	-	-	10	1	1	-	3	19	Whibley(C) Wheeler(T) Rowell(T)
25	22	Rosslyn Park	A	Won	-	3	-	1	15	-	1	-	2	10	Whibley(P) Duggan(2T) Barker(T)
26	29	HEADINGLEY	H	Won	1	4	-	1	25	-	-	1	1	6	Whibley(C,P) Duggan(2T) Wheeler(T) Bann(2T)
27	Feb 3	ROYAL NAVY	H	Won	-	3	-	1	15	-	1	-	1	7	Whibley(P) Duggan(T) Barker(T) Wheeler(T)
28	5	LONDON SCOTTISH	H	Won	-	1	-	2	10	1	-	-	1	9	Whibley(2P) Duggan(T)
29	12	NEWPORT	H	Won	-	3	-	3	21	1	-	-	1	9	Whibley(3P) Duggan(2T) Jones(T)
	16	MOSELEY	H		Cancelled Strike										
30	19	Wasps	A	Won	3	1	-	1	25	-	-	-	1	3	Hall(T) Whibley(T,3C,P) Barker(T) Adey(T)
31	26	NORTHAMPTON	H	Lost	1	-	-	3	15	3	-	-	2	24	Whibley(C,3P) Hall(T)
32	Mar 4	HARLEQUINS	H	Won	2	-	-	1	15	-	2	-	-	8	Whibley(2C,P) Duggan(T) Barker(T)
	8	LOUGHBOROUGH COLLEGE	H		Cancelled										
	11	Coventry	A		Cancelled										
33	18	ROYAL AIR FORCE	H	Won	2	8	-	2	50	-	-	-	3	9	Whibley(2C,2P) Duggan(3T) Hall(T) Barker(2T) Jones(T) Allen(T) Mortimer(T) Forfar(T)
	22	Gloucester	A		Cancelled										
34	25	Sale	A	Drew	-	1	-	3	13	-	1	-	3	13	Whibley(3P) Watson(T)
35	Apr 1	BIRKENHEAD PARK	H	Won	8	1	-	2	58	1	-	-	1	9	Whibley(8C,2P) Money(T) Hall(T) Barker(3T) Jones(2T) Wheeler(T) Bann(T)
36	3	FYLDE	H	Won	2	3	-	2	30	1	-	-	2	12	Whibley(2P) Jackson(T) Barker(T,2C) Pickering(T) Shaw(T) Joyce(T)
37	4	WILMSLOW	H	Won	3	1	1	-	25	-	-	-	-	0	Jackson(T) Yandle(D) Barker(T) Allen(T) Wheeler(3C) Matthews(T)
38	8	Llanelli	A	Lost	-	1	-	-	4	1	-	-	3	15	Duggan(T)
39	15	NOTTINGHAM	H	Won	4	4	-	-	40	-	-	-	3	9	Cooper(T,3C) Duggan(2T) Barker(2T) Wheeler(2T,C) Matthews(T)
40	22	Newport	A	Won	2	1	1	2	25	-	2	-	1	11	Barker(2T) Hall(T) Jones(D) Wheeler(2C,2P)
41	29	Hartlepool Rovers	A	Won	2	-	-	2	18	-	2	-	1	11	Duggan(2T) Wheeler(2C,2P)

INDIVIDUAL APPEARANCES 1971-1972

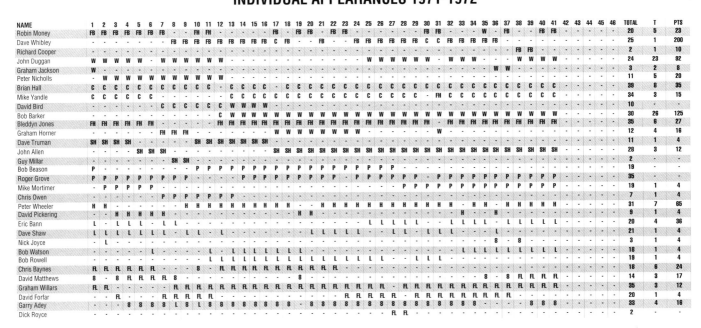

NAME	1	2	3	4	5	6	7	8	9	10	11	12	13	14	15	16	17	18	19	20	21	22	23	24	25	26	27	28	29	30	31	32	33	34	35	36	37	38	39	40	41	42	43	44	45	46	TOTAL	T	PTS
Robin Money	FB	FB	FB	FB	FB	FB	FB	-	-	FH	FH	-	-	-	-	-	FB	-	FB	FB	-	FB	FB	-	-	-	-	-	-	FB	FB	-	-	-	W	-	FB	-	-	FB	FB	-	-	-	-	-	20	5	23
Dave Whibley	-	-	-	-	-	-	-	FB	FB	FB	FB	FB	FB	FB	FB	FB	C	FB	-	-	FB	-	-	FB	FB	FB	FB	FB	FB	C	C	FB	FB	FB	FB	FB	-	-	-	-	-	-	-	-	-	-	25	1	200
Richard Cooper	-	-	-	-	-	-	-	-	-	-	-	-	-	-	-	-	-	-	-	-	-	-	-	-	-	-	-	-	-	-	-	-	-	-	-	-	-	FB	FB	-	-	-	-	-	-	-	2	1	10
John Duggan	W	W	W	W	W	-	W	W	W	W	W	W	-	-	-	-	-	-	-	-	-	-	-	-	W	W	W	W	W	W	-	W	W	W	-	-	-	W	W	W	W	-	-	-	-	-	24	23	92
Graham Jackson	W	-	-	-	-	-	-	-	-	-	-	-	-	-	-	-	-	-	-	-	-	-	-	-	-	-	-	-	-	-	-	-	-	-	-	W	W	-	-	-	-	-	-	-	-	-	3	2	8
Peter Nicholls	-	W	W	W	W	W	W	W	W	W	W	W	-	-	-	-	-	-	-	-	-	-	-	-	-	-	-	-	-	-	-	-	-	-	-	-	-	-	-	-	-	-	-	-	-	-	11	5	20
Brian Hall	C	C	C	C	C	C	C	C	C	C	C	-	C	C	C	C	-	C	C	C	C	C	C	C	C	C	C	C	C	C	C	C	C	C	C	C	C	C	C	C	C	-	-	-	-	-	39	8	35
Mike Yandle	C	C	C	C	C	C	-	-	-	-	-	-	C	C	C	C	C	C	C	C	C	C	C	C	C	C	C	C	C	-	FH	C	C	C	C	C	C	C	C	C	C	-	-	-	-	-	34	3	15
David Bird	-	-	-	-	-	-	C	C	C	C	C	C	W	W	W	W	-	-	-	-	-	-	-	-	-	-	-	-	-	-	-	-	-	-	-	-	-	-	-	-	-	-	-	-	-	-	10	-	-
Bob Barker	-	-	-	-	-	-	-	-	-	-	-	C	W	W	W	W	W	W	W	W	W	W	W	W	W	W	W	W	W	W	W	W	W	W	W	W	W	W	W	W	W	-	-	-	-	-	30	26	125
Bleddyn Jones	FH	FH	FH	FH	FH	FH	-	-	-	-	-	FH	FH	FH	FH	FH	FH	FH	FH	FH	FH	FH	FH	FH	FH	FH	FH	FH	FH	FH	-	FH	FH	FH	FH	FH	FH	FH	FH	FH	FH	-	-	-	-	-	35	6	27
Graham Horner	-	-	-	-	-	-	FH	FH	FH	-	-	-	-	-	-	-	W	W	W	W	W	W	W	W	-	-	-	-	-	-	W	-	-	-	-	-	-	-	-	-	-	-	-	-	-	-	12	4	16
Dave Truman	SH	SH	SH	SH	-	-	-	-	-	SH	SH	SH	SH	SH	SH	SH	-	-	-	-	-	-	-	-	-	-	-	-	-	-	-	-	-	-	-	-	-	-	-	-	-	-	-	-	-	-	11	1	4
John Allen	-	-	-	-	SH	SH	SH	-	-	-	-	-	-	-	-	-	SH	SH	SH	SH	SH	SH	SH	SH	SH	SH	SH	SH	SH	SH	SH	SH	SH	SH	SH	SH	SH	SH	SH	SH	SH	-	-	-	-	-	28	3	12
Guy Millar	-	-	-	-	-	-	-	SH	SH	-	-	-	-	-	-	-	-	-	-	-	-	-	-	-	-	-	-	-	-	-	-	-	-	-	-	-	-	-	-	-	-	-	-	-	-	-	2	-	-
Bob Beason	P	-	-	-	-	-	-	-	-	P	P	P	P	P	P	P	P	P	P	P	P	P	P	P	P	P	P	-	-	-	-	-	-	-	-	-	-	-	-	-	-	-	-	-	-	-	19	-	-
Roger Grove	P	P	P	P	P	P	P	P	P	-	-	-	-	P	P	P	P	P	P	P	P	P	-	P	P	P	P	P	P	-	P	P	P	P	P	P	P	P	P	P	P	-	-	-	-	-	35	-	-
Mike Mortimer	-	P	P	P	P	P	-	-	-	-	-	-	-	-	-	-	-	-	-	-	-	-	-	-	-	-	-	P	P	P	P	P	P	P	P	P	P	P	P	P	P	-	-	-	-	-	19	1	4
Chris Owen	-	-	-	-	-	-	P	P	P	P	P	P	P	-	-	-	-	-	-	-	-	-	-	-	-	-	-	-	-	-	-	-	-	-	-	-	-	-	-	-	-	-	-	-	-	-	7	1	4
Peter Wheeler	H	H	-	-	-	-	-	-	H	H	H	H	H	H	H	H	H	H	-	-	H	H	H	H	H	H	H	H	H	H	H	H	-	H	H	-	H	H	H	H	H	-	-	-	-	-	31	7	65
David Pickering	-	-	H	H	H	H	H	-	-	-	-	-	-	-	-	-	-	-	H	H	-	-	-	-	-	-	-	-	-	-	-	H	-	-	-	H	-	-	-	-	-	-	-	-	-	-	9	1	4
Eric Bann	L	-	L	L	L	-	L	L	-	-	-	-	-	-	-	-	-	-	-	-	-	-	-	-	L	L	L	L	L	-	-	L	L	L	L	-	L	L	L	L	L	-	-	-	-	-	20	4	36
Dave Shaw	L	L	L	L	L	L	L	-	L	L	-	L	-	-	-	-	-	-	-	L	L	L	L	L	-	-	L	L	-	L	L	L	-	-	-	L	-	-	-	-	-	-	-	-	-	-	21	1	4
Nick Joyce	-	L	-	-	-	-	-	-	-	-	-	-	-	-	-	-	-	-	-	-	-	-	-	-	-	-	-	-	-	-	-	-	-	-	-	8	-	8	-	-	-	-	-	-	-	-	3	1	4
Bob Watson	-	-	-	-	-	L	-	-	-	-	L	-	L	L	L	L	L	L	L	-	-	-	-	-	-	-	-	-	-	-	-	-	L	L	L	L	L	L	L	L	L	-	-	-	-	-	18	1	4
Bob Rowell	-	-	-	-	-	-	-	-	-	-	L	L	L	L	L	L	L	L	L	L	L	L	L	L	L	L	-	-	L	L	L	-	-	-	-	-	-	-	-	-	-	-	-	-	-	-	19	1	4
Chris Baynes	FL	FL	FL	FL	FL	FL	-	-	-	8	-	FL	FL	FL	FL	FL	FL	FL	FL	FL	FL	FL	-	-	-	-	-	-	-	-	-	-	-	-	-	-	-	-	-	-	-	-	-	-	-	-	18	6	24
David Matthews	8	-	8	FL	FL	FL	FL	8	-	-	-	-	-	-	-	-	-	-	8	-	-	-	-	-	-	-	-	-	-	-	-	-	-	-	8	-	8	FL	FL	FL	FL	-	-	-	-	-	14	3	17
Graham Willars	FL	FL	-	-	-	-	-	FL	FL	FL	FL	FL	FL	FL	FL	FL	FL	FL	FL	FL	FL	FL	FL	FL	FL	FL	-	FL	FL	FL	FL	FL	FL	FL	FL	FL	FL	FL	FL	FL	FL	-	-	-	-	-	35	3	12
David Forfar	-	-	FL	-	-	-	FL	FL	FL	FL	FL	-	-	-	-	-	-	-	-	-	-	-	FL	FL	FL	FL	FL	-	FL	FL	FL	FL	FL	FL	FL	FL	FL	-	-	-	-	-	-	-	-	-	20	1	4
Garry Adey	-	-	-	8	8	8	8	L	8	L	8	8	8	8	8	8	8	8	-	8	8	8	8	8	8	8	8	8	8	8	8	8	8	8	-	-	-	-	8	8	8	-	-	-	-	-	33	4	16
Dick Royce	-	-	-	-	-	-	-	-	-	-	-	-	-	-	-	-	-	-	-	-	-	-	-	-	-	-	FL	FL	-	-	-	-	-	-	-	-	-	-	-	-	-	-	-	-	-	-	2	-	-

1 game: Keith Fielding W(6), Roy French H(8), John Lacey L(9), D.Morley P(23), Peter Riley 8(2), Phil Vesty P(30)

LEICESTER FOOTBALL CLUB 1970-71
Back: H.W. Sibson (Team Hon.Sec), A.S. Thorpe (Hon.Tres), Dr.H.P. Hughes (President), P. Nicholls, C.J. Baynes,
R.G. Barker, C.J. Adey, E.E. Bann, D.M. Shaw, R.J. Arneil, R. Beason, H.V. White (Coach), J.D. Day (Hon.Sec).
Middle: B.P. Hall, P.J. Wheeler, R.V. Grove, J.A. Allen (Capt), D.J. Matthews, M.J. Yandle, G.G. Willars, M.J. Duggan.
Front: D.W. Bird, R.S. Money, J.J. Elliott, B. Jones.

LEICESTER FOOTBALL CLUB 1971-72
Back: J.D. Day (Hon.Sec), H.V. White (Coach), M.J. Yandle, P. Nicholls, B.P. Hall, R. Watson, G.J. Adey, D.J. Matthews,
M.R. Mortimer, R.E. Rowell, R.G. Barker, G. Horner, J.T.W. Berry (President), H.W. Sibson (Team Hon.Sec).
Middle: P.J. Wheeler, G.G. Willars, R.V. Grove (Capt), R. Beason, R.S. Money.
Front: B. Jones, J.A. Allen.

NO	DATE		OPPONENTS	V	RES	FOR				PTS	AGAINST				PTS	SCORERS
						G	T	D	P		G	T	D	P		
1	Sep	2	BEDFORD	H	Won	3	1	-	1	25	-	-	-	2	6	Whibley(3C,P) Barker(T) Wheeler(T) Baynes(T) Willars(T)
2		9	BATH	H	Won	2	4	-	2	34	-	1	-	-	4	Whibley(2C,2P) Barker(2T) Yandle(T) Jones(T) Baynes(T) Willars(T)
3		16	LIVERPOOL	H	Won	7	5	-	1	65	-	-	-	1	3	Whibley(7C,P) Barker(3T) Duggan(T) Allen(T) Wheeler(2T) Rowell(T) Baynes(T) Adey(2T) Willars(T)
4		20	Nottingham	A	Won	2	2	-	2	26	1	-	-	2	12	Whibley(2C,2P) Duggan(2T) Jones(T) Churchward(T)
5		23	Harlequins	A	Won	5	-	-	-	30	2	-	-	2	18	Whibley(5C) Yandle(T) Hall(T) Duggan(T) Bann(T) Baynes(T)
6		27	Nuneaton (RFUP)	A	Won	1	2	-	3	23	2	1	-	2	22	Money(T) Duggan(T) Whibley(C,3P) Barker(T)
7		30	Percy Park	A	Won	3	2	-	2	32	2	-	1	1	18	Whibley(3C,2P) Barker(T) Hall(T) Duggan(2T) Shaw(T)
8	Oct	7	Coventry	A	Lost	-	-	-	2	6	5	3	-	1	45	Whibley(2P)
9		14	RICHMOND	H	Won	5	2	-	2	44	-	1	-	1	7	Whibley(T,5C,2P) Barker(2T) Duggan(T) Bann(2T) Adey(T)
10		21	NORTHAMPTON	H	Lost	1	-	-	2	12	1	1	1	3	22	Whibley(C,2P) Hall(T)
11		25	OXFORD UNIVERSITY	H	Won	4	3	-	-	36	-	-	-	1	3	Whibley(T,2C) Weinberg(2T) Barker(T) Young(T) Wheeler(T,2C) Bann(T)
12		28	Swansea	A	Lost	2	1	-	3	25	3	3	-	1	33	Whibley(2C,3P) Duggan(2T) Jones(T)
13	Nov	4	Gloucester	A	Drew	1	1	-	1	13	-	1	-	3	13	Whibley(C,P) Barker(2T)
14		11	CAMBRIDGE UNIVERSITY	H	Won	2	4	-	-	28	-	1	-	2	10	Whibley(2C) Duggan(T) Yandle(T) Barker(T) Jones(T) Mortimer(T) Forfar(T)
15		18	Newport	A	Lost	1	3	-	2	24	4	2	-	-	32	Whibley(C,2P) Duggan(T) Weinberg(T) Barker(T) Wheeler(T)
16		25	Moseley	A	Lost	1	1	-	2	16	1	1	1	2	19	Ingleby(C,2P) Mortimer(T) Baynes(T)
17	Dec	2	WATERLOO	H	Won	4	-	-	2	30	1	-	-	2	12	Ingleby(T,4C,2P) Barker(T) Baynes(2T)
18		9	BLACKHEATH	H	Won	4	2	-	1	35	-	-	-	-	0	Money(T) Duggan(3T) Ingleby(4C,P) Barker(T) Willars(T)
19		16	Bristol	A	Lost	-	1	-	1	7	-	2	1	-	11	Ingleby(P) Willars(T)
20		23	Bedford (RFU1)	A	Won	1	3	-	1	21	-	2	-	3	17	Duggan(T) Barker(T,C) Wheeler(T,P) Willars(T)
21		27	BARBARIANS	H	Won	2	2	-	2	26	1	1	-	2	16	Old(C) Barker(C,2P) Allen(T) Wheeler(T) Adey(T) Willars(T)
22		30	CARDIFF	H	Lost	1	1	-	1	13	2	2	-	3	29	Barker(T,C,P) Baynes(T)
23	Jan	6	Bath	A	Lost	-	-	-	-	0	5	3	-	-	42	
24		15	GLOUCESTER	H	Won	2	2	-	-	20	-	-	-	2	12	Nicholls(T) Barker(T) Horner(T) Ingleby(2C) Mortimer(T)
25		21	Bedford	A	Lost	1	-	-	1	9	3	4	-	1	37	Barker(T) Ingleby(C,P)
26		25	ROYAL NAVY	H	Won	3	-	-	1	29	1	-	-	2	12	Money(T) Duggan(T) Ingleby(2C) Horner(T) Wheeler(T) Bann(C,P) Adey(T)
27		27	ROSSLYN PARK	H	Won	1	1	-	1	13	-	2	-	1	11	Whibley(C,P) Bann(T) D.J.Matthews(T)
28	Feb	3	Hinckley (RFU2)	A	Won	1	1	-	2	16	-	1	-	-	4	Whibley(C,2P) Wheeler(T) Bann(T)
29		10	NEWPORT	H	Won	3	-	1	2	27	-	-	-	1	3	Money(D) Duggan(2T) Ingleby(3C,2P) Barker(T)
30		17	WASPS	H	Lost	-	1	-	-	4	-	1	-	2	10	Allen(T)
31		20	MOSELEY	H	Lost	-	-	1	2	9	1	2	-	-	14	Ingleby(2P) Hillicker(D)
32		23	Northampton	A	Lost	-	-	-	2	12	1	4	-	-	22	Ingleby(2C) Bann(T) Adey(T)
33	Mar	3	HARLEQUINS	H	Lost	2	-	-	3	21	2	1	-	3	25	Ingleby(2C,3P) Willars(T) Adey(T)
		7	LOUGHBOROUGH COLLEGE	H		Cancelled											
34		10	Sale (RFUQF)	A	Lost	-	-	-	-	0	-	1	1	-	7	
35		16	ROYAL AIR FORCE	H	Won	4	2	-	5	47	2	1	-	1	19	Money(T) Duggan(T) Yandle(2T) Ingleby(T,4C,5P) Bann(T)
36		21	RUGBY	H	Won	3	1	-	4	34	1	3	-	1	21	Yandle(T) Ingleby(3C,4P) Barker(T) Wheeler(T) Bann(T)
37		24	LLANELLI	H	Won	1	-	-	5	21	-	2	-	1	11	Duggan(T) Ingleby(C,5P)
38		28	Headingley	A	Won	4	1	-	2	34	-	1	-	2	10	Duggan(T) Yandle(T) Ingleby(T,4C,2P) Barker(T) Bann(T)
39		31	Nuneaton	A	Won	2	-	-	3	21	-	-	-	1	3	Ingleby(2C,3P) Jones(T) Wheeler(T)
40	Apr	7	Birkenhead Park	A	Drew	-	1	-	2	10	-	1	-	2	10	Ingleby(2P) Ringer(T)
41		11	SALE	H	Won	3	1	-	-	22	-	1	-	1	7	Ingleby(3C) Barker(T) Jones(2T) Roy.French(T)
42		14	BIRMINGHAM	H	Won	2	1	-	1	19	-	1	-	1	7	Nicholls(T) Ingleby(2C,P) Barker(T) Ringer(T)
43		21	Broughton Park	A	Won	1	1	-	-	10	1	-	-	1	9	Barker(T) Edwards(T) Old(C)
44		23	Fylde	A	Won	-	2	-	2	14	-	-	-	-	12	Yandle(T) Old(2P) Wheeler(T)
45		24	Wilmslow	A	Lost	-	1	-	2	10	-	1	1	3	16	Barker(T) Old(2P)
46		28	HARTLEPOOL ROVERS	H	Won	-	3	-	1	15	-	1	-	1	7	Duggan(T) Barker(T) Wheeler(P) Watson(T)

INDIVIDUAL APPEARANCES 1972-1973

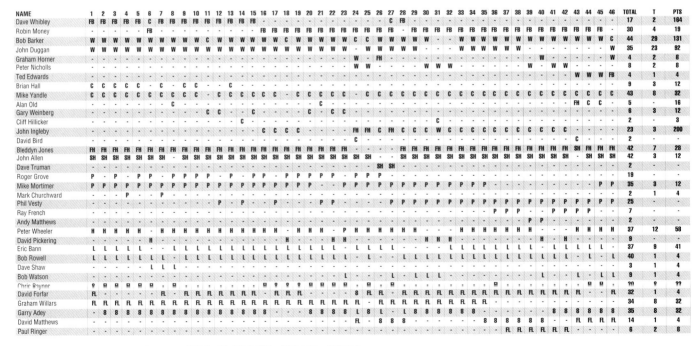

NAME	TOTAL	T	PTS
Dave Whibley	17	2	164
Robin Money	30	4	19
Bob Barker	44	29	131
John Duggan	35	23	92
Graham Horner	4	2	8
Peter Nicholls	8	2	8
Ted Edwards	4	1	4
Brian Hall	9	3	12
Mike Yandle	43	8	32
Alan Old	5	-	16
Gary Weinberg	6	3	12
Cliff Hillicker	2	-	3
John Ingleby	23	3	200
David Bird	2	-	-
Bleddyn Jones	42	7	28
John Allen	42	3	12
Dave Truman	2	-	-
Roger Grove	19	-	-
Mike Mortimer	35	3	12
Mark Churchward	2	1	4
Phil Vesty	25	-	-
Ray French	7	-	-
Andy Matthews	2	-	-
Peter Wheeler	37	12	58
David Pickering	9	-	-
Eric Bann	37	9	41
Bob Rowell	40	1	4
Dave Shaw	3	1	4
Bob Watson	9	1	4
Chris Baynes	29	9	??
David Forfar	32	1	8
Graham Willars	34	8	32
Garry Adey	35	8	32
David Matthews	14	1	4
Paul Ringer	6	2	8

1 game: Bob Beason P(2), Roy French H(41)[1T-4], Graham Jackson W(18), Guy Millar SH(8), Bob Williams W(32), Jeff Young W(11)[1T-4]

NO	DATE		OPPONENTS	V	RES	FOR					AGAINST					SCORERS
						G	T	D	P	PTS	G	T	D	P	PTS	
1	Sep	1	Bedford	A	Lost	2	-	-	1	15	4	2	-	1	35	Duggan(T) Ingleby(2C,P) Adey(T)
2		5	NOTTINGHAM	H	Won	-	-	-	4	12	-	-	-	3	9	Ingleby(4P)
3		8	BATH	H	Won	1	1	-	2	16	-	-	-	1	3	Ingleby(C,2P) Barker(T) B.Jones(T)
4		11	FIJI ISLANDS	H	Won	1	1	-	4	22	1	2	-	1	17	Barker(T) Ingleby(C,4P) Wheeler(T)
5		15	Liverpool	A	Won	2	1	-	1	19	-	-	-	1	3	Nicholls(T) Ingleby(2C,P) B.Jones(T) Adey(T)
6		22	Harlequins	A	Won	3	3	-	1	33	-	-	-	1	3	Nicholls(T) Ingleby(T,3C,P) B.Jones(T) Mortimer(T) Forfar(T) Adey(T)
7		29	Saracens	A	Won	1	1	-	2	16	-	1	-	2	10	Ingleby(C,P) Hall(2T) Old(P)
8	Oct	3	RANDWICK	H	Won	1	-	1	2	15	1	1	-	-	10	Money(D) Ingleby(C) B.Jones(T) Wheeler(2P)
9		6	COVENTRY	H	Lost	1	1	1	1	16	2	1	-	2	22	Ingleby(C,P) Old(T,D) Wheeler(T)
10		13	Richmond	A	Won	1	1	1	1	16	-	-	-	-	0	Duggan(T) Hall(D) Ingleby(C,P) Adey(T)
11		20	Northampton	A	Lost	-	-	-	1	7	3	2	-	1	26	Ingleby(P) Hall(T)
12		24	Oxford University	A	Drew	-	4	-	-	16	1	1	-	2	16	Duggan(T) Holley(T) Barker(T) Wheeler(T)
13		27	SWANSEA	H	Drew	1	-	-	5	21	-	3	-	3	21	Ingleby(C,5P) B.Jones(T)
14	Nov	3	GLOUCESTER	H	Lost	-	-	-	2	6	-	2	-	7	29	Ingleby(2P)
15		6	Northampton (RFU1)	A	Lost	-	-	-	2	6	1	1	-	4	22	Ingleby(2P)
16		10	Cambridge University	A	Won	3	-	-	2	24	1	-	-	-	6	Ingleby(3C,2P) Wheeler(T) Adey(2T)
17		17	FYLDE	H	Won	3	3	-	1	33	-	1	-	2	10	Nicholls(T) Ingleby(3C,P) Hall(T) B.Jones(T) Allen(T) Bann(T) Forfar(T)
18		24	MOSELEY	H	Lost	-	1	-	3	13	-	3	-	4	24	Duggan(T) Ingleby(3P)
	Dec	1	Waterloo	A		Cancelled Frost										
19		8	Blackheath	A	Won	1	1	-	2	16	1	-	-	-	6	Old(C,2P) Wheeler(T) Bann(T)
20		15	BRISTOL	H	Won	2	2	-	-	20	-	-	-	1	3	Duggan(T) Old(2C) Barker(2T) Allen(T)
21		22	London Welsh	A	Won	2	-	-	2	18	2	-	-	-	12	Money(T) Old(2C,2P) Adey(T)
22		27	BARBARIANS	H	Lost	-	1	-	1	7	2	1	-	-	16	Duggan(T) Old(P)
23		29	HEADINGLEY	H	Won	2	1	-	2	22	-	3	-	1	15	Money(T) Ingleby(T,2C,2P) Marshall(T)
24	Jan	5	Bath	A	Lost	-	-	-	1	3	1	2	-	2	20	Barker(P)
25		12	Gloucester	A	Lost	1	1	-	-	10	1	3	1	2	27	Wheeler(C) Marshall(2T)
26		19	BEDFORD	H	Won	1	2	-	2	20	-	-	-	2	6	Reeve(T) Barker(C,2P) Needham(T) Bann(T)
27		26	Rosslyn Park	A	Lost	-	-	-	1	3	1	3	-	-	18	Old(P)
		30	ROYAL NAVY	H	Cancelled											
28	Feb	2	LONDON SCOTTISH	H	Won	-	-	-	5	15	-	-	-	3	9	Barker(5P)
		9	Newport	A		Cancelled Waterloggd										
29		16	Wasps	A	Lost	-	-	-	-	0	1	1	-	1	13	
		20	Moseley	A		Cancelled Floodl.ban										
30		23	NORTHAMPTON	H	Won	1	-	-	3	15	-	-	-	3	9	Old(T,C,3P)
31	Mar	2	HARLEQUINS	H	Lost	1	-	-	1	9	1	1	-	1	13	Barker(C,P) Horner(T)
32		9	Coventry	A	Won	1	6	1	1	36	2	1	-	-	16	Hall(2T) Barker(2T,D) Old(T,P) Wheeler(T,C) Willars(T)
		12	LOUGHBOROUGH COLLEGE	H		Cancelled										
33		15	ROYAL AIR FORCE	H	Lost	-	1	-	1	7	1	-	1	1	12	Barker(P) Needham(T)
34		20	Rugby	A	Drew	1	-	-	2	12	1	-	-	2	12	Hall(T) Old(C,2P)
35		23	Sale	A	Lost	-	2	-	3	17	1	1	1	4	25	Nicholls(2T) Old(3P)
36		26	LOUGHBOROUGH COLLEGE	H	Won	2	3	-	2	30	1	-	-	1	9	Money(T) Barker(T,2C,2P) Allen(2T) P.Ringer(T)
37		30	Llanelli	A	Won	-	2	-	1	11	-	1	-	2	10	Barker(P) B.Jones(T) F.Jones(T)
38	Apr	6	BIRKENHEAD PARK	H	Won	2	3	-	1	27	-	1	1	3	16	Reeve(T) Wheeler(2C,P) Bann(2T) Adey(2T)
39		13	Middlesbrough	A	Won	1	2	-	1	17	-	1	-	-	4	Old(P) Hall(T) Barker(2T) Wheeler(C)
40		15	Gosforth	A	Lost	2	-	-	2	18	3	1	-	2	28	Barker(T) Old(2C,2P) Joyce(T)
41		16	Harrogate	A	Won	6	5	-	-	56	-	1	-	2	10	Money(T) Duggan(3T) Thomas(2T) Reeve(T) B.Jones(T) Mortimer(T) Rowell(T) Joyce(T) Wheeler(6C)
42		20	Bristol	A	Lost	-	2	-	-	8	1	5	-	1	29	Hall(T) Reeve(T)
43		27	NUNEATON	H	Won	3	3	-	2	36	-	-	-	1	3	Duggan(2T) Barker(T) Wheeler(3C,2P) Mortimer(T) Marshall(T) Penalty Try

INDIVIDUAL APPEARANCES 1973-1974

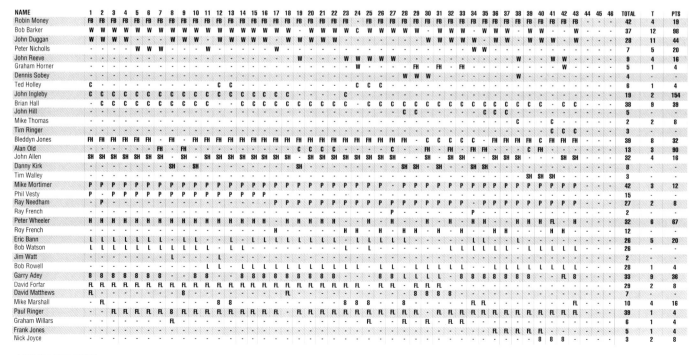

1 game: Steve Solomons FB(24)

LEICESTER FOOTBALL CLUB 1972-73
Back: A.S. Thorpe (Hon.Tres), J.D. Day (Hon.Sec), M.J. Duggan, G. Horner, D.J. Forfar, C.J. Baynes, R. Watson, P.N. Vesty,
M.R. Mortimer, G.J. Adey, D.J. Matthews, R.E. Rowell, J.T.W. Berry (President), H.V. White (Coach), H.W. Sibson (Team Hon.Sec).
Middle: J.A. Allen, M.J. Yandle, G.G. Willars (Capt), P.J. Wheeler, R.S. Money.
Front: B.P. Hall, N. Edwards, B. Jones, R.G. Barker.

LEICESTER FOOTBALL CLUB 1973-74
Back: H.V. White (Coach), H.W. Sibson (Team Hon.Sec), M.J. Duggan, R. Watson, G.J. Adey, M.R. Mortimer, D.J. Forfar,
M. Marshall, J.A. Allen, J.T.W. Berry (President), J.D. Day (Hon.Sec).
Middle: R.E. Needham, B. Jones, R.S. Money, P.J. Wheeler (Capt), R.G. Barker, R.E. Rowell, T. Ringer.
Front: P. Ringer, B.P. Hall.

NO	DATE	OPPONENTS	V	RES	FOR G	FOR T	FOR D	FOR P	FOR PTS	AGAINST G	AGAINST T	AGAINST D	AGAINST P	AGAINST PTS	SCORERS
1	Sep 7	BEDFORD	H	Won	1	1	-	3	19	1	-	-	2	12	Wheeler(T,C,3P) P.Ringer(T)
2	14	Bath	A	Lost	1	-	-	1	9	1	-	1	2	15	Hall(T) Wheeler(C,P)
3	21	LIVERPOOL	H	Won	3	4	1	-	37	-	-	-	2	6	Money(D) B.Jones(T) Wheeler(2T,3C) Watson(3T) Adey(T)
4	25	Nottingham	A	Won	-	1	1	1	10	-	-	-	1	3	Duggan(T) Allen(D) Wheeler(P)
5	28	Harlequins	A	Lost	-	1	-	2	10	3	2	-	2	32	Wheeler(2P) Mortimer(T)
6	Oct 2	Nuneaton	A	Won	1	2	-	4	26	-	1	-	2	10	Kirk(T) Wheeler(C,4P) Marshall(T) Forfar(T)
7	5	Coventry	A	Lost	-	-	-	1	3	1	1	1	-	13	Wheeler(P)
8	12	RICHMOND	H	Lost	-	-	-	3	9	1	1	-	2	16	Wheeler(3P)
9	19	NORTHAMPTON	H	Drew	1	1	-	1	13	-	1	-	3	13	Wheeler(C,P) Adey(T) Willars(T)
10	23	OXFORD UNIVERSITY	H	Won	1	2	-	2	20	-	1	1	2	13	Duggan(T) Reeve(T) Wheeler(C,2P) Willars(T)
11	26	Swansea	A	Lost	-	1	-	1	7	1	-	-	1	9	Allen(P) Forfar(T)
12	Nov 2	Gloucester	A	Lost	-	1	-	1	7	1	-	1	5	24	Wheeler(P) Adey(T)
13	9	CAMBRIDGE UNIVERSITY	H	Won	1	1	-	2	16	1	1	-	-	10	Hill(T) Allen(C,2P) Adey(T)
14	16	Newport	A	Lost	1	-	-	1	9	2	3	-	-	24	Duggan(T) Wheeler(C,P)
15	23	MOSELEY	H	Lost	-	1	-	-	4	2	1	1	1	22	Reeve(T)
16	29	SARACENS	H	Won	1	1	-	-	10	1	-	-	-	6	Holley(T) Hall(C) Adey(T)
17	Dec 7	WATERLOO	H	Won	1	3	-	1	21	1	-	-	1	9	Reeve(2T) B.Jones(2T) Wheeler(C,P)
18	14	BLACKHEATH	H	Lost	1	1	-	1	13	1	4	-	1	25	Duggan(2T) Allen(C,P)
19	21	Bristol	A	Lost	-	1	-	2	10	2	-	-	1	15	Money(T) Barker(2P)
20	27	BARBARIANS	H	Lost	-	1	-	-	4	2	7	-	1	43	Duggan(T)
21	28	Headingley	A	Lost	-	-	-	1	3	1	3	-	2	24	Wheeler(P)
22	Jan 4	BATH	H	Won	1	2	-	-	14	-	-	-	1	3	Duggan(T) Hall(C) Reeve(T) Ray.French(T)
23	8	ROYAL NAVY	H	Won	-	3	-	3	21	-	1	-	1	7	Duggan(T) Hall(T) Reeve(T) Wheeler(3P)
24	11	GLOUCESTER	H	Won	1	-	-	4	18	-	1	-	-	4	Duggan(T) Wheeler(C,4P)
25	18	Bedford	A	Lost	2	1	-	1	19	1	2	2	1	23	Duggan(2T) Barker(T,2C,P)
26	25	ROSSLYN PARK	H	Won	1	-	-	2	12	1	-	-	-	6	Burwell(T) Wheeler(C,2P)
	Feb 1	London Scottish	A		Cancelled Waterloggd										
27	8	NEWPORT	H	Lost	-	-	-	2	6	-	1	-	2	10	Wheeler(2P)
28	15	WASPS	H	Lost	1	1	-	4	22	1	1	-	5	25	Barker(T,C,4P) Burwell(T)
29	19	MOSELEY	H	Lost	1	-	-	1	9	1	3	-	3	27	Barker(T,C,P)
30	22	Northampton	A	Lost	-	-	-	2	6	1	2	-	2	20	Barker(2P)
31	Mar 1	HARLEQUINS	H	Lost	1	-	-	1	9	2	-	-	1	15	Duggan(T) Barker(C,P)
32	8	NEATH	H	Won	1	1	-	3	19	-	-	-	2	6	Barker(T,C,3P) Kempin(T)
	11	LOUGHBOROUGH COLLEGE	H		Cancelled Waterloggd										
	14	ROYAL AIR FORCE	H		Cancelled Waterloggd										
33	19	RUGBY	H	Won	3	1	-	1	25	-	-	-	-	0	Duggan(T) Bracewell(T) Barker(T,3C,P) Forfar(T)
34	22	Sale	A	Lost	-	-	-	-	0	2	2	-	1	23	
35	29	ORRELL	H	Won	1	1	-	1	13	-	-	-	3	9	Bracewell(T) Barker(C,P) F.Jones(T)
36	31	GOSFORTH	H	Won	2	-	2	-	18	2	-	-	1	15	Money(2D) Bracewell(T) Barker(T,C) Allen(C)
37	Apr 5	Birkenhead Park	A	Won	2	1	-	1	19	1	1	-	1	13	Barker(2C,P) Bracewell(2T) Allen(T)
38	12	BRISTOL	H	Lost	-	1	-	2	10	-	-	-	4	12	Nicholls(T) Barker(P) Wheeler(P)
39	19	Fylde	A	Won	1	3	-	1	21	2	1	-	1	19	Money(T) Bracewell(T) Barker(T) B.Jones(T) Wheeler(C,P)
40	26	MIDDLESBROUGH	H	Won	-	3	-	3	21	1	2	-	1	17	Barker(T) Wheeler(T,3P) Adey(T)

INDIVIDUAL APPEARANCES 1974-1975

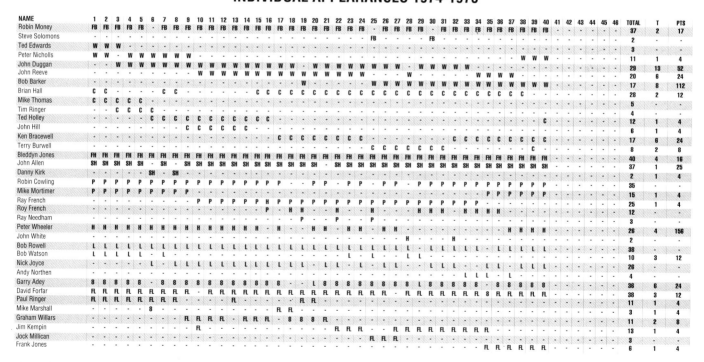

NAME	1	2	3	4	5	6	7	8	9	10	11	12	13	14	15	16	17	18	19	20	21	22	23	24	25	26	27	28	29	30	31	32	33	34	35	36	37	38	39	40	41	42	43	44	45	46	TOTAL	T	PTS
Robin Money	FB	FB	FB	FB	FB	-	FB	FB	FB	FB	FB	FB	FB	FB	FB	FB	FB	FB	FB	FB	FB	FB	FB	FB	-	FB	FB	FB	FB	-	FB	FB	FB	FB	FB	FB	FB	FB	FB	FB	-	-	-	-	-	-	37	2	17
Steve Solomons	-	-	-	-	-	-	-	-	-	-	-	-	-	-	-	-	-	-	-	-	-	-	-	-	FB	-	-	-	-	FB	-	-	-	-	-	-	-	-	-	-	-	-	-	-	-	-	2	-	-
Ted Edwards	W	W	W	-	-	-	-	-	-	-	-	-	-	-	-	-	-	-	-	-	-	-	-	-	-	-	-	-	-	-	-	-	-	-	-	-	-	-	-	-	-	-	-	-	-	-	3	-	-
Peter Nicholls	W	W	-	W	W	W	W	W	W	-	-	-	-	-	-	-	-	-	-	-	-	-	-	-	-	-	-	-	-	-	-	-	-	-	-	-	-	W	W	W	-	-	-	-	-	-	11	1	4
John Duggan	-	-	W	W	W	W	W	W	W	W	W	W	W	W	W	W	W	W	-	W	W	W	W	W	W	W	W	-	W	W	W	W	W	-	-	-	-	-	-	-	-	-	-	-	-	-	29	13	52
John Reeve	-	-	-	-	-	-	-	-	-	W	W	W	W	W	W	W	W	W	W	W	W	W	W	W	-	-	-	W	-	-	-	-	-	W	W	W	W	-	-	-	-	-	-	-	-	-	20	6	24
Bob Barker	-	-	-	-	-	-	-	-	-	-	-	-	-	-	-	-	-	-	W	-	-	-	-	-	W	W	W	W	W	W	W	W	W	W	W	W	W	W	W	W	-	-	-	-	-	-	17	8	112
Brian Hall	C	C	-	-	-	-	C	C	-	-	-	-	-	-	C	C	C	C	C	C	C	C	C	C	C	C	C	C	C	C	C	C	C	C	C	C	C	C	-	-	-	-	-	-	-	-	28	2	12
Mike Thomas	C	C	C	C	C	-	-	-	-	-	-	-	-	-	-	-	-	-	-	-	-	-	-	-	-	-	-	-	-	-	-	-	-	-	-	-	-	-	-	-	-	-	-	-	-	-	5	-	-
Tim Ringer	-	-	C	C	C	C	-	-	-	-	-	-	-	-	-	-	-	-	-	-	-	-	-	-	-	-	-	-	-	-	-	-	-	-	-	-	-	-	-	-	-	-	-	-	-	-	4	-	-
Ted Holley	-	-	-	-	-	C	C	C	C	C	C	C	C	C	C	C	-	-	-	-	-	-	-	-	-	-	-	-	-	-	-	-	-	-	-	-	-	-	-	C	-	-	-	-	-	-	12	1	4
John Hill	-	-	-	-	-	-	-	-	C	C	C	C	C	C	-	-	-	-	-	-	-	-	-	-	-	-	-	-	-	-	-	-	-	-	-	-	-	-	-	-	-	-	-	-	-	-	6	1	4
Ken Bracewell	-	-	-	-	-	-	-	-	-	-	-	-	-	-	-	-	C	C	C	C	C	C	C	C	-	-	-	-	-	-	-	C	C	C	C	C	C	C	C	C	-	-	-	-	-	-	17	6	24
Terry Burwell	-	-	-	-	-	-	-	-	-	-	-	-	-	-	-	-	-	-	-	-	-	-	-	-	C	C	C	C	C	C	C	-	-	-	-	-	-	-	C	-	-	-	-	-	-	-	8	2	8
Bleddyn Jones	FH	FH	FH	FH	FH	FH	FH	FH	FH	FH	FH	FH	FH	FH	FH	FH	FH	FH	FH	FH	FH	FH	FH	FH	FH	FH	FH	FH	FH	FH	FH	FH	FH	FH	FH	FH	FH	FH	FH	FH	-	-	-	-	-	-	40	4	16
John Allen	SH	SH	SH	SH	SH	-	SH	-	SH	SH	SH	SH	SH	SH	SH	SH	SH	SH	SH	SH	-	SH	SH	SH	SH	SH	SH	SH	SH	SH	SH	SH	SH	SH	SH	SH	SH	SH	SH	SH	-	-	-	-	-	-	37	1	25
Danny Kirk	-	-	-	-	-	SH	-	SH	-	-	-	-	-	-	-	-	-	-	-	-	-	-	-	-	-	-	-	-	-	-	-	-	-	-	-	-	-	-	-	-	-	-	-	-	-	-	2	1	4
Robin Cowling	P	P	P	P	P	P	P	P	P	P	P	P	P	P	P	P	P	-	-	P	P	-	P	P	-	P	P	-	P	P	P	P	P	P	P	P	P	P	P	P	-	-	-	-	-	-	35	-	-
Mike Mortimer	P	P	P	P	P	P	P	P	P	-	-	-	-	-	-	-	-	-	-	-	-	-	-	-	-	-	-	-	-	-	-	-	-	-	P	P	P	P	P	P	-	-	-	-	-	-	15	1	4
Ray French	-	-	-	-	-	-	-	-	-	P	P	P	P	P	P	H	P	P	P	P	P	P	P	P	P	P	P	P	P	P	P	P	P	P	-	-	-	-	-	-	-	-	-	-	-	-	25	1	4
Roy French	-	-	-	-	-	-	-	-	-	-	-	-	-	-	-	P	-	H	H	-	-	H	-	-	H	-	-	-	H	H	H	-	H	H	H	H	-	-	-	-	-	-	-	-	-	-	12	-	-
Ray Needham	-	-	-	-	-	-	-	-	-	-	-	-	-	-	-	-	-	-	P	-	-	P	-	-	P	-	-	-	-	-	-	-	-	-	-	-	-	-	-	-	-	-	-	-	-	-	3	-	-
Peter Wheeler	H	H	H	H	H	H	H	H	H	H	H	H	H	H	H	-	H	-	-	H	H	-	H	H	-	H	H	-	-	-	-	-	-	-	-	-	H	H	H	H	-	-	-	-	-	-	26	4	156
John White	-	-	-	-	-	-	-	-	-	-	-	-	-	-	-	-	-	-	-	-	-	-	-	-	-	-	-	H	-	-	-	H	-	-	-	-	-	-	-	-	-	-	-	-	-	-	2	-	-
Bob Rowell	L	L	L	L	L	L	L	L	L	L	L	L	L	L	L	L	L	L	L	L	L	L	L	L	L	L	L	L	-	L	L	L	L	L	-	L	L	L	L	L	-	-	-	-	-	-	38	-	-
Bob Watson	L	L	L	L	L	-	L	-	-	-	-	-	-	-	-	-	-	-	-	-	-	-	L	-	L	-	-	L	L	-	-	-	-	-	-	-	-	-	-	-	-	-	-	-	-	-	10	3	12
Nick Joyce	-	-	-	-	-	L	-	L	L	L	L	L	L	L	L	L	L	L	L	-	L	L	-	L	-	L	L	-	-	L	L	L	-	-	L	L	-	L	L	L	-	-	-	-	-	-	26	-	-
Andy Northen	-	-	-	-	-	-	-	-	-	-	-	-	-	-	-	-	-	-	-	-	-	-	-	-	-	-	-	-	-	-	-	-	L	L	L	-	L	-	-	-	-	-	-	-	-	-	4	-	-
Garry Adey	8	8	8	8	8	-	8	8	8	8	8	8	8	8	8	8	8	-	-	L	8	8	8	8	8	8	8	8	L	8	8	8	8	8	-	8	8	8	8	8	-	-	-	-	-	-	36	6	24
David Forfar	FL	FL	FL	FL	FL	FL	FL	FL	FL	-	FL	FL	FL	FL	FL	FL	FL	FL	FL	FL	FL	FL	FL	FL	FL	FL	-	FL	FL	FL	FL	FL	FL	FL	8	FL	FL	FL	FL	FL	-	-	-	-	-	-	38	3	12
Paul Ringer	FL	FL	FL	FL	FL	FL	FL	FL	-	-	-	-	FL	-	-	-	-	-	FL	FL	-	-	-	-	-	-	-	-	-	-	-	-	-	-	-	-	-	-	-	-	-	-	-	-	-	-	11	1	4
Mike Marshall	-	-	-	-	-	8	-	-	-	-	-	-	-	-	-	-	FL	FL	-	-	-	-	-	-	-	-	-	-	-	-	-	-	-	-	-	-	-	-	-	-	-	-	-	-	-	-	3	1	4
Graham Willars	-	-	-	-	-	-	-	-	FL	FL	FL	FL	-	FL	FL	FL	-	8	8	8	FL	-	-	-	-	-	-	-	-	-	-	-	-	-	-	-	-	-	-	-	-	-	-	-	-	-	11	2	8
Jim Kempin	-	-	-	-	-	-	-	-	-	FL	-	-	-	-	-	-	-	-	-	-	-	FL	FL	FL	-	-	FL	FL	FL	FL	FL	FL	FL	FL	FL	-	-	-	-	-	-	-	-	-	-	-	13	1	4
Jock Millican	-	-	-	-	-	-	-	-	-	-	-	-	-	-	-	-	-	-	-	-	-	-	-	-	FL	FL	FL	-	-	-	-	-	-	-	-	-	-	-	-	-	-	-	-	-	-	-	3	-	-
Frank Jones	-	-	-	-	-	-	-	-	-	-	-	-	-	-	-	-	-	-	-	-	-	-	-	-	-	-	-	-	-	-	-	-	-	-	FL	FL	FL	FL	FL	FL	-	-	-	-	-	-	6	1	4

1 game: Angus Collington 8(29), John Ingleby FB(6), Jez Krych P(18), Charlie Tassell P(28), Tim Walley SH(21)

1975-1976

NO	DATE		OPPONENTS	V	RES	FOR G	FOR T	FOR D	FOR P	FOR PTS	AGAINST G	AGAINST T	AGAINST D	AGAINST P	AGAINST PTS	SCORERS
1	Sep	6	Bedford	A	Lost	-	-	-	4	12	3	-	-	2	24	Flint(4P)
2		10	NUNEATON	H	Won	4	4	-	2	46	-	-	-	1	3	Denner(P) Duggan(T) Barker(T) Flint(T,4C,P) Kenney(2T) Mortimer(T) Kempin(2T)
3		13	BATH	H	Won	5	1	-	1	37	-	1	-	1	7	Duggan(2T) Barker(T) Flint(5C,P) Allen(T) Wheeler(T) Bann(T)
4		20	Mountain Ash	A	Won	2	1	-	2	22	-	1	-	5	19	Bracewell(T) Dodge(T) Flint(2C,2P) Bann(T)
5		27	Harlequins	A	Lost	-	2	-	3	17	5	3	-	1	45	Barker(T) Flint(3P) Wheeler(T)
6	Oct	4	COVENTRY	H	Lost	2	-	-	2	18	1	4	1	2	31	Hall(T) Dodge(2C) Barker(T) Flint(2P)
7		11	Richmond	A	Lost	-	2	-	2	14	1	2	1	1	20	Duggan(T) Flint(2P) Wheeler(T)
8		18	Northampton	A	Lost	1	-	-	2	12	2	1	1	3	28	Flint(C,2P) Wheeler(T)
9		22	Oxford University	A	Lost	1	2	-	1	17	4	3	-	1	39	Barker(T) Flint(C,P) Walley(T) Mortimer(T)
10		25	SWANSEA	H	Lost	-	-	-	2	6	2	1	-	3	25	Dodge(2P)
11	Nov	1	GLOUCESTER	H	Lost	1	-	-	2	12	1	1	-	4	22	Hall(T) Dodge(P) Barker(C,P)
12		8	Cambridge University	A	Lost	-	-	-	1	3	2	4	-	-	28	Dodge(P)
13		15	EASTERN SUBURBS	H	Won	2	1	-	2	22	-	3	-	1	15	Hall(T) Barker(T,2C,2P) Marshall(T)
14		22	Liverpool (JPC1)	A	Lost	-	1	-	1	7	-	1	-	2	10	Dodge(P) Barker(T)
15		29	SARACENS	H	Won	6	1	-	-	40	-	1	-	-	4	Duggan(T) Dodge(T,2C) Barker(3T,4C) B.Jones(T) Forfar(T)
16	Dec	6	Waterloo	A	Lost	-	1	-	1	7	-	1	-	3	13	Duggan(T) Barker(P)
17		10	NOTTINGHAM	H	Won	-	1	-	2	10	-	-	-	2	6	Dodge(T,P) Barker(P)
18		13	Blackheath	A	Won	1	1	1	-	13	-	2	-	-	8	Duggan(T) Hall(D) Barker(C) Kenney(T)
19		20	BRISTOL	H	Won	-	2	-	3	17	1	1	-	2	16	Rose(3P) Dodge(T) Duggan(T)
20		27	BARBARIANS	H	Lost	-	2	-	1	11	2	2	-	-	20	Rose(P) Dodge(T) Rowell(T)
21	Jan	2	Bath	A	Won	2	-	-	-	12	-	-	-	1	3	Denner(2C) Dodge(T) Forfar(T)
22		10	Gloucester	A	Won	1	-	-	1	9	-	1	-	-	4	Denner(C,P) Joyce(T)
23		16	BEDFORD	H	Won	2	1	-	4	28	2	-	1	1	18	Rose(2C,4P) Duggan(T) Dodge(T) Kempin(T)
24		24	Rosslyn Park	A	Lost	-	1	-	1	7	1	2	1	3	26	Barker(T,P)
		31	London Welsh	A		Cancelled										
	Feb	4	ROYAL NAVY	H		Cancelled										
25		7	LONDON SCOTTISH	H	Won	2	2	-	1	23	-	1	-	-	4	Duggan(2T) Barker(2C,P) Wheeler(T) Joyce(T)
26		14	Newport	A	Lost	1	1	-	2	16	5	2	-	-	38	Barker(C,2P) Rowell(T) Kempin(T)
27		18	HEADINGLEY	H	Won	3	-	-	2	24	1	-	-	-	6	Dodge(2T) Barker(T,3C,2P)
28		21	Wasps	A	Drew	-	1	-	2	10	-	1	-	2	10	Barker(2P) Marshall(T)
29		24	NOTTINGHAM (MCCP)	H	Won	4	1	1	-	31	-	-	-	3	9	Rose(4C,D) Barker(T) Kenney(T) Ray.French(T) Millican(2T)
30		28	NORTHAMPTON	H	Won	-	3	1	3	24	1	-	-	2	12	Rose(T,3P) Duggan(T) Barker(D) Kenney(T)
31	Mar	2	MOSELEY	H	Lost	-	1	-	1	7	1	1	-	1	13	Barker(P) White(T)
32		5	HARLEQUINS	H	Lost	1	-	-	-	6	1	4	-	2	28	Barker(C) Collington(T)
33		9	WESTLEIGH (JPCP)	H	Won	-	1	1	4	19	-	-	1	4	15	Rose(D,4P) Cowling(T)
34		13	Coventry	A	Lost	-	1	-	-	4	2	1	-	2	22	Barker(T)
35		16	ROYAL AIR FORCE	H	Won	1	5	-	1	29	-	1	-	1	7	Rose(P) Hall(T) Barker(2T,C) White(T) Collington(T) Millican(T)
36		20	C.A.S.G. Paris	A	Won	1	2	2	-	20	-	2	-	-	8	Money(2D) Holley(T) Reeve(T) B.Jones(C) Willars(T)
		23	LOUGHBOROUGH COLLEGE	H		Cancelled										
37		27	SALE	H	Lost	-	4	-	-	16	3	-	-	-	18	Reeve(2T) Barker(T) Kempin(T)
38		30	Burton-on-Trent	A	Won	2	3	-	2	30	2	-	-	1	15	Reeve(T) Barker(2T,2C,2P) Millican(T) Collington(T)
39	Apr	3	BIRKENHEAD PARK	H	Won	2	-	-	2	18	1	2	-	-	14	Hall(T) Barker(T,2C,2P)
40		10	Kettering (JPCP)	A	Won	-	2	-	2	14	-	-	-	2	6	Reeve(T) Barker(2P) Ray.French(T)
41		17	Middlesbrough	A	Lost	1	-	-	1	9	1	1	-	3	19	Dodge(T,C,P)
42		19	Gosforth	A	Lost	1	-	-	1	9	1	3	-	3	27	Dodge(C) Barker(T,P)
43		20	Harrogate	A	Won	1	2	-	1	17	-	-	-	1	3	Duggan(T) Barker(C,P) Walley(T) Roy.French(T)
44		24	FYLDE	H	Won	1	1	-	4	22	-	1	-	3	13	Bracewell(T) Barker(C,P) Dodge(3P) Kempin(T)
45	May	1	Rugby	A	Lost	-	2	-	1	11	-	-	-	4	12	Hall(T) Barker(P) Adey(T)

INDIVIDUAL APPEARANCES 1975-1976

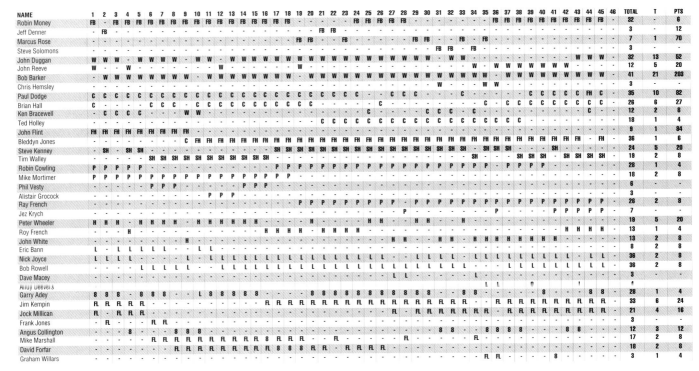

NAME	1	2	3	4	5	6	7	8	9	10	11	12	13	14	15	16	17	18	19	20	21	22	23	24	25	26	27	28	29	30	31	32	33	34	35	36	37	38	39	40	41	42	43	44	45	46	TOTAL	T	PTS
Robin Money	FB	-	FB	FB	FB	FB	FB	FB	FB	FB	FB	FB	FB	FB	FB	FB	FB	FB	-	-	-	-	-	FB	FB	FB	FB	FB	-	-	-	-	-	-	-	FB	FB	FB	FB	FB	FB	FB	FB	FB	FB	-	32	-	6
Jeff Denner	-	FB	-	-	-	-	-	-	-	-	-	-	-	-	-	-	-	-	-	-	FB	FB	-	-	-	-	-	-	-	-	-	-	-	-	-	-	-	-	-	-	-	-	-	-	-	-	3	-	12
Marcus Rose	-	-	-	-	-	-	-	-	-	-	-	-	-	-	-	-	-	-	FB	FB	-	-	FB	-	-	-	-	-	FB	FB	-	-	FB	-	FB	-	-	-	-	-	-	-	-	-	-	-	7	1	70
Steve Solomons	-	-	-	-	-	-	-	-	-	-	-	-	-	-	-	-	-	-	-	-	-	-	-	-	-	-	-	-	-	-	FB	FB	-	FB	-	-	-	-	-	-	-	-	-	-	-	-	3	-	-
John Duggan	W	W	W	-	W	W	W	W	-	W	W	-	W	W	W	W	W	W	W	W	W	W	W	W	W	W	W	W	W	W	-	W	W	-	-	-	-	-	-	-	-	-	W	W	W	-	32	13	52
John Reeve	W	-	-	W	-	-	-	-	-	-	-	W	-	-	-	-	-	-	W	-	-	-	-	-	-	-	-	-	-	-	-	-	-	W	-	W	W	W	W	W	W	W	-	-	-	-	12	5	20
Bob Barker	-	W	W	W	W	W	W	W	W	-	W	W	W	W	W	W	W	W	-	W	W	W	W	W	W	W	W	W	W	W	W	W	W	W	W	-	W	W	W	W	W	W	W	W	W	-	41	21	203
Chris Hemsley	-	-	-	-	-	-	-	-	-	-	-	-	-	-	-	-	-	-	-	-	-	-	-	-	-	-	-	-	-	-	W	-	-	-	W	W	-	-	-	-	-	-	-	-	-	-	3	-	-
Paul Dodge	C	C	C	C	C	C	C	C	C	C	C	C	C	C	C	C	C	C	C	C	C	C	C	C	-	-	C	C	C	-	-	-	C	-	-	-	-	-	C	C	C	C	C	FH	C	-	35	10	82
Brian Hall	C	-	-	-	-	C	C	C	-	C	C	C	C	C	C	C	C	C	C	C	-	-	-	-	-	C	-	-	-	-	-	-	-	-	C	-	C	C	C	C	C	C	C	C	C	-	26	6	27
Ken Bracewell	-	C	C	C	C	-	-	-	W	W	-	-	-	-	-	-	-	-	-	-	-	-	-	-	C	-	-	-	-	C	C	C	-	C	-	-	-	-	-	-	-	-	-	C	-	-	12	2	8
Ted Holley	-	-	-	-	-	-	-	-	-	-	-	-	-	-	-	-	-	-	-	-	C	C	C	C	C	C	C	C	C	C	C	C	C	C	C	C	C	C	-	-	-	-	-	-	-	-	18	1	4
John Flint	FH	FH	FH	FH	FH	FH	FH	FH	FH	-	-	-	-	-	-	-	-	-	-	-	-	-	-	-	-	-	-	-	-	-	-	-	-	-	-	-	-	-	-	-	-	-	-	-	-	-	9	1	84
Bleddyn Jones	-	-	-	-	-	-	-	-	C	FH	FH	FH	FH	FH	FH	FH	FH	FH	FH	FH	FH	FH	FH	FH	FH	FH	FH	FH	FH	FH	FH	FH	FH	FH	FH	FH	FH	FH	FH	FH	FH	FH	FH	-	FH	-	36	1	6
Steve Kenney	-	SH	-	SH	SH	-	-	-	-	-	-	-	-	-	-	-	SH	SH	SH	SH	SH	SH	SH	SH	SH	SH	SH	SH	SH	SH	SH	SH	SH	-	SH	SH	SH	-	-	-	SH	-	-	-	-	-	24	5	20
Tim Walley	-	-	-	-	-	SH	SH	SH	SH	SH	SH	SH	SH	SH	SH	SH	-	-	-	-	-	-	-	-	-	-	-	-	-	-	-	-	-	SH	-	-	-	SH	SH	SH	-	SH	SH	SH	SH	-	19	2	8
Robin Cowling	P	P	P	P	P	-	-	-	-	-	-	-	-	-	-	-	P	P	P	P	P	P	P	P	P	P	P	P	P	P	P	P	P	P	P	-	P	P	P	P	-	-	-	-	-	-	28	1	4
Mike Mortimer	P	P	P	P	P	P	P	P	P	P	P	P	P	P	P	P	P	P	-	-	-	-	-	-	-	-	-	-	-	-	-	-	-	-	-	-	-	-	-	-	-	-	-	-	-	-	18	2	8
Phil Vesty	-	-	-	-	-	P	P	P	-	-	-	-	-	P	P	P	-	-	-	-	-	-	-	-	-	-	-	-	-	-	-	-	-	-	-	-	-	-	-	-	-	-	-	-	-	-	6	-	-
Alistair Grocock	-	-	-	-	-	-	-	-	-	-	P	P	P	-	-	-	-	-	-	-	-	-	-	-	-	-	-	-	-	-	-	-	-	-	-	-	-	-	-	-	-	-	-	-	-	-	3	-	-
Ray French	-	-	-	-	-	-	-	-	-	-	-	-	-	-	-	-	-	-	P	P	P	P	P	P	P	P	P	P	-	P	P	P	P	P	P	P	P	P	P	P	P	P	P	P	P	-	26	2	8
Jez Krych	-	-	-	-	-	-	-	-	-	-	-	-	-	-	-	-	-	-	-	-	-	-	-	-	-	-	-	P	-	-	-	-	-	-	-	P	-	-	-	-	P	P	P	P	P	-	7	-	-
Peter Wheeler	H	H	H	-	H	H	H	H	-	H	H	H	H	H	H	-	-	-	-	H	-	-	-	-	H	H	-	-	H	H	-	-	H	-	-	-	-	-	-	-	-	-	-	-	-	-	19	5	20
Roy French	-	-	-	H	-	-	-	-	-	-	-	-	-	-	-	H	H	H	H	-	H	H	H	H	-	-	-	-	-	-	-	-	-	-	-	-	-	-	-	-	-	H	H	H	H	-	13	1	4
John White	-	-	-	-	-	-	-	-	H	-	-	-	-	-	-	-	-	-	-	-	-	-	-	-	-	-	H	H	-	-	H	H	-	H	H	H	H	H	H	H	H	-	-	-	-	-	13	2	8
Eric Bann	L	-	L	L	L	L	L	-	-	L	L	-	-	-	-	-	-	-	-	-	-	-	-	-	-	-	-	-	-	-	-	-	-	-	-	-	-	-	-	-	-	-	-	-	-	-	8	2	8
Nick Joyce	L	L	L	L	-	-	-	-	L	-	L	L	L	L	L	L	L	L	L	L	L	L	L	L	L	L	-	-	L	L	L	L	-	L	L	L	L	L	L	L	L	L	-	L	L	-	36	2	8
Bob Rowell	-	-	-	-	L	L	L	L	L	-	-	L	L	L	L	L	L	L	L	L	L	L	L	L	L	L	L	L	L	L	L	L	L	-	-	-	L	L	L	L	L	L	L	L	L	-	36	2	8
Dave Macey	-	-	-	-	-	-	-	-	-	-	-	-	-	-	-	-	-	-	-	-	-	-	-	-	-	-	L	L	-	-	-	-	-	L	-	-	-	-	-	-	-	-	-	-	-	-	3	-	-
Andy Beevers																																			L	L			[illegible]				[illegible]				[illegible]		
Garry Adey	8	8	8	-	8	8	8	-	-	L	8	8	8	8	8	-	-	-	-	8	8	8	8	8	8	8	8	8	8	8	-	-	8	8	-	-	-	-	-	8	-	-	-	8	8	-	28	1	4
Jim Kempin	FL	FL	FL	FL	FL	-	-	-	-	-	-	-	-	-	-	FL	FL	FL	FL	FL	FL	FL	FL	FL	FL	FL	FL	FL	FL	FL	FL	FL	FL	-	-	FL	FL	FL	FL	FL	FL	FL	FL	FL	FL	-	33	6	24
Jock Millican	FL	-	FL	FL	FL	-	-	-	-	-	-	-	-	-	-	-	-	-	-	-	-	-	-	-	-	-	FL	-	FL	FL	FL	FL	FL	FL	FL	-	FL	FL	FL	FL	FL	FL	FL	FL	FL	-	21	4	16
Frank Jones	-	FL	-	-	-	FL	FL	-	-	-	-	-	-	-	-	-	-	-	-	-	-	-	-	-	-	-	-	-	-	-	-	-	-	-	-	-	-	-	-	-	-	-	-	-	-	-	3	-	-
Angus Collington	-	-	-	8	-	-	-	8	8	8	-	-	-	-	-	-	-	-	-	-	-	-	-	-	-	-	-	-	-	-	8	8	-	-	8	8	8	8	-	-	-	8	8	-	-	-	12	3	12
Mike Marshall	-	-	-	-	-	FL	FL	FL	FL	FL	FL	FL	FL	FL	FL	8	FL	FL	FL	-	-	FL	-	-	-	-	-	FL	-	-	-	-	-	FL	-	-	-	-	-	-	-	-	-	-	-	-	17	2	8
David Forfar	-	-	-	-	-	-	-	FL	FL	FL	FL	FL	FL	FL	FL	FL	8	8	8	FL	FL	-	FL	FL	FL	FL	-	-	-	-	-	-	-	-	-	-	-	-	-	-	-	-	-	-	-	-	18	2	8
Graham Willars	-	-	-	-	-	-	-	-	-	-	-	-	-	-	-	-	-	-	-	-	-	-	-	-	-	-	-	-	-	-	-	-	-	-	FL	FL	-	-	-	-	8	-	-	-	-	-	3	1	4

2 games: John Allen SH(1,3)[1T-4], Ray Needham P(9,10), Andy Northen L(2,33)
1 game: Larry Parkes C(36), Bob Watson L(8)

LEICESTER FOOTBALL CLUB 1974-75
Back: R.J. Willcox (President), H.V. White (Coach), M.R. Mortimer, G.G. Willars, Roy French, Ray French, B.P. Hall, J. Reeve,
J.S. Kempin, J.A. Allen, R.J. Cowling, A.S. Thorpe (Hon.Tres), J.D. Day (Hon.Sec), H.W. Sibson (Team Hon.Sec).
Middle: G.J. Adey, R.S. Money, R.G. Barker, P.J. Wheeler (Capt), F. Jones, N.J. Joyce, R.E. Rowell.
Front: K. Bracewell, B. Jones, P. Nicholls, E.R. Holley, D.J. Forfar.

LEICESTER FOOTBALL CLUB 1975-76
Back: H.V. White (Coach), R.J. Willcox (President), M.R. Mortimer, B.P. Hall, G.J. Adey, J.G. Millican, N.J. Joyce, D.J. Forfar,
R.J. Cowling, J.S. Kempin, J.A. Allen (Hon.Tres), J.D. Day (Hon.Sec), H.W. Sibson (Team Hon.Sec).
Middle: M.J. Duggan, P.J. Wheeler, R.G. Barker, R.S. Money (Capt), R.E. Rowell, M. Marshall, P.W. Dodge.
Front: E.R. Holley, T.A. Walley, S. Kenney, B. Jones, Ray French.

NO	DATE		OPPONENTS	V	RES	FOR					AGAINST					SCORERS
						G	T	D	P	PTS	G	T	D	P	PTS	
1	Sep	1	SOLIHULL (MCCF)	H	Won	4	3	-	1	39	-	-	-	-	0	Rose(4C,P) Barker(T) Dodge(T) Hall(2T) Reeve(T) Wheeler(T) Kempin(T)
2		4	BEDFORD (MMT)	H	Won	4	1	-	2	34	1	1	-	1	13	Rose(4C,2P) Hall(T) Kenney(T) Rowell(T) Joyce(T) Kempin(T)
		8	Saracens	A		Cancelled Hard pitch										
3		11	Bath	A	Lost	1	1	-	-	10	1	1	1	2	19	Rose(C) Ray.French(T) Kempin(T)
4		18	MOUNTAIN ASH	H	Won	5	3	-	1	45	-	-	-	1	3	Rose(2T,5C,P) Reeve(T) Barker(3T) Adey(2T)
5		21	BIRMINGHAM (MMT)	H	Won	4	1	-	3	37	1	-	-	3	15	Rose(4C,3P) Duggan(T) Barker(T) Kenney(T) Wheeler(T) Joyce(T)
6		25	Harlequins	A	Won	1	2	-	3	23	-	1	-	-	4	Rose(C,3P) Dodge(T) Kenney(2T)
7	Oct	2	Coventry (MMT)	A	Lost	2	-	-	1	15	1	-	1	3	18	Rose(T,2C,P) Jones(T)
8		9	RICHMOND	H	Won	2	-	-	4	24	1	-	-	2	12	Holley(T) Barker(2C,4P) Kenney(T)
9		16	NORTHAMPTON (MMT)	H	Won	3	4	-	2	40	-	1	-	3	13	Duggan(T) Parkes(T) Barker(T,3C,2P) Kenney(T) Wheeler(2T) Ray.French(T)
10		20	OXFORD UNIVERSITY	H	Won	5	1	-	4	46	-	2	-	-	8	Hare(5C,4P) Dodge(T) Barker(T) Kenney(2T) Cowling(T) Beevers(T)
11		23	Swansea	A	Won	1	-	-	3	15	-	-	-	3	9	Hare(C,3P) Forfar(T)
12		30	Nottingham (MMT)	A	Won	1	1	-	3	19	1	-	-	-	6	Hare(C,3P) Barker(T) Wheeler(T)
13	Nov	6	Gloucester	A	Lost	1	-	-	2	12	1	2	-	-	14	Hare(C,2P) Duggan(T)
14		13	CAMBRIDGE UNIVERSITY	H	Won	4	-	1	2	33	-	-	-	-	6	Hare(T,4C,D,2P) Duggan(T) Barker(T) Kenney(T)
15		20	Wasps	A	Won	-	1	-	-	7	-	-	-	-	0	Hare(P) Duggan(T)
16		27	MOSELEY (MMT)	H	Lost	-	-	-	2	6	1	1	-	3	19	Hare(2P)
	Dec	4	Wakefield (JPC1)	A		Cancelled Snow										
		11	Wakefield (JPC1)	A		Cancelled Frost										
17		18	BRISTOL	H	Won	-	1	-	1	7	-	-	-	1	3	Rose(P) Dodge(T)
18		28	BARBARIANS	H	Won	1	-	-	2	12	-	2	-	-	8	Hare(C,2P) Dodge(T)
19	Jan	1	BATH	H	Won	2	2	-	-	20	-	1	-	-	4	Rose(2C) Duggan(T) Dodge(T) Hall(T) Kenney(T)
20		8	GLOUCESTER	H	Lost	1	1	-	-	10	2	1	1	2	25	Hare(C) Hall(T) White(T)
21		14	Bedford	A	Lost	-	-	-	-	0	1	3	-	-	18	
22		19	ROYAL NAVY	H	Won	3	1	-	1	25	-	-	-	2	6	Hare(3C,P) Duggan(T) Hall(2T) Adey(T)
23		22	Wakefield (JPC1)	A	Won	1	2	-	1	17	-	-	-	2	6	Hare(P) Duggan(T) Dodge(T,C) Rowell(T)
24		29	LONDON WELSH	H	Won	1	1	-	3	19	1	1	-	-	10	Dodge(C,3P) Newton(T) Wheeler(T)
25	Feb	5	London Scottish	A	Lost	-	-	-	-	0	-	3	-	1	15	
26		12	Moseley (JPC2)	A	Lost	-	-	-	3	9	2	2	-	1	23	Hare(3P)
27		16	Headingley	A	Won	1	1	-	2	16	-	-	-	4	12	Hare(T,C,2P) Duggan(T)
28		18	C.A.S.G. PARIS	H	Won	2	4	-	-	28	-	1	-	-	4	Duggan(2T) Dodge(2C) Parkes(T) Burwell(T) White(2T)
29		26	Northampton	A	Won	2	2	-	1	23	-	-	-	1	3	Hare(2C,P) Duggan(T) Kenney(T) Joyce(T) Kempin(T)
30	Mar	2	Nuneaton (MMT)	A	Won	3	2	-	2	32	1	-	-	-	6	Hare(T,3C,2P) Duggan(T) Hall(T) Kenney(T) Redfern(T)
31		5	HARLEQUINS	H	Lost	1	1	-	2	16	1	3	1	2	27	Hare(C,2P) Burwell(T) Ray.French(T)
32		12	COVENTRY	H	Won	1	-	-	6	24	-	1	-	2	10	Hare(C,6P) Dodge(T)
33		18	LOUGHBOROUGH COLLEGE	H	Won	-	2	-	2	14	-	-	-	1	3	Hare(2P) Dodge(T) Burwell(T)
34		26	Sale	A	Won	2	2	-	1	23	-	2	-	2	14	Hare(T,2C,P) Duggan(2T) Forfar(T)
35	Apr	2	Birkenhead Park	A	Lost	-	-	-	1	3	1	-	1	-	9	Hare(P)
36		9	RUGBY (MMT)	H	Won	4	1	-	1	31	-	-	-	3	9	Money(2T) Duggan(2T) Dodge(4C,P) Adey(T)
37		11	GOSFORTH	H	Lost	-	-	-	2	6	2	-	1	1	18	Dodge(2P)
38		16	Bristol	A	Lost	1	-	-	1	9	2	1	-	-	16	Holley(C,P) Reeve(T)
39		23	Moseley	A	Lost	-	-	-	1	3	2	1	-	-	16	Hare(P)
		30	MIDDLESBROUGH	H		Cancelled Middx.viis										

INDIVIDUAL APPEARANCES 1976-1977

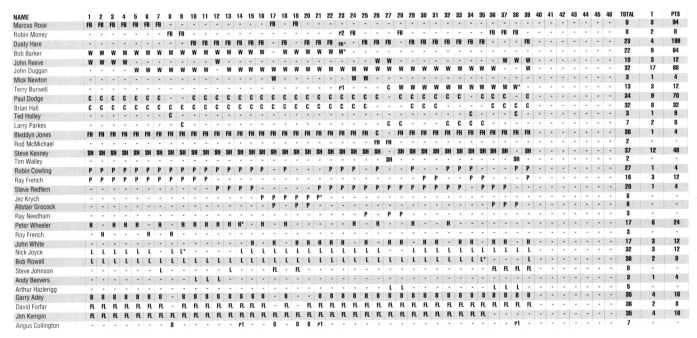

1 game: Mike Marshall P(35), Jock Millican FL(8), John Hawes H(35), D.Webb H(38), Graham Willars FL(9)

LEICESTER FOOTBALL CLUB 1976-77
Back: H.W. Sibson (Team Hon.Sec), J.D. Day (Hon.Sec), J.A. Allen (Hon.Tres), T.R. Burwell, R.J. Cowling, P.J. Wheeler, N.J. Joyce, G.J. Adey, S.P. Redfern, R.J. Willcox (President), H.V. White (Coach).
Middle: B.P. Hall, M.J. Duggan, R.G. Barker, R.E. Rowell (Capt), J.S. Kempin, P.W. Dodge, D.J. Forfar.
Front: W.H. Hare, B. Jones, S. Kenney, J.R. White.

RFU Merit Tables - Midlands Division 1976-77

		P	W	D	L	F	A	PTS	%
1	Moseley	6	6	-	-	178	39	12	100.00
2	**LEICESTER**	8	6	-	2	214	99	12	75.00
3	Coventry	8	5	-	3	160	118	10	62.50
4	Bedford	8	4	-	4	164	167	8	50.00
	Northampton	6	3	-	3	101	104	6	50.00
6	Nottingham	8	3	-	5	128	185	6	37.50
7	Birmingham	6	2	-	4	100	116	4	33.33
8	Nuneaton	7	2	-	5	60	182	4	28.57
9	Rugby	7	1	-	6	40	135	2	14.29

NO	DATE		OPPONENTS	V	RES	FOR					AGAINST					SCORERS
						G	T	D	P	PTS	G	T	D	P	PTS	
1	Sep	3	Bedford (MMT)	A	Lost	1	1	-	3	19	1	8	-	-	38	Hare(C,3P) Rose(T) Barker(T)
2		6	NUNEATON (MMT)	H	Won	6	3	-	1	51	-	1	-	2	10	Hare(6C,P) Rose(2T) Hall(T) Barker(4T) White(T) Joyce(T)
3		10	BATH	H	Won	3	3	-	3	39	1	2	-	4	26	Hare(3C,3P) Rose(2T) Hall(2T) Dodge(T) Kenney(T)
4		14	Birmingham (MMT)	A	Won	2	1	1	3	28	1	-	-	1	9	Hare(2C,D,3P) Barnwell(2T) Forfar(T)
5		17	LIVERPOOL	H	Won	4	2	-	1	35	-	-	-	1	3	Hare(4C,P) Dodge(T) Barker(2T) Kenney(T) Joyce(T) Parkes(T)
6		20	Sheffield	A	Won	6	2	-	1	47	-	-	-	1	3	Hare(6C,P) Barker(4T) Kenney(T) Redfern(T) Johnson(T) Parkes(T)
7		24	Harlequins	A	Won	1	2	-	3	23	-	2	-	3	17	Hare(C,3P) Barker(2T) Smith(T)
8	Oct	1	COVENTRY (MMT)	H	Won	1	2	-	2	20	-	-	-	2	6	Hare(T,C,2P) Barnwell(T) Barker(T)
9		8	Richmond	A	Lost	-	-	-	2	6	1	-	-	1	9	Hare(2P)
10		15	Northampton (MMT)	A	Lost	1	1	-	-	10	2	2	-	2	26	Hall(T) Barker(C) Collington(T)
11		19	Oxford University	A	Won	1	2	-	-	14	1	-	-	1	9	Duggan(T) Dodge(C) Barker(T) Jones(T)
12		22	SWANSEA	H	Won	4	-	-	3	33	1	1	1	1	16	Duggan(T) Dodge(C,2P) Hall(T) Barker(T,3C,P) Johnson(T)
13		29	Saracens	A	Drew	2	1	-	1	19	2	1	-	1	19	Hare(2C,P) Duggan(2T) McMichael(T)
14	Nov	5	GLOUCESTER	H	Won	3	1	-	2	28	2	-	-	1	15	Hare(3C,2P) Barker(T) Redfern(T) Joyce(T) Smith(T)
15		12	Cambridge University	A	Won	5	1	-	1	37	1	-	-	3	15	Hare(5C,P) Duggan(2T) Hall(T) Wheeler(T) Redfern(2T)
16		15	NOTTINGHAM (MMT)	H	Won	4	6	1	2	57	1	-	-	-	6	Hare(T,4C,D,2P) Duggan(2T) Hall(2T) Barker(3T) Kenney(T) Adey(T)
17		19	WASPS	H	Won	-	2	1	3	20	1	-	-	2	12	Hare(T,D,3P) Barker(T)
18		26	SALE	H	Won	3	2	-	-	26	1	-	-	2	12	Hare(3C) Duggan(T) Barker(T) Kenney(T) White(T) Smith(T)
19	Dec	3	WATERLOO	H	Won	1	2	-	-	14	-	-	-	1	3	Money(T) Burwell(T) Needham(C) Johnson(T)
20		10	Blackheath	A	Lost	-	2	-	2	14	1	1	-	3	19	Reichwald(T) Barker(T,2P)
21		17	BRISTOL	H	Won	-	1	-	5	19	1	-	2	-	14	Barker(T,5P)
22		27	BARBARIANS	H	Lost	1	-	-	-	6	2	-	-	-	12	Hare(T,C)
23		31	HEADINGLEY	H	Won	1	1	1	3	22	-	1	-	2	10	Hare(C,D,3P) Barker(T) Barnwell(T)
24	Jan	7	Bath	A	Lost	2	1	-	-	16	3	1	2	-	28	White(T) Needham(2C) Joyce(T) Smith(T)
25		14	Gloucester	A	Lost	1	-	-	-	6	4	3	-	1	39	Hare(C) Kempin(T)
26		20	BEDFORD	H	Won	1	-	-	2	12	-	-	-	2	6	Barker(C,2P) Jones(T)
		21	C.A.S.G. Paris	A		Cancelled										
27		28	HARTLEPOOL ROVERS (JPC1)	H	Won	-	-	-	3	9	-	-	-	1	3	Hare(3P)
28	Feb	1	ROYAL NAVY	H	Drew	-	-	-	-	0	-	-	-	-	0	
		4	LONDON SCOTTISH	H		Cancelled Frost										
		11	Newport	A		Cancelled Frost										
		15	SALE	H		Cancelled										
		18	Fylde	A		Cancelled Frost										
29		25	ROSSLYN PARK (JPC2)	H	Won	2	1	-	3	25	-	1	-	4	16	Hare(2C,3P) Barker(T) Kenney(T) Forfar(T)
30	Mar	4	HARLEQUINS	H	Lost	2	2	-	-	20	3	1	-	-	22	Hare(2C) Duggan(T) Reichwald(T) Hall(T) Joyce(T)
31		11	NORTHAMPTON (JPCQF)	H	Won	-	2	-	4	20	-	2	1	-	11	Hare(2P) Dodge(2P) Joyce(T)
32		14	LOUGHBOROUGH COLLEGE	H	Won	2	2	-	2	26	2	2	-	1	23	Duggan(T) Barker(2C,2P) Jones(T) Hazlerigg(T) Adey(T)
33		17	ROYAL AIR FORCE	H	Won	3	3	-	-	30	1	-	-	-	6	Barnwell(4T) Parkes(T) Barker(T,3C)
34		25	Neath	A	Lost	-	-	-	-	0	-	2	-	1	11	
35		27	Maesteg	A	Won	2	-	-	1	15	1	-	-	-	6	Hare(T,2C,P) Dodge(T)
36	Apr	1	COVENTRY (JPCSF)	H	Won	1	1	2	3	25	1	1	-	2	16	Hare(C,D,3P) Dodge(T) Reichwald(D) Jones(T)
37		8	Bristol	A	Lost	-	-	-	-	0	2	2	-	1	23	
38		15	Gloucester (JPCF)	A	Lost	-	-	-	1	3	1	-	-	-	6	Hare(P)
39		22	MOSELEY (MMT)	H	Won	2	-	1	2	21	1	-	-	3	15	Hare(2C,D,2P) Duggan(T) Jones(T)
40		26	Rugby (MMT)	A	Lost	1	1	-	1	13	1	2	-	1	17	Hare(C,P) Wheeler(T) Collington(T)
41		29	NORTHERN	H	Won	2	-	-	3	21	1	1	-	2	16	Hare(T,2C,3P) Dodge(T)

INDIVIDUAL APPEARANCES 1977-1978

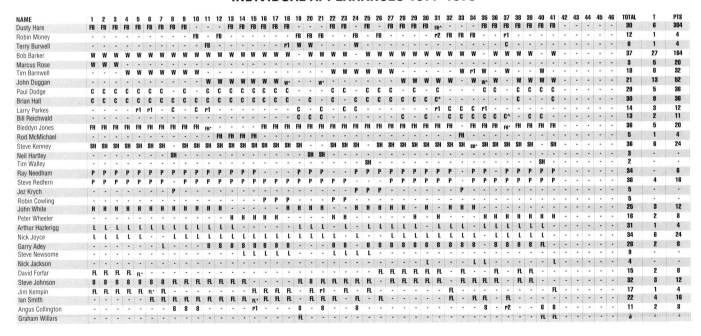

1 game: Alistair Grocock P(36), Neil Holloway P(33), Alistair Meldrum L(26), Bob Rowell L(41), Kevin Steptoe L(6), Paul Strickland FL(37), Ian Tomalin W(19)

LEICESTER FOOTBALL CLUB 1977-78

Back: H.W. Sibson (Team Hon.Sec), J.D. Day (Hon.Sec), J.A. Allen (Hon.Tres), M.J. Duggan, S.P. Redfern, A.P. Collington, S.R. Johnson, A.G. Hazlerigg, G.J. Adey, R.E. Needham, I.R. Smith, H.V. White (Coach), K.R. Kinder (President).

Front: W.H. Hare, R.S. Money, J.R. White, T.A. Walley, N.A. Jackson, B.P. Hall (Capt), R.G. Barker, N.J. Joyce, S. Kenney, P.W. Dodge.

RFU Merit Tables - Midlands Division 1977-78

		P	W	D	L	F	A	PTS	%
1	Bedford	8	7	-	1	209	94	14	87.50
2	Moseley	8	5	1	2	206	81	11	68.75
3	Coventry	8	5	1	2	142	93	11	68.75
4	Northampton	6	4	-	2	91	74	8	66.67
5	**LEICESTER**	**8**	**5**	**-**	**3**	**219**	**127**	**10**	**62.50**
6	Birmingham	7	3	-	4	92	105	6	42.86
7	Rugby	8	3	-	5	76	172	6	37.50
8	Nuneaton	7	1	-	6	57	226	2	14.29
9	Nottingham	8	-	-	8	74	194	0	0.00

1978-1979

NO	DATE	OPPONENTS	V	RES	FOR G	T	D	P	PTS	AGAINST G	T	D	P	PTS	SCORERS
1	Sep 2	BEDFORD (MMT)	H	Won	3	1	-	5	37	2	-	-	-	12	Hare(3C,5P) Duggan(T) Dodge(T) Hall(T) Barnwell(T)
2	5	Nuneaton (MMT)	A	Won	-	6	1	2	33	1	-	-	-	6	Hare(T,D,2P) Duggan(T) Barnwell(2T) Kenney(T) Wheeler(T)
3	9	Bath	A	Won	2	1	1	2	25	-	-	-	2	6	Hare(2C,D,2P) Duggan(T) Joyce(T) I.R.Smith(T)
4	13	BIRMINGHAM (MMT)	H	Won	3	2	-	3	35	1	-	1	2	15	Hare(3C,3P) Cowling(T) Wheeler(T) Joyce(T) Johnson(T) I.R.Smith(T)
5	16	LONDON WELSH	H	Lost	-	-	1	3	12	2	-	-	2	18	Hare(D,3P)
6	23	Harlequins	A	Lost	-	-	1	2	9	3	-	-	1	21	Hare(D,2P)
7	30	SARACENS	H	Won	2	4	-	2	34	1	-	-	1	9	Hare(2C,2P) Duggan(2T) Dodge(2T) Burwell(T) Johnson(T)
8	Oct 7	Coventry (MMT)	A	Lost	1	2	-	3	23	3	-	-	3	27	Hare(T,C,3P) Hall(T) Wheeler(T)
9	14	RICHMOND	H	Won	1	-	-	2	12	-	-	-	-	0	Hare(C,2P) Duggan(T)
10	21	NORTHAMPTON (MMT)	H	Won	3	2	-	2	32	-	-	-	2	6	Hare(T,3C,2P) Duggan(T) Burwell(T) Wheeler(T) Collington(T)
11	25	OXFORD UNIVERSITY	H	Won	3	3	-	1	33	1	-	1	2	15	Hare(3C,P) Burwell(T) Dodge(T) White(T) Joyce(T) I.R.Smith(2T)
12	28	Swansea	A	Lost	-	-	1	3	12	1	-	2	3	21	Hare(3P) Cusworth(D)
13	Nov 4	Gloucester	A	Won	-	-	2	1	9	-	1	-	1	7	Hare(2D,P)
14	11	CAMBRIDGE UNIVERSITY	H	Won	4	1	-	2	34	-	1	-	1	7	Hare(4C,2P) Burwell(T) Hall(T) Newton(T) Kenney(T) Collington(T)
15	18	Wasps	A	Lost	-	2	-	2	14	3	3	-	2	36	Key(2P) Burwell(T) Parkes(T)
16	25	MOSELEY (MMT)	H	Won	2	-	-	1	15	-	1	-	2	10	Barnwell(2T) Cusworth(2C,P)
	28	Nottingham (MMT)	A		Cancelled Frost										
	Dec 2	Waterloo	A		Cancelled Frost										
17	9	BLACKHEATH	H	Won	2	3	1	1	30	-	-	-	-	0	Hare(2C,D,P) Duggan(T) Hall(T) Barnwell(T) Kenney(2T)
18	15	Bristol	A	Lost	2	-	-	1	15	2	-	-	2	18	Hare(2C,P) Barnwell(T) White(T)
19	23	London Welsh	A	Lost	1	-	-	-	6	1	-	-	2	12	Hare(C) Dodge(T)
20	27	BARBARIANS	H	Won	2	-	-	2	18	1	-	-	-	6	Hare(2C,2P) Johnson(T) Adey(T)
	30	Headingley	A		Cancelled Frost										
	Jan 6	BATH	H		Cancelled Frost										
	13	GLOUCESTER	H		Cancelled Frost										
21	20	Bedford	A	Lost	-	2	-	-	8	1	1	-	-	10	Newton(T) Needham(T)
22	27	NORTHAMPTON (JPC1)	H	Won	2	2	1	2	29	-	-	-	1	3	Hare(T,2C,2P) Burwell(T,D) Barnwell(T) Adey(T)
23	Feb 3	London Scottish	A	Won	3	1	1	3	34	-	-	-	-	0	Hare(2T,3C,3P) Parkes(T) Barnwell(T) Cusworth(D)
	10	NEWPORT	H		Cancelled Frost										
	17	FYLDE	H		Cancelled Frost										
24	24	BROUGHTON PARK (JPC2)	H	Won	1	3	1	3	30	-	1	1	-	7	Hare(C,D,3P) Dodge(T) Cusworth(T) Adey(T) I.R.Smith(T)
25	28	ROYAL NAVY	H	Won	1	3	-	1	21	-	-	1	-	3	Hare(C,P) Barnwell(T) Cusworth(T) Joyce(T) Kempin(T)
26	Mar 3	HARLEQUINS	H	Won	5	-	-	1	33	-	-	-	1	3	Hare(5C,P) Newton(T) Barnwell(T) Cusworth(T) Kenney(T) Kempin(T)
27	10	Northampton	A	Lost	-	-	-	3	9	-	1	2	2	16	Dodge(3P)
	13	LOUGHBOROUGH COLLEGE	H		Cancelled Frost										
	16	ROYAL AIR FORCE	H		Cancelled Frost										
28	24	Bedford (JPCQF)	A	Won	1	1	-	4	22	1	-	-	2	12	Hare(T,C,4P) Burwell(T)
29	31	RUGBY (MMT)	H	Won	5	1	-	3	43	-	-	-	3	9	Hare(5C,3P) Barnwell(2T) Cowling(T) Kempin(T) Adey(T) Johnson(T)
30	Apr 7	Wasps (JPCSF)	A	Won	4	4	-	1	43	-	1	-	1	7	Hare(T,4C,P) Newton(2T) Burwell(T) Barnwell(2T) Redfern(T) Collington(T)
31	14	NEATH	H	Won	2	1	-	3	25	2	-	-	1	15	Hare(2C,3P) Burwell(T) Kenney(T) Johnson(T)
32	16	MAESTEG	H	Won	1	2	1	3	26	1	-	-	1	9	Hare(P) Dodge(C,2P) Cusworth(D) White(2T) I.R.Smith(T)
33	21	Moseley (JPCF)	A	Won	1	-	1	2	15	1	-	1	1	12	Hare(C,D,2P) Kenney(T)
34	28	Moseley	A	Lost	-	2	-	-	8	-	2	-	2	14	White(2T)

INDIVIDUAL APPEARANCES 1978-1979

NAME	1	2	3	4	5	6	7	8	9	10	11	12	13	14	15	16	17	18	19	20	21	22	23	24	25	26	27	28	29	30	31	32	33	34	35	36	37	38	39	40	41	42	43	44	45	46	TOTAL	T	PTS
Dusty Hare	FB	FB	FB	FB	FB	FB	FB	FB	FB	FB	FB	FB	FB	FB	-	-	FB	FB	FB	FB	-	FB	FB	FB	FB	FB	-	FB	FB	FB	FB	FB*	FB	-	-	-	-	-	-	-	-	-	-	-	-	-	29	8	350
Andy Key	-	-	-	-	-	-	-	-	-	-	-	-	-	-	FB	FB	-	-	-	-	FB	-	-	-	-	-	FB	-	-	-	-	-	-	FB	-	-	-	-	-	-	-	-	-	-	-	-	5	-	6
Tim Barnwell	W	W	W	W	W	W	W	W	W	W	-	W	W	-	W	W	W	W	W	W	W	W	W	W	W	W	-	W	W	W	-	W	W	W	-	-	-	-	-	-	-	-	-	-	-	-	30	15	60
John Duggan	W	W	W	W	-	-	W	W	W	W	W	W	W	W	-	W	W	W	W	W	-	W	-	-	-	-	-	-	-	-	W	W^	-	-	-	-	-	-	-	-	-	-	-	-	-	-	20	8	32
Bob Barker	-	-	-	-	W	W	-	-	C	C	W	-	-	-	W	-	-	-	-	-	-	-	-	-	-	-	W	-	-	-	-	r1	-	-	-	-	-	-	-	-	-	-	-	-	-	-	8	-	-
Mick Newton	-	-	-	-	-	-	-	-	-	-	-	-	-	W	-	-	-	-	-	-	W	-	W	W	W	W	W	W	W	W	W	-	W	W	-	-	-	-	-	-	-	-	-	-	-	-	13	5	20
Paul Dodge	C	C	C	C	C	C	C	C	-	FH	C	C	C	-	-	-	C	-	C	C	-	C	-	C	-	-	FH	C	C	C	C	C	C	-	-	-	-	-	-	-	-	-	-	-	-	-	24	6	41
Brian Hall	C	C	C	C	C	C*	-	C	-	-	-	-	-	C*	-	C	C	C	-	-	-	-	-	-	-	-	-	-	-	-	-	-	-	C	-	-	-	-	-	-	-	-	-	-	-	-	12	4	16
Terry Burwell	-	-	-	-	-	-	C	r2	C	C	C	C	C	C	C	C	-	C	C	C	C	C	C	C	C	C	C	C	C	C	C	C	C	C	-	-	-	-	-	-	-	-	-	-	-	-	27	9	39
Larry Parkes	-	-	-	-	-	-	-	-	-	-	-	-	-	-	C	-	-	-	-	-	C	-	C	-	C	C	C	-	-	-	-	-	-	-	-	-	-	-	-	-	-	-	-	-	-	-	6	2	8
Dick Peters	-	-	-	-	-	-	-	-	-	-	-	-	-	r1	-	-	-	-	-	-	-	-	-	-	-	-	-	-	-	-	-	-	-	r1	-	-	-	-	-	-	-	-	-	-	-	-	2	-	-
Bleddyn Jones	FH	FH	FH	FH	FH	FH	-	-	-	-	-	-	-	-	-	-	-	-	-	-	-	-	-	-	-	-	-	-	-	-	-	-	-	-	-	-	-	-	-	-	-	-	-	-	-	-	6	-	-
Bill Reichwald	-	-	-	-	-	r1	FH	FH	FH	-	FH	-	-	-	FH	-	-	-	-	-	-	-	-	-	-	-	-	-	-	-	-	-	-	-	-	-	-	-	-	-	-	-	-	-	-	-	6	-	-
Les Cusworth	-	-	-	-	-	-	-	-	-	-	-	FH	FH	FH	-	FH	FH	FH	FH	FH	FH	FH	FH	FH	FH	FH	-	FH	FH	FH	FH	FH	FH	FH	-	-	-	-	-	-	-	-	-	-	-	-	21	3	28
Steve Kenney	SH	SH	SH	SH	SH	SH	SH	SH	SH	SH	SH	SH	SH	SH	SH	SH	SH	SH	SH	SH	SH	SH	SH	SH	SH	SH	SH	SH	-	SH	SH	SH	SH	-	-	-	-	-	-	-	-	-	-	-	-	-	32	7	28
Tim Walley	-	-	-	-	-	-	-	-	-	-	-	-	-	-	-	-	-	-	-	-	-	-	-	-	-	-	-	-	SH	-	-	-	-	SH	-	-	-	-	-	-	-	-	-	-	-	-	2	-	-
Robin Cowling	P	P	P	P	P	P	P	P	P	P	P	P	P	P	-	-	-	-	P	P	-	P	-	P	P	P	P	P	P	P	P	P	P	P	-	-	-	-	-	-	-	-	-	-	-	-	28	2	8
Ray Needham	P	P	P	P	P	P	P	P	P	P	-	P	P	P	P	P	P	P	P	P	P	P	P	P	P*	-	-	-	-	-	-	-	-	-	-	-	-	-	-	-	-	-	-	-	-	-	24	1	4
Neil Holloway	-	-	-	-	-	-	-	-	-	-	P	-	-	-	-	-	-	-	-	-	-	-	-	-	-	-	-	-	P	-	-	-	-	P	-	-	-	-	-	-	-	-	-	-	-	-	3	-	-
Jez Krych	-	-	-	-	-	-	-	-	-	-	-	-	-	-	P	P	P	P	-	-	P	-	P	-	-	-	-	-	-	-	-	-	-	-	-	-	-	-	-	-	-	-	-	-	-	-	6	-	-
Steve Redfern	-	-	-	-	-	-	-	-	-	-	-	-	-	-	-	-	-	-	-	-	-	-	-	-	-	P	P	P	-	P	P	P	P	-	-	-	-	-	-	-	-	-	-	-	-	-	7	1	4
Peter Wheeler	H	H	H	H	H	H	H	H	-	H	-	H	H	-	-	-	H	-	H	H	-	H	-	H	-	-	-	H	H	H	-	-	H	-	-	-	-	-	-	-	-	-	-	-	-	-	20	4	16
John White	-	-	-	-	-	-	-	-	H	-	H	-	-	H	-	H	-	H	-	-	H	-	H	-	H	H	H	-	-	-	H	H	-	H	-	-	-	-	-	-	-	-	-	-	-	-	13	6	24
Nigel Gillingham	L	L	L	L	L	L	L	L	-	L	-	L	L	L	-	-	L	-	-	-	-	-	-	-	-	-	-	-	-	-	-	-	-	-	-	-	-	-	-	-	-	-	-	-	-	-	13	-	-
Nick Joyce	L	-	L	L	L	-	-	-	L	L	L	L	-	-	L	L	L	L	L	L	L	L	L	L	L	L	L	L	L	L	L	L	L	L	-	-	-	-	-	-	-	-	-	-	-	-	28	4	16
Arthur Hazlerigg	-	L	-	-	-	L	L	L	L	-	L	-	L	L	L	L	-	L	L	L	L	L	L	L	L	L	L	L	L	L	L	L	L	L	-	-	-	-	-	-	-	-	-	-	-	-	27	-	-
Garry Adey	8	8	8	8	8	8	-	8	-	-	-	-	-	-	-	8	8	8	8	8	-	8	8	8	8	-	8	8	8	8*	-	8	8	8	-	-	-	-	-	-	-	-	-	-	-	-	23	4	16
Steve Johnson	FL	FL	FL	FL	FL	FL	FL	FL^	FL	FL	-	FL	FL	FL	FL	FL	FL	FL	FL	FL	-	FL	FL	FL*	-	-	-	-	FL	FL	FL*	-	FL	-	-	-	-	-	-	-	-	-	-	-	-	-	26	5	20
Ian Smith	FL	FL	FL	FL	FL	FL	FL	FL*	FL	FL	FL	FL	FL	-	-	FL	FL	FL*	FL	FL	-	FL	FL	FL	FL	FL	FL	FL	-	FL	-	FL	FL	FL	-	-	-	-	-	-	-	-	-	-	-	-	29	6	24
Angus Collington	-	-	-	-	-	-	8	-	8	8	8	8	8	8	8	-	-	r1	-	-	8	-	-	r1	-	8	-	-	-	r1	8	-	-	-	-	-	-	-	-	-	-	-	-	-	-	-	14	3	12
Jim Kempin	-	-	-	-	-	-	-	r1	-	-	FL*	-	-	-	-	-	-	-	-	-	FL	-	-	-	FL	FL	FL	FL	FL	-	FL	FL	-	FL	-	-	-	-	-	-	-	-	-	-	-	-	11	3	12
Paul Strickland	-	-	-	-	-	-	-	-	-	-	r1	-	-	-	-	-	-	-	-	-	FL	-	-	-	-	-	-	-	-	-	-	-	-	-	-	-	-	-	-	-	-	-	-	-	-	-	2	-	-
Graham Smith	-	-	-	-	-	-	-	-	-	-	-	-	-	FL	FL	-	-	-	-	-	-	-	-	-	-	-	-	-	-	-	-	-	-	-	-	-	-	-	-	-	-	-	-	-	-	-	2	-	-
Nick Jackson	-	-	-	-	-	-	-	-	-	-	-	-	-	-	-	-	-	-	-	-	-	-	-	-	r1	-	-	-	-	-	r1	-	-	-	-	-	-	-	-	-	-	-	-	-	-	-	2	-	-

1 game: Chris DeLuca H(15), Kelvin Wilford r2(32)

RFU Merit Tables - Midlands Division 1978-79

		P	W	D	L	F	A	PTS	%
1	Coventry	8	7	-	1	193	94	14	87.50
2	**LEICESTER**	**7**	**6**	**-**	**1**	**218**	**85**	**12**	**85.71**
3	Nottingham	7	5	-	2	103	48	10	71.43
4	Moseley	6	4	-	2	163	66	8	66.67
	Northampton	6	4	-	2	70	86	8	66.67
6	Rugby	7	2	-	5	86	175	4	28.57
7	Bedford	8	2	-	6	112	135	4	25.00
8	Birmingham	6	1	-	5	68	142	2	16.67
9	Nuneaton	7	-	-	7	36	218	0	0.00

Paul Dodge - the popular Tigers centre scored 41 points in 24 appearances during 1978-79.

NO	DATE		OPPONENTS	V	RES	FOR G	T	D	P	PTS	AGAINST G	T	D	P	PTS	SCORERS
1	Sep	1	Bedford (MMT)	A	Won	3	1	-	4	34	-	-	1	3	12	Hare(2T,3C,4P) Woodward(T) Needham(T)
2		4	NUNEATON (MMT)	H	Won	2	1	-	2	22	1	-	-	1	9	Hare(2C,2P) Barnwell(2T) Wheeler(T)
3		8	BATH	H	Lost	-	-	1	2	9	1	1	-	-	10	Hare(D,2P)
4		12	BIRMINGHAM (MMT)	H	Won	3	5	-	-	38	-	-	-	-	0	Duggan(T) Woodward(4T,2C) Cusworth(C) Forfar(T) Jackson(T) Key(T)
5		15	LONDON WELSH	H	Won	1	-	-	7	27	2	1	-	3	25	Woodward(T) Cusworth(C,7P)
6		22	Harlequins	A	Won	3	-	-	1	21	-	-	-	2	6	Hare(3C,P) Burwell(T) I.R.Smith(2T)
7		29	Saracens	A	Won	1	-	1	2	15	1	1	-	1	13	Hare(C,D,2P) Kenney(T)
8	Oct	6	COVENTRY (MMT)	H	Won	2	1	-	3	25	-	-	-	1	3	Hare(2C,3P) Duggan(T) Hall(T) Barnwell(T)
9		13	Richmond	A	Won	3	1	1	1	28	1	-	-	1	13	Hare(3C,D,P) Duggan(T) Woodward(T) Barnwell(2T)
10		20	Northampton (MMT)	A	Won	5	3	-	-	42	-	1	-	-	4	Hare(2T,5C) Dodge(T) Woodward(2T) Barnwell(2T) Cusworth(T)
11		24	Oxford University	A	Won	1	-	1	3	18	2	-	-	1	15	Hare(C,D,3P) Barnwell(T)
12		27	SWANSEA	H	Lost	-	-	-	4	12	4	-	-	1	27	Hare(4P)
	Nov	5	GLOUCESTER	H		Cancelled										
13		10	Cambridge University	A	Won	5	1	-	-	34	-	-	-	-	0	Duggan(T,5C) Duggan(2T) Cusworth(T) Wheeler(T) Gillingham(T)
14		13	Nottingham (MMT)	A	Won	3	1	2	-	28	-	2	-	-	8	Hare(T,3C,D) Dodge(T) A.K.Williams(T) Cusworth(D) Redfern(T)
15		17	WASPS	H	Won	2	2	-	1	23	-	1	-	-	4	Hare(2C,P) Woodward(T) Burwell(T) Wheeler(2T)
16		23	Moseley (MMT)	A	Lost	-	-	-	2	6	1	1	-	1	13	Dodge(2P)
17	Dec	1	WATERLOO	H	Won	2	-	1	1	18	1	1	1	2	13	Hare(2C,P) Dodge(T) Cusworth(T,D)
18		8	Blackheath	A	Won	2	-	-	4	24	-	-	-	2	6	Hare(2C,4P) Hall(T) Woodward(T)
19		15	BRISTOL	H	Won	1	1	2	2	22	1	2	-	-	14	Hare(C,D,2P) Woodward(T) Cusworth(D) Gillingham(T)
20		22	London Welsh	A	Won	-	-	2	2	12	-	-	-	2	6	Hare(D,2P) Cusworth(D)
21		27	BARBARIANS	H	Lost	-	2	-	-	8	1	-	-	1	9	Burwell(T) Adey(T)
22		29	HEADINGLEY	H	Won	8	1	1	-	55	-	-	-	1	3	Hare(T,8C) Duggan(T) Dodge(T) Woodward(2T) Barnwell(2T) Poulson(D) Kenney(T) I.R.Smith(T)
23	Jan	5	Bath	A	Won	2	1	-	2	22	1	-	-	2	12	Key(2C,2P) Burwell(T) Cowling(T) I.R.Smith(T)
24		12	Gloucester	A	Lost	-	-	1	4	15	-	2	1	3	20	Key(4P) Poulson(D)
		18	BEDFORD	H		Cancelled										
25		26	ORRELL (JPC1)	H	Won	-	1	2	2	16	-	1	-	1	7	Hare(2P) Cusworth(2D) I.R.Smith(T)
26	Feb	2	LONDON SCOTTISH	H	Won	1	2	-	-	14	-	-	1	2	9	Manship(C) Hall(T) Barnwell(2T)
27		9	Newport	A	Won	1	1	1	1	16	1	2	-	-	14	Woodward(T) Cusworth(T,C,D,P)
28		16	HARTLEPOOL ROVERS	H	Won	2	1	-	3	25	-	-	-	2	6	A.K.Williams(T) Cusworth(2C,3P) Gillingham(T) I.R.Smith(T)
29		23	Moseley (JPC2)	A	Won	-	2	1	2	17	-	1	-	1	7	Dodge(2P) Burwell(T) Cusworth(D)
30		27	ROYAL NAVY	H	Won	3	9	-	-	54	-	-	-	1	3	Hare(C) Duggan(3T) Dodge(T) Burwell(T) Cusworth(2C) Kenney(T) Cowling(T) Wheeler(T) Johnson(2T) Collington(T) Jackson(T)
31	Mar	1	HARLEQUINS	H	Won	5	3	1	3	54	-	1	-	2	10	Duggan(T) A.K.Williams(2T) Cusworth(2T,5C,D,3P) Redfern(T) Gillingham(T) Joyce(T)
32		8	LONDON SCOTTISH (JPCQF)	H	Won	1	1	1	3	22	-	-	-	-	0	Hare(C,3P) Cusworth(T,D) I.R.Smith(T)
33		11	LOUGHBOROUGH COLLEGE	H	Won	4	1	1	1	34	-	-	-	2	6	Burwell(T) Cusworth(4C,D,P) Kenney(2T) Collington(2T)
34		14	ROYAL AIR FORCE	H	Won	4	2	-	2	38	-	-	-	-	0	Duggan(2T) Burwell(2T) Cusworth(4C,2P) Redfern(T) Collington(T)
35		22	SALE	H	Won	3	-	-	2	24	-	1	-	1	7	Hare(3C,2P) Duggan(T) Dodge(2T)
36		29	Harlequins (JPCSF)	A	Won	-	1	-	4	16	-	-	1	2	9	Hare(4P) Dodge(T)
37	Apr	5	Neath	A	Won	-	1	-	2	10	-	-	-	2	6	Burwell(T) Cusworth(2P)
38		7	Pontypool	A	Lost	1	1	-	1	13	-	-	2	5	21	Barnwell(T) Cusworth(C,P) Gillingham(T)
39		12	Bristol	A	Lost	1	1	-	1	13	1	1	-	2	16	Hare(C,P) Dodge(T) Johnson(T)
40		19	London Irish (JPCF)	A	Won	-	-	3	4	21	1	-	-	1	9	Hare(D,4P) Cusworth(2D)
41		26	MOSELEY	H	Lost	2	2	-	-	20	2	-	1	4	27	Hare(T,2C) Cowling(T) Joyce(T) Jackson(T)
42		29	Rosslyn Park	A	Lost	2	-	-	1	15	1	-	-	4	18	Hare(T,2C,P) Cusworth(T)

INDIVIDUAL APPEARANCES 1979-1980

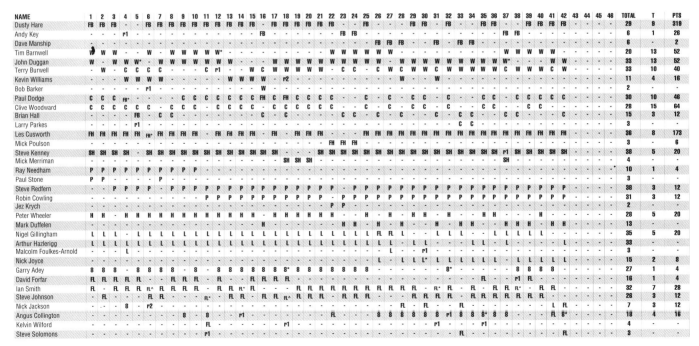

1 game: Ian Bridgewood H(3), Phil Smith FH(11), Tim Walley SH(5), Graham Willars r1(42), David Williams W(14)

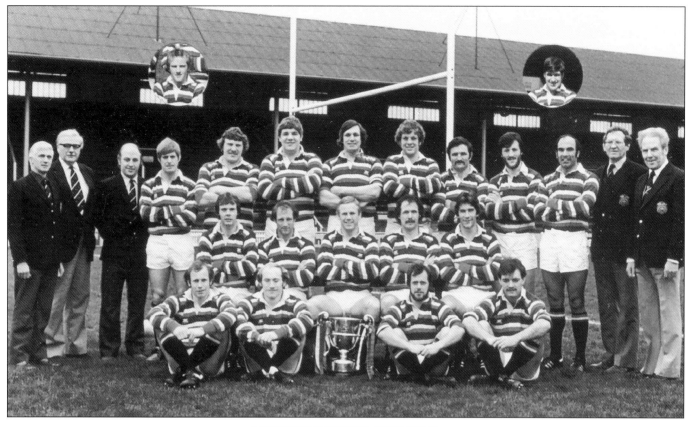

LEICESTER FOOTBALL CLUB 1979-80
Back: H.V. White (Coach), E.C. Lacey (President), J.A. Allen (Hon.Tres), B.P. Hall, S.P. Redfern, N.J. Joyce, G.J. Adey,
A.P. Collington, R.J. Cowling, I.R. Smith, M.J. Duggan, J.D. Day (Hon.Sec), J.T. Thomas (Team Hon.Sec).
Middle: C.R. Woodward, W.H. Hare, P.J. Wheeler (Capt), T.R. Burwell, P.W. Dodge.
Front: R.C. Barnwell, L. Cusworth, S. Kenney, M. Duffelen.
Inset: M.J.P. Merriman, S.R. Johnson.

1980 Tour - Australia and Fiji

v QUEENSLAND	v EASTERN SUBURBS	v RANDWICK	v LAUTOKA	v FIJI COMBINED SERVICES	v FIJI CHAIRMAN'S XV
Dusty Hare 2C	Andy Key 1T	Dusty Hare 1C,1D,5P	Dusty Hare 1C,2D	Andy Key	Dusty Hare 3P
John Duggan	Kevin Williams 1T	Kevin Williams	John Duggan	Tim Barnwell 1T	Tim Barnwell
Paul Dodge	Terry Burwell	Paul Dodge	Larry Parkes	Larry Parkes	Paul Dodge
Brian Hall1	Larry Parkes	Terry Burwell	Andy Key	Terry Burwell	Terry Burwell
Tim Barnwell	Tim Barnwell 1T	Tim Barnwell	Kevin Williams	Kevin Williams	Kevin Williams
Les Cusworth	Les Cusworth 3C,2P	Les Cusworth 1D	Paul Dodge	Les Cusworth 1T	Les Cusworth 1D
Steve Kenney	Mick Merriman	Steve Kenney	Mick Merriman	Steve Kenney	Mick Merriman
Ray Needham	Paul Stone	Paul Stone	Ray Needham	Ray Needham	Paul Stone
John White	Mark Duffelen	John White 1T	Mark Duffelen	John White	Peter Wheeler*
Steve Redfern	Ray Needham	Steve Redfern	Steve Redfern	Steve Redfern	Steve Redfern
Nick Joyce*	Nigel Gillingham1	Nick Joyce	Nick Joyce*	Nick Jackson	Nick Joyce
Nigel Gillingham	Nick Jackson	Nick Jackson	Nick Jackson	Garry Adey	Nick Jackson
Steve Johnson	Steve Johnson*	Steve Johnson*	David Forfar	Steve Johnson*	David Forfar1
Garry Adey 2T	Angus Collington	Garry Adey	Angus Collington	David Forfar	Garry Adey
Ian Smith	David Forfar	Ian Smith 1T	Ian Smith 1T	Ian Smith1	Steve Johnson
Terry Burwell rep 1	Nick Joyce rep 1			Nick Joyce rep 1	Angus Collington rep 1
Lost 12-22	*Won 24-3*	*Won 31-19*	*Won 12-6*	*Won 8-4*	*Won 12-0*
Tigers:2G	*Tigers:3G 2PG*	*Tigers:1G 1T 2DG 5PG*	*Tigers:1G 2DG*	*Tigers:2T*	*Tigers:1DG 3PG*
Queensland:2G 1T 2PG	*E.Suburbs:1PG*	*Randwick:1G 1T 3PG*	*Lautoka:1G*	*Fiji C.S:1T*	*Fiji Chair:Nil*
6 Aug 1980	*10 Aug 1980*	*13 Aug 1980*	*16 Aug 1980*	*20 Aug 1980*	*23 Aug 1980*

RFU Merit Tables - Midlands Division 1979-80

		P	W	D	L	F	A	PTS	%
1	**LEICESTER**	7	6	-	1	195	49	12	85.71
2	Northampton	8	6	-	2	125	98	12	75.00
3	Moseley	7	4	2	1	77	56	10	71.43
4	Bedford	8	5	-	3	178	117	10	62.50
	Coventry	8	5	-	3	138	125	10	62.50
6	Birmingham	6	2	-	4	68	114	4	33.33
7	Nottingham	8	2	1	5	104	136	5	31.25
8	Nuneaton	8	1	1	6	70	151	3	18.75
9	Rugby	6	-	-	6	50	159	0	0.00

1980-1981

NO	DATE		OPPONENTS	V	RES	FOR G	FOR T	FOR D	FOR P	PTS	AGAINST G	AGAINST T	AGAINST D	AGAINST P	PTS	SCORERS
1	Sep	2	Nuneaton (MMT)	A	Won	-	1	-	2	10	-	-	-	2	6	Hare(2P) Barnwell(T)
2		6	BEDFORD (MMT)	H	Won	5	1	-	3	43	-	-	-	2	6	Hare(5C,3P) Barnwell(2T) Gillingham(T) Johnson(T) Adey(T) Smith(T)
3		10	IRISH WOLFHOUNDS	H	Won	1	1	-	-	10	-	-	-	2	6	Hare(T,C) Woodward(T)
4		13	Bath	A	Lost	-	1	-	-	4	-	1	1	2	13	Dodge(T)
5		17	BIRMINGHAM (MMT)	H	Won	5	-	-	2	36	1	-	-	2	12	A.K.Williams(T) Cusworth(2T,5C,2P) Kenney(T) Johnson(T)
6		20	LONDON WELSH	H	Won	4	-	1	1	30	1	-	-	3	15	Hare(4C,D,P) A.K.Williams(T) Kenney(T) Gillingham(T) Adey(T)
7		27	Harlequins	A	Won	6	-	-	3	45	1	-	-	3	15	Hare(T,6C,3P) Woodward(T) Dodge(T) Barnwell(T) Needham(T) Gillingham(T)
8	Oct	4	Coventry (MMT)	A	Won	1	1	-	4	22	1	1	1	2	19	Hare(C,4P) A.K.Williams(T) Dodge(T)
9		11	RICHMOND	H	Won	3	2	-	4	38	-	-	-	2	6	Hare(T,3C,4P) Dodge(2T) Barnwell(T) Joyce(T)
10		18	NORTHAMPTON (MMT)	H	Won	3	1	-	1	25	3	-	1	-	21	Hare(T,3C,P) Woodward(T) Cusworth(T) Kenney(T)
11		22	ROMANIA	H	Lost	-	1	-	1	7	3	3	1	2	39	Hare(P) A.K.Williams(T)
12		25	QUEENSLAND	H	Won	1	-	2	3	21	1	-	-	1	9	Hare(C,2D,3P) A.K.Williams(T)
13	Nov	1	Gloucester	A	Lost	-	1	-	-	4	2	4	1	-	31	Dodge(T)
14		8	CAMBRIDGE UNIVERSITY	H	Won	5	2	2	2	50	-	1	-	1	7	Hare(3T,5C,2P) A.K.Williams(T) Woodward(D) Dodge(T) Cusworth(D) Redfern(T) Knowles(T)
15		11	NOTTINGHAM (MMT)	H	Won	2	2	-	1	23	-	1	-	2	10	Hare(2C,P) A.K.Williams(T) Joyce(T) Jackson(T) Knowles(T)
16		15	Wasps	A	Won	-	-	2	4	18	-	-	2	2	12	Hare(4P) Cusworth(2D)
17		22	MOSELEY (MMT)	H	Drew	-	1	1	1	10	-	1	-	2	10	Hare(P) Barnwell(T) Cusworth(D)
18		29	SARACENS	H	Won	2	1	-	2	22	1	1	-	1	13	Dodge(T,2C,2P) Barnwell(2T)
19	Dec	6	Waterloo	A	Won	1	3	1	2	27	-	1	-	1	7	Key(T) Hall(T) Dodge(C) Cusworth(D,2P) Kenney(T) Joyce(T)
20		13	BLACKHEATH	H	Won	5	1	1	3	46	1	-	-	1	9	Key(T) A.K.Williams(T) Poulson(T,D) Merriman(T,5C,3P) Joyce(T) Johnson(T)
21		20	Bristol	A	Won	-	-	1	2	9	-	-	-	2	6	Poulson(D) Merriman(2P)
22		29	BARBARIANS	H	Lost	4	-	-	-	24	1	4	-	2	28	Hare(4C) A.K.Williams(T) Woodward(T) Wheeler(T) Smith(T)
23	Jan	3	BATH	H	Won	1	1	-	1	13	-	2	-	1	11	Key(C,P) Jackson(T) Smith(T)
24		10	GLOUCESTER	H	Won	1	2	-	-	14	1	-	-	1	9	Barnwell(T) Cusworth(T,C) Redfern(T)
		16	Bedford	A		Cancelled										
25		24	Roundhay (JPC3)	A	Won	2	1	2	4	34	-	-	1	-	3	Hare(2C,4P) Dodge(D) Barnwell(T) Cusworth(T,D) Cowling(T)
26		31	BALLYMENA	H	Won	3	3	-	3	39	-	1	1	-	7	Hare(3C,3P) A.K.Williams(T) Woodward(2T) Dodge(T) Smith(2T)
27	Feb	7	London Scottish	A	Won	1	3	2	2	30	-	1	-	1	7	Hare(C,2P) A.K.Williams(T) Cusworth(T,2D) Knowles(T) Collington(T)
28		14	NEWPORT	H	Won	3	1	-	5	37	-	-	-	2	6	Hare(3C,5P) Kenney(T) Wheeler(2T) Johnson(T)
29		18	ROYAL NAVY	H	Won	2	1	-	2	22	1	-	1	1	12	Key(P) A.K.Williams(T) Cusworth(2C,P) Jackson(T) Johnson(T)
30		21	London Welsh	A	Lost	-	1	-	2	10	6	1	1	1	46	A.K.Williams(T) Key(2P)
31		28	BRISTOL (JPC4)	H	Won	2	-	-	5	27	-	2	-	2	14	Hare(2C,5P) A.K.Williams(T) Smith(T)
32	Mar	7	HARLEQUINS	H	Won	3	2	-	1	29	-	-	-	2	6	Key(3C,P) Burwell(T) Barnwell(T) Jackson(T) Collington(T) Smith(T)
33		14	SALE (JPCQF)	H	Won	1	-	1	4	21	-	1	-	1	7	Hare(C,4P) A.K.Williams(T) Cusworth(D)
		17	LOUGHBOROUGH COLLEGE	H		Cancelled Rain										
34		20	ROYAL AIR FORCE	H	Won	1	4	-	-	22	-	-	-	1	3	Manship(C) A.K.Williams(T) Barnwell(T) Joyce(T) Johnson(2T)
35		28	Sale	A	Lost	-	-	-	2	6	-	3	1	-	15	Hare(2P)
36	Apr	4	London Scottish (JPCSF)	A	Won	-	-	2	4	18	-	-	1	3	12	Hare(4P) Cusworth(2D)
37		10	Pontypridd	A	Lost	1	-	-	-	6	1	4	1	-	25	Hare(T,C)
38		18	NEATH	H	Won	2	1	-	2	22	-	-	1	-	3	Hare(2C,2P) Barnwell(T) Wheeler(T) Johnson(T)
39		20	PONTYPOOL	H	Won	3	-	-	-	18	1	1	1	-	13	Hare(3C) Dodge(T) Adey(T) Smith(T)
40		25	Moseley	A	Won	2	2	-	2	26	1	1	-	1	13	Hare(T,2C,2P) Newton(2T) Smith(T)
		28	ROSSLYN PARK	H		Cancelled										
41	May	2	Gosforth (JPCF)	A	Won	2	1	-	2	22	1	-	-	3	15	Hare(T,2C,2P) Barnwell(T) Kenney(T)

INDIVIDUAL APPEARANCES 1980-1981

NAME	1	2	3	4	5	6	7	8	9	10	11	12	13	14	15	16	17	18	19	20	21	22	23	24	25	26	27	28	29	30	31	32	33	34	35	36	37	38	39	40	41	42	43	44	45	46	TOTAL	T	PTS
Dusty Hare	FB	FB	FB	FB	-	FB	FB	FB	FB	FB	FB	FB	FB	FB	FB	FB	FB*	-	-	-	-	FB	-	-	FB	FB	FB	FB	-	-	FB	-	FB	-	FB	FB	FB	FB	FB	FB	FB	-	-	-	-	-	30	10	358
Dave Manship	-	-	-	-	-	-	-	-	-	-	-	-	-	-	-	-	-	-	-	-	-	-	-	-	-	-	-	-	-	FB	-	-	-	FB	-	-	-	-	-	-	-	-	-	-	-	-	2	-	2
Tim Barnwell	W	W	W	W	W	W	W	W	W	W	W	W	W	W	W	W	W	W	W	-	-	W	W	W	W	W	W	W	W	W	W	W	W	W	W	W	W	W	W	-	W	-	-	-	-	-	38	14	56
Kevin Williams	W	W	W	W	W	W	W	W	W	W	W	W	W	W	W	W	W	W	-	W	W	W	-	W	W	W	W	W	W	W	W	W	W	W	W	W	W	W	W	-	W	-	-	-	-	-	38	16	64
Mick Newton	-	-	-	-	-	-	-	-	-	-	-	-	-	-	-	-	-	-	W	W	W	-	-	-	-	-	-	-	-	-	-	-	-	-	-	-	-	r1	r1	W	-	-	-	-	-	-	6	2	8
David Williams	-	-	-	-	-	-	-	-	-	-	-	-	-	-	-	-	-	-	-	-	-	-	W	-	-	-	-	-	-	-	-	-	-	-	-	-	-	-	-	W	-	-	-	-	-	-	2	-	-
Terry Burwell	C	C	C	C	-	-	-	-	-	-	-	-	-	-	-	-	r1	-	-	C	C	-	C	C	-	-	-	-	C	C	-	C	-	C	-	-	C	C*	-	-	-	-	-	-	-	-	15	1	4
Clive Woodward	C	C	C*	-	C	C	C	C	C	C	C	C	C	C	C	C	C	-	-	-	-	C	-	-	C	C	C	C	-	-	C	-	C	-	-	C*	-	FH	FH*	-	C	-	-	-	-	-	27	6	27
Andy Key	-	-	r1	-	FB	-	-	-	-	-	-	-	-	-	-	-	-	FB	FB	FB	FB	-	FB	FB	-	-	-	-	FB	FH	-	FB	-	-	-	-	-	C	C	C	-	-	-	-	-	-	14	2	31
Paul Dodge	-	-	-	C	-	C	C	C	C	C	C	C	C	C	C	C	C	C	C	-	-	C	-	-	C	C	C	C	-	-	C	-	C	-	C	C	C	-	C	C	C	-	-	-	-	-	28	10	55
Brian Hall	-	-	-	-	C	-	-	-	-	-	-	-	-	-	-	-	-	C	C	-	C	-	C	C	-	-	-	-	C	C	-	C	-	C	C	r1	-	-	-	-	-	-	-	-	-	-	12	1	4
John Cooke	-	-	-	-	-	-	-	-	-	-	-	-	r2	-	-	-	-	-	-	C	-	-	-	-	-	-	-	-	r1	-	-	-	-	-	-	-	-	-	-	-	-	-	-	-	-	-	3	-	-
Les Cusworth	FH	FH	FH	FH	FH	FH	FH	FH	FH	FH	FH	FH	FH	FH	FH	FH	FH	-	FH	-	-	FH	-	FH	FH	FH	FH	FH	FH*	-	FH	-	FH	FH	-	FH	FH	-	-	FH	FH	-	-	-	-	-	32	6	88
Mick Poulson	-	-	-	-	-	-	-	-	-	-	-	-	-	-	-	-	-	FH	-	FH	FH	-	FH	-	-	-	-	-	-	-	-	-	-	-	-	-	-	-	-	-	-	-	-	-	-	-	4	1	10
Ian Dodson	-	-	-	-	-	-	-	-	-	-	-	-	-	-	-	-	-	-	-	-	-	-	-	-	-	-	-	-	-	-	-	FH	-	-	FH	-	-	-	-	-	-	-	-	-	-	-	2	-	-
Steve Kenney	SH	SH	SH	SH	SH	SH	SH	SH	SH	SH	SH	SH	SH	SH	SH	SH	SH	SH	SH	-	-	SH	SH	-	SH	SH	SH	SH	SH	SH	SH	SH	SH	SH	SH	SH	SH	-	SH	SH	SH	-	-	-	-	-	37	6	24
Mick Merriman	-	-	-	-	-	-	-	-	-	-	-	-	-	-	-	-	-	-	-	SH	SH	-	-	SH	-	-	-	-	-	-	-	-	-	-	-	-	-	SH	-	-	-	-	-	-	-	-	4	1	29
Ray Needham	P	P	P	P	-	-	P	P	P	P	-	-	P	-	-	-	-	-	-	P	P	-	-	-	r1	-	r1	-	-	-	-	-	-	-	-	-	-	-	-	-	-	-	-	-	-	-	13	1	4
Steve Redfern	P	P	P	P	P	P	P	P	P	P	P	P	-	P	P	P	P	P	P	-	-	P	P	P	P	P	P	P	P	P	P	P	P	P	-	P	P	P	-	P	P	-	-	-	-	-	36	2	8
Paul Stone	-	-	-	-	P	P	-	-	-	-	-	-	-	-	-	-	-	-	-	-	-	-	-	-	-	-	-	-	-	-	-	-	-	-	-	-	-	-	-	-	-	-	-	-	-	-	2	-	-
Robin Cowling	-	-	-	-	-	-	-	-	-	-	P	P	P	P	P	P	P	P	P	P	P	P	P	P	P	P	P	P	P	P	P	P	P	P	P	P	P	-	P	P	P	-	-	-	-	-	30	1	4
Wayne Richardson	-	-	-	-	-	-	-	-	-	-	-	-	-	-	-	-	-	-	-	-	-	-	-	-	-	-	-	-	-	-	-	-	-	-	P	-	-	P	P	-	-	-	-	-	-	-	3	-	-
Mark Duffelen	H	H	H	H	-	H	H	H	-	H	H	H	H	-	-	-	-	-	-	-	-	-	-	-	-	-	-	-	-	-	-	-	-	-	-	-	-	-	-	-	-	-	-	-	-	-	11	-	-
Chris Tressler	-	-	-	-	H	-	-	-	H	-	-	-	-	H	H	H	-	H	-	H	H	-	H	H	-	-	-	-	H	H	-	H	-	H	H	-	-	-	-	H	-	-	-	-	-	-	16	-	-
Peter Wheeler	-	-	-	-	-	-	-	-	-	-	-	-	-	-	-	-	H	-	H	-	-	H	-	-	H	H	H	H	-	-	H	-	H	-	-	H	H	H	H	-	H	-	-	-	-	-	14	4	16
Nick Jackson	L	r1	-	-	r1	-	r1	-	-	-	-	-	-	-	FL*	-	L	L	L	L	L	L	L	L	L	L	L	L	L	L	L	L	L	8	8	L	L	L	L	L	L	-	-	-	-	-	30	4	16
Nick Joyce	L	L	L	L	-	L	L	L	L	-	L	L	-	L	L	L	L	L	L*	L	L	L	L	L	L	L	L	L	L	L	L	L	L	L	L	L	-	L	L	L	L	-	-	-	-	-	37	5	20
Nigel Gillingham	-	L	L	L	L	L	L	L	-	L	L	L	L	L	L	L*	-	-	-	-	-	-	-	-	-	-	-	-	-	-	-	-	-	-	-	-	-	-	-	-	-	-	-	-	-	-	14	3	12
Malcolm Foulkes-Arnold	-	-	-	-	L	-	-	-	L	L	-	-	L	-	-	r1	-	-	-	-	-	-	-	-	-	-	-	-	-	-	-	-	-	-	-	-	-	-	-	-	-	-	-	-	-	-	5	-	-
Dean Waddingham	-	-	-	-	-	-	-	-	-	-	-	-	-	-	-	-	-	-	r1	-	-	-	-	-	-	-	-	-	-	-	-	-	-	L	L	-	L	-	-	-	-	-	-	-	-	-	4	-	-
Garry Adey	8	8	8	8	-	8	8	8	8	8	8	8	8	8*	-	-	-	-	-	-	-	-	-	-	-	-	-	-	-	-	-	-	-	-	-	-	-	-	8	8	8	-	-	-	-	-	16	3	12
David Forfar	FL	-	-	-	FL	-	-	FL	FL	FL	FL	-	FL^	-	-	-	-	-	-	-	-	-	-	-	-	-	-	-	-	-	-	-	-	-	-	-	-	-	-	-	-	-	-	-	-	-	7	-	-
Steve Johnson	FL	FL	FL	FL	FL	FL	FL*	-	-	-	FL	FL	FL*	-	-	FL	FL	FL	FL	FL	FL	FL	FL	FL	FL	FL*	-	FL	FL	FL	FL	-	FL	FL	FL	FL	-	FL	-	FL	FL*	-	-	-	-	-	32	8	32
Ian Smith	-	FL*	FL	FL	-	FL	FL	FL	FL	FL	-	FL	-	-	-	-	FL	FL	FL	-	FL	FL	FL	FL	FL	FL	FL*	FL	FL	FL	FL	FL	FL	-	FL*	FL	FL	FL	FL	FL	FL	-	-	-	-	-	32	9	36
Angus Collington	-	-	-	-	8	-	-	-	-	-	-	-	-	FL	8	8	8	8	8	8	8	8	8	8	8*	8	8	8	8	8	8	8	8	-	-	8^	-	8	-	-	r1	-	-	-	-	-	24	2	8
Steve Solomons	-	-	-	-	-	-	-	-	-	-	-	-	r1	-	-	-	-	-	-	r1	-	-	-	-	-	-	-	-	-	-	-	-	-	-	-	-	-	-	-	-	-	-	-	-	-	-	2	-	-
Mac Knowles	-	-	-	-	-	-	-	-	-	-	-	-	-	FL	FL	FL	-	-	-	FL	-	-	-	-	-	r1	FL	-	-	-	-	FL	-	-	-	r2	FL	-	FL	-	-	-	-	-	-	-	10	3	12
M.Nangrave	-	-	-	-	-	-	-	-	-	-	-	-	-	r1	-	-	-	-	-	-	-	-	-	-	-	-	-	-	-	-	-	-	-	-	-	-	-	-	-	-	-	-	-	-	-	-	1	-	-
Duncan Black	-	-	-	-	-	-	-	-	-	-	-	-	-	-	r1	-	-	-	-	-	-	-	-	-	-	-	-	-	-	-	-	-	-	FL	-	-	8	-	-	-	-	-	-	-	-	-	3	-	-
Dave Gavins	-	-	-	-	-	-	-	-	-	-	-	-	-	-	-	-	-	-	-	-	-	-	-	-	-	-	-	-	-	-	-	-	-	-	r1	-	-	-	-	-	-	-	-	-	-	-	1	-	-

LEICESTER FOOTBALL CLUB 1980-81

Back: J.D. Day (Hon.Sec), J.T. Thomas (Team Hon.Sec), R.E. Needham, S.R. Johnson, A.P. Collington, W.P. Richardson, N.A. Jackson, N.J. Joyce, G.J. Adey, S.P. Redfern, I.R. Smith, E.C. Lacey (President), H.V. White (Coach).
Middle: A.M. Key, A.K. Williams, S. Kenney, W.H. Hare, P.J. Wheeler (Capt), R.J. Cowling, C.R. Woodward, R.C. Barnwell, T.R. Burwell.
Front: M.J.P. Merriman, C.J. Tressler.
Inset: L. Cusworth.

RFU Merit Tables - Midlands Division 1980-81

		P	W	D	L	F	A	PTS	%
1	LEICESTER	7	6	1	-	169	84	13	92.86
2	Moseley	8	6	1	1	186	71	13	81.25
3	Bedford	8	5	-	3	95	104	10	62.50
4	Nottingham	7	3	2	2	102	86	8	57.14
5	Coventry	8	3	1	4	147	97	7	43.75
	Nuneaton	8	3	1	4	69	64	7	43.75
	Northampton	8	3	1	4	119	136	7	43.75
8	Birmingham	7	1	-	6	48	190	2	14.29
9	Rugby	7	-	1	6	56	159	1	7.14

NO	DATE		OPPONENTS	V	RES	FOR					AGAINST					SCORERS
						G	T	D	P	PTS	G	T	D	P	PTS	
1	Sep	5	Bedford (MMT)	A	Won	3	1	-	2	28	-	1	-	-	4	Hare(3C,2P) Woodward(T) Dodge(T) Barnwell(T) Wheeler(T)
2		8	NUNEATON (MMT)	H	Won	3	2	1	3	38	-	-	-	1	3	Hare(3C,3P) A.K.Williams(T) Barnwell(2T) Cusworth(D) Black(2T)
3		12	BATH	H	Won	4	2	1	3	44	-	-	-	2	6	Hare(4C,D,3P) A.K.Williams(T) Woodward(T) Dodge(T) Merriman(T) Wheeler(T) Johnson(T)
4		16	Birmingham (MMT)	A	Won	11	3	-	-	78	-	2	-	-	8	Hare(3T,11C) Dodge(T) Woodward(2T) Barnwell(2T) Cusworth(3T) Johnson(T) Black(T) Smith(T)
5		19	LONDON WELSH	H	Won	-	4	-	1	19	1	-	-	-	6	Hare(P) A.K.Williams(T) Dodge(T) Wheeler(T) Joyce(T)
6		26	Harlequins	A	Won	4	4	1	2	49	1	-	-	2	12	Hare(4C,2P) Dodge(T) Barnwell(2T) Cusworth(D) Merriman(T) Black(2T) Cooke(2T)
7	Oct	3	COVENTRY (MMT)	H	Won	2	1	-	4	28	-	-	-	2	6	Hare(2C,4P) Woodward(T) Barnwell(2T)
8		10	Richmond	A	Drew	-	-	-	2	6	-	-	-	2	6	Hare(2P)
9		16	Northampton (MMT)	A	Lost	-	-	1	1	6	2	1	1	1	22	Poulson(D,P)
10		24	SWANSEA	H	Lost	2	-	-	-	12	-	1	2	3	19	Hare(2C) Woodward(T) Whitcombe(T)
11		31	Saracens	A	Won	3	1	-	4	34	1	2	-	-	14	Hare(T,3C,4P) Evans(T) Barnwell(T) Smith(T)
12	Nov	7	GLOUCESTER	H	Lost	-	-	-	3	9	-	-	1	3	12	Hare(3P)
13		14	Cambridge University	A	Won	1	-	1	1	12	1	-	-	1	9	Hare(T,C,P) Cusworth(D)
14		17	Nottingham (MMT)	A	Won	1	1	1	1	16	-	-	-	1	3	Hare(C,D,P) Evans(2T)
15		21	WASPS	H	Won	3	-	1	2	27	1	-	1	3	18	Hare(3C,D,2P) Evans(T) Woodward(T) Barnwell(T)
16		25	AUSTRALIA	H	Lost	-	-	3	2	15	1	-	1	3	18	Hare(2D,2P) Cusworth(D)
17		28	MOSELEY (MMT)	H	Won	1	1	2	2	22	2	-	-	1	15	Hare(C,2P) Evans(T) Woodward(2D) Smith(T)
18	Dec	5	WATERLOO	H	Won	5	1	2	3	49	-	-	-	1	3	Hare(T,5C,D,3P) Woodward(T) Dodge(2T,D) Jackson(T) Collington(T)
		12	Blackheath	A		Cancelled										
		19	BRISTOL	H		Cancelled Frost										
		29	BARBARIANS	H		Cancelled										
19	Jan	2	Bath	A	Drew	1	-	-	1	9	-	-	-	3	9	Hare(C,P) Youngs(T)
		9	Gloucester	A		Cancelled Snow/frost										
		15	BEDFORD	H		Cancelled Snow/ice										
20		17	Torquay Athletic	A	Won	6	2	-	-	44	-	1	-	-	4	Hare(T,6C) Evans(T) Hall(T) Barnwell(T) Youngs(2T) Gillingham(T) Smith(T)
21		23	HARTLEPOOL ROVERS (JPC3)	H	Won	4	5	-	3	53	2	1	-	1	19	Hare(T,4C,3P) Evans(T) Dodge(T) Barnwell(T) Youngs(2T) Deacon(T) Johnson(T) Smith(T)
22		30	London Welsh	A	Won	1	1	-	4	22	-	1	-	1	7	Hare(T,C,4P) Evans(T)
23	Feb	6	LONDON SCOTTISH	H	Won	2	1	-	1	19	-	-	1	1	6	Hare(2C,P) Hall(T) Barnwell(T) Smith(T)
24		13	Newport	A	Lost	1	-	-	3	15	1	1	-	2	16	Hare(C,3P) Woodward(T)
25		20	Orrell	A	Lost	-	1	-	-	4	1	-	-	2	12	Hall(T)
26		27	Northampton (JPC4)	A	Won	1	2	-	3	23	-	1	-	2	10	Hare(T,C,3P) Evans(T) Barnwell(T)
27	Mar	3	ROYAL NAVY	H	Won	-	2	-	3	17	1	-	1	1	12	Evans(T) Barnwell(T) Poulson(3P)
28		5	HARLEQUINS	H	Lost	-	1	-	1	7	1	1	-	1	13	Poulson(T,P)
29		13	GOSFORTH (JPCQF)	H	Won	1	-	1	3	18	1	-	-	1	9	Hare(C,3P) Cusworth(D) Smith(T)
30		16	LOUGHBOROUGH COLLEGE	H	Won	-	-	-	4	12	1	-	-	1	9	Hare(4P)
31		19	ROYAL AIR FORCE	H	Won	4	-	-	3	33	-	-	-	3	9	Hare(2C,3P) Evans(T) Barnwell(T) Cusworth(2C) Collington(T) Smith(T)
32		23	RUGBY	H	Won	1	4	-	2	28	-	1	-	1	7	Dodson(T) Barnwell(T) Poulson(C,2P) Collington(T) Black(T) Smith(T)
33		27	SALE	H	Won	-	2	-	2	14	1	1	-	-	10	Dodge(2P) Poulson(T) Marriott(T)
34	Apr	3	Moseley (JPCSF)	A	Lost	-	1	-	-	4	-	-	2	2	12	Cusworth(T)
35		10	Neath	A	Won	3	1	-	1	25	-	2	-	2	14	Hall(T) Poulson(2T,3C,P) Youngs(T)
36		12	Pontypool	A	Lost	2	1	-	-	16	3	2	-	2	32	Woodward(T,C) Cusworth(C) Youngs(2T)
37		17	Bristol	A	Lost	-	1	-	-	4	4	2	1	1	38	Dodson(T)
38		20	BARBARIANS	H	Won	6	-	-	-	36	4	2	-	-	32	Hare(6C) A.K.Williams(T) Barnwell(T) Cusworth(T) Wheeler(T) Smith(2T)
39		24	Moseley	A	Lost	1	-	-	1	9	4	-	2	-	30	Hare(C,P) Hall(T)
40		30	Ballymena	A	Won	1	-	1	4	21	1	3	-	-	18	Hare(C,D,4P) Barnwell(T)

INDIVIDUAL APPEARANCES 1981-1982

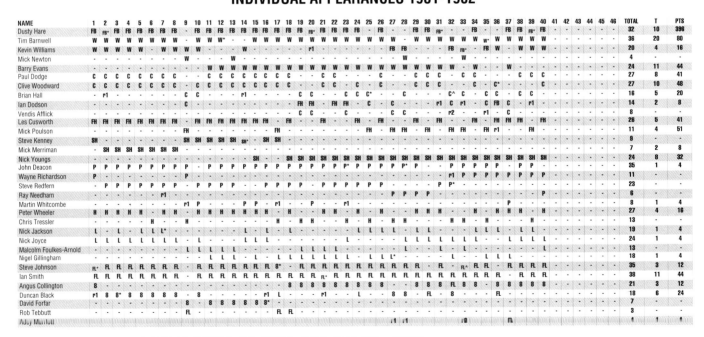

2 games: John Cooke r1(6,12)[2T-8], Arthur Hazlerigg L(8,9), Andy Key W*(6)FB(9), Stuart Redfern P(30,31), Dean Waddingham L(2,4), David Williams r1(25)W(35)
1 game: Mac Knowles FL*(9), Dave Manship FB(25), Dean Richards 8(35), Paul Stone r1(3)

LEICESTER FOOTBALL CLUB 1981-82
Back: H.W. Sibson (President), J.D. Day (Hon.Sec), N.G. Youngs, A.P. Collington, I.R. Dodson, P.W. Dodge,
I.R. Smith, N.A. Jackson, N.J. Joyce, N.K. Gillingham, S.P. Redfern, S. Kenney, W.P. Richardson, J. Deacon,
J.T. Thomas (Team Hon.Sec), H.V. White (Coach).
Middle: A.K. Williams, W.H. Hare, S.R. Johnson (Capt), R.C. Barnwell, L. Cusworth.
Front: B.P. Hall, P.J. Wheeler, C.J. Tressler, D. Black.

1982 Tour - Zimbabwe

v MASHONALAND	v MATABELELAND	v ZIMBABWE	v ZIMBABWE MIDLANDS XV	v ZIMBABWE
Kevin Williams	Kevin Williams	Kevin Williams	Kevin Williams.1T	Kevin Williams
Barry Evans	Barry Evans	Terry Burwell	Barry Evans 2T	Barry Evans
Ian Dodson	Terry Burwell	Ian Dodson 2C,1P	Terry Burwell	Ian Dodson
Brian Hall	Vendis Afflick 1T	Brian Hall	Vendis Afflick 1T	Brian Hall
Tim Barnwell 2T	Tim Barnwell 2T	Tim Barnwell 1T	Tim Barnwell 1T,1C	Tim Barnwell
Mick Poulson 2C,1D	Ian Dodson 2C,3P	Mick Poulson1 1P	Ian Dodson 1T,4C	Mick Poulson 1C,1D,2P
Nick Youngs	Steve Kenney	Steve Kenney	Nick Youngs 2T	Nick Youngs
John Deacon	John Deacon	John Deacon	Wayne Richardson	John Deacon
Chris Tressler 1T	David Thomas	Chris Tressler	David Thomas	Chris Tressler
Martin Whitcombe	Wayne Richardson	Martin Whitcombe	Martin Whitcombe	Martin Whitcombe
Nick Joyce	Nick Joyce	Nick Joyce	Malcolm Foulkes-Arnold 1T	Nick Joyce
Nick Jackson 1T	Malcolm Foulkes-Arnold	Malcolm Foulkes-Arnold	Nick Jackson	Malcolm Foulkes-Arnold
Steve Johnson*	Steve Johnson*	Steve Johnson*	Duncan Black	Steve Johnson* 1T
Angus Collington	Duncan Black	Duncan Black 1T	Angus Collington	Duncan Black
Ian Smith	Rob Tebbutt	Ian Smith 1T	Rob Tebbutt	Ian Smith
	Ian Smith rep 1	Barry Evans rep 1	Nick Joyce rep 1	Nick Jackson rep 1
			Ian Smith rep 2	Steve Kenney rep 2

Lost 23-28	*Won 25-12*	*Won 22-18*	*Won 46-0*	*Drew 15-15*
Tigers:2G 2T 1DG	*Tigers:2G 1T 3PG*	*Tigers:2G 1T 2PG*	*Tigers:5G 4T*	*Tigers:1G 1DG 2PG*
Mashonaland:2G 1T 4PG	*Matabeleland:1G 2PG*	*Zimbabwe:6PG*	*Z.Midlands:Nil*	*Zimbabwe:2G 1PG*
24 Jul 1982	*27 Jul 1982*	*31 Jul 1982*	*4 Aug 1982*	*7 Aug 1982*

RFU Merit Tables - Midlands Division 1981-82

		P	W	D	L	F	A	PTS	%
1	LEICESTER	7	6	-	1	216	61	12	85.71
	Coventry	7	6	-	1	152	65	12	85.71
3	Moseley	7	5	-	2	130	92	10	71.43
4	Bedford	7	4	1	2	122	82	9	64.29
5	Nottingham	7	4	-	3	96	82	8	57.14
6	Northampton	6	3	-	3	103	55	6	50.00
7	Birmingham	8	2	-	6	71	217	4	25.00
8	Nuneaton	7	1	1	5	47	135	3	21.43
9	Rugby	8	-	-	8	30	207	0	0.00

NO	DATE		OPPONENTS	V	RES	FOR					AGAINST					SCORERS
						G	T	D	P	PTS	G	T	D	P	PTS	
1	Sep	4	BEDFORD (MMT)	H	Won	3	1	-	2	28	-	-	-	5	15	Dodge(C) Cusworth(2C,2P) Foulkes-Arnold(T) Black(T) Johnson(T) Smith(T)
2		7	Nuneaton (MMT)	A	Won	3	5	-	1	41	-	2	-	1	11	A.K.Williams(2T) Dodge(T,P) Barnwell(2T) Cusworth(3C) Black(T) Johnson(T) Smith(T)
3		11	Bath	A	Lost	1	-	-	3	15	3	-	-	2	24	Dodge(C) Cusworth(3P) Collington(T)
4		14	BIRMINGHAM (MMT)	H	Won	3	-	-	-	18	-	-	-	1	3	D.Williams(2T) Cusworth(3C) Smith(T)
5		18	LONDON WELSH	H	Lost	2	-	-	1	15	1	2	1	-	17	Hare(2C,P) Steve.Redfern(T) Johnson(T)
6		25	Harlequins	A	Won	3	2	-	1	29	2	1	-	3	25	Hare(2C) Dodge(C,P) Cusworth(2T) Kenney(T) Wells(2T)
7	Oct	2	Coventry (MMT)	A	Won	-	2	-	2	14	1	-	-	2	12	Hare(2P) Kenney(T) Whitcombe(T)
8		9	RICHMOND	H	Won	2	-	-	3	21	-	2	-	-	8	Hare(2C,3P) Wheeler(T) Johnson(T)
9		16	NORTHAMPTON	H	Won	-	3	-	1	15	1	1	-	-	10	D.Williams(T) Barnwell(2T) Dodson(P)
10		20	OXFORD UNIVERSITY	H	Won	4	2	-	3	41	-	-	-	1	3	Hare(4C,3P) Evans(2T) Barnwell(T) Cusworth(T) Black(T) Collington(T)
11		23	Swansea	A	Lost	1	-	-	3	12	3	2	-	1	29	Hare(3P) Cusworth(D)
		27	RANDWICK	H		Cancelled										
12		30	SARACENS	H	Won	7	-	-	3	51	1	-	2	1	15	Hare(7C,3P) Evans(T) Hall(T) Dodge(2T) Barnwell(T) Youngs(T) Jackson(T)
13	Nov	6	Cardiff	A	Lost	-	-	-	3	9	4	2	-	-	32	Hare(3P)
14		13	CAMBRIDGE UNIVERSITY	H	Won	4	2	-	2	38	1	-	-	-	6	Hare(4C,2P) Evans(T) Barnwell(T) Kenney(2T) Johnson(2T)
15		17	NOTTINGHAM (MMT)	H	Won	1	1	-	4	22	-	-	-	3	9	Hare(C,4P) Evans(T) Steve.Redfern(T)
16		20	Wasps	A	Lost	-	1	-	1	7	-	-	-	5	15	Hare(T) Cusworth(P)
17		27	MOSELEY (MMT)	H	Won	1	1	-	4	22	1	-	-	3	15	Hare(C,4P) Cusworth(T) Richards(T)
18	Dec	1	Gloucester	A	Won	2	-	-	3	21	-	1	1	1	10	Hare(T,2C,3P) Woodward(T)
19		4	Waterloo	A	Won	-	1	-	2	10	-	-	-	3	9	Hare(2P) Barnwell(T)
20		11	BLACKHEATH	H	Won	2	1	-	4	28	1	-	-	5	21	Hare(2C,4P) Whitcombe(T) Richards(T) Tebbutt(T)
21		18	Bristol	A	Lost	-	-	1	1	6	1	3	-	1	21	Poulson(D,P)
22		29	BARBARIANS	H	Won	2	3	-	4	36	1	1	-	2	16	Hare(2C,4P) Evans(3T) Cusworth(T) Kenney(T)
23	Jan	1	BATH	H	Won	2	-	1	2	21	1	-	-	1	9	Hare(T,2C,2P) Evans(T) Cusworth(D)
24		8	GLOUCESTER	H	Won	1	2	-	3	23	1	-	-	1	9	Barnwell(T) Poulson(C,3P) Kenney(T) Johnson(T)
25		14	Bedford	A	Won	1	1	-	1	13	-	-	-	1	3	Evans(T) Poulson(C,P) Richards(T)
26		22	HIGH WYCOMBE (JPC3)	H	Won	4	5	-	1	47	2	-	-	2	18	Hare(2T,4C,P) Evans(T) Barnwell(3T) Kenney(T) Wheeler(T) Foulkes-Arnold(T)
27		29	London Welsh	A	Lost	-	-	-	4	12	1	1	1	4	25	Hare(4P)
28	Feb	5	London Scottish	A	Won	1	-	-	4	18	1	-	-	2	12	Evans(T) Poulson(C,4P)
29		12	NEWPORT	H	Won	3	-	-	1	21	1	-	-	1	9	Hare(3C,P) Cusworth(2T) Youngs(T)
30		19	ORRELL	H	Won	2	-	-	2	18	1	-	-	2	12	Hare(2C,2P) Johnson(T) Richards(T)
31		26	WAKEFIELD (JPC4)	H	Won	4	-	-	2	30	1	2	-	-	14	Hare(4C,2P) Evans(T) Woodward(T) Barnwell(T) Richards(T)
32	Mar	2	ROYAL NAVY	H	Won	3	1	-	-	22	-	-	-	-	0	Evans(T) Barnwell(T) Cusworth(3C) Joyce(T) Smith(T)
33		5	HARLEQUINS	H	Lost	-	-	-	1	3	-	1	-	3	13	Cusworth(P)
34		12	HARLEQUINS (JPCQF)	H	Won	2	-	1	1	18	-	1	-	-	4	Hare(2C,P) Cusworth(D) Youngs(2T)
35		15	LOUGHBOROUGH COLLEGE	H	Won	6	1	-	2	46	1	2	1	2	17	Evans(2T) D.Williams(T) Cusworth(6C,2P) Foulkes-Arnold(T) Collington(T) Smith(2T)
36		18	ROYAL AIR FORCE	H	Won	2	4	-	2	34	-	-	-	-	0	Poulson(C,2P) Bates(T) Burwell(T) Barnwell(T) Cusworth(C) Kenney(T) D.Williams(2T)
37		26	London Scottish (JPCSF)	A	Won	4	-	2	-	30	-	-	-	1	9	Hare(4C,D) Evans(T) Barnwell(T) Cusworth(T,D) Richards(T)
38		29	RUGBY (MMT)	H	Won	4	5	-	3	53	-	-	-	1	3	Evans(4T) Dodge(C) D.Williams(2T) Cusworth(3C,3P) Foulkes-Arnold(T) Marriott(T) Dexter(T)
39	Apr	2	NEATH	H	Won	1	3	-	1	21	-	-	-	1	6	Cusworth(T,C,P) Youngs(T) Stuart.Redfern(T) Smith(T)
40		4	PONTYPOOL	H	Lost	1	-	-	-	6	-	2	1	3	20	Cusworth(C) Marriott(T)
41		12	Northampton	A	Lost	1	-	-	1	9	-	-	2	4	18	Cusworth(C,P) Youngs(T)
42		16	Maesteg	A	Won	1	2	1	-	17	1	1	-	1	13	Evans(T) Barnwell(T) Cusworth(C,D) Youngs(T)
43		23	Moseley	A	Won	3	2	-	1	29	-	1	-	2	10	Evans(T) Woodward(2T) Cusworth(3C,P) Tebbutt(T) Poulson(T)
44		30	Bristol (JPCF)	A	Lost	1	1	-	4	22	3	-	-	2	28	Evans(T) Cusworth(C,4P) Smith(T)

INDIVIDUAL APPEARANCES 1982-1983

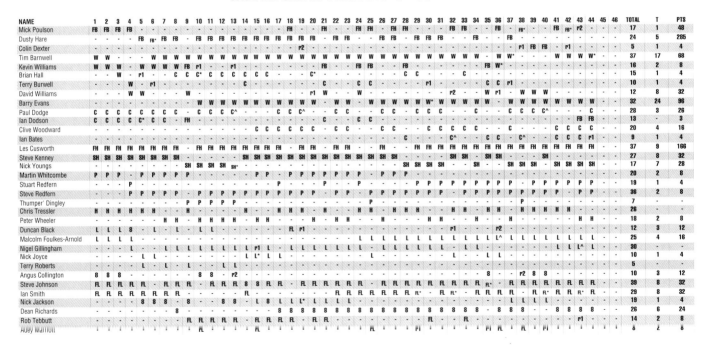

3 games: Vendis Afflick C(9,39,40), John Deacon P(1,2,3)
2 games: Tommy Lawton FL(14,19), Wayne Richardson P(32,42)
1 game: Claude Gerald r2(40), Jez Krych P(14), John Wells FL(6)[2T-8]

LEICESTER FOOTBALL CLUB 1982-83

Back: R. Beason (Hon.Tres), H.W. Sibson (President), G.G. Willars (Coach), W.H. Hare, N.A. Jackson, N.K. Gillingham, M.V. Foulkes-Arnold, S.P. Redfern, I.R. Smith, M. Whitcombe, P.J. Wheeler, J.A. Allen (Hon.Sec), J.T. Thomas (Team Hon.Sec).

Middle: R.C. Barnwell, M. Poulson, P.W. Dodge, D. Richards, S.R. Johnson (Capt), S.B. Redfern, B.J. Evans, C.J. Tressler, R.S. Tebbutt, C.R. Woodward.

Front: A.K. Williams, S. Kenney, L. Cusworth, N.G. Youngs.

RFU Merit Tables - Midlands Division 1982-83

		P	W	D	L	F	A	PTS	%
1	**LEICESTER**	7	7	-	-	198	68	14	100.00
2	Coventry	8	7	-	1	184	74	14	87.50
3	Moseley	8	5	1	2	181	82	11	68.75
4	Northampton	7	4	-	3	148	85	8	57.14
5	Bedford	8	4	1	3	118	93	9	56.25
6	Nottingham	8	4	-	4	167	113	8	50.00
7	Nuneaton	8	2	-	6	56	181	4	25.00
8	Birmingham	8	1	-	7	35	189	2	12.50
9	Rugby	8	-	-	8	58	260	0	0.00

1983-1984

NO	DATE		OPPONENTS	V	RES	FOR					AGAINST					SCORERS
						G	T	D	P	PTS	G	T	D	P	PTS	
1	Sep	3	Bedford (MMT)	A	Won	10	2	-	-	68	-	-	-	1	3	Dodson(T) A.K.Williams(2T) Dodge(T) Woodward(T) Evans(3T) Cusworth(10C) Tressler(T) Marriott(T) Dexter(T) Black(T)
2		6	NUNEATON (MMT)	H	Won	5	5	-	3	59	-	1	-	-	4	Dexter(T) Evans(4T) A.K.Williams(T) Cusworth(T,5C,3P) Stuart.Redfern(T) Foulkes-Arnold(T) Black(T)
3		10	BATH	H	Won	-	-	-	6	18	-	-	2	3	15	Cusworth(6P)
4		14	ZIMBABWE	H	Won	2	2	-	3	29	-	-	-	4	12	Dodson(T) Evans(T) A.K.Williams(T) Cusworth(2C,3P) Stuart.Redfern(T)
5		17	LONDON WELSH	H	Won	-	2	1	1	14	-	-	1	2	9	Evans(T) Dodge(P) Cusworth(D) Youngs(T)
6		21	BIRMINGHAM (MMT)	H	Won	4	1	-	4	40	-	-	-	1	3	Hare(4C,4P) A.K.Williams(2T) Gillingham(2T) Black(T)
7		24	Harlequins	A	Won	2	2	-	-	20	3	-	-	-	18	Hare(2C) Dodge(2T) Poulson(T) Youngs(T)
8	Oct	1	COVENTRY (MMT)	H	Won	3	3	1	2	39	-	-	-	3	9	Dodson(T) Dexter(T) Dodge(T,3C,2P) Cusworth(T,D) Youngs(T) Tebbutt(T)
9		8	Richmond	A	Won	-	1	-	2	10	-	-	-	-	0	Hare(2P) Evans(T)
10		15	Northampton	A	Won	1	4	-	1	25	-	-	-	-	0	Dodson(C) Evans(T) Cusworth(P) Walker(T) Richards(2T) Tebbutt(T)
11		19	Oxford University	A	Won	5	-	1	1	36	-	1	-	1	7	Dodge(T,5C,P) Cusworth(T) Smith(2T) Poulson(D) Penalty Try
12		22	SWANSEA	H	Won	4	2	-	3	41	-	-	-	1	3	Hare(T,4C,3P) A.K.Williams(T) Evans(T) Youngs(T) Marriott(T) Smith(T)
13		29	Saracens	A	Won	8	1	1	2	61	-	1	1	1	10	Hare(T,8C,2P) Underwood(3T) Cusworth(D) Youngs(2T) Stuart.Redfern(T) Whitcombe(2T)
14	Nov	5	CARDIFF	H	Won	2	2	-	3	29	1	3	-	2	24	Hare(2C,3P) Evans(T) Underwood(T) Youngs(T) Smith(T)
15		12	Cambridge University	A	Won	2	5	-	1	35	1	1	-	2	16	Cave(T) Evans(3T) Dodge(2T,C) Cusworth(C,P) Black(T)
16		15	Nottingham	A	Won	-	2	2	2	20	-	-	-	3	9	A.K.Williams(T) Bates(T) Poulson(2D,2P)
17		19	WASPS	H	Lost	2	-	-	2	18	1	2	-	3	23	Hall(T) Poulson(2C,2P) Whitcombe(T)
18		26	Moseley	A	Won	2	-	-	1	15	-	-	-	2	6	Hare(2C,P) Evans(T) Foulkes-Arnold(T)
19	Dec	3	GLOUCESTER	H	Won	2	-	-	6	30	2	2	-	-	20	Hare(2C,6P) Underwood(2T)
20		10	Blackheath	A	Lost	-	-	1	-	3	3	-	-	1	21	Cusworth(D)
21		17	BRISTOL	H	Lost	1	-	-	2	12	-	3	-	1	15	Hare(C,2P) Marriott(T)
22		28	BARBARIANS	H	Won	1	3	1	3	30	2	2	-	2	26	Hare(C,3P) Evans(T) Underwood(2T) Cusworth(D) Youngs(T)
23		31	London Welsh	A	Won	-	1	1	3	16	-	2	-	2	14	Hare(3P) Cusworth(D) Richards(T)
24	Jan	7	Bath	A	Lost	-	-	-	-	0	-	2	1	1	14	
25		14	Gloucester	A	Lost	2	-	-	3	21	-	4	-	2	22	Woodward(T) Cusworth(2C,3P) Richards(T)
		21	BEDFORD	H		Cancelled Frost										
26		28	Coventry (JPC3)	A	Lost	-	-	-	3	9	-	1	-	3	13	Hare(3P)
27	Feb	4	LONDON SCOTTISH	H	Lost	-	-	-	4	12	2	1	-	-	16	Dodson(4P)
28		11	Newport	A	Won	1	1	2	1	19	2	-	-	1	15	Hare(C,P) Evans(T) Underwood(T) Cusworth(2D)
29		18	Orrell	A	Lost	-	2	-	-	8	1	-	-	5	21	Dodson(T) Richardson(T)
30		25	ROSSLYN PARK	H	Won	1	4	-	1	25	1	1	2	-	16	Hare(C,P) Evans(T) Cusworth(2T) Richards(2T)
31	Mar	3	HARLEQUINS	H	Won	4	2	-	1	35	1	2	-	2	20	Dodson(2C,P) Evans(T) Pell(T,2C) Kenney(T) Gillingham(T) Foulkes-Arnold(T) Richards(T)
32		10	BEDFORD	H	Won	8	1	-	4	64	-	-	-	3	9	Hare(8C,4P) Evans(T) Woodward(T) Underwood(3T) Youngs(2T) Joyce(T) Richards(T)
33		13	LOUGHBOROUGH COLLEGE	H	Won	2	2	-	2	26	1	-	-	1	9	Dodson(C,2P) Bates(T) Pell(C) Foulkes-Arnold(T) Richards(2T)
34		16	ROYAL AIR FORCE	H	Won	1	5	-	-	26	-	-	-	1	3	Dodson(T) Evans(2T,C) A.K.Williams(T) Black(2T)
35		24	SALE	H	Won	1	4	-	1	25	-	1	-	2	10	Gerald(2T) Cusworth(C,P) Wheeler(T) Richardson(T) Foulkes-Arnold(T)
36		31	Headingley	A	Lost	-	-	-	1	3	-	-	-	4	12	Dodson(P)
37	Apr	7	WATERLOO	H	Drew	-	-	1	5	18	1	3	-	-	18	Pell(5P) Pell(D)
38		11	MOSELEY (MMT)	H	Won	3	1	-	3	31	2	1	-	2	22	Hare(3C,3P) A.K.Williams(2T) Pell(T) Tressler(T)
39		14	Bristol	A	Lost	1	1	1	1	16	5	1	-	3	43	Hare(P) A.K.Williams(2T) Cusworth(C,D)
40		21	Neath	A	Lost	3	-	-	2	24	3	1	1	1	28	Hare(3C,2P) Dexter(T) Hall(T) A.K.Williams(T)
41		23	Pontypool	A	Lost	-	-	-	-	0	1	1	1	2	19	

INDIVIDUAL APPEARANCES 1983-1984

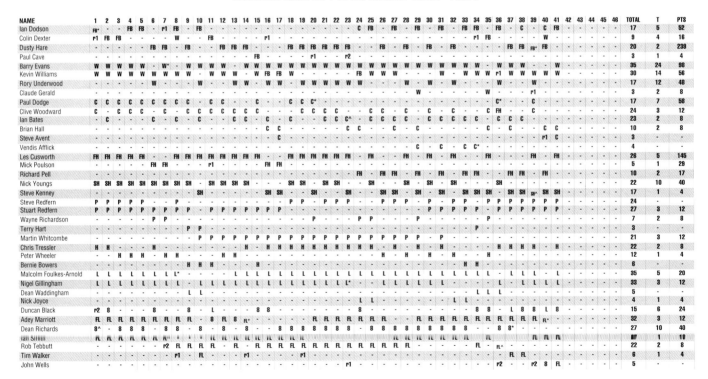

2 games: Lewis Clifford r1(37)H(40), Tommy Lawton L(9,12), Gareth Williams SH(15,24)

LEICESTER FOOTBALL CLUB 1983-84
Back: G.G. Willars (Coach), R. Beason (Hon.Tres), J.A. Allen (Hon.Sec), P.J. Wheeler, D. Richards,
P.W. Dodge, T.M. Walker, S.P. Redfern, M.V. Foulkes-Arnold, N.K. Gillingham, D. Black, M. Whitcombe,
W.H. Hare, P. Herbert (President), J.T. Thomas (Team Hon.Sec).
Middle: S.B. Redfern, A.N. Marriott, A.K. Williams, S. Kenney, I.R. Smith (Capt), C.J. Tressler,
B.J. Evans, I. Bates, R.S. Tebbutt, C.R. Woodward.
Front: I.R. Dodson, I. Pell.

1984 Tour - Middle East

GULF XV	v SOUTH GULF SELECT XV
Dusty Hare 7C	Ian Dodson 3C
Barry Evans 1T	Barry Evans 1T
Paul Dodge 1T	Paul Dodge
Ian Dodson	Brian Hall
Kevin Williams 1T	Colin Dexter 1T
Les Cusworth 2T	Dusty Hare 1C
Steve Kenney 2T	Nick Youngs 1T
Martin Whitcombe	Martin Whitcombe 1T
Peter Wheeler	Chris Tressler 1T
Wayne Richardson 1T	Terry Hart
Tom Smith	Tom Smith
Malcolm Foulkes-Arnold 1T	Malcolm Foulkes-Arnold 2T
Adey Marriott	Tim Walker
John Wells 1T	John Wells 1T
Ian Smith*	Ian Smith* 1T
Won 54-3	*Won 44-3*
Tigers:7G 3T	*Tigers:4G 5T*
Gulf XV:1PG	*S.Gulf:1PG*
27 Apr 1984	*29 Apr 1984*

RFU Merit Tables - Midlands Division 1983-84

		P	W	D	L	F	A	PTS	%
1	LEICESTER	5	5	-	-	237	41	10	100.00
2	Coventry	8	6	1	1	155	95	13	81.25
3	Nottingham	6	4	1	1	141	48	9	75.00
4	Moseley	8	5	-	3	142	95	10	62.50
5	Northampton	7	4	-	3	132	94	8	57.14
6	Nuneaton	8	4	-	4	109	163	8	50.00
7	Bedford	8	2	-	6	91	162	4	25.00
8	Birmingham	7	1	-	6	48	178	2	14.29
9	Rugby	7	-	-	7	64	243	0	0.00

1984-1985

NO	DATE	OPPONENTS	V	RES	FOR G	FOR T	FOR D	FOR P	FOR PTS	AGAINST G	AGAINST T	AGAINST D	AGAINST P	AGAINST PTS	SCORERS
1	Sep 1	BEDFORD (MMT)	H	Won	2	2	1	5	38	-	-	-	4	12	Hare(2C,5P) Evans(T) Cusworth(D) Steve.Redfern(2T) Penalty Try
2	4	Nuneaton (MMT)	A	Won	2	3	-	2	30	-	-	-	2	6	Hare(2C,2P) Gerald(T) Cusworth(T) Hartley(T) Black(T) Dodson(T)
3	8	Bath	A	Lost	1	-	-	-	6	1	2	-	1	17	Underwood(T) Cusworth(C)
4	12	BIRMINGHAM (MMT)	H	Won	5	2	-	1	41	-	1	-	-	4	Hare(5C,P) Williams(T) Woodward(T) Dexter(T) Hartley(T) Stuart.Redfern(T) Tressler(T) T.Smith(T)
5	15	LONDON WELSH	H	Won	1	-	1	3	18	-	-	1	2	9	Hare(C,3P) Cusworth(T,D)
6	22	Harlequins	A	Won	2	1	-	3	25	1	-	-	3	15	Hare(2C,3P) Underwood(2T) Steve.Redfern(T)
7	29	SARACENS	H	Won	1	1	-	4	22	1	-	1	2	15	Hare(C,4P) Williams(T) Dodge(T)
8	Oct 6	Coventry (MMT)	A	Won	4	2	-	2	38	-	-	-	2	6	Hare(4C,2P) Williams(T) Dexter(T) Youngs(T) Foulkes-Arnold(T) Wells(2T)
9	13	RICHMOND	H	Won	6	1	-	5	55	3	-	-	1	21	Hare(6C,5P) Evans(2T) Williams(T) Youngs(T) Stuart.Redfern(2T) Wells(T)
10	20	NORTHAMPTON (MMT)	H	Won	2	-	-	4	24	-	1	-	-	4	Hare(2C,4P) Youngs(2T)
11	24	OXFORD UNIVERSITY	H	Won	3	2	-	-	26	1	-	-	1	9	Pell(C) Woodward(C) Williams(T) Cusworth(C) Kenney(2T) Wells(T) I.R.Smith(T)
12	27	Swansea	A	Lost	1	-	1	1	12	2	1	1	2	25	Hare(C,P) Cusworth(D) Roy(T)
13	Nov 3	Cardiff	A	Lost	1	3	-	1	21	4	5	-	1	47	Hare(T,C,P) Williams(T) Dexter(2T)
14	10	CAMBRIDGE UNIVERSITY	H	Won	2	3	1	2	33	1	-	-	1	9	Afflick(T) Harris(2C,D,2P) Stuart.Redfern(T) Wells(3T)
15	13	NOTTINGHAM (MMT)	H	Won	-	-	1	3	12	-	-	-	2	6	Hare(D,3P)
16	17	Wasps	A	Drew	-	1	1	3	16	-	1	1	3	16	Harris(P) Woodward(D) Underwood(T) Pell(2P)
17	24	MOSELEY (MMT)	H	Lost	1	1	-	3	19	2	1	-	2	22	Hare(C,3P) Youngs(T) Robb(T)
18	Dec 1	Gloucester	A	Lost	2	-	-	1	15	4	1	-	3	37	Hare(2C,P) Harris(T) Richards(T)
19	8	BLACKHEATH	H	Won	4	5	-	2	50	1	2	-	-	14	Hare(T,4C,2P) Evans(4T) Underwood(2T) Cusworth(T) Richards(T)
20	15	Bristol	A	Won	1	2	-	-	14	-	1	-	-	4	Hare(T,C) Evans(2T)
21	22	London Welsh	A	Lost	1	2	-	1	17	2	1	-	3	25	Hare(C,P) Evans(T) Underwood(T) Tressler(T)
22	27	BARBARIANS	H	Won	4	2	-	1	35	-	2	-	1	11	Hare(4C,P) Evans(T) Williams(T) Cusworth(2T) Richards(T) I.R.Smith(T)
	Jan 5	Ballymena	A	Cancelled Frost											
23	12	GLOUCESTER	H	Won	2	-	1	4	27	-	-	1	1	6	Hare(T,2C,D,4P) Williams(T)
24	19	BEDFORD	H	Won	2	2	-	-	20	-	-	-	-	0	Hare(2C) Evans(2T) Cusworth(T) Richards(T)
25	26	BRISTOL (JPC3)	H	Won	4	1	1	4	43	-	1	-	-	4	Hare(4C,4P) Williams(T) Woodward(D) Underwood(4T)
26	Feb 2	London Scottish	A	Won	1	1	2	1	19	1	1	-	-	10	Evans(2T) Harris(C,P) Cusworth(2D)
	9	NEWPORT	H	Cancelled Frost											
	16	ORRELL	H	Cancelled Frost											
27	23	Liverpool (JPC4)	A	Won	3	1	2	3	37	-	-	-	3	9	Hare(3C,3P) Evans(2T) Underwood(T) Cusworth(2D) Wells(T)
28	Mar 2	HARLEQUINS	H	Won	3	2	2	1	35	1	1	-	3	19	Hare(T,3C,D,P) Woodward(T) Cusworth(T,D) Stuart.Redfern(T) Richards(T)
29	9	Coventry (JPCQF)	A	Drew	-	1	-	2	10	1	1	-	-	10	Hare(2P) Dodge(T)
30	12	LOUGHBOROUGH COLLEGE	H	Won	4	3	1	1	42	-	-	-	1	3	Hare(T,4C,P) Harris(D) Youngs(3T) Foulkes-Arnold(T) Steptoe(T) Richards(T)
31	15	ROYAL AIR FORCE	H	Won	3	5	-	-	38	-	-	-	1	3	Hare(3C) Harris(T) Williams(2T) Youngs(T) Richardson(T) Steptoe(T) Richards(T) I.R.Smith(T)
32	20	ROYAL NAVY	H	Won	5	1	-	2	40	2	1	-	-	16	Hare(5C,2P) Evans(T) Afflick(T) Dodge(T) Youngs(T) Collington(2T)
33	23	Sale	A	Lost	-	-	-	1	3	-	-	-	3	9	Hare(P)
34	30	HEADINGLEY	H	Lost	-	-	1	2	9	1	1	-	1	13	Hare(2P) Harris(D)
35	Apr 6	NEATH	H	Won	3	-	1	1	24	-	2	-	3	17	Hare(3C,P) Dexter(T) Cusworth(D) Youngs(T) Stuart.Redfern(T)
36	8	PONTYPOOL	H	Lost	-	-	-	2	6	1	1	1	3	22	Hare(2P)
37	13	BRISTOL	H	Lost	-	-	-	5	15	-	3	2	1	21	Hare(5P)
38	20	Gosforth	A	Won	1	1	1	2	19	-	1	1	1	10	Harris(C,2P) Cusworth(D) Youngs(T) Wells(T)
39	27	Moseley	A	Lost	1	-	-	1	9	1	1	-	-	10	Hare(C,P) Harris(T)

INDIVIDUAL APPEARANCES 1984-1985

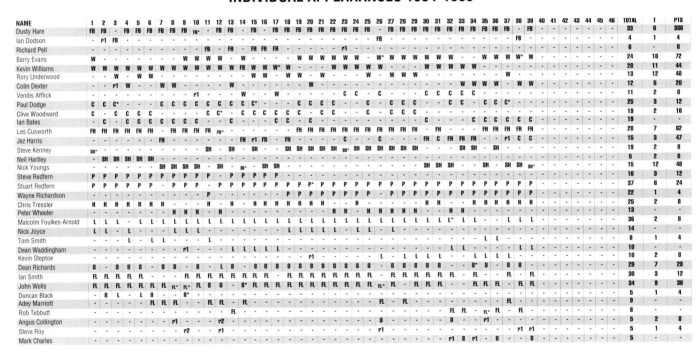

NAME	1	2	3	4	5	6	7	8	9	10	11	12	13	14	15	16	17	18	19	20	21	22	23	24	25	26	27	28	29	30	31	32	33	34	35	36	37	38	39	40	41	42	43	44	45	46	TOTAL	T	PTS
Dusty Hare	FB	FB	-	FB	FB	FB	FB	FB	FB	FB*	-	FB	FB	-	FB	-	FB	FB	FB	FB	FB	FB	FB	FB	FB	-	FB	FB	FB	FB	FB	FB	FB	FB	FB	FB	FB	-	FB	-	-	-	-	-	-	-	33	6	386
Ian Dodson	-	r1	FB	-	-	-	-	-	-	-	-	-	-	-	-	-	-	-	-	-	-	-	-	-	-	FB	-	-	-	-	-	-	-	-	-	-	-	FB	-	-	-	-	-	-	-	-	4	1	4
Richard Pell	-	-	-	-	-	-	-	-	-	-	FB	-	FH	-	FH	FH	FH	-	-	-	-	-	r1	-	-	-	-	-	-	-	-	-	-	-	-	-	-	-	-	-	-	-	-	-	-	-	6	-	8
Barry Evans	W	-	-	-	-	-	-	-	W	W	W	W	-	W	-	-	-	-	W	W	W	W	W	W	-	W*	W	W	W	W	W	W	-	-	W	W	W	W*	W	-	-	-	-	-	-	-	24	18	72
Kevin Williams	W	W	W	W	W	W	W	W	W	W	W	W	W	FB	W	W	W*	W	-	-	-	W	W	W	W	W	-	-	-	W	W	W	W	W	-	-	-	-	-	-	-	-	-	-	-	-	28	11	44
Rory Underwood	-	-	W	-	W	W	-	-	-	-	-	-	-	-	W	W	-	W	W	-	W	-	-	-	W	-	W	W	W	-	-	-	-	-	-	-	W	-	-	-	-	-	-	-	-	-	13	12	48
Colin Dexter	-	-	r1	W	-	-	W	W	-	-	-	-	W	-	-	-	-	-	-	W	-	-	-	-	-	-	-	-	-	-	-	-	W	W	W	W	-	W	W	-	-	-	-	-	-	-	12	5	20
Vendis Afflick	-	-	-	-	-	-	-	-	-	r1	-	-	-	W	-	-	W	-	-	-	-	-	C	C	-	C	-	-	-	C	C	C	C	C	-	-	-	-	-	-	-	-	-	-	-	-	11	2	8
Paul Dodge	C	C	C*	-	-	-	C	C	C	C	C	C	C	C	C*	-	-	-	C	C	C	C	-	-	C	-	C	C	C	-	-	C	C	-	C	C	C*	-	-	-	-	-	-	-	-	-	25	3	12
Clive Woodward	C	-	C	C	C	C	-	-	-	-	C	C*	-	C	C	C	C	C	C	-	C	C	-	-	C	-	C	C	C	-	-	-	-	-	-	-	-	-	-	-	-	-	-	-	-	-	19	2	16
Ian Bates	-	C	-	C	C	C	C	C	C	C	-	-	C	-	-	-	C	C	-	C	-	-	-	-	-	-	-	-	-	C	-	-	-	C	C	C	C	C	C	-	-	-	-	-	-	-	19	-	-
Les Cusworth	FH	FH	FH	FH	FH	FH	-	FH	FH	FH	FH	FH^	-	-	-	-	-	-	FH	FH	FH	FH	FH	FH	FH	FH	FH	FH	FH	-	FH	-	-	-	FH	FH	FH	FH	FH	-	-	-	-	-	-	-	28	7	62
Jez Harris	-	-	-	-	-	-	FH	-	-	-	-	-	-	FH	r1	FB	-	FH	-	-	-	-	C	-	-	C	-	-	-	FH	C	FH	FH	FH	-	-	r1	C	C	-	-	-	-	-	-	-	15	3	47
Steve Kenney	SH*	-	-	-	-	-	-	-	-	-	SH	-	SH	-	SH	-	-	SH	SH	SH	SH	SH	SH*	SH	SH	SH	SH	SH	SH	-	-	-	SH	SH	-	SH	-	-	-	-	-	-	-	-	-	-	19	2	8
Neil Hartley	-	SH	SH	SH	SH	SH	-	-	-	-	-	-	-	-	-	-	-	-	-	-	-	-	-	-	-	-	-	-	-	-	-	-	-	-	-	-	-	-	-	-	-	-	-	-	-	-	5	2	8
Nick Youngs	-	-	-	-	-	-	SH	SH	SH	SH	-	SH	-	SH^	-	SH	SH	-	-	-	-	-	-	-	-	-	-	-	-	SH	SH	SH	-	-	SH	-	SH	SH	SH*	-	-	-	-	-	-	-	15	12	48
Steve Redfern	P	P	P	P	P	P	P	P	P	P	P	-	P	P	P	P	P	-	-	-	-	-	-	-	-	-	-	-	-	-	-	-	-	-	-	-	-	-	-	-	-	-	-	-	-	-	16	3	12
Stuart Redfern	P	P	P	P	P	P	-	P	P	P	-	P	P	P	P	P	P	P	P	P	P*	P	P	P	P	P	P	P	P	P	P	P	P	P	P	P	P	P	P	-	-	-	-	-	-	-	37	6	24
Wayne Richardson	-	-	-	-	-	-	-	-	-	-	P	-	-	-	-	-	-	P	P	P	P	P	P	P	P	-	P	P	P	P	P	P	P	P	P	P	P	P	P	-	-	-	-	-	-	-	22	1	4
Chris Tressler	H	H	H	H	H	H	H	-	-	-	H	-	H	-	H	H	H	H	H	H	H	-	-	H	-	-	-	-	-	H	H	-	-	H	H	H	H	H	H	-	-	-	-	-	-	-	25	2	8
Peter Wheeler	-	-	-	-	-	-	-	H	H	H	-	H	-	-	-	-	-	-	-	-	-	H	H	-	H	H	H	H	H	-	-	H	H	-	-	-	-	-	-	-	-	-	-	-	-	-	13	-	-
Malcolm Foulkes-Arnold	L	L	L	-	L	L	L	L	L	L	L	L	L	L	L	L	L	L	L	L	L	L	L	L	L	L	L	L	L	L	L	L*	L	L	-	-	L	L	L	-	-	-	-	-	-	-	36	2	8
Nick Joyce	L	L	-	L	-	-	-	L	L	L	-	-	-	-	-	-	-	L	L	L	L	L	-	L	L	-	L	-	-	-	-	-	-	-	-	-	-	-	-	-	-	-	-	-	-	-	14	-	-
Tom Smith	-	-	-	L	-	L	L	-	-	-	L	-	-	-	-	-	-	-	-	-	-	-	-	-	-	-	-	-	-	-	-	-	-	-	L	L	-	-	-	-	-	-	-	-	-	-	6	1	4
Dean Waddingham	-	-	-	-	-	-	-	-	r1	-	-	-	L	L	L	L	L	-	-	-	-	-	-	-	-	-	-	-	-	-	-	L	L	-	-	-	-	L	L	-	-	-	-	-	-	-	10	-	-
Kevin Steptoe	-	-	-	-	-	-	-	-	-	-	-	-	-	-	-	-	-	-	-	r1	-	-	-	-	-	L	-	L	L	L	L	-	-	L	L	L	L	-	-	-	-	-	-	-	-	-	10	2	8
Dean Richards	8	-	8	8	8	-	8	8	-	8	-	L	8	-	8	8	8	8	8	8	8	8	8	8	8	-	8	8	8	8	8	-	-	8*	8	-	8	8	-	-	-	-	-	-	-	-	29	7	28
Ian Smith	FL	FL	FL	FL	FL	-	-	-	FL	FL	FL	FL	FL	FL	FL	FL	-	FL	FL	FL	FL	FL	FL	FL	FL	-	FL	FL	FL	FL	FL	FL	-	FL	-	-	FL	-	FL	-	-	-	-	-	-	-	30	3	12
John Wells	FL	FL	FL	FL	FL	FL	FL	FL*	FL^	FL	8	8	-	8*	FL	FL	FL	FL	FL	FL	FL	FL	FL	FL	FL	FL^	FL	-	FL	FL	FL	-	-	FL	FL	FL	-	FL	FL	-	-	-	-	-	-	-	34	9	36
Duncan Black	-	8	L	-	L	8	-	-	8*	-	-	-	-	-	-	-	-	-	-	-	-	-	-	-	-	-	-	-	-	-	-	-	-	-	-	-	-	-	-	-	-	-	-	-	-	-	5	1	4
Adey Marriott	-	-	-	-	-	FL	FL	FL	-	-	FL	FL	-	FL	-	-	-	-	-	-	-	-	-	-	-	FL	-	FL	-	-	-	-	-	-	-	-	FL	-	-	-	-	-	-	-	-	-	9	-	-
Rob Tebbutt	-	-	-	-	-	-	-	-	-	-	-	-	FL	-	-	-	-	-	-	-	-	-	-	-	-	-	-	-	-	-	-	FL	FL	-	FL*	FL	-	FL	-	-	-	-	-	-	-	-	6	-	-
Angus Collington	-	-	-	-	-	-	-	r1	-	-	-	r2	-	-	-	-	-	-	-	-	-	-	-	-	-	8	-	-	-	-	-	8	-	-	r1	-	-	-	-	-	-	-	-	-	-	-	5	2	8
Steve Roy	-	-	-	-	-	-	-	-	r2	-	-	r1	-	-	-	-	-	-	-	-	-	-	-	-	-	r1	-	-	-	-	-	-	-	-	-	-	-	r1	r1	-	-	-	-	-	-	-	5	1	4
Mark Charles	-	-	-	-	-	-	-	-	-	-	-	-	-	-	-	-	-	-	-	-	-	-	-	-	-	-	-	-	-	-	-	r1	8	r1	-	8	-	-	8	-	-	-	-	-	-	-	5	-	-

2 games: Claude Gerald r1(1)W*(2)[1T 4], Nick Jackson FL(17)L(22), Graham Robb r1(17)C(24)[1T 4], Martin Whitcombe P(7,26)
1 game: Steve Avent C(16), Lewis Clifford H(14), Ray French P(12), Terry Hart r1(14), Lyndsey Stratton FL(33), Tim Walker r2(26), Graham Willars r2(14)

LEICESTER FOOTBALL CLUB 1984-85
Back: G.G. Willars (Coach), J.T. Thomas (Team Hon.Sec.), P. Herbert (President), P.J. Wheeler,
P.W. Dodge, J.M. Wells, M.V. Foulkes-Arnold, D. Richards, W.P. Richardson,
S.B. Redfern, I. Bates, R. Beason (Hon.Tres.), J.A. Allen (Hon.Sec.).
Front: C.R. Woodward, W.H. Hare, L. Cusworth, B.J. Evans,
I.R. Smith (Capt), J.C. Harris, S. Kenney, N.G. Youngs, C.J. Tressler.

1985 Tour - France

v CHAMBERY	v ST CLAUDE
Peter Sly	Colin Dexter2
Mark Cleaver	Mark Cleaver
Ian Bates	Ian Bates
Graham Robb 1T	Vendis Afflick
Colin Dexter2	John Wood
Phil Kendall 1C	Phil Kendall 1C
Darren Grewcock	Steve Kenney
Martin Whitcombe3	Stuart Redfern
Chris Tressler1	Bernie Bowers1
Wayne Richardson	Wayne Richardson
Dean Waddingham	Dean Waddingham
Dean Richards	John Wells 1T
John Wells	Rob Tebbutt
Mark Charles	Dean Richards 1T
Ian Smith*	Ian Smith*
Bernie Bowers rep 1	Chris Tressler rep 1
Vendis Afflick rep 2	Peter Sly rep 2
Stuart Redfern rep 3	

Lost 6-32
Tigers:1G
Chambery:4G 2T
10 May 1985

Lost 10-13
Tigers:1G 1T
St Claude:1G 1T 1PG
12 May 1985

RFU Merit Tables - Midlands Division 1984-85

		P	W	D	L	F	A	PTS	%
1	Nottingham	8	7	-	1	236	51	14	87.50
	Moseley	8	7	-	1	227	81	14	87.50
3	**LEICESTER**	**7**	**6**	**-**	**1**	**202**	**60**	**12**	**85.71**
4	Coventry	7	4	-	3	148	123	8	57.14
5	Northampton	8	4	-	4	111	137	8	50.00
6	Bedford	7	2	-	5	84	158	4	28.57
7	Nuneaton	8	2	-	6	93	150	4	25.00
8	Rugby	7	1	-	6	43	169	2	14.29
9	Birmingham	8	1	-	7	68	283	2	12.50

NO	DATE		OPPONENTS	V	RES	FOR					AGAINST					SCORERS
						G	T	D	P	PTS	G	T	D	P	PTS	
1	Sep	7	Bedford	A	Won	5	4	-	2	52	-	-	-	2	6	Hare(3T,5C,2P) Evans(3T) Woodward(2T) Williams(T)
2		10	NUNEATON	H	Won	2	3	-	2	30	-	-	-	4	12	Hare(2C,2P) Evans(T) Woodward(T) Williams(T) Davidson(T) Wells(T)
3		14	BATH	H	Lost	1	-	-	3	15	5	1	-	2	40	Hare(C,3P) Evans(T)
4		18	Birmingham	A	Won	3	3	-	1	33	-	-	-	2	6	Hare(T,3C,P) Williams(2T) Cusworth(T) Redfern(T) Whitcombe(T)
5		21	London Welsh	A	Won	3	2	-	4	38	1	-	-	3	15	Hare(3C,4P) Redfern(T) Davidson(T) Richards(2T) Tebbutt(T)
6		28	Harlequins	A	Won	2	1	-	1	19	1	-	-	1	9	Hare(2C,P) Youngs(2T) Tebbutt(T)
7	Oct	5	COVENTRY	H	Won	5	-	-	4	42	1	1	-	2	16	Hare(T,5C,4P) Williams(T) Youngs(T) Wells(T) Tebbutt(T)
8		12	Richmond	A	Won	3	-	-	3	27	-	1	1	2	13	Hare(2C,3P) Evans(T) Cusworth(C) Foulkes-Arnold(T) Wells(T)
9		19	Northampton	A	Tale	-	2	-	2	14	1	-	-	-	6	Hare(2P) Wells(T) Tebbutt(T)
10		23	Oxford University	A	Won	4	2	-	-	32	-	1	-	1	7	Hare(4C) Burnhill(T) Cusworth(T) Kenney(T) Richards(3T)
11		26	SWANSEA	H	Won	2	-	-	2	18	-	1	-	2	10	Hare(T,2C,2P) Tebbutt(T)
12	Nov	2	CARDIFF	H	Lost	2	-	-	1	15	1	2	1	1	20	Hare(2C,P) Tressler(T) Davidson(T)
13		9	Cambridge University	A	Won	3	1	1	2	31	1	-	-	1	9	Hare(3C,D,2P) Dexter(T) Youngs(T) Richards(2T)
14		12	Nottingham	A	Won	1	-	-	3	15	1	-	-	1	9	Hare(C,3P) Evans(T)
15		16	WASPS	H	Won	1	1	-	3	19	1	-	-	-	6	Hare(C,3P) Youngs(2T)
16		23	Moseley	A	Lost	-	-	-	2	6	-	, 1	-	1	7	Hare(2P)
17		30	Saracens	A	Won	4	3	-	-	36	2	-	-	-	12	Hare(T,4C) Pell(2T) Youngs(T) Wells(T) Richards(2T)
18	Dec	7	GLOUCESTER	H	Lost	-	-	-	3	9	1	-	-	3	15	Hare(3P)
19		14	Blackheath	A	Won	-	1	-	4	16	1	-	-	2	12	Hare(4P) Evans(T)
20		21	BRISTOL	H	Won	4	-	-	2	30	3	1	-	1	25	Hare(4C,2P) Evans(T) Burnhill(T) Richards(2T)
21		28	BARBARIANS	H	Lost	2	1	-	-	16	2	1	-	1	19	Hare(C) Burnhill(T) Youngs(2T) Harris(C)
22	Jan	4	HEADINGLEY	H	Won	2	2	-	1	23	-	1	-	1	7	Hare(2C,P) Dodge(2T) Davidson(T) Penalty Try
23		11	Gloucester	A	Lost	1	1	-	-	10	-	3	-	1	15	Hare(C) Evans(T) Richards(T)
24		18	BEDFORD	H	Won	3	3	-	1	33	-	-	-	1	3	Dodson(3C) Evans(2T) Dodge(P) Burnhill(T) Youngs(T) Richards(2T)
25		25	Coventry (JPC3)	A	Won	1	-	2	3	21	-	2	1	1	14	Hare(C,3P) Evans(T) Cusworth(2D)
26	Feb	1	LONDON SCOTTISH	H	Won	3	-	1	1	24	-	-	-	-	0	Hare(3C,P) Dodge(D) Tebbutt(2T) Penalty Try
27		8	NORTHAMPTON	H	Won	2	1	-	3	25	-	3	1	-	15	Hare(2C,3P) Dodge(T) Cusworth(T) Tebbutt(T)
		15	Orrell	A		Cancelled Frost										
		22	Broughton Park (JPC4)	A		Cancelled										
		26	ROYAL NAVY	H		Cancelled Frost										
	Mar	1	HARLEQUINS	H		Cancelled										
		8	Coventry	A		Cancelled										
28		9	Broughton Park (JPC4)	A	Won	7	1	-	-	46	-	-	-	2	6	Hare(7C) Evans(T) Youngs(T) Tressler(T) Foulkes-Arnold(T) Wells(T) Richards(3T)
		11	LOUGHBOROUGH COLLEGE	H		Cancelled										
29		14	ROYAL AIR FORCE	H	Won	6	4	-	-	52	2	-	-	1	15	Hare(T,6C) Evans(2T) Burnhill(3T) Williams(T) Davidson(T) Charles(2T)
30		22	Harlequins (JPCQF)	A	Won	2	-	-	1	15	-	2	-	-	8	Hare(2C,P) Cusworth(T) Richards(T)
31		29	Neath	A	Won	2	-	-	1	15	-	2	-	1	11	Hare(2C,P) Evans(T) Charles(T)
32		31	Pontypool	A	Lost	-	-	1	1	6	3	3	-	3	39	Dodge(P) Harris(D)
33	Apr	5	BATH (JPCSF)	H	Lost	-	-	-	2	6	-	1	-	2	10	Hare(2P)
34		12	Bristol	A	Lost	-	-	-	1	3	3	2	-	1	29	Hare(P)
35		19	GOSFORTH	H	Won	7	2	-	2	56	1	-	-	3	15	Hare(T,7C,2P) Evans(2T) Burnhill(T) Williams(T) Harris(T) Kenney(T) Richards(2T)
36		26	MOSELEY	H	Lost	1	-	-	4	18	2	1	-	1	19	Hare(C,4P) Kenney(T)

INDIVIDUAL APPEARANCES 1985-1986

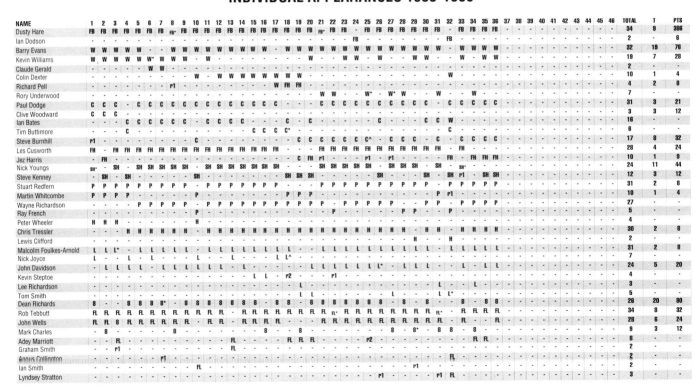

NAME	1	2	3	4	5	6	7	8	9	10	11	12	13	14	15	16	17	18	19	20	21	22	23	24	25	26	27	28	29	30	31	32	33	34	35	36	37	38	39	40	41	42	43	44	45	46	TOTAL	T	PTS
Dusty Hare	FB	FB	FB	FB	FB	FB	FB	FB*	FB	FB	FB	FB	FB	FB	FB	FB	FB	FB	FB	FB	FB*	FB		FB	FB	FB	FB	FB	FB	FB	FB			FB	FB	FB											34	9	386
Ian Dodson																								FB										FB													2		6
Barry Evans	W	W	W	W	W			W	W	W	W	W	W	W	W	W		W	W	W	W	W	W	W	W	W	W	W	W	W	W		W	W	W	W											32	19	76
Kevin Williams	W	W	W	W	W	W*	W	W	W		W										W			W			W				W			W		W											19	7	28
Claude Gerald							W	W																																							2		
Colin Dexter								W		W	W	W	W	W	W	W																		W													10	1	4
Richard Pell									r1								W	FH	FH																												4	2	8
Rory Underwood																					W	W		W*		W*	W		W			W														7		
Paul Dodge	C	C	C		C	C	C	C	C	C	C	C	C	C	C	C	C	C				C	C	C	C	C	C	C	C	C	C		C	C	C	C											31	3	21
Clive Woodward	C	C	C																																												3	3	12
Ian Bates				C	C	C	C	C	C		C	C	C	C				C		C									C					C	C	W												16		
Tim Buttimore					C										C	C	C	C*															C														6		
Steve Burnhill	r1							C											C	C	C	C	C	C^		C	C	C		C			C	C	C	C											17	8	32
Les Cusworth	FH		FH	FH	FH	FH	FH	FH	FH	FH	FH	FH	FH	FH	FH	FH			FH	FH	FH	FH	FH	FH	FH	FH	FH	FH		FH																	28	4	24
Jez Harris			FH															C	FH	r1				r1				FH		FH	FH	FH	FH														10	1	9
Nick Youngs	SH*		SH		SH	SH	SH	SH	SH		SH	SH	SH	SH	SH	SH			SH	SH	SH	SH	SH		SH	SH	SH		SH		SH*																24	11	44
Steve Kenney		SH		SH						SH									SH	SH	SH					SH				SH		SH	r1		SH	SH											12	3	12
Stuart Redfern	P	P	P	P	P	P	P	P	P		P	P	P	P	P	P	P	P				P	P	P	P	P	P	P	P	P	P		P		P	P											31	2	8
Martin Whitcombe	P	P	P	P						P									P	P													P	r1													10	1	4
Wayne Richardson					P	P	P	P	P		P	P	P	P	P	P	P	P	P	P		P	P	P	P		P	P		P					P	P											27		
Ray French																												P	P		P																4		
Peter Wheeler	H	H	H							H																																					4		
Chris Tressler				H		H	H	H	H		H	H	H	H	H	H	H	H	H	H	H	H	H		H	H	H	H		H					H												30	2	8
Lewis Clifford																																	H		H												2		
Malcolm Foulkes-Arnold	L		L*		L	L	L	L		L	L		L	L	L	L	L	L		L		L	L	L	L	L	L	L	L	L	L		L	L	L	L											31	2	8
Nick Joyce	L			L		L			L			L			L			L	L^																												7		
John Davidson		L	L	L		L	L	L	L		L	L	L					L				L	L	L	L	L	L	L*		L	L				L	L											24	5	20
Kevin Steptoe																L	L	r2				r1																									4		
Lee Richardson																								L									L		L	L*											3		
Tom Smith																								L	L					L				L	L*												5		
Dean Richards	8			8	8	8	8*		8	8	8	8	8	8		8	8		8		8	8	8	8	8	8		8		8					8	8											26	20	80
Rob Tebbutt	FL	FL		FL	FL	FL	FL	FL	FL	FL		FL	FL	FL	FL	FL	FL	FL	FL	FL	FL	FL	FL	FL	FL	FL	FL	FL	R*	FL	FL	FL															34	8	32
John Wells	FL	FL	8	FL	FL	FL	FL	FL	FL		FL	FL	FL		FL	FL	FL	FL	FL	FL	FL	FL	FL	FL	FL	FL	FL	FL		FL				FL		FL											28	6	24
Mark Charles		8						8									8		8										8		8*		8	8	8												9	3	12
Adey Marriott														FL			FL	FL	FL									r2																			8		
Graham Smith			r1											FL																																	2		
Angus Collington							r1																									FL															2		
Ian Smith											FL																								r1												2		
Lyndsey Stratton																											r1							r1	FL												3		

1 game: Neil Beazley r1(18), Darren Grewcock SH(34), Kevin McDonald r1(6)

LEICESTER FOOTBALL CLUB 1985-86

Back: G.G. Willars (Coach), J.T. Thomas (Team Hon.Sec), J.M. Wells, D. Richards, M.V. Foulkes-Arnold, J. Davidson, W.P. Richardson, S.B. Redfern, R. Beason (President), J.A. Allen (Hon.Sec), R.J. Farrands (Hon.Tres).

Middle: A.K. Williams, S. Kenney, P.W. Dodge, L. Cusworth (Capt), W.H. Hare, C.J. Tressler, B.J. Evans, R.S. Tebbutt.

Front: I. Bates, S.B. Burnhill.

John Smith's National Merit Tables - Division A 1985-86

		P	W	D	L	F	A	PTS	%
1	Gloucester	9	8	-	1	170	120	16	88.89
2	Nottingham	7	5	-	2	146	82	10	71.43
	Wasps	7	5	-	2	123	104	10	71.43
4	**LEICESTER**	**10**	**7**	-	**3**	**213**	**133**	**14**	**70.00**
5	Bath	6	3	-	3	142	73	6	50.00
	Harlequins	4	2	-	2	74	52	4	50.00
7	Bristol	7	3	-	4	117	120	6	42.86
	London Scottish	7	3	-	4	81	139	6	42.86
9	Sale	5	2	-	3	63	97	4	40.00
	Gosforth	5	2	-	3	52	109	4	40.00
11	Moseley	9	2	-	7	102	156	4	22.22
12	Headingley	8	-	-	8	77	175	0	0.00

NO	DATE		OPPONENTS	V	RES	FOR G	T	D	P	PTS	AGAINST G	T	D	P	PTS	SCORERS
1	Sep	6	BEDFORD	H	Won	2	1	-	2	22	-	1	1	1	10	Hare(2C,2P) Evans(2T) Dodge(T)
2		9	Nuneaton	A	Won	5	4	-	1	49	-	-	-	2	6	Hare(T,5C,P) Williams(T) Underwood(4T) W.P.Richardson(T) Richards(2T)
3		13	Bath	A	Lost	-	-	-	1	3	-	-	-	2	6	Hare(P)
4		17	BIRMINGHAM	H	Won	13	2	-	3	95	1	-	-	-	6	Hare(2T,13C,3P) Evans(T) Dodge(T) Buttimore(T) Youngs(4T) Redfern(T) Davidson(T) Charles(T) Tebbutt(3T)
5		20	LONDON WELSH	H	Won	9	3	-	1	69	-	1	-	-	4	Hare(9C,P) Evans(2T) Underwood(4T) Youngs(T) Redfern(T) Tressler(T) W.P.Richardson(T) Richards(2T)
6		27	Harlequins	A	Lost	1	-	1	1	12	-	2	1	3	20	Hare(C,P) Cusworth(D) Penalty Try
7	Oct	4	Coventry (JSA)	A	Won	1	1	-	1	13	-	-	-	4	12	Hare(C,P) Cusworth(T) Richards(T)
8		11	RICHMOND	H	Won	3	-	-	6	36	1	1	-	3	19	Hare(3C,6P) Evans(T) Dodge(T) Cusworth(T)
9		18	NORTHAMPTON	H	Won	2	-	-	4	24	-	-	1	4	15	Hare(2C,4P) Richards(2T)
10		22	OXFORD UNIVERSITY	H	Won	3	3	-	1	33	1	1	-	2	16	Hare(3C,P) Evans(T) Youngs(T) Roberts(T) Richards(3T)
11		25	Swansea	A	Won	1	1	1	-	13	-	2	-	1	11	Hare(C) Dodge(T) Cusworth(D) Richards(T)
12	Nov	1	Cardiff	A	Lost	1	1	-	-	10	-	1	-	4	16	Hare(C) Redfern(T) Wells(T)
13		4	FIJI BARBARIANS	H	Won	6	-	-	1	39	1	2	-	-	14	Hare(6C,P) Lane(T) Dodge(T) Buttimore(T) Williams(2T) Grewcock(T)
14		8	NOTTINGHAM (JSA)	H	Won	-	-	-	3	9	-	-	-	1	3	Hare(3P)
15		12	Cambridge University	A	Won	4	2	-	-	32	1	1	-	-	10	Lane(T) Buttimore(T) Underwood(T) Cusworth(4C) Clifford(T) French(T) I.R.Smith(T)
16		15	Wasps (JSA)	A	Won	-	2	1	2	17	1	1	-	1	13	Hare(2P) Cusworth(D) Youngs(T) Richards(T)
17		22	MOSELEY (JSA)	H	Won	1	1	-	4	22	-	-	-	2	6	Hare(C,4P) Richards(2T)
18		29	SARACENS (JSA)	H	Won	-	1	-	5	19	1	1	-	2	16	Hare(5P) Burnell(T)
19	Dec	6	Gloucester	A	Lost	1	-	-	-	6	3	5	-	1	41	Hare(C) Penalty Try
20		13	BLACKHEATH	H	Won	-	2	1	2	17	-	1	1	1	10	Hare(2P) Harris(D) Youngs(T) Charles(T)
21		20	Bristol	A	Lost	1	-	-	1	9	2	6	-	1	39	Hare(C,P) Marriott(T)
22		27	BARBARIANS	H	Lost	2	-	-	2	18	2	1	-	2	22	Hare(T,2C,2P) Richards(T)
23	Jan	3	Headingley	A	Won	3	1	-	-	22	2	1	-	1	19	Hare(3C) Dexter(T) Youngs(T) Povoas(2T)
24		10	GLOUCESTER (JSA)	H	Lost	-	-	-	4	12	-	2	1	1	14	Hare(4P)
		16	Bedford	A		Cancelled										
25		24	Metropolitan Police	A	Won	4	3	1	-	39	-	-	-	-	0	Dodson(C) Underwood(T) Cusworth(T,3C,D) Redfern(T) Foulkes-Arnold(T) Richards(2T) Tebbutt(T)
		31	Rosslyn Park (JPC3)	A		Cancelled										
26	Feb	7	London Scottish (JSA)	A	Drew	-	-	1	3	12	1	-	1	1	12	Hare(3P) Harris(D)
27		14	Rosslyn Park (JPC3)	A	Won	1	-	1	3	18	1	-	-	3	15	Hare(C,3P) Cusworth(D) Povoas(T)
28		21	ORRELL (JSA)	H	Won	-	3	-	6	30	2	1	1	1	22	Hare(T,6P) Dexter(T) Kenney(T)
29		28	GOSFORTH (JPC4)	H	Won	1	1	1	2	19	-	-	-	2	6	Hare(C,2P) Evans(T) Cusworth(D) Charles(T)
30	Mar	7	HARLEQUINS (JSA)	H	Won	2	-	-	2	18	-	2	-	-	8	Hare(2C,2P) Kenney(T) Tebbutt(T)
31		14	Bristol (JSA) & (JPCQF)	A	Won	-	2	1	2	17	-	1	-	1	7	Hare(2P) Dexter(T) Cusworth(T,D)
32		18	N.ZEALAND BARBARIANS	H	Lost	-	-	-	1	3	2	3	1	2	33	Hare(P)
33		20	LOUGHBOROUGH COLLEGE	H	Won	6	2	-	-	44	1	1	1	1	16	Hare(6C) Dodge(T) Dexter(2T) T.Smith(T) Wells(T) Richards(3T)
34		28	Wasps (JPCSF)	A	Lost	-	-	-	2	6	1	1	-	1	13	Hare(2P)
35	Apr	4	Waterloo	A	Won	1	-	2	1	15	-	-	-	3	9	Hare(C,P) Cusworth(2D) Charles(T)
36		11	BRISTOL	H	Lost	1	2	-	3	23	2	2	-	3	29	Hare(C,3P) Bates(T) Burnhill(2T)
37		18	NEATH	H	Lost	-	-	2	2	12	1	2	-	1	17	Hare(2P) Cusworth(2D)
38		20	PONTYPOOL	H	Won	4	1	1	2	37	1	-	-	2	12	Hare(4C,D,2P) Buttimore(2T) Dexter(T) Burnell(T) Povoas(T)
39		25	Moseley	A	Lost	-	-	-	2	6	2	1	1	1	22	Hare(2P)

INDIVIDUAL APPEARANCES 1986-1987

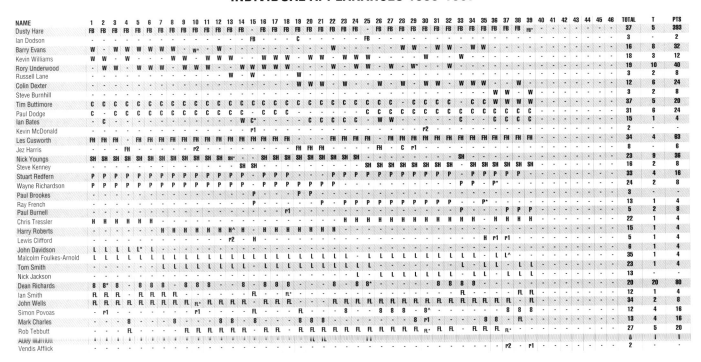

NAME	1	2	3	4	5	6	7	8	9	10	11	12	13	14	15	16	17	18	19	20	21	22	23	24	25	26	27	28	29	30	31	32	33	34	35	36	37	38	39	40	41	42	43	44	45	46	TOTAL	T	PTS
Dusty Hare	FB	FB	FB	FB	FB	FB	FB	FB	FB	FB	FB	FB	FB	-	FB	FB	FB	FB	FB	FB	FB	FB	FB	-	FB	FB	FB	FB	FB	FB	FB	FB	FB	FB	FB*	-	-	-	-	-	-	-	-	-			37	5	393
Ian Dodson	-	-	-	-	-	-	-	-	-	-	-	-	FB	-	-	-	C	-	-	-	-	-	FB	-	-	-	-	-	-	-	-	-	-	-	-	-	-	-	-								3	-	2
Barry Evans	W	-	W	W	W	W	W	W	-	W^	-	W	-	-	-	-	-	-	-	-	-	W	-	-	-	-	-	W	W	-	W	W	-	W	W	-	-	-	-							16	8	32
Kevin Williams	W	W	-	W	-	-	W	W	-	W	W	W	-	-	W	W	W	-	W	W	-	W	W	W	-	W	W	W	-	W	-	-	W	-	W	-	W	-	-							18	3	12
Rory Underwood	-	W	W	-	W	W	W	-	W	W	W	-	-	W	W	W	W	W	-	W	-	W	W	W	-	W	-	W*	-	W	-	W	-	W	-	-	-	-	-							19	10	40
Russell Lane	-	-	-	-	-	-	-	-	-	-	-	-	W	-	W	-	-	-	-	W	-	-	-	-	-	-	-	-	-	-	-	-	-	-	-	-	-	-	-							3	2	8
Colin Dexter	-	-	-	-	-	-	-	-	-	-	-	-	-	-	-	-	-	-	W	W	W	-	W	-	-	W	-	W	-	-	W	W	-	W	W	-	W	-							12	6	24
Steve Burnhill	-	-	-	-	-	-	-	-	-	-	-	-	-	-	-	-	-	-	-	-	-	-	-	-	-	-	-	-	-	-	-	-	-	-	W	W	-	W	-							3	2	8
Tim Buttimore	C	C	C	C	C	C	C	C	C	C	C	C	C	C	C	C	C	C	C	C	C	C	C	C	C	-	C	C	C	C	-	C	C	W	W	W	W	-	-							37	5	20
Paul Dodge	C	-	C	C	C	C	C	C	C	C	C	C	-	C	C	C	-	-	-	-	-	C	C	C	C	C	C	C	C	C	C	C	C	C	C	C	-	-	-							31	6	24
Ian Bates	-	C	-	-	-	-	-	-	-	-	-	-	W	C*	-	-	-	-	C	C	C	C	C	-	W	W	-	-	-	C	-	-	C	-	C	C	C	-	-							15	1	4
Kevin McDonald	-	-	-	-	-	-	-	-	-	-	-	-	-	r1	-	-	-	-	-	-	-	-	-	-	-	-	-	-	-	-	r2	-	-	-	-	-	-	-	-							2	-	-
Les Cusworth	FH	FH	FH	-	FH	FH	FH	FH	FH	FH	FH	FH	FH	FH	FH	FH	FH	-	-	FH	FH	FH	FH	-	FH	FH	FH	FH	FH	FH	FH	FH	FH	FH	FH	-	-	-	-							34	4	63
Jez Harris	-	-	-	FH	-	-	-	-	-	-	-	r2	-	-	-	-	-	-	FH	FH	FH	-	-	FH	-	C	r1	-	-	-	-	-	-	-	-	-	-	-	-							8	-	6
Nick Youngs	SH	SH	SH	SH	SH	SH	SH	SH	SH	SH	SH	SH	SH	SH*	-	-	SH	SH	SH	SH	SH	SH	SH	SH	SH	-	-	-	-	SH	-	SH	SH	SH	SH	SH	SH	-	-							23	9	36
Steve Kenney	-	-	-	-	-	-	-	-	-	-	-	-	-	-	SH	SH	-	-	-	-	-	-	-	-	-	SH	SH	SH	SH	SH	SH	SH	-	SH	SH	SH	SH	-	-							16	2	8
Stuart Redfern	P	P	P	P	P	P	P	P	P	P	P	P	P	-	P	P	P	-	P	P	P	-	-	P	P	P	P	P	P	P	P	P	-	P	P	P	P	-	-							33	4	16
Wayne Richardson	P	P	P	P	P	P	P	P	P	P	P	P	P	-	P	P	P	P	P	P	P	-	-	-	-	-	-	-	-	-	P	P	P*	-	-	-	-	-	-							24	2	8
Paul Brookes	-	-	-	-	-	-	-	-	-	-	-	-	P	-	-	-	-	-	P	P	-	-	-	-	-	-	-	-	-	-	-	-	-	-	-	-	-	-	-							3	-	-
Ray French	-	-	-	-	-	-	-	-	-	-	-	-	-	P	-	-	-	-	-	-	-	P	-	P	P	P	P	P	P	P	-	-	-	-	P*	-	-	-	-							13	1	4
Paul Burnell	-	-	-	-	-	-	-	-	-	-	-	-	-	-	-	r1	-	-	-	-	-	-	-	-	-	-	-	-	-	-	P	-	-	-	-	P	P	P	-							5	2	8
Chris Tressler	H	H	H	H	-	H	H	-	-	-	-	-	-	-	-	-	-	-	-	-	H	H	H	H	H	H	H	H	H	H	-	-	-	-	-	-	-	-	-							22	1	4
Harry Roberts	-	-	-	-	-	-	H	H	H	H	H	H	H^	H	-	H	H	H	H	H	H	H	-	-	-	-	-	-	-	-	-	-	-	-	-	-	-	-	-							15	1	4
Lewis Clifford	-	-	-	-	-	-	-	-	-	-	-	-	r2	-	H	-	-	-	-	-	-	-	-	-	-	-	-	-	-	-	-	H	r1	r1	-	-	-	-	-							5	1	4
John Davidson	L	L	L	L	L	L*	-	L	-	-	-	-	-	-	-	-	-	-	-	-	-	-	-	-	-	-	-	-	-	-	-	-	-	-	-	-	L	L^	-							6	1	4
Malcolm Foulkes-Arnold	L	L	L	L	-	L	L	L	L	L	L	L	L	L	L	L	L	L	L	L	L	L	-	L	L	L	L	L	L	L	L	L	L	-	L	L	L	L	-							35	1	4
Tom Smith	-	-	-	-	-	-	-	-	L	L	L	L	L	-	L	L	L	-	L	L	L	L	L	L	L	L	L	L	L	-	-	-	-	-	L	-	L	L	-							23	1	4
Nick Jackson	-	-	-	-	-	-	-	-	-	-	-	-	-	-	-	-	-	-	-	-	-	-	-	L	L	L	L	L	L	L	L	L	L	-	-	-	-	-	-							13	-	-
Dean Richards	8	8*	8	-	8	8	8	-	8	8	8	-	-	8	-	8	8	8	-	-	8	-	8	8*	-	-	-	-	-	-	8	8	8	-	-	-	-	-	-							20	20	80
Ian Smith	FL	FL	FL	-	FL	FL	FL	-	-	-	-	-	-	FL	-	-	FL	-	FL*	-	-	-	-	-	-	-	-	-	-	-	-	-	FL	-	-	-	FL	FL	-							12	1	4
John Wells	FL	FL	FL	FL	FL	FL	FL	FL	FL	FL	FL	FL	-	FL	FL	FL	-	FL	FL	FL	-	FL	FL	FL	FL	FL	FL	FL	FL	FL	FL	FL	FL	FL	FL	FL	FL	-	-							34	2	8
Simon Povoas	-	r1	-	-	-	-	-	8	-	-	r1	-	-	-	FL	-	-	-	8	-	-	8	-	8	8	8	-	8^	-	-	-	-	-	8	8	8	-	-	-							12	4	16
Mark Charles	-	-	-	8	-	-	-	8	-	-	8	8	-	8	-	-	-	8	8	8	-	-	-	-	-	-	8	r1	-	-	8	8	-	FL	-	-	-	-	-							27	5	20
Rob Tebbutt	-	-	FL	-	-	-	-	FL	FL	FL	FL	FL	-	FL	FL	FL	-	FL	FL	FL	-	FL	FL	FL	FL	R*	-	FL	FL	FL	FL	R*	-	-	-	-	-	-	-							13	4	18
Adey Marriott	-	-	-	-	-	-	-	-	-	-	-	-	-	-	-	-	FL	FL	-	-	-	FL	-	-	-	-	-	-	-	-	-	-	-	-	-	-	-	-	-							6	1	4
Vendis Afflick	-	-	-	-	-	-	-	-	-	-	-	-	-	-	-	-	-	-	-	-	-	-	-	-	-	-	-	-	-	-	-	-	-	-	r2	-	r1	-	-							2	-	-

1 game: Paul Coltman P(39), Darren Grewcock r1(13)[1T-4], Phil Mann L(15), Lee Richardson r1(4), Graham Willars r1(35)

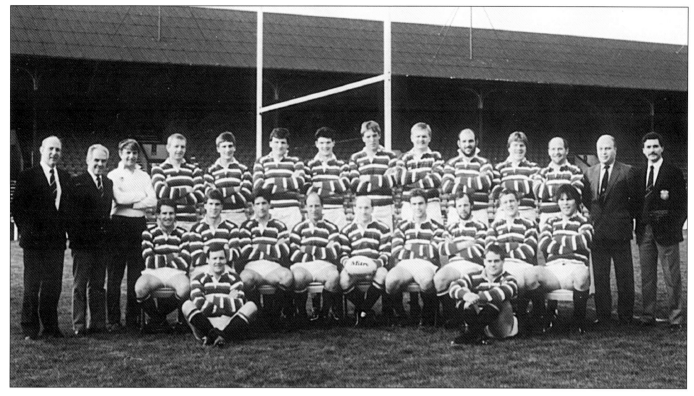

LEICESTER FOOTBALL CLUB 1986-87
Back: R. Beason (President), J.T. Thomas (Team Hon.Sec), G.G. Willars (Coach),
D. Richards, C.D. Dexter, M.V. Foulkes-Arnold, M.R. Charles, T. Smith, N.A. Jackson, W.P. Richardson,
S.B. Redfern, Ray French, J.A. Allen (Hon.Sec), R.J. Farrands (Hon.Tres).
Middle: T.J. Buttimore, B.J. Evans, P.W. Dodge, W.H. Hare, L. Cusworth (Capt), I. Bates, S. Kenney, R.S. Tebbutt, J.M. Wells.
Front: C.J. Tressler, H. Roberts.

1987 Tour - Australia and Singapore

v WESTERN AUSTRALIA	v W.AUSTRALIA PRESIDENT'S XV	v MANLY	v PONSONBY	v QUEENSLAND	v SINGAPORE C.C.
Dusty Hare 1C,3P	Paul Dodge1*	Dusty Hare 3C,1P	Jez Harris 2C,2P	Dusty Hare1 1P	Les Cusworth*
Barry Evans	Tim Buttimore	Barry Evans	Barry Evans 1T	Tim Buttimore	Barry Evans 3T
Paul Dodge* 1T	Ian Bates 1T	Ian Bates	Paul Dodge*	Paul Dodge*	Ian Bates 1T
Tim Buttimore	Steve Burnhill	Tim Buttimore	Steve Burnhill	Ian Bates	Steve Burnhill 2T
Steve Burnhill 1T	Colin Dexter 1T	Colin Dexter	Colin Dexter	Colin Dexter	Colin Dexter 3T
Les Cusworth	Jez Harris 3C,2P	Les Cusworth*	Les Cusworth	Les Cusworth	Jez Harris 8C
Nick Youngs	Steve Kenney	Nick Youngs 1T	Steve Kenney	Nick Youngs 1T	Steve Kenney
Paul Burnell	Stuart Redfern	Paul Burnell1	Stuart Redfern	Stuart Redfern	Stuart Redfern
Chris Tressler	Harry Roberts	Chris Tressler 1T	Harry Roberts	Chris Tressler	Harry Roberts 1T
Wayne Richardson	Ray French	Wayne Richardson	Wayne Richardson	Ray French2	Wayne Richardson
Phil Mann	Phil Mann	Tom Smith	Phil Mann	Phil Mann	Malcolm Foulkes-Arnold 1T
Malcolm Foulkes-Arnold1	Tom Smith	Malcolm Foulkes-Arnold	Tom Smith	Malcolm Foulkes-Arnold	Tom Smith
Adey Marriott	John Wells 1T	Adey Marriott	John Wells	John Wells	Adey Marriott 1T
Mark Charles2	Simon Povoas 1T	Simon Povoas 1T	Simon Povoas 3T	Mark Charles 1T	Simon Povoas
Ian Smith	Rob Tebbutt	Rob Tebbutt	Ian Smith	Rob Tebbutt	Ian Smith
John Wells rep 1	Dusty Hare rep 1	Stuart Redfern rep 1		Jez Harris rep 1 1C	Tim Buttimore rep 1 1T
Tom Smith rep 2				Wayne Richardson rep 2	
				Adey Marriott rep 3	
Lost 19-26	*Won 28-10*	*Won 21-10*	*Won 26-17*	*Lost 13-37*	*Won 68-0*
Tigers:1G 1T 3PG	*Tigers:3G 1T 2PG*	*Tigers:3G 1PG*	*Tigers:2G 2T 2PG*	*Tigers:1G 1T 1PG*	*Tigers:8G 5T*
W.Australia:2G 2T 2DG	*W.A.Pres.:1T 2PG*	*Manly:1G 1T*	*Ponsonby:N/A*	*Queensland:4G 1T 3PG*	*Singapore:Nil*
2 Aug 1987	*4 Aug 1987*	*9 Aug 1987*	*12 Aug 1987*	*16 Aug 1987*	*18 Aug 1987*

John Smith's National Merit Tables - Division A 1986-87

		P	W	D	L	F	A	PTS	%
1	Bath	7	6	-	1	178	65	12	85.71
2	**LEICESTER**	**10**	**7**	**1**	**2**	**153**	**103**	**15**	**75.00**
3	Moseley	10	6	1	3	107	133	13	65.00
4	Nottingham	7	4	1	2	92	71	9	64.29
5	Bristol	10	5	-	5	170	126	10	50.00
	Gloucester	8	4	-	4	106	95	8	50.00
7	Sale	7	3	-	4	82	136	6	42.86
8	Coventry	11	4	-	7	145	189	8	36.36
9	Wasps	6	2	-	4	109	94	4	33.33
	Harlequins	6	2	-	4	59	82	4	33.33
11	Orrell	7	2	-	5	67	145	4	28.57
	London Scottish	7	1	1	5	84	113	3	21.43

1987-1988

NO	DATE		OPPONENTS	V	RES	FOR					AGAINST					SCORERS
						G	T	D	P	PTS	G	T	D	P	PTS	
1	Sep	5	Bedford	A	Won	2	2	1	2	29	1	-	-	1	9	Hare(2C,D,2P) Evans(T) Bates(T) Tebbutt(T) Penalty Try
2		8	NUNEATON	H	Won	8	1	-	-	52	-	-	-	-	0	Dodge(2T) Buttimore(T) Burnhill(T) Dexter(2T) Harris(8C) Povoas(T) Tebbutt(2T)
3		12	BATH (CL)	H	Won	-	3	1	3	24	1	1	1	-	13	Hare(3P) Dexter(T) Cusworth(T,D) Harris(T)
4		19	LONDON WELSH	H	Lost	-	-	-	2	6	-	-	-	3	9	Nockles(P) Dodge(P)
5		26	Harlequins (CL)	A	Won	1	-	1	1	12	1	-	-	1	9	Hare(C,D,P) Evans(T)
6	Oct	3	COVENTRY (CL)	H	Won	2	2	1	3	32	1	1	-	2	16	Hare(2C,3P) Burnhill(T) Cusworth(D) Kenney(T) Richardson(T) Charles(T)
7		10	Richmond	A	Won	1	2	-	2	20	-	-	-	2	6	Hare(C,2P) Cusworth(T) Kenney(T) Richards(T)
8		17	Northampton	A	Won	5	2	-	3	47	-	-	-	-	0	Hare(5C,3P) Evans(3T) R.Underwood(T) Cusworth(T) Redfern(T) Richards(T)
9		21	Oxford University	A	Won	-	2	-	3	17	-	-	-	2	6	Evans(2T) Harris(3P)
10		24	SWANSEA	H	Lost	-	-	-	3	9	1	2	-	1	17	Hare(3P)
11		31	Llanelli	A	Lost	2	-	1	-	15	1	2	1	1	20	Hare(2C) Buttimore(T) R.Underwood(T) Cusworth(D)
12	Nov	7	CARDIFF	H	Won	1	-	1	6	27	1	1	2	1	19	Hare(C,D,6P) Richards(T)
13		10	CAMBRIDGE UNIVERSITY	H	Won	7	4	-	2	64	1	-	-	-	6	Hare(7C,2P) Bates(2T) Buttimore(T) Dexter(3T) Roberts(T) Foulkes-Arnold(T) T.Smith(T) Wells(T) Povoas(T)
14		14	Nottingham (CL)	A	Won	-	1	1	5	22	-	1	1	2	13	Hare(5P) Cusworth(D) Richards(T)
15		21	WASPS (CL)	H	Won	-	-	1	3	12	-	-	-	3	9	Hare(3P) Cusworth(D)
16		28	Moseley (CL)	A	Won	2	-	-	3	21	-	-	-	1	3	Hare(2C,3P) Evans(T) Richards(T)
17	Dec	5	GLOUCESTER	H	Won	1	1	-	3	19	2	-	-	-	12	Hare(C,3P) Evans(T) Povoas(T)
18		12	Blackheath	A	Won	1	1	1	1	16	2	-	1	-	15	Harris(T,C,D,P) Kenney(T)
19		19	BRISTOL (CL)	H	Won	1	-	-	3	15	-	1	-	2	10	Hare(C,3P) Evans(T)
20		28	BARBARIANS	H	Won	6	3	-	-	48	4	-	1	1	30	Hare(T,6C) Evans(T) Buttimore(T) R.Underwood(T) Youngs(T) Redfern(T) Wells(T) Richards(T) Thornley(T)
21	Jan	2	HEADINGLEY	H	Won	5	1	-	-	37	-	-	-	2	6	Hare(5C) Dexter(T) Harris(D) Youngs(T) Mann(T) Povoas(2T) Penalty Try
22		9	Gloucester	A	Lost	-	1	-	4	16	3	3	-	-	30	Hare(4P) Kenney(T)
23		16	BEDFORD	H	Won	5	3	-	-	42	1	-	1	-	9	Hare(5C) Evans(2T) Bates(T) Youngs(3T) Roberts(T) Povoas(T)
24		23	Rosslyn Park (JPC3)	A	Won	1	-	-	3	15	-	-	-	-	0	Hare(C,3P) Thornley(T)
25		30	London Welsh	A	Won	5	2	-	1	41	1	-	-	-	6	Hare(5C,P) Evans(2T) R.Underwood(T) Cusworth(T) Youngs(T) Richards(T) Penalty Try
	Feb	3	TOULON	H	Cancelled											
26		6	LONDON SCOTTISH	H	Won	4	1	-	2	34	1	-	1	2	15	Evans(T) Harris(4C,2P) Kenney(T) Povoas(3T)
27		13	BATH (JPC4)	H	Lost	1	-	-	-	6	-	1	1	2	13	Hare(C) Youngs(T)
28		20	Orrell (CL)	A	Lost	-	-	-	2	6	4	-	-	2	30	Hare(2P)
29		27	NORTHAMPTON	H	Won	4	2	-	1	35	-	-	-	3	9	Hare(4C,P) R.Underwood(4T) Dexter(T) Roberts(T)
30	Mar	5	Saracens	A	Won	2	1	1	3	28	-	2	-	-	8	Hare(2C,3P) Harris(D) Grewcock(T) Roberts(T) Tebbutt(T)
31		8	ROYAL AIR FORCE	H	Won	8	-	1	-	51	-	-	-	-	0	Hare(8C) Evans(T) Dexter(2T) Harris(T,D) Grewcock(T) Charles(T) Tebbutt(2T)
		12	Coventry	A	Cancelled										'	
		15	LOUGHBOROUGH COLLEGE	H	Cancelled Frost											
32		18	LANSDOWNE	H	Won	3	5	-	-	38	1	1	-	1	13	Hare(3C) Evans(T) Bates(T) Harris(T) Kenney(T) Roberts(T) Charles(2T) Grewcock(T)
33		26	SALE (CL)	H	Won	5	-	-	4	42	1	-	-	3	15	Hare(5C,4P) Evans(T) Bates(T) Charles(3T)
34	Apr	2	Ballymena	A	Won	-	1	-	5	19	2	1	-	-	16	Hare(5P) Gerald(T)
35		4	WATERLOO (CL)	H	Won	4	-	1	4	39	2	-	-	1	15	Hare(4C,4P) Evans(T) R.Underwood(T) Cusworth(D) Thornley(T) Penalty Try
36		9	Bristol	A	Won	-	-	3	2	15	-	-	1	3	12	Hare(2P) Cusworth(3D)
37		16	GOSFORTH	H	Won	9	2	1	-	65	-	-	-	-	0	Harris(T,9C,D) R.Underwood(3T) Redfern(T) Wells(T) Richards(3T) Tebbutt(T) Grewcock(T)
38		23	MOSELEY	H	Won	4	2	1	2	41	-	-	-	1	3	Harris(4C,D,2P) Bates(T) Dexter(2T) Thornley(3T)

INDIVIDUAL APPEARANCES 1987-1988

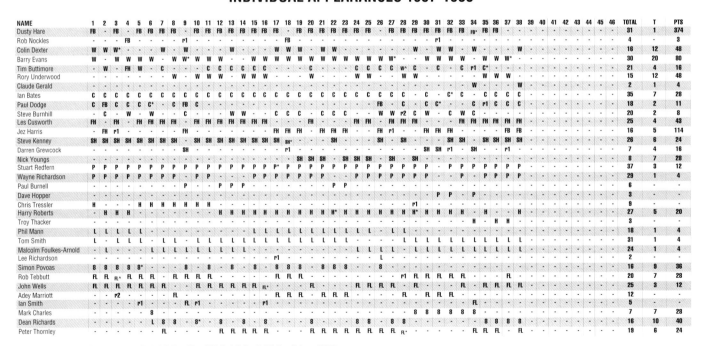

1 game: G Collins r1(22), Paul Coltman P(31), Alex Gissing I (9), Russell Lane W(7), Kevin McDonald r1(6), Tony Underwood W(22)

LEICESTER FOOTBALL CLUB 1987-88

Back: J.T. Thomas (Team Hon.Sec), J.A. Allen (Hon.Sec), C.J. Tressler, S.B. Redfern,
S.J. Povoas, T. Smith, M.V. Foulkes-Arnold, M.R. Charles, C.D. Dexter, P.J. Mann, J.M. Wells,
H. Roberts, K.P. Andrews (President), R.J. Farrands (Hon.Tres).

Front: J.C. Harris, T.J. Buttimore, I. Bates, B.J. Evans, P.W. Dodge (Capt), L. Cusworth, S. Kenney, R.S. Tebbutt, S.B. Burnhill.

Courage League - National Division 1 1987-88

		P	W	D	L	F	A	PTS	PD
1	**LEICESTER**	10	9	-	1	225	133	37	92
2	Wasps	11	8	1	2	218	136	36	82
3	Harlequins	11	6	1	4	261	128	30	133
4	Bath	11	6	1	4	197	156	30	41
5	Gloucester	10	6	1	3	206	121	29	85
6	Orrell	11	5	1	5	192	153	27	39
7	Moseley	11	5	-	6	167	170	26	-3
8	Nottingham	11	4	1	6	146	170	24	-24
9	Bristol	10	4	1	5	171	145	23	26
10	Waterloo	10	4	-	6	123	208	22	-85
11	Coventry	11	3	1	7	139	246	21	-107
12	Sale	11	-	-	11	95	374	11	-279

1988-1989

NO	DATE		OPPONENTS	V	RES	FOR G	T	D	P	PTS	AGAINST G	T	D	P	PTS	SCORERS
1	Sep	3	BEDFORD	H	Won	3	1	1	5	40	1	1	-	-	10	Hare(3C,5P) Evans(T) R.Underwood(T) Cusworth(T,D) West(T)
2		10	WASPS (CL)	H	Won	-	-	-	5	15	-	-	1	1	6	Hare(5P)
3		17	Northampton	A	Won	2	3	-	2	30	2	1	-	1	19	Hare(T,2C,2P) Youngs(T) Richards(3T)
4		24	Liverpool St Helens (CL)	A	Won	2	2	-	1	23	1	-	-	2	12	Hare(2C,P) R.Underwood(T) Reid(T) Richards(T) Thornley(T)
5	Oct	1	Coventry	A	Won	7	-	-	1	45	-	1	-	1	7	Hare(2T,7C,P) Evans(2T) R.Underwood(T) Youngs(T) Richards(T)
6		8	ORRELL (CL)	H	Lost	-	-	-	5	15	3	-	-	3	27	Hare(5P)
7		15	Swansea	A	Lost	-	1	1	3	16	3	2	1	2	35	Evans(T) Harris(D,3P)
8		18	OXFORD UNIVERSITY	H	Won	1	-	1	5	24	-	1	1	1	6	Hare(C,5P) Harris(D) T.Smith(T)
9		22	Nottingham (CL)	A	Drew	1	-	-	2	12	-	-	-	4	12	Hare(C,2P) Evans(T)
10		30	LLANELLI	H	Lost	-	-	-	5	15	2	2	-	3	29	Hare(5P)
11	Nov	5	Cardiff	A	Lost	3	-	-	2	24	3	2	-	-	26	Hare(T,3C,2P) Evans(T) T.Underwood(T)
12		8	Cambridge University	A	Won	1	2	-	3	23	2	-	-	3	21	Hare(C,3P) Warwood(T) Kenney(T) Thornley(T)
13		12	Waterloo (CL)	A	Won	2	4	1	1	34	1	1	1	3	22	Harris(2C,P) Evans(T) Cusworth(T,D) Kardooni(T) Redfern(T) Richards(2T)
14		19	ROSSLYN PARK (CL)	H	Won	1	1	-	6	28	1	-	-	3	15	Hare(T,C,6P) Warwood(T)
15		26	HARLEQUINS (CL)	H	Lost	3	-	-	1	21	3	1	1	2	31	Hare(T,3C,P) T.Underwood(T) Kardooni(T)
16	Dec	3	GLOUCESTER	H	Won	-	1	1	4	19	-	1	1	2	13	Hare(D,4P) T.Underwood(T)
17		10	BLACKHEATH	H	Won	2	1	-	2	22	1	-	1	1	12	Hare(2C,2P) Warwood(T) McDonald(T) Penalty Try
18		17	Richmond	A	Won	1	1	-	2	16	-	1	-	1	7	Hare(C,2P) Gerald(2T)
19		28	BARBARIANS	H	Lost	1	1	-	3	19	4	3	-	-	36	Hare(C,3P) Evans(T) Kardooni(T)
20		31	Nuneaton	A	Won	3	3	1	2	39	1	1	-	1	13	Hare(T,3C,2P) Bates(T) Dexter(T) Harris(T,D) Grant(2T)
21	Jan	7	HEADINGLEY	H	Won	7	2	-	1	53	-	1	-	1	7	Hare(3T,7C,P) Evans(T) Dodge(T) T.Underwood(T) Wells(T) Grant(T) I.R.Smith(T)
22		14	Gloucester (CL)	A	Lost	-	-	-	-	0	-	7	-	-	28	
23		20	Bedford	A	Won	1	1	-	2	16	-	-	-	1	3	Hare(C,2P) Bates(T) T.Underwood(T)
24		28	Liverpool St Helens (PC3)	A	Won	3	1	4	1	37	-	-	-	2	6	Hare(3C,P) Evans(T) Cusworth(T,4D) Kardooni(2T)
25	Feb	4	NORTHAMPTON	H	Won	5	3	-	-	42	-	2	-	-	8	Hare(T,5C) Evans(3T) T.Underwood(T) Grant(T) I.R.Smith(T) Poole(T)
26		11	Rosslyn Park (PC4)	A	Won	1	2	-	3	23	1	-	-	1	9	Hare(C,3P) Evans(T) Wells(T) I.R.Smith(T)
27		14	ROYAL AIR FORCE	H	Won	2	4	-	2	34	1	-	1	1	12	Gerald(T) T.Underwood(T) Harris(2C,2P) Kenney(T) T.Smith(T) I.R.Smith(T) Dexter(T)
28		18	MOSELEY	H	Won	3	-	-	3	27	1	1	-	-	10	Hare(3C,3P) Evans(2T) Penalty Try
29		25	WASPS (PCQF)	H	Won	-	1	2	4	22	-	-	-	4	18	Hare(4P) T.Underwood(T) Cusworth(2D)
30	Mar	4	SARACENS	H	Won	2	1	-	3	25	-	-	-	2	6	Hare(2C,3P) T.Smith(T) Marriott(T) Grant(T)
31		11	BRISTOL (CL)	H	Won	-	1	1	2	13	1	-	1	1	12	Hare(2P) Evans(T) Cusworth(D)
		14	LOUGHBOROUGH COLLEGE	H	Cancelled											
32		25	Harlequins (PCSF)	A	Won	1	1	1	1	16	-	1	-	1	7	Hare(T,C,P) Cusworth(D) Kardooni(T)
33		27	BALLYMENA	H	Won	1	-	-	5	21	-	2	-	3	17	Hare(C,5P) I.R.Smith(T)
34	Apr	1	London Scottish	A	Won	2	2	-	-	20	2	-	-	1	15	Gerald(T) R.Underwood(T) Harris(2C) Redfern(T) Grant(T)
35		8	Moseley (CL)	A	Lost	-	1	-	3	13	2	1	-	2	22	Hare(3P) Grant(T)
36		15	Gosforth	A	Won	5	2	-	3	47	1	2	-	-	14	Hare(5C,3P) Evans(2T) Dodge(T) Bates(2T) Thacker(T) Richards(T)
37		22	BATH (CL)	H	Won	1	-	-	3	15	-	3	-	-	12	Liley(3P) McDonald(T) Harris(C)
38		29	Bath (PCF)	A	Lost	-	-	-	2	6	-	1	-	2	10	Hare(2P)

INDIVIDUAL APPEARANCES 1988-1989

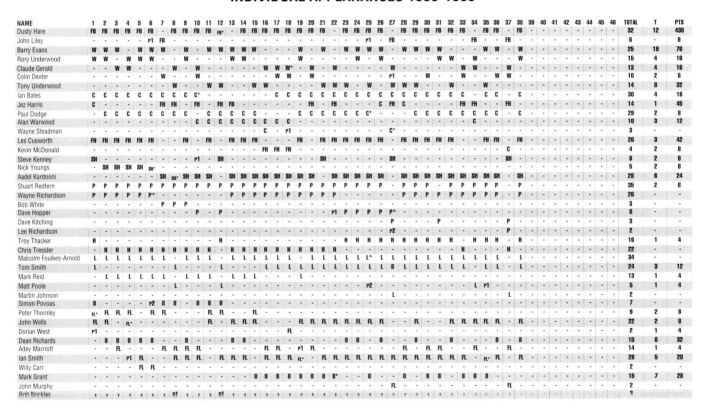

1 game: Paul Coltman P(11), Alex Gissing L(37), Nick Jackson 8(37), Andy Key C(37)

LEICESTER FOOTBALL CLUB 1988-89
Back: J.A. Allen (Hon.Sec), R.J. Farrands (Hon.Tres), I. Bates, A.N. Marriott, T. Smith,
M. Grant, M.V. Foulkes-Arnold, D. Richards, J.M. Wells, W.P. Richardson, S.B. Redfern,
D.J. Matthews (Coach), A. Foster (Coach), J.T. Thomas (Team Hon.Sec).
Front: A. Kardooni, C.J. Tressler, C. Gerald, J.C. Harris, T. Underwood,
P.W. Dodge (Capt), L. Cusworth, I.R. Smith, B.J. Evans, R. Underwood.

1989 Tour - U.S.A.

v VAIL	v DENVER BARBARIANS	v U.S.A.EAGLES
John Liley 3T,2C	Jez Harris 6C,1P	John Liley 1C,2P
Kevin McDonald	Kevin McDonald 3T	Claude Gerald 1T
Alan Warwood	Ian Bates 1T	Paul Dodge*
Paul Dodge*	Alan Warwood	Ian Bates
Claude Gerald 2T	Andy Key1	Jez Harris
Jez Harris 2C	Les Cusworth* 1D	Les Cusworth
Aadel Kardooni	Steve Kenney	Aadel Kardooni
Dave Kitching	Stuart Redfern	Stuart Redfern
Troy Thacker	Chris Tressler 1T	Troy Thacker
Lee Richardson 2T	Dave Kitching	Lee Richardson
Matt Poole	Matt Poole	Malcolm Foulkes-Arnold
Tom Smith	Malcolm Foulkes-Arnold 1T	Tom Smith
John Wells	John Wells	John Wells
Mark Grant 3T	Simon Povoas 1T	Simon Povoas
Ian Smith	Adey Marriott	Ian Smith1
	Paul Dodge rep 1	Adey Marriott rep 1
Won 48-0	*Won 46-16*	*Lost 12-24*
Tigers:6G 4T	*Tigers:6G 1T 1DG 1PG*	*Tigers:1G 2PG*
Vail:Nil	*Denver Bar:1T 1DG 3PG*	*Eagles:N/A*
13 Aug 1989	*17 Aug 1989*	*20 Aug 1989*

Courage League - National Division 1 1988-89

		P	W	D	L	F	A	PTS	PD
1	Bath	11	10	-	1	263	98	20	165
2	Gloucester	11	7	1	3	215	112	15	103
3	Wasps	11	7	1	3	206	138	15	68
4	Nottingham	11	6	1	4	142	122	13	20
5	Orrell	11	6	1	4	148	157	13	-9
6	**LEICESTER**	**11**	**6**	**1**	**4**	**189**	**199**	**13**	**-10**
7	Bristol	11	6	-	5	188	117	12	71
8	Harlequins	11	5	-	6	194	184	10	10
9	Rosslyn Park	11	5	-	6	172	208	10	-36
10	Moseley	11	3	-	8	113	242	6	-129
11	Waterloo	11	1	1	9	120	235	3	-115
12	Liverpool St Helens	11	1	-	10	116	254	2	-138

NO	DATE		OPPONENTS	V	RES	FOR G	T	D	P	PTS	AGAINST G	T	D	P	PTS	SCORERS
1	Sep	2	PONTYPRIDD	H	Won	2	2	2	5	41	1	3	-	-	18	Liley(2T,2C,5P) Dodge(T) T.Underwood(T) Cusworth(2D)
2		9	Wasps (CL)	A	Lost	1	-	-	2	12	1	2	-	5	29	Liley(C,2P) Kardooni(T)
3		16	NORTHAMPTON	H	Won	3	1	-	4	34	-	-	-	4	12	Liley(3C,4P) Gerald(T) Sandford(T) Poole(T) Povoas(T)
4		23	BEDFORD (CL)	H	Won	5	6	1	1	60	-	-	-	1	3	Liley(3T,5C,P) T.Underwood(T) Bates(T) R.Underwood(2T) Cusworth(D) Wells(2T) Povoas(T) I.R.Smith(T)
5		30	Llanelli	A	Lost	3	-	-	-	18	1	3	1	2	27	Liley(3C) R.Underwood(2T) Povoas(T)
6	Oct	7	COVENTRY	H	Won	2	2	-	5	35	-	-	-	2	6	Liley(T,2C,5P) Bates(T) R.Underwood(T) Povoas(T)
7		14	Orrell (CL)	A	Lost	-	1	1	1	10	4	-	-	3	33	Liley(P) T.Underwood(T) Harris(D)
8		24	Oxford University	A	Won	2	3	-	2	30	1	-	1	2	15	Liley(2C,2P) Evans(T) Cusworth(T) Tebbutt(T) Povoas(2T)
9		28	NOTTINGHAM (CL)	H	Won	2	-	-	1	15	-	-	1	1	6	Liley(2C,P) Redfern(T) Penalty Try
10	Nov	3	CARDIFF	H	Won	2	2	-	1	23	1	-	1	2	15	Liley(2C,P) Evans(T) Bates(T) Kardooni(T) I.R.Smith(T)
11		7	CAMBRIDGE UNIVERSITY	H	Won	3	-	-	3	27	1	-	-	1	9	Harris(3C,3P) Redfern(T) Thacker(T) Povoas(T)
12		11	SARACENS (CL)	H	Won	2	4	-	2	34	-	-	-	2	6	Liley(2T,2C,2P) T.Underwood(T) R.Underwood(T) Thacker(T) Povoas(T)
13		18	Rosslyn Park (CL)	A	Won	-	5	-	1	23	1	-	1	-	9	Liley(P) Evans(2T) Sandford(2T) Povoas(T)
14		25	Harlequins (CL)	A	Lost	-	-	-	4	12	1	-	1	2	15	Liley(4P)
15	Dec	2	Gloucester	A	Lost	1	1	-	1	13	2	1	-	1	19	Key(C,P) Sandford(2T)
16		9	Blackheath	A	Won	3	1	-	-	22	1	1	-	-	10	Key(3C) Gerald(2T) McDonald(T) Povoas(T)
17		16	RICHMOND	H	Won	3	5	-	2	44	1	-	-	2	12	Liley(3C,2P) McDonald(T) Sandford(2T) Redfern(T) Poole(T) Marriott(T) Povoas(T) I.R.Smith(T)
18		27	BARBARIANS	H	Won	3	2	-	2	32	2	1	-	-	16	Liley(3C,2P) Evans(T) R.Underwood(2T) Kenney(T) I.R.Smith(T)
19		30	NUNEATON	H	Won	2	2	-	2	26	2	1	-	1	19	Liley(T,2C,2P) Gerald(T) Povoas(2T)
20	Jan	6	Headingley	A	Won	2	-	1	2	21	2	-	-	-	12	Liley(2C,2P) Cusworth(D) Gissing(T) Povoas(T)
21		13	GLOUCESTER (CL)	H	Lost	-	1	-	4	16	2	2	-	2	26	Liley(4P) R.Underwood(T)
22		19	Bedford	A	Won	9	-	-	-	54	-	-	-	-	0	Liley(9C) Evans(T) Gerald(3T) Kenney(T) W.P.Richardson(T) Gissing(T) Povoas(2T)
23		27	London Welsh (PC3)	A	Won	6	1	-	1	43	-	-	-	1	3	Liley(6C,P) Cusworth(2T) Wells(2T) Povoas(3T)
	Feb	3	Northampton	A		Cancelled Rain										
24		10	WEST HARTLEPOOL (PC4)	H	Won	5	1	-	3	43	-	-	-	5	15	Liley(2T,5C,3P) R.Underwood(T) Thacker(T) Gissing(T) Povoas(T)
25		13	ROYAL AIR FORCE	H	Won	5	10	-	-	70	-	1	-	-	4	Harris(3T,2C) Evans(5T) Buttimore(T,C) Key(2T) Cusworth(2C) Kardooni(3T) Gissing(T)
26		16	Moseley	A	Won	-	1	1	3	16	-	-	-	2	6	Liley(3P) Cusworth(D) Poole(T)
27		24	Northampton (PCQF)	A	Lost	-	1	-	1	7	-	2	-	5	23	Liley(P) Evans(T)
28	Mar	3	Rugby	A	Won	4	2	-	1	35	-	1	-	-	4	Liley(4C,P) Evans(T) Buttimore(T) Cusworth(T) Kardooni(2T) Poole(T)
29		6	LOUGHBOROUGH COLLEGE	H	Won	4	1	-	2	34	-	-	-	1	3	Liley(T,4C,2P) Evans(2T) Thacker(T) Tebbutt(T)
30		10	Bristol (CL)	A	Won	1	1	-	1	13	-	2	-	1	11	Liley(C,P) Evans(T) Bates(T)
31		16	Nottingham	A	Lost	-	-	-	-	0	-	1	-	2	10	
32		24	SALE	H	Won	2	1	-	4	28	1	-	-	1	9	Liley(2C,4P) Buttimore(T) Kardooni(T) Povoas(T)
33		31	MOSELEY (CL)	H	Won	4	2	-	2	38	2	2	-	-	20	Liley(T,4C,2P) Gerald(3T) Kardooni(2T)
34	Apr	7	LONDON SCOTTISH	H	Won	7	6	-	-	66	2	-	-	-	12	Liley(T,7C) Gerald(3T) Buttimore(T) R.Underwood(5T) Hopper(T) Povoas(T)
35		14	Ballymena	A	Won	6	3	-	-	48	1	1	-	-	10	Liley(2T,6C) Sandford(2T) Key(T) Kardooni(2T) Tebbutt(T)
36		21	GOSFORTH	H	Won	6	3	-	1	51	-	1	-	1	7	Liley(T,6C,P) Evans(T) Bates(T) Gerald(T) Cusworth(T) Kardooni(2T) Povoas(2T)
37		28	Bath (CL)	A	Lost	1	-	-	3	15	3	2	-	-	26	Liley(T,C,3P)

INDIVIDUAL APPEARANCES 1989-1990

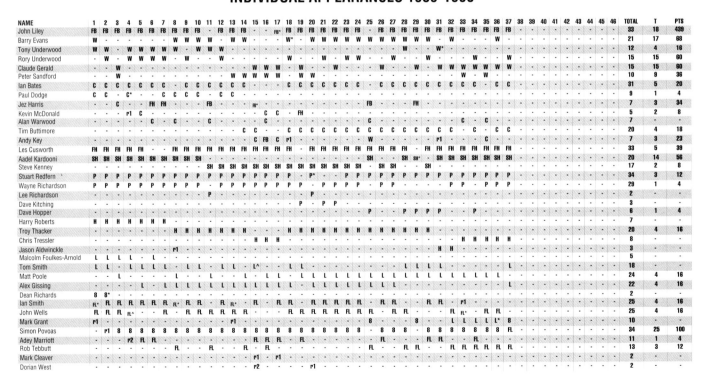

1 game: Paul Grant r1(36), John Murphy FL(29), Steve Wills r1(29)

LEICESTER FOOTBALL CLUB 1989-90

Back: J.A. Allen (Hon.Sec), R.J. Farrands (Hon.Tres), B.T.C. Small (President), I. Bates, R.S. Tebbutt, A.N. Marriott, T. Smith, A. Gissing, M.D. Poole, J.M. Wells, S.J. Povoas, W.P. Richardson, S.B. Redfern, D.J. Matthews (Coach), A. Foster (Coach), J.T. Thomas (Team Hon.Sec).
Middle: T.J. Buttimore, J.C. Harris, A. Kardooni, S. Kenney, T. Underwood, D. Richards (Capt), L. Cusworth, B.J. Evans, I.R. Smith, R. Underwood.
Front: C. Gerald, J.G. Liley.

Courage League - National Division 1 1989-90

		P	W	D	L	F	A	PTS	PD
1	Wasps	11	9	-	2	250	106	18	144
2	Gloucester	11	8	1	2	214	139	17	75
3	Bath	11	8	-	3	258	104	16	154
4	Saracens	11	7	1	3	168	167	15	1
5	**LEICESTER**	**11**	**6**	**-**	**5**	**248**	**184**	**12**	**64**
6	Nottingham	11	6	-	5	187	148	12	39
7	Harlequins	11	6	-	5	218	180	12	38
8	Orrell	11	5	-	6	221	132	10	89
9	Bristol	11	4	-	7	136	144	8	-8
10	Rosslyn Park	11	4	-	7	164	243	8	-79
11	Moseley	11	2	-	9	138	258	4	-120
12	Bedford	11	-	-	11	70	467	0	-397

NO	DATE		OPPONENTS	V	RES	FOR					AGAINST					SCORERS
						G	T	D	P	PTS	G	T	D	P	PTS	
1	Sep	1	BEDFORD	H	Won	7	3	-	1	57	-	-	-	2	6	Liley(T,7C,P) T.Underwood(2T) Bates(2T) R.Underwood(2T) B.A.Smith(T) Richards(T) Back(T)
2		4	ROMANIA	H	Won	-	-	1	4	15	-	-	3	1	12	Liley(D,4P)
3		8	Cardiff	A	Lost	1	-	-	1	9	3	2	1	2	35	Liley(C,P) Wells(T)
4		15	NORTHAMPTON	H	Won	-	2	-	6	26	-	-	-	1	3	Liley(6P) Bates(T) T.Smith(T)
5		22	GLOUCESTER (CL)	H	Won	1	-	-	4	18	-	-	-	2	6	Liley(C,4P) Richards(T)
6	Oct	6	Wasps (CL)	A	Won	1	1	-	4	22	-	-	-	4	12	Liley(C,4P) Gissing(T) T.Smith(T)
7		13	NOTTINGHAM (CL)	H	Won	1	1	1	4	25	-	-	-	3	9	Liley(C,4P) B.A.Smith(T,D) Key(T)
8		20	Rosslyn Park (CL)	A	Lost	2	-	-	1	15	-	2	1	2	17	Liley(2C,P) Wills(T) Bates(T)
9		23	OXFORD UNIVERSITY	H	Won	1	2	-	3	23	1	1	1	3	22	Wills(C,3P) Cleaver(2T) Sandford(T)
10		27	SARACENS (CL)	H	Won	3	2	-	1	29	-	-	-	2	6	Liley(3C,P) Sandford(T) Dodge(T) R.Underwood(T) Wright(T) Wells(T)
11	Nov	3	MOSELEY	H	Lost	-	1	-	2	10	-	1	-	4	16	Wright(2P) Wright(T)
12		6	Cambridge University	A	Won	1	1	-	4	22	-	1	-	2	10	Liley(C,4P) Dodge(T) Marriott(T)
13		10	Liverpool St Helens (CL)	A	Won	3	1	-	2	28	-	1	-	1	7	Liley(T,3C,2P) Sandford(T) R.Underwood(T) Richards(T)
14		17	BATH (CL)	H	Lost	-	-	-	1	3	-	-	-	3	9	Liley(P)
15		24	Bath (PC3)	A	Won	1	-	-	2	12	-	-	-	-	0	Liley(C,2P) B.A.Smith(T)
16	Dec	1	Gloucester	A	Lost	-	3	-	1	15	2	-	-	2	18	Sandford(T) Harris(P) Gissing(T) T.Smith(T)
		8	BLACKHEATH	H			Cancelled										
17		15	BRISTOL	H	Won	2	2	-	2	26	-	-	-	1	3	Sandford(T) Key(T) Harris(2C,2P) Gissing(T) Penalty Try
18		22	Coventry	A	Won	2	3	-	1	27	-	-	1	-	3	Liley(2T,2C,P) T.Underwood(T) Buttimore(T) R.Underwood(T)
19		27	BARBARIANS	H	Lost	2	-	-	3	21	3	2	-	-	26	Liley(2C,3P) T.Underwood(T) R.Underwood(T)
20		29	Nuneaton	A	Won	3	2	1	1	32	1	-	-	-	6	Liley(3C,P) T.Underwood(T) Bates(T) Dodge(T) Sandford(T) Harris(D) Gissing(T)
21	Jan	5	HEADINGLEY	H	Won	3	2	-	1	29	-	-	-	2	6	Wills(T) B.A.Smith(T,3C,P) Gissing(T) Grant(2T)
22		12	Northampton (CL)	A	Won	1	4	1	1	28	3	-	-	-	18	Liley(T,C,P) Bates(T) R.Underwood(3T) B.A.Smith(D)
23		18	Bedford	A	Won	5	2	-	1	41	-	1	-	1	7	Key(T) Bates(T) Harris(T,5C,P) Hamilton(T) Gissing(T) T.Smith(T) Grant(T)
24		26	WASPS (PC4)	H	Lost	-	1	-	3	13	-	-	-	5	15	Liley(3P) T.Underwood(T)
25	Feb	2	WAKEFIELD	H	Won	-	2	-	3	17	-	2	-	-	8	McAdam(T) Harris(3P) Back(T)
		9	ORRELL (CL)	H			Cancelled										
		16	RUGBY	H			Cancelled										
26		23	London Welsh	A	Won	6	5	-	1	59	-	-	-	1	3	Liley(2T) T.Underwood(2T) Dodge(T) Bates(T) R.Underwood(T) B.A.Smith(6C,P) Tressler(T) T.Smith(2T) Richards(T)
27	Mar	2	Richmond	A	Won	3	4	-	2	40	2	-	-	2	18	Wills(T) Bates(T) Key(T) Harris(3C,2P) Gissing(T) Povoas(2T) Tebbutt(T)
28		5	LOUGHBOROUGH COLLEGE	H	Won	7	3	-	1	57	1	1	-	1	13	Liley(T,7C,P) Wigley(T) Sandford(T) Kardooni(2T) Tressler(T) Gissing(T) T.Smith(T) Richards(T) Penalty Try
29		9	Bristol (CL)	A	Lost	-	-	1	1	6	-	1	2	-	10	Liley(P) B.A.Smith(D)
30		16	Nottingham	A	Won	-	1	-	3	13	1	-	-	2	12	Liley(3P) Cleaver(T)
31		23	HARLEQUINS (CL)	H	Lost	-	-	1	3	12	1	-	2	1	15	Liley(3P) Harris(D)
32		30	COVENTRY	H	Won	-	3	-	1	15	1	-	-	2	12	Liley(P) Harris(T) Kardooni(T) Rowntree(T)
33	Apr	1	WASPS	H	Won	4	-	-	5	39	2	-	-	2	18	Wills(T) Dodge(T) Harris(4C,5P) Kardooni(T) Back(T)
34		6	Saracens	A	Won	1	1	-	-	10	1	-	-	-	6	Liley(C) T.Underwood(T) R.Underwood(T)
35		13	LONDON IRISH	H	Won	6	3	-	2	54	1	1	-	2	16	T.Underwood(T) Sandford(2T) Harris(6C,2P) Kardooni(T) Rowntree(T) Wells(T) Grant(T) Back(T) Penalty Try
36		20	ORRELL (CL)	H	Won	1	-	-	3	15	1	-	-	2	12	Harris(C,3P) Richards(T)
37		27	Moseley (CL)	A	Won	6	1	1	-	43	2	1	-	1	19	Liley(6C) T.Underwood(2T) Dodge(T) R.Underwood(3T) Harris(D) Wells(T)

INDIVIDUAL APPEARANCES 1990-1991

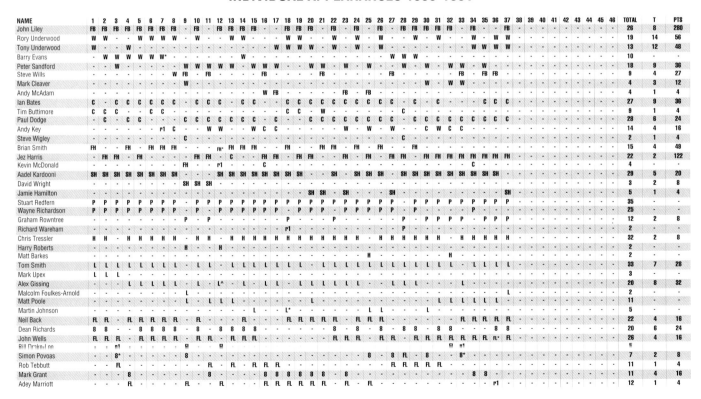

1 game: Paul Brookes P(9), Paul Hillyer H(3), Ian Smith r2(12)

LEICESTER FOOTBALL CLUB 1990-91
Back: J.A. Allen (Hon.Sec), B.T.C. Small (President), S.B. Redfern, W.P. Richardson, M.D. Poole, T. Smith, J.M. Wells,
G.C. Rowntree, A.N. Marriott, J.T. Thomas (Team Hon.Sec), D.J. Matthews (Coach), A.O. Russ (Director of Coaching).
Middle: P. Sandford, C.J. Tressler, J.C. Harris, S.R. Wills, D. Richards (Capt), A.M. Key,
P.W. Dodge, N.A. Back, R. Underwood, I. Bates.
Front: A. Kardooni, T. Underwood.

1991 Tour - Canada

v EDMONTON	v ALBERTA	v BRITISH COLOMBIA	v B.COLOMBIA PRESS XV
John Liley* 3C,4P	John Liley1 1C,2P	Steve Wills 1C,3P	John Liley 1C,3P
Steve Hackney 1T	Steve Hackney 1T	Steve Hackney 1T	Steve Hackney
Ian Bates	Ian Bates	Ian Bates	Steve Wills
Steve Wigley 1T	Laurence Boyle	Laurence Boyle	Laurence Boyle
Mark Cleaver	Steve Wills	Mark Cleaver	Mark Cleaver
Dave Wigley 1T	Jez Harris	Dave Wigley 1T	Jez Harris
Aadel Kardooni1	Jamie Hamilton	Aadel Kardooni*	Aadel Kardooni
Darren Eagland	Graham Rowntree	Darren Eagland	Graham Rowntree
Matt Barkes	Paul Hillyer	Paul Hillyer	Paul Hillyer 1T
Wayne Richardson2	Richard Wareham	Richard Wareham	Richard Wareham
Alex Gissing	Martin Johnson	Alex Gissing	Alex Gissing
Matt Poole	Matt Poole	Martin Johnson	Matt Poole
Adey Marriott	John Wells*	Simon Povoas	John Wells*
Simon Povoas	Mark Grant	Mark Grant 1T	Simon Povoas
Bill Drake-Lee	Neil Back 1T	Adey Marriott	Neil Back
Jamie Hamilton rep 1	Mark Cleaver rep 1		
Graham Rowntree rep 2			
Won 30-18	**Won 16-9**	**Won 23-18**	**Lost 15-19**
Tigers:3G 4PG	Tigers:1G 1T 2PG	Tigers:1G 2T 3PG	Tigers:1G 3PG
Edmonton:2G 2PG	Alberta:1G 1PG	B.C.:1G 4PG	B.C.Press:1T 5PG
14 Aug 1991	17 Aug 1991	20 Aug 1991	23 Aug 1991

Courage League - National Division 1 1990-91

		P	W	D	L	F	A	PTS	PD
1	Bath	12	11	-	1	280	104	22	176
2	Wasps	12	9	1	2	252	151	19	101
3	Harlequins	12	8	-	4	267	162	16	105
4	**LEICESTER**	**12**	**8**	**-**	**4**	**244**	**140**	**16**	**104**
5	Orrell	12	7	-	5	247	105	14	142
6	Gloucester	12	6	-	6	207	163	12	44
7	Rosslyn Park	12	6	-	6	216	174	12	42
8	Nottingham	12	6	-	6	138	194	12	-56
9	Northampton	12	5	1	6	149	254	11	-105
10	Saracens	12	5	-	7	151	228	10	-77
11	Bristol	12	4	1	7	135	219	9	-84
12	Moseley	12	1	1	10	113	244	3	-131
13	Liverpool St Helens	12	-	-	12	88	349	0	-261

NO	DATE		OPPONENTS	V	RES	FOR					AGAINST					SCORERS
						G	T	D	P	PTS	G	T	D	P	PTS	
1	Sep	7	Bedford	A	Won	2	1	-	3	25	1	-	-	4	18	Liley(2C,3P) Bates(T) Boyle(T) Gissing(T)
2		14	CARDIFF	H	Won	1	2	-	3	23	2	-	-	2	18	Liley(T,C,3P) Wells(T) M.Grant(T)
3		21	Northampton	A	Lost	1	2	-	1	17	2	-	-	3	21	Liley(C,P) Hackney(T) Povoas(T) Back(T)
4		24	NORTHERN DIVISION	H	Lost	-	-	-	1	3	3	1	-	2	28	Liley(P)
5		28	Headingley	A	Won	7	4	-	-	58	-	1	-	2	10	Liley(T,7C) Hackney(2T) Harris(T) Hamilton(T) Smith(2T) Povoas(4T)
6	Oct	5	COVENTRY	H	Lost	1	2	-	2	20	1	1	1	3	22	Wills(C) Harris(2P) Povoas(2T) Drake-Lee(T)
		12	Bristol	A		Cancelled										
7		19	GLOUCESTER	H	Lost	1	-	1	1	12	1	1	1	3	22	Sandford(T) Harris(C,D,P)
8		22	Oxford University	A	Won	1	1	-	1	13	2	-	-	-	12	Liley(C,P) Garforth(T) M.Grant(T)
9		26	Sale	A	Lost	1	-	-	1	9	-	-	1	3	12	Liley(C,P) Smith(T)
10	Nov	2	Moseley	A	Lost	-	-	1	4	15	1	1	-	2	16	Liley(4P) Harris(D)
11		5	CAMBRIDGE UNIVERSITY	H	Won	2	3	-	1	27	1	-	-	2	12	Liley(2C,P) Evans(T) Tressler(T) Richards(T) Back(2T)
12		16	Gloucester (CL)	A	Lost	-	-	-	1	3	2	-	-	3	21	Liley(P)
13		23	WASPS (CL)	H	Won	1	1	3	4	31	-	-	-	4	12	Liley(C,4P) R.Underwood(T) Harris(3D) Wells(T)
14		30	Fylde (PC3)	A	Won	3	4	-	-	34	-	-	-	2	6	Liley(3C) Kardooni(T) Wells(2T) Richards(2T) Back(T) Penalty Try
15	Dec	7	Nottingham (CL)	A	Won	2	-	1	4	27	-	2	-	2	14	Liley(2C,4P) R.Underwood(2T) Harris(D)
		14	ROSSLYN PARK	H		Cancelled										
16		21	Saracens (CL)	A	Won	1	2	-	2	20	1	-	-	1	9	Liley(C,2P) Hackney(T) Wells(T) Back(T)
17		27	BARBARIANS	H	Lost	2	-	-	3	21	3	2	-	1	29	Liley(2C,3P) R.Underwood(2T)
18	Jan	4	LONDON IRISH (CL)	H	Won	4	3	-	4	36	-	1	1	2	13	Liley(T,4C) Hackney(3T) R.Underwood(2T) Richards(T)
19		11	Bath (CL)	A	Lost	-	-	-	2	6	3	4	-	1	37	Liley(2P)
20		18	BEDFORD	H	Won	4	3	-	3	45	1	-	-	6	24	Wills(4C,3P) Hackney(2T) Sandford(T) Kardooni(T) Gissing(T) M.Grant(2T)
		25	Waterloo (PC4)	A		Cancelled										
21	Feb	1	WAKEFIELD	H	Won	5	3	-	2	48	2	2	-	-	20	Liley(2T,5C,2P) Hackney(T) Warwood(T) Kardooni(2T) Povoas(2T)
22		8	Waterloo (PC4)	A	Won	1	2	-	2	20	1	-	-	2	12	Liley(C,2P) Garforth(T) Richards(2T)
23		15	NUNEATON	H	Won	5	5	-	-	50	1	-	-	-	6	Liley(T,5C) Hackney(2T) Sandford(2T) Harris(T) Kardooni(2T) Redfern(T) Smith(T)
24		22	Newcastle Gosforth (PCQF)	A	Won	1	1	-	-	10	-	-	-	-	0	Liley(C) Kardooni(T) Penalty Try
25		29	Orrell (CL)	A	Lost	-	-	-	3	9	-	3	-	3	21	Liley(3P)
26	Mar	3	LOUGHBOROUGH COLLEGE	H	Won	3	3	-	3	39	1	1	-	-	10	Wills(T,3C,3P) Key(T) Rowntree(T) Povoas(3T)
27		7	RICHMOND	H	Won	6	2	1	1	50	2	1	1	-	19	Liley(T,6C,P) Hackney(3T) Bates(2T) Harris(D) Garforth(T) Gissing(T)
28		14	BRISTOL (CL)	H	Won	-	4	-	3	25	1	-	1	-	9	Liley(3P) T.Underwood(T) Boyle(T) Ainscough(T) Garforth(T)
29		21	ROSSLYN PARK (CL)	H	Won	7	-	-	3	51	2	1	-	-	16	Liley(2T,7C,3P) R.Underwood(3T) Ainscough(T) Kardooni(T)
30		28	Harlequins (CL)	A	Lost	1	1	-	1	13	1	2	-	2	20	Wills(C,P) Povoas(T)
31	Apr	4	Harlequins (PCSF)	A	Lost	1	-	-	1	9	1	-	-	3	15	Liley(T,C,P)
32		7	NORTHAMPTON (CL)	H	Lost	1	1	-	3	19	1	1	-	4	22	Liley(C,3P) Harris(T) Grewcock(T)
33		11	LIVERPOOL ST HELENS	H	Won	12	7	-	-	100	-	-	-	-	0	Liley(C) Hackney(3T) Boyle(T) T.Underwood(6T) Ainscough(T,11C) Grewcock(3T) Wells(T) Drake-Lee(T) Wills(2T) Marriott(T)
34		18	BALLYMENA	H	Won	3	1	-	-	22	-	-	-	1	9	Key(T) Sandford(T) Ainscough(T,3C) Garforth(T)
35		20	Wasps	A	Lost	-	-	-	2	6	1	1	-	3	19	Harris(2P)
36		25	RUGBY (CL)	H	Drew	3	1	-	-	22	-	1	-	6	22	Liley(3C) T.Underwood(2T) Bates(T) R.Underwood(T)

INDIVIDUAL APPEARANCES 1991-1992

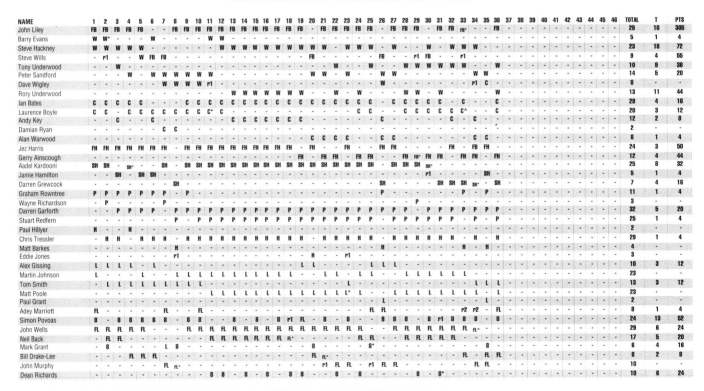

1 game: Ben Brier FL(6), Ashley Johnson FH(8), Andy McAdam FB(35), Sam Quick FL(8), Tom Reynolds W(35), Alan Royer r1(4), Ian Smith FL(9)[1T-4], Richard Wareham P(1)

LEICESTER FOOTBALL CLUB 1991-92

Back: J.A. Allen (Hon.Sec), G.G. Willars (President), T. Underwood, S.T. Hackney, M.D. Poole, M.O. Johnson, A. Kardooni, S.B. Redfern, D.J. Garforth, I.R. Smith (Coach), A.O. Russ (Director of Coaching), J.T. Thomas (Team Hon.Sec).
Front: P. Sandford, D. Richards, S.J. Povoas, L.S. Boyle, J.M. Wells (Capt), J.C. Harris, I. Bates, C.J. Tressler, J.G. Liley.

Courage League - National Division 1 1991-92

		P	W	D	L	F	A	PTS	PD
1	Bath *	12	10	1	1	277	126	20	151
2	Orrell	12	10	-	2	204	95	20	109
3	Northampton	12	9	1	2	209	136	19	73
4	Gloucester	12	7	1	4	193	168	15	25
5	Saracens	12	7	1	4	176	165	15	11
6	**LEICESTER**	**12**	**6**	**1**	**5**	**262**	**216**	**13**	**46**
7	Wasps	12	6	-	6	177	180	12	-3
8	Harlequins	12	5	1	6	213	207	11	6
9	London Irish	12	3	3	6	147	237	9	-90
10	Bristol	12	4	-	8	192	174	8	18
11	Rugby	12	2	3	7	124	252	7	-128
12	Nottingham	12	2	1	9	133	204	5	-71
13	Rosslyn Park	12	-	1	11	111	258	1	-147

* 1pt deducted

1992-1993

NO	DATE		OPPONENTS	V	RES	FOR						AGAINST					SCORERS
						G	T	D	P	PTS		G	T	D	P	PTS	
1	Sep	1	Sheffield	A	Won	3	-	1	1	27		1	-	-	-	7	Liley(3C,P) Hackney(T) J.C.Harris(D) Kardooni(T) Poole(T)
2		5	ENGLAND XV	H	Lost	-	1	-	2	11		1	1	1	1	18	Liley(2P) Hackney(T)
3		9	LEICESTERSHIRE XV	H	Won	3	2	1	2	40		1	2	-	1	20	Kilford(3C) Reynolds(T) Boyle(2P) I.Harris(T,D) Grewcock(T) Murphy(T) Drake-Lee(T)
4		12	MEDIOLANUM MILAN	H	Won	4	-	-	4	40		3	-	-	1	24	Liley(4C,4P) Hackney(T) Garforth(T) Povoas(T) N.D.Richardson(T)
5		19	London Irish (CL)	A	Won	3	-	-	3	30		-	1	-	3	14	Liley(T,3C,3P) T.Underwood(T) N.D.Richardson(T)
6		26	GLOUCESTER (CL)	H	Won	2	1	-	1	22		1	1	-	3	21	Liley(2C,P) Hackney(T) Kardooni(T) N.D.Richardson(T)
7	Oct	3	Wasps (CL)	A	Lost	1	-	-	2	13		-	1	-	3	14	Liley(C,2P) Potter(T)
8		10	WEST HARTLEPOOL (CL)	H	Won	1	1	-	3	21		-	1	-	1	8	Liley(T,C,3P) Potter(T)
9		17	Moseley	A	Lost	-	1	-	3	14		2	-	1	1	20	Kilford(P) Sandford(T) J.C.Harris(2P)
10		20	OXFORD UNIVERSITY	H	Won	3	-	-	2	27		-	-	-	5	15	Kilford(3C,2P) Hackney(T) Eagland(T) M.O.Johnson(T)
11		24	London Scottish (CL)	A	Won	1	1	-	2	18		-	1	1	1	11	Liley(C,2P) T.Underwood(T) Poole(T)
12		31	SARACENS (CL)	H	Won	3	-	1	2	30		-	-	-	1	3	Liley(3C,2P) R.Underwood(T) J.C.Harris(D) Cockerill(T) Penalty Try
13	Nov	3	Cambridge University	A	Lost	-	3	-	1	18		2	-	-	3	23	Kilford(2T,P) Drake-Lee(T)
14		7	Orrell	A	Won	2	2	-	3	33		1	1	-	2	18	Liley(2T,2C,3P) Kilford(T) Sandford(T)
15		13	NORTHAMPTON	H	Won	2	1	-	3	28		-	-	-	1	3	Liley(2C,3P) Hackney(T) Bates(T) Poole(T)
16		21	BATH (CL)	H	Lost	-	-	-	1	3		-	2	-	1	13	Liley(P)
17		29	London Scottish (PC3)	A	Won	2	-	1	1	20		-	1	1	1	11	Liley(T,2C,P) Hackney(T) J.C.Harris(D)
18	Dec	5	Gloucester	A	Lost	-	2	1	-	13		3	3	-	-	36	Sandford(2T) J.C.Harris(D)
		12	Blackheath	A		Cancelled												
19		28	BARBARIANS	H	Won	4	2	-	1	41		-	4	-	1	23	Liley(T,4C,P) T.Underwood(T) R.Underwood(T) Grewcock(T) Garforth(T) Wells(T)
	Jan	2	LEEDS	H		Cancelled Frost												
20		9	Northampton (CL)	A	Won	1	-	-	2	13		1	1	-	-	12	Liley(C,2P) Back(T)
21		15	Bedford	A	Won	1	-	1	2	16		1	-	-	2	13	Liley(T,C,2P) J.C.Harris(D)
22		23	Nottingham (PC4)	A	Won	2	1	-	3	28		-	-	-	1	3	Liley(2C,3P) R.Underwood(T) T.Underwood(T) Back(T)
23		30	Coventry	A	Won	3	2	-	2	37		2	-	-	1	17	Kilford(2T) T.Underwood(T) Boyle(T) J.C.Harris(3C,2P) Garforth(T)
24	Feb	6	ROSSLYN PARK	H	Won	3	5	1	1	52		1	-	-	1	10	Liley(2T,3C,P) Hackney(T) Potter(T) Sandford(T) J.C.Harris(D) Kardooni(T) Rowntree(T) Povoas(T)
25		13	ORRELL (CL)	H	Won	-	-	-	3	9		-	-	-	-	0	Liley(3P)
26		20	Nuneaton	A	Won	3	8	-	-	61		1	1	-	2	18	Liley(3C) Hackney(4T) Boyle(T) Sandford(3T) Kardooni(T) Back(2T)
27		27	EXETER (PCQF)	H	Won	4	9	-	1	76		-	-	-	-	0	Liley(2T,4C,P) T.Underwood(3T) Potter(T) R.Underwood(T) Cockerill(T) Povoas(T) Richards(2T) Back(T) Grewcock(T)
	Mar	2	LOUGHBOROUGH COLLEGE	H		Cancelled												
28		5	MOSELEY	H	Won	-	2	-	5	25		-	1	-	-	5	Liley(5P) Kardooni(T) Povoas(T)
29		13	Bristol (CL)	A	Lost	1	-	-	1	10		1	1	-	1	15	Liley(C,P) Kardooni(T)
30		19	Nottingham	A	Won	1	4	-	-	27		1	-	-	-	7	Liley(C) Kilford(T) Boyle(2T) Sandford(T) Hopper(T)
31		27	HARLEQUINS (CL)	H	Won	2	-	1	2	23		-	-	-	-	0	Liley(2C,2P) J.C.Harris(D) Povoas(T) N.D.Richardson(T)
32	Apr	3	Richmond	A	Won	1	2	1	2	29		-	-	-	1	15	Liley(T,C,3P) Hackney(T) Bates(T) Green(T)
33		10	NORTHAMPTON (PCSF)	H	Won	2	1	1	2	28		-	-	-	2	6	Liley(2C,2P) J.C.Harris(D) Richards(T) Back(T) Boyle(T)
34		12	WASPS	H	Won	-	1	-	3	14		-	-	-	2	13	Green(3P) C.A.P.Johnson(T)
35		17	SALE	H	Won	4	3	-	-	43		-	1	-	1	8	Kilford(2T,4C) Hackney(T) Evans(T) Sandford(T) Rowntree(T) N.D.Richardson(T)
36		24	Rugby (CL)	A	Won	2	1	2	1	28		-	1	-	-	5	Kilford(P) T.Underwood(T) R.Underwood(T) J.C.Harris(2C,2D) Grewcock(T)
37	May	1	Harlequins (PCF)	A	Won	2	-	1	2	23		1	-	-	3	16	Liley(2C,2P) Potter(T) J.C.Harris(D) M.O.Johnson(T)

INDIVIDUAL APPEARANCES 1992-1993

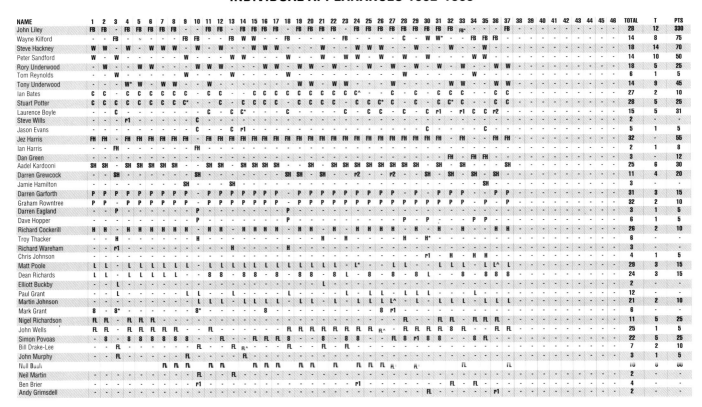

1 game: Paul Dodge r1(32), Malcolm Foulkes-Arnold L(34), Niall Griffiths P(34), Steve Harris r1(26), Derek Jelly P*(36), Wayne Richardson r2(14), Roy Robson 8(13), Stuart Towns rf(9), Toby White r2(26), Steve Wigley C(34)

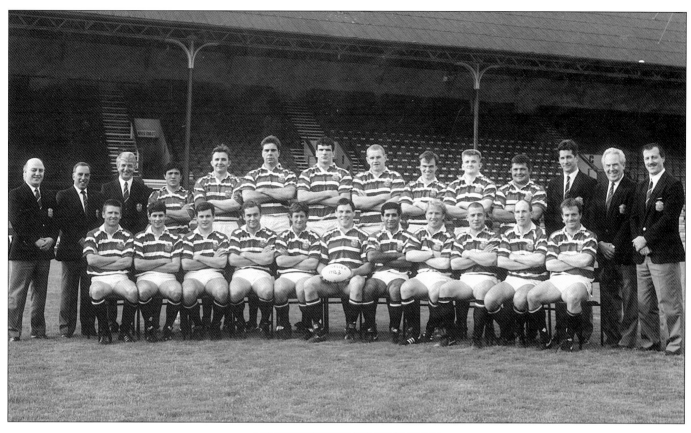

LEICESTER FOOTBALL CLUB 1992-93
Back: J.A. Allen (Hon.Sec), A.O. Russ (Director of Coaching), G.G. Willars (President),
T. Underwood, S.J. Povoas, M.D. Poole, M.O. Johnson, D. Richards, S.T. Hackney, G.C. Rowntree,
D.J. Garforth, P.W. Dodge (Coach), J.T. Thomas (Team Hon.Sec), I.R. Smith (Coach).
Front: P. Sandford, W.A. Kilford, S. Potter, I. Bates, J.C. Harris, J.M. Wells (Capt), A. Kardooni, N.A. Back, R. Cockerill, J.G. Liley, L.S. Boyle.

1993 Tour - South Africa

v W.PROVINCE DEFENCE XV	v GARDENS TECH	v NATAL DEVELOPMENT XV	v ZULULAND REGIONAL XV	v NATAL SELECTORS XV
John Liley 8C,2P	Wayne Kilford	John Liley 7C,3P	Wayne Kilford	John Liley 3P
Tom Reynolds 1T	Peter Sandford 1T	Wayne Kilford	Dave Wigley1 1T	Wayne Kilford1
Stuart Potter 1T	Stuart Potter	Ian Bates	Ian Bates	Jez Harris
Ian Bates	Laurence Boyle1	Stuart Potter 1T	Stuart Potter	Stuart Potter 1T
Peter Sandford	Dave Wigley	Dave Wigley 1T	Peter Sandford 1T	Dave Wigley
Jez Harris 1D	Niall Malone 1C,1P	Jez Harris	Niall Malone 1C,1P	Niall Malone
Aadel Kardooni2 1T	Darren Grewcock 1T	Darren Grewcock 1T	Aadel Kardooni	Aadel Kardooni
Derek Jelly 1T	Graham Rowntree	Derek Jelly	Graham Rowntree	Graham Rowntree
Richard Cockerill1	Chris Johnson	Richard Cockerill	Chris Johnson	Richard Cockerill
Darren Garforth 1T	Wayne Richardson	Wayne Richardson1	Darren Garforth	Darren Garforth
Alex Gissing 1T	Alex Gissing	Paul Grant 2T	Alex Gissing2	Tom Smith
Tom Smith	Paul Grant	Tom Smith 1T	Matt Poole	Matt Poole
John Wells*	Ben Brier	Bill Drake-Lee 1T	Ben Brier	John Wells*
Paul Grant	John Wells* 1T	John Wells	Tom Smith	Nigel Richardson
Nigel Richardson 1T	Bill Drake-Lee 1T	Ben Brier2	Neil Back	Neil Back
Chris Johnson rep 1 3T	Jez Harris rep 1	Darren Garforth rep 1	John Liley rep 1	Peter Sandford rep 1
Darren Grewcock rep 2		Nigel Richardson3 rep 2	Paul Grant rep 2	
		Chris Johnson rep 3		
Won 75-3	*Won 25-0*	*Won 58-8*	*Won 15-8*	*Won 14-13*
Tigers:8G 2T 1DG 2PG	*Tigers:1G 3T 1PG*	*Tigers:7G 3PG*	*Tigers:1G 1T 1PG*	*Tigers:1T 3PG*
W.P.Defence:1PG	*Gardens Tech:Nil*	*Natal B:1T 1PG*	*Zululand:1T 1PG*	*Natal:1G 2PG*
7 Aug 1993	*11 Aug 1993*	*14 Aug 1993*	*17 Aug 1993*	*20 Aug 1993*

Courage League - National Division 1 1992-93

		P	W	D	L	F	A	PTS	PD
1	Bath	12	11	-	1	355	97	22	258
2	Wasps	12	11	-	1	186	118	22	68
3	**LEICESTER**	12	9	-	3	220	116	18	104
4	Northampton	12	8	-	4	215	150	16	65
5	Gloucester	12	6	-	6	173	151	12	22
6	Bristol	12	6	-	6	148	169	12	-21
7	London Irish	12	6	-	6	175	223	12	-48
8	Harlequins	12	5	1	6	197	187	11	10
9	Orrell	12	5	-	7	175	183	10	-8
10	London Scottish	12	3	1	8	192	248	7	-56
11	Saracens	12	3	-	9	137	180	6	-43
12	West Hartlepool	12	3	-	9	149	236	6	-87
13	Rugby	12	1	-	11	104	368	2	-264

1914-15 v BARBARIANS	v BARBARIANS	1939-40 v THE REST
C. Freer	Fred Mellor	Ernie Watkin 1T, 1C
C. L. Curie	F. R. Broadley	Ken Cooke 1T
Ken Wood	Percy Lawrie	J. R. Preston
Percy Lawrie 2C	C. L. Curie	S. D. Pearce
H. K. Pearce 2T	H. Hirst	
'Tim' Taylor	'Tim' Taylor	James Taylor 1C, 1D
'Pedlar' Wood 2T	'Pedlar' Wood	Eric Bevins
Harry Lawrie 1C	A. V. Manton 1T	Denis Bolesworth
George Ward	A. Kitchener	George Ridgway
Gil Hopkins	A. J. Osbourne	Jim Stapleton
Jimmy Allen 1T	J. Morris	Peter Jerwood 1P
A. E. G. Bowell	S. Livingstone	Fred Doe 1T
Charlie Cross	Gil Hopkins	Tom Berry
G. P. Baines	G. P. Baines	G. A. Lebens
	George Ward	
Won 21-6	**Drew 3-3**	**Won 20-6**
Tigers: 3G 2T	*Tigers: 1T*	*Tigers: 2G 1T 1DG 1PG*
Barbarians: 2T	*Barbarians: 1T*	*The Rest: 1T 1PG*
2 Jan 1915	*27 Mar 1915*	*2 Sep 1939*

WARTIME FIXTURES

The Barbarians played six War Service games in the season 1914-15, two of these featured Leicester and were played at Welford Road in aid of charity.

The game on January 2nd was staged "for encouragement of recruiting and in aid of patriotic funds", with each team playing one man short. The game on March 27th was again played "for encouragement of local recruiting", and the total proceeds of the match were donated to the Leicester Royal Infirmary. The matches took place largely because of the patriotic drive of Edgar Mobbs of the Barbarians and Tom Crumbie the Leicester secretary.

Leicester should have met Bedford on 2nd September 1939 in the first game of the 1939-40 season, but owing to the impending Second World War and the difficulty of travel only one member of the opposition - Vic Lyttle the Irish international - turned up. A hurriedly arranged Rest XV was assembled and played a 13 a side match with Leicester.

SOURCES OF INFORMATION

The Club's official archives have been used wherever possible to correct long standing reporting errors contained in the newspaper reports of the day. The *Leicester Mercury* archives and notebooks have also been examined for transcription accuracy.

Local Newspapers

Leicester Mercury	1880 to date
Leicester Daily Post	1880 to March 1921
Leicester Echo	Dec 1883 to March 1884
Leicester Evening Standard	October 1885 to July 1886
Leicester Saturday Herald	Jan 1887 to August 1899
Leicester Guardian	Oct 1891 to December 1906
(became the *Wyvern* in 1899)	
Leicester Daily Express	June 1892 to October 1895
Leicester Evening News	April 1903 to October 1905
Leicester Evening Mail	May 1910 to Nov 1963
Sports Mercury	January 1919 to date
Football Mail	Sept 1919 to Nov 1963
(became the *Sports Mail* in Mar 1931)	

National Newspapers

The Times
The Sportsman
The Field
The Sporting Life
The Golden Penny
Numerous other regional newspapers

A-Z STOP PRESS:

The following biographical detail on British Lion and Tigers player Billy Wallace has been unearthed, since the Celebrated Tigers section was compiled.

WALLACE, William
b. Tynemouth, Northumberland, 25.4.1905
d. Burton-on-Trent, 20.8.1960
Educated: Giggleswick School
Clubs: Percy Park, Leicester
Debut: *13.2.1923 v Racing Club de France (A), Lost 9-19*
Last Game: *20.3.1929 v Bristol (A), Lost 8-14*
CAPS: British Isles (1) 1924

Billy Wallace represented his native Northumberland as a speedy winger which led to him being selected to tour South Africa with the British Isles in 1924 when only 19. He played in the first Test at Durban but, though he was named reserve wing, never gained an international cap for England. Billy was a mining engineer at Sedghill Colliery and later became manager at Halls Colliery at Swadlincote, Derbyshire.
Apps: 10   Points: 39   Scoring: 13T

THE SEASON BY SEASON RECORD 1880-1993

SEASON	PLD	W	D	L	LEICESTER T	C	PG	DG	PTS	OPPONENTS T	C	PG	DG	AGST	PLYRS
1880/81	17	9	5	3	21	8	0	2	43	15	6	0	1	30	55
1881/82	19	9	2	8	20	5	0	1	33	31	13	0	1	60	55
1882/83	14	8	2	4	24	6	0	3	45	12	5	0	1	25	47
1883/84	21	13	3	5	34	12	0	5	73	22	9	0	0	40	27
1884/85	18	8	1	9	14	6	0	6	44	19	6	0	1	34	39
1885/86	14	8	2	4	17	5	0	1	30	12	6	0	3	33	39
1886/87	17	8	5	4	39	19	0	4	89	17	9	0	0	35	29
1887/88	21	11	3	7	45	19	0	3	92	20	9	1	2	47	37
1888/89	33	11	7	15	53	13	1	4	94	61	18	1	4	112	57
1889/90	27	5	2	20	25	8	1	1	46	81	29	1	1	144	73
1890/91	25	18	2	5	60	28	3	5	137	30	15	0	4	72	41
1891/92	31	15	2	14	58	29	0	0	203	49	17	0	2	157	57
1892/93	36	16	5	15	63	17	4	12	237	66	30	1	4	241	61
1893/94	37	23	3	11	68	29	3	3	283	32	16	1	5	151	46
1894/95	38	26	3	9	130	59	3	7	545	20	8	1	4	95	48
1895/96	39	23	6	10	106	47	3	5	441	27	6	4	2	113	59
1896/97	39	27	5	7	95	36	1	4	376	26	9	1	1	103	43
1897/98	38	31	0	7	116	48	3	9	489	24	11	4	1	110	39
1898/99	44	28	4	12	124	53	6	16	560	43	17	2	7	197	51
1899/00	36	25	3	8	98	41	3	14	441	38	15	2	5	170	43
1900/01	37	24	2	11	96	38	5	13	431	37	10	1	4	150	40
1901/02	35	21	3	11	79	23	3	10	332	35	13	4	2	151	52
1902/03	36	26	1	9	117	42	4	10	487	43	10	2	4	171	45
1903/04	39	19	3	17	81	25	3	9	338	69	25	3	4	282	47
1904/05	37	21	6	10	94	34	3	1	363	46	17	2	5	198	55
1905/06	37	17	6	14	49	16	4	5	211	60	25	4	6	266	60
1906/07	33	16	5	12	68	22	7	0	269	38	8	4	1	146	42
1907/08	36	18	4	14	87	32	4	3	349	56	26	6	5	258	59
1908/09	41	27	1	13	112	45	3	10	472	55	20	8	8	260	57
1909/10	39	24	5	10	109	45	6	2	441	52	21	4	1	214	40
1910/11	42	23	6	13	134	37	15	5	539	59	21	6	5	256	52
1911/12	39	21	2	16	117	43	7	3	469	65	24	5	3	270	46
1912/13	41	29	3	9	154	65	8	5	636	69	25	8	2	289	44
1913/14	39	21	3	15	98	40	8	3	410	73	18	5	3	282	50
1914/15	2	1	1	0	6	3	0	0	24	3	0	0	0	9	22
1918/19	19	12	0	7	77	35	2	3	319	28	8	2	4	121	62
1919/20	41	27	1	13	192	71	10	2	756	68	26	6	5	294	61
1920/21	41	31	2	8	151	69	9	6	640	77	24	6	7	325	44
1921/22	44	29	4	11	140	50	8	4	560	61	25	8	6	281	47
1922/23	45	30	5	10	129	55	18	8	582	62	19	6	9	278	67
1923/24	46	24	3	19	102	51	24	4	496	106	39	5	7	438	84
1924/25	40	27	3	10	107	47	14	6	479	77	28	6	4	320	57
1925/26	41	22	4	15	96	49	17	5	456	85	29	15	3	369	58
1926/27	41	23	1	17	123	56	15	0	526	73	37	4	12	353	54
1927/28	39	21	4	14	123	63	13	3	546	75	23	4	5	302	47
1928/29	38	16	1	21	94	41	11	1	401	83	38	13	4	380	61
1929/30	39	26	3	10	119	42	14	7	511	71	29	13	3	322	54
1930/31	39	23	4	12	118	45	10	9	510	72	36	6	3	318	54
1931/32	38	18	6	14	89	30	10	5	377	74	42	8	4	346	60
1932/33	37	23	0	14	93	38	10	9	420	69	38	8	6	331	67
1933/34	43	25	1	17	100	36	15	16	481	79	40	6	10	374	76
1934/35	44	26	4	14	109	50	6	10	484	64	26	7	6	289	79
1935/36	38	15	3	20	59	29	16	11	326	82	27	7	7	349	84
1936/37	39	14	2	23	70	28	12	9	338	95	37	11	10	432	59
1937/38	38	16	2	20	67	25	28	4	351	97	41	10	1	407	53
1938/39	36	20	3	13	83	31	20	6	395	74	36	16	3	354	56
1939/40	1	1	0	0	3	2	1	1	20	1	0	1	0	6	

SEASON	PLD	W	D	L	LEICESTER T	C	PG	DG	PTS	OPPONENTS T	C	PG	DG	AGST	PLYRS
1945/46	34	16	2	16	49	16	17	3	242	58	23	13	2	278	53
1946/47	32	18	1	13	72	31	13	6	341	50	20	15	6	258	46
1947/48	38	17	1	20	83	37	20	8	415	77	40	18	11	409	49
1948/49	37	16	1	20	57	18	27	10	318	75	30	19	8	366	51
1949/50	39	15	1	23	47	18	24	7	270	77	36	18	6	375	47
1950/51	38	23	2	13	85	41	22	13	442	55	23	24	6	301	34
1951/52	35	16	2	17	66	29	21	9	346	53	30	20	4	291	34
1952/53	35	15	3	17	65	19	23	5	317	62	31	22	4	326	45
1953/54	37	22	2	13	83	34	20	10	407	74	24	25	6	363	41
1954/55	40	21	2	17	86	41	36	2	454	89	36	29	4	438	40
1955/56	41	17	2	22	68	31	30	7	377	82	28	23	9	398	42
1956/57	43	18	6	19	77	38	25	1	385	79	31	34	6	419	42
1957/58	39	14	6	19	60	29	29	3	334	85	34	24	4	407	43
1958/59	38	19	5	14	73	32	31	5	391	62	27	27	4	333	39
1959/60	40	22	4	14	74	29	48	8	448	68	27	33	6	375	48
1960/61	42	24	2	16	86	50	38	6	490	65	20	29	3	331	41
1961/62	41	22	2	17	84	53	42	4	496	69	36	25	10	384	47
1962/63	31	21	1	9	66	35	23	2	343	49	12	18	6	243	40
1963/64	41	26	3	12	91	44	36	2	475	54	25	23	5	296	40
1964/65	41	20	2	19	76	41	40	3	439	91	40	19	7	431	42
1965/66	44	30	1	13	102	42	35	3	504	50	25	20	3	269	35
1966/67	46	33	2	11	98	40	39	6	509	44	16	29	9	278	43
1967/68	41	23	4	14	96	41	34	4	484	60	25	27	9	338	42
1968/69	43	27	4	12	122	48	56	9	657	81	40	38	7	461	41
1969/70	44	26	3	15	123	57	48	8	651	101	49	46	8	563	44
1970/71	45	23	2	20	116	54	63	3	654	86	36	49	6	495	38
1971/72	41	26	3	12	123	54	59	4	789	59	31	64	5	505	38
1972/73	46	29	2	15	148	87	72	2	988	99	46	59	6	683	41
1973/74	43	24	3	16	104	49	71	4	739	80	34	69	4	607	37
1974/75	40	19	1	20	72	31	60	4	542	80	37	61	7	598	41
1975/76	45	23	1	21	107	51	70	6	758	101	46	73	6	733	43
1976/77	39	26	0	13	105	64	67	1	752	55	24	46	6	424	39
1977/78	41	27	2	12	122	71	66	7	849	79	40	55	4	573	40
1978/79	34	24	0	10	106	57	69	13	784	40	28	43	9	372	36
1979/80	42	33	0	9	129	79	79	23	980	43	22	60	8	420	40
1980/81	41	33	1	7	121	78	82	18	940	63	28	57	16	527	40
1981/82	40	27	2	11	124	78	75	16	925	61	35	53	13	512	43
1982/83	44	33	0	11	139	87	87	7	1,012	64	35	74	10	578	41
1983/84	41	28	1	12	144	83	83	13	1,030	70	33	68	9	577	41
1984/85	39	26	2	11	129	78	79	18	963	64	31	57	9	516	46
1985/86	36	26	0	10	122	84	65	5	866	63	33	50	4	480	42
1986/87	39	26	1	12	118	79	76	14	900	74	30	61	10	569	41
1987/88	38	32	0	6	145	100	81	18	1,077	49	32	43	11	422	40
1988/89	38	28	1	9	110	67	98	14	910	76	38	56	9	575	45
1989/90	37	28	0	9	172	101	67	6	1,109	60	33	52	6	480	41
1990/91	37	28	0	9	130	74	79	7	926	43	26	59	11	434	43
1991/92	36	21	1	14	142	83	61	7	938	66	39	72	6	576	47
1992/93	37	30	0	7	122	66	70	13	991	52	26	47	4	465	51
OFF-SEASON TOURS															
1980	6	5	0	1	10	7	10	5	99	7	4	6	0	54	
1982	5	3	1	1	20	12	7	2	131	6	5	13	0	73	
1984	2	2	0	0	19	11	0	0	98	0	0	2	0	6	
1985	2	0	0	2	3	2	0	0	16	8	5	1	0	45	
1987	6	4	0	2	28	18	9	0	175	12	7	5	2	100	
1989	3	2	0	1	18	13	3	1	106	1	0	3	1	40	
1991	4	3	0	1	9	6	12	0	84	5	4	12	0	64	
1993	5	5	0	0	24	17	10	1	187	3	1	5	0	32	

Since 1980 Leicester have tried to arrange overseas tours in the summer every two years, the venues above were as follows, 1980-Australia and Fiji; 1982-Zimbabwe; 1984-Bahrain and Dubai; 1985-France; 1987-Australia, New Zealand and Singapore; 1989-United States; 1991-Canada; 1993-South Africa.

LEICESTER'S RECORD AGAINST ALL OPPONENTS

There follows a complete list of the 253 different opponents Leicester have met. If there have been more than FOUR games between the clubs, then a summary of the record appears in the table below, if they have met less than this then a further list follows this table.

Notes: *Bedford Swifts and Bedford Rovers merged to form Bedford in 1886/87: Devonport Albion and Plymouth merged to become Plymouth Albion by 1919/20: Gosforth became Newcastle-Gosforth in 1990/91: Liverpool became Liverpool St Helens in 1986/87.*

OPPONENTS	FIRST MEET	PLD	HOME W	D	L	F	A	AWAY W	D	L	F	A	OVERALL W	D	L	F	A
Aberavon	1899/00	11	6	1	1	83	29	0	1	2	19	34	6	2	3	102	63
The Army	1918/19	9	6	0	2	109	54	1	0	0	22	3	7	0	2	131	57
Ashby-de-la-Zouch	1889/90	6	4	0	0	42	1	2	0	0	9	0	6	0	0	51	1
Ballymena	1980/81	6	3	0	0	82	33	3	0	0	88	44	6	0	0	170	77
Barbarians	1909/10	75	31	5	39	997	1,136	-	-	-	-	-	31	5	39	997	1,136
Bath	1913/14	128	54	1	8	1,003	451	23	7	35	624	739	77	8	43	1,627	1,190
Bective Rangers	1893/94	11	6	2	2	125	32	0	0	1	11	16	6	2	3	136	48
Bedford	1886/87	138	57	3	12	1,385	573	29	6	31	830	654	86	9	43	2,215	1,227
Bedford Grammar School	1882/83	29	10	0	6	139	63	11	0	2	114	40	21	0	8	253	103
Birkenhead Park	1904/05	101	38	3	9	789	419	26	6	19	566	442	64	9	28	1,355	861
Birmingham	1972/73	12	9	0	0	359	65	3	0	0	139	23	12	0	0	498	88
Blackheath	1891/92	85	33	0	9	687	324	23	2	18	460	474	56	2	27	1,147	798
Bradford	1920/21	9	5	0	0	135	46	3	1	0	63	40	8	1	0	198	86
Bridgwater	1895/96	13	6	0	1	171	39	4	1	1	84	21	10	1	2	255	60
Bristol	1897/98	150	48	4	17	891	591	23	5	53	596	1,038	71	9	70	1,487	1,629
Burton-on-Trent	1880/81	45	16	4	4	289	56	11	3	7	211	73	27	7	11	500	129
Cambridge University	1899/00	72	25	4	7	644	313	15	1	20	450	535	40	5	27	1,094	848
Cardiff	1889/90	83	17	5	20	337	388	1	3	37	243	678	18	8	57	580	1,066
Cheltenham	1895/96	23	11	1	1	238	57	3	2	5	47	42	14	3	6	285	99
Coventry	1880/81	201	57	8	32	1,128	727	38	11	55	880	996	95	19	87	2,008	1,723
Devonport Albion	1895/96	33	8	1	7	86	97	0	3	14	30	161	8	4	21	116	258
Edgbaston Crusaders	1881/82	11	8	0	0	86	5	1	1	1	4	7	9	1	1	90	12
Edinburgh Royal High Sch.	1898/99	5	3	1	1	56	15	-	-	-	-	-	3	1	1	56	15
Exeter	1898/99	35	6	1	0	147	0	17	3	8	334	168	23	4	8	481	168
Fylde	1965/66	11	6	0	0	139	61	5	0	0	108	73	11	0	0	247	134
Gloucester	1891/92	162	53	2	27	928	693	15	4	61	544	1,169	68	6	88	1,472	1,862
Gosforth	1969/70	13	7	0	1	281	76	3	0	2	115	94	10	0	3	396	170
Guy's Hospital	1892/93	9	6	1	1	108	34	0	0	1	5	6	6	1	2	113	40
Handsworth	1890/91	10	9	0	0	184	9	1	0	0	12	4	10	0	0	196	13
Harlequins	1895/96	141	39	5	26	977	629	32	3	36	866	910	71	8	62	1,843	1,539
Hartlepool Rovers	1895/96	25	15	0	0	292	73	4	1	5	91	73	19	1	5	383	146
Headingley	1905/06	62	27	2	6	710	253	14	1	12	380	235	41	3	18	1,090	488
Kettering	1880/81	13	5	1	1	22	5	2	3	1	28	16	7	4	2	50	21
Leicestershire XV	1890/91	11	11	0	0	255	52	-	-	-	-	-	11	0	0	255	52
Liverpool	1960/61	11	5	0	0	159	21	3	0	3	85	57	8	0	3	244	78
Llanelli	1896/97	62	20	3	8	362	184	3	2	26	168	427	23	5	34	530	611
London	1906/07	6	6	0	0	123	40	-	-	-	-	-	6	0	0	123	40
London Irish	1922/23	10	5	0	0	172	35	5	0	0	73	37	10	0	0	245	72
London Scottish	1904/05	60	23	2	5	517	211	16	2	12	402	355	39	4	17	919	566
London Welsh	1902/03	49	27	0	7	568	240	11	0	4	334	193	38	0	11	902	433
Loughborough College	1953/54	31	28	1	2	710	239	-	-	-	-	-	28	1	2	710	239
Manchester	1896/97	34	19	0	1	400	92	10	1	3	187	97	29	1	4	587	189
Manningham	1887/88	6	0	0	3	4	28	0	0	3	4	25	0	0	6	8	53
Middlesex Hospital	1945/46	8	8	0	0	131	42	-	-	-	-	-	8	0	0	131	42
Moseley	1880/81	157	47	6	19	1,060	578	43	3	39	799	709	90	9	58	1,859	1,287
Mountain Ash	1896/97	5	3	0	0	62	8	1	0	1	22	30	4	0	1	84	38
Neath	1908/09	28	11	2	3	203	119	3	0	9	91	200	14	2	12	294	319
Newport	1889/90	121	19	6	32	452	527	5	2	57	410	1,117	24	8	89	862	1,644
Northampton	1880/81	183	63	12	19	1,292	640	34	6	49	861	941	97	18	68	2,153	1,581
Northern	1925/26	7	4	0	0	104	35	2	0	1	33	19	6	0	1	137	54
Nottingham	1884/85	39	20	0	0	397	85	13	2	4	298	138	33	2	4	695	223
Nuneaton	1880/81	96	50	3	2	1,225	271	33	0	8	717	254	83	3	10	1,942	525
Old Belvedere	1956/57	5	1	0	0	18	5	0	0	4	26	65	1	0	4	44	70

OPPONENTS	FIRST MEET	PLD	HOME W	D	L	F	A	AWAY W	D	L	F	A	OVERALL W	D	L	F	A
Old Blues	1923/24	14	13	0	1	242	90	-	-	-	-	-	13	0	1	242	90
Old Edwardians	1888/89	31	15	2	5	258	52	4	2	3	27	41	19	4	8	285	93
Old Merchant Taylors	1892/93	14	10	0	4	173	73	-	-	-	-	-	10	0	4	173	73
Orrell	1974/75	13	6	0	1	116	89	1	0	5	70	135	7	0	6	186	224
Oxford University	1903/04	72	23	0	14	562	395	14	3	18	400	432	37	3	32	962	827
Penarth	1894/95	8	5	1	1	105	28	0	0	1	9	20	5	1	2	114	48
Percy Park	1899/00	8	5	0	0	116	18	2	1	0	43	28	7	1	0	159	46
Plymouth	1900/01	20	6	3	1	72	22	0	3	7	36	86	6	6	8	108	108
Plymouth Albion	1919/20	86	35	2	6	667	250	25	4	14	495	344	60	6	20	1,162	594
Pontypool	1913/14	10	2	0	3	70	75	0	0	5	38	135	2	0	8	108	210
Richmond	1898/99	78	33	0	6	882	320	21	2	16	443	373	54	2	22	1,325	693
Rosslyn Park	1928/29	44	25	1	3	481	224	7	1	7	173	166	32	2	10	654	390
Royal Air Force	1918/19	54	41	2	11	1,093	396	-	-	-	-	-	41	2	11	1,093	396
Royal Navy	1919/20	14	13	1	0	334	87	-	-	-	-	-	13	1	0	334	87
Rugby	1881/82	84	35	2	5	708	183	22	7	13	394	253	57	9	18	1,102	436
Rushden	1880/81	17	5	3	1	32	8	3	3	2	21	18	8	6	3	53	26
St Bartholomew's Hospital	1892/93	5	5	0	0	93	7	-	-	-	-	-	5	0	0	93	7
St Thomas' Hospital	1892/93	5	3	1	1	62	7	-	-	-	-	-	3	1	1	62	7
Sale	1890/91	35	25	0	1	489	164	2	1	6	95	137	27	1	7	584	301
Saracens	1962/63	27	15	0	0	360	118	10	2	0	278	113	25	2	0	638	231
Stratford-upon-Avon	1888/89	11	6	0	1	134	23	2	0	2	41	31	8	0	3	175	54
Swansea	1896/97	115	19	13	26	433	463	7	3	47	344	821	26	16	73	777	1,284
Swinton	1888/89	11	1	1	6	16	59	0	0	3	0	35	1	1	9	16	94
United Services	1905/06	12	7	0	0	115	26	2	1	2	37	33	9	1	2	152	59
Wakefield	1921/22	5	4	0	0	125	42	1	0	0	17	6	5	0	0	142	48
Wasps	1957/58	41	14	0	5	347	215	11	3	8	293	247	25	3	13	640	462
Watcyn Thomas XV	1958/59	11	9	0	2	178	91	-	-	-	-	0	9	0	2	178	91
Waterloo	1929/30	51	22	2	7	543	301	12	1	7	271	184	34	3	14	814	485
West Hartlepool	1901/02	12	6	0	2	155	58	2	1	1	28	16	8	1	3	183	74

OTHER OPPONENTS PLAYED LESS THAN FIVE TIMES:

Alberta(1991 W1)
Altrincham(1896/97 W1)
Ambleside(1893/94 W1)
Aspatria(1896/97 D1)
Australia(1981/82 L1)
Australian Forces(1918/19 L1)

Bedford Rovers(1880/81 W2)
Bedford Swifts(1884/85 W2)
Bedford & District XV(1918/19 W1)
Belgrave(1902/03 W1)
Belgrave Premier Works(1912/13 W1)
Belgrave St Peter's(1898/99 W1)
Bridgend(1912/13 W2,L1)
British Police(1956/57 W1)
British Colombia(1991 W1)
British Colombia Press XV(1991 L1)
Bromsgrove(1890/91 W1)
Broughton Park(1968/69 W4)
Broughton Rangers(1892/93 W1,L1)
Burfield Rangers(1894/95 W1)
Burton Anglesey Rovers(1880/81 W1)

Camp Hill Old Edwardians(1901/02 W1)
Canadian Forces(1918/19 W1)
Cardiff Harlequins(1888/89 W1,L1)
Carlisle(1898/99 W1)
C.A.S.G. Paris(1975/76 W2)
Castleford(1901/02 W4)
Chambéry(1985 L1)
Cinderford(1909/10 W3,D1)
Combined Services(1969/70 D1)
Coventry Excelsior(1892/93 W1)
Cross Keys(1923/24 W1,L1)
Croydon(1903/04 W2)

Denver Barbarians(1989 W1)
Derby Wanderers(1883/84 W2)
Derbyshire(1884/85 L1)
Dukinfield(1891/92 W1)

Eastern Suburbs(1975/76 W2)
East Sheen(1893/94 L1)
Edmonton(1991 W1)
The 18 of Town & District(1888/89 L1)
England XV(1930/31 L2)
England M.G.C.(1918/19 W1)

Fettes-Lorettonians(1904/05 W1,D1,L2)
Fiji Islands(1973/74 W1)
Fiji Barbarians(1986/87 W1)
Fiji Chairmans XV(1980 W1)
Fiji Combined Services(1980 W1)
Five Ways Old Edwardians(1898/99 W4)

Gardens Tech(1993 W1)
Glasgow University(1911/12 W1)
Gulf XV(1984 W1)

Halifax(1894/95 W1,L1)
Hampstead(1896/97 W1)
Harrogate(1970/71 W3)
Heriotonians(1924/25 W1,L1)
High Wycombe(1982/83 W1)
Hinckley(1972/73 W1)
Huddersfield(1894/95 D1,L1)

Irish Wolfhounds(1966/67 W2,L1)

Jedforest(1913/14 W1)
Jesus College,Oxford(1896/97 W1)

Keighley(1899/00 W1)
Kendal(1910/11 W1)
Kent Wanderers(1892/93 W1,L1)
Kirkstall(1900/01 W2,D1)

Lancaster(1896/97 W1)
Lansdowne(1898/99 W1,D1,L1)
Lautoka(1980 W1)
Leamington(1881/82 W2)

Leeds(1894/95 L1)
Leicestershire Presidents XV(1967/68 W1)
1st Leicestershire Regiment(1908/09 W1)
3rd Leicestershire Regiment(1918/19 W1)
4th Leicestershire Regiment(1918/19 W1)
Leicester Crusaders(1890/91 W4)
Leicester & District(1969/70 W3)
Leicester Past(1884/85 L1)
Leicester Swifts(1888/89 W3)
Leicester Victoria(1880/81 W2)
Lennox(1900/01 W1)
Littleborough(1896/97 W1)
Liverpool St Helens(1988/89 W4)
Llwynypia(1898/99 W3,D1)

Machine Gun Corps(1918/19 W1)
Maesteg(1961/62 W4)
Manchester Free Wanderers(1889/90 W3,L1)
Manly(1987 W1)
Maoris(1926/27 L1)
Market Harborough(1880/81 W1)
Mashonaland(1982 L1)
Matabeleland(1982 W1)
Mediolanum Milan(1992/93 W1)
Metropolitan Police(1986/87 W1)
Middlesbrough(1973/74 W1)
Middlesex Wanderers(1894/95 W1)
Midlands XV(1901/02 W2)
Moseley Harlequins(1888/89 W1)
Moseley Woodstock(1884/85 W4)
Mossley(1889/90 W1,L1)

Natal Selectors XV(1993 W1)
Natal Development XV(1993 W1)
Newbold on Avon(1911/12 W2)
Newbridge(1964/65 W1,L1)
New Brighton(1969/70 W3)
Newcastle Gosforth(1991/92 W1)
New Zealand(1905/06 L2)
New Zealand Barbarians(1986/87 L1)

New Zealand M.G.C.(1918/19 W1)
New Zealand Services(1918/19 L2)
Northampton Unity(1887/88 W1)
Northern Division(1991/92 L1)
North of Ireland(1970/71 W1)

Oldham(1888/89 L3)
Old Leysians(1893/94 L1)
Olney(1897/98 W1)

Pendleton(1892/93 L1)
Penygraig(1890/91 W2,L1)
Peterborough & District(1887/88 W1)
Pill Harriers(1921/22 W1)
Ponsonby(1987 W1)
Pontefract(1893/94 W1)
Pontypridd(1894/95 W2,L2)
Portsmouth(1896/97 W2)

Queensland(1980 W1,L2)

Racing Club de France(1922/23 W2,L2)
Randwick(1973/74 W2)
The Rest(1939/40 W1)
Richmond & Blackheath XV(1945/46 W1)
Romania(1956/57 W1,D1,L1)
Roundhay(1980/81 W1)
Royal Naval Division(1918/19 L1)
Rugby B.T.H.(1922/23 W3)
Rugby Rovers(1880/81 W2,D1,L1)

St Claude(1985 L1)
St Helens(1891/92 L1)
St Mary's Hospital(1948/49 L1)
Salford(1892/93 D1,L1)
Sheffield(1921/22 W4)
Singapore Cricket Club(1987 W1)
Solihull(1976/77 W1)
South African Forces(1918/19 L1)
South Gulf Select XV(1984 W1)

South Northamptonshire(1892/93 W1)
South Warwickshire Rovers(1883/84 W2)
Stafford(1883/84 W1)
Stamford(1882/83 W1)
Stoneygate(1893/94 W3)
Stourbridge(1891/92 W1)
Stroud(1967/68 W1,L1)

Torquay Athletic(1963/64 W2)
Town & Country Colts(1888/89 W1)
Treherbert(1898/99 W4)
The 20 of Town & District(1886/87 W1)

U.S.A.Eagles(1989 L1)

Vail(1989 W1)

Walkden(1891/92 L1)
Western Australia Presidents XV(1987 W1)
Western Australia(1987 L1)
Western Province Defence XV(1993 W1)
Westleigh(1975/76 W1)
Wilmslow(1969/70 W1,L2)
Wolverhampton(1895/96 W1)
Wolverton(1890/91 W2)
Worcester(1894/95 W1)
Wortley(1895/96 W1)

York(1892/93 W1)
Yorkshire(1918/19 W1)

Zimbabwe(1982 W2,D1)
Zimbabwe Midlands XV(1982 W1)
Zululand Regional XV(1993 W1)

THE TOTAL RECORD	PLD	WON	DREW	LOST	FOR	AGST
Home games	2,179	1,554	134	491	33,996	15,736
Away games	1,677	710	126	841	17,903	17,890
All games	**3,856**	**2,264**	**260**	**1,332**	**51,899**	**33,626**

INDIVIDUAL RECORDS
THE 300 CLUB

NAME	CAREER	GAMES
David Matthews	**1955/56-1973/74**	**502**
Sid Penny	1895/96-1910/11	491
John Allen	1960/61-1975/76	457
Doug Norman	1919/20-1932/33	453
Paul Dodge	1975/76-1992/93	437
'Dusty' Hare	1976/77-1988/89	394
'Pedlar' Wood	1906/07-1922/23	388
Garry Adey	1966/67-1980/81	381
Steve Kenney	1975/76-1989/90	365
Les Cusworth	1978/79-1989/90	365
George Ward	1909/10-1925/26	361
Jacky Braithwaite	1895/96-1906/07	359
Billy Foreman	1893/94-1905/06	358
Bob Rowell	1961/62-1977/78	355
Peter Wheeler	1969/70-1985/86	349
Sid Matthews	1897/98-1907/08	340
Tom Bleasdale	1949/50-1963/64	340
Graham Willars	1959/60-1986/87	338
Bleddyn Jones	1969/70-1978/79	333
Frank Chawner	1948/49-1963/64	331
Ian Smith	1977/78-1991/92	331
Denis Bolesworth	1936/37-1954/55	330
Ralph Buckingham	1924/25-1934/35	325
Stuart Redfern	1981/82-1991/92	324
Bob Barker	1968/69-1979/80	320
Percy Lawrie	1907/08-1923/24	318
Brian Hall	1970/71-1984	312
John Duggan	1969/70-1980	302

Billy Foreman held the club appearance record between 1899 and 1906.

Breaking the club appearance record: W A Sheffield 16th game 26.11.1881; John Parsons 99th game 14.1.1888; W R Porter 113th game 19.1.1889; Arthur McKechnie 169th game 20.2.1892; Billy Foreman 216th game 14.10.1899; Sid Penny 359th game 1.12.1906; David Matthews 492nd game 21.4.1973.

174 players have made over one hundred first team appearances, 40 went on to complete 200 games, and the 23 *(left)* made the 300 club.

Graham Willars has the longest Tigers playing career, 27 years 169 days, during which time the Tigers played 1,154 games; his final three appearances were all as a replacement. If however, you remove these Graham's career is still the longest at 18 years 194 days, just a week longer than David Matthews' career, and in terms of games is 787 against 779.

EVER PRESENT SEASONS
1883/84 - W A Sheffield; 1885/6 - W A Sheffield & Jack Lovett; 1887/8 - John Parsons; 1890/1 - Arthur McKechnie; 1893/4 - J Touhey; 1898/9 - Alf Butlin & W F Lincoln; 1900/1 - Alf Butlin & John Garner; 1901/2 - Jacky Braithwaite & Sid Penny; 1902/3 - Sid Matthews; 1904/5 - Sid Matthews; 1908/9 - 'Pedlar' Wood; 1922/3 - Teddy Haselmere; 1929/30 - Ernie Coleman; 1930/1 - Doug Norman; 1937/8 - Bill Bainbridge; 1948/9 - Denis Bolesworth; 1950/1 - Denis Bolesworth & Harry Sibson; 1951/2 - Gwynne Lawrence & Bill Moore; 1954/5 - John Jenkins; 1956/7 - John Thompson; 1957/8 - John Thompson; 1958/9 - Rex Skelton; Tom Bleasdale & Gordon Almey; 1961/2 - Colin Martin & David Matthews; 1962/3 - Frank Chawner & David Matthews; 1964/5 - Peter Edwards; 1968/9-John Allen & David Matthews; 1974/5 - Bleddyn Jones.

David Matthews is the only one to have three times played all the games in a season, although Sheffield, Butlin, Sid Matthews, Bolesworth and Thompson did so twice.

The most appearances in a season is 45 by **Teddy Haselmere** in 1922/3, followed by Alf Butlin and W F Lincoln in 1898/9, John Allen in 1970/1 and Bob Barker in 1972/3 - all with 44.

SUCCESSIVE APPEARANCES

109	David Matthews	14.1.1961	to	7.12.1963
103	John Thompson	3.4.1956	to	29.11.1958
75	Rex Skelton	27.12.1957	to	5.12.1959
74	Frank Chawner	21.10.1961	to	30.10.1963
70	Doug Norman	11.1.1930	to	28.11.1931
70	Peter Edwards	7.12.1963	to	15.9.1965
68	Alf Butlin	28.12.1897	to	30.9.1899
68	Jacky Braithwaite	3.11.1900	to	11.10.1902

James Bainbridge played only 41 games for the Club - all consecutively from 3.4.1937 to 19.4.1938.

Sid Matthews played in 127 out of 128 possible games between 19.4.1902 and 9.12.1905, only missing the match at Swansea on 30.1.1904, making sequences of 63 and 64 successive games. Denis Bolesworth is the only other player with two separate sequences of fifty consecutive games in a career.

MOST PLAYERS IN A SEASON
84 players were used in the 46 games of the 1923/24 season, and this was matched in 1935/36 when only 38 games were played. 79 players were used in the 44 game season of 1934/35.

LEAST PLAYERS IN A SEASON
Only 27 players were used in the 1883/84 season of 21 games, 29 were used in the 17 game 1886/87 season, and 34 players were used in both the 1950/51 and 1951/52 seasons with 38 and 35 games respectively.

FEWEST PLAYERS IN A GAME

There have 30 occasions that Leicester have played a complete game a player short, six times there have been two players short, and once on 31.3.1888 they were three players short, but on 9.12.1882 they played away to Stamford with only eleven men (and they still won easily!) Most of these occasions were in the early days, the last time was 2.9.1939 just as war was to break out; prior to this it was 21.2.1920 at home to Richmond.

Conversely though on 27.12.1884 at home to Bedford Swifts, Gilbert scored a try and Parsons a drop goal, before it was realised Leicester had been playing with sixteen men! Accordingly the game was halted, the extra man dismissed, and all previous Leicester scores were struck from the record. Leicester later went on to win by one goal to nil.

THE FAMILY CONNECTION

FATHER & THREE SONS - Tom Berry with sons David, John and Richard.

FATHER & TWO SONS - Percy Oscroft with sons A & Donald; Brian Wigley with sons Dave & Steve.

FATHER & SON - James Bainbridge with son Bill; Alf Bates with son E; Nick Drake-Lee with son Bill; Mike Gavins with son Dave; H C Harrison with son Mike; Maurice Key with son Andy; Percy Lawrie with son Gordon; John Quick with son Sam; Bernard Vesty with son Phil.

FOUR BROTHERS - Charles, Cecil, Victor & George Beamish [Victor & George (31)]

THREE BROTHERS - David, John & Richard Berry [David & Richard (5), John & Richard (1)]; Charlie, Frank & John Cramphorn [Charlie & John (1), Frank & John (1)]; Phil, Arthur & Ron Palmer [Arthur & Ron (4)]

TWO BROTHERS - Trevor & John Allen (1); Percy & Shirley Atkins (4); LB & RO Baillon; Jack & Ron Ball; CC & JL Barker (3); William & Walter Buckler (1); G & Dick Cattell (2); Percy & Tom Clarke; Ted & Rupert Cooke (40); Morgan & Phil Crowe (2); Harry & JG Edmiston (2); JJM & BHL Ewin (1); Ray & Roy French (23); Alf & Tom Goodrich (74); Paul & Mark Grant (5); OJ & L Hargrave (1); Geoff & Frank Herbert (42); Ernest & Harold Hind (53); Tom & A Hogarth (2); John & Dick Jackett (32); Arthur & Frank Jones (83); Percy & Harry Lawrie (129); Jim & Will Leather; Kenneth & Donal McAlpin (8); David & Andy Matthews (5); Stephen & Graham Meikle (1); Bill & Jeff Moore; Steve & Stuart Redfern (45); Wayne & Lee Richardson (6); Paul & Tim Ringer (7); Claude & Harold Sambrook (30); Brian & Bob Small (14); Paddy & AE Swain; 'Tim' & 'Sos' Taylor (186); John & Bill Thompson; Eric & Trevor Thorneloe (1); Rory & Tony Underwood (30); Willie & Charlie Watts (4); Dave & Steve Wigley (1); Harry & E Wilkinson (9); 'Pedlar' & Frank Wood (9); F & G Wright (1); CHL & E Wynne(3)

Note: *The figures in parentheses are how many times they appeared together in the same team.*

Bill Moore is also a grandson of Billy Foreman

Another Berry brother, Michael has appeared for the Extras and Richard & David are twin brothers.

David Palmer, the son of another brother Ralph has also appeared.

The last time two separate sets of brothers appeared in the same team was on 1.12.1928 when the Cramphorn and Beamish brothers played against the Harlequins.

Frank Jones played for Tigers 83 times alongside his brother Arthur.

LANDMARKS

QUICKEST

The quickest to achieve 50 first team appearances is **Mike Yandle** in only 406 days; in terms of games played J Wilkinson the full-back in the twenties only missed one Leicester game in his first 58. **Mike Yandle** also holds the record for 100 appearances with 2 years 151 days; 'Pedlar' Wood only missed five games during his first 100. **Bleddyn Jones** is the quickest to 200 games with 5 years 54 days, whilst Alf Butlin missed just 13 Leicester games in attaining 200 personal appearances. **Bleddyn Jones** was also the quickest to 300 games in 7 years 327 days, with 'Pedlar' Wood missing only 25 Tigers games in his 300.

SLOWEST

Andy Key took 12 years 118 days and 509 Tigers matches to play in 50 games himself. **Charlie Cross** took 12 years 167 days to play in 100 games, **'Tim' Taylor** took 13 years 103 days to make 200 appearances, and **Denis Bolesworth** 16 years 52 days to play in 300 games.

AGE

Although very little information exists on the exact birthdates of many of the early Tigers, one of the youngest would have to be **Paul Dodge** who was only 17 years 103 days old when he made his first-team debut, and 18 when he made his 50th appearance, 20 on his 100th, 23 on his 200th and only 27 on his 300th.

Graham Willars is probably the oldest Tiger (when he appeared as a replacement) at 47 years 135 days, but the oldest Tiger in a starting line-up is likely to be **'Pedlar' Wood** who played his last game at age 40 years 290 days. Charlie Cross was 35 years 55 days old when he played his 50th game, and 36 years 264 days when he made his 100th appearance.

The oldest on debut is likely to be **Alf Brice** who against Headingley on 1 January, 1909 was aged 37 years, 100 days.

Edward Whetstone - finished a winner in 47 of his 61 Tigers games.

TRY ON DEBUT

180 players have scored a try on their first appearance for the Tigers, a hat-trick of tries on debut has been achieved on the following six occasions:

'Knott'	v Bedford(H)	6.3.1889
Jack Miles	v Handsworth(H)	9.9.1899
A Francis	v Headingley(A)	1.1.1923
J J M Ewin	v Manchester(A)	1.1.1930
Graham Meikle	v Barbarians(H)	27.12.1933
S G Walker	v Exeter(A)	23.4.1935

MOST POINTS ON DEBUT

22 (5C,4PG)	**Dusty Hare**	**v Oxford Univ.(H)**	**20.10.1976**
13 (3T,1DG)	Graham Meikle	v Barbarians(H)	27.12.1933
12 (4PG)	John Flint	v Bedford(A)	6.9.1975

CAPTAINS

Percy Lawrie captained the Tigers an incredible 163 times, winning a record 106 and losing a record 48 games (Sid Matthews also lost 48 of his matches as captain). The only other captain with over 100 victories is Les Cusworth who won 101 times in 130 games. Dean Richards has the best winning percentage (22 wins in 28 games), and W R Porter has the worst losing percentage with 24 losses in only 35 games.

In 6 games Frank Tarr never led the team to victory, whereas Nigel Gillingham and J W Symington won all four of their matches in charge.

RESULTS

Of players that have made a minimum of 50 appearances, nine have been on the winning side in more than 75% of their Tigers careers. **Martin Johnson** has won 43 of his 53 games and has the best percentage. The others are Alastair Smallwood, Harry

Roberts, Matt Poole, Clive Woodward, Mark Grant, Les Cusworth, Kevin Williams and Edward Whetstone.

Paul Stone won all of his nine Tigers games, and Mick Merriman was never on the losing side in 18 appearances. Troy Thacker has won 41 of his 47 games.

The most wins were gained by Paul Dodge with 316 in 437 games, the most draws were obtained by Sid Penny with 45 in 491 appearances.

On the other hand, nine players have lost more than half of their games for the Tigers. Allan Towell lost 51 of his 93 games and has the worst percentage, followed by, John Stevens, David Brook, Brian A F Smith, Danny Rees, Dick Jackett, Ronnie Tudor, Bob Stirling and Peter Thorneloe.

W S Sheppard, J Sutcliffe and David Walker all lost each of their four Tigers games, and Paul Ash was never on the winning side in his 6 games.

The most losses as a Tiger is attributed to David Matthews with 176 in his 502 games.

REPLACEMENTS

Substitutions for injured players were first allowed in the 1976/77 season, although J C K Campbell was replaced by Haydn Thomas at Blackheath on 14.12.1946 a few minutes after the start because Thomas was late in arriving. Since then 106 different players have been involved in 323 replacements. **Angus Collington** leads the appearances as a replacement with 18, followed by Adrian Marriott with 16, Jez Harris with 10, and Terry Burwell and Ian Smith with nine each. S Roy made all his five appearances as a replacement, D Peters both of his, and eight other players have made their only appearance as a replacement.

The Tigers have used three replacements in the same game on three occasions, all coincidentally whilst on tour: 10.5.1985 against Chambry, France; 16.8.1987 against Queensland, Australia; 14.8.1993 against Natal Development XV, South Africa.

22 replacements have scored tries, Darren Grewcock getting four, Colin Dexter, Adrian Marriott and Chris Johnson three. Chris Johnson is the only one to have scored a hat-trick of tries as a replacement against Western Province Defence on 7.8.1993; John Cooke in 1981/82, David Williams in 1982/83 and Steve Wills in 1991/92 scored two tries in the same game.

In terms of players being replaced Ian Smith leads this category with 25 games cut short through injury. Dusty Hare with 17, Paul Dodge 14, Steve Johnson 13, John Wells 12 and Barry Evans 11, follow him.

HALF-BACK PARTNERSHIPS

Billy Foreman and **Jacky Braithwaite** partnered each other at half-back 236 times for Leicester. The next most experienced partnerships are Les Cusworth & Steve Kenney with 193, 'Tim' Taylor & 'Pedlar' Wood with 188, Bleddyn Jones & John Allen 186, and Les Cusworth & Nick Youngs with 111, the only pairings with over one hundred games. Cusworth and Mick Merriman won 12 and drew one in their 13 combined games, and Toone and Wynne lost all six in 1892/93.

EXPERIENCE

The most experienced Tigers starting lineup of all time is the one which beat Headingley 53-7 at Welford Road on 7.1.1989, it was as follows;

Dusty Hare (381 games); Barry Evans (218), Paul Dodge (383), Ian Bates (138), Tony Underwood (7); Les Cusworth (317), Steve Kenney (345); Stuart Redfern (214), Chris Tressler (191), Wayne Richardson (150), Malcolm Foulkes-Arnold (235), Tom Smith (81), John Wells (145), Mark Grant (7), Ian Smith (287)

For a grand total of 3,099 games between them.

If you exclude the very first season, and the first seasons after the World Wars then the least experienced team was fielded at Welford Road on 9.9.1992, when the Tigers defeated a Leicestershire XV 40-20;

Wayne Kilford (1); Tom Reynolds (2), Laurence Boyle (24), Stuart Potter (3), Peter Sandford (44); Ian Harris (1), Darren Grewcock (18); Darren Eagland (3), Troy Thacker (42), Darren Garforth (35), Elliott Buckby (1), Paul Grant (4), John Murphy (14), Mark Grant (47), Bill Drake-Lee (15)

A grand total of only 254 appearances.

It is a strange coincidence that Mark Grant appears in both the above teams.

REFEREES

A number of ex-Tigers have gone on to referee Leicester games, amongst these are Dan Ellwood, B H L Ewin, Brian Gray, Teddy Haselmere, A O Jones, Stephen Meikle, Jack Miles, Bill Moore, Percy Oscroft, Peter Tahany, Gordon Vears, and W W Wakefield. Also Cyril Gadney (brother of Leicester captain Bernard) refereed 16 Tigers games.

E B Holmes of Moseley has refereed the most with 73 games, followed by another Moseley man Gil Evans with 63, and Albert Freethy the Welsh international referee with 62. The Tigers won all eight games under the control of G C Cromwell from 1978-83, and lost only one of 15 games when David Matthews (of the Liverpool Society) was in charge. Leicester also only lost one of A Browning's 31 games in charge before the First World War.

SENDINGS OFF

Player	Club/Opponents	Date	Referee
Dick Hellings	Llwynypia(H)	26.12.1901	Gil Evans
Harry Lawrie	v Harlequins(A)	9.3.1912	H A Taylor
Pedlar Wood	v Newport(H)	14.2.1914	E Browning
A C Bell	Newport(H)	14.2.1914	" (2)
R Allison	Cardiff(H)	29.11.1919	A J Trollope
Llewellyn Jones	Swansea(H)	5.11.1921	J Welshman
S C Craven	Cardiff(H)	10.11.1928	E Browning
D McArthur	Cardiff(H)	10.11.1928	" (2)
Ron Richards	Swansea(H)	5.1.1935	R I Scorer
Gordon Almey	v Llanelli(A)	21.11.1959	F Croster
E J F Stephens	Gloucester(H)	11.1.1969	M Walker
Bob Rowell	v Llanelli(A)	18.4.1970	D M Davies
John Dawson	v Harlequins(H)	6.3.1971	M Walker
Bruce Wilson	Harlequins(H)	6.3.1971	" (2)
Paul Ringer	v Northampton(A)	20.10.1973	D Howard
B Holt	Coventry(A)	5.10.1974	N Sanson
Nick Joyce	v Northampton(A)	22.2.1975	R Quittenton
Robin Cowling	v Fylde(A)	19.4.1975	A Welsby
Bob Rowell	v Fylde(A)	19.4.1975	" (2)
Steve Redfern	v London Welsh(H)	29.1.1977	K Lockerbie
Chris Howcroft	London Welsh(H)	29.1.1977	" (2)
Micky Skinner	Blackheath(H)	13.12.1980	F A Howard
Jim Sydall	Waterloo(A)	4.12.1982	D J Matthews
Nick Jackson	v Bath(H)	1.1.1983	Ron Mayo
Nigel Fox	Northampton(A)	15.10.1983	Ron Mayo
Jock Ross	London Welsh(A)	31.12.1983	Ron Mayo
Nigel Benzani	Pontypridd(H)	2.9.1989	Tony Sparks
Steve Binnington	Bedford(H)	23.9.1989	K McCartney
Paul Ashmead	Gloucester(H)	26.9.1992	D J Matthews
David Hinkins	Bristol(A)	13.3.1993	Colin High

FIRST-CLASS CRICKETERS

The following Tigers played First-Class cricket:
J N Beasley, R B Bruce-Lockhart, J W Burdett, H L V Day, K D Downes, E D Dynes, R D M Evers, H W F Franklin, F Geeson,

H German, R A Gerrard, C Gimson, W H Hare, R E Hemingway, A E Hind, F S Hodder, P P Hope, A O Jones, R Joyce, J King, H E Kingston, C J King-Turner, L Kirk, P H Konig, A S McIntyre, D Moeller, J Morton, F C W Newman, A G B Old, H R Orr, D S Oscroft, P W Oscroft, H G Owen-Smith, G A Palmer, J Powers, H L Price, S T A Radcliffe, H Rotherham, G H Salmon, K J F Scotland, G Shingler, W A Sime, J W D Smith, W A Smith, F W Stocks, J A S Taylor, J A C Thornton, H G Topham, D F Walker, L F Ward, S R Wright. In addition R H Hincks and A E Wright appeared for Leicestershire before the County attained First-Class status in 1894.

THE ACCUMULATORS
500 CAREER POINTS

	Gm	T	PT	Con	Pen	DG	GM	Pts
Dusty Hare	**394**	**87**	**-**	**779**	**820**	**47**	**-**	**4,507**
John Liley	131	51	-	265	243	1	-	1,478
Harold Day	212	108	-	281	81	4	2	1,151
Bob Barker	320	158	-	92	107	2	-	1,117
Les Cusworth	365	66	-	100	65	96	-	947
Percy Lawrie	318	206	-	23	9	9	-	727
Barry Evans	265	169	-	1	-	-	-	678
John Duggan	302	158	1	-	-	-	-	608
Mike Gavins	121	5	-	107	119	2	-	592
Peter Wheeler	349	66	1	61	69	-	-	589
Doug Prentice	239	60	-	133	43	-	-	575
Paul Dodge	437	93	1	33	40	3	-	567
Arthur Jones	224	39	-	113	20	37	3	563
Colin Martin	272	13	-	126	88	-	-	555
Keith Chilton	144	26	-	91	95	2	-	551
George Cullen	180	66	1	77	57	9	-	550
Jez Harris	161	18	-	92	58	38	-	544
Teddy Haselmere	180	136	1	35	6	8	-	528

In all fifty players have amassed over 200 pts each.
Breaking the points scoring record: John Parsons 10 pts 18.3.1882; Ted Cooke 151 pts 27.12.1895; Archie Field 158 pts 17.2.1897; A O Jones 177 pts 12.3.1898; Harry Wilkinson 360 pts 8.9.1900; A O Jones 475 pts 21.3.1903; Percy Lawrie 564 pts 16.10.1920; Harold Day 728 pts 11.4.1925; Dusty Hare 1,152 pts 19.4.1980.

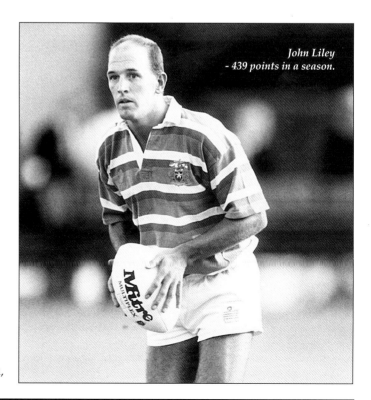

John Liley - 439 points in a season.

Frank Jackson - 6 tries against St. Bart's.

MOST POINTS IN A SEASON:

439 (18T,89C,63PG)	**John Liley**	**1989/90**
438 (12T,60C,89PG,1DG)	Dusty Hare	1988/9

31 different players have scored 100 points or over in a season, with Dusty Hare achieving the mark in each of his thirteen seasons with the club. Indeed he accumulated in excess of 200 points in all but his first season (finishing with 199 after missing the first 9 games playing for Nottingham). Harold Day achieved the hundred on seven occasions (all successive), and Bob Barker six times.

MOST POINTS IN A GAME:

43	**Dusty Hare**	**Birmingham(H)**	**17.9.1986**
34	Dusty Hare	Birmingham(A)	16.9.1981
31	Teddy Haselmere	Burton-on-Trent(H)	4.10.1919
31	John Liley	Rosslyn Park(H)	21.3.1992
30	Les Cusworth	Harlequins(H)	1.3.1980

The most points by an individual contributing all Leicester's points in a game is 19 (1T,5PG) by Bob Barker at home to Bristol on 17.12.1977

MOST SUCCESSIVE POINTS SCORING GAMES

'Dusty' Hare scored points in 183 successive games for which he was selected in the starting lineup between 17.12.1983 and the end of his career at Twickenham on 29.4.1989. He did however come on as a replacement for Paul Dodge in Australia on 4.8.1987, and did not score any points, therefore strictly speaking the above record is actually broken into two separate runs of 118 and 65 games. John Liley extended his own run to 96 games after the recent South African tour, but failed to score in his replacement appearance against Zululand. Marcus Rose scored points in each of his 19 games, whilst Howard Deacon has played in the most games (29) without ever scoring a point.

THE FINISHERS
75 CAREER TRIES

	Gm	T	PT	TPG
Percy Lawrie	**318**	**206**	**-**	**0.65**
Barry Evans	265	169	-	0.64
John Duggan	302	158	1	0.52
Bob Barker	320	158	-	0.49
Harry Wilkinson	233	153	-	0.66
Teddy Haselmere	180	136	1	0.76
David Matthews	502	119	-	0.24
Ralph Buckingham	325	117	-	0.36
Harold Day	212	108	-	0.51
'Pedlar' Wood	388	102	-	0.26
'Tim' Taylor	294	97	-	0.33
Dean Richards	218	97	-	0.44
Rory Underwood	151	95	-	0.63
Tim Barnwell	189	95	-	0.50
Paul Dodge	437	93	1	0.21
Dusty Hare	394	87	-	0.22
Ewart Farndon	183	86	-	0.47
David Bird	285	86	-	0.30
Billy Foreman	358	85	-	0.24
Ernest Hind	127	81	-	0.64
Jack Miles	93	75	-	0.81

43 different players have scored over fifty tries each.
Breaking the try scoring record: W A Sheffield 10 tries 8.12.1883; Sherrard Coleman 20 tries 29.10.1887; Bob Hesmondhalgh 32 tries 26.10.1895; Billy Foreman 34 tries 17.2.1897; Harry Wilkinson 50 tries17.9.1898; Percy Lawrie 154 tries 26.12.1918.

MOST TRIES IN A SEASON:

59	**Teddy Haselmere**	**1919/20**
37	Harry Wilkinson	1898/9
37	Ernest Hind	1902/3

21 players have scored over twenty tries in a season, Percy Lawrie did it six times (five in succession), Harry Wilkinson five (all consecutive), and Bob Barker four times.

MOST TRIES IN A GAME:

7	**Alastair Smallwood**	**Manchester(H)**	**30.12.1922**
6	Bobby Lewis	Worcester(H)	2.3.1895
6	Frank Jackson	St Bartholomew's(H)	20.1.1896
6	Ernest Hind	Belgrave(H)	21.3.1903
6	Tony Underwood	Liverpool St Helens(H)	11.4.1992

Five tries in a game have been recorded by Teddy Haselmere (3 times); Ernest Hind (twice); and Ally Nutt, A O Jones, Barry Evans and Rory Underwood (once each).

Four tries in a game were scored by 29 players; Haselmere and Harry Wilkinson topping the list with 5 times, followed with Rory Underwood on 4 occasions.

Hat-tricks have been scored by 116 different players; by Percy Lawrie on ten occasions, Haselmere nine, Jack Miles, John Duggan and Barry Evans with seven, whilst Harry Wilkinson, Ted Flewitt, David Senior, Bob Barker, Dean Richards, and Rory Underwood have achieved hat-tricks on six separate occasions. Chris Johnson uniquely scored a hat-trick as a replacement against Western Province Defence on 7.8.1993.

MOST SUCCESSIVE GAMES WITH A TRY

8	**Percy Lawrie (12T)**	**19.11.1911**	**to**	**28.12.1911**
7	Ted Flewitt (10T)	28.12.1929	to	1.2.1930
7	Percy Lawrie			

Tries in six successive games have been recorded by John Charles, Frank Jackson, Percy Lawrie (twice), John Liley, Jack Miles, Alexander Obolensky and David Senior.

MOST GAMES WITHOUT A TRY

241	**Bobby Barr**	**(3.11.1928 to 15.4.1939)**	*His complete career*
251	Claude Sambrook	(12.9.1921 to 3.3.1928)	*His complete career*
150	Mick Walker	(20.9.1958 to 3.12.1966)	*His last 150 games*
149	Sid Penny	(23.11.1901 to 17.3.1906)	
148	John Garner	(6.4.1895 to 5.11.1900)	*His first 148 games*

THE KICKERS
100 CAREER CONVERSIONS

	Gm	Con	CPG
Dusty Hare	**394**	**779**	**1.98**
Harold Day	212	281	1.33
John Liley	131	265	2.02
Doug Prentice	239	133	0.56
Colin Martin	272	126	0.46
J.W.Bream	101	125	1.24
Arthur Jones	224	113	0.50
Mike Gavins	121	107	0.88
Les Cusworth	365	100	0.27

MOST CONVERSIONS IN A SEASON:

89	**John Liley**	**1989/90**
79	Dusty Hare	1985/6

MOST CONVERSIONS IN A GAME:

13	**Dusty Hare**	**Birmingham(H)**	**17.9.1986**
11	Dusty Hare	Birmingham(A)	16.9.1981
11	Gerry Ainscough	Liverpool St Helens(H)	11.4.1992
10	John Greenwood	Richmond(H)	21.2.1920
10	Les Cusworth	Bedford(A)	3.9.1983

50 CAREER PENALTY GOALS

	Gm	PG	PPG
Dusty Hare	**394**	**820**	**2.08**
John Liley	131	243	1.85
Mike Gavins	121	119	0.98
Bob Barker	320	107	0.33
Keith Chilton	144	95	0.66
Colin Martin	272	88	0.32
Harold Day	212	81	0.38
Dave Whibley	45	75	1.67
John Ingleby	45	70	1.55
Peter Wheeler	349	69	0.20
Les Cusworth	365	65	0.18
Jez Harris	161	58	0.36
George Cullen	180	57	0.32

MOST PENALTY GOALS IN A SEASON:

89	**Dusty Hare**	**1988/9**

Dusty Hare has the top seven seasonal totals in this category

MOST PENALTY GOALS IN A GAME:

7	**Les Cusworth**	**London Welsh(H)**	**15.9.1979**

10 CAREER DROP GOALS

	Gm	DG	GPD
Les Cusworth	**365**	**96**	**3.80**
Dusty Hare	394	47	8.38
Jez Harris	161	38	4.23
Arthur Jones	224	37	6.05
Mel Channer	127	26	4.88
Charlie Slow	98	24	4.08
Jacky Braithwaite	359	15	23.93
John Parsons	113	13	8.69
Robin Money	258	12	21.50
Mick Poulson	43	11	3.91
Harry Greenlees	153	10	15.30

The most recent 'extra time' game.

MOST DROP GOALS IN A SEASON:

13	**Les Cusworth**	**1979/80**

MOST DROP GOALS IN A GAME:

4	**Les Cusworth**	**Liverpool St Helens(A)**	**28.1.1989**
3	Mel Channer	Bath(H)	13.9.1947
3	Les Cusworth	Bristol(A)	9.4.1988
3	Jez Harris	Wasps(H)	23.11.1991

SCORING IN EVERY WAY IN A GAME:

Date	Opponents	Name
23.3.1901	Nuneaton(H)	A.O.Jones
15.4.1950	Nuneaton(H)	George Cullen
1.11.1964	Old Belvedere(A)	Keith Chilton
15.9.1969	Irish Wolfhounds(H)	Arthur Chapman
13.11.1976	Cambridge University(H)	Dusty Hare
15.11.1977	Nottingham(H)	Dusty Hare
9.2.1980	Newport(A)	Les Cusworth
1.3.1980	Harlequins(H)	Les Cusworth
5.12.1981	Waterloo(H)	Dusty Hare
12.1.1985	Gloucester(H)	Dusty Hare
2.3.1985	Harlequins(H)	Dusty Hare
12.12.1987	Blackheath(A)	Jez Harris

PENALTY TRIES

Thirty penalty tries have been awarded to the Tigers. The following eight have been awarded to an individual, as he was the person who was impeded in "The act of scoring" as the law states. These eight have been included as tries in individual career records.

6.9.1919	Bath(H)	E E Haselmere
4.12.1954	Waterloo(H)	G H Cullen
27.9.1958	Harlequins(A)	H G Jessop
4.4.1970	Birkenhead Park(A)	M J Yandle
15.4.1972	Nottingham(H)	P J Wheeler
28.10.1972	Swansea(A)	M J Duggan
1.10.1983	Coventry(H)	N G Youngs
6.11.1990	Cambridge University(A)	P W Dodge

A GAME OF TWO HALVES

The Tigers have only once totalled over 50 points in the first-half of a game, 58 on 11.4.1992 against Liverpool St Helens in the club's record score. In the second half of a game they have achieved this on three occasions. In consecutive games against Birmingham and London Welsh at Welford Road on 17th and 20th September 1986, they amassed 64 and exactly 50 respectively. The third time was again exactly 50 points on 7.4.1990 against London Scottish, taking the score from 16-0 at half time to 66-12.

The most points conceded by half time was 28 inflicted by Bath on 6.1.1973 on the way to the record defeat of 42-0, whilst the most points conceded in a second half was 39 on 14.4.1984 against Bristol.

The biggest turnaround was being 4-15 down at half time resulting in a win of 37-15 on 12.11.1977 against Cambridge University. The worst reversal was a half time lead of 11-5 turning into a 11-36 loss on 8.11.1969 again versus Cambridge University.

CURTAILED GAMES

5.11.1881 v Kettering(A), Leicester left the field 5 minutes early because of a dispute over a try; Result a 0-0 draw.

9.2.1884 v Kettering(H), both teams left the field due to numerous disputes; Result Won 1G-0

2.4.1887 v Nottingham(A), Leicester left the field because of a dispute over a try; Result Lost 1T-1G & 3T

31.10.1896 v Old Edwardians(A), abandoned after 66 minutes due to bad light; Result Won 8-3

5.4.1947 v Bristol(A), abandoned after 64 minutes due to mud and rain; Result Lost 0-6

18.2.1977 v CASG Paris(H), abandoned after 69 minutes due to rain; Result Won 28-4

18.9.1985 v Birmingham(A), abandoned after 70 minutes due to bad light; Result Won 33-6

In addition the following games were started agreeing to play only 25 minutes each way due to conditions:

26.12.1891 v Leicester Swifts(H), late arrival; Result Won 4-0

18.11.1893 v Rugby(H), snow; Result Won 3-0

22.12.1934 v London Welsh(H), fog; Result Won 8-0

15.3.1947 v Cardiff(A), snow; Result Lost 5-17

AFTER EXTRA TIME

Four Tigers games have required extra time to be played to decide a winner, in each instances 10 minutes each way was played:

21.3.1891 v Old Edwardians(H), 4-4 at full time in the Semi-Final of the Midland Counties Cup; Result Won 7-4

20.3.1897 v Coventry(A), 3-3 at full-time in the 2nd Round of the Midland Counties Cup; Result Won 6-3

30.3.1901 v Moseley at Rugby, 3-3 at full-time in the final of the Midland Counties Cup; Result Won 8-3

4.4.1981 v London Scottish(A), 12-12 at full-time in the Semi-Final of the John Player Cup; Result Won 18-12

MIDLAND COUNTIES CUP RECORD

Season	Furthest Reached	Opponents	Result
1881-82	1st Round	Edgbaston Crusaders(A)	Lost 0-5
1882-83	2nd Round	Moseley(A)	Lost 0-7
1883-84	2nd Round	Rushden(A)	Drew 0-0
1884-85	1st Round	Moseley(A)	Lost 0-8
1885-86	2nd Round	Coventry(A)	Lost 0-6
1886-87	Semi Final	Rugby(A)	Lost 0-3
1887-88	Semi Final	Burton(H)	Drew 0-0
1888-89	Final	Moseley (at Coventry)	Lost 0-6
1889-90	1st Round	Stratford-upon-Avon(A)	Lost 0-13
1890-91	Final	Coventry (at Rugby)	Lost 0-8
1891-92	3rd Round	Old Edwardians(A)	Lost 0-21
1892-93	2nd Round	Coventry(H)	Lost 0-12
1893-94	Final	Coventry (at Rugby)	Lost 0-11
1894-95	Semi Final	Moseley(A)	Lost 0-11
1895-96	3rd Round	Moseley(A)	Lost 0-3
1896-97	Semi Final	Old Edwardians(H)	Lost 0-3
1897-98	Final	Moseley (at Coventry)	Won 5-3
1898-99	Final	Nuneaton (at Coventry)	Won 20-3
1899-00	Final	Moseley (at Coventry)	Won 13-4
1900-01	Final	Moseley (at Rugby)	Won 8-3
1901-02	Final	Moseley (at Coventry)	Won 5-0
1902-03	Final	Rugby (at Coventry)	Won 18-0
1903-04	Final	Moseley (at Burton)	Won 13-3
1904-05	Final	Nottingham (at Coventry)	Won 31-0
1905-06 to 1907-08	Did Not Compete		
1908-09	Final	Coventry (at Nottingham)	Won 8-3
1909-10	Final	Coventry (at Nuneaton)	Won 8-6
1910-11	4th Round	Coventry(A)	Lost 6-21
1911-12	Final	Coventry (at Rugby)	Won 16-0
1912-13	Final	Belgrave Premier Works(H)	Won 39-8
1913-14	Semi Final	Coventry(H)	Lost 0-8

RFU KNOCKOUT CUP

1971-72	1st Round	Nottingham(A)	Lost 3-10
1972-73	Quarter Final	Sale(A)	Lost 0-7
1973-74	1st Round	Northampton(A)	Lost 6-22
1974-75	Did Not Compete		

JOHN PLAYER CUP

1975-76	1st Round	Liverpool(A)	Lost 7-10
1976-77	2nd Round	Moseley(A)	Lost 9-23
1977-78	Final	Gloucester(Twickenham)	Lost 3-6
1978-79	Final	Moseley(Twickenham)	Won 15-12
1979-80	Final	London Irish(Twickenham)	Won 21-9
1980-81	Final	Gosforth(Twickenham)	Won 22-15
1981-82	Semi Final	Moseley(A)	Lost 4-12
1982-83	Final	Bristol(Twickenham)	Lost 22-28
1983-84	3rd Round	Coventry(A)	Lost 9-13
1984-85	Quarter Final	Coventry(A)	Draw 10-10
1985-86	Semi Final	Bath(H)	Lost 6-10
1986-87	Semi Final	Wasps(A)	Lost 6-13
1987-88	4th Round	Bath(H)	Lost 6-13

PILKINGTON CUP

1988-89	Final	Bath(Twickenham)	Lost 6-10
1989-90	Quarter Final	Northampton(A)	Lost 7-23
1990-91	4th Round	Wasps(H)	Lost 13-15
1991-92	Semi Final	Harlequins(A)	Lost 9-15
1992-93	Final	Harlequins(Twickenham)	Won 23-16

Tigers' Records

SEASONAL RECORDS

CLUB RECORDS (All records relate to a season of 30 games or more)

	MOST			LEAST		
	All games	Home games	Away games	All games	Home games	Away games
Games Played:	46 1923/4	29 1892/3	23 1973/4			
	46 1966/7	29 1893/4	23 1975/6			
	46 1972/3	29 1968/9				
Wins:	33 1966/7	25 1966/7	16 1979/80	11 1888/9	9 1952/3	1 1888/9
	33 1979/80					
	33 1980/1					
	33 1982/3					
Defeats:	23 1936/7	11 1892/3	16 1970/1	6 1987/8	1 7 times	3 1893/4
	23 1949/50	11 1949/50				3 1987/8
Draws:	7 1888/9	5 1931/2	4 4 times			
Points scored:	1,109 1989/90	738 1987/8	458 1992/3	94 1888/9	82 1888/9	12 1888/9
Points conceded:	733 1975/6	331 1974/5	427 1975/6	95 1894/5	25 1896/7	37 1894/5
Points Difference:	655 1987/8	499 1987/8	221 1990/1	-105 1949/50	-41 1949/50	-135 1975/6
		499 1989/90				
Tries scored:	192 1919/20	135 1919/20	69 1912/3	47 1949/50	25 1949/50	7 1888/9
Tries conceded:	106 1923/4	58 1968/9	68 1923/4	20 1894/5	7 1896/7	6 1894/5
					7 1897/8	
Conversions scored:	101 1989/90	78 1987/8	41 1985/6	13 1888/9	9 1945/6	Nil 1892/3
					9 1952/3	
Conversions conceded:	49 1969/70	30 1968/9	32 1969/70	6 1895/6	1 1895/6	2 1894/5
			32 1972/3			
Penalty Goals scored:	98 1988/9	64 1988/9	41 1979/80			
Penalty Goals conceded:	74 1982/3	40 1973/4	40 1975/6			
Drop Goals scored:	23 1979/80	12 1898/9	13 1979/80			
Drop Goals conceded:	16 1980/1	9 1955/6	10 1980/1			
Goals from a Mark scored:	3 1908/9					
Goals from a Mark conceded:	2 1894/5					

SEQUENCES
ALL GAMES-
Most Consecutive Wins:

17	27.3.1967	to	4.10.1967
16	3.9.1983	to	15.11.1983
15	17.4.1897	to	13.11.1897
15	27.2.1988	to	1.10.1988

Most Consecutive Defeats:

9	27.9.1947	to	15.11.1947
8	20.1.1890	to	1.3.1890
8	27.9.1975	to	8.11.1975

Most Consecutive Draws:

3	22.1.1887	to	12.2.1887

Most Consecutive Games Unbeaten:

18	27.3.1967	to	7.10.1967

Most Consecutive Games Without a Win:

13	6.10.1888	to	22.12.1888
11	27.9.1947	to	6.12.1947

HOME GAMES ONLY-
Most Consecutive Wins:

21	1.2.1902	to	10.1.1903
20	7.1.1989	to	30.12.1989
16	30.9.1978	to	4.9.1979
16	9.10.1982	to	2.3.1983

Most Consecutive Defeats:

6	28.1.1937	to	6.3.1937
5	4.10.1947	to	29.11.1947
5	30.11.1957	to	11.1.1958
5	13.2.1965	to	13.3.1965

Most Consecutive Draws:

2	on nine occasions

Most Consecutive Games Unbeaten:

34	1.1.1896	to	6.3.1897
32	29.11.1924	to	20.2.1926

Most Consecutive Games Without a Win:

7	24.12.1892	to	11.2.1893

AWAY GAMES ONLY-
Most Consecutive Wins:

9	3.9.1983	to	26.11.1983
9	7.9.1985	to	12.11.1985
8	9.12.1950	to	24.3.1951
8	1.9.1979	to	13.11.1979

Most Consecutive Defeats:

13	27.10.1926	to	16.4.1927
13	3.10.1970	to	10.4.1971
10	23.3.1889	to	1.3.1890
10	30.3.1907	to	14.12.1907

Most Consecutive Draws:

3	20.11.1886	to	12.2.1887

Most Consecutive Games Unbeaten:

9	3.9.1983	to	26.11.1983
9	7.9.1985	to	12.11.1985

Most Consecutive Games Without a Win:

15	14.1.1928	to	8.12.1928
14	23.3.1889	to	11.10.1890

TEAM MATCH SCORING
CLUB RECORDS:
Most Points Scored:

100-0	Liverpool St Helens(H)	11.4.1992
95-6	Birmingham(H)	17.9.1986
78-8	Birmingham(A)	16.9.1981
76-0	Exeter(H)	27.2.1993

(Pilkington Cup Quarter Final)

Most Points Conceded:

5-50	Cardiff(A)	15.11.1947
21-47	Cardiff(A)	3.11.1984
10-46	London Welsh(A)	21.2.1981

Worst Defeats:

5-50	Cardiff(A)	15.11.1947
0-42	Bath(A)	6.1.1973
0-39	London Scottish(A)	7.12.1907
6-45	Coventry(A)	7.10.1972
4-43	Barbarians(H)	27.12.1974

Most Tries Scored:

19	Liverpool St Helens(H)	100-0	11.4.1992
19	Bedford XV(H)	71-0	15.2.1919
17	Burfield Rangers(H)	71-0	8.9.1894
17	Newbold-on-Avon(H)	65-0	23.3.1912

Most Tries Against:

11	Blackheath(A)	0-37	13.2.1892
11	Neath(A)	6-37	26.11.1923
11	Cardiff(A)	5-50	15.11.1947
10	Cambridge University(A)	11-36	8.11.1969

The Barbarians have three times scored nine tries at Welford Road in 1953, 1969 and 1974.

Most Conversions Scored:

13	Birmingham(H)	95-6	17.9.1986
12	Liverpool St Helens(H)	100-0	11.4.1992
11	Birmingham(A)	78-8	16.9.1981

All nine Tigers tries at Bedford on 19.1.1990 were successfully converted.

Most Conversions Against:

7	Cardiff(A)	5-50	15.11.1947

Most Penalty Goals:

7	London Welsh(H)	27-25	15.9.1979

Most Penalty Goals Against:

7	Gloucester(H)	6-29	3.11.1973

Most Drop Goals:

4	Liverpool St Helens(A)	37-6	28.1.198

(John Player Cup)

Most Drop Goals Against:

3	Bath(A)	13-17	30.3.1937
3	Bedford(H)	11-20	3.9.1955
3	Romania(H)	15-12	4.9.1990

Missed Conversions:

12	Bedford XV(H)	71-0	15.2.1919

On 27.12.1904 at Home to Rugby only one try in eleven was converted.

Missed Conversions Against:

9	Neath(A)	6-37	26.11.1923

All eight conversions attempted at Pontypool on 2.2.1914 were missed.

COMBINED RECORDS (BOTH SIDES)

Points:	101	Leicester 95, Birmingham 6	17.9.1986
Tries:	19	Leicester 19, Liverpool St H 0	11.4.1992
	19	Leicester 19, Bedford XV 0	15.2.1919
Conversions:	14	Leicester 13, Birmingham 1	17.9.1986
Pen Goals:	10	Leicester 7, London Welsh 3	15.9.1979
Drop Goals:	5	Leicester 3, Bath 2	13.9.1947
	5	Leicester 3, Plymouth Alb. 2	16.9.1950

COURAGE LEAGUE RECORDS

RESULTS GRID	1987/8 1st	1988/9 6th	1989/90 5th	1990/1 4th	1991/2 6th	1992/3 3rd	P	W	D	L	F	A
Bath	24-13H	15-12H	15-26A	3-9 H	6-37 A	3-13 H	6	2	-	4	66	110
Bedford			60-3 H				1	1	-	-	60	3
Bristol	15-10H	13-12H	13-11A	6-10 A	25-9 H	10-15A	6	4	-	2	82	67
Coventry	32-16H						1	1	-	-	32	16
Gloucester		0-28 A	16-26H	18-6 H	3-21 A	22-21H	5	2	-	3	59	102
Harlequins	12-9 A	21-31H	12-15A	12-15H	13-20A	23-0 H	6	2	-	4	93	90
Liverpool St.H.		23-12A		28-7 A			2	2	-	-	51	19
London Irish					36-13H	30-14A	2	2	-	-	66	27
London Scottish						18-11A	1	1	-	-	18	11
Moseley	21-3 A	13-22A	38-20H	43-19A			4	3	-	1	115	64
Northampton				28-18A	19-22H	13-12A	3	2	-	1	60	52
Nottingham	22-13A	12-12A	15-6 H	25-9 H	27-14A		5	4	1	-	101	54
Orrell	6-30 A	15-27H	10-33A	15-12H	9-21 A	9-0 H	6	2	-	4	64	123
Rosslyn Park		28-15H	23-9 A	15-17A	51-16H		4	3	-	1	117	57
Rugby					22-22H	28-5 A	2	1	1	-	50	27
Sale	42-15H						1	1	-	-	42	15
Saracens			34-6 H	29-6 H	20-9 A	30-3 H	4	4	-	-	113	24
Wasps	12-9 H	15-6 H	12-29A	22-12A	31-12H	13-14A	6	4	-	2	105	82
Waterloo	39-15H	34-22A					2	2	-	-	73	37
West Hartlepool						21-8 H	1	1	-	-	21	8

PLAYERS CHART	1987/8	1988/9	1989/90	1990/1	1991/2	1992/3	G	T	C	PG	DG	PTS
Gerry Ainscough					6 8		6	2	-	-	-	8
Neil Back				9 -	10 4	8 5	27	2	-	-	-	9
Ian Bates	10 4	7 -	11 8	11 8	11 4	11 -	61	6	-	-	-	24
Laurence Boyle					7 4	4 -	11	1	-	-	-	4
Paul Burnell	1 -						1	-	-	-	-	-
Steve Burnhill	5 4						5	1	-	-	-	4
Tim Buttimore	7 -		4 -	2 -			13	-	-	-	-	-
Willy Carr		1 -					1	-	-	-	-	-
Mark Charles	2 16						2	4	-	-	-	16
Richard Cockerill						12 5	12	1	-	-	-	5
Les Cusworth	9 19	10 10	10 3				29	2	-	-	8	32
Colin Dexter	2 4	1 -					3	1	-	-	-	4
Paul Dodge	5 -	10 -	6 -	9 8			30	2	-	-	-	8
Bill Drake-Lee					1 -		1	-	-	-	-	-
Barry Evans	8 20	8 12	5 12	5 -	1 -		27	11	-	-	-	44
M Foulkes-Arnold	4 -	10 -	2 -	1 -			17	-	-	-	-	-
Darren Garforth					11 4	12 -	23	1	-	-	-	4
Claude Gerald		3 -	2 12				5	0	-	-	-	12
Alex Gissing		1 -	7 -	8 4	2 -		18	1	-	-	-	4
Mark Grant		4 4	3 -		1 -	1 -	9	1	-	-	-	4
Paul Grant						2 -	2	-	-	-	-	-
Darren Grewcock					2 4	1 5	3	2	-	-	-	9
Andy Grimsdell					1 -		1	-	-	-	-	-

PLAYERS CHART	1987/8	1988/9	1989/90	1990/1	1991/2	1992/3	G	T	C	PG	DG	PTS
Steve Hackney					9 16	7 5	16	5	-	-	-	21
Jamie Hamilton				1 -	1 -		2	-	-	-	-	-
Dusty Hare	10 126	8 97					18	2	22	56	1	223
Jez Harris	2 4	3 9	1 3	6 17	6 16	12 16	30	2	6	4	11	65
Dave Hopper		1 -	1 -				2	-	-	-	-	-
Nick Jackson		1 -					1	-	-	-	-	-
Derek Jelly						1 -	1	-	-	-	-	-
Martin Johnson		1 -			10 -	8 -	19	-	-	-	-	-
Aadel Kardooni		7 8	6 12	10 -	10 4	11 10	44	8	-	-	-	34
Steve Kenney	9 4	1 -	5 -				15	1	-	-	-	4
Andy Key		1 -		3 4	6 -		10	1	-	-	-	4
Wayne Kilford						2 3	2	-	-	1	-	3
Dave Kitching		2 -	1 -				3	-	-	-	-	-
John Liley		2 9	11 126	11 110	11 125	11 106	46	14	68	94	-	476
Kevin McDonald	1 -	1 4	1 -				3	1	-	-	-	4
Phil Mann	6 -						6	-	-	-	-	-
Adey Marriott	3 -	3 -	2 -	1 -	2 -		11	-	-	-	-	-
John Murphy		1 -			1 -		2	-	-	-	-	-
Matt Poole		1 -	4 -	3 -	11 -	10 5	29	1	-	-	-	5
Stuart Potter						11 10	11	2	-	-	-	10
Simon Povoas	4 -	1 -	11 12		8 4	8 5	32	5	-	-	-	21
Stuart Redfern	10 -	9 4	10 4	12 -	12 -		53	2	-	-	-	8
Mark Reid		7 4					7	1	-	-	-	4
Dean Richards	5 8	6 12	1 -	12 12	5 4	10 -	39	9	-	-	-	36
Lee Richardson		1 -					1	-	-	-	-	-
Nigel Richardson						4 15	4	3	-	-	-	15
Wayne Richardson	9 4	9 -	10 -	8 -	1 -		37	1	-	-	-	4
Harry Roberts	8 -		3 -				11	-	-	-	-	-
Graham Rowntree				4 -		11 -	15	-	-	-	-	-
Peter Sandford		3 8		2 8			5	4	-	-	-	16
Brian Smith				7 13			7	1	-	-	3	13
Ian Smith	2 -	7 -	9 4				18	1	-	-	-	4
Tom Smith	9 -	3 -	8 -	12 4	1 -		33	1	-	-	-	4
Rob Tebbutt	6 -		3 -	3 -			12	-	-	-	-	-
Troy Thacker		2 -	6 4				8	1	-	-	-	4
Peter Thornley	5 4	4 4					9	2	-	-	-	8
Chris Tressler	2 -	9 -	2 -	12 -	12 -		37	-	-	-	-	-
Rory Underwood	5 4	7 4	8 16	12 32	8 36	10 10	50	25	-	-	-	102
Tony Underwood		3 4	4 12	3 8	6 12	6 15	22	12	-	-	-	51
Alan Warwood		3 4	1 -				4	1	-	-	-	4
John Wells	8 -	7 -	9 8	12 8	10 8	10 -	56	6	-	-	-	24
Bob White		1 -					1	-	-	-	-	-
Steve Wills				2 4	2 9		4	2	1	1	-	13
David Wright				1 4			1	1	-	-	-	4
Nick Youngs	1 -	3 -					4					
Penalty Tries	- 4		- 4	'		- 5		3			-	13

Tigers' Records

INTERNATIONALS

Niall Malone became the 159th international to play for the Tigers, including four who played for various British teams but not for their individual countries. However, only 64 of these were members of the Leicester club whilst they won at least one cap, including three who were British internationals. The following table lists all of the internationals who have made at least one appearance for the Tigers. The affiliation column reflects which club(s) the player in question was at when he was awarded his international caps. If Leicester figure as one of those clubs then the caps won whilst at the individual clubs appear in brackets after the club name.

Robin Cowling - England

Name	Affiliation	Caps		Seasons
C D Aarvold	Cambridge University/			
	Headingley/Blackheath	16	E	1928-33
M Abraham	Bective Rangers	5	I	1912-14
G J Adey	Leicester	2	E	1976
R J Arneil	Edinburgh Academicals (8)	22	S	1968-69
	Leicester (10)		S	1970-71
	Northampton (4)		S	1972
W R Arnold	Swansea	1	W	1903
A Ashworth	Oldham	1	E	1892
A P Atkins	Bective Rangers	1	I	1924
J R Auty	Headingley	1	E	1935
A Baker	Neath	5	W	1921-23
R J Barr	Leicester	3	E	1932
C E St J Beamish	North of Ireland/Harlequins(2)	12	I	1933
	Leicester (6)		I	1934-35
	North of Ireland (4)		I	1936-38
G R Beamish	Coleraine (3)	25	I	1925
	Leicester (11)		I	1928-30
	London Irish (5)		I	1931
	Leicester		I	1932-33

Name	Affiliation	Caps		Seasons
J A Beattie	Hawick	23	S	1929-36
B B Bennetts	Penzance	2	E	1909
J T W Berry	Leicester	3	E	1939
G E Beynon	Swansea	2	W	1925
A W Black	Edinburgh University	6	S	1947-50
A F Blakiston	Northampton/			
	Blackheath/Liverpool	17	E	1920-25
E E Booth	Otago	3	N	1906-07
I J Botting	Oxford University	2	E	1950
J Braithwaite	Leicester	1	E	1905
A Brice	Aberavon/Cardiff	18	W	1899-04
R Bruce-Lockhart	Cambridge Univ./London Scottish	3	S	1937-39
J C R Buchanan	Stewart's Melville F P/Exeter	16	S	1921-25
R A Buckingham	Leicester	1	E	1927
A G Bull	Northampton	1	E	1914
A P Burnell	London Scottish	25	S	1989-93
D A Campbell	Cambridge University	2	E	1937
R H B Cattell	Blackheath	7	E	1895-00
R J Collopy	Bective Rangers	13	I	1923-25
W P Collopy	Bective Rangers	19	I	1914-24
P B Coote	Leicester	1	I	1933
I D F Coutts	Old Alleynians	2	S	1951-52
R J Cowling	Leicester	8	E	1977-79
M P Crowe	Lansdowne	13	I	1929-34
P M Crowe	Blackrock College	2	I	1935-38
L Cusworth	Leicester	12	E	1979-88
J Davey	Redruth	2	E	1908-09
W J N Davis	Bessbrook/Edinburgh University	9	I	1890-95
H L V Day	Leicester	4	E	1920-26
D D Dobson	Oxford University/Newton Abbot	6	E	1902-03
P W Dodge	Leicester	32	E	1978-85
A O Dowson	Moseley	1	E	1899
N J Drake-Lee	Leicester	8	E	1963-65

Paul Dodge - England

Martin Johnson - England.

Name	Affiliation	Caps		Seasons
E J Jackett	Leicester	13	E	1905-09
J L Jenkins	Aberavon	2	W	1923
L H Jenkins	Monmouth Tech/Newport	5	W	1954-56
M O Johnson	Leicester	1	E	1993
C W Jones	Bridgend	3	W	1920
K J Jones	Newport	44	W	1947-57
W Jones	Cardiff	2	W	1898
G H Keeton	Richmond	3	E	1904
T A Kemp	Cambridge University/			
	St Mary's Hospital/Richmond	5	E	1937-48
D A Kendrew	Woodford (2)	10	E	1930
	Leicester (8)		E	1933-36
A L Kewney	Rockcliff (4)	16	E	1906
	Leicester (12)		E	1909-13
J R Lawrie	Melrose (8)	11	S	1922-23
	Leicester (3)		S	1924
P W Lawrie	Leicester	2	E	1910-11
J M C Lewis	Cardiff	11	W	1912-23
R Leyland	Waterloo	3	E	1935
V J Lyttle	Belfast College/Bradford	3	I	1938-39
K R MacDonald	Stewart's Melville F P	6	S	1956-57
N G Malone	Oxford Univ/London Irish	2	I	1993
E J Massey	Leicester	3	E	1925
G W C Meikle	Waterloo	3	E	1934
S S C Meikle	Waterloo	1	E	1929
E J S Michie	Aberdeen Univ/Aberdeen GSFP/			
	London Scottish	15	S	1954-57
J H Miles	Leicester	1	E	1903
J G Millican	Edinburgh University	3	S	1973

Name	Affiliation	Caps		Seasons
P E Dunkley	Harlequins	6	E	1931-36
J Duthie	West Hartlepool	1	E	1903
J C M Dyke	Penarth	1	W	1906
J H Eddison	Headingley	4	E	1912
B J Evans	Leicester	2	E	1988
J L Farrell	Bective Rangers	29	I	1926-32
K J Fielding	Loughborough Colleges/Moseley	10	E	1969-72
J E Forrest	Glasgow Academicals	3	S	1932-35
D G Francis	Llanelli	2	W	1919-24
A E Freear	Lansdowne	3	I	1901
K C Fyfe	Cambridge University/			
	Sale/London Scottish	10	S	1933-39
B C Gadney	Leicester (13)	14	E	1932-37
	Headingley (1)		E	1938
M N Gavins	Leicester	1	E	1961
R A Gerrard	Bath	14	E	1932-36
J L Giles	Coventry	6	E	1935-38
H D Greenlees	Leicester	6	S	1927-30
J E Greenwood	Cambridge University (9)	13	E	1912-14
	Leicester (4)		E	1920
W H Hare	Nottingham (1)	25	E	1974
	Leicester (24)		E	1978-84
T M Hart	Glasgow University	2	S	1930
W T Havard	Llanelli	1	W	1919
D St G Hazell	Leicester	4	E	1955
M M Henderson	Dunfermline	3	S	1937
A E Hind	Leicester	2	E	1905-06
J M Hodgson	Northern	7	E	1932-36
T B Hogarth	Hartlepool Rovers	1	E	1906
G Holford	Gloucester	2	E	1920
J P Horrocks-Taylor	Cambridge University (2)	9	E	1958
	Leicester (5)		E	1961-63
	Middlesbrough (2)		E	1964
T F Huskisson	Old Merchant Taylors	8	E	1937-39

Steve Redfern - England

Name	Affiliation	Caps		Seasons
W K T Moore	Leicester	7	E	1947-50
E Morgan	Swansea	4	W	1914
M C Morrison	Royal High School F P	23	S	1896-04
K D Mullen	Old Belvedere	25	I	1947-52
E Myers	Bradford	18	E	1920-25
J B Nelson	Glasgow Academicals	25	S	1925-31
E S Nicholson	Oxford University (3)	5	E	1935
	Leicester (2)		E	1936
D J Norman	Leicester	2	E	1932
A L Novis	Army/Blackheath	7	E	1929-33
A Obolensky	Oxford University	4	E	1936
R V M Odbert	Royal Air Force	1	I	1928
A G B Old	Middlesbrough (5)	16	E	1972
	Leicester (6)		E	1973-74
	Middlesbrough (4)		E	1975-76
	Sheffield (1)		E	1978
W L Oldham	Coventry	2	E	1908-09
A J F K O'Reilly	Old Belvedere (20)	29	I	1955-59
	Leicester (2)		I	1959-60
	Old Belvedere (6)		I	1961-63
	London Irish (1)		I	1970
H G Owen-Smith	Oxford Univ./St Mary's Hosp.	10	E	1934-37
S H Penny	Leicester	1	E	1909
D G Perry	Bedford	15	E	1963-66
F D Prentice	Leicester	3	E	1928
H L Price	Oxford University (2)	4	E	1922
	Leicester (2)		E	1923

Peter Wheeler - England.

Mike Wade - England

Name	Affiliation	Caps		Seasons
S P Redfern	Leicester	1	E	1984
D Rees	Swansea	5	W	1900-05
J S R Reeve	Harlequins	8	E	1929-31
D Richards	Leicester	34	E	1986-92
P Ringer	Ebbw Vale/Llanelli	8	W	1978-80
J D Robins	Birkenhead Park/Bradford	11	W	1950-53
D N Rocyn-Jones	St Mary's Hospital	1	W	1925
W M H Rose	Cambridge U/Harlequins	10	E	1981-87
R E Rowell	Leicester	2	E	1964-65
R F Russell	Leicester	1	E	1905
G A Sanderson	Royal High School F P	4	S	1907-08
K J F Scotland	Heriot's FP/Cambridge Univ/			
	London Scottish(18)	27	S	1957-61
	Leicester (4)		S	1962
	Heriot's/Aberdeenshre (5)		S	1963-65
C F Slow	Leicester	1	E	1934
A M Smallwood	Cambridge University (2)	14	E	1920
	Leicester (12)		E	1921-25
B A Smith	Queensland	6	A	1987
	Oxford University (5)	9	I	1989-90
	Leicester (4)		I	1991
R V Stirling	Leicester (13)	18	E	1951-53
	Wasps (5)		E	1954
G S Sturtridge	Victoria	9	A	1929-33

Nick Youngs - England.

BRITISH LIONS

Martin Johnson became the thirteenth member of the Leicester club to represent a British team in a Test Match abroad. Altogether 36 players who have made at least one appearance for the Tigers were British international players.

C D Aarvold	Blackheath	5	1930 NZ,A
R J Arneil	Edinburgh Academicals	4	1968 SA
G R Beamish	Leicester	5	1930 NZ,A
A W Black	Edinburgh University	2	1950 NZ
A F Blakiston	Blackheath	4	1924 SA
A P Burnell	London Scottish	1	1993 NZ
J Davey	Redruth	1	1908 NZ
D D Dobson	Oxford University	4	1904 A
P W Dodge	Leicester	2	1980 SA
J L Farrell	Bective Rangers	5	1930 NZ,A
J L Giles	Coventry	2	1938 SA
J M Hodgson	Northern	2	1930 NZ
J P Horrocks-Taylor	Leicester	1	1959 NZ
E J Jackett	Leicester	3	1908 NZ
F S Jackson	Leicester	1	1908 NZ*
M O Johnson	Leicester	2	1993 NZ
K J Jones	Newport	3	1950 NZ
E Morgan	Swansea	2	1908 NZ
M C Morrison	Royal High School FP	3	1903 SA
K D Mullen	Old Belvedere	3	1950 NZ,A
A L Novis	Blackheath	3	1930 NZ,A
W L Oldham	Coventry	1	1908 NZ
A J F K O'Reilly	Old Belvedere	10	1955 SA
			1959 A,NZ
F D Prentice	Leicester	2	1930 NZ,A
J S R Reeve	Harlequins	4	1930 NZ,A

Name	Affiliation	Caps		Seasons
J S Swan	St Andrew's University/			
	London Scottish/Coventry(16)	17	S	1953-57
	Leicester (1)		S	1958
F N Tarr	Oxford University (3)	4	E	1909
	Leicester (1)		E	1913
F Taylor	Leicester	2	E	1920
F M Taylor	Leicester	1	E	1914
A C Towell	Leicester (1)	2	E	1948
	Bedford (1)		E	1951
R Underwood	Leicester	56	E	1984-93
T Underwood	Leicester	4	E	1992-93
M R Wade	Cambridge University	3	E	1962
W W Wakefield	Harlequins/Cambridge Univ. (16)	31	E	1920-23
	Leicester (4)		E	1924
	Harlequins (11)		E	1925-27
E J Walton	Oxford Univ/Castleford	4	E	1901-02
G Ward	Leicester	6	E	1913-14
J A Waters	Selkirk	16	S	1933-37
W J Watts	Llanelli	1	W	1914
R H G Weighill	Harlequins	4	E	1947-48
A Wemyss	Gala/Edinburgh Wanderers	7	S	1914-22
P J Wheeler	Leicester	41	E	1975-84
H Whitley	Northern	1	E	1929
F L Williams	Cardiff	14	W	1929-33
G W Wood	Leicester	1	E	1914
C R Woodward	Leicester	21	E	1980-84
S T H Wright	Stewart's Melville F P	1	S	1949
W Yiend	Gloucester/Hartlepool Rovers	6	E	1889-93
N G Youngs	Leicester	6	E	1983-84

Clive Woodward - England and British Lions.

Dusty Hare - an unlucky British Lions tourist.

SUMMARY OF TIGERS INTERNATIONALS

	Players	Caps	Try	Con	PG	DG	Pts
England	51	403	68	28	86	6	592
Ireland	5	30	1	4	1	2	20
Scotland	5	24	-	2	3	-	13
British	13	41	1	4	-	-	13
Total	**64**	**498**	**70**	**38**	**90**	**8**	**638**

INTERNATIONAL CAPTAINS

ENGLAND-
J E Greenwood (4 in 1920), W W Wakefield (4 in 1924),
B C Gadney (8 between 1934-36), D A Kendrew (2 in 1935),
P J Wheeler (5 in 1983-84), P W Dodge (7 in 1985)
BRITISH-
F D Prentice (2 in 1930)

MOST PLAYERS IN A TEST MATCH

Seven
England v Ireland at Twickenham on 18.2.1984
(6 in starting line-up plus a replacement)

Six
England v New Zealand at Twickenham on 19.11.1983
England v France at Parc des Princes on 3.3.1984
England v Wales at Twickenham on 17.3.1984

Between 3.1.1976 and 18.1.1986 the Tigers supplied at least one international to every England team (54 matches). Also since 3.1.1976 only three England teams in the last 109 have contained NO Leicester representatives, 15.2.1986 against Scotland at Murrayfield (when Rory Underwood was selected but failed a fitness test), and both Tests on the Argentinian tour on 28.7.1990 and 4.8.1990 (when Leicester had contributed three members to the tour squad - John Liley, Matt Poole and Tony Underwood).

MOST PLAYERS IN A BRITISH ISLES TEAM

Three
v South Africa at Port Elizabeth on 28.6.1980
v New Zealand at Wellington on 26.6.1993
v New Zealand at Auckland on 3.7.1993

UNLUCKY TOURISTS

The following players went on Test Match playing tours abroad whilst playing members of the Leicester club, but did not gain an international cap on that tour.

ENGLAND TOURS:

Dave Whibley	1972 to South Africa
Paul Dodge	1984 to South Africa
Nick Youngs	1984 to South Africa
Tim Buttimore	1988 to Australia and Fiji as a replacement playing 2 games
John Liley	1990 to Argentina, playing 4 games
Matt Poole	1990 to Argentina, playing 3 games
Tony Underwood	1990 to Argentina, playing 3 games

BRITISH ISLES TOURS:

Douglas Kendrew	1930 to New Zealand & Australia
Rodger Arneil	1971 to Australia & New Zealand
Alan Old	1974 to South Africa, playing in 4 games
Dusty Hare	1983 to New Zealand, playing in 6 games
Clive Woodward	1983 to New Zealand, playing in 7 games
Tony Underwood	1993 to New Zealand, playing in 6 games

D Richards	Leicester	6	1989 A
			1993 NZ
J D Robins	Birkenhead Park	5	1950 NZ,A
K J F Scotland	Cambridge University	5	1959 A,NZ
T W Smith	Leicester	2	1908 NZ*
R Underwood	Leicester	6	1989 A
			1993 NZ
W Wallace	Percy Park	1	1924 SA*
J A Waters	Selkirk	1	1938 SA
P J Wheeler	Leicester	7	1977 NZ
			1980 SA
H Whitley	Northern	3	1924 SA
K B Wood	Leicester	2	1910 SA*
C R Woodward	Leicester	2	1980 SA

Note: * denotes a player who was never capped by his home country.

Leicester Tigers.

British airways
The world's favourite airline.

South Gulf Select XV
V
Leicester Tigers

Sunday 29th April, 1984
at
DUBAI EXILES GROUND
Kick off - 7.30 pm

Sponsored by

British airways

A Sunday Rugby programme from 1984.

SUNDAY RUGBY

The following Tigers games were played on a Sunday, but only seven of these games took place in England:

18.11.1956	Old Belvedere(A)	Lost 3-23
16.11.1958	Old Belvedere(A)	Lost 3-14
1.11.1964	Old Belvedere(A)	Lost 14-16
31.10.1965	Old Belvedere(A)	Lost 6-12
21.11.1971	Nottingham(A) *(RFU Cup)*	Lost 3-10
16.1.1972	Bedford(H)	Lost 10-19
21.1.1973	Bedford(A)	Lost 9-37
10.8.1980	Eastern Suburbs(A)	Won 24-3
17.1.1982	Torquay Athletic(A)	Won 44-4
29.4.1984	South Gulf Select XV(A)	Won 44-3
12.5.1985	St Claude(A)	Lost 10-13
9.3.1986	Broughton Park(A) *(J P Cup at Headingley)*	Won 46-6
2.8.1987	Western Australia(A)	Lost 19-26
9.8.1987	Manly(A)	Won 21-10
16.8.1987	Queensland(A)	Lost 13-37
30.10.1988	Llanelli(H)	Lost 15-29
13.8.1989	Vail(A)	Won 48-0
20.8.1989	U S A Eagles(A)	Lost 12-24
29.11.1992	London Scottish(A) *(Pilkington Cup)*	Won 20-11

PLAYER IDENTIFICATION

The numbering of players in international matches was first adopted on a regular basis in 1920/21, the Leicester forwards first regularly wore letters in the 1926/27 season. A report in *The Birmingham Post* on the 6th October 1926 of the match against Bath, stated that "Leicester's forwards were picked out easily as their jerseys were decorated with large bold letters - A to G." The reporter continued, "it struck me that the use of the numerals for

the men in the rear would have completed a capital scheme which one would thoroughly commend to other clubs, the lettering, in particular, being of great service to all those who wanted to appreciate who was who in the tight and loose."

The lettering was by 1931/32 eventually extended to cover the whole team however, the policy for other clubs changed, some which had originally worn letters now favoured numbers, and this became the standard means of identification.

Tradition at Leicester remains, and now only they and Bristol still wear letters, although both have slight variations. Bristol letter their players the opposite way around with the full-back wearing 'A' through to the open-side flanker who is 'O'. Leicester exchange numbers for letters throughout with one eccentric exception; the number-eight forward wears 'G', and the usual number seven wears 'H'!

HOME GROUNDS: BELGRAVE CRICKET & CYCLE GROUND

The ground, situated a mile north of the city on Belgrave Road, opened in 1880. It was a first class general sports arena, oval in shape, covering ten acres with a running and cycle track encircling it. There was a grandstand on the left hand side looking from Belgrave Road, and a refreshment room placed centrally on the main road frontage. As it was surrounded by a high brick wall admission charges could be made to all games (2d in 1880/81).

Leicester played there in three separate spells; in 1880/81 it was their first ground, but as it was so far from the centre of Leicester that the team could not readily be associated with the city, so the club decided to move after only half a season. They returned in 1882/83 for one season, but as gate receipts had fallen from £5 to £2 the club decided to move again. Their final spell was between 1888/89 and 1891/92, when a dispute over the lease soured relations between the Belgrave Road Ground Company and the club.

The ground was used by many local sporting clubs, among them Leicester Fosse in 1887/88, and in June 1881 Sixteen of Leicestershire took on an All England XI at cricket. However, the ground only had a short life, as in 1901 houses, shops and part of the British United Shoe Machinery factory were built on the site. Now the area is bordered by Roberts Road, Buller Road and Macdonald Road.

Leicester's record:
Played 84; Won 48; Drew 10; lost 26

VICTORIA PARK

Victoria Park was used as a racecourse until the track moved to Oadby in 1883, hence the park was often referred to by locals as the Racecourse ground. In 1866/67 an area in the centre of the racecourse was levelled making it suitable for sports, primarily cricket. A large ornamental Victorian pavilion was built about 1860, with a viewing balcony on the second floor, which served the players and privileged spectators. Situated on the edge of the present car park, slightly to the right of the entrance from Granville Road, it was partly destroyed by a German land-mine in 1940.

Leicester used the ground in two spells; the first from January 1881 ended after one and a half seasons because as the ground was not enclosed charges could not be made for admission. During their second spell at Victoria Park between 1883/84 and 1887/88 Leicester developed a large following which moved with them back to the Belgrave Road ground in 1888.

Leicester's record:
Played 57; Won 41; Drew 5; lost 11

The Victoria Park Racecourse Pavilion in 1870.

WELFORD ROAD

Looking to the future the club could see they needed a ground of their own, so in December 1891 they accepted the offer from Leicester Corporation for a ten year lease on an acre of land between Welford Road and Aylestone Road, just outside the City boundary. In March 1892 the lease was signed and work began immediately; £1,100 was spent preparing an entirely new playing area, and permission was given to transfer the stand erected on the Belgrave Cricket & Cycle Ground to the new site. The new Aylestone Road ground, as it was called for the first few weeks, was officially opened on 10 September 1892 with a game against the Leicestershire Rugby Union.

In 1893 the Pavilion was enlarged at a cost of £80 to £90 to provide additional accommodation for between 400 and 500 people. On the South side of the ground a stand 45 feet by 30 feet was erected to seat a further 600 members. A year later a scoreboard was purchased for the sum of £5 and installed at the Welford Road end of the ground.

Photographs are in existence which show the ground as it was at the turn of the century, but the earliest structure which still remains today is the Clubhouse. Opened in 1909, as indicated by the inscription above the old players' entrance on Aylestone Road, it cost £1,150 and contained dressing rooms, referees' room, committee room, and groundsmen's facilities, with a gymnasium on the first floor. (Prior to this teams used to change "over the road" at the Bedford Hotel in Aylestone Road.)

The next major project undertaken by the then Honorary Secretary, Tom Crumbie, was the rebuilding of the Members' Stand (which had been moved in 1899 when the ground capacity was 19,800, with over 3,000 seated). It was first used in 1913, but was not officially opened until after the end of the First World War in December 1918, having cost approximately £13,000.

Development continued with another new stand (subsequently renamed the Crumbie stand after his death in 1928) which was completed at a cost of £27,000. It was opened on 2nd October 1920 by the then President of the Rugby Union, Ernest Prescott.

Having spent the equivalent of £2 million in modern values in a twenty-five year period, financial problems meant that for a further 30 years, no further development could be undertaken by the club. During this difficult period Eric Thorneloe was at the helm, and after his death in August 1959 two clocks were erected (one on the Crumbie stand, and one on the Members' stand) in his memory. These were unveiled by Tom Voyce (ex-Gloucester and England, then president of the RFU) at the game against Northampton in October 1960.

In the summer of 1964 floodlights were erected and were first used in the game against a Midlands XV on 8th October. In the close season of 1970 the restructuring of the Clubhouse took place, including new function facilities upstairs, with an extra changing room and office downstairs. The banking at the Aylestone Road end of the ground was also levelled to give extra car parking space.

In 1975 the decision was taken to further extend the Clubhouse facilities to provide additional dressing rooms as well as a kitchen, and more modern members' facilities. The cost of £19,000 was raised by public appeal over a three year period. In 1978 the Crumbie stand was re-roofed, and the Clubhouse work was completed in time for it to be re-opened by Herbert Waddell, President of the Barbarians, before their fixture in December that year. Prior to this on 6th September 1977 a new scoreboard was unveiled, a gift of the Loughborough building materials firm run by the Adey family.

With the success of the team in the mid to late seventies especially in the John Player Cup coupled with a steady increase in membership, finance was generated to commence the repair to the fabric of the ground. Over a ten year period £82,000 was spent on a major repair programme which included roofing the two stands as well as re-cladding the whole of the rear elevation of the stands.

Major works during the same period cost a total of £200,000, this included new seats, floodlights, pitch covers, Clubhouse extension and turnstiles.

In 1985 work commenced on improved changing and medical facilities under the Crumbie Stand (previously let out for industrial purposes). This comprised of dressing rooms with associated baths and showers for up to four teams, a referees' room, medical room, weights room and groundsmen's facilities. At a cost of £120,000 they were first used on 14 September. This move allowed additional bar facilities to be incorporated in the Clubhouse.

After the Bradford Football ground tragedy and the subsequent Popplewell enquiry, it became clear that in view of its total capacity of 16,800 (with seating for 9,600) the ground would eventually be designated under the Safety of Sports Grounds Act. In the Autumn of 1985, emergency work was undertaken to carry out the fire prevention measures to ensure that the ground conformed to the Act for the major matches of that season. It was agreed that the capacity be reduced to 15,200 and work costing £57,000 was completed in time for that years' Barbarians fixture.

Phase II of the work was carried out in the summer of 1986, which included new crush barriers on the Crumbie terracing and replacement of the concrete steps. This was completed by the end of September at a cost of £130,000.

Work continues throughout each off-season to maintain and upgrade the facilities at Welford Road so that it remains the foremost rugby ground outside Twickenham.

WELFORD ROAD RECORDS

6 internationals have been staged on the ground:
8th February 1902 - England 6, Ireland 3
9th January 1904 - England 14, Wales 14
10th February 1906 - England 6, Ireland 16
30th January 1909 - England 22, France 0
10th February 1923 - England 23, Ireland 5 in the last England home international played away from Twickenham until Wembley was used against Canada in 1992
13th October 1991 - New Zealand 31,
Italy 21 - in the 2nd World Cup

Leicester's record:
Played 2,031; Won 1,461; Drew 119; Lost 451;
For 33,240; Against 15,412

Individual records:
Sid Penny is the only one to have played over 300 games for the Tigers at Welford Road, finishing with 301. David Matthews 282, Doug Norman 265, John Allen 252, Billy Foreman 233, Pedlar Wood 227, Paul Dodge 225, Jacky Braithwaite 217, George Ward 212, Dusty Hare 208 and Sid Matthews 205 follow him.

Most Wins: Sid Penny 231 of 301
Most Draws: Sid Penny 45 of 301
Most Defeats: Denis Bolesworth 72 of 185
Larry Parkes won all of his seventeen Tigers games at Welford Road, and O Wynne never won in 7 outings.

Percy Lawrie - 148 tries at Welford Road for Leicester.

Top points scorers:

	Gms	T	Con	PG	DG	GM	Pts
Dusty Hare	**208**	**41**	**487**	**493**	**25**	**-**	**2,692**
Harold Day	136	77	193	59	3	2	812
John Liley	61	31	140	131	1	-	806
Bob Barker	174	104	71	73	1	-	763
Percy Lawrie	183	148	12	6	5	-	506

Most tries: Lawrie 148 in 183 games, Harry Wilkinson 117 in 145 games, Bob Barker 104 in 174 games are the only ones to have scored over 100 tries.
Most Drop Goals: Les Cusworth dropped 37 goals in 188 games at Welford Road for the Tigers.

WELFORD ROAD RECREATION GROUND

Six games have been played at the 'Reccy', later known as Nelson Mandela Park.
vs Rosslyn Park 24 January 1959 - frost at Welford Road - Won 8-6
vs R A F 26 January 1961 - frost at Welford Road - Lost 6-11
vs London Irish 23 December 1967 - straw at Welford Road in preparation for the visit of the Barbarians - Won 17-0
vs Manchester 27 April 1968 - Welford Road seeded for next season - Won 13-6
vs Wasps 17 February 1973 - frost at Welford Road - Lost 4-10
vs Richmond 9 October 1976 - Noon kick-off North Midlands vs Argentina same day at Welford Road - Won 24-12

COVERT LANE, SCRAPTOFT

One Tigers home game has been played at Stoneygate RFC, Covert Lane because Welford Road was being used for the Midlands Counties game against the touring New Zealanders on the same day.
28 October 1967 - vs Cheltenham - Lost 8-11

The authors would like to express sincere thanks
to all those companies and individuals
whose subscriptions to this book helped make
publication possible.

BRAY & BRAY SOLICITORS

1, 3 & 5 Welford Road

Leicester LE2 7AN

CARL ZEISS LIMITED

P.O. Box 78 Woodfield Road

Welwyn Garden City

Herts AL7 1LU

CARLSBERG-TETLEY MIDLAND & WALES

Blakelands House. 400 Aldridge Road

Perry Barr, Birmingham B44 8BH

CLARK'S ROVER

St. John's

Narborough

Leicester LE9 5BS

DOWNES DYES & AUXILIARIES LTD

84 - 86 Barkby Road

Leicester LE4 7LF

IMPRESS (LEICESTER) LTD

8 Morris Road

Leicester LE2 6BR

RUGBY PROGRAMME CLUB

9 Pine Close

Thornbury

Bristol BS12 1AS

SYTNER of LEICESTER

929, Loughborough Road

Rothley

Leicester LE7 7NH

1 J. TUDOR THOMAS	53 W.H. COCKERILL, Birstall, Leicester
2 ROY D. JACKSON	54 ROY SAUNDERS, Netherhall Estate, Leicester
3 JOHN A. ALLEN	55 DEAN RAMSDALE, Melton Mowbray, Leics
4 ANTHONY E. HOPKINS	56 DON RADCLIFFE, Thurcaston, Leicester
5 ANTHONY O. RUSS	57 GRAHAM STRONG, Rowley Fields, Leicester
6 IAN R. SMITH	58 ALAN FOSSEY & HAZEL HILL, Glenfield, Leicester
7 ERIC C. LACEY	59 T.E. BANBURY, Langham, Rutland
8 PETER W.G. TOM	60 DANIEL J. ABELL, Crowthorne, Berkshire
9 GRAHAM G. WILLARS	61 LEN W. MINOR, LAVINIA VENABLE, Leire, Leics
10 DEAN RICHARDS	62 DONALD MICHAEL SIMPSON, Great Glen, Leicester
11 PAUL W. DODGE	63 R.W. ATKINSON, Great Bowden, Leics
12 DEREK LIMMAGE	64 IAN COCKERILL, Hugglescote, Leics
13 JOHN M. WELLS	65 MAUREEN SMITH, Hugglescote, Leics
14 BRIAN T.C. SMALL	66 TIM ASHURST, Shepshed, Leics
15 RAYMOND E. NEEDHAM	67 DESMOND WRIGHT, Anstey, Leicester
16 KEVIN P. ANDREWS	68 CRAIG KING, Leicester
17 STUART FARMER, Hinckley, Leicestershire	69 JOHN P.N. LANGFORD, Oadby, Leicester
18 DAVID HANDS, Fordingbridge, Hampshire	70 JAMES C. CRAIG, Groby, Leicester
19 JOHN M. JENKINS, Bow Street, Wales	71 KEVIN POLE, Blaby, Leicester
20 GILLIAN & BRIAN BATES, King's Norton, Birmingham	72 Mrs S.E. BUSBY, Ratby, Leicester
21 GERALD TOON, Scraptoft, Leicester	73 M.J. GAINSFORD, Burbage, Leics
22 DAVID CHRISTOPHER GASK, Rothley, Leicester	74 JOHN D. WRIGHT, Glenfield, Leicester
23 EAMON, JANICE & CONOR HEIGHWAY, Thurmaston, Leicester	75 DAVID JOHN WARD, Leicester
24 BOBBY BASKCOMB, Worth Matravers, Dorset	76 SIMON KEMP, Eaton, Grantham, Lincs
25 BERYL & WALTER FARMER, Nuneaton, Warwicks	77 LAURENCE FENTON, Narborough Road South, Leicester
26 LAURENCE MAXWELL ABNEY GRIFFITHS, Stonesby, Leics	78 Mrs JUNE P. KEANE, Cosby, Leicester
27 DOROTHY LESLIE SMITH, Melton Mowbray, Leics	79 J.T. GARNER, Thurlaston, Leicester
28 JULIA & EDWARD, Clarendon Park, Leicester	80 STEPHEN PAGE, Quorn, Leics
29 PAULINE CRAMPHORN, Leicester	81 FIONA CARSTAIRS, Aylestone, Leicester
30 JOHN HARRIS, Enfield, Middlesex	82 Mr & Mrs DEWDNEY, Aylestone, Leicester
31 ANDREW MAYFIELD, Woodloes Park, Warwick	83 Mrs D. KING, Crown Hills, Leicester
32 ALAN JACKSON, Radcliffe-on-Trent, Notts	84 A.L. SHORE, Thurnby, Leicester
33 PAUL HERON, Burbage, Hinckley	85 BERNARD ALAN BROWN, Rothley, Leics
34 RICHARD TAYLOR, Leicester	86 IAN BROWN, Rothley, Leics
35 WILLIAM J.C. REED, Desford, Leics	87 ROGER MICHAEL DICKMAN, Birstall, Leicester
36 PETER BAXTER, Leicester	88 MARTIN DICKMAN, Birstall, Leicester
37 GLYNN ALLEN, Narborough, Leics	89 Prof. PETER SWALLOW, Fleckney, Leicester
38 SHIRLEY JAMES SMITH, Narborough, Leics	90 J.R. HOLDRIDGE, Countesthorpe, Leicester
39 IAN SMITH, Coalville, Leics	91 JENNIFER METCALF, Melton Mowbray, Leics
40 R.J. COLEBURNE, Kirby Muxloe, Leics	92 PETER DIXON, Englefield Green, Surrey
41 ROBERT I. SMART, Oadby, Leicester	93 B.E. WARREN, Burton upon Trent, Staff
42 ARTHUR FLETCHER, Queniborough, Leics	94 ALEC HADEN, Enderby, Leicester
43 JAMES SMITH, Stoke Albany, Market Harborough, Leics	95 DAVE SMITH, Oadby, Leicester
44 R.M. POTTER, Gorleston, Great Yarmouth, Norfolk	96 STAFFORD ROBERT BUCK, Fleckney, Leicester
45 STEVE WHATNALL, Ellistown, Leics	97 HOWARD IMBER, Grantham, Lincs
46 AMP WHATNALL, Whitwick, Leics	98 TREVOR D. HAYES, East Challow, Oxon
47 JOANNE K. TAYLOR, Leicester	99 P.D. HIND, Thurmaston, Leicester
48 CLIVE DOUTHWAITE, Leicester	100 CUNNINGTON & COMPANY, New Walk, Leicester
49 STUART FRASER, Enderby, Leicester	101 CHRISTOPHER ASHTON, Blaby, Leicester
50 MICHAEL N. JORDAN, East Goscote, Leics	102 S.D. WILLIAMS, Groby, Leicester
51 TREVOR PAYNE, Glen Parva, Leicester	103 TERENCE JAMES GREAVES, Leicester
52 JOHN PARKER, Wigston, Leicester	104 DAVID JONES, Stoneygate, Leicester

105	IAIN SELKIRK, Market Bosworth, Warwickshire
106	RICHARD J. PELL, Bedford
107	A. HARLOW, Kettering, Northamptonshire
108	GRAHAM JOHN BLACKWELL, Netherhall Estate, Leicester
109	C.J. CHORLTON, Buckland, Aylesbury, Bucks
110	PAUL H. KIRK, Braunstone Town, Leicester
111	ATHOL JAMIESON, Brizlincote, Burton upon Trent
112	RUSSELL KNELL, Woodhouse Eaves, Leics
113	TERRY MASON, Leicester
114	CLIVE WOOD, Aylestone, Leicester
115	K. HYLTON HERRICK, Stoneygate, Leicester
116	PETER COLIN WARD, Glenfield, Leicester
117	L.J.P. SAMBROOK, Mountsorrel, Leicester
118	N. MORETON, Nuneaton, Warwickshire
119	MALCOLM JOHNSON, Northampton
120	KARL STEVENS, Ibstock, Leics
121	MALCOLM JOSEPH SHAW, Leicester
122	F.G. HUGHES, Stamford, Lincolnshire
123	DORIS MAUD HUGHES (nee MATTS), Stamford, Lincs
124	ROBERT THOMAS ARGUILE, Market Harborough, Leics
125	MIKE HOLT, Barwell, Leicester
126	C.A. FLOWER, Loughborough, Leics
127	JULIAN A. RICHARDSON, South Wigston, Leics
128	P.J.K. STONEHOUSE, Selston, Nottinghamshire
129	ANDREW WHITMAN, Chiswick, London
130	PETER WHITMAN, York
131	MARY & PETER KNIGHT, Derby
132	JOHN M TANSEY, Stoneygate, Leicester
133	GEORGE R. HOVELL, Leicester
134	PETER & BEVERLEY MAYNE, Houghton on the Hill, Leics
135	JAMES RUDMAN, Melton Mowbray, Leics
136	JOHN DARMON, Nuneaton, Warwickshire
137	E.G. WELBOURNE, Leamington Spa, Warwickshire
138	M.G. WELBOURNE, Horfield, Bristol
139	K.L. PEARSON, Market Harborough, Leics
140	MIKE & KAZIE POLE, Whetstone, Leics
141	SPENCER PARRY, Aylestone, Leicester
142	M.S. BAILEY, Barrow upon Soar, Leics
143	R. OAKLEY
144	A.S. WEBSTER
145	H.H. OAKLEY
146	ANDREW SHEFFIELD, Leicester Forest East
147	IAN C.S. SHEPHERD, High Wycombe, Bucks
148	STEVEN SHARP, Whetstone, Leicester
149	CLIVE GEORGE PICKFORD, Hinckley, Leics
150	P.J. WILKINSON, Thurnby, Leicester
151	MARTIN CROSSLEY, Leicester
152	RACHEL MARIE TALLIS, Earl Shilton, Leics
153	SIMON ALASTAIR MORTON, Whetstone, Leicester
154	PETER DALE, Leicester
155	ANDREW WYE, Birstall, Leicester
156	ANDY LARRAD, Aylestone, Leicester
157	T.A. HOWORTH, Great Glen, Leics
158	IVOR GEORGE SUTTON, Leicester
159	KING FREEMAN, Chartered Accountants, Leicester
160	IAN GIBSON-LEITCH, Nottingham
161	ROBIN A. GILLIVER, Earl Shilton, Leics
162	RONALD STRAHAN CASS, South Wigston, Leics
163	RICHARD GEARY, Thurcaston, Leics
164	MICHAEL DARCH, Wigston, Leicester
165	KAREN PALMER, Burbage, Leicestershire
166	PHILIP JELLEY, Syston, Leicester
167	COLLEEN SHUTE, Enderby, Leicester
168	JOHN M. MASTERS, Ashby de la Zouch, Leics
169	DEREK WOOD, Wigston Harcourt, Leics
170	JOHN G. MAWBY, Arnesby, Leicestershire
171	MICHAEL S. EVANS, Loughborough, Leics
172	TERENCE TREVOR JOY, Four Pools, Evesham, Worcs
173	PETER SHAW, Pinkneys Green, Maidenhead, Berks
174	WILLIAM ROBERT WHITE, Kegworth, Leicestershire
175	IAN McALPINE, Peatling Parva, Lutterworth, Leics
176	DOROTHY MARSH, Oadby, Leicester
177	VERNON ADAMS, Willoughby Waterleys, Leics
178	M.C. WALE, Nuneaton, Warwickshire
179	RAYMOND H. HOBELL, Leicester
180	SID CHAMBERLAIN, Glenfield, Leicester
181	DENNIS A. LAMBERT, Noctorum, Birkenhead
182	R. ELLIS, Wigston Fields, Leicester
183	RICHARD AGG, Great Glen, Leicester
184	DEREK & VALERIE JOYCE, Leicester
185	CHERYL WRIGHT, Newtown Linford, Leics
186	IAN JAMES BUSWELL, Abbey Rise East, Leicester
187	DEREK STANIFORTH, Leicester
188	EDWARD E. WOODS, Willoughby Waterleys, Leics
189	DENIS BIRCH, Earl Shilton, Leics
190	DAVID BROOKS, Thurmaston, Leicester
191	R.J GOODACRE, Bradford on Avon, Wiltshire
192	JASON PEACH, Barwell, Leics
193	J.J. STONE, Oadby, Leicester
194	ROY ANTCLIFFE, Leicester
195	R.O. BIGNELL, Hinckley, Leics
196	DAVID ARIS, Coalville, Leicester
197	RAYMOND J. MORRIS, Leicester Forest East
198	G.L. KIMBERLEY, Cropston, Leicester
199	M.R. CHARLES, Cropston, Leicester
200	C.J. FRANK, Leicester
201	DIANE THOMPSON, Woodgate, Leicester
202	HOWARD CANNING, Braybrooke, Mkt Harborough
203	HELEN COLEMAN, Birstall, Leicester
204	OLIVER MARK PERKINS, Countesthorpe, Leicester
205	DAVID GALLAGHER, Crag Bank, Carnforth, Lancs
206	MALCOLM DERRICK SHORT, Millfield Farm, Leicester
207	BRIAN MARCH, Thornton, Leicestershire
208	Mrs E.M. INGREY, Glenfield, Leicester

Subscribers

209 SAMANTHA D. DOLMAN, Winshill, Burton upon Trent

210 RON CARTER, Repton, Derbyshire

211 JOHN MICHAEL GRANT, Stoneygate, Leicester

212 ROSS IAN GRANT, Stoneygate, Leicester

213 EVELYN GRACE GRANT, Knighton, Leicester

214 JACK COE, Birstall, Leicester

215 RICHARD ASHCROFT, Cape Town, South Africa

216 MAURICE PAWLEY, Broughton Astley, Leics

217 Dr. MARTIN K. PAWLEY, Radyr, Cardiff

218 MICHAEL J. PAWLEY B.D.S., Cotham, Bristol

219 GARY DAVID MARS, Burleigh Grange, Loughborough

220 D.J. KILSBY, Blaby, Leicester

221 ERIC E. FLACK, Oadby, Leicester

222 RACHEL MARSHALL, Peatling Magna, Leics

223 Mr & Mrs A.E. BROWN, Aylestone, Leicester

224 DAVID NOEL JACKSON, Barton-in-the-Beans, Leics

225 NORMAN JOHN BAUM, Leicester

226 ALAN THOMAS, Galley Common, Nuneaton

227 NATHAN THOMAS, Stoney Stanton, Leicester

228 JOHN FOSS, Bushby, Leicestershire

229 S.A. COOPER, Leicester

230 LUCY FLETCHER, Broughton Astley, Leics

231 Mrs E.A. HAYDN (nee CRAMPHORN), Wigston Magna, Leics

232 OWEN LAWRENCE, Groby, Leicester

233 JEFFREY S.L. SCAIFE, Kibworth, Leics

234 JEAN P. WOODCOCK, Glen Parva, Leicester

235 ALAN GODDARD, Braunstone Frith, Leicester

236 MARTIN BALLARD, Leicester

237 CHRISTOPHER L. DUPOND, Clifton Hampden, Abingdon, Oxon

238 C.W.E. HAINES, Birstall, Leicester

239 STÉPHANE JACQUES PANDIT, Groby, Leicester

240 IAN R. JOHNSON, Oadby, Leicester

241 M. BONSER, Hambleton, Oakham, Rutland

242 IAN STUART, Orton Malborne, Peterborough

243 ROSIE & MICHAEL WOOD, Stoney Stanton, Leicester

244 TREFOR JONES, Barwell, Hinckley, Leics

245 STEPHEN L. KISBY, Oadby, Leicester

246 ROY GUISE WILSON, Leicester

247 KEITH WORTH, Glinton, Peterborough

248 F.N. TAYLOR, Houghton-on-the-Hill, Leicester

249 Mrs WINIFRED WEBSTER, Leicester

250 WALTER HIGGINS, OBE, JP, Great Glen, Leics

251 IAN HIGGINS, Cupar, Fife

252 TONY HIGGINS, Stow on the Wold, Glos

253 ROBERT STAINES, Leire, Leicestershire

254 JULIAN P. GILLESPIE, Birstall, Leicester

255 Mrs EILEEN B. JACKSON, Wigston, Leicester

256 J.C. STEVENS, Oakham, Rutland

257 Miss R.G. HALFORD, Lower Swainswick, Bath, Avon

258 D.J. SHIELDS, Loughborough, Leics

259 MARTIN R. BLEE & JEAN McCAULEY, Boston, Lincs

260 BOB GOODMAN, Navenby, Lincolnshire

261 JOHN COLTMAN, Glenfield, Leicester

262 MARK O'NEILL, Edmondthorpe, Melton Mowbray

263 PETER WILSON, Clarendon Park, Leicester

264 S.A. TOACH, Leicester

265 MICHAEL GARRATT, West Knighton, Leicester

266 RICHARD GARRATT, Wigston, Leicester

267 TIMOTHY ODAMS, Oadby, Leicester

268 IAN C. MORRIS, Leicester Forest East

269 R.M. MUDDIMER, Billesdon, Leics

270 NIGEL BRISTOWE, Hathern, Loughborough, Leics

271 ANNE FOWELL, Leicester

272 ANTHONY & HEATHER BIRR, Birstall, Leicester

273 ROBERT G. DICKINS, Wigston, Leicester

274 RICHARD M. GASCOIGNE, Knighton, Leicester

275 ANN DAVISON, Leicester

276 CLIVE STACE, Ullesthorpe, Leicestershire

277 R.O. CAVE, Harpenden, Hertfordshire

278 ROY BLYTH, Somerby, Leicestershire

279 B.P. CLARKE, Wigston Fields, Leicester

280 GARY MORRISON, West Knighton, Leicester

281 RUSSELL MORRISON, West Knighton, Leicester

282 ALISTAIR GRAHAM HAMPSON, Whetstone, Leicester

283 SCOTT BROWNLOW, Thringstone, Leicester

284 SIMON COLE, Alvechurch, Worcerstershire

285 DAVID JAMES BULLOCK, Melton Mowbray, Leics

286 R. TITLEY, Oadby, Leicester

287 F.M.T. ASHLEY, Moira, Swadlincote, Derbyshire

288 J.W. BAKER, Newton Harcourt, Leics

289 ROY W. WINTER, Leicester

290 PETER JOHN HUBBARD & SALLY WADSWORTH, Hove, Sussex

291 CAROL SUSAN MAISEY, Lower Parkstone, Poole, Dorset

292 RONALD SCOTTON, Burbage, Hinckley, Leics

293 GEORGE COSTELLO, Great Glen, Leicester

294 LEE WHITEHOUSE, Earl Shilton, Leics

295 ANDREW REDPATH, Jedburgh, Roxburghshire

296 RAMON V. MARTIN, Leicester

297 SIMON D. MARTIN, Leicester

298 IAN RICHARDSON, Glenfield, Leicester

299 STUART & BRUCE KIRK, Wednesfield, Wolverhampton

300 JOHN B. HAWKES, Stoneygate, Leicester

301 JAMES J. HAWKES, Oadby, Leicester

302 DAVID NEVILLE, Burbage, Leicester

303 MATTHEW COLIN HASELTON, Flitwick, Bedford

304 D.W. CLARKE, West Knighton, Leicester

305 MARTIN PRINCE, Scraptoft, Leicester

306 J.T.M. UNDERWOOD, Leicester Forest East

307 HOWARD J. ARCHER, Ratby, Leicestershire

308 BRIAN ALFRED BATES, Earl Shilton, Leicestershire

309 ANTHONY JOHN HARRISON, Hugglescote, Leics

310 N.H. HARTLEY, Wigston, Leicester

311 JOHN D. STAPLEY, Wormley, Hertfordshire

312 R.A. OWENS, Hinckley, Leics

Subscribers

313 JOY M. & NORMAN MATTHEWS, Thurmaston, Leicester
314 KEITH PALMER, South Wigston, Leicester
315 COLIN GOLDING, Broughton Astley, Leics
316 KEITH GEORGE WILTSHIRE, Wigston, Leics
317 JULIA GRUNDY, Kilby, Leicester
318 B.A.F. SMITH
319 RICHARD PETER EVERETT
320 RICHARD J.F. DALE, DALES ESTATE AGENTS, Leicester
321 BARRY MAY, Loughborough, Leics
322 CATHERINE FOWELL, Oadby, Leicester
323 KENNETH WARD, Aylestone, Leicester
324 D.R. LANGLEY, Holme-next-the-sea, Norfolk
325 ANDREW NICHOLAS ROSE, Grantham, Lincs
326 RICHARD S. ROBINSON, Wigston, Leics
327 ELAINE NICHOLLS, Dilton Marsh, Wiltshire
328 CYNTHIA TOMLINSON, Market Cross, Mountsorrel, Leics
329 GARY CLARKE, Leicester
330 CHRIS BREWIN, Broughton Astley, Leicester
331 GRAHAME CARTER, Leicester
332 AUBREY W. STEVENSON, Knighton, Leicester
333 LAWRIE SIMPKIN, Rothley, Leicester
334 PETER BATES, Oadby, Leicester
335 DEREK A. PERRY, Leicester
336 MICHAEL & JILLIAN HAWKES & FAMILY, Stoneygate, Leicester
337 Mr & Mrs H.A. HAWKES, Skegness, Lincolnshire
338 Dr. JOHN BATTERBEE, Bavel, Holland
339 SIMON J. BATTERBEE, Chicago, U.S.A.
340 ALAN THOMAS FORD, Leicester Forest East
341 IAN STAPLEFORD, Wallington, Fareham, Hants
342 J.A.D. HAWKER, Thurnby, Leicester
343 JEAN & BILL CLAYTON, Cropston, Leicestershire
344 MARK R.M. COLE, Braiswick, Colchester, Essex
345 JOHN POPE, Market Bosworth, Nuneaton, Warwicks
346 J.K. HOLYOAK, Leicester
347 P.A. STEPHENSON, Leicester
348 DAVID STANYER, Leicester
349 PHILIP A. NORTON, Knighton, Leicester
350 JOHN L. WEST, Wigston Harcourt, Leicester
351 R.J. HUTCHINSON, POWDRILLS, Croft, Leics
352 Mrs AMY PEPPER, Brampton, Huntingdon, Cambs
353 ERIC M. FAULCONBRIDGE, Sileby, Leicestershire
354 R.F. GAMBLE, Leicester
355 ANTHONY & LINDA TAYLOR, Lutterworth, Leics
356 STEPHEN ILIFFE, Southgate, London
357 D.A. ILIFFE, Oakham, Rutland, Leics
358 A. YOUNGJOHNS, Mowsley, Lutterworth, Leics
359 ANDREW D. NOBLE, Aspley Guise, Bucks
360 MATT PRATT, Wigston, Leicester
361 FIONA SANDERS, St. James Park, Salford, Lancs
362 PAUL ATKINS, Wigston Fields, Leicester
363 BARRY & JUDITH WILKINS, Syston, Leics
364 R.J. & S. POYNTER, Swinstead, Grantham, Lincs

365 JOHN W. WATERS, Leicester
366 JEFFREY ROSENTHAL, Leicester
367 K.R. GREEN, Leicester Forest East
368 W.G. SMITH, Stoney Stanton, Leicestershire
369 DAVID C. COLTON, Brackla, Bridgend, Mid-Glamorgan
370 STEPHEN AGAR, South Kilworth, Lutterworth, Leics
371 DAVE & CHRIS ALLSOP, Putney, London
372 SIMON NOAKES, Leicester
373 J. BALL, Kirby Muxloe, Leicester
374 JONATHAN COX, Oadby, Leicester
375 Dr. HENRY PIERCE HUGHES, Loughborough, Leics
376 ANDY JACKSON, Sapcote, Leicestershire
377 BRUCE SCOTT, Sapcote, Leicestershire
378 MICK RICHARDSON, Sapcote, Leicestershire
379 S.P HIND, Leicester
380 R.W. HIND, Fleckney, Leicester
381 BEN E. WARREN, Newton Solney, Staffs
382 HOWARD M. WELLINGS, Loughborough, Leics
383 BARRY MEADOWS, Hinckley, Leics
384 Mr E.P. & Mrs S.P. GOULD, Cropston, Leicester
385 ANDREW & JOE CHAMBERLAIN, Wimbledon, London
386 PAUL ROBSHAW, Cropston, Leicester
387 PETER R.S. WAITE, Great Bowden, Leics
388 JOHN OWEN CHIVERS, Bearwood, Bournemouth, Dorset
389 ALAN HOLLINGWORTH, Ratby, Leics
390 Miss J.M. VALE, Rearsby, Leicester
391 MIKE MORTIMER, Littlethorpe, Leicester
392 Dr. P.G.F.SWIFT, Stoneygate, Leicester
393 W.A. TOONE, Billesdon, Leics
394 JOHN BOWLER, Loughborough, Leics
395 PAUL S. BONNETT, Bushby, Leicestershire
396 R.I. MacPHERSON-RAIT, Gilmorton, Leics
397 Mrs MARY E. REEVES, Birstall, Leicester
398 DAVID J.N. SPARROW, Sutton Bonington, Loughboro', Leics
399 HAYDN GEORGE THOMAS, Ravenhill, Swansea
400 J. WHITE, Oostkamp, Belgium
401 D.K. TROTTER, Queniborough, Leicester
402 PETER WILSON, Stoneygate, Leicester
403 STEPHEN JOHN CONLON, Groby, Leicester
404 R. CHERRY, Anstey, Leicester
405 PETER ENGLISH, Leicester
406 Mrs MAVIS EVANS, Hinckley, Leics
407 PETER HARRISON, Leicester
408 B.R. BIRCH, Hinckley, Leics
409 NORMAN CURTIS, Glenfield, Leicester
410 A.R. HAMBLY M.B.E., Nether Broughton, Leics
411 ROBERT LESLIE MATTS, Anstey, Leicester
412 Prof. ROBIN C. FRASER, Leicester
413 BARRY GOULD, Evington, Leicester
414 Mr & Mrs M.W. BUSSEY, Rowley Fields, Leicester
415 MICHAEL & ISABEL CLARKE, Thrussington, Leics
416 JOHN ATKINSON, Market Bosworth, Warwickshire

417	ADRIAN A. BENTLEY, Market Harborough, Leics	469	CLIVE H. PALMER, Swannington, Leicestershire
418	EDWARD BROUGHTON, Burton on the Wolds, Leics	470	MARTIN (MUSH) CORY, South Wigston, Leicester
419	MICHAEL J.S. ROBERTS, Stamford, Lincs	471	STEWART O. SMITH, Evington, Leicester
420	CHARLES EARP, Earl Shilton, Leics	472	MARK JENNINGS, Enderby, Leicester
421	MARK WOODLAND, Oadby, Leicester	473	ROGER FRENCH, Moreton Morrell, Warwicks
422	PAUL GIBSON, Oadby, Leicester	474	MICHAEL IRVING, Dorridge, Solihull, West Midlands
423	G.P.C. VALLANCE, Widmerpool, Nottingham	475	MARK INGRAM, Fradswell, Stafford
424	TIM R. HUTCHINS, Oakham, Rutland, Leics	476	H. FRANKS, Willington, Derby
425	LORNA JANE COOPER, Thurmaston, Leicester	477	DAVID ROGERS, Rugby, Warwickshire
426	JOHN C. TURNER, Wigston Magna, Leicester	478	TIM KILBY, Barrow upon Soar, Leics
427	KEITH FAULKES, Thurmaston, Leicester	479	R.H. NEWMAN, Groby, Leicester
428	S.S. GODDARD, Leicester	480	DAVID HIGGINS, Little Milton, Oxon
429	Mrs J.P. WOODCOCK, Glen Parva, Leicester	481	STEPHEN WINCH, Leicester
430	RUTH BATES, Burbage, Hinckley, Leics	482	W.B. CHORLTON, Castle Bytham, Lincs
431	PETER JONES, Barwell, Leicester	483	PAUL J. GRIBBELL, Groby, Leicester
432	VIC & MARGARET IRONMONGER, Leicester	484	A.D. CLEWLOW, Kilby, Leicester
433	J. DOLAN, Wigston Magna, Leicester	485	LEONARD SWANWICK, South Kilworth, Leics
434	PETER ROWE, Westerham, Kent	486	DUNCAN J. CHANDLER, South Wigston, Leicester
435	JAMES BUTTERFIELD, Normanton on the Wolds, Notts	487	PHILIP HENDERSON, Loughborough, Leics
436	AMY SWINFEN, South Kilworth, Leics	488	J.S. BLEBY, Countesthorpe, Leicester
437	JOCK MILLICAN, Edinburgh	489	NORMAN H. LOAKES, Ingleton, Carnforth, Lancs
438	MICHAEL R. MARSHALL, Thurmaston, Leicester	490	NEIL JALLAND, Sileby, Leicestershire
439	STEPHEN C. MARSHALL, Thurmaston, Leicester	491	F. THISTLETHWAITE, Leicester
440	VANESSA MARSHALL, Thurmaston, Leicester	492	MICHAEL W. SIMMS-REEVE, Duston, Northampton
441	STUART F. BALMFORTH, Barton-in-Fabis, Notts	493	MICHAEL TOWE, Burbage, Leicester
442	JOHN F. THOMPSON	494	J. CRAIG, Leicester
443	G.P.B. MUTTER, London SW1	495	GARY SHELLARD, East Farndon, Leicestershire
444	ANNETTE HALES, Thurnby Lodge, Leicester	496	DARREN SYMES-GOODMAN, Loughborough, Leics
445	S.W. CHAPMAN, Anstey, Leicester	497	STEPHEN SYMES-GOODMAN, Loughborough, Leics
446	JOAN FARAM, Barrow-on-Soar, Leics	498	CARL SYMES-GOODMAN, Groby, Leicester
447	P.H. KONIG, Gressenhall, Norfolk	499	MARTIN WALL, Fleckney, Leicester
448	B.J. SMITH, Wallington, Surrey	500	PAUL SHAW, Leamington Spa, Warwicks
449	JOHN GRAHAM WILSON, Leicester	501	Mrs J.L. BILSBORROW, Marlow, Bucks
450	DON KENDALL, Birstall, Leicester	502	P. SQUIRES, Knighton, Leicester
451	KEITH MARK STEPHENSON, Desford, Leics	503	J.A. LEDDINGTON, Glen Parva, Leicester
452	A.B. HINE, Clarendon Park, Leicester	504	JIM FORD, Hallaton, Leicestershire
453	L. GLOVER & Co. (LEICESTER) LIMITED, Leicester	505	WILLIAM WREGLESWORTH, Cossington, Leicester
454	D.T. McSWEENEY, Houghton on the Hill, Leics	506	IAN SOUTHWELL, Dingley, Leicestershire
455	ADAM WALTON, Humberstone Cottage, Old Humberstone,	507	MARK COLEMAN, Littlethorpe, Leicester
456	R.F. PERKINS, Ashton,Stamford, Lincs	508	IAN FRASER, Ashby de la Zouch, Leics
457	TREVOR LOYDALL, Clifton, Beds	509	PETE DOWELL, Barlestone, Nuneaton, Warwicks
458	ROY LEATHERLAND, Wigston, Leicester	510	Dr. C.J. SHARPLES, Royal Air Force, Wansford, Cambs
459	Mrs PAULA SMITH, South Wigston, Leicester	511	CHRIS BULL, Monkspath, Solihull
460	GAIL STEVENSON-FREER, Countesthorpe, Leicester	512	SUE BULL, Monkspath, Solihull
461	GEOFF STEVENSON, Glen Parva, Leicester	513	DONALD ERIC BEVINS, Oswestry, Shropshire
462	R. IVAN SMITH, Oakham, Rutland, Leics	514	C.K. ELLIOTT, Market Bosworth, Warwicks
463	B.B. KNIGHT, Burton Joyce, Nottinghamshire	515	DAVID R. SHAW, Edwalton, Nottingham
464	J.C.P. ARNOLD, Syston, Leicester	516	NIGEL J. ROBINSON, Bromham, Bedford
465	JOHN ALLISON, Leicester	517	NEIL TURNER, Aylestone, Leicester
466	NORMAN PYNE, Thurmaston, Leicester	518	HERBERT VICTOR WHITE, Wellington, Somerset
467	Gp. Capt. N. ADAMS (Retd.), Eckington, Pershore, Worcs	519	A.N. ODAMS, Leicester
468	Mr & Mrs D. YORK, Braunstone Town, Leicester	520	ALEC DAVID MOORE, Bilbrook, Codsall, Wolverhampton

521 PETER JAMES WILKINS, Wigston Magna, Leicester

522 JOHN PATRICK WISEHALL (J.P. & P.A. WISEHALL) Whitwick

523 Mr & Mrs B.E. SPENCE, Evington, Leicester

524 A.G. JONES, Middle Barton, Chipping Norton, Oxon

525 G.C. MORTON, South Wigston, Leicester

526 JOHN A. MOTE, Broughton Astley, Leicester

527 GEOFFREY A. BELL, Wigston, Leicester

528 ROBIN MONEY, Holmes Chapel, Cheshire

529 FIONA ELIZABETH WILKINSON, Alveston, Bristol

530 TONY FREEMAN, Wigston, Leicester

531 B.C. GADNEY, Aldeburgh, Suffolk

532 MAUREEN & JOHN SAUNDERS, Glenfield, Leicester

533 ERIC WILLIAM BIRK, Welton, Lincoln

534 PHILIP R. POWELL, Rothley, Leicester

535 ALAN SMITH, Anstey, Leicester

536 JIM CORKILL, Welford, Northamptonshire

537 ANDREW M.S. HALES, Oadby, Leicester

538 ARTHUR LEONARD MURGATROYD, Cosby, Leicester

539 DAVID KING, South Woodham Ferrers, Essex

540 JULIAN R. BRANSTON, Thurcaston, Leicester

541 GRUFFYDD MORGAN-JONES, Syston, Leicester

542 PETER, THERESA & JACQUELINE THOMAS, Derby

543 JOHN FEEHALLY, Houghton on the Hill, Leics

544 R.J. PARSONS, Leicester

545 LOUISE & MARK JACKSON, Paignton, Devon

546 DAVID PRICE, Braunstone, Leicester

547 MATTHEW FERGUSON, Thurlaston, Leicester

548 ARTHUR PROUD, Keresley, Coventry

549 GRAHAM P.G.S. PULFREY, Crieff, Scotland

550 DAVID JAMES CASTLEDINE, St. Brelade, Jersey

551 J.C. JACKSON, Glen Parva, Leicester

552 A. JONATHAN SMITH, Oadby, Leicester

553 ROY CLARK, Glen Parva, Leicester

554 PETER J. NICHOLLS, Bramcote, Nottingham

555 MARTIN PRICE, Bruntingthorpe, Leics

556 Mr & Mrs E.J. ROUND, Southwell, Notts

557 PHILLIP BOTT, East Goscote, Leicester

558 ARTHUR A. MOLD, Market Harborough, Leics

559 ANDY COLLINS, Glenfield, Leicester

560 GORDON & SHEILA HARRISON, Mountsorrel, Leics

561 WAYNE GADSBY, Coalville, Leicester

562 IAIN WATSON, WINGPLAY LTD, Leicester

563 FRED CORK, Streetly, West Midlands

564 N.J. STONE, Leicester

565 M.C. STOTT, Claybrooke Magna, Leics

566 DAVID M. TARRY, Leicester

567 ALAN P. O'SULLIVAN, Birstall, Leicester

568 BILL WOOD, Oadby, Leicester

569 W.J.A. DALY, Ratby, Leicester

570 DAVID W. BLAIR, Oadby, Leicester

571 TREVOR E. SNOWDEN, Enderby, Leicester

572 JIM PARSONS, Lapworth, Warwickshire

573 FREDERICK F. SMITH, Maxey, Peterborough

574 MICHAEL G. HEARTH, Kibworth Beauchamp, Leicestershire

575 DAVID HAMPSON, Kingsbury, Tamworth, Staffs

576 D.R.C. SCHWARZ, Ordsall, Retford, Notts

577 ANDREW MURFIN, Blyth Hall, Nr. Worksop, Notts

578 LEWIS HIPWELL SMITH, Leicester

579 ALAN K. SHORE, Oadby, Leicester

580 IVOR GEORGE SUTTON, Western Park, Leicester

581 MARK BEATTY, Cheddleton, Leek, Staffs

582 D.J. MATTHEWS, Barrow, Oakham, Rutland

583 ANDY DABSON, Oadby Grange, Leicester

584 JIM RUDKIN, Waltham on the Wolds, Leics

585 JANE & MARK SHARMAN, Glenfield, Leicester

586 A.G. WOODWARD, Wigston Harcourt, Leicester

587 RICHARD STACE, Ullesthorpe, Leics

588 DARRELL A. WHITAKER, Sileby, Leics

589 TONY MALCOLM SCOTT, Hathern, Leics

590 HEIDi LOUISE SCOTT, Hathern, Leics

591 G.J.W. & Mrs B.E. TOVEY, Kingsbury, Tamworth, Staffs

592 G.E. PARREY, Nuthall, Nottingham

593 GRAHAM G. WILLARS, Oadby, Leicester

594 MAURICE S. TIMSON, Cosby, Leicester

595 PETER MacLENNAN, Easton on the Hill, Lincs

596 BRYAN R. FOSTER, Hinckley, Leics

597 Dr. PETER J.B. HUBNER, Kirby Muxloe, Leicester

598 D. STOTT, Abington, Northampton

599 DAVID JONES, Oadby, Leicester

600 JOHN APPLEBY, Oadby, Leicester

601 W.J.S. BOOTON, Evington, Leicester

602 MICHAEL C. MARTIN, Hungarton, Leicester

603 GERALD BENNETT, Glenfield, Leicester

604 KELVIN J. SMITH, Rothley, Leicester

605 PAUL J. WILCOCK, Amersham, Bucks

606 R.F.C. TAYLOR, Egmond aan Zee, Nederland

607 A. TEKELL, Fenstanton, Cambs

608 IAN C. JONES, Spondon, Derby

609 RICHARD P. JONES, St. Johns Wood, London

610 C.G. HARRISON & Miss T.H. COOKE, Quorn, Leics

611 R.N. AVERY, Queniborough, Leics

612 NORMAN W. LEWIN, Leicester

613 JOHN L. BAGLEY, Burntwood, Walsall, W. Mids

614 P.E. OUGH, Tilton on the Hill, Leics

615 R. ATTWOOD, Mountsorrel, Leics

616 CHRISTOPHER HATTON, Melton Mowbray, Leics

617 ROY FOX, Aylestone, Leicester

618 KEITH J. LOND, Anstey Heights, Leicester

619 RON CURSLEY, Torquay, Devon

620 PETER B.L. THORNELOE, Brixham, South Devon

621 DENNIS WILLIAM BENNETT, Great Glen, Leicester

622 FRANK STEPHENSON, Desford, Leicester

623 JOHN SANDERS, Wigston, Leicester

624 HUGH HANSFORD, Birstall, Leicester

625 NICOLA JONES, Great Glen, Leicester	677 MARK PRESTON, Aylestone, Leicester
626 A.J. & P.M. BAMFORD, Market Bosworth, Warwicks	678 JACK PALEY, Ratby, Leicestershire
627 JOHN GASCOYNE, Castle Bytham, Lincs	679 RORY CLEARY, Loughborough, Leics
628 RICHARD PAWLEY, Thurcaston, Leicester	680 M.S. BEVAN, Earl Shilton, Leics
629 DEREK P. BOWEN, Burbage, Leics	681 ED TITLEY, Oadby, Leicester
630 JAMES BULL, Scraptoft, Leicester	682 CLARE HANLEY, Western Park, Leicester
631 DENIS W. FULFORD, Groby, Leicester	683 M.J. HARRISON, Thrussington, Leics
632 M.J. GARFORTH, Exhall, Coventry	684 R.W. MURGATROYD, Leicester
633 JOHN BARRELL, Leicester	685 STEPHEN CONDON, Petts Wood, Orpington, Kent
634 Mrs S. ROBINSON, Hinckley, Leics	686 N.J. JOYCE, Waltham on the Wolds, Leics
635 J. SWIFT, Hinckley, Leics	687 CLIVE HAWLEY, Evington, Leicester
636 A.R. WILDMAN, Enfield, Middlesex	688 NORMAN C. BOWLER, Braybrooke, Leics
637 MICHAEL FRANCKS, Hinckley, Leics	689 ROBERT I. NORMAN, Evington, Leicester
638 GEORGE & SHEILA HOPKINS, Okehampton, Devon	690 ANDREW MATTHEWS, Barrow, Nr. Oakham, Rutland
639 DAVID B. GREEN, Oadby, Leicester	691 E.A. BRAZIER, Birstall, Leicester
640 COLIN J. HEBBORN, Northorpe, Bourne, Lincs	692 GRAHAM HOWSON, Syston, Leics
641 DEREK J. GREEN, Tilton on the Hill, Leics	693 NEIL JOHN, Swithland, Leicester
642 MARTIN G. BOWRON, Ashby de la Zouch, Leics	694 TIM McMAHON, South Witham, Lincoln
643 DEREK T. SMITH, Leicester	695 C.E. SMITH, Smeeton Westerby, Leics
644 JOHN ROBERT WOODLAND, Humberstone, Leicester	696 J.P. HORROCKS-TAYLOR, Nunthorpe, Middlesbrough
645 CHARLES SMITH, Thorpe Satchville, Leics	697 ERIC HEYS, Leicester
646 THOMAS BARTON, Knighton, Leicester	698 CHARLES H. NUTT, Stoke on Trent, Staff
647 G. NEVITT, Gaulby, Leicester	699 J.R. MALLETT, Oadby, Leicester
648 NICOLA JANE STEVENS, Croft, Leicester	700 A.K. WILLIAMS, Shangton, Leics
649 ARTHUR IAN BURTON, Kirby Muxloe, Leicester	701 TREVOR ALLEN, Woodhouse Eaves, Leics
650 REGINALD WOODWARD, Aylestone, Leicester	702 ANDY COX, Burbage, Hinckley, Leics
651 CLIFFORD E. MASON, Knighton, Leicester	703 NEIL S. IBBETSON, Sketchley Lane, Hinckley
652 R.J. WILSON, Groby, Leicester	704 DENNIS & RITA BARTON, Wigston, Leicester
653 MICHAEL HARRISON, East Goscote, Leicester	705 RAE MARSHALL, Flitton, Bedfordshire
654 COLIN A. WOLVERSON, West Parley, Ferndown, Dorset	706 E.J.W. VENABLE, Leicester
655 STEVEN WRIGHT, Wigston, Leicester	707 DOUG BROWN, Keyworth, Nottingham
656 CHRIS PERKINS, Fleckney, Leicester	708 TIM BARSON, Netherhall, Leicester
657 C.F. ELLIOTT, Broughton Astley, Leicester	709 MICHAEL E. NEAL, Portishead, Bristol
658 MICK JOHNSON, Anstey, Leicester	710 M. KENDRICK, Enderby, Leics
659 W.C. SUTTON, Loughborough, Leics	711 P. LEACH, Oadby, Leicester
660 J.A. ALLEN, Leicester	712 PAUL ASH, Cheadle Hulme, Cheshire
661 DEREK EDWARD EATO, Cosby, Leicester	713 STEVEN TANSER, Birstall, Leicester
662 CHRISTOPHER BOWEN-JONES, Leicester	714 JOSEPH KRYCH, Stanton under Bardon, Leics
663 Mr & Mrs J.T. GILFORD, Braunstone, Leicester	715 LISA JANE SHARRATT, Hinckley, Leics
664 PETER WORRALL, Kirby Muxloe, Leicester	716 J. ELDERS, Melton Park, Newcastle upon Tyne
665 TREVOR IRELAND, Leicester	717 JONATHAN D. VARLEY, Groby, Leicester
666 ADAM IRELAND, Littlethorpe, Leicester	718 PETER HOLDRIDGE, Countesthorpe, Leicester
667 RICHARD JOHNSON, Leicester Forest East	719 NATALIE FREEMAN, Markfield, Leicester
668 NEVILLE CHADWICK PHOTOGRAPHY, Wigston, Leicester	720 KENNETH J. LAMBDEN, Bardon Hill, Coalville, Leics
669 A.M. & Mrs D. BOX, Burton Lazars, Leics	721 B.T. WIGLEY, Lutterworth, Leics
670 BRIAN HYDE, Clarendon Park, Leicester	722 DAVID JOHNSON, Market Harborough, Leics
671 DAVID A BRANT, Stoney Stanton, Leicester	723 R. BUCKLEY, Oadby, Leicester
672 PETER BRENNAN, Enderby, Leicester	724 Dr. P.H. WINSON, Thame, Oxon
673 DAVID N. BROOKS, Brixworth, Northamptonshire	725 CHRIS CARTER, Hathern, Leicestershire
674 STEPHEN TUDOR, Panshanger, Welwyn Garden City, Herts	726 L.H. WIGHTMAN, Maidstone, Kent
675 PETER M. COX, Melton Mowbray, Leics	727 J. WIGHTMAN, Burbage, Leicestershire
676 A.J.P. BRIGGS, Braunstone, Leicester	728 JOHN WHITTAKER, Durham City

729 COLIN HILL, Kirkham, Preston, Lancs

730 ION C.W. HILL, Sparham, Norwich, Norfolk

731 CHRISTOPHER A. SIMS, Bracon Ash, Norwich, Norfolk

732 ALAN STYLES, Coalville, Leicestershire

733 JOHN TAYLOR, Ravenstone, Leicestershire

734 J.W. WALKLEY, Asfordby, Leicestershire

735 ROBERT DAVID MATTHEWS, Welford on Avon, Warwicks

736 IAN DODSON, South Wigston, Leicester

737 LEONARD WILKINSON, Leicester

738 MARK WALKER, Hilsea, Portsmouth

739 DAVID DALBY, Knighton, Leicester

740 PETER LOAKE, Market Harborough, Leics

741 GILLIAN L. MOSS-WAGHORN, Polesworth, Staffs

742 B.C. BAILEY, Oakham, Rutland

743 ANDREW J. MIDDLETON, Birstall, Leicester

744 JOHN EVERITT, Wigston Magna, Leicester

745 VICTOR WATTS, Melton Mowbray, Leics

746 Mrs J.E. SANDERSON, Croft, Skegness, Lincs

747 PAUL J. GRANT, Langrick, Boston, Lincs

748 TREVOR T. JORDAN, South Wigston, Leicester

749 PETER J. LOWETH, Wigston, Leicester

750 D. BOLESWORTH, Rock, Wadebridge, Cornwall

751 BOB WILLIAMS, Wildmoor, Bromsgrove, Worcs

752 TERRY GRETTON, Ibstock, Leicestershire

753 PHILIP SIMPSON, Swadlincote, Derbyshire

754 IAN ROBERT SMITH, Uppingham, Rutland

755 SIDNEY HERBERT HULL, Wigston Magna, Leicester

756 ANDREW WEATHERBY, Fleckney, Leicester

757 G.A. KIND, Radbrook Green, Shrewsbury, Salop

758 GRAHAM M. KING, Sutton Coldfield, W. Midlands

759 NEIL ANTHONY & VICTORIA ANN CARTWRIGHT, Blaby

760 JOHN L. SKINNER, Leicester

761 FIONA SMART, Oadby, Leicester

762 DAVID PRIMROSE, Melton Mowbray, Leics

763 STANLEY HERBERT SAUNDERS, Leicester

764 KEN HUGHES, Harlow, Essex

765 R.E. GATE, Ripponden, Sowerby Bridge, Yorks

766 Mr & Mrs A.W. BROWN, Whitwick, Leicester

767 M.A. BAILEY, Hinckley, Leics

768 JOHN LABAND, Glenfield, Leicester

769 F.G. MORLEY, Teigh, Oakham, Rutland

770 CLIFFORD JON OAKES, Wigston, Leicester

771 DEREK SHAW, Hinckley, Leics

772 D.A. GREWCOCK (Tamworth) & A. MERRIMAN (Oadby)

773 Dr. JOHN T. QUICK, Crows Nest, Australia

774 CATHERINE ILLSLEY, Thurnby, Leicester

775 DAVID ROSS, Polesworth, Tamworth, Staffs

776 CHRISTOPHER C. WATSON, Kegworth, Derbyshire

777 PETER JOHN STEVENS, Wellingborough, Northants

778 CHRISTOPHER JAMES STEVENS, Burbage, Leics

779 CHRISTOPHER J. BELLAMY, Knighton, Leicester

780 ROSS MICHAEL CHARLTON, Market Harborough, Leics

781 K.J. NORMAN, Barrow on Soar, Leics

782 PETER JAMES ALDWINCKLE, Calverton, Notts

783 MARTIN L.V. DALE, Ickenham, Middlesex

784 J.R. BARNWELL, Leicester

785 TERRY DONOVAN, Hinckley, Leics

786 D.L. CARBY, Queniborough, Leicester

787 WILLIAM JAMES COULSEY, Knighton, Leicester

788 SCOTT GAVIN WORTHY, Beaumont Leys, Leicester

789 K. NICHOLAS, Sanderstead, Surrey

790 FRANK FIELD, Olney, Buckinghamshire

791 MALCOLM T. BOTT, Thurmaston, Leicester

792 CLIVE HARRISON, Croft, Leicester

793 R.W.S. RODWELL, Aylestone, Leicester

794 J. GREAVES, Blackpool, Lancashire

795 JANE A. SMITH, Beaumont Leys, Leicester

796 DAVID RHODES, Great Glen, Leicester

797 LEE S. JONES, Lincoln

798 NORMAN JONES, Oadby, Leicester

799 JAN KITCHEN, Wigston Meadows, Leicester

800 ROLAND GODDARD, Oadby, Leicester

801 FRED LEE, Knighton, Leicester

802 ROSS ALTHORNE, Nassington, Peterborough

803 DOUGLAS PAUL SMITH, Leicester

804 J.H. FORD, Kirby Muxloe, Leicester

805 R.A. PADMORE, Solihull, West Midlands

806 R. THIRLBY, Glenfield, Leicester

807 KEVIN SMITH, Leicester

808 ADRIAN WILKINS, Leicester

809 ROBERT H. TURNELL, Stoneygate, Leicester

810 IAN JARVIS, Barrow upon Soar, Leicester

811 G.S.M. YOUNG, Raskelf, North Yorkshire

812 JOHN R. HOLLIS, Long Clawson, Leicestershire

813 ROLAND, A. EDWARDS, Ashby-de-la-Zouch, Leics

814 MICHAEL NEIL GAVINS, Manton, Oakham, Leics

815 DARREN & LESLEY BOWERS, Leicester

816 KIERON PATRICK MALLOY, Rothwell, Northants

817 STUART CHRISTOPHER LONIE, Aylesham, Canterbury, Kent

818 W.G. BEYNON, Desford, Leicestershire

819 JEREMY NICHOLAS HALL, Hinckley, Leics

820 JOHN ERNEST HALL, Hinckley, Leics

821 DONNA EASINGWOOD, Syston, Leicester

822 PAUL EASINGWOOD, Syston, Leicester

823 ROBIN HILL, Tunbridge Wells, Kent

824 DEV DZIEWULSKI, Stoneygate, Leicester

825 DAVID BRANKIN-FRISBY

826 MICHAEL BRANKIN-FRISBY

827 RUPERT BRANKIN-FRISBY

828 DAVID E. MOSELEY, Whitwick, Leics

829 ANDREW HURST, Market Harborough, Leics

830 J. MAURICE THORNELOE, Dedworth, Windsor, Berks

831 ANN LAVERACK, Louth, Lincolnshire

832 DAVID JOHN PENNY, Owston, Oakham, Rutland, Leics

Subscribers

833 ROBERT S. WATSON, Leicester Forest East

834 Mrs FREDA WALLACE, Burton upon Trent, Staffs

835 A.M. JONES, Hinckley, Leicestershire

836 JENNIFER M. SMITH, Oadby, Leicester

837 MARTYN R. SLATTER, Glen Parva, Leicester

838 A.C. ROBERTS, Shepshed, Leicestershire

839 CHRIS STANYON, Cranford, Northamptonshire

840 KATIE STANYON, Cranford, Northamptonshire

841 ROB HINXMAN, Leicester

842 PHILIP HALLAM, Coalville, Leicester

843 KAREN, TONY, ERIKA & CRAIG STEPHENS, Lutterworth

844 ANDY BEEVERS, Wigston, Leicester

845 ANDREW HARRISON, Lilbourne, Rugby, Warwicks

846 ALAN R. BURDETT, Hinckley, Leics

847 JEFFERY A. SABIN

848 DAVID JOHN CORE, Melton Mowbray, Leics

849 WILLIAM D. MOORE

850 DAVID ROSE, Frolesworth, Leics

851 FRANK ROSE

852 DAVID LENG, Braunstone, Leicester

853 LEIGH R. PEARCE, Quorn, Leicestershire

854 DAVE LEWIS, Ise Village, Kettering, Northants

855 KENNETH HARRY NEWCOMBE, Radcliffe on Trent, Notts

856 ANDREW DAVID NEWCOMBE, Radcliffe on Trent, Notts

857 STEPHEN PHILIP NEWCOMBE, Radcliffe on Trent, Notts

858 BAS FORGHAM, Hugglescote, Leicestershire

859 H.E. RIDDINGTON, Thurcaston, Leicester

860 NEIL DOUGLAS FOWLER, Jesmond, Newcastle upon Tyne

861 RICHARD JOHN WARREN, Wigston, Leicester

862 JONATHAN COLTON (Wm. Colton & Sons) Leicester

863 JULIE COOKE, Leicester

864 ROBERT FORD, Cosby, Leicester

865 TIM WALLEY, Leicester

866 ANDREW ABBOTT, Leicester

867 JOHN MARK MELFORT SHARMAN, Leicester

868 PETER LLOYD, Allesley, Coventry, Warwicks

869 A.J. McQUILLAN, Badsey, Evesham, Worcs

870 R.E. BASTOCK, Leicester

871 DAVID METCALF, Leicester

872 QUENTIN & VELTA WOODHOUSE, Birstall, Leicester

873 HUGH OLIVER (H & S SHOES), Allandale Road, Leicester

874 CHRIS WARD

875 NEIL WALKER

876 JOHN HALLETT, Birstall, Leicester

877 G.S. WHITE, Braunstone, Leicester

878 W.M. ALLEN, Fen Ditton, Cambridge

879 DONNA K. WATMORE, Kingsway, Leicester

880 GRAHAM FACER, Countesthorpe, Leicester

881 KEITH BENTLEY ELECTRICAL, Clarendon Park, Leicester

882 GRAHAM "C.I.D." SMITH, Wigston, Leicester

883 LESLIE WALTON, Leicester

884 RICHARD MORRIS, Oadby, Leicester

885 CHARLIE BRODERICK, Foxton, Leicestershire

886 DAVE & MO LACEY, Aylestone, Leicester

887 MICHAEL WHITMORE, Evington, Leicester

888 ROGER BUNKER - Happy 50th Birthday Dad! (Chris)

889 TUDOR LLOYD WOOLMAN M.B.E., Plymouth

890 FRANK HENRY SPENCE, Aylestone, Leicester

891 T.F.S. RODWELL, Aylestone, Leicester

892 JUSTINE BOWERS, Kilby, Leicester

893 JONES & DUFFIN SOLICITORS, Narborough Rd, Leicester

894 ALAN THOMAS BEYNON JONES, Burnham Market, Norfolk

895 RAYMOND F. BOOT, Leicester

896 CANDIDA F.V. BASKCOMB, Melbourne, Australia

897 DAVID & JEANETTE STANHOPE, Leicester

898 DENNIS W. FREER, Willoughby Waterleys, Leicester

899 J.G. MARSLAND, Ashby Magna, Lutterworth, Leics

900 PETER NEGUS, Barton under Needwood, Staffs

901 I.E. FRASER, Ashby de la Zouch, Leicestershire

902 PETER & JANE KINAL, Oakham, Leicestershire

903 VINCE & ELIZABETH FOLEY, Cricklade, Swindon, Wilts

904 PAUL M. SIMPSON, Countesthorpe, Leicestershire

905 ANDREW M. SIMPSON, Great Glen, Leicestershire

906 GERRY LOXLEY, Quorn, Leicestershire

907 HELEN BROOKS, Hanwell, London

908 DEREK PAYNE, Wigston, Leicester

909 KEITH WILLIAMS, Hamilton, Leicester

910 JULIAN B. BASKCOMB, Clarendon Park, Leicester